Psychotherapy in Independent Practice: Current Issues for Clinicians

Psychotherapy in Independent Practice: Current Issues for Clinicians

Robert D. Weitz

The Haworth Press, Inc.
New York • London

Psychotherapy in Independent Practice: Current Issues for Clinicians has also been published as *Psychotherapy in Private Practice*, Volume 10, Numbers 1/2 1992.

The Haworth Press, Inc., 10 Alice Street, Binghamton, NY 13904-1580 USA

Library of Congress Cataloging-in-Publication Data

Psychotherapy in independent practice : current issues for clinicians / [edited by] Robert D. Weitz.
p. cm.
Has been published as Psychotherapy in private practice, v. 10, no. 1/2 1992.
Includes bibliographical references.
ISBN 1-56024-232-9 (hardback : alk. paper)
1. Psychotherapy – Congresses. 2. Psychotherapy – Practice – Congresses. I. Weitz, Robert D. (Robert Daniel)
[DNLM: 1. Psychotherapy – education – United States. 2. Psychotherapy – methods. 3. Psychotherapy – organization & administration – United States. W1 PS86M v. 10 no. 1/2]
RC475.5.P77 1992
616.89'14 – dc20
DNLM/DLC
for Library of Congress

92-1637
CIP

Psychotherapy in Independent Practice: Current Issues for Clinicians

Psychotherapy in Independent Practice: Current Issues for Clinicians

CONTENTS

∞ ALL HAWORTH BOOKS & JOURNALS ARE PRINTED ON CERTIFIED ACID-FREE PAPER

Psychotherapy in Independent Practice: Current Issues for Clinicians

ABOUT THE EDITOR

Robert D. Weitz, PhD, a pioneer and innovator in the private practice of professional psychology, has maintained an independent practice for nearly fifty years during his long and distinguished career. He was a prime founder of the Graduate School of Applied and Professional Psychology at Rutgers University and the Florida School of Professional Psychology, now under the aegis of Nova University. At the Florida School of Professional Psychology, he served as the first President and Dean. Dr. Weitz has been honored by the New Jersey State Senate, the New Jersey Psychological Association, the American Society of Psychologists in Private Practice, the American Psychological Association's Divisions of Independent Practice and Clinical Psychology, and has been elected to the National Academies of Practice. He has extensive background as a lecturer and workshop leader, and has presented more than 1200 educational programs to lay and professional groups. Currently, his major therapeutic interest is the application of hypnosis in the treatment of neurotic depression, anxiety states, and psychophysiological disorders. Presently semi-retired, Dr. Weitz conducts a part-time practice in Boca Raton, Florida.

SYMPOSIUM: PSYCHOTHERAPISTS IN INDEPENDENT PRACTICE AND IN MANAGED HEALTH CARE SETTINGS: A COMPARISON

Overview and Introduction

Carol Shaw Austad

OVERVIEW. This four part article is concerned with how health care delivery settings (private sector versus managed health care), affect psychotherapists' practice style. Following general comments about the revolution in the American health care delivery system and its effects upon psychotherapy, individual clinicians from the disciplines of nursing and counseling psychology compare their personal experiences of working in both HMOs and private practice. In the final section, data from interviews with 43 HMO psychotherapists are summarized. Those with private practice experience reported that some of the ways in which their practice styles differed between the two settings were as follows: flexibility and limitations of treat-

Carol Shaw Austad, PhD, is Assistant Professor, Central Connecticut State University and Staff Psychologist, HMO, Community Health Care Plan, New Haven, CT.

ment parameters; financial incentives, dealing with therapeutic dependency; therapist's awareness of time; freedom of patient selection; messages of health; therapist's activity level in the transference; collaboration of mental health professionals; and history taking. The authors conclude that in order to be fully understood, psychotherapy must be studied within its environmental context, or "ecological niche." Defining appropriate treatment parameters (the quality, quantity, and cost effectiveness) of psychotherapy as well as consideration of the positive effects of managed health care upon the evolution of psychotherapy should be considered.

INTRODUCTION

Psychotherapy does not take place in a vacuum. The environment influences its delivery and its deliverer. For example, how is a person affected by being in a gorgeous open wheat field? Or sitting in a thick, lush, cool dark forest beside a gurgling brook? Or crossing a busy city intersection? Few people would deny that the environment influences a person's internal state. So, too, does the setting affect the therapist. How does a psychotherapist feel when treating patients in a setting which endorses long term, psychoanalytic care? Or in a Community Mental Health Center adhering to a community treatment model? In a private practice? In a managed health care setting? In order to understand the psychotherapeutic process, it is best considered as possessing an "ecological niche," a place which contains not only a given entity, but all factors that impinge upon and influence it. Since psychotherapy is a form of health care, the factors which influence general health care, also have an effect upon it. Figure 1 illustrates factors which directly influence the health care system and thus, psychotherapy.

At this very moment, American health care is in a revolution (Starr, 1986). It is becoming a consumer good in which the payers (patient, government, employers, insurers) are worried about how much they are spending (Goldsmith, 1984). Runaway costs are forcing non-medical people to say to medical people "Justify your treatments, your costs, and your charges." Just as medical care is conducted in new systems, so is psychotherapy being conducted in non-traditional settings called "Managed Health Care" (Lee, 1987), which now come in so many shapes and forms – Health Maintenance

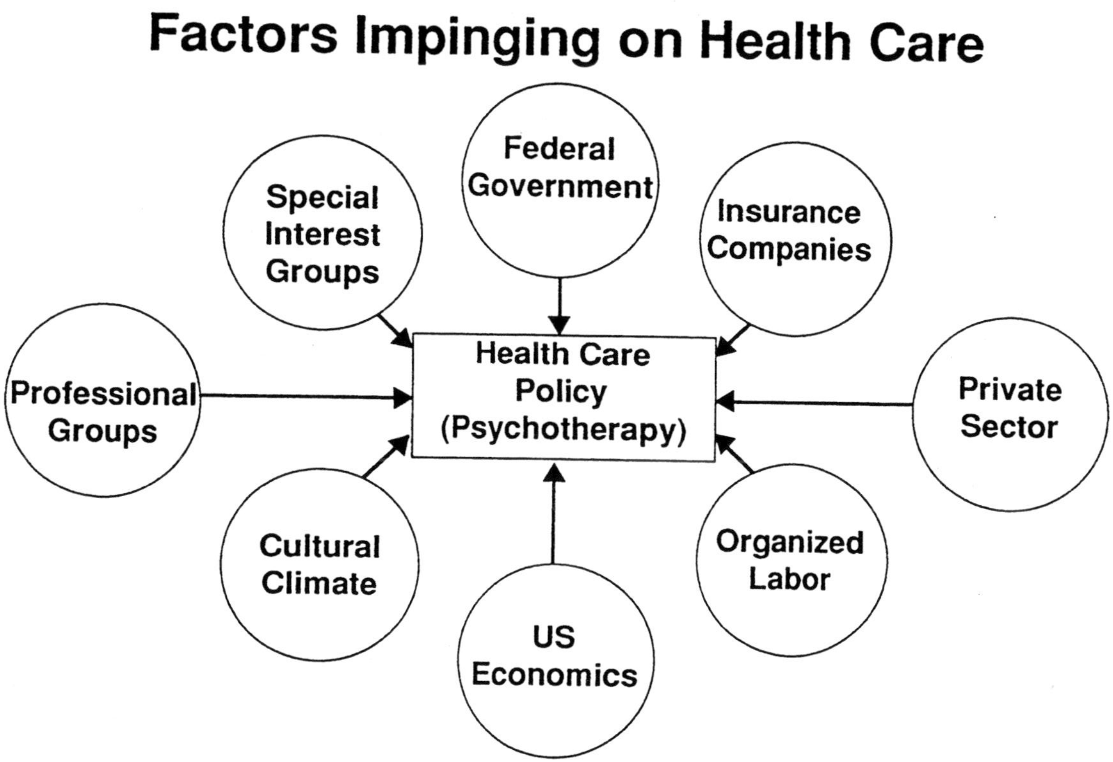

FIGURE 1. Factors which are impinging upon health care which indirectly affect the practice of psychotherapy are many.

Organizations (HMOs), Preferred Provider Organizations (PPOs), Mental Health Maintenance Organizations (MHMOs), etc., that a dictionary is needed to define and describe the variations on prepaid health care that now exist.

The once very private psychotherapeutic dyad, which occurred between two people behind closed doors with no other party impinging upon the interaction, is coming under close scrutiny. Since the psychotherapist collects a fee, and since the fee is not typically absorbed solely by the patient, a third party – the payer – whether it be government, employer, or insurance plan, is in the room. The only way to chase this presence away is to have the patient pay out of pocket. If this is the case, will a consumer (provided he or she is able) value psychotherapy services to such a degree that he or she will directly pay expenses in the same way that indemnity plan payers have in the past? Figure 2 illustrates how familiar factors, as well as some unrealized variables, directly impinge upon and affect the psychotherapeutic dyad.

It is the premise of this paper that in today's psychotherapeutic world, managed health care is influencing the practice of psychotherapy. And often times the psychotherapist is not consciously aware of how.

Research which explores the thoughts, feelings, and wisdom of psychotherapists in differing health care delivery settings can help in understanding how psychotherapy is being changed because part of its ecological niche, the health care delivery system, is in a state of revolution. The therapist in the managed health care setting – the staff model HMO in particular, is in a unique position to be involved in and perform such research. The HMO setting can bring about rapid clinical maturation and seasoning because models of therapy taught in graduate schools are often not adequate to deal with the heterogeneity of patients and problems found in the HMO. The therapist is often left to his or her own devices and must often face, handle, and deal with a sea of clinical predicaments that may take his or her private practitioner counterpart many more years to experience.

Goldfried and Padawer (1982) point out that clinicians often recognize that their particular frame of reference is not always congruent with their clinical observations. They add that there is a clini-

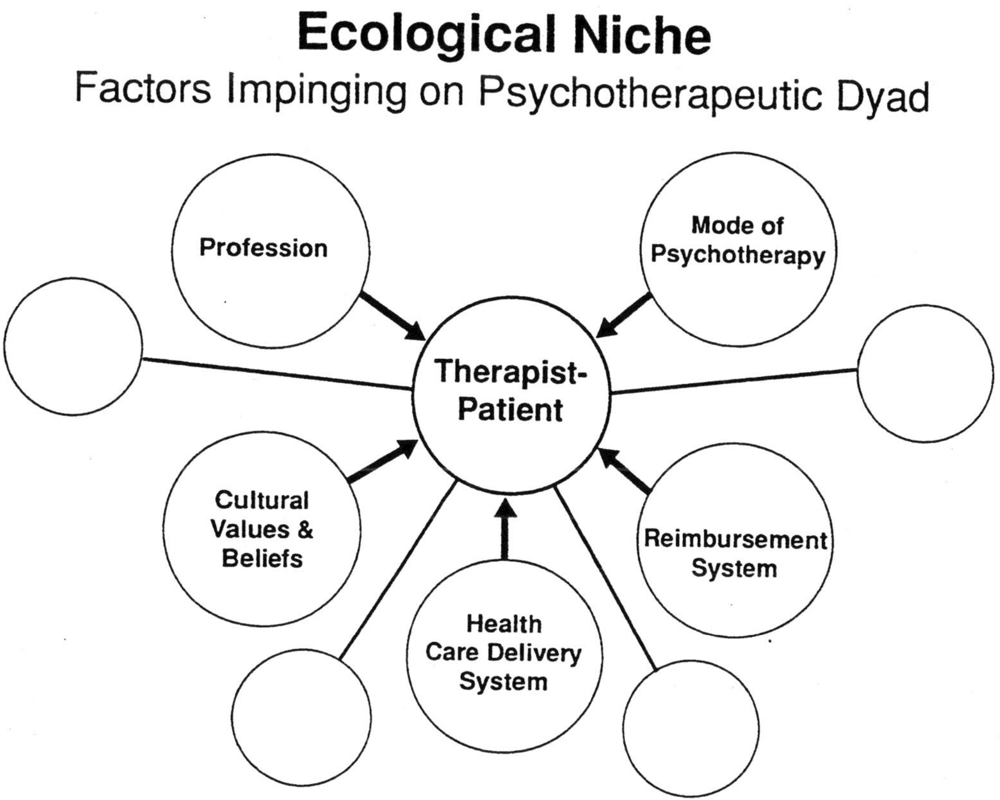

FIGURE 2. Psychotherapy occurs in an environmental setting or "ecologicalniche" in which many factors, known and unknown (blank circles), affect its delivery.

cian/researcher gap in the study of psychotherapy which should be closed by gathering clinical observations from experienced therapists who act as problem finders and can offer a very rich source of hypotheses to pursue in research. Furthermore, mental health care is dispensed to many people from managed health care settings, who might not be receiving it if they were not in a managed health care plan. Whether managed health care is perceived negatively or not, its presence is inevitable. Is it possible to view it as force with much positive potential? The HMO therapist holds the accumulated secrets of the hearts and souls of many. This resource should not go untapped.

In hopes of promoting a greater understanding of how psychotherapy delivered within the context of private practice differs from that delivered in the HMO, the next segments of this paper describe the subjective impressions of HMO psychotherapists about how the managed health care and private practice differentially affect their practice style. These subjective reports are followed by a report of a study in which 43 HMO psychotherapists were interviewed. This is not a well controlled empirical study, but an attempt to gather some meaningful data based upon clinical observation which will promote further empirical observations and study.

REFERENCES

Goldsmith, J. (1984) Death of a paradigm: the challenge of competition. *Health Affairs*, Fall.

Goldfried, M. & Padawer, W. (1982) Current status and future directions in psychotherapy. In Goldfried, M. R. (Ed.) *Converging Themes in Psychotherapy*. New York, Springer Publishing, 3-52.

Starr, P. (1984) *The Social Transformation of American Medicine*. New York: Basic Books.

Working Both in Private Practice and in the HMO

Nina Steefel

Working half time in my own private practice and half time in a staff model HMO has brought me the advantages of each and minimized many of the disadvantages.

My training in graduate school provided a broad theoretical base and also included a wide variety of practicum experiences. Among these experiences were several years as a therapist in an Adlerian family therapy center and extensive work using cognitive/behavioral techniques.

In 1981 I opened my private practice in Connecticut, and I was in full-time practice until two years ago. This practice is broadly based and has included testing and evaluations, a contract to work with Veterans with PTSD, some clinical supervision and psychotherapy around a variety of issues facing individuals, couples and families.

My work at the HMO is focussed on children twelve and under and therefore also includes work with parents and families.

For this talk I have looked at both my private practice and the HMO work from three different aspects:

I practice and business management concerns
II therapy issues
III professional/collegial relationships

Nina Steefel, PhD, is on the Faculty at Central Connecticut State University and Staff Psychologist, HMO, New Haven, CT. She is also in private practice, Hamden, CT.

I. While building my private practice I learned a lot about negative cash flow and fixed costs, the anxiety of establishing a referral base, the expense of support staff (and therefore how to do without it), and the crazy ways work hours can expand and spread through the day and the night.

But at the same time, building a private practice taught me economic reality, allowed me autonomy and forced on me the assumption of responsibility for the management of time and of practical business problems. All of this brought the pleasure and the confidence of having control over my work life.

From a practical business point of view, the HMO work has some built in advantages. There is a predictable salary with benefits, business expenses are taken care of, clients are waiting, support staff is present and work hours are defined. Rather than take these things for granted, I appreciated them and also knew something about the kinds of decisions which underlie providing them.

II. In private practice, it is you and your client (and in reality, to some extent, the third party payer) who set the parameters for treatment. The clients I accept, the number of sessions, the type of therapy, the cost . . . are all negotiable. Full accountability lies with me, the psychologist, which allows great freedom along with the responsibility.

A disadvantage in private practice is that it's also true that for many people it is difficult to "take the big step" into therapy. Therefore they postpone seeking help until things feel really unbearable to them, and they then have to struggle with the decision of whom to see, build up courage to call that person or to be referred, and then come to a new place to find the therapist.

In the HMO parameters are set by the management's definition of the benefit package. Cost, number of sessions, client load, etc., are all established for you. The parameters encourage short term, efficient and intermittent styles of treatment. Client loads can get heavy at times and the pace of work and pressures of back to back scheduling can be intense.

But an advantage in the HMO is that, given the unity of the medical and mental health services, primary care physician referrals, at least for children, frequently come earlier in the course of problems and allow an easy flow of care between physician and mental health worker.

III. In private practice there is always a danger of isolation, and isolation can lead to a distorted view of oneself and one's work. Consultation and support frequently are not quickly available; but with experience and discipline it is possible to space appointments to allow relief from constant client work, to schedule time with colleagues for consultation and support and to break the work schedule for needed variety, relaxation and exercise.

In the HMO setting there are colleagues and opportunities for group supervision; support and consultation are nearby from other mental health professionals and from medical staff. Colleagues are available for letting off steam and griping.

In conclusion, I am glad that I had the experience in private practice before I began to work in the HMO. I had chosen private practice because I wanted autonomy, flexibility and variety. Adding part time work in an HMO to my private practice has allowed me a measure of security and support as well. In private practice I became confident in my therapy skills and grew in my management ability. My experience gave me a basis for choosing among the various managed health care arrangements in my geographic area.

> First, I chose a staff model HMO rather than an arrangement where I would see health plan patients in my private office.
>
> Second, I chose a setting where I would be doing both evaluation and treatment of my client, and where clients could continue to see me as they moved in and out of therapy unless they chose to be referred. This allowed a relationship comparable to that in private practice.
>
> Third, I chose a setting where there was flexibility, in practice, even though the HMO had defined strict limitations for the mental health benefits.
>
> Fourth, I chose a setting where the mental health staff is headed by a psychologist.

My experience has given me the firm belief that it is up to psychologists and other mental health professionals to become involved and actively to influence the maturing of managed mental health care. In order to continue to be able to provide good mental health services for clients and to incorporate what we have learned about healthy work situations for therapists, we must participate in change rather than merely react to it.

From HMO to Private Practice

Karen Henault

At the time I began working in a prepaid group health practice in 1973 little was known about the practice of psychotherapy in this type of setting and there was even less information available in the literature. Community Health Care Plan, CHCP, a staff model HMO in New Haven, CT was in existence for approximately two years when I joined the staff and had an enrollment of 10,000 members. The mental health staff was composed of two half-time psychiatric social workers and a half-time psychiatrist. I became the first full-time employee, and was hired, in part, because of my recent experience in an inpatient crisis intervention and brief treatment unit at the local community mental health center. At the time I left the HMO, fourteen years later, the enrollment had grown to approximately 50,000 members with a Mental Health Department of 16 full-time equivalent staff.

In 1973 I was four years out of a psychodynamically oriented graduate program in psychiatric nursing and had limited experience beyond graduate training in actually doing psychotherapy, particularly of a long term nature.

Needless to say, therefore, my predominant non-academic learning and experience in psychotherapy has been in the context of a managed health care system.

I would like to briefly discuss this experience, sharing with you what I feel are the positive highlights of therapy in this type of setting and how they have influenced my private practice.

HMO psychotherapy emphasizes close collaboration and consul-

Karen Henault, MSN, is in private practice and a Psychiatric Nurse, Connecticut Valley Hospital, Wellingford, CT.

tation with primary care providers. Most referrals are initiated by the patient's internist, either by his suggestion or initiative or by the patient requesting a referral. Physicians have always played an active role in the treatment of emotional problems of their patients, from being interested and listening, offering support, to prescribing and monitoring psychotropic medication. With the physician's active involvement in their patients' lives, the therapist often starts working with the patient with some knowledge and insights gleaned by the physician.

In order to provide an effective service to its enrollees, and in consideration of staff resources and overall cost effectiveness, the HMO's benefit package has generally been 20 psychotherapy sessions per calendar year. Certainly, when I first heard this, I had questions about this amount. It was contrary to everything I had learned. I do believe the idea of 20 sessions being sufficient is a difficult concept to understand when one's training and prior experiences have been centered around a long-term model. However, from my own experience and from observing others as they have joined the staff of the HMO, after at least several months, one begins to develop a conceptual understanding of how this model works and to see that it is very effective for the majority of patients receiving therapy in the HMO.

What has evolved over time, and is now well documented in the literature, is a problem-focused short term therapy that calls for an integrated eclectic approach. Cummings has recommended brief intermittent psychotherapy throughout the life cycle. When initially interviewing a patient, while developing a psychodynamic formulation, the therapist assertively focuses on the immediate issues that have brought the person to seek help at this time. When this immediate problem is resolved the therapist and patient can view their work as finished—for the time being. Patients will often initiate this by saying something like, "I'm feeling better, do you think I need to keep coming to see you"; or "I'd like to try handling this on my own now."

At CHCP we began to call this Installment Therapy. Sessions would end, but the patient would be invited to return should problems occur again. Therapy is open-ended, the relationship is not terminated. Many patients do return, some in several months, some after a year or two for another installment or series of sessions. After working in this setting for a while the therapist develops a sense of how effective this can be. One can readily reestablish the working relationship and do very meaningful and therapeutic work.

Another principle of HMO therapy is the flexible timing of sessions. After the initial assessment patients may be scheduled every two weeks or in a frequency that seems appropriate for each person, taking into consideration their personal needs and the degree of difficulty they are experiencing. With this flexibility in timing, and the concept of installment therapy many patients are able to receive care over a long period of time. I worked with many patients over a several year period, seeing them approximately 12-15 times per year.

One woman, diagnosed as having chronic schizophrenia was first referred when her husband died suddenly of a cerebral hemorrhage in 1974. Although this woman had had several psychiatric hospitalizations in her life, she had none in the thirteen years that we worked together.

This case characterizes another area in which one's practice is strongly influenced in the HMO setting. Easy access, early rapid intervention, and crisis intervention are crucial concepts in a good managed health care setting. The therapist is immediately and frequently available to the patient (daily, if necessary) until the crisis is contained.

Another of my HMO patients was referred by her physician with approximately six months of complaints of headaches, fatigue and irritability with a negative medical workup. Kathy described multiple problems; dissatisfaction with her marriage, always feeling overwhelmed and in chaos. She stated her children had become very demanding and she was often angry and yelling at them. She had particular concerns regarding her oldest daughter's severe learning disabilities and felt that she could no longer cope with the special needs of this child. She frequently thought of just leaving home, so that her family, particularly her husband, would have to fend for themselves.

She was developing neurovegetative symptoms of depression and was struggling with these feelings which were fairly foreign to her. After 3-4 sessions it became evident that what was underlying this symptom picture was an ever increasing belief and preoccupation in her own imminent death. Kathy was approaching her 39th birthday, and in time was able to relate these feelings to her mother's death at age 39 when Kathy was the same age as the oldest daughter. With this insight she improved rapidly and shortly thereafter stopped treatment. She returned several months later to focus on some concerns regarding her marriage and after several bi-weekly sessions she joined a woman's group that I had recently formed. Time does not allow me to elaborate further on this case. I hope I have been able to provide you with a meaningful example of HMO work.

There are drawbacks to working in a managed care setting. Clinicians are always busy, and when a former patient calls in a crisis, you may end up seeing them on a lunch hour, or working later than usual in order to rapidly contain things and avoid a costly hospitalization. You could be fully booked for the next two or three weeks and suddenly receive several new referrals. To accommodate these new patients you then are forced to look very carefully at your current case load to see who may be seen less frequently in order to free up some clinical time. For the most part, however, I feel the HMO model works very well for both the therapist and patient even though there are times when one feels particularly pressured and overworked.

In my private practice my therapeutic style differs very little from the HMO model. Rapid and easy access helps keep a business going. I maintain a collaborative relationship with other mental health colleagues which decreases the sense of isolation of working independently while providing me with the opportunity for continued professional growth. Ongoing consultation with referral sources ensures more comprehensive care for my patients and encourages more referrals. A flexible timing of sessions and installment therapy concepts work well; with patients feeling that they are receiving an individualized treatment approach that meets both their emotional and fiscal needs.

In summary, in my private practice I feel I now have a comfortable, well integrated, eclectic blend of techniques. I am more relaxed and in control of how I can accommodate referrals without having to worry about a rapid turnover of my current caseload. Frequency of sessions and length of treatment is determined primarily by myself and the patient and not by a third party, the HMO or managed care system. However, this oversight or review process is becoming more prevalent in the private sector as well, so it appears to be in my best interest to continue working with the principles and techniques developed in the HMO. I feel strongly that this can be accomplished and that my patients are receiving a timely and highly individualized psychotherapeutic experience.

Techniques in Independent Practice and Managed Health Care: Interviews with 43 HMO Psychotherapists

Carol Shaw Austad
Thomas Morgan
Lisa Holstein

METHOD

Subjects

Letters requesting participation in a study about HMO psychotherapists were mailed to all staff model HMOs in the Northeastern area of the United States listed in the Group Health Association National Directory (1988). Of the plans that replied affirmatively, appointments were set up to interview individual therapists who volunteered to participate. Subjects were also recruited from a national psychotherapy conference by placing a request for subjects on a bulletin board. A total of 43, (21 male/22 female) subjects, were recruited from a total of ten HMOs. The sample contained 20 Ph.D. psychologists, 1 psychiatrist, 13 masters level social workers, 4 psychiatric nurses, and 5 others (masters prepared therapists).

Carol Shaw Austad, PhD, is Assistant Professor, staff psychologist, HMO: Community Health Care Plan, at Central Connecticut State University, New Haven, CT. Thomas Morgan, PhD, is Staff Psychologist, HMO: Community Health Care Plan, New Haven, CT. Lisa Holstein is a graduate student, Central Connecticut State University.

Procedure

Each of the therapists were asked a number of questions. Amongst them were "Do you have a private practice?" Therapists who answered affirmatively, were asked, "How does your practice style differ in the HMO and in your private practice (if it does)?"

The interviews were tape recorded and transcribed. The answers were placed into categories by two raters. When the raters did not agree upon a category, a third rater was called in, and the response was placed into the category in which there was agreement amongst two out of three raters.

RESULTS AND DISCUSSION

Twenty-nine or 67.4% of therapists had both private practice and HMO experience. Three therapists practiced in both settings but claimed there was no difference in the way they practiced between settings. Twenty-six or 60.4% of the HMO therapists were concurrently or had previously been involved in private practice and indicated that their practice style differed in the respective settings. All therapists gave examples of ways in which their styles differed in the two settings and Table I illustrates the nature of these differences.

More than thirty percent of the therapists felt that private practice allowed them to be more flexible or open ended in the scheduling, focus and timing of psychotherapy, and 11.5% believed private practice allowed the therapist to be more selective about which patients he or she chose to see. Illustrative quotes are as follows:

> I'm more relaxed . . . about the time limit in private practice . . . and less likely to think about ending at a specific time.
>
> I don't feel compelled to just manage the case. I can work with the families. I feel freer to do certain things.
>
> . . . I have more leeway . . . If I'm going to see somebody who has really severe or long term problems that's going to need longer term therapy, I think it's easier to give that in my private practice. Like I have somebody that has severe anorexia nervosa in my private practice and I certainly feel I'll see

How Does Your Practice Style Differ? (N = 26)

Between Private Practice and HMO

Differences	Percentage	Differences	Percentage
1. More Flexibility in Private Practice (Scheduling, Time, Focus, Open Ended)	30.7%	5. Patient Selection (More Selective in Private Practice)	11.5%
2. Financial Incentives (Keep Patients Longer in Private Practice)	15.4%	6. More Limited Services at HMO	7.7%
3. Independence - Dependence (More Dependence in Private Practice; Less in HMO)	15.4%	7. Message of Health Greater at HMO	3.8%
		8. More Active in Manipulating Transference in HMO	3.8%
4. Awareness of Time (Greater in HMO than Private Practice)	11.5%	9. Safer at HMO Due to Collaboration	3.8%
		10. Less Historical at HMO	3.8%

TABLE I.

> that person for a long period of time and also schedule her for extra sessions if I feel that's necessary . . . my schedule here would not permit that.

Financial incentives operated in private practice to keep patients in therapy longer for 15.4% of the therapists. Quotes from subjects illustrate this opinion:

> . . . if you only work in private practice there is a huge temptation to make sure you are making enough money. Here whether you are seeing 50 patients or one patient you are making the same salary so there is no unconscious agenda on my part to hold onto people and make them into chronic emotional people who feel that without the therapist they drift.
>
> I keep people longer in my private practice setting. I keep people as long as they want to come . . . it's kind of a luxury. I don't think my work is any better in my private practice than in my HMO setting . . . it is a more leisurely pace. And I'm more motivated by money in my private practice than I am at the HMO.

Fostering greater independence in HMO work than in private was reported by 15.4% of the therapists. Example replies were as follows:

> . . . in private practice I would keep my clients for as long as they wanted to come and as long as I felt they were getting something out of it. And I don't think I was promoting independence in the same way that I do here . . .
>
> I don't always feel I need to see a patient every week . . . that's something I learned from the HMO . . . patients I think can adjust on their own. I force dependency less than . . . in my previous work. So I think those are . . . advantages of HMO work that I think I picked up in private practice.
>
> Clearly there is an incentive to keep patients which is completely reversed here. It's dirty talk, but that's the fact of it . . . For me personally . . . just holding people that aren't moving anywhere gets . . . boring and depressing. I . . . feel I'm going

> to collect my share of the dependent people that don't want to move on anyway. I don't want that to be a large percentage of my practice. I'd much rather be proactive and . . . reaching for people that are ready to change and move . . .

A greater awareness of how time affects treatment as well as a press to work faster at the HMO (11.5%) and more active manipulation of the transference (3.8%) at the HMO were reported by 15.3% of the therapists.

Practicing in the HMO meant dealing with more limited services (7.7%) and taking less history and background from patients (3.8%) for 11.5% of the therapists.

HMO therapists reported that they used messages of greater health at the HMO than they typically used in private practice (3.8%). Increased safeguarding of patient welfare and higher quality assurance due to the opportunities for collaboration and observation (3.8%) were seen as affecting practice style of 7.7% of the therapists.

When asked what tips might be useful to psychotherapists who were beginning to work at the HMO, the interviewees replied with the advice summarized in Table II.

CONCLUSIONS

Psychotherapists do perceive themselves as changing their practice style contingent upon the context in which they perform psychotherapy. It is not possible to generalize from this small, perhaps unrepresentative sample of HMO psychotherapists, to all psychotherapists, but the results make salient key points in the controversy around the issues of whether the HMO or private practice is a more favorable treatment setting. The findings point to the importance of studying the two major questions which arise:

1. How do we, as mental health professionals, define standards of necessary and sufficient treatment. How do we specify "overtreatment" versus "undertreatment." How do we analyze the ecological factors which affect the psychotherapist and the psychotherapy? For example, private practitioners with long term therapeutic orientation accuse managed care therapists of cutting quality to save

Tips for HMO Therapists

1. Set Boundaries/Limits
2. Take Care of Yourself
3. Be Flexible
4. Pace Yourself/ Start Slowly
5. Use Clinical Supervision
6. Investigate the Model
7. Know Short Term Therapy
8. Get Variety into the Job
9. Don't Stay in the HMO too Long
10. Stick it Out for 2 - 3 Years
11. Get More Training
12. Develop Realtionships with Medical Staff

TABLE II

costs. HMO therapists accuse long term therapists of elongating the course of therapy for their own financial gain. Financial incentives are ecological variables which potentially influence length of treatment. It is only natural that if an environment furnishes a financial incentive to provide more, the therapist might tend to elongate treatment; but if there is a financial incentive to provide less, then the therapist might tend to shorten treatment. We must find a way to openly and honestly discuss how financial incentives affect practice style. The majority of credentialed psychotherapists are highly ethical, well intended professionals who keenly desire to help their patients. If payment affects practice style unconsciously, acknowledgement of how cost affects practice style may be one of the keys to establish what is NECESSARY AND SUFFICIENT, GOOD QUALITY treatment versus LUXURY treatment. Thus, we need to identify the characteristics of good therapy by understanding how financial incentives, as well as length and quality, interact to affect therapists' practice style.

2. What is the relationship of intensity and duration of psychotherapy contact to the dimension of independence versus dependence? Fostering dependency is an essential therapeutic tool in many models of traditional psychotherapy. In HMO therapy, it may be considered of less value, and discouraged, not encouraged. Whereas the private practitioner who adheres to a long term model seems to feel that the dependency is an essential instrument, some HMO therapists indicate that a message of greater health for the patient exists when dependency is discouraged. These diametrically opposed views are accentuated within these differing settings. Which orientation has more value remains to be seen and much discussion and study should revolve around such issues.

By bringing questions such as these to consciousness and by encouraging questioning and open dialogue, managed health care, a controversial entity, can be viewed as a catalyst, a friend to the evolution of today's psychotherapy. Managed health care settings, according to LaCourt (1988), can represent both danger and opportunity. While all of the dangers have been stressed and are well known, the opportunities can be used to the advantage of both practitioner and patient. Managed health care COULD provide us with:

1. rich sources of clinical data for research through long term records on normal populations;
2. integration and cross fertilization of psychotherapy disciplines (while psychiatry and psychology battle about turf, the HMO fosters collaboration);
3. exposure to common frameworks but a diversity of disciplines;
4. a place to derive a greater understanding of the models of psychotherapy and of the motivation of psychotherapists;
5. an opportunity to provide psychotherapy for many individuals who would not have it because they either could not afford the co-pay of an indemnity plan, or would have less likely been referred by a solo practice physician than their HMO primary care physician.

REFERENCES

Goldfried, M. R. & Padawer, W. (1982) Current status and future directions in psychotherapy. In Goldfried, M. *Converging Themes in Psychotherapy*. New York, Springer Publishing Co.

Goldsmith, J. (1984, Fall) Death of a paradigm: The challenge of competition. *Health Affairs*.

Group Health Association of America (1988) *Directory of HMOs*. Washington, D.C.

LaCourt, M. (1988) The HMO Crisis: Danger/Opportunity. *Family Systems Medicine*, Vol. 6., (1), 80-93.

Lee, F. (1987) Purchasers address escalating psychiatric and substance abuse utilization. *Employee Benefits Journal*, March, p. 9-12.

Starr, P. (1982) *The Social transformation of American Medicine*. New York, Basic Books, Inc.

Managed Health Care: Boon or Bane of Psychologists in Private Practice?

Louis J. DeStefano

After having heard my colleagues speak, I would like to first make a few general comments. It may not have been made clear, but we've all known each other for close to six years and all worked at the same HMO, Community Health Care Plan (CHCP) in New Haven, Connecticut for some period of time from 1984-1988.

Last night, while eating at a local restaurant, we discussed what we were going to say today. It was remarkable that there was a lack of consensus about the issues involved in the comparison of independent practice and managed health care. For example, we could not agree upon whether it was acceptable to see a private patient for longer than he or she needed to be as long as the patient was willing to pay. We were split 50-50 on this issue. We also could not agree about whether our styles of practice differed in independent practice vs. the HMO.

As I look at my fellow panel members, I realize that none of us are currently employed full-time at CHCP. We have each come up with our own solutions to a very difficult problem – and that is: how to maintain both one's livelihood and sanity in a highly competitive mental health market. In the Greater New Haven area, the private practice market is oversaturated with a great number of mental

---

Louis J. DeStefano, PhD, is Assistant Professor, Department of Psychiatry, Cornell University Medical College, Westchester Division, The New York Hospital and is in private practice, North Haven, CT.

Presented as discussant in symposium: A Comparison: Psychotherapists in Independent Practice and Managed Health Care. American Psychological Association Convention, New Orleans, August 14, 1989.

health professionals affiliated with Yale University; and HMO's of various types have well-penetrated the area. Therefore, establishing a solo private practice is a nearly impossible task. And, working for an HMO full-time over many years also does not seem possible.

Although Dr. Austad's study, which she presented earlier is just a beginning, it does give us some valuable information about the feelings of HMO psychotherapists about their work. It is a sad commentary on the HMO that most respondents to the survey felt that working full-time at an HMO over a long period wasn't possible due to the inevitable burnout. HMO therapists felt one could only stay employed by the HMO for four years, on average.

Following Dr. Austad's study, one might conclude that working at an HMO part-time is preferable. In fact 26 of the 43 respondents were engaged in some private practice. However, if I were the manager of an HMO Mental Health Service, I would prefer that my employees were full-time for a couple of reasons: firstly, if a therapist works part-time in private practice and part-time at the HMO, the therapist will develop a two-tiered system of care: the "paying clients" and the "nonpaying clients." Also, since the HMO Mental Health Service provides crisis intervention to stabilize patients to avert hospitalization, a full-time staff ensures continuity of care. As the manager of an HMO Mental Health Service, I would want an exclusive contract with my employees.

To remedy a difficult situation, I would propose that HMO therapists be paid more (so they wouldn't feel compelled to "moonlight") and, if the HMO were large enough, I would vary the role of the therapist to include a variety of activities such as research, administration and supervision rather than only psychotherapy hour after hour.

What leads to such burnout among HMO therapists? One major problem is the lack of control over one's own caseload. Since CHCP began to experience financial difficulties in 1986, the mental health staff size has remained constant, while the enrollment in the HMO and the number of referrals continued to grow. Since CHCP is a closed-panel HMO, the mental health clinicians must see all patients who are referred to them. Another factor which led to burnout at CHCP was the on-call system. If your patient called "urgent visit" at any time of the day or night, you, the therapist, were called first. If you were unreachable, the call was referred to the "on-call" mental health clinician. A third factor which fostered burnout was the policy of not hospitalizing psychotic or suicidal patients unless they were an imminent danger to themselves or others. We saw these patients three to five times per week during the crisis period. This crisis intervention is being done on top of an already large caseload.

I'd like to make a few more general comments before proceeding to each speaker's presentation:

None of the speakers spoke about the unique opportunity presented at the HMO of collaborating closely with psychiatrists and internists in developing the patient's treatment plan, including psychotropic medications. At a time when many psychologists are pushing for the prescription privilege, the HMO provides valuable on-the-job training in psychopharmacology.

Earlier, I spoke about the differences in the styles of therapists depending upon whether they are seeing patients in a managed care or a fee-for-service setting. We, as psychologists should not forget that, from a behavioral perspective, we are modified by the reinforcement schedule of the payment system. Economic considerations are the driving force in both the fee-for-service and managed care systems. We cannot be so blind or so idealistic to think that we are above such considerations. However, for the seasoned HMO therapist, my sense is that therapy styles will converge and be consistent in the managed care and the fee-for-service settings.

Now, I would like to comment on each speaker's presentation:

Dr. Austad talks about the "ecological niche" in which psychotherapy takes place. Again, the behavioral contingencies of the environment affects the practice of psychotherapy. The psychotherapist is not always aware of the factors affecting his or her work. Observations that are made based on clinical experience need to be verified empirically.

Dr. Austad's study is the first to survey the attitudes of mental health practitioners in staff-model HMO's. More research needs to be done in this area. It might be interesting to survey the attitudes of psychologists in full-time independent practice and compare them to the HMO therapists. For HMO therapists' attitudes toward independent practice may not be generalizable to independent practitioners, since the HMO therapist is not doing independent practice full-time, and furthermore, the HMO therapist may be a "different animal" than the independent practitioner.

Ms. Karen Henault, a clinical nurse specialist in psychiatry described the structure and the framework of CHCP. Ms. Henault had more than 14 years of experience as an HMO psychotherapist. She saw the evolution of the Mental Health Service from a consultation and liaison service with the primary care physicians at one site to a large clinical service providing direct care to thousands of enrollees spread over nine sites. Ms. Henault did not speak about the tremendous toll that the chronically mental ill patient can have on the HMO therapist. The way that the CHCP Mental Health Service operated, if the patient was once assigned to you, he or she would continue to be yours as long as you continued to be employed by the HMO, and the patient continued to be enrolled in the Plan.

As the HMO therapist's practice "matures," there occurs what we called "the silting" effect. As the healthier and more acute patients got well and terminated therapy, one would be left with an increasingly higher percentage of chronic patients. For example, after working at CHCP for nearly five years and seeing several hundred patients, more than half of my caseload was composed of "chronic patients." Perhaps, a utilization review committee could be set up to review the chronic patient's cases and recommend referral to group psychotherapy or termination of psychotherapy.

Our next speaker, Dr. Nina Steefel started in full-time private practice, then consulted for CHCP and finally accepted a half-time position with CHCP. Although Dr. Steefel says that in continuing her private practice and working for the HMO, she has "the best of both worlds," I wonder if this was a conscious decision on her part or was it economic necessity? The highly competitive private practice market in the New Haven area and the rapidly changing mental health reimbursement systems necessitate diversifying into many different clinical activities in order to survive these difficult times.

The question of whether to participate in managed health care systems is not a simple answer for the private practitioner. It depends on: Which HMO? What is the structure of the HMO? What is the reimbursement system? Does the therapist have control over his or her caseload? How are on-call responsibilities handled?

Private practitioners need to carefully evaluate all of these many factors and decide which HMO's to join. With the rising enrollment in HMO's, not too far into the future private practitioners in most areas of the country will find that participation in some type of HMO will be necessary. Gathering the requisite information will help the practitioner to make the best, informed decisions.

SYMPOSIUM: LIABILITY RISKS IN TREATING DANGEROUS AND ABUSIVE PATIENTS

Liability Risks in Treating Dangerous Patients: Introduction

Leon VandeCreek

INTRODUCTION

The treatment of patients who pose threats of harm to others is an area of expanding liability for psychotherapists. In instances of potential physical assault, therapists must determine how to defuse the danger, and they may need to consider warning a potential victim. When the threat of suicide is present, the therapist should act to protect the patient's life, although as yet there is no legal mandate to warn third parties.

The following three papers were presented as part of a Sympo-

Leon VandeCreek, PhD, is Chairperson, Department of Psychology, Indiana University of Pennsylvania.

Presented at the 97th Annual Convention of the American Psychological Association, New Orleans, LA, August, 1989.

sium presented at the 1989 Annual Convention of the American Psychological Association. The Symposium was entitled "Liability Risks in Treating Dangerous and Abusive Patients." The first paper, by Solomon Fulero, describes recent developments in court cases in the area of duty to protect. The article by David Shapiro describes recent efforts to provide statutory immunity for clinicians who work with dangerous patients. Finally, the article by Knapp and VandeCreek discusses the potential application of duty-to-protect principles to HIV-positive patients.

Recent Developments in the Duty to Protect

Solomon M. Fulero

The California Supreme Court decided the now-famous case of *Tarasoff v. Regents of the University of California et al.*, in 1976. In brief, the case involved the killing of a young woman by her ex-boyfriend, who had been a patient of the University Counseling Center. The woman's parents sued, alleging negligence (for a fascinating discussion of the facts, see Winslade & Ross, 1983; for the text of the judicial opinion, see Cohen, 1979). The case was heard a total of four times at various levels of the California legal system, coming before the California Supreme Court twice *(Tarasoff I*, 1974; *Tarasoff II*, 1976).

In *Tarasoff I*, the court found the defendants liable for negligence on a theory of failure to warn, holding that "public policy favoring protection of the confidential character of patient-psychotherapist relationships must yield in instances in which disclosure is essential to avert danger to others; the protective privilege ends where the public peril begins" *(Tarasoff I*, 1974). Upon rehearing, the decision was upheld, although the theory was modified somewhat. This time, the court ruled that when a therapist determines, or should have determined, that a patient presents a serious danger of violence to another, the therapist "bears a duty to exercise reasonable care to

---

Solomon M. Fulero, PhD, is Professor in the Department of Psychology, Sinclair College, Dayton, OH.

The author thanks Lynda Olsen-Fulero for her constructive editorial comments. Requests for reprints should be sent to Solomon M. Fulero, Department of Psychology, Sinclair College, Dayton, OH 45402.

protect the foreseeable victim of that danger" (*Tarasoff II*, 1976; see Fulero, 1988 for further discussion of the issues and of reactions to the decision).

In this paper, I will address the trends or themes in the recent cases dealing with a mental health professional's duty to protect third parties from harm at the hands of a potentially dangerous client. A list of most of the reported cases related to or based on *Tarasoff* up to June, 1987 is presented in the Appendix of Fulero (1988). Fulero argued that the legal key to the *Tarasoff* decision appears to be Sections 315 and 319 of the American Law Institute's Restatement of Torts 2d (1965), sections that were explicitly considered by the California Supreme Court in its decision. Section 315 provides that there is no duty to control a person's conduct so as to prevent him from causing physical harm to another unless (a) a special relation exists between the actor and that person which imposes a duty on the actor to control the person s conduct, or (b) a special relation exists between the actor and the potential victim giving him a right to protection. Section 319 provides that one who takes charge of a person whom he knows or should know to be likely to cause bodily harm to others if not controlled is under a duty to exercise reasonable care to control that person to prevent him from doing such harm. It is clear from a survey of the *Tarasoff* cases around the country that many of the courts have viewed duty to protect cases as dealing with the question of whether or not Sections 315 and 319 are applicable in their jurisdiction.

In recent *Tarasoff* cases, seven issues have been addressed. First, can a mental health professional be held liable where the claim is that he or she "should have known" of a client's dangerousness? Second, what is the standard of care against which a mental health professional's actions are to be measured? Third, does *Tarasoff* imply an affirmative duty involuntarily to commit a potentially dangerous client? Fourth, does the doctrine protect the client as well as third parties? Fifth, what liability might accrue to a professional who breaches confidence and acts to protect a third party? Sixth, to what extent does the *Tarasoff* duty apply to mental health professionals other than psychiatrists and psychologists, or even to nonprofessionals? Finally, is property damage covered under a *Tarasoff* duty to protect, or only bodily harm?

"Should have known" cases. First, there are clearly times when the mental health professional does not have *actual* knowledge of the client's dangerousness. Does liability exist anyway if it can be shown that he or she "should have known?" Three such cases have been decided, and all indicate that the answer is "yes," if the plaintiff can indeed prove that the professional should have known. In *Jablonski by Pahls v. United States*, (1983), a federal court applying California law found a psychiatrist liable where he failed to warn his client's live-in girlfriend that she was in danger from him. The court ruled that despite a lack of a specific threat against a specific person, the fact that the client had attempted to rape the victim several weeks earlier and had previously served five years in prison for the rape of his spouse, coupled with the psychiatrist's apparent failure to obtain the patient's prior records, indicated that the psychiatrist should have been able to predict the danger to her and should have warned her about it. In *Bardoni v. Kim*, (1986), a Michigan case, a claim against a psychiatrist for failing to warn his client's family members of the client's potential dangerousness to them was allowed to proceed to trial, where the claim was based on a "should have known" allegation rather than on actual knowledge. The court set forth a two-step test in such cases. In order to prevail, a plaintiff must be able to establish (a) that the target of the patient's violence was identified or readily identifiable, and (b) that the psychiatrist should have known, according to the standards of his profession, that the specific person was the target of his patient's serious threat of violence. Using such a standard, a federal court in Michigan found that in a case where a recently released mental patient killed his mother, the psychiatrist was not liable, since the evidence did not support the claim that he "should have known" of the patient's dangerousness *(Soutear v. United States*, 1986).

The standard of care. The second issue addressed in recent *Tarasoff* cases is the question of the standard of care against which a mental health professional's actions are to be measured. In a recent and very important case out of Ohio, the Ohio Supreme Court has indicated that a psychiatrist will not be held liable for the violent acts of a voluntarily hospitalized mental patient after discharge if (a) the patient did not manifest violent propensities while being hospitalized and there was no reason to suspect the patient would become violent after discharge, (b) a thorough evaluation of the patient's propensity for violence was conducted, taking into account all relevant factors, and a good faith decision was made by the psychiatrist that the patient had no violent propensity, or (c) the patient was diagnosed as having violent propensities and, after a thorough evaluation of the severity of the propensities and a balancing of the patient's interests and the interests of potential victims, a treatment plan was formulated in good faith which included discharge of the patient. The case is *Littleton v. Good Samaritan Hospital*, (1988), and it involved the death of a two-and-one-half-month old girl from an overdose of aspirin administered by her mother, a recently released psychiatric patient. The staff psychiatrist, who had been found liable by a jury for failing to protect the child, was given a new trial under the "professional judgment" standard set forth by the court.

The professional judgment standard evolved from cases in New York state dating back to 1898, and it now applies to all cases of professional malpractice. Psychiatrists in New York have been held not liable under this rule for diagnostic decisions, treatment decisions, release decisions, and decisions not to admit to a hospital, as long as a "good faith" and "reasonable" evaluation of relevant factors is made (see cases cited in *Littleton*). In four other recent applications of the rule, two New York courts, in *Mohan v. Westchester County Medical Center* (1988) and *Schrempf v. New York*, (1985), a Colorado court, in *Perreira v. State*, (1989), and a North Carolina federal district court, in *Currie v. United States*, (1986), found no liability on the part of mental health professionals where decisions either to release (in *Mohan* and *Perreira*) or not to commit (in *Schrempf* and *Currie*) were made in accord with a good faith or professional judgment standard. Even in the much-maligned Nebraska federal case of *Lipari v. Sears, Roebuck & Company* (1980), the court noted that no liability would ensue if the mental health professional could show that "due care" was taken. A mere "error in judgment" would not be sufficient basis for the establishment of liability.

Duty to commit. The *Currie* case also addressed the third of the recent issues, which is the question of whether or not *Tarasoff* implies an affirmative duty involuntarily to commit a potentially dangerous client. In *Currie*, a VA patient shot and killed a co-worker.

Shortly before the shooting, the patient threatened to blow up the building where he worked. The company alerted the therapist, who tried unsuccessfully to convince the patient to commit himself for treatment. The therapist warned authorities after determining that the patient could not be committed involuntarily under North Carolina law, and warned the employer of the threats twice. The District Court found that the therapist was not liable for damages, since accepted professional judgment and practice were followed. However, the decision also asserted that the duty to protect third parties may imply a duty to commit. The implications of this case were so distressing that the American Psychological Association filed an *amicus* brief arguing that discretion to commit is not a duty to do so, and that the ruling was unsound as a matter of law and policy. On appeal, the Fourth Circuit Court of Appeals upheld the district court, and ruled specifically that a competent therapist would not be held to have a duty involuntarily to commit a patient. At least three other states (New York, Michigan, and Louisiana) and the federal Eighth Circuit Court of Appeals have refused to impose liability where steps were not taken either to convince an outpatient voluntarily to commit himself or involuntarily to commit him (*Schrempf v. State of New York*, 1985, *Hinkleman v. Borgess Medical Center*, 1987, *Newton v. Department of Health and Human Resources*, (1988), *Abernathy v. United States*, 1985). The only case finding a duty to commit is *Schuster v. Altenberg*, (1988), a Wisconsin case in which a psychiatrist was sued by the spouse and paralyzed daughter of a patient killed in an automobile accident for allegedly failing to warn the patient's family of her dangerous condition and for failure to seek her commitment. The Wisconsin Supreme Court considered the reasoning of the *Currie* court, but disagreed, noting that expert testimony might well show that a therapist exercising reasonable care and professional judgment with respect to a duty to protect should have initiated commitment proceedings. The logic of the *Schuster* court on this matter seems much more persuasive, and is consistent with the APA's reasoning in their *amicus* brief in *Currie*. That is, it seems that under a standard of "professional judgment," it could well be the case that a failure to commit might lead to liability. However, such a failure to commit is best understood as a deviation from the standard of care rather than as a duty question.

Who is protected. The fourth issue that has come up in the *Tara-*

soff cases is whether the doctrine protects the client as well as third parties. That is, does a mental health professional have a duty to protect his or her client under *Tarasoff*? The answer from the cases is clearly no. The doctrine as enunciated in the Restatement of Torts refers only to bodily harm to third parties, and not to the client. Thus, in *Bellah v. Greenson*, (1977), one of the earliest California cases to be decided after *Tarasoff*, the Court held that the duty to protect does not extend either to cases of suicide or to damage to property. Similarly, in *Stepakoff v. Kanter* (1985), the Massachusetts Supreme Court found no duty to protect a patient from suicide. In *Cole v. Taylor* (1981), the Iowa court held that there was no liability where a patient committed a murder and her husband sued the psychiatrist for allegedly failing to prevent the patient from committing the murder, since *Tarasoff* deals only with the duty owed to third parties. However, in an interesting twist, in *Thomasson v. Diethelm*, (1984), an Alabama court dismissed a suit by a respiratory therapist against two physicians who called her to provide treatment to a patient with hepatitis, which she later contracted. That court ruled that there was a duty owed only to patients, and failure to warn her of the hepatitis did not constitute medical malpractice under state statutory law. The *Tarasoff* case was not addressed (and perhaps was not raised), and so common-law tort principles were not discussed.

Liability for breach. The fifth issue to arise is the question of the liability of a mental health professional who actually does act on the duty to protect. In a lower court decision in Pennsylvania, *Hopewell v. Adebimpe*, (1981), a psychiatrist was found liable for breach of confidentiality where he wrote a letter to his client's employer disclosing her remark to him that if harassment on the job did not cease, she would "blow up and hurt someone seriously." Though there is no published opinion, it appears that the psychiatrist was unable to articulate clear clinical justification for his warning. In another case, *Davis v. Monsanto Co.*, (1986), a West Virginia federal court found that a therapist was not liable for invasion of privacy for informing a patient's employer of imminent danger to the patient's wife and his fellow employees, citing a doctrine of "qualified privilege." This doctrine has five elements: (a) good faith, (b) a legitimate interest or duty to be furthered by the statement, (c) a statement limited in scope to that purpose, (d) a proper occasion, and (e) communication in a proper manner and to proper parties only (see Krauskopf & Krauskopf, 1965). In Ohio, case law has carved out such an exception for disclosures "necessary to protect individual or public welfare" (see *Jones v. Stanko*, 1928), and courts in other states are likely to follow suit if given the right case.

Applicability of duty to others. The sixth issue is the extent to which the *Tarasoff* duty applies to mental health professionals other than psychiatrists and psychologists. This issue was addressed by the Vermont Supreme Court in the case of *Peck v. Counseling Service of Addison County, Inc.* (1985; see Stone, 1986 for an in-depth discussion of the case). In *Peck*, a patient made a threat to "get back at his father" by burning down his barn. After securing a promise not to do it, the therapist concluded that Peck would not act out. Six nights later, Peck burned down the barn, which was located only 130 feet from the family residence. The parents sued the Center, claiming negligence on the basis of "the prevailing standards of the mental health profession." The Vermont Supreme Court, in reversing the trial court's dismissal of the case, held that "a mental health professional who knows or, based upon the standards of the mental health profession, should know that his or her patient poses a serious risk of danger to an identifiable victim has a duty to exercise reasonable care to protect him or her from that danger."

The most important aspect of the *Peck* case is that the duty to protect was extended to all mental health professionals (here, the therapist was a certified counselor with an M.A. in educational psychology). Normally, a mental health professional is held to the standard expected of his or her own discipline, but in an organized setting such as a community mental health center, all mental health professionals may be held to some hybrid, "universal" standard. For example, in *Peck* expert testimony indicated that Peck's epilepsy would have influenced a psychiatrist's judgment as to whether he could control himself. While the defendants argued that a counselor with no medical training could not be held to that standard, the Court noted that there was no formal procedure or policy for intra-staff consultation in dangerous patient cases, and found liability nonetheless. Clearly, close coordination across disciplines is critical in such cases (Fulero, 1988).

One might also question whether a *Tarasoff* duty to warn might apply to other professionals outside of mental health fields, such as attorneys. Indeed, Mills (1985) has suggested that even though the *Tarasoff* court based its creation of a duty to protect partly on the assertion that the "special nature" of the therapeutic relationship made the disclosure of certain things more likely and that therapists have expertise in assessing states of mind, such professionals as clergy, employers, judges, probation and parole officers, teachers, general physicians, police, and attorneys all may obtain information from or about individuals that might include threats or the fact of danger. Further, one could argue that such professionals would be equally competent at assessing or predicting dangerousness. Mills advocates legislatively extending *Tarasoff* to require individuals without clinical training who, while acting in an official capacity, believe that another is going to commit a violent or dangerous act, to make a reasonable effort to notify law enforcement officials and the potential victim, if his or her identity is known (Mills, 1985). A growing number of cases have attempted to hold just such individuals liable under *Tarasoff* reasoning. These include probation and parole officers (see, e.g., *Division of Corrections v. Neakok*, 1986, *Sterling v. Bloom*, 1986, *Johnson v. State of California*, 1968, *Reiser v. District of Columbia*, 1978), police officers who fail to arrest a drunk driver who later causes accident or injury (see, e.g., *Ashburn v. Anne Arundel County*, 1986, *Bailey v. Town of Forks*, 1984, *Irwin v. Town of Ware*, 1982), prosecuting attorneys (see, e.g, *Seibel v. City and County of Honolulu*, 1979), physicians who fail to warn the patient of the effect of taking or discontinuing various medications on their driving (see, e.g., *Gooden v. Tips*, 1983, *Myers v. Quesenberry*, 1983, *Duvall v. Goldin*, 1984, *Welke v. Kuzilla*, 1985), or who are not psychiatrists but work in emergency room settings (see, e.g., *Paul v. Plymouth General Hospital*, 1987).

Some cases have been filed against non-professionals based on a *Tarasoff* argument. For example, in *Rozycki v. Peley*, (1984), the parents of a group of minor boys brought suit against the wife of the pedophile who sexually abused the boys, alleging that she knew of her husband's pedophilia and failed to warn the parents or the children of the danger to them. The New Jersey Superior Court ruled that no such duty exists for laypersons, who cannot be held to the higher standard of care reserved for professionals. In *Mangeris v. Gordon* (1978), a taxi driver drove a passenger to and from a massage parlor. The passenger robbed and killed the driver, whose family sued the parlor, alleging that they knew about and failed to warn the driver or to report to the police that the passenger was a fugitive and had committed violent acts. No liability was found, as the parlor did not have the requisite "special relationship" with the driver or with the passenger that is required to create a duty to warn or otherwise protect a third party.

Property damage. The seventh and last issue is whether or not property damage is covered under a *Tarasoff* duty to protect. The *Peck* court in Vermont held that property damage alone could be sufficient for liability (see also *Knight v. Michigan*, 1983). The court reasoned that "arson is a violent act and represents a lethal threat to human beings who may be in the vicinity of the conflagration." This leaves open the question of whether property damage completely separate from any risk of harm to people, such as taking a sledgehammer to someone's car, would be compensable.

CONCLUSION

It seems clear that the issues raised by the *Tarasoff* decision will continue to generate litigation, legislation, and controversy for some time. However, a number of recent decisions have begun to tackle some of the thorny questions raised by the establishment of a duty to protect third parties, and the new cases, coupled with a spate of recent legislative action, should define the boundaries of the duty more clearly over the next five years.

In particular, I would predict that there will be continued attempts to extend the *Tarasoff* principle to other situations or professional relationships, such as that of attorney and client. There will also be more attempts to apply the duty to protect to non-professionals. Why not, for example, hold parents liable for failure to warn a babysitter of a child's nasty disposition and proclivity to dangerous antics (see *Ellis v. D'Angelo*, 1953, for a case in which such liability was found). Indeed, as this broadening of the duty to protect occurs, it will be largely outside the view of mental health professionals, since it will not be seen as relevant to them. In addition, as more states begin to adopt statutes that more precisely define the scope of the duty to protect, cases will increasingly focus on interpreting and "fine-tuning" the statutes rather than on common-law principles or sections of the Restatement of Torts. This will have the effect of making the cases appear somewhat more mundane and less revolutionary, since the major parameters of the duty have already been established. Last, and most importantly, the professional judgment standard enunciated in the *Littleton* case will be adopted by other states. It will become the key to the determination of professional liability in *Tarasoff* situations, and perhaps in mental health malpractice generally. The adoption of this standard will not only more sharply focus the issue of liability, but will also decrease the number of cases in which it is found.

REFERENCES

American Law Institute (1965). *Restatement of Torts 2d., Vol. 2.* St. Paul, MN: American Law Institute.

Cohen, R. (1979). *Malpractice: A guide for mental health professionals.* New York: Free Press.

Fulero, S. (1988). *Tarasoff:* Ten years later. *Professional Psychology: Research and Practice, 19,* 184-190.

Krauskopf, J. & Krauskopf, C. (1965). Torts and psychologists. *Journal of Counseling Psychology, 12,* 227-237.

Mills, M. (1985). Expanding the duties to protect third parties from violent acts. In S. Rachlin (Ed.), *Legal encroachment on psychiatric practice* (pp. 61-68). San Francisco: Jossey-Bass.

Stone, A. (1986). Vermont adopts *Tarasoff:* A real barn-burner. *American Journal of Psychiatry, 143,* 352-355.

Winslade, W. & Ross, J. (1983). *The insanity defense.* New York: Scribner's.

Cases cited:

Abernathy v. United States, 773 F.2d 184 (8th Cir. 1985).

Ashburn v. Anne Arundel County, 510 A.2d 1078 (Md. 1986).

Bailey v. Town of Forks, 688 P.2d 526 (Wash.App. 1984).

Bardoni v. Kim, 390 N.W.2d 218 (Mich.App. 1986).

Bellah v. Greenson, Cal.App.3d, 141 Cal.Rptr. 92 (1977).

Cole v. Taylor, 301 N.W.2d 766 (Iowa 1981).

Currie v. United States, 644 F.Supp. 1074 (M.D.N.C. 1986), affirmed on other grounds, 836 F.2d 209 (4th Cir. 1987).

Davis v. Monsanto Co., 627 F.Supp. 418 (S.D.W.Va. 1986).
Division of Corrections v. Neakok, 721 P.2d 1121 (Alaska 1986).
Duvall v. Goldin, 362 N.W.2d 775 (Mich.App. 1984).
Ellis v. D'Angelo, 116 Cal.App.2d 310, 253 P.2d 675 (1953).
Goodin v. Tips, 651 S.W.2d 364 (Tex.App. 1983).
Hinkelman v. Borgess Medical Center, 403 N.W.2d 547 (Mich.App. 1987).
Hopewell v. Adebimpe, Pa. Ct. Common Pleas (1981).
Irwin v. Town of Ware, 467 N.E.2d 1292 (Mass. 1983).
Jablonski by Pahls v. United States, 712 F.2d 391 (9th Cir. 1983).
Johnson v. State of California, 69 Cal.2d 782, 447 P.2d 352, 73 Cal. Rptr. 240 (1968).
Jones v. Stanko, 118 Ohio St. 147, 160 N.E. 456 (1928).
Knight v. Michigan, 335 N.W.2d 481 (Mich.App. 1983).
Littleton v. Good Samaritan Hospital, 39 Ohio St. 3d 86, 529 N.E. 2d 449 (1988).
Lipari v. Sears, Roebuck & Company, 497 F.Supp.185 (D.Neb. 1980).
Mangeris v. Gordon, 580 P.2d 481 (Nev. 1978).
Mohan v. Westchester County Medical Center, 535 N.Y.S.2d 431 (A.D. 2 Dept. 1988).
Myers v. Quesenberry, 193 Cal.Rptr. 733 (Cal.App. 4 Dist. 1983).
Newton v. Department of Health and Human Resources, 536 So.2d 560 (1988).
Paul v. Plymouth General Hospital, 408 N.W.2d 492 (Mich. App. 1987).
Peck v. Counseling Service of Addison County, 499 A.2d 422 (Vt.1985).
Perreira v. State, 768 P.2d 1198 (Colo. 1989).
Rieser v. District of Columbia, 563 F.2d 462 (D.C. Cir. 1977), modified on other grounds en banc, 580 F.2d 647 (1978).
Rozycki v. Peley, 489 A.2d 1272 (N.J. Super. 1984).
Schrempf v. State of New York, 486 N.Y.S.2d 1010 (A.D. 4 Dept. 1985), reversed, 496 N.Y.S.2d 973, 487 N.E.2d 883 (1985).
Schuster v. Altenberg, 424 N.W.2d 159 (Wis. 1988).
Seibel v. City and County of Honolulu, 602 P.2d 532 (Haw. 1979).
Soutear v. United States, 646 F.Supp. 646 (E.D. Mich. 1986).
Stepakoff v. Kanter, 473 N.E. 2d 1131 (Mass. 1985).
Sterling v. Bloom, 723 P.2d 755 (Idaho 1986).
Tarasoff v. Regents of the University of California, 118 Cal.Rptr. 129, 529 P.2d 533 (1974) (Tarasoff I).
Tarasoff v. Regents of the University of California, 17 Cal.3d 425, 551 P.2d 334 (1976) (Tarasoff II).
Thompson v. County of Alameda, 614 P.2d 728 (Cal. 1980).
Welke v. Kuzilla, 375 N.W.2d 403 (Mich.App. 1985).

Statutory Solutions to Liability in Duty to Protect Situations

David L. Shapiro

The most recent of the duty-to-protect statutes was adopted in Maryland on July 1, 1989. While it has loosely been called a "duty-to-warn" bill, its more accurate title is "Mental Health Care Providers: Limits on Liability." It represents an important step forward in this critically important area. Duty-to-protect situations have been terribly misunderstood by the vast majority of mental health professionals. The Maryland bill represents an attempt by mental health professionals to inform courts of law about the realities of dealing with potentially violent patients.

Because of the vast profusion of case law that has been spawned since the original *Tarasoff* case in California in 1974, thirteen states have now enacted duty-to-warn or duty-to-protect statutes which supersede case law. Maryland's is the latest to be enacted, and is in many ways the most sophisticated. Virtually all of these statutes provide some protection from liability for therapists in duty-to-protect situations (Knapp, VandeCreek, & Shapiro, in press). They are based on a model law that was proposed by APA and thus share many common ingredients. Of interest is the fact that the original APA model proposal included the concept of the clinician working out a treatment plan which in his or her opinion would mitigate or reduce the likelihood of acting out. Establishing and documenting

---

David L. Shapiro, PhD, is in private practice specializing in Forensic Psychology with offices in Baltimore, MD and Washington, DC.

such a treatment plan was to be one of the ways that the clinician could avoid potential liability. This eventually was dropped from the APA proposal because it was believed that this would not "sell." In point of fact, this is precisely the provision which was included in the new Maryland law.

Most of the state statutes define foreseeability of threat in terms of the threat being communicated verbally, or in writing, or through conduct or behavior. The statutes also identify ways for the therapist to discharge the duty so as to avoid incurring liability. There are some major problems in some of the original bills. Several have a "rush to judgment" quality about them because that duty can be discharged by warning the police or the victim, or initiating civil commitment. However, they do not encourage a comprehensive assessment of the potential for violence and do not provide protection for a variety of other therapeutic options, such as voluntary hospitalization, increasing medication, increasing the number of therapy sessions, bringing the intended victim into the session, or referring the patient for medication. Both of these shortcomings, are remedied by the current bill in Maryland.

All of the state statutes, except Kansas and Ohio, define foreseeability and ways to discharge that duty. Ten states define foreseeability as "a threat to an identifiable victim." The Louisiana statute adds that a threat is foreseeable if it is "coupled with an apparent intent and availability of a means to carry out the threat." New Hampshire includes as threatening behavior, "a serious threat of substantial damage to real property." Ten states allow for discharging the duty through warning the potential victim or notifying the police. The Kentucky statute states that if the victim is not identifiable, then the duty can be discharged by notifying the police, while if the victim is identifiable, then apparently he or she should be notified. Five states allow for the discharge of duty through civil commitment, and the State of Colorado allows, in addition to notifying the victim and the police or initiating civil commitment, "other appropriate action," which is apparently unspecified.

Most of the statutes have the following provisions in common. First, the threat to do bodily harm against a third party must be verbalized or articulated by the patient and communicated to the therapist and must name an identifiable third party. This avoids putting the therapist in the predicament of being expected to predict future violent behavior on the basis of conjecture. The therapist, in each of these statutes, must also be convinced that the threat is a genuine one. Most of the statutes, as noted above, allow for the discharge of duty by notification of the authorities, notification of the intended victim or initiation of civil commitment proceedings. Up to this point, the bill in Maryland is identical to previous bills.

Where the Maryland statute goes beyond the others is that it also allows the discharge of duty by the mental health professional through the undertaking of a treatment plan which, in the opinion of the mental health professional, will serve to mitigate or lessen the likelihood of violent acting-out. This is the only statute which has a provision for discharging the duty through a treatment plan, though as noted before, this was part of the original APA model proposal. The treatment plan proviso is of particular importance because it allows the therapist to act as a therapist rather than as a mere extension of law enforcement authorities. It essentially gives the therapist the flexibility of handling the crisis situation in any way which he or she feels is clinically justified, providing that the strategy is clearly documented and based on a comprehensive assessment and treatment plan.

The critical issue becomes whether or not the intervention strategy is based on a clear-cut assessment and treatment plan. This is the only statute that recognizes a point implicit in many recent court decisions: That the relevant standard of care is not the accurate prediction of violent behavior, but rather the performance of a comprehensive assessment so that the way the clinician handles the threat of violence is rational, and coherent, and follows logically from the assessment.

Even going back as far as the final *Tarasoff* decision in 1976, the court noted that warning an intended victim is only one of many possible options within the treatment situation, that the duty was to protect the intended victim against violent behavior. Many clinicians do not realize that there were two separate *Tarasoff* decisions. The initial decision, in 1974, did indeed articulate a duty to warn as a cause of action. Based on briefs filed after this decision, the court reversed its original stand and in 1976 articulated the standard of "duty to protect." The duty to protect gave the clinician a variety of options in protecting the intended victim, basically indicating that anything that is clinically justified within a given situation would be appropriate. In other words, depending on the circumstances, when a therapist is confronted by a patient threatening violent behavior, the therapist might (a) increase the number of therapy sessions, (b) refer the patient for medication evaluation, (c) increase the amount of medication, (d) hospitalize the patient voluntarily, (e) hospitalize the patient involuntarily, (f) bring the intended victim into the therapy session, (g) notify the law enforcement authorities, or (h) warn the intended victim. Any of these would be appropriate as long as the therapist could justify, with reference to the assessment and treatment plan, why he or she was taking one course of action and not another. Whatever course of action was taken would be subject to change based on the situation at any given point in time.

As noted earlier, the majority of case law in this area recognizes that the relevant standard of care is doing the comprehensive assessment, developing a treatment plan based on that assessment, and finally following the treatment plan. Courts are aware that clinicians cannot accurately predict violent behavior; and except in a very few instances, courts have not held clinicians to such a standard. The need for careful assessment and treatment plans, of course, also points to the importance of keeping careful notes, perhaps the best insurance against being successfully sued in a malpractice case (Soisson, VandeCreek, & Knapp, 1987).

Most therapists see the profusion of case law, subsequent to *Tarasoff* as somewhat threatening. However, in many of the cases, there are some important issues which have not been emphasized often.

In *Thompson v. County of Alameda* (1980), and subsequently in *Brady v. Hopper* (1983), the courts recognized that there was no duty unless there was a specifically named, readily identifiable, third party.

In *Lipari v. Sears* (1980), the court ruled that in the absence of an identifiable victim, the therapist could be held liable for possible harm to the public at large. However, this case really does not create an unmanageable burden for therapists. The patient in this case had a history of violent behavior during periods of psychotic decompensation. Given the fact that he was undergoing such a decompensation, it is not unreasonable to expect that an accurate assessment would foresee another round of violent behavior. The therapist in question had not taken adequate steps to control that behavior. That is, the therapist permitted the patient to be discharged against medical advice, rather than initiating civil commitment procedures.

A Pennsylvania case, *Hopewell v. Adibempe* (1987), is an illustration in how not to warn an intended victim. The therapist in this case was treating a woman who made some threats about blowing up her place of employment. Apparently, the therapist did not take the threats seriously but was so fearful of being sued that he disclosed the woman's threats to her employer without telling her that he was planning to do so. He was sued successfully for breach of confidentiality. The therapist did not know that there was no duty-to-warn case law in the State of Pennsylvania at the time.

In the case of *Petersen v. Washington* (1983), there is much unfortunate wording which makes the case sound like it is a duty-to-warn situation. The court stated that the therapist must take reasonable precautions to "protect anyone who might foreseeably be in danger." If one reads the actual case, however, one finds that it is actually neither a duty-to-warn nor duty-to-protect case, but one involving negligent release. The therapist failed to adequately assess the risk of the patient acting-out and failed to take precautions against the patient doing so. The patient in question was demonstrating exceedingly bizarre behavior the very day prior to his discharge, and the bizarre behavior was highly related to the behavior which brought him into the hospital in the first place.

In the case of *Peck v. Counseling Service of Addison County* (1985), a therapist was held liable for failure to take reasonable precautions to prevent her patient, a mentally retarded and epileptic young man, from setting his father's barn on fire. This court extended the duty-to-protect doctrine to property damage. However, the court also raised an important additional issue, namely that given the patient's history of alcohol abuse, a seizure disorder, mental retardation, and assaultive behavior, the therapist might have been practicing out of the bounds of her competence by not obtaining independent consultation, or not obtaining prior records. She had merely obtained a promise from the patient that he would not burn down his father's barn, but she failed to consult with her supervisors.

The case of *Jablonski v. United States* (1983), presents a rather ominous precedent, suggesting that even if a direct threat is not made, an intended victim would be reasonably foreseeable if he or she fit the profile of prior victims. However, even in this case, the court commented on the necessity for a comprehensive assessment. In this case the psychiatric staff did not consult or review prior medical records and did not pay attention to the concerns of the police who brought Mr. Jablonski to the hospital. This, once again, reflects the court's awareness of the need for a comprehensive assessment.

Two recent cases, one from the Fourth Circuit Court of Appeals and another from the District of Columbia Circuit, illustrate these observations even further. In *Currie v. United States* (1987), the court held that a Veterans Administration Hospital was not libel essentially because the staff members had acted in good faith in managing the patient. The patient, a Viet Nam veteran suffering from post-traumatic stress disorder, had threatened to destroy the IBM Building. The staff at the Veterans Administration who were treating the patient at the time became very concerned, carefully evaluated the veteran psychiatrically and psychologically, held staff conferences, consulted with outside colleagues, and ultimately concluded that the patient did not satisfy the criteria for involuntary civil commitment. They, therefore, felt that they needed to warn the staff at IBM, which they did. When the patient subsequently did act out, the family of one of the victims sued, but the court, both at the trial court level and at the appellate level, held that the hospital was not negligent because the hospital had adhered to the relevant standard of care, namely the performance of the comprehensive assessment.

In a similar manner, in the case from the DC Circuit, *White v. United States* (1986), the patient, Dwayne White, had discussed in psychotherapy fantasies of hurting his wife. The therapist had determined, based on a careful assessment, and consultation with a supervisor and colleagues, and comprehensive psychological testing, that this was an isolated fantasy that could be dealt with in psychotherapy, rather than requiring a breach of the confidentiality to warn the victim. White subsequently did injure his wife. The court held that the therapist was not liable because she had adhered to the relevant standard of care, namely, once again, the performance of a comprehensive assessment.

CONCLUSION

The Maryland statute is the only one to date which explicitly incorporates the thinking in these various court decisions that as long as therapists carefully think through the issues, do a comprehensive assessment, and base their treatment plans on that assessment, they should be insulated from liability. This does not, of course, mean that a victim's family or a victim might not initiate a lawsuit, but rather that the likelihood of that lawsuit succeeding would be minimal, since the therapist did adhere to the relevant standard of care for the profession. In order to demonstrate malpractice, in other words, the plaintiff must always demonstrate that the therapist had deviated from an established standard of care. It should also be noted that in the new law in Maryland, consistent with other state statutes, if confidentiality is breached, and a victim is warned, and the violence does not occur, the therapist is immune from liability for the breach of the confidentiality.

The Maryland bill is an important step forward and should provide a great deal of comfort to the clinicians who have been running scared because of the profusion of case law in the duty-to-protect area. Hopefully, other states that are considering duty-to-protect statutes will consider this bill in their review. It also is of some comfort and satisfaction that despite the reservations initially shown by APA, mental health professionals in Maryland were able to "sell" to the legislature the idea of a treatment plan being part of the statute. The statute should ultimately remind the therapist of a statement made in the *Tarasoff* case: "A therapist can be wrong without being negligent."

REFERENCES

Brady v. Hopper, 570 F. Supp. 1333 (D. Colo. 1983).
Currie v. United States, 836 F.2d 209 (4th Cir. 1987).
Hopewell v. Adibimpe. (1982). *Pittsburgh Legal Journal*, *130*, 107-109, No. G.D. 78-28756 (Common Pleas of Allegheny Co.).
Jablonski v. United States, 712 F.2d 391 (9th Cir. 1983).
Knapp, S., VandeCreek, L., & Shapiro, D. (in press). Statutory remedies to the "Duty to Protect": A reconsideration. *Psychotherapy*.
Lipari v. Sears, 479 F. Supp. 185 (D. Neb. 1980).
Peck v. Counseling Service of Addison County, Inc., 499 A.2d 422 (Vt. 1985).
Petersen v. Washington, 671 P.2d 230 (Wash. 1983).
Soisson, E., VandeCreek, L., & Knapp, S. (1987). Thorough record keeping: A good defense in a litigious era. *Professional Psychology*, *18*, 498-502.
Tarasoff v. Regents of the University of California, 13 Cal.3d 177, 529 P.2d 533 (1974) *vacated*, 17 Cal. 3d 425, 551 P.2d 334 (1976).
Thompson v. County of Alameda, 614 P.2d 728 (1980).
White v. United States, 780 F.2d 97 (D.C. Cir. 1986).

Public Policy Issues in Applying the "Duty to Protect" to HIV-Positive Patients

Samuel Knapp
Leon VandeCreek

Acquired Immune Deficiency Syndrome (AIDS) is the most dangerous epidemic of the twentieth century. Any "magic bullet" cure or vaccine for AIDS, however, is likely to be decades away. The Human Immunodeficiency Virus (HIV), the precursor for AIDS, is most commonly transmitted through intimate sexual contact, especially unprotected anal intercourse, through intravenous drug use, or through birth from mother to child. Consequently, the optimal way to stop the spread of AIDS is through encouraging persons to change high-risk behaviors.

Currently about 100,000 Americans are infected with AIDS (CDC, 1989). In addition, it is estimated that between 1 to 1.5 million Americans have the HIV infection and will develop AIDS or AIDS Related Complex (ARC) in the next decade.

AIDS AND CONFIDENTIALITY

The spread of AIDS has led to questions regarding the limits of confidentiality in the psychotherapeutic relationship. This issue is

---

Samuel Knapp, PhD, is Professional Affairs Officer of the Pennsylvania Psychological Association.

Leon VandeCreek is Chairperson of the Indiana University of Pennsylvania Department of Psychology.

The views expressed do not necessarily represent those of the Pennsylvania Psychological Association.

especially important when the HIV-positive patient is engaging in high risk behavior with a partner who is unaware of the partner's infectious status. The question of limited disclosure with HIV-positive patients involves the collision of two important values: protection of the privacy of the patient, and protection of the welfare of the community. HIV-positive patients have an even greater need for protection of the privacy of their communications than other psychotherapy patients. HIV patients usually belong to high-risk groups such as gays or drug abusers who already suffer social stigma because of their lifestyle. In addition, many members of the public have an unrealistic fear of HIV contagion and consequently discriminate against HIV-positive persons.

On the other hand, AIDS is a catastrophic, chronic, and eventually fatal condition that can be prevented only by eliminating high risk behavior. Psychotherapists may have a responsibility to protect identifiable victims from contracting the HIV infection.

How should a psychotherapist respond to a patient who, in the course of psychotherapy, discloses that he or she tests HIV positive? The patient may also reveal that he or she has an identifiable sexual or needle sharing partner who is not aware of this infection. Does the psychotherapist have an obligation to warn the identifiable partner?

Fortunately, anecdotal reports suggest that effective psychotherapy can encourage many HIV infected persons to reveal their infection voluntarily to significant others (Howe, 1988; Perry, 1989). A patient's revealing information about endangering a partner within psychotherapy is a healthy sign of legitimate concern for another person. It is likely that this concern can usually be mobilized so that patients will warn their partners voluntarily. In addition, research indicates that persons who want to change their high risk behavior and stop endangering others, can do so with proper treatment (e.g., Kelly & St. Lawrence, 1988).

Nevertheless, it is feared that some patients will not voluntarily disclose their status to their partners (Kegeles, Catania, & Coates, 1988). Consequently, psychotherapists rightfully ask whether the "duty to protect" doctrine enunciated in *Tarasoff v Regents of the University of California* (1976), applies to HIV-positive persons. Specifically, should psychotherapists consider warning identifiable victims of the infectious status of a partner when the patient refuses to do so?

DOES THE "DUTY TO PROTECT" DOCTRINE APPLY?

According to *Tarasoff*, confidentiality within psychotherapy is to be valued highly, but is never absolute. Instead, confidentiality is measured against the degree of threat to specific individuals. "The protective privilege ends where the public peril begins" (*Tarasoff*, p. 337).

Of course, the *Tarasoff* decision did not require that psychotherapists always warn the intended victim. Instead, the *Tarasoff* decision held that the duty to protect can be discharged in a variety of ways, "including warning the intended victim or others likely to apprise the victim of the danger, notifying the police, or taking whatever steps are reasonably necessary under the circumstances" (p. 334). Notifying the police would not be a reasonable option in protecting an identifiable victim about possible HIV infection, but notifying public health authorities might be.

Since the California Supreme Court decided *Tarasoff*, 14 states have passed "duty to protect" statutes that define or limit the potential liability of psychotherapists under the duty to protect (Knapp, VandeCreek, & Shapiro, in press). As a rule these statutes apply to potentially assaultive patients only and would not necessarily be applicable to persons who pose a danger to others through infectious diseases.

Arguments in Favor of Applying Tarasoff Duty to Protect

Nevertheless, it can be argued a doctrine similar to a duty to protect would apply to HIV-positive persons who endanger others. *Tarasoff* and other decisions regarding the duty to protect were based on long-standing precedents dealing with the duty of physicians to protect third persons from infectious diseases (e.g., *Simonson v. Swenson*, 1920; *Skillings v. Allen*, 1919; *Wojcik v. Aluminum Co. of America*, 1959). The application of the duty to warn with

AIDS would not be so much an extension of *Tarasoff*; rather, *Tarasoff* is an extension of a long legal tradition dealing with the duty to warn third persons of infectious diseases.

Those who favor applying a duty to protect doctrine with AIDS also emphasize the public safety rationale as a compelling reason why it should apply to persons who are HIV positive. Although confidentiality is to be valued highly and every attempt should be made to effect a voluntary disclosure, it is argued that the therapist has a duty to act to protect members of the public (Bisbing, 1988; Council on Ethics and Judicial Affairs of the American Medical Association, 1988; Eth, 1988; Gostin & Curran, 1987; Kaplan, Sager, & Schiavi, 1985, 1986; Peter & Sanchez, 1987; Rosencranz & Lavey, 1987; Walters, 1988).

Evaluation of Arguments Against Applying a Duty to Protect Doctrine

Those who argue against the application of a duty to protect to HIV-positive patients have emphasized five points: (a) the difficulty in identifying potential victims (Perry, 1989), (b) the difficulty in predicting imminent harm (Girardi, Keese, Traver, & Cooksey, 1988), (c) the apparent inappropriateness of requiring psychotherapists to make *medical* decisions about AIDS (Girardi, Keese, Traver, & Cooksey, 1988), (d) the argument that the potential victim likely knew the dangers of the high risk behaviors and participated voluntarily (Perry, 1989), and (e) that the maintenance of absolute confidentiality "would reduce the overall spread of HIV and thereby more effectively protect the general public" (Perry, 1989, p. 159; see also Girardi, Keese, Traver, & Cooksey, 1988). Each of these reasons will be evaluated below.

Identifiable Victims

The *Tarasoff* decision only creates a duty when there is an identifiable victim. Applying a similar duty to protect doctrine to HIV-positive patients would be appropriate only when sexual or drug partners are readily identifiable. The *Tarasoff* court stated that

> It would be unreasonable to require the therapist to interrogate the patient to discover the victim's identity or to conduct an independent investigation but . . . there may be cases in which a moment's reflection will reveal the victim's identity; hence [the] matter is one which depends on the circumstances of each case. (p. 336)

However, it is likely that at least one or some partners may be identifiable readily; so this argument cannot be used to support the general non-application of a duty to protect.

Infectiousness Is Too Hard to Predict

Difficulty in predicting dangerousness is not a legitimate argument either. Admittedly, it is difficult to predict transmission of the HIV virus. The ability of AIDS to be transmitted varies according to many factors such as the practice of vaginal versus anal intercourse, the effective use of condoms, the presence of coexisting sexually transmitted diseases, and the state of the immune system of the potential victim (Friedland & Klein, 1987).

Nevertheless, the *Tarasoff* court held that "the therapist need only exercise that reasonable degree of skill, knowledge and care ordinarily possessed and exercised by members of the profession under similar circumstances" (p. 336). Although psychotherapists may have an imperfect ability to predict the infectiousness of the sexual or needle sharing behavior, they are required to use whatever knowledge exists to make a reasonable prediction.

Non-Medical Psychotherapists Should Not Assess the Dangerousness of Infections

The argument is made that non-medical psychotherapists should not be liable for assessing the danger from AIDS because it is a medical condition and not a psychological disorder. Girardi, Keese, Traver, and Cooksey (1988) argued that

> People do not go to psychotherapists to be diagnosed, tested or treated for AIDS. They go to psychotherapists in order to deal with emotional problems, behavioral problems and conditions of the mind. (p. 17)

This argument does not appear compelling. Although non-medical psychotherapists may not diagnose AIDS, they should know more about the behaviors that lead to its transmission than the laboratory or medical personnel who identify the virus. Psychologists do not have to be experts in guns or ballistics in order to conclude that patients are serious in their intent to shoot someone. Similarly, they do not have to be able to diagnose the HIV infection to know that certain behaviors place another person at risk of infection.

The Victim Should Know the Risk Without Being Warned

A fourth argument is that the potential victim should have known about the risks and therefore engaged in the high-risk behavior voluntarily. This argument could apply to some partners, but not likely to all. It is true that sharing needles and engaging in casual sex, especially involving unprotected anal intercourse, are risky behaviors. But some post-*Tarasoff* courts have concluded that the duty to protect should apply even when partners already know of the potential dangers (e.g., *Jablonski v. United States* 1983). Such courts have argued that a warning from a professional would more clearly underscore the danger to the potential victim. In addition, some partners of HIV-positive persons live under the "illusion of monogamy" or "illusion of safety" because they trusted the word of a partner and, not recognizing their behaviors as being of high-risk, they have been lulled into a false sense of security. The duty to protect might apply to these identifiable victims who had no reason to believe that they were assuming risks.

Public Safety Is Better Protected by Absolute Confidentiality

The final argument against the application of a duty to protect is that the shield of absolute confidentiality would eventually lead to better protection for the public. It is argued that a duty to protect, even if narrowly limited to identifiable victims like the original *Tarasoff* decision, would drive HIV-infected persons from psychotherapy, closing the window of opportunity to assist them in changing high-risk behaviors. Although one potential victim may have been saved by a warning, the original patient who drops out of therapy, it is argued, may continue to engage in high-risk behaviors and infect others (Perry, 1989). This shield of absolute confidentiality is especially important because the populations most at risk of HIV infection today include gays and drug abusers who have traditionally felt alienated from the mainstream of society and from traditional psychotherapy.

Furthermore, other persons who are HIV positive may be deterred from seeking psychotherapy if absolute confidentiality is not assured (Girardi, Keese, Traver, & Cooksey, 1988). "The real battle against the spread of HIV involves individuals who do not seek our help to reduce their risk behaviors" (Perry, p. 160).

Although we have no data either supporting or contradicting this final argument, it appears to have some face validity.

CONCLUSIONS AND RECOMMENDATIONS

Perhaps the most important questions to be answered in regard to the application of a duty to protect doctrine to HIV-positive persons concern which policy best protects the public. Will the public be best protected by applying the duty to protect to HIV-positive patients who threaten others? Or will the public be best protected by providing an absolute shield of confidentiality?

Public policy decisions should not, however, be made by the courts. Instead, they properly belong to the legislature where the merits of the issue can be discussed in public debate. In the meantime, the courts will have to decide these issues on the basis of common law precedents which, in our analysis, strongly favor application of a duty to protect to HIV-positive persons who pose a risk to infect others.

We should not wait for the courts to resolve this issue through case law. Instead, we need to determine the optimal approach through statutory change.

In our view, the optimal strategy would be to promote legislation that would allow psychotherapists the discretion to warn identifiable victims, but not require them to do so. This would allow psychotherapists to continue to work with HIV-positive patients and attempt to get them to alter high-risk behaviors. At the same time it would permit psychotherapists to use their discretion for situations in which behavior change is unlikely to occur and issuing a warning to an identifiable victim is the only means to protect an identifiable potential victim.

These laws could either allow psychotherapists, after exhausting attempts to encourage a voluntary disclosure by the patient, to make the warning themselves or to report the infectious status to a public health agency which could then implement the warning.

Although we recommend a carefully delineated exception to confidentiality described above, we believe this exception should occur only in the context of laws assuring privacy for HIV-positive persons. A strong AIDS confidentiality law has been enacted in California (California Statutes, Health and Safety Code, Division 1.1, chapter 1.20, section 199.25). This law, however, provides for discretion and immunity for warning potential victims only to physicians and not to non-medical psychotherapists. The public welfare would be enhanced by providing a similar warning mechanism for non-medical psychotherapists within these statutes.

Until the legal obligations are clarified, we can give no blanket recommendation to psychotherapists caught in this legal and ethical dilemma. Fortunately, many psychotherapists can avoid this dilemma by encouraging patients to disclose their infection status voluntarily. The psychotherapist may be able to increase the likelihood of such disclosures by developing a good relationship with the patient, involving the intended victim in psychotherapy, and speaking frankly and knowledgeably to the patient about the risks involved.

Because most laws presently provide no guidance when such a voluntary disclosure is not forthcoming, psychotherapists are placed in a difficult situation. They could have legal liability if they warned a potential victim or they could have legal liability if they did not issue such a warning. Psychotherapists should seek consultation to help them formulate an ethical response consistent with their values.

REFERENCES

Bisbing, S. (1988). Psychiatric patients and AIDS: Evolving law and liability. *Psychiatric Annals*, *18*, 582-586.

Council on Ethical and Judicial Affairs, American Medical Association. (1988). Ethical issues involved in the growing AIDS crisis. *Journal of the American Medical Association*, *259*, 1360-1361.

CDC (1989). Update: Acquired Immunodeficiency Syndrome—United States,

1981-1988. *Journal of the American Medical Association, 261*, 2609, 2613, 2617.

Eth, S. (1988). The sexually active, HIV infected patient: Confidentiality versus duty to protect. *Psychiatric Annals, 18*, 571-576.

Friedland, G., & Klein, R. (1987). Transmission of the human immunodeficiency virus. *New England Journal of Medicine, 317*, 1125-1135.

Girardi, J., Keese, R., Traver, L. B., & Cooksey, D. (1988). Psychotherapist responsibility in notifying individuals at risk for exposure to HIV. *The Journal of Sex Research, 25*, 1-27.

Gostin, L., & Curran, W. (1987). AIDS screening, confidentiality, and the duty to warn. *American Journal of Public Health, 77*, 361-365.

Howe, E. (1988). Ethical aspects of military physicians treating service persons with HIV/Part Three: The duty to protect third parties. *Military Medicine, 153*, 140-144.

Jablonski v. United States, 712 F.2d 391 (9th Cir. 1983).

Kaplan, H., Sager, C., & Schiavi, R. (1985). Editorial: AIDS and the sex therapist. *Journal of Sex and Marital Therapy, 12*, 210-214.

Kaplan, H., Sager, C., & Schiavi, R. (1986). Editorial: Preventing the spread of AIDS. *Journal of Sex and Marital Therapy, 12*, 159-164.

Kegeles, T., Catania, J., & Coates, T. (1988). Intentions to communicate positive HIV antibodies status to sex partners [Letter to the Editor]. *Journal of the American Medical Association, 259*, 216-217.

Kelly, J., & St. Lawrence, J. (1988). *The AIDS Health Crisis.* NY: Plenum.

Knapp, S., VandeCreek, L., & Shapiro, D. (in press). Statutory remedies to the "duty to protect." *Psychotherapy: Theory, Research, and Practice.*

Perry, S. (1989). Warning third parties at risk for AIDS: APA's policy is a barrier to treatment. *Hospital and Community Psychiatry, 40*, 158-161.

Peter, A., & Sanchez, H. (1987). The therapist's duty to disclose communicable diseases. *Western State University Law Review, 14*, 465-478.

Rosencranz, H., & Lavey, H. (1987). Treating patients with communicable diseases: Limiting liability for physicians and safeguarding the public health. *Saint Louis University Law Journal, 32*, 75-101.

Simonson v. Swenson, 177 N.W. 831 (1920).

Skillings v. Allen, 173 N.W. 663 (1919).

Tarasoff v. Regents of the University of California et al., 551 P. 2d 334 (1976).

Walters, L. (1988). Ethical issues in the prevention and treatment of HIV infection and AIDS. *Science, 219*, 597-603.

Wojcik v. Aluminum Co. of America, 183 NYS 2d 351 (1959).

SYMPOSIUM: ALTERNATE TREATMENT METHODS FOR REDUCING MARITAL VIOLENCE

Introduction: Treatment Approaches at Various Stages in Abusive Relationships

Robert Geffner

A major problem facing our society in recent years is family violence; several governmental agencies have now labeled family violence as an epidemic due to the large prevalence rates (nearly one in every four families). Clinicians are also reporting that clients involved in abusive relationships comprise a larger percentage of their caseload than previously. However, few training programs or workshops are devoted to specific techniques or strategies for treating these clients. Thus, the purpose of a symposium that was presented

Robert Geffner, PhD, is Associate Professor of Psychology at the University of Texas at Tyler and is Director of the Family Violence and Treatment Program. He also maintains a private practice.

Presented at the Annual Mid-Winter Meeting of Divisions 29, 42 and 43 of the American Psychological Association, Orlando, FL, March, 1989.

to the Midwinter Conference of Divisions 29, 42, and 43 of the American Psychological Association in 1989 was to discuss specific approaches and practical suggestions for treating those who are involved in various stages of abusive relationships. The following three articles are taken from the presentations at this symposium.

The first article focuses on comprehensive family therapy with abusive couples in various stages of crisis. This approach is based upon the use of a re-parental bond in a therapeutic stance and fear-of-loss techniques. Using healthy/remedial re-parenting, the therapist can focus on gaps in family-of-origin issues by varying paradoxical, cognitive-behavioral, and directive techniques. The abuse is reduced as the intrapersonal and interpersonal dynamics change. Conjoint therapy is often utilized in this approach. The authors founded and direct The Institute for Comprehensive Family Therapy in Spring House, Pennsylvania. This institute is a post-graduate training center for family therapists. The Kirschners have written a book concerning their approach (Kirschner & Kirschner, 1986), and are involved in numerous workshops concerning the treatment of dysfunctions in the family. Specific suggestions for using these therapy techniques are presented.

The second article focuses on abusive couples who are in the process of separation/divorce or contemplating such action. There has been substantial debate as to whether mediation can be successful for couples who have a history of spouse abuse. The major issue involves power since mediation often assumes a relatively equal distribution of power. Thus, mediation with these couples must include techniques to empower the victim of abuse while reducing the intimidation of the abuser. This can be accomplished when certain guidelines are followed in the treatment of these couples. Specific mediation techniques for identifying and working with these couples is presented. The author is founder and director of the Family Violence Research and Treatment Program at the University of Texas at Tyler. This program includes research and treatment for spouse abuse and sexual abuse as well as a national clearinghouse for all aspects of family violence. The *Family Violence Bulletin* is published quarterly by this clearinghouse. Geffner has also been a co-author of two treatment manuals for reducing spouse abuse (Mantooth, Geffner, Franks, & Patrick, 1987; Franks, Geffner, Laney, Mantooth, & McGaughey, 1988) as well as several book chapters.

The final article focuses on treatment techniques for battered women in the aftermath stage of the violence. Once the risk of violence in a relationship has been reduced, either by separation/divorce or with therapy, the victims must deal with several issues as part of their own healing and recovery. Specific techniques are presented for reducing post-traumatic stress disorder, improving self-esteem, and constructively dealing with the victim's anger. The author is the director of the Family Violence Program at Nova University in Fort Lauderdale, Florida. This is an applied clinical research program, and she is the director of clinical training. Dutton-Douglas has written several chapters concerning the treatment of battered women, and she is the author of a recent book entitled, "Psychological Trauma of Women Battering: Assessment and Treatment."

The authors of the three articles are experienced clinicians who have treated violent couples in a variety of settings; as stated above, two are also researchers who direct family violence programs in different universities. Even though the approaches of each are somewhat different, and each article focuses on different stages of abusive relationships, common themes are apparent. The crucial issues consist of helping both the abuser and the abused deal with power, control and intimidation so that both are empowered in appropriate ways. The goal of all three approaches is to reduce the abusiveness and intimidation so that re-victimization does not occur.

Comprehensive Family Therapy in the Treatment of Spouse Abuse

Diana Adile Kirschner
Sam Kirschner

JoAnn, a young attractive social worker of Italian descent in her early 30's was on the phone, sobbing. "I asked Frank about his car business and he started screaming and slapped me" she whispered. Her therapist (the senior author) asked where Frank, her husband of the past three years, was. "He's in the living room and I'm afraid" she replied. The therapist couldn't blame her.

JoAnn was but one of approximately 3-4 million women who are abused by husbands, ex-husbands, paramours and boyfriends in this country each year according to the National Center on Women & Family Law in New York City. A number of researchers including Martin (1976) and Dobash & Dobash (1977) have suggested that sexual inequality in society is a primary factor in wife battering. Because of this societally condoned inequality, men have used violence as a means of maintaining control and power over their wives. The literature on family violence has shown that there are both individual and systemic contributors to spouse abuse. For example, Bandura's frustration-aggression model (1973) has been offered as an example of how men have learned how to be aggressive as a way of dealing with frustration and anger. Walker (1979), on the other hand, has used Seligman's "learned helplessness" concept to explain how women have learned to stay in abusive relationships by maintaining impotent positions relative to the abuser.

Diana Adile Kirschner, PhD, and Sam Kirschner, PhD, are in private practice, at the Institute for Comprehensive Family Therapy, Spring House, PA.

A number of systemic concepts have also been offered as explanations for the maintenance of family violence. Kalmuss (1984) has argued that spouse abuse is transmitted through an inter-generational process in which children who were either abused and/or witnessed intra-marital violence have a greater likelihood of becoming spouse abusers themselves. Other systemic theorists have scrutinized the feedback mechanisms of the couple's interactional patterns. In this view, victims inadvertently tend to reinforce the violent behavior by either becoming more compliant or by not punishing the abuser for his actions (Giles-Sims, 1983). As a result, violence becomes a primary way of establishing homeostasis in the couple.

From a treatment standpoint, therefore, both individual and systemic issues need to be addressed in order to change the historic patterns of violence and to help establish more productive ways of relating.

Comprehensive Family Therapy, (CFT), the approach used in the case of JoAnn and Frank, is an integration of individual, marital, and family therapy which seems to show promise in the treatment of spouse abuse. In the treatment, each spouse is worked with individually while couples' work is done in conjoint sessions. In a book we have co-authored, *Comprehensive Family Therapy* (Kirschner & Kirschner, 1986) we describe three key strategies in the work: (1) the therapist assumes the role of a healing, reparental figure who is empowering to both the man and the woman; (2) the therapist uses a fear-of-loss strategy to reverse the balance of power in the relationship and, (3) the therapist mobilizes the spouses' resources for healing and reparenting each other so that they can escape the repetitive and painful dramas from the past that they tend to play out together.

Because of time considerations, today's discussion will outline only the first two strategies. Let's start with number one: The therapist assumes the role of a healing transference figure with each spouse. This is necessary because, as the literature suggests, spouses who enter therapy with spouse abuse as the presenting problem suffer from severe individual problems in addition to their marital dysfunction. The abused woman often has strong fears of abandonment and of being alone, which keep her in the relationship. She may experience herself as weak and worthless, and often expresses responsibility for causing her companion's violent behavior. She is frequently out of touch with her anger and has not developed her own goal-directed instrumentality or power in the world. In the abused woman, anger is often turned inward with the result that she experiences pervasive and chronic depressive feelings and exhibits all the symptoms of "learned helplessness." Oftentimes, her mother had a similar kind of gender identification as a weak impotent woman and behaved in accordance with rigid role prescriptions in her marriage. In JoAnn's case, her mother was an overweight depressed housewife for whom she had little respect. Her mother had suffered for 40 years with her father's periodic alcoholic rages.

The male abuser may also present with strong fears of abandonment. His gender identification is typically that of the "macho" man who denies his own "femininity." Feelings of emotional vulnerability are taboo for him as he strives to prove his potency and masculinity through excessive demands and bullying of the spouse. Supporting this pattern of behavior, of course, is his profound sense of weakness and fear of being found out as an "imposter," that is as a weak man.

In our case, Frank showed a similar pattern of intrapsychic conflict and interpersonal dysfunction. When he was growing up, both of his parents had preferred his older brother to him. He received attention by being the "bad boy." His father was mostly distant except when he became verbally and physically abusive to Frank. Frank's mother was weak in relation to his father and would not protect Frank. She remained a distant figure in Frank's life. Thus, Frank's models for living and loving involved for the most part either emotional disengagement or the contact of abusive punishment.

Frank was initially highly mistrustful of the therapist. When JoAnn had first consulted Diana about her stormy marriage – Frank had been quite threatened. He had called to say that he was angry about her "messing" with his marriage and that if anything went wrong he would be sure to make trouble for her with her "boss" and anyone else he could think of. Frank was a tall strapping Italian man, also in his 30's, a man given to anger, threats and shady practices in the used car business he had started in the previous year. Diana had to engage him in the treatment by taking initiative in courting and bonding him.

You might ask: Why invest in having Frank join in treatment? It has been our experience in Comprehensive Family Therapy that the therapist can fulfill the clients' dual goals of stopping the violence while avoiding marital breakup if both husband and wife participate in treatment. Quite often if the woman enters treatment alone, and the husband is not engaged, she may become empowered and will not tolerate the violence. Unfortunately, this may not result in a rebirth of the marriage but rather in its demise. The ensuing breakup, especially where there are children, will result in further heartbreak and economic and social hardships. Thus, our goal in CFT is ideally to treat both of the spouses and their marital transactions as well. Of course, in instances of extreme violence with danger to life and limb, we counsel women to simply disappear and leave the marriage. The husband is not engaged in treatment.

This paper describes an approach useful for less severe abuse. In these milder to moderate cases, the strategy is to engage both spouses in individual and couples therapy with the same practitioner. In the individual sessions the therapist helps repair the deficits in the self created in the families of origin of each spouse. Typically, with the abused woman, the therapist provides a corrective mothering experience. She bonds as a caring empathic authority figure who also models toughness and strength. She actively prizes the woman to build the self-esteem and empowerment so vital for her escape from the helpless victim role.

In individual sessions with JoAnn, Diana began to function as a strong mother figure. She empathized and held her as she wept and expressed her self-hatred after Frank's violent episodes. She also modeled anger and instrumentality by talking about how she would feel and behave if someone tried to abuse her. As the relationship unfolded Diana began to compare JoAnn with a beautiful orchid. In one session she brought her an orchid to concretize the metaphor. As Diana talked with her about the kind of caring behaviors she deserved from Frank, she was simultaneously demonstrating those behaviors to her. JoAnn's self-esteem increased. After 13 months of weekly individual treatment, she became more assertive, asked her boss for a raise, and wound up being promoted at work. JoAnn began to dress more fashionably and displayed greater confidence in her speech and posture.

As we had mentioned before, Diana had to take the initiative in reaching out to engage Frank in treatment. After securing JoAnn's approval, she used the strategy of commiserating with him about his marriage. By telephone she sympathetically asked Frank about his complaints about JoAnn, who in her own passive aggressive way, had really hurt him. Diana invited him to "tell more about her screw ups" and he jumped at the opportunity. She was thus able to transition him into treatment, where he spent three sessions enumerating his laundry list of complaints. In this empathic context, Frank began to relax and bond with Diana as a potential ally. Meanwhile, Diana filled JoAnn in on what she was saying to Frank lest he undermine Diana's relationship with her by suggesting that Diana was more sympathetic to him and that everything was her fault.

In the next phase of the dyadic work with Frank, he opened up even further. He shared pivotal and painful early familial experiences in which his father had repeatedly abused him. Frank confessed that he, like his father, had a "monster" inside him, a monster he was afraid of and could not control. Like most other abusers, Frank was starved for a relationship in which he could talk openly and honestly about himself without feeling weak and impotent. Frank began to respect Diana and enjoyed coming to sessions. At some points in the therapy, he was even more enthusiastic about attending sessions than JoAnn. Little by little Diana was able to validate his experiences and feelings and prize his hidden vulnerable self. As a new kind of father figure she talked with him about being a "real man"—one who has balls enough to express himself—that is his emotions, frustrations, and needs honestly without recourse to violence.

After a year of weekly individual sessions, Diana had Frank practice asking for attention and nurturance in role plays in which she either took his role or that of JoAnn. In the former instance, she modeled for him how a man can ask for what he needs or express his anger appropriately while simultaneously putting Frank in the "female" role which helped him get in touch with his feminine side. Both the behavioral rehearsal and reeducative aspects of the role plays helped reduce Frank's anxiety such that he began to express both his frustrations and his wants in a clearer non-threatening way.

We will return to this case shortly, but first let us examine how the individual therapeutic relationships are related to and are necessary for implementing the second strategy in CFT, that is, the fear-of-loss strategy. In this maneuver, the therapist uses the spouses' fears of abandonment to fuel personal and interpersonal growth. Carefully, utilized by a skilled clinician the fear-of-loss strategy appears to be successful in ultimately stopping abusive behavior. There are three prerequisite conditions which must be met before using the fear-of-loss strategy. They are: (1) the woman has to become personally empowered in terms of her assertiveness and instrumentality; (2) the man has begun to accept and express his feelings of vulnerability and neediness; (3) both spouses have to be closely bonded to the therapist. The individual reparental work is organized around these three prerequisites. The spouses are strengthened both behaviorally and emotionally. The therapist's dyadic bond with each spouse tends to have a stabilizing effect which helps to contain anxiety. This prepares the couple for the inevitable separation maneuvers which usually occur at some point in treatment.

In these fear-of-loss maneuvers the therapist works to reverse the power structure of the relationship by encouraging the woman to take the upper hand and discipline her husband through a strategic use of abandonment. The tactics range on a continuum that includes sleeping in another room, refusing sex, leaving for a night or a weekend, legally separating for a month to a year or even filing for divorce. In each case the therapist can select a fear-of-loss maneuver based on the couple's history and tolerance for anxiety. Often the therapist can start with a less threatening maneuver based on the couple's own wishes or prior attempts at fear-of-loss. If this is not effective, she can then escalate to a stronger maneuver. In general the maneuver should be strong enough to let the abuser know his wife means business, but not so strong as to destroy all hope for the marriage. The maneuvers are designed to fully empower the wife so that she can use her anger in a way that frees her from her sense of impotence in the marriage, and to motivate the husband to grow out of his infantile behavior. The fear-of-loss strategy alters the contingencies which have supported violence since it is so aversive and punitive to the abuser. As the homeostasis is upended, real change can occur in the couple.

Let us now return to our case. After 10 months of treatment, JoAnn started the fear-of-loss process when she indicated that she did not have sex with Frank for 3 days after one of his outbursts. Diana seized on that and suggested that after the next outburst she not only refuse sex, but sleep in the spare bedroom as well. After JoAnn actually moved to the other bedroom, Frank became more conciliatory and they had some long talks together.

However, Diana knew that the movement wasn't enough, and in couples sessions starting at around the 16 month period she began talking with the couple about stronger fear-of-loss maneuvers. In these sessions she spoke with Frank about exerting greater self-discipline and framed JoAnn's sleeping in the other room as "doing him a favor," i.e., helping him to learn self-discipline. JoAnn spoke about how she had felt good about herself when she had moved to the other room. Both spouses also commented about the new feelings of closeness which had resulted. Diana then used the opportunity to suggest that they should contract to escalate the consequences of any further violent behavior. She asked JoAnn to have a packed suitcase in the trunk of her car so that she could actually leave and go to a hotel if Frank's monster re-appeared. She instructed her to select an expensive hotel in which she could pamper herself to the hilt to make up for the monster's abuse.

In the holding and steadying environment which Diana was providing, Frank actually could rise above his abandonment anxiety and agree that this plan was a fair one. We must point out here that this contract would have been impossible if Diana had not secured a strong therapeutic bond with both JoAnn and Frank. Instead JoAnn would have collapsed at the thought and Frank would have had a violent fit and threatened both JoAnn and Diana right there in the session.

A few months thereafter, JoAnn's resolve was tested. JoAnn had decided to confront Frank, for the first time, about some illegal business practices. He had reacted initially by demeaning her verbally and then when she had persisted, Frank had slapped her. But this time, JoAnn was not simply to cower in fear. She quickly walked out of the house with her packed bag and spent the night at a hotel. JoAnn called Diana and she applauded her strength and told her not to return until Frank had agreed to stop his infantile behavior.

Twenty minutes later, Diana heard a phone call come in. It was Frank who was quite upset. "She left" he said. Diana answered, "What did you expect? Two months ago, we all agreed that the violence had to stop and you heard me instructing her to leave if it happened again." "Yeah, but I never believed she would," said the despondent caller. Diana's voice had a tough edge when she said: "She's doing you a favor, helping you learn to control yourself. She's gotten much stronger and she won't take any more crap, Frank. In fact, if you choose to let the monster live, she would probably leave you altogether at this point."

"I'd die without her" Frank replied. He then proceeded to ask for an emergency session with Diana the next morning in order to "Kill off the monster once and for all." In the session the next day he did a very touching gestalt role play using an empty chair. He played himself and the "monster."

In the role play he discovered that the monster was mostly an overwhelmed little boy who felt he could never be heard or understood by a woman. At a critical juncture, Diana stepped in and became the "woman" in the role play, assuring him, like a benevolent mother figure that she could hear him and that what he had to do was to talk openly and assertively about his feelings.

JoAnn came in for a session with Frank the next day. Frank apologized and swore that he would not abuse her physically again. JoAnn explained that he had in fact promised this before, but this time something seemed quite different, – Frank seemed more open, more pained, and more sincere. JoAnn had informed Frank that if, in fact, he was abusive again, she would leave for a month. Although she was frightened, JoAnn was expressing a sense of pride and strength like never before. Diana applauded her new sense of personal power and her effective discipline of Frank. The couple had begun to show a level of respect and a mature dialogue in their interactions that they had never shown before. Up to this point Diana had conducted only sporadic couples sessions. With the new maturity in their relationship she was able to work with Frank and

JoAnn as a couple on a bimonthly basis. They continued in treatment and the physical violence never again recurred.

CAUTIONS AND CONTRAINDICATIONS

The triangular work and fear-of-loss strategy we have described is not for use with more dangerous cases of abuse. In these extreme cases, as we have already indicated, Comprehensive Family Therapy is aimed first and foremost at protecting the safety of the abused woman and her children. The therapist will encourage legal separations, restraint orders, and the use of women's shelters where necessary. In such cases the therapist usually works only with the battered woman.

In addition, even when working with mild to moderate spouse abuse, the fear-of-loss strategy should not be used by the novice clinician, because separating spouses arouses the deepest feelings and terrors of abandonment. There are several dangers to its use:

1. The couple may collude by clinging to each other and scapegoating the therapist as the one who has failed and terminate treatment.
2. The separation may arouse profound negative transference on the part of the abuser. In this state he may threaten the practitioner either physically, verbally, or legally.
3. Use of fear-of-loss maneuvers without careful assessment of the unique needs of the couple could lead to the dissolution of the marriage. For instance, if the abuser's mother died when he was quite young, the use of a fear-of-loss maneuver like JoAnn's night at the hotel might recreate too much of the abuser's original abandonment trauma. The abuser would then fall into depression rather than mobilizing inner reserves for self exploration and self control. The whole marital transaction would then shift to a more distant mode, with greater risk of marital break-up.
4. The separation may exacerbate the abusive acting out so that it becomes severe.

In the hands of the seasoned clinician, however, judicious and careful use of the fear-of-loss maneuver can disrupt the homeostatic patterns of the couple and create opportunities for real change. As seen in the case study described above, both the individual members of the couple and their relationship itself can be positively transformed. The abusive patterns, the shame, the self-hatred and the guilt tend to abate and are replaced by a more mature, respectful relating and higher self-esteem for both partners.

REFERENCES

Bandura, A. (1973). *Aggression–A social learning analysis*. Englewood Cliffs, NJ: Prentice-Hall.

Dobash, R., & Dobash, R.P. (1977). Love, honor, and obey: Institutional ideologies and the struggle for battered women. *Contemporary Crisis*, *1*, 403-415.

Giles-Sims, J. (1983). *Wife battering: A systems theory approach*. New York: Guilford Press.

Kalmuss, D. (1984). The intergenerational transmission of marital aggression. *Journal of Marriage and the Family*, *47*, 11-19.

Kirschner, D.A., & Kirschner, S. (1986). *Comprehensive family therapy: An integration of systemic and psychodynamic treatment models*. New York: Brunner/Mazel.

Martin, D. (1976). *Battered wives*. San Francisco: Glide Press.

Walker, L.E. (1979). *The battered woman*. New York: Harper & Row.

Guidelines for Using Mediation with Abusive Couples

Robert Geffner

This article focuses on techniques and issues concerning couples during and after separation or divorce. In addition, the specific emphasis is on those couples who were abusive during their marriage. It should be noted that marital abuse usually refers to those situations in which the husband battered the wife since this is the most typical type of violence that occurs in these relationships. The treatment that occurs during divorce or separation is normally thought of as mediation or divorce counseling. When doing this type of counseling, it is important to be aware of the prevalence of abuse in relationships. It appears, from recent statistics (Straus & Gelles, 1986), that at least one in four marriages involve abuse. This implies that there is a good chance that many couples who enter mediation or divorce counseling were violent during their relationship. It is therefore vital to check for this in the initial sessions. It is also important to obtain background information, especially concerning the families of origin of the couples. This should include information concerning possible abuse (i.e., whether they were abused or witnessed abuse as children, and whether any abuse or intimidation was present in their marriage), any alcoholism in their families of origin, and how much social interaction or social isolation occurred.

Research indicates that some characteristics are present in both the batterer and the battered woman (e.g., Geffner, Jordan, Hicks,

---

Robert Geffner, PhD, is Director, Family Violence Research and Treatment Program, University of Texas at Tyler.

Copies of this article can be obtained from Robert Geffner, PhD, Director, Family Violence Research and Treatment Program, UT-Tyler, Tyler, TX 75701.

& Cook, 1985). Both partners are likely to have low self-esteem and to be dependent. These factors are probably why the fear-of-loss strategy is so important and such a powerful motivator as well, as indicated by the Kirschners in the preceding article. Both partners are likely to be hostile, depressed, impulsive, aggressive, socially isolated, and have poor communication. Alcohol use is also a strong characteristic of both partners (Geffner et al., 1985; Hamberger & Hastings, 1986). It should be noted, however, that the presence of these characteristics does not explain causation. If a client was battered for many years, it is probable that s/he would develop many of these characteristics. It is important, however, for the clinician to realize that these characteristics are present since they play an important role in mediation and divorce counseling.

The idea of co-dependency appears to be popular and somewhat of a fad with the general public of late, but marital and family therapists have treated dysfunctional families for a long time (i.e., both partners exhibiting negative, self-defeating interactional behavior patterns developed as a result of dysfunction in their families of origin). Witnessing abuse or being abused as a child is still one of the strongest risk factors for becoming an abuser or for being in an abusive relationship (Hotaling & Sugarman, 1986). Therefore, the mediator should be aware that certain characteristics may be present in these couples and may need to be treated.

For example, if mediation or divorce counseling is to be conducted, a crucial issue is the batterer's strong need for power and control. The mediator should determine whether the battered woman appears to have what is now popularly termed "Battered Woman Syndrome" (Walker, 1984). This is similar to a type of post-traumatic stress disorder where the victim exhibits many symptoms of fear and intimidation, and may have incorporated a victim profile.

Thus, it is very important to determine whether the characteristics exist by doing individual intakes at the beginning of mediation or divorce counseling. Individual interviews are mandatory, not only to obtain the history and general information, but to determine what has occurred in the relationship with respect to abuse and intimidation. Unfortunately, many mediators do not do this, and some never learn whether a woman had been battered, especially since both batterers and battered women often tend to minimize or deny the abuse (Sedlak, 1988).

IDENTIFYING ABUSIVE RELATIONSHIPS

It is important to find out whether both parties actually want to participate in the mediation, and whether there are safety issues that must be considered. Therefore, the type of abuse (i.e., physical battering, verbal degradation, emotional intimidation, or sexual abuse), if any, that may have occurred in the relationship must be determined first.

In order to accomplish this, there are a series of questions that the clients are asked in individual sessions. If there is a discrepancy in answers between the husband and wife, research findings suggest that the woman should be believed if she reports that she was abused (Rosenbaum & O'Leary, 1981). In order to identify possible victims of abuse and to obtain relevant background information, a structured set of interview questions has been designed (Geffner & Pagelow, 1989). Either client may state that no abuse had occurred if this is the only manner in which such a question is directly asked. Therefore, the questionnaire includes many other aspects of abuse, such as a history of possible childhood abuse, background information, marital interactions, current and past feelings (e.g., fear or anger), threats, injuries, actions directed at children or pets, alcohol use, social isolation, and police or legal intervention. The questionnaire is reproduced in Figure 1.

Jealousy is one of the highlighted questions since it is a very important predictor of abuse. Another important question concerns a possible "Jekyll and Hyde" personality. This is important to know because often a batterer can sit in the room, be charming, and carry out a friendly conversation. This type of behavior may make it more difficult to recognize such a person as a batterer. Battered women may answer "no" to many of the other questions in the questionnaire while responding affirmatively to the question concerning different personalities in their partners.

It is very important to identify and understand the degree of fear and intimidation that may be present. This type of pressure can be overt or covert. The question concerning injury to pets is important because some abusers perform such acts to intimidate the victims (e.g., "This will happen to you if you say anything or refuse to do what I want."). Another example is the destruction of property (e.g., punching a hole in the wall with his fist). Threats of injury or even of kidnapping the children must be taken very seriously. In fact, some women are killed when they try to leave the relationship or file for divorce (Browne, 1987). There are batterers who have kidnapped their children and would not return them immediately even with a court order. As stated previously, power and control are the crucial issues for the batterer.

Figure 1

*Spouse Abuse Identification Questionnaire**

Robert Geffner, Ph.D. & Mildred Pagelow, Ph.D., 1989

__ How old were you at the time of your marriage?
__ Have you changed locations or residences frequently?
__ Are either you or your spouse extremely religious?
__ Were either you or your spouse physically abused in childhood?
__ Were either of you emotionally abused during childhood?
__ Were either of you sexually abused during childhood?
__ Was there a history of violence in either of your families?
__ If so, was the violence directed at the children, or was it directed at one parent by the other?
__ Did either your spouse's or your parents abuse alcohol?
__ Does your spouse treat his parents roughly or disrespectfully?
__ Has your spouse ever hit his parents, brothers, or sisters?
__ Has your spouse ever threatened to harm you?
__ Are your spouse's problems usually blamed on you or others?
__ Have you been attacked or blamed when your spouse got angry?
__ Are you afraid of your spouse's temper?
__ When drinking, does your spouse get rough or violent?
__ Has your spouse ever deliberately hurt you?
__ Did your spouse ever hit a former spouse or lover?
__ Has your spouse ever deliberately hurt or killed a pet?
__ Does your spouse have a Dr. Jekyll and Mr. Hyde personality?

__ Do you usually give in to settle arguments?
__ Are your children afraid when your spouse is angry?
__ Do the children have emotional or school problems?
__ Do the children display extremes in behavior?
__ Does any child assume a parental role in the family by waiting on you or caring for younger siblings?
__ Have you felt free to invite family or friends to visit you?
__ Are you socially active or more socially isolated?
__ Does your spouse listen in when you're talking on the phone?
__ Has your mail been opened before you receive it?
__ Do you select your own clothes?
__ Does your spouse insist on going everywhere with you?
__ Is your spouse suspicious of your every move?
__ Is your spouse an extremely jealous person?
__ Has your spouse accused you of having an affair? Have you?
__ Has your spouse ever forced you to have sex even though you did not want to?
__ Have you ever called, or thought of calling, the police because an argument was getting out of control?
__ Have your neighbors or friends ever called the police?
__ If the police were called, was your spouse arrested or given a citation?
__ Does your spouse ever threaten to take the children where you could not find them? Did this ever occur?
__ Do you feel safer when I talk with you alone?

*The ideas for this questionnaire originated in a subcommittee of the Domestic Violence/Family Court System Committee of the Los Angeles, Calif. Conciliation Court.

SAFETY ISSUES AND APPROPRIATENESS OF MEDIATION

It is very important for those conducting mediation or any type of divorce counseling to be trained in identifying and treating abusive couples. The potential dangerousness of abusers must be kept in mind. In addition, protective orders and legal restraints are not necessarily that effective. In fact, several newspaper articles during a recent two-week period in different states contained stories about women who had obtained restraining or protective orders, but their husbands or ex-husbands had shot them anyway. The mediator should be aware that the protection of a battered woman can be a serious concern.

The first task, then, is to determine whether the couple want individual counseling, reconciliation, or mediation/divorce counseling. If both have independently stated that they desire mediation (or that it is court-mandated), that the abused partner is willing and able to participate, and that it appears that any attempts at intimidation would be manageable, then mediation may be an appropriate approach. If they decide, for example, that they may want to try to reconcile, then we would refer them to another one of our treatment programs that focuses on reducing spouse abuse in a relationship (Geffner & Pagelow, In Press). This may be a conjoint treatment program (Geffner, Mantooth, Franks, & Rao, In Press) or one for each separately to eliminate the violence and intimidation (e.g., Franks, Geffner, Laney, McGaughey, & Mantooth, 1988). Our programs are quite comprehensive and include a variety of approaches (Mantooth, Geffner, Franks, & Patrick, 1987).

If they decide to proceed with the divorce or separation, then the mediator should be aware that the clients may have different agendas. Her agenda may be to leave the abusive relationship, to be "free" with her children, to be safe, and to just end the relationship. She may not even be thinking about long-term effects nor long-term consequences, and she may not be aware of nor understand her long-term needs. She may have been living in fear for a long time, may still be afraid, and this fear and her safety may have been her primary concerns. It may be necessary for the mediator to help her determine her long-term needs.

The abuser often has a strong need to maintain power and control. That is what occurred in the relationship, often led to the abuse, and usually maintained the abuse. Just because the abused woman or somebody else (e.g., a judge or attorney) has decided that they will divorce, that may not have changed his needs. In most cases, he may not be able to eliminate nor stop her from getting a divorce. However, many batterers have used violence or threats when this situation arises. Recent research by Browne and Williams (1989) has shown that more batterers have killed their spouses during this time period, and that these types of incidences are increasing. It may be that a batterer finally realizes in many of these cases that he cannot stop the divorce. As his power and control are threatened, then he may escalate the violence. However, abusers usually realize that they can no longer control their wives directly nor continue to beat them, so they then attempt to control other aspects of the woman's life, such as the finances and the property, or they try to gain control of the children. Therefore, these are the areas that must be dealt with in mediation.

It is important that the mediator/divorce counselor be familiar with the power and intimidation that abusers use. If the mediator takes a purely neutral stance, which is what is usually encouraged with mediation, then the abused woman has lost ground. She is in an unbalanced position already and does not have the equal bargaining power that mediation assumes. If this is the case, then mediation per se would not be recommended because the battered woman would be in a less powerful position with respect to the batterer. This not only creates an unfair situation, but it can be dangerous for the woman or her children.

In one extreme case in California, the mediator was not trained in handling abusive situations, did not determine whether the relationship had been abusive, and never found out that there had been prior restraining orders and threats of violence (Brodeur & Downey, 1987). The woman was in the process of filing for a divorce and trying to get her life together without her husband, but she was still very intimidated and insecure. After a few sessions, the mediator encouraged the woman to start dating her husband again. In addition, the batterer eventually convinced the woman to give up custody of her two older sons (with the endorsement of the mediator). About a month afterward, the husband, in a fit of rage, shot all three children and himself. The older child and the husband died immediately, the youngest child was finally released from the hospital physically healed, and the middle child was permanently disabled and is still confined to a wheelchair. The woman is now raising the two children. She has appeared on television programs to try to make mediators aware of the potential dangers that can occur.

MODIFIED MEDIATION

The role of the trained mediator is usually to be able to be neutral and help the couple. However, since the power is not equivalent in abusive relationships, true mediation in its literal sense cannot occur. Modified mediation or divorce counseling can occur if the mediator can balance the power so that the situation does become truly neutral. It should be noted that this type of divorce counseling is still being considered modified mediation for the purposes of this article even though it may not meet the "pure" definition of mediation.

The mediator may have to encourage and role model ways of dealing with the possible intimidation and control that the batterer may be attempting to exert. A good mediator can actually be a good role model for the woman in diffusing an abuser's anger and dealing with him in an assertive manner while making sure that her needs are being protected. She can observe the techniques and learn to become more assertive. It is important not to get misled by a batterer's "charm," since some are excellent manipulators. Mediators sometimes are lured into a subtle conspiracy of silence if they are not aware of the situation. In addition, many battered women have been intimidated and will portray themselves as very helpless; it is very easy to overemphasize this as well.

It is important to evaluate these situations and to determine how free the woman actually is to express her feelings and opinions openly in front of the man. If she is not able to be open, is too intimidated, or has much less control, then one must seriously consider whether mediation is appropriate. In these situations, we will not begin nor continue mediation if there is not a sufficient balance of power. We will refer them to individual therapy, especially if we are concerned that her safety needs are not being met or that her safety may really be in jeopardy if we continue this process. That is why it is very important for mediators to have the power and authority of the court to counteract an abuser's attempts at control. It is important that the mediator not be involved in their joint or individual therapy. We keep these roles separate.

CONDUCTING MODIFIED MEDIATION

If we believe that actual or modified mediation can occur, then one of the first topics that we deal with is the living arrangements. In some cases, the only way the woman was able to escape the abuse was to leave her house and go to a shelter or elsewhere. Working out some type of mutually fair and reasonable living arrangements for the adults and the children may be a high priority. The next step is the care and visitation of the children. This usually has to be worked out in a very structured, very detailed fashion. When we get involved with formerly abusive relationships, we emphasize detailed structure, even the hours of the day that phone calls will be allowed. We have observed situations in which phone calls became intimidating and an abuser maintained control because the woman was supposed to be at home for eight hours in case he happened to call to talk to the children. Therefore, we specify the hours that she will be home that is convenient for both schedules. It is then up to him to call during that time period if he so desires. If he calls outside of that time period and she is not there, then that is his problem. We make sure that all these arrangements are agreed to in writing, and we have both of them sign them. This is helpful if the case goes back to court later.

Another area of concern is conversion changes in children, especially in older boys. In one case, an 11 year-old boy had observed the abuse of the mother by the father, and had seen his father threaten his mother with a knife when they lived together. However, he had a strong need for the father's attention, approval, and acceptance. During a two-year divorce period, this boy had a complete conversion in attitude. By the time the case went into court, he had stated that it was the mother who had attacked the father with the knife. If the boy had not been interviewed at the beginning of treatment and the story had not been in the therapy notes, it would have been more difficult to show the court how this boy had essentially been "brainwashed" and converted by his father. This identification and conversion process is a common phenomenon that is now being reported by other clinicians and researchers.

We have also seen this conversion process with younger children after kidnapping incidents by the abusers. In fact, in one particular situation, the husband left with their son when the wife had filed for divorce; she did not know where they were for a week. It took five weeks to regain custody of her son as various motions were filed in the courts; she was only able to see her son a few times during this period. By the time that the 4 year-old boy was returned, he was very aggressive and antagonistic toward his mother and grandmother. He was kicking and biting even though this behavior had not occurred prior to the kidnapping. We later learned that during the kidnapping time period, the father had told the boy that the mother did not love the boy and that she did not want him; the father had completely alienated his son against the mother. A year of counseling was needed to undo some of the boy's trauma from this situation.

Financial support is another key issue. If the woman has been intimidated and battered, then she often does not have resources for her "new" life. The mediator will probably need to help with arrangements for her initial support. This is probably a sensitive issue because money and property are important expressions of a batterer's power. Dividing property is one of the most difficult areas to mediate due to the manipulation and control that most batterers attempt to exert. Sometimes this manipulation is subtle; being prepared for this situation may help mediators reduce their own frustration.

For example, in the kidnapping case reported above, the father (an abuser during the marriage) moved back into their house since the mother had moved out for her own protection. She then decided to let him keep the house, but she wanted her possessions, clothes, and furniture returned. She had owned some of the furniture prior to the marriage. The attorneys acted as mediators in this case, with court approval, but it still required eight months before she was able to obtain many of her possessions. She had an itemized list of her property, but her husband stated that he had already returned everything that she owned. It was very difficult to "prove" who was correct since she had stated that she still had not received everything but her property was no longer in the home. He also stated that much of her furniture had been sold prior to their separation. Follow-up later revealed that he had "sold" much of her property to his relatives as a way of getting back at her for filing the divorce. As stated previously, the batterer's need for power and control may be so strong that it can influence all aspects of mediation.

An important role of the mediator is to help the couple discuss the various alternatives and options that are available to them. Brainstorming and providing suggestions in a very problem-solving fashion is sometimes a difficult task. If the woman has been abused, then she has not usually had decision-making power. Therefore, mediation can teach her these skills through role modeling. Since the abuser has not often been placed in a position where he was required to problem-solve without complete authority and power, he must also learn new techniques. The main role of the mediator may be to help each party suggest alternatives for visitation, property division, financial arrangements, and other issues, to discuss the advantages and disadvantages of each suggestion, and to help them arrive at reasonable solutions and compromises. It is important to have the woman list the pros and cons of the various suggestions, and then to have the man do the same. If the mediator believes they have not listed all alternatives, additional probing may be necessary until it does appear that everything is in the open, including a good description of the advantages and disadvantages of each option. Decisions can then be made.

Again, the mediator must balance the power differential. The man may state, "well this is the option we are going to follow," and the woman may say "okay, I don't want to deal with it." It is then up to the mediator to ensure that such "solutions" are not merely accepted and that decisions are *mediated*. This is the reason that one of our initial questions was, "Do you give in to settle arguments?" It is important to be aware of this, and then to continue to probe so that the formerly abused woman actively takes part in the mediation.

The major emphasis of mediation is on conflict resolution. One goal, then, is to encourage compromises that neither party may strongly desire but that both can live with. A trial period is then recommended. It is made clear to both parties that this is a trial and error approach; if the agreement does not work for either party, then we always have the option to return and renegotiate. This negotiation and renegotiation is new for people in battering situations, especially for the woman. She has usually been conditioned that certain actions are going to be followed once they have been decided, whether or not they work and are beneficial. It is very important to introduce the notion that decisions can be changed. Even the batterers have some difficulty adjusting to this idea of decision change, unless of course it was at their instigation. The mediator must emphasize this process repeatedly. It is important to make sure that both parties understand the ramifications of their agreements. Having both people explain in their own words what they think they are agreeing to and the possible consequences is an important but often overlooked step to accurate and mutual communication, and for successful mediation. If either party does not understand completely, then the communication process is initiated again.

JOINT CUSTODY

An issue related to mediation is joint custody. As with mediation, this type of arrangement is being recommended in many states. I am generally in favor of joint custody, as are many other psychologists. However, I am not usually in favor of joint custody in abusive relationships because joint custody assumes an equal bargaining, mutual decision-making position similar to that required in true mediation. If the couple are not to the point where the woman has become assertive and the man is able to deal appropriately with her assertiveness, then joint custody could be prolonging the couple's problems for years because the power confrontations are perpetuated. Some divorced couples have never psychologically divorced. Even though they may have legally divorced several years previously, have remarried, and have new families, they continue to argue about their children, decisions, or various property issues.

In one case, a couple had not only been divorced for eight years, but they had both remarried and there were stepfamilies within the stepfamilies. However, they still argue about every decision concerning the children. This case seems to return to court on a yearly basis, and two mediators have already withdrawn from the case during the past three years. The children have been trapped in the middle by their parents' fighting; the youngest child has become anorexic because she cannot handle the pressure. The mediation was finally eliminated, and the adults are no longer treated conjointly. The adults have their own therapists, and I am treating the children. This appears to have reduced the manipulation. As with mediation, in those situations where power and control are crucial issues and the potential for violence and intimidation is high, then joint custody is not usually recommended.

PARENT ALIENATION SYNDROME

A problem that has occurred in many of the cases where abuse had been present involves parent alienation syndrome. It is very frustrating for the therapist to be trying to mediate these complex situations and later learn that one parent is alienating the children against the other parent. This counteracts and sabotages mediation. However, this is not unusual in abusive relationships, and can be attempted by either parent.

One particular case involved a couple and their two children. They were court-ordered into mediation in order to deal with visitation issues and the daughter's fear of her father. In this case, the formerly abused woman sabotaged the mediation. She was alienating her 12 year-old daughter against her father. To his credit, he had entered individual therapy after his divorce in order to eliminate his own abusive tendencies (verbal abuse and intimidation were involved). He had made excellent progress during a year in therapy and was attempting to deal appropriately with his ex-wife and his children. He was also beginning to incorporate constructive parenting techniques and to communicate openly without the use of power or intimidation, something he had not done in the marriage.

He and his ex-wife had already been to four therapists without success. Family therapy, reframing, and paradoxical techniques did not seem to be eliminating the negative comments and resentment the woman was directing toward her ex-husband, and the pressure that she was directing toward her daughter. The woman's anger and resentment resulting from the power-oriented, abusive marriage was understandable, but it had become self-defeating for her and was creating severe difficulties for her child. The 12 year-old daughter was developing such serious emotional problems as a result of this pressure by her mother that the mother was finally informed by the mediator that the mediator would have to recommend to the court that the daughter be removed from the mother's custody for the child's protection if the situation did not improve. When another counselor was alone with both parents and the daughter in an informal setting later that day (i.e., monitoring visitation at a restaurant), the mother told her daughter in front of the others that because of her father's complaints, the daughter would be forcibly taken from her and put in a foster home. Needless to say, the parent alienation syndrome escalated and the daughter became hysterical, screaming at her father and blaming him even though he had no involvement in this recommendation. In fact, the mother was aware that he was not involved in this decision. The mediator finally did inform the court that the daughter was being severely harmed emotionally in the mother's possession. However, the mother fled the state with the daughter before the court could act. It is still pending.

This is an unfortunate example of mediation, combined with parent alienation syndrome, doing more harm than good due to the abuse of power of one of the parents. However, in this case it was the formerly abused woman who had not adequately dealt with her own resentment, and was now becoming abusive. This case is much more unusual since it was the woman who was now abusing her power rather than the man. A mediator must be prepared for all situations.

CONCLUSION

Thus, the key issues of concern for mediating formerly abusive relationships are power and control. It is important for mediators to try to empower all parties such that re-victimization does not occur. Modified mediation can accomplish this if conducted by properly trained professionals who are familiar with spouse abuse treatment as well as mediation techniques. It is also important for mediators to be aware of abuse, be able to identify these relationships, and be aware of the guidelines concerning the appropriateness of using mediation with abusive or formerly abusive couples. Mediators must recognize that it is not always a good idea to use a mediation approach with all couples. If mediation is to be used with couples when abuse has occurred in the marriage, then it is important to overcome the intimidation and to balance the power. The mediator must have the safety of a formerly battered woman as the prime objective, and must be cautious about the appropriateness of using this approach. However, a modified mediation approach can be helpful at times in reaching productive outcomes with some of these couples. When this occurs, the intergenerational transmission of abuse has a better chance of being eliminated.

REFERENCES

Brodeur, N. & Downey, C. (1987). Father shoots 3 sons, killing 1, then takes his own life in south county. *Orange County Register*. (August 18), A1-A2.

Browne, A. (1987). *When battered women kill*. New York: Free Press.

Browne, A., & Williams, K. R. (1989). Exploring the effect of resource availability and the likelihood of female-perpetrated homicides. *Law and Society Review*, *23*, 75-94.

Franks, D., Geffner, R., Laney, N., McGaughey, L., & Mantooth, C. (1988). *Help end abusive relationship tendencies (HEART): A personal growth program manual for battered and formerly battered women*. Tyler, TX: University of Texas at Tyler Press.

Geffner, R. A., Jordan, K., Hicks, D., & Cook, S. K. (1985, August). Psychological characteristics of violent couples. In R. A. Geffner (Chair), *Violent couples: Current research and new directions for family psychologists*. Symposium conducted at the annual meeting of the American Psychological Association, Los Angeles.

Geffner, R., Mantooth, C., Franks, D., & Rao, L. (In Press). A psychoeducational, conjoint therapy approach to reducing family violence. In P. L. Caesar & L. K. Hamberger (Eds.), *Therapeutic interventions with batterers: Theory and practice*. New York: Springer.

Geffner, R., & Pagelow, M. (1989). *Identification of victims of spouse abuse*. Unpublished questionnaire, University of Texas, Tyler, TX.

Geffner, R., & Pagelow, M. D. (In Press). Treatments for spouse abuse. In R. T. Ammerman & M. Hersen (Eds.), *Treatment of family violence: A sourcebook*. New York: John Wiley & Sons.

Hamberger, L. K., & Hastings, J. (1986). Personality correlates of men who abuse their partners: A cross-validation study. *Journal of Family Violence*, *1*, 323-345.

Hotaling, G. T., & Sugarman, D. B. (1986). An analysis of risk markers in husband to wife violence: The current state of knowledge. *Violence and Victims*, *1*, 101-124.

Mantooth, C. M., Geffner, R., Franks, D., & Patrick, J. (1987). *Family preservation: A treatment manual for reducing couple violence*. Tyler, TX: University of Texas at Tyler Press.

Rosenbaum, A., & O'Leary, K. D. (1981). Marital violence: Characteristics of the abusive couples. *Journal of Consulting and Clinical Psychology*, *49*, 63-71.

Sedlak, A. J. (1988). Prevention of wife abuse. In V. B. Van Hasselt, R. L. Morrison, A. S. Bellack, & M. Hersen (Eds.), *Handbook of family violence* (pp. 457-481). New York: Plenum.

Straus, M. A., & Gelles, R. J. (1986). Societal change and change in family violence from 1975 to 1985 as revealed by two national surveys. *Journal of Marriage and the Family*, *48*, 465-479.

Walker, L. E. (1984). *The battered woman syndrome*. New York: Springer.

Treating Battered Women in the Aftermath Stage

Mary Ann Dutton-Douglas

The problem of abuse in intimate relationships has become more widely recognized today largely as a function of the battered woman's movement which also has been instrumental in establishing shelters to safely house battered women and their children. Battered women's shelters and grass roots programs have been essential in providing aide to battered women and their children in the immediate crisis of the physical, sexual, and emotional abuse they experience. However, for a variety of reasons, a significant number of women who experience abuse in their intimate relationships do not become involved with services provided through a battered woman's shelter. Even for those women who do seek shelter services, the psychological aftermath of the abuse often continues long after they leave the shelter even when the violence has stopped or the relationship has ended. This paper addresses clinical intervention with battered women after the immediate crisis of the abuse has passed. A framework for conceptualizing stages of intervention and for integrating multidisciplinary efforts is discussed.

The problem of domestic violence centers around the issues of power and control; major themes of intervention with battered women can be described as empowerment and autonomy. Interlocking components of the therapeutic process have been described previously as Crisis, Transition, and Recovery phases (Douglas, 1987). During the crisis stage the primary issues of intervention focus on physical safety, whether by escape from impending violence or by reduction of suicidal and/or homicidal potential as a

Mary Ann Dutton-Douglas, PhD, is Professor in the School of Psychology, Nova University, Fort Lauderdale, FL.

means of escaping further victimization. Psychotic or extreme dissociative reactions to the trauma of victimization also require immediate intervention.

The Transition phase of intervention involves decision-making and problem-solving. Examples of these issues include whether to leave the relationship (temporarily or permanently), to file for divorce, to obtain a restraining order, to locate alternative housing, employment, and/or child care, to file legal charges, etc. This component of intervention requires the clinician to have knowledge of the availability of social service, legal, and other community resources as well as information about the pragmatics of accessing those resources. Working with victims requires both a multidisciplinary effort and helping professionals who can facilitate the integration of the necessary components of that effort.

The primary focus of this paper is on the final component of intervention with battered women, the Recovery phase. Recovery can only truly begin after the perceived threat of continued violence ceases. It is important to distinguish the battered woman's perception of threat from the actual occurrence of violence. In some relationships the typical cycle of violence may be 3, 6, 12 months or more in duration. The absence of violence at a given point in time may only mean that the usual point in the cycle where violence occurs has yet to be reached again following the previous episode. Alternatively, the cycle may have shifted due to some legal, social service, mental health intervention or personal effort by the battered woman, but she may still perceive the threat of violence and thus maintain her perception of continued danger.

Psychotherapy provides one avenue of recovery for the battered woman; alternative routes may be equally as effective, such as the healing environment of a feminist support system. It is my view that a combination of efforts can provide the most powerful healing effect.

Post-traumatic therapy typically presumes the cessation of the trauma prior to the onset of therapy, although the trauma may have included multiple exposures typical, for example, of the experience of combat veterans. Although post-traumatic therapy can begin from the immediate post-trauma point of crisis (e.g., rape, disaster, and accident victims) or at some later point (e.g., combat veterans or adult survivors of incest), the impact of continued threat of victimization has not yet been fully addressed (e.g., child incest victims or battered women when contact with the offender is ongoing). To reiterate, my view is that the Recovery phase of intervention cannot adequately begin until the threat of continued abuse has ceased. For some battered women that point has occurred prior to their seeking help, but for most it does not occur until some later point, if at all. In contrast, intervention with the Crisis and Transition components most often begins when the battered woman still faces some level of danger.

The Recovery phase of intervention addresses the whole range of traumatic effects of victimization. The universal and normal response to victimization includes both an intrusion/repetition and a denial/numbing component (Janoff-Bulman, 1985). Differences in the course of recovery for battered women related to such factors as duration and number of repeated occurrences of victimization, severity of abuse, perception of lethal potential, etc. have yet to be determined. Recovery may be complicated by factors which render the victim more vulnerable and less able to cope effectively once the abuse ceases. These factors may include inadequate social support and economic resources, other life stressors, and a history of prior victimization.

Post-traumatic Stress Disorder (PTSD; DSM-IIIR) includes three basic symptom patterns: intrusive recollections and experiences of the trauma, numbing or constricted affect and focus, and a lowered threshold for anxious arousal (Ochberg, 1988). Common emotional reactions characteristic of post-traumatic reactions include anger/rage, grief/depression/sadness, fear/anxiety, and shame. A distinction should be made between formal diagnostic criteria for PTSD, as is currently identified in DSM-IIIR, and other common psychological correlates of victimization, e.g., substance abuse, eating disorders, etc.

Recovery phase intervention includes four components: (1) working through the trauma, (2) decreasing specific symptom patterns, (3) cognitive restructuring, and (4) rebuilding a new life. Previous literature about post-traumatic therapy (cf. Curtois, 1988; Ochberg, 1988) has described the importance of therapeutically reenacting the trauma toward the goal of integration with the victim's current life. For battered women, the traumatic experiences are likely to have been many and varied in their content, requiring focus on multiple traumatic experiences in the context of her history of abuse. Three processes are important to the "working through" component of treatment. First, decreasing in measured doses the avoidance and numbing of the experience is important to facilitate recall of the traumatic event(s) and/or the emotional responses to them. Naming and acknowledging the trauma and its source is important for decreasing the patterns of denial. Other strategies which can be adopted for the purpose of work through the traumatic experience include gestalt techniques, imagery, journaling, bodywork, and hypnosis. A second and crucial phase of treatment is developing strategies to cope with intrusive recollections of the traumatic experience through nightmares, dreams, and flashbacks, for example. Coping with recollections and measuring the dosage of the emotional content accompanying them can be facilitated by careful timing of the efforts toward reducing denial, education concerning the normalcy of various emotional responses, building strong support systems outside the therapeutic relationship, relaxation and stress-management training, and a focus on self-nurturing and caretaking. Finally, the goal of this component of intervention is to integrate the trauma into the formerly battered woman's current life so she can continue her life without her battering history dominating her day-to-day experience. Validating and providing empathy for the negative aspects of the battering is essential. Also important is naming the growth and positive aspects which have resulted from her attempts to deal with the battering. This work can provide a perspective which transforms the woman from a victim to a survivor. However, a caution is in order; without the validation of the victimization, this approach can too easily function to revictimize the battered woman.

Addressing symptom patterns is a second component of the Recovery Phase of treatment. Common problems associated with victimization, not all of which are explicitly identified as components of PTSD, include eating and sleep problems, somatic complaints, dissociative responses, confusion and memory impairment, paranoid-like thinking, substance abuse, panic attacks and other anxiety-related problems, child abuse and other aggressive behaviors, self-mutilation and other self-destructive behaviors, low self-esteem and other indicators of depression. Although many therapeutic approaches may be used to address these symptom patterns, the common element which is very important in addressing these problem areas is the context in which they are framed. Identifying the problem areas as functionally related to the victimization "normalizes" the symptoms as coping and survival strategies or as "normal" reactions to trauma. It is important for the therapist to work with the client to establish boundaries where there is risk of further harm, e.g., child abuse, suicide, self-mutilation or other self-destructive behavior. Methods adjunctive to therapy may also be helpful in reducing symptoms patterns, such as 12-step programs (e.g., AA, NA, OA, ACOA).

Changing dysfunctional cognitions is a third component of the recovery phase. It is important to recognize that many of these cognitions may have developed as a function of stereotypic sex-role socialization which has detrimental effects especially for women. Developing an awareness of basic human rights is also important, including the right not to be abused, the right to experience and express one's feelings, the right to control one's own body, etc. The popular concept of "codependency" describes an over-focus/responsibility on others and an under-focus/responsibility on self. The effects of this framework, learned from socialization both in a sexist society and a dysfunctional family environment, is to render women generally, and battered women in particular, less able to effectively care for themselves and more at risk for victimization by others. An important goal in this component of treatment is to increase the battered woman's ability to distinguish those events which in fact she can control, e.g., her own behavior, from those which she cannot, e.g., her partner's battering behavior. Increasing choice-making and taking responsibility for one's own behavior is the core to the concept of empowerment.

Finally, rebuilding a new life is the final component of the Recovery Phase of treatment. Going on with one's life is the major goal; skill development to facilitate both autonomy/independence and interdependence/connectedness may be useful. Helping the formerly battered woman to identify risk and/or vulnerabilities for revictimization is important. Strategies for decreasing risks include developing the ability to establish clear boundaries and increasing one's awareness of other's subtle controlling behavior before it reaches proportions of greater abuse. Healing in the formerly abusive relationship is essential to full recovery if the battered woman is planning to continue her relationship with her partner. Couple therapy is important here, but only following both the battered woman's and the batterer's successful treatment in their respective therapies. Trust building is one of the major components to address within conjoint therapy.

To conclude, clinical intervention with battered women needs to be focused on the specific phase of the victimization and/or recovery process which matches her current experience and be coordinated with intervention from other disciplines, e.g., law, medicine, etc. The Crisis, Transition, and Recovery phases of treatment are important to distinguish, but with the recognition that the client may recycle through various phases repeatedly, thus requiring considerable flexibility in treatment methods. Finally, a note about therapists engaging in this work. Clinical intervention with victims is exceptionally emotionally demanding. I believe that it is particularly critical for the therapist to utilize strong peer support networks in order to avoid burnout and maintain a mentally healthy perspective in this very difficult work.

REFERENCES

Douglas, M. A. (1987). Battered woman syndrome. In D. J. Sonkin (Ed.), *Domestic violence on trial: Psychological and legal dimensions of family violence*. New York: Springer.

Curtois, C. C. (1988). *Healing the incest wound: Adult survivors in therapy*. New York: W. W. Norton & Co.

Janoff-Bulman, R. (1985). The aftermath of victimization: Rebuilding shattered assumptions. In C. R. Figley (Ed.), *Trauma and its wake*. Vol. 1. New York: Brunner/Mazel.

Ochbert, F. M. (1988). *Post-traumatic therapy and victims of violence*. New York: Brunner/Mazel.

SYMPOSIUM: POST-DOCTORAL TRAINING FOR THE SPECIALTY OF PSYCHOTHERAPY

Introduction

Alvin R. Mahrer

Neither psychology, psychiatry, social work, nor any other psychotherapy-related profession formally acknowledges a specialty of psychotherapy—although each defends its right to train psychotherapists, and each formally recognizes other specialties. Neither within nor across the several psychotherapy-related professions is there a recognized program of education and training or accreditation and certification for a specialty of psychotherapy or even for the professional practice of psychotherapy.

The purpose of this symposium is (a) to update and review the current status of postdoctoral training in psychotherapy, (b) to propose minimal standards for postdoctoral training in psychotherapy,

---

Alvin R. Mahrer, PhD, is Professor of Psychology at the School of Psychology, and Director of the Centre for Psychological Service, University of Ottawa.

Presented at the 97th Annual Meeting of the American Psychological Association, New Orleans, LA August 1989.

(c) to propose a mandated specialty of psychotherapy, and (d) to highlight the implications for the psychotherapy-related professions, licensing and accreditation, education and training, and also for the development of a specialty of psychotherapy.

Postdoctoral Training for the Preparation and Regulation of Professional Psychologists

Ronald E. Fox

The proper education and training of psychotherapists is a broad topic that extends well beyond the boundaries of psychology to the numerous other professions that also provide psychotherapeutic services to their clients. Because I have neither the knowledge nor the inclination to discuss other professions and what they should do, I will restrict my observations to the profession of psychology.

In the course of this paper I will argue that psychotherapy should be seen as a specialty in professional practice and that training for that specialty should be offered, primarily, at the postdoctoral level. However, it is difficult to imagine the profession of psychology being able to deal with the matter of a psychotherapy specialty without resolving some of the constraints which currently are operative. The following sections present some of those constraints and suggest some possible solutions.

DEFINING A SPECIALTY IN PSYCHOLOGY

1. The principle difficulty in establishing a psychotherapy specialty may be the lack of agreement among professional psychologists regarding what constitutes a practice specialty and how such practice should be recognized. The APA recognizes four specialties

---

Ronald E. Fox, PhD, is Dean of the School of Professional Psychology, Wright State University, Dayton, OH.

through the development of guidelines for practice in clinical, counseling, school, and industrial/organizational psychology. The American Board of Professional Psychology currently recognizes six specialties: clinical, counseling, school, industrial and organization, clinical neuropsychology, and forensic. However, in its accreditation process, APA's Committee on Accreditation has developed procedures for evaluating programs only in the specialties of clinical, counseling, and school psychology. So, according to our current "official" processes, psychology has either 3, 4, or 6 specialties, and that's all. To further confound the issue, APA (in contrast to other learned professions), does not accredit schools or departments as generic entities but rather recognizes specialty programs within each department or school. If a school or department wishes to have accredited programs in counseling, clinical and school psychology, it would be required to submit to three separate evaluations but would never be evaluated as a psychology department or school per se. This situation would be analogous to medical schools being separately accredited for family practice, surgery, psychiatry, internal medicine, obstetrics and gynecology, ophthalmology, etc., etc., etc., without there being any accreditation for medical schools per se. Medical Schools are accredited to educate physicians, not specialists, just as dental schools are accredited to educate dentists not orthodontists or oral surgeons, and law schools are accredited to educate attorneys, not criminal lawyers or tax attorneys. Other professions educate students for generic practice and license them for the same thing. Specialization is left in the hands of specialty boards. We've gotten the whole thing backwards in psychology and ultimately we will have to do something about it. The accreditation of programs by specialties leaves our professional in the peculiar position of training psychologists only as specialists while licensing them generically. We train clinical psychologists, or school psychologists or counseling psychologists, but we only license people as psychologists.

2. Before finally resolving specialty training issues, it may be necessary to change the nature of doctoral level education itself. I believe that education at the doctoral level should be generic rather than specialty oriented. Although *some* specializations could begin

in the last year of the doctoral programs, the education of qualified specialists should be left to specifically recognized, well-developed postdoctoral programs.

The field of professional psychology is changing rapidly and is faced with what amounts to a knowledge explosion in theories, models, and tactics for the application of psychological knowledge to the improvement of human functioning and coping skills. My daughter currently is finishing her final year in preparation for becoming a child clinical psychologist, and one of my sons is a practicing clinical neuropsychologist. Over the past decade, his specialty area has become so sophisticated that they speak a whole different language than what my generation learned. Only twenty-five years ago, graduate programs were still teaching students to administer the Bender-Gestalt test as a rough screening device to detect "organicity." Today, neuropsychologists regard such practice as somewhat analogous to using a thermometer to detect viral pneumonia. I find it difficult to even talk with my son in any specific manner about his clinical work. I do not have the knowledge. The assessment techniques used today are complex, the knowledge required to interpret them properly is beyond the ken of most psychologists, and the ability to specify the area of malfunctioning in the brain is far more precise than any of us imagined possible only a few generations of students ago. Recently I talked with a neurosurgeon who makes extensive use of neuropsychological expertise, often even deciding whether or not to do surgery depending on the results obtained. Neuropsychologists know how to use assessment instruments that are more accurate than many physical assessment tools, are relatively inexpensive to administer, and pose no risks to the patient. Knowledgeable neurosurgeons see them as very plausible consultants not only in diagnosis but in rehabilitation. Many psychologists, trained prior to the rapid growth of this relatively new specialty, have had to obtain retraining to equip themselves to utilize the new assessment instruments. I could give other examples, but, the point is that if students are not to be trained for obsolescence, they must have a broad knowledge of the entire spectrum of psychological theory and practice. The profession will flourish only if it is able to provide those entering the profession with a comprehensive general education in a rapidly expanding discipline that will enable them to adopt and grow as new opportunities develop.

To implement a change to generic professional education at the doctoral level would require a significant change in the mission of the Committee on Accreditation. There no longer would be separate accreditation for clinical, counseling, and school programs within larger training settings. Rather, each training entity would be accredited in its entirety. There should be one set of accreditation standards developed to answer the single question of whether the school (or department) provides quality generic education and training for the practice of psychology.

3. Regardless of whether specialty training occurs at the predoctoral or postdoctoral level, we still face the problem of recognizing a specialty when we see one. I believe that specialty areas in professional psychology should be redefined along functional lines. In the aftermath of World War II, psychologists began to establish careers for themselves in increasing numbers in nonacademic settings. Clinical, counseling and school psychology derive simply from the names of organizational structures in which new applied psychologists were struggling to apply their new skills: clinics, counseling centers, and schools. These are locations not specialties.

Indeed, it should be apparent that there is much overlap in the functions performed by professional psychologists in these areas (clinical, counseling, school). For example, I challenge the reader to give me a meaningful and convincing explication of the difference between clinical and counseling psychology. Particularly in large eastern cities of the U.S., it is common to find people trained as school psychologists who are practicing as psychoanalysts because that is what they were educated to do.

I believe that it is time to break out of thought patterns that accept definitions that have grown fortuitously during the years of our immaturity. True specialties should not be distinguished from each other by the settings in which they are practiced. We will have to give considerable thought to how we wish to define a true specialty in psychotherapy. Some of our colleagues already argue that psychoanalysis is a specialty. Others see cognitive therapy as a specialty. In addition, we already have training institutes and programs under varying auspices providing extensive training experiences in gestalt therapy, family therapy, group therapy, and a host of others. Which of these are true specialties and which are simply variants or sub-specialties of an over-arching specialty? To my mind, psychotherapy is the specialty and most of the others are sub-specialties; some of the others are simply special proficiencies. But that is only an opinion. I believe it to be an opinion based on logic, but then logic has never characterized the development of our discipline. Psychologists are worse than economists in this regard. If you have on hand six economists you will have six different theories to account for every observable financial phenomenon; seven, if one of them went to Harvard. Psychologists develop a new theory of therapy every time one of our practitioners hits upon an apparently new phenomenon, even when what has happened is that the new theorist has simply rediscovered an old theory, which he or she never learned, and so concludes it must be new. We are one of the few professions I know of that has a penchant for independently and repeatedly re-discovering gravity and then giving a different name (and calling for different training) to each discovery.

Specialties should be characterized largely by a unique domain of knowledge, a set of general and specific paradigms, and the intervention strategies flowing from these paradigms.

The full implications of moving from current definitions of specialties in psychology to a new group of functionally defined specialties would be awesome. If professional psychology training programs were to provide effective generic training, they would have to develop curricula that would ensure that doctoral students were given the beginnings of effective knowledge and skills in each specialty. Accreditation guidelines would have to be changed so that the Committee on Accreditation would review a program's capabilities to provide comprehensive, generic training which would be an important standard for approval. In addition, licensing procedures would have to be changed. Young psychologists choosing not to practice a specialty would need to be trained to carry out, with reasonable capability, all of the basic skills that characterize professional psychology, and the licensing process would have to evaluate whether such a level of accomplishment had indeed been reached. If we move in this general direction, we eventually should look forward to seeing specialty training for the general practice of psychology.

SPECIALTY TRAINING IN PSYCHOLOGY

Where should it take place? I have argued that specialty training, typically amounting to two years of full-time effort, should be provided in approved, comprehensive psychological service centers (PSCs). For 25 years, Albee (1964) has been calling attention to the fact that applied psychology can never reach its fullness as a profession as long as its new members are trained primarily in settings that are directed by members of other professions and receive large portions of their education and supervision from members of those professions.

The profession must take control over the entire sweep of the predoctoral and postdoctoral training of its neophytes. In addition, the profession most assume responsibility for delivering a full range of services and for developing alternative models for the delivery of those services. Unless and until these training and service responsibilities are accepted, psychology will remain an ancillary profession. It will not be an easy task to develop the numbers of complex PSCs that we will need. In effect, I am talking about developing a whole, largely new psychological delivery system. In the Fall of 1989, the School of Professional Psychology at Wright State University will dedicate the new Ellis Institute for Human Development. Designed to serve as the clinical teaching, research and service arm of the School, the new Institute has outpatient and day-care facilities, hut no 24-hour capabilities for clients who need such services. It is a small building (20,000 sq. feet) to serve a small school (115 doctoral students) but it cost $3,000,000 to build, another $300,000 to equip (partially), and $350,000 per year to operate (and that's not inclusive of professional practitioners, students, and postdoctoral residents). That's cheap as such things go. The Wright State University School of Medicine, when it was established about 15 years or so ago, spent over 50 million dollars for additions to various hospitals in the city to support clinical teaching and research and in addition gets a regular clinical teaching subsidy from the state to help support those buildings and services on an ongoing basis. So my School has its little building, but none of the other ten psychology programs in the state has one. None of them receives a regular clinical teaching subsidy from the state. Any one of the seven state-supported medical schools in the state receives many times the public support of all of the psychology programs combined. If psychology really is to realize its potential as a profession, and resolve some of our chronic problems and deficiencies in training, then it must stop being such pikers and "go for the gold."

The development of comprehensive psychological service centers is necessary, not only to further the political end of bringing about the final emergence of professional psychology as an autonomous profession, but also to provide a focus for specialty training for young members of our discipline. Such centers, if managed appropriately, would (a) provide quality training over a minimum of a two-year period to new graduates desiring specialty training, (b) provide at least a modest stipend to those in residency training—enough to make the idea of specialty training economically viable and reasonably attractive, and (c) ensure that graduates would enter the community with sufficient professional contacts, clients, knowledge, skills and visibility to establish themselves as specialists.

Another one of our current customs that, in my opinion, interferes with the proper development of post-doctoral specialty training, is the fact that most states' licensure laws require two years of experience, one of which must be postdoctoral. This policy seems to be another anachronism, held over from our past, that has become enshrined in practice without any serious review of its implications. Reflection should indicate that the requirement that graduates of training programs must have another full year of supervised training before they are ready to practice clearly implies that our training programs not only fail to prepare their graduates for adequate entry-level functioning, but, indeed, are not even held responsible for doing so! It further implies that someone else in some other setting has the responsibility for completing the preparation of new practitioners. Yet there exists no organized system of postdoctoral training centers nor any agreed-upon criteria regarding the nature of such training. This is one of those more destructive and insidious requirements which we impose on our new graduates. It leaves them open to exploitation with very little real protection. I know of state systems, Ohio being one of them, which simply use new graduates as cheap professional labor (and to build a recruiting pool for positions requiring licensure). In many instances (and I believe it to be the majority of instances) the "supervision" provided is perfunctory at best. I know of group practices that regularly hire new graduates to do regular clinical work for low wages in return for marginal supervision that meets the letter, but not the spirit, of the psychology board's supervisory requirements. In some instances, young psychologists' stipends are reduced if the patient load goes down—an arrangement that may border on fee splitting. What kind of introduction to professional practice is this for our new graduates? What kind of example does this set? Since many of these agencies and groups advertise themselves as providing "postdoctoral training," what kind of image are we creating as to what postdoctoral training (specialty training) is all about? How long can we tolerate this kind of abuse?

Instead of attempting to compensate for deficiencies in training by requiring that new graduates undergo another year of training with someone, somewhere, psychology should move to become a mature profession by maintaining, as do many other professions, that the role of professional education is to prepare graduates for the assumption of full professional responsibility upon receipt of the terminal degree. If new graduates were made eligible for licensure upon obtaining the doctoral degree, the clear message would be given to training programs that they are expected to ensure that their graduates are capable of independent practice.

The incorporation of such a change in licensure requirements would have extensive repercussions. It would necessitate changes in graduate curricula and it would create a new standard by which to judge professional programs: the ability of their graduates to achieve licensure.

CREDENTIALITY SPECIALTIES

Eligibility for receipt of a specialty diploma from entities such as the American Board of Professional Psychology, should be based upon possession of a license to practice psychology in one or more states, *and* possession of a certificate of completion of a postdoctoral training sequence in that specialty issued by an accredited, comprehensive psychological service center.

The examination for the issuance of a specialty diploma by a specialty board or boards should be based upon assessment of the candidates: (a) capability of performing the practice functions of the specialty, (b) knowledge of the theories, models, intervention strategies, and relevant research findings in the specialty area, and (c) capacity to deal with the legal and ethical issues likely to arise in the course of practice of the specialty.

CLOSING

Psychotherapy is a highly technical specialty that deserves recognition as such, in my opinion. I believe that it is properly taught, like other specialties, *primarily* at the postdoctoral level; but in order to implement proper specialty training in our field, some basic changes are needed in current policies and regulations. The changes needed are complex and the problems in resolving them are not simple ones. However, I also agree with H. L. Mencken who once observed that some problems are so difficult that they can't be solved in a million years, unless someone thinks about them for 5 minutes.

REFERENCE

Albee, G. (1964, June). A declaration of independence for psychology. *Ohio Psychologist*, pp 60-64.

Postdoctoral Education and Training for the Practice of Psychotherapy

Alvin R. Mahrer

What kind of education and training would qualify a person for the practice of psychotherapy? According to the postdoctoral plan to be proposed, the psychotherapist has a doctorate (not a masters degree), in any of the psychotherapy-related professions (such as psychology, medicine, social work, or any other psychotherapy-related profession), and a diploma from a postdoctoral training center in psychotherapy certifying satisfactory completion of a program designed to provide qualified knowledge and competence in a designated psychotherapy.

This plan lacks the enthusiastic support of, and may even contravene some entrenched, intransigent, intractable convictions of, the psychotherapy-related professions, their certification and regulatory boards, those involved in graduate education and training in each of the psychotherapy-related professions, those who cherish a particular kind of doctorate or masters degree, those in postgraduate training programs, those committed to distinguishing between psychotherapy, counseling, psychoanalysis, casework, and similar terms, and those for whom the field of psychotherapy lacks an adequate base of knowledge, competencies, and skills in the first place. It

---

Alvin R. Mahrer, PhD, is affiliated with the University of Ottowa.

This article is based on an address from a symposium on postdoctoral training for the speciality on psychotherapy, at the 1989 meeting of the American Psychological Association in New Orleans, and is an extension of an article in the October, 1989 issue of the Canadian Journal of Counselling.

Special appreciation is extended to Drs. Ronald E. Fox, Stanley R. Graham, and Arnold A. Lazarus for their helpful comments.

Correspondence concerning this article should be addressed to Alvin R. Mahrer, Ph.D., School of Psychology, University of Ottawa, Canada, K1N 6N5.

seems that this plan does not enjoy a broad base of enthusiastic support.

Accordingly, the postdoctoral plan could use some arguments on its behalf. If you are even moderately cordial to the following arguments, then the subsequent section introduces provisional minimal standards for discussion, modification, and adoption by postgraduate and postdoctoral training centers in psychotherapy, and the final section outlines some of the implications of this plan for the field of psychotherapy and the psychotherapy-related professions.

EIGHT SUPPORTING ARGUMENTS

1. None of the Psychotherapy-Related Professions Recognize the Existence of the Practice or Speciality of Psychotherapy

Psychotherapy is a nonexistent, unrecognized practice for which about a dozen professions provide education and training to thousands of practitioners to enable them to offer a nonexistent, unrecognized service to multitudes of patients and clients.

The American Board of Professional Psychology (1978) recognizes and credentials several specialities, but psychotherapy is not one of them. The American Psychological Association's Subcommittee on Specialization outlined steps enabling subgroups to seek formal designated specialities (Sales, 1985; Sales, Bricklin & Hall, 1983,1984), but again psychotherapy is not a formal speciality in psychology, and the same holds true in psychiatry (Paris, Kravitz, & Prince, 1986), social work, and all other psychotherapy disciplines and professions. After all, it is difficult to establish standards of training for a practice or speciality that is not generally recognized as having formal existence.

2. The Best Word for It Is "Psychotherapy"

The word "psychotherapy" is used in countless publications, hundreds of conferences and meetings, thousands of academic courses, dozens of associations, and in identifying the practice of many thousands of professionals. Nevertheless, there is trouble when powerful groups are intent on distinguishing between psychotherapy and counseling, guidance, case work, psychoanalysis, rehabilitation, and loads of related words. I believe that the best word for it is "psychotherapy" even though the mere intent to distinguish psychotherapy from any of these other words is doomed to success. For example, if you are inclined, you can successfully distinguish between psychotherapy, counseling, and guidance (e.g., Bedal, 1981; Belkin, 1975; Eberlin, 1981; Hamilton, 1977; Hewer, 1972; Lewis, 1970; Manning & Cates, 1972; Pallone, 1977; Wrenn, 1977) so as to enable a formal organization such as the Canadian Guidance and Counselling Association to extend squatter's rights over a huge territory by defining counselling as ". . . a complex human activity which has as its goal the giving of aid by one person to another in the solution of the latter's life problems" (Peavy, Robertson, & Westwood, 1982, p. 136).

Using similar strategies, each profession can claim a part of the pie by limiting "psychoanalysis" to credentialed psychoanalysts, while the field of rehabilitation prefers to speak of rehabilitation therapy, education identifies school counseling, social workers want to call it case work, theology uses the phrase pastoral counseling, and psychology cherishes *psycho*therapy. Nevertheless, of all the words and terms, I suggest that the best word for it is "psychotherapy," and I will use that word as the overall umbrella for the whole family of related terms.

3. Psychotherapy Is the Collective Property of Many Professions and Disciplines, None of Whom has Exclusive Rights of Ownership

Whether we call it psychotherapy, counseling, or whatever, there are many professions and disciplines among those who originated and developed it, study and research it, teach and train and supervise it, and especially who practice it. There are the professions and disciplines of medicine, education, social work, sociology, psychiatry, psychology, theology, human relations, nursing, counseling, communication, and others.

Throughout the world, there are hundreds of postgraduate training centers, in all sorts of psychotherapies, that accept for training members of virtually all these professions and disciplines (Mahrer,

1987; Mahrer & Boulet, 1989; Matarazzo, 1965a, 1965b, 1977; Saslow & Matarazzo, 1962), yet ". . . what seems to get aired in public is each profession's belief that it is the only suitable profession for providing psychotherapeutic or counseling services" (Fretz & Mills, 1980, p.176). Even more, each of these professions and disciplines firmly insists that proper education and training requires a core foundation in that profession and discipline (Holt, 1965; Mahrer, 1987; Matarazzo, 1977). I respect all these claims in submitting that psychotherapy is the collective property of many professions and disciplines, none of whom has exclusive rights of ownership.

4. There Are No Generally Recognized Standards for the Practice or Speciality of Psychotherapy

There are no generally recognized standards for the practice of psychotherapy, for designating a speciality of psychotherapy, or for certifying qualified knowledge and competence in psychotherapy. Psychotherapy is not a recognized speciality in psychology (American Board of Professional Psychology, 1978; Sales, 1985; Sales, Bricklin, & Hall, 1983,1984), in psychiatry (Paris, Kravitz, & Prince, 1986), nor in any other profession. In the words of John Warkentin, a fellow of both the American Psychological Association and the American Psychiatric Association, "As psychotherapy is practiced in America today, there exist no standards of training, function, or responsibility on which psychotherapists generally agree" (1971, p. 107).

Nor are there any generally recognized standards for certifying knowledge and competence in psychotherapy. In sharp contrast to licensing examinations for the practice of medicine, dentistry and, to some extent, educational and school counseling (cf. Brown, Sewall, & Linstrom, 1977; Jones, 1976), state licensing examinations in psychology do not assess knowledge and competency in the practice of psychotherapy (Hogan, 1979; Koocher, 1979; Strupp, Butler, & Rosser, 1988). "The most widely used exam probably is an irrelevant instrument for assessing competency to practice" (Fox, Kovacs, & Graham, 1985, p. 1048); ". . . no state presently requires the competence of psychologists to be evaluated" (Fretz &

Mills, 1980, p. 12; cf. Shaw & Dobson, 1988). The Council for the National Register of Health Service Providers in Psychology is explicit that the register "was not designed nor does it purport in any way to evaluate the quality or competence of the services provided by anyone listed or not listed in the register" (1978, p. vii), and the APA Task Force on the Evaluation, Training, and Service in Psychology (1982) candidly states ". . . there is no evidence that any specific educational or training program or experience is related to professional competence" (p. 2). All in all, there are no generally recognized standards for the practice or speciality of psychotherapy.

5. Psychotherapy Is a Speciality Within and Across Established Professions and Disciplines

The practice of psychotherapy is best understood as a speciality within and across the various psychotherapy-related professions and disciplines. Under this proposition, the practitioner says that my profession or discipline is education (or psychology or medicine or social work), and my specialization is in the practice of psychotherapy. This leaves quite intact each profession's and each discipline's efforts to maintain, for example, that ". . . counseling psychology is a *bonafide* discipline (which) has a complex interdisciplinary relationship with better established disciplines such as education, psychiatry, sociology and psychology" (Friesen, 1983, pp. 147-148). On the other hand, this proposition is in distinct contrast to efforts to elevate psychotherapy to the status of an independent profession of its own (Holt, 1965, 1971).

6. The Provision of Qualified Knowledge and Competence in Psychotherapy Is the Job of Postgraduate Rather Than Pregraduate Training Programs

Most of the leading figures across the psychotherapy-related professions concur that graduation from masters or doctoral programs does not ensure qualified knowledge and competence for the practice of psychotherapy. "It is generally acknowledged that predoctoral training is not sufficient to guarantee a high level of competence in professional functioning" (Lewinsohn & Pearlman, 1972,

p. 48). What is more, it is ". . . quite doubtful that the clinical training such programs would offer could be improved in quality and quantity to the extent that is needed (for the practice of psychotherapy)" (Holt, 1965, p. 82; cf. Kovaks, 1965; McConnell, 1984).

If adequate education and training for the practice of psychotherapy does not occur in doctoral programs, it is to be acquired in the postdoctoral period wherein formal recognition by, for example, the American Psychological Association stops and formal recognition by licensing and certification bodies starts:

> Although the American Psychological Association (APA) currently recognizes no formal training requirements beyond the Ph.D. degree and offers no standards or guidelines for postdoctoral training, an examination of state licensing and certification laws clearly indicates that postdoctoral training is quickly becoming the norm rather than the exception for psychology doctorates pursuing state licensure . . . (Plante, 1988, p. 251)

Where is the doctoral graduate to gain qualified education and training in psychotherapy? Perhaps the answer lies in the postgraduate training programs that are the established tradition in such clinical professions as medicine and dentistry (Mahrer, 1987, 1989a, 1989b; Matarazzo, 1987). In psychology there are already powerful groups lobbying that ". . . relatively general training be given at the predoctoral level and more specialized training at the postdoctoral level" (Sheridan et al., 1988, p. 3; cf. Lange, 1972; Stigal, 1988) in specialities such as health psychology (Sheridan et al., 1988; Olbrisch et al., 1985; Stone, 1983), community psychology (Silverman & Fourcher, 1975), pediatric psychology (Routh, 1977), and internships in all specialities (Belar, 1988; Plante, 1988; Toye & Pierce, 1987). If you want qualified knowledge and competence in psychotherapy, the place to go is the postgraduate training center, even though ". . . psychology today does not have a societal or a professional requirement or a mechanism under and through which to begin to *mandate* additional education and training" (Matarazzo, 1987, p. 373).

7. Postgraduate Training Centers in Psychotherapy Are Plentiful and Thriving

Both in terms of the sheer number of centers and number of persons in training, postgraduate training centers in psychotherapy are plentiful and thriving. The American Psychological Association's Division of Psychotherapy published a directory of postdoctoral training centers in psychotherapy for psychologists (Rachman & Kauff, 1972), listing 18 in 1964, 34 in 1965, and 54 in 1972. Among all training centers, those in psychoanalysis are currently the most popular, according to a survey of these programs in 23 countries (Fichter & Wittchen, 1980). The American Academy of Psychoanalysis lists 45 training centers and approximately 2500-3500 currently enrolled physicians; the American Psychoanalytic Association estimates approximately 4000 graduates of psychoanalytic institutes; and estimates of the number of current Jungian analytic trainees are in the 1900-2500 range. As an example of the popularity of psychoanalytic training, there are approximately 150 psychologists currently enrolled in the Postdoctoral Program in Psychotherapy and Psychoanalysis of New York University.

The same picture holds for other approaches. The 1988 Gestalt Directory lists 49 training centers and approximately 2000 current trainees, and notes that this is a very conservative estimate since many Gestalt centers are not included in the directory. The Bulletin of the International Institute for Bioenergetic Analysis lists 42 postgraduate training centers, and the American Society of Clinical Hypnosis (1988) indicates that specialized postgraduate training is provided to approximately 500 professionals annually. Including training centers in client-centered, rational-motive, experiential, cognitive behavior, transactional analysis, and other therapies, the picture is of plentiful and thriving postgraduate training in psychotherapy.

8. There Are No Uniform Minimal Standards of Postgraduate Education and Training in Psychotherapy

Unfortunately, these postgraduate training centers accept no across-the-board minimal standards. Even within similar approaches, there is substantial variability, and across approaches the variability is exceedingly widespread. Nor are there any viable movements in the direction of establishing uniform minimal standards across all or most postgraduate training centers in psychotherapy.

Whether or not you are persuaded by these eight arguments, they pave the way for the consideration of minimal standards of postdoctoral training in psychotherapy.

THE POSTDOCTORAL PLAN: MINIMAL STANDARDS OF POSTDOCTORAL TRAINING IN PSYCHOTHERAPY

These minimal standards are proposed as a friendly provisional beginning toward much needed discussion and consideration among those who are involved in any kind of postgraduate education and training in any kind of psychotherapy, from psychoanalytic to Gestalt, Adlerian to cognitive behavior, integrative-eclectic to experiential, client-centered to rational-emotive. They are also addressed toward psychotherapy practitioners, those involved with graduate education and training in the psychotherapy-related professions, and toward the psychotherapy-related professions themselves, including their accrediting, regulating, certifying, and licensing boards and agencies.

A Doctorate in a Psychotherapy-Related Profession

Admission requires a doctorate in any psychotherapy-related profession. While this is a blockbuster issue, wherein any arguments favoring the doctorate have easily been countered by powerful arguments favoring the masters degree, the doctorate is preferred on the basis of three admittedly vulnerable considerations. One is that the doctorate is the highest academic degree across all of the psychotherapy-related professions. It is the accepted practitioner degree in medicine and, to a large extent, psychology, although the masters is the accepted practitioner degree in many other psychotherapy-related professions, and is a solidly acceptable admission degree in a majority of postgraduate psychotherapy training centers. Second, an impressively large proportion of the distinguished theoreticians, researchers, and exemplars in psychotherapy possess this higher degree. Third, I believe that the acrimonious, long-standing antagonism between those favoring the masters degree has better chances of long-term resolution by adopting the doctorate as the degree of choice for admission to postgraduate training in psychotherapy. At the very least, this is specific enough for purposes of discussion.

The Mandate

Each postdoctoral training center accepts the mandate of providing qualified and specialized knowledge and competence in the practice of a designated approach or approaches to psychotherapy (Herron, Borello, & Trubowitz, 1977; Matarazzo, 1987).

Administrative Independence and Representativeness

Whether free-standing or university-based, the training center is to be administratively independent of any single psychotherapy-related profession, notably medicine or psychology, and may be conjointly administered by several psychotherapy-related professions, schools, faculties, or departments (Holt, 1965; Keller & Baumann, 1986; Prokasy, 1986; Shakow, 1971). Similarly, the faculty is to be reasonably representative of the various psychotherapy-related professions (Belar, 1987).

The Program

The provisional program was arrived at from careful study of the minimum requirements of the programs of 100 postgraduate centers and institutes offering education and training in a broad diversity of approaches to psychotherapy, psychoanalysis, and counseling. Many of the programs exceed these proposed minimal requirements, and many fall short. The aim was to provide a set of provisional requirements that best represented a balanced compromise among the actual requirements used by most of the training programs, and, therefore, a reasonable agenda for discussion and modification. Accordingly, the program is to include a minimum of at least 1000 hours, distributed over at least two years, designed to accommodate the working professional (Matarazzo, 1987; Ross, 1974), and comprising the following minimal requirements:

1. Personal therapy (100 hours). Each trainee is to receive a minimum of 100 hours of personal therapy in the designated approach (cf. Kubie, 1971).
2. Direct practice (400 hours). Each trainee is to complete a minimum of 400 hours of direct practice in the designated approach.
3. Supervision (200 hours). Each trainee is to receive a minimum of 200 hours of individual or small-group supervision of their direct practice.
4. Listening/observing exemplars (100 hours). Each trainee is to accrue a minimum of 100 hours of listening to and/or observing the therapeutic work of exemplars, including direct observation, audiotapes, and videotapes.
5. Didactic courses and seminars (200 hours). Each trainee is to receive a minimum of 200 hours of didactic courses and seminars in the following areas as related to the therapeutic approach: (a) history and background; (b) philosophical and theoretical foundations; (c) theory of practice; (d) methods and procedures; and (e) special topics.
6. Examination of knowledge and competence. Each trainee is to receive a formal examination of depth and breadth of knowledge, and level of skills and competencies (British Psychological Society, 1981; Fordyce & Meier, 1987; McClelland, 1973).

Under this proposed plan, a psychotherapist would be understood as a professional who has a doctorate in any of the psychotherapy-related professions, and a diploma from a postdoctoral training center certifying satisfactory completion of a minimum of two years and 1000 hours of training, and the achievement of certified, qualified knowledge and competence in a designated psychotherapeutic approach.

IMPLICATIONS FOR THE FIELD OF PSYCHOTHERAPY

It is not likely that the next few years will see any substantial movement toward any set of common minimal standards among the various postgraduate training centers in psychotherapy. But part of the enthusiasm or reluctance to move in this direction is based on the likely consequence on the field of psychotherapy, and therefore a few of these might be anticipated.

1. For the first time, there would be a set of generally accepted standards for the education and training of psychotherapists. Within and across the several psychotherapy-related professions, with all their various degrees and programs, and within and across the many different kinds of postgraduate programs, the standards are so exceedingly variable as to be virtually nonexistent. If most of the postgraduate training centers and institutes could adopt uniform standards, we could finally point to these as the guidelines for the education and training for the qualified practice of psychotherapy.

2. It is likely that there will be a growing sense of identity among those whose speciality is the practice of psychotherapy (Herron, Borello, & Trubowitz, 1977; Holt, 1971; Kubie, 1971). Nevertheless, rather than foreseeing the emergence of an independent profession, the likelihood is of a shared speciality of psychotherapy while preserving the professional identification with the larger disciplines of psychology, medicine, social work, education, or any of the other psychotherapy-related professions.

3. Especially with regard to licensing and certification, the American Psychological Association continues its long struggle to resolve the antinomy between the doctorate and the master's degree (Colliver, Havens, & Wesley, 1985; Fox, Kovacs, & Graham, 1985; Perlman, 1985a, 1985b; Woods, 1971), while it is ". . . clear that tens of thousands of masters-level personnel, from hundreds of programs, are working in the field of psychology" (Dale, 1988, p. 589). In the field of psychotherapy, the traditional practitioner degree is the masters in such professions as social work, education, and counseling, as well as many others. It is likely that all the psychotherapy-related professions and their graduate training programs will be sharply affected depending on whether postgraduate training

centers continue to accept both the doctorate and the master's degree or, as is proposed here, the doctorate emerges as the degree of choice. In either case, the implications will likely be far-reaching.

4. If postgraduate training centers are the place to go for qualified education and training in psychotherapy, this will exert strong impacts on both masters and doctoral graduate programs in all the psychotherapy-related professions to follow the medical model of core, generic, foundational predoctoral education followed by specialized postdoctoral training. In psychology, as in all the psychotherapy-related professions, the likely consequence will tend to support those who favor core, generic, foundational graduate education, and will not support those espousing more specialized graduate training (Caddy & Lapointe, 1984; Dörken & Cummings, 1977; Peterson, 1982, 1985; Stricker, 1975), including specialized graduate education and training in health psychology, school psychology, cognitive, forensic, pediatric, community, rehabilitation, industrial and organizational psychology, neuropsychology, psychophysiology, psychopharmacology, and other predoctoral specialities.

5. Similarly, it is likely that graduate internship, residency, and field training will also become more core, generic, and foundational, followed by postgraduate specialization, in accord with the established tradition in psychiatry (Katz, 1984) and reflected in current trends in psychology where, for example, the National Conference on Internship Training in Psychology (Belar et al., 1987) called for a two-year internship with the second as a more advanced, specialized, postdoctoral year (Belar, 1988; Plante, 1988; Toye & Pierce, 1987).

6. One of the blockbuster implications will involve the accreditation, certification, licensing, and mandating of the postdoctoral training centers and the practice of psychotherapy. While each of the psychotherapy-related professions currently accredits its own graduate education and licenses or certifies its own practitioners, it is likely that the future will see the emergence of a single overall organization responsible for accrediting its member postdoctoral training centers, and for determining the standards for the certification and licensing of the practice of psychotherapy. The way has been paved by organizations in other countries such as the Federal

Republic of Germany, the Netherlands, England, and Norway where there is a recognised distinction ". . . between university training and subsequent curricula for specialization in psychotherapy outside the university" (Fichter & Wittchen, 1980, p. 19). These organizations are responsible for their own self-imposed standards ". . . in the Netherlands by the Dutch Organization for Psychology and in Norway by the State Center for Medical Postgraduate Training" (Fichter & Wittchen, 1980, p. 19), in the Federal Republic of Germany by three organizations responsible for the provision of postgraduate training in the various psychotherapeutic approaches (Brengelmann & Wittchen, 1986), and in England by the British Psychological Society's (1981) standards for approving "postqualification" programs in psychotherapy. The likelihood is a growing rapprochement between postgraduate training centers self-imposing their own minimal standards, and the several psychotherapy-related professions working together toward mutually agreed-upon minimal standards for postgraduate standards of education and training for the practice of psychotherapy.

7. Psychotherapy is a unique field of practice if only because it cuts across a number of psychotherapy-related professions and disciplines, has so many different approaches, and has so many different graduate and postgraduate settings and sites for its education and training. It is hoped that one implication is the launching of constructive discussion toward a set of minimal standards of postgraduate education and training for the practice of psychotherapy.

REFERENCES

American Academy of Psychoanalysis (1988). Training facilities in psychoanalysis. 30 East 40th Street, New York, New York 10016.

American Board of Professional Psychology (1978). *Policies and Procedures for the Creation of Diplomates in Professional Psychology*. Washington, DC: American Board of Professional Psychology.

American Psychological Association (1982). *Report of the task force on the evaluation of education, training, and service in psychology*. Washington, DC: American Psychological Association.

American Society of Clinical Hypnosis (1988). Membership information. 2250 East Devon Avenue, Des Plaines, Illinois 60018.

Bedal, C.L. (1981). The education of school counsellors in Canada. *Canadian Counsellor, 15*, 115-118.

Belar, C.D. (1987). The current status of predoctoral and postdoctoral training in health psychology. In G.C. Stone, S.M. Weiss, J.D. Matarazzo, N.E. Miller, J. Rodin, C.D. Belar, M.J. Follick, & J.E. Singer (Eds.), *Health Psychology: A Discipline and a Profession* (pp. 325-334). Chicago: The University of Chicago Press.

Belar, C.D., Bieliauskas, L.A., & Larsen, K.G. (1987). *Proceedings: National Conference on Internship Training in Psychology*. Baton Rouge, LA: Land and Land.

Belkin, G. (1975). *Practical Counselling in Schools*. Dubuque, IA: W.C. Brown.

Bernstein, B. & Lecompte, C. (1976). An integrative competency-based counsellor education model. *Counsellor Education and Supervision*, *16*, 26-35.

Brengelmann, J.C. & Wittchen, H.U. (1986). Professional psychology and private health services: Developing trends in the Federal Republic of Germany. *American Psychologist*, *41*, 306-308.

British Psychological Society (1981). Criteria for the assessment of postqualification courses for applied psychologists in psychological therapy. *Bulletin of the British Psychological Society*, *34*, 130.

Brown, D., Sewall, T., & Lindstrom, J. (1977). *Handbook of Certification/Licensure Requirements for School Psychologists*. Washington: National Association of School Psychology.

Caddy, G.R. & LaPointe, L.L. (1984). The training of professional psychologists: Historical developments and present trends. In G.S. Tryon (Ed.), *Professional Practice of Psychology* (pp. 218-233). Norwood, NJ: Ablex.

Colliver, J.A., Havens, R.A., & Wesley, R.M. (1985). Doctoral and masters-level clinical psychologists and MSWs in public mental health settings: A nationwide follow-up. *Professional Psychology: Research and Practice*, *16*, 634-640.

Council for the National Register of Health Service Providers in Psychology (1978). *National Register of Health Service Providers in Psychology*. Washington, DC: National Register of Health Service Providers in Psychology.

Dale, R.H.I. (1988). State psychological associations, licensing criteria, and the "master's issue." *Professional Psychology*, *19*, 589-593.

Dörken, H. & Cummings, N.A. (1977). A school of psychology as innovation in professional education: The California School of Professional Psychology. *Professional Psychology*, *8*, 129-148.

Eberlin, L.E. (1981). School trustees vs. counsellor educators: A reaction to the Jevne report. *Canadian Counsellor*, *15*, 68-69.

Fichter, M.M., & Wittchen, H.U. (1980). Clinical psychology and psychotherapy: A survey of the present state of professionalization in 23 countries. *American Psychologist*, *35*, 16-25.

Fordyce, W.E. & Meier, M.J. (1987). Respecialization and continuing education for health psychology. In G.C. Stone, S.M. Weiss, J.D. Matarazzo, N.E. Miller, J. Rodin, C.D. Belar, M.J. Follick, & J.E. Singer (Eds.), *Health Psychology: A Discipline and a Profession* (pp. 403-412). Chicago: University of Chicago Press.

Fox, R.E., Kovacs, A.L., & Graham, S.R. (1985). Proposals for a revolution in the preparation and regulation of professional psychologists. *American Psychologist, 40*, 1042-1050.

Fretz, B.R. & Mills, D.H. (1980). *Licensing and Certification of Psychologists and Counsellors*. San Francisco: Jossey-Bass.

Friesen, J.D. (1983). Counselling psychology: A discipline. *Canadian Counsellor, 17*, 147-154.

Gestalt Directory (1988). The Center for Gestalt Development, P.O. Box 990, Highland, New York 12528.

Hamilton, M. (1977). Graduate training and professional identity. *The Counseling Psychologist, 7*, 26-29.

Herron, W.G., Borello, J., & Trubowitz, J. (1977). The value of postdoctoral training for the practice of psychotherapy. *Journal of Contemporary Psychotherapy, 9*, 95-99.

Hewer, V. (1972). Identity and the psychological practitioner. *Professional Psychology, 3*, 241-250.

Hogan, D.B. (1979). *The Regulation of Psychotherapists: Vol. 1. A Study in the Philosophy and Practice of Professional Regulation*. Cambridge, MA: Ballinger.

Holt, R.R. (1965). Psychotherapy as an autonomous profession. *Preconference Materials for the Conference on the Professional Preparation of Clinical Psychologists* (pp. 81-83). Washington, DC: American Psychological Association.

Holt, R.R. (1971). Summary and prospect: The dawn of a new profession. In R.R. Holt (Ed.), *New Horizon for Psychotherapy* (pp. 312-411). New York: International Universities Press.

International Institute for Bioenergetic Analysis (1988). Bulletin. 144 East 34th Street, New York, New York 10016.

Jevne, R. (1981). Counsellor competencies and selected issues in Canadian counsellor education. *Canadian Counsellor, 15*, 57-63.

Jones, L. (1976). A national survey of the program and enrollment characteristics of counsellor education programs. *Counsellor Education and Supervision, 15*, 166-177.

Katz, P. (1984). *The Role of the Psychotherapies in the Practice of Psychiatry*. Ottawa: Scientific Council, Canadian Psychiatric Association.

Keller, M.L. & Baumann, L.J. (1986). Further comments on psychology and nursing. *American Psychologist, 41*, 1169-1170.

Koocher, G.P. (1979). Credentialing in psychology: Close encounters with competence? *American Psychologist, 34*, 694-702.

Korman, M. (1974). National conference on levels and patterns of professional training in psychology. *American Psychologist, 29*, 441-449.

Kovacs, A.L. (1965). Training in clinical psychology: A view of future prospects. *Preconference Materials for the Conference on the Professional Preparation of Clinical Psychologists* (pp. 83-86). Washington, DC: American Psychological Association.

Kubie, L.S. (1971). A doctorate in psychotherapy: The reasons for a new profession. In R.R. Holt (Ed.), *New Horizon for Psychotherapy* (pp. 11-36). New York: International Universities Press.

Lange, J. (1972). Post-doctoral training: A time for change? *Menninger Perspective, 3*, 13-16.

Lewinsohn, P.M. & Pearlman, S. (1972). Continuing education for psychologists. *Professional Psychology, 3*, 48-52.

Lewis, E. (1970). *The Psychology of Counseling*. New York: Holt, Rinehart and Winston.

Mahrer, A.R. (1987). If there really were a speciality of psychotherapy: Standards for postdoctoral training in psychotherapy. *The Humanistic Psychologist, 15*, 83-94.

Mahrer, A.R. (1989a). *Experiencing: A Humanistic Theory of Psychology and Psychiatry*. Ottawa: University of Ottawa Press. (Original work published 1978).

Mahrer, A.R. (1989b). *The Integration of Psychotherapies: A Guide for Practicing Therapists*. New York: Human Sciences Press.

Mahrer, A.R. & Boulet, D.B. (1989). The postdoctoral plan for the education and training of counsellors. *Canadian Journal of Counselling, 23*, pp. 27-39.

Manning, T. & Cates, J. (1972). Specialization within psychology. *American Psychologist, 27*, 462-467.

Matarazzo, J.D. (1965a). A postdoctoral residency program in clinical psychology. *American Psychologist, 20*, 432-439.

Matarazzo, J.D. (1965b). Postdoctoral residency program in clinical psychology. *Preconference Materials for the Conference on the Professional Preparation of Clinical Psychologists* (pp. 71-73). Washington, DC: American Psychological Association.

Matarazzo, J.D. (1977). Higher education, professional accreditation, and licensure. *American Psychologist, 32*, 854-859.

Matarazzo, J.D. (1987). Postdoctoral education and training of service providers in health psychology. In G.C. Stone, S.M. Weiss, J.D. Matarazzo, N.E. Miller, J. Rodin, C.D. Belar, M.J. Follick, & J.E. Singer (Eds.), *Health Psychology: A Discipline and a Profession* (pp. 371-388). Chicago: University of Chicago Press.

McClelland, D.C. (1973). Testing for competence rather than intelligence. *American Psychologist, 28*, 1-14.

McConnell, S.C. (1984). Doctor of Psychology degree: From hibernation to reality. *Professional Psychology: Research and Practice, 15*, 362-370.

Olbrisch, M.E., Weiss, S.M., Stone, G.C., & Schwartz, G.E. (1985). Report of the National Working Conference on Education and Training in Healthy Psychology. *American Psychologist, 40*, 1038-1041.

Pallone, N. (1977). Counseling psychology: Toward an empirical definition. *Counseling Psychology, 7*, 29-32.

Paris, J., Kravitz, H., & Prince, R. (1986). Report: Conference on key issues in postgraduate psychiatric education in Canada. *Canadian Journal of Psychiatry, 31*, 705-707.

Peavy, R.V., Robertson, S., & Westwood, M. (1982). Guidelines for counsellor education in Canada. *Canadian Counsellor, 16*, 135-143.

Perlman, B. (1985a). A national survey of APA-affiliated master-level clinicians: Description and comparison. *Professional Psychology: Research and Practice, 16*, 553-564.

Perlman, B. (1985b). Training and career issues of APA-affiliated master-level clinicians. *Professional Psychology: Research and Practice, 16*, 753-767.

Peterson, D.R. (1982). Origins and development of the Doctor of Psychology concept. In G.R. Caddy, D.C. Rimm, H. Watson, & J.H. Johnson (Eds.), *Educating Professional Psychologists* (pp. 19-38). New Brunswick, NJ: Transaction Books.

Peterson, D.R. (1985). Twenty years of practitioner training in psychology. *American Psychologist, 40*, 441-451.

Plante, T.G. (1988). Postdoctoral training in clinical psychology: As amorphous as an inkblot. *Professional Psychology: Research and Practice, 19*, 251-253.

Prokasy, W.F. (1986). Preparation and regulation of professional psychologists. *American Psychologist, 41*, 1176-1177.

Rachman, A.W. & Kauff, P.F. (1972). *Directory of postgraduate psychotherapy training facilities*. Washington, DC: Division of Psychotherapy, American Psychotherapy Association.

Ross, A.O. (1974). Continuing professional development in psychology. *Professional Psychology, 5*, 122-128.

Routh, D.K. (1977). Postdoctoral training in pediatric psychology. *Professional Psychology, 8*, 145-150.

Sales, B. (1985). Specialization: Past history and future alternatives. *The Clinical Psychologist, 38*, 48-52.

Sales, B., Bricklin, P., and Hall, J. (1983). *Manual for Identification and Continued Recognition of Proficiencies and New Specialities in Psychology*. Washington, DC: American Psychological Association.

Sales, B., Bricklin, P., and Hall, H. (1984). *Specialization in Psychology: Principles*. Washington, DC: American Psychological Association.

Saslow, G., & Matarazzo, J.D. (1962). A psychiatric service in a general hospital: A setting for social learning. *International Journal of Social Psychiatry, 8*, 5-18.

Shakow, D. (1971). Patterns of institutional sponsorship. In R.R. Holt (Ed.), *New Horizon for Psychotherapy* (pp. 194-208). New York: International Universities Press.

Shaw, B.F. & Dobson, K.S. (1988). Competency judgements in the training and evaluation of psychotherapists. *Journal of Consulting and Clinical Psychology, 56*, 666-672.

Sheridan, E.P, Matarazzo, J.D., Boll, T.J., Perry, Jr., N.W., Weiss, S.M., & Belar, C.D. (1988). Postdoctoral education and training for clinical service providers in health psychology. *Health Psychology, 7*, 1-17.

Silverman, W.H. & Fourcher, L.A. (1975). A developmental approach to post-doctoral training in community psychology. *Professional Psychology*, *6*, 344-349.

Stigall, T.T. (1988). A new look at graduate education for practice. *The Psychotherapy Bulletin*, *23*, 18-20.

Stone, G.C. (Ed.) (1983). Proceedings of the National Working Conference on Education and Training in Health Psychology. *Health Psychology*, *2*, 1-153, supplement section.

Stricker, G. (1975). On professional schools and professional degrees. *American Psychologist*, *30*, 1062-1066.

Strupp, H.H., Butler, S.F., & Rosser, C. (1988). Training in psychodynamic therapy. *Journal of Consulting and Clinical Psychology*, *56*, 689-695.

Toye, R.C. & Pierce, P.S. (1987). Addressing the statutory requirements of a postdoctoral year of experience in clinical psychology. *Professional Psychology: Research and Practice*, *18*, 3-4.

Warkentin, J. (1971). An ideal training program for psychotherapists. In R.R. Holt (Ed.), *New Horizon for Psychotherapy* (pp. 105-123). New York: International Universities Press.

Woods, P.J. (1971). A history of APA's concern within the master's degree: Or, "discharged with thanks." *American Psychologist*, *26*, 696-707.

Wrenn, G. (1977). Landmarks and the growing edge. *The Counseling Psychologist*, *7*, 10-13.

SYMPOSIUM: THE ROLES OF PSYCHOLOGISTS IN HEALTH CARE

Psychological Practice in Hospitals

Jack G. Wiggins

Psychologists and hospitals are not very well acquainted with one another. This is especially true in hospitals without psychiatric or alcoholism units. This will change because of economic factors affecting hospitals and psychologists alike. New laws, government regulations, and changes in private health insurance benefits force all participants to reassess their positions in the reform of the health care system. New alliances are likely to be created to assure economic survival.

The health care market has been disrupted by a variety of cost cutting techniques. The Diagnostic Related Group (DRG) prospective reimbursement system for Medicare caused Ohio hospitals to lose $53 million in 1988. These losses reflect the national trend and

---

Jack G. Wiggins, PhD, is in private practice in Cleveland, OH.

Presented at the meeting of the American College of Health Executives, Chicago, IL, February-March, 1990.

are projected to have increased in 1989. Losses from Medicare payments are forcing hospitals into a new industry of "community based services for chronically ill people." As a result, hospitals are building and affiliating with nursing homes to control their costs of long term inpatient care. They are also expanding their home health care programs and hiring case managers for services to the chronically ill ambulatory patient. Not only are inpatient days being reduced, but the use of a wide variety of outpatient diagnostic services for pre-admission screening are increasing. Furthermore, outpatient treatment services are being used to eliminate the use of inpatient hospital care entirely.

Mental health services in acute medical hospitals are also being curtailed significantly. Ten years ago the average length of stay (LOS) was 22 days in a psychiatric unit. Now the average LOS is fourteen days or less for most hospitals with a target of nine days for Schizophrenia. Greater emphasis is being placed on outpatient psychiatric and psychological services. Ironically, at this same time, insurers are placing more stringent controls on the utilization of mental health benefits, especially psychological services. Since mental health costs constitute 13% of claims dollars paid, both inpatient and outpatient psychiatric claims have become a special target of the MBA cost-cutters.

Psychology, although originally pressed into service in State and Veterans Administration Mental Hospital Programs, has for the last forty years focused on outpatient acute mental health care. This population tended to be younger and more ambulatory than that typically served by hospitals. As a result, psychologists showed little interest in providing services in acute care general hospitals until Medicaid created a market for psychiatric services in community hospitals in the mid 60's. As community based hospitals began to develop psychiatric and alcoholism units, psychologists began to look to hospitals as a place for care for their most disturbed patients. When psychologists found that the JCAHO (formerly JCAH) rules limited their participation on the staffs of hospitals an antitrust suit was filed. This suit resulted in the JCAHO rules regarding hospital staff privileges being modified to allow each hospital to set its own rules according to state law. This change greatly accelerated the use of hospitals by psychologists in private practice. Currently there are about 50,000 psychologists practicing in the mental health arena compared to about 40,000 psychiatrists. Psychologists are also the largest doctoral level provider group of outpatient psychotherapeutic services in the United States. Psychologists have become involved with hospitals more frequently and significant numbers have joined hospital staffs.

Psychological practice in hospitals has heightened the turf battle between psychiatry and psychology. As a result, hospital privileges have been limited in scope for psychologists since they are frequently characterized as a psychiatric look alike. Because of the turf issues, hospitals have proceeded cautiously in accepting psychologists on hospital staffs. This is because hospital administrations do not have a full appreciation of the wide variety of services psychologists provide to bed patients and to ambulatory patients *who are not psychiatrically* disordered. Psychological care to non-psychiatrically disordered populations is the major issue upon which I wish to focus attention. It is a given that psychologists have a significant contribution to make to mentally disordered as well as chemically dependent patients. However, these constitute only a small portion of the services psychologists render in hospitals. Each service psychology delivers in hospital must be judged on its own merits and must be clearly differentiated from psychiatry.

Reductions in reimbursement from third party payers have caused psychologists to seek new markets for their services. Hospitals expanding into outpatient and home health care have called upon psychologists to provide services not currently offered by the hospitals. Thus, hospitals and psychologists have found a natural alliance which has been a long time in coming. Recently, Dr. Ludwigsen and I were asked to write a chapter in a book regarding the different kinds of services psychologists offer in hospitals. We found that psychologists are routinely rendering 20 different services in hospitals. These include: Alcoholism and substance abuse, cancer counseling, cardiac rehabilitation, eating disorder management, elderly and retirement counseling, emergency room consultation, health promotion, home health care, neuropsychological assessments, nursing home preadmission screening, pain management, pre-employment screenings, preoperative counseling, psychiatric counseling, rehabilitation of victims of stroke and those in prolonged rehabilitation programs, sexual dysfunction counseling, sleep disorders, specialized outpatient programs such as phobic clinics, weight loss programs, etc. Psychologists have become an integral part of nearly every department or division in hospitals and are not restricted to departments of psychiatry.

The alliance between hospitals and psychologists has been strengthened by psychologists' recent inclusion as independent providers under Medicare as of July 1, 1990. It is anticipated that this will increase psychology's involvement in hospital practice because their services are reimbursable under Medicare. Also self-regulation through behavioral management of physical conditions will be more necessary as rehabilitation shifts from inpatient care to community based care.

Let me offer some observations about how psychologists can be of assistance to the hospital population. Many bed patients in hospitals are elderly and become depressed. Lifetime incidence for experiencing anxiety or depression is estimated to be 25 percent for individuals without a chronic medical condition and 42 percent for those with a chronic health problem. The elderly are often taking a combination of cardiac, antihypertensives, insulin as well as other specialized medications which complicate psychopharmacology. Furthermore, the elderly do not necessarily respond well to psychotropic medication and are subject to a higher incidence of falling and breaking bones as a result of being on psychotropic medication. In such situations, psychotherapy may be the treatment of choice. A recent study of psychotherapy found it to be as effective as antidepressants in treatment of the less severely depressed. At one time we thought that the elderly were not amenable to psychological treatment. My experience on a rehabilitation unit where the average age was 73, has taught me otherwise. The elderly respond well both to group and individual psychotherapy provided by experts. They, being older and wiser, do not necessarily respond well to unskilled counseling by well intended but untrained hospital employees. The elderly do respond to the attention and helpfulness of young hospital employees but often there is little carry-over into the home situation. Unless there is psychological intervention that affects attitudes which motivate the individual toward self help and personal fulfillment, medical regimens learned in the hospital are apt to be ignored and medication schedules forgotten.

Recovery from a serious injury or illness is devastating enough and requires *professional* counseling. Recently through serendipity Spiegal found that women with metastasized breast cancer who received professional assistance in a group setting had survival rates nearly twice as long as those of controls who did not participate in these activities (36 to 19 months). Psychological interventions do improve the quality of care. Similarly, cardiac surgery patients receiving professional counseling reduced their stays in hospitals by two days as a result of psychological intervention. For those cardiac patients who are on a Medicare DRG payment schedule, this can make the difference between profit and loss for a hospital.

Psychological diagnostic and treatment techniques are very versatile and are adaptable to the unique needs of special populations. One example are services to workers who have been injured on the job and are subject to prolonged recovery and rehabilitation. These individuals often experience personal depression during this period and are dependent upon their families for emotional support. However, long delays in payment by Workers Compensation programs frequently create additional stress and anxiety within the family. The average length of time between incurred service and payment for that service in Ohio is 110 days. This period of uncertainty is devastating upon the patient and their family. The Ohio Injured Workers Association was recently formed to deal with this problem by setting up self help programs. The Ohio Injured Workers Association embarked on a program with area hospitals to educate injured workers about their rights and benefits. Hospitals can practice enlightened self interest by providing literature to injured workers defining their rights and opportunities for treatment. This educational material can help the injured worker and their family locate other assistance that they will need during their recovery and rehabilitation. By informing the injured worker and their family and setting up support groups for them, the hospital can often recover payments more promptly because they get greater cooperation from the injured workers and their families. Psychologists are routinely involved with Workers Compensation, Bureaus of Vocational Rehabilitation, as well as Social Security Disability Determinations. Thus they are ideally situated to serve patients injured at work and facilitate the educative and restorative functions these individuals need.

In addition to providing services to injured workers, psychologists have also helped hospitals select their work force. Psychologists evaluate professional personnel from top management down and throughout the entire hospital employment program. Hospitals are just now learning that psychologists can also help them promote the pre-employment physicals that corporations require. Psychological assessment of personnel has given major corporations a significant advantage in attracting the talent and personal stability of their employees over those recruited by smaller firms. Corporations with 200 employees or less frequently do not have a personnel department let alone a nurse on their staff. These smaller corporations are most likely to use hospitals for pre-employment physicals. Smaller companies are now becoming sophisticated enough to use psychological testing to help them screen employees for alcoholism and substance abuse as well as suitability for the work for which they are to be hired. By providing psychological assessment for the small companies, hospitals can help small firms become more economically competitive and grow. This tends to increase the utilization of hospital services as well as provide additional revenue for the hospital. Hospitals tend to have a profit margin of 20-30% from professional staff services. The margin of profit in pre-employment screening tends to be even higher. Other high profit areas for hospitals which involve the skills of psychologists include pain management, sleep disorders, sexual dysfunction and weight loss and weight maintenance functions.

In order for hospitals to survive and remain profitable, it will be necessary for them to provide health services in larger proportion to younger and healthier populations. Hospitals have tended to emphasize critical care to the aged and dying. Now, a major portion of the health benefits under Medicare are paid out in the last six months of life and in the last two weeks of life, in particular. Health care costs are not as much of a problem to Medicare as are the high costs of dying. Providing high tech services to the dying is being called into question not only by the economists but by those interested in the ethics of health as well. The Hospice concept is growing and will be a major factor in the health care system in the next millennium. We can anticipate hospitals developing hospice units. As most people are aware, psychology comes from the Greek word meaning "psyche" or "soul" and "logos" meaning "the study of." Most are not aware that "psyche" is also the Greek word for butterfly. The metamorphosis of the butterfly was used as an allegory for the transmigration of the soul. Psychologists trained in family systems are uniquely qualified to assist families in making the decisions about continuing medical care for loved ones, as well as helping in the bereavement process.

In concluding I have a few observations about psychology and hospitals. Psychology has transformed itself from its academic, philosophical beginnings to a neuroscience connecting physiology with human experience and the adjustments to life circumstances. In the last *thirty years* a significant portion of the practice of psychologists has turned to the amelioration and adjustment of not only the mental health, but of the physical health of the American public. We have joined hands with our medical colleagues in outpatient services. In the last *fifteen years* psychologists have been providing services not just to the physically healthy but also to medically unstable bed patients. Psychological evaluations and treatments have helped patients take better care of their health needs. Psychology and hospitals have joined together to do this. While it is a recent beginning, I believe that it is mutually advantageous and one that will continue to grow and flourish.

Psychologists: An Essential Component to Cost-Effective, Innovative Care

Nicholas Cummings

ARGUMENTS FOR THE FINANCIAL EFFICACY OF PSYCHOLOGICAL SERVICES IN HEALTHCARE SETTINGS

The "healthcare revolution" has produced a new array of health and mental health service delivery systems. In light of these changes, a thorough understanding of the evidence for the financial efficacy of psychological services in health settings is critical for the healthcare industry, for service providers, for patients, and for policy-makers.

Psychotherapy Key to Effective Healthcare Planning

Cummings and VandenBos (1981) summarized the twenty-year Kaiser-Permanente research experience demonstrating the financial efficacy of psychological services in healthcare settings (see Chart 1 attached). Despite an initial view of mental health services as a less costly "dumping ground for hypochondriacs," twenty-five years of

---

Nicholas Cummings, PhD, is Chairman and CEO, American Biodyne, Inc., 400 Oyster Point Boulevard, Suite 218, South San Francisco, CA 94080.

Presented to The American College of Healthcare Executives, February 28 and March 1, 1990.

CHART 1. Potential for Reduction in Medical Claims. Decline in Medical Utilization During Year of Intervention.

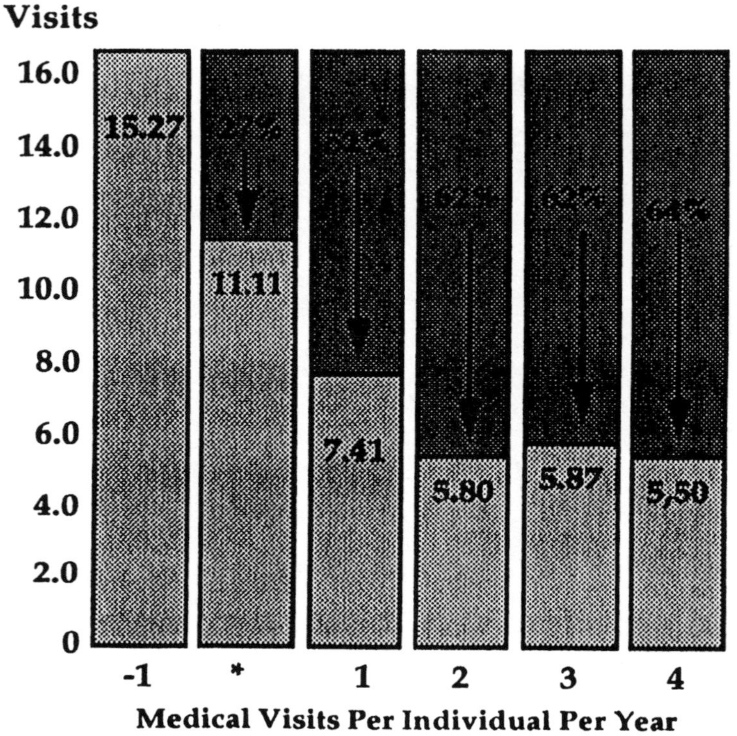

Kaiser Permanente data
Period 1974-1979
Sample based on 4,166 subscribers
Population sample withdrawn from 187,300

research has led to the conclusion that no comprehensive prepaid system can survive financially without a psychotherapy benefit.

The Somatization Cycle

For example, early investigations confirmed that 60% of all physician visits were for patients without a confirmable physical or biological problem. Add to this figure the visits by patients with

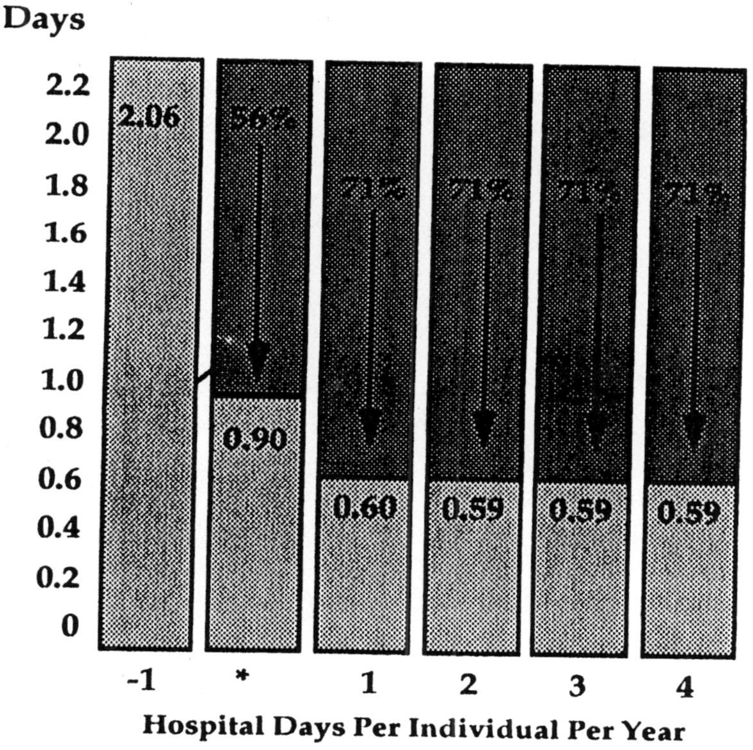

stress-related illnesses (e.g., peptic ulcer, ulcerative colitis, hypertension, etc.) and the total approaches 80-90% (cf. Shapiro, 1971). Subsequent research has demonstrated that turning 60-90% of all M.D.'s into psychotherapists (in order to handle the emotionally distressed) was not necessary since a relatively small number of psychotherapists can effectively ameliorate these patients.

Once these patients enter the somatization cycle, there is a burgeoning symptomology. This results because the original stress problems still exists despite the physician's best efforts to treat the resulting physical complaint. Patients who enter this cycle move from one physician to another thereby instituting a new round of ineffectual diagnostic tests and medical utilization. In similar fashion, stress may impact an existing physical illness, exacerbating the symptomology and increasing its duration.

The Intertwining of Psychotherapy and Medical Utilization

Follette and Cummings (1967) compared the number and type of medical services used for the year preceding and for five years following psychotherapy for three groups of randomly selected patients: patients who had one interview only, those who were treated by brief therapy (mean of 6.2 interviews), and those who were cared for under a program of long-term therapy (mean of 34 interviews), as well as a control group without therapy based on the initial distress. The results were as follows:

- Persons in emotional distress were higher utilizers of both inpatient (hospitalization) and outpatient medical facilities than the health plan average.
- There were significant declines in medical utilization by those emotionally distressed patients who received psychotherapy.
- These declines remained constant during the five years following termination of psychotherapy.
- The most significant declines occurred in the second year following termination of psychotherapy; patients with only one session or with brief therapy (2-8 sessions) did not require additional sessions to maintain lowered medical utilization.
- Patients seen two years or more in continuous psychotherapy demonstrated no overall decline in outpatient utilization (therapy visits supplanted medical visits). However, even these latter declined in inpatient utilization—from several times the plan average initially down to the plan average. Thus even long term therapy is cost effective in reducing medical utilization when applied only to those patients that need it and should receive it.
- Cummings and Follette (1968) also concluded that in a prepaid plan that already employs educative techniques to both patients and physicians along with a range of psychological services, the number of subscribers seeking psychotherapy at a

given time reaches an optimal level and remains constant thereafter.

- Over a five-year period, 85% of patients were seen for 15 or fewer sessions (mean of 8.6), and achieved a satisfactory state of well-being that continued into the eighth year after termination of therapy.

The Kaiser-Permanente medical cost-offset results have been extensively replicated in a variety of healthcare delivery systems with an overall "best estimate" of between 10% and 30% in cost savings; savings increase as interventions are tailored to the effective treatment of stress.

Psychotherapy and the Physically Ill Patient

In addition to somaticizing patients, there are also patients whose physical illness is either a source of stress, or for whom stress has contributed to or complicates the illness. A third category is the patient who experiences no discomfort, but for whom medical evaluation establishes the existence of illness (e.g., hypertension). Mechanic (1966) estimated that these three categories suggest that 95% of all medical-surgical patients could benefit from psychological interventions resulting in reduced medical costs.

An extensive literature documents the effectiveness of psychological interventions with chronic diseases such as diabetes, ischemic heart disease, airway diseases, and hypertension. These interventions reduce reliance on medications, numbers of hospital days post-surgery, and physician office visits. The potential savings in workmen's compensation costs can be even greater as a result of behavioral outpatient pain treatment programs.

In light of the fact that inflation in healthcare is about 9% per year and the fact that inflation in mental healthcare is almost double at 16.5% per year due to increased hospitalization, any health system that does not include comprehensive mental health services will pay for stress-related conditions through over-utilization of its medical services. Psychologists have developed an impressive array of targeted, brief interventions focused on specific psychological conditions that aid in addressing these inflationary trends.

Brief, Targeted Therapy Techniques: Biodyne, a Case Study

Psychologists have developed and innovated brief intermittent therapy throughout the life cycle as a proven outpatient alternative to the over-hospitalization of emotionally disturbed adults, adolescents, and substance abusers. Biodyne, a psychology-driven managed mental health organization, using a wide array of protocols, has achieved what is regarded as the lowest psychiatric and substance abuse hospitalization in the nation while maintaining the highest standards in quality of care. In one market, the 178,000 enrollees averaged 114 hospital days per year per 1000 enrollees. Through application of its managed care techniques and clinical protocols, Biodyne reduced the rate of inpatient days to 4 per 1000 enrollees per year, demonstrating what can be accomplished through the application of state of the art psychological services.

It is important to note that the Biodyne Model of triaging somaticizers out of the medical system was not developed as a cost-containment procedure. Rather it was developed first to bring therapeutic effectiveness and relief from pain, anxiety and depression to the patient in psychological distress. In cases of physical illness, the psychologist accepts the illness as a given and concentrates on the patient's reaction to the condition (depression, rage, despair) and to neurotic conflicts that may be impeding recovery. The Biodyne Model of care was developed as part of an effective comprehensive mental health treatment system, and only then was it discovered that it was also cost-effective in terms of reducing medical costs.

Today, Biodyne provides comprehensive managed mental healthcare services as an instrumental part of a comprehensive health plan program to almost two million health plan members throughout the United States.

CONCLUSION

- Persons in emotional distress over-utilize medical services
- 60% of all physician visits are by patients with no physical disease
- Psychological Intervention can reduce outpatient utilization by 50-65%

- Psychological intervention can reduce medical-surgical hospitalization by 60-75%
- With focused, targeted psychological intervention, 85% of patients can be helped with *brief* therapy

Psychologists: An Essential Component to Hospital Health Care

Kris R. Ludwigsen

Since the early 1950's, psychologists have served on the staffs of Veterans Administration Hospitals, state mental hospitals, mental retardation facilities and, more recently, private psychiatric hospitals. However, despite indications that 60% of visits to physicians are for somatized emotional problems (Cummings, 1986), there has been little involvement of psychology in general medical and acute care hospitals. Although the number of psychologists in hospital practice has been increasing, hospital practice by psychologists has been on a very limited scale in comparison with the need for inpatient psychological services. Hospitals are discovering that psychological treatment is increasingly important in enhancing quality of patient care, in reducing length of stay, and in developing new programs to meet the needs of patients.

There are several reasons why psychological treatment is particularly needed in hospitals in the 1990's. First, psychological treatment can reduce medical overutilization through treating the underlying problem. Cummings (1986) reports that 60% of visits to physicians in an HM0 were by patients without a diagnosable physical problem, i.e., for somatized emotional disorders. There is considerable evidence that emotional disorders masquerade as physical conditions which the physician attempts to treat through appropriate

---

Kris R. Ludwigsen is affiliated with the Oak Grove Hospital and he is in private practice in Berkely, CA.

Correspondence concerning this article should be addressed to Kris R. Ludwigsen, 142 Alvarado Rd., Berkeley, CA 94705.

medication, physical therapy, etc., without improvement. The conscientious physician then often orders additional, costly diagnostic tests while the underlying problem remains untreated (Cummings, 1990). Physical symptoms are often the tip of the iceberg, where psychological issues are the underlying essential cause of the disorder. Cummings reports that such patients have nine times the average per capita utilization of health care services.

Psychological issues are usually complicating factors in stress-related disorders such as ulcers, hypertension, cardiac arrhythmias, asthma, etc. Today, admissions to general, acute care hospitals are primarily for stress-related disorders versus the infectious disorders of the early 20th century (Richards, 1987). Adding stress-related illnesses to somatized physical disorders increases the total to 80-90% of physical conditions where the underlying psychological issues must be addressed for effective treatment. Psychologists are the only health providers whose training focuses on the physiological, social, cognitive and emotional bases of behavior, thus making them best trained to diagnose and treat the underlying psychological complications. Cummings (1986) found that appropriate psychotherapy reduced medical overutilization as much as 79%.

Psychological treatment can reduce length of stay. In myocardial infarction, psychotherapy dealing with the associated anxiety and depression was found to significantly reduce the number of days hospitalized, days in intensive care, and days on the cardiac monitor versus no treatment (Gruen, 1975). Similarly, Mumford, Schlesinger, and Glass (1982), in a review of 13 studies, reported that psychological intervention, on the average, reduced days hospitalized post-surgery or post-heart attack by approximately two days from an average length of stay of 9.2 days. Pre and postoperative psychotherapy dealing with the associated anxiety, fear and depression has been found to reduce recovery from surgery, reduce complications and to facilitate compliance with hospital procedures.

Over the past 15 years the field of health psychology has focused specifically on psychological intervention in the amelioration of physical disorders. Psychologists have been involved in cardiac rehabilitation, weight loss programs and eating disorders, cancer counselling, emergency room consultation, pain management, rehabilitation of physical injuries, sleep disorders and neuropsychological assessment. Psychologists have addressed the needs of stroke victims, patients with colostomies, complications of labor and delivery, and other medical problems, thus improving cooperation with the treatment regimen. One such patient, a 16 year-old boy with a serious renal condition was required to take 50 pills per day to prevent renal failure. His chronic noncompliance was becoming life-threatening. The psychologist consulted determined that the patient's mother had died from an overdose of prescription medicines mixed with alcohol and that the father secretly feared that "the doctors might be making a mistake." When these fears were identified and successfully challenged in family therapy, the patient overcame his resistance and began to take better care of his own medical needs (Libow, 1985).

Psychological issues often underlie the patient's decision to sue the hospital. Appropriate psychological intervention can reduce risk management, liability and malpractice costs. As an example, the wife of a retired military member was referred to a psychologist for intractable neck and shoulder pain which had been unameliorated by physical therapy. Psychotherapy revealed the patient to be a hostile-dependent individual with considerable denied anger toward her husband; and marital therapy was initiated to deal with these issues. Shortly thereafter, the husband had a heart attack, was rushed to the nearest Veterans Administration Hospital and subsequently died. The patient's neck and shoulder pain vanished following the death of her husband, thus substantiating the psychological cause. However, her anger and dependency were transferred to the VA hospital which she then sued for not preventing her husband's death. Dealing with the underlying psychological issues can reduce the incidence of inappropriate lawsuits for hospitals and their staffs in addition to addressing the underlying patient issues (Ludwigsen, 1990).

Psychologists perform a valuable service in addressing the psychosocial aspects of physical as well as mental illness. These issues are often unidentified in more traditional approaches to treatment in general, acute care hospitals. Schlesinger, Mumford, Glass, Patrick, and Sharfstein (1983), found that mental health services, plus treatment for physical disorders decreased hospital costs at a level equal to, or greater than, the cost of the mental health services, demonstrating again that physical disorders involve psychological issues which must be addressed for medical treatment to be effective.

Since the 1950's, psychologists have substantially expanded their range of roles within the hospital to include hospital administrator, clinical services director, program director, quality assurance coordinator, dual diagnosis director, director of training, hospital owner, independent contractor of services, e.g., biofeedback, stress management, etc., and admitting clinician. There are many opportunities for private practitioners to establish relationships with hospitals for mutual benefit. One psychologist developed a group therapy approach for chronic pain, utilizing a coping skills program in his private practice. The program was subsequently marketed to a local hospital and integrated into the pain management program in an inpatient rehabilitation unit in a general hospital (Cole, personal communication, February 28, 1989 and March 1, 1989). In addition, psychologists affiliated with hospitals do research, conduct program evaluation and provide consultation-liaison as well as community outreach, marketing and organizational development (Wiggins & Ludwigsen, in press).

There is emerging evidence that psychologists can be a significant source of referrals for hospitals. Dafter and Freeland (1988) conducted a survey (n = 71). Psychologists' referrals accounted for 48 inpatient days each, or approximately $27,500.00 per psychologist for the receiving hospital, based on Blue Cross estimated daily charges of $573.00 per day.

In addition, trends in hospital health care strongly favor the introduction of psychological treatment. The hospital as a health care institution has passed through several phases in its evolution. Hospitals began as larger public infirmaries for the indigent. Quality of care was improved by the nursing profession and by physicians who viewed the hospital as the most appropriate setting to bring together patients and technological resources for medical research and education. Thus, the hospital became the "temple of health care" (Newman, 1990) consuming 70% of medical reimbursement. The pressure to reduce these costs over the past several years has resulted in hospitals becoming increasingly competitive for the business of the health care consumer while striving to reduce length of stay. As a result, hospitals are assessing community needs and are developing inpatient, outpatient, and aftercare programs to meet them, as a community resource. One hospital in a large metropolitan area offers a chemical dependency treatment program marketed specifically to the white-collar cocaine addict working in the Financial District.

Secondly, health care consumers are increasingly more knowledgeable and less dependent in their role as patients. The earlier, more authoritarian "doctor knows best" mode is being replaced by the patient-provider partnership model where the role of the hospital, HMO or provider becomes educating the patient to assume responsibility for his health. Heart disease can be substantially prevented by stress management treatment and behavioral weight control treatment. In VA hospitals, stress is being placed on maintaining a healthy life-style through eliminating smoking and other addictions, maintaining good nutrition and compliance with outpatient treatment recommendations. While due in part to the need to reduce hospital utilization, this approach reflects a significant shift from the *disease model* to the *patient education* approach to health care. Preparing patients to assume responsibility for understanding and managing their physical and mental problems will become the prevailing philosophy of inpatient treatment due to increasing pressures to decrease length of stay and support alternative modes of care delivery, which hospitals are developing as adjuncts. Psychologists are the only health care providers whose training emphasizes the cognitive-behavioral approach designed to identify dysfunctional attitudes and correct maladaptive behaviors. Thus, psychological treatment is the philosophy most responsive to the needs of hospitals and their patient-consumers in the '90's and beyond. Hospitals are moving toward a more democratic model of health care, a model where the hospital and community are partners paralleling the patient-provider partnership in individual treatment. Patient needs, community needs and health care economics increasingly indicate that psychologists have a key role to play, not only in implementing the patient education approach to health care and preventative health maintenance, but also in introducing a unique philosophy of treatment which better addresses the needs of hospitals moving into the 21st century.

REFERENCES

Cummings, N.A. (1986). The dismantling of our health system: Strategies for the survival of psychological practice. *American psychologist*, *41*, 426-431.

Cummings, N.A. (1990, February). *Psychologists: An essential component to cost-effective innovative care*. Paper presented at the meeting of the American College of Health Care Executives. Chicago, IL.

Dafter, R., & Freeland, G. (1988, December). Psychologists' unrealized power in the mental health marketplace. *The California Psychologist*, p. 14.

Gruen, W. (1975). Effects of brief psychotherapy on recovery. *Journal of Consulting and Clinical Psychotherapy*, *43*, 223-232.

Libow, J. (1985). Care of critically and chronically ill adolescents in a medical setting. In M.P. Mirkin and S.L. Koonan, (Eds.). *Handbook of adolescents and family therapy*, (pp. 89-105). New York: Gardner Press.

Ludwigsen, K.R. (1990, February). Psychologists; An essential component of hospital health care. Paper presented to the meeting of the American College of Health Care Executives. Chicago, IL.

Mumford, E., Schlesinger, H.J., & Glass, G.V. (1982). The effects of psychological intervention on recovery from surgery and heart attacks: An analysis of the literature. *American Journal of Public Health*, *72*, 141-151.

Newman, R. (1990, February). Independent practice in hospitals: A cornerstone for professional legitimacy. *Hospital Progress Notes*, pp. 3-4.

Richards, S.A. (1987). Health care in the 80's and beyond. *Psychotherapy in private practice*, *5*(1), 39-45.

Schlesinger, H.J., Mumford, E., Glass, G.V., Patrick, C., & Sharfstein, S. (1983). Mental health treatment and medical care utilization in a fee-for-service system: Outpatient mental health treatment following the onset of a chronic disease. *American Journal of Mental Health*, *73*, 422-429.

Wiggins, J.G., & Ludwigsen, K.R. (in press). Marketing psychological services in hospitals. In J. Sweet, R. Rozensky & S. Tovian (Eds.) *Handbook of clinical psychology in medical settings*. New York: Plenum.

SYMPOSIUM: ECLECTIC USES OF METAPHOR IN PSYCHOTHERAPY

The Use of Metaphor in Rational-Emotive Psychotherapy

Raymond A. DiGiuseppe
J. Christopher Muran

Metaphorical communication is usually not perceived as being a major component of cognitive-behavioral psychotherapies. Cognitive approaches to psychotherapy are usually perceived as cold, rational, logical analyses of clients' problems or the rote learning of self-statements to guide behavior. Since cognitions are generally

---

Raymond A. DiGiuseppe, PhD, is Associate Professor and Director of School Psychology Graduate Program, St. John's University and Director of Research and Training at the Institute for Rational Emotive Therapy. J. Christopher Muran, MA, is a doctoral candidate at Hofstra University, Hempstead, NJ and a Psychology Intern at the Institute for Rational Emotive Therapy, New York, NY.

Requests for reprints should be addressed to the first author at Department of Psychology, St. John's University, Jamaica, NY 11439.

An abbreviated version of this paper was presented at the 96th Annual Convention of the American Psychological Association, Atlanta, GA, August 1988.

considered to affect language and to be affected by it (Clark and Clark, 1977), language and linguistic systems, such as metaphor, have become central to the restructuring of maladaptive cognitions. A great number of approaches to cognitive restructuring have been well-described and provide the cognitive-behavioral therapist with ample alternatives to challenge client's dysfunctional or maladaptive thinking (e.g., Dryden and Golden, 1986; Freeman, 1987). The explicit use of metaphor has been mentioned as one such approach (e.g., Beck and Emery, 1985; Guidano and Liotti, 1983; Walen, DiGiuseppe, and Wessler, 1980). For example, Wessler and Wessler (1980) outlined the therapeutic value of relating various stories, songs, parables, witty sayings, poems, aphorisms, and jokes to clients. Also, Dryden (1986) described the use of active visual methods and visual models to convey the impossibility of assigning a global rating to oneself and the dysfunctionality of low frustration tolerance.

RET AND METAPHOR

As a cognitive-behavioral approach, Rational-Emotive Therapy (RET) not only involves the uncovering of dysfunctional thinking or irrational beliefs that lead to emotional and behavioral disturbances, but also includes the active disputation of those cognitions and the establishment of more functional and rational thoughts. Language plays a pivotal role in both the expression and restructuring of thought. While language and thought are not synonymous, they are seen as interdependent in many ways. Greatly influenced by General Semantics (Korzybski, 1933), rational-emotive theory regards language as having a great impact on the structuring of cognitive processes (Ellis, 1962). RET aligns itself most closely with the position of Vygotsky (1962) and Luria (1969) that linguistic meanings are central to thought and semantic analysis is key to understanding thought.

In RET, cognitive restructuring frequently involves altering the language and meaning that clients apply to the organization and understanding of their world. Without linguistic communication, without the direct and clear exchange of meanings based on a shared system of symbols, psychotherapy, according to rational-emotive theory, becomes a near impossible task. Metaphor is seen as a discrete symbol system within language (Ortony, 1975; Petrie, 1979) that functions comparably to other linguistic systems in the communicative process. Ordinary or normal usage in language and metaphor are considered continuous phenomena, involving common cognitive and linguistic properties. Rational-emotive theory agrees with the perspective of a number of scholars (Miller, 1979; Paivio, 1979; Rumelhart, 1979) who see no psychological correlate or cognitive basis for the distinction between metaphor and ordinary language in terms of comprehension. In other words, the underlying processes required to understand one are the same as those required to understand the other.

RET approaches cognitive restructuring in terms of the hypothetico-deductive model in the philosophy of science (DiGiuseppe, 1986; Ellis, 1962; 1979). It recognizes irrational beliefs involving demandingness as personal paradigms, similar to Kelly's (1955) concept of personal construct and parallel to Kuhn's (1970) idea of paradigm in the history of science. These paradigms are considered to be underlying assumptive constructs or theories that people generate to explain and maneuver their way in the world, which are comparable to Piagetian schemata and to concepts presented by other cognitive-behavior theorists (Guidano and Liotti, 1983; Mahoney, 1980). They are hypothesized to influence perceptual, evaluative, and inferential processes. The therapeutic implications of this conceptualization in terms of developing disputational strategies can be summed up in the following requisites: (1) challenge an existing paradigm on logical, empirical, and heuristic grounds and (2) provide an alternative paradigm that is logically and empirically sound and functional (DiGiuseppe, 1986).

Metaphor is regarded as playing an important role in the formulation and transmission of new paradigms; in fact, according to Kuhn (1979), along with a number of others (Boyd, 1979; Petrie, 1979), metaphor lies at the heart of paradigm change. What makes metaphor effective in paradigm shifts is characterized by the interaction view of metaphor (Black, 1979) that something new is created when a metaphor is understood; that metaphor is in effect an epistemic device or additive instrument of knowledge which creates similarities and generates different alternatives to perceive and organize the world (Boyd, 1979; Eco, 1984; Jaynes, 1976; Ricoeur, 1977; Schon, 1979).

CONSTRUCTING A PSYCHOTHERAPEUTIC METAPHOR

Metaphor typically involves abstracting a concept from a topic that the client knows well. A metaphor for that concept is then applied by analogue to a new arena to help explain or construct an experience in a different arena. For example, a client with athletic experience or interest recently asked his therapist for more direction and specific advice on how to respond to some practical problems. The therapist looked for a way to explain a therapist's role; that is, a therapist teaches clients skills to help solve life's problems without making the actual decisions for clients. The metaphor of "coach" then came to the therapist's mind and he explained to the client that a therapist was like a coach, teaching skills and making sure that the athlete practices. A coach, however, cannot compete for the athlete. A therapist can likewise teach a client what steps to go through to make decisions, but cannot make them for the client. Here, the abstract concept embodied in a familiar arena (i.e., a coach in athletics) was applied to a new arena (i.e., a therapist in therapy) to help the client understand a new concept (i.e., the therapist's role).

How to choose the most forceful strategy for disputing any particular irrational belief or dysfunctional schema in a given clinical context often involves a creative search for metaphors that seem to have symbolic significance or personal meaning for the client and, therefore, has high persuasive impact. This search may sometimes simply involve joining a client's own use of metaphor and reframing it according to a particular disputational strategy. In sum, the rules in selecting a metaphor for use in therapy are as follows: (1) clearly define the concept that you wish to communicate or teach; (2) attend to the client's language and search for an arena which the client understands and has comfortably mastered; (3) search for an analogue construct in the client's arena of knowledge which includes the core elements of the concept that you wish to teach; and (4) if none exists or comes to mind, start over with a new arena about which the client has knowledge.

METAPHOR AS MNEMONIC

Clinical experience suggests that clients are initially overwhelmed by disputation and fail to remember all the relevant disputes to their irrational beliefs and to recall the new rational beliefs. Metaphor ameliorates this process because of its heuristic value, i.e., its usefulness in learning. Ortony (1975) has indicated the memorability, the compactness, and the vividness in his general facilitation view of metaphor, which research has supported (Reynolds and Schwartz, 1983). Further, Paivio (1979) has described metaphor in his dual-coding approach as having a mnemonic function that allows for the synchronous organization of information into large, integrated chunks. Accordingly, its imagistic system facilitates concept acquisition and the speed and flexibility of accessing information from long-term memory. Its verbal system contributes to an orderly, logical sequence in the flow of ideas, particularly in terms of making a relevant interpretation of a metaphor. Therefore, the use of metaphor in disputation is a highly salient and compact way of organizing information about oneself and the environment and processing information for coping with life and solving problems. Metaphor also requires the active engagement of the listener for its understanding that enhances the learning of new material, such as new paradigms (Guidano and Liotti, 1983; Petrie, 1979).

THERAPEUTIC IMPLEMENTATION OF METAPHOR

A major problem with metaphor is the assumption of shared meaning. Since the therapist applies by analogue the meaning of the metaphor to a new arena, the client may not initially extract the same abstract concept from the metaphor that the therapist intended. Therefore, to ensure that the appropriate concept is communicated, after presenting a metaphor, the RET therapist will frequently ask clients to restate it in their own words. They are directly questioned on their own understanding of the metaphor, on how it relates to the desired behavior and/or emotional change. They are also asked to imagine the range of situations where they see it as applicable. Often, it may be necessary that the therapist explain the meaning, the value, and the applicability of the metaphor and then model its use in various stressful situations. The therapist will then typically repeat the metaphor where appropriate over several sessions and have clients practice imagining the metaphor as a homework assignment between sessions so that the metaphor becomes a conditioned coping or problem-solving strategy and part of a client's habitual way of thinking. It is a main tenet of RET that therapeutic gains or paradigmatic shifts usually come after repeated and forceful attempts at disputing and through repeated rehearsal and practice of a new rational perspective. The rehearsal of the metaphor is similar to the rehearsal of self-statements in Cognitive-Behavior Modification (Meichenbaum, 1977; Novaco, 1975) and the conditioning of imagery in Systematic Desensitization (Wolpe, 1969). The frequent and repeated presentation of a particular metaphor will also serve to break down the resistance of a client in certain cases.

RATIONALE FOR THE RET USE OF METAPHOR

The explicit nature of the RET approach to metaphorical communication is due in great part to the assessment by a number of linguists and psychologists that metaphor can be potentially harmful (Fraser, 1979; Petrie, 1979; Pylyshyn, 1979; Reddy, 1979; Schon, 1979). Specifically, they suggest that metaphor can encourage sloppy thought by acting as a substitute for hard analytic thought and that metaphor can be taken in so many ways that the possibility of mistakes abounds. Subsequently, if we grant the possible misuse and misleadingness of metaphor, recognize the interpretive contribution of the receiver's own knowledge and experience, and assume the end of communication is the exchange of shared meaning, it follows that we ought to communicate metaphorically for increased memorability and guard against misleading interpretations by later making the implicit meaning of the metaphor explicit.

In contrast to the Ericksonian conceptualization (Bandler and Grinder, 1975; Barker, 1985; Erickson and Rossi, 1976/1980; Lankton and Lankton, 1983), the rational-emotive use of metaphor is neither seen nor used as a two-level means of communication involving implicit messages that are slipped into the unconscious mind via implication and connotation and that subsequently interrupt maladaptive behavior patterns. Rather, it is used as a direct method of communication that is actively employed by the therapist in that the message and meaning is clearly conveyed to the client and then questioned to ensure the accuracy of the communicative process. Metaphor is considered a discrete symbol system, functioning comparably to other linguistic systems and involving the same psychological processes. Consequently, rational-emotive theory rejects the Freudian/Jungian notion of metaphor as the language of the unconscious (Freud, 1965; Jung, 1961) and the Ericksonian notion of metaphor (Erickson and Rossi, 1979) as mediated by right-brain processes, but rather supports Paivio's (1979) dual-coding approach to metaphor and maintains that metaphorical communication involves the integration of whole brain processes. This seems to be substantiated by research literature that suggests that there is bilateral hemispheric involvement in both imagistic and emotive processing (Danesi, 1984; Ehrlichman and Barrett, 1983; Izard, 1988).

Because of its well acknowledged implicit and elusive nature, i.e., because metaphor typically involves meaning explicit to the speaker and implicit to the hearer, we believe that it is crucial in psychotherapy to establish explicitly shared meaning to ensure that the intended meaning is being communicated. As Small and Manthei (1986) emphasized, it is important to guard against therapist vagueness and to reduce discrepancy between intended and actual messages of the therapist; with such discrepancies, clients are often "left feeling at best unsure and confused, and at worst resentful and distrustful. To overcome this, therapists should always say exactly what they mean" (p. 410), which highlights Carkhuff's (1971) position that concreteness, genuineness, and immediacy should be central to the therapeutic message. We believe that clients should not be expected to generate their own meaning from the metaphor which may very well be irrelevant and unhelpful to their presenting problem and ongoing experience; nor should the meaning of metaphoric symbols be assumed to be implicitly shared, which seems to be loosely based on failed Lamarckian logic (Gould, 1987). Insight is also not considered automatic or necessarily sufficient for change in RET, as it is in psychoanalysis; instead, active application of the insight plays a pivotal part in the change process.

EXAMPLES OF METAPHOR IN RET

Metaphor in RET is usually used to meaningfully convey (1) the relationship between cognitions, emotions, and behavior, (2) the illogical and anti-empirical bases of maladaptive thoughts, and (3) the lack of heuristic value in maintaining such thoughts. To begin with, rational-emotive therapists typically present their clients with the simple conceptual schema of the ABC's of RET, where A stands for activating event, B stands for belief system, and C stands for emotional and behavioral consequences. To further illustrate this relationship, the following metaphorical example may be provided:

> Suppose you are driving, and you come to a red light. Does this make you stop? If red lights make you stop, you would brake at all red lights, not just those in traffic signals. And if all red traffic lights made you stop, no one would ever go through them or get traffic tickets for doing so. Do you always stop when you come to a red traffic light? No, not always. Perhaps it is the wee hours of the morning, and the streets are deserted. Perhaps you are in a great hurry. Perhaps you are driving to the hospital with your wife, whose labor pains are two minutes apart. In other words, red lights do not always make us behave in a predictable fashion. Other factors can intervene, and these are our attitudes or cognitions about the event—the way we interpret it. (Walen, DiGiuseppe, and Wessler, 1980, p.15)

Another metaphorical approach that concretely and causally relates the effects of the construct of absolute demandingness on emotional disturbance involves describing an emotional upset as a great building where an absolute demand is the cornerstone. Each of these examples help clients to better conceptualize their problem, to see the relationship between how they think, feel, and behave, and to subsequently generate an appropriate disputational strategy.

As for a metaphorical approach that empirically disputes maladaptive thinking, one example involves challenging the cognitive distortion of overgeneralization and the irrational belief of global rating by asking clients to attempt to assign a comprehensive rating to a basket of fruit. Clients are encouraged to actively explore the components of the fruit basket while attempting to assign a global rating to it and to recognize the complexibility and impossibility of applying a general label to something comprised of many elements. Another empirical example involves showing clients who procrastinate and evidence low frustration tolerance that while they think what they are avoiding is hard, it is even harder if they do not do it. This can be accomplished by representing difficult tasks as weeds in that "they grow taller, the roots go deeper, and they spread out to ever and ever wider areas if they are not attacked when detected" (Hauck, 1980, p. 138). A challenge to the arbitrary inference that one's predicament is entirely hopeless may involve the story of two frogs Pierre and Jean-Paul who are held separately in two tall jars of milk. Pierre infers that his future is indeed bleak, paddles a short while, then gives up and drowns. Jean-Paul, on the other hand, refuses to readily accept such a sad fate and paddles vigorously and thoroughly, subsequently turning the milk into butter and creating a means of escape (R. Yeager, personal communication, August 6, 1988). Such a story not only emphasizes the importance of persisting against all apparent odds, but also it can be used to highlight the importance of working very hard at disputing irrational beliefs in the face of the most ominous activating events.

To dispute the illogic of the irrational belief of dogmatism or demandingness, the rational-emotive therapist may use the metaphor that conjures up the image of Mickey Mouse as "the Sorcerer's Apprentice" cloaked in oversized wizardly garb with his hands raised, his fingers outstretched, as he grandiosely and magically attempts to alter his world to the dramatically reverberating sound of the musical score. When clients start irrationally demanding that they, others, or the world absolutely must be or must treat them a certain way, they are humorously reminded that they are doing their Mickey Mouse impersonation again. Another metaphorical example that redresses demandingness, with a touch of humor, may involve suggesting to a client:

> You seem to be using the Reverse Golden Rule. Remember the Golden Rule? Do unto others as you would have them do unto you? The Reverse Golden Rule says others should do unto me as I do unto them. (Walen, DiGiuseppe, and Wessler, 1980, p. 31)

Aside from implying that clients are grandiosely setting themselves up like God by establishing commandments, this metaphor also challenges the irrational belief that there should be an implicitly guaranteed fairness or reciprocity in human relations. The use of humor is seen as undermining what Ellis (1977) has described as a major cause of emotional disturbance, that is, taking life and oneself all too seriously. Also, humor can evoke positive emotions within a therapeutic session, which has been implicated in facilitating cognitive processes involved in problem-solving, learning, and memory (Izard, 1988). In yet another example, with a client who demonstrates a dire need for love, an effective dispute may involve elaborately juxtaposing an addiction to heroin and a fancy for chocolate and then posing the question, "Which, do you think, is the healthier love?" Finally, when facing clients who incessantly rate themselves according to their acts and apparently adopt a "You are only as good as your last performance!" philosophy, a therapist can suggest humorously that they have taken the George Steinbrenner/"What have you done for me lately?" approach to human worth. And where has that logic gotten the New York Yankees lately?

A metaphorical example of disputing the heuristic value of maintaining irrational beliefs is highlighted by an illustration that Albert Ellis often gives to his clients:

> Suppose you believe right now there is a red devil, an invisible red devil, standing behind you, and he is going to jab you up the ass with a pitchfork every time you make a mistake. How would you feel? . . . You'd be off the wall! But you've invented a red devil. None exists. But you've invented a red devil who is going to jab you with a pitchfork for every error. And the red devil is you. (Bernard, 1986, pp. 93-4)

Ellis goes on to show a client via this metaphor how dysfunctional it is to create and maintain red devils or irrational beliefs, how such thoughts will only prove to be the undoing of the client in the long-run. Also, with a client who comes in self-downing and self-damning regarding past mistakes, a sports analogy may prove effective if it has appropriate special meaning for the client. For example, Kenny Stabler was known as one of the best two-minute quarterbacks in the game of football. There were many times when he would commit a number of miscues throughout a ballgame—an interception in the first quarter, a fumble in the second, and another interception in the third; however, when it came to the final two minutes and there was still a chance to win, did he concentrate on his screw-ups, did he obsess over what he should have done? No, he rather focused on the task at hand, probably realizing that there was no heuristic value in lamenting over what has passed when there was still a game to be won. Such a metaphor is particularly effective with depressed clients whose goals are still in reach, but who have paralyzed themselves with self-pity and self degradation. This metaphor can also be elaborated on to point out a plan of action; for example, Stabler never resorted to the bomb in driving for a touchdown, but rather threw short outlet passes, taking small sure steps toward the goal and using the time wisely.

CONCLUSIONS

Following Jaynes' (1976) formulation, metaphor within the RET framework simply serves a twofold purpose of (1) describing an experience or idea, which may then (2) generate new patterns of awareness. This new awareness is then actively directed by the rational-emotive therapist toward changing behavior and affect to more adaptive forms, and not necessarily counted upon to "interrupt" dysfunctional behavior and emotions on its own. In Kuhnian terms, the metaphor fosters a paradigm shift. It both challenges a personal paradigm that is illogical, anti-empirical, and dysfunctional and offers an alternative paradigm that proves to be more adaptive for the client, allowing the client to better organize and maneuver in the world. Because it involves both imagistic and verbal processes, metaphor also facilitates acquisition, retention, and recall of the new paradigm.

In sum, RET adopts the interaction view of metaphor. It not only recognizes and employs metaphor as an epistemic and heuristic device but also recognizes and guards against its potential misuse and misleadingness. Further, it respects the arbitrary nature of language and meaning as related to thought that is emphasized in General Semantics, as well as the definitive aspect of communication theory that the meanings exchanged via symbol systems had better be shared or made explicit in order to be clearly communicated (Gordon, 1984). Therefore, rational-emotive use of metaphor seems the more logical and efficient use in that it accurately acknowledges the nature of communication, language, and metaphor.

REFERENCES

Bandler, R. and Grinder, J. (1975). *The Patterns of the Hypnotic Techniques of Milton H. Erickson, M.D. Vol. I*. Palo Alto, CA: Behavior and Science Books.

Barker, P. (1985). *Using Metaphors in Psychotherapy*. New York: Brunner/Mazel.

Beck, A. and Emery, G. (1985). *Anxiety Disorders and Phobias: a Cognitive Perspective*. New York: Basic Books.

Bernard, M. (1986). *Staying Rational in an Irrational World*. Vic, Australia: McCulloch Publishing in association with The Macmillan Company.

Black M. (1979). More about metaphor. In A. Ortony (ed.), *Metaphor and Thought* (pp. 19-43). New York: Cambridge University Press.

Boyd R. (1979). Metaphor and theory change: what is metaphor for. In A. Ortony (ed.), *Metaphor and Thought* (pp. 356-408). New York: Cambridge University Press.

Carkhuff, R.R. (1971). *The Development of Human Resources*. New York: Holt, Rinehart, and Winston.

Danesi, M. (1984). Lateralization, affect, metaphors, and language use. *Interfaces*, 11 (2), 41-46.

DiGiuseppe, R. (1986). The implication of the philosophy of science for rational-emotive theory and therapy. *Psychotherapy*, 23 (4), 634-639.

Dryden, W. (1986). Vivid methods in Rational-Emotive Therapy. In Ellis, A. and Grieger, R., *Handbook of Rational-Emotive Therapy Vol. II* (pp. 221-245). New York: Springer Publishing.

Dryden, W. and Golden, W. (1986). *Cognitive-Behavioural Approaches to Psychotherapy*. London: Harper and Row.

Eco, U. (1984). *Semiotics and the Philosophy of Language*. Bloomington, IA: Indiana University Press.

Ehrlichman, H. and Barrett, J. (1903). Right hemispheric specialization for mental imagery: A review of the evidence. *Brain and Cognition*, 2 (1), 55-76.

Ellis, A. (1962). *Reason and Emotion in Psychotherapy*. Secaucus, NJ: Lyle Stuart.

Ellis, A. (1977). Fun as psychotherapy. In A. Ellis and R. Grieger (eds.), *Handbook of Rational-Emotive Therapy* (pp. 262-270). New York: Springer.

Ellis, A. (1979). Rational-emotive therapy as a new theory of personality and therapy. In A. Ellis and J. Whitely (Eds.), *Theoretical and Empirical Foundations of Rational-Emotive Therapy*. Monterey, CA: Brooks/Cole.

Ellis, A. and Dryden, W. (1987). *The Practice of Rational-Emotive Therapy*. New York: Springer.

Erickson, M.H. and Rossi, E. (1976/80). Two-level communication and the microdynamics of trance and suggestion. In E. Rossi (ed.), *The Collected Pacers of Milton H. Erickson on Hypnosis. Vol. I. The Nature of Hypnosis and Suggestion* (pp. 108-132). New York: Irvington.

Erickson, M.H. and Rossi, E. (1979). *Hypnotherapy: An Exploratory Casebook*. New York: Irvington.

Fraser, B. (1979). The interpretation of novel metaphors. In A. Ortony (ed.), *Metaphor and Thought* (pp. 172-185). New York: Cambridge University Press.

Freeman, A. (1987). Cognitive therapy: an overview. In A. Freeman and V. Greenwood (eds.), *Cognitive Therapy: Application in Psychiatric and Medical Setting* (pp. 19-35). New York: Human Sciences Press.

Freud, S. (1965). *The Interpretation of Dreams*. New York: Avon Books. (First German edition, 1900.)

Galin, D. (1974). Implications for psychiatry of left and right specialization. *Archives of General Psychiatry*, 31, 527-583.

Gordon, G.N. (1984). Communication. *The New Encyclopedia Britannica: Macropedia Vol. IV*. Chicago, IL: Encyclopedia Britannica.

Gould, S.J. (1987). Freud's phylogenetic fantasy. *Natural History*, 96 (12), 10-16.

Guidano, V.F. and Liotti, G. (1983). *The Cognitive Processes and Emotional Disorders*. New York: Guilford.

Hauck, P.A. (1980). *Brief Counseling with RET*. Philadelphia, PA: The Westminster Press.

Izard, C. (1988, August). The structure and functions of human emotions. *G. Stanley Hall Lecture*, Series 8, presented at the 96th Annual Convention of the American Psychological Association, Atlanta, Georgia.

Jaynes, J. (1976). *The Origins of Consciousness in the Breakdown of the Bicameral Mind*. New York: Houghton Mifflin.

Jung, C. (1961). *Memories, Dreams, Reflections*. New York: Vintage Books.

Kelly, G. (1955). *The Psychology of Personal Constructs*. New York: W.W. Norton.

Korzybski, A. (1933). *Science and Sanity*. San Francisco: International Society of General Semantics.

Kuhn, T. (1970). *The Structure of Scientific Revolutions*. Chicago: Chicago University Press.

Kuhn, T. (1979). Metaphor in science. In A. Ortony (ed.), *Metaphor and Thought* (pp. 409-419). New York: Cambridge University Press.

Lankton, S.R. and Lankton, C.N. (1983). *The Answer Within: A Clinical Framework of Ericksonian Hypnotherapy*. New York: Brunner/Mazel.

Luria, A. (1969). Speech and the formation of mental processes. In M. Cole and I. Malzman (eds.), *A Handbook of Contemporary Soviet Psychology*. New York: Basic Books.

Meichenbaum, D. (1977). *Cognitive Behavior Modification*. New York: Plenum.

Miller G. (1979). Images, models, similes, and metaphors. In A. Ortony (ed.), *Metaphor and Thought* (pp. 202-250). New York: Cambridge University Press.

Novaco, R. (1975). *Anger Control: the Development and Evaluation of an Experimental Treatment*. Lexington, MA: Heath and Co.

Ortony, A. (1975). Why metaphors are necessary and not just nice. *Educational Theory*, 25, 45-53.

Ortony, A. (1979). Metaphor: a multidimensional problem. In A. Ortony (ed.), *Metaphor and Thought* (pp. 1-16). New York: Cambridge University Press.

Paivio, A. (1971). *Imagery and Verbal Processes*. New York: Holt, Rinehart, and Winston.

Paivio, A. (1979). Psychological processes in the comprehension of metaphor. In A. Ortony (ed.), *Metaphor and Thought* (pp. 150-171). New York: Cambridge University Press.

Petrie, H.G. (1979). Metaphor and learning. In A. Ortony (ed.), *Metaphor and Thought* (pp. 438-461). New York: Cambridge University Press.

Pylyshyn, Z.W. (1979). Metaphorical imprecision and the "Top-Down" research strategy. In A. Ortony (ed.), *Metaphor and Thought* (pp. 420-436). New York: Cambridge University Press.

Reddy, M.J. (1979). The conduit metaphor: a case of frame conflict in our language about language. In A. Ortony (ed.), *Metaphor and Thought* (pp. 284-324). New York: Cambridge University Press.

Ricoeur, P. (1977). *The Rule of Metaphor: Multi-Disciplinary Studies of the Creation of Meaning in Language*. Toronto: University of Toronto Press.

Rumelhart, D.E. (1979). Some problems with the notion of literal meanings. In A. Ortony (ed.), *Metaphor and Thought* (pp. 78-90). New York: Cambridge University Press.

Sadock, J.M. (1979). Figurative speech and linguistics. In A. Ortony (ed.), *Metaphor and Thought* (pp. 46-63). New York: Cambridge University Press.

Schon, D.A. (1979). Generative metaphor: a perspective on problem-setting in social policy. In A. Ortony (ed.), *Metaphor and Thought* (pp. 254-283). New York: Cambridge University.

Small, J.J. and Manthei, R.J. (1986). The language of therapy. *Psychotherapy*, 23, 395-404.

Sticht, T.G. (1979). Educational uses of metaphor. In A. Ortony (ed.), *Metaphor and Thought*. New York: Cambridge University Press.

Vygotsky (1962). *Language and Thought*. New York: Cambridge, MA: MIT Press.

Walen, S., DiGiuseppe, R., and Wessler, R. (1980). *The Practitioner's Guide to Rational-Emotive Therapy*. New York: Oxford University Press.
Wessler, R.R. and Wessler, R.L. (1980). *The Practice and Principles of Rational-Emotive Therapy*. London: Jossey-Bass.
Wolpe, J. (1969). *The Practice of Behavior Therapy*. New York: Pergamon Press.

Humor as Metaphor

Don-David Lusterman

A metaphor is a word or figure of speech which compares one thing to another by speaking of the one as though it were the other. Unlike its cousin, the simile, a metaphor does not use any word of comparison, such as "like" or "as," and therein lies its special power. If a man says of his work, "Everyday I go off to do battle," he is speaking metaphorically, and the metaphor says volumes about his experience of work. In fact, metaphor touches us at such a deep level because it avoids the logical, sequential thinking of the simile, which merely equates one thing with another.

The power of metaphor is that it traverses boundaries. It is a form of linguistic and experiential transformation. In fact, the two Greek words that form the word metaphor are meta (to go over, or beyond) and pherein (to carry, or bear), suggesting that the power of metaphor is that it can carry us beyond our immediate level of perception.

Metaphor has a disarming quality. If one compares two things, that is to say, make a simile, it is easy enough to challenge the comparison on the basis of its imperfection. "An apple is like an orange" may elicit the response, "yes—but one is red, the other is orange," or, "one is a citrus fruit, the other is not." A simile, then, may promote "yes—but" thinking. One frequently notes the dangers of simile in family or couples therapy, where one person often accuses the other of being "just like your mother (brother, father, etc.)." Clearly, such similes tend to invite disqualification. A metaphor, on the other hand, goes beyond simple logic, and therefore is less likely to call forth logical defenses.

Don-David Lusterman, PhD, is in private practice, Baldwin, NY.

Milton Erickson was particularly noted for his use of metaphor. A famous example is that of a purportedly psychotic patient who claimed to be Jesus. "I hear you are a carpenter" said Erickson. "Will you help me build same shelves?" (Haley, 1973). Soon Erickson had his patient so overburdened with various carpentry assignments that he not only refused to continue his woodworking, but he also ceased claiming that he was Jesus. Erickson's metaphoric thinking is effective because it transcends logical limits (how can I convince this man that he is not Jesus) and instead continues the patient's own metaphor, merely intensifying it by moving to the thought, "If he is Jesus, he is a carpenter." If one accepts that he is Jesus, it is irrefutable that he is a carpenter, and quite unlikely that, as Jesus, he would refuse the request to help someone in need.

Madanes (1981) has pointed out that systems can themselves be viewed as metaphors. "For example," she writes, "a wife who vomits compulsively may be expressing disgust at her husband." This sensitivity to the metaphoric nature of the symptom can lead the therapist to new and slightly altered metaphors that challenge the metaphor by which the system is operating. Bateson, Jackson, Haley and Weakland (1956) published a groundbreaking paper, "Towards a Theory of Schizophrenia." With the benefit of hindsight, it is now generally accepted that, while they believed they were theorizing about the etiology and treatment of schizophrenia, their major contribution was instead to sensitize us to the nature of communication, and particularly, to the power of metaphor.

They observed that metaphor is an "indispensable tool of thought and expression – a characteristic of all human communication, even that of the scientist. The conceptual models of cybernetics and the energy theories of psychoanalysis are, after all, only labeled metaphors. The peculiarity of the schizophrenic is not that he uses metaphors, but that he uses unlabeled metaphors."

I mentioned earlier the disarming quality of metaphor. This is true either if the metaphor is presented to a person or system, as happens in the therapeutic encounter, or if a particular metaphor has come to dominate the life of a person or system. It is important to remember that the power of metaphor cuts both ways – the power to hurt or to help. The early work of the MRI team, Selvini-Polazzoli and her group and others in implementing the theorizing of Bateson and his group is well-known. The general term "paradoxical thinking" has become a kind of short-hand symbol for all those theorists who struggle to find ways to rescue their patients from the grip of the often destructive metaphors by which they live.

Humor, like metaphor, has a disarming quality. Although laughter is such an important part of life, it has received relatively scant attention in the psychological literature. Mahrer and Gervaize (1984), however, undertook a comprehensive review of the issue of strong laughter in therapy. They concluded that laughter which is a singular, discrete event in the session and is marked by strength, high energy and intensity, is a welcome and desirable event. Such laughter is valuable for several reasons: It may indicate a positive shift in the patient's self-concept or self-perspective. It may heighten feelings. It may move the patient towards healthier goals. It may also strengthen the patient-therapist relationship through increased warmth and reduced emotional distance. They then list a number of therapeutic methods for eliciting strong laughter. Curiously, the telling of a joke is not included.

The use of jokes may have important functions in helping patients to be released from the grip of oppressive metaphors. Such Jokes, of course, find their way into therapy because the therapist feels that they are evocative of the oppressive metaphor, and may produce change. The telling of a joke in therapy is akin to storytelling as practiced by Erickson (1976). It is playful, tends to catch the listener unawares, and because it is unexpected in the context of therapy, may increase alertness, thus encouraging some interruption of the existing cognitive frame.

A mother and father in their late fifties came to therapy with their 26-year-old son, who was still living at home. He had dropped out of some of the best colleges, and had lived at home since the age of twenty, never holding a job for more than a few days, and frequently unemployed. After a number of sessions in which the family had demonstrated quite well how much they could stick together in disqualifying one rational suggestion after another on my part, I suddenly found myself very bored and uninterested. As I listened to them drone on, an old joke came to my mind. I found myself inquiring if they had ever heard the story about Mrs. Cohen.

One day Mrs. Cohen pulled up to a plush hotel in Florida. As she went to the desk, she was greeted by the manager, who noticed that her chauffeur had gone to the back seat of her limo, picked up her very handsome son, and deposited him on a chair in the lobby. What a handsome young son you have, Mrs. Cohen, said the manager, and how sad it is that he can't walk. What do you mean, can't walk, replied Mrs. Cohen. Thanks to God, he doesn't have to.

There was general laughter, followed by silence. The family began to play with the story. Mother, at first, laughed and said that she couldn't see what was so terrible about that—he was in the lap of luxury. The young man didn't think it was so funny. He wondered what life would be like for the young man as he got older. If the legs weren't used for long enough, he thought, wouldn't they begin to atrophy? The father said he felt kind of like the chauffeur. Having enjoyed a good laugh, we went on with the session.

Interestingly enough, the family returned to the theme of this joke frequently in subsequent meetings. The young man said to his mother one day—"Don't Mrs. Cohen me." Sometimes she would herself allude to the "Mrs. Cohen fallacy." Father wondered when the boy would regain the use of his legs. After a few months, the young man got a full-time job, and a bit after, an apartment of his own. A follow-up call revealed that, after a year, he was maintaining his new-found independence.

A young couple in their early thirties entered therapy because of marital problems. He was a rather demanding and perfectionistic mate, although he felt that he was very empathic and supportive. His approach to the marriage was very serious, and she stolidly resisted his pleas for lengthy conversations about their relationship, where it was going, why it wasn't better than it was, and so forth. The more he would pursue her with requests for heart-to-heart talks, the more she would distance herself. He felt extremely put-upon, because he believed he was trying so hard to make things work, and she so frequently rebuffed him. I asked if I had ever told them about Moish.

Moish was a good and a God-fearing man. His religion demanded that he pray three times a day, but Moish prayed constantly. Moish did many good deeds. Nonetheless, tragedy continually dogged him. His business failed, the dog died, he got boils, and developed a bad case of gas. One day, he cried out to the Lord. "What is it with you? I do nothing but good deeds. I think only of others. You ask me to pray three times a day, and I pray constantly. What is wrong?" The voice of the Lord replied loud and clear: "Moish, you nudge too much!"

The couple was much amused by this story. Curiously, the husband did not become defensive, but began to observe the effect of what they began to call his "Moishisms" on her distancing behavior. Again, the story became a new part of the couple's interaction, a new metaphor that helped them to reconstruct their own reality in a more productive way. One of her observations was that it made her nervous to be put in the position of God, and this caused her to feel even more distant. They began to focus instead on what was good in their marriage, and in particular, what good friends they were. Both agreed that sharing what they each liked about the marriage was much more enjoyable than endless attempts to analyze it. Both agreed that intimacy increased.

I have cited two examples of the use of jokes in therapy, and described jokes as a particular type of metaphoric intervention. I am in no way suggesting that there is a need for a new therapeutic modality henceforth to be known as Joke Therapy. It is simply useful to remember that an appropriate joke, growing out of the patient, couple or family's metaphoric bind, may be a useful way of introducing therapeutic change.

As with any intervention, there are certain qualifications to be met. First, the therapist must enjoy telling jokes. Second, the therapist should be sure that the joke is, indeed, motivated by the therapeutic situation, and not by a personal need for attention on the part of the therapist. Finally, the patient, or the system, may or may not find the joke funny, or may not find it helpful. Good comics know that if you have to explain it, it isn't funny. The same holds true for jokes in therapy. If they are not responded to, that is fine too. But if their "message" is belabored by the therapist, they may have precisely the reverse of the desired effect. They may be turned from metaphor to simile, and engender the very resistance that we would like to avoid.

REFERENCES

Bateson, G., Jackson, D., Haley, J. & Weakland, J. (1956). Toward a theory of schizophrenia. *Behavioral Science*, *1*, 251-264.

Erickson, E., Rossi, E. & Rossi, S. (1976). *Hypnotic Realities* (p. 225). NY: Irvington Publishers.

Haley, J. (1973). *Uncommon Therapy: The Psychiatric Techniques of Milton H. Erickson: M.D.* (p. 214). NY: W. W. Norton.

Madanes, C. (1981). *Strategic Family Therapy* (p. 32). San Francisco: Jossey-Bass.

Mahrer, A. & Gervaize, P. (1984). An integrative review of strong laughter in psychotherapy: What it is and how it works. *Psychotherapy*, *21*, 510-516.

The Use of Dreams and the Dream Metaphor in Cognitive-Behavior Therapy

Arthur Freeman
Suzanne Boyll

In 1897, Freud presented the first of a series of lectures on the interpretation of dreams to the Vienna Lodge of B'nai Brith (an organization of Jewish laymen) (Bakan, 1958, 1975, p. 48). Because his theories were considered unsavory by the medical establishment, Freud had few other professional outlets where he could discuss his theoretical and conceptual notions about psychopathology, psychotherapy, and psychic mechanisms. The basic premise of his early lectures and his later elaborations through several editions of his classic "Interpretation of Dreams" (1900), was that the dream was the "royal road to the unconscious." Dreams, according to Freud, involve wish fulfillment. The dream becomes the pathway to satisfy the desires of the id, allowing accumulated energies to be discharged. The dream becomes the way of fulfilling desires that cannot otherwise be fulfilled during the waking life (Frager, 1976). This window into the unconscious allows the skilled psychoanalytic interpreter to understand the interplay of the patient's psychic structures. The patient's defenses, and the conflicts that were the basis of the patient's dysfunctional or maladaptive behaviors, affect, and thoughts could all be understood by the careful and systematic psychoanalytic interpretation of the patient's dreams.

Arthur Freeman, EdD, is affiliated with the Department of Psychiatry, Cooper/Hospital University Medical Center, Camden, NJ.

Suzanne Boyll, PhD, is affiliated with the LaSalle University, Philadelphia, PA.

Dreams are not, however, the sole province of Freudian psychoanalysis but have been an important part of psychotherapeutic treatment since the early pioneering days of Freud, Adler, and Jung, or the later psychoanalytically derived Gestalt therapy of Fritz Perls. Despite various disagreements on the specific foci or overall goals of psychotherapeutic treatment, all of the pioneers agreed on the importance, if not the primacy, of the dream as one of the most important and essential psychotherapeutic tools. There was general agreement that through the dream work, the therapist could understand the workings of the patient's unconscious, give voice to conflicts as yet unspoken, or dynamics not fully understood. Dreams were, therefore, an expected part of the psychoanalytic/psychotherapeutic process, and production and recollection of the dreams were an important part of the therapeutic material. In fact, the patients who did not report their dreams or claimed that they did not dream, were seen as resisting the analytic work. As the dreams might reflect the symbolized turmoil of the primitive personality structures, dreams were, for Freud, the normal person's loss of reality. They were a psychotic-like state that allowed the dreamer to speak and consort with persons long dead or who were fantasy objects, or be involved with persons or events never experienced in life (Freud, 1940). Fine (1979), a Freudian analyst, reports a number of studies that . . . . "have failed to demonstrate clear-cut differences between the dreams of schizophrenics and non-schizophrenics" thereby tending to . . . . "confirm Freud's position that the dream is a 'normal psychosis,' to which every individual regresses during the night" (p. 254).

For Jungians, the dream symbol was important as it reflected not only the personal unconscious of the individual, but also the collective unconscious of the society. Jung's understanding of dream symbols were later used in his analysis of the symbols inherent in folklore, mythology, primitive and contemporary religious symbols, and in artwork. Dreams were, for Jung, a bridge between conscious and unconscious process. Jung focused on the form and content of the dream and moved away from the psychoanalytic reliance on free association to the dream symbols (Frager, 1976). Jung stated, "Free association will bring out all my complexes, but hardly ever the meaning of a dream. To understand the dream's meanings I must stick as close as possible to the dream images" (Jung, 1934, p. 29).

For Adler, however, the patient's dream life corresponded directly and entirely to the dreamer's world picture or life style (Adler, 1923). Adler (1927) stated: "The purpose of dreams must be in the feelings they arouse. The dream is only the means, the instrument to stir up feelings" (p. 127). This was in direct conflict with the Freudian notion of the dream as being specifically focused on the unconscious and not on the conscious.

For Perls, originally trained as a psychoanalyst, but who later developed his own school of Gestalt therapy, dreams were "existential messengers which can help us to understand what unfinished situations we are carrying around with us, what we are missing in our lives, what we are avoiding doing, and how we are avoiding and disowning parts of ourselves" (Frager, 1976, p. 183).

Research has demonstrated that nightly dreams are part of the human condition, whether remembered or not, though studies on the use of dreams in psychotherapy have, for the most part been limited to descriptive and case study approaches (Weiss, 1986). He further states, "Research on dreams and psychotherapy is still in its infancy stages at this point (p. 36).

Therapists of all theoretical orientations will affirm that dreams are commonly mentioned in the course of therapy, and, in fact, for some patients, their extreme anxiogenic or depressogenic dreams may be the reason for seeking therapy. The uncomfortable affective and cognitive residue of the dream, may lead to sleep avoidance, thereby causing sleep deprivation and the consequent difficulties.

The non-psychoanalytic therapist's dilemma in using dreams was well stated by Shonbar (1968) when she wrote "She further confounded me by reporting a dream one day. As a client-centered therapist I'd had little experience with dreams . . . When my patient told me her dream I felt handcuffed; my limited armamentarium gave me no way to deal with it meaningfully, apart from a comment on the mood or feeling of the dream. I felt as if something valuable had been brought into the room and just shoved aside into a corner—or, more properly, that it lay between us untouched, thus depriving her of its potential value." The cognitive behavioral therapist is often at the disadvantage described by Shonbar, in that he or she is generally not oriented or trained to use the dream as grist for the therapeutic mill. In fact, training in the use and understanding (if not the interpretation) of dreams has not been a part of the traditional training of behavioral or cognitive behavioral therapists. An examination of several basic behavioral and cognitive behavioral texts finds no references to dreams, dreaming, or the use of dreams in the therapeutic process (Bandura, 1969; Bellack, Hersen, & Kazdin, 1991; Freeman, Pretzer, Fleming, & Simon, 1990; Lazarus, 1971; Martin & Pear, 1971; Masters, Burish, Hollon, & Rimm, 1987; Persons, 1989; Vallis, Howes, & Miller, 1991; Walen, Hauserman, & Lavin, 1977). We would explain this in several ways: (1) Many CBT therapists coming from predominantly behaviorally oriented training programs will, in all likelihood, have had little or no supervision, required readings, or training in the use of dreams in therapy. (2) Since dreams have no direct behavioral component, these therapists might have been taught that dreams ought to be totally avoided as therapeutic material. (3) Those CBT therapists with psychodynamic training may have refrained from using dream material in therapy as a way of further distancing themselves from their early psychodynamic influences. (4) Some CBT therapists may have avoided using dreams in therapy because of their belief that dream work is simply of no value (Ellis & Harper, 1975). Regardless of the reasons, the avoidance of dream work as part of cognitive behavioral therapy will result in the loss of extremely valuable cognitive and affective data. The dream can be a valuable tool in the overall CBT armamentarium, and a fruitful area for exploration in CBT (Mahoney, 1974). In a statement reminiscent of Adler, Weiss states (1986) "Dreams can be viewed as part of the continuity between sleeping and waking phenomena and reflect waking concerns and styles." Further, ". . . . dreams are influenced by waking conditions and are not just random, meaningless activity" (p. 36).

Our goal in this paper is to offer a rationale, specific guidelines, and ways of integrating dreams and the dreams metaphor into the broader CBT context. The first modern cognitive-behavioral outline for dreamwork was formulated by Beck (1971) in one of his early papers. Historically, this paper was an important transitional work as Beck began his shift from his earlier psychoanalytic training and practice and was beginning to formulate his ideas for his Cognitive Therapy. His dream work was based on a combination of his early classical psychoanalytic training, and on his extensive clinical experience which demonstrated the potential value of the dream. He regarded dreams as "a kind of biopsy of the patient's psychological process." The patient's dreams were seen to be idiosyncratic and dramatized the cognitive triad, that is, the patient's view of self, the world and experience, and the future posited by Beck as one of the three basic elements in depression, along with the cognitive distortions and the schema (Beck, Rush, Shaw, & Emery, 1979). Given that the dream material reflected the triad, it would follow that the dream would also embody the patient's cognitive distortions relative to those three areas. By understanding the triadic elements, the therapist could begin to develop a treatment protocol for treating the patient's depression (Freeman & Davis, 1990; Freeman et al., 1990). The dream material essentially reflected the patient's waking problems (Beck & Ward, 1961).

Two types of dream content have been differentiated by psychoanalytic writers, manifest content and latent content. The manifest content is the way the dream appears to the dreamer (a much more direct and conscious focus), while the latent content consists of the associated thoughts and memories that are triggered by the dream (a much more unconscious focus). The latent content, according to psychodynamic theory, contains the "repressed" or hidden meaning that is available only upon psychoanalytic interpretation. From the classical psychoanalytic perspective, the manifest content can, in fact, be discarded as cover, introductory or stimulus material, with the latent content being the true "essence" of the dream. The latent content is uncovered by the analyst's interpretations of the dream symbols and of the patient's associations to the dream symbols. (Of course, one might argue that as soon as the patient identifies a symbol and discusses and describes associations to the dream symbols, the previously latent content becomes manifest and should therefore be discarded.) The primary focus on the latent content shifted attention away from the manifest content and the manifest content was virtually ignored by analysts (Fine, 1979). A more contemporary psychoanalytic view is that much of the psychodynamic information is available from the manifest dream content. In fact, Erikson (1954) makes the point that by focusing on latent or unconscious symbols and their meaning, the therapist may lose much of the important meaning(s) of the dream. The therapist's interpretation may not only be off of the target, but may move the cognitive stream in ways the therapist may see as essential although the patient does not see that direction.

THE COGNITIVE PERSPECTIVE

It is necessary to view dreams as reflecting the cognitions and affective responses of waking experience and of the patient's life in general. Beck (1976) points out that concentrating on the manifest content of dreams is far more satisfactory than attempting to infer underlying processes which may be vague or unreachable. Since the manifest content is readily available to the dreamer and can be reported to the therapist, it is available for immediate use in the therapy session. Utilizing material that is readily available, the patient can obtain a sense of mastery and self-knowledge without depending on the therapist to interpret the symbolism of the dream. Beck states: "If the patient has a dream in which he perceives other people as frustrating him, it would be more economical to simply consider this conception of people as being frustrating rather than to read into the dream an underlying 'masochistic wish'" (p. 180). Further, Beck (1967) found that "dream themes are relevant to observable patterns of behavior" (p. 181), and that "dreams were analogous to the kind of suffering the depressed patient experienced in his waking life" (p. 208). Of course, dreams differ from the waking cognitions by the relative absence of external input. They are the product of the dreamer's internal world, but maintain an essential continuity with the waking thought process. In studying typical dreams of psychiatric patients, Ward, Beck, and Roscoe (1961) and Beck and Ward (1961) found dream themes characteristic of the particular disorder manifest in the patient's waking experience. Beck (1967) states: "In the course of the psychotherapy of patients with neurotic-depressive reactions, it was noted that there was a high incidence of dreams with unpleasant content" (p. 170). As treatment progresses, and the individual is better able to meet and overcome the day-to-day problems of life, the dream content will change to reflect the waking changes. As patients who previously may have had dreams of helplessness or failure to progress in treatment, their dreams begin to reflect their mastery. This process can be seen quite clearly in the case of a 27-year-old graduate student who had been procrastinating over completion of his dissertation for over a year. The material to be written was laid out on his desk. He had conducted the research and analyzed the data but was unable to complete the appropriate charts, tables, and interpretive prose. His waking cognitions tended to minimize his accomplishments with his typical thought pattern revolving around his inability to successfully complete the dissertation and the likelihood that he would never earn the doctorate, the relative lack of value of the dissertation to the literature of the field, the perceived huge flaws in the experimental design, and the social concerns about how the dissertation would be received and reviewed by colleagues, etc. In addition, there was his perfectionism that demanded that his dissertation be seen as one that would earn a Nobel prize for content and a Pulitzer prize for style. Chief among his basic beliefs were ideas about his lack of worth. His worth and value as a human being were centered, according to his belief system, on his productivity. Since he was worthless, he believed that any product of his must thereby be tainted and similarly worthless. In a circular manner, if his work was seen as valuable or successful it could not, by virtue of his flaws, be used to contradict his idea that he was worthless. As the days grew to weeks, the weeks to months, the individual had numerous anxiety dreams that would cause him to wake several times during the night with a "sense of dread." The thought that accompanied the dream, though the exact content of each dream was not always clear, was "I've got to get going, the material is sitting there waiting to be worked on . . . . but I can't work on it, I can't do it." The most common dream themes were of work uncompleted, and uncompletable. Several dreams were sexual in nature where sexual relationships were never consummated after much foreplay. The cognition associated with the dreams was "I can't finish anything." The goals in therapy were to take both a cognitive and a behavioral focus. The cognitive focus was on the thoughts surrounding personal efficacy, personal worth and ability to succeed. The behavioral focus involved a graded task approach to the completion of the project, through activity scheduling, and mastery and pleasure activities. As the student actively tested and challenged the various dysfunctional cognitions in the course of therapy while simultaneously working on the dissertation in small bits, the frequency of the anxiety dreams diminished. He experienced a growing sense of mastery, by understanding that the dissertation needed only to be appropriate and acceptable rather than perfect. As a consequence, the amount of work produced increased, until the individual, toward the completion of the dissertation, experienced no more anxiety dreams. On follow-up at six-month intervals over the next three years, the individual reported that anxiety dreams were experienced only in those situations where he had procrastinated and not completed required work, and that the anxiety dream became a signal for him to either organize or increase his efforts. In the final three-year follow-up, the individual reported that when he was awakened by a fearful dream in the middle of the night, rather than lying awake and ruminating, he would resolve to take concrete and positive action in the morning to resolve whatever issue existed as a source of anxiety. The anxiety dream in this case became a trigger for his success, not simply an aversive stimulus.

Although having made the statement that the dream material is idiosyncratic to the dreamer, Adler (1927) went on to offer several common dream themes that he viewed as extensions of the individual's waking cognitions, behavior, and lifestyle. For example, dreams of falling might represent a loss of status or prestige, while dreams of flying might represent activity, ambition, or a sense of looking forward. Dreams about dead people might reflect the fact that the dreamer has not "buried" the person and is still under his or her influence. It is essential, however, that the CB therapist avoid the pitfall of universal dream symbols, e.g., a certain symbol always having the same meaning. The therapist must work to understand the dream content and the broader dream themes in the context of the patient's life, experience, and base of knowledge. For example, two individuals may dream of cats. For one individual the dream is a pleasant one with associations about a favorite cat they had as a pet in childhood, how soft and cuddly cats are, and how cats are quite nice. For the other individual cats are a disliked or feared animal that scratches and bites. They are seen as too autonomous and independent, unlike dogs who are perceived as loyal.

Since the dream is not fettered by the constraints of the waking state, e.g., attending to necessary or vital circumstances such as watching the road while driving, the dreamer is freer to express a broad range of ideas, utilize magical thinking, and to be as creative and inventive as possible. Some dreams may, as indicated above, goad the person into action, and may presage activities. The dream may then have some small predictive value. The use of this less restrained cognitive stream can be a value to the therapist. In keeping all possible avenues opened for data collection in the therapy the dream can add immeasurably to the therapy work. It should be stressed that not all patients will come in reporting their dreams. It would be valuable for the therapist to suggest (but not require) that the patient record and report their dreams, so as to be better prepared to deal with them when offered. One can simply leave a pad on the bedside table for the recording of dreams upon waking. One more formalized technique for dream recording has been developed by Delaney (1991). She suggests that a dream journal be started for the recording of the dreams and the associated cognitions. The following format can be used (Delaney, 1991, pp. 20-21).

DATE. Be sure to record the date of each entry. (This helps to record the sequence of particular dreams.)

DAY NOTES. Before going to sleep, record three or four lines describing, in broad strokes, the activities of the day. Emphasize any particularly emotional or troubling aspects of the day. (This can allow a day/night interface.)

TITLE OF DREAM. Leave a blank line between the day notes and the dream record. This will allow you to give the dream a title. (The title or label can help to remember the dream and to later look for recurring themes.)

THE DREAM. Write down every detail and feeling that can be recalled upon waking. (This recording is the raw data to be processed later using a five column technique.)

COMMENTARY. This space can be used to record thoughts, feelings, and physiological responses (sweating, heart racing, urge to urinate, etc.). Also, any feelings, or impressions about the dream upon waking can be recorded here. (This space, and any additional pages can be used to make notes about the "dream interview" where the dream material is examined.)

Delaney (1991) also includes a category of "incubation question" (p. 20). This involves writing a short, focused question prior to sleep that will be repeated over, and over again as the dreamer falls asleep in an attempt to target a helpful dream that can help to resolve an issue in waking life. Inasmuch as the literature on dream problem-solving is anecdotal, not empirical, it is a category that we generally omit the question, using the spontaneously produced dream content.

The dream interview is a technique for examining the dream either in the therapy session or as homework. Delaney (1991) states, "To give the dreamer an effective forum in which to speak for herself, my method involves setting up a dream interview in which the dreamer is questioned by a friend, colleague, or dream analyst who pretends to come from another planet. The would-be interpreter becomes an interviewer who will be curious to discover what life is like seen through the eyes of the dreamer. . . . The interviewer then asks the dreamer to define and describe the images as if she were describing them to someone who has never heard of them before" (p. 37). The description should focus on the physical setting of the dream (my apartment; the beach; an open field), any sensory impressions (we were cold; it smelled bad), the major and minor action (while I was walking, there were birds flying around my head), the objects (there were three classic cars, all 1957 Chevies; a couch covered in plastic), the cast of characters (my brother was there along with my boss, and Charlton Heston), and the feelings (I was sad; we just kept laughing with joy). Following the description, the interviewer recapitulates the descriptions to the dreamer asking if the description reminds the dreamer of any person, situation, or events in life thereby bridging the sleep-waking experience. The final step is to have the dreamer connect and summarize the images, bridges settings and cast of the dream and to identify any dream themes.

The Daily Record of Dysfunctional Thoughts (Beck et al., 1979; Freeman et al., 1990), perhaps better known as the Dysfunctional Thought Record (DTR) (Figure 1), is an ideal format for exploring

FIGURE 1. Adaptation of the Dysfunctional Thought Record.

SITUATION	EMOTIONS	THOUGHTS	ADAPTIVE RESPONSES
Write out the dream	Identify emotions	Write out associations to the dream	Restructure, reframe, re-image the dream material

the dream content, and making changes to the cognitions and mood evoked during the interview.

The dream is recorded in column 1 under situation.

The emotions attendant to the dream are recorded in column 2. The amount of emotion, from 0-100 is rated as baseline data.

The related associations and images are recorded in column 3. The degree of belief or endorsement of an idea can also be rated as baseline data.

A particular part of the dream image or thought can be targeted for testing or challenge in column 4. Using the traditional CT techniques (Beck et al., 1979; Freeman et al., 1990) the ideas can be challenged and modified.

The baseline emotional weighting (column 2) and the degree of belief or endorsement of an idea (column 3) can be rerated.

SUMMARY OF COGNITIVE DREAM WORK

The following summary guidelines have been developed to assist the clinician in utilizing dreams within the context of CBT.

1. The dream needs to be understood in thematic and contextual terms, rather than symbolic terms. The particular images and ideas expressed by patients in their dream can be taken at face value. The dreams are not necessarily cognitive transformations that are representations of something else, but stand within the context of the life themes or schema of the patient. The search for symbols may, in fact, distract from the dream work. As the therapist might continue to search for the "true meaning" expressed in the dream symbols, he or she may begin to stray from a basic understanding of the individual. Even Freud would probably have agreed that at times a cigar might be a cigar and nothing more. The question that the therapist can ask is how this dream material inconsistent or is consistent with the patient's life, conflicts, successes or failures.

2. The thematic content of the dream is idiosyncratic to the dreamer and must be viewed within the context of the dreamer's life. In maintaining the cognitive continuum from waking to sleep,

we are able to view the dream as part of the overall life experience. Dreams are not isolated phenomena and need to be connected to the patient's current concerns. What a particular dream experience means must be seen in the overall view of life maintained by the patient.

3. The specific language and imagery are important to the meaning. The words, voice tone, visual images, and quality of language very much influence the affect being expressed. By using the dreamer's words and symbols, we can better understand his or her dream interest. A dream image of being alone in a large stadium conveys a very different sense from being alone in a small room. Having a lover whisper in one's ear differs from having a lover scream insults in one's ear.

4. The affective responses to the dreams can be seen as similar to the dreamer's affective responses in waking situations. Happiness, anxiety, depression, or any of the range of emotional responses would be the same in dreaming or waking situations. The affective residue responses or residue of the dream can be dealt with as in any waking emotional response.

5. The particular length of the dream is of lesser import than the content. Since we dream in images and pictures, a dream image or fragment may be exceptionally brief but have tremendous emotional impact. For example, a fragment of image where the dreamer sees her child lying dead on the street in front of a car can produce a sense of terror that persists well into the following day.

6. The dream is a product of, and the responsibility, of the dreamer. The particular material that the dreamer chooses to include in the dream, while possibly being a product of the previous day's experience, still becomes a function of, and idiosyncratic to the dreamer. For example, a patient reported a dream of his boss being cruel to him. The affective experience was first fear, and then anger that the boss had intruded on his sleep. As the patient spoke about the boss, he became angry that even his time at home was not safe. The therapist reminded the patient that the boss did not intrude on his dream or his leisure time. Instead, it was the patient who carried a mental representation of the boss with him wherever he went. While there may be been reality issues related to the boss, his

intrusion on the dream needed to be identified clearly as a product of the dreamer.

7. Dream material is amenable to the same cognitive restructuring as are any automatic thoughts. Dreams can be reworked to arrange affect shifts, alternative outcomes, or new solutions. By utilizing the Dysfunctional Thought Record (Figure 1) dreams can be restructured with appropriate disputation and rational challenges to the dysfunctional dream material. The dream can be written down as the incident, with an assessment of the nature and degree of the emotional response, followed by the dysfunctional thinking expressed in the dream, and degree of belief in the dysfunctional dream material. The patient can then learn to dispute the dysfunctional themes embodied in the dream, and to change his or her affective response to the dream as a result.

8. Dreams can be used when the patient appears "stuck" in therapy. Practicing the process of adaptive responding on the patient's dreams can assist the patient in building further skills to deal rationally with dysfunctional thinking. When the particular direction or momentum of therapy seems lost, the dream material can be a valuable adjunctive tool providing an arena for practice. Patients often readily accept the use of dreams because they are so personal and such a familiar part of their experiences.

9. Dreams cannot become the sole focus of the session and need to be dealt with as part of the agenda setting. An active dreamer may wish to use the entire therapy hour to discuss several dreams. The therapist needs to be judicious in using dreams in the session, so that the exclusion of other important material does not occur.

10. Images, like dreams can also be valuable as metaphorical material. The therapist can, of course, utilize imagery and imaginal restructuring as a major tool for both dream related images and waking images (Edwards, 1989). The use of imagery, like the use of dreams, can add immeasurably to the therapy. Since few patients can describe symptoms without describing accompanying images, the image is a ready, accessible entry point for cognitive intervention. Images may be visual, auditory, gustatory, or olfactory. Images may utilize an economy of words, but they provide a directness of meaning and a vivid affective experience for the patient.

The affect-laden image can often penetrate the depression and isolation of the lonely patient. The image-maker does not always have to be the patient, since the therapist can suggest images and imagining techniques to effectively break through a number of symptoms. Images can be made evocative through the inclusion of multisensory elements. Beck, Laude, and Bohnert (1974) observed that with the onset or exacerbation of anxiety, many patients have thoughts or visual fantasies revolving around the theme of danger. The anxiety, they conclude, was a direct result of the visualization of the danger-laden image. Their observations have direct implications for the treatment of anxiety. The therapist does not have to be the image-maker, but can call upon the patient to produce the images. The imaging can become part of the homework assignment arrived at between the patient and the therapist. The patient can be asked to develop a number of images that help focus on the particular symptoms currently being addressed in treatment.

Using the above-mentioned guidelines, the following cases demonstrate the use of dreams in CT.

Case 1 – A 31-year-old woman reported the following dream: "I was sitting on the couch in my living room when this huge snake came at me from out of the opposite wall near the ceiling line. It struck at me with incredible speed, not allowing me to move away. It sank its fangs into my arm. All I could do was look at it and comment aloud on the pain and the fact that it was biting me. I woke up feeling anxious and frightened. It was a scary dream." The basic cognitive elements involved were her helplessness and inability to react, her passivity in response to being attacked, and her feelings of anxiety when placed in a position that required direct action. These cognitions paralleled her dysfunctional cognitions in the waking state. She was extremely effective on the job but often felt anxious when called upon to be assertive. She more generally took a passive approach, and then being angry at herself for not being more assertive. The therapist helped her to restructure the experience by asking the patient what she might have done differently in the dream. Her initial response was that she could do very little, that she was at the mercy of her dream content (cognitions). The therapist emphasized that since she was the sole producer, director, stage manager, and casting director (after all, she recruited the snake), she could recast or restructure the scene as she wished. At first, she restructured the dream tentatively, by visualizing herself trying to hold something over the snake hole in the wall (a "finger-in-the-dike" response); a response that she quickly indicated would probably fail because of the strength of the snake. With further encouragement and some modeling on the therapist's part, she restructured the scene so that she immediately severed the snake's head. (When she protested that she did not have a knife, it was pointed out that the knife could come from the same source as the snake, her imagination.) As she restructured the dream scene to one of her taking greater control and asserting herself, there was a rapid affect shift from anxiety to relief. Another technique used was to have the patient revisualize the dream but for the primary purpose of altering the negative elements. The snake could become a Sesame Street character, or the patient could offer the snake a treat or erect a transparent shield. In restructuring the dream, a positive outcome can always be effected (Leurner, 1969).

Case 2 – A 24-year-old female graduate student reported the following dream fragment: "I woke up early one morning. I was at my parent's home. I went downstairs and saw my boyfriend's car parked by my garage. I felt annoyed because he didn't ask for permission, or tell me he was going to do it." The affect associated with the dream was anger and the major cognition was of helplessness. The associated information elicited involved an ongoing conflict over her sexual relationship with her boyfriend. She felt that he would often appear to be unaware of her needs or was insensitive to her feelings. His demands took precedence, which she allowed, and she experienced anger and depression as a result. In this brief dream fragment, the basic themes are the patient's loss of control and her subsequent anger, and of her being taken for granted. In restructuring the dream, the patient attempted a number of strategies in dealing with the unwanted car. She first tried locking the garage doors, thus forcing the boyfriend to park out in the cold. This strategy set up a situation where he had to ask to be allowed to park in the garage. Further images included demanding that she be informed of his desire to park, discussing his parking as part of a mutual decision and even having him park on her demand. As she discussed the various strategies that she might have used in the dream, there was a rather rapid affect shift, resulting from the dream restructuring. She experienced a sense of pleasure and satisfaction that helped her to resolve that she would not allow herself to be used any longer. Utilizing the restructured images in her dream, she was able to begin asserting herself in the relationship with her boyfriend.

Case 3—A 34-year-old woman who had successfully been through a course of cognitive therapy aimed at reducing depression and anxiety relative to her work situation returned for therapy specific to an ongoing sexual problem. The problem had been a secondary item on the agenda of the earlier course of treatment. The patient was well socialized to cognitive therapy and to use of the various techniques. Among the first interventions of the session were attempts at imaging. The patient reported that she had great difficulty in imaging and would often find herself distracted by any one of a number of work or home related issues. This was especially true in sexual situations, where she found herself very quickly and easily distracted. Due to the distractibility, she and her husband had fewer and fewer sexual contacts, which had the consequence of marital conflict. She reported that she would often reject certain dreams, because as a feminist, she could not accept the males in a superior position. Any dreams that involved sadism or masochism were likewise rejected because she was by nature and belief, nonviolent. And if the fantasy involved a man or men other than her husband, she would reject that, too, because she believed in monogamous relationships. As we discussed the dismissal of images and the resultant distracting effect she commented, "My God, I only allow myself politically correct dreams and fantasies." Indeed, she severely limited the range of her fantasies and her sexual responses as well. As she could accept and challenge the dysfunctional notion that her dreams and fantasies must be politically correct, she was able to gain a greater freedom and sense of control over her fantasies, her body, and her sexual relationships. The patient severely limited herself to only the "right kinds of dreams and fantasies," rejecting other themes as inappropriate or wrong. As the patient began to realize that her fantasies and images did not have to be acted out, she could then indulge her fantasies and enjoy them more fully.

SUMMARY

The present paper deals with the use of dreams and the associated images in the context of cognitive behavioral therapy. Dreams have historically been an important part of the psychotherapeutic process. The therapist trained in cognitive behavioral therapy is frequently not trained or prepared to work with dreams in psychotherapy and may lose valuable opportunities to tap the richness of imagery offered in dreams. The cognitive model sees the dreamer as idiosyncratic and the dream as a dramatization of the patient's view of self, world, and future, subject to the same cognitive distortions as the waking state. The following guidelines can be set for C-B dream work: (1) The dream needs to be understood in thematic rather than symbolic terms. (2) The thematic content of the dream is idiosyncratic to the dreamer and must be viewed within the context of the dreamer's life. (3) The specific language and images of the dream are important. (4) The affective responses to the dreams can be seen as similar to the dreamer's affective response in waking situations. (5) The particular length of the dream is of lesser import than the content. (6) The dream is a product of, and the responsibility of the dreamer. (7) Dream material is amenable to the same cognitive restructuring as any automatic thoughts. (8) Dreams can be used when the patient appears "stuck" in therapy. (9) Dreams cannot become the sole focus of the session and need to be dealt with as part of the agenda. (10) Imagery, associated with the dreams can be quite useful in the therapeutic work.

The cognitive therapist can enrich his or her armamentarium by including dreams and imagery as part of the psychotherapeutic collaborative process. They offer an opportunity for the patient to understand his or her cognitions as played out on the stage of the imagination and to challenge or dispute those depressogenic thoughts, with a resultant positive affect shift. The dream would not then necessarily be the royal road to the unconscious, but rather the more commonly traveled route toward the individual's conscious understandings of personal, family, cultural, religious, and gender-related schema.

REFERENCES

Adler, A. (1927). *The practice and theory of individual psychology*. New York: Harcourt, Brace & Co.

Bakan, D. (1958/1975). *Sigmund Freud and the Jewish Mystical Tradition*. Boston: Beacon.

Bandura, A. (1969). *Principles of behavior modification*. New York: Holt, Rinehart, and Winston.

Beck, A. T. (1971). Cognition, affect and psychopathology. *Archives of General Psychiatry*, 24, 495-500.

Beck, A. T. (1967). *Depression: Clinical, experimental, and theoretical aspects*. New York: Harper & Row, 1967. (Republished as Depression: Causes and treatment. Philadelphia: University of Pennsylvania Press, 1972.)

Beck, A. T., Laude, R., & Bohnert, M. (1974). Ideational components of anxiety neurosis. *Archives of General Psychiatry*, 31, 319-325.

Beck, A. T., Rush, A. J., Shaw, B.F., & Emery, G. (1979). *Cognitive therapy of depression*. New York: Guilford Press.

Beck, A.T., & Ward, C.H. (1961). Dreams of depressed patients: Characteristic themes in manifest content. *Archives of General Psychiatry*, 5, 462-467.

Bellack, A.S., Hersen, M., & Kazdin, A.E. (1991). *International handbook of behavior modification and therapy*, Second edition. New York: Plenum.

Delaney, G. (1991). *Break through dreaming: How to tap the power of your 24-hour mind*. New York: Bantam.

Ellis, A., & Harper, R.A. (1975). *A new guide to rational living*. Englewood Cliffs, N.J.: Prentice-Hall.

Erikson, E. (1954). The dream specimen of Psychoanalysis. *JAPA*, 2, 5-56.

Fine, R. (1979). *A History of psychoanalysis*. New York: Columbia University Press.

Freeman, A. (1979). The use of dreams and imagery in cognitive therapy. In G. Emery, S. Hollon, & R. Bedrosian. *New directions in cognitive therapy*. New York: Guilford.

Freeman, A. & Davis, D.D. (1991). Cognitive therapy of depression. In A.S. Bellack, M. Hersen, & A.E. Kazdin. *International handbook of behavior modification and therapy*, Second edition. New York: Plenum.

Freud, S. (1909). *Interpretation of dreams. Standard edition*, London: Hogarth Press, Vols 4-5.

Freud, S. (1949). *An outline of psychoanalysis*. New York: Norton.

Lazarus, A.A. (1971). *Behavior therapy and beyond*. New York: McGraw-Hill Book Co.

Leurner, H. (1969). Guided affective imagery (GAI): A method of intensive psychotherapy. *American Journal of Psychotherapy*, 23, 4-22.

Mahoney, M. (1974). *Cognitive behavior therapy*. Cambridge, Mass.: Ballinger.
Martin, G. & Pear, J. (1978). *Behavior modification: What it is and how to do it*. Englewood Cliffs, NJ: Prentice-Hall.
Masters, J.C., Burish, T.G., Hollon, S.D., & Rimm, D.C. (1987). *Behavior therapy*. New York: Harcourt, Brace, Jovanovich.
Persons, J. (1989). *Cognitive therapy in practice*. New York: Norton.
Shonbar, R. (1968). Confessions of an ex-nondirectivist. In E. Hammer (Ed.), *Use of interpretation in treatment*. New York: Grune & Stratton.
Vallis, T.M., Howes, J.L., & Miller, P.C. (1991). *The challenge of cognitive therapy*. New York: Plenum.
Walen, S., Hauserman, N.M., & Lavin, P.J. (1977). *Clinical guide to behavior therapy*. Baltimore: Williams & Wilkins.
Ward, C.H., Beck, A.T., & Roscoe, E. (1961). Typical dreams: Incidence among psychiatric patients. *Archives of General Psychiatry*, 5, 606-615.
Weiss, L. (1986). *Dream analysis in psychotherapy*. New York: Pergamon.

Discussant Comments from Eclectic Uses of Metaphor in Psychotherapy

J. Marvin Eisenstadt

We have an overflow crowd here and nine hours have been devoted at this convention to metaphors. It seems it is an important topic, but that shouldn't surprise us. Metaphors have been around ever since the beginning of time probably. Aristotle (1984) in his *Rhetoric* discussed the topic.

Language is designed to make life coherent and meaningful. It orders our experience in a way that is satisfying to us. Language represents knowledge that can be transmitted from one person to another. It has been remarked that any communication may not accomplish what the speaker intends. The explicit message as has been mentioned will try for clarity and attempt to evoke a rational, intelligible response from the listener. However, in the figure of speech of the metaphor you want to attempt something that's implicit. The danger there is that you may not communicate what you want to communicate to the listener. And it may be rejected by the listener not only because they don't understand what you are saying, but, what may be worse, they do understand it, and they don't like the message that you are sending to them.

In the use of paradoxical approaches you have the situation that

J. Marvin Eisenstadt is Chief Psychologist of the Central Nassau Guidance and Counseling Services of Hicksville, NY. He also conducts a private practice in Syosset, NY.

Presented at the 96th Annual Convention of the American Psychological Association, Atlanta, GA, August 1988.

there is a disguised truth that you are trying to get the patient to understand. You want to compel that logic or that truth of a new conception that they would ordinarily reject. Now they are at least compelled to listen to it and give it some kind of a careful, respectful hearing. It is designed to disrupt what already is and create a new potential of what can be for the patient. By definition a metaphor cannot be completely analyzed. We have heard how you would have to rehearse and dispute with the patient in order to get them to believe the same point of view that you have. The advantage of the metaphor is that you avoid confrontation and avoid the logical "yes, but" that may arise. In terms of the eclectic uses of metaphor, I am not going to attempt to recapitulate all of the speakers. Not only because I am not wise enough to do so, but the time is too limited. I will point out to you that all of us who leave here today heard Suzanne Boyll speaking for Dr. Arthur Freeman refer to "parking his car in her garage." The phrase will be something that you will take away from this symposium. It is a shorthand way to understand something. Or "don't Mrs. Cohen me" will give us something that Dr. Don-David Lusterman has left with us. "Flew into a rage" might capture something for you after hearing Dr. David Rouzer. And "how's Mickey doing?" may have some new meaning as explained by Dr. Ray DiGiuseppe. We don't know if it will or will not. It is an empirical question that would have to be decided in an individual discussion with each of you.

The idea of a metaphor in terms of psychotherapy is that it induces change. It has the potential to produce a new insight. It could lead to increasing understanding and wisdom. It has several features that's kind of nifty for the therapist. For example, one is that it's short and sweet. When you say, "how's Mickey doing?" you don't have to give a long speech. You instantaneously capture something in a way that is quick. It may be more effective than a long winded big sentence that may not communicate what you want anyway. It has also been mentioned it is a wonderful mnemonic device, a memory aid. If you say something that is short, it tends to be remembered, as you all know. It is something that can be taken away with you.

It also can serve to free up the therapy. When things get a little stale, you can always mention a joke, a metaphor, or a story that will get the dialogue moving again. As therapists we understand this is a very valuable commodity. It is an enriched armamentarium that we have. Therapy needs to have many metaphors.

There are certain dangers I want to point out to you in using metaphors. The first one is that you take an educated guess when you use a metaphor. You hope that there is a shared knowledge between you and the listener which may or may not build understanding. I think in terms of, let's say, "a wild goose chase." Now that metaphor may have a lot of meaning for all of us, but frankly I have never seen a wild goose, and I don't know if any of you have either. I don't know exactly what a wild goose does when it chases.

Sometimes it can be quite trivial. What you are communicating is not really worth being communicated, although it may sound quite good. Also the real issue is not whether to use a metaphor or not to use a metaphor, but rather the choice of the metaphor that we use. We all agree, the masters of our field, the Milton Ericksons, the Jay Haleys, the Albert Ellises, are people that know how to use something that really works. Maybe in the hands of somebody else it may not work as well or it may not work at all. Certainly the choice that we make and the cleverness with which we pick the metaphor to communicate something to the individual is really what is at the heart of the discussion.

A metaphor may be misleading or even worse may interfere with acquiring new knowledge or insight. If the therapist uses the wrong metaphor it may blind the patient. It can be used in such a way that it ceases to be a figure of speech, but rather becomes a confirmed reality which may turn out to be incorrect. Moreover, the reaction you hope for may not be the reaction you get from the patient. You think you have just made a meaningful, insightful commentary, but what was heard was a colorful, meaningless rhetoric, a mere literary device of a poetic, perhaps misguided psychotherapist.

It is necessary for science to progress from metaphor to algebra. From the art of therapy we have to achieve a science of therapeutics. The key question to be asked is does this intervention, this comment, this metaphor, facilitate or interfere with the discovery of wisdom? In writing about the blues singer, Bessie Smith, in a column entitled "My heart's on fire but my love is icy cold," one of my favorite writers, Murray Kempton, captured the main requirement for all communicators. He said what was needed was "to distill a complexity into the sparest of direct statements and still preserve intact its paradox" (Kempton, 1987). I wish you all success in accomplishing this difficult task.

REFERENCES

Aristotle (1984). Rhetoric, Book III, 1410b. In J. Barnes (Ed.), *The complete works of Aristotle: The revised Oxford translation* (Vol. 2, pp. 2250-2252). Princeton, NJ: Princeton University Press.

Barker, P. (1985). *Using metaphors in psychotherapy*. New York: Brunner/Mazel.

Beier, E.G. (1987). Metaphors as tools in psychotherapy. (Review of *Using metaphors in psychotherapy*.) *Contemporary Psychology*, 32, 174-175.

Efran, J.S. & Alexander, K.J. (1988). Childish or childlike metaphors? Therapy with Sammy the elephant. (Review of *Therapeutic metaphors for children and the child within*.) *Contemporary Psychology*, 33, 265.

Eisenstadt, M., Haynal, A., Rentchnick, P., & de Senarclens, P. (in press). *Parental loss and achievement*. Madison, CT: International Universities Press.

Kempton, M. (1987, July 5). My heart's on fire but my love is icy cold. *Newsday*, *Ideas*, p. 6.

Lakoff, G. & Johnson, M. (1980). *Metaphors we live by*. Chicago: University of Chicago Press.

Mills, J. C. & Crowley, R.J. (1986). *Therapeutic metaphors for children and the child within*. New York: Brunner/Mazel.

Sapir, J.D. & Crocker, J.C. (Eds.). (1977). *The social use of metaphor: Essays on the anthropology of rhetoric*. Philadelphia, PA: University of Pennsylvania Press.

Spence, D. P. (1987). *The Freudian metaphor: Toward paradigm change in psychoanalysis*. New York: Norton.

Stein, H. F., & Apprey, M. (1987). *From metaphor to meaning: Papers in psychoanalytic anthropology*. Charlottesville: University Press of Virginia.

RECOMMENDED BOOKS, TEXTS AND MONOGRAPHS

COME HERE! GO AWAY: STOP RUNNING FROM THE LOVE YOU WANT. Ralph Earle and Susan Meltsner. *New York: Pocket Books: Simon Schuster, 1991, 257 pp., $19.95.*

Intimacy, its discovery, development and maintenance is the central theme of human relationships. This self-help book is rich with simply written illustrations, and easy to understand points. Seven prerequisites for intimacy listed are trust, self-worth, positive regard for others, interdependence, tolerance for conflict, ambiguity and imperfection, self-disclosure, courage and having an intimacy role model. There are self-rating scales for each of these areas.

Clarification of certain patterns of disrupted intimacy and directions to overcome these problems are provided. Identification of intimacy paradoxes and writing a prescription for positive change are outlined. The steps in making these changes are likened to learning dance steps. Several suggestions are made on self-worth, trust, and courage with valuable exercises clearly described.

There is a recommended auxiliary reading list provided. Resource organizations are indexed to assist the reader find groups to facilitate their development of intimacy.

The authors are generous with information which can be followed by a diligent reader. Therapists will find this patient guide a useful adjunct to their interventions with individuals who have problems developing and maintaining intimacy.

Jack G. Wiggins, PhD
Psychological Development Center
Cleveland, Ohio

COPING WITH ETHICAL DILEMMAS IN PSYCHOTHERAPY. Martin Lakin. *New York and London: Pergamon Press, 1991, $35.00 hardcover, $17.95 softcover.*

This book's central thesis is that ethical problems are part and parcel of the ". . . ambiguous nature of therapy contact and interactions." The intended audience for this includes practitioners, teachers and supervisors of therapy as well as trainees in clinical psychology, clinical social work, counseling, psychiatry and individuals in cognate fields who aim to produce therapeutic change.

The book is divided into eight themes (chapters) which include ethical dilemmas in the therapeutic relationship (e.g., informed consent, confidentiality, therapist responsibilities), values of psychotherapies and psychotherapists, ethical issues in cross-gender and cross-cultural therapy (e.g., feminist perspective, African-American perspective, psychopolitical therapies), modality-linked ethical dilemmas (dyadic, group, family/marital, organizational intervention), supervision of therapy, teaching of ethical awareness, legal aspects of psychotherapy practice and continuing education for ethical practice.

For this book the author interviewed 50 clinicians, clinical psychologists, clinical social workers, counselors and psychiatrists about their own ethical dilemmas. Illustrative case material are included to highlight ethical problems for clients who are self referred outpatients. Specifically excluded, according to the author, are ethical problems involving long term hospitalized patients and organically impaired individuals.

What are the strengths of this brief volume? I was impressed by the high quality of the vignettes presented and found them to be challenging, thought provoking and stimulating. Dr. Lakin gives excellent coverage to such topics as informed consent, legal issues, supervision and countertransference and numerous other themes of great value to clinicians. The "modalities" chapter stands out in that many discussions on ethics limit their efforts to dyadic therapy. The discussion of ethical dilemmas of group psychotherapists, family/marital therapies and interventions in organizations provide helpful guidelines to those involved in the interventions. This section includes a discussion of quasi-therapeutic groups such as self-help or support groups which should be of interest to many. The suggestions for workshops are well delineated and provide constructive hints for teachers of ethics. I also liked the discussion concerning ambivalence about ethics instruction (recognizing that ethics is a required course for graduate students in APA approved programs). In addition, I found the section on values in psychotherapy particularly instructive. The author points out, for example, that little is written about therapy from a consumer's perspective especially with a view toward selecting the appropriate therapy, though there have been some recent efforts at delineating how one should choose a therapist.

What is missing from this book? First of all there is no discussion about the relationship of assessment to psychotherapy. Dr. Lakin does mention the Osheroff case (patient treated with psychoanalysis for depression at Chestnut Lodge) but there is no mention of assessment even though differential diagnosis was the hotly debated issue in that case. This reader is left with the impression that assessment is not part of therapy, does not need ethical review or is simply unimportant. Therapists are not supposed to practice beyond their competence yet how is this decided? Is that not an ethical issue worth discussing in depth? The book gives brief mention to questions of whether or not the therapist is the "right" person for a given client, what kinds of treatment should be proposed and the alternatives to that treatment. But there is no direct discussion of assessment. Certainly for the psychologists, having knowledge of and competence to use assessment techniques is important for practice (Bennett, Bryant, VandenBos & Greenwood. 1990). The book excludes coverage of ethical problems for hospitalized long term patients but there is no discussion of ethical issues concerning voluntary hospitalization and ethical issues concerning the side effects of medications are also not to be found. I find that strange in a book which aims to be helpful to psychiatrists, aside from the raging debate about prescription privileges among psychologists.

Second, concerns about target populations are also not covered, despite the NIMH initiative concerning the seriously mentally ill, the homeless and other populations. What about issues concerning the elderly, the physically handicapped, the retarded, substance abusers, etc.? Does psychotherapy with these individuals involve ethical dilemmas? Are there any ethical dilemmas concerned with managed care? With practitioners who use anatomically detailed dolls in therapy with abused children? Are there ethical concerns related to therapy with court referred clients?

Third, it would have been helpful to discuss instances when ethics and the law are in conflict. For example, does the duty to protect require a therapist to inform partners of HIV positive clients when that client does not engage in safe sex practices? Or, it might have been helpful to discuss the ethical dilemmas involved in being called to testify in court about a client (with that client's permission) when you are convinced that testifying will be harmful to that individual.

I recognize that no one book can fully cover all the issues relating to ethics but, in my opinion, more consciousness raising would have been helpful.

As it stands, this book is a perfectly good introduction to therapy as usual. It seems to limit itself to "office counseling" as physicians like to call it, or general casework or outpatient therapy with the not too seriously disturbed. That is certainly a modal approach. On the other hand the field of therapy is moving toward increasing specialization and this raises additional ethical dilemmas.

Despite the limitations discussed above, Lakin's book is a well written introduction to ethical dilemmas for students in training. Practitioners will also find this book to be useful.

Norman Abeles, PhD
Professor of Psychology and
Director, Psychological Clinic
Michigan State University
East Lansing, MI 48824

REFERENCE

Bennett, Bruce, Bryant, B., VandenBos, Gary, & Greenwood, Addison (1990). *Professional Liability and Risk Management*. Washington, DC: American Psychological Association.

WOMEN OVER FORTY, VISIONS AND REALITIES. Jean Dresden Grambs (Ed.). *New York: Springer, 1989, 254 pp., $35.95 hardcover, $21.95 softcover.*

In "Women Over Forty" Jean Grambs has assembled and organized a formidable range of facts and research findings on the aging women, admirable in its thoroughness. What makes this slim volume so engrossing, however, over and above its scholarliness, is the wise, sensitive and penetrating commentary interwoven with the presentation of factual material. This is a book which speaks to lay and professional alike, regardless of age and gender. It brings together and illuminates the full range of issues salient to women reaching middle age and the years beyond.

Grambs confronts and analyzes each issue in turn, often expressing appropriate dismay and anger at the blatantly sexist neglect, distortion and ignorance which have obstructed the valid examination of these issues in past years. No pat solutions or "pop" advice giving are to be found in this volume. However, what *is* striking on almost every page is hard evidence of the trivialization and, even more damaging, the misinformation which has served to obscure the truths fundamental to the lives of aging women, to this day. Little significant research data were to be found before the '80s. Dominant opinion on such basic issues as health, family relationships, differing cultural patterns, as well as the normal emotional and physical surrounds of the aging process itself, were pervaded with sexism and superstitious beliefs. The "explosion" of data generated largely by women researchers in the '80s and synthesized by Jean Grambs in this volume is, she feels, a wholly constructive byproduct of the women's movement. The first edition of "Women Over Forty," (1981) of which this is a much enlarged revision, has grown out of the author's work at the Center for Aging at the University of Maryland, which began in the late '70s.

The longevity of women has long been known to be greater than that of men, but as Grambs says, the meaning of this fact has only recently been examined. The urgency of conducting a serious examination of this and the other basic facts of life as they relate to aging women is brought into high relief by the exponential, continuing increase in our aging population.

With continually increasing social awareness, enhanced by the sense of their own individual and group strength, Grambs predicts, in her final summing up:

> There are many reasons to predict that the world of older women in the next century will be better than many women experience today – assuming no great economic or nuclear catastrophe. Older women will be healthier, wealthier and wiser. And, there will be so many of them that they can have a major influence on public policy.

Much of this optimistic prediction and dissemination depends on the expanded production of better research on every aspect of women's lives and throughout the life span. What we know about older persons in general is too little compared to what we know about infancy, for instance. Women must be aggressive and vigilant in their insistence that research in every discipline include women and, when the subjects of study are both male and female, that the results are analyzed by gender.

The human life span has a finite limit as far as we now know, but with adequate understanding of the aging process in both women and men and of the social context in which this takes place we can do far more than we now do to vastly improve the quality of life of the final decades.

I see this as a fitting conclusion to a highly interesting and scholarly volume which should serve as a reference source for research data and as an inspiration, not only for women over forty, but for individuals of all ages and genders.

Helen M. Strauss, PhD
Private Practice
West Orange, N.J.
Facility, Institute of Psychoanalysis and Psychotherapy of New Jersey

ACTING ASSERTIVELY AT WORK: A SELF-HELP MANUAL. Mary Valentich and James Gripton. *Calgary, Canada: Faculty of Social Work, The University of Canada, 1990, 85 pp., $9.95.*

The authors of this concise and very readable manual entitle the second chapter, "Assertiveness Is Old Hat." Yet, they point out that despite the popularity of assertiveness training for nearly two decades, learning to be assertive in the work context can be helpful in avoiding or limiting the degree of tension, frustration, guilt, or even depression individuals may experience as a result of going head-to-head with a difficult work situation.

They begin by defining assertiveness and making clear differentiations between assertiveness and aggressiveness. This is followed by a discussion of the risks and benefits of being assertive. Operating from a rational-emotive framework, they present their thesis: that understanding problem situations and espousing ideas that are rational, testable, specific, and relative will allow people to deal most effectively with work problems. A schema is offered which involves identifying and challenging self-defeating ideas, changing feelings, and behavior. An important component of this process is practice. To this end, the authors offer many examples of problem situations, self-defeating ideas, negative feelings, and unassertive behavior as well as self-enhancing ideas and assertive actions. Similarly, the manual is chock-full of practice opportunities, including an entire chapter at the end of the book with exercises (i.e., keeping weekly assertiveness logs; muscle relaxation; etc.

While this manual may seem to oversimplify, at times, the task at hand (something the authors acknowledge), its strength is its clarity, brevity, and the ease with which it can be read and put into practice. It can certainly be a useful adjunct for therapists working with patients who are experiencing work-related assertiveness problems.

Steven Korner, PhD
Associate Professor
Doctoral Program in Child-Clinical Psychology and Coordinator,
School Psychology Program
Department of Counseling Psychology
Seton Hall University
South Orange, New Jersey

ONE COUPLE: FOUR REALITIES . . . MULTIPLE PERSPECTIVES ON COUPLE THERAPY. Richard Chasin, Henry Grunebaum, and Margaret Herzig. *New York: Guilford Press, 1990, 420 pp., $35.00.*

"Larry and Jennifer" were videotaped having therapy sessions with Peggy Papp, James Framo, Norman and Betty Paul, and Carlos Sluzki, at Cambridge Hospital in 1983 as part of the Harvard Couple Therapy Conference. The videotaped sessions had subsequent professional showings in San Francisco, Boston, and New York. As the couple became "older and more visible in their professions . . . the couple was unlikely to allow further showings of the tapes . . . and the videotapes were retired in favor of this book." In an age when "progress" is associated with clearer, more immediate visual experiences, the broad and thoughtful integration of theory and transcript woven throughout this book creates a new paradigm for "progress" in therapeutic pedagogy.

The four therapists give prototypical demonstrations of their therapy style. Peggy Papp presents one of her classic structured fantasies exercises. Framo works with the wife and her family of origin. Paul's transgenerational approach is filled with creative uses of the videotape. Of particular interest were the use of audio and visual "enabling tapes." Each stimulus tape presents a vivid sample of a universal human experience (e.g., rejection by a spouse or parent; terror at the prospect of a family encounter, etc.) and is listened to by the couple to "sanction and evoke suppressed emotional experiences." The use of enabling tapes appears to be a potent tool for breaking through resistance as well as modeling the level of discourse that facilitates brief therapy work. Sluzki artfully demonstrates the power of well known systemic techniques such as joining strategies, reframing strategies, and mind reading dissections. The four presentations are instructive and interesting but clearly geared to professionals who are already familiar with their techniques.

To my surprise, I enjoyed the second half of the book, where a variety of couple perspectives are presented and discussed in relation to "Larry" and "Jennifer," as much, if not more, than the first half. There are chapters on object relation approaches, "fairness" in therapy with couples, treating communication problems from a behavioral perspective, the experience of women in marriage, the power of therapist fantasies to aid or interfere with couples' work, and a well needed chapter on eclecticism. Grunebaum wrote a wonderful chapter on the nature of marital bonds and why people stay married. His final evaluation provides an uplifting metaphor for use with clients: "I also believe that there is a basic human tendency that manifests itself in our admiration of synthesis. In art and literature, this is reflected in our esteem for great artists like Rembrandt and Shakespeare, for instance, and the same holds true for our evaluation of relationships. We may envy a passionate love affair, but we admire two people who have integrated many facets of their life together over time (333-334)." In an age where "adjustment" is again more valued than "change," this chapter helps provide a meta frame for many of the other points made in the book.

The couple have follow up reports at six months and six years, and there is an invaluable appendix on the clinical and ethical issues involved with demonstration interviews and teaching tapes. Overall, this is a book that could serve as a guide for how to create powerful training conferences, a stimulus book for peer supervisory groups, or a "how-to" manual on conceptualizing and treating couples in crisis. I found myself picking it up after I had already read it, a reliable indicator that I've found a real gem!

Linda Berg-Cross, PhD
Howard University
Washington, DC

BIOCHEMICAL

SAUNDERS GOLDEN SUNBURST SERIES

CONCEPTS

ROBERT W. McGILVERY, Ph.D.
Professor of Biochemistry
University of Virginia
School of Medicine

W. B. SAUNDERS COMPANY
Philadelphia London Toronto

W. B. Saunders Company: West Washington Square
Philadelphia, Pa. 19105

1 St. Anne's Road
Eastbourne, East Sussex BN21 3UN, England

833 Oxford Street
Toronto, M8Z 5T9, Canada

Library of Congress Cataloging in Publication Data

McGilvery, Robert W

Biochemical concepts.

(Saunders golden series)
Includes index.

1. Biological chemistry. I. Title

QH345.M23 574.1'92 74-6690

ISBN 0-7216-5914-4

Biochemical Concepts ISBN 0-7216-5914-4

Last digit is the print number: 9 8 7 6 5 4 3 2

PREFACE

A Note to the Student

My hope is that this book will provide you a readable, but still rather complete, survey of the way in which the functions of all kinds of living organisms depend upon the properties and reactions of chemical compounds. You will do better if you have had some rudimentary encounters with organic compounds and with the nature of living cells, but almost any introductory courses, even at the high-school level, will suffice. No other scientific background is necessary, and I think you will be rather pleased to see how an understanding of apparently complex behavior is well within your grasp.

However, I don't think you will be bored if you are one of those with extensive background and high talent. Most of the book covers fundamental information that is necessary for any comprehension of biochemistry, but some parts are designed for efficient use of available time by students of different interest or backgrounds. The objective is to make the book useful to many students and many instructors without becoming condescending or trivial.

A word on organization. Each chapter begins with a summary of the major points made in the chapter. I suggest that you read it before tackling the main text, but without worrying about anything that is not immediately clear, and that you return to it after finishing the chapter so as to check the completeness of your understanding.

The chapters close with questions, which do not cover all of the factual details, but which are used to emphasize some points, and to show you how to utilize the facts in reasoning about new situations. Here again, I think you will be pleased to see what you can do.

Acknowledgments

Everyone knows that the success of any male textbook author hinges upon the presence of a wife or daughter. I fortunately had both, and would have been totally disorganized without the tactful assistance of Alice and Elizabeth McGilvery.

Those of my associates at the University of Virginia who have been both willing and able to answer quick inquiries are too many to list, but I must give special recognition to Dr. Gerald Goldstein for pointing out in detail why the second draft of Chapter 5 wouldn't do. (He didn't see the final version, and therefore bears no blame for its shortcomings.) Colleagues from other institutions who willingly gave information or the use of material include: Drs. Helmut Beinert, Ernest J. Briskey, Robert K. Crane, Herbert C. Dessauer, Richard E. Dickerson, Lewis C. Mokrasch, Dominick J. Paolillo, Jr., and Lester J. Reed.

Drs. Eddie C. Smith and Roberts A. Smith provided extensive discussions of the teaching of biochemistry in chemistry departments that were most helpful.

At the W. B. Saunders Company, I am very grateful for the light and deft editorial touch of Joseph J. Freedman. William F. Brothers, Jr. translated my sketches into finished drawings, and the chemical formulas and diagrams were set by Graphic Services, Inc. Their work speaks for itself.

Addenda

The following miscellaneous points were inadvertently omitted during revision of the text:

The Svedberg unit (S). The relative masses of macromolecules of similar composition are frequently compared by spinning solutions of them in a centrifuge, and measuring the velocity at which they move through the solution. The velocity per unit of applied centrifugal force is the sedimentation constant for the molecules, customarily expressed in Svedberg units, where one Svedberg unit equals 10^{-13} second.

This is a pragmatic comparison of relative size, because the force acting on a molecule depends not only upon the centrifugal field, but also upon the apparent "density" of the molecules (the mass per effective volume) compared to the density of the solvent. Furthermore, the velocity at which friction against the solvent just counterbalances the applied force depends upon the shape of the molecule; those that are round move faster than long, thin molecules of equal volume and mass because they have less surface area.

Even so, the Svedberg unit is valuable for comparing molecules, or even complex particles, when accurate molecular weights are not known. It is important to have in mind that S values, unlike molecular weights, are not additive. The union of two 5S particles does not create a 10S particle. (Two cannonballs glued together do not sink twice as fast as one alone.)

As a rough guide, the corresponding sedimentation constants and masses, in daltons, of spherical protein molecules are as follows: 2S—10,000; 4S—50,000; 8S—160,000, and 16S—400,000.

Histones. Histones are relatively small basic proteins (rich in arginine and lysine residues) that are associated with DNA in chromosomes. They are believed to be involved in the regulation of the cell cycle, but their specific function is unknown.

Coding and the nature of amino acids. The genetic code has evolved so as to minimize the consequences of mutations. Substitution of one base for another in a coding triplet frequently creates a codon for either the same amino acid, or another with a similar side chain. This may be seen by comparing codons in the same rows and columns of the top part of the codon dictionary on p. 36.

For example, altering the first base in the codon A-U-C for isoleucine will result in the appearance of leucine (C-U-C), valine (G-U-C), or phenylalanine (U-U-C) in the corresponding position of a peptide chain. Altering the third base, will continue to result in the appearance of isoleucine (A-U-A or A-U-U) or of methionine (A-U-G) in the corresponding position.

Show for yourself how this applies by comparing structure and codons for aspartate and asparagine, glutamate and glutamine, lysine and arginine, tyrosine and phenylalanine, glycine and alanine, and serine and threonine.

R. W. McGilvery

CONTENTS

THE PROTEINS

PART 1

PROTEIN STRUCTURE

CHAPTER 1

THE NATURE OF PROTEINS

THE CONCEPTS

Composition. Proteins are the molecules whose chemical properties create most biological functions. They are polymers of amino acids. Each of the amino acids from which they are made contains an ammonium group and a carboxylate group, which serve as connectors for linking the molecules into long chains. Amide bonds are formed between the ammonium nitrogen of one amino acid and the carboxylate group of the next. Such linear polymers are called peptide chains, and proteins are sometimes made from one, sometimes from more, peptide chains. The differences in proteins come from differences in amino acid composition of their peptide chains. Proteins are made from 20 amino acids containing different substituent groups, or side chains, that are not involved in the polymerization of the peptide chains. A peptide chain therefore has an arrangement of chemical groups along its length that depends upon the kinds of amino acids from which it was made, and the order in which they were put together. Changing this sequence, or primary structure, of the peptide creates new arrangements of chemical groups and changes the properties of the peptide. Some arrangements have the special reactivities we call biological function.

Folding of Peptide Chains. Part of the specific arrangement of chemical groups in a protein comes from the way in which the peptide chains are folded upon themselves. The regular repetition of structure in the peptide backbone by itself tends to cause a regular displacement in space of successive amino acids; such regular displacements create spirals sometimes called secondary structures. Among the spirals found in proteins are an arrangement known as the α-helix, and special cases known as pleated sheets, constructed as if adjacent spirals had been stretched out into parallel zigzag arrays. Both of these structures involve the regular formation of hydrogen bonds between amide groups in the peptide backbone. However, the formation of regular spirals is often prevented by the presence of particular amino acids with side chains that do not fit easily into the spiral geometry, or that develop additional bonding forces favoring some more irregular, although definite, structure.

Side Chains and Bonding. The spatial arrangement of peptide chains in proteins sometimes appears random, but it isn't. A particular peptide chain will nearly always fold in a particular way that results in the greatest summation of bonding forces, not only within the molecule itself, but also involving the surrounding water. Where do these forces originate?

Some amino acids have hydrocarbon, or other non-polar, side chains, which create forces of particular importance because they cannot interact strongly with water. Such side chains tend to aggregate; it requires work to disperse them because water loses some freedom for random motion near hydrophobic groups and assumes a more ordered, ice-like structure of greater energy content.

Other amino acids have side chains containing N or O atoms, and folding the peptide backbone so as to bring these atoms into positions where they can form hydrogen bonds sometimes results in a more stable structure. Similarly, some of these side chains have negatively charged carboxylate groups, and others have positively charged ammonium groups. These charges sometimes help stabilize arrangements that bring opposite charges near each other and that separate like charges.

The result of these various effects frequently is a protein molecule in which the peptide chains are folded in such a way as to pack the interior of the molecule with amino acid residues bearing non-polar side chains, and to have all of the charged side chains on the surface in contact with water.

Bends in the Peptide Chain. The creation of particular shapes is also promoted by the occurrence of sharp bends in the peptide chains. Some of the bends are due to the presence of the amino acid, proline, in which the amino nitrogen is part of a ring that tends to force a change of direction. Other bends result from the presence of glycine, which has no side chain and therefore permits the peptide backbone to be folded back upon itself very tightly. However, many bends result only because their presence is necessary for the largest possible summation of forces between different parts of the peptide chain, thereby creating a molecule of lowest energy content.

The first part of our study of the chemistry of living organisms will be mainly concerned with an exploration of the proteins, including their nature, their formation, and the kinds of functions they carry out. We begin in this way because the proteins are the chemical compounds truly characteristic of life. They determine our metabolism, form our tissues, give us motion, carry compounds from one part of the organism to another, and protect us from deleterious invasion. Even the heredity of an organism is nothing more than an expression of its ability to make various kinds of proteins at different rates.

Proteins are made by polymerizing amino acids, so let us start our story by examining the essential nature of these building blocks.

THE NATURE OF AMINO ACIDS

The amino acids found in proteins are all α-amino acids, with ammonium groups and carboxylate groups attached to the same carbon atom; here is the simplest, **glycine,** in which the remaining substituents on that carbon atom are hydrogen atoms:

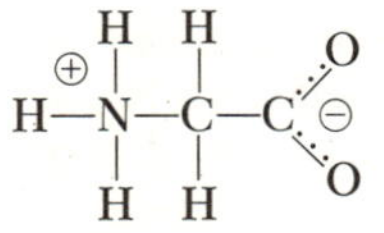

or $^{\oplus}H_3N—CH_2—COO^{\ominus}$

glycine

The molecule is shown in two ways, the first indicating the position of every bond, and the second utilizing a common kind of shorthand notation in which substituent hydrogen atoms are lumped together without indicating the bonds, and the individual C=O bonds also are not drawn.

Why is this molecule called an amino acid? Well, the original investigators thought that the structure looked like this:

$$H_2N—CH_2—COOH$$

with an authentic amino group and carboxyl group, which made it both an amine and a carboxylic acid. We have known better for many decades, but it is very difficult to change established usage, even when the usage is clearly wrong; the compound is still written this way by many.

Amino Acids as Acids and Bases. Both the ammonium and the carboxylate groups of an amino acid equilibrate with protons in water in the same qualitative way as do similar groups occurring separately in other compounds:

$$R—NH_2 + H^{\oplus} \longrightarrow R—NH_3^{\oplus}$$

$$R—COOH \longrightarrow R—COO^{\ominus} + H^{\oplus}$$

The position of equilibrium for each of these two reactions will depend upon the concentration of H^+, which is near that of pure water, 10^{-7} M, in most living cells. It so happens that the equilibrium position for both reactions lies far to the right under those circumstances. It is therefore quite true that amino acids are amphoteric compounds, that is, they are capable of acting both as acids and as bases; but it is the charged ammonium group that is the acid capable of donating protons, and it is the charged carboxylate group that is the base capable of accepting protons:

$$H_2N—CH_2—COO^{\ominus} \xleftarrow{-H^{\oplus}} {}^{\oplus}H_3N—CH_2—COO^{\ominus} \xrightarrow{+H^{\oplus}} {}^{\oplus}H_3N—CH_2—COOH$$

(A more extensive discussion of the acid-base behavior of amino acids is given in the Appendix, p. 479.)

Amino Acids as Stereoisomers. The next most simple amino acid, **alanine,** has one more carbon atom than does glycine:

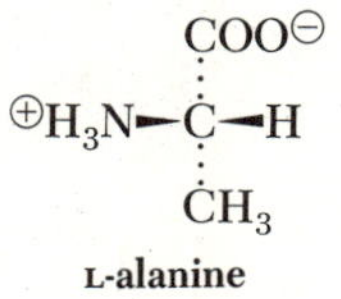

L-alanine

Notice that the figure specifies an arrangement of groups about the α-carbon atom by broad arrows going from the groups closest to us and by dotted lines coming from the more distant groups.

We recall from organic chemistry that four different substituents can be placed on one carbon atom in two arrangements that are mirror images, or enantiomers, of each other. The two forms are also known as optical isomers because they cause the plane of polarization of light to rotate in opposite directions upon passing through the compounds. The isomer that is shown in the figure as designated as L-alanine; its mirror image is D-alanine.

It so happened that evolution proceeded in a way involving the incorporation of L-alanine, but not of D-alanine, into proteins. It is not clear what determined this particular choice. Meteorites contain equal amounts of the two isomers, which seems to indicate there is no cosmological preference for the formation of one isomer over the other, and it may only be chance that primitive organisms began the selective use of the L-compound.

In any event, not only alanine but all of the amino acids (except glycine) that are incorporated into proteins are of the L-family, in which the arrangement of groups around the α-carbon atom is the same as the arrangement in L-alanine. Glycine is an exception because it has no asymmetric carbon atom, and therefore exists only in a single form.

As a matter of convenience, we shall want to draw optical isomers with ordinary symbols, and shall use the standard convention for this purpose in which vertical bonds are imagined as being behind the plane of the paper, and horizontal bonds in front. Here are some ways of presenting L-alanine according to this convention:

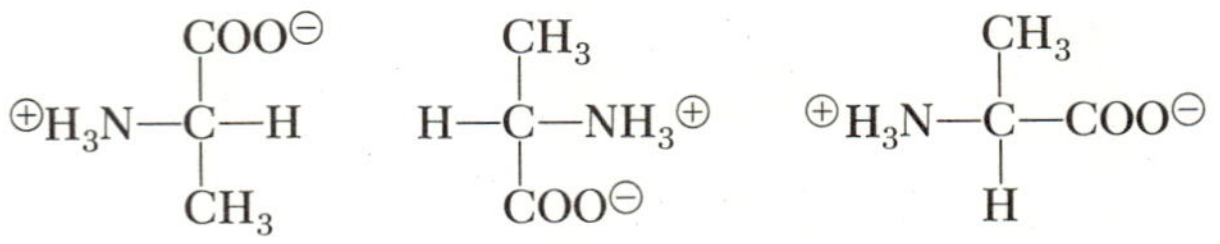

Stereoisomerism is also considered in the Appendix (p. 483).

PROTEINS AS POLYPEPTIDES: POLYMERS OF AMINO ACIDS

The ammonium and carboxylate groups found in each amino acid are the connectors used to link the amino acids together into linear polymers known as peptide chains. The ammonium group of one amino acid combines with the carboxylate group of another to create an amide bond between the two amino acid residues. Figure 1–1

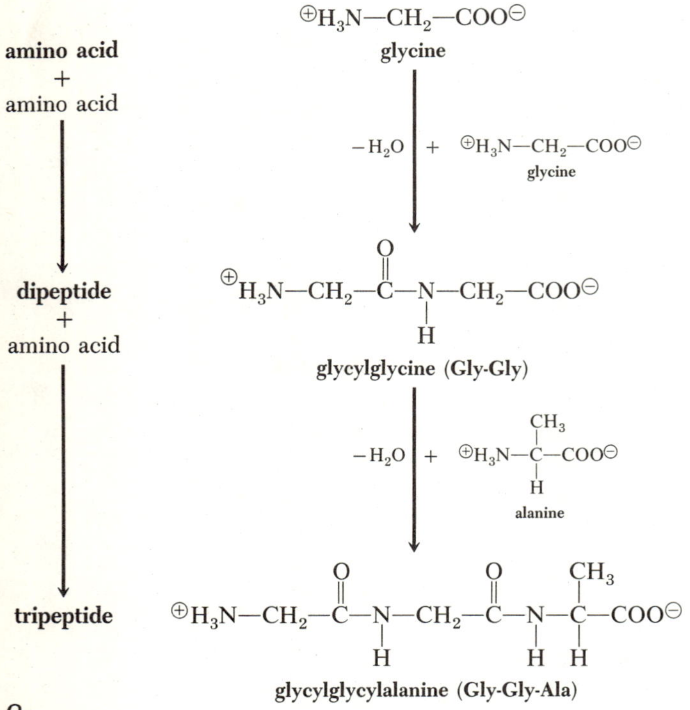

Figure 1–1 Peptides are amides formed between the carboxylate group of one amino acid and the ammonium group of another. The resultant peptides are named from the ammonium end (the N-terminal) in terms of the constituent amino acid residues.

shows the formal combination of two molecules of glycine to create the dipeptide, glycylglycine, and the further formal addition of a molecule of alanine to create the tripeptide, glycylglycylalanine. (We shall see in the next chapter how such combinations are actually made by organisms.)

The addition of amino acids can be continued, with the formation of a tetrapeptide, then a pentapeptide, and so on, until finally a large polypeptide is created, because at each stage the growing chain still has an ammonium group on one end (the N-terminal), and a carboxylate group on the other (the C-terminal). The polypeptide that is made has a backbone of repeating amide groups, to which are attached the side chains characteristic of the constituent amino acids, such as the methyl group that is the side chain of alanine.

If the polypeptide created in this way is large enough, we call it a protein. In short, proteins are made from one or more long chains of amino acids linked by amide bonds, commonly called peptide bonds. We speak of amino acid residues in proteins, meaning the groups formed from amino acids by the formal loss of water during peptide bond formation.

Primary Structure of Peptides. Proteins are made by polymerizing 20 different amino acids into peptide chains. (The amino acids are listed in the Appendix, p. 480, and we shall also encounter them earlier in our discussion.) Each of these amino acids has an ammonium group and a carboxylate group, which are used in the formation of amide bonds, but each, with the exception of glycine, also has some additional organic substituent on the α-carbon that is not involved in amide bond formation. The nature of a peptide depends upon its amino acid composition—the number of each kind of amino acid molecule used to form the peptide and the order in which they are put together. It is the arrangement of substituent chemical groups represented by this primary structure of the peptide chain that creates the specific chemical reactivities of biological function. We shall see that a general understanding of these arrangements and the way in which they are created is well within our grasp.

Number of Different Peptides. Although there are only 20 different kinds of amino acids from which proteins are made, there is no danger of exhausting the possible primary structures for the creation of new proteins. A protein made by combining only 100 amino acid molecules is quite small as proteins go, and yet 20 different amino acids can be combined 100 at a time in 20^{100} different ways. This number is so large that every single protein molecule conceivable in our universe, existing now or at any time in the past, could be unique without using any more than an infinitesimal portion of the possibilities.

In fact, every protein molecule is not unique. A single organism makes many identical molecules of most kinds of proteins within it, and other individual organisms of the same species also make many of these kinds of molecules. In other words, one human contains many protein molecules identical to molecules found in another human; indeed, their common humanity is a result of this fact. Similarly, one red oak tree contains proteins identical to those in another red oak tree. However, it is entirely likely that humans and red oak trees have no kinds of protein molecules in common; their functions are too different to be served in exactly the same way. Proteins are made to satisfy these diverse needs by varying the way in which the 20 kinds of amino acids are put together, and the specification of these variations is a major part of the heredity of the organism.

Proteins as Macromolecules

Proteins are large molecules, macromolecules, and their size is a biologically important attribute, because it prevents them from leaking out of cells through the plasma membrane. Proteins with molecular weights in the range of 100,000 to 300,000 are common, and only a few have molecular weights as low as 10,000. Each amino acid residue added to a growing peptide chain contributes between 57 and 186 daltons* to its mass. A protein molecule with a mass near 100,000 daltons, which is not at all large, requires approximately 900 amino acid molecules for its formation.

THE SPATIAL ARRANGEMENT OF PEPTIDE CHAINS

The character of a protein hinges upon the arrangement in space of its constituent chemical groups. How does this arrangement occur? One factor is the nature of the peptide backbone; there are favored orientations for a bare peptide skeleton. The other factor is the primary structure; varying sequences of amino acids create varying forces because of the different side chains. The remainder of this chapter is concerned with understanding these factors.

The Peptide Bond

Let us examine the amide linkage, the peptide bond, that always occurs between amino acid residues in a polypeptide. The critical fact is that it has some double bond character. We draw it as:

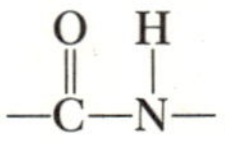

when it would be more realistic to draw it as:

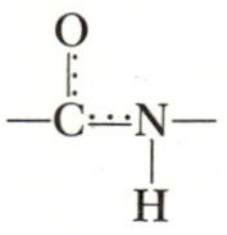

The important consequence of this double bond character is that it freezes the entire amide group in a single plane. Slight deviations can occur, but for our purposes the planar configuration may be regarded as nearly fixed. The only possibilities for free rotation in the peptide backbone occur at the two bonds on the α-carbon atoms.

In other words, the arrangement in space of the backbone of a peptide chain is nearly completely defined by two angles of rotation on each α-carbon atom (Fig. 1–2), which are named **Ramachadran angles** after the man who made a systematic study of the consequences of changing their values. These angles provide a handy way of defining the spatial orientation of amino acid residues in a peptide backbone. The actual numbers need not concern us, but we ought to note that they are not randomly scattered among all possible values. Some angles do not occur because steric hindrance prevents the particular orientation; adjacent carbonyl oxygen atoms collide before the angle can be reached. In addition, there are some orientations that occur much more frequently than others equally free of steric hindrance, and we shall see that the favored configurations permit the formation of additional forces between parts of the peptide chain.

---

*The dalton is the weight of a molecule expressed in atomic mass units based on ^{12}C. That is, one atom of this isotope has a mass of 12 daltons.

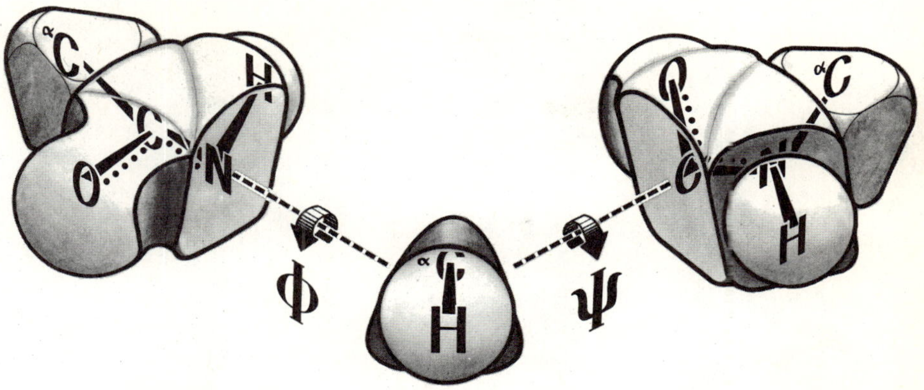

Figure 1-2 Free rotation of a peptide chain occurs only around the bonds joining the nearly planar amide groups to the α-carbons. The angles of rotation, known as Ramachadran angles, therefore determine the spatial orientation of the peptide chain. Each angle is 180° as illustrated.

Secondary Structures: Helix and Sheet

A long repeating polymer of any kind will tend to form a coil. Why is this so? Because any repetitious displacement in space travels a spiral path. Imagine a polypeptide made of one kind of amino acid. Each residue in the middle of the chain is exposed to much the same environment as its neighbors. Therefore, they will tend to form the same Ramachadran angles relative to each other; the peptide backbone will be regularly bent in the same way. It so happens that particular spiral arrangements are quite common parts of protein molecules.

The particular spiral formed will depend upon the forces determining the Ramachadran angles. When we explore secondary and other structures in protein molecules, we are also of necessity examining the forces that favor particular orientations of the molecules. What forces are available to fix the conformation of a peptide chain? Among the most important are the small forces of the sort that prevent gases from obeying simple laws—the forces that formerly were lumped together as van der Waal's forces. Such forces can frequently be neglected in describing the behavior of isolated small molecules containing few atoms, but they are important factors in determining the configuration of large molecules, in which the sum of small forces affecting each atom becomes a large total force confined within a single molecule. Let us explore some of these forces, and the shapes they tend to create.

Hydrogen Bonds. Atoms of hydrogen bound to oxygen or nitrogen atoms form additional weak bonds with other atoms of oxygen or nitrogen. Now, the peptide backbone contains —NH— and —C═O groups, which tend to form hydrogen bonds:

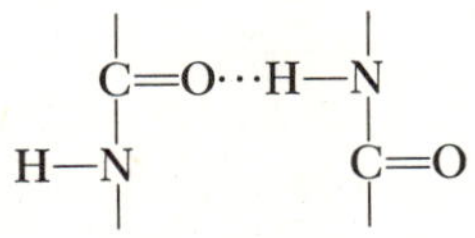

Since nearly every amino acid residue contains these groups, the peptide chain will tend to form some shape such that every carbonyl oxygen and every amide nitrogen in the peptide backbone is linked by hydrogen bonds. It turns out that there are two important ways in which this can be done with many kinds of peptide chains.

α-Helix. One of the ways to create all possible hydrogen bonds with a peptide backbone is to twist it into a right-handed screw, known as the α-helix, so that the —NH group of an amino acid is hydrogen-bonded to the C═O group of the fourth

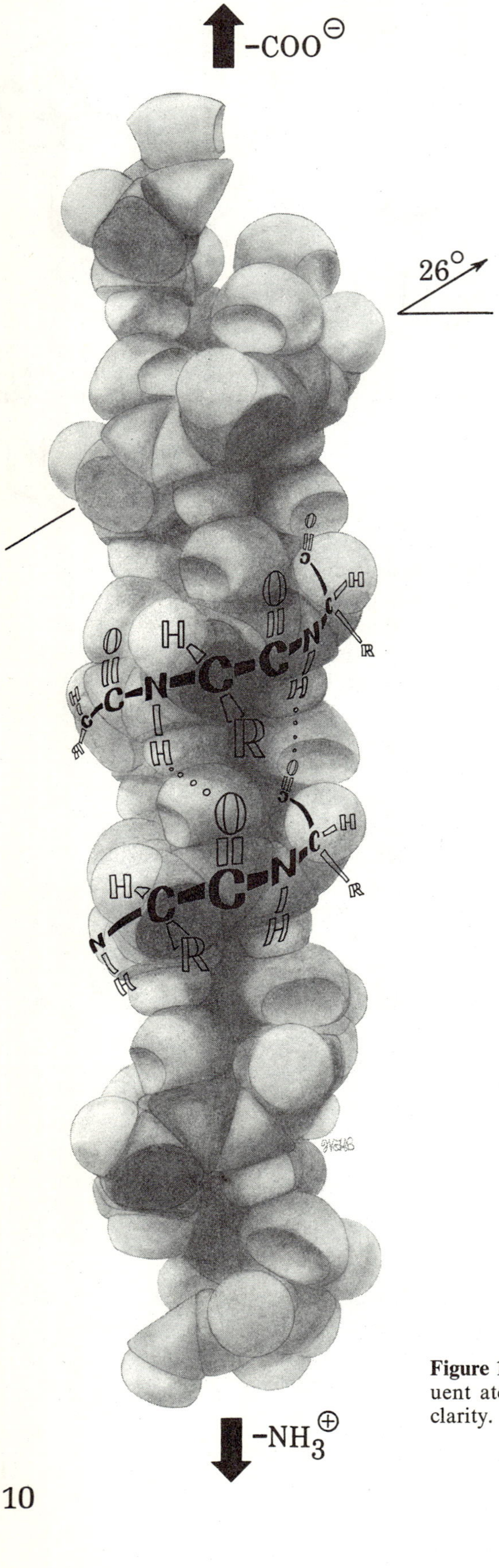

Figure 1-3 A model of an α-helix, showing the positions of the constituent atoms. The side chains of the amino acids have been omitted for clarity.

following residue (Fig. 1–3), which is now on an adjacent turn of the helix. As the figure shows, the α-helix is a structure in which the peptide backbone forms a cylinder coated with amino acid side chains extending outwards from the axis. It is apparent that this structure is especially suitable for creating long fiber-like molecules, but segments of the α-helix are also used as part of the structure of nearly spherical molecules.

β-STRUCTURE. Another way to form all possible hydrogen bonds with the peptide backbone is to stretch out the peptide chain to maximum extension and then to fold segments back on themselves so that hydrogen bonds form between adjacent chains. This makes the anti-parallel pleated sheet, also known as the β-structure. (A somewhat similar structure can be made from adjacent chains that run in the same direction; this is the parallel pleated sheet, or β_P-structure.) A striking characteristic of the β-structure is the appearance of alternate side chains on opposite sides of the sheet (Fig. 1–4). Silk is made from stacks of pleated sheets, but fragments of this structure are also part of many nearly spherical protein molecules.

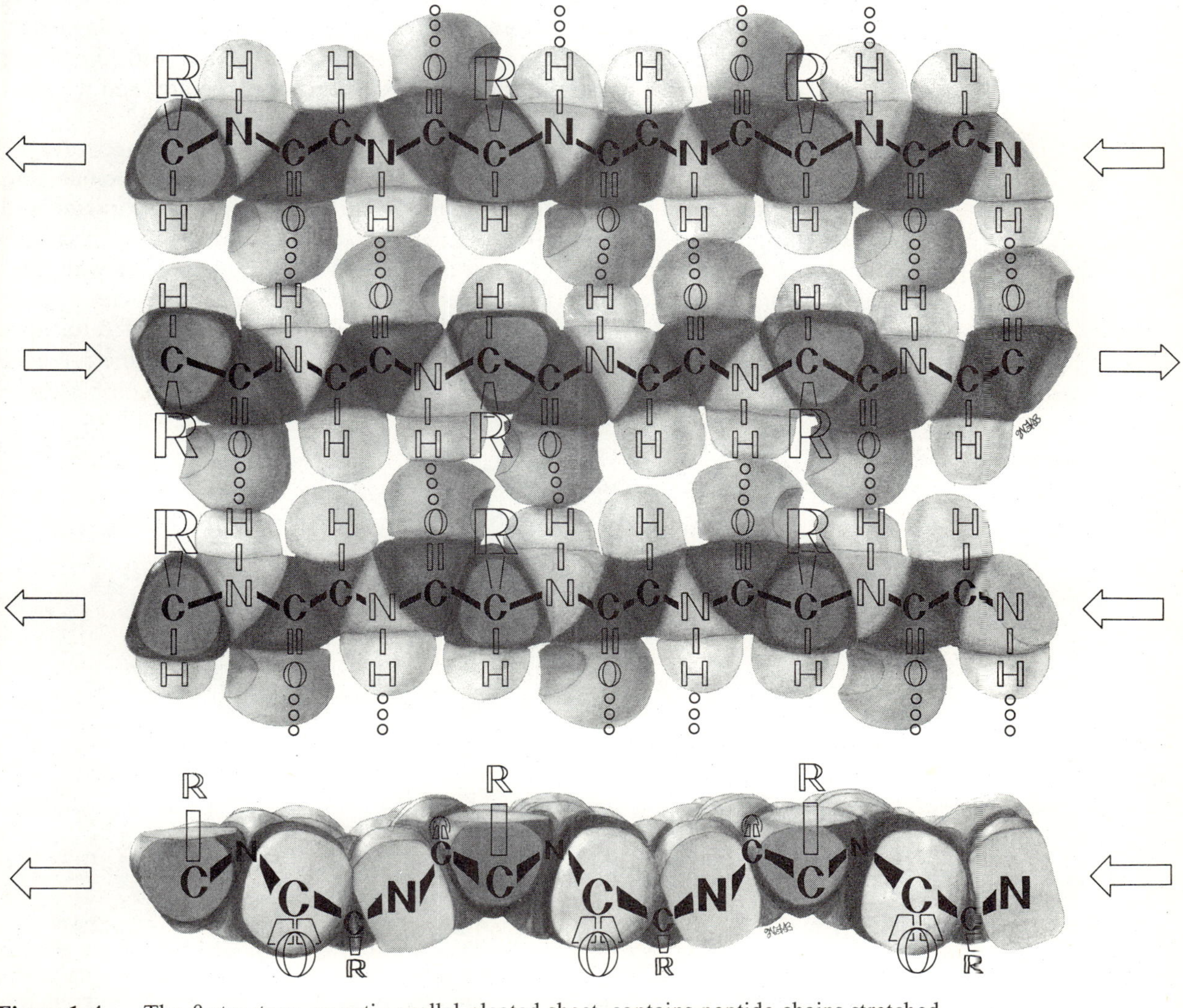

Figure 1–4 The β-structure, or anti-parallel pleated sheet, contains peptide chains stretched to nearly maximum extension and bonded side-by-side. However, adjacent chains run in opposite directions. The result is alternating rows of side chains on each side of a sheet of peptides, viewed face-on (*top*) and edge-on (*bottom*).

Dispersion Forces. These forces, also known as London forces, make molecules tend to nestle together. They arise from electronic vibrations that stabilize complementary areas of charge in neighboring molecules or parts of the same molecule, thereby creating a weak attraction of unlike charges. These forces tend to eliminate holes between atoms, and favor structures in which atoms either are tightly packed, or are open enough to admit solvent molecules that will completely fill the gaps. According to one estimate, this kind of bonding is greatest in proteins when a α-helix is formed. However, the unfortunate truth is that, while we know dispersion forces exist, their magnitude in protein molecules is unknown.

Forces Affecting Side Chains

So far, we have mainly considered bonding forces affecting the peptide backbone, and tending to create regularly repeating structures, such as the α-helix and the pleated sheets. Yet we know that forces affecting only the peptide backbone cannot be determining factors in fixing biological function, because it is the nature of the sequence of amino acids, the difference in the order of occurrence of the various side chains, that makes one protein different from another. It therefore follows that forces involving the side chains must be the important factors in fixing protein structure, and we must examine specific amino acids to see how they act. What are these forces?

Hydrogen Bonds. Some side chains have groups capable of forming hydrogen bonds, such as the hydroxyl groups found in the side chains of **serine, threonine,** and **tyrosine** (Fig. 1–5), and the amide groups found in the side chains of **asparagine** and **glutamine.** The presence of residues of these amino acids in a peptide chain creates a possibility, although not a necessity, for the formation of hydrogen bonds with their side chains. An excellent example occurs in molecules of hemoglobin. The peptide chains of hemoglobin are coiled into segments of α-helix, which are nestled together into a compact shape. One of the forces creating that shape results from the presence of a tyrosyl residue in a segment of helix near the C-terminal of the chains, because

Hydroxyl-substituted amino acids:

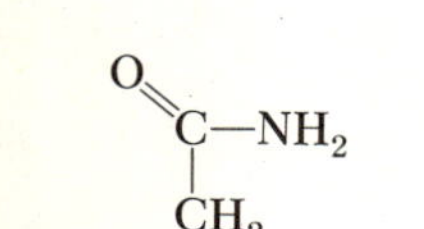
L-serine

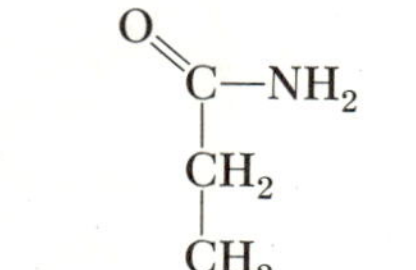
L-threonine

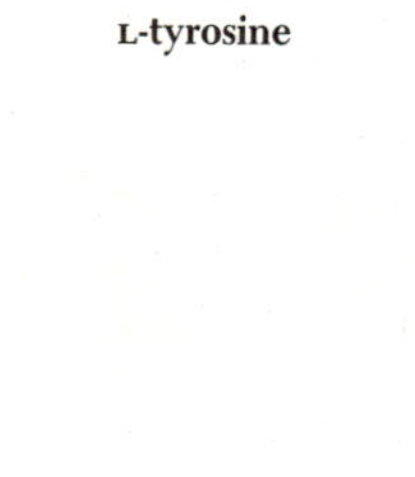
L-tyrosine

Amide-substituted amino acids:

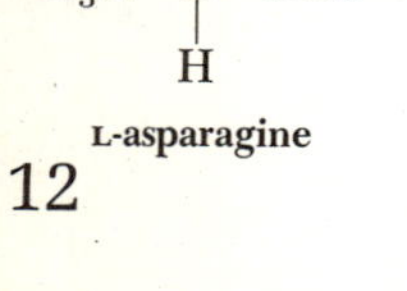
L-asparagine

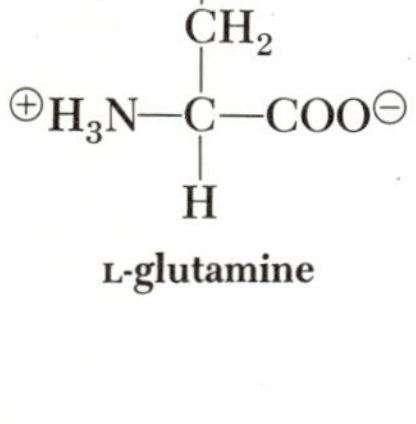
L-glutamine

Figure 1–5 The side chains of some amino acids contain hydroxyl groups; others contain amide groups. These groups often participate in the formation of hydrogen bonds between segments of peptide chains.

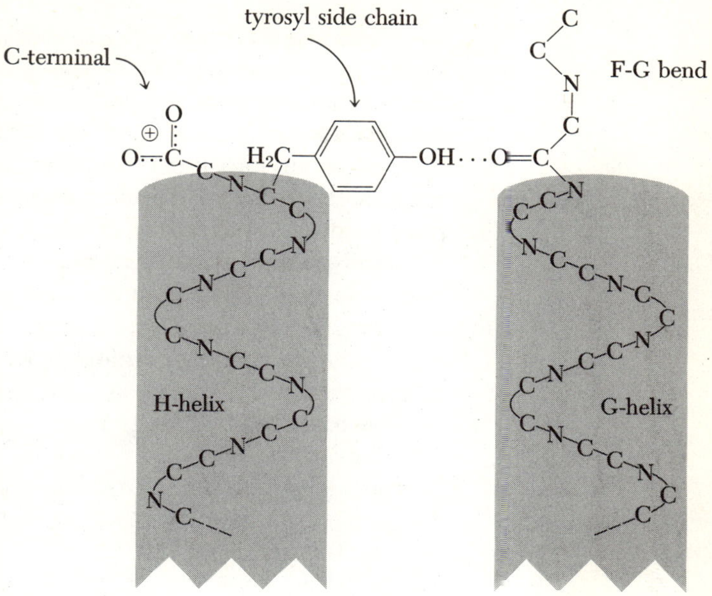

Figure 1-6 The peptide chains of hemoglobin are coiled into segments of α-helix, designated by capital letters. The transport of oxygen by hemoglobin depends upon the presence of a tyrosyl residue in the H-helix (near the C-terminal of the peptide) that forms a hydrogen bond with the adjacent G-helix.

it forms a hydrogen bond through its hydroxyl groups when brought in proximity with the peptide backbone of an adjoining segment of helix (Fig. 1–6), and the bond helps to keep the two segments together.

Hydrophobic Bonds. One of the major forces affecting the shape of proteins comes from the tendency of non-polar side chains, such as alkyl or aromatic groups, to cluster together in the interior of a molecule exposed to water. The force comes, not from the specific attraction of such chains for each other, but from the propensity of surrounding water to resist being forced into ordered structures by the presence of the non-polar groups. The so-called hydrophobic bond is really an association created by spurned water, and it is the same kind of force that causes insoluble oils to form compact spheres upon suspension in water. How does this happen?

Molecules of water have a strong tendency to form hydrogen bonds with each other, as is shown by the release of heat when water freezes into the fixed lattice of ice. There is an opposing tendency of all molecules to stay dispersed, to be random and unordered. This tendency, measured as entropy, is increased by a rise in temperature. The two effects just balance at the melting point. At higher temperatures, hydrogen bonds persist for shorter and shorter times; each molecule becomes more and more promiscuous.

A non-polar molecule introduced into liquid water represents a eunuch at an orgy. Since it cannot form hydrogen bonds or other bonds created by polarity, neighboring water molecules lose some of their possibilities for random union, and associate with each other longer than they would in the absence of the non-polar intruder. However, this longer association represents greater order, a step toward freezing into ice, and we have already said that creation of such order at temperatures above the melting point can be accomplished only by introduction of energy. It follows that dispersing non-polar molecules in water requires energy, and the non-polar molecules will aggregate when left to themselves so as to diminish their surface area, thereby diminishing the number of water molecules with hindered random associations.

Hydrophobic Bonds in Proteins. Nearly all proteins contain many amino acid residues with hydrophobic side chains, but they also contain others with polar groups, and the peptide backbone itself is a polar arrangement. Molecules like this, with mixed polar and non-polar regions, will tend to fold in such a way as to place the non-polar constituents on the inside, away from surrounding water, and have all of the polar regions on the surface where they can interact with water molecules and diminish any tendency toward ice formation. The separation is not complete in proteins; either some non-polar side chains can be exposed without significant development of hydrophobic forces, or it is not possible to fold the peptide chain in such a way as to eliminate them without opposing other, greater forces. However, the tendency for separation by degree of polarity is quite real, and there are only a few examples of proteins having charged groups buried in the interior. The tendency for separation by degree of polarity appears to be one of the most important forces causing a peptide chain of a given primary structure to fold in the specific way necessary to make a functional molecule.

Non-polar Amino Acid Side Chains. What are the amino acids bearing non-polar side chains? The prominent examples are shown in Figure 1–7 along with values for the relative hydrophobic character of their side chains. (These numbers are estimates of the additional energy, in joules per mole, required to move the side chain portion of each molecule from a non-polar solvent to water.) **Tryptophan, phenylalanine,** and **tyrosine** have aromatic rings that not only provide rather bulky non-polar groups, but are also capable of forming π-bonds. The rings tend to stack in parallel arrays with themselves or with other aromatic compounds. Tryptophan is the most non-polar of the amino acids, but it is also the least abundant, and it appears to be used mainly for special spacing of chains, and as a participant in some catalytic mechanisms. Phenylalanine and tyrosine are used as more general structural elements in proteins. (The hydroxyl group of tyrosine is usually hydrogen-bonded in the interior, thereby diminishing its polarity.)

Isoleucine, leucine and **valine** are non-polar amino acids with branched hydrocarbon side chains. They are common constituents of proteins, in which they provide different arrangements of hydrophobic volume with which to pack interior crannies. Finally, **methionine** has a side chain with a methyl thioether group. It is used to make particular structures, but it is also involved in catalytic mechanisms (p. 164).

Amino Acids with Polar Side Chains. The most hydrophilic, or water-loving, of the amino acid residues are those with net charges—those with ionic side chains. (They also can form hydrogen bonds.) **Aspartic acid** and **glutamic acid** have carboxyl groups in the side chain that ionize almost completely in neutral solution to form the corresponding negatively-charged aspartate and glutamate ions (Fig. 1–8).

Positive charges are carried by the side chains of **lysine** and of **arginine** in neutral

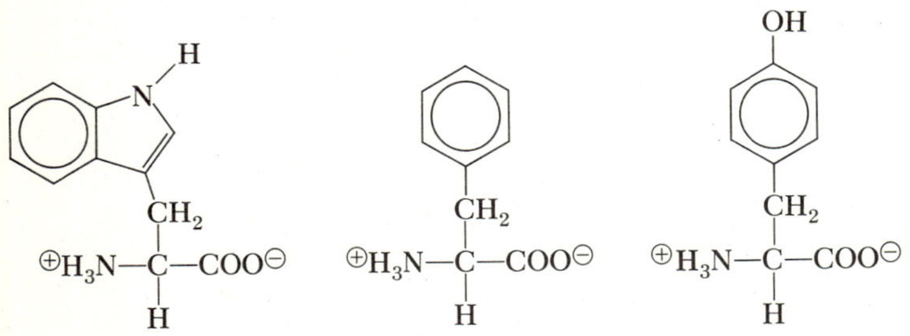

L-tryptophan 14,000 | **L-phenylalanine** 10,500 | **L-tyrosine** 9600

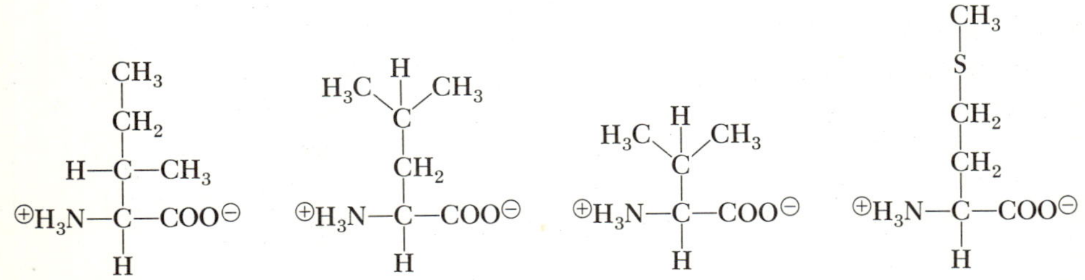

L-isoleucine ~10,000? | **L-leucine** 7500 | **L-valine** 6300 | **L-methionine** 5500

Figure 1–7 Amino acids with bulky, hydrophobic side chains. When tyrosyl residues are exposed to water, the phenolic hydroxyl group partially ionizes to make the residue polar, but the group forms hydrogen bonds or is otherwise prevented from ionizing when the residue is buried.

Figure 1-8 Amino acids with charged side chains. These residues are strongly hydrophilic, and are almost invariably exposed at the surface of proteins.

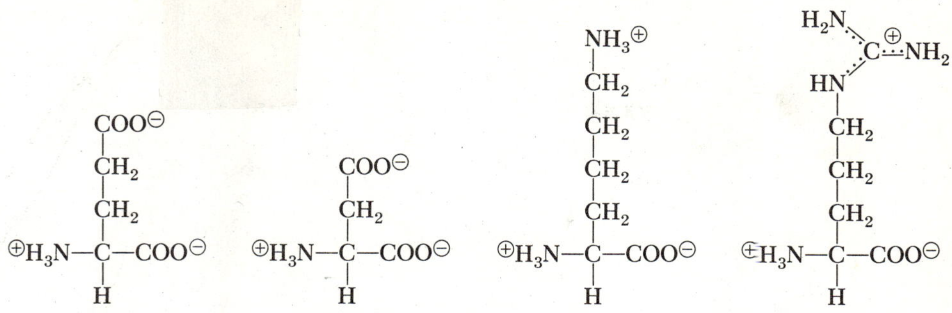

L-glutamate L-aspartate L-lysine L-arginine

solution, also shown in Figure 1-8. The concentration of H^+ must drop below 10^{-10} M before half of the side chain ammonium groups of lysine residues will lose H^+, and the guanidinium group of arginine will lose H^+ only in strongly alkaline solutions, because guanidine and substituted guanidino compounds are very strong bases, and will take up H^+ nearly as readily as does OH^- itself.

Some amino acid residues have side chains with more feeble polarity, favoring association with water, but not such strong associations as to preclude burial in the interior. We have already seen glutamine and asparagine; their amide groups have no net charge, but are polar enough to resist burial. The hydroxymethyl group of serine conveys a polar character favoring exposure at the surface, but this effect is frequently counteracted by the formation of interior hydrogen bonds. Threonine has an additional methylene group to convey hydrocarbon character, and its side chain is therefore feebly hydrophobic.

Determination of Tertiary Structure

We have at this point gone over most of the forces acting on peptides; some involve the peptide backbone, some the side chains, and some both. All of our knowledge at this point supports the notion that peptides assume the shape that creates the maximum forces, or, put another way, that involves the greatest loss of energy in creating the shape. (There are some qualifications; it may be in some cases that the arrangement of the very lowest energy content forms so slowly that some other, more rapidly equilibrating conformation is the most stable practical form. The principle that the biologically functional molecule is the one that forms spontaneously is not violated by such circumstances.)

Let us look at a simple-minded example to show how the amino acid sequence might influence arrangement of the peptide chain. Suppose that we have a peptide chain with a repeating sequence of lysyl, glycyl, glutamyl, and leucyl groups:

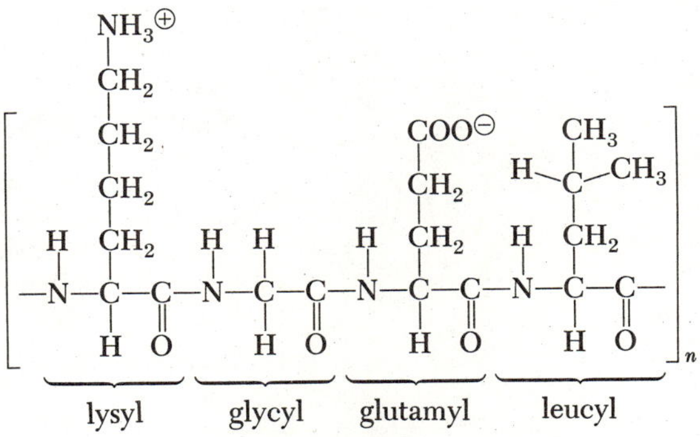

$[\text{Lys-Gly-Glu-Leu}]_n$

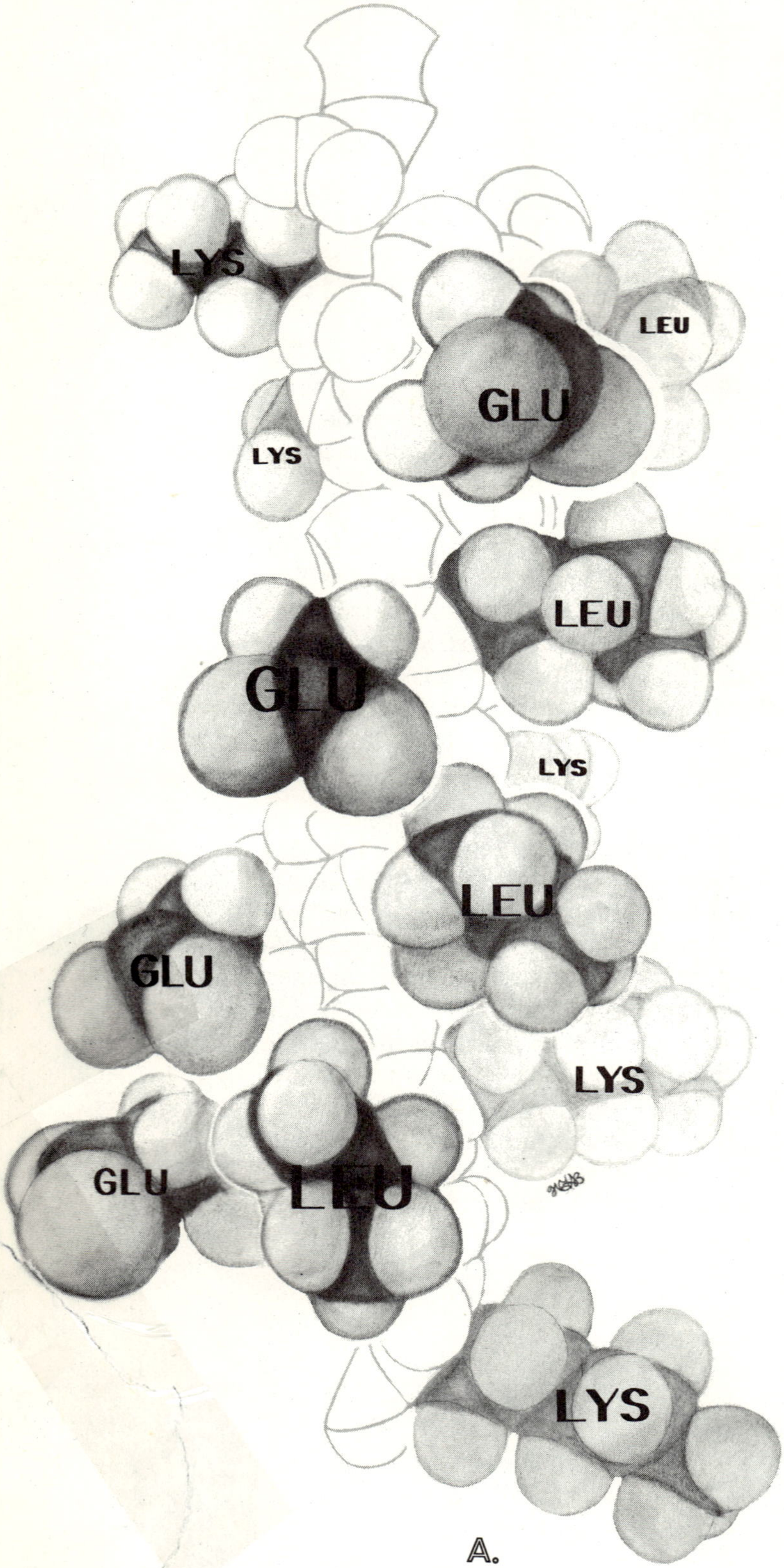

Figure 1-9 Demonstration of the effect of amino acid composition on secondary structures. Models of a peptide composed of repeating units of lysyl, glycyl, glutamyl, and leucyl groups, $(\text{Lys-Gly-Glu-Leu})_n$, are folded into α-helix and β-structures. *A*. The resultant helix is substituted with like residues in spiral bands. There is no predominantly hydrophobic face to cause association with other hydrophobic molecules, but the bands of groups bearing like charges make the configuration less probable. *B*. The pleated sheet made from the same peptide chain has quite different properties. The polar groups are on one side in a checkerboard lattice of positive and negative charges, while the uncharged groups are on the other side. This sheet will not exist in water by itself, but it may form back-to-back dimers or associate with other non-polar regions so as to bury the non-polar face.

Illustration continued on opposite page.

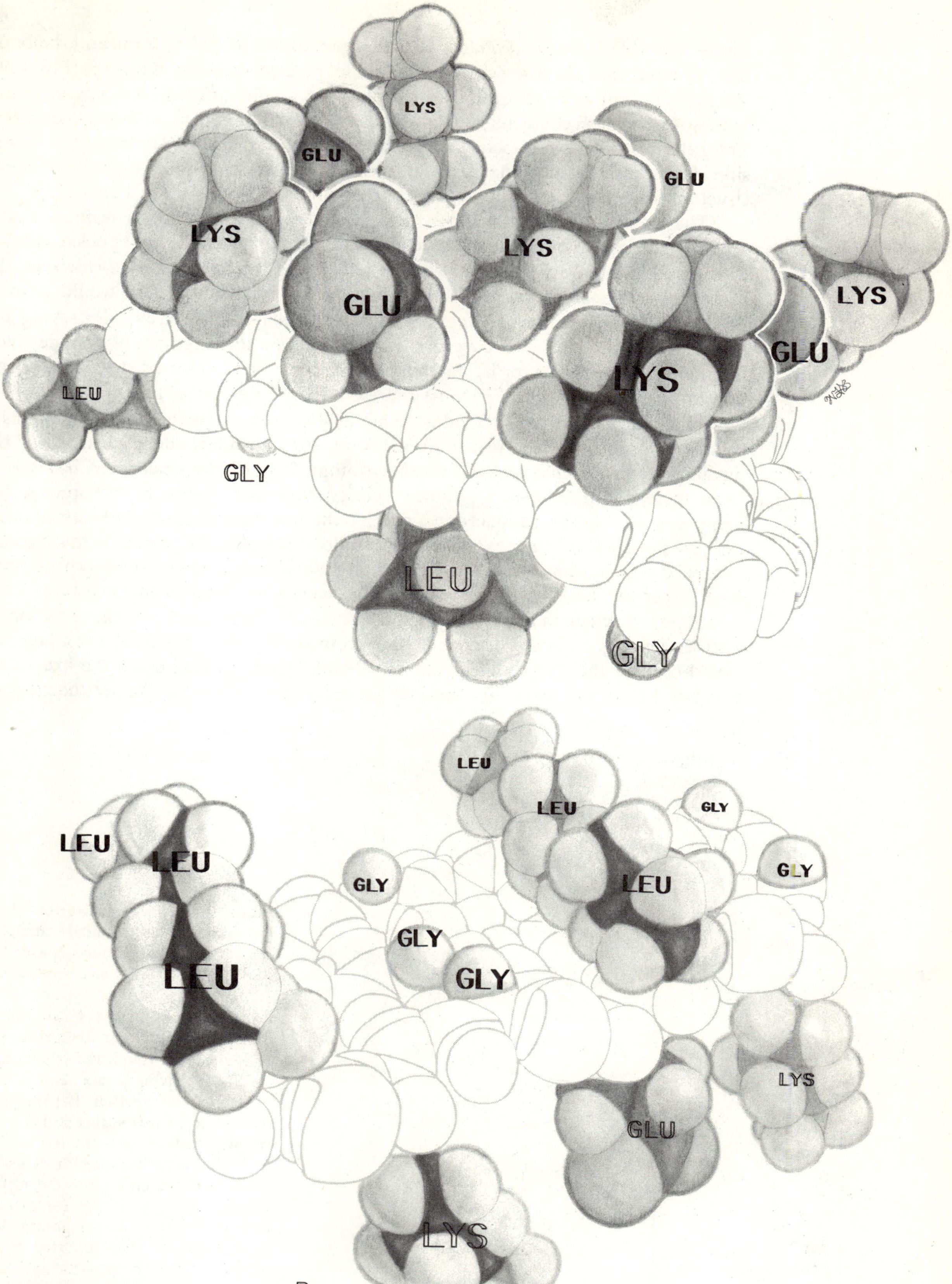

Figure 1-9 (*Continued*) B.

Let us see what happens if chains of this sequence are folded to form an α-helix on the one hand, and the β-structure (anti-parallel pleated sheet) on the other (Fig. 1–9). We can see right away that the two structures are totally different, not only in shape, but also in chemical character; they present entirely different faces to the surroundings. The helix distributes non-polar and polar residues all over its surface, and it brings side chains carrying like charges near each other. It doesn't seem to be a probable structure for a peptide of this sequence to assume.

The pleated sheet, on the other hand, has its non-polar and polar residues neatly separated on opposite sides of the sheet. In addition, the polar side has opposite charges distributed in an almost perfect lattice of alternating cation and anion. However, the massively non-polar opposite face couldn't exist as such in water. It would have to be covered, perhaps by bending the molecule upon itself, thereby destroying the β-structure at the hinge; by covering the face with another segment of peptide chain of different composition; or by back-to-back stacking of two pleated sheets, non-polar side to non-polar side. Any of these represent a modification of the molecule.

The point is that the particular amino acid sequence specified here, simple as it is, creates problems, each of a different kind, for the independent existence of the regular structures. Let us consider another example in which the α-helix may be favored. Once more, the α-helix is a cylinder studded with side chains. It so happens that non-polar residues can be spaced in a peptide chain at intervals such that they all occur near the same side of the helix. It is then possible to construct the protein so that another non-polar region forms a snug fit with the non-polar side of the helix, thereby generating both dispersion forces and hydrophobic interactions to maintain the structure.

A peptide chain in human hemoglobin illustrates the point. A portion of the amino acid sequence is plotted in Figure 1–10 so as to show the distribution of residues that would occur if the chain folded into an α-helix. One is looking down the axis of the resultant helix, with successive residues spaced at 100° intervals. We see that there is

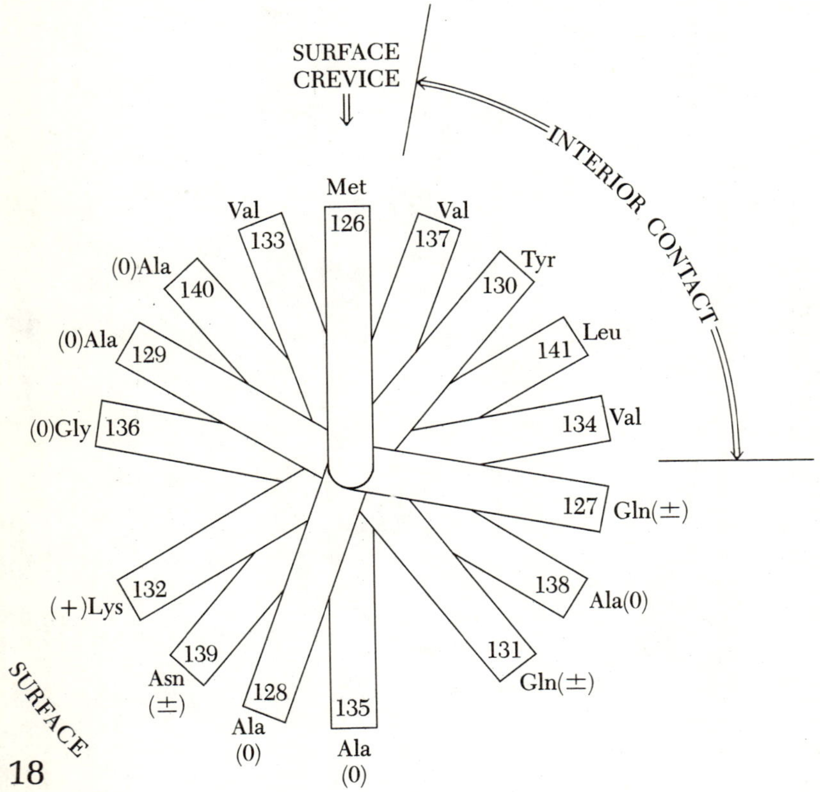

Figure 1–10 Visualization of the spacing of amino acid side chains on the surface of an α-helix is aided by plotting the amino acid sequence at 100° intervals, as if one were looking down the axis of the helix. Shown here is the resultant distribution of residues 126 through 141 of a peptide chain in a hemoglobin, and it may be seen by inspection that the helix formed from this segment has a hydrophobic face suitable for contact with the non-polar interior of a molecule, with the balance of the surface containing polar groups for association with water. This segment does in fact form a helix oriented as described within the protein molecule.

indeed a non-polar strip centered near 1 o'clock on the diagram. One can infer from this the actual facts: This segment of peptide occurs as an α-helix, with the non-polar strip buried in contact with other non-polar parts of the peptide chain. The remaining face of the helix represents part of the surface of the hemoglobin molecule, with the polar groups of that face in contact with water. In sum, this small portion of the peptide chain illustrates the way in which the amino acid sequence causes the entire hemoglobin molecule to form a particular three-dimensional shape through burial of non-polar regions and surface exposure of polar groups.

Non-ordered Tertiary Structure. The formation of the maximum bonding forces can't be accomplished for most primary structures by the extensive combination of secondary structures such as the helix or pleated sheet. Most proteins contain large regions in which the peptide chain appears to be bent in a random way, like a crushed coat-hanger. It is this complex folding that creates biological function by making a particular arrangement of chemically reactive groups. The irregular shapes are, of course, not random, but represent the configuration bringing the largest combinations of internally interacting groups into contact, while at the same time minimizing ordering of the solvent. The creation of such shapes often involves the formation of sharp bends in the peptide chain. What makes these bends? Do they form in a particular place because the portions of peptide chain thereby brought together have an especially strong affinity for each other, or do some parts of the peptide chain have a strong tendency to form bends, thereby creating a preference for structures containing these bends?

Both of these circumstances are true. The presence of a sharp bend attests the development of stronger forces due to the bend. These forces may develop between parts of the chain away from the bend, or they may develop at the bend itself, or they may represent a combination of both effects.

HELIX BREAKERS. One of the ways to force a bend is to insert amino acid residues that can't participate in the formation of regular structures.

Proline is an amino acid in which the amino nitrogen is part of a ring, and a peptide bond created from this secondary amine lacks the hydrogen atom used for bond formation in the helix or pleated sheet:

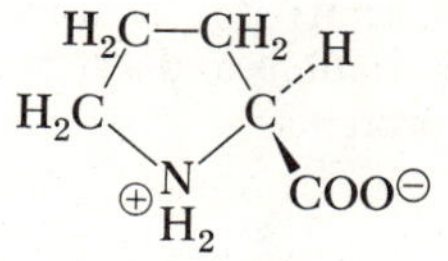

L-proline

These factors prevent prolyl residues from participating in α-helix formation beyond the first turn, and insertion of the amino acid in a peptide therefore also causes an obligatory interruption of a helix.

3_{10} BENDS. The presence of glycine, with no side chain, also favors the formation of bends, which may be interruptions of helices or may occur in other parts of the chain. One of the reasons is that the lack of a side chain permits tight packing of the peptide backbone—the peptide chain can double back on itself without interference by side chains. Indeed, there is a specific structure that is possible only with glycyl residues, which is known as a 3_{10} bend because it represents one turn of a helix with 3 residues per turn in which hydrogen bonds close a ring of 10 atoms. (An α-helix is a 3.6_{13} helix by this notation.)

However, there is another variant of the 3_{10} bend, shown in Figure 1–11, that does not require the presence of glycyl groups for its formation, and this makes the final point. Some bends occur without any apparent deviation in amino acid composition at the point of flexure; they occur because folding the molecule at that particular

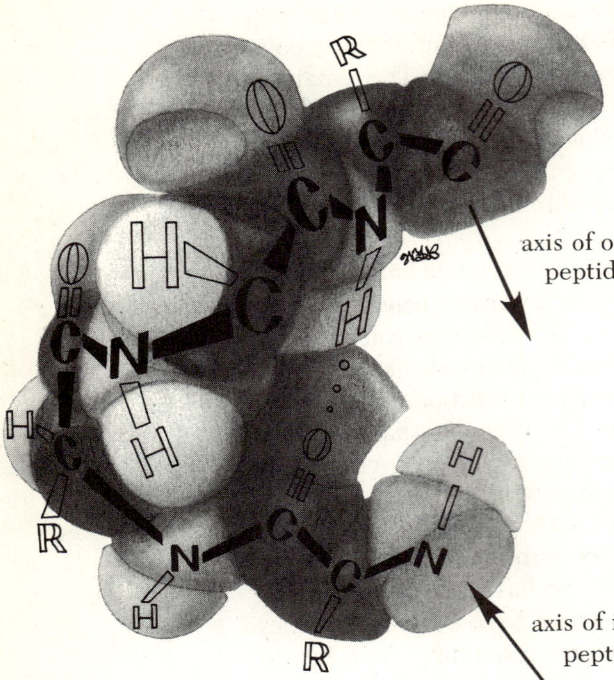

Figure 1-11 Peptide chains can form a sharp bend with a hydrogen bond between the carbonyl oxygen of one residue and the amino hydrogen of the third following residue. The bend resembles a segment of a 3_{10} helix, which is not stable, but one twist can be stabilized if sufficient bonds form in the remainder of the molecule as a result of the bend. Another variant of the bend occurs in which the chain is twisted in the opposite direction, but this is possible only at a glycyl group, owing to steric hindrance from the side chain of other amino acid residues.

point will result in stronger bonds between the parts of the molecule brought into proximity by the bend than would be the case if the molecule were folded elsewhere. A fold occurs because it results in a greater discharge of energy than would result from other possible structures.

FURTHER READING

R. E. Dickerson and I. Geis, The structure and action of proteins, Harper and Row (1969). A readable guide with excellent illustrations and a stereo supplement showing spatial orientation of peptide chains in various proteins.

QUESTIONS

1. Write a structural formula for alanylalanylglycine, and show how this tripeptide can act both as an acid and as a base.
2. Show how the side chains of threonine, of serine, or of glutamine might form hydrogen bonds to stabilize the position of an adjacent peptide backbone.
3. Why do glycyl residues disrupt an α-helix, but have no effect on the formation of a pleated sheet?
4. Trace the spacing of Figure 1-10 and use it to plot the arrangement of the following peptide chain in the form of an α-helix: —Phe—Glu—Gly—Ile—Lys—Ala—Val—Leu—Asn—Arg—Met—. Which of these have non-polar side chains? Is there a likely face for interior bonding on this helix? Which groups are almost certainly in contact with surrounding water? Which groups carry a negative charge in neutral solution? Which groups carry a positive charge in neutral solution?
5. What are Ramachadran angles, and what do they specify?
6. What is proline, and what effect does it have upon the arrangement of a peptide backbone?
7. The presence of a residue of what amino acid sometimes favors the formation of 3_{10} bends? Why?
8. Why do some peptides form regular secondary structures, and others form seemingly random arrangements of the backbone?

CHAPTER 2

NUCLEIC ACIDS AND INFORMATION

THE CONCEPTS

The ability to synthesize definite amounts of peptides with specific amino acid composition constitutes most of the heredity of an organism. The information necessary for the syntheses and their control is contained within molecules of nucleic acids.

Nature of Nucleic Acids. Nucleic acids are like peptides in being linear polymers with different substituents scattered along the backbone. The nucleic acid backbone consists of molecules of 5-carbon sugars joined by forming esters with phosphoric acid. The substituents on the backbone consist of various nitrogenous heterocyclic compounds, termed the bases of the nucleic acids, also attached to the sugar molecules.

Nucleotides and Nucleosides. The repeating unit of a nucleic acid therefore is a combination of a nitrogenous base, a sugar, and phosphoric acid, known as a nucleotide, and a nucleic acid is a polynucleotide. A base-sugar combination without the phosphoric acid is a nucleoside, so a nucleotide may be regarded as a nucleoside phosphate.

DNA Composition. Deoxyribonucleic acids contain the sugar, 2′-deoxyribose, in the backbone; the substituent bases scattered along the backbone are the purines, adenine and guanine, and the pyrimidines, cytosine and thymine. Therefore, DNA may be regarded as a polymer of the corresponding deoxynucleosides, deoxyadenosine, -guanosine, -cytidine, or -thymidine, linked by phosphoric acid between the sugar moieties.

Triplet Coding. DNA molecules are the primary sources of genetic information which is contained in the order of arrangement of the four bases along the nucleic acid backbone. Three consecutive nucleotides constitute a triplet that defines one amino acid. There are 64 possible triplets; three are used for punctuation of the genetic message, and each of the remainder represents only one amino acid, although one amino acid may be defined by more than one triplet.

Complementary Bases. The bases of DNA have the property of forming hydrogen bonds with each other in the combinations adenine-thymine and cytosine-guanine, and this property is the basis for the transmittal and utilization of genetic information. The association of complementary bases by hydrogen bond formation is the means by which one specific pattern of base arrangements creates another specific pattern.

Double Helix and Antiparallel Strands. DNA is composed of two strands of polynucleotide, with the bases in one strand represented by their complements in the other strand. The two strands therefore associate into a particular helical structure that permits each base to bond with its complement in the other strand. The strands of this double helix are antiparallel; that is, the sugar groups of the backbone are connected in opposite directions. Successive complementary pairs of bases therefore represent one nucleotide forward on one strand, and one nucleotide back on the other, in formal nomenclature. When cells divide, new DNA is formed by replication of both strands so as to provide daughter cells with the same informational molecules.

Ribonucleic Acids. During the life of a cell, the information contained in its DNA is transcribed in the form of ribonucleic acids for transient use. These ribonucleic acids differ from DNA in that they contain ribose as a sugar, and the pyrimidine uracil is used as a complement of adenine. They are made only as complements of one strand of DNA, and therefore do not occur as a double helix. The coding for peptide sequence contained in DNA is specifically transcribed in messenger ribonucleic acids (mRNA), with each amino acid represented by a triplet of successive nucleotides representing antiparallel complements of the strand in DNA from which it was transcribed. The mRNA triplets are known as codons for the amino acid, whereas the

antiparallel complements, such as occur in one strand of DNA, are called anticodons. One molecule of mRNA usually contains the coding for a single peptide chain, in contrast to molecules of DNA, which carry a large fraction, sometimes all, of the genetic information in a cell.

"A common observation is that cats give birth to cats. Cats have been up to this for centuries all the world over. Furthermore, there is no documented instance of a cat giving birth to anything else. This is the primary observation of the science of heredity."*

The ability of living organisms to generate organisms much like themselves is one of their most obvious characteristics. We now have a good general idea of how this is done, even though the details are known only in untested speculations. The notion was offered in the first chapter that the inherent form of an organism and the responses it makes to changes in the environment (in other words, its heredity) are mainly determined by the nature of the proteins it contains. (We shall see as we go along that even the quantity of particular proteins is determined in most instances by the presence of still other proteins.)

Since the character of a particular protein is fixed by the order of the constituent amino acids in its peptide chain, it is logical to infer that the heredity of an organism is its capacity to construct peptide chains with particular sequences of amino acids. A concept of heroic simplicity! But is it correct? All of the evidence at hand seems to say that it is close to the complete truth. A particular fertilized ovum will become a cat because it turns out peptide chains that form the structures, carry out the functions, and regulate the entire transformation from a slow-moving single cell into a yowling, spitting adult. In this and the following chapters, we shall see how these chains are made.

Magnitude of Inheritance. How many different proteins must be made during the life of an organism? Viruses require very few, because they depend upon other living cells to act as hosts and carry out most of the functions necessary for their survival. Those organisms that must have a more complete complement of functions require many more proteins. Current estimates range around 3000 different proteins required to make a typical micro-organism, such as the bacterium *Escherichia coli,* and 10,000 different proteins to form a human.

INFORMATION AND NUCLEIC ACIDS

Put in an abstract way, most of the heredity of an organism consists of information for the construction of peptide chains, and reproduction involves the transmittal of that information from the parent cell to the daughter cell. Both the transmittal and the utilization of information are accomplished by the means of nucleic acids. We shall see that the mechanism of information transfer represents another example of the use of specific spatial patterns of chemical groups.

The nucleic acids are macromolecules, even larger than the corresponding proteins, and therefore have ample bulk to carry information in the form of arrangements of chemical groups with a complexity comparable to that of arrangements of amino acids in proteins. Before turning to a more detailed examination of the nucleic acids, let us get a general idea of their participation in the flow of genetic information (Fig. 2–1).

The original reservoir of genetic information in the cell is contained in polymers known as **deoxyribonucleic acids (DNA),** which are made from four compounds ar-

*F. W. Stahl, The mechanics of inheritance, 2nd. ed., Prentice-Hall (1969).

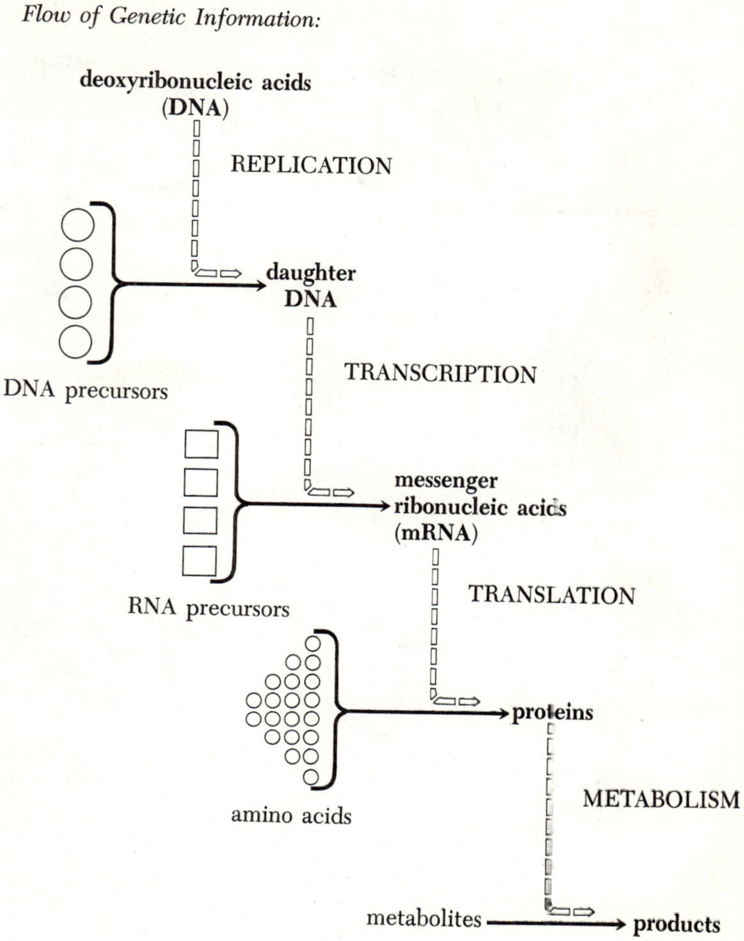

Figure 2-1 Genetic information in the form of deoxyribonucleic acids (DNA) is used to direct the replication of the DNA for creation of new cells. The information is transcribed within a cell as messenger ribonucleic acids (mRNA), the information of which is used to direct the synthesis of peptides from amino acids. Some of the peptides form conformations that catalyze or direct the catalysis of the reactions constituting the metabolism of the cell.

ranged in particular order. Copies are made of these polymers during the process of cell division so that newly formed cells contain the same information. New cells therefore obtain information by replication of DNA.

The information obtained in DNA is used during the lifetime of each cell to direct the formation of proteins within the cell. To protect the DNA molecules, which are the source of all information for every descendant of the cell, they are used only as a master copy, and information is transcribed from them by the formation of **messenger ribonucleic acids (mRNA),** which are also built from four components, but of somewhat different chemical nature than those used in forming DNA. The assembly of these ribonucleic acids occurs in proximity to molecules of DNA, and they are put together in patterns dictated by the arrangement of the constituents of DNA, so they also carry the same information, but in a modified way.

The information on mRNA molecules is then translated into the assembly of amino acids to make particular proteins. This translation of information involves the use of patterns created by the arrangement of the four components in mRNA along its chain to fix the sequence in which 20 amino acids will be linked together in peptides.

Once the peptides are formed, they can perform their specific biological functions. These functions, which are the ultimate expression of the original genetic information, frequently involve the catalysis of the many chemical reactions involved in metabolism—the processes by which incoming compounds are utilized and ultimately converted to products that are excreted.

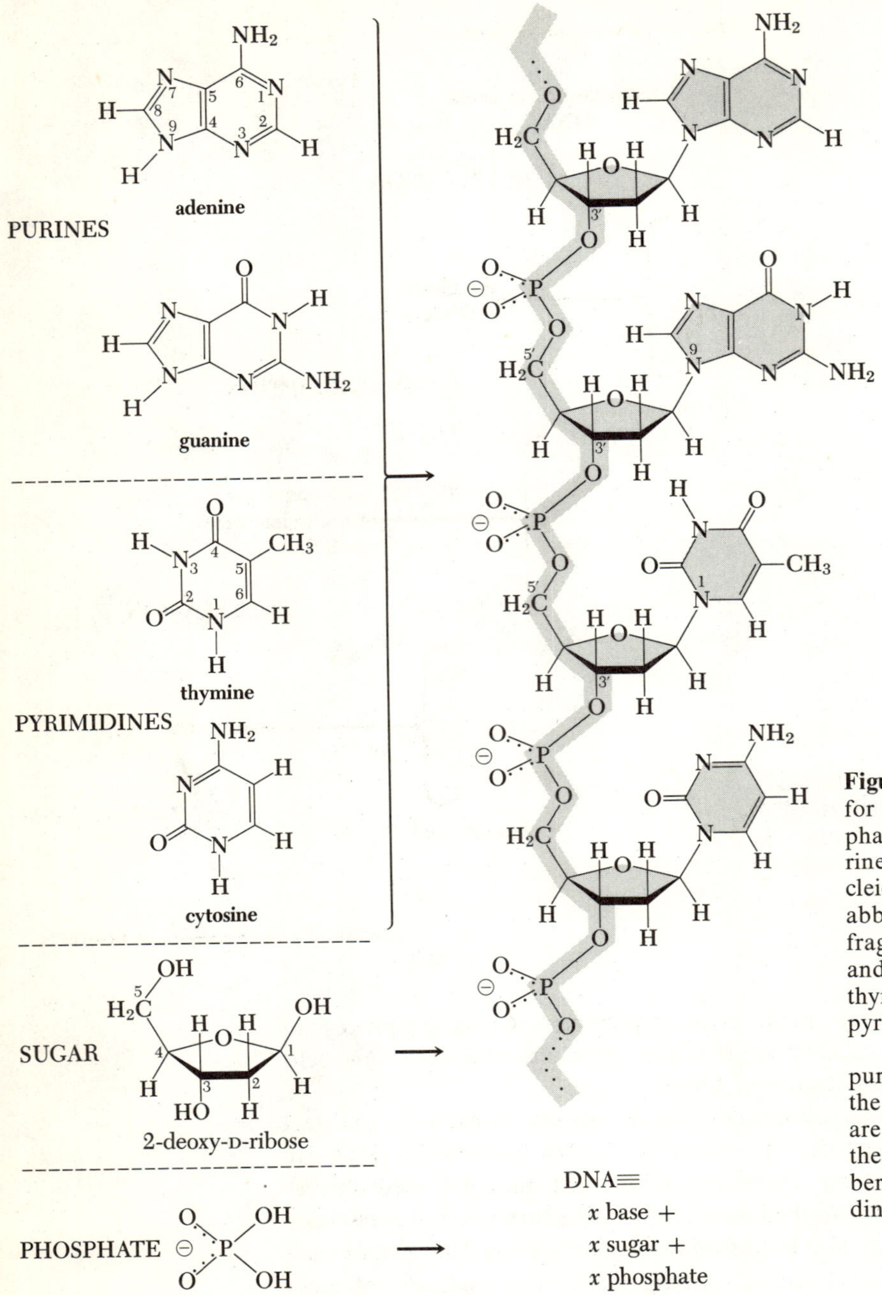

Figure 2-2 The formal stoichiometry for the combination of inorganic phosphate (P_i), 2-deoxy-D-ribose, and purines or pyrimidines into deoxyribonucleic acid (DNA). The conventional abbreviation for the polynucleotide fragment shown is dA-G-T-C-. Adenine and guanine are substituted purines; thymine and cystosine are substituted pyrimidines.

The numbering of atoms in ribose, purines, and pyrimidines is shown. In the nucleotides, the atoms of the sugar are designated 1′, 2′, etc., to distinguish these positions from the similarly numbered positions on the purine or pyrimidine rings.

The Information in DNA. The genetic information necessary for the construction of peptides is contained in deoxyribonucleic acids in the form of specific arrangements of chemical substituents. These substituents are provided by heterocyclic compounds known as **purines** and **pyrimidines** (Fig. 2–2), which are attached to the sugar portion of repeating backbones in the molecule. The backbones are made by linking molecules of the sugar, **2-deoxy-D-ribose,** by the formation of ester bridges between the molecules with phosphoric acid. DNA is therefore made from repeating units, known as **nucleotides,** which contain a nitrogenous heterocyclic compound combined with a sugar and phosphate. DNA is thus an example of a polynucleotide.

Bases and Coding in DNA. The purines of DNA are **adenine** and **guanine,** and the pyrimidines are **cytosine** and **thymine,** as shown in the figure. We shall follow custom in referring to these compounds as the "bases" of the nucleic acids, even though some behave as acids in neutral solution.

The only structural variable along the polynucleotide chain of DNA is the location of the four bases, and it is the arrangement of these particular parts of the structure that indicates the sequence in which amino acids are ultimately to be put together to made peptides. It has been recognized for some time that the coding for amino acids must involve the particular arrangement of at least three successive bases along the DNA chain. The reason for this is that four bases taken two at a time could only yield 4^2 (or 16) different combinations, and there are 20 different amino acids to be coded. However, there are 64 possible combinations of four bases taken three at a time, and experimentation has shown that **triplets** of successive bases are indeed the elements of information specifying particular amino acids to be incorporated into proteins.

Nomenclature. Before going further, let us examine how the structures of nucleic acids are designated. Nucleic acids are polymers of nucleotides (base-sugar-phosphate), and nucleotides are also described as nucleoside phosphates, a **nucleoside** being the base-sugar combination. If the sugar is 2-deoxyribose, then deoxy- is used as a prefix. Thus, the nucleosides of DNA are **deoxyadenosine, deoxyguanosine, deoxycytidine,** and **deoxythymidine.** (Caution: It was formerly believed that thymine occurred only in DNA, and many biochemists still use the term thymidine without the deoxy prefix to describe the deoxynucleoside. It takes time to discard even such obvious anachronisms; semantic booby traps are among the perils of a growing science, but logic often prevails in the end.)

The position of the phosphoryl ester bond on each sugar residue is specified by a numeral. Thus, 5′-deoxyadenosine monophosphate has the phosphate ester group on the fifth carbon of the deoxyribose portion of deoxyadenosine.

In designating the order of the bases in nucleic acids, the nucleosides are abbreviated A, G, C, or T, with d- as a prefix for deoxynucleosides. When occurring in free form, MP is used as an abbreviation for monophosphate. Thus, dG is deoxyguanosine; 3′-dGMP is deoxyguanosine esterified with phosphate on the third carbon of the deoxyribose. We shall later see that the nucleotides involved in metabolic reactions are usually 5′-phosphate esters of nucleosides, and the abbreviation is understood to designate only the 5′-ester when no number appears. Thus, **AMP, ADP,** and **ATP** are understood as meaning **adenosine 5′-monophosphate, adenosine 5′-diphosphate,** and **adenosine 5′-triphosphate,** respectively, which are made with adenine linked to ribose and one, two, or three phosphate groups. (These compounds are discussed more fully on p. 144.)

The order of the nucleosides in nucleic acids is indicated simply by separating their abbreviations with hyphens, except that terminal phosphate groups are indicated by the letter p. For example, d-pA-T-C indicates a deoxynucleotide chain in which deoxyadenosine, deoxythymidine, and deoxycytidine are linked in that order. Now, the links involve the 5′-carbon of one nucleoside and the 3′-carbon of the next. The convention is to specify them so that the 5′-linkage is to the left of each nucleoside. Thus, in our example the chain begins with a terminal phosphate on the 5′-carbon of deoxyadenosine. The hyphen after A indicates that the 3′-carbon of deoxyadenosine is linked to the 5′-carbon of the next nucleoside, which is deoxythymidine in this case. The next hyphen indicates that the 3′-carbon of deoxythymidine is linked to the 5′-carbon of deoxycytidine. The lack of any symbol after the C indicates that the 3′-hydroxyl group of deoxycytidine is not substituted with anything.

Complementary Bases. It so happens that the DNA from most cells is made of two strands twisted into a **double helix** (Fig. 2–3). Each base in one strand is attached to a base in the other strand by hydrogen bonds. The ability of certain pairs of bases to form these hydrogen bonds is the foundation for the transmission of genetic information.

The bases of DNA that can bond with each other in this way are adenine with thymine, and guanine with cytosine (Fig. 2–4). We say that adenine and thymine are complementary, and guanine and cytosine are complementary, because they tend to associate by the formation of hydrogen bonds. The principle is so fundamental to the mechanics of reproduction and protein synthesis that we appear safe in saying that these particular purines and pyrimidines are used because they have the structures necessary for the formation of the double helix and can also participate in the metabolic reactions we shall consider later.

DNA twists into a double helix because it is made of two kinds of strands, each

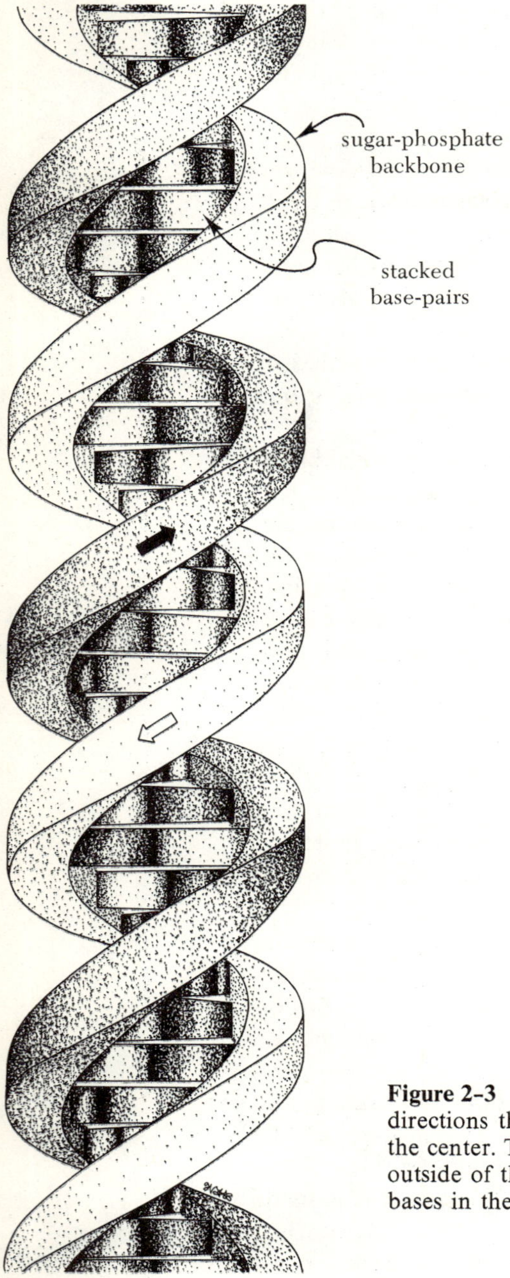

Figure 2–3 DNA is composed of two polynucleotide strands running in opposite directions that twist into a double helix so as to bring the bases into contact in the center. The sugar phosphate ester backbones of the strands are exposed on the outside of the helix. Ten pairs of nucleotide residues, with their associated paired bases in the center, form one complete turn of the helix.

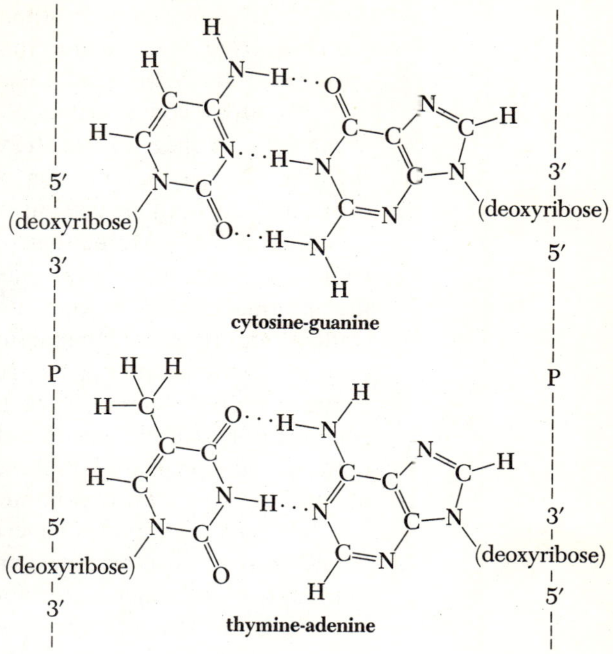

Figure 2-4 Hydrogen bonding of complementary bases between adjacent nucleic acid strands. The symbols are spaced to scale the actual positions of the atoms. Note the opposing directions of the phosphodiester bonds in the two strands being linked. Modified from Pauling and Corey, Arch. Biochem. Biophys., 65:164 (1956).

having an arrangement of bases that is the complement of the other. The most stable conformation will therefore be one that brings all of the bases on one strand in contact with all of the bases on the other strand in such a way that the complements will bond with the least strain, and this conformation is the double helix.

The two strands of the double helix are actually twisted in opposition, so that one of the strands viewed from a particular end will have the phosphates linking the sugars 5′-sugar-3′-phosphate-5′-sugar-3′-phosphate, while the other strand viewed in that way will have the phosphate linkages in the order 3′-sugar-5′-phosphate-3′-sugar-5′-phosphate. This creates a problem in communication, because the first strand can be designated as it stands according to the rules, but the latter strand must be named backwards (Fig. 2-5). The physical fact is simple enough. If one has the segment d(—T—A—C—) on one strand, the other strand will have the complementary nucleosides dA,

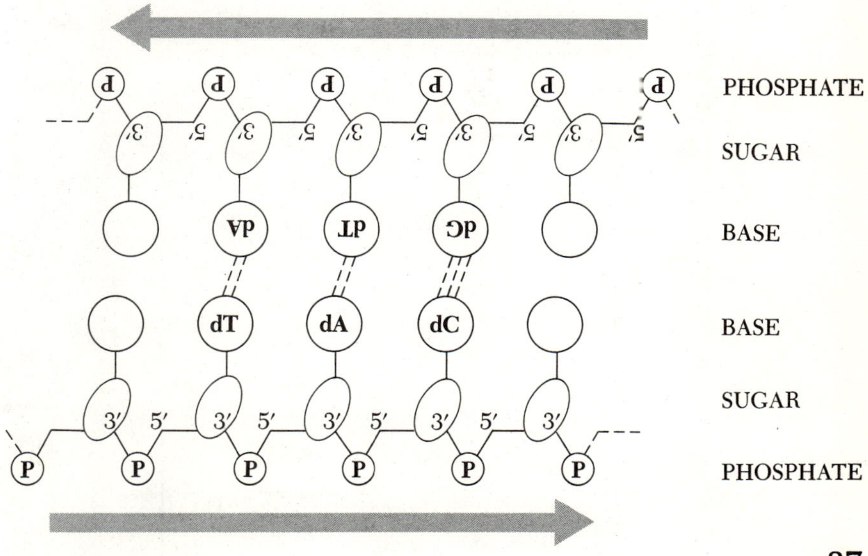

Figure 2-5 Each succeeding base in a strand of DNA has a complementary base in the corresponding position of the other strand. This is not evident from the nomenclature of the strands, which requires that the base sequence be listed from the 5′-end of each strand.

dT, and dG in the same positions viewed from one end; since the phosphate linkages are connecting them in the opposite direction, the complement of d(—T—A—C—) must be formally specified backwards as d(—G—T—A—).

One of the consequences of base-pairing, which can be used as a test for its likely occurrence, is that double-stranded DNA contains equal amounts of adenine and thymine, and equal amounts of guanine and cytosine, even if the four bases are distributed in random fashion in one strand.

Size of DNA Molecules. DNA typically occurs in long lengths of double helix, which are coiled and super-coiled into compact structures. A single molecule contains the information for making many peptide chains *via* messenger RNA, but it also contains information for making other nucleic acids, and for regulating the rate of protein synthesis; perhaps it contains some segments that serve only a structural purpose. Indeed, some bacteria have only one molecule of DNA containing all of their genetic information; these double-stranded molecules have molecular weights greater than 10^9, and would be millimeters long if they could be stretched out—thousands of times greater than the diameter of the bacteria in which they are packed.

Similarly, eukaryotes have molecules of double-stranded DNA that may run the length of their chromosomes, and which would be centimeters in length if stretched out. There is still much uncertainty about the molecular arrangement of chromosomes, but even minimum estimates for eukaryotic DNA range around 10^{10} molecular weight.

Cistrons and Genes. Geneticists introduced the term *gene* to describe the minimum component of heredity that could be altered (mutated). The introduction of experimental methods permitting the assignment of location of specific genetic traits on the length of a chromosome led to the introduction of *cistron* as a word describing such chromosomal segments bearing fundamental genetic information. The two terms describe somewhat the same operational properties; today they are both frequently represented in molecular terms as a segment of DNA that is transcribed into messenger RNA as a unit, although "cistron" is frequently further limited to a segment of DNA containing information for the formation of one polypeptide chain.

RIBONUCLEIC ACIDS

The ribonucleic acids (RNA) differ from deoxyribonucleic acids in two important respects. One is the presence of **D-ribose,** rather than 2′-deoxy-D-ribose, as the sugar in the constituent nucleotides. The other is the use of **uracil** as a base in place of thymine:

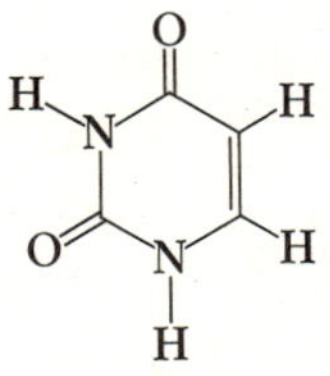

uracil

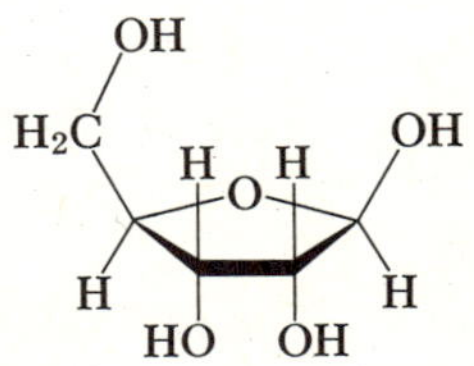

β-D-ribose

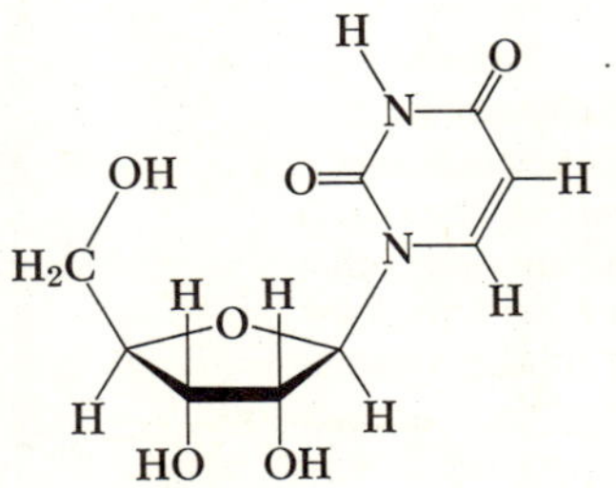

uridine

The nucleoside made by combining uracil and ribose is **uridine** (U); molecules of RNA completely complementary to DNA can be made by linking only A, C, G, and U with phosphate bridges, because uracil is like thymine in forming complementary hydrogen bonds with adenine.

We shall see in the next chapter how the ability of RNA to form complementary bonds is used in transcribing DNA as RNA and in translating the sequence of nucleotides in RNA into a sequence of amino acids in a peptide. All of these activities involve only a single strand of RNA. Double-stranded RNA is known to occur only in some viruses, in which it serves the same genetic function as does double-stranded DNA in higher organisms.

Coding in Messenger RNA

Messenger RNA is the particular kind of RNA carrying information for peptide sequence; each successive triplet of nucleotides along an mRNA chain represents a particular amino acid. These triplets, known as **codons** for the amino acids, are laid down as complements of the sequence in a DNA strand. The complementary, antiparallel sequences in DNA corresponding to the codons in mRNA are known as **anticodons.** (It may seem odd that the sequence in the parental DNA strand is not called the codon, but coding was first studied in mRNA, and the implications were not thought through.) This point is pursued in more detail in the next chapter.

Since the base arrangement in mRNA is used for coding a sequence of amino acids, it does not contain any systematic sequences of complements that might cause internal bonding in one molecule. A strand of mRNA therefore does not exist in any fixed compact structure.

FURTHER READING

F. W. Stahl, The mechanics of inheritance, 2nd. ed., Prentice-Hall (1969). The title is self-descriptive.

H. R. Mahler and E. H. Cordes, Biological chemistry, 2nd. ed., Harper and Row (1971). For the student desiring a detailed summary of the chemical and physical properties of the nucleic acids.

QUESTIONS

1. As the terms are ordinarily used, what compound is being synthesized, and what compound acts as a source of information during transcription? During translation? During replication?
2. How do molecules of DNA and of messenger RNA differ in
   a. chemical composition?
   b. 3-dimensional structure?
   c. content of cistrons?
3. Use the principles of nomenclature illustrated in the text to deduce what is meant by d-(pppG-Tp).
4. What would be the sequence of nucleosides, as read from the 5′- end, in the segment of a DNA strand complementary to the sequence d(—T—A—G—C—) in the other strand?
5. What is the difference between a purine and a pyrimidine? Which of the complementary pairs adenine-thymine, adenine-uracil, and cytosine-guanine represent bonding between purines, between pyrimidines, or between a purine and a pyrimidine?
6. If a certain segment of one strand of DNA contains approximately 2100 residues of dA, 1800 residues of dT, 2300 residues of dG, and 2500 residues of dC, how can it be true that a double helix including that segment will have equal amounts of dA and dT, and equal amounts of dG and dC? What are the expected numbers of residues of each deoxynucleoside in the double helix?

CHAPTER 3

UTILIZATION OF GENETIC INFORMATION

THE CONCEPTS

The construction of peptide chains in response to instructions contained in DNA involves the participation of three different kinds of structures containing RNA. These include ribosomes, which are the organelles on which peptides are made; transfer RNAs, which carry amino acids to the site of synthesis; and messenger RNAs, which carry the actual information on the desired amino acid sequence.

Transcription. All of the kinds of RNA required for peptide synthesis are assembled by successive addition of nucleotides with bases complementary to the bases in a strand of DNA. DNA therefore contains information for the direct assembly of the RNA components of the apparatus for protein synthesis, as well as for the primary structure of the peptides to be made by the apparatus. The precursors of RNA are nucleoside triphosphates (adenosine, guanosine, cytidine, or uridine triphosphates), which are attached to the growing RNA chain by the action of an RNA polymerase. The reaction involves loss of two of the phosphate atoms as inorganic pyrophosphate (PP_i).

Refinement of RNA. RNA chains are made with sequences of nucleotides at the beginning and end that are unnecessary for the function of the molecule; these redundant sequences are removed after the molecules are made. Some of these sequences may be necessary for the recognition of the beginning and end of genetic messages in the DNA. Others act as spacers between functional portions of the RNA, so that a single strand of RNA may contain several functional segments. Ribosomal and transfer RNAs are also further modified by the substitution of additional chemical groups on their constituent bases and by occasional rearrangement of nucleoside structures.

Ribosomes. Ribosomes are aggregates of many proteins with RNA. They are made by joining two subunits; the smaller contains one piece of RNA, and the larger contains two similar pieces in both prokaryotic and eukaryotic cells, with an additional piece of unknown function in the eukaryotic cells. The three ubiquitous pieces of ribosomal RNA are made in identical quantities because they are formed as segments of a single strand of RNA, with the spacer sequences later cleaved to liberate the three functional fragments of the original molecule. These fragments then associate with various proteins, which include enzymes catalyzing peptide synthesis, to form the complete ribosomal subunits.

Translation. The translation into a sequence of amino acids of the genetic message brought to the ribosomes on messenger RNA is accomplished through the recognition of successive codons on mRNA by transfer RNA (tRNA) molecules that also carry the amino acids corresponding to the codon. Recognition involves binding between the mRNA codon and a complementary anticodon in specific tRNA molecules. Growth of the peptide chain is in the direction of the carboxyl terminal, so previously synthesized peptide is added to the amino group of each new amino acid carried to the ribosome. The growing peptide is therefore always carried on the tRNA molecules that brought in the most recently added amino acid.

The ribosomes, along with the attached peptide chain and tRNA molecules, move down the length of messenger RNA as the codon sequences are translated into amino acid sequences. There is room on most mRNA molecules for several ribosomes at once, so synthesis of several identical molecules of peptide may be proceeding simultaneously on one molecule of mRNA.

Transfer RNA. The process of translation hinges on the performance of several functions by molecules of transfer RNA, which consist of chains of somewhat less than 100 nucleotides containing complementary sequences that cause the molecules to fold into specific configurations. These configurations include a particular location for the anticodon near the center of the molecule, a location at the 3′ terminus for binding the amino acid to be transported, a specific

sequence of nucleotides that is recognized by an enzyme that attaches one, and only one, of the 20 amino acids to a particular RNA, and a surface facilitating binding to the active sites of ribosomes.

Replication. **Genetic information is transferred from one generation of cells to another by the formation of new strands of DNA. The replication of DNA involves the separation of the double helix, and the binding of complementary deoxyribonucleoside triphosphates to each of the separated strands, followed by union of the nucleotides catalyzed by a DNA polymerase. However, the first step in replication is the formation of a complementary strand of RNA in the same way that transcription begins. After this strand becomes some 40 to 50 nucleotides long, a DNA polymerase then begins to add deoxyribonucleotides to create a DNA strand.**

Later steps in replication involve hydrolyzing the RNA spacers, filling the gaps with additional deoxyribonucleotides, and finally uniting the segments by the action of a ligase. The result of this is the laying down of a new strand on each of the parent strands of DNA, so that each of the new double helical molecules, although identical to the other in composition, contains one parent strand and its new complement. Replication in this way is said to be semi-conservative in terms of the parent molecules.

Let us first take an overall view of the use of genetic information, and then examine the steps in the process in more detail. The way in which the information in DNA is used to cause the synthesis of particular proteins is summarized in Figure 3–1. The necessary components include a molecule of DNA and three kinds of RNA molecules (along with several protein catalysts, or enzymes, that are not shown). Information transfer begins with the use of one DNA strand as a pattern, or template, on which complementary bases are combined to create messenger RNA. Messenger RNA therefore contains the same information present in the DNA strand on which it is made, except that the information is represented by an antiparallel, complementary sequence of bases.

The information in mRNA is used to assemble amino acids in a specific sequence, but the sites of peptide synthesis are structures known as **ribosomes,** which are small particles that also contain ribonucleic acids, along with some of the enzymes required for peptide synthesis. (The ribonucleic acids in ribosomes do not carry information on peptide sequences.) Peptide synthesis occurs when ribosomes combine with molecules of mRNA. (There is room for several ribosomes in one strand of mRNA, and such clusters are known as **polysomes.**) In prokaryotes, ribosomes become fixed to growing threads of mRNA before they are even completed and released from the DNA template, but the ribosomes of eukaryotes are in the cytoplasm while mRNA is made on DNA in the nucleus. The completed mRNA molecules must pass out of the nucleus into the cytoplasm before they can be used to direct the construction of peptide chains.

As Figure 3–1 shows, utilization of the information in mRNA to determine amino acid sequence in peptides involves still other kinds of nucleic acids, known as **transfer RNAs (tRNA),** which are relatively small molecules that also attach to the ribosomes. However, tRNA molecules have a specific three-dimensional conformation, and each kind contains a triplet of bases in a particular location where bonds can form with complementary triplets on the messenger RNA also bound to the ribosome. The result is that the messenger RNA-ribosome complex will strongly bond only those molecules of tRNA bearing anticodons for a particular triplet on the segment of mRNA in contact with the ribosome. Furthermore, each kind of tRNA has a particular kind of amino acid attached to it. That is, a tRNA molecule is recognized by particular enzymes that catalyze the attachment of one, and only one, amino acid to that kind of tRNA.

Here we have it. The molecules of tRNA constitute the dictionary for translating the base sequence of polynucleotide chains into the amino acid sequence of polypeptide chains; each molecule of tRNA has a triplet matching a particular base arrangement on mRNA, and the molecule is also recognized by specific enzymes that attach a particular amino acid to it. (The point of attachment of the amino acid is

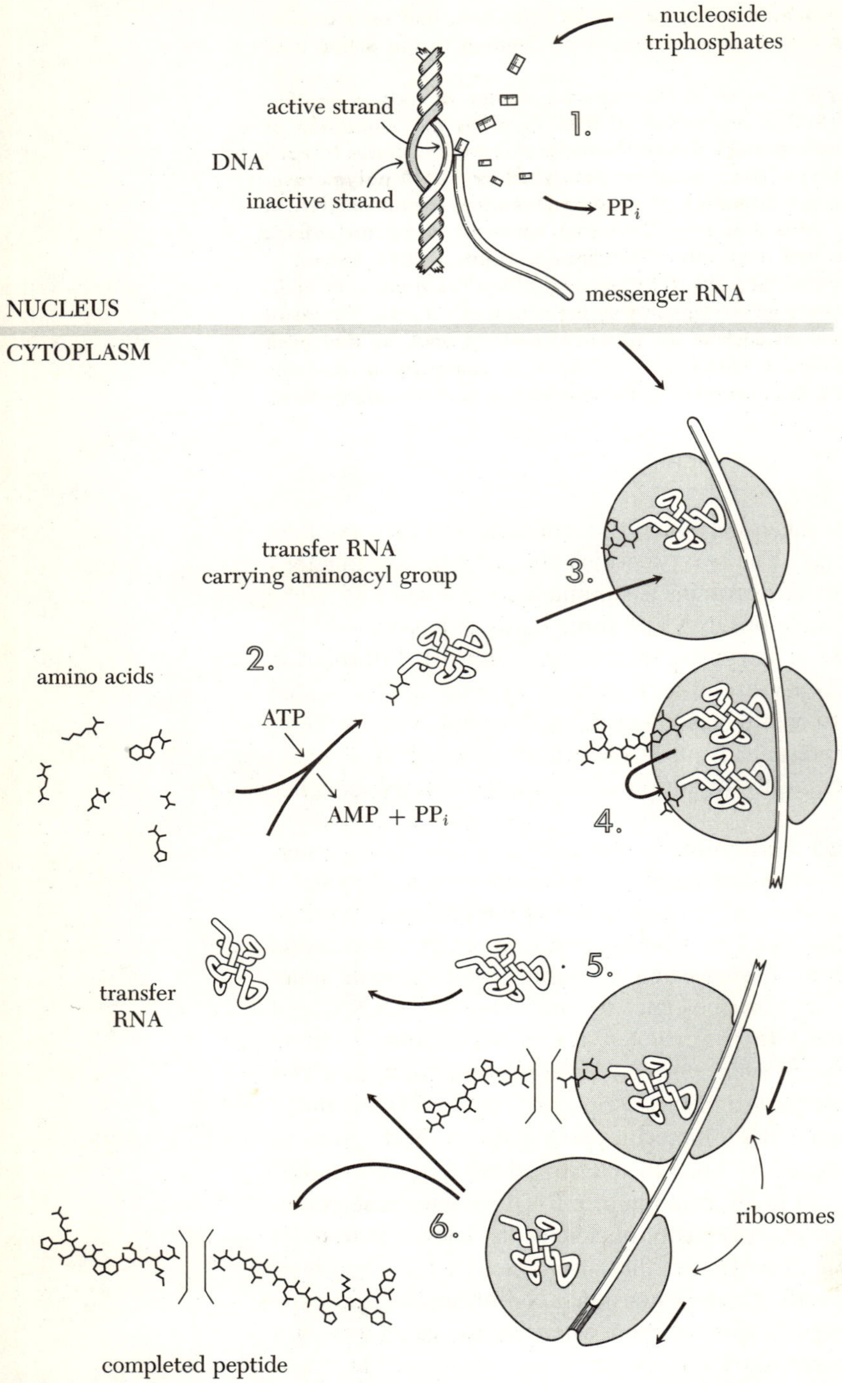

Figure 3-1 Schematic summary of protein synthesis. *Top, step 1.* A molecule of DNA in the nucleus unfolds, and one of its strands is used as a template to direct the formation of messenger RNA from nucleoside triphosphates, which lose inorganic pyrophosphate (PP_i) as they attach to the growing RNA chain. The completed mRNA moves to the cytoplasm (bottom), where it binds ribosomes into a polysome, and acts as a template for protein synthesis.

The following steps are shown on separate ribosomes for clarity, but in fact they are repeated in sequence on each ribosome. The successive ribosomes grow longer and longer peptide chains as they move down the molecule of mRNA.

Step 2. Meanwhile, amino acids are combined with specific molecules of transfer RNA (tRNA) in the cytoplasm by a reaction that also involves the cleavage of adenosine triphosphate (ATP) into adenosine monophosphate (AMP) and PP_i.

Step 3. The tRNA molecules, carrying the amino acids in the form of aminoacyl groups, diffuse to the polysome, where the growing peptide chain is on another molecule of tRNA already attached. The incoming tRNA, which bears the next group required for the growing peptide (in this case a leucyl residue), has the proper configuration to complex with mRNA on the ribosome.

Step 4. When the proper tRNA is in place, the peptide chain is transferred onto the amino group of the new residue brought in by tRNA, so that the chain is now one residue longer.

Step 5. When the transfer of the previous step is completed, the previously bound tRNA no longer carries a peptide chain and is free to dissociate from the ribosome, returning to the mixed pool of tRNA in the soluble cytoplasm, where it is available for transport of another molecule of its specific amino acid. The ribosome now moves along the mRNA molecule to the position where the placement of the next amino acid will be directed.

Step 6. Steps 3, 4, and 5 are repeated. As each amino acid residue adds to the peptide chain, the ribosome moves down the mRNA molecule. When a ribosome has reached the end of the molecule, the peptide is completed and is detached into the soluble cytoplasm. The ribosome itself can then move free of the mRNA and be available for attachment to the beginning of yet another molecular of mRNA (not shown).

not the location of the coding triplet, but at one end of the polynucleotide chain.) The result of all this is the transport, in correct order, of amino acids by tRNA molecules to sites on the ribosome where catalysts cause them to be joined into finished peptide chains. This is the general outline; now let us consider the events in a little more detail.

TRANSCRIPTION

Transcription is the process of constructing ribonucleic acids complementary to the base sequence in a strand of DNA. We have emphasized the construction of messenger RNA, which carries the coding for the formation of peptides, but the DNA also bears information for the construction of all kinds of ribonucleic acids, including those found in ribosomes **(ribosomal RNA, rRNA)** and the different kinds of transfer RNA.

The formation of the ribonucleic acids requires the presence of an enzyme, RNA polymerase, as a catalyst, and the triphosphates of each of the nucleosides to be incorporated into RNA. The mechanism of formation of the ribonucleic acids involves the progressive movement of the polymerase down a strand of DNA. The bases of

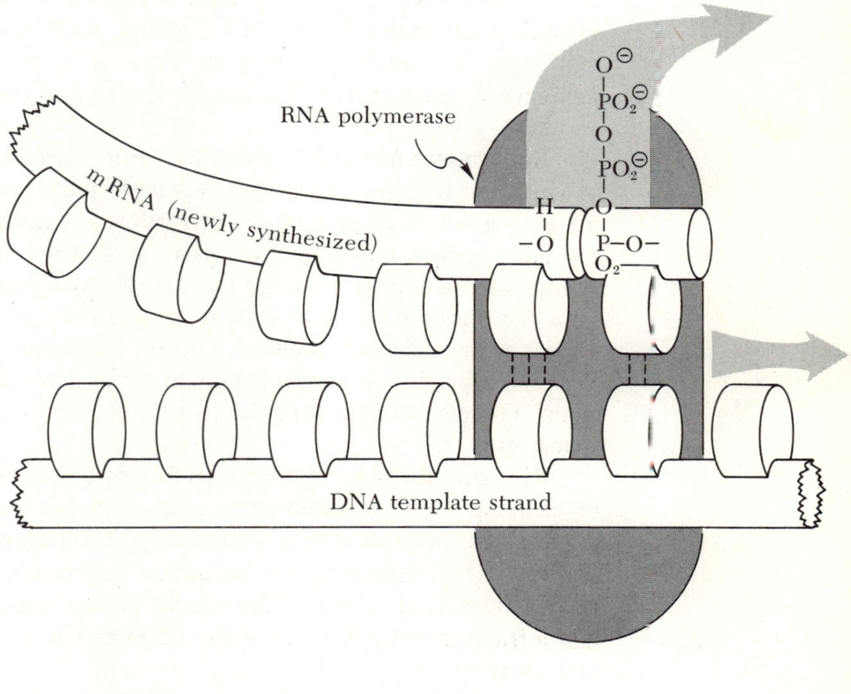

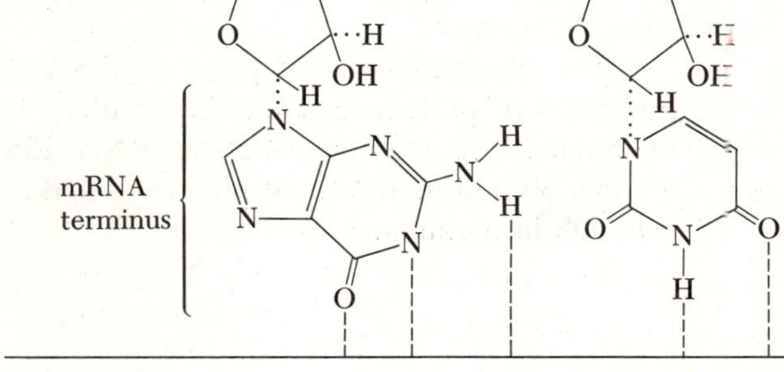

Figure 3-2 Ribonucleic acid chains are built by successive additions of nucleoside phosphate residues obtained from nucleoside triphosphates that contain bases complementary to successive bases on a strand of DNA, which acts as a template. The transfer of the nucleoside phosphate residue to the growing RNA chain liberates inorganic pyrophosphate into solution.

the nucleoside triphosphates in solution form complementary bonds with the bases of the deoxyribonucleoside phosphate residues in the DNA:

adenine in ATP binds with thymine of dT residues in DNA
cytosine in CTP binds with guanine of dG residues in DNA
guanine in GTP binds with cytosine of dC residues in DNA
uracil in UTP binds with adenine of dA residues in DNA.

The binding of complementary bases is the essential part of information transfer, but the actual construction of the ribonucleic acids involves the linkage of the bound nucleotides with the loss of inorganic pyrophosphate (Fig. 3–2).

The RNA polymerase reaction explains how the arrangement of nucleotides in DNA determines the arrangement of nucleotides in the various kinds of RNA, but there are some interesting problems yet remaining. It is not known exactly how the reaction of RNA polymerase is made to begin and end at particular points on the DNA strands. Each molecule of DNA contains the information for many different RNA molecules, so there must be some kind of a spacer arrangement, some particular sequence of nucleotides, that signals the end of one molecule and the beginning of another.

Refinement of RNA Molecules. It may well be that there are only a few points at which transcription of a given DNA molecule is interrupted, and that RNA is initially made as giant molecules, containing information for many different functions, which are later broken down by hydrolysis at selected points into pieces, each of which contains the complete message for, say, a given peptide, or which constitutes a given kind of transfer RNA. It is known, for example, that messenger RNA molecules first appear with nucleotide sequences on the beginning and end of the molecule that are cleaved before the molecule begins to act as a template for the building of a peptide chain. These seemingly superfluous portions of the chain may be the remnants of the spacer groups.

Ribosomal RNA. The process of refinement of the structure of ribonucleic acids by cleaving portions of the chain after synthesis is especially clear in the case of the nucleic acids incorporated into ribosomes. The ribosomes are particles to which mRNA and the tRNA molecules bearing amino acid residues attach while peptide chains are being constructed. The particles consist of two pieces, each of which contains proteins and a fragment of RNA. All of the ribosomes in a cell appear to be alike in structure and composition.

It turns out that the ribosomal RNA is transcribed in a single piece. (There are many portions of DNA containing the information for making rRNA in a single cell, that is, the genes for rRNA are repeated, but each of these portions signals the creation of the same kind of rRNA, barring mutations.) This long precursor molecule consists of three pieces that are incorporated into ribosomes, with spacer sequences between the pieces; these spacer sequences are discarded (Fig. 3–3). In the bacterium *E. coli,* the single transcriptional unit is hydrolyzed to form 16S, 23S, and 5S pieces, and the cleavage of the RNA into these pieces begins before transcription is completed on the DNA. Eukaryotes also make a single transcriptional unit, but it passes intact into the nucleolus of the cell, where it is then broken into 18S, 28S, and 7S pieces, which have the same function as the corresponding pieces in the prokaryotes, although each is somewhat larger.

The intermediate sized piece of rRNA (16S or 18S) is combined with about 20 molecules of protein to make the smaller ribosomal particle (30S in *E. coli,* 40S in mammals). The other two pieces of rRNA (23S + 5S, or 28S + 7S) are combined with another 30-odd molecules of protein to make the larger ribosomal particle (50S in *E. coli,* 60S in mammals).

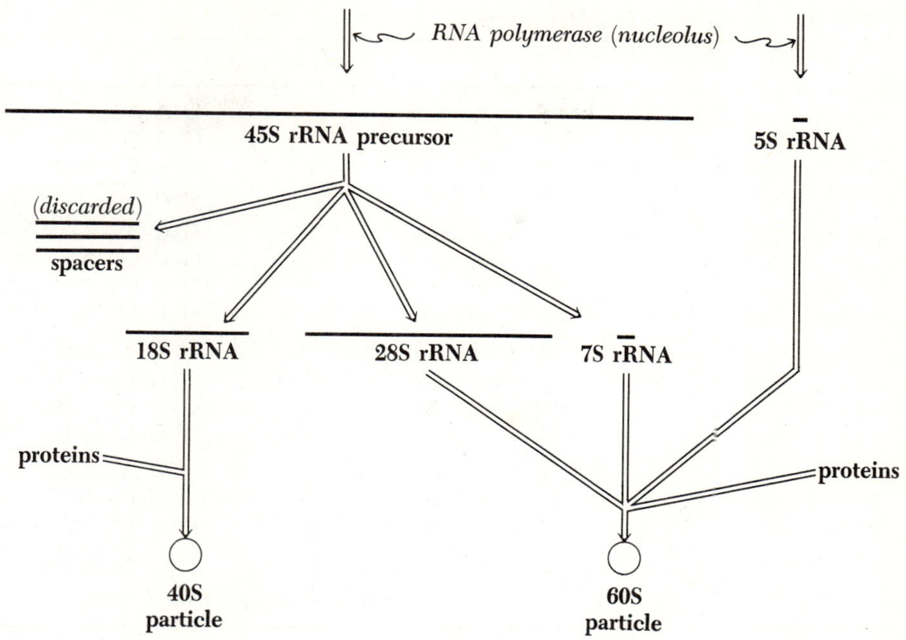

Figure 3-3 Three of the separate molecules of RNA that are used as structural elements in forming ribosomes are synthesized as a single long molecule in which the functional portions are separated by spacer sequences of nucleotides. The spacers are removed by selective hydrolysis of the polynucleotide so as to liberate the three final molecules. One of these, 18S rRNA, reacts with proteins to form the 40S ribosomal particle of eukaryotic cells. The 7S and 28S rRNA molecules react with other proteins and a separately synthesized 5S rRNA ribosomal particle. (The various molecules and particles are somewhat smaller in prokaryotic cells.)

TRANSLATION

Transfer RNA Coding. The amino acids are brought to the site of peptide formation on the ribosome by attachment to molecules of tRNA. These RNA molecules are relatively small, containing about 80 nucleotides, whereas mRNA molecules must contain three nucleotides for each amino acid in the peptide for which they code, and are therefore sometimes thousands of nucleotide residues in length.

There is at least one kind of transfer RNA specific for each of the 20 amino acids, but more than one kind of tRNA is sometimes used for a particular amino acid. The reason for this has to do with the nature of the coding dictionary. There are 64 different ways in which the four bases can be arranged in triplets, but only 20 amino acids. Each of the 64 different triplets possible in messenger RNA is used to convey information, as is summarized in Table 3–1. Three of the 64 combinations are apparently used for punctuation; they signal the end of a peptide chain whenever they occur. Each of the other 61 combinations in mRNA is a signal for the insertion of a particular amino acid, and no other. It is evident, as we can see from the table, that some amino acids are coded by more than one triplet. (The code is said to be degenerate, because there is not a one-to-one correlation in translation, but this is not to be taken as an indication of genetic sloppiness. The meaning of the code is precise, even though redundant.)

For each of the 61 possible codons in mRNA designating an amino acid, there must be a kind of tRNA molecule containing an anticodon that will bind to the codon. This does not mean that there are 61 separate kinds of tRNA, because it so happens that exact complements in tRNA are required only for the first two nucleosides of a triplet in mRNA. With certain of the bases, there is sufficient permissible wobble in the third position to permit binding with more than one kind of anticodon nucleoside. For example, a molecule of tRNA with an anticodon beginning with G will bind codons ending in either U or C, if the other two positions of the triplet are exact complements (remember that the first position of an anticodon matches the third position of a codon,

TABLE 3-1 MESSENGER RNA CODONS

Listed by Codon

A-A-A—Lys	C-A-A—Gln	G-A-A—Glu	U-A-A—Term*
A-A-G—Lys	C-A-G—Gln	G-A-G—Glu	U-A-G—Term*
A-A-C—Asn	C-A-C—His	G-A-C—Asp	U-A-C—Tyr
A-A-U—Asn	C-A-U—His	G-A-U—Asp	U-A-U—Tyr
A-C-A—Thr	C-C-A—Pro	G-C-A—Ala	U-C-A—Ser
A-C-G—Thr	C-C-G—Pro	G-C-G—Ala	U-C-G—Ser
A-C-C—Thr	C-C-C—Pro	G-C-C—Ala	U-C-C—Ser
A-C-U—Thr	C-C-U—Pro	G-C-U—Ala	U-C-U—Ser
A-G-A—Arg	C-G-A—Arg	G-G-A—Gly	U-G-A—Term*
A-G-G—Arg	C-G-G—Arg	G-G-G—Gly	U-G-G—Trp
A-G-C—Ser	C-G-C—Arg	G-G-C—Gly	U-G-C—Cys
A-G-U—Ser	C-G-U—Arg	G-G-U—Gly	U-G-U—Cys
A-U-A—Ile	C-U-A—Leu	G-U-A—Val	U-U-A—Leu
A-U-G—Met	C-U-G—Leu	G-U-G—Val	U-U-G—Leu
A-U-C—Ile	C-U-C—Leu	G-U-C—Val	U-U-C—Phe
A-U-U—Ile	C-U-U—Leu	G-U-U—Val	U-U-U—Phe

Listed by Amino Acid

Ala—G-C-A	Gly—G-G-A	Leu—C-U-A	Thr—A-C-A
G-C-G	G-G-G	C-U-G	A-C-G
G-C-C	G-G-C	C-U-C	A-C-C
G-C-U	G-G-U	C-U-U	A-C-U
Arg—A-G-A	Gln—C-A-A	U-U-A	Trp—U-G-G
A-G-G	C-A-G	U-U-G	Tyr—U-A-C
C-G-A	Glu—G-A-A	Met—A-U-G	U-A-U
C-G-G	G-A-G	Phe—U-U-C	Val—G-U-A
C-G-C	His—C-A-C	U-U-U	G-U-G
C-G-U	C-A-U	Pro—C-C-A	G-U-C
Asp—G-A-C	Ile—A-U-C	C-C-G	G-U-U
G-A-U	A-U-U	C-C-C	Term*—U-A-A
Asn—A-A-C	A-U-A	C-C-U	U-A-G
A-A-U	Lys—A-A-A	Ser—A-G-C	U-G-A
Cys—U-G-C	A-A-G	A-G-U	
U-G-U		U-C-A	
		U-C-G	
		U-C-C	
		U-C-U	

*Term are terminator codons.
Note that amino acids within a block of codons, or in the corresponding position in the same row or column of blocks, are interchangeable by substitution of one nucleotide.

and vice versa). This means that such a molecule of tRNA will carry the appropriate amino acid when either of two codons appears on mRNA. Since all codons differing only in C or U in the terminal positions represent the same amino acid, there are a number of instances in which one kind of tRNA will do the job.

To take a different example, anticodons beginning with C will form complements only with codons ending with G, so every triplet with such a codon must have a kind of tRNA that binds specifically with it.

Special features of tRNA. Transfer RNA molecules differ from those of mRNA in that only one triplet is used in the transfer of genetic information; the other parts

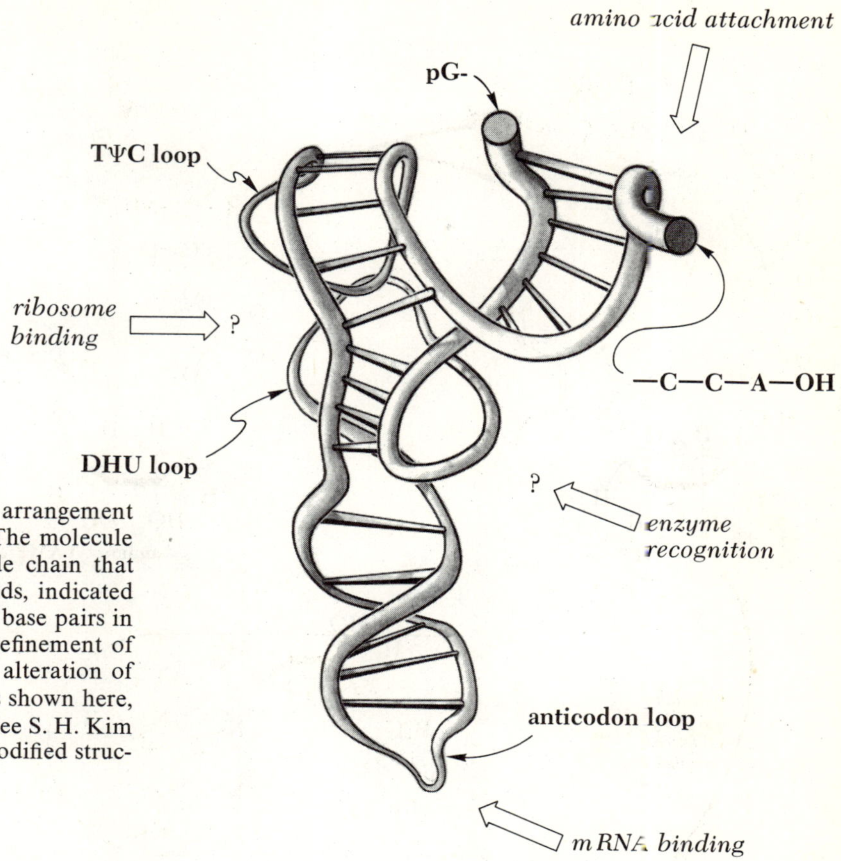

Figure 3-4 The three-dimensional arrangement of a transfer RNA (tRNA) molecule. The molecule is composed of a single polynucleotide chain that is folded back upon itself to form bonds, indicated by cross-bars, between complementary base pairs in different portions of the chain. Later refinement of the structural analysis has led to some alteration of the positions of the bonds from what is shown here, but the principal features are correct. (See S. H. Kim et al., Science, 185:435 (1974) for the modified structure.)

of the molecule are used to form bonds with ribosomes or with enzymes responsible for attaching the specific amino acid to be transported. The result is that the molecules must be folded into a specific three-dimensional conformation, creating a pattern of substituent groups that can be "recognized" for each of these separate functions. The specific conformation is created through some complementary sequences within the single nucleotide chains of tRNA (Fig. 3-4). Now, when a single chain contains a sequence of complementary bases, the chain will tend to fold upon itself to permit these bases to bond with each other, and this is what happens to tRNA. The molecules fold into a compact form with the anticodon, which occurs near the center of the chain, exposed for binding on one face, and with the tail of the molecule exposed for attachment of the amino acids. This tail is the same in all kinds of tRNA because it always has the same function.

Various kinds of tRNA appear to have similar shapes, but they also differ in an important way. Part of the exposed face is used to bind a specific enzyme that is responsible for the attachment of a particular amino acid. We see that there are some critical recognition problems here that must be resolved smoothly if the genetic information is to be translated accurately into peptide sequences. Each molecule of tRNA must have two distinctive areas of nucleotide sequence used to form specific bonds. One of these areas includes the anticodon that binds specific codons on mRNA. The other area forms bonds with an enzyme that catalyzes the association of one kind of amino acid with the particular tRNA. On the other hand, the tails of all tRNA molecules have the same —C—C—A terminus for attachment of the aminoacyl group (Fig. 3-5),

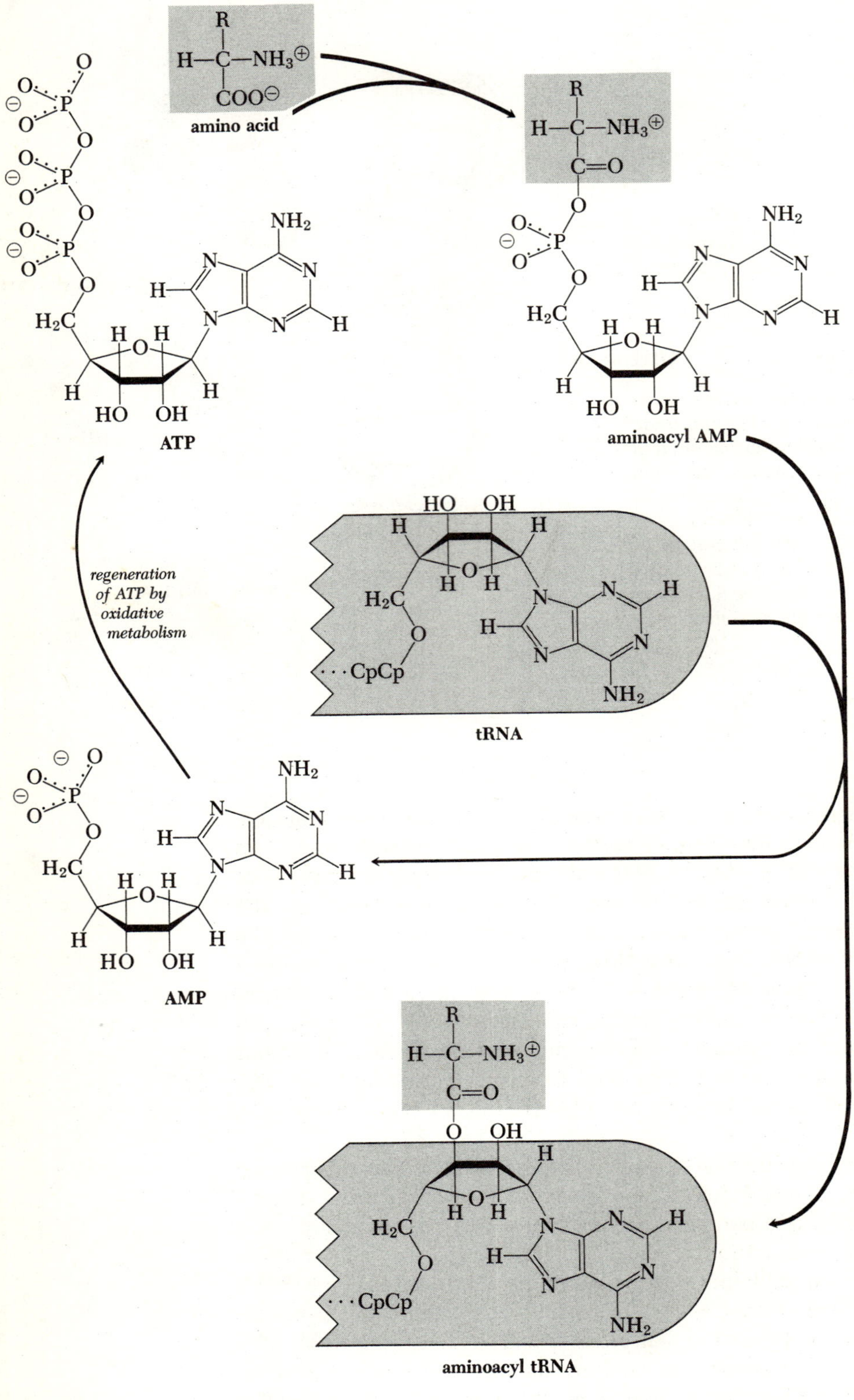

Figure 3–5 The formation of an aminoacyl tRNA involves a reaction between the proper amino acid and adenosine triphosphate (*top*), releasing PP_i and forming the aminoacyl adenosine monophosphate, which is a mixed anhydride of carboxylic and phosphoric acids. The aminoacyl group is then transferred to the terminal ribosyl moiety of the corresponding tRNA (*lower right*). The group is shown on the 3′ oxygen (*bottom center*), but there is in fact an equilibration between the 2′ and 3′ positions. The AMP that is released (*center left*) is phosphorylated by the processes of oxidative metabolism, generating the original ATP.

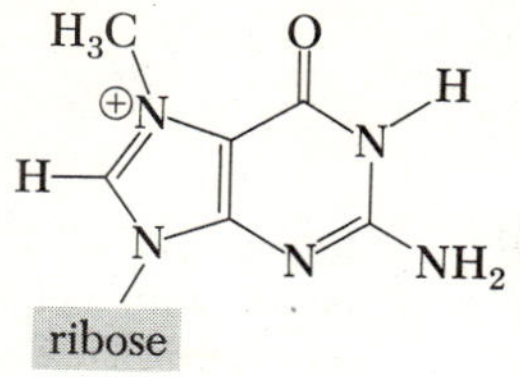

7MG
7-methylguanosine

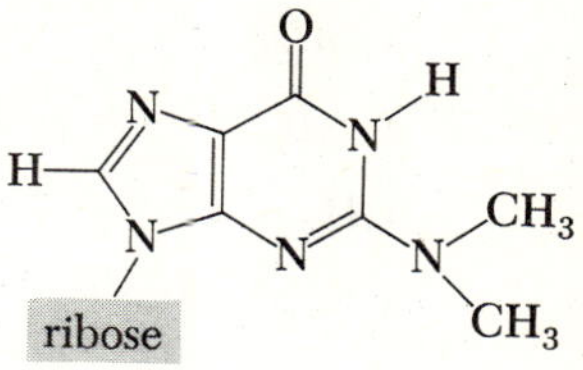

DMG
N^2-dimethylguanosine

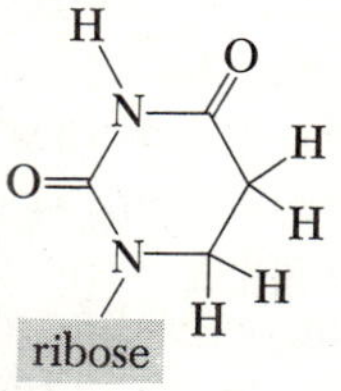

DHU
5,6-dihydrouridine

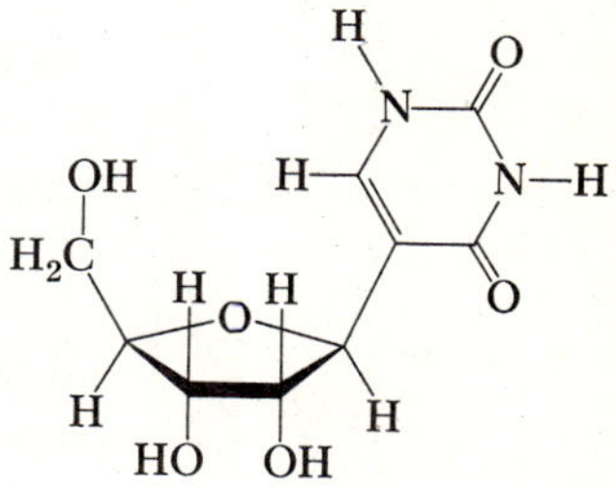

Ψ
pseudouridine

Figure 3–6 A few of the modified bases occurring in tRNA.

because this location must be "recognized" on every kind of tRNA by one enzyme that makes a peptide from the attached group.

Similarly, the enzyme catalyzing the attachment of an amino acid to a particular kind of tRNA must have two binding sites, one for associating with the recognition sites on the tRNA and the other for binding a particular amino acid and catalyzing its attachment to the tRNA. It is specific attachment between enzyme and tRNA that provides the necessary correlation between codon-anticodon bonding, which occurs separately, and the trapping of the intended amino acid from the mixture in solution in the cell.

Modified Bases. The development of the specific binding sites in tRNA requires chemical modification of some of the bases in the molecule. It is not necessary for our purposes to recite all of the known examples. They include such changes as the addition of methyl groups to guanine rings, the reduction of uracil rings, and the rearrangement of uridine (Fig. 3–6). The changes occur after the fundamental base sequence is transcribed from DNA, and this sequence carries in itself the determinants of which bases will be modified, so the late modifications do not violate our principle that the character of all of the nucleic acids is determined by the sequence in DNA.

MECHANISM OF TRANSLATION

Chain Initiation. Let us now outline the major events in translation. Suppose that a particular molecule of messenger RNA contains the information for the construction of a peptide beginning with the sequence Val-Leu-Ser. . . . The first requirement for proper translation is identification of the starting point, and this is accomplished by beginning the coding of all peptides with the triplet A-U-G-. This is a codon for methionine, but it also acts as an initiating codon. When it occurs at the beginning of the coding for a peptide, it serves as a specific point of attachment for the small ribosomal particle (30S or 40S), and for special **initiator tRNA** molecules, which carry

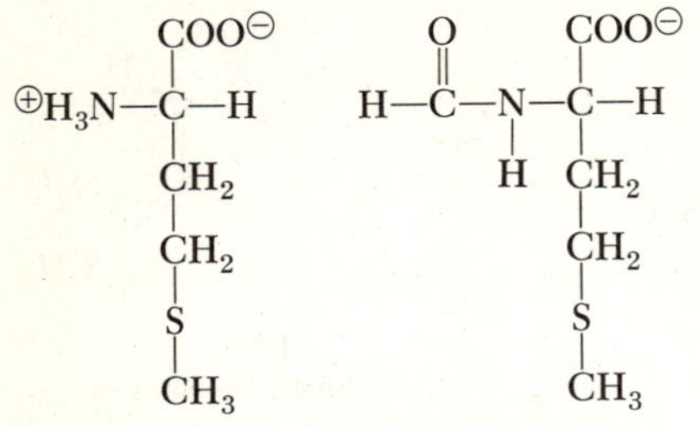

L-methionine N-formyl-L-methionine

Figure 3–7 The specification of amino acid sequence in mRNA always begins with a codon for methionine. Initiation of peptide synthesis begins by attachment of a special initiator tRNA that carries methionine in eukaryotes and N-formylmethionine in prokaryotes.

methionine in eukaryotes, or the N-formyl derivative of methionine in prokaryotes (Fig. 3–7). No matter what the intended final peptide sequence may be, its formation begins with the attachment of a methionyl residue, either as it is, or as the N-formyl derivative. Here, then, is how it begins (Fig. 3–8).

Step 1. A complex forms between a special **initiator protein,** an initiator tRNA carrying a methionyl residue, and a molecule of guanosine triphosphate (GTP). The complex then binds to the initial methionine codon (A-U-G) on a molecule of mRNA attached to a small ribosomal particle.

Step 2. A complete ribosome is then formed by association of a large particle. The formation of the complete ribosome places the initiator tRNA with its attached methionyl residue on a peptide binding site. (This, and the following diagrams, illustrate principles; they are not drawings of actual molecules.)

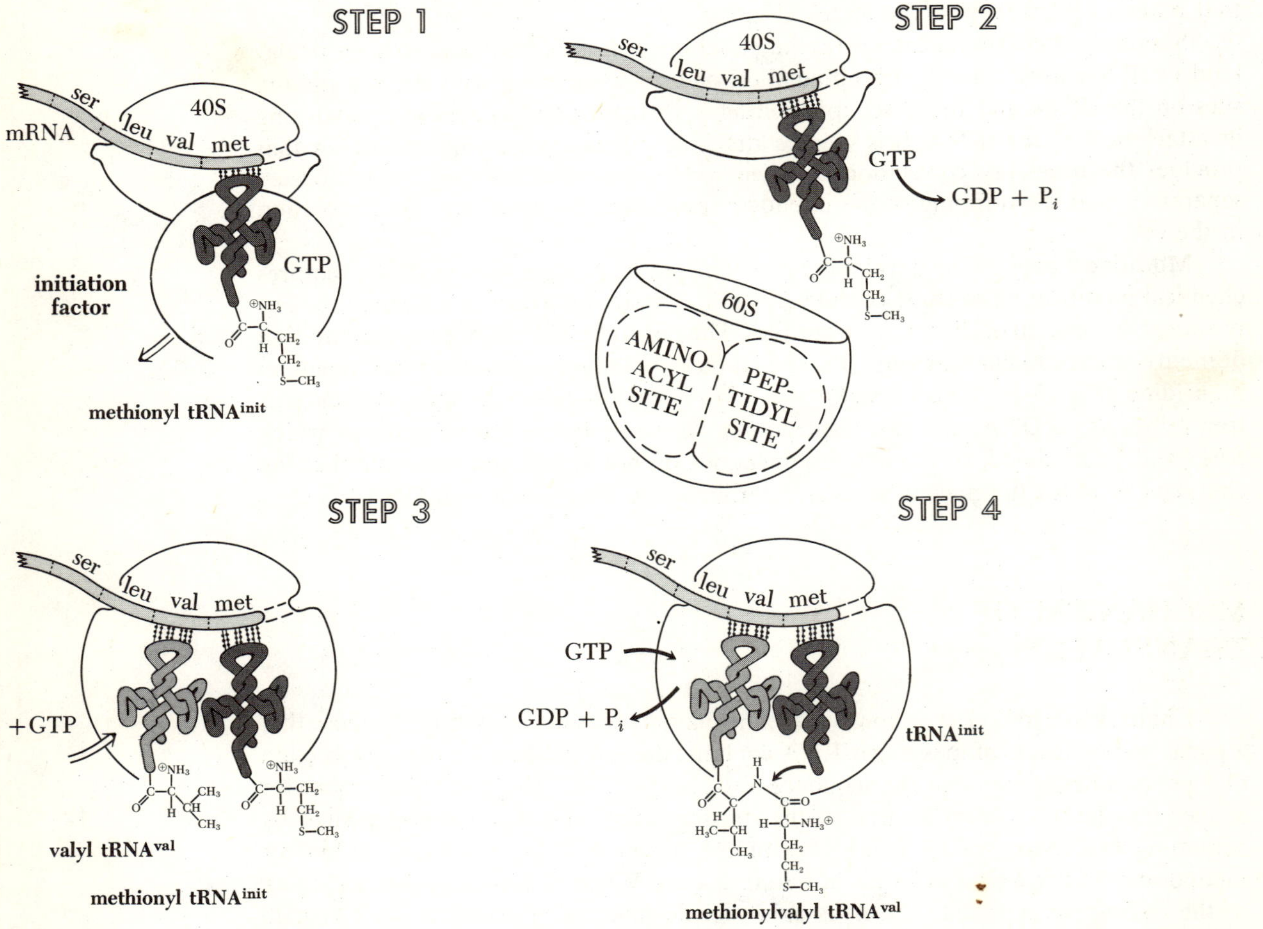

Figure 3–8 Steps in protein synthesis. *Illustration continued on opposite page.*

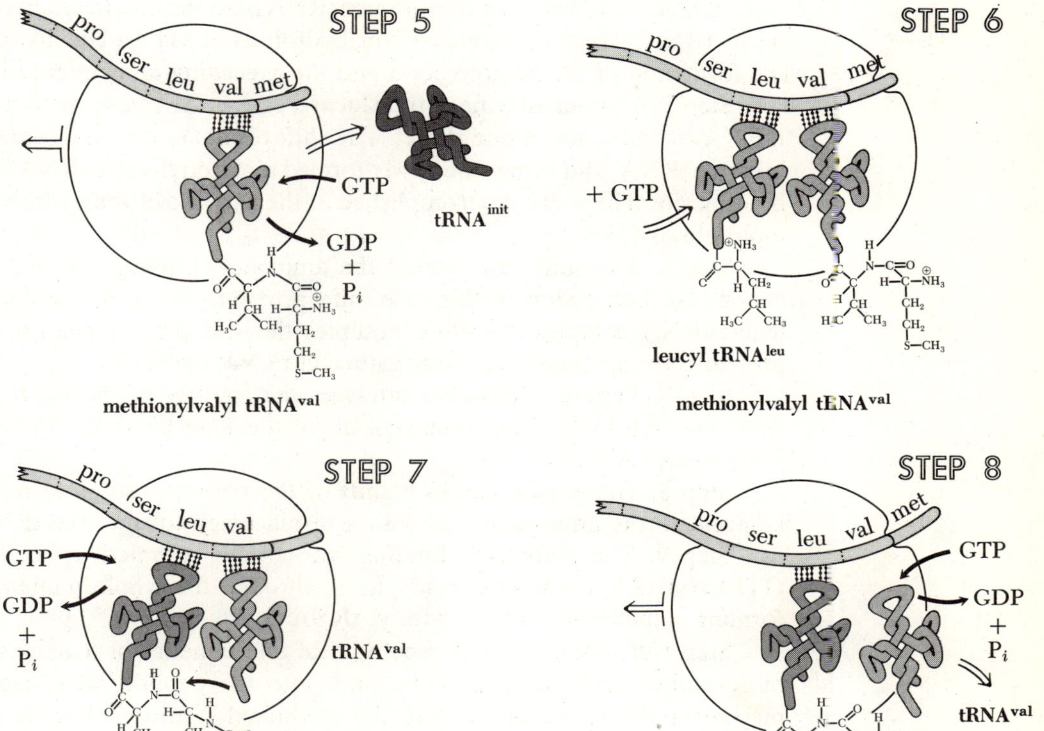

Figure 3-8 *(Continued)*

Step 3. An adjacent aminoacyl-binding site is now filled by a valyl-specific tRNA which binds to the valyl codon on mRNA. The attachment involves a complex of tRNA and GTP with a specific **elongation protein** (not shown).

Step 4. An enzyme, **peptide synthetase,** in the ribosome catalyzes the transfer of the methionyl residue from the initiator tRNA onto the amino group of the valyl residue on its tRNA. There is a concomitant hydrolysis of GTP. (This hydrolysis drives both the formation of the peptide bond and the preceding attachment of the valyl tRNA.)

Step 5. Another enzyme, a **translocase,** causes the ribosome to shift on its attached mRNA by the space of one triplet. The shift results in the dissociation of the now-free initiator tRNA, and brings the newly formed methionyl-valyl-$tRNA^{Val}$ onto the peptide binding site. The move is accomplished at the expense of the hydrolysis of still another molecule of GTP.

Step 6. The shift has vacated the aminoacyl binding site and brought the next codon, the Leu codon in this case, into proximity to it. An elongation factor-GTP-leucyl-tRNA complex therefore occupies the site. The elongation factor is another protein forming complexes with aminacyl tRNA molecules.

Step 7. Peptide synthetase catalyzes the transfer of the methionylvalyl residues from the $tRNA^{Val}$ to the amino group of the leucyl residue, thereby creating Met-Val-Leu-$tRNA^{Leu}$.

Step 8. Translocase causes a shift of the ribosome so as to bring the Ser codon adjacent to the aminoacyl site, with a displacement of the free $tRNA^{Val}$.

Step 9. The aminoacyl binding site is now occupied by an elongation factor-GTP-seryl tRNA complex, ready to go through the whole sequence of steps again, forming a methionylvalylleucylseryl-$tRNA^{Ser}$.

Step 10ff (not shown). A repetition of the sequence of reactions causes more and more amino acids residues to be built into the peptide, as coded by the attached messenger RNA. At some point, the methionyl residue is lost by hydrolysis, so the constant use of a special initiating methionyl codon does not require that all finished peptides begin with methionine. Finally, the ribosome encounters one of the terminating codons, which trips the action of a protein catalyzing the hydrolysis of the finished peptide from its attached tRNA, releasing it into solution to carry out its biological function.

REPLICATION OF DNA

New molecules of DNA are created to enable cell division. Cells undergo a cycle of growth (Fig. 3–9) that begins with the synthesis of new cell constituents, especially DNA and the associated histones (S-phase), followed by assembly of the previously existing and newly synthesized DNA into chromosomes and the formation of the mitotic apparatus (G_2-phase). Mitosis and cell division (M or D phase) then occurs, creating two cells where one existed. The new cells then go through a period of expression of phenotype—they do their thing, as it were. This G_1 phase is absent in many bacteria, which are either in a quiescent state (G_0) in the absence of essential nutrients, or are actively dividing, but the interphase is the predominant phase in eukaryotic cells.

The formation of new DNA proceeds so as to give both daughter cells the same information found in the parent cell. We saw that DNA ordinarily is a double helix formed between complementary strands. The process of replication involves nothing more than the separation of these strands and the synthesis of a new complement to each. Suppose we say that in one segment of the original pair there is an active strand, from which RNA molecules are transcribed, and a complementary strand. When these are separated, and new strands are made by joining complementary bases next to each

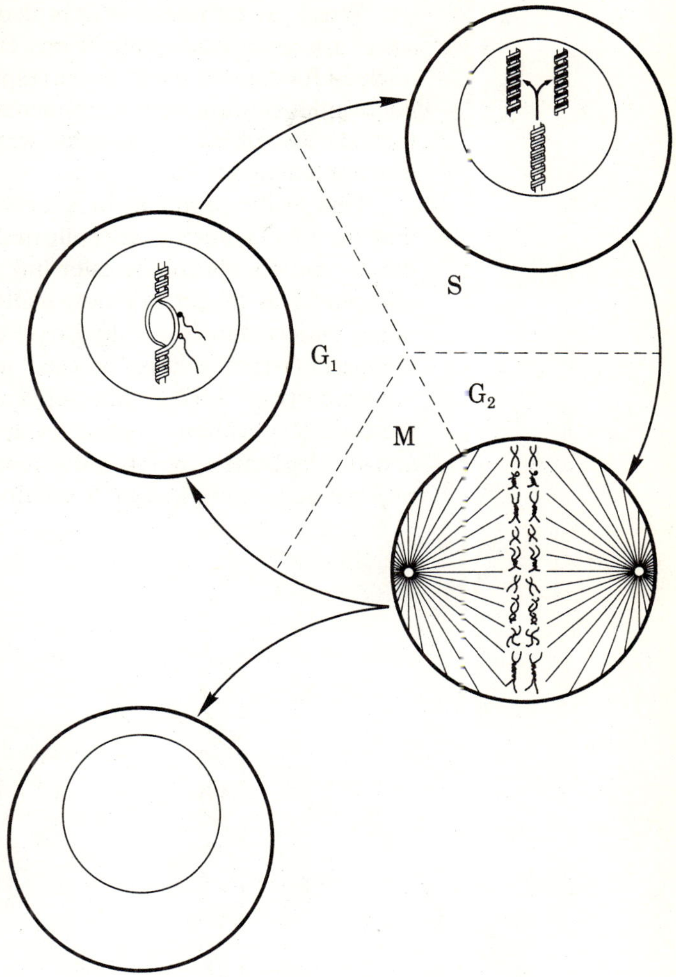

Figure 3-9 Cells undergo a cycle of growth beginning with mitosis in which new cells are formed (M-phase). The new cells synthesize proteins as required to grow and carry out their functions (G_1 phase), until they prepare for another division by beginning DNA replication (S-phase). Another growth phase (G_2) creates the proteins and RNA necessary for the following mitosis (M) that splits the cell into two daughter cells.

of the parent strands, what will we have? The original active strand will be associated with a new complementary strand. However, the original complementary strand will now be associated with a new strand made of complements to its bases. That is, there will now be a new active strand associated with the old complementary strand (Fig. 3-10). In sum, two new molecules of DNA have been made, each containing one of the original parent strands and one newly synthesized strand.

Mechanism of Replication. The actual mechanism for making new molecules of DNA is still in dispute. It apparently begins with a separation of the two strands of DNA that are to be replicated. This may be visualized for eukaryotic cells, which have long linear DNA molecules that may be untwisted, but prokaryotic cells often have molecules of DNA closed into a circle after the insertion of additional twists to create supercoiling (Fig. 3-11). Such molecules must be "nicked," that is, the chain must be cleaved by hydrolysis, at one or more points before the strands can be separated. Replication proceeds in both directions from the points of strand separation.

Once strand separation is achieved, the initial step apparently involves the formation of short pieces of RNA containing 50 to 100 nucleotides complementary to the DNA sequence, beginning at fixed replication points of uncharacterized structure. This step may be a specialized version of ordinary transcription by RNA polymerase. In any event, ribonucleotides are initially required for the formation of polymers of deoxyribonucleotides!

When the formation of complementary chains is well underway, a DNA polymerase comes into action and begins extending the chain by the addition of deoxyribonucleotides derived from the corresponding deoxynucleoside triphosphates. The added nucleotides contain bases complementary to the bases of the DNA chains upon which they are assembled, in the same way that transcription of RNA involves the bonding of complementary bases.

One of the problems in understanding the replication of DNA concerns the fact that the two chains being replicated are joined in opposite directions with respect to the 3′- and 5′- phosphate ester linkages. Since replication using the nucleoside 5′-triphosphates as precursors most likely involves the addition of the nucleoside 5′-phosphate moiety onto the 3′-hydroxyl end of a growing chain, the replication of one of the parent strands must proceed toward the fork at which the parent strands are untwisted (Fig. 3–12), while replication of the other strand can proceed away from the fork. Replication proceeds at approximately 1 nm per minute in most organisms, and the replication points are a few tens of micrometers apart, so replication usually requires something less than a half-hour.

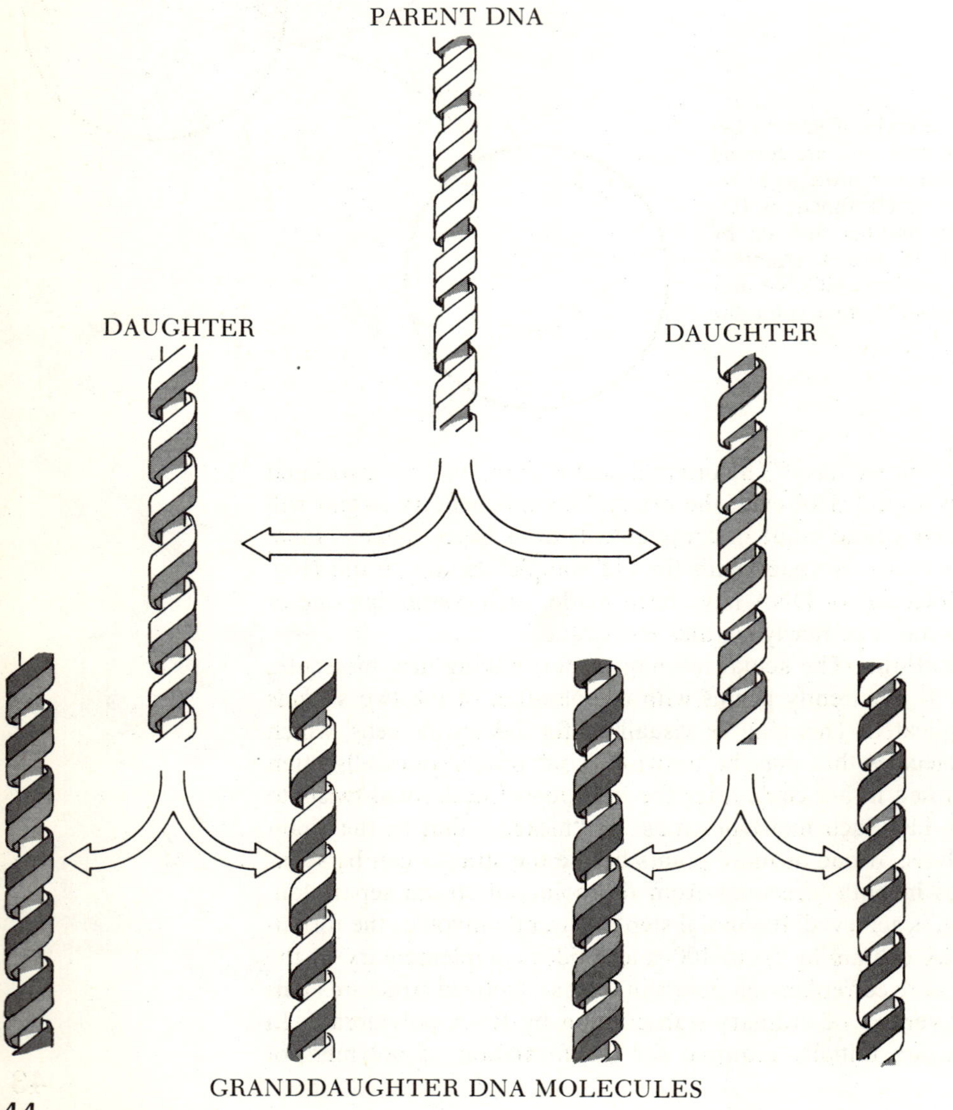

Figure 3–10 Replication of DNA proceeds by a semi-conservative mechanism in which a new complementary strand is synthesized to match each parent strand. The daughter DNA molecules in each generation therefore contain one parent strand and one new strand.

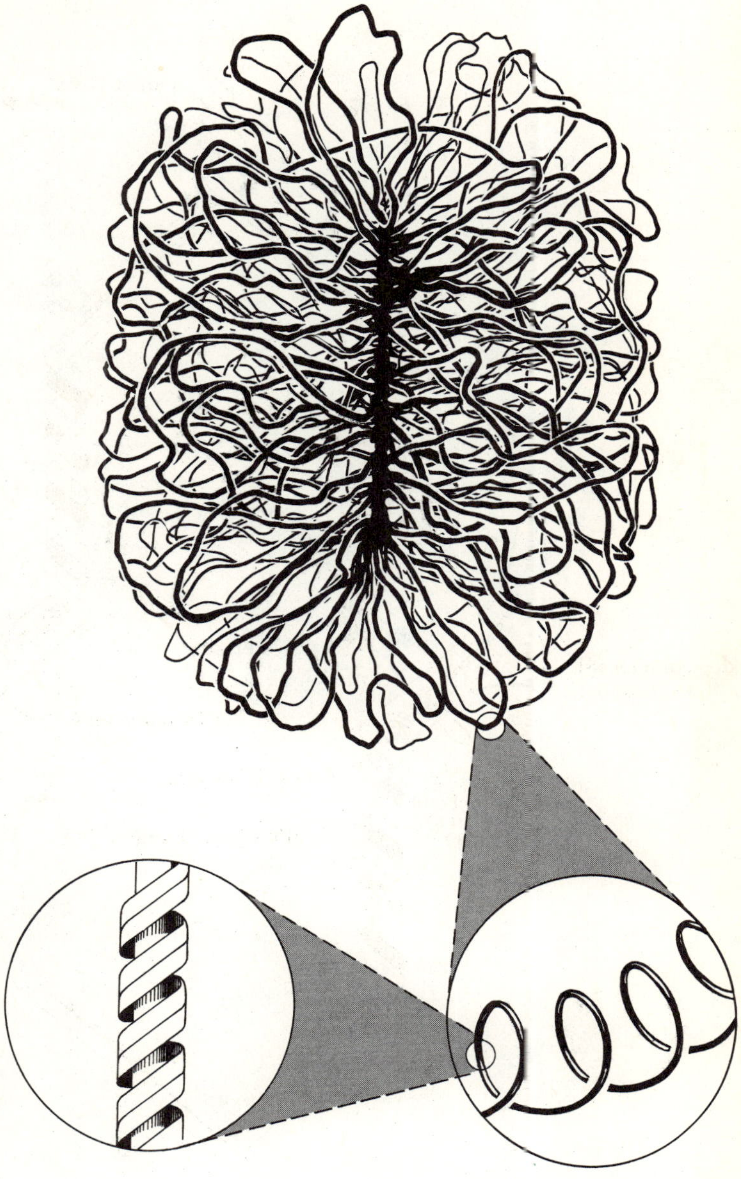

Figure 3–11 Possible structure of the *E. coli* chromosome. The DNA is a single circular molecule that is pinned in some 50 tangled loops to a central core, giving a relatively compact form. The DNA strands are twisted into supercoils (*lower right*), and the strand itself is the familiar double helix (*lower left*).

At some point in the process, the segments of RNA that join the newly formed pieces of DNA are removed by hydrolysis, leaving unconnected segments of DNA (these are known as Okazaki pieces, after a principal discoverer). These segments contain between several hundred and a few thousand nucleotides, so they are not small except in comparison to a complete DNA molecule, which is millimeters in length in prokaryotes, and centimeters in length in eukaryotes. (The molecules are too thin and folded upon themselves to be visible. Chromosomes are composed of one or more double strands of DNA that run the full length of each chromosomal segment, along with several protein components.)

The Okazaki pieces are then joined, first by the action of an additional DNA polymerase that fills in the gaps with complementary deoxynucleotides, and second by the action of a ligase that closes the final gap in the chain. The polymerase involved here was formerly believed to be the enzyme mainly responsible for replication, but

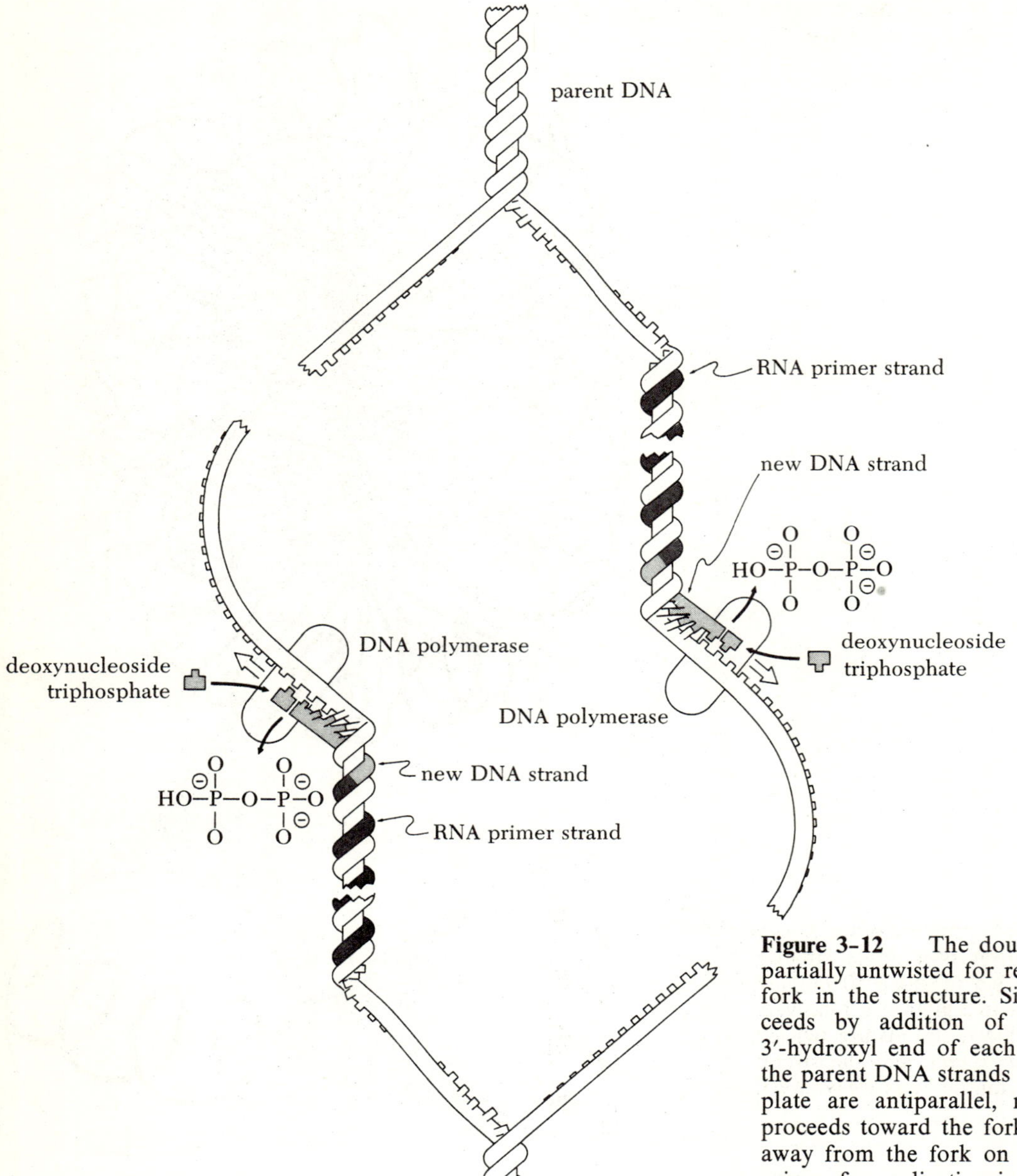

Figure 3–12 The double helix of DNA is partially untwisted for replication, creating a fork in the structure. Since replication proceeds by addition of nucleotides to the 3′-hydroxyl end of each growing chain, and the parent DNA strands being used as a template are antiparallel, new chain synthesis proceeds toward the fork on one strand and away from the fork on the other. An RNA primer for replication is first made from nucleoside triphosphates complementary to the DNA sequence, followed by a shift to the use of deoxynucleoside triphosphates to create new DNA. The RNA sequence at the beginning of the chain is later removed, and the gaps between the DNA segments are closed by further addition of deoxynucleotides (not shown).

most people now think that it is primarily concerned with finishing short gaps in the DNA chain, such as those that occur between Okazaki pieces, and also gaps created by the repair of damaged portions of DNA. Repair involves hydrolysis of neighboring nucleotides to remove the damage, and resynthesis of the affected part of the chain.

Modification of Completed DNA. There is minor modification of some of the bases in completed DNA, mostly involving the addition of methyl groups to form bases such as 5-methylcytosine. Such modifications have been shown to be a protective mechanism in some prokaryotes through the creation of distinctive recognition sites at particular portions of the chain. The organisms contain hydrolytic enzymes that attack DNA molecules not containing the distinctive bases at particular points, and this is a means of removing foreign molecules of DNA that get into the cell and would otherwise be replicated along with the previously existing DNA.

FURTHER READING

O. L. Miller, Jr., The visualization of genes in action, Sci. Amer., 228:34 (March, 1973). Superb electron micrographs showing transcription and translation actually underway. Not to be missed.

S. H. Kim, G. J. Quigley, F. L. Suddath, et al., Three-dimensional structure of yeast phenylalanine transfer RNA: Folding of the polynucleotide chain, Science, 179:285(1973). An account of important current work.

See also references at end of Chapter 2.

QUESTIONS

1. The anticodon in a particular tRNA specific for tyrosine is G-U-A, read from the 5′ end. What would be the corresponding codon in mRNA, the corresponding sequence in the template strand of DNA, and in the other strand of DNA, all read from the 5′ end?
2. One of the peptide chains in adult human hemoglobin begins with the amino acid sequence Val-Leu-Ser. Why does the formation of this peptide begin by transferring a methionyl group?
3. Since every possible triplet of bases in mRNA may be used to code for an amino acid or for termination of a peptide chain, does every triplet of bases throughout the length of DNA designate an amino acid to be incorporated into a peptide? Explain.
4. Why is it commonly true that bacterial DNA can't be replicated until one of the strands has been nicked (cleaved by hydrolysis), whereas it may be true that eukaryotic DNA can be replicated without nicking a strand?
5. Why does replication proceed in opposite directions on the two strands of DNA?
6. In what kind of nucleic acids does pseudouridine appear?
7. How does specific association of a particular amino acid with a particular codon in mRNA occur?

CHAPTER 4

MODIFYING PEPTIDE CHAINS

THE CONCEPTS

Some proteins are made of peptide chains that undergo covalent alterations after the formation of the primary structure. These alterations include modification of the amino acid side chains and removal of portions of the original peptide chains by hydrolysis. The alterations are accomplished by enzymes that respond only to particular sequences of amino acids, so even the alterations are the result of the primary structure that is determined by the genetic information contained in DNA.

Disulfide Bonds. Cysteine is an amino acid with a sulfhydryl (thiol) group in its side chain. Segments of peptide chain can be held in proximity by oxidizing a pair of sulfhydryl groups to form a disulfide bridge. These bridges frequently form at random among all available cysteine residues, but they rapidly equilibrate by cleavage and reconstruction to yield the most stable protein structure.

Insulin. A combination of disulfide formation and chain refinement by hydrolysis creates the hormone insulin. Insulin is originally made as a single chain that is fixed in a particular shape through the formation of disulfide bridges. It is then possible to remove a central portion of the peptide chain by hydrolysis without serious disruption of the conformation, thereby creating biological activity. The effect of the discarded spacer segment is to hold the two active segments together until they are linked by disulfide bridges, thereby creating a structure not attainable by spontaneous association of the active segments.

Collagen. Rigid, insoluble fibers of collagen are important components of many kinds of connective tissue in animals. The fibers are made by association of rod-like molecules of tropocollagen, which are long tight coils of three peptide chains. Tropocollagen assumes that shape because much of its length contains glycine as every third amino acid residue. Glycine has no side chain to impede tight packing, and the favored conformation is a triple helix that brings glycyl residues from the three chains into contact. The formation of the triple helix is favored by initial association of the peptide chains owing to amino acid sequences near one end. These sequences are discarded by hydrolysis after the triple helix forms.

Oxidation of Collagen. The conversion of tropocollagen to collagen fibers involves the formation of covalent cross-links between the tropocollagen rods. These cross-links are made by oxidizing lysyl side chains to aldehydes, which then condense, either with similar aldehydes or with unmodified lysyl side chains on adjacent molecules, to form covalent bonds.

Residues of proline and of lysine are also oxidized in collagen to form substituent hydroxyl groups. The resultant hydroxylysine residues are a point of attachment for carbohydrate groups, but the function of the abundant residues of hydroxyproline, which are characteristic of collagen, is not known.

Fibrin. Fibrin is a protein that forms an insoluble lattice during the clotting of blood, and the creation of fibrin involves both the partial hydrolysis of precursor fibrinogen and the formation of cross-links. Hydrolysis removes a negatively charged segment of peptide that prevents association of protein molecules. When association does occur, it is reinforced by the creation of cross-links involving the substitution of a side chain amino group on one molecule for the amide nitrogen in a glutamine residue on another molecule. The result is an amide bond linking molecules.

Phosphoproteins. Some proteins are modified by attaching phosphate ester groups to side chains of serine or threonine residues in peptides. Phosphorylation is often used as a device for regulating the biological activity of proteins through the resultant changes in conformation, but phosphoproteins are also useful as sources of nutrition. Birds secrete a phosphoprotein,

vitellin, in the yolk of eggs, and mammals secrete casein, another phosphoprotein, in their milk. In addition to supplying amino acids and phosphate, casein also binds calcium ion for transport from the mother to the infant *via* milk.

The synthesis of proteins is not always completed by formation of the primary structure through translation of messenger RNA, even though the amino acid sequence contains all of the information needed to determine the character of the final molecule. Many proteins are composed of peptides that have been modified, sometimes by reactions changing the covalent nature of the amino acid residues in the chains, and other times by removing portions of the chains through hydrolysis. We shall examine in this chapter several proteins that illustrate various ways in which these modifications are made. Let us begin by considering the formation of a hormone, insulin, which involves both covalent modification of amino acid residues and refinement of the peptide structure by hydrolysis.

SYNTHESIS OF INSULIN

The pancreas of higher animals contains cells with the primary function of synthesizing insulin. Insulin is a peptide that promotes the utilization of glucose by skeletal muscles and other tissues. This and other functions will be discussed at later points; we are now interested in the synthesis of the hormone because it illustrates two important ways in which the original sequence of amino acids translated from a messenger RNA molecule can be altered to create biological activity.

Creation of Disulfide Bridges. Insulin is first made in the form of a single peptide chain, known as **proinsulin.** The number of amino acid residues in proinsulin varies from one animal to another, but it ranges between 80 and 90 in the known examples. The peptide contains six residues of cysteine, which is the amino acid with a sulfhydryl group in its side chain. The sulfhydryl group has a special function in fixing the spatial arrangement of peptide chains because two of these groups can be oxidized to create a disulfide bridge (Fig. 4-1). Since the disulfide linkage is a covalent bond, it can be used to hold two segments of peptide chain in a fixed conformation. The cysteine residues in proinsulin are used for this purpose, and they are oxidized to create three disulfide bridges in the molecule.

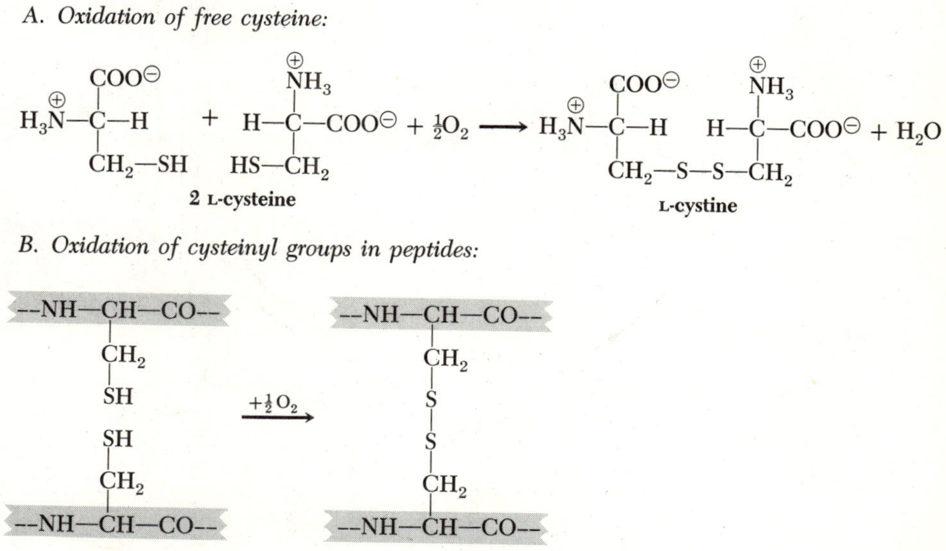

Figure 4-1 *A.* The oxidation of the sulfhydryl groups in free cysteine forms cystine, which contains a disulfide bridge. *B.* When two cysteinyl residues occur in different segments of a peptide chain, they may be oxidized to form a disulfide bridge that holds the two segments near each other.

Oxidation of Sulfhydryl Groups. The formation of disulfide bridges in peptides involves two steps. The first step is the oxidation of the sulfhydryl groups to create disulfides. How this is accomplished in most tissues is not known, but the reaction in the pancreas involves the oxidized form of a tripeptide, glutathion (Fig. 4-2). The reaction may be regarded as a hydrogen exchange, with the hydrogen atoms on cysteine residues in proinsulin transferred to the disulfide bridge of oxidized glutathione.

Disulfide Exchange. The next step in the formation of disulfide bonds in proteins is a rearrangement of the bonds so as to arrive at the most stable structure. The initial formation of disulfide bonds may occur at relatively random locations as the peptide chain twists about upon itself. However, the bonds migrate from one position to another by a disulfide exchange reaction, also shown in Figure 4-2. Such exchange reactions involve a sulfhydryl group on the enzyme catalyzing the reaction.

The important feature of the rearrangement of disulfide bonds, according to present belief, is that it will continue in a more or less random way, but it is like all chemical processes in that it will proceed in the direction favoring the most stable structure. That is, when the disulfide bonds are formed that make the most compact structure, or the structure with the strongest chemical bonding of all kinds between portions of the peptide chain, those disulfide bonds will tend to remain fixed. Their formation is favored by the position of equilibrium for all of the resultant bonding reactions.

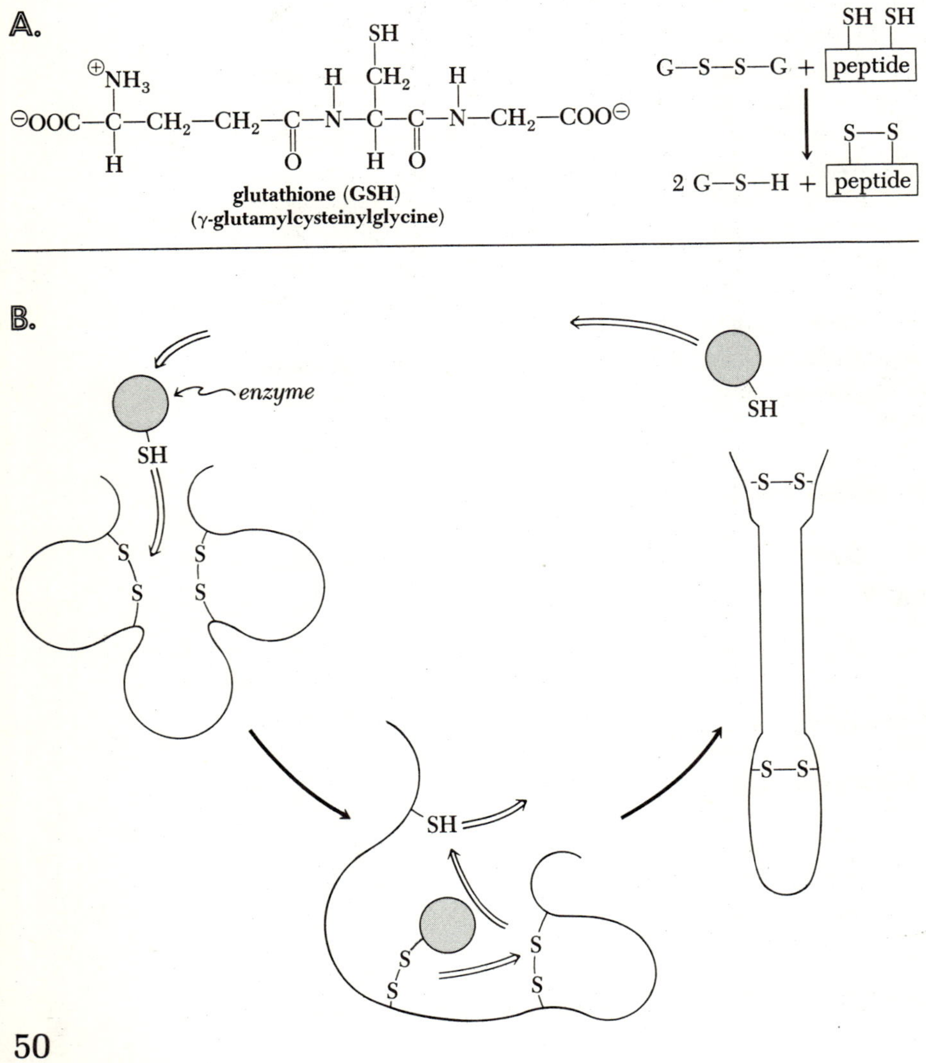

Figure 4-2 *A.* Disulfide bridges are formed in proinsulin by the reaction of two sulfhydryl groups with oxidized glutathione, which is a disulfide. The glutathione is reduced to its sulfhydryl form by oxidizing the cysteinyl groups to their disulfide form. *B.* Disulfide bridges are rearranged by reaction with a sulfhydryl-containing enzyme that splits the various disulfide bonds and reforms them. Successive recombinations occur until the arrangement of the peptide chain with the lowest energy content (greatest internal bonding) is achieved.

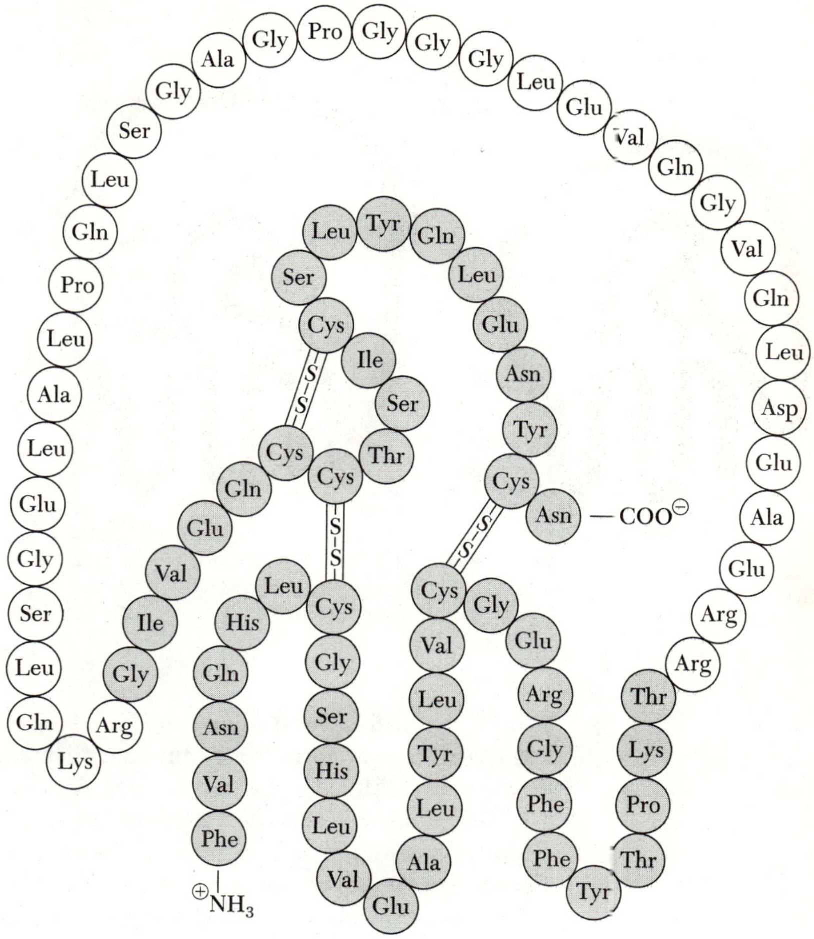

Figure 4-3 The primary structure of human proinsulin. The formula is arranged to show the position of the disulfide bridges, and is not an indication of conformation.

In any event, the proinsulin peptide chain does bend into a conformation that leads to the formation of three particular disulfide bonds between various portions of the chain (Fig. 4–3), and it is an example of a quite common phenomenon in protein synthesis—the development of disulfide bridges in a protein molecule to supplement the forces created by the primary sequence of amino acids in maintaining a particular three-dimensional conformation.

Hydrolysis of the Peptide. Even with the development of the disulfide bridges, the proinsulin peptide has none of the biological action characteristic of insulin. In order to create insulin, a segment is removed from the middle of the peptide by hydrolysis (Fig. 4–4). The result is the creation of two shorter peptide chains held together by disulfide bonds, and this new molecule is insulin. The connecting segment is of no further value and is destroyed. Here we see an example of a second important way in which newly synthesized peptide chains are altered to become biologically active—the hydrolysis of segments of the peptide chain.

Purpose of the Mechanism. If the completed insulin molecule is reduced so as to convert the disulfide bonds back to pairs of sulfhydryl groups, the two peptides completely separate. If this mixture of two peptides is then re-oxidized so as to create new disulfide bridges, very few of the peptides combine in such a way as to rebuild a functional insulin molecule.

We can see now why insulin is synthesized in the way it is. The activity of the peptides as a hormone hinges on the formation of a particular conformation, which

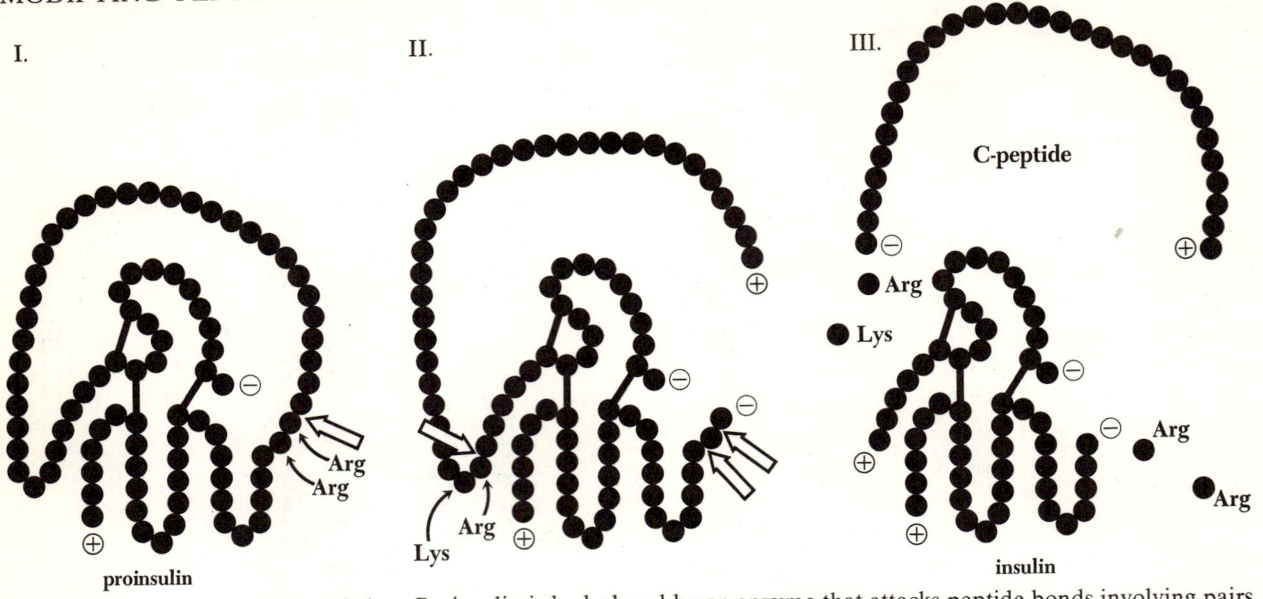

Figure 4–4 Proinsulin is hydrolyzed by an enzyme that attacks peptide bonds involving pairs of arginyl and lysyl residues. A segment of the single peptide chain is removed by the resultant hydrolyses, leaving the two remaining segments joined by disulfide bridges; the result is active insulin.

is held in position by disulfide bridges. However, this conformation is not one that will spontaneously form from a mixture of the constituent peptides. (This is partly true because it is difficult to get separate molecules to associate in a defined way.)

The problem is solved by first synthesizing the desired peptides as parts of a single chain held together by additional amino acid residues. The residues of cysteine have a much greater chance of assuming the most stable conformation when they are kept in proximity as components of a single molecule, and it may be that the connecting peptide is also constructed with an amino acid sequence that aids the stabilization of an active conformation. The result is that what are to be the finished peptide chains of insulin are held in an active conformation by the connecting segment of proinsulin while the disulfide bonds are formed. Once those bonds are created, the connecting segment can be discarded, and the active conformation will still be held in position by the disulfide bridges.

COLLAGEN

Some of the most striking examples of the modification of the primary sequence of peptides occur in the formation of proteins in connective tissues. (We shall say more about connective tissues in Chapter 29.) The most abundant of these proteins is collagen. Varieties of collagen occur in many animals; indeed, it is the most abundant protein in the entire body of vertebrates. Collagen forms fibers that are used as structural elements in the organism. Structural elements must have a low solubility in water, and frequently must have mechanical strength. It is desirable for the organism to resist the slings and arrows of outrageous fortune, and it is imperative that it not thaw and resolve itself into a dew.

Both of these desirable properties are contributed by collagen. It is an insoluble molecule made into rigid rods that serve to stiffen a variety of tissues. For example, a felt-like mat of these fibers occurs in the deep layer of the skin, resisting tearing without loss of flexibility. Collagen is the principal protein in cartilage, and it makes up about a third of the total solid matter in bone. The cornea of the eye is constructed largely from alternating stacks of collagen fibers. The different properties of these various tissues come in part from other components, but also from the particular way in which collagen fibers are arranged within the tissue.

Events in Collagen Synthesis

Formation of the Collagen Peptide. The synthesis of collagen begins with the formation of the primary structure—the amino acid sequence—in response to information on messenger RNA. The synthesis occurs on ribosomes in the ordinary way, utilizing amino acids obtained from cytosol, and the resultant single peptide chains are released into solution. Events occurring after the formation of the peptide chains are responsible for the transition from soluble peptides into rigid rods.

Unusual Glycine Content. An important part of the assembly of collagen fibers results from the unusual amino acid composition of the peptide chains. Glycine, the smallest amino acid, is incorporated into every third position in the interior part of the chains. Approximately one position in every five is occupied by a prolyl residue. The balance of the positions are filled with various amino acids specific for the particular peptide chain; the collagens of mammals contain two different peptide chains, with two out of every three chains being one kind ($\alpha 1$), and the remaining chain being another kind ($\alpha 2$), so that the chain formula for collagen is expressed $(\alpha 1)_2(\alpha 2)$, but each of these chains has the same arrangement of glycyl residues in its interior and the high proportion of prolyl residues.

Coiling of Peptide Chains. We have seen that peptide chains fold in such a way as to create the maximum bonding force. How is this done with the distinctive amino acid composition seen in collagen? The many prolyl residues in themselves would prevent the formation of an α-helix. It turns out that the maximum bonding is developed by forming a **triple helix,** a coil of three peptide chains, with each of these chains twisted one turn for each three residues (Fig. 4–5). This kind of tight twist brings each of the glycyl residues to the same side of the peptide chain. Since glycyl residues have no side chains other than a hydrogen atom, the coiled peptide chain is completely bare on one side of its central portion. This permits three of the coils to be further twisted together, so as to pack the bare sides of the coil against one another in the interior of a rope-like structure.

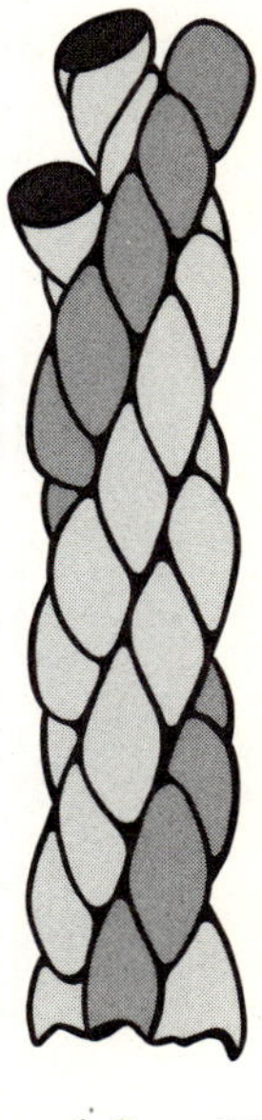

Figure 4–5 The strands of collagen are in a triple helix. Each of three peptide chains is individually coiled in a left-handed helix, and the three together are twisted in a right-handed helix. There are 10 turns in the individual chains per turn of the triple helix.

Hydroxylation of Amino Acid Residues. Even before the primary sequence of the peptide chain has been completed on the ribosomes, some of the amino acid residues begin to be modified by oxidations that form hydroxyl groups. Enzymes are present that oxidize some prolyl groups to **hydroxyprolyl** groups, and a few lysyl groups are also oxidized to create **hydroxylysyl** groups (Fig. 4–6). Does this violate the principle that the nature of peptides is determined by the coding in DNA? No, it does not, because the enzymes catalyzing these reactions are themselves built according to instructions in DNA so as to attack only prolyl and lysyl residues in particular situations, that is, those residues with particular combinations of neighboring amino acids. Therefore, the susceptibility of prolyl and lysyl residues to hydroxylation is determined by the amino acid sequence, which in turn is fixed by DNA, and it follows that the information in DNA determines the ultimate position of hydroxyprolyl and hydroxylysyl residues in collagen peptides, even though there is no specific genetic coding for these amino acids.

About half of the prolyl residues in the original sequence are hydroxylated while the peptide chain is being completed. Analysis of these unusual hydroxyprolyl residues is used as a measure of collagen content, since their only other occurrence is as minor

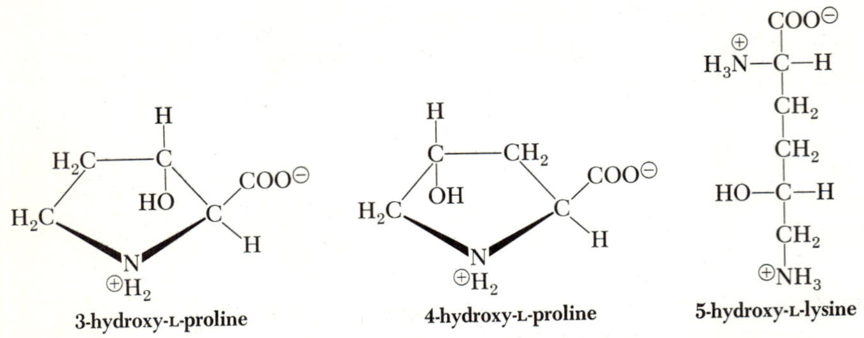

Figure 4–6 Some of the residues of proline and lysine in the growing procollagen peptides are hydroxylated. The 4-hydroxyproline is much more common than the 3-isomer.

components of other connective tissue proteins. The function of these many hydroxyl groups is not clear, although they may be involved in interactions of the collagen fibers with surrounding elements of connective tissue, as we shall discuss in Chapter 32. However, the hydroxylysyl residues have a very particular function. They serve as a point of attachment for sugar residues. Collagen is an example of a **glycoprotein**—a protein containing attached carbohydrate to modify its character. However, the presence of the carbohydrate does not appear to be a crucial factor in determining the nature of collagen, and we shall discuss other examples of glycoproteins later.

Refinement of the Peptide Chain. The peptide chains in collagen are like those in insulin, in that they are synthesized with extra sequences of amino acid residues that are important for the initial generation of the desired conformation. These **procollagen** peptides have a mass greater than 115,000 daltons, whereas the finished $\alpha 1$ peptide has a mass of 95,000 daltons. The extra section of peptide, with a mass of 20,000 daltons, apparently serves at least two functions. First, it brings the three peptides into an alignment facilitating formation of the compact triple helix in the finished molecule; this is deduced from the fact that peptides separated from finished collagen molecules spontaneously associate much too slowly to account for the observed rates of collagen synthesis by fibroblasts. Second, the extra pieces probably aid in keeping the procollagen molecule in solution for export from the cell; the conversion to the insoluble collagen fibers takes place outside the cell. (Indeed, the formation of insoluble polymers inside the cell would undoubtedly kill it.)

Once procollagen is secreted by the cell, the redundant segments of the peptide chain are removed by hydrolysis to create **tropocollagen,** the actual building block of collagen fibers.

Pyroglutamyl Terminal. Hydrolysis of the terminal amino acid sequences from procollagen occurs next to glutamyl groups; however, the resultant tropocollagen peptides do not have glutamate as the N-terminal amino acid residue, because there is still a further modification of the structure. N-terminal glutamate residues frequently cyclize to form a heterocyclic group variously named as a residue of pyroglutamate, oxoproline, or pyrrolidone carboxylate (Fig. 4–7). Regardless of name, the upshot is that collagen peptides have no terminal amino group.

Cross-linking Tropocollagen. The final, and a critical, part of collagen synthesis

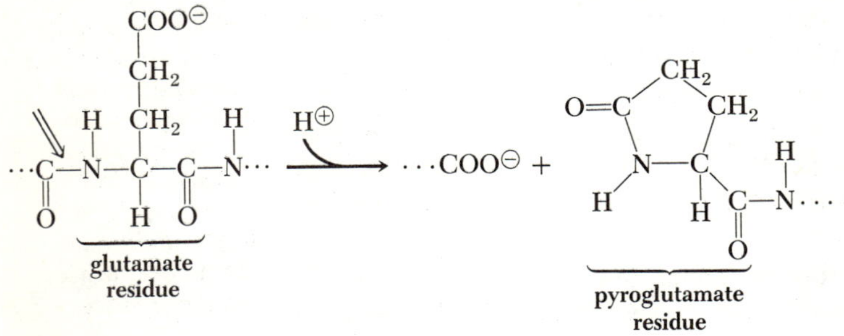

Figure 4–7 Hydrolysis of peptide bonds involving the amino group of glutamate or glutamine residues does not result in liberation of the amino group. Ring closure with the side-chain carboxylate group occurs to form a residue of pyroglutamate, which has no free amino group.

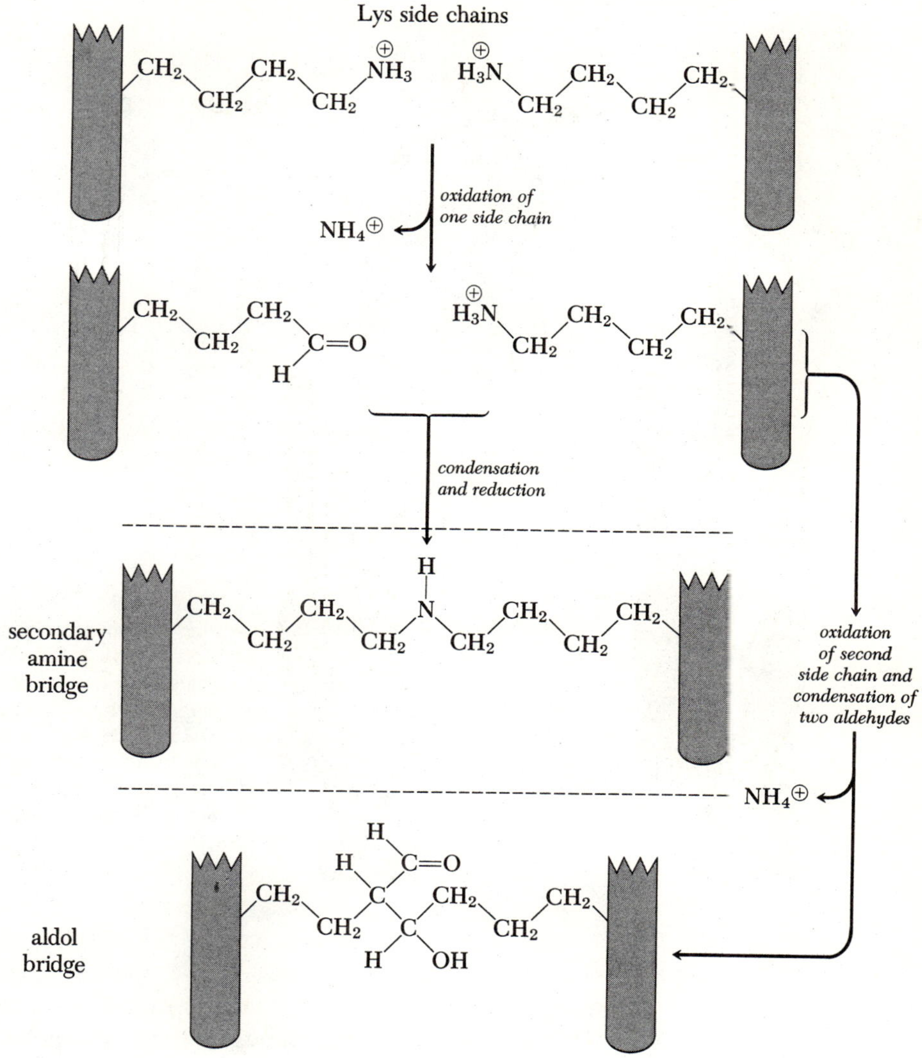

Figure 4–8 Covalent bonds are formed between the separate peptide chains of collagen by oxidizing a lysyl side chain to an aldehyde, which then condenses with another lysyl side chain or aldehyde group in various ways, two of which are shown.

is the formation of covalent cross-links between peptide chains so as to bind them into a rigid, strong rod. These cross-links are made by oxidizing some of the residues of lysine and hydroxylysine in the chains, with the loss of ammonia, to the corresponding aldehydes. We know from organic chemistry that aldehydes can participate in a variety of condensation reactions, and the side chain aldehydes created by oxidation of tropocollagen are no exception. They form many kinds of bonds between adjacent peptide chains (Fig. 4–8). Some are made by aldol condensations between two aldehyde side chains; others involve the combination of aldehydes with amino groups contributed by unmodified lysyl residues to form **aldimines.** (Aldimines and analogous **ketimines** are commonly known as **Schiff's bases.**) We shall see many other important examples of these structures.

Not only does the creation of all these covalent linkages between peptides serve to fix the triple helical structure, but the bonds also can shift so as to link peptides in separate tropocollagen molecules (Fig. 4–9), and this is an important factor in making a strong collagen fiber. The long, linear tropocollagen molecules tend to associate side-by-side, as is commonly the case with molecules of that shape. The associations

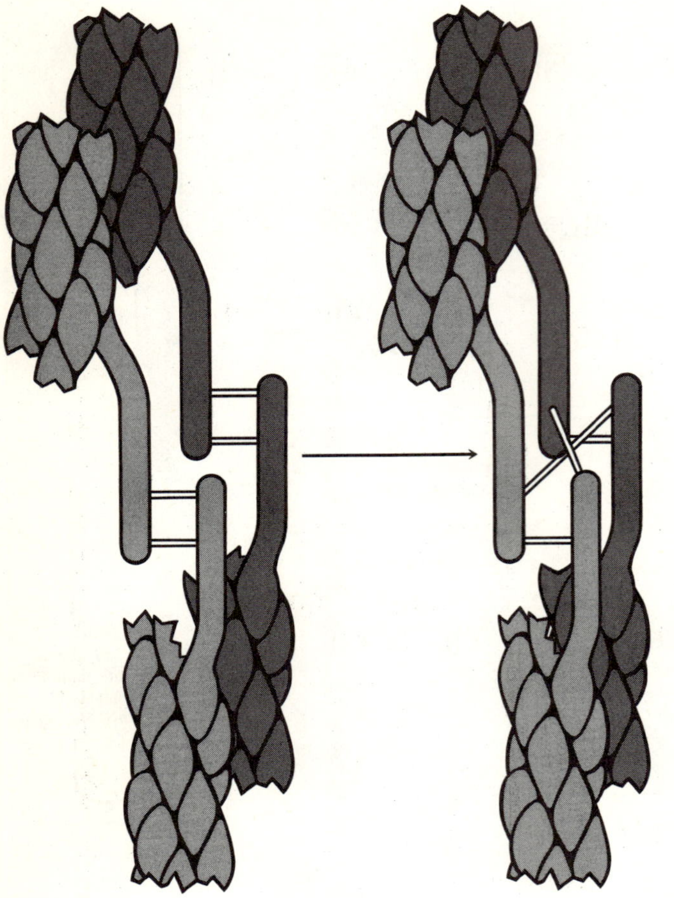

Figure 4-9 Adjacent molecules of tropocollagen may be covalently linked in a collagen fiber by a shift of bonds between subunits. The diagram indicates only one of the three peptide strands in each tropocollagen molecule. The principle is that the linkages between aldehydes within a molecule may open and reform with aldehydes from the adjacent molecule, but the exact position and number of these bonds is not known.

are not very strong, but the weak interactions between tropocollagen molecules need hold them in position only long enough for the covalent cross-links to be formed, which then give the fibers their great strength.

An Experimental Red Herring. It is well to be reminded occasionally that even very good scientists can be misled, so let us finish our discussion of collagen with a small tale of experimental problems. Hydroxylamine can be used to disrupt ester bonds under conditions in which amides do not react. When the reagent was applied to tropocollagen under these conditions, the molecule was disrupted into several large pieces. This led to the conclusion that the tropocollagen fiber, some 300 nm long, was actually composed of four to six pieces, linked head to tail by ester bonds. However, later observations were more and more inconsistent with the notion of subunits in the tropocollagen chains, and the discrepancy between these observations and the preceding conclusion were both puzzling and a source of irritation until one investigator had the happy notion that the observations on the effect of hydroxylamine were correct, but the conclusion was wrong. The upshot was the discovery of previously unrecognized behavior of amino acids; hydroxylamine cleaves peptide bonds between asparagine and glycine residues under conditions thought to be specific for esters. The reason this phenomenon had not previously been noticed was that Asn-Gly bonds are not very common in proteins, but the high proportion of Gly in collagen insures that it contains nearly all permutations of combinations of other amino acid residues with glycyl residues.

FIBRIN CLOTS

Another example of the modification of peptide chains through hydrolysis and subsequent formation of cross-links occurs during the clotting of blood. The formation of blood clots is a complex process, in which the agglomeration of platelets, which are small cells in the blood, is an important part. The platelets become enmeshed in a tangled lattice made by association of molecules of a protein, fibrin, and this is the part of clot formation with which we are immediately concerned.

The story begins in the liver, which makes three long peptide chains, α, β, and γ; two of each of these associate to make a fibrinogen molecule, which therefore has six peptide chains: $\alpha_2\beta_2\gamma_2$. As is commonly the case with proteins that are to be secreted, molecules of sugar derivatives are added to the peptide chains, so fibrinogin is a glycoprotein, but this fact is not important to our story. (The presence of the carbohydrate groups apparently stabilizes circulating proteins, and protects them from removal by scavenging processes, which also occur in the liver.) What is important is that the N-terminal portions of two of the fibrinogen peptides contain an abundance of negatively charged residues—residues that repel each other. The fibrinogen molecule is kept from flying apart because several cysteinyl residues, not far from the end, form disulfide bonds to hold the chains together. However, the existence of the excess negative charge on one region of the molecule evidently is what prevents the long fibrinogen rods from associating prematurely into insoluble aggregates.

Action of Thrombin. The formation of a clot involves the removal of the negatively charged tails on fibrinogen so that the molecules can associate. How does this occur? When a tissue is damaged, a complex sequence of events occurs that culminates in the formation of an enzyme known as thrombin. Thrombin catalyzes the hydrolysis of α and β fibrinogen peptides at a point some 10 to 20 residues removed

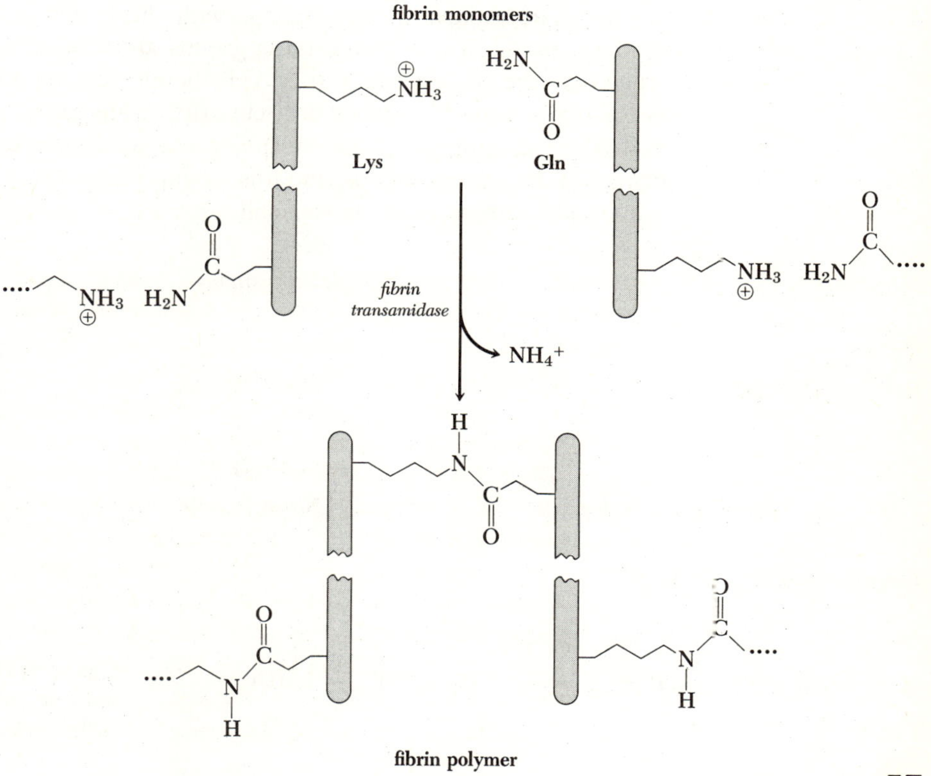

Figure 4-10 The formation of a fibrin polymer involves reaction between lysyl and glutaminyl residues on separate monomer molecules, with a substitution of the amino group on the lysyl side chain for the ammonia moiety of the carboxamide group on the glutaminyl side chain. The result is the formation of amide bonds between monomers and the liberation of ammonia.

from the N-terminal. (The number varies in fibrinogens from different mammals. The bond cleaved lies between Arg and Gly groups, so that Gly always becomes the N-terminal residue of the remaining peptide chains, but this also is not an important part of the story.) The removal of these short segments of peptide, known as fibrinopeptides A and B, also removes most of the excess negative charges from the ends of the chain. The remaining part of the molecule, which is now a fibrin monomer, is only slightly smaller than the original fibrinogen, but the loss of charge permits fibrin molecules to associate to an extent not possible with fibrinogen.

Cross-linking of Fibrin. Simple hydrolysis of fibrinogen permits association of fibrin monomers, but polymerization of the monomers is like the conversion of tropocollagen to collagen, in that the monomers are linked by the formation of covalent bonds. The result in the case of fibrin is a strong lattice. The formation of the covalent cross-links involves a residue of lysine in one monomer, and a residue of glutamine in another (Fig. 4–10). The amino group of the lysyl chain is exchanged for the amide nitrogen of the glutaminyl residue, with release of the amide nitrogen as an ammonium ion.

Here we see the use of lysyl side chains to form bonds between peptides in a different way than occurs in the formation of collagen; no oxidation of the lysyl chains is necessary.

PHOSPHORYLATION OF PROTEINS: CASEIN

We shall encounter many examples of modification of proteins through addition of chemical groups. We have already mentioned the addition of molecules of sugar derivatives to form **glycoproteins.** Fats and related compounds can be added to create **lipoproteins.** Smaller groups may also be added. For example, some side chains may be methylated or acetylated (Fig. 4–11). Another important modification is the addition of phosphate groups in ester linkage with the hydroxyl groups of seryl or threonyl residues. As the figure shows, these groups are formed by a transfer of a phosphate group onto the peptide chain from ATP, thereby leaving adenosine diphosphate (ADP) as the other product. (We shall discuss such transfers of phosphate in great detail in Part III.) The addition of the phosphate groups usually causes changes in the conformation of the peptide chains, and it is an important means of controlling the biological activity of some proteins, as we shall later see.

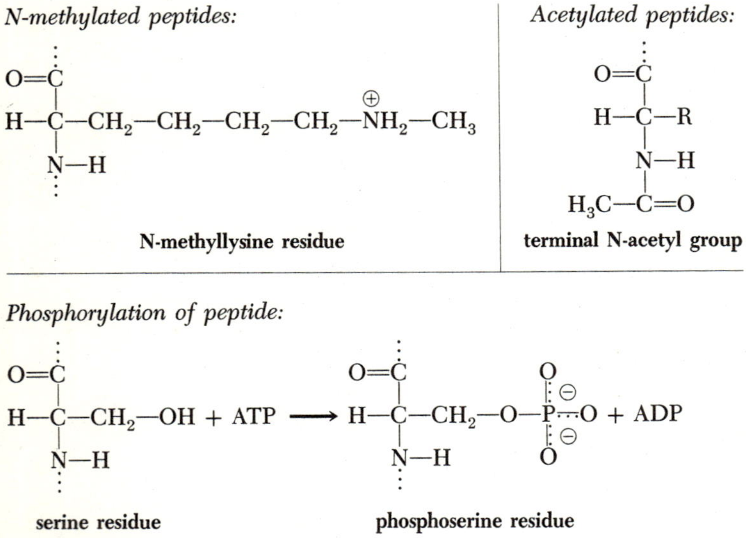

Figure 4–11 Amino acid residues in some peptides are modified by methylation, acetylation, or phosphorylation.

However, the best known example of a **phosphoprotein** is casein in milk; casein has no special biological activity, but it is of importance to mammals as a primordial nutrient for suckling infants. Humans also modify it to please adults in the form of cheese.

Casein is actually a mixture of proteins, and it is more proper to speak of the caseins in milk. The caseins supply a major part of the amino acids from which infants make proteins. There are many different peptides composing these caseins, some with few attached phosphate groups and others with several. Proline constitutes 0.2 of the amino acid residues in some caseins, and this may contribute to an important property of the molecules—the lack of highly ordered internal structure, which facilitates attack by digestive enzymes in the infant.

Since caseins are phosphoproteins, they also supply the infant with its phosphate requirement, in addition to amino acids. Beyond that, the caseins are built so as to associate into micelles that include substantial amounts of chelated Ca^{2+}. The character of these particles is not known in detail, but it appears that some of the different caseins are synthesized primarily to stabilize the micelles, and to prevent formation of insoluble aggregates of calcium-linked phosphoproteins in the milk. Like many secreted proteins, some of the casein peptides have attached carbohydrates, and the notion that these groups contribute to stabilization of proteins is strengthened by the fact that digestion of casein in the stomach of infants begins with a partial hydrolysis that removes the glycopeptide portions of the molecules. When this happens, the remaining complexes of calcium phosphopeptide agglomerate into a soft clot, or curd. In sum, casein is a protein constructed primarily to function as a food for suckling mammalian infants. (The yolk of bird eggs contains another phosphoprotein, vitellin, to nourish growing embryos.)

FURTHER READING

C. B. Anfinsen, Principles that govern the folding of peptide chains, Science, 181:223 (1973). Nobel lecture by the man who first clearly described the rearrangement of disulfide bonds.

D. F. Steiner, W. Kemmler, J. L. Clark, et al., The biosynthesis of insulin, p. 175 in v. 1, sect. 7 of Handbook of physiology. N. Freinkel and D. F. Steiner, eds., American Physiological Society (1972). Clear description in a generally useful treatise on insulin and its function.

K. A. Piez, The chemistry and biology of collagen, p. 101 in Current topics in biochemistry, C. B. Anfinsen, R. F. Goldberger, and A. N. Schachter, eds., Academic Press (1972).

QUESTIONS

1. Why is the presence of a large concentration of aspartyl groups in a peptide chain believed to diminish the likelihood of association of molecules? Would a large concentration of lysyl groups have a similar effect?
2. A certain protein dissociates into three different peptide chains under conditions causing the reduction of disulfide bonds to sulfhydryl groups. When the chains are combined under conditions favoring the renewed formation of disulfide bridges, the original protein is not recovered. How, then, can the cell have synthesized the protein?
3. What is the difference in structure between the α-helix, the double helix involved in transfer of genetic information, and the triple helix found in a connective tissue protein?
4. What is the origin of aldehyde groups on side chains in tropocollagen peptides? Show how they are used to form aldols and aldimines for cross-links. How do these cross-links differ from those created from the same amino acid residue in fibrinogen?
5. What kind of reaction do the formations of insulin, of collagen, and of fibrin have in common?
6. Why is a supply of maternal phosphate necessary for the provision of calcium to a suckling infant?

PART 2

SPECIFIC BINDING BY PROTEINS

CHAPTER 5

ANTIBODIES

THE CONCEPTS

All biological functions of proteins require the formation of bonds between the proteins and other molecules. Although most functions involve further events, binding is always a prelude to any changes caused by the protein; this is especially well illustrated by the action of antibodies, which are built specifically to form strong bonds with foreign compounds, such as those on the surface of invading microorganisms. A compound provoking the formation of an antibody that will bind to it is an antigen; the formation of an antibody-antigen complex is a prelude to the removal or destruction of the antigen.

Antibodies are globulins, which means that they are soluble in dilute salt solutions but are precipitated at higher concentrations still insufficient to precipitate albumins. They are also gamma globulins, migrating the least rapidly of the blood proteins when placed in an electric field. (Such electrophoresis separates serum albumin, and α- and β-globulins.)

Antibodies are made from two heavy peptide chains and two light chains that form Y- or T-shaped molecules held by disulfide bridges. Successive portions of two neighboring chains are folded into compact domains that serve different functional purposes. The domains at the end of limbs of the Y are made from variable regions of the peptide chains, in which the amino acid composition of each kind of antibody is unique. The variable region contains certain segments that frequently have different amino acid residues in different antibodies; hot spots in these hypervariable regions are nearly always different. These hypervariable segments comprise the active site for antigen binding.

The remainder of each peptide chain is made of a constant region that has the same amino acid composition in all antibodies of a given class. The constant region comprises at least three domains, one of which is used to attach carbohydrate, which apparently protects the protein from early destruction. The constant domains also include signalling sites that are changed by the formation of an antibody-antigen complex so as to provoke subsequent events in the immune

response. These events may include lysis of invading cells, attraction of white blood cells, liberation of additional antibody, and inflammation.

Antibodies are probably synthesized by translation of mRNA in the usual way, with refinement of the peptide by partial hydrolysis. However, the mRNA for one antibody chain is derived from two genes, one for the constant region and one for the variable region, according to present belief. The mechanism of its formation is not known. Each lymphocyte has the capacity to form both variable and constant regions for various types of light and heavy chains, but it suppresses the transcription of mRNA for all but one set.

Something happens during the development of the lymphocyte population from the original germ cells that causes changes in the DNA coding for the hypervariable segments, and different antibodies may arise by uncontrolled mutations.

We have seen how proteins are made, and have some general idea of their structures; now let us see how they work. The biological functions of proteins hinge on their ability to form specific bonds with other compounds. Nothing more is required for the simplest sort of function. For example, the strong association of a compound with a protein may be used to form structural elements, or to remove the compound. In any event, there is a certain degree of implied stability in functions dependent only upon simple association. The union is intended to persist for a substantial period of time. We saw this in the use of casein in milk as a device for exporting calcium ions from the mother to the infant. This is one-time formation of a chelate; there is no provision for releasing the calcium and using the casein over again. The association of casein and calcium persists until the milk is transferred to the infant, which digests the complex and destroys it.

Antibodies and Antigens. We have more elegant examples of the proteins made to form specific complexes. Antibodies (Ab) are proteins constructed to form complexes with specific compounds. The compounds provoking the formation of antibodies are antigens (Ag), and the two combine to form antigen-antibody complexes (Ab-Ag). Compounds foreign to the organism, especially the polypeptide and carbohydrate polymers occurring on the surface of invading microorganisms, are frequently good antigens, and the formation of an antigen-antibody complex facilitates their removal or destruction.

THE NATURE OF ANTIBODIES

Antibodies as Globulins

Antibodies are commonly referred to as **immunoglobulins,** and also as **gamma-globulins.** The terms arise from general classifications of proteins made on the basis of *in vitro* behavior, rather than biological function or chemical composition, but it is still advisable to know their origin.

Albumins and Globulins. Early biochemists classified globular proteins on the basis of solubility, especially in salt solutions of varying concentrations. Albumins are soluble in solutions ranging from those with no salt to those of high concentration (saturated NaCl, for example), whereas globulins are substantially less soluble at very low and high salt concentrations, although they are soluble at intermediate values, such as 0.15 M NaCl. (0.15 M NaCl has roughly the same osmotic pressure as human blood; clinicians refer to it as normal saline.) These solubility properties have little to do with function, but provide a basis for partial purification of proteins in the laboratory.

γ-Globulins and Other Serum Proteins. Proteins can sometimes be separated in solution by applying an electric field to make them migrate, a technique known as electrophoresis. The proteins in blood plasma can be separated into five major fractions in this way; most of the albumin molecules migrate near the same velocity,

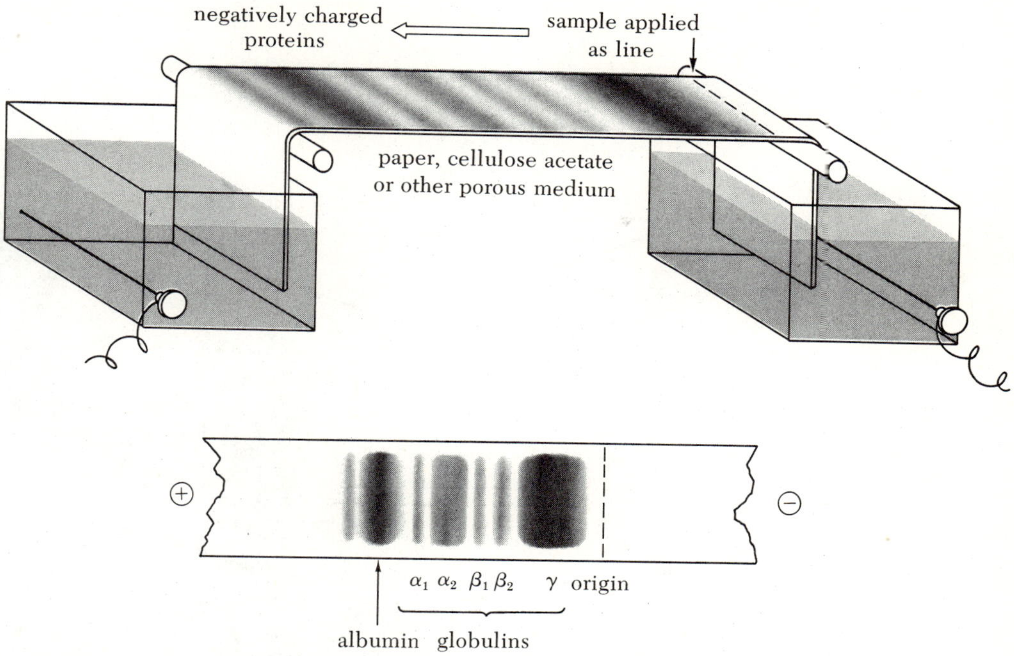

Figure 5-1 (*Top*) Zone electrophoresis. A strip of porous material (e.g., paper or cellulose acetate) is saturated with a buffer solution and suspended between two containers of buffer that are fitted with inert electrodes. The sample containing a mixture of proteins is applied as a thin stripe; those proteins having different net charges separate when a voltage is applied. The buffer is usually made sufficiently alkaline to create a net negative charge on most proteins. Those with the most charges migrate most rapidly. (*Bottom*) Results of electrophoretic separation of the proteins in human serum.

and a protein involved in blood clotting (fibrinogen) also appears as a single component, but there are three major groups of globulins, designated as α-, β-, and γ-, on the basis of the relative velocity of their migration in the electric field (Fig. 5-1). The γ-globulin fraction was found to consist mainly of circulating antibodies, and gamma-globulin began to be applied as a general designation for antibodies even though some have electrophoretic mobilities corresponding to α- or β-globulins.

We shall encounter the plasma proteins repeatedly. They are the proteins in the fluid, or extracellular, part of the blood. Most of them are still in solution in the serum that is expressed after blood clots, and are therefore also known as serum proteins. Plasma albumin is a carrier for a variety of substances, including fatty acids; the α-globulins include a number of other transport proteins, and the β-globulins include lipoproteins with fat and other non-polar compounds attached.

Chemical Composition of Antibodies

Heavy Chains and Light Chains. Antibody molecules are made from equal amounts of two kinds of peptide chains. One, known as the heavy chain, is at least twice the length of the light chain, sometimes more. (Some types of antibodies include additional small connecting chains.) A prototype antibody consists of pairs of identical heavy chains and light chains, with each light chain associating with one half of a heavy chain, and the remaining halves of the heavy chains associating with each other. The result is the creation of a Y- or T-shaped molecule (Fig. 5-2) with an axis of symmetry. (Rotating one half of the molecule 180° superimposes it on the other half.)

Domains. Successive segments of the light and heavy chains coil to form compact

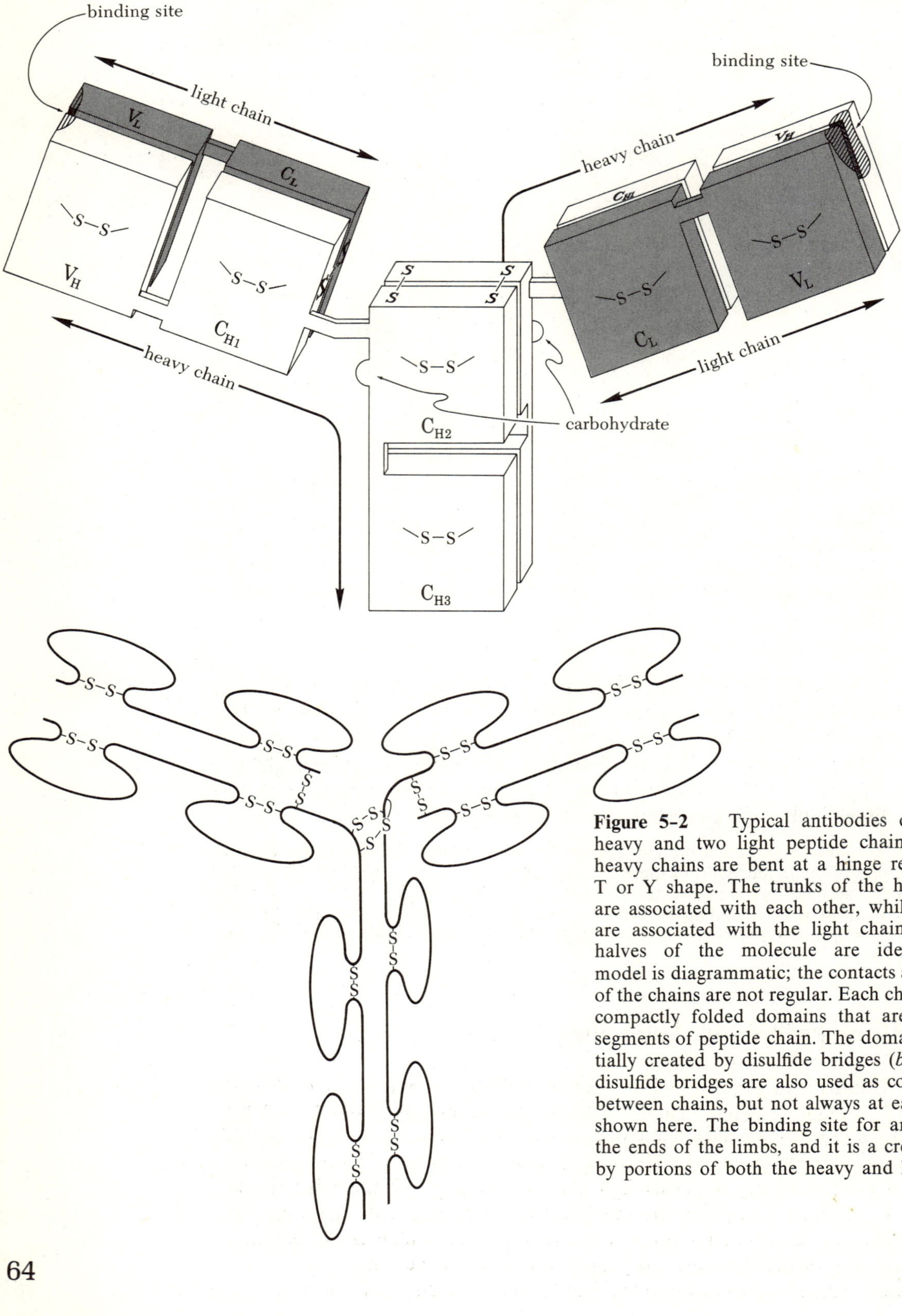

Figure 5-2 Typical antibodies contain two heavy and two light peptide chains. The two heavy chains are bent at a hinge region into a T or Y shape. The trunks of the heavy chains are associated with each other, while the limbs are associated with the light chains. The two halves of the molecule are identical. The model is diagrammatic; the contacts and surfaces of the chains are not regular. Each chain contains compactly folded domains that are linked by segments of peptide chain. The domains are partially created by disulfide bridges (*bottom*), and disulfide bridges are also used as covalent links between chains, but not always at each position shown here. The binding site for antigens is at the ends of the limbs, and it is a crevice walled by portions of both the heavy and light chains.

structures, each containing somewhat over 100 amino acid residues. The structure is held in place by disulfide bonds formed both within the coil of each chain and also between the chains. These structures formed by paired coils are believed to represent domains of the molecule that may have distinct functions in the immune response. For example, antibodies are like secreted proteins in general; they contain attached carbohydrate that is believed to stabilize the molecule against destruction, but the carbohydrate is attached to only one of the domains formed by the heavy chains.

Constant and Variable Regions. The concept of domains is furthered by the observation that many antibodies, although differing in their specificity toward different antigens, have identical amino acid composition in successive segments of their respective light and heavy chains, except in the segments constituting the ends of the limbs. Most of an antibody molecule therefore is made of a constant region with the same amino acid composition as is in many molecules of totally different reactivity toward antigens. The different immune response comes from changes in the amino acid composition of the one variable domain on each limb.

Classes of Immunoglobulins. There are different general types of antibodies to fulfill different functions. Some circulate in the body fluids, others are involved in cellular immune responses, and still others are secreted at surfaces exposed to external substances. The differences arise by changes in the constant regions, especially in the heavy chains. All antibodies containing similar constant regions constitute a class. There are five different heavy chain classes and two light chain classes. (Molecules differing in only one or two residues are regarded as mutants of the same class.)

The general classes determined by the heavy chain are designated IgA, IgD, IgE, IgG, and IgM, with the corresponding types of heavy chains designated as α, δ, ϵ, γ, or μ. The light chains are κ or λ. An IgG molecule, for example, may contain either two κ chains or two λ chains, but it will always have two γ chains. Some pertinent properties of the various classes of immunoglobulins are listed in Table 5-1.

IgG is the principal class of circulating antibodies, mainly responsible for promoting engulfment of foreign particles by white blood cells (phagocytosis) and for setting in motion other processes for destroying foreign organisms.

IgA, found in secretions, contains two extra peptides, a small joining link and a secretory component. The joining link apparently promotes the association of two of the usual Y-shaped antibody monomers, each composed of two heavy and two light chains, into dimers for secretion. IgA provides defense against entry of organisms through external membranes.

IgM also contains a single joining link, but it appears to promote the formation of pentameters—five of the Y-shaped monomers linked in a circle (Fig. 5-3). This large macroglobulin is made by the same cells that make IgG, and it appears that antibody response first involves a stimulation of the formation of IgM, followed by the incorporation of the same binding sites in IgG molecules.

TABLE 5-1 CLASSES OF IMMUNOGLOBULINS

name	IgA	IgD	IgE	IgG	IgM
molecular weight	390K (dimer)	178K	188K	146K	880K (pentamer)
heavy chain	α	δ	ϵ	γ	μ
% carbohydrate	5–10	10	12	2.5	5–10
typical serum concentration ($g\ l^{-1}$).	1.8	0.03	0.0003	12	1.0

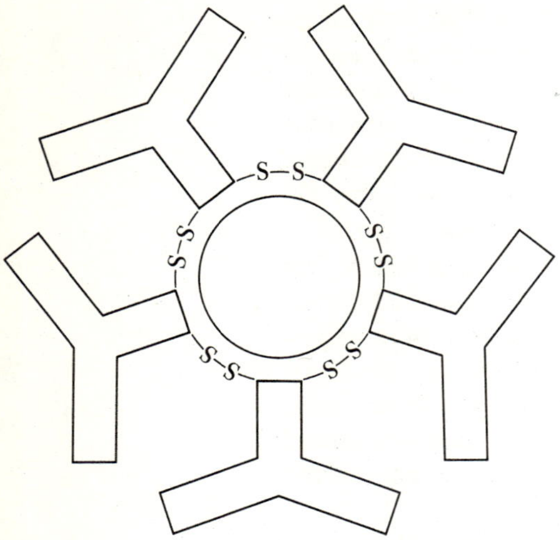

Figure 5-3 IgM is a pentamer of Y-shaped molecules linked by disulfide bridges around a core. (The trunk of the molecule is presumably bent back upon itself in a way not shown, since the linking disulfides occur in the center of the trunk. The actual shape of the molecule is not clear.)

IgE appears to be the antibody responsible for hypersensitive reactions such as allergic asthma and dermatitis. Little is known about the function of IgD.

FUNCTION OF ANTIBODIES

Binding of Antigens

Hypervariable Regions and Hot Spots. The binding sites of antibodies—the locations at which they form strong associations with antigens—are in the variable regions of the light and heavy chains. Antibody molecules that differ in their specificity toward antigens also differ in the amino acid sequence of the first 110 residues from the N-terminus. However, some portions of this variable region are much more variable

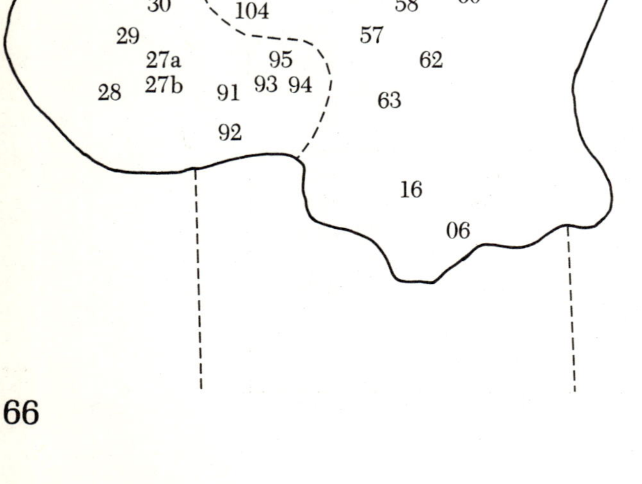

Figure 5-4 The actual profile of the end of an antibody limb. The orientation of the limb is indicated by the bottom dashed lines. The numbers indicate the spatial arrangement of the corresponding hypervariable residues in the light and heavy chains, and therefore show the location of the antigen binding site.

than others, and the positions likely to differ are known as hypervariable regions, with some hot spots that are almost certain to have different amino acid residues in different antibodies. Most immunochemists believe that these hypervariable regions, especially the hot spots, constitute the specific binding sites even though they represent less than 1% of the total amino acid residues. This view is given strong support by the demonstration of the hypervariable region in the end of the limbs on one antibody (Fig. 5-4).

Variable Regions. The remainder of the variable region has the same amino acid composition in many different antibodies, which constitute sub-classes within the general classes as determined by the constant regions of the chains. What is the purpose of these areas of the peptide? The formation of a binding site depends not only upon the insertion of particular amino acid residues in the hypervariable portion of the chain, but it also depends upon the chain being folded so as to bring the hypervariable residues into position where they can form bonds with a foreign substance. They must be reasonably close together, and accessible at the surface of the molecule. Therefore, most of the so-called variable region is not so variable because it must produce a similar conformation in related immunoglobulins. Such differences in amino acid sequence that occur in the variable regions outside of the hypervariable locations evidently cause the necessary changes in folding so as to bring the active sites of the various sub-classes of antibodies into being.

Role of Glycine. The notion of a particular location of residues in the hypervariable region being required for activity as a binding site is supported by the common occurrence of residues of glycine in the variable region. (Recall that glycine favors disruption of α-helices, and it has no side chain to cause steric hindrance.) Glycine invariably occurs at a position near the hottest spot, and there are several other positions near hypervariable segments where it frequently occurs. The presence of glycine would promote a freedom of orientation of the hypervariable residues, permitting them to be arranged in the most favorable grouping for binding of particular antigens. That is, the forces affecting specific side chains can become predominant.

Divalent Antibodies and Polyvalent Antigens. The presence of two identical binding sites in an antibody molecule is a critical feature. Each antibody molecule can link two molecules of antigen. However, a principal purpose of the immune system is to protect against the invasion of microorganisms. The surface of microorganisms is huge in molecular terms, containing many identical regions of peptides and carbohydrate polymers. An antibody capable of binding one of these locations will also be able to bind many parts of the cell surface. Put another way, a microorganism is polyvalent in terms of most specific antigenic sites, so that many identical antibody molecules will bind to the surface of one cell. Since each antibody molecule has a second site that can form bonds with another antigen, the result is the formation of a lattice of cells (or other particles) held together by antibody molecules (Fig. 5-5).

Specificity of Antigens. Figure 5-5 also illustrates another way in which lattices can be constructed by antigen-antibody interactions. Different parts of the surface of a foreign macromolecule may be bound by different antibodies, so that antigen molecules linked by antibodies reacting with one site may be linked to other antigen molecules by another kind of antibody reacting with a second site. As few as seven amino acid residues or carbohydrate units in an exposed portion of a macromolecule may be sufficient to be recognized by an antibody. (This does not mean that peptide made only of seven amino acid residues will act as an antigen—the residues must be held in specific and stable conformation through the interactions of longer segments of adjoining peptide chains.) For example, injection of myoglobin from sperm whale muscles into rabbits causes the appearance in the rabbits of at least four anti-sperm whale myoglobins. Each antibody appears to be specific to a sequence of seven residues occurring on one of the external corners of myoglobin. (Myoglobin is muscle hemo-

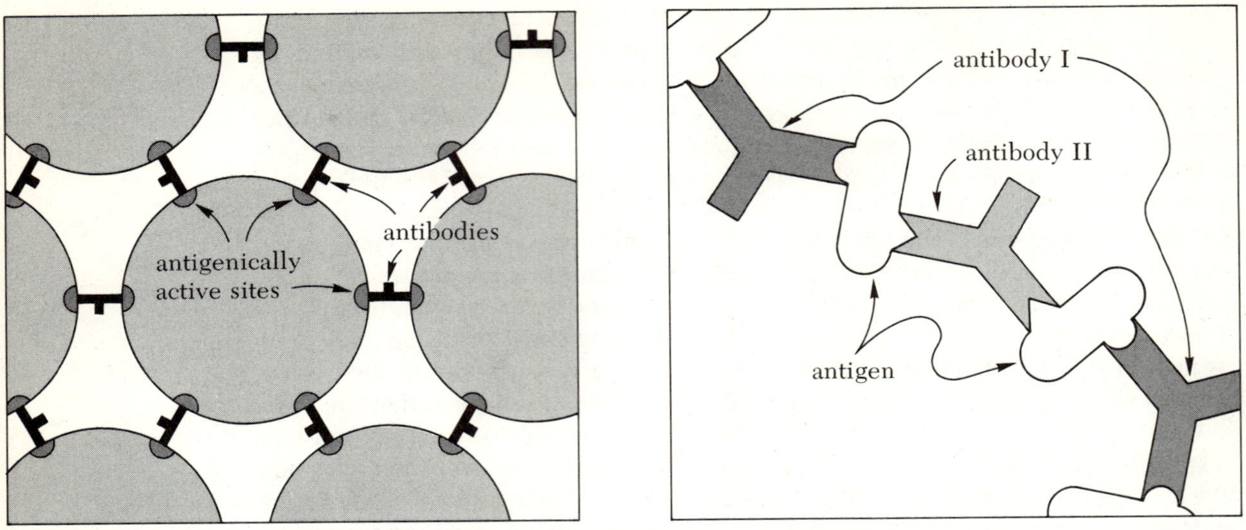

Figure 5-5 (*Left*) Cells and other large antigens usually contain many identical antigenic sites. The divalent antibodies may therefore link the antigens into a three-dimensional lattice. (*Right*) Lattices may also be formed with smaller antigens that contain different antigenic sites through combination with different antibodies.

globin; it is a single peptide chain that binds oxygen in muscles, and more will be said about it in the next chapter. It is abundant in whale muscles.)

Disposition of Antigen-Antibody Complexes

The primary purpose of the antigen-antibody interaction is to rid the organism of a threat. The antigen-antibody lattice will often grow in the test tube until the complex becomes large enough to form precipitates. This **precipitin reaction** is a valuable tool for visual demonstration of the presence of specific antibodies or antigens in the laboratory, but such a capillary-clogging event would not be a good way for disposal of antigens in the body.

The immune response is too complex for even a general outline here, but we ought to note that it appears to involve the other domains of the antibody molecule beyond the variable domain and the secretory domain. The binding of an antigen apparently causes the conformation of some of the constant domains to change, and the change acts as a signal. (We shall see better-defined examples of regulation by conformational changes in the following chapters.) One result is an activation of the **complement** system of blood. This is a group of proteins that acts in a sequential way, after being triggered by the presence of an antigen-antibody complex, to lyse antigenic cells, attract the host's white blood cells (macrophages), and cause the release of still more antibody.

It appears that the variable portion of the antibody molecule acts only as a lookout, putting the finger on strange substances; a domain in the constant region of the molecule gives the password during transport outside the cell, and another domain in the constant region whistles for the cops once the alarm is raised.

FORMATION OF ANTIBODIES

How Many Antibodies? Current estimates are that a human can form 1,000,000 different kinds of antibody molecules, containing 2,000,000 different kinds of peptide chains. Where do the translational instructions for all of these peptides come from? We noted earlier that all of human heredity may consist of instructions for some 10,000 different proteins. It is therefore ridiculous by current notions to think that the fertilized ovum contains a DNA molecule corresponding to each antibody that the adult will make. If different antibodies do reflect the presence of different DNA, at least part of the difference must arise after the fusion of germ cells. Much speculation has been given to the extent and the mechanism of these hypothetical somatic mutations in the antibody-forming cells. Let us examine some of the more likely ideas and their basis.

One Polypeptide from Two Genes. Analysis of the inheritance of immunoglobulin chains developed the startling conclusion that the amino acid composition of the constant and variable regions of one chain is not inherited as a unit. Identical variable regions may be found on different constant regions, and vice versa. This is true of both the light and the heavy chains. The easiest way to explain these observations is to assume that the constant and variable portions are made from information coded in separate segments of DNA. That is, genes for the two portions of what is to be a single polypeptide chain are in different parts of DNA, and the formation of a messenger RNA molecule for that chain involves the sequential translation of two genes. Either the separated segments of DNA must somehow come into head-to-tail contact for transcription, or there must be some sort of carrier that moves incomplete mRNA from one site of transcription to another (Fig. 5–6).

Multiple Genes. If each peptide in an immunoglobulin is coded by two genes, the possibilities for different immunoglobulins are multiplied by the permutations of these two genes. According to current views, there are independent sites for the inheritance of each of the two light chain types and a separate site for the inheritance of the heavy chains. However, several different genes are believed to be present at each site. Suppose that there are sequences of nucleotides in DNA designating five different variable regions and three different constant regions in a light chain. It is then possible to form 15 different types of light chain. Considering the various combinations of light chains and heavy chains, it is possible to imagine the construction of a few thousand different sub-types of immunoglobulins from genetic information.

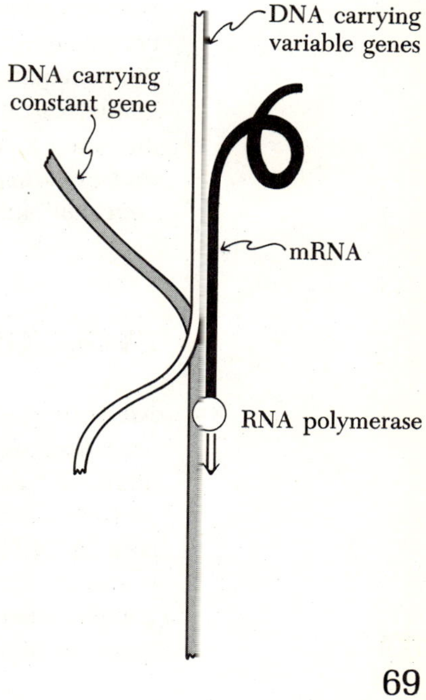

Figure 5-6 The messenger RNA specifying the sequence of an antibody peptide chain is created by transcription of two genes, one for the constant region and one for the variable region. It is not known how the transcription is shifted from one segment of DNA to another without interruption of the mRNA, but it may involve physical proximity of the two DNA segments, so the RNA polymerase may easily shift from one to the other.

However, this is a considerable distance from the one million distinct antibodies that are believed to be formed by one human.

Formation of Specific Binding Sites. The great diversity of antibodies requires the formation of an average of at least several hundred different hypervariable sequences in each of the sub-types of immunoglobulins created by genetic information. Since an individual can create the same antibody over many years, it seems likely that each antibody is specified by a particular kind of DNA molecule. The problem then becomes one of explaining the appearance of many different kinds of DNA after fertilization. We have many ingenious hypotheses on the way in which this occurs, but little proof. Many believe that the lymphocyte is deliberately constructed to be susceptible to mutation by having a relatively short lifetime with a consequent rapid formation of DNA when compared to other cell lines.

Provocation of Synthesis. In any event, the higher animals develop a population of lymphocytes composed of many clones, perhaps a million. (A **clone** is a group of cells or organisms with an identical heredity. Identical twins initially constitute a clone.) Each lymphocyte has the genetic capability of producing any one of perhaps a few thousand different combinations of light and variable regions, but something has happened so that it will form only one combination, and the selected variable region contains a hypervariable region highly specific to particular structures.

A virgin lymphocyte remains in a quiescent state unless it encounters some antigen that fits its binding site. The cell is then stimulated to form IgG for secretion and to divide. Division continues to expand the clone so long as there is still excess antigen to react with the lymphocyte surface. When it is gone, the cells become memory cells, waiting in increased number for a further appearance of the particular antigen to provoke a new outpouring of IgG.

Tumors of Lymphocytes. Our knowledge of immunoglobulins is to a considerable extent based on tragic misfortune. Some people develop tumors of plasma cells, or **multiple myeloma,** with the formation of large numbers of a single clone of cells, which elaborate a specific immunoglobulin. Such people frequently excrete light chains in their urine, which were named **Bence-Jones protein,** after their discoverer. The importance of these abnormal proteins is that an afflicted individual excretes a single specific protein, whereas antibodies against highly purified antigens are mixtures arising from the recognition of different aspects of the same antigen by different clones of lymphocytes. Information on the sequence of amino acids in immunoglobulins, with the concomitant elucidation of the variable, hypervariable, and constant regions, was made possible by the existence of myeloma immunoglobulins. Unfortunately, there has not yet been a specific example in which it has been possible to find an antigen that fits a myeloma clone, so investigation of binding is still limited to the less clean "normal" antibodies created in response to exposure to a known antigen.

EVOLUTION OF IMMUNOGLOBULINS

All of the light chains and heavy chains found in immunoglobulins apparently arose from a single ancestor, perhaps half the length of the present light chains. How is this deduced? Certain homologies in amino acid sequence become apparent upon comparison of the segments of light chains and heavy chains enclosed in disulfide loops (Fig. 5–7). That is, the various segments have similar amino acid composition at some positions. The similarity is increased if one inserts gaps in some of the chains, a process known as maximizing the homology. Such a procedure is logical from an evolutionary point of view, because deletion of amino acids by mutation is an expected event.

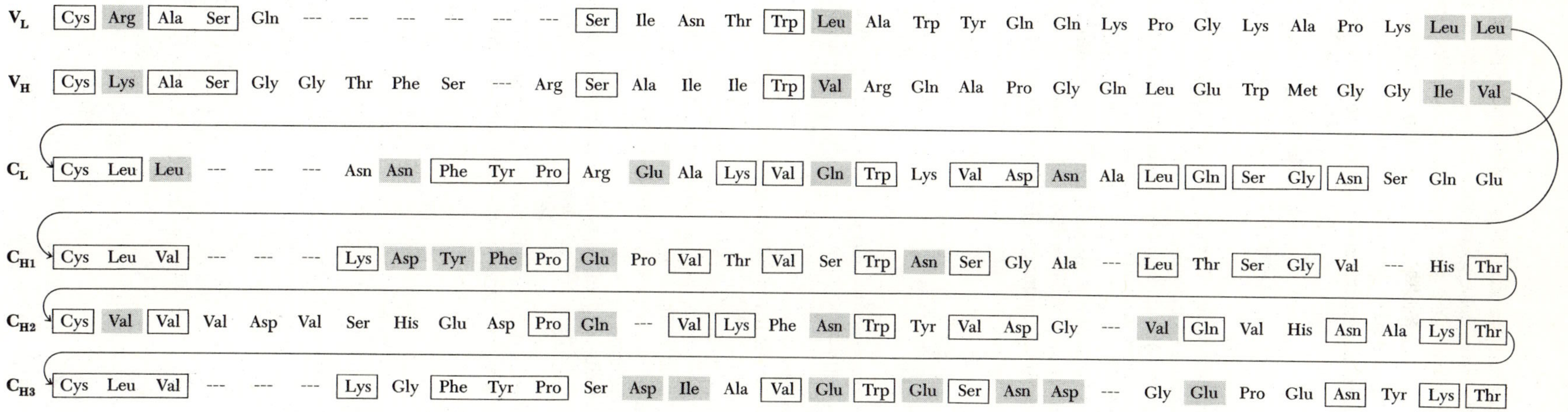

Figure 5-7 The demonstration of common evolutionary origin of segments of peptide chains involves a side-by-side comparison of their sequences. Here we have the initial portions of the sequence of six domains in an antibody—the two variable regions, the constant light chain region, and the three domains of the constant heavy chain region. Gaps are inserted as required in the sequence to obtain the greatest similarity between the sequences, a process known as maximizing the homology. Identical amino acid residues are indicated here by boxes, and residues with side chains of similar properties are indicated by shading. We see some indication that the two variable regions had a common origin, and considerable evidence that the four constant domains had a common origin. (Comparison of additional examples of antibodies would show that some of the similarities in structure indicated here are fortuitous occurrences of particular residues, but sufficient homologies remain to demonstrate the common origin.)

Two homologous segments can be found in light chains, four in γ heavy chains, and five in μ heavy chains. The simplest explanation is that there was originally a gene coding for a shorter segment of peptide that became duplicated, both by end-to-end repetition in a continuous strand, and also by formation of similar genes in different strands. After duplication, the various genes underwent independent mutations to develop separate coding for the constant and variable regions of the various chains.

FURTHER READING

N. K. Jerne, The immune system, Sci. Amer., 229:52 (July, 1973). An excellent general account.

G. M. Edelman, Antibody structure and molecular immunology, Science, 180:830 (1973). The Nobel Prize lecture by one of the authorities. More readable than most.

E. Haber et al., Two genes, one polypeptide chain, Federation Proc., 31:176 (1972). A symposium, in which the papers by L. E. Hood (p. 177) and by F. W. Putnam et al. (p. 193) are most useful to the general reader desiring more detailed information.

E. F. Osserman, Plasma cell dyscrasias, p. 1574 in P. G. Beeson and W. McDermott, Cecil-Loeb Textbook of medicine, 13th ed., W. B. Saunders (1971). For those with an interest in medical problems.

QUESTIONS

1. Three solutions containing protein are available. Upon diluting a portion of the solutions ten-fold with distilled water, a precipitate forms in tube A. Upon making portions of the solution 4 M to sodium chloride, precipitates form in tubes A and C. Classify the respective proteins as albumins or globulins.
2. Proteins with which of the following chain compositions do not occur as effective antibodies: (a) $\kappa_2\alpha_2$, (b) $\kappa_2\lambda_2$, (c) $\lambda_2\gamma_2$, (d) $\alpha_2\gamma_2$. Why?
3. Since mutations can occur in any position on DNA, the persistence of a particular amino acid residue during the evolution of a protein indicates that a change would impair the survival or reproduction of the animals in which it occurs. With this in mind, explain why a glycine residue always occurs at a particular position in the variable region of all immunoglobulin peptides of known structure.
4. What is the function of the amino acid residues in the hypervariable positions of immunoglobulins? What is the function of the other residues in the variable regions? In the constant regions?
5. Why is it that univalent antigens, that is, those with only one site capable of stimulating antibody formation, do not form precipitates with the corresponding antibodies?

233

CHAPTER 6

BINDING FOR TRANSPORT

THE CONCEPTS

Transport by Simple Binding. Simple combination of a molecule with a carrier protein is useful only for transport with high concentration gradients. Myoglobin carries oxygen within muscle fibers in this way.

Transport by Conformational Change. Effective transport frequently requires the carrier protein to release the transported molecule more readily upon exposure to conditions at the biological destination of the molecule. Such carrier proteins are constructed so as to change their conformation in response to a signal represented by a different concentration of some compound at the destination. Hemoglobin changes its conformation so as to release oxygen at the peripheral tissues, and this change is promoted by three separate signals.

Subunit Cooperativity in Hemoglobin. Hemoglobin has four separate peptide chains, each approximately the same size and shape as the single chain in myoglobin. Each chain in hemoglobin or myoglobin is wrapped around a heme molecule, which is a ferrous-porphyrin chelate. Combination with O_2 causes a displacement of the iron atom and the adjacent peptide chain. Relief of this displacement by loss of oxygen has little effect on isolated single chains, which combine tightly with oxygen at low concentrations. However, relief of displacement by loss of O_2 from a complete hemoglobin molecule disturbs the association of its four chains so that they snap into a new arrangement with a low affinity for oxygen, and more O_2 is released. The loss of oxygen therefore acts as a signal for the release of additional oxygen, and the subunits of hemoglobin are therefore said to exhibit positive cooperativity. (Negative cooperativity would be shown by stronger retention of the remaining bound molecules when one is lost.)

Bohr Effect. Hemoglobin also releases more oxygen upon exposure to increased H^+ concentrations, as in heavily working muscles. It does so because the shift in conformation upon releasing oxygen causes hemoglobin to take up H^+, and increased H^+ therefore promotes the shift.

Diphosphoglycerate Effect. Hemoglobin also releases more oxygen upon exposure to increased concentrations of 2,3-diphosphoglycerate, a compound that prevents the shift of conformation necessary for combination with oxygen. The amount of 2,3-diphosphoglycerate in the red blood cell increases when it is necessary for oxygen to be released more completely, as in exposure to high altitudes or in other conditions in which less oxygen is being carried.

Membrane Structure. Biological membranes separate different chemical environments in organisms. The membranes have proteins on their surfaces and non-polar lipids in their cores. The principal lipids (fat-like substances) present are phospholipids, which form bilayers with polar phosphate and amino groups on the outside and with long hydrocarbon tails toward the interior. While some compounds leak through biological membranes by simple diffusion, with a rate dependent only on concentration gradient, most require a carrier to cross the lipid core.

Transport Across Membranes. Some carriers simply facilitate diffusion by combining equally readily with a compound on either side of the membrane; the transported compound is therefore bound more often on the side of higher concentration and released more often on the side of lower concentration. Other membrane carriers are able to actively transport one compound against its concentration gradient, that is, from a region of low concentration to a region of high concentration. This is possible because they also transport a second compound in the direction favored by its concentration gradient. In effect, the active transport of the first compound is being driven by the facilitated diffusion of the second compound. The two compounds may be transported in the same direction by a symport mechanism, or in opposite directions by an antiport mechanism. Other mechanisms of active transport involve coupling transport with some additional chemical reaction, such as the hydrolysis of adenosine triphosphate or an actual modification of the compound being transported.

TRANSPORT THROUGH CONFORMATIONAL CHANGES

Some proteins are constructed so that they will act as carriers for the movement of compounds in the organism. The transport may be within a cell, across a cell membrane, or between cells *via* the circulation, but transport in any case involves picking up at one site and letting go at another. Transport therefore is not like the simple binding of antigen and antibody, in which the object is to make a tight and relatively permanent combination of the two molecules. Effective transport often requires a more complex kind of behavior from the carrier protein, so that the association of the protein with the transported molecule is strong at the source of supply of the molecule, and is weak at its biological destination. How can the strength of association between a carrier and its transported molecule be made to vary at different locations within the organism? The variation in binding strength is accomplished by constructing the protein carrier so that it changes its shape when the biological destination is reached, with this conformational change weakening the bonds between the carrier and the molecule being transported.

Signal for Conformational Change. The carrier protein assumes a shape favorable for binding at one location and a shape unfavorable for binding at another location because there is some difference in the chemical environment at the two locations. The protein "knows" when the destination of the transported compound has been reached only because it encounters a different set of conditions. At least one chemical compound that interacts with the carrier protein must be present in different concentrations at the origin and the destination, so that the concentration differences can act as a signal to cause the alteration in conformation.

TRANSPORT OF OXYGEN BY HEMOGLOBIN

Nature of Oxygen Transport

Every educated person knows that oxygen is transported in the blood of higher animals by combination with hemoglobin, but fewer know that the muscles of these animals contain another hemoglobin, known as **myoglobin,** that also binds oxygen. Hemoglobin can effectively transport oxygen in the blood because it undergoes a conformational change when it gains oxygen. Myoglobin does not undergo a conformational change upon combination with oxygen, and it is used mainly for speeding the diffusion of oxygen within a muscle fiber and for the storage of oxygen within the muscles. (The storage function is especially important in diving animals, which have high concentrations of myoglobin in their muscles.) The differences in action of myoglobin and hemoglobin therefore provide an excellent example of the way in which conformational changes can be used to broaden the usefulness of binding by proteins. Let us first see what these functional differences are, and then examine how they come about.

Combination of Myoglobin and Oxygen. Molecules of myoglobin (Mb) and oxygen combine to form oxymyoglobin in a simple reaction, which is described by an ordinary equilibrium constant:

$$Mb + O_2 \longrightarrow MbO_2 \qquad K_{eq} = \frac{[MbO_2]}{[Mb][O_2]}$$

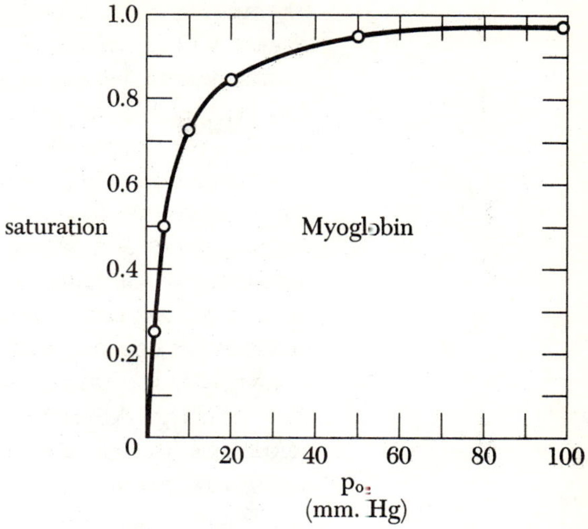

Figure 6–1 The saturation of a carrier with oxygen when the reaction between them has a simple equilibrium. Myoglobin, the hemoglobin of muscle, combines with oxygen in this way.

In a reaction of this sort, the amount of myoglobin that is combined with oxygen (that is, the **saturation** of myoglobin with oxygen) increases in a simple hyperbolic way as the concentration of oxygen increases (Fig. 6–1). When oxygen is first introduced into a solution of pure myoglobin, it combines readily, but more and more oxygen is required to create additional oxymyoglobin as the ratio of the concentration of oxymyoglobin to that of free myoglobin increases.

Myoglobin can function as a carrier of oxygen within muscle fibers because there is a sharp gradient of oxygen concentration between the surface of the fibers and the mitochondria, which are the organelles in which oxygen is consumed. (The utilization of oxygen by mitochondria is the principal topic of Chapter 10.) The concentration at the cell surface, expressed in terms of the pressure of oxygen gas in equilibrium with the solution, is 40 mm Hg at rest, and it may go as low as 10 mm Hg during severe exercise. We see from Figure 6–1 that 70% to 90% of the myoglobin will be combined with oxygen under these conditions.

The mitochondria of working muscles use oxygen so rapidly that the concentration in their vicinity is estimated to be between 0.5 and 2 mm of Hg, and only 10% to 25% of myoglobin will be combined with oxygen at these low concentrations. This being so, myoglobin molecules that have spontaneously associated with oxygen near the cell surface will lose the oxygen when their random diffusion carries them near mitochondria, and this is an important mechanism for moving oxygen through the muscle fibers. At a given moment, half or fewer of the myoglobin molecules are combined with oxygen in a working muscle. Those near mitochondria have little oxygen, while those near the surface are almost saturated. (It may seem strange that the small oxygen molecule doesn't diffuse very rapidly by itself. It can, but the solubility of oxygen in water is so low that the flux of dissolved oxygen is about the same as the flux of the slower moving, but more concentrated, oxymyoglobin molecules.)

Combination of Hemoglobin and Oxygen. Myoglobin operates efficiently as a carrier without conformational change because there is a 10-fold or greater concentration gradient for oxygen within the cells. Now let us consider the transport of oxygen within the circulation.

In order to maintain the concentration gradient for oxygen within the muscle fibers, oxygen must be delivered to their surface at a relatively high concentration, for example, 40 mm Hg at rest. However, oxygen is available to the circulation in the lungs at only

100 mm Hg. (The atmospheric partial pressure is near 160 mm Hg, but the air in the **alveoli,** which are the sacs of the lung in contact with the capillary bed, does not fully exchange with the atmosphere during respiration, and alveolar air is also lighter because it is warmer.) Hemoglobin is built to combine with oxygen in a complex way, so that it will lose oxygen at a relatively high partial pressure (Figure 6–2). The plot of saturation versus concentration is **sigmoidal,** rather than hyperbolic. It is as if the loss (or gain) of one oxygen promoted, rather than impeded, the further loss (or gain) of additional oxygen. When the erythrocytes (red blood cells) are squeezed through the capillaries of the lung, the hemoglobin within them becomes almost completely saturated with oxygen. Upon delivery to the peripheral tissues through the heart, the erythrocytes come in contact with regions of lower oxygen concentration. Hemoglobin is constructed so that it is approximately 75% saturated with oxygen at a partial pressure of 40 mm Hg; therefore, blood carried from the lungs to resting muscles releases an amount of oxygen equivalent to approximately one-quarter of the total amount hemoglobin can carry.

When muscles work very hard, and the partial pressure of oxygen at their surface falls owing to the great consumption by the mitochondria, hemoglobin is driven to release more oxygen. For example, at 10 mm Hg, hemoglobin is only 10% saturated with oxygen, and hemoglobin can therefore release nearly all of its bound oxygen to muscles doing maximum work.

The Bohr Effect. The hemoglobin molecule is also constructed to respond to an additional signal, so that some oxygen can be released without the partial pressure falling to very low values. We shall see that hard-working muscles tend to produce lactic acid. The resultant increase in H^+ concentration weakens the affinity of hemoglobin for oxygen, so that more is released at a given partial pressure. This is so because hemoglobin and H^+ associate more strongly than do oxyhemoglobin and H^+. When the basic form of hemoglobin is removed by combination with H^+, the resultant fall in concentration causes more of the basic form of oxyhemoglobin to dissociate into oxygen and free hemoglobin (Fig. 6–3). The decline in oxygen affinity with increasing acidity is known as the Bohr effect.

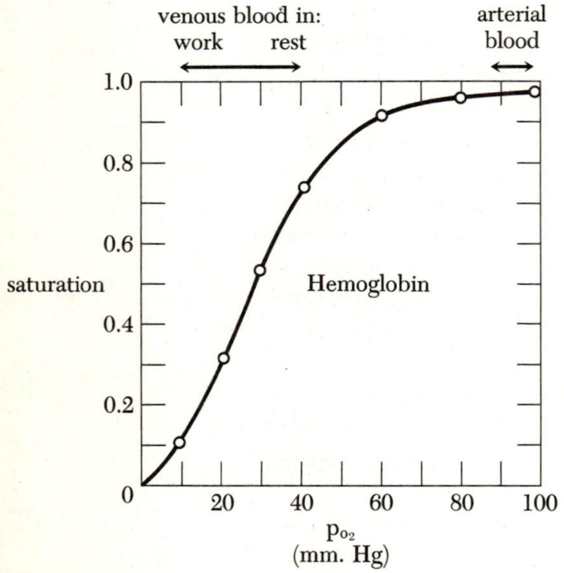

Figure 6–2 The saturation of hemoglobin A_1 exposed to varying partial pressures of oxygen. At the top are shown ranges of oxygen tension found in venous blood of adult humans at work and at rest, and in the arterial blood. The oxygen tension of arterial blood does not vary widely with exercise.

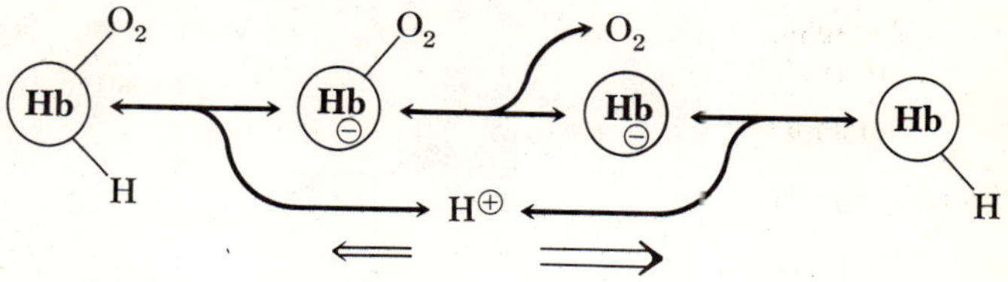

Figure 6-3 Free hemoglobin binds H^+ more tightly than does oxyhemoglobin. A rise in the concentration of H^+ therefore causes an increased release of O_2 to create more free hemoglobin.

Mechanism of Oxygen Transport

Heme as a Prosthetic Group. Hemoglobin and myoglobin can bind oxygen because they contain heme groups, which are chelates of ferrous ions with a **porphyrin** (Fig. 6-4). Here we have an illustration of another important principle: Proteins may be constructed so as to bind other compounds that are used as tools to carry out

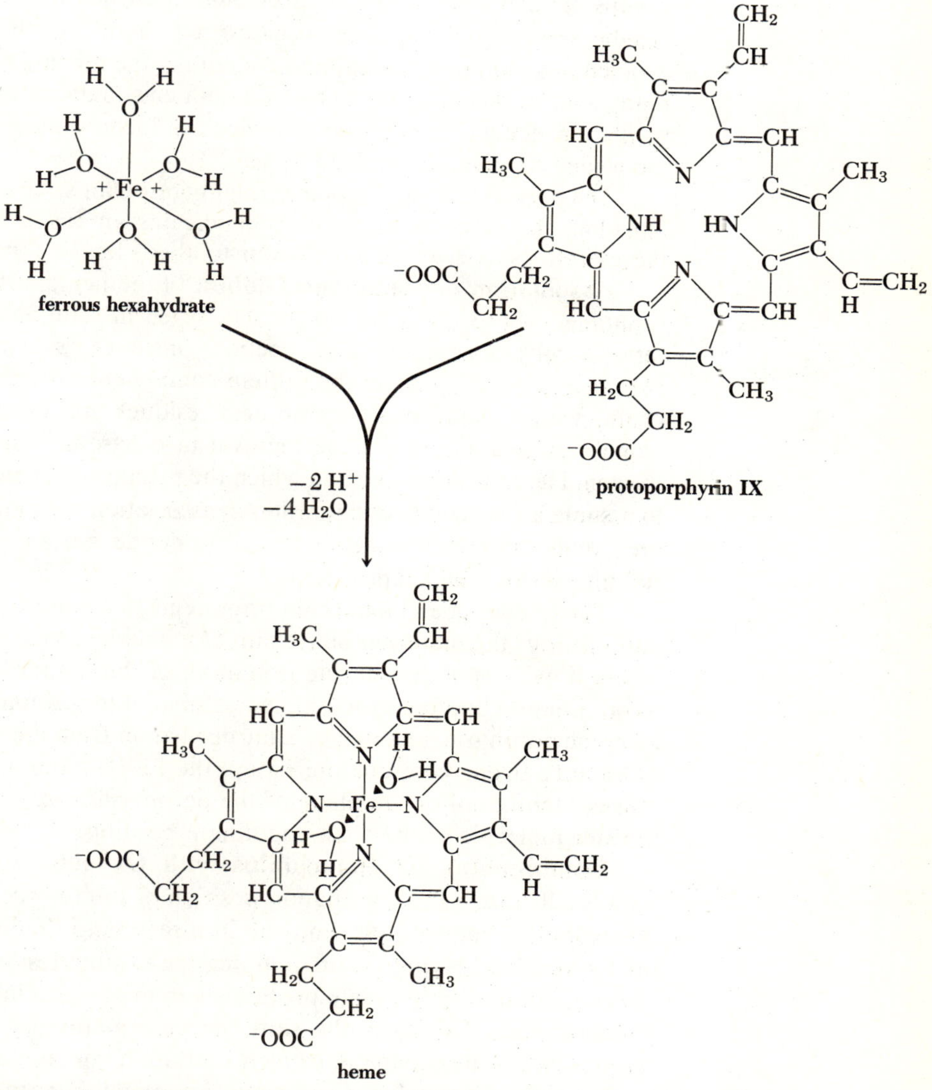

Figure 6-4 The formal stoichiometry of the combination of ferrous ion and protoporphyrin IX to form heme.

L-histidine
(His)

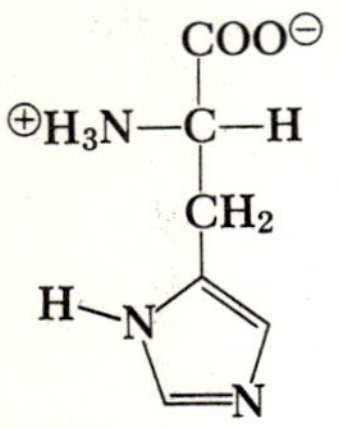

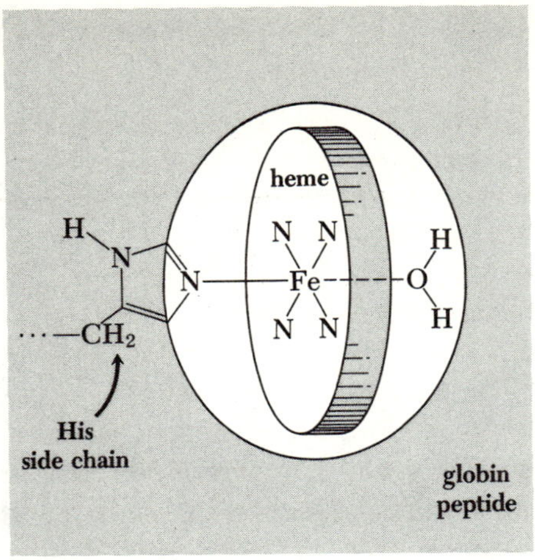

Figure 6–5 Schematic illustration of heme in a pocket formed by the globin peptide. A histidyl side chain from the globin acts as an additional ligand for the iron atom in heme. The free amino acid, histidine, is shown at the left.

particular functions, because the twenty amino acid residues do not provide chemical groups of sufficient variety to participate in all biological reactions. When a function can be served only by some structure not found in the amino acids, proteins have evolved so as to bind a compound containing the missing structure. We shall encounter many such compounds in connection with enzymatic catalysis; now we are concerned with a particular example, heme, which is incorporated by globin peptides to form molecules capable of binding oxygen.

The porphyrin ring is a planar, highly resonant structure, with four nitrogen atoms fixed in the center at a spacing that creates an especial affinity for iron atoms; it therefore acts as a tetradentate (four-toothed) ligand for iron.

Association of Heme and Globin. Free heme, a ferrous-porphyrin chelate, is spontaneously oxidized by molecular oxygen in solution to form **hemin,** which is the ferric-porphyrin complex. This reaction consumes oxygen, rather than transporting it. However, globin, which is the protein component of hemoglobin, is made of peptide chains with a sequence of amino acid residues that causes the chain to fold around heme groups and prevent the removal of electrons from the heme iron to attached oxygen. Here we have a case in which the primary structure of the peptides is designed to assume a particular configuration in association with another compound, heme, and the bonds between the heme and the peptide are an important part of the forces stabilizing the final shape.

The folding of a globin chain traps heme in a pocket lined with non-polar residues, and it brings the **imidazole** side chain of a **histidyl** group in the peptide into a position where it will complex with the iron atom of the heme (Fig. 6–5). Iron ordinarily has a coordination number of six; in hemoglobin four positions are filled by nitrogen atoms from the porphyrin, and one by a nitrogen atom from the histidyl group. In the absence of another strong coordinating group, the Fe(II) atom assumes a high-spin state and moves slightly out of the plane of the porphyrin ring, with perhaps weak bonding of a water molecule at the sixth coordinate position.

Combination of Hemoglobins with Oxygen. Oxygen, with its π electrons, readily fills the sixth coordination position of the ferrous iron atom in hemoglobin or myoglobin. When this happens, the iron reverts to the low spin state and moves into the plane of the porphyrin ring, pulling the histidyl residue with it. The resultant shift of configuration of the single peptide chain in myoglobin has no further consequences of importance. However, the shift in conformation of the chain in hemoglobin is responsible for its sigmoidal oxygen saturation curve and the Bohr effect. This comes about because hemoglobin molecules are made from two different peptide chains, α and β, which have surfaces built to associate with each other as $\alpha\beta$ pairs; two such pairs combine to make hemoglobin. A complete hemoglobin molecule in the higher animals is therefore a tetramer, $\alpha_2\beta_2$, with each of the four chains containing a heme group and capable of binding oxygen. The peptides of myoglobin and hemoglobin coil around heme in a very similar way, but the hemoglobin peptides are constructed with "sticky" exterior surfaces—regions with non-polar amino acid residues folded in complementary shapes—that cause the peptides to associate.

COOPERATIVITY OF HEMOGLOBIN CHAINS. The presence of more than one subunit in a protein molecule makes it possible (but not obligatory) for it to associate in a complex way with other molecules. This is so because the binding of one molecule on one subunit (for example, the binding of one O_2 molecule on one subunit of hemoglobin) can change the remaining subunits so that they bind additional molecules more or less easily. If the binding of the first molecule makes it easier for subsequent molecules to be bound, the protein is said to exhibit **positive cooperativity.** If the initial binding makes it more difficult to bind additional molecules, it is said to exhibit **negative cooperativity.** The binding of oxygen to hemoglobin is an example of positive cooperativity, because it requires a smaller increase in oxygen concentration to bind the second, third, and fourth oxygen molecules than would be predicted from the concentration required to bind the preceding molecules in simple equilibria.

The positive cooperativity comes about in this way. The hemoglobin molecule can exist in a somewhat strained structure in which the heme crevices of some, probably two, of the subunits do not readily admit molecular oxygen, and the remaining crevices are closed, or nearly so, to oxygen. It can also exist in a more relaxed structure, in which the β-subunits slide toward each other, and the heme crevices are more freely accessible to oxygen. Deoxyhemoglobin is locked in the strained configuration by **salt bridges,** that is, combinations of negatively and positively charged side chains from the different subunits (Fig. 6–6). (These salt bridges are forces present at the surface of the chains in addition to the normal non-polar interactions at the interior contacts.)

As oxyhemoglobin is delivered from the lungs to the tissues, the first and then the second molecule of oxygen are detached. However, the removal of each molecule causes the corresponding iron atom to move out of the plane of its porphyrin ring and displace the attached histidyl residue. The resultant disturbance in the configuration of the peptides brings the groups forming salt bridges closer together until there is a sudden shift, a snap, from the relaxed to the strained configuration, with the salt

Figure 6–6 (*Right*) The α- and β-peptides of hemoglobin are locked together by salt bridges, and a tyrosyl residue near the C-terminal is partially buried to form a hydrogen bond between helical segments (Fig. 1–6, p. 13). Combination with oxygen changes the position of the chains (*left*) enough so that the tyrosyl residue snaps out of its pocket, and the salt bridges are broken. The β-peptides can then slide toward each other in a more relaxed configuration that permits easier combination with additional oxygen. (Modified from R. E. Dickerson, Ann. Rev. Biochem., 41:815 (1972).)

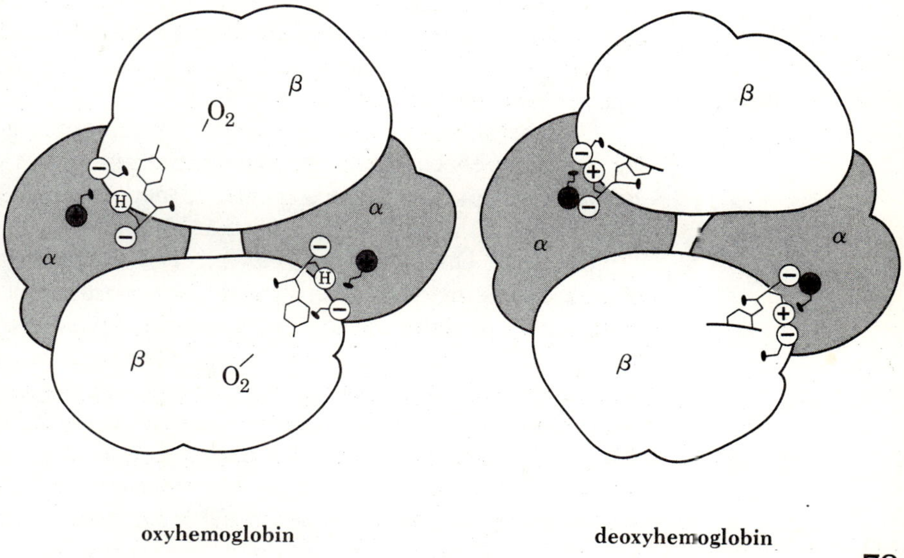

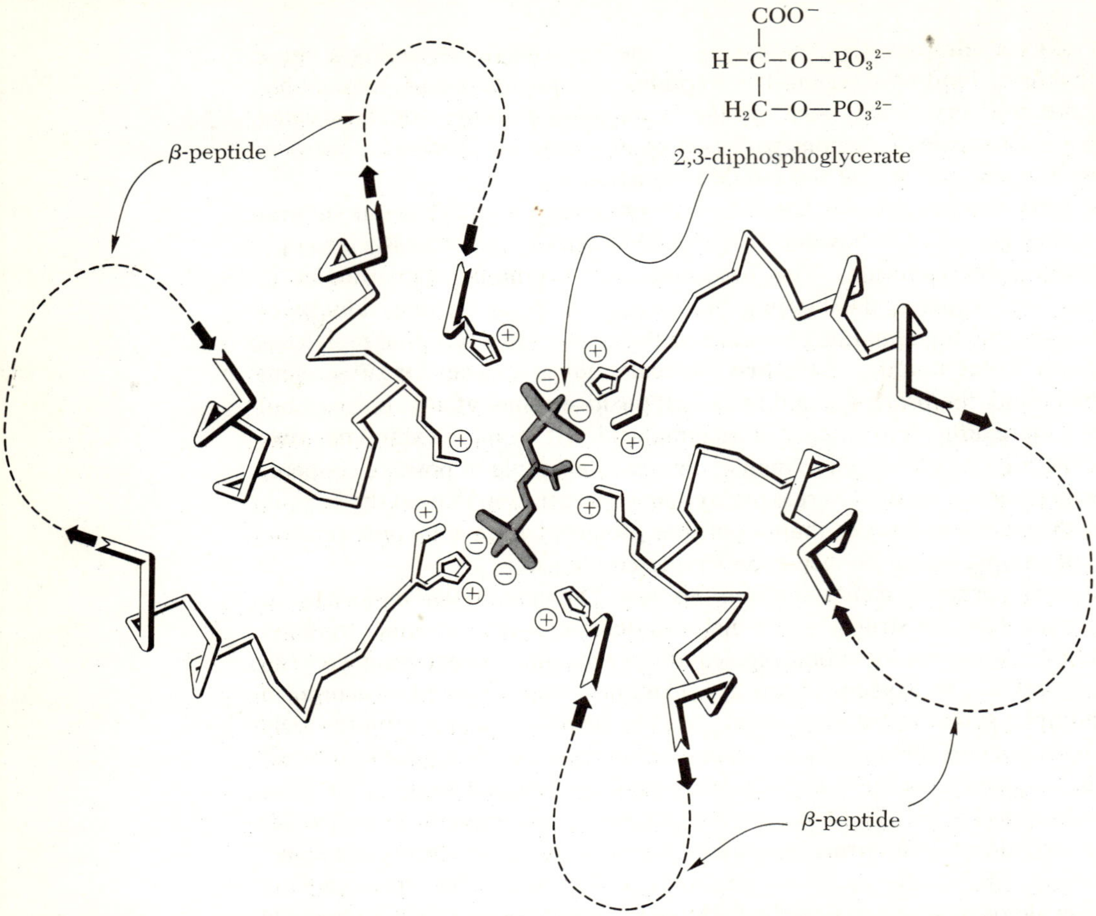

Figure 6-7 2,3-Diphosphoglycerate, with its five negative charges, combines with positively charged side chains on the β-peptides of hemoglobin to keep them apart in the tense, deoxygenated configuration. The compound therefore diminishes the affinity of hemoglobin for oxygen. (Adapted from A. Arone, Nature, 237:146 (1972).)

bridges clicking into place. This shift to the weakly-binding tense structure causes oxygen to be expelled, even though the oxygen tension is still relatively high.

The reverse sequence occurs when venous blood reaches the lungs. When a molecule of deoxyhemoglobin acquires two oxygen molecules, it suddenly snaps into the relaxed configuration, which readily binds two more oxygen molecules at the concentrations necessary to affix the first two.

The break in salt linkages caused by the binding of oxygen also is responsible for the Bohr effect. When the ammonium groups are removed from associated carboxylate groups, they have a greater tendence to lose H^+, and this is why oxyhemoglobin behaves as a stronger acid than does deoxyhemoglobin.

Role of Diphosphoglycerate. The hemoglobins of some animals, including man, are constructed so as to regulate oxygen transport in still an additional way. The erythrocytes of these animals contain concentrations of 2,3-diphosphoglycerate (Fig. 6-7) roughly equal to the concentration of hemoglobin, and their hemoglobin molecules are constructed so that positively charged side chains from the β-subunits are in a position to react with the negative charges on the 2,3-diphosphoglycerate. However, this can happen only when the molecule is in the tense configuration, with the β-subunits moved apart. Indeed, the combination with 2,3-diphosphoglycerate forces the subunits into an even more unfavorable location for combination with oxygen.

The result of this interaction is that diphosphoglycerate must be expelled from the molecule before oxygen can combine. The higher the concentration of diphosphoglycerate, the higher the oxygen concentration must be in order to form oxyhemoglobin. To state the physiological function more accurately, the higher the concentration of diphosphoglycerate, the less the oxygen that can be retained at a given partial pressure. Since the resultant loss of affinity has less effect on the saturation of hemoglobin in the lungs, the increase in diphosphoglycerate serves mainly to increase the loss of oxygen to the tissues. Adjustments in its concentration serve to adapt the organism to changes in altitude, or to lung damage, or to other conditions affecting the oxygen supply.

TRANSPORT BY PLASMA PROTEINS

We shall see as we go along that many of the other proteins in the blood are also involved in transport of nutrients and other compounds between tissues. For example, plasma albumin binds fatty acids, and carries these fuels to the muscles. Other proteins are designed to transport minor mineral nutrients, such as copper or iron, and still others transport hormones. The way in which these proteins pick up and release their burdens is not nearly as well defined as it is with hemoglobin.

TRANSPORT ACROSS MEMBRANES

The Nature of Biological Membranes

The periphery of a cell and its interior organelles are defined by membranes. The important feature of a membrane is that it has a sidedness—it separates different environments. It follows that a membrane must have a selective permeability toward different compounds, so that some compounds move across the membrane much faster than others in order to create these different environments.

The separation of the solutions on the two sides of a biological membrane, and the consequent regulation of the passage of molecules through it, is substantially aided by the general character of the membranes. They are essentially composed of two sheets of protein molecules separated by a non-polar lipid core. Let us first define the lipids.

Nature of Lipids. The lipids are the fat-like substances of organisms (Fig. 6–8). They include the **fats** themselves (**triglycerides**), which are esters of **glycerol** and alkyl carboxylic acids (the **fatty acids**); the **steroids,** which are polycyclic hydrocarbons, usually substituted with only a few oxygen atoms; and the **phospholipids.** The phospholipids, which are the major constituents of the lipid core of membranes, may be regarded as fats in which one of the fatty acids has been replaced by a phosphoric acid group, also esterified with an amine-substituted alcohol. We shall consider all of these compounds in more detail later.

The important thing for now is to recognize that phospholipids have a charged end and a long non-polar tail, which gives them a detergent action. Such molecules spontaneously form **bilayers** in aqueous solution, with the charged ends oriented toward the water on each side, and the hydrocarbon tails directed toward each other in the center (Fig. 6–9). The membranes also contain varying amounts of cholesterol.

Membrane Proteins. The detailed architecture of the protein components of membranes is not known. Since the interior lipid core is fluid, it seems likely that the two protein surfaces are stabilized by connecting links going through the core. (The

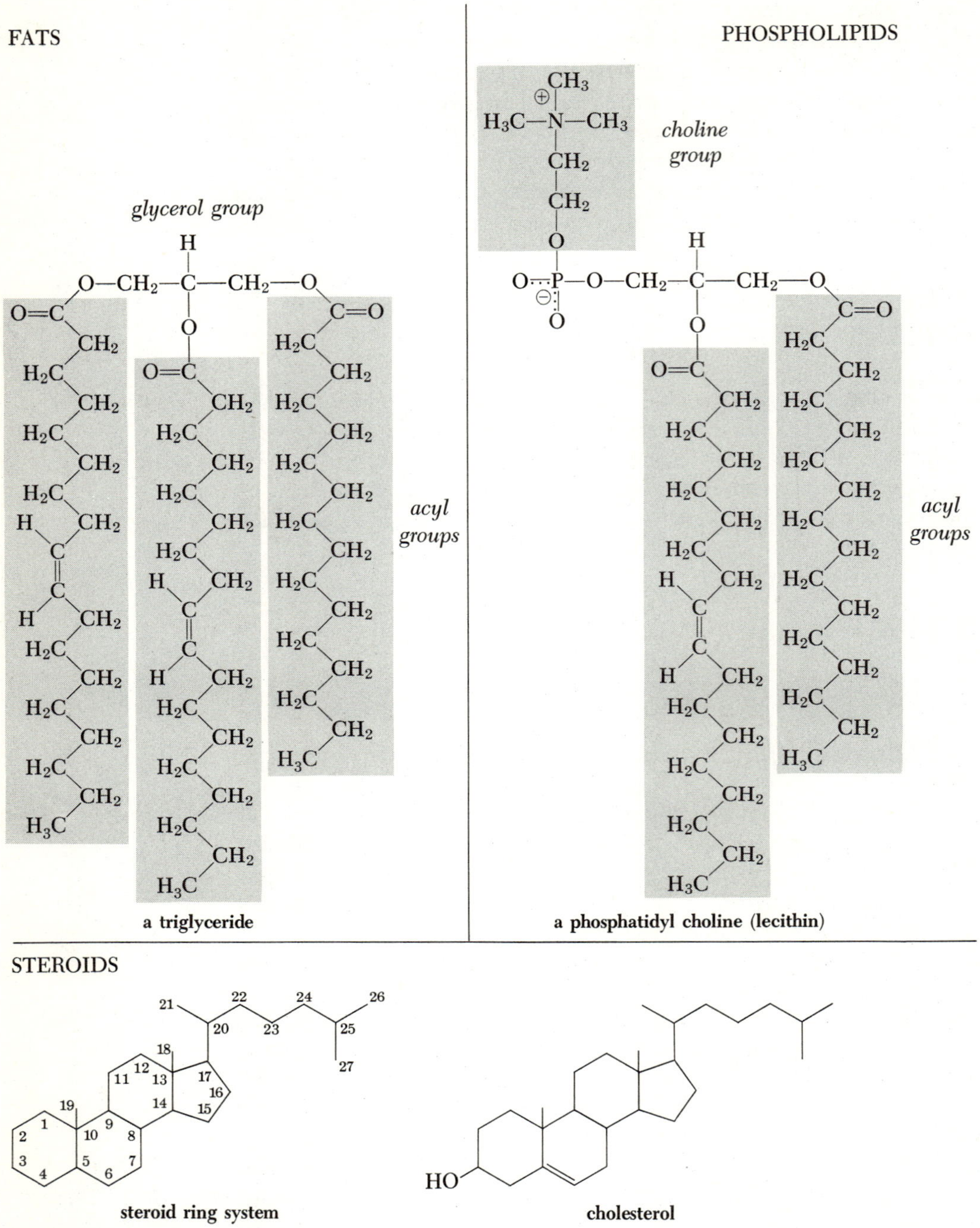

Figure 6-8 Typical lipids.

molecular composition of membrane lipids is adjusted in various organisms to maintain the liquid state of the core at the normal environmental temperatures.)

Transport Mechanisms

Passive Diffusion. Since the chemical environment differs on the two sides of biological membranes, there is a concentration gradient for many compounds across

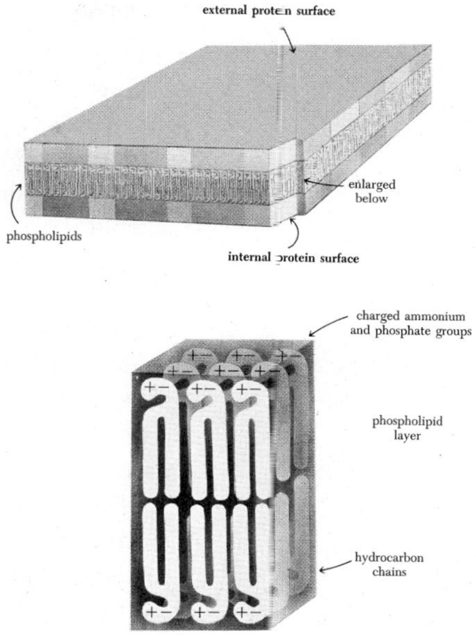

Figure 6-9 Biological membranes are modified bilayers. The simplest bilayer structure, first recognized by J. J. Danielli, has a hydrophobic core mainly composed of the hydrocarbon tails of phospholipids and hydrophilic faces composed of proteins bound to the polar head groups of the phospholipids. The inner and outer faces of membranes have different proteins attached, and various kinds of protein form pillars (not shown) that cross the hydrophobic core between the polar surfaces. The nature of these proteins differs from one kind of membrane to another.

the membrane. If the membrane is leaky for a given compound, it will diffuse faster from the side of higher concentration to the side of lower concentration than it does in the reverse direction, and there will be net movement across the membrane. Movement of this sort is believed to occur with Na^+ across the **plasma membrane** (the outside membrane) of most mammalian cells. The concentration of Na^+ is higher outside than it is inside, and there is a constant leakage by passive diffusion into the cell. (The concentration gradient is maintained by pumping Na^+ out by a completely different mechanism.)

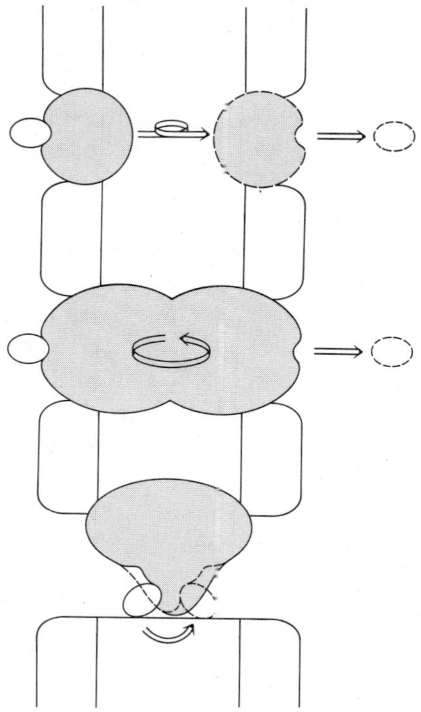

Figure 6-10 Many substances can cross membranes only by attachment to a protein carrier. In theory, the carrier may act by actually moving from one side of the membrane to another (*top*), by rotating within the membrane (*middle*), or by shifting conformation in a way that exposes the binding site alternately to the inside or the outside phase. The actual mechanism is yet to be seen, but in any case, this simple facilitated diffusion will result only in net transport from the side of higher concentration to the side of lower concentration.

The distinguishing features of passive transport are that it can occur only from high concentrations to low concentrations, and that the rate at which it occurs is dependent on the concentration differences across the membrane. The greater the concentration gradient, the faster the diffusion.

Facilitated Diffusion. Organisms have evolved a means of regulating the movement of compounds across membranes in response to a concentration gradient by incorporating carrier proteins into the membrane. These proteins have the function of specifically binding particular compounds and of moving within the membrane in such a way as to expose the binding site on both sides of the membrane (Fig. 6–10). Again, the exact details of the mechanism are not known. It may be that the carrier protein rotates within the membrane, moves in a linear direction, or does some combination of the two. It is even conceivable that some carrier proteins are built as a bridge across a membrane, with multiple binding sites along which the transported molecule is passed as in a bucket brigade.

An excellent example of facilitated diffusion is the movement of **glucose,** the principal sugar in blood, into most cells of the higher animals. The concentration of glucose is greater in the blood than it is within muscle cells, for example, and it moves into the muscle by facilitated diffusion. This movement represents consecutive equilibria:

$$\begin{array}{ccc} \textbf{glucose}_{out} + \textbf{carrier}_{out} & \longleftrightarrow & \textbf{glucose} - \textbf{carrier}_{out} \\ \updownarrow & & \updownarrow \\ \textbf{glucose}_{in} + \textbf{carrier}_{in} & \longleftrightarrow & \textbf{glucose} - \textbf{carrier}_{in} \end{array}$$

(In the case of the carrier, out or in represents exposure of the binding sites on one side of the membrane or the other, not physical displacement from the membrane.)

Three important characteristics of facilitated diffusion can be deduced from this mechanism. Since it depends upon binding of the transported molecule to a particular protein, the binding can be made specific to a few compounds, perhaps only one, whereas the presence of an open hole in the membrane would permit any compound of similar size to diffuse. Furthermore, the strength of binding and the rate at which the carrier functions can be altered by changes in the conformation of the carrier owing to the presence of some third compound. This may be the mechanism, for example, by which the hormone insulin regulates the flow of glucose into muscle cells. Finally, the rate of transport does not continue to increase as the concentration gradient is increased. Although the amount of glucose-carrier complex formed on the outside increases with increasing concentration of glucose, and the amount of glucose released on the inside increases as its internal concentration becomes lower, there is a limited amount of carrier available. As the concentration of glucose rises on the outside, the carrier becomes nearly saturated with glucose, and further increases in concentration make little difference. The rate of transport therefore approaches a maximum velocity that depends upon the amount of carrier present, as well as upon its inherent kinetic properties (Fig. 6–11).

Active Transport. Active transport is the ability to move a compound from a region of lower concentration to a region of higher concentration. The transport against a concentration gradient cannot proceed by itself; it must be a part of a larger process that is proceeding toward equilibrium.

Symport-Antiport Mechanisms. One way in which active transport can be accomplished is to couple the movement of one compound against a concentration gradient to the movement of another compound with an even greater concentration gradient. This is done by making a single carrier protein bind two molecules for

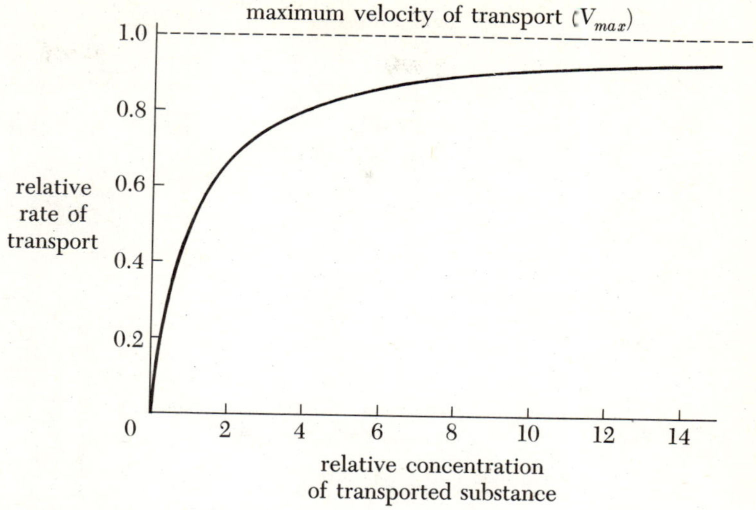

Figure 6–11 The kinetics of facilitated diffusion. As the concentration gradient across a membrane rises, the rate of transport increases toward a theoretical maximum velocity obtained by always having the carrier occupied by a transported molecule.

transport. If the carrier normally transports both molecules in the same direction across a membrane, it is said to be a symport mechanism; if they are transported in opposite directions, it is an antiport mechanism (Fig. 6–12).

Many microorganisms and the mucosal cells of vertebrate intestines are able to take up glucose even though the concentration inside the cell is greater than the concentration outside. The advantage is that the cells are in effect licking the plate to get the last available bit of this primary fuel from the environment. The active transport of glucose is frequently driven by the simultaneous carriage of Na^+ into the cells. A single carrier molecule combines with both a glucose molecule and a Na^+ ion, and the carrier is built so that it readily shifts binding sites from one side of the membrane to the other if, and only if, it has both Na^+ and glucose attached (Fig. 6–13). The cells have a lower concentration of Na^+ inside than they do outside, so there is a greater tendency for Na^+ to be released on the inside, as in facilitated diffusion. However, the release of Na^+ weakens the binding of glucose, and it will also be released even though the concentration inside may be greater than the concentration outside. The favorable gradient of Na^+ concentration is driving glucose against its unfavorable gradient by this symport mechanism.

Other Mechanisms. Active transport is also accomplished by coupling the

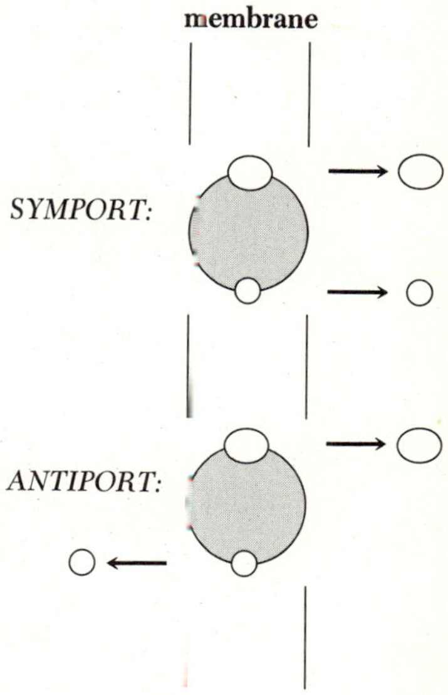

Figure 6–12 A carrier may be constructed to transport two different molecules, either in the same direction, or in opposite directions, across the membrane. If the concentration gradient is sufficiently high for one of the molecules, its transport by either the symport or the antiport mechanism can drive the transport of the other molecule against a concentration gradient.

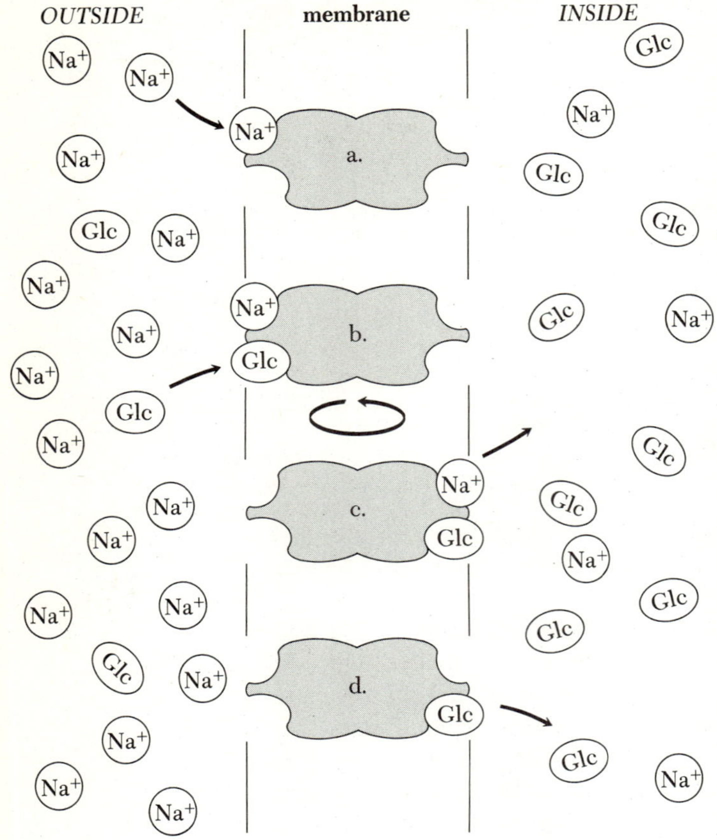

Figure 6–13 Glucose is concentrated in the intestinal mucosa by a symport mechanism involving the simultaneous movement of Na^+. Both Na^+ and glucose must be bound to the carrier before it will shift position so as to expose the binding sites to the opposite side of the membrane. (The shift is shown as a rotation, but the real mechanism is not known.) The high concentration gradient for Na^+ from the outside (the lumen of the intestine) to the inside of the mucosal cells enables glucose to be concentrated to an equally large gradient in the opposite direction.

movement of a compound to a variety of other reactions. For example, we shall see that the concentration of Na^+ is kept high outside of many cells, and the concentration of K^+ is kept high inside the cells, through a **Na^+-K^+ pump** that is driven by the simultaneous hydrolysis of ATP, much in the way that protein synthesis is driven by the hydrolysis of nucleotides. Active transport may also be accomplished by **group translocations,** in which the molecule to be transported is modified through chemical reactions as it crosses the membrane. The modification removes the compound and creates another compound that cannot pass through the membrane. This process maintains a concentration gradient into the cell for the original material by transforming it into another compound of higher concentration, which can be used in the cell metabolism. Some microorganisms take up glucose by mechanisms of this sort, and we shall discuss specific examples later.

FURTHER READING

R. E. Dickerson, X-Ray studies of protein mechanisms, Ann. Rev. Biochem., 41:815 (1972). See pages 818–827 for a description of sub-unit interactions in hemoglobin by the master of lucid exposition on protein conformations.

M. F. Perutz, Stereochemistry of cooperative effects in hemoglobin, Nature, 228:726 (1970). A more detailed description of the action of hemoglobin than is contained in Dickerson's article, but also more difficult to follow.

L. E. Hokin, ed., Metabolic Transport, vol. 6 of Metabolic Pathways, 3rd ed., Academic Press (1972). More technical descriptions of various kinds of transport mechanisms. Heavy work.

QUESTIONS

1. Explain how myoglobin and hemoglobin work in tandem for effective oxygen transport, with particular reference to the oxygen concentration at the surface of the muscle fibers.
2. Many mutations in the structure of hemoglobin molecules have been discovered in humans, and the effects of these mutations are often instructive. For example:

   (a) Explain why the replacement of a residue of phenylalanine at position 42 of the β-chain, which is a position in the lining of the heme pocket, with a residue of serine creates a molecule in which the heme is readily oxidized to hemin.

   (b) Explain why replacement of one amino acid residue with another in the regions where subunits contact each other frequently causes the association with oxygen to become more hyperbolic and stronger.
3. What is the advantage of the Bohr effect to the organism?
4. Consider the origin of the Bohr effect and of the sigmoidal oxygen association curve of hemoglobin, and then offer an explanation of the inability of hemoglobin to display these effects when the H^+ concentration is displaced markedly from physiological values.

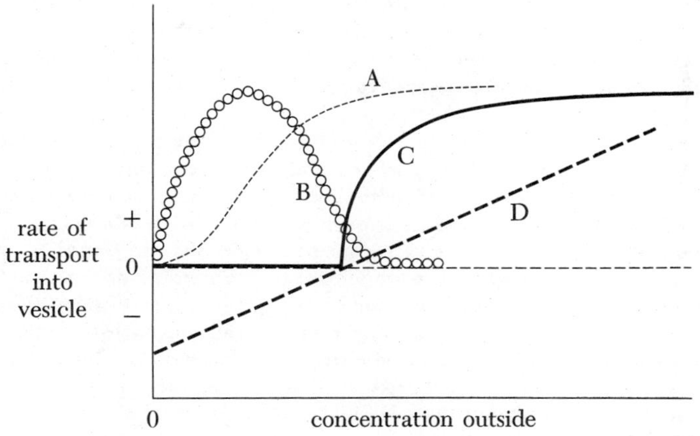

5. The above sketch shows the initial rate of transport of four different substances into vesicles prepared by homogenizing a biological membrane. The interior of the vesicles contains the same solution in each case, but the initial concentration of the respective compounds on the outside is varied.

   (a) Which compound crosses the membrane by passive diffusion?

   (b) Which crosses by facilitated diffusion?

   (c) Which crosses by an active transport mechanism exhibiting positive cooperativity?

   (d) Which crosses by an active transport mechanism exhibiting negative cooperativity?

   (e) Which shows the same behavior as the mechanism for transport of glucose into muscles?

CHAPTER 7

ENZYMES: BINDING FOR CATALYSIS

THE CONCEPTS

An enzyme is a protein that combines with one or more compounds in such a way that the compound undergoes a specific reaction at a much more rapid rate than it would by itself. Enzymes are like other proteins in that they have primary sequences causing them to fold into a particular configuration in which their reactive groups are spaced so as to create their biological activity.

The reactive groups of an enzyme have two functions. One function is to bind compounds of particular kinds in proximity to the site where catalysis occurs, and an enzyme therefore has a specificity for only a limited number of compounds. Some enzymes are so highly specific that they catalyze the reaction of only one or two physiological compounds. The compounds that are bound in an effective way are said to be substrates for the enzyme. The specificity comes about from the complementary spatial arrangements of substrates and enzyme.

The second function of the reactive groups on the enzyme is to provide the actual catalytic mechanism. This involves a change in conformation of the enzyme-substrate complex which stretches the bonds of the substrate into more reactive configurations. The enzyme also provides conventional catalytic groups of the sort seen in other organic reactions (general acids, general bases, and nucleophilic centers), but the enzyme has the advantage of effective spacing of the groups next to the affected compound.

The mammalian pancreas secretes proteases, which are enzymes catalyzing the hydrolysis of interior peptide bonds in proteins, as a part of the apparatus for digesting foods. The proteases illustrate many of the general features of enzyme action and some of the specific mechanisms occurring in many, but not all enzymes. Each protease is specific for particular kinds of peptides because it has a crevice built to accommodate particular kinds of side chains on the peptides to be digested. Each has a seryl group to act as a nucleophilic center for splitting the peptide bond, and the effectiveness of this center is augmented through bonding to histidyl and aspartyl side chains, which act as general acids and bases in the catalytic mechanism.

The proteases are secreted in an inactive form, so as to protect the pancreatic cells that form them from digestion. These proenzymes, or zymogens, are activated by cleaving small segments of peptides. The cleavage occurs at a point such that a new electrostatic bond is created, which changes the conformation of the remaining large portion of the peptide so as to bring the groups forming an active site into proper position. The sequence of cleavages forming active proteases begins only after the pancreatic secretion reaches the small intestine.

Enzymes are proteins constructed to catalyze reactions of other compounds. They bind specific compounds in much the same way as do other proteins. However, enzymes are different from the other proteins in that the complex of bound compound and protein can assume a new configuration, in which the bound compound is modified so that it becomes a new compound upon release from the enzyme. The enzyme then reverts to its original form. It is this capacity to catalyze the myriads of chemical reactions that occur in living organisms that gives the enzymes special importance among the proteins. Much of the heredity of an organism consists of instructions for building enzymes, thereby determining the nature and the rate of the reactions constituting the metabolism of the organism. A surprising number of the biological responses to change in environment are also due to changes in the enzymatic* constitution of the organism.

General Nature of Enzymes. There is nothing mysterious about enzymes and the way in which they catalyze reactions. They are composed of the same 20 amino acids found in other proteins, and assume characteristic shapes dictated by the sequence of amino acids. As with other proteins, the molecule may be made from pieces of α-helix, parallel or anti-parallel pleated sheets, or unordered sequences. It is not yet possible to predict what kinds of molecular architecture have been evolved to do a particular job. Enzymes catalyzing similar reactions may have seemingly unrelated molecular structures, or may bear such close resemblance that it is almost certain they have evolved from common precursors. Even so, there is no known instance, and no reason to expect such an instance to appear, in which the catalysis of a reaction by an enzyme involves any kind of reaction or general principle that is not also illustrated by ordinary organic reactions.

SPECIFICITY OF ENZYMES

Even though enzymes are constructed from prosaic chemical groups behaving in their customary way, catalysis by enzymes differs from ordinary catalysis in important respects. Being proteins, the reactive groups of enzymes are spaced in closely defined positions, and this geometric specificity permits a degree of control over the catalytic process that is not seen with ordinary catalysts.

Substrate Binding. The compounds whose reactions are catalyzed by enzymes are said to be substrates for the enzyme:

$$\text{substrates (S)} \xrightarrow{\text{enzyme (E)}} \text{products (P)}$$

Enzymatic catalysis begins with the formation of bonds between a substrate and the enzyme:

$$\mathrm{E + S \longrightarrow ES}$$

Since the groups on the enzyme that form the bonds are fixed in space, it follows that the enzyme must be built to react with particular kinds of substrates; its geometric specificity creates a substrate specificity. An enzyme may be highly specific, with reactive groups that fit only one or a few very closely related compounds, or it may have a broad specificity, catalyzing the reaction of a wide variety of compounds containing a similar group in one portion of the molecule.

Specificity of Proteases. Some appreciation of the meaning of enzyme specificity and its origin can be obtained by examining the proteases secreted by the mammalian pancreas. These are enzymes that aid digestion by hydrolyzing peptide bonds in proteins (protein + ase = proteinase = protease). They are examples of a general class of enzymes catalyzing hydrolytic cleavage of esters and amides, known as **hydrolases** (hydrolysis + ase), and more specifically are **endopeptidases,** enzymes catalyzing the hydrolysis of interior peptide bonds in peptide chains. (**Exopeptidases** catalyze the hydrolysis of terminal peptide bonds, liberating one free amino acid at a time. The

*Some people, especially the English, use *enzymic* as the adjective form of the word enzyme.

combined action of exo- and endopeptidases results in the total cleavage of ingested proteins into free amino acids for absorption into the blood.)

The pancreas produces three different endopeptidases, each of which has the same general structure and uses the same catalytic mechanism to catalyze the same general reaction:

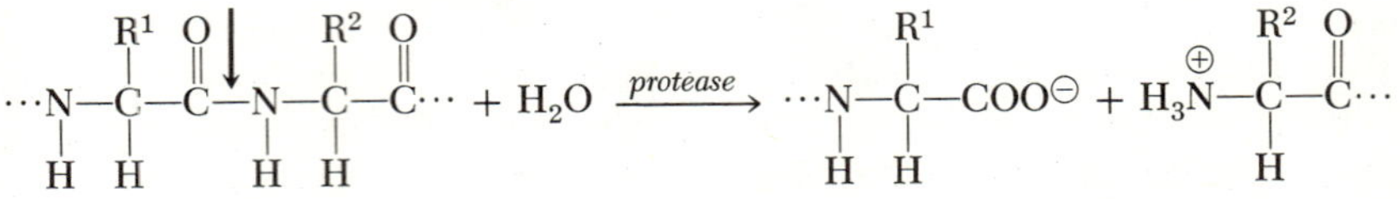

These three enzymes are respectively named **trypsin, chymotrypsin,** and **elastase.** (Trypsin and chymotrypsin are old names, applied before the suffix -ase was invented as a general designation for enzymes. Elastase was originally thought to be an enzyme specifically designed to attack elastin, a protein found in connective tissues, but it is now known to have a general function.)

The differences in the three proteases lie in the nature of the peptides they will attack. Trypsin catalyzes the hydrolysis of peptides made from the carboxyl group of arginine or lysine (Fig. 7-1). Chymotrypsin attacks peptides made from the carboxyl group of amino acids with bulky non-polar side chains, especially the aromatic amino acids, phenylalanine, tyrosine, or tryptophan. Elastase preferentially attacks peptides made from the carboxyl group of neutral, small amino acids, especially alanine, and works best when there is a succession of such acids in a chain.

Function of Protease Specificity. The peptide bonds that are attacked by proteases lie between amino acid residues, and these residues differ in the nature of their side chains. In order for catalysis to occur, as we shall shortly see, the amide groups being hydrolyzed must be brought into proximity with groups in the enzyme so as to form bonds favoring hydrolysis. In order to create the close fit, with the correct orientation of groups, the neighboring parts of the substrate molecule being attacked must not get in the way. In other words, there is a steric factor involved, and peptide bonds will not be hydrolyzed by an enzyme unless the shape of the enzyme permits the amide bond being attacked, along with its neighboring side chains, to come into contact with the active site on the enzyme.

Beyond mere avoidance of steric hindrance, close contact between the neighboring parts of the substrate and the enzyme has a more positive effect in promoting catalysis. By increasing the affinity of enzyme for substrate, such bonds make it possible for enzyme and substrate to combine at low concentrations. For example, some bacteria have proteases with broad specificity, which attack most kinds of peptides. However, these proteases require substrates to be present at 1000 times the concentration neces-

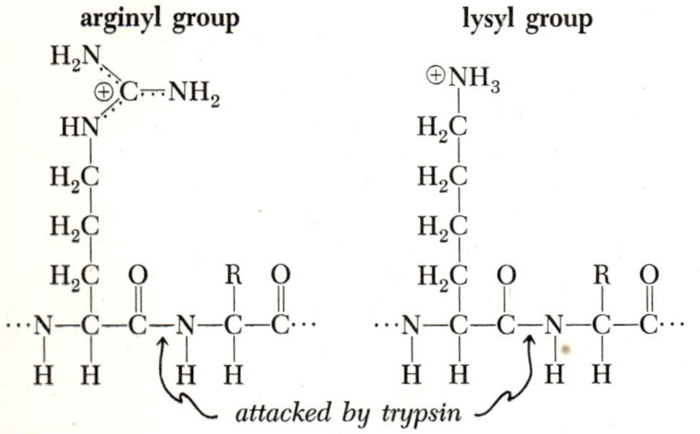

Figure 7-1 Trypsin specifically hydrolyzes positively charged arginyl and lysyl peptides.

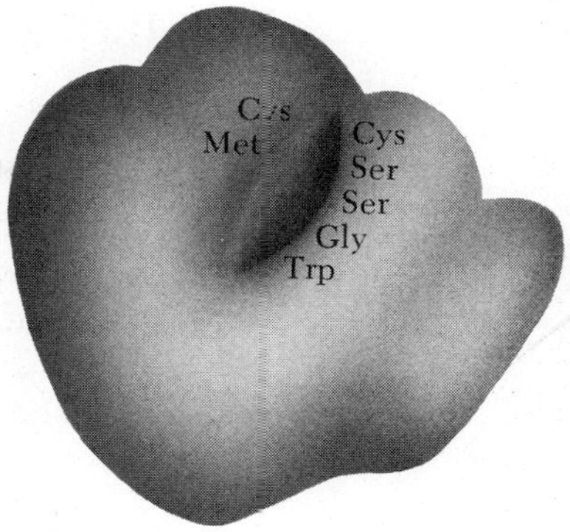

Figure 7-2 Peptides must fit in an overhanging crevice in the chymotrypsin molecule in order to be hydrolyzed. The crevice is lined with non-polar or feebly polar residues, as shown here in surface projection, that favor entry of peptides with hydrophobic side chains, such as those of the aromatic amino acids.

sary for equally rapid hydrolysis by the more specific proteases of the higher organisms, which have more binding sites to hold the substrate.

Even the proteases of broad specificity must make some contact with the peptide chain beyond the amide group being attacked. We know that this is so because they will not catalyze the hydrolysis of all amides, and the reason it is so is that some kind of orienting forces are needed to place the amide group in the proper position for catalysis.

Finally, we shall see throughout the remainder of the book what is not so obvious in the case of the proteases: The development of specific enzymes permits tightly controlled metabolic sequences, in which a compound with a particular group will react, but other compounds with the same group will not, because they differ in other respects, and are therefore not substrates for the same enzyme.

ORIGIN OF PROTEASE SPECIFICITY. The necessary contacts between an enzyme and its substrates are usually created because the enzyme folds in such a way as to form a crevice into which the substrate fits; the crevice also contains the catalytic groups. This is the circumstance in the proteases. The peptide chains of chymotrypsin, trypsin, and elastase are all folded to form a crevice. In the case of chymotrypsin, the crevice is lined with non-polar side chains arranged in such a way that peptides also having non-polar side chains, especially the aromatic side chains, will fill the crevice and orient the amide group that is to be hydrolyzed toward a catalytic site, which is discussed in the next section (Fig. 7-2). Chymotrypsin will not hydrolyze peptides constructed from the carboxyl group of aspartate, glutamate, asparagine, glutamine, arginine, and lysine, because these polar side chains will not freely enter the non-polar crevice on the enzyme. Trypsin, on the other hand, has a structure almost identical to that of chymotrypsin with one important exception. A residue of aspartate is substituted for a residue of serine in the lining of the base of the crevice into which the substrate side chain fits. The insertion of this negatively charged residue destroys the hydrophobic character of the crevice; negatively charged side chains (Asp or Glu) won't enter because of charge repulsion, and trypsin is in fact highly specific for hydrolysis of peptides constructed from the carboxyl groups of arginine or lysine, because the side chain of these amino acids contains a positive charge. The substrate crevice of trypsin is built so as to bring the negative charge of the enzyme's aspartyl group into close proximity to the positive charge on an arginyl or lysyl peptide entering the crevice as a substrate.

Elastase has the same sort of crevice found in chymotrypsin, but the entrance is partially blocked by the insertion of residues of valine and threonine at positions occupied by glycine in trypsin and chymotrypsin. The result is that elastase will accept only peptides with uncharged small side chains, such as alanyl peptides.

MECHANISM OF CATALYSIS

Enzymes and Activation Energy. A remarkable thing about enzymes is that they can make a reaction proceed at a brisk rate under mild conditions even though the same reaction is ordinarily so slow as to be regarded as non-existent in neutral solutions at modest temperatures (0° to 40°). For example, we need not worry about the spontaneous hydrolysis of the proteins in our carcasses, even though the equilibrium position is far in the direction of amino acids, because the molecular orbitals favoring rupture of the peptide bond are only rarely occupied. We say that hydrolysis of peptide bonds has a high activation energy under physiological conditions, and if it were not so, organisms made of proteins wouldn't exist. On the other hand, bonds in these proteins are rapidly hydrolyzed in the presence of the pancreatic endopeptidases. The overall nature of the reaction is not changed by the enzymes; the position of equilibrium is still the same, and the enzymes only make the reaction go toward equilibrium faster. They do this by changing the nature of the molecular orbitals; in other words, enzymes lower the activation energy for a reaction (Fig. 7–3).

The Catalytic Process

Enzymes lower the activation energy and make reactions go faster because they form a complex with the substrate that can shift to a new conformation, in which the bonds of the substrate portion of the complex are strained into more reactive positions. A configuration of the substrate that is improbable by itself becomes a favored configuration because it can react better with the enzyme. This active intermediate can revert back to the original enzyme-substrate conformation, or may undergo further conformation change to become an enzyme-product complex. An enzymatic reaction therefore becomes a succession of at least these reversible steps:

$$E + S \rightleftharpoons E\text{-}S \rightleftharpoons E\text{-}M \rightleftharpoons E\text{-}P \rightleftharpoons E + P$$

in which M is the intermediate form of the substrate.

There are two ways in which the formation of bonds between the enzyme and the substrate can contribute to the catalytic mechanism. Groups on the enzyme and the substrate may interact during transient steps in what may be regarded as true catalysis. Groups on the enzyme may also behave as participants in the reaction, with the formation of covalent intermediates between the substrate and enzyme that can actually be isolated under experimental conditions, although they do not persist in physiological circumstances. Again, we can gain a better picture of these functions by examining the action of the pancreatic proteases.

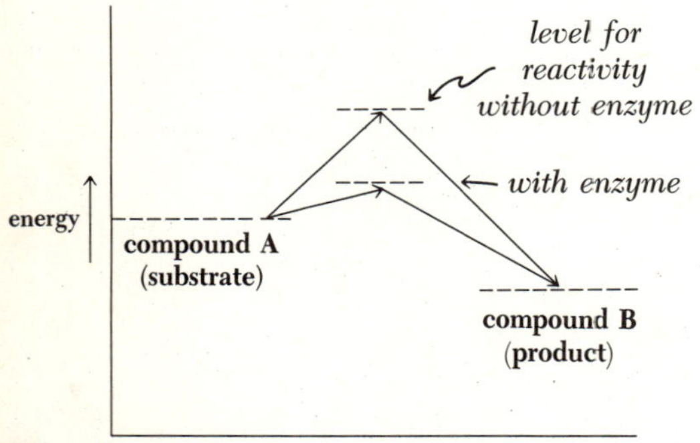

Figure 7–3 The combination of a compound with an enzyme enables the formation of a reactive configuration at an energy state lower than the energy state necessary for reaction of the compound by itself. The position of equilibrium is not affected, since the substrate and the product are the same in either case, but the activation energy is lowered by the use of the enzyme.

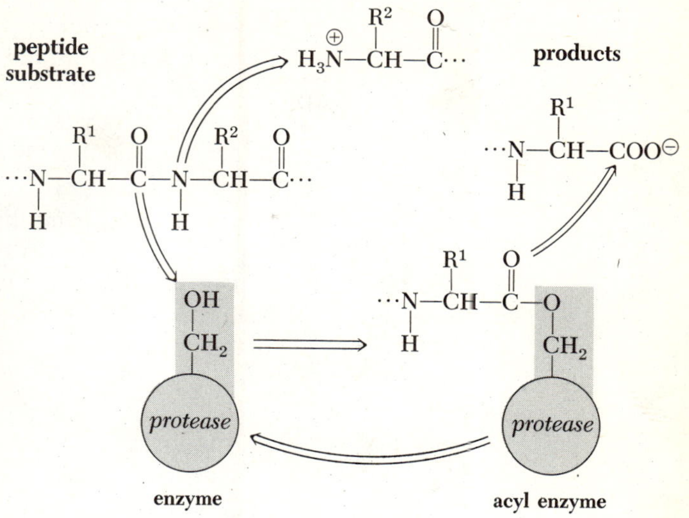

Figure 7-4 The mechanism of the serine proteases. A peptide bond is cleaved by transferring the acyl group to a seryl hydroxyl group on the enzyme, releasing the newly-created amino group. The acyl enzyme is then hydrolyzed to release a newly-created carboxylate group, restoring the enzyme to its original form.

Mechanism of Endopeptidases

Role of Seryl Groups. The pancreatic endopeptidases are examples of a large class of hydrolases that attack amides and esters by using a seryl side chain on the enzyme for nucleophilic attack, with the acyl group of the substrate being temporarily bound in ester linkage to the seryl group (Fig. 7–4). The seryl group is also an important nucleophilic participant in the action of many other enzymes catalyzing group transfers.

Role of Histidyl Group; Acid-Base Catalysis. The mechanism of many reactions catalyzed by enzymes involves the addition and removal of protons, and the enzyme facilitates these proton exchanges by providing acidic or basic groups to act as donors or acceptors. Enzymes are akin to the general acid and general base catalysts necessary for many organic reactions, but enzymes have the advantage that the catalytic groups are held in proximity to the substrate, and the substrate is held in a position favoring strong bonding with these groups.

The imidazole group in the side chain of histidine residues is perhaps the most widely used group for catalyzing reactions by proton transfer. This is so because the dissociation constant of the acidic form (imidazolium ions) is near 10^{-7}, or roughly the same as the concentration of H^+ in water. The histidyl side chains therefore exist with roughly half in the acidic form and half in the basic form in neutral solutions (Fig. 7–5), and this dual nature permits the group to be used as a catalyst in either direction. If a reaction is catalyzed by a general acid mechanism, the reverse of a reaction must be catalyzed by a general base mechanism. Since enzymes catalyze a

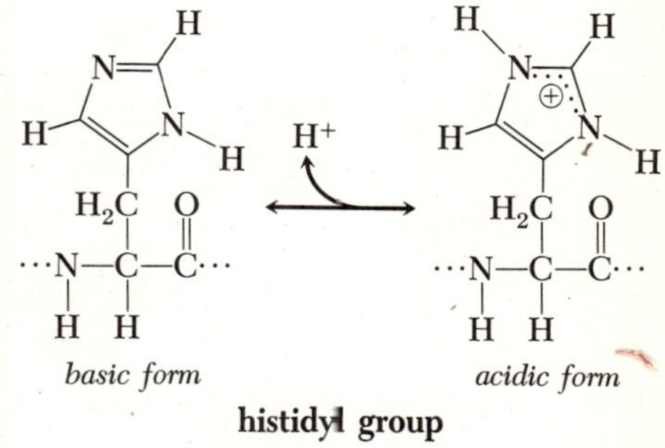

Figure 7-5 The acidic and basic forms of a histidyl group. The acidic form contains a charged imidazolium group.

reaction in either direction, and many enzymatic reactions are in fact reversible under varying physiological conditions, it is not very profitable to classify enzymes as general acids or general bases in catalysis.

Role of Aspartyl Group and the Catalytic Mechanism. Other groups in enzymes can also act as general acids or bases. These probably include the ammonium and carboxylate groups that occur at the ends of the peptide chains, the ammonium group on the lysyl side chains, and the carboxylate groups on the aspartyl and glutamyl side chains (Fig. 7–6). It so happens that the pancreatic endopeptidases use both the imidazole group of histidine, and the carboxylate group of aspartate. The aspartyl residue in question is buried deep within the enzyme, but this is not a violation of the principle that charged groups cannot be buried, because the carboxylate side chain is hydrogen-bonded to three other side chains, with an almost complete loss of charged character!

The histidyl group, aspartyl group, and seryl group that are involved in the catalytic mechanism are arranged in such a way that the imidazole side chain is placed as a bridge between the carboxylate and alcohol groups of the respective amino acid residues (Fig. 7–7). The presence of the bridge has the effect of creating a sink for electrons drawn from the seryl group, thereby making it a much more powerful nucleophilic reagent. This is so because the principal catalytic steps—removing the acyl group from the substrate, transferring it to the seryl group on the enzyme, and then transferring it to water—can be accomplished mainly by moving electrons from one position to another in the enzyme-substrate complexes. Moving electrons is much easier than moving atoms; even though the fine details of the rearrangements catalyzed by the endopeptidases are not known, it is easy to see how the reaction is made to go faster by the presence of the many groups in the enzyme at locations where they fit the intermediate activated forms of the substrate.

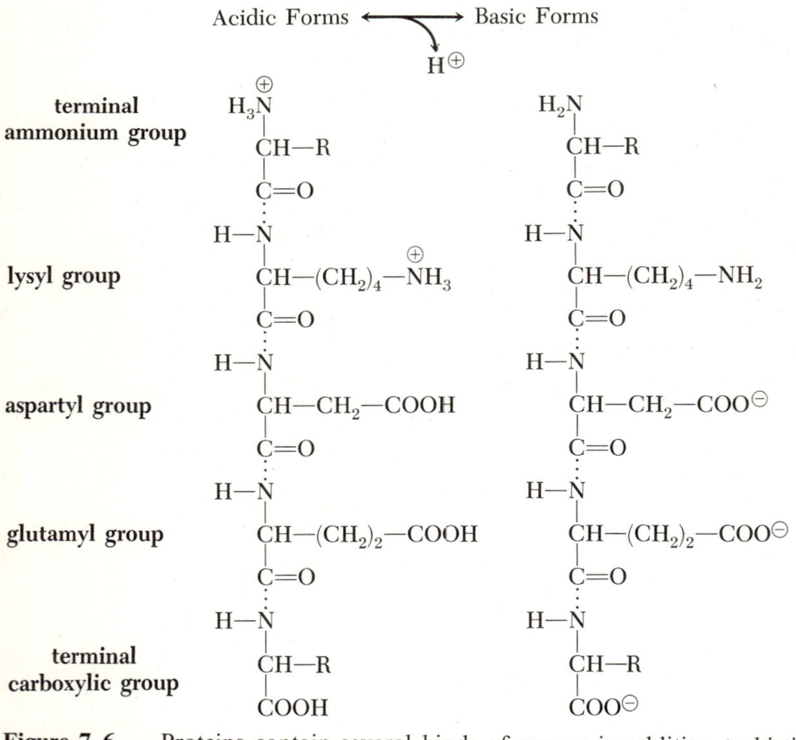

Figure 7–6 Proteins contain several kinds of groups in addition to histidyl groups that may participate in acid-base catalysis by donating or accepting protons.

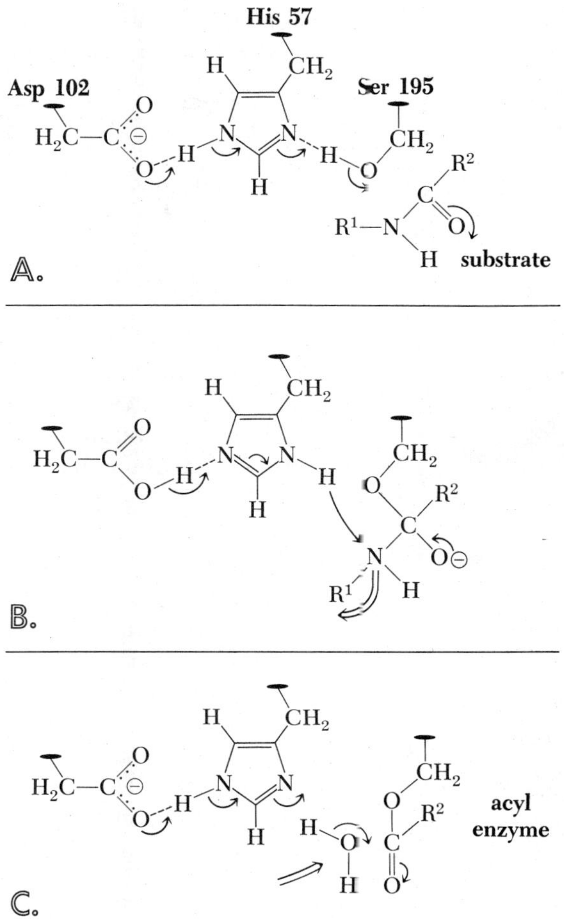

Figure 7–7 The seryl group of the proteases is activated for nucleophilic attack on a peptide bond through hydrogen bonding to neighboring histidyl and aspartyl side chains. The mechanism may involve a shift of bonds causing the aspartyl residue to alternate between its charged and uncharged forms, as shown, but this interpretation is not universally accepted.

Effect of H^+ Concentration

A typical enzyme has a pH optimum; that is, it catalyzes its reaction most effectively at a certain concentration of H^+ (Fig. 7–8). There are several reasons for this kind of behavior. One is that the rate of reactions involving acid-base catalysis is dependent upon the concentrations of the acidic and basic forms of groups in both the enzyme and the substrate, and the equilibrium between these forms depends upon the concentration of H^+. Another is that the total conformation of the enzyme molecule necessary for catalysis sometimes depends upon the existence of electrostatic charges. An attraction between an ammonium group and a carboxylate group, for example,

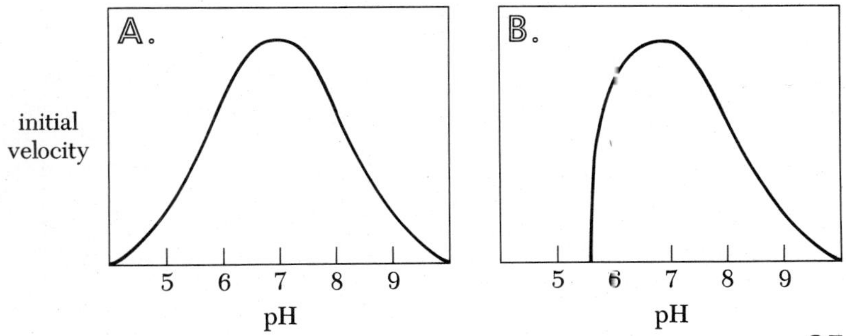

Figure 7–8 The effect of pH on the rate of enzymatic reactions. *A.* The enzyme is stable over the pH range tested, and the mechanism of catalysis requires both acidic and basic groups. *B.* The mechanism is similar to that of the above enzyme, but the transition temperature for disruption of the enzyme's structure falls at pH 5.7 below the temperature used for assay.

won't be present at extremely low or extremely high concentrations of H^+, because one or the other group will lose its charge:

$$R'\text{—}NH_3^+ \longrightarrow R\text{—}NH_2 + H^+, \quad \text{or} \quad R\text{—}COO^- + H^+ \longrightarrow R\text{—}COOH$$

Hydrogen bond formation may also be prevented at extreme H^+ concentrations.

Effect of Temperature

Denaturation. Reactions catalyzed by enzymes are like other reactions in that the rate is increased by increasing temperatures—up to a point. Beyond a critical range, the **transition temperature,** the activity of an enzyme declines sharply (Fig. 7-9). Not only enzymes but nearly all proteins lose conformation readily above certain temperatures. When thermal energy becomes great enough to cause the rupture of a few bonds, the neighboring bonds are weakened, and the whole molecule becomes unzippered. This gross loss of conformation is known as denaturation of the protein.

Function and Critical Temperature. It happens that most of the proteins in an organism become denatured at temperatures only a few degrees above the environmental temperature of the organism. For example, the critical temperature for denaturation to proteins in mammals is frequently between 50° and 55°, only 10 to 15° above the usual cellular temperature. Dr. R. L. Biltonen points out that this may be a necessary condition for effective use of enzymes. A rock-like solidity of conformation may be incompatible with the action of enzymes, which requires that some bonds in the structure of the protein shift during catalysis. In other words, Biltonen is saying that biological activity may require tickling the tiger to a rippling alertness that is not far removed from a destructive frenzy.

PROENZYMES

The pancreatic endopeptidases illustrate another important aspect of the enzymes: Some enzymes are menaces to the organisms that synthesize them. It wouldn't do to have the proteases fully active inside the cells of the pancreas, and precautions are taken to insure that they do not become active. To begin, the pancreas does not synthesize chymotrypsin, elastase, or trypsin; instead, it synthesizes precursors of these

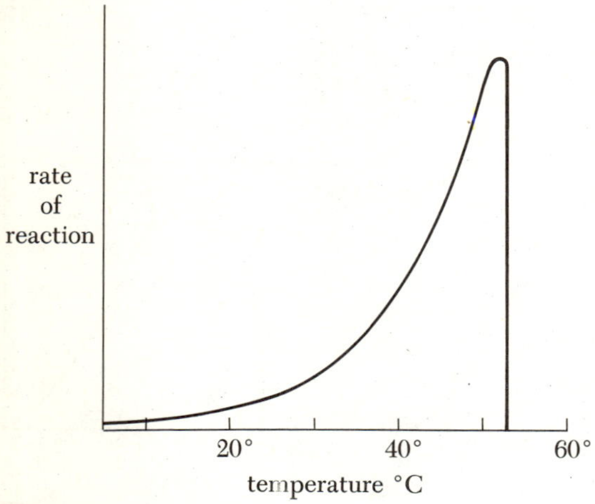

Figure 7-9 Enzymatic reactions are like most reactions in that their rates accelerate as the temperature rises above the freezing point. However, unlike most reactions, the rate abruptly falls to low values when the temperature is reached that causes disruption of the conformation of the enzyme.

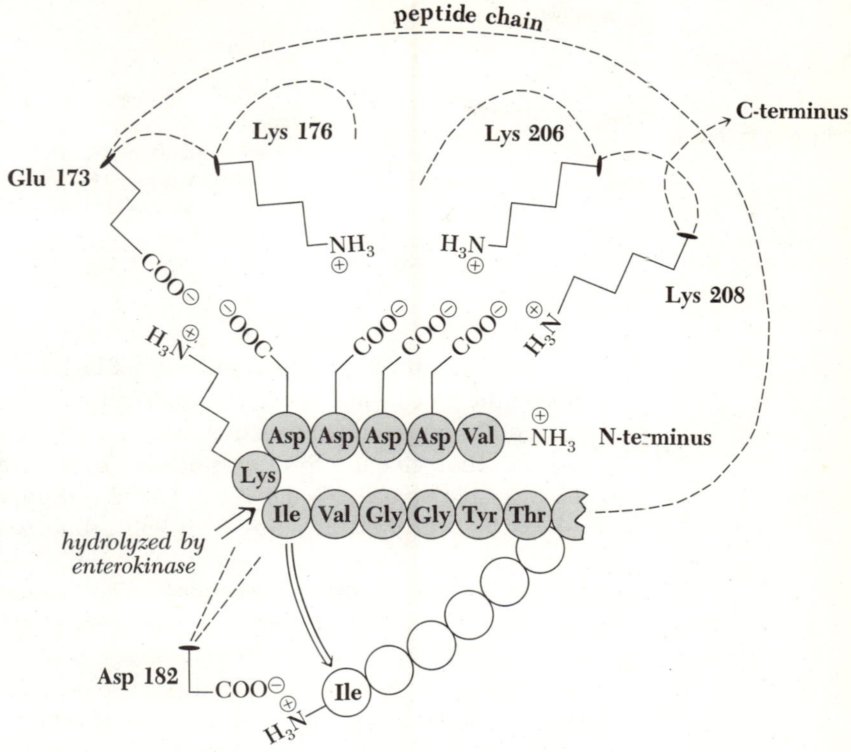

Figure 7-10 The conversion of trypsinogen to active trypsin involves the cleavage of a lysyl bond six residues removed from the N-terminal. These six residues are held in a particular location by electrostatic bonds. When the remainder of the chain is released by hydrolysis, it swings to a new position that enables the enzyme to be active.

enzymes in the form of peptides that have no enzymatic activity. Such precursors are said to be **proenzymes,** or **zymogens;** the proenzymes of the pancreatic endopeptidases are named chymotrypsinogen, trypsinogen, and proelastase. (The pro--ase form is used for all newer discoveries.)

It is only after the proenzymes have been safely secreted and removed from the cell that steps are taken to convert them to their active form. We have here one more example of the synthesis of peptides with redundant sequences of amino acid residues that must be removed before the peptide can assume the biologically active conformation. The proenzymes must be partially hydrolyzed before they can become enzymes.

Activation of Trypsin. Trypsinogen leaving the pancreas is exposed to an enzyme, **enterokinase,** secreted by the intestinal mucosa. Now, the amino acid sequence of trypsinogen in various species begins with one to three non-polar amino acid residues followed in each case by the sequence -Asp-Asp-Asp-Asp-Lys-. The next residue is either Ile or Val. Enterokinase is an endopeptidase built to attack specifically peptide bonds preceded by this unusual Asp_4Lys peptide. Hence, it cleaves off the initial portion of the peptide chain in trypsinogen, thereby removing a collection of negatively charged residues, and exposing the positively charged ammonium group of what is now a terminal isoleucyl or valyl group. The molecule is built so that this new positive charge is attracted to a negative charge on still another aspartyl residue, which was formerly repelled in trypsinogen by the negative charges of the terminal sequence (Fig. 7-10). The important thing about the movement to make an electrostatic bond is that it brings the seryl, histidyl, and aspartyl groups that constitute the catalytic site near each other in the interior of the molecule. (The aspartyl residue of the active site is not the same residue involved in the conformational change just discussed.) The action of enterokinase in partially hydrolyzing trypsinogen therefore directly causes the formation of the active site characteristic of trypsin.

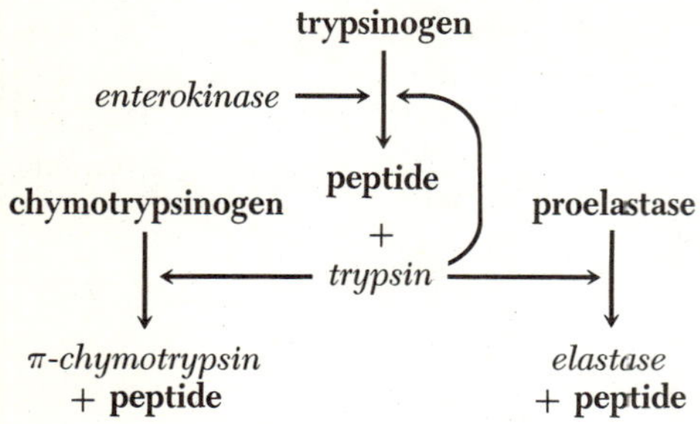

Figure 7-11 Active trypsin is formed by the action of enterokinase, and then catalyzes its own formation. It also catalyzes the partial hydrolysis of chymotrypsinogen and proelastase that creates active chymotrypsin and elastase.

Activation of Chymotrypsin and Elastase. Once trypsin is formed, it in turn attacks the proenzyme forms of chymotrypsin and elastase also present in the pancreatic juice, and converts them to active forms by hydrolysis of particular peptide bonds (Fig. 7-11). Active chymotrypsin also attacks itself to remove further small peptides, but the principle involved is the same. The chymotrypsinogen peptide is built so as to be subject to hydrolysis at points that will produce a conformation active as an endopeptidase.

Activation of other Enzymes. The production of proenzymes that are later converted to active enzymes as a protective regulatory device is not limited to the digestive enzymes. We have already noted that the process of blood clotting involves an attack on proteins in the blood plasma by hydrolytic enzymes. These enzymes are also secreted into the blood in the form of proenzymes, which are converted to their active forms only upon the initiation of a complex series of events after injury to a blood vessel or cells within the blood. The activation of enzymes is a special case of general modification of proteins after formation of the primary structure, which we discussed in Chapter 4.

FURTHER READING

Structure and function of proteins at the three-dimensional level, Cold Spring Harbor Symp. Quant. Biol., vol. 36 (1971). Contains a number of excellent drawings of the structure of many kinds of enzymes and other proteins, including detailed technical discussions of catalysis and the action of proteases.

P. D. Boyer, ed., Hydrolysis: peptide bonds, vol. 3 of The Enzymes, 3rd ed., Academic Press (1971). See especially D. M. Blow, The structure of chymotrypsin, p. 185; G. P. Hess, Chymotrypsin—chemical properties and catalysis, p. 213; B. Keil, Trypsin, p. 250; and B. S. Hartley and D. M. Shotton, Pancreatic elastase, p. 323. Clearer than usual for professional-level discussions.

H. R. Mahler and E. H. Cordes, Biological chemistry, 2nd ed., Harper & Row (1971). See Chapter 7, Mechanism of enzyme action, for a more detailed and frequently relevant discussion of the general subject.

QUESTIONS

1. Draw the structural formulas of the acidic and the basic forms of residues of histidine, glutamic acid, and lysine in peptide chains.
2. Three residues of aspartic acid are known to be required for the action of trypsin; two of these also serve the same function in chymotrypsin. Explain the function of each residue in trypsin, and explain why one is missing from chymotrypsin.
3. Draw the structural formulas of valine and glycine, and explain why the presence of one or the other at the entrance of the substrate crevice accounts for the different specificities of chymotrypsin and elastase.

4. The conversion of the respective proenzymes to active trypsin, chymotrypsin, and elastase involves similar events. However, the formation of active trypsin is a key to the activation of the other two. What is peculiar about trypsinogen, compared to the other proenzymes, that makes its conversion to trypsin the triggering event?
5. (a) Sketch the structural formula of the seryl-bound intermediate when chymotrypsin attacks a tyrosyl-leucyl bond in the middle of a peptide.
   (b) Does the enzyme-substrate complex have greatest energy content during the formation of the seryl-bound intermediate or after the intermediate is formed? Explain.
6. Would you expect trypsin, chymotrypsin, or elastase to be the most useful experimental tool for reproducible cleaving a protein of unknown amino acid sequence into segments of definite composition? Why?

CHAPTER 8

COENZYMES AND VITAMINS

THE CONCEPTS

Coenzymes are prosthetic groups that provide additional chemical structures to promote enzymatic reactions. Some are tightly bound to a particular apoenzyme peptide; others migrate freely from one enzyme to another and behave more like recycling substrates than as components of proteins.

Group Transfer. Some transfers of chemical groups from one compound to another are catalyzed without the aid of coenzymes. We saw the use of serine residues for transferring acyl groups. Lysine residues can be used in a similar way for transferring aldehyde or ketone groups through the intermediate formation of Schiff's bases. Schiff's bases are aldimines or ketimines, —N=C—, here joining the nitrogen of a lysyl side chain to the carbon of a carbonyl group. Biological condensations involving carbonyl compounds are frequently catalyzed by this kind of mechanism.

Other group transfers require coenzymes. Transaminations, which involve an exchange of amino and carbonyl functions between two carbon chains, utilize both a lysyl group on the enzyme and pyridoxal phosphate, which provides an aldehyde group for the initial formation of an aldimine required for the exchange. Carboxylases, which catalyze the formation of carboxylate groups by attachment of CO_2 to a carbon chain, frequently require both lysyl groups and biotin. Biotin is a coenzyme specifically utilized for transfer of carboxylate groups. Carboxylases have two active sites, one for attachment of CO_2 to biotin at the expense of ATP hydrolysis, and one for transfer of the resultant carboxylate group to the acceptor substrate. The function of the lysine residue in this case is to provide a long side chain by which the coenzyme can be attached securely to the apoenzyme and still be free to move from one site to another.

Metalloproteins. The biotin-coupled carboxylases are also examples of enzymes requiring bound metal ions for activity. The metal, Mn^{2+} or Zn^{2+}, binds the acceptor substrate to the enzyme during the carboxylate transfer. The carboxylases also require magnesium ions to form a chelate with ATP ($MgATP^{2-}$) and to activate the site of the initial reaction in which CO_2 is affixed to biotin. Enzymes catalyzing transfer of phosphate from nucleotides commonly require the presence of Mg^{2+}.

Oxidation-Reductions. The oxidation of a compound is a reaction in which atoms of oxygen are added to it, atoms of hydrogen are removed from it, or electrons are removed from it. The reduction of a compound is the reverse of any of these processes. Most biological oxidations and reductions require the presence of either a coenzyme or a metallic ion in addition to the groups provided by amino acid side chains.

Nicotinamide Nucleotides. Nicotinamide adenine dinucleotide (NAD) and a phosphorylated derivative (NADP) are used by every organism to transfer hydride ions ($H:^-$). Many of the enzymes utilizing the coenzymes catalyze the reversible oxidation of an alcoholic hydroxyl group to a carbonyl group. Each reaction resulting in the reduction of NAD to NADH must be matched by another reaction utilizing NADH to reduce a substrate and regenerate NAD.

The coenzymes freely dissociate from the various enzymes, so all reactions catalyzed by enzymes utilizing NAD tend to equilibrate. However, similar reactions catalyzed by enzymes utilizing NADP represent another set, equilibrating only among themselves. The isolation of these two sets is the reason for the evolution of two similar nucleotides.

Flavoproteins. Other enzymes catalyze transfer of hydrogen atoms, either singly or in pairs, by the use of tightly bound riboflavin monophosphate (FMN) or riboflavin adenine dinucleotide (FAD). These are stronger oxidizing agents and are used mainly to transfer hydrogen atoms to another coenzyme or metallic ion. Some catalyze the direct attack of substrates by molecular oxygen, with the production of hydrogen peroxide. These flavoprotein oxidases are

mainly found in organelles known as peroxisomes, and are used to destroy potentially toxic compounds or to generate hydrogen peroxide for other purposes.

Hemoproteins. The oxidation and reduction of the iron atom in some hemoproteins is used for electron transfer. These proteins include the cytochromes, involved in fuel metabolism; catalase, which decomposes hydrogen peroxide; and peroxidases, which utilize hydrogen peroxide to form structural components and to destroy foreign organisms engulfed by leucocytes.

Metalloproteins. Electrons can also be transferred through ions of metals such as Fe, Cu, Mn, and Mo that are directly attached to peptide chains. Some enzymes containing Cu catalyze direct oxidations by O_2. Many different proteins contain iron in association with a sulfide lattice; these non-heme iron proteins vary from powerful oxidizing agents to powerful reducing agents. Other proteins contain Fe or Mo in association with flavoproteins, with both the metal and the flavin involved in electron transfer.

Dietary Requirements. The trace metals required for oxidation-reduction reactions must be supplied from the diet. In addition, riboflavin is required by all animals, and some animals also require a source of nicotinate in order to make the coenzymes containing these components.

It was noted in the discussion of hemoglobin that the side chains of amino acids do not provide all of the kinds of chemical groups required for biological reactions. Proteins are sometimes built so as to incorporate other compounds containing additional kinds of structures that will facilitate particular reactions. Compounds added to an enzyme in this way are said to be **coenzymes,** or **prosthetic groups.** ("Prosthetic group" is a term also applied to other kinds of proteins; heme is a prosthetic group in hemoglobin as well as in enzymes that we shall encounter later. "Coenzyme" and "prosthetic group" are used interchangeably for tightly bound compounds that participate in enzymatic function; loosely bound ones are always called coenzymes.) The peptide portion of an enzyme that requires a coenzyme for its function is called an **apoenzyme.**

COENZYMES AND GROUP TRANSFERS

Many coenzymes are involved in moving groups of atoms from one compound to another. First, let it be emphasized that many group transfers are catalyzed by enzymes that do not contain any structures other than amino acid residues. The endopeptidases we considered in the previous chapter are classed as hydrolases, but we saw that in fact they catalyze the transfer of acyl groups from amines to water, via seryl groups on the enzyme. We shall see the transfer of phosphate groups by a similar mechanism.

Group Transfer on Lysyl Residues

Aldimines and Ketimines—Schiff's Bases. Other amino acid residues can be called into play for group transfer. For example, the enzyme **fructose diphosphate aldolase** catalyzes the reversible cleavage of a six-carbon diphosphate ester into two three-carbon monophosphate esters (Fig. 8–1). This is an important reaction in sugar metabolism, as we shall see later, but it is introduced now to illustrate the combination of lysyl side chains on an enzyme with carbonyl groups, and the use of the combination for a group transfer reaction involving a ketone. Aldehydes and ketones are frequently involved in metabolic reactions, and one of the things they do that is of importance is to combine with amines to form either an aldimine or a ketimine. These important intermediates are also known as Schiff's bases. In the example at hand, the aldolase has a lysyl residue that reacts specifically with the ketone group of **dihydroxyacetone phosphate.** (The catalytic mechanism, not shown, also involves a histidyl residue.)

The Aldol Condensation. Another important characteristic of aldehydes and

MECHANISM: **amine + ketone ⟷ ketimine**

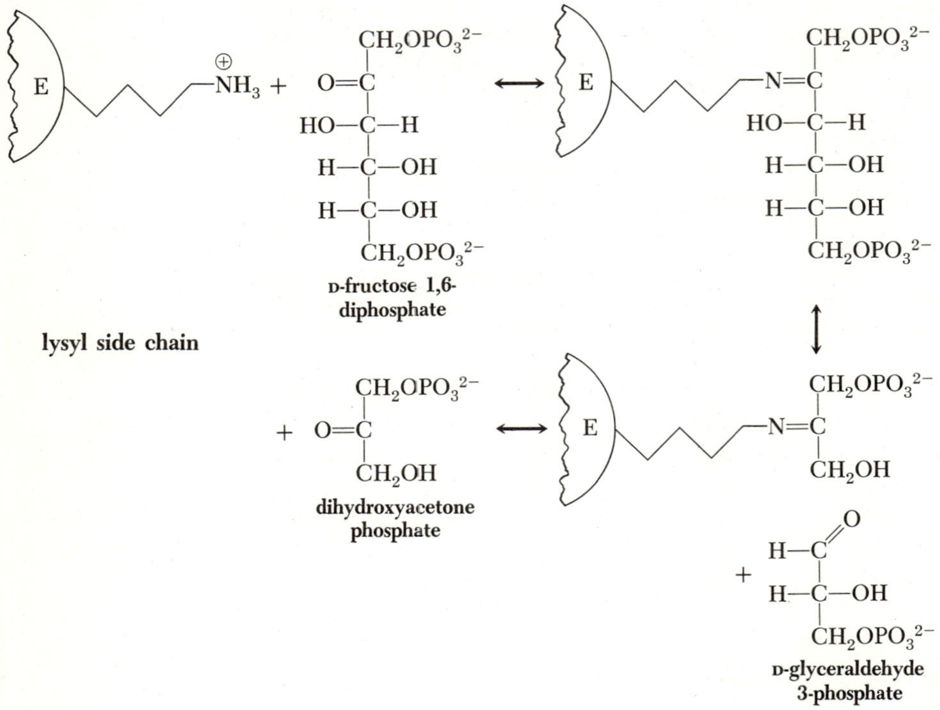

OVERALL REACTION: **alcohol + aldehyde ⟷ aldol**

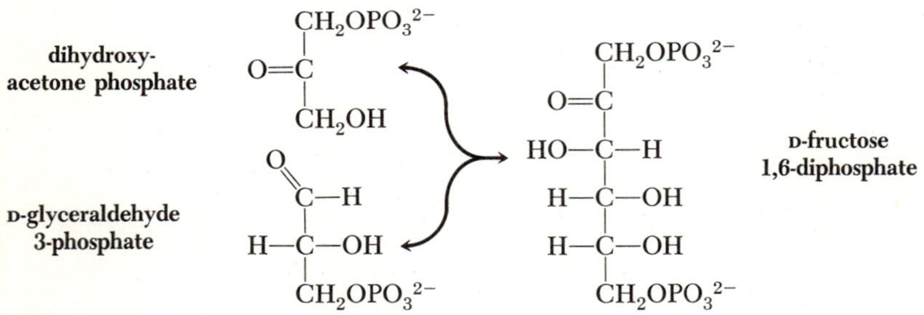

Figure 8–1 The action of fructose-diphosphate aldolase involves a condensation between a substrate ketone group and the amino group of a lysyl side chain on the enzyme to form a ketimine, or Schiff's base. The substrate is thereby activated for a cleavage, or the reverse condensation. The condensation is a variant of a typical aldol condensation, in which the effect is the addition of a methylene group across the carbonyl group of an aldehyde.

ketones that is frequently exploited in metabolism is that they readily condense, either with themselves or with many other compounds. An example, well known to the organic chemist, is the aldol condensation. Fructose diphosphate aldolase catalyzes the transfer of dihydroxyacetone phosphate from its own lysyl residue to an aldehyde, **glyceraldehyde 3-phosphate.** Taken overall, the reaction is a typical aldol condensation. The initial formation of the ketimine facilitates the condensation (or the reverse cleavage) under mild physiological conditions.

Transamination

A type of reaction of great importance in metabolism involves an exchange of an amino group and a carbonyl oxygen between two compounds:

$$\mathrm{H-\overset{R}{\underset{R}{C}}-\overset{\oplus}{N}H_3 + O=\overset{R'}{\underset{R'}{C}} \longleftrightarrow \overset{R}{\underset{R}{C}}=O + H_3\overset{\oplus}{N}-\overset{R'}{\underset{R'}{C}}-H}$$

For example, we shall shortly consider the mechanism of an **aspartate aminotransferase** that catalyzes the equilibration of these amino acids and their corresponding 2-oxo analogues:

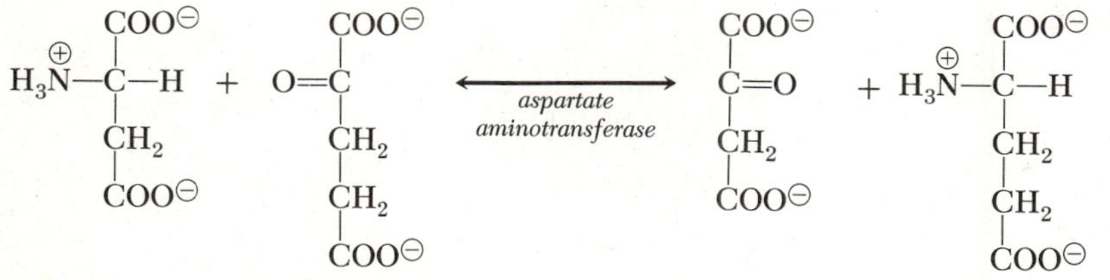

L-aspartate α-ketoglutarate oxaloacetate L-glutamate

Pyridoxal Phosphate as Coenzyme. The aminotransferases are built to bind pyridoxal phosphate (Fig. 8–2), which participates in the reaction as a coenzyme. This compound contributes an aldehyde group, which is not available on any amino acid side chains, as a reactant. The remainder of the molecule serves to potentiate the mechanism in which this group participates, and also contributes identifying groups. As Figure 8–2 shows, pyridoxal phosphate combines with the peptide chains of an aminotransferase by forming an aldimine linkage with a lysyl side chain. In principle, any aldehyde or ketone could combine with this side chain, and there are many such carbonyl compounds involved in metabolism. Likewise, pyridoxal phosphate could combine through its aldehyde carbon with any amino group on any protein. However, the construction of the enzyme with a site that binds one particular aldehyde, pyridoxal phosphate, in proximity to one particular lysyl group insures that the catalytically active combination will be favored over possible union with other compounds.

The Mechanism of Transamination. Catalysis by the aminotransferases hinges upon the fact that an aldimine or ketimine can be formed more rapidly by exchange of an amine or carbonyl compound for the corresponding part of a pre-existing aldimine or ketimine than it can by union of separated amine and carbonyl compounds. The aldimine formed by the combination of pyridoxal phosphate and a lysyl group on the enzyme's peptide chain provides the pre-existing aldimine for the exchange. The reaction then proceeds as shown in Fig. 8–3.

A. A molecule of L-glutamate collides with the enzyme and is bound, probably by its carboxylate groups, so that its ammonium group is near the aldimine structure on the enzyme.

B. The double bond shifts from the lysyl group to the glutamate, releasing the lysyl ammonium group and forming the aldimine of glutamate.

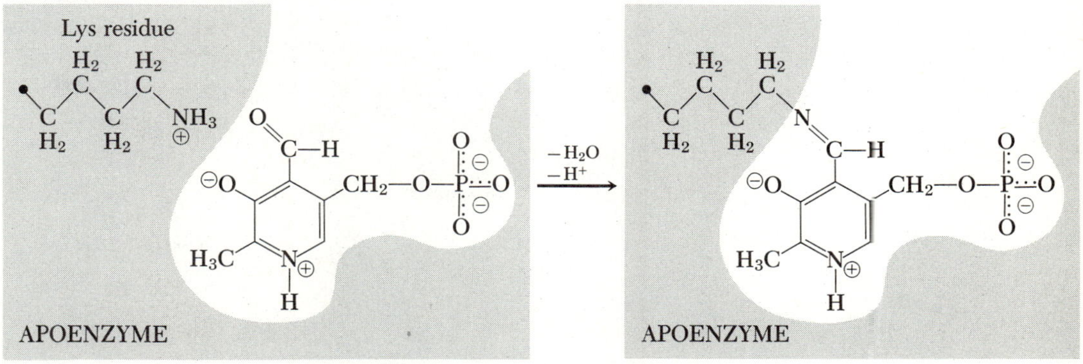

aldehyde + amine ⟶ aldimine

Figure 8-2 Aminotransferases contain a coenzyme, pyridoxal phosphate; the aldehyde group of the coenzyme combines with a lysyl group on the enzyme to form an aldimine, another type of Schiff's base.

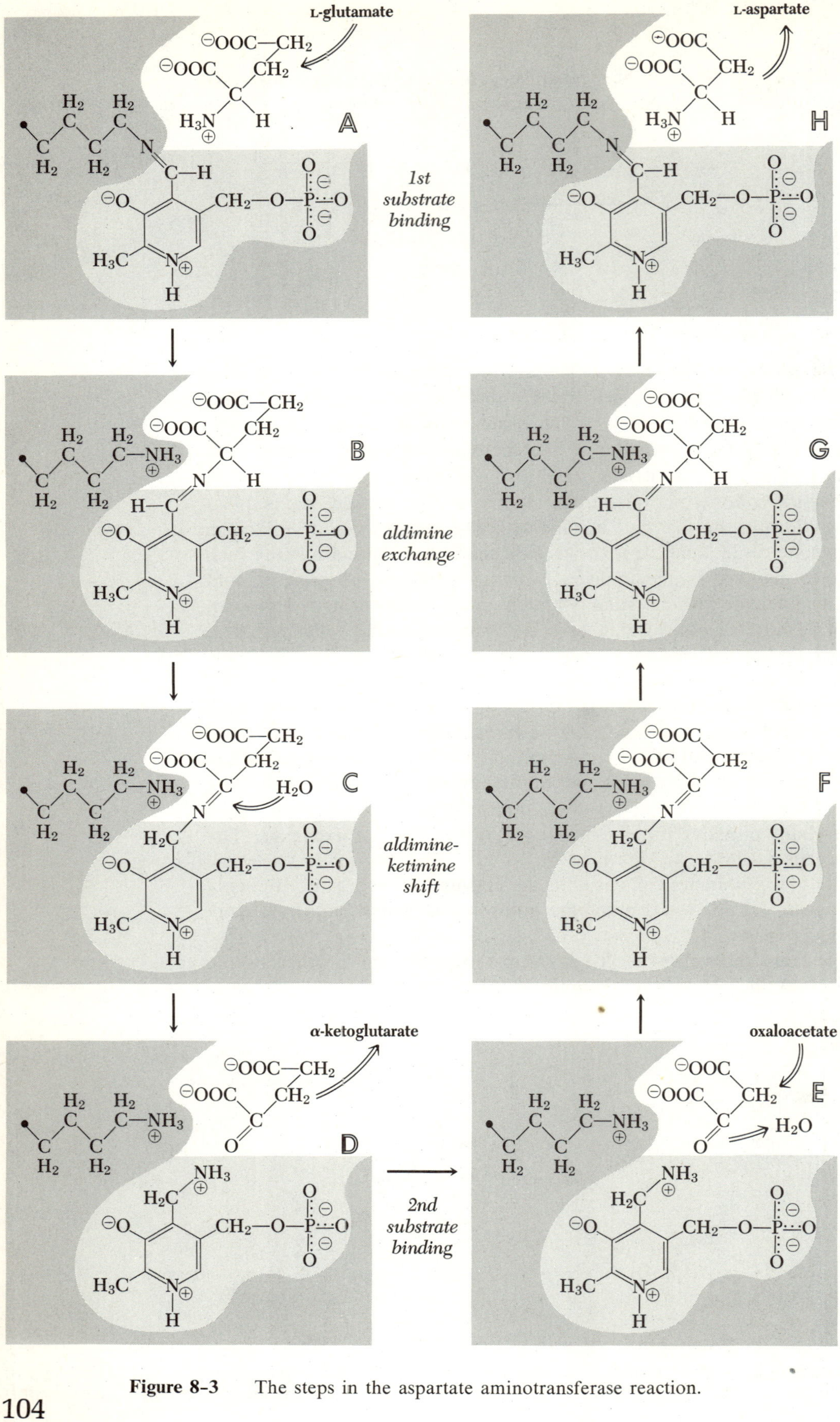

Figure 8-3 The steps in the aspartate aminotransferase reaction.

C. The double bond shifts, forming a ketimine. This is the rate-limiting step, which appears to be catalyzed by proton exchange with a neighboring histidyl side chain.

D. The ketimine is hydrolyzed to form α-ketoglutarate and pyridoxamine phosphate. The α-ketoglutarate is free to dissociate, but the pyridoxamine phosphate is still held to the enzyme by the other groups on the molecule. (However, the loss of the covalent binding makes it experimentally easier to dissociate coenzyme and apoenzyme at this stage, and this has aided the discovery of the mechanism of the reaction.)

E. A molecule of oxaloacetate combines with the protein, also by attachment of carboxylate groups.

F. A ketimine is formed between the oxaloacetate and the pyridoxamine phosphate.

G. The double bond again shifts, now forming the aldimine of L-aspartate and pyridoxal phosphate.

H. The aldimine double bond shifts from the nitrogen of L-aspartate to the lysyl residue on the protein, leaving L-aspartate free to dissociate and restoring the original condition of the enzyme so that it can begin the whole process over again with a new molecule of L-glutamate.

The mechanism can operate in the exact reverse of the steps given, so that one can start with L-aspartate + α-ketoglutarate and arrive at L-glutamate + oxaloacetate.

The sequence details only the actual organic reactions (i.e., those in which there is a change in covalent bonding) and does not describe the electron shift responsible for catalysis. This has not been established with certainty, but there is some evidence that at least one histidyl residue is involved, and that the catalysis is of an acid-base type.

Pyridoxine Compounds as Vitamins. In addition to being the first example of a coenzyme we have discussed, pyridoxal phosphate is also the first example of a compound for which a precursor must be supplied in the human diet because the entire compound cannot be synthesized by human tissues from common metabolic intermediates.

Coenzymes frequently contain structures not found in ordinary metabolites and behave as catalysts in the sense that they are eventually recovered in their original form. Therefore, they need not be present in high concentrations in the tissues, any more than the apoenzyme need be. We have noted the widespread occurrence of transamination reactions among plants and animals. Most other kinds of enzymatic reactions, with the necessary coenzymes, also have a wide occurrence.

Putting these facts together, it is easy to rationalize the evolutionary truth—organisms whose principal nutrition is supplied by tissues from other organisms frequently have lost their ability to synthesize the structural elements of coenzymes. If the structure is unusual, it need not be made for the quantitatively important metabolic reactions, in which moles of compounds may be handled per day, and its sole function may be in the coenzyme. But only a small amount of coenzyme is required, and if the structure is constantly appearing in dietary compounds, its synthesis becomes unnecessary. Therefore, mutations deleting some of the reactions peculiar to the formation of coenzymes will not cause the death of the animal, and may even give it some advantage by making room in the cell for increased amounts of the enzymes that are absolutely necessary to form other compounds.

When such a deletion has occurred, and small amounts of the necessary organic structure must be supplied in the diet, the dietary compound is a vitamin. The formation of every coenzyme does not require a vitamin, but all vitamins for which the biological function has been exactly established are known to be required because they are used to form coenzymes.

The substituted pyridine ring of pyridoxal phosphate is an example of a structure that cannot be synthesized by vertebrates, and its dietary precursors are lumped together as **vitamin B_6,** which includes **pyridoxal, pyridoxamine,** and the corresponding alcohol, **pyridoxine:**

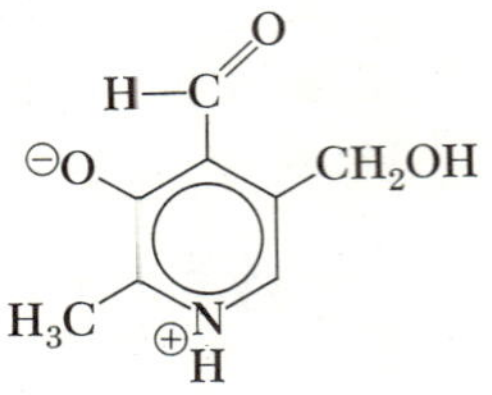

pyridoxal

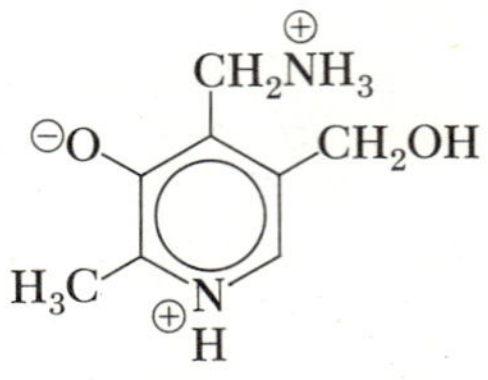

pyridoxamine

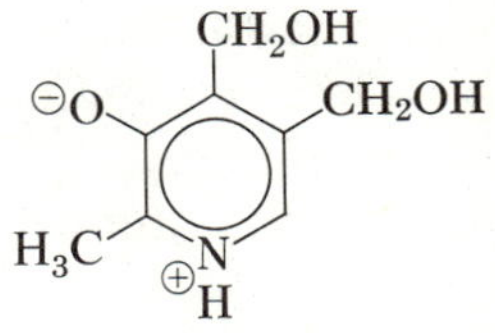

pyridoxine

Biotin and Carboxylases

Some enzymes catalyze the incorporation of CO_2 into substrates as carboxylate groups, and contain a coenzyme, biotin, to participate in the catalysis. Such incorporations occur on a carbon adjacent to a carbonyl group; a typical, and important, example is the conversion of the 2-oxo acid anion, **pyruvate,** to the corresponding 2-oxo dicarboxylic acid anion, **oxaloacetate** (Fig. 8–4).

Transfer of Biotin Between Active Sites. One of the important features of carboxylases utilizing biotin is that they contain two active sites. One of the sites catalyzes the formation of a carboxylate group on the biotin molecule from bicarbonate, which is accompanied by a hydrolysis of ATP to drive the reaction, much in the way that hydrolysis of nucleoside triphosphates is used to drive the various steps of protein synthesis. The second active site catalyzes the transfer of the carboxylate group from biotin to pyruvate. It is apparent that the biotin molecule must be able to move from site to site without being lost into solution. This is accomplished by attaching the coenzyme by amide linkage to a lysyl side chain in one of the peptides in the carboxylase (Fig. 8–5). The result is that a string of 10 atoms connects the active rings of the coenzyme to the peptide backbone. Five of these atoms are contributed by the lysyl side chain, and the other five come from the coenzyme. The string of atoms is free to rotate over the surface of the enzyme, thereby carrying the ring structure with attached carboxylate group from one site to another. Here then is another function for lysyl residues in proteins; they are sometimes used to bind coenzymes or substrates in strong covalent linkage and still permit movement across the enzyme surface so as to come in contact with different sites.

Pyruvate Carboxylase as a Metalloprotein. ROLE OF MANGANOUS ION. Pyruvate carboxylase is also an excellent example of an enzyme containing tightly bound metallic ions. Manganous ions are present in pyruvate carboxylase prepared from vertebrate tissues, while zinc is present in a yeast preparation. The metallic ion is present

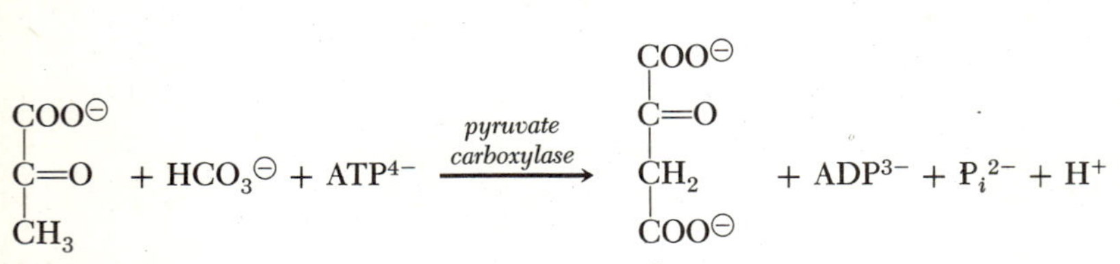

pyruvate **oxaloacetate**

Figure 8–4 Pyruvate may be carboxylated to form oxaloacetate.

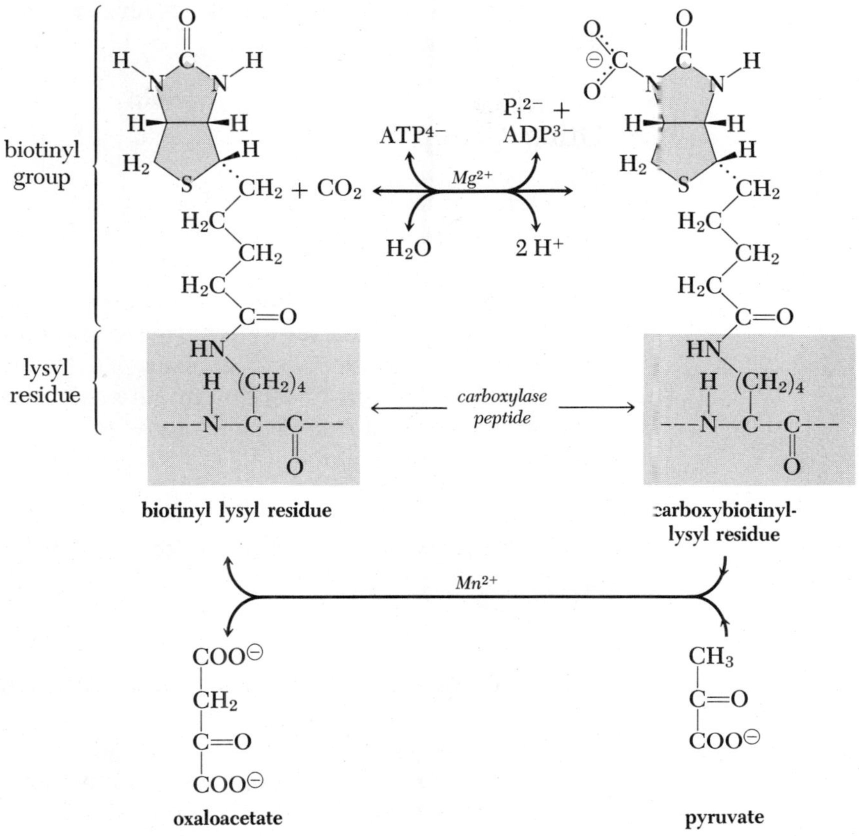

Figure 8-5 The mechanism of pyruvate carboxylase involves a biotinyl group attached to a lysyl residue. The biotinyl group is carboxylated at the expense of high-energy phosphate. The carboxyl group can then be transferred to pyruvate without further expenditure of ATP.

at the active site where pyruvate is carboxylated, and its function is to hold the substrate in position and facilitate the reaction.

ROLE OF MAGNESIUM IONS. Pyruvate carboxylase also requires the presence of magnesium ions for activity, but these are necessary for the initial step in which the carboxyl group is added to biotin from bicarbonate with an accompanying hydrolysis of ATP. Magnesium is often required by enzymes catalyzing phosphate transfers. It may be used to form a complex either with the substrate or with the enzyme, and the ion serves both purposes in this instance. The active form of ATP involved in the pyruvate carboxylase reaction is the complex, **$MgATP^{2-}$**; this is frequently true of reactions requiring ATP, although this special form of the substrate is usually not specified in describing the reaction. In addition, pyruvate carboxylase requires the presence of free Mg^{2+}, presumably to bind a substrate to the enzyme peptide.

Biotin as a Vitamin. Higher animals have lost the ability to synthesize the fused rings of biotin, and the compound must be supplied in the diet. Biotin is attached to the appropriate apoenzymes (the peptide portion of the enzyme) by amide bonds. The bonds cannot be created spontaneously, and cells have still another enzyme that utilizes ATP as a means of driving the formation of biotin-apoenzyme amide linkages. These strong covalent bonds are not readily broken; therefore, the amount of biotin present in the organism need only be equivalent to the number of active sites on the biotin-containing carboxylases, and it is lost only slowly. The miniscule losses and the small content in tissues make the requirement low, and biotin deficiency only occurs under rare circumstances in humans. (One of the circumstances is an appetite for raw eggs. Eggs, for unknown reasons, contain a small protein known as **avidin,** which has a very high affinity for biotin. Frequent consumption of raw eggs may result in an unprofitable passage of most of the biotin, as an avidin complex, from the entrance to the exit of the gastrointestinal tract.)

Other Group Carriers

Other coenzymes that are used as group carriers can be more profitably considered in connection with the reactions in which they participate. For example, we shall consider:

Thiamin Pyrophosphate. This coenzyme, made from the thiamine in the diet, carries two-carbon aldehyde units during important reactions involved in carbohydrate metabolism in both plants and animals.

Coenzyme A and Phosphopantetheine. These coenzymes, which contain **pantothenic** acid derived from the diet, act as acyl carriers, and are involved in the oxidations of all metabolic fuels.

OXIDATION-REDUCTION REACTIONS AND COENZYMES

The Nature of Oxidations and Reductions

Let us briefly review oxidation-reduction reactions before considering the biological examples. Three kinds of oxidations are important for our purposes:

(1) Addition of Oxygen. Combination with elemental oxygen is an oxidation, and this was the original meaning of the word. A compound is said to be oxidized when its relative content of oxygen is increased, but oxidations are not to be confused with hydrations, in which water is added.

This is an oxidation of an organic compound:

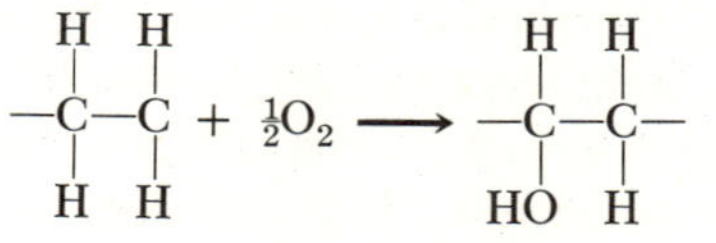

This is a hydration and not an oxidation:

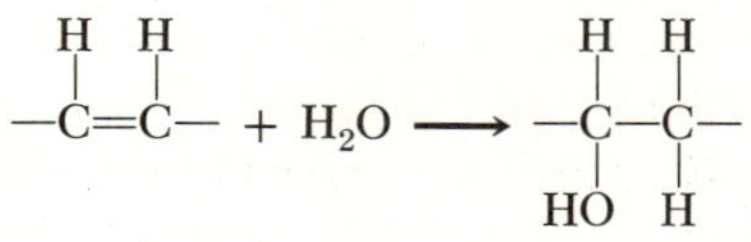

(2) Dehydrogenations. A compound may also be oxidized by the removal of hydrogen, including both the proton and its associated electron. These dehydrogenations are not to be confused with simple ionizations of acids.

This is an oxidation:

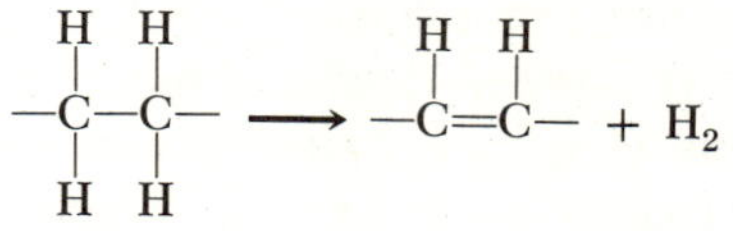

This is an oxidation:

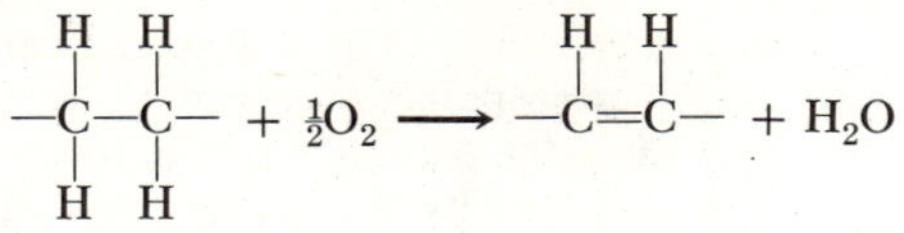

(*Notice that this reaction creates the starting material for the hydration given above—the compound with the double bond is already as oxidized as is the corresponding alcohol.*)

This is also an oxidation:

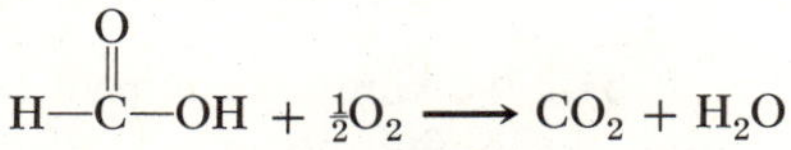

This is an ionization, and not an oxidation:

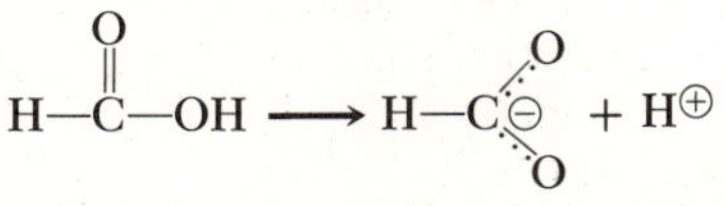

(*Only a proton is liberated here, and the corresponding electron is retained in the organic anion.*)

(3) Electron Transfer. A compound may be oxidized by a simple removal of electrons with a concomitant increase in positive charge. In this case, there must be another compound present to accept electrons, and this compound is said to be **reduced** by the gain of electrons. (The name came from the practice of reducing metallic oxide ores to the free metals.)

This is an oxidation-reduction:

$$Fe^{3+} + Cu^{+} \longrightarrow Fe^{2+} + Cu^{2+}$$

In this case, the cuprous ion is being oxidized by the ferric ion. The ferric ion is being reduced by the cuprous ion. We can say that the ferric ion is an oxidizing agent, which becomes reduced when it oxidizes other compounds. The cuprous ion is a reducing agent, which becomes oxidized when it reduces other materials.

The idea that every oxidation must be accompanied by a reduction, and vice versa, has been extended from the simple example we have here to other cases in which it is not obvious. Thus, we say that oxygen is reduced when it adds to organic compounds in the way illustrated in example (1) above, or hydrogen is being reduced in the first reaction given under example (2), while the carbon skeleton is being oxidized. The terminology is somewhat of a formalism in these cases, but the value of the practice will become more apparent as we become familiar with the actual sequences of biological oxidations, in which similar final results are sometimes achieved by the use of differing types of oxidations.

Coenzymes in Oxidations and Reductions

A fundamental feature of biological oxidations and reductions is that only a few coenzymes are used as oxidizing or reducing agents for a wide variety of organic compounds. The coenzymes become reduced when they act as oxidizing agents in any one of many reactions, and become oxidized when they act as reducing agents in still another set of reactions. Since each coenzyme undergoes both oxidation and reduction, it really is a device for coupling the oxidation of one set of compounds with the

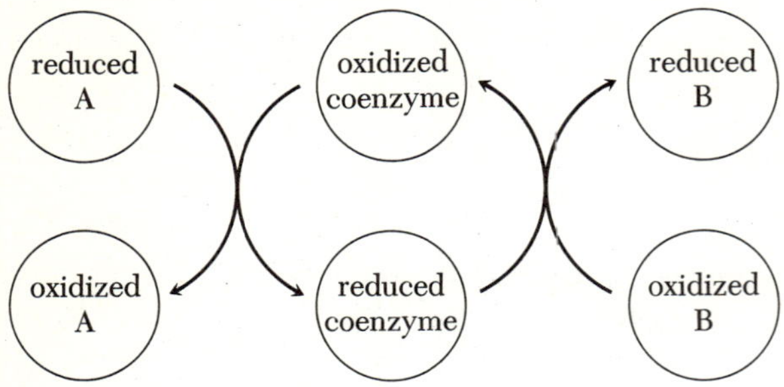

Figure 8-6 The use of the same coenzyme for different oxidation-reduction reactions serves to couple the reactions. That is, the oxidation of one substrate will cause the reduction of another by increasing the concentration of the reduced coenzyme and lowering the concentration of its oxidized form.

reduction of another set (Fig. 8-6). Five kinds of coenzymes are widely used in oxidations and reductions, stretching the definition of a coenzyme a little: nicotinamide nucleotides, flavins, quinones, hemins, and metallic ions. We shall also encounter other, more specialized, examples as we go along.

Nicotinamide Nucleotides

Oxidized and Reduced NAD. Every living organism utilizes **nicotinamide adenine dinucleotide (NAD)** in its oxidized and reduced forms. The name implies its structure, in which nucleotides containing nicotinamide and adenine are linked through a pyrophosphate bond:

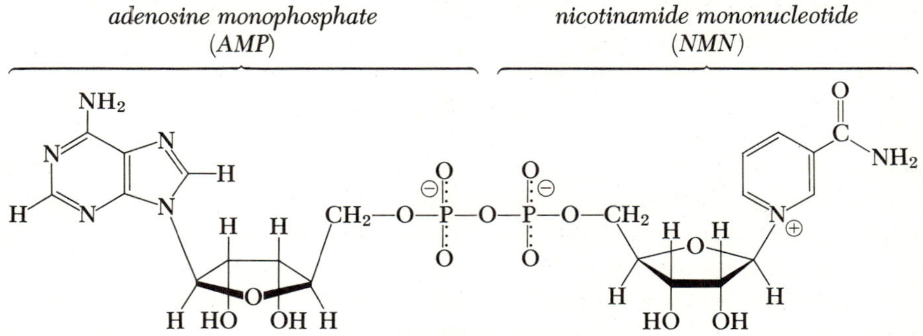

nicotinamide adenine dinucleotide
(NAD)

The pyridine ring of nicotinamide is the part of the molecule that changes during oxidation and reduction (Fig. 8-7); the combination of nicotinamide with ribose creates a quaternary nitrogen with a positive charge in the ring, and the nucleotide is a stronger oxidizing agent than free nicotinamide itself. As Figure 8-7 shows, the reduction of NAD requires the addition of a **hydride ion**—a proton with two electrons—and the

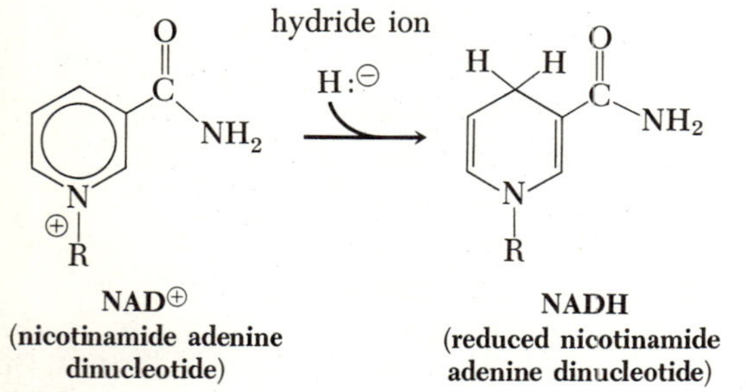

Figure 8-7 NAD is reduced to NADH by the transfer of a hydride ion from a substrate being oxidized.

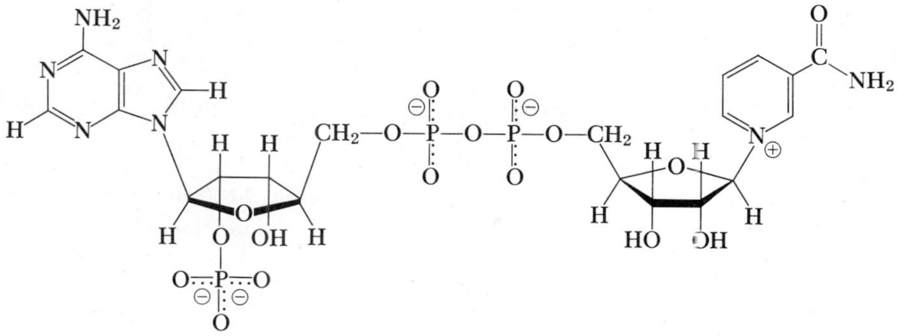

Figure 8-8 Nicotinamide adenine dinucleotide phosphate (NADP) differs from NAD only in the presence of an additional phosphate ester group on the 3′-carbon of the adenosine moiety.

nucleotide loses its positive charge in the process. The hydride ion is contributed by a substrate being oxidized, and is later added to another substrate being reduced.

NADP and Coenzyme Specificity. The reactive nicotinamide ring is only a small portion of the bulky NAD molecule. The remainder of the molecule consists of groups that serve to affix the compound to the proper enzymes. We noted the principle earlier in the discussion of pyridoxal phosphate—the additional structures of the molecule serve to bind it in a distinctive way to specific enzymes. The principle is especially well illustrated here because there is a second nicotinamide adenine dinucleotide that occurs widely; it differs from NAD only in that it contains an additional phosphate group esterified to the 2′-hydroxyl group of the adenine nucleotide portion of the molecule (Fig. 8-8). This **nicotinamide adenine dinucleotide phosphate (NADP)** has properties as an oxidizing agent that are almost identical to those of NAD, but the presence of the extra phosphate group makes the two coenzymes identifiable by separate sets of enzymes. The result is that, although many compounds undergo quite similar reactions associated with nicotinamide nucleotides, a particular oxidation can be coupled only with a particular reduction if both of the enzymes involved can utilize the same nucleotide (Fig. 8-9).

Alcohol Dehydrogenases. The action of the nicotinamide nucleotides is especially well illustrated by their participation in the interconversion of alcohols and the corresponding carbonyl compounds (Fig. 8-10). We shall encounter many examples of this kind of reaction, some involving primary alcohols and aldehydes, and others involving secondary alcohols and ketones. In either case, the substrates frequently have other substituent groups in addition to the hydroxyl or carbonyl functions, so that we don't think of them in the first instance as alcohols, aldehydes, or ketones, but the interconversion reaction is still the same.

MECHANISM OF ALCOHOL DEHYDROGENASES. The transfer of a hydride ion from the substrate to the nicotinamide ring is believed to result from an initial loss of a proton to a histidyl group in the enzyme (Fig. 8-11). The nicotinamide ring is believed to be made a more powerful electrophilic group because of bonding between it and

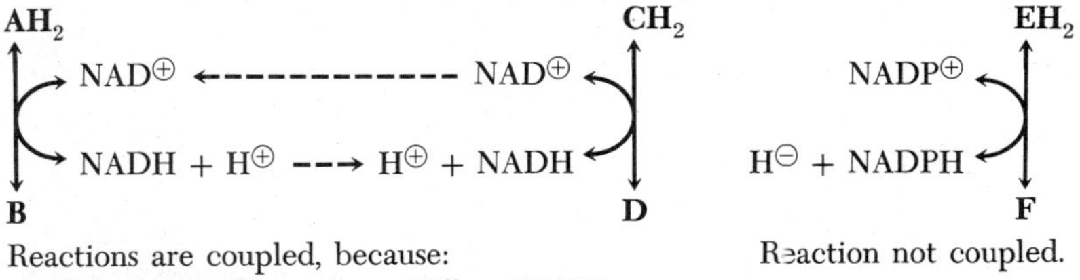

Reactions are coupled, because:

$$\text{“AH}_2\text{” + NAD}^{\oplus} \longleftrightarrow \text{“B” + NADH}$$
$$\text{“D” + NADH} \longleftrightarrow \text{“CH}_2\text{” + NAD}^{\oplus}$$
$$\textit{SUM: } \text{“A” + “D”} \longleftrightarrow \text{“B” + “C”}$$

Figure 8-9 The use of both NAD and NADP permits similar reactions to be maintained at different oxidation-reduction equilibria. All reactions involving NAD tend to equilibrate, but will not affect similar reactions catalyzed by enzymes specific for NADP.

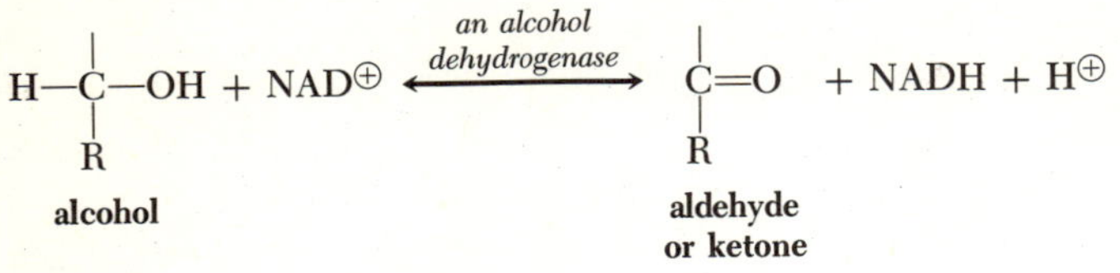

Figure 8-10 The oxidation of an alcohol group to a carbonyl group by NAD (or NADP) is one of the most common reactions in metabolism.

a lysyl group. In any event, it has been clearly established that one of the two hydrogens involved in the interconversion of alcohols and carbonyl compounds is transferred directly to or from the nicotinamide ring, while the other is released or picked up as a proton. Both of the electrons being transferred go with the nicotinamide-bound hydrogen.

FORMAL REPRESENTATION. Since the nicotinamide ring is the only portion of the coenzymes that changes upon reaction, it is common to show only the net charge in this part of the molecule when formally balancing reactions. Thus, the reduction of acetaldehyde to ethanol by NADH that is catalyzed by the alcohol dehydrogenase in yeast, and the reverse oxidation of ethanol back to acetaldehyde by NAD that is catalyzed by the alcohol dehydrogenase in human liver, can be represented by:

$$\underset{\textbf{acetaldehyde}}{C_2H_4O} + NADH + H^+ \longleftrightarrow \underset{\textbf{ethanol}}{C_2H_6O} + NAD^+$$

(The plus sign is omitted when the acronym NAD is used in text, as it is in this sentence.)

DISSOCIATION OF COENZYMES. The nicotinamide nucleotides are relatively loosely

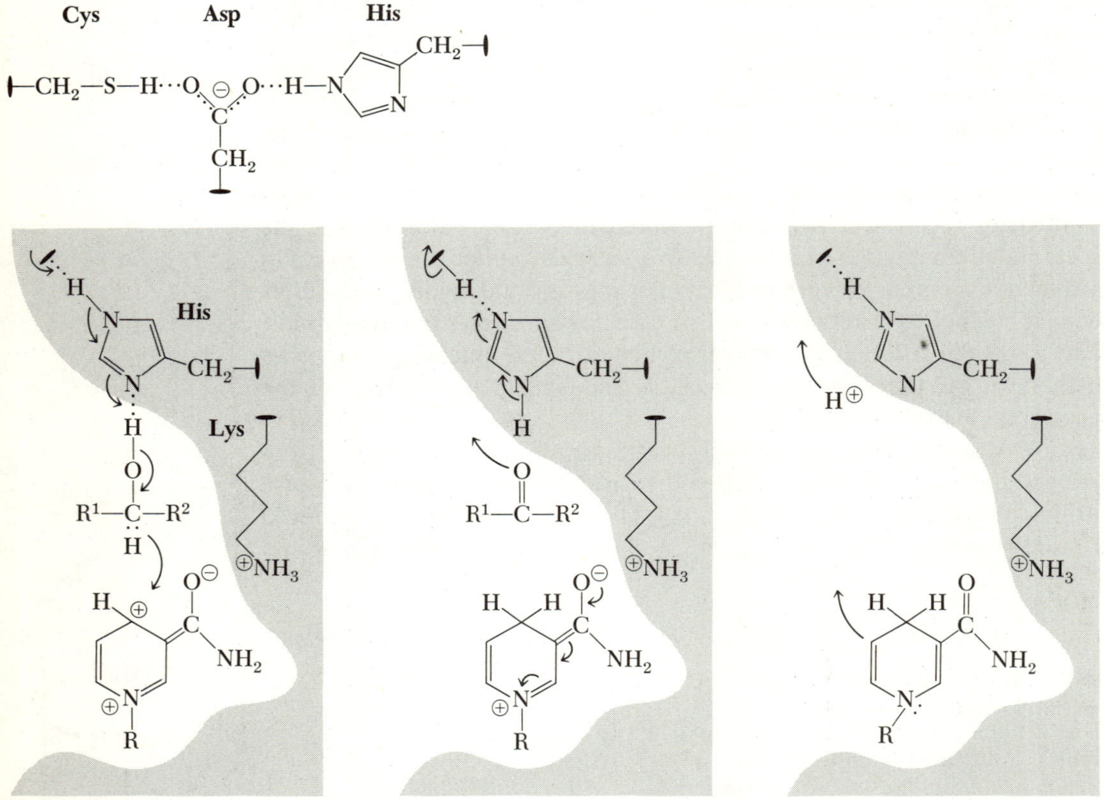

Figure 8-11 Many, if not all, of the NAD-coupled dehydrogenases attacking alcohol groups contain a hydrogen-bonded triad of cysteine, aspartate, and histidine residues. (Compare the serine proteases, p. 95.) The histidyl group acts as an acid-base catalyst in promoting the reversible transfer of a hydride ion from the substrate to NAD. A lysyl group in the coenzyme binding site makes NAD more electrophilic.

bound to the dehydrogenase peptides, so that a molecule of coenzyme does not "belong" to a particular molecule of enzyme in the same way that a molecule of biotin, for example, is associated with a molecule of pyruvate carboxylase. The dissociation of the nicotinamide nucleotides is an important part of their function, because it enables them to act as carriers for hydrogen atoms from one enzyme to another. In order for one molecule of coenzyme to act as an oxidizing agent in one reaction and a reducing agent in another, either the enzymes responsible for the two reactions must be physically close, or the coenzyme itself must be free to move from one enzyme to another. Since the nicotinamide nucleotides are used to equilibrate dozens of reactions, it would not be feasible to have all of the corresponding enzymes in close contact, and the enzymes have been evolved so as to share a common pool of coenzyme molecules that circulate among the various apoenzymes.

Flavoproteins

Some of the enzymes catalyzing oxidation-reduction reactions are flavoproteins, and have a bright yellow color (flavus = yellow) owing to the presence of either **riboflavin 5′-phosphate** (Fig. 8–12), also known as **flavin mononucleotide (FMN),** or **flavin adenine dinucleotide (FAD).** (Both of these names are technically wrong, because riboflavin is not a nucleoside. Why isn't it?)

The flavoproteins are a versatile group of enzymes. Some form quite stable free radicals, with the flavin reduced by only one electron. Such a free radical may act as a reducing agent by alternating with the fully oxidized form, or as an oxidizing agent by alternating with the fully reduced form (Fig. 8–13), with only one electron being transferred at a time in either case. Other flavoprotein enzymes never form the free radical, and use two electrons to change the fully oxidized to the fully reduced form.

Function of Flavoproteins. The flavin coenzyme is tightly bound to the apoenzyme in most flavoproteins. Consequently, these proteins are mainly used to transfer hydrogen atoms and the associated electrons between other coenzymes, or from a substrate to another coenzyme. (In mechanistic terms, there is no distinction between a substrate and a dissociable coenzyme, but there is a functional distinction because the supply of substrate is continually replenished from external sources, whereas the

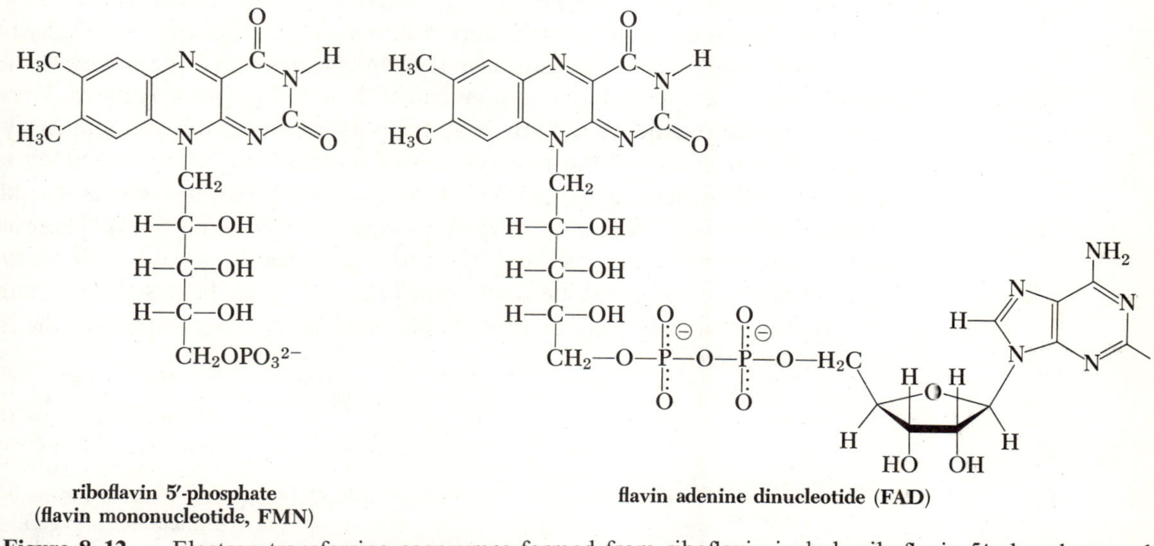

Figure 8–12 Electron-transferring coenzymes formed from riboflavin include riboflavin 5′-phosphate and flavin adenine dinucleotide (FAD). Riboflavin 5′-phosphate is often called flavin mononucleotide (FMN).

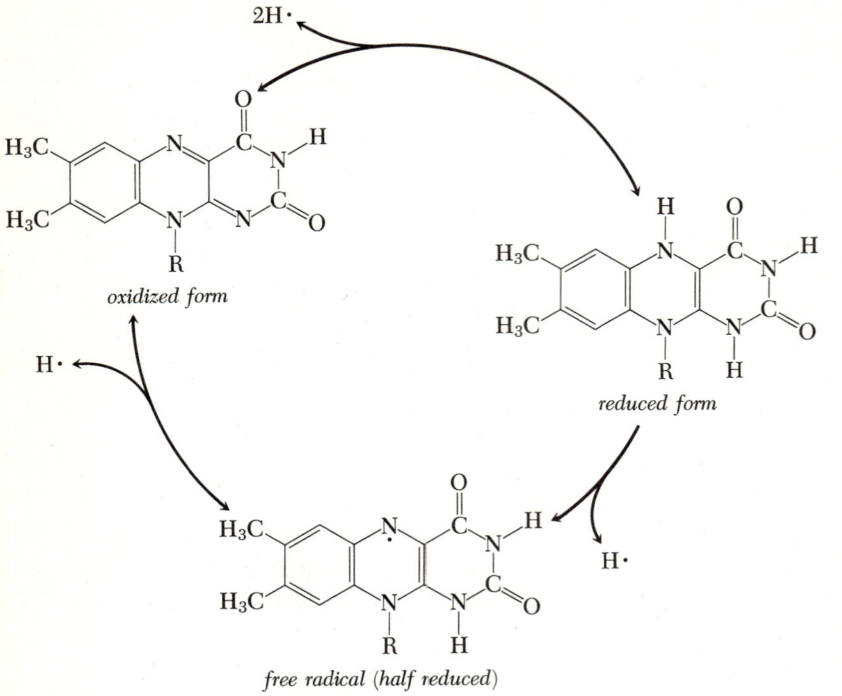

Figure 8-13 The flavin coenzymes may carry two electrons (*top*) or one electron (*bottom*). When transporting one electron, they may oscillate between the oxidized and half-reduced forms, or between the half-reduced and fully-reduced forms.

supply of a coenzyme is relatively constant over short periods.) Most of the flavoproteins are stronger oxidizing agents than are the protein-bound nicotinamide nucleotides, and are therefore used for reactions such as the oxidation of part of an alkyl chain to an ethylenic bond:

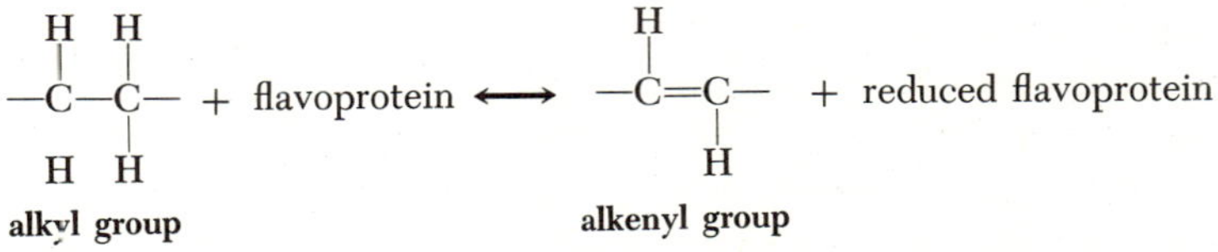

Flavoprotein Oxidases. We shall treat the transfer of electrons from flavoproteins to other carriers in Chapter 11. In some cases, molecular oxygen is used as a sink for electrons. When electrons are transferred directly from a substrate to O_2 by the action of a flavoprotein, one of the products is **hydrogen peroxide.** The organelles known as **peroxisomes** in animal cells contain several of these flavoprotein oxidases. The apparent purpose of the organelles is to dispose of potentially noxious compounds by a direct oxidation. For example, the peroxisomes of mammalian liver and kidney contain a D-amino acid oxidase, a flavoprotein that specifically oxidizes the unnatural isomer of amino acids with molecular oxygen, producing H_2O_2 (Fig. 8-14). These unnatural amino acid isomers are generated by some microorganisms, and some peptides containing them are known to be toxic; that is, they are antibiotics. It is presumed that they are automatically degraded by the peroxisomes in order to prevent the formation of toxic products.

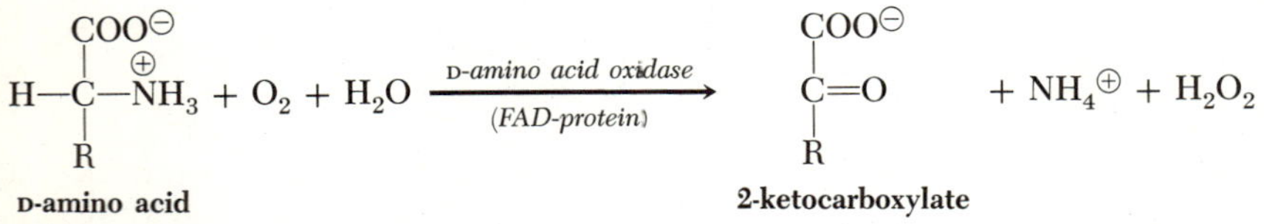

Figure 8-14 D-Amino acid oxidase, a flavoprotein, catalyzes the oxidative deamination of D-amino acids by molecular oxygen, with the production of hydrogen peroxide.

Quinones

The quinone-hydroquinone interconversion is well known to organic chemists in general, and to photographic chemists in particular. Coenzymes containing a quinone structure are used for transferring hydrogen atoms and associated electrons through the hydrophobic core of membranes. We shall later spend considerable time on the function of the **ubiquinones,** also known as **coenzymes Q,** and on the function of **plastoquinones.** These are quinones with varying lengths of polyprenyl tail attached (Fig. 8–15). Ubiquinones are involved in fuel metabolism, and the similar plastoquinones participate in photosynthesis.

Hemoproteins

We have already considered hemoglobin, in which the ferrous atom of the heme group retains its valence during ordinary function. However, this behavior is unusual among the hemoproteins. Most are constructed to participate in oxidation-reduction reactions through a change in the valence of the constituent iron atom.

Cytochromes. The cytochromes are membrane-associated hemoproteins used in transferring electrons from one carrier to another, both in the oxidation of fuels and in photosynthesis, as well as in subsidiary synthetic reactions. Particular examples will be discussed as we encounter their functions.

Catalase. Catalase is a hemoprotein present in high concentrations in peroxisomes to degrade hydrogen peroxide:

$$H_2O_2 \longrightarrow H_2O + \tfrac{1}{2}O_2$$

The purpose evidently is only to remove this dangerous byproduct of the reactions catalyzed by the flavoprotein oxidases.

Peroxidases. The peroxidases are hemoproteins that catalyze the utilization of hydrogen peroxide for the oxidation of substrates:

$$AH_2 + H_2O_2 \longrightarrow A + 2H_2O$$

The reactions of the peroxidases, like the reactions of the flavoprotein oxidases that produce H_2O_2, are not a part of the routes of fuel metabolism; they are used for

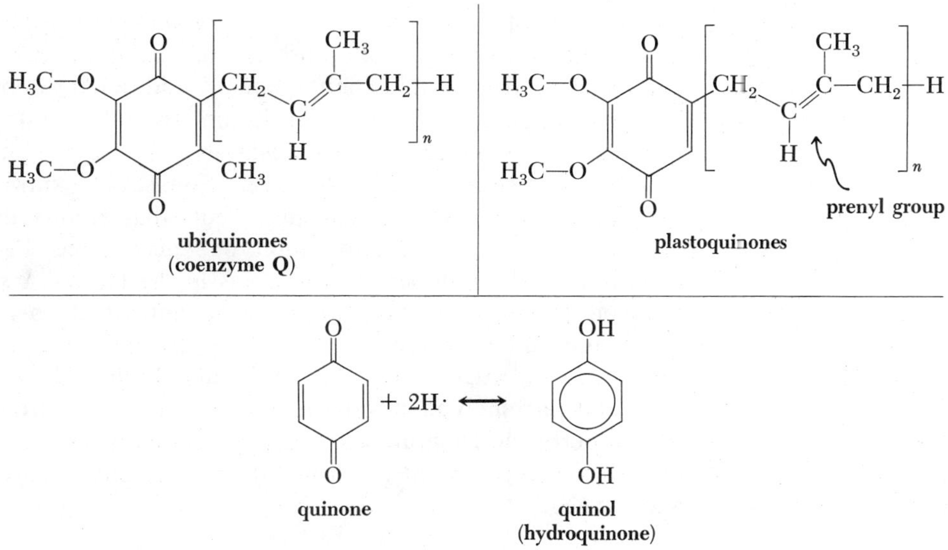

Figure 8–15 Quinones with long polyprenyl tails are used for electron transfers. Ubiquinones occur in mitochondria and are used in the combustion of fuels; plastoquinones occur in chloroplasts of plants and are used in photosynthesis. The reduction of a quinone creates a hydroquinone, or quinol. Electrons may also be transferred one at a time with the use of an intermediate free radical (not shown).

synthesis of some compounds, and for protective purposes. The enzymes are especially effective in oxidizing phenols, and this action is utilized in the formation of structural components of insects and plants (Chapter 29).

HALIDE ACTIVATION BY PEROXIDASES. Some peroxidases in animal cells are capable of converting halide ions to an active state so that they behave in some ways as if they were converted to hypohalite, although the ion is not released as such:

$$X^- + H_2O_2 \longrightarrow OX^- + H_2O$$

For example, a peroxidase in the **thyroid gland** is responsible for activating iodide so that tyrosyl residues are iodinated to create the hormone, **thyroxine.** This same mechanism is apparently responsible for the ability of **leukocytes,** the white blood cells that engulf foreign particles, to kill microorganisms that they have ingested. The leukocytes create H_2O_2 by the action of a flavoprotein, NADPH oxidase:

$$\text{NADPH} + H^+ + O_2 \longrightarrow \text{NADP}^+ + H_2O_2$$

(The NADPH is created by a special route of carbohydrate metabolism considered in Chapter 21.) The intermediate H_2O_2 is then used by a myeloperoxidase (that is, a peroxidase occurring in myelocytes) to activate chloride ions, followed by still unknown reactions that result in the death of the microorganism. (The greenish hue of purulent discharge ought to be admired—it is due to the myeloperoxidase in the leukocytes fighting the infection.)

Metalloproteins

Some enzymes catalyzing oxidation-reduction reactions use metallic ions directly linked to the apoenzyme for the transfer of electrons. The ions most frequently involved are those of iron and copper. There are even a few examples of cuproproteins that catalyze the direct oxidation of substrates without the formation of H_2O_2. Other examples of metalloproteins that we shall later encounter include the following:

Iron-Sulfide Proteins. Plants, animals, and many microorganisms contain proteins that bind iron atoms in a lattice of sulfur atoms; these proteins are often called **non-heme iron proteins** to distinguish them from the proteins containing iron chelated to porphyrins. The structure has been worked out in detail for **ferredoxins,** which are involved in photosynthesis and in bacterial metabolism. Part of the sulfur in the ferredoxin lattice comes from inorganic sulfide, and part from cysteinyl groups in the peptide chain (Fig. 8–16). There are many additional examples of proteins containing iron and sulfide in varying amounts in similar kinds of linkages. It is evidently possible to modify the structure in such a way as to cause profound changes in the affinity for electrons, because these proteins vary from strong oxidizing agents with high affinity for an electron, to strong reducing agents that readily discharge an electron. It is probable that all are built to handle one electron per Fe-S lattice in the molecule, regardless of the number of iron atoms in the lattice. A similar protein involved in nitrogen fixation by microorganisms also contains at least one molybdenum atom.

Metalloflavoproteins. Some enzymes transfer electrons through both flavin coenzymes and attached metallic ions. Examples include ferroflavoproteins, containing iron, and ferromolybdoflavoproteins, containing both iron and molybdenum atoms.

Superoxide Dismutases. Perhaps the most diverse use of metallic ions is seen in the enzymes catalyzing the dismutation of superoxide ions to form hydrogen peroxide and oxygen:

$$2(\cdot O_2^-) + 2H^+ \longrightarrow H_2O_2 + O_2$$

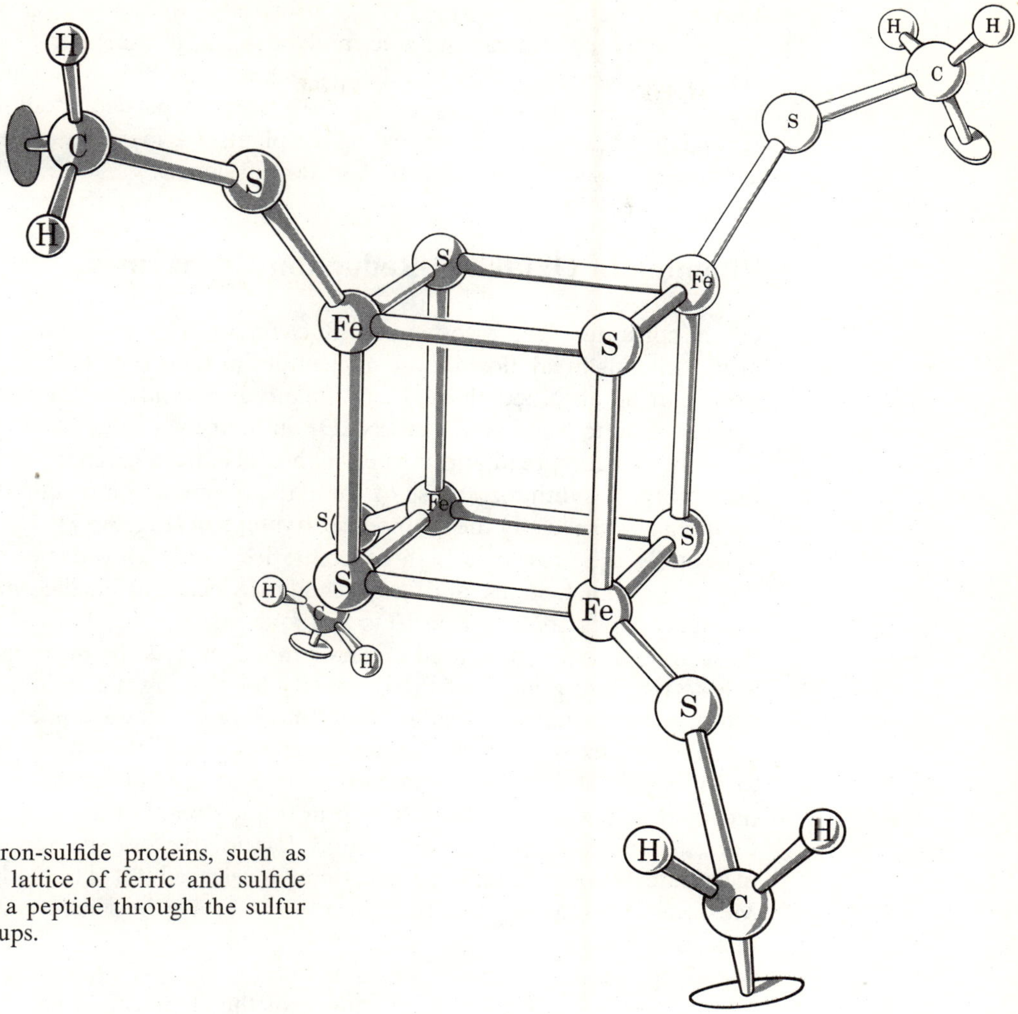

Figure 8–16 The iron-sulfide proteins, such as ferredoxins, contain a lattice of ferric and sulfide ions that is bonded to a peptide through the sulfur atoms of cysteinyl groups.

Some bacteria and the mitochondria of eukaryotic cells (Chapter 11) contain Mn^{2+} in the richly violet enzyme catalyzing this reaction. Some bacteria also contain another enzyme catalyzing the same reaction, but which has Fe^{3+} attached. Eukaryotic cells contain still another kind of superoxide dismutase, blue-green in color, which contains both Cu^{2+} and Zn^{2+}.

FUNCTION OF SUPEROXIDE DISMUTASE. The superoxide radical is created as a minor byproduct of the action of some oxidases, especially the metalloflavoproteins. It is dangerously reactive, and cells built to live in oxygen atmospheres therefore contain the dismutase necessary to eliminate it. It is believed that evolution of this enzyme was a necessary prerequisite for continued survival of organisms when oxygen began to appear in the atmosphere.

Dietary Metal Requirements. It is apparent that the metals necessary for the maintenance of enzymatic activity must be supplied in the diet. Non-marine animals require relatively large amounts of dietary sodium, potassium, magnesium, and calcium to maintain the effective concentrations of these loosely bound ions, but only small quantities of more tightly chelated ions are required to replace daily losses. Humans require, on the average, several milligrams of iron per day because they contain large amounts of hemoglobin which is lost in variable amounts, even without injury. The requirements for manganese, zinc, molybdenum, and copper are so small, although real, that deficiencies owing to a dietary lack are very rare in humans. Plants sometimes are affected by a lack of one or more elements in particular soils, which in turn can cause deficiencies in herbivores eating the plants. Farmers therefore pay more attention to these so-called trace elements than do physicians.

Vitamins in Oxidation-Reduction Coenzymes

Nicotinate. The nicotinamide nucleotides are constituents of every living organism. Animals break down these nucleotides in their ingested food so that the components can be absorbed through cell membranes, and use the resultant nicotinate or nicotinamide to build NAD and NADP in their own cells. Even though these nucleotides are so widespread and in such high concentrations, many animals have retained the ability to synthesize most of their requirement for nicotinate from other body components, especially the amino acid **tryptophan** (Fig. 8–17). The reason is that these nucleotides are present in high concentrations, only an order of magnitude less than the adenine nucleotides, and they readily dissociate from the enzymes into solution. The daily losses are therefore 10 to 100 fold greater than those of most vitamins. Only those animals with an assured dietary supply, such as the meat-eating cats, have been able to risk losing much of their capacity for making nicotinate. (Animals in general can make nicotinamide residues from nicotinate.) Non-ruminant herbivores, such as guinea pigs, have an uncertain dietary supply, and they have retained the capacity to synthesize their total requirements. Man is on the borderline. He can make sufficient nicotinate if his diet is relatively rich in tryptophan, but this is not true in some cases. For example, corn (maize) is not only low in tryptophan, but also low in available nicotinate. (However, sufficient nicotinate is released if it is treated with alkali. Modern Mexicans, presumably like their ancestors, survive in a corn culture by treating the meal with lime.)

Nutritionists list nicotinate as a human vitamin under the euphemism **niacin,** coined to avoid any nasty connotations of the chemical name.

Riboflavin. Since the flavin coenzymes are tightly bound to the corresponding apoenzymes, there is no need for high concentrations of the free coenzymes in tissues, and the losses are also low—probably no greater than a few milligrams per day in an adult human. The coenzymes occur in all cells because their functions are fundamental to metabolism. The low demand and wide availability of these compounds has made their synthesis by animals unnecessary, and the enzymes responsible for synthesis have been discarded. The absorption of riboflavin either present in the diet or manufactured by bacteria in the gut is therefore an absolute necessity for survival of animals. However, riboflavin deficiency is rarely seen in humans except with diets so sparse as to provoke symptoms of deficiency of many dietary components.

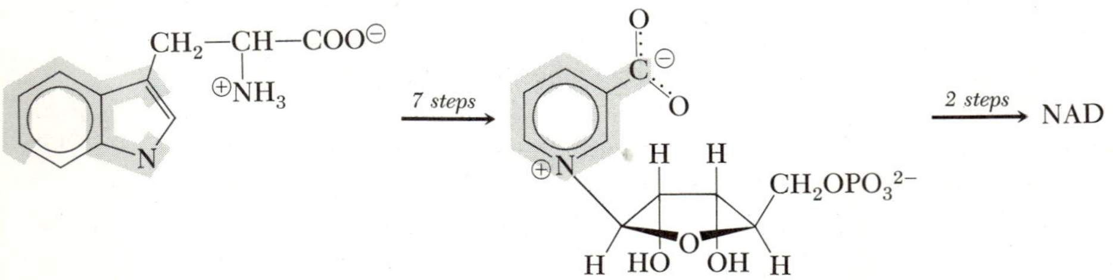

tryptophan

nicotinate mononucleotide

Figure 8–17 The nicotinate portion of NAD is formed from tryptophan. Those animals unable to catalyze this reaction at an effective rate require a source of nicotinate in their diets.

FURTHER READING

C. Y. Lai and B. L. Horecker, Aldolase: a model for enzyme structure-function relationships, Essays in Biochem., 8:149 (1972).

E. E. Snell and S. J. Di Mari, Schiff base intermediates in enzyme catalysis, 2:355 in P. D. Boyer, ed., The enzymes, 3rd ed., Academic Press (1970).

H. R. Mahler and E. H. Cordes, Biological chemistry, 2nd ed., Harper & Row (1971). See Chapter 14 for detailed discussion of oxidation-reduction reactions and the coenzymes involved.

J. M. McCord, B. B. Keele, Jr., and I. Fridovich, An enzyme-based theory of obligate anaerobiosis: The physiological function of superoxide dismutase, Proc. Natl. Acad. Sci. U. S., 68:1024 (1971).

J. Moss and M. D. Lane, The biotin-dependent enzymes, Adv. Enzymol., 35:321 (1971).

QUESTIONS

1. A lysyl group in a peptide contains an amino group that is (a) attached to a four-carbon chain, (b) equilibrated with the ammonium form, and (c) capable of forming a Schiff's base. Reasoning by analogy from known reactions, which of these properties is likely to be of paramount importance to (1) an enzyme catalyzing the transfer of a three-carbon ketone group from one carbon chain to another, (2) an enzyme catalyzing the hydrolysis of an ester, (3) an enzyme catalyzing the oxidation of an alcohol by NAD, and (4) an enzyme complex containing three different active sites that interact with a single coenzyme molecule?
2. Which coenzyme, if any, is a likely participant in each of the following reactions?

a. $$H_3C{-}\overset{\displaystyle O}{\overset{\|}{C}}{-}X + HCO_3^{\ominus} + ATP \longrightarrow {}^{\ominus}OOC{-}CH_2{-}\overset{\displaystyle O}{\overset{\|}{C}}{-}X + ADP + P_i$$

b. $${}^{\ominus}OOC{-}CH_2{-}CH_2{-}COO^{\ominus} \longrightarrow {}^{\ominus}OOC{-}CH{=}CH{-}COO^{\ominus}$$

c. $$HOOC{-}CH_2{-}CH_2{-}COOH \longrightarrow {}^{\ominus}OOC{-}CH_2{-}CH_2{-}COO^{\ominus} + 2H^{\oplus}$$

d. $${}^{\ominus}OOC{-}\underset{\displaystyle OH}{\underset{|}{C}H}{-}CH_2{-}COO^{\ominus} \longrightarrow {}^{\ominus}OOC{-}\underset{\displaystyle O}{\underset{\|}{C}}{-}CH_2{-}COO^{\ominus}$$

e. $${}^{\ominus}OOC{-}CH{=}CH{-}COO^{\ominus} + H_2O \longrightarrow {}^{\ominus}OOC{-}\underset{\displaystyle OH}{\underset{|}{C}H}{-}CH_2{-}COO^{\ominus}$$

f. 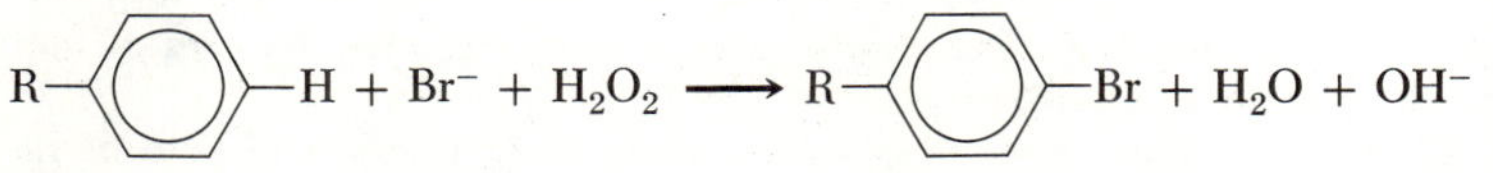

3. How does the binding of iron in non-heme iron proteins differ from that in the cytochromes?
4. Why is Cu also necessary in superoxide dismutase molecules that contain Zn, when the enzyme in some organisms contains either Mn or Fe alone?
5. Some organisms lack superoxide dismutase, but can survive only in specialized ecological niches. What environmental quality would be necessary for their survival?
6. Are quinones mainly involved in group transfers or in oxidation-reduction reactions? Show the transition that quinones undergo when they act as coenzymes.
7. Does each of the following prosthetic groups transfer the equivalent of a single electron or of two electrons?
   (a) NADPH
   (b) FAD
   (c) hemin
   (d) ubiquinone
   (e) coenzyme Q
   (f) FMN

CHAPTER 9

REGULATION OF RATES OF ENZYMATIC REACTIONS

THE CONCEPTS

Regulation by Substrate Concentration. The rates of enzymatic reactions in an organism are controlled so as to carry out its external functions effectively without large changes in composition. Enzymes are often self-regulating to a certain extent because changes in substrate concentration cause corresponding changes in the rates of their reactions. An increased supply of a compound therefore causes an increased rate of its removal.

Michaelis-Menten Kinetics. The response of a simple enzyme to changes in substrate concentration is described in terms of the maximum velocity (V_{max}) it would achieve if saturated with substrate and the substrate concentration required to reach half of the maximum velocity. That concentration is known as the Michaelis constant (K_M).

The Michaelis constant is greater for an enzyme with less affinity for its substrate. Enzymes are frequently constructed so that their Michaelis constants are roughly comparable to the physiological concentrations of their substrates.

Various mathematical manipulations to achieve linear plots, such as the Lineweaver-Burk plot, are used to estimate values of K_M from experimental kinetic data. Full appreciation of the kinetic responses requires V_{max} for both the forward and reverse reactions and K_M values for all substrates in both directions, because the product of an enzymatic reaction is a substrate in its own right for the reverse reaction, and it also acts as an inhibitor of the forward reaction by competing with the substrate for the active site on the enzyme. By constructing enzymes with different affinities for the various reactants, they can be made to catalyze a reaction better when concentrations cause reaction toward equilibrium from one direction than they do when reaction occurs from the other direction. The kinetic effects influence only the rate of approach to equilibrium, not the position of equilibrium.

Homotropic Kinetics. Some enzymes have a sigmoidal response of rate of reaction to substrate concentration. Such enzymes contain several subunits with active sites of catalysis, which interact much as do the subunits of hemoglobin, so that the binding of substrate to one active site increases the affinity of the next active site for the substrate. This positive cooperativity is especially valuable in controlling the rate of irreversible reactions, because the sigmoidal response permits the reaction to be shut off before the substrate is totally consumed. The response to fluctuations in substrate concentration can also be made very sensitive over the steep portion of the curve.

Regulation by Inhibition and Activation. Metabolic sequences are also controlled by building key enzymes to interact with other metabolites that activate or inhibit the enzymes. Sequences used for a single purpose may be controlled by negative feedback, in which a final product of the sequence inhibits the first enzyme in the sequence by which it is formed. The product shuts off its own formation as its concentration rises, and thus prevents the accumulation of intermediates not used for any other purpose. Activating an enzyme is also useful; for example, the accumulation of an intermediate in energy production from glucose activates an enzyme that causes the excess glucose to be stored as fat.

Allosteric Mechanisms. Control is sometimes exerted through simple competitive inhibitors, which resemble the substrate sufficiently to combine with the active site on an enzyme; but regulation by other metabolite effectors usually involves construction of an additional binding

site for the effector on the regulated enzyme. The combination of the effector with the enzyme changes its conformation and thereby modifies its catalytic properties, changing K_M, V_{max}, or both. If the enzyme is a multi-subunit enzyme exhibiting the sigmoidal response of homotropic interactions, the presence of the effector may diminish the interactions so that the subunits are independently active, or it may increase the interactions so that even more substrate is required for effective catalysis. Effectors may also modify the conformation of enzymes that have ordinary Michaelis-Menten kinetics so as to alter the affinity for substrate and catalytic ability. They sometimes cause subunits to aggregate into polymeric enzymes or cause multi-subunit molecules to dissociate, with only one or the other form being active.

Rate-Limiting Step. **Regulation of metabolic sequences usually, but not always, occurs at an irreversible step catalyzed by an enzyme with the smallest V_{max} of any in the sequence. Such a step is said to be rate-limiting because it causes an accumulation of compounds preceding its reaction in the sequence, and a disappearance of compounds involved in following reactions. Changing the activity of the rate-limiting enzyme is the only way of causing a proportionate change in the steady-state rate of the entire sequence under these conditions.**

Enzymes cause reactions that would not otherwise occur to a significant extent; this is the qualitative aspect of function, which we have been considering. However, the actual velocities of the reactions catalyzed, the quantitative aspect, is equally important. Each enzymatic reaction in the large collection constituting the metabolism of an organism proceeds at a rate that is automatically adjusted to carry out the functions of the organism and at the same time to maintain the essential nature of the organism. The mechanisms responsible for this all-important regulation of the rates of individual reactions are the topic of this chapter.

REGULATION BY SUBSTRATE CONCENTRATION

The fundamental control of metabolism comes from a simple response of enzymes to changes in the concentration of their substrates. When the substrate concentration rises, the reaction goes faster in most cases. The increased rate of removal of the substrate prevents further rise in its concentration. The organism is somewhat comparable to a succession of tanks connected by pipes, with food funneled in at one end and the excreta discharged at the other. When the flow into a tank increases, the level in the tank rises until the rate of flow out of the tank matches the flow into the tank.

Michaelis-Menten Kinetics

Single Substrate. The simplest sort of quantitative behavior is seen with enzymes containing a single active site that combines with only one substrate molecule. When the concentration of the product of the reaction is kept so low that the tendency for it to occupy the active site in place of the substrate is negligible, the velocity of the reaction varies with changing substrate concentrations in the manner shown in Figure 9–1.

MAXIMUM VELOCITY; SUBSTRATE SATURATION. We see from the figure that the velocity of the reaction approaches a limiting value as the substrate concentration rises. This maximum velocity of the enzyme (V_{max}) is reached when the enzyme is **saturated** with substrate; that is, when the molecules of substrate are so abundant that one will immediately combine with the active site on a molecule of enzyme at the moment of release of product. The concentration of free enzyme is negligible when it is saturated with substrate. Saturation and maximum velocity are theoretical limits that could be reached only at infinite substrate concentrations, but they are useful expressions of the capacity for catalysis, which can be estimated mathematically.

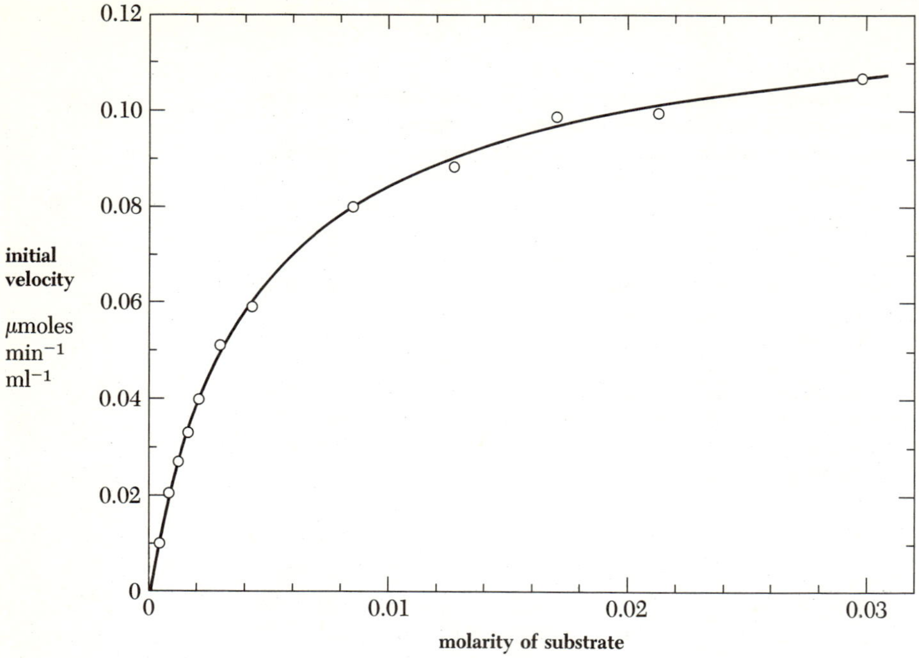

Figure 9-1 Measured values of the initial velocity of an enzymatic reaction with varying concentrations of substrate. The scatter apparent at the higher substrate concentrations amounts to 2 per cent of the highest velocity, which is quite good for measurements of most enzymes with standard techniques.

V_{max} and Enzyme Concentration. The maximum velocity is actually a relative measure of the concentration of an enzyme present, expressed in terms of its catalytic ability. Velocities are usually given in terms of concentration per unit time. The common **enzyme unit** (E.U.) has dimensions of micromoles of substrate consumed per minute, so an expression of V_{max} in micromoles consumed per volume per minute is the same as an expression of enzyme units per volume: µmoles/min/volume = E.U./volume.

The V_{max} of a reaction in a tissue is directly proportional to the concentration of molecules of enzyme in the tissue, but the effectiveness of individual molecules as catalysts differs among enzymes, so the proportionality of V_{max} and molecular concentration is not the same for all enzymes. Put another way, if the V_{max} values for two different enzymatic reactions are identical in a solution, then the capacity for catalysis by each enzyme is the same, but the number of molecules of each enzyme required to achieve that capacity is not the same. However, doubling the number of molecules of enzyme, whatever that number may be, doubles the V_{max} in each case.

MICHAELIS-MENTEN EQUATION. Michaelis and Menten reported in 1913 that the actual velocity of an enzymatic reaction can be expressed in a simple way as a fraction of the maximum velocity dependent upon the substrate concentration:

$$v = \frac{V_{max}S}{K_M + S}$$

in which v = initial velocity, V_{max} = maximum velocity, K_M = a constant, known as the Michaelis constant, and S = concentration of substrate. (The initial velocity is the velocity after equilibration of enzyme and substrate upon mixing under experimental conditions, but before significant formation of product.)

Significance of K_M. Most enzymes in biological systems are not functioning under the limiting conditions described by the simple Michaelis-Menten equation. Even so, it is a starting point for tackling the real behavior of any enzyme. One reason is the character of the Michaelis constant, K_M. It is easy to show that K_M is identical to the substrate concentration at which the velocity of the reaction is half of its maximum:

$$\text{if } S = K_M, \text{ then } v = \frac{V_{max}K_M}{K_M + K_M} = \frac{V_{max}K_M}{2K_M} = \frac{V_{max}}{2}$$

The definition of K_M as the substrate concentration necessary to achieve $\frac{1}{2}V_{max}$ has theoretical significance for some more complicated enzymes, and is a useful qualitative index for physiological performance of all enzymes. A high value of K_M means low affinity of the enzyme for the substrate and vice versa.

The extent to which the capacity for catalysis is being used depends upon the relationship of the actual substrate concentration in a cell to the K_M value of the enzyme. It so happens that many enzymes are constructed to have K_M values near the physiological concentrations of their substrates, thereby achieving an optimum balance between effectiveness as a catalyst and self-regulation. (If the K_M is very low compared to the substrate concentration, then the enzyme will always be nearly saturated, and variations in substrate concentration will have little effect. If the K_M is very high, the enzyme will have maximum sensitivity to changes in substrate concentration, but will be functioning at only a small fraction of its catalytic capacity.)

Lineweaver-Burk Plot. The Michaelis constant is one of the parameters frequently determined for enzymes because of its importance in assessing physiological function. A common way to do this for enzymes with simple kinetics is to rearrange the Michaelis-Menten equation so as to give a linear plot, named a Lineweaver-Burk plot after the men best known for developing this type of analysis. (The manipulation is elementary, but realization of the need for it was not so obvious in their time.) Upon inversion and rearrangement of the equation, we have:

$$\frac{1}{v} = \frac{K_M + S}{V_{max}S} = \frac{K_M}{V_{max}} \times \frac{1}{S} + \frac{1}{V_{max}}$$

If we now take $1/v$ and $1/S$ as our variables, we have a simple linear equation of the type $y = ax + b$, which can be solved by graphical analysis (Fig. 9–2). The intercept on the ordinate is the reciprocal of V_{max} and the intercept on the abscissa is the reciprocal of $-K_M$, so both of these constants can be estimated. Various other linear permutations of the Michaelis-Menten equation have been devised to give the same result without the crowding of the data points seen in Fig. 9–2, but modern computer programs do even better.

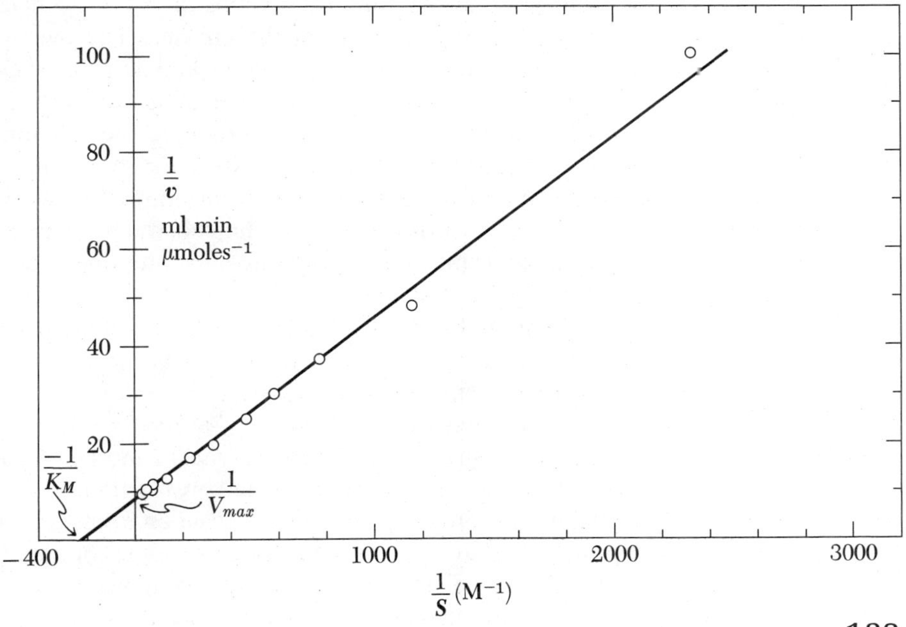

Figure 9–2 A Lineweaver-Burk plot of the data from Figure 9–1. Note the gross scatter of values obtained at low substrate concentrations (high values of $1/S$), which were not evident in the steeply rising portion of the regular plot given in Figure 9–1.

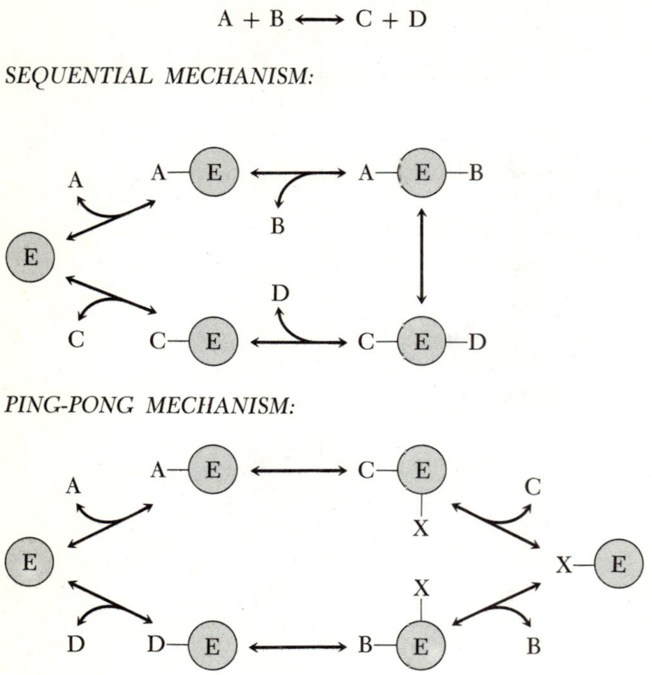

Figure 9-3 Two of the possible mechanisms by which an enzyme may react with two substrates.

Two or More Substrates. Many enzymatic reactions involve more than one substrate: $\mathbf{A + B \xrightarrow{E} P}$, or $\mathbf{A + B \xrightarrow{E} P + Q}$, and so on. The initial velocity of these reactions will depend upon the concentration of each of the different substrates, and the actual form of the equation describing the initial velocity depends upon the mechanism of the reaction. For example, two substrates may react in a sequential fashion, with both becoming attached to the enzyme before any products are formed (Fig. 9-3). On the other hand, the substrates may react in a ping-pong mechanism, in which one substrate reacts with the enzyme and dissociates into one product, leaving some functional group from the substrate attached to the enzyme. The attached group is then transferred to the second substrate so as to make the second product, thereby releasing the original form of the enzyme. The overall result seems similar, but the two mechanisms have quite different kinetic properties.

If a large excess of all but one of the substrates is added to a multi-substrate enzyme, variation of the concentration of the remaining substrate affects the initial velocity in the way we have described for single-substrate reactions, and the K_M for that substrate can be determined from simple Lineweaver-Burk plots. The process can be repeated in turn for each of the substrates. (This kind of analysis is valid only if the high concentration of any one substrate does not change the catalytic properties of the enzyme in some way.)

Effect of Product. Simple Michaelis-Menten kinetics are based upon the assumption that the reverse reaction can be neglected, and this is usually not true in biological systems. Enzymes catalyze the attainment of an equilibrium, and we noted earlier that what we call product of an enzymatic reaction in one circumstance may behave as substrate for the same enzyme in another circumstance, when the net reaction goes in the opposite direction. The construction of an enzyme can do nothing about changing the direction in which a reaction goes; a reaction has a certain position of equilibrium that is fixed by the character of the compounds participating in the reaction, and the enzyme can only accelerate the approach toward the equilibrium.

However, enzymes can be constructed so that they will accelerate the approach toward equilibrium much more effectively in one direction than in the other. In other words, an enzyme may be built to function briskly when the concentrations of reactants favor a reaction in the "right" direction (the direction promoting proper biological function), and to drag its feet, catalyzing the reaction only slowly, in the "wrong" direction when concentrations favor the reverse reaction. On the other hand, some enzymes are built as strict neutrals and facilitate an approach to equilibrium from either direction with equal verve.

THE HALDANE RELATIONSHIP. The way in which enzymes are made to differ in their relative ability to catalyze the forward or the reverse reaction is by constructing them to have different affinities for the various reactants. Since the rates of forward and back reactions must be equal at equilibrium concentrations, it follows that a change in the affinity for substrate, tending to change the rate of a reaction because of a change in the degree of saturation, must be counterbalanced by an opposing change in the V_{max} of the enzyme. This truism is expressed formally by the Haldane relationship:

$$K_{eq} = \frac{V_F K_B}{V_B K_F}$$

in which V_F, K_F and V_B, K_B are the respective maximum velocities and Michaelis constants for the forward and back reactions.

Homotropic Kinetics

Some enzymes are constructed with multiple subunits, each with a catalytic site, that interact with each other so as to create more complex responses to changes in

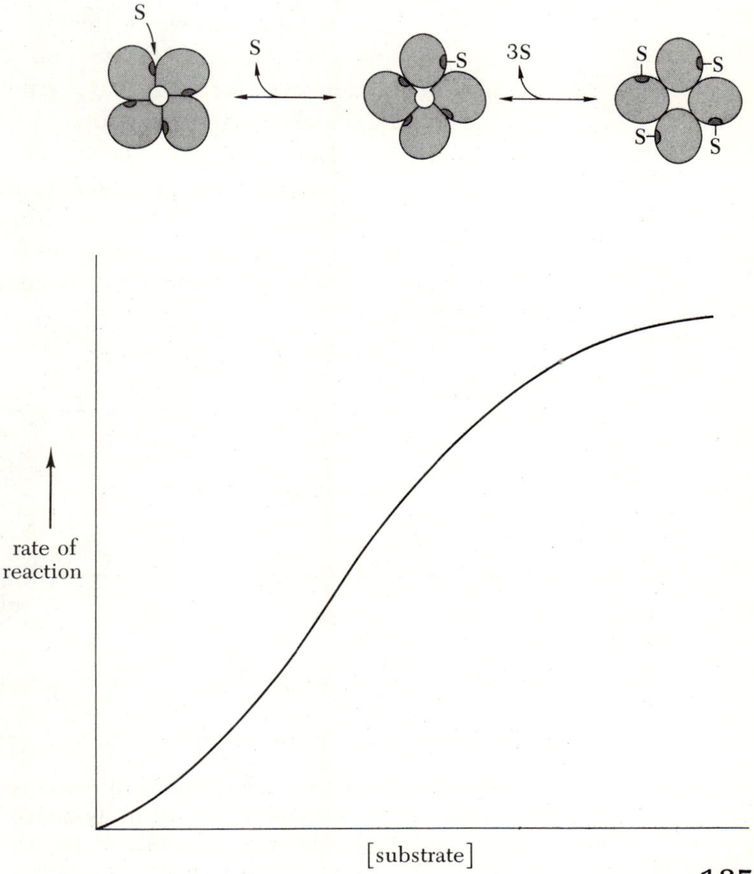

Figure 9-4 Enzymes that are constructed with multiple subunits may exhibit complex kinetics, such as the positive cooperativity shown here. In this example, formation of a tetramer creates a conformation in which access to the catalytic site is impeded (*upper left*). When the substrate concentration is elevated enough to stabilize a combination with one of the subunits in a more open form (*top center*), the remaining subunits can more readily combine with substrate and form a totally reactive tetramer (*upper right*). The result is a sigmoidal response of rate of reaction to substrate concentration (*bottom*).

substrate concentration (Fig. 9–4). Such enzymes display **positive cooperativity** of the same sort seen with hemoglobin. The binding of one or more molecules of substrate stabilizes a new conformation in which the affinity for the substrate is increased at the remaining binding sites.

Physiological Implications. An enzyme with homotropic interactions cannot effectively catalyze its reaction until the substrate concentration has built up to a level approaching the steep portion of the velocity-concentration curve. This is an especially desirable property for enzymes catalyzing reactions in which the position of equilibrium is far in the direction of the product. Suppose that the equilibrium ratio of [**P**]/[**S**] is 10,000 for the reaction: **S** $\longrightarrow$ **P.** It would be very difficult to maintain a reasonable concentration of **S** in the presence of an enzyme actively catalyzing this reaction. We shall see that one compound frequently is a substrate for several enzymes, and it is undesirable to allow it to be depleted by a single reaction.

The problem is solved by constructing the enzyme from several identical subunits that interact with each other so that the enzyme fails to be an effective catalyst when the substrate concentration drops below a certain range. The system tends to be self-adjusting with respect to maintenance of substrate concentration, even though the substrate participates in an effectively irreversible reaction.

REGULATION BY INHIBITION AND ACTIVATION

Enzymes may combine with compounds other than the substrates in a way that affects the rate of the catalytic reactions. These effectors, or modulators, may be inhibitors, which slow the reaction, or activators, which make the reaction go faster. To appreciate the purpose of the mechanisms we shall discuss, let us examine some of the kinds of physiological situations in which they are used.

Negative Feedback. The synthesis of components of the organism frequently involves sequences of reactions that are not used for any other purpose. For example, the formation of the purines incorporated into nucleotides begins with common metabolites used for many purposes. The synthesis proceeds by adding one group at a time, forming intermediates that are good for nothing except making a purine nucleotide. Each of the steps in the formation requires an enzyme. The problem is how to regulate the rate of a long sequence of reactions so as to produce enough purine nucleotides, but not too much, and without ever accumulating the otherwise useless intermediate compounds.

Rather than regulating each reaction involved in such long sequences, the problem

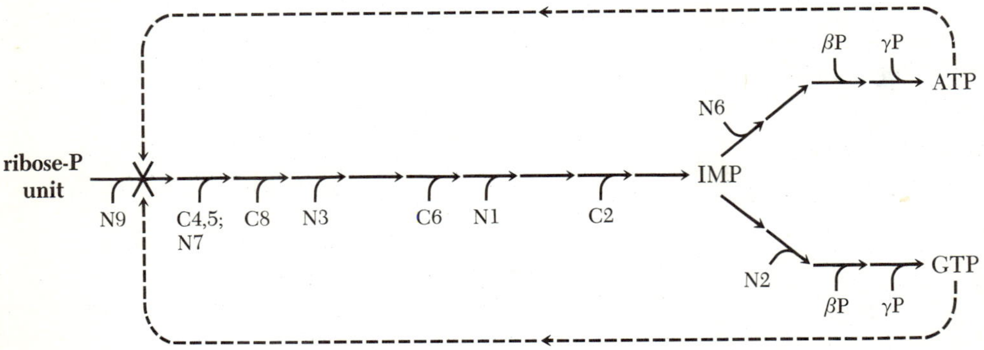

Figure 9–5 The purine component of purine nucleotides is assembled one piece at a time on a ribose phosphate unit. The numbers of the successively added atoms indicate their positions in the completed molecule. This long sequence is regulated through feedback inhibition of the first reaction by the final products, thereby preventing accumulation of the many intermediates.

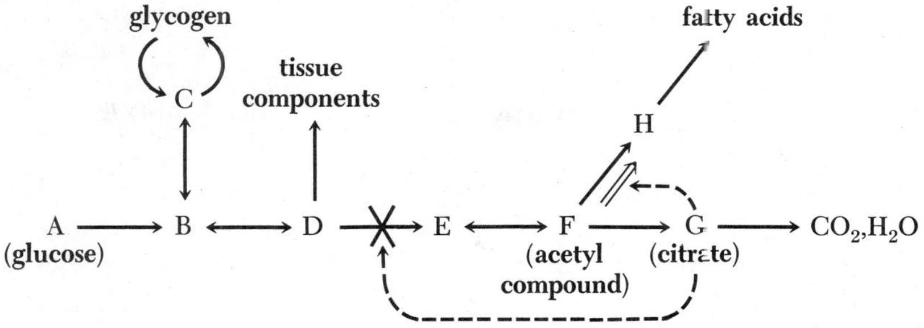

Figure 9-6 Glucose entering cells is used to form a variety of compounds, including stored glycogen, tissue components, and fatty acids. A portion is oxidized to CO_2 and H_2O as a source of energy in many cells. The formation of citrate is necessary for the oxidation, and if it accumulates beyond the requirements for oxidation, it shuts off its own formation at an earlier step. However, the regulation does not prevent the use of glucose for storage as glycogen or for forming other tissue components. Citrate also accelerates the formation of fatty acids, which tends to diminish citrate accumulation.

is solved by making the ultimate products of the sequence, the purine nucleotides themselves, inhibitors of the first reaction peculiar to purine synthesis (Fig. 9–5). (The reactions are described in Chapter 26.) When ATP and GTP are in short supply, the initial enzyme is not inhibited, and a flow of substrate begins through the long series of enzymatic reactions that ultimately result in the formation of more ATP and GTP. When the supply is adequate, the initial enzyme is inhibited, and all of the intermediate reactions also slow down because the enzymes run out of substrates. The general process by which a compound inhibits its own formation is called "negative feedback" after a term borrowed from electronics.

Glucose Utilization. The sugar glucose is the principal fuel for many cells, and it is also the precursor for a variety of other compounds. A simplified diagram of its metabolism is shown in Figure 9–6. (The actual routes occupy the next section of the book. We are here concerned with a principle rather than with the compounds themselves.) The initial steps in glucose metabolism involve the successive formation of compounds that can also be used as precursors of a stored polymer of glucose (glycogen) and of constituents of connective tissue. However, most of the glucose is either oxidized to CO_2 and H_2O or converted to fatty acids for storage and later use as a fuel. The choice between immediate combustion and storage as fat is made after glucose is converted to acetyl groups in an intermediate compound (designated F in the diagram).

It is to the advantage of the organism to have a capability for rapid oxidation of glucose by the sequence going to CO_2 and H_2O when the demand for energy is high, and yet not waste glucose when the demand for energy is low. At the same time, the initial reactions in glucose metabolism must be permitted to continue because they provide precursors for the formation of other cellular constituents.

One of the ways in which the problem is solved is by making the first compound that is peculiar to the oxidative route a negative modulator of glucose metabolism. This compound is designated G in the diagram. It does not affect the first two enzymes that make compounds also used for other purposes, but it is an inhibitor of the next enzyme, which initiates the long sequence arriving at the acetyl groups that either are used directly as a fuel or are stored as fats.

The negative modulation acting by itself would tend to shut off the utilization of glucose for either combustion or storage of fat at any time the demand for energy was low. Why? Because a low energy demand would cause slow combustion. Slow combustion leads to an accumulation of compound G, and this accumulation shuts off an early step in the metabolism of glucose.

However, it is not desirable to have fat storage prevented when there is an excess of available glucose. This is circumvented by making the negative modulator of glucose metabolism also act as a positive modulator of the conversion of acetyl groups (compound F) to fatty acids. Compound G therefore accelerates the removal of its own precursor by diverting it to another route. It thus tends to lower its own concentration to the extent that fatty acids can be formed.

The overall result is that an accumulation of compound G will indeed slow the metabolism of glucose, but only to the point at which its rate matches the rate at which fatty acids are synthesized. Here we see a more sophisticated example of control, in which negative feedback of one route is counterbalanced by activation of another. A high capability for oxidizing glucose as a fuel is kept under leash without preventing the same reactions from being used for other purposes.

Competitive Inhibition

One of the important ways of inhibiting an enzyme is through the use of a compound other than the substrate that also will occupy the active site. We have already seen how the product of a reaction competes with the substrate for binding to the active site, in addition to its effect in speeding the reverse reaction; but a competitive inhibitor need not undergo a reaction in order to be bound.

Indeed, the most effective competitive inhibitors are found among compounds that sufficiently mimic a substrate so that they are bound by the same groups on the enzyme, but lack the particular structures that undergo reaction. Since such compounds are not destroyed by the enzyme, a smaller quantity is often required to maintain an effective concentration over a long period.

Kinetics of Competitive Inhibition. The hallmark of competitive inhibition is the competition implied in the name. Increasing the substrate concentration can overcome the effects of the inhibitor, so that an infinite substrate concentration (in the presence of finite amounts of inhibitor) would still result in the same maximum velocity, because a substrate molecule would immediately occupy any vacant active site before the inhibitor molecules could reach it. This theoretical circumstance can be projected in a practical way by making standard Lineweaver-Burk plots in the presence and absence of inhibitor. If the inhibition is competitive, all of the lines intersect at $1/S = 0$ ($S = \infty$), and $1/v = 1/V_{max}$ at that point (Fig. 9-7). If the lines do not intersect, then the inhibitor and the substrate are not in simple competition for the active site, and the character of the enzyme must be changed in some different way by the presence of the inhibitor compared to the change caused by the presence of the substrate.

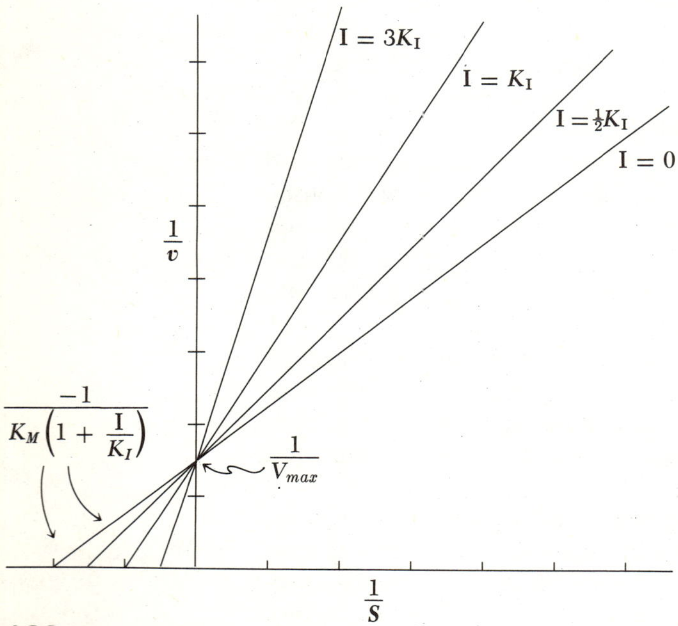

Figure 9-7 Lineweaver-Burk plots obtained with varying concentrations, *I*, of a purely competitive inhibitor. There is a single intercept on the ordinate because V_{max} is the same in all cases, but the intercept on the abscissa changes.

Allosteric Mechanisms

Allosteric effects are the modification of the rate of an enzymatic reaction through a change in conformation caused by a combination with some effector. The homotropic reactions are a specialized example in which one molecule of substrate acts as an effector for enzymatic attack on another molecule of substrate. The term is not restricted to enzymes; indeed, the combination of hemoglobin with oxygen is taken as a classical example of an allosteric mechanism of the homotropic variety.

The key to allosteric effects is the change in conformation. The peptide subunits have a different geometry in the effector-enzyme or effector-enzyme-substrate complex than they do in the free enzyme or enzyme-substrate complex. In some cases, the effector combines with the enzyme and causes the change in conformation. In other cases, the enzyme equilibrates between two conformations and the effector will combine with only one, thereby stabilizing it. The result is the same in either case.

Heterotropic Modification of Substrate Binding. Many key enzymes are regulated through combination with effectors that are bound at sites other than the active catalytic site. The enzymes are constructed in such a way that their conformation is altered by the presence of the bound effector. When the enzymes are composed of more than one subunit, the interactions between these subunits will be modified by the conformational changes. Since the modified interaction is brought about by a compound other than the substrate, it is said to be a heterotropic interaction. Negative feedback and modulations of fuel metabolism frequently involve heterotropic interaction, with the effector being a distant participant in the metabolic sequence.

We have already seen that interaction between subunits of a multi-subunit enzyme results in a sigmoidal response of velocity to substrate concentration. (Such a response is seen only in multi-subunit enzymes.) A heterotropic effector simply changes that interaction, so its effect frequently is to alter the apparent K_M without substantial change in the V_{max} of the enzyme (Fig. 9–8). If the effector is an activator, it may diminish interacting constraints on catalysis so that each subunit of the enzyme acts as an isolated molecule with simple Michaelis-Menten kinetics. If it is an inhibitor, it may stabilize the interactions so that even more substrate is required to overcome them.

The binding site for the effector need not be on the same subunit as the active

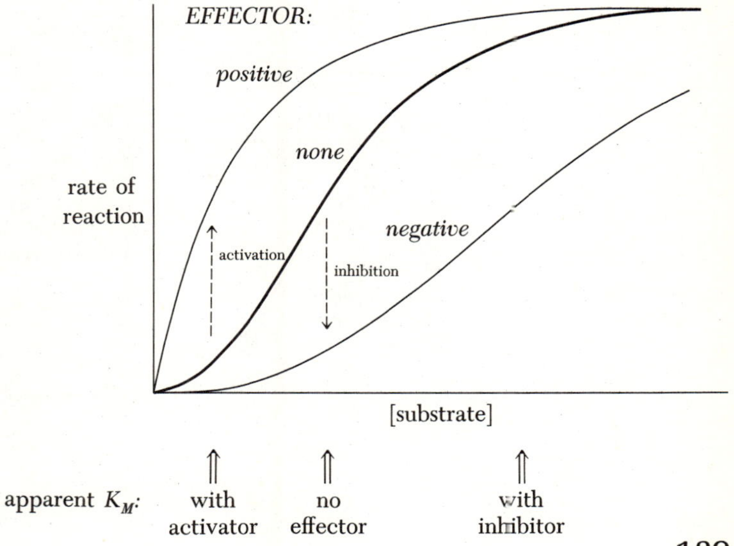

Figure 9–8 Some enzymes are built to bind compounds at sites other than the catalytic sites so as to alter the rate of reaction. Such heterotropic effectors frequently alter the K_M of the enzyme without substantial effect on V_{max}, and sometimes do so by eliminating homotropic interactions so that the enzyme shows simple Michaelis-Menten kinetics.

site. Many examples are known of enzymes that are aggregates of separate catalytic and regulating subunits, all interacting.

Other Allosteric Mechanisms. Conformational changes caused by the presence of an effector may have effects other than modification of homotropic interactions. The change may diminish or increase the rate of a reaction catalyzed by an enzyme with a single peptide chain, either by changing its substrate affinity or by altering V_{max}.

A conformational change can alter the tendency of molecules of an enzyme to aggregate. Cases are known in which a polymer of an enzyme is the active form, and others in which the polymer is inactive. Effectors promoting aggregation therefore are activators in some cases and inhibitors in others.

THE CONCEPT OF THE RATE-LIMITING STEP

An important principle in understanding metabolic regulation is the idea that one reaction in a sequence may be governing the rate of the entire sequence. Such a reaction is referred to as the rate-limiting step.

Consider the sequence:

$$\mathrm{A} \xrightarrow{E_1} \mathrm{B} \xrightarrow{E_2} \mathrm{C} \xrightarrow{E_3} \mathrm{D} \xrightarrow{E_4} \mathrm{E} \xrightarrow{E_5} \mathrm{F}$$

Let us presume the following: (1) compound A is being supplied at a constant concentration; (2) compound F, the product of the sequence, is being removed in such a way as to hold its concentration constant; (3) the equilibrium constant for each of the individual reactions is identical; (4) all of the enzymes involved have identical Michaelis constants; and (5) the maximum velocity of all of the enzymes is identical, except that E_3, the enzyme catalyzing C $\longrightarrow$ D, has a substantially lower V_{max} than the others.

Now let us set up a hypothetical case in which a cell begins with concentrations of all of the intermediates equal to the concentration of the starting material (Fig. 9–9). What will happen? There is a large difference in concentrations between E and F, so the last reaction will proceed rapidly. This will drop the concentration of E, so the conversion of D to E will accelerate, thus lowering the concentration of D. This will tend to accelerate the conversion of C to D, but there is less of this enzyme, so the conversion will be accelerated less by the same fall in product concentration. The result will be that the drop in concentrations of D and E will continue and eventually cause the conversion of D $\longrightarrow$ E $\longrightarrow$ F to slow down. The reaction C $\longrightarrow$ D does not

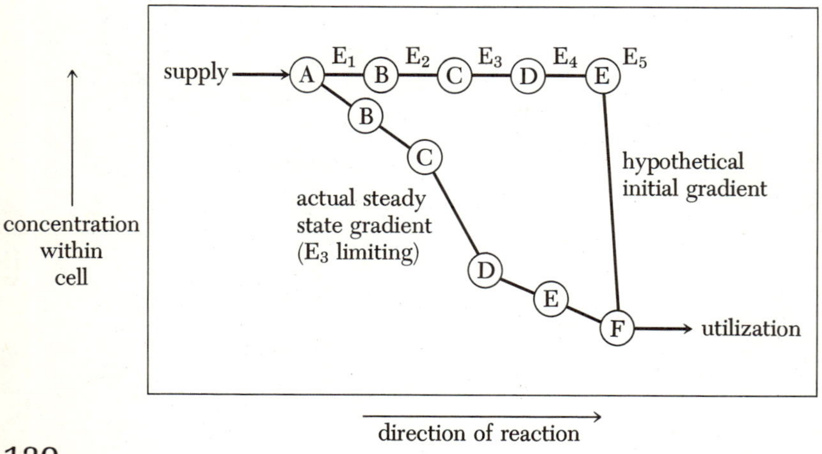

Figure 9–9 When substrates are flowing through a sequence of reactions, the substrate for the enzyme with the lowest V_{max} will tend to pile up, so the ratio of concentrations of substrates and products will be farther from an equilibrium ratio for this rate-limiting step than it will be for other reactions in the sequence. Changes in the activity of the rate-limiting enzyme will therefore have a greater effect on the overall flow than changes in the activity of other enzymes.

cause as sharp a drop in the concentrations of B and C, because the reactions A $\longrightarrow$ B $\longrightarrow$ C are being catalyzed by more active enzymes, and *it takes less difference in concentration to make these reactions go fast enough to replace the C being removed.*

The end result is the attainment of concentrations such that all of the reactions are proceeding at the same rate, and in this **steady state** the difference in concentrations of substrate and product for the example we are using will be greatest for the reaction with the least active enzyme.

If all are now proceeding at the same rate, why are we justified in calling E_3 rate-limiting? Suppose that the activity of this enzyme is increased by an increased concentration of an activator. There will be a corresponding increase in the rate of conversion of C $\longrightarrow$ D, less difference in concentration between these two compounds, and a corresponding increase in rate of all of the other reactions in the sequence. On the other hand, if the activity of one of the other enzymes was increased little would happen, because the difference in concentrations is already small between their substrates and their products.

It ought not be assumed from this example that the substrate concentration is always much larger and the product concentration is always much smaller for rate-limiting reactions than for neighboring reactions. The equilibrium constants and kinetic parameters for neighboring reactions in a sequence are rarely identical, as we have assumed. It is the degree of displacement from the equilibrium values that is greater for the rate-limiting step, which is frequently, but not always, an essentially irreversible reaction.

The idea of a rate-limiting step therefore is that the rate of an entire sequence is fixed by the activity of the single enzyme that has the lowest V_{max}.

FURTHER READING

R. W. McGilvery, Biochemistry, A functional approach, W. B. Saunders (1970). Chapter 7 contains a more extensive discussion of measurement of enzymatic activity, and the effect of product concentration.

H. R. Mahler and E. H. Cordes, Biological chemistry, 2nd ed., Harper & Row (1971). Chapter 6 contains a thorough discussion of enzyme kinetics for those with a mathematical bent and strong interest.

P. D. Boyer, The enzymes, Academic Press (1970). Chapters discussing regulatory mechanisms are in vol. 1, and those discussing kinetics are in vol. 2. Discussions at the professional level.

QUESTIONS

1. The relative initial velocities of the reaction of a certain enzyme under experimental conditions with changing substrate concentration, but without added product, were as follows:

$$[S] = 4 \quad 5 \quad 6 \quad \text{millimolar}$$
$$v = 1 \quad 2 \quad 3 \quad \text{nmoles/ml/sec}$$

   Is this enzyme displaying Michaelis-Menten kinetics? How do you know?
2. Protease A has a K_M for its substrate of 3 micromolar. Protease B has a K_M for the same substrate of 1.2 millimolar.
   (a) Which protease has the higher affinity for its substrate?
   (b) Which protease is more likely to be highly specific for the substrate?

(c) If 3 E.U. of each protease are added to 9 micromolar solutions of the substrate, in which solution will the substrate be more rapidly destroyed?
(d) If both enzymes have the same V_{max} for a given quantity of enzyme, which enzyme has the greater affinity for the products of hydrolysis of a substrate?

3. Which of the following conditions are associated with competitive inhibition?
   (a) Presence of more than one subunit in the enzyme.
   (b) A change in the apparent K_M for the substrate.
   (c) A change in the V_{max}.
   (d) Sigmoidal response of velocity to substrate concentration.
   (e) Presence of separate binding site for inhibitor.
4. Which of the conditions listed in Question 3 are associated with heterotropic interactions?
5. After steady state is established in a sequence of reactions, does the slowest reaction then occur before, at, or after the rate-limiting step, or do all reactions proceed at the same rate?

THE CARBON CYCLE

BACKGROUND

We shall be concerned with metabolism throughout most of the remainder of the book. Metabolism is the sum of the thousands of reactions by which compounds are created and destroyed in living organisms. Most of these compounds contain carbon, and it is therefore fitting that we have at least a general idea of the source of the carbon used in the growth and maintenance of living things, and the fate of the carbon when they die.

A schematic outline of the major forms in which carbon occurs on the face of the earth, and of the rate of flow of carbon from one form to another, is shown on the next page. The values given are necessarily only rough estimates, but they are still valuable for reasoning about our planet.

Perhaps the most striking aspect of the carbon cycle is the small fraction of the carbon available at the earth's surface that is present as living tissue compared to the rate at which these tissues consume or produce carbon compounds. This is especially true in the case of the sea. The large and long-lived trees on the land contain a more impressive quantity of carbon, but even this is a small fraction of the total available in the seas and the atmosphere.

The high rate of flow of carbon through living organisms comes about because it is a necessary part of the production of energy in these organisms. The primary source of the energy in green plants is absorbed sunlight, but the utilization of this energy hinges on the formation of compounds that can be made to react in a way that will perform chemical or mechanical work. In this respect, the plants are like the animals in that their major source of energy frequently becomes the combustion of organic compounds with molecular oxygen. We shall discuss how this occurs in the succeeding chapters.

The left-hand part of the figure depicts events on the land, where land plants have removed an amount of carbon equal to more than half of the carbon remaining in the atmosphere. Dead tissues accumulate in the soil and on the surface until the rate of their decomposition balances the rate at which they are deposited. Decomposition of dead tissues returns CO_2 to the atmosphere, but the plants themselves also return CO_2 by oxidizing part of their substance: animals are a small but significant factor in disposing of the plant tissues. For example, humans can take credit for disposing through their own metabolism of nearly $\frac{1}{1000}$ of the total CO_2 fixed per year by plants; however, they also add $\frac{1}{7}$ as much to the atmosphere as the plants removed through their combustion of carbon fixed long ago in sediments. (The fossil fuels and the balance of photosynthesis are discussed in Chapter 17.)

The major reservoir of CO_2 for the atmosphere is in the sea, as illustrated in the right-hand portion of the figure. There is a rapid equilibration between the air and the surface of the sea, and a less rapid exchange with the large reserves in the deep waters. Any vision of the sea as a rich biological soup is readily dispelled by noting how little living tissue it contains. The rate of decomposition of dead tissue is much slower in the sea than it is on the land, so more accumulated before the rate of decomposition balanced the rate of formation.

Much of the carbon present at the surface of the earth is fixed in the continental sediments, partly as coal, oil, and other deposits of reduced carbon compounds, but mostly as mineral carbonates. Some of this carbon probably will never participate in anything resembling a cycle, because there is no reason to expect all sediments to be reworked during the habitable lifetime of the earth.

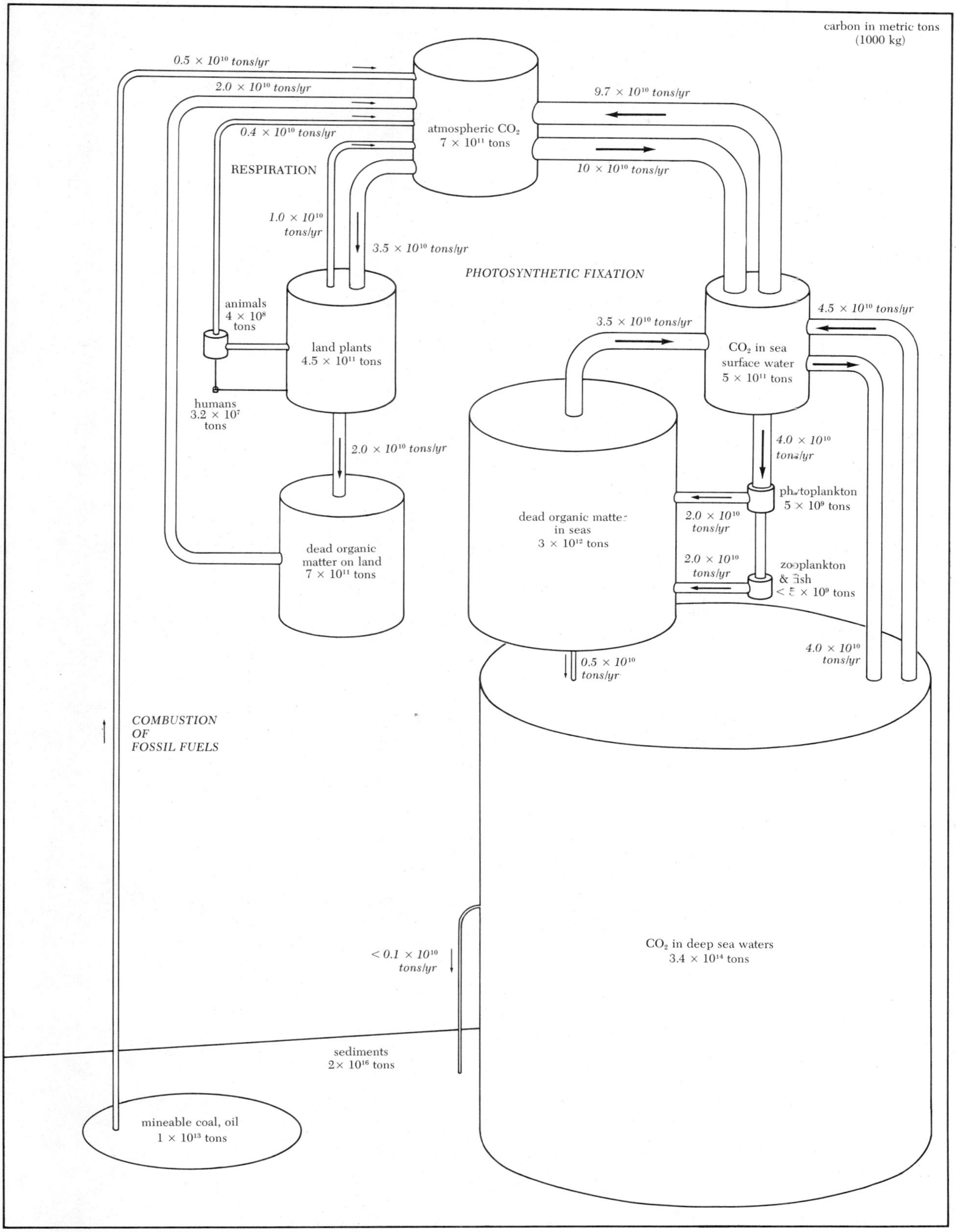

carbon in metric tons (1000 kg)
0.5 × 10¹⁰ tons/yr
2.0 × 10¹⁰ tons/yr
0.4 × 10¹⁰ tons/yr
atmospheric CO_2 7 × 10¹¹ tons
9.7 × 10¹⁰ tons/yr
10 × 10¹⁰ tons/yr
RESPIRATION
1.0 × 10¹⁰ tons/yr
3.5 × 10¹⁰ tons/yr
PHOTOSYNTHETIC FIXATION
animals 4 × 10⁸ tons
land plants 4.5 × 10¹¹ tons
humans 3.2 × 10⁷ tons
4.5 × 10¹⁰ tons/yr
3.5 × 10¹⁰ tons/yr
CO_2 in sea surface water 5 × 10¹¹ tons
2.0 × 10¹⁰ tons/yr
4.0 × 10¹⁰ tons/yr
phytoplankton 5 × 10⁹ tons
dead organic matter in seas 3 × 10¹² tons
2.0 × 10¹⁰ tons/yr
dead organic matter on land 7 × 10¹¹ tons
2.0 × 10¹⁰ tons/yr
zooplankton & fish
0.5 × 10¹⁰ tons/yr
4.0 × 10¹⁰ tons/yr
COMBUSTION OF FOSSIL FUELS
< 0.1 × 10¹⁰ tons/yr
CO_2 in deep sea waters 3.4 × 10¹⁴ tons
sediments 2× 10¹⁶ tons
mineable coal, oil 1 × 10¹³ tons

PART 3

ENERGY FOR BIOLOGICAL WORK

CHAPTER 10

BIOLOGICAL ENERGETICS AND MOTILITY

THE CONCEPTS

Free Energy and Equilibrium. Every compound has a chemical potential for doing work, or free energy, which depends upon the nature of the compound and which increases as the logarithm of the concentration. Reactions can proceed only in a direction that creates compounds of lower chemical potential; that is, all real reactions involve a loss of free energy and can do work. The amount of work that can be done depends upon how far the concentrations of the reactants and products are from equilibrium. When compounds of inherently high chemical potential are converted to products of inherently low chemical potential, the position of equilibrium will lie far in the direction of the products.

Exergonic and Endergonic Reactions. Reactions that liberate free energy are said to be exergonic, and all real reactions are exergonic. Hypothetical reactions that consume free energy are said to be endergonic. The reversal of a real reaction is always endergonic under the same conditions at which the real reaction occurs. Although endergonic reactions do not exist as such, it is convenient to treat biological processes as the sum of endergonic and exergonic processes. For example, the oxidation of fuels and photosynthesis would be highly exergonic processes if they occurred in isolation; the combination of amino acids into proteins by the loss of water, the concentration of compounds by cells, and muscular contraction would be highly endergonic processes by themselves. The destructive exergonic processes are sometimes referred to as catabolism, and the synthetic endergonic processes are referred to as anabolism.

Coupling Exergonic and Endergonic Processes. The metabolism of organisms is constructed so that what would be highly exergonic processes are coupled to otherwise endergonic processes. Coupling is accomplished by modifying exergonic processes such as fuel

oxidation so that they form ATP from ADP and P_i, and also modifying endergonic processes such as amino acid synthesis so that they consume ATP and convert it back to ADP and P_i. The endergonic processes driven by ATP hydrolysis then become exergonic in themselves. The formation and destruction of ATP functions as a device for transferring energy from one process to another.

Energy-Rich Phosphates. **ATP is an effective medium for transferring energy because it contains pyrophosphate bonds. These bonds, which represent the formation of an anhydride of phosphoric acid, have relatively high standard free energies of formation. (The standard free energy of a reaction is proportional to the logarithm of the equilibrium constant and provides a means of comparing the change in inherent chemical potential of various reactions.) Compounds containing pyrophosphate linkages are said to be high-energy, or energy-rich, phosphates. Ester linkages of phosphoric acid, such as the bond between adenosine and phosphate, have much lower standard free energies of formation, and are said to be low-energy bonds. The coupling of ATP formation to the oxidation of fuels diminishes the dissipation of free energy. The high chemical potential of the resultant pyrophosphate is sufficient for its cleavage to drive anabolic processes and muscular contraction, and to create concentration gradients.**

The High-Energy Phosphate Pool. **Other nucleoside triphosphates, such as guanosine triphosphate (GTP), uridine triphosphate (UTP), and cytidine triphosphate (CTP), are also used in metabolic reactions, which sometimes involve cleavage of the triphosphates to the diphosphates with the liberation of inorganic phosphate (P_i) and sometimes to the monophosphates with the liberation of inorganic pyrophosphate (PP_i). These diphosphates and monophosphates are converted back to the corresponding triphosphates by transfer to them of the terminal phosphate of ATP through reactions catalyzed by nucleoside diphosphate or nucleoside monophosphate kinases. The ADP that is produced can in turn be converted back to ATP in coupled exergonic processes.**

Phosphagens. **Muscles require a large supply of immediately available high-energy phosphate for quick contractions, and this is provided by a store of another type of compound, the phosphagens. Phosphagens are amides of phosphoric acid with substituted guanidinium compounds, such as creatine. Phosphocreatine is formed by a reversible transfer of phosphate from ATP catalyzed by creatine kinase. Any tendency for the concentration of ATP to fall as it is used in muscular contraction is resisted by a transfer of phosphate from phosphocreatine to the ADP that is formed.**

Muscular Contraction. **Muscles are composed of fibers, which are in turn made from bundles of myofibrils. The myofibril may be regarded as an end-to-end structural polymer of sarcomeres. Each sarcomere contains terminal round plates of protein known as the Z-band, from which bristles of thin filaments protrude toward each other. The thin filaments are overlapped by thick filaments. Forces developed between the thin filaments and the thick filaments pull the thin filaments toward each other by increasing their overlaps with the thick filaments. The result is contraction of the sarcomere.**

Myosin and Actin. **The thick filaments are made from bundles of myosin, a protein with a long shaft and a globular head. The head has sites that catalyze the hydrolysis of ATP and that bind to the thin filaments. The thin filaments are composed in turn of a spiral chain of globular beads of actin. The beads of this protein are spaced out along still another long molecule of protein, tropomyosin. The head of the myosin molecule clasps actin in two conformations, one in which the head combines with the magnesium chelate of ADP (MgADP) and is extended from its connected shaft, and the other in which it is bent back upon the shaft, thereby moving the attached actin. Movement is ordinarily prevented by an inhibitory component, known as troponin. When an impulse reaches the muscle fiber from a motor nerve, Ca^{2+} is released and combines with the troponin so as to remove it from the inhibitory site between myosin and actin. This also releases the MgADP and permits the myosin head to pull the actin into a new position. Once this is done, the head then catalyzes the hydrolysis of MgATP, forming more MgADP and reverting to its extended or relaxed shape. The result is the hydrolysis of ATP for each cycle of contraction and relaxation by each myosin molecule in the fiber. The shortening of a sarcomere involves the "walking" of each myosin molecule in a thick filament from one turn of chain of actin beads to another, and the energy for the walk comes from the hydrolysis of ATP to ADP and P_i.**

Author's Note on Units

Biological energy exchanges are expressed in this book in terms of joules. This will be no problem to beginning students who are not very familiar with the concepts, but will be an obstacle to advanced students and instructors who customarily use calories. The choice was made, not to be unusual, but because the joule has all the advantages over the calorie that the other units of the International System have over their empirically related counterparts, such as the inch and pound. Scientific editors and other responsible people are pressing for general use of the International System at this time. It would be especially advantageous to discard anomalous units such as the calorie, Angstrom, parsec, and so on, before the general public in the United States and Canada is trained to think in metric terms.

One calorie is 4.183 joules.

The advantage of the joule is that it makes it easy to think about the interconversion of heat, mechanical work, and electrical energy. The **joule** is the energy expended in moving an object one meter with a force of one newton, and the **newton** is the force required to accelerate one kilogram by one meter per second per second. The expenditure of a joule per second is a power of one **watt.**

ENERGY TRANSFER THROUGH PHOSPHATES

Exergonic and Endergonic Reactions

Energy and Equilibrium. We learned from general chemistry that all chemical reactions proceed in such a way as to change the concentrations of reactants and products toward an equilibrium value. It follows from this that if a reaction is occurring, the concentrations of reactants—the materials that are disappearing in the reaction—must be greater than the equilibrium value, and the concentrations of the products of the reaction—the materials that are being formed—must be less than the equilibrium value.

We also learned from general chemistry that each compound involved in a reaction has a **chemical potential**—a capacity for doing work—that depends upon the logarithm of the concentration of the compound. When a reaction is at equilibrium, the chemical potentials of the products equal the chemical potentials of the reactants. This being so, real reactions, in which the chemical potential of the reactants is greater than the equilibrium value and the chemical potential of the products is less than the equilibrium value, must always liberate **free energy,** which is another way of saying that they have the capacity to perform work under the conditions of uniform temperature and pressure existing in biological systems.

Meaning of Exergonic and Endergonic. Since real reactions always liberate free energy, they are said to be exergonic. A reaction that takes up free energy is an endergonic reaction, but reactions that do this don't exist as independent entities. Why do we waste time defining something that exists only in theory? We do so because it turns out to be a handy device for reasoning about some complex reactions that can be imagined to be made up of at least two components. We treat many real biological reactions as the sum of a highly exergonic reaction, producing lots of free energy, and an endergonic reaction, which consumes part, but not all, of that free energy. Enough free energy must be liberated so that the overall result is at least somewhat exergonic, and therefore can occur as a real reaction.

This brings us onto more familiar ground, because we are taught from an early age that we burn fuels, not only for the energy with which to move, but also for the energy necessary for the building of tissues and the like. This isn't too far from the truth; the major defect of the notion is its tendency to equate the concept of energy with a concrete physical entity that can be transferred in a bundle from one reaction to another. The concept is a very useful abstraction, but still an abstraction.

Biological Examples. What are these exergonic and endergonic reactions, or rather the exergonic and endergonic components of biological reactions? Here are some conspicuous examples:

Exergonic (energy-producing)	Endergonic (energy-consuming)
Oxidation of fuels (carbohydrates, fats, and proteins)	Mechanical movement
Photosynthesis	Synthesis of cellular constituents
Fermentations	Creation of concentration gradients
	Storage of fuels

Anabolism and Catabolism. The exergonic components characteristically have large equilibrium constants, and would cause a "wasteful" liberation of free energy if they occurred by themselves. Their sum is sometimes referred to as catabolism—the disruptive component of metabolism. The endergonic components characteristically cannot occur by themselves, and have equilibrium constants less than one. The sum of these synthetic processes is sometimes referred to as anabolism.

Driving Endergonic Reactions with Exergonic Reactions

Impracticality of Isolated Exergonic Reactions. Since the free energy liberated during a reaction depends only upon the distance from equilibrium at which it occurs, in principle any reaction could be made mildly exergonic by adjusting the concentrations of reactants and products so as to be slightly displaced from the equilibrium condition. In fact, this cannot be done for many reactions. Those reactions listed as exergonic have such high equilibrium constants that only unmeasureable amounts of starting material exist at equilibrium. They represent a sort of chemical overkill in which the reaction can be unnecessarily complete for biological purposes.

For example, the oxidation of the sugar, glucose, is a very common reaction in many organisms. In the test tube, occurring by itself, it has a very high equilibrium constant:

$$\text{glucose } (C_6H_{10}O_6) + 6\ O_2 \longrightarrow 6\ CO_2 + 6\ H_2O$$

$$K_{eq} = \frac{[CO_2]^6[H_2O]^6}{[\text{glucose}][O_2]^6} = 10^{495}$$

It isn't possible to bring this system to equilibrium in real terms. At the highest concentration of water and CO_2 we can achieve, the calculated equilibrium concentration of glucose and oxygen is such that only one molecule of each could exist in a sphere with a diameter some 50 times that of the solar system.

Impracticality of Isolated Endergonic Reactions. On the other hand, the reactions listed as endergonic have very low equilibrium constants in water, and it would require impossibly large concentrations of starting materials to make them proceed to even a small extent. Consider an equilibrium involving a peptide chain that is 100 identical amino acid residues long, its constituent amino acids, and water:

$$100 \text{ amino acids} \longrightarrow \text{peptide} + 99 \text{ water}$$

$$K_{eq} = \frac{[\text{peptide}]}{[\text{amino acid}]^{100}} = 10^{-33}$$

When water is a reactant or a product, it is common practice to calculate an "equilibrium constant" that includes the concentration of water, 55.6 M, since it is always near the same value in dilute solutions. In the example here, the stated equilibrium constant is the true value for the entire reaction already divided by $(55.6)^{99}$.

We have already seen in Chapter 3 that amino acids are not made by this simple reaction, but let us consider why. A concentration of 0.01 M is a high value to expect for most intracellular constituents, including amino acids, and even if we take this extreme estimate, not even one molecule of peptide would be formed in an entire universe of solution by merely reversing hydrolysis. Indeed, we noted in discussing proteolytic enzymes that equilibration with water proceeds toward the hydrolysis of peptides, not toward their creation. Something else must be done if the formation of peptides from amino acids is to be feasible.

Coupling Endergonic Reactions to Exergonic Reactions. The biological problem is one of somehow combining wildly exergonic reactions, such as the oxidation of glucose, with impossibly endergonic reactions, such as the combination of amino acids into a peptide. It isn't a simple matter of having the two sets of reactions going in the same solution. We could make a solution of glucose, oxygen, and amino acids, along with appropriate catalysts, and find carbon dioxide being vigorously evolved from the oxidation of the sugar while the amino acids sit there essentially unchanged. Once more, energy is not a concrete thing that is automatically transferred from compounds of high chemical potential to those of low potential.

However, there is a way in which the oxidation of glucose can be made to drive endergonic reactions, and that is to modify both of the reactions so as to involve an additional compound that is produced by one and consumed by the other. We have already seen one of the most common of the modifications in connection with peptide synthesis. The formation of peptides involves not only a combination of amino acids, but also a sequence of reactions in which the nucleotides, ATP and GTP, are cleaved:

$$\textbf{amino acid} + \textbf{ATP} + \textbf{tRNA} \longrightarrow \textbf{aminoacyl-tRNA} + \textbf{AMP} + \textbf{PP}_i$$

$$n(\textbf{aminoacyl-tRNA} + \textbf{GTP}) \xrightarrow[mRNA]{ribosomes} \textbf{peptide} + n(\textbf{GDP} + \textbf{P}_i)$$

It is the exergonic cleavage of the nucleotides that converts what would be an endergonic formation of peptides into an exergonic combination. If the ATP and GTP being consumed for peptide synthesis are now remade in conjunction with the oxidation of glucose, the synthesis of peptides will be effectively driven by the oxidation of glucose, and this is exactly what happens.

We can make a general picture that applies to all metabolic processes:

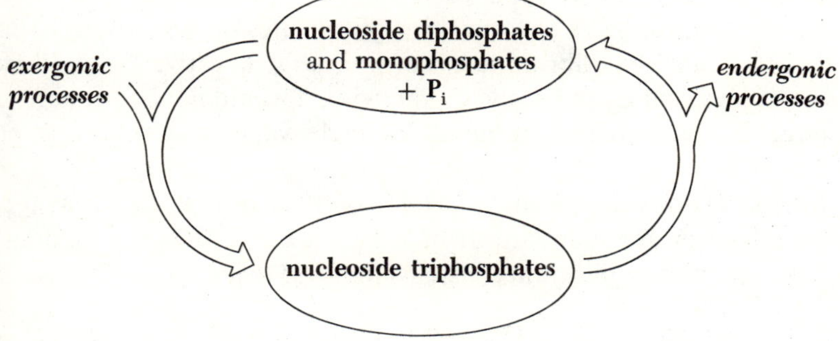

What would be highly exergonic processes, such as the oxidation of glucose, are modified so that nucleoside diphosphates and monophosphates are phosphorylated to create nucleoside triphosphates. This diminishes the liberation of free energy that ordinarily accompanies the oxidation of glucose.

The nucleoside triphosphates are then used in otherwise endergonic reactions, and are cleaved in these reactions to the corresponding diphosphates or monophosphates.

The overall effect is as if there was a direct transfer of energy, but the real mechanism is the modification of the exergonic reactions so as to create products of higher chemical potential, and to use these products as reactants in the formerly endergonic reactions. The exergonic and endergonic processes became coupled through the involvement of the same nucleotides in both processes, which therefore have the function of energy carriers.

ENERGY-RICH PHOSPHATES

Standard Free Energies and Equilibrium Constants. Before going further, let us refresh our memory on the meaning of standard free energies as opposed to actual free energies. Standard free energy is a means of comparing the potential energy of different chemical reactions. It is the calculated free energy change at defined standard concentrations, which are taken to be 1 M for all products and reactants. This maneuver makes the **standard free energy change, ΔG^0,** become a logarithmic function of the equilibrium constant:

$$\begin{aligned}\Delta G^0 &= -RT\ln K_{eq} = -8.314 \times 2.303\, T\log K_{eq}\\ &= -5706 \log K_{eq} \text{ joules mole}^{-1} \text{ at } 25^\circ \text{ C}\end{aligned}$$

where R is the gas constant, and T is the temperature in degrees Kelvin. (1 joule = 0.239 calories.) Figure 10–1 plots this relationship.

Use of Standard Free Energy Values. The principal value for our purposes of using standard free energies rather than equilibrium constants for comparing reactions comes from the logarithmic function. The standard free energy for the sum of two reactions is the sum of the standard free energies for the individual reactions, a characteristic that is especially useful in reasoning about biological systems, which have long sequences of consecutive reactions. If, for example, one knows the individual standard free energy changes for A $\longrightarrow$ B, B $\longrightarrow$ C, and C $\longrightarrow$ D, then the value for A $\longrightarrow$ D is the sum of these individual values. (Of course, if one has the corresponding equilibrium constants in exponential form, one can also obtain the overall equilibrium constant by merely adding exponents, but many people are more accustomed to think in terms of standard free energy changes.)

Hydrolysis of ATP. If we think on it a moment, we can see that the hydrolysis of the nucleoside triphosphates to form the diphosphates or monophosphates must be reactions that have high equilibrium constants, or large negative standard free energy changes, when they occur by themselves; otherwise, it would not be possible to produce feasible exergonic reactions by combining these cleavages with otherwise endergonic reactions.

ATP can be hydrolyzed through several routes involving the cleavage of P—O bonds, some of which are summarized in Figure 10–2. The corresponding standard free energy changes and equilibrium constants for these reactions at 25 °C are as follows:

Reaction	$\Delta G^{0'}$ (joules/mole)	K'_{eq}
$ATP^{4-} + H_2O \longrightarrow ADP^{3-} + P_i^{2-} + H^+$	−40,600	1.3×10^7
$ADP^{3-} + H_2O \longrightarrow AMP^{2-} + P_i^{2-} + H^+$	−38,100	4.7×10^6

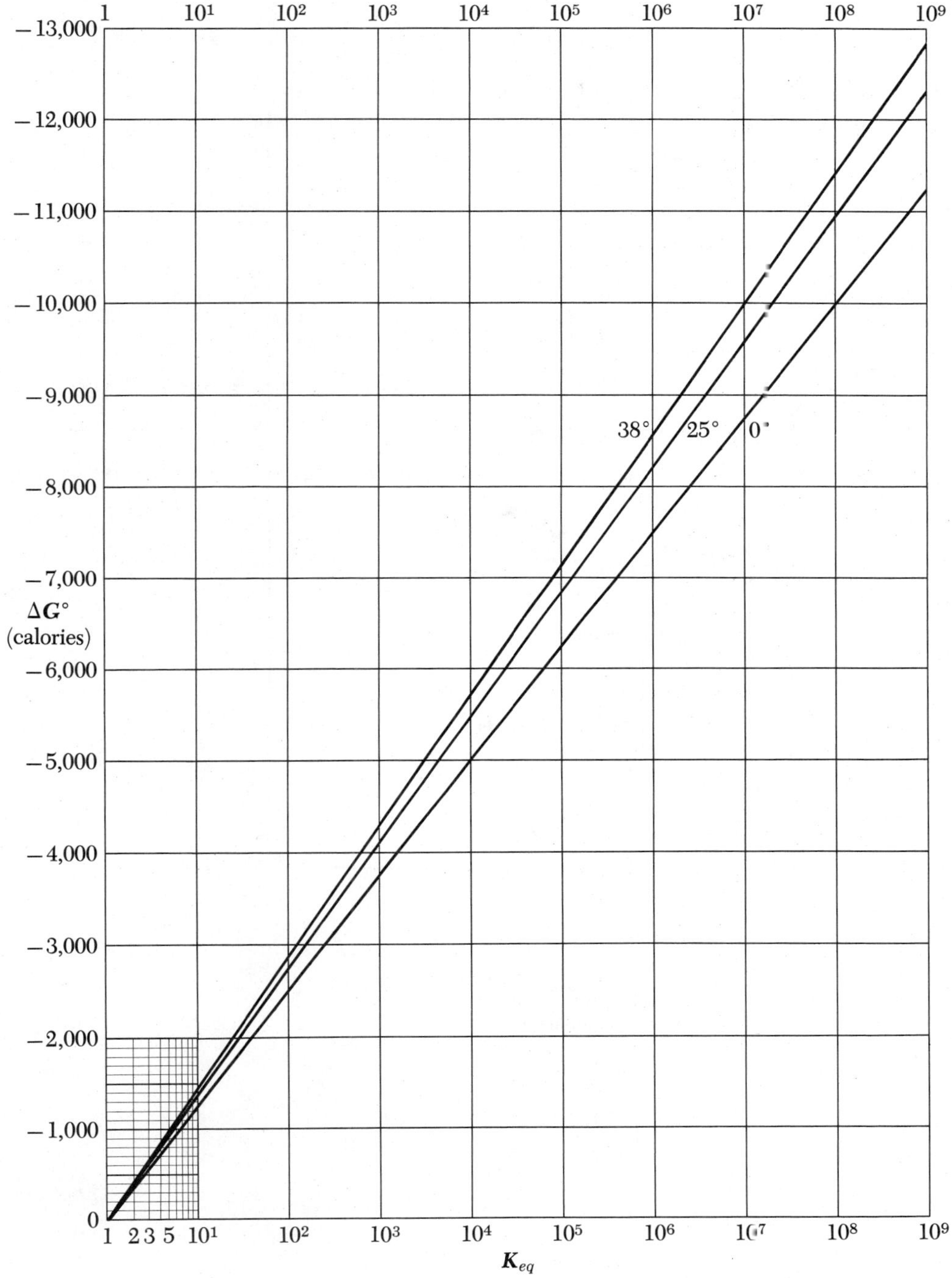

Figure 10–1 The relation of standard free energy change and equilibrium constant at three temperatures. The ΔG^0 scale is linear; the K_{eq} scale is logarithmic. The same plot relates positive free energy changes and the reciprocal of the corresponding equilibrium constant.

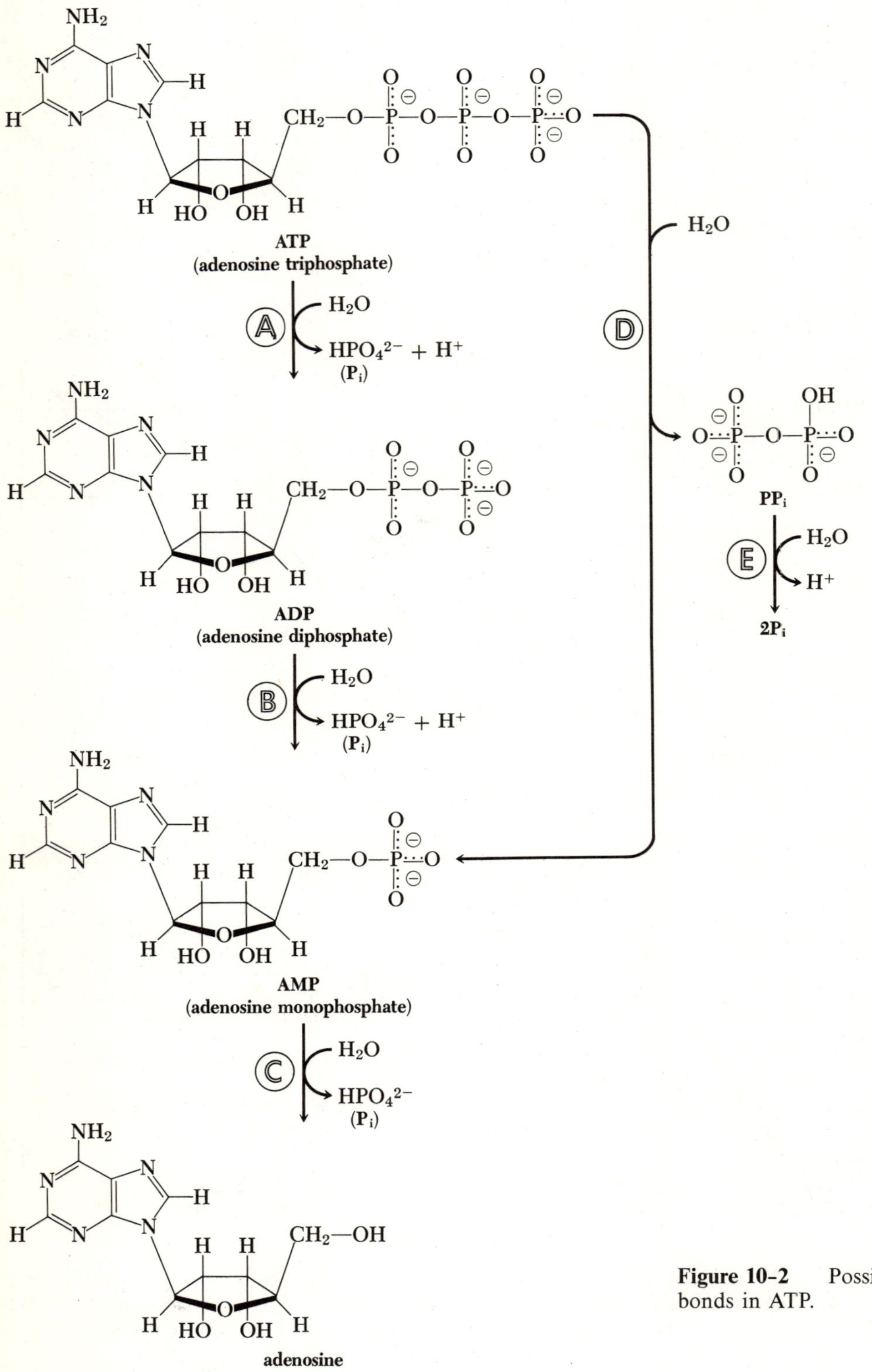

Figure 10–2 Possible hydrolyses of phosphate bonds in ATP.

$ATP^{4-} + H_2O \longrightarrow AMP^{2-} + PP_i^{3-} + H^+$	−43,500	4.2×10^7
$PP_i^{3} + H_2O \longrightarrow 2P_i^{2-} + H^+$	−35,100	1.4×10^6
$AMP^{2-} + H_2O \longrightarrow A + P_i^{2-}$	−12,600	1.6×10^2

P_i and **PP_i** are abbreviations for inorganic orthophosphate and pyrophosphate, respectively. The corresponding ionic forms that are most abundant at pH 7.4 are HPO_4^{2-} and $HP_2O_7^{3-}$.

The prime marks on the symbols for the standard free energy change and the equilibrium constant signify that these values apply to some empirical conditions; in this case, they were determined at a concentration of H^+ of $10^{-7.4}$ M (pH 7.4), and a concentration of Mg^{2+} of 10^{-4} M. The concentration of magnesium ion is important because it forms complexes with the phosphates, thereby altering the apparent equilibrium. The empirical equilibrium constants are calculated with the total nucleotide concentrations, including all ionic forms and the magnesium complexes.

The reactions are given here, and in most of the book, in terms of the predominant free ionic form present at pH 7.4, even though 0.9 of the ATP exists as the Mg complex. This is done in order to simplify recognition of reactions involving H^+. It is rather difficult to see what is going on when all of the ionic species are specified. For example, here is the hydrolysis of ATP at pH 7.4 and 0.5 mM Mg^{2+} expressed in a more rigorous way:

$$0.88\ MgATP^{2-} + 0.014\ HATP^{3-} + 0.106\ ATP^{4-} + H_2O \longrightarrow 0.40\ MgADP^{-} + 0.06\ HADP^{2-} + 0.54\ ADP^{3-} + 0.04\ MgHPO_4 + 0.10\ H_2PO_4^{-} + 0.86\ HPO_4^{2-} + 0.44\ Mg^{2+} + 0.85\ H^+$$

Ester *vs.* Anhydride Phosphates. We see right away that there is something different about the hydrolysis of the phosphate of AMP, which forms free adenosine. If we look at the structures shown in Figure 10–2, we see that it alone represents the hydrolysis of a phosphate ester, a compound formally made from alcohol (adenosine) and an acid (phosphoric acid). The other hydrolyses all represent the cleavage of an oxygen bridge between two phosphorus atoms, in other words, the cleavage of a **pyrophosphate** bond.

Formally, pyrophosphoric acid is an acid anhydride; it represents the combination of two molecules of phosphoric acid with the loss of water. More molecules of phosphoric acid may be added with the further loss of water to made extended chain polyphosphoric acids, which are polyanhydrides:

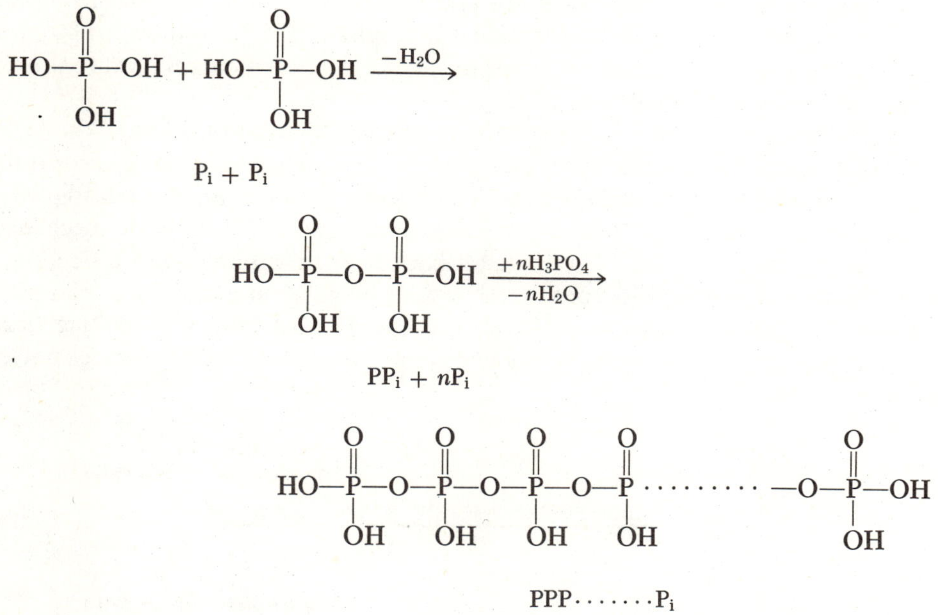

High-Energy, or Energy-Rich, Phosphates. We see by comparing the table and Fig. 10–2 that the standard free energy is quite highly negative in each case in which a pyrophosphate bond is hydrolyzed. For this reason, such bonds and the compounds that contain them are said to be energy-rich or high-energy. (Some physical chemists become quite upset by this usage, believing the terms imply that the liberated free energy is concentrated in the bond or that the compounds are activated to unusual energy states, and neither of these conditions occurs. Most people who use the terms understand that they simply designate bonds or compounds with large standard free energies of hydrolysis, and this free energy change is the result of the changes in chemical potential of all components of the system, including water and the hydrogen ion.)

Bonds are sometimes designated with a squiggle symbol if their cleavage by hydrolysis has a large negative standard free energy change. Thus, ATP might be designated as A—P∼P∼P, because the final two bonds are of the energy-rich anhydride type, while the bond between adenosine and phosphorus is of an ordinary ester type. (We shall later see that there are other kinds of groups in addition to phosphate groups that are attached by energy-rich bonds in the sense that their hydrolysis has a large equilibrium constant.)

The Phosphate Pool

The conclusion we have reached is that pyrophosphates, especially the nucleoside pyrophosphates, act as a sort of medium of exchange for energy among reactions, being formed by what would otherwise be highly exergonic reactions, and being cleaved to drive what would otherwise be endergonic processes.

Adenine Nucleotides. The nucleotides that are most commonly used to couple endergonic and exergonic processes are the adenosine phosphates. Thus, we shall see that the oxidation of fuels, photosynthesis, and related exergonic processes are coupled to the formation of ATP from ADP, whereas the formation of many compounds involves the simultaneous conversion of ATP to ADP or AMP, along with P_i or PP_i.

Other Nucleotides. We know that nucleotides are required as precursors of nucleic acids. We also saw that guanosine triphosphate (GTP) is used as an energy source for peptide synthesis and the movement of ribosomes in addition to its function as precursor for RNA. We shall later see syntheses that require still other nucleoside triphosphates as energy carriers. Cytidine triphosphate (CTP), uridine triphosphate (UTP), and even deoxythymidine triphosphate (dTTP) are sometimes used to provide energy for particular syntheses.

REGENERATION OF TRIPHOSPHATE BY NUCLEOSIDE DIPHOSPHOKINASE. When CTP, GTP, UTP, and other triphosphates are used to drive reactions, they are converted to their diphosphates or monophosphates. The monophosphates are also released when nucleic acids are destroyed. It is therefore necessary that there be some mechanism for converting the mono- and diphosphates back to their triphosphates for re-use, if metabolism is to continue. Most of the conversions hinge upon a transfer of phosphate from ATP. For example, there is a relatively non-specific nucleoside diphosphate kinase that catalyzes the reversible transfer of a phosphate group from ATP to various nucleoside diphosphates:

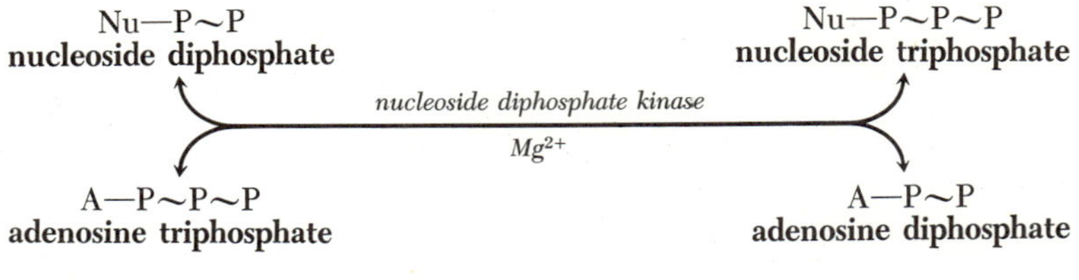

The effect of the action of this enzyme is to make the ratio of concentrations of the triphosphates and diphosphates nearly the same for all the nucleotides.

NUCLEOSIDE MONOPHOSPHATE KINASES. Similarly, there are nucleoside monophosphate kinases in the soluble cytoplasm that catalyze the transfer of a phosphate group from ATP to various nucleoside monophosphates:

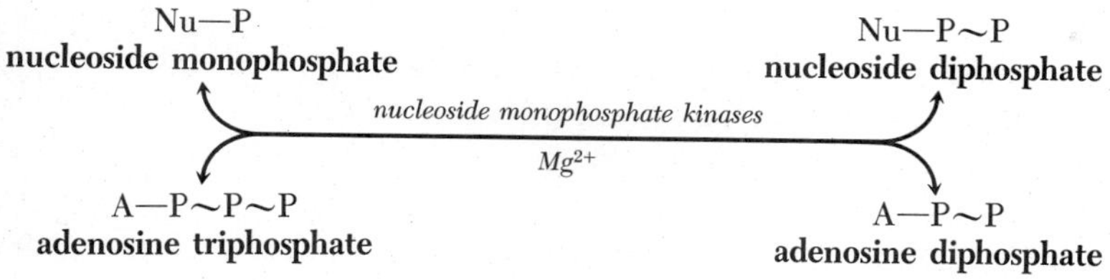

There are several enzymes of limited specificity for particular monophosphates (a GMP kinase, a CMP kinase, and so on), and the AMP kinase is of particular importance because of the involvement of the adenosine phosphates in so many processes. It is the most active of the monophosphate kinases, and catalyzes the reaction:

$$\text{ATP} + \text{AMP} \longleftrightarrow 2\ \text{ADP}$$

We see that it would require two phosphorylations to convert the resultant ADP completely to ATP. Therefore, we can make a mental reminder that any reaction forming AMP from ATP is effectively spending 2 moles of high-energy phosphate per mole of AMP formed, because it will take an additional mole of ATP to convert the resultant AMP back to ADP before it can be further phosphorylated to regenerate the original ATP.

Complete Interrelationships. The interplay between these various high-energy phosphates is summarized in Figure 10–3. The involvement of ATP in the re-phosphorylation of the other kinds of nucleotides effectively means that the expenditure of any of the high-energy phosphates for endergonic processes, as represented on the right of the figure, is equivalent to the conversion of ATP to ADP, even though the rates of these processes may be independently regulated. The ultimate result in each case is the replenishment of the high-energy phosphate through the action of highly exergonic processes that are coupled to the phosphorylation of ADP, as shown on the left.

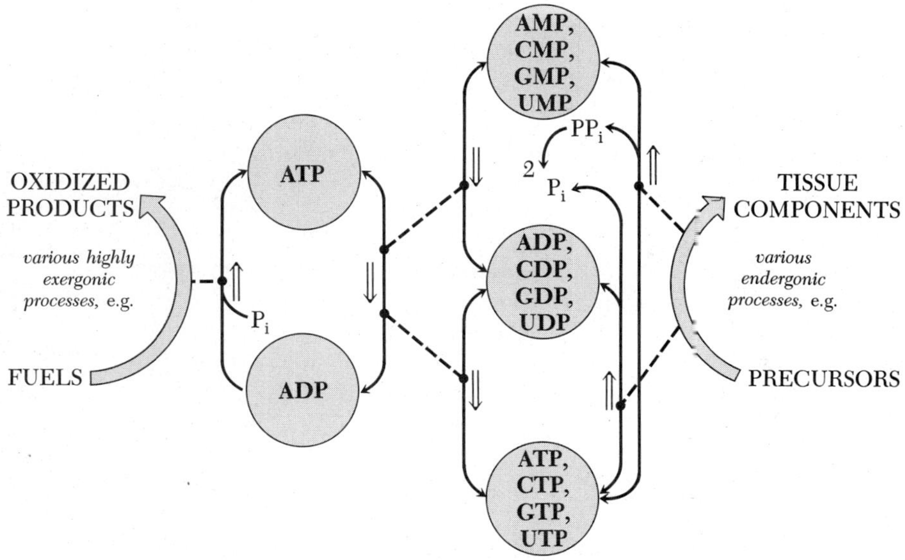

Figure 10–3 The nucleotide phosphate pool. Exergonic processes, such as the oxidation of fuels, drives the phosphorylation of ADP to form ATP (*left*). The ATP is used in turn to phosphorylate nucleoside monophosphates to form nucleoside diphosphates, and to phosphorylate nucleoside diphosphates to form nucleoside triphosphates. The nucleoside triphosphates are used to drive various endergonic processes, such as the formation of tissue components from precursors. In doing so, either a phosphate or a pyrophosphate group is split from the nucleoside triphosphate.

Phosphagens. The concentrations of the nucleoside di- and triphosphates represent only a small reserve for the energy requirements of cells. These compounds are intermediates, not stored fuels. Typical concentrations in cells range around several millimoles of ATP, tenths of a millimole of ADP, and 0.01 (or less) of a millimole of AMP per kilogram of active tissue (excluding gross structural components such as cartilage in animals, extracellular structures in protists, and woody tissue in plants). The concentrations of the guanine, cytosine, and uracil nucleotides are typically a tenth or less of that of the adenine nucleotides. The lack of reserves of high-energy phosphate is no problem for cells that require only relatively slow acceleration of ATP-consuming processes, because the ATP-producing reactions can be accelerated at the same pace. However, the muscles of animals represent a special case, in which the tissues have evolved to give rapid responses. Quick contraction of muscles represents a prompt demand on high-energy phosphate of greater magnitude than can be met by any reasonable metabolic capacity for generating ATP. For example, a man can expend as much as 6 mmoles of ATP per kg of muscle per second in a sudden burst of activity, but the maximum production, which only occurs after several seconds delay, is 1 mmole kg^{-1} s^{-1}. The quick contraction can occur only at the expense of high-energy phosphate already at hand.

If the necessity for high-energy phosphate were the only consideration, the need could be met by simply increasing the ATP concentration in the tissue. However, this would affect the rate of all of the processes in which ATP is involved, and cause an intolerable disruption of the general metabolism. Hence, different compounds have been evolved to serve as a high-energy phosphate store. These compounds are known collectively as the phosphagens, and they are substituted phosphoguanidinium compounds (Fig. 10–4). (These compounds are named both as the phosphoguanidines and as the guanidine phosphates. For example, phosphocreatine and creatine phosphate mean the same thing. The nomenclature of phosphorus compounds is a mess.)

Phosphocreatine is the phosphagen found in most vertebrates and in some invertebrates. **Phosphoarginine** is found in many other invertebrates. The other compounds listed occur in fewer phyla.

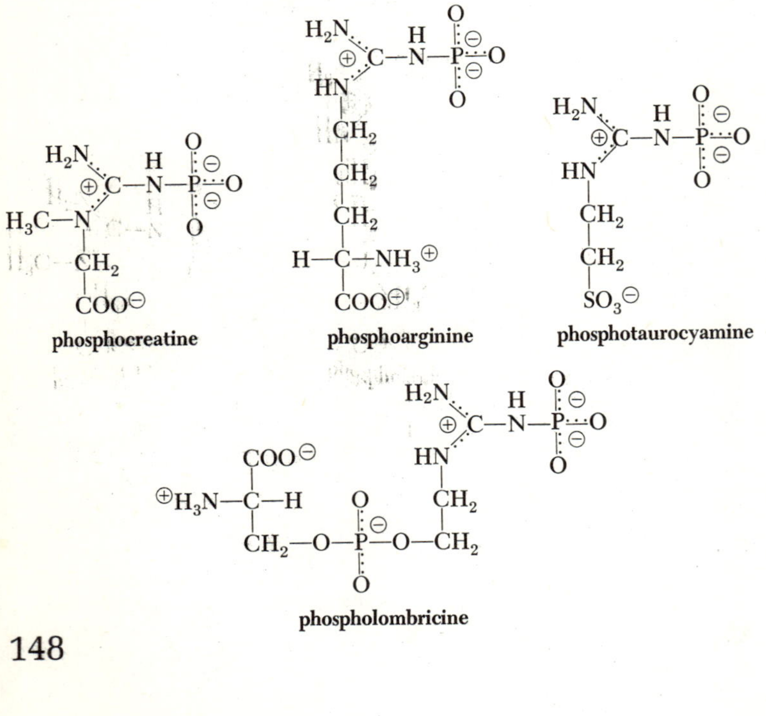

Figure 10–4 The phosphagens are guanidinio compounds that are phosphorylated as a means of storing high-energy phosphate, especially in muscles. The compounds used as phosphagens differ in various phyla.

The phosphagens typically occur in tens of millimoles per kilogram of muscle. (They also occur in brain, presumably to protect this vital tissue from an accidental transitory lack of ATP.) Their function as energy stores hinges upon enzymes that catalyze the equilibration with ADP, such as the creatine kinase found in mammalian muscles and brain:

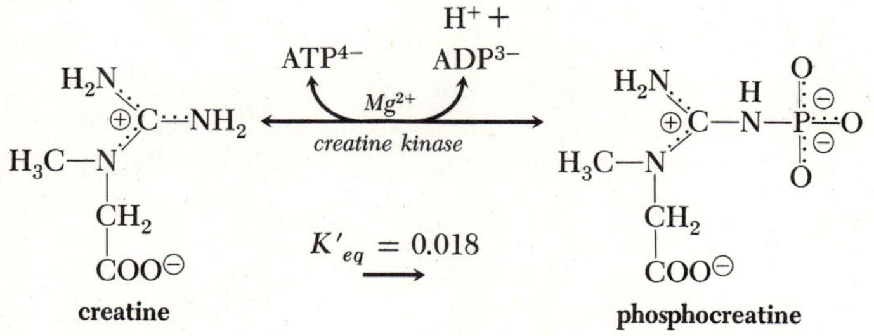

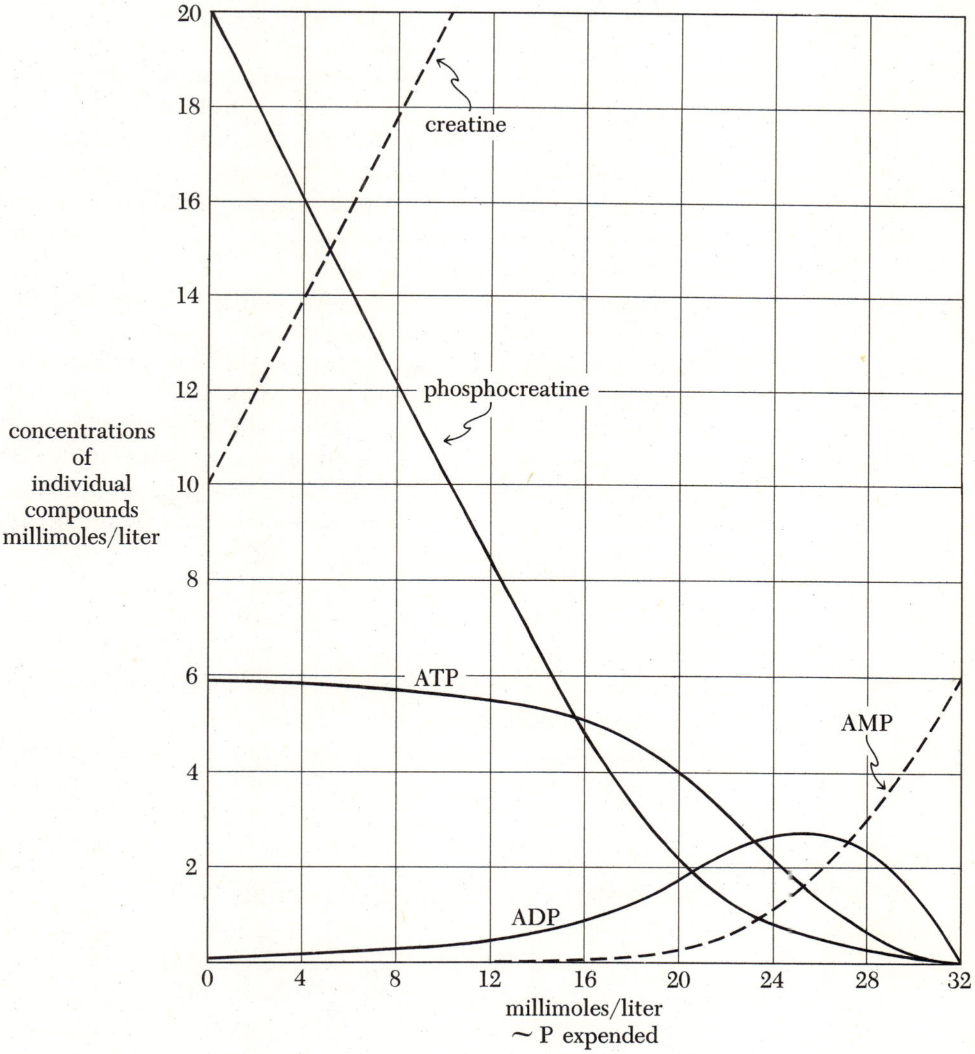

Figure 10-5 The changes in the concentrations of phosphocreatine, creatine, and the adenine nucleotides as high-energy phosphate is expended in a contracting muscle. Most of the early discharge is at the expense of phosphocreatine, and a sharp fall in the concentration of ATP, with corresponding rises in the concentrations of ADP and AMP, does not occur until much of the phosphocreatine is gone. (Adapted from calculations of McGilvery and Murray, J. Biol. Chem., 249:5845 (1974).)

Superficially, it might appear that the quoted equilibrium constant of 0.018 would mean that only a small fraction of the total creatine could be in the phosphorylated form. This is not so, because the reactions forming ATP can build up the ratio (ATP)/(ADP) to values greater than 100 in resting muscles, and this is sufficient to make the ratio (phosphocreatine)/(creatine) equal to 2.

Figure 10–5 illustrates what happens in these circumstances when there is a demand for high-energy phosphate for muscular contraction. The demand is supplied almost completely by phosphocreatine under physiological conditions, with a relatively small decline in the concentration of ATP and a small increase in the concentration of AMP, since the AMP kinase reaction will also be at equilibrium. The quantity of AMP becomes significant only when the store of phosphocreatine is nearly completely exhausted.

UTILIZATION OF ATP FOR MOTILITY

One of the most important requirements for the generation of energy in the form of ATP comes from its utilization in physical movement. We comprehend this most readily in the case of the higher animals, and indeed we must always have in mind the fact that the contraction of striated muscles is the greatest potential load on the ATP supply in most animals. For example, even a human of sedentary habits can easily expend ATP for muscular contraction at a more than ten-fold greater rate than it is used for all other purposes at rest.

However, this is a specialized example of a general phenomenon that occurs in all kinds of organisms. Biological motility is seen in such things as the whipping of flagella, the stroking of cilia, the folding of leaves, and the movement of chromosomes during cell division, along with other internal changes in shape and position of intracellular organelles. It now appears that the energy for all these motions may be obtained from the cleavage of ATP. This doesn't mean that complex events like the movement of amoeba proceed in exactly the same way as does the relatively simple contraction of a rabbit's hind leg, but only that there may be a similar pulling together of the parts involved in each case.

ATP-supported motility is an example of a transduction, a conversion of energy from one form to another. One begins with ATP and an extended structure, and ends with a contracted structure and the appearance of ADP and P_i. The free energy of hydrolysis of ATP is being used to change shape. How this is done is still not understood in even rough outline for many of the examples listed above. The most nearly complete picture has been developed for the striated muscle of animals, so let us look at this tissue in some detail.

The Nature of Striated Muscles

Fibers and Fibrils. The skeletal muscles of vertebrates, the flight muscles of insects, and the like are made by the fusing of cells into fibers. These fibers are surrounded by connective tissue that joins at the ends into a link to the skeleton or other part to be moved, and the motion is created by a shortening of the fibers. The fibers may be regarded as multinucleated cells, but they are packed so tightly with still smaller fibrous structures, known as **myofibrils,** that the nuclei and the mitochondria appear only along the edges (Fig. 10–6). We have already discussed the function of the nuclei, and shall talk about the role of the mitochondria in the formation of ATP

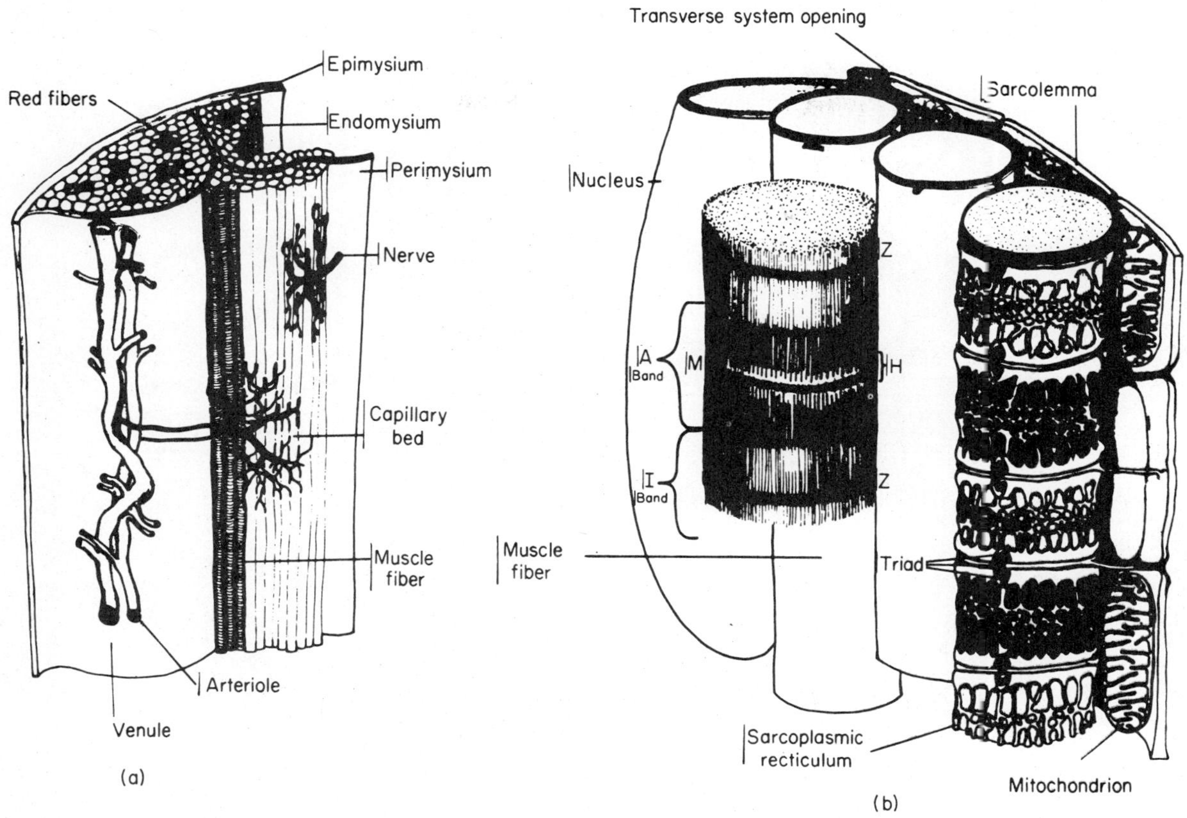

Figure 10–6 Drawing of the arrangement of fibers in a typical muscle (*left*), and of the myofibrils within a fiber (*right*). The capital letters refer to the various bands seen by microscopists. The sarcoplasmic reticulum is the arrangement of passageways through which Ca^{2+} is discharged to initiate contraction. Mitochondria are seen at the right hand side. (Drawings by H. Swatland in E. J. Briskey and T. Fukazawa, Myofibrillar proteins of skeletal muscle, Adv. Food Res., 19:279 (1971). Copyright Academic Press, Inc., and reproduced by permission.)

in the next chapter. Right now, we are concerned with the myofibrils, because these are the elements of the cell that actively contract so as to shorten the fibers.

Thick and Thin Filaments. The myofibrils are stacked bundles of rod-like filaments of molecular diameters. The myofibrils are divided crosswise by rigid, thin circular plates of protein known as the **Z-bands,** which have thin filaments bristling out in a lengthwise direction from each face. The Z-bands are spaced along the myofibril so that there is some distance between the successive free ends of the thin filaments in a relaxed muscle. These free ends are overlapped by a second set of filaments, the thick filaments. (The overlapping regions add to the banded appearance of the fibrils which led to the name *striated muscles.*) Contraction occurs because the thin filaments are drawn toward each other over these thick filaments, thereby pulling the Z-bands together. The facing thin filaments with their overlapping thick filaments and attached Z-band plates constitute the elementary functional structure of the muscle, the **sarcomere.** Of course, the sarcomere is not an independent entity, since each Z-band belongs to adjacent sarcomeres, but the term is still useful.

The myofibrils are bounded and penetrated by a network of tubular passages known as the **sarcoplasmic reticulum,** which carries the signal for contraction to the filaments, as we shall shortly see.

In sum, a skeletal muscle fiber is a bundle of a few thousand myofibrils that run its length. Each myofibril is in turn an end-to-end stack of a few thousand sarcomeres,

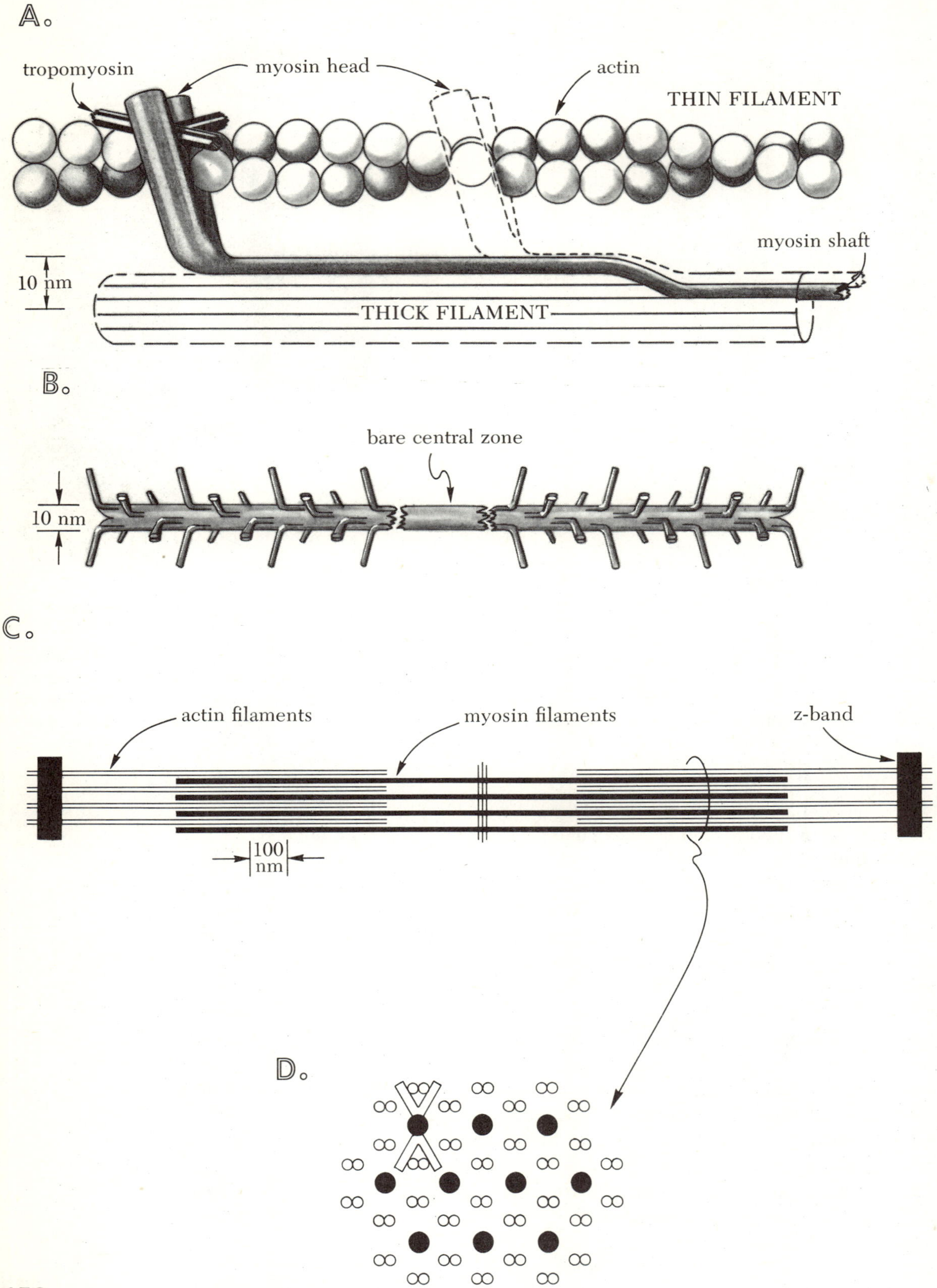

Figure 10-7 *See opposite page for legend.*

and each sarcomere is a bundle of a few thousand filaments, and these filaments are the actual contractile elements of the muscle.

Myosin and Actin. Contraction occurs because of the development of forces between the thick and the thin filaments, which is another way of saying that bonds are formed and displaced between the molecules comprising the filaments. As we might suspect, these specifically oriented bonds are created by the presence of particular proteins in the filaments.

The proteins that beome linked to cause contraction are myosin in the thick filaments and actin in the thin filaments (Fig. 10–7). Myosin is a club-shaped molecule with a thin shaft and a globular two-part head, made principally from two identical peptide chains, although there are small additional peptide chains in the head. The two long peptides are twisted into super-coiled α-helices to form the shaft, with the ends of the chain rolled up into more globular form to make the heads.

Isolated myosin catalyzes the hydrolysis of ATP:

$$ATP^{4-} + H_2O \longrightarrow ADP^{3-} + H^+$$

In other words, it behaves as an **adenosinetriphosphatase,** or **ATPase.** The catalytic site is in the head of the molecule; the shaft of the molecule is used only for structural purposes, with the shafts stacked in parallel to form the body of the thick filaments. (Of course, there must be important bonds formed between the shafts; otherwise the filaments would pull apart upon development of the contractile force.) The heads are directed toward opposite ends of the thick filament from its middle.

Muscular contraction also involves another property of the globular head of myosin, which is its ability to combine with actin in the thin filaments. Actin is a protein composed of globular units that combine into long coiled strands, somewhat like a double chain of beads. Each bead is composed of identical peptide chains which do not cross from one bead to the next. Instead, the beads are held together by bonds between the peptides.

The thin filaments appear to be spaced out by molecules of still another protein, **tropomyosin,** which, like the body of myosin, is a long, thin shaft made from a super-coiled pair of α-helices, and it may be that the actin-myosin bonds are formed only adjacent to a particular position on tropomyosin.

The Mechanism of Contraction

The Moving Parts. The fundamental action of contraction is a binding of the actin chains by the globular head of myosin, followed by a movement of the head

---

Figure 10–7 *A.* The thin filaments of myofibrils are composed of double-helical chains of beads bound to threads of tropomyosin molecules. Each bead is an actin molecule. The beads are clasped by the forked heads of myosin molecules, which protrude from thick filaments. The thick filaments are bundles of the shafts of myosin molecules, and contraction involves a bending back of the myosin heads relative to the shafts.

B. The forked myosin heads protrude from the thick filaments at 120° intervals in a helical arrangement so that successive heads clasp thin filaments at this spacing around the surface of the thick filament.

C. The actin filaments are attached to plates (Z-bands) with their free ends clasped by thick filaments. Seen in cross-section, the thin filaments are in hexagonal array around the thick filaments. Only one pair of myosin heads is indicated. The spacing of heads is such that each successive pair of actin beads is probably clasped by heads from one of the thick filaments near it.

relative to the shaft that pulls the actin chain into a new position. (The shaft of myosin appears to have two elastic positions where bending can occur to shorten the over-all length.) Since the two ends of the thick filaments are pulling in opposite directions on the corresponding sets of thin filaments, the result is that the thick filaments do not move. The two sets of thin filaments are instead pulled toward each other along the thick filaments. This displacement is accompanied by a release of ADP and P_i.

Calcium Ions Trigger Contraction. Another important fact is that contraction is initiated by the release of calcium ions from the sarcoplasmic reticulum. The nerve impulse to the muscle that signals for contraction causes a traveling wave of changing ion concentration on the reticulum, and this traveling wave results in the discharge of Ca^{2+} from combination with the principal protein in the reticulum. (As soon as the wave has passed, the reticulum begins to bind Ca^{2+} once more, and the binding is done at the expense of ATP. This utilization of ATP is not to be confused with much greater utilization for the contractile mechanism itself. However, it is important; a graduate student at Duke University was afflicted with a painless, but paralyzing, continued contraction of his muscles upon exercise. He was found to have muscles with a diminished ability to concentrate discharged Ca^{2+} back into his sarcoplasmic reticulum.)

The triggering by calcium hinges upon the action of a protein complex, **troponin.** Troponin contains a peptide that inhibits the combination of actin and myosin, and therefore keeps the fiber in a relaxed state. It also contains another peptide that will overcome this inhibition, provided that Ca^{2+} is present. The action of troponin also requires in some way the presence of tropomyosin, which we noted may act as a spacer for the active sites on the thin filaments.

Sequence of Events in Contraction. To put this information together into a more understandable whole, let us visualize one of the possible mechanisms by which contraction could occur, with the qualification that it not be swallowed intact as a proven series of events.

As is shown in Figure 10–8, a relaxed muscle appears to be one in which the active sites of actin and myosin are in proximity, but are kept separated by a binding of MgADP and P_i, along with the inhibitory component of troponin.

The discharge of Ca^{2+} from the sarcoplasmic reticulum in response to nervous stimulation causes the activating component of troponin to somehow withdraw the inhibitory component. This is not too hard to imagine. A related calcium-binding protein from carp has been shown to have a cage of negative side-chains from glutamate and aspartate around the calcium ion. The formation of this cage could easily draw together parts of the protein molecule, and thereby expose new sites, or shift the position of existing ones.

The withdrawal of the inhibitory protein enables myosin and actin to combine, with the displacement of ADP and P_i from the binding site. Their combination causes the conformation of the myosin globular head to change so that it rotates back on the shaft, drawing the actin along with it. This is the power stroke.

The new conformation is such that the myosin head has a greater affinity for MgATP than it does for actin; in other words, MgATP displaces actin from myosin. (One of the differences of the physiological activity of myosin compared to the test tube ATPase activity is that it has an absolute requirement for magnesium ions.) The combination of MgATP with the active site results in the cleavage of the ATP component to form ADP and P_i. This results in the return of the conformation of the myosin head to the relaxed form, in which the head is brought into proximity with a new combining site on the thin filaments, where the sequence can be repeated to advance the thin filament another notch.

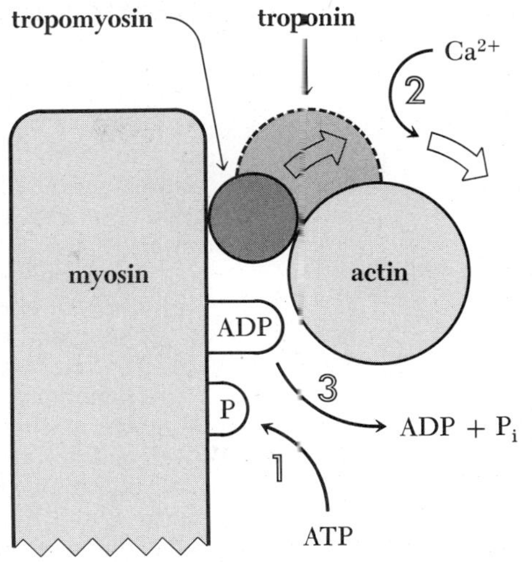

Figure 10-8 Diagrammatic outline of postulated events during muscular contraction.
1. ATP reacts with the myosin heads of a contracted fibril; the resultant ADP remains bound to the phosphorylated myosin, which is converted to a relaxed conformation, representing a high-energy state. Threads of tropomyosin fall between the relaxed myosin and actin in the absence of calcium ions so as to prevent their association.
2. The location of tropomyosin is determined by an association with troponin. Troponin binds calcium ions that are released upon stimulation of the muscle and shifts conformation so as to move the tropomyosin threads from between actin and myosin.
3. The combination of actin and myosin causes the removal of the phosphate group and ADP from myosin. Myosin can then return to its contracted configuration, which will react again with ATP to start the entire sequence again. The result is a repeated shortening of the fibril as long as Ca^{2+} is present.

Why doesn't the thin filament slip backwards during part of the sequence when there is no bonding between actin and myosin? It doesn't because the thick filament is coated with a whole array of myosin heads, and not all of them are in any part of the cycle at once. Complete combination of the myosin heads with thin filaments is believed to be the cause of the extreme contraction (rigor mortis) in the muscles of dead animals.

Once more, the critical feature of this sequence for our purposes is that motion represents the effective hydrolysis of ATP into ADP and P_i, and motion is therefore one of the major drains on the high-energy phosphate pool, a drain that requires replacement through the processes discussed in the next chapters.

FURTHER READING

P. D. Boyer, H. A. Lardy, and K. Myrbäck, eds., The enzymes, 2nd edition, Academic Press (1960). The following articles are of interest:
- M. J. Johnson, Enzyme equilibria and thermodynamics, 3:407. Written by one of the pioneers in applying clear thinking to the subject. Directed toward the beginning professional student.
- R. M. Bock, Adenine nucleotides and properties of pyrophosphate compounds, 2:3. Detailed summary.

F. Lipmann, Metabolic generation and utilization of phosphate bond energy, Advances Enzymol., 1:99 (1941). The classic introduction of the concept.

J. M. Murray and A. Weber, The cooperative action of muscle proteins, Sci. American, 230:59 (1974). Readable account of recent experimentation and speculations on mechanism.

T. D. Pollard and R. R. Weihing. Actin and myosin and cell movement, CRC Critical Rev. Biochem., 2:1 (1974). Review of motile mechanisms in some cells other than muscle fibers.

QUESTIONS

1. The "Calorie" used in describing the potential energy of foods is really a kilocalorie. (a) If a cooking oil yields 9 "Calories" per gram upon metabolism, what is the yield in joules per gram? (b) If a man liberates 12 megajoules of energy per day, what should be his "caloric intake" in dietitian's terms to maintain his body weight?
2. Which, if any, of the following indicators will tell you that a reaction cannot proceed as given?
   (a) The standard free energy change is positive.
   (b) The free energy change is positive.
   (c) The equilibrium constant is less than one.
   (d) The reaction is exergonic.
3. It is sometimes said that all reactions are reversible. Cite an example of a reaction that is clearly not reversible in any real sense.
4. We shall see that many cells oxidize fatty acids as a means of generating high-energy phosphate. Would the equilibrium constant for this process be higher, lower, or about the same as the equilibrium constant for the oxidation of fatty acids without the generation of high-energy phosphate?
5. Identify the "low-energy" bonds (those that have standard free energies of hydrolysis less than 20 kJ mole^{-1}) and the "high-energy" bonds in the following structure:

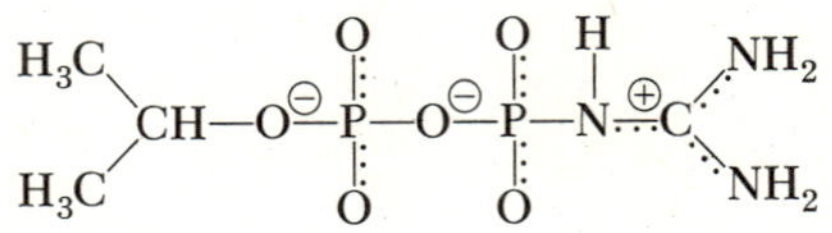

6. The oxidation of glucose causes the phosphorylation of ADP to form ATP. Show how the presence of nucleoside diphosphate kinase and UMP kinase enables the same phosphorylation also to result in the conversion of UMP to UTP.
7. What is the net reaction of muscular contraction? Of muscular contraction and creatine kinase acting in concert?
8. What compound disappears most rapidly from mammalian skeletal muscles during the maximum effort that can be carried out in 2 seconds?
9. Most of the ATP in cells exists in what ionic form?
10. What is the function of Ca^{2+} in muscular contraction?
11. Which of the following is shortened by the largest fraction of its length during contraction: (a) the sarcomere; (b) the thick filament; (c) the thin filament; (d) the actin molecule; (e) the myosin molecule; (f) the tropomyosin molecule?

CHAPTER 11

THE COUPLING OF PHOSPHORYLATION TO OXIDATION

THE CONCEPTS

The aerobic organisms, which include the higher plants, many protists, and the animals, generate most of their ATP by oxidative phosphorylation. Oxidative phosphorylation is the production of ATP from ADP and P_i in association with the transfer of electrons to molecular oxygen. It occurs in membranes, either the plasma membrane in bacteria or the inner membrane of mitochondria in plants and animals.

A single pathway is used for oxidative phosphorylation, even though fuels such as the fats or sugars undergo combustion in a sequence of many small steps involving dozens of different intermediate metabolites. The existence of the common pathway means that the number of moles of high-energy phosphate generated per atom of oxygen consumed, the P:O ratio, is about the same (2.8 to 3.0) with all the common fuels.

It is possible to use the same pathway for handling electrons from a variety of substrates because many of the substrate dehydrogenases use NAD as a coenzyme, so that the electrons from all sorts of compounds appear as NADH. The electrons can then be transferred from NADH to O_2 by a single sequence of reactions, regardless of their origin. ATP is produced in association with this common sequence.

The oxidation of NADH by O_2 in membranes is broken into several steps so that the potential energy can be used to drive the formation of 3 moles of ATP per mole of NADH oxidized. The initial steps, which cause the formation of one molecule of ATP per pair of electrons transferred, involve the oxidation of NADH by ubiquinone. The transfer is catalyzed by an NADH dehydrogenase complex, which contains both riboflavin 5′-phosphate and non-heme iron as electron carriers.

The ubiquinol created by the first sequence is then re-oxidized by cytochrome c in a sequence causing the formation of a second molecule of ATP. This sequence involves transfers of electrons through two other cytochromes, b and c_1, as well as non-heme iron, on the way to c.

The final sequence involves the oxidation of reduced cytochrome c by molecular oxygen, with the formation of a third molecule of ATP. This sequence utilizes cytochromes $a + a_3$, a copper-containing complex that is also known as cytochrome oxidase.

The oxidation of some substrates by ubiquinone is not sufficiently exergonic to sustain the generation of a molecule of ATP, and the oxidation therefore could not occur if electrons were transferred from these substrates to NAD within mitochondria. Such substrates, which include acyl compounds that are oxidized to the corresponding unsaturated enoyl derivatives, are therefore attacked by dehydrogenases that contain FAD or FMN as oxidants, rather than NAD. The electrons are transferred in these cases directly to ubiquinone, bypassing the phosphorylation apparatus. The P:O ratio for the oxidation of these substrates is 2.0 rather than the 3.0 seen when NAD is involved.

The phosphorylations accompanying electron transfer may require the existence of a membrane to create the high-energy state that is used to drive phosphorylation. Some believe that the entire process is a chemical coupling, in which the electron transfers create some covalent compounds with high-energy bonds that are cleaved by phosphate to form high-energy phosphate, which is then transferred to ADP, creating ATP. Others believe in a chemiosmotic process, which hinges on the creation of a concentration gradient for H^+ across the membrane, with the

resultant concentration and potential differences forcing some unknown intermediate into a high-energy configuration within the membrane. Whatever the mechanism, it is clear that the energy obtained from electron transfers may be used directly to cause other ions, such as K^+ or Ca^{2+}, to move against a concentration gradient across the membrane, in addition to its use in generating ATP from ADP and P_i. Consumption of the high-energy intermediate for these purposes usually is substantially less than the consumption for the generation of ATP, so we shall mainly be concerned with the flux of high-energy phosphate in discussing energy transfers.

Since the transfer of electrons from substrates to O_2 can occur only in association with the conversion of ADP and P_i to ATP in membranes carrying out oxidative phosphorylation in an efficient way, it follows that O_2 will be consumed only when ADP is available. In other words, oxygen consumption would stop if all of the ADP were converted to ATP. Oxygen consumption doesn't stop completely in aerobic organisms because they are always doing something that requires ATP—synthesizing cell constituents, changing shape, moving, and the like. The use of ATP in driving endergonic processes involves the formation of ADP. The rate of oxygen consumption is geared to the rate at which ADP is being made available. The greater the work load, the greater the oxygen consumption.

Aerobic organisms are killed by failure of oxidative phosphorylation. The failure may come about by lack of oxygen (suffocation) or by inhibitors that prevent some step in the process. Inhibitors of interest include cyanide, the fish and insect poison rotenone, the barbiturates, and some antibiotics that are made by microorganisms to protect themselves from other microorganisms.

We have developed at this point the idea that living organisms can go about their business of growing, reproducing, and moving because the chemical reactions involved in these events include the cleavage of pyrophosphate bonds in ATP or in other nucleoside triphosphates that are equilibrated with ATP. The other side of life that isn't so obvious includes the means of generating the pyrophosphate bonds that are being expended to look alive.

More than half of the pyrophosphate bonds in the entire biomass are created by the reaction of fuels with molecular oxygen. We shall see in Chapter 17 that some ATP is also formed when the fuels and oxygen are created by photosynthesis, but more ATP is generated during the later recombination of fuels and oxygen. The formation of ATP by phosphorylation of ADP is a concomitant of the combustion of fats, of carbohydrates, and even of proteins. The total oxidation of a typical fat and a typical sugar, glucose, goes like this in the laboratory:

$$\text{(fat)} \quad C_{55}H_{102}O_6 + 77\tfrac{1}{2}\,O_2 \longrightarrow 55\,CO_2 + 51\,H_2O$$
$$\text{(glucose)} \quad C_6H_{12}O_6 + 6\,O_2 \longrightarrow 6\,CO_2 + 6\,H_2O$$

We shall see that these reactions are modified in tissue so as to cause the phosphorylation of a large number of molecules of ATP per molecule of fuel consumed; the overall biological processes can be approximated by these equations:

$$\text{(fat)} \quad C_{55}H_{102}O_6 + 77\tfrac{1}{2}\,O_2 + 437\,(ADP^{3-} + P_i^{2-} + H^+) \longrightarrow 55\,CO_2 + 437\,ATP^{4-} + 488\,H_2O$$

$$\text{(glucose)} \quad C_6H_{10}O_6 + 6\,O_2 + 36\,(ADP^{3-} + P_i^{2-} + H^+) \longrightarrow 6\,CO_2 + 36\,ATP^{4-} + 42\,H_2O$$

How is this accomplished? Each of these processes must represent the summation of many individual reactions, because hundreds of molecules simply don't collide simultaneously in one grand reaction. There is a clue buried in the equations. Suppose that we calculate the number of molecules of high-energy phosphate produced per atom of oxygen consumed; this ratio, abbreviated as the **P:O ratio,** is commonly used as an index of the efficiency of energy conversion in oxidative metabolism. We find that it is 2.82 when fats are oxidized and 3.00 when glucose is oxidized. These values are nearly the same, and the reason is that most of the phosphorylations are associated with the consumption of oxygen. The same mechanism of generating high-energy phosphate is used over and over again regardless of the nature of the fuel being burned.

The association of the utilization of oxygen and the phosphorylation of ADP is known as oxidative phosphorylation, and it constitutes the principal source of high-energy phosphate for nearly all animals, and also for plants during the dark hours.

General Nature of Oxidative Phosphorylation

A fundamental feature of oxidative phosphorylation is this: Only a few coenzymes are used as oxidizing agents for a wide variety of organic compounds. The coenzymes become reduced when they are involved in any one of these many reactions, and the reduced forms of the coenzymes are mainly re-oxidized by transferring electrons from them to molecular oxygen in aerobic organisms. These transfers of electrons are made through particular intermediates, and they are the reactions used to drive the phosphorylation of ADP (Fig. 11–1).

Essentially there is one set of enzymes catalyzing a sequence of reactions through which electrons removed from a variety of organic substrates are fed, one pair at a time, to reduce molecular oxygen. Since the substrates are oxidized in small steps with only two electrons or two hydrogen atoms being removed at a time, a long series of reactions is required before the last carbon and hydrogen atoms of the original fuel appear as CO_2 and H_2O. These more complicated sequences will concern us in the following chapter; we are here concerned with one of the major purposes for which they exist—the transfer of electrons to oxygen so as to cause the formation of ATP.

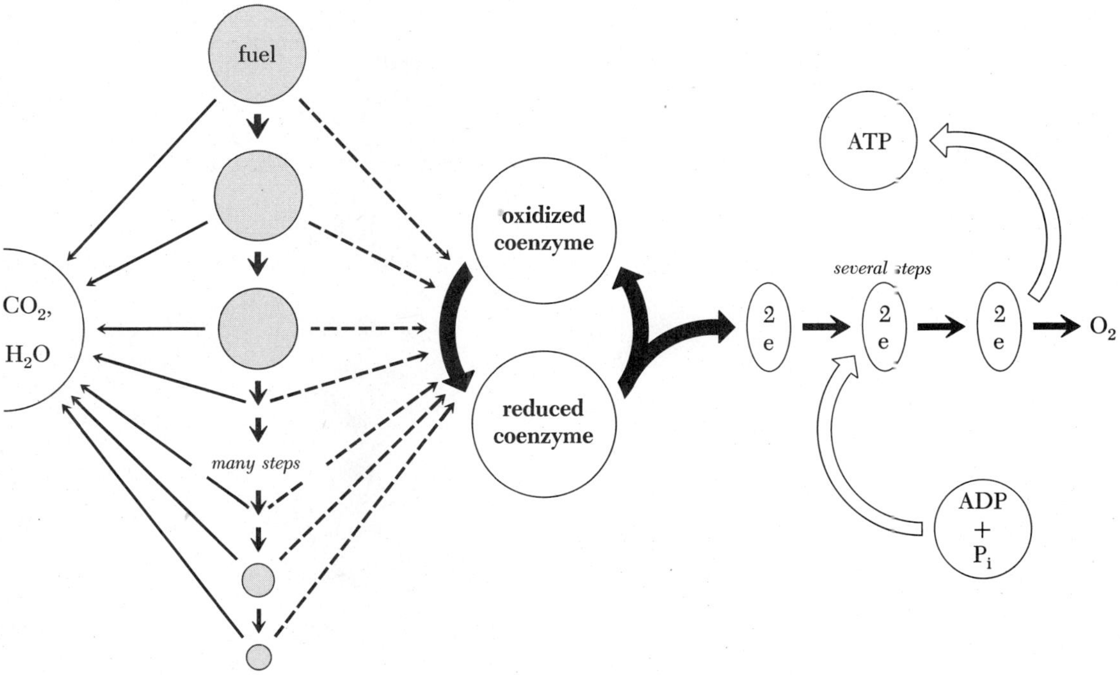

Figure 11-1 Many different fuels can be attacked by the same oxidized coenzymes. The fuels are chipped away, two electrons at a time, with their substance gradually appearing as CO_2 and H_2O. The coenzymes become reduced, and their oxidized form is regenerated by the transfer of electrons to molecular oxygen through several intermediate carriers. These transfers are highly exergonic by themselves, and are used to drive the phosphorylation of ADP to form ATP.

The Role of Membranes. The process of oxidative phosphorylation is localized in membranes in all kinds of cells in which it occurs. In the case of bacteria, it occurs in the cytoplasmic membrane, which is the innermost of the envelopes enclosing the cell. In the eukaryotes, which include the fungi, the higher plants, and the animals, oxidative phosphorylation occurs in the inner membranes of mitochondria.

MITOCHONDRIAL MEMBRANES. A mitochondrion consists of two sacs, one inside the other. The outer membrane is relatively unwrinkled, but the inner membrane has bulges into the center of the mitochondrion. The number and shape of these bulges, which are known as **cristae,** varies from one kind of a cell to another, even in the differing cells of the same organism (Fig. 11–2), but in all cases the membrane is continuous and encloses a matrix that is richly packed with enzymes, including several that catalyze the transfer of hydrogen from substrates to coenzymes. However, it is the inner membrane itself, not the matrix, that contains the enzymes responsible for transferring electrons to oxygen in association with the phosphorylation of ADP, and the inner membrane also has some of the enzymes acting on the organic substrates, as well. This explains why mitochondria in cells with a high capacity for utilizing oxygen, such as those in repeatedly contracting muscles, have many cristae. The folds provide a means of increasing the amount of inner membrane and its associated enzymes in a given volume of mitochondria.

STRUCTURE OF PHOSPHORYLATING MEMBRANES. The plasma membranes of oxygen-utilizing bacteria and the inner membranes of mitochondria are like most other biological membranes in that they consist of a phospholipid core, coated on either side with a layer of protein. However, they differ from other membranes in that the inner side of the core is studded with globular particles of protein (Fig. 11–3) that are believed to contain the enzymes necessary for phosphorylation of ADP. The enzymes catalyzing the electron transfers are believed to be within complexes that traverse the lipid core.

THE ELECTRON TRANSFERS

The reaction of a typical substrate with molecular oxygen involves enough change in chemical potential to sustain the formation of two or three molecules of ATP for each atom of oxygen consumed (equivalent to four or six molecules per molecule of O_2). However, it is practical to make only one molecule of ATP at a time, and it is therefore necessary for the transfer of the electrons from substrate to oxygen to be broken up

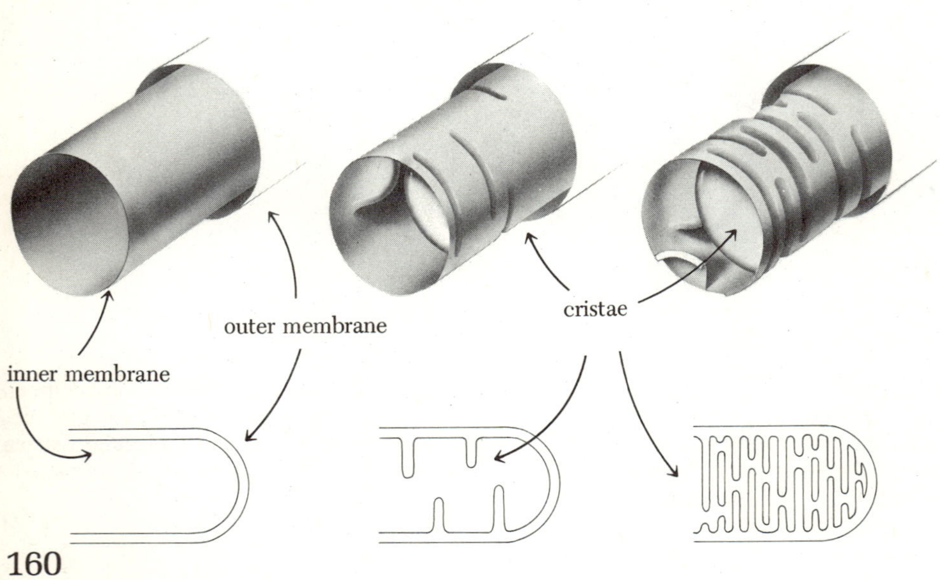

Figure 11–2 Idealized gross structure of mitochondria, shown in cutaway view at the top and in longitudinal section at the bottom. The structure is made from two concentric bags, and the membrane comprising the inner bag may be indented into ridges, tubes, or pouches, called cristae. As shown, there may be few cristae, or there may be so many that they nearly fill the interior, with cross-sections appearing to have nearly even laminations.

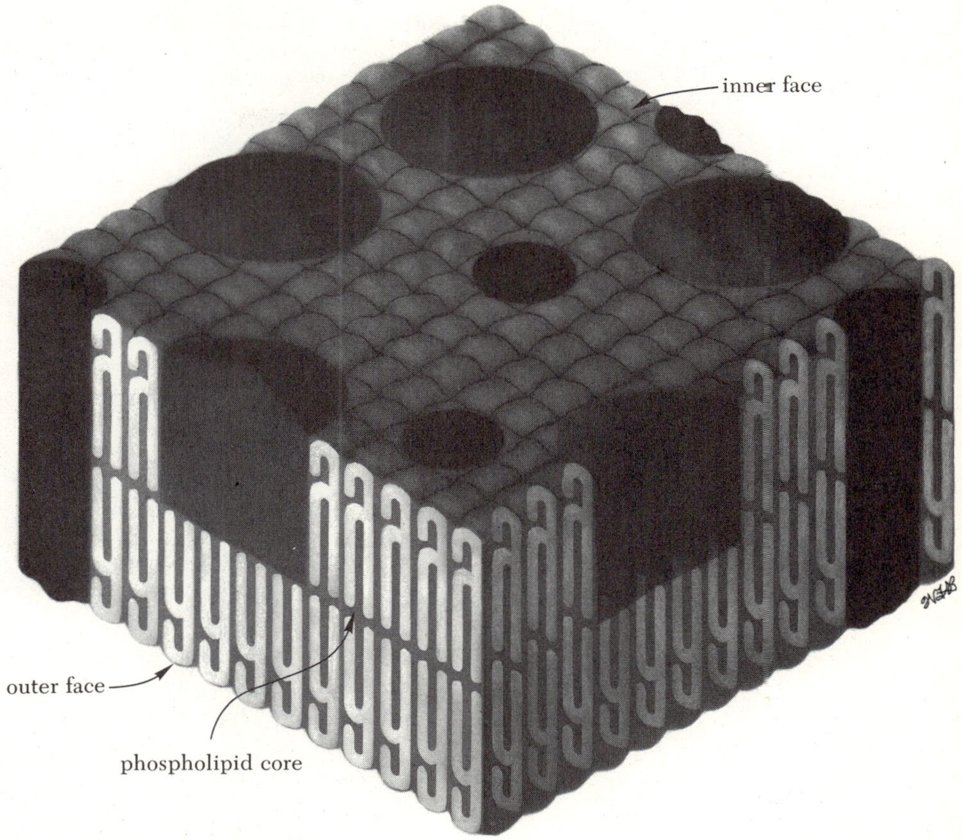

Figure 11-3 The lipid core of the inner mitochondrial membrane is believed by many to be traversed by protein complexes that contain some of the electron-transferring components, and to contain other protein complexes, such as the apparatus of oxidative phosphorylation, floating on the inner surface. (The protein layers on the two faces are not shown.)

into a number of steps, if the greatest possible amount of ADP is to be converted to ATP. In effect, the electrons are transferred to successively more powerful oxidizing agents until they finally reach molecular oxygen, so that a sequence is created in which three parts are exergonic enough to support the formation of ATP. This is good for the organism, but hard on the student, because such sequences must inherently involve a number of different compounds in order to create the succession of increasingly more powerful oxidants.

However, the action of this seemingly formidable array of coenzymes and prosthetic groups is not at all difficult to understand, because it involves nothing more than sequences of oxidation-reductions, each of which can be represented as:

$$\text{reduced A} + \text{oxidized B} \longrightarrow \text{oxidized A} + \text{reduced B}$$

All we must do is describe the successive components that are oxidized and reduced in turn, as is sketched in Figure 11-4.

Substrate Dehydrogenases in the Matrix. Many of the electrons that are transferred to oxygen in the inner membrane originate from substrate in the matrix. In order to appreciate how this occurs, let us consider a typical and important example. We shall repeatedly encounter compounds that contain hydroxyl groups (in other words, substituted alcohols), and we saw in Chapter 8 how alcohols are oxidized by NAD (or NADP) through the action of specific dehydrogenases. A specific example is the oxidation of an important compound, L-malate, which is the anionic form of a dicarboxylic

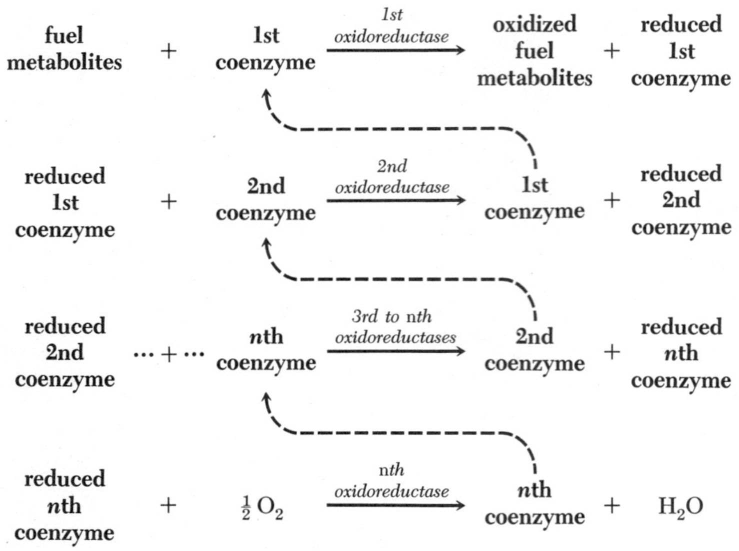

Figure 11-4 The combustion of fuels does not involve direct reactions of the intermediate metabolites with oxygen. Electrons are passed from the metabolites to O_2 through several coenzymes so that the resultant release of energy can be utilized to generate ATP. When a metabolite is oxidized by a coenzyme, the resultant reduced coenzyme becomes a substrate for a second oxidoreductase, and the reduced second coenzyme created in this reaction is the substrate for a third oxidoreductase, and so on until electrons finally arrive at O_2.

acid, malic acid, that also contains a hydroxyl group. (We shall encounter L-malate and its oxidation repeatedly.)

MALATE DEHYDROGENASE. The hydroxyl group of L-malate is attacked by malate dehydrogenase in the mitochondrial matrix, which catalyzes the removal of two hydrogen atoms from the compound (Fig. 11-5). One of these hydrogen atoms appears as

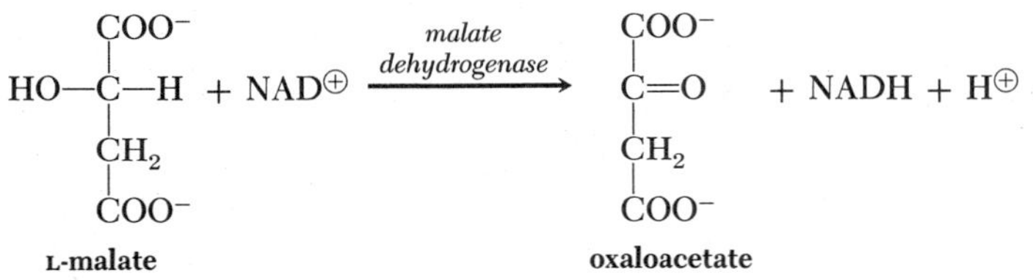

Figure 11-5 L-Malate is oxidized to oxaloacetate by the action of malate dehydrogenase in the matrix of mitochondria.

a proton, but the other is transferred as a **hydride ion, H:⁻**, to NAD. The net result of the malate dehydrogenase reaction therefore is to convert L-malate to the more oxidized compound **oxaloacetate,** by oxidizing an alcohol group to a carbonyl group; this is accomplished by simultaneously reducing NAD, with the formation of NADH and an accompanying proton. The systematic name of the enzyme, **L-malate: NAD oxidoreductase,** is therefore a little more descriptive of its action.

NADH Dehydrogenase and Ubiquinone. Since the electrons from many substrates in addition to malate are used to form NADH, the further disposal of these electrons and the concomitant phosphorylations involve a common pathway for the oxidation of NADH, which is catalyzed by a complex of proteins on the matrix-facing surface of the mitochondrial inner membrane. The electron-transferring components of the complex are collectively known as NADH dehydrogenase; the complex uses ubiquinone as the acceptor for the electrons removed from NADH.

The route for handling the hydrogen atoms and associated electrons obtained from substrates such as L-malate now looks like this:

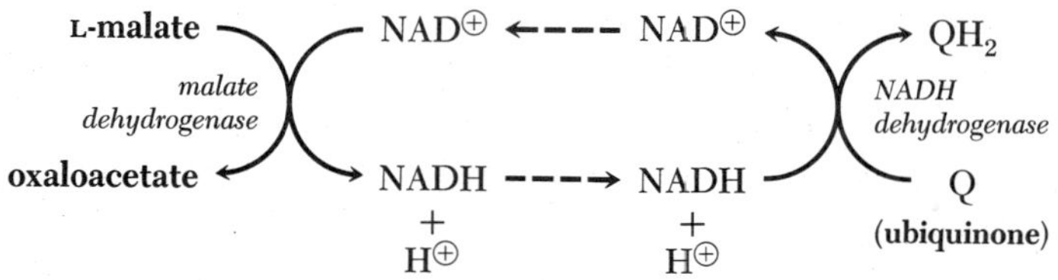

We can state this overall process in a shorthand way by simply indicating the progressive reductions with arrows:

$$\text{malate} \longrightarrow \text{NAD} \longrightarrow \text{ubiquinone}$$

meaning that hydrogen atoms from malate are used to reduce NAD, and then are removed from the resultant NADH to reduce ubiquinone.

The overall reaction of the NADH dehydrogenase is simple enough, but the enzyme is really a complex containing several components. The study of this enzyme and the other components of the electron transport chain is a formidable problem that has challenged some of the most able experimentalists for decades. (It has also produced some of the most confusing literature in all of biochemistry; progress has been painfully slow, and yet it is documented by a huge volume of papers.) The problem is that the components of the chain are also components of the inner membrane. In order to study them individually, the membrane must be destroyed. There is always the danger that the pieces of the membrane one isolates are artifacts—chance aggregations of compounds that aren't physically associated in the intact membrane. There is also the danger that the fragmentation has caused the loss of some key intermediate or critical architectural feature so that the experimentally determined path of electron transfer is quite different from the biological path. Furthermore, the restoration of biological activity frequently requires careful reconstruction of an association between lipid and protein.

However, there are some important certainties about NADH dehydrogenase that deserve attention. One is that the catalytic protein of the complex contains **riboflavin 5′-phosphate** as a coenzyme. The complex also contains **non-heme iron** atoms. Some are bound to the flavoprotein, which is therefore a ferreflavoprotein, but more are present in a separate ferreprotein.

At least some of the iron atoms are involved in the transfer of electrons, so the action of NADH dehydrogenase probably involves at least three oxidation-reduction steps:

$$\text{NADH} \longrightarrow \text{riboflavin 5'-phosphate} \longrightarrow \text{non-heme iron} \longrightarrow \text{ubiquinone}$$

but it is not possible to describe the exact nature of the steps.

Other Flavoprotein Dehydrogenases. There are other flavoprotein dehydrogenases on the matrix surface of the inner mitochondrial membrane that directly remove hydrogen atoms from fuel metabolites and transfer them to ubiquinone. Many of the enzymes, but not all, are specific for saturated acetyl compounds, which are oxidized to the corresponding unsaturated derivatives:

$$\underset{\textbf{acyl derivative}}{R{-}CH_2{-}CH_2{-}\overset{\overset{\displaystyle O}{\|}}{C}{-}X} + \underset{\textbf{ubiquinone}}{Q} \xrightarrow[\ ]{\textit{(flavoprotein) dehydrogenase}} \underset{\textbf{enoyl derivative}}{R{-}CH{=}CH{-}\overset{\overset{\displaystyle O}{\|}}{C}{-}X} + \underset{\textbf{ubiquinol}}{QH_2}$$

Why aren't the electrons transferred from these substrates to NAD in the way we described for malate dehydrogenase, since the overall reaction is an oxidation by ubiquinone in either case? The explanation is simple. We shall see that the transfer of electrons to ubiquinone *via* NADH is coupled to the generation of ATP from ADP and P_i. The oxidation of some substrates by ubiquinone is not sufficiently exergonic to support the generation of ATP. Therefore, the dehydrogenases attacking these substrates have been constructed to use the more powerful flavin oxidants with direct transfer of electrons to ubiquinone, thereby bypassing the endergonic phosphorylation step that accompanies transfer of electrons to ubiquinone *via* NADH.

The essential point is that electrons from substrates are used to reduce ubiquinone by one of two kinds of routes. In one of these, the substrates utilize NAD, and the transfer of electrons from the resultant NADH to ubiquinone in the inner mitochondrial membrane results in the generation of one molecule of ATP per pair of electrons transferred. The other kind of route involves a direct transfer by a ferreflavoprotein enzyme complex from the substrate to ubiquinone without the involvement of NAD or the generation of ATP. Reduced ubiquinone (**ubiquinol,** QH_2) produced by either route is re-oxidized in the same way.

Oxidation of QH_2 by Cytochromes. Electrons are removed from ubiquinol and transferred to molecular oxygen by the sequential reduction and oxidation of iron atoms in a series of hemoproteins, the cytochromes.

Why should there be several cytochromes, which differ in the nature of the peptide chains and of the hemin prosthetic group? Once again, it is to provide a series of increasingly more powerful oxidizing agents so that the flow of electrons can be broken into two sequences, each of which is accompanied by the formation of ATP from ADP and P_i. The various cytochromes are designated by letters.* The **cytochromes b** have the same iron-protoporphyrin IX complex found in hemoglobin, and there are no covalent bonds to the peptide chains. The **cytochromes c** also have the same prosthetic group, except that the vinyl side chains of the porphyrin are added to cysteinyl side chains of the accompanying peptide, creating covalent **thioether** bonds between the porphyrin and the peptide chain. The **cytochromes a** contain iron-porphyrins with a formyl group (—CH=O) in the side chains.

There can be several different proteins in each class of cytochromes, depending upon the nature of the peptide chains and any other associated materials. Thus we have **cytochrome c,** a quite small protein with a molecular weight near 13,400, and **cytochrome c_1,** with a molecular weight near 60,000 per hemin group. The hemin group of cytochrome c is in a deep crevice in the peptide, with the coordinating positions of the iron atom filled by histidyl and methionyl side chains (Fig. 11–6). The exact conformation of the other cytochromes is not known.

It has therefore been possible to evolve cytochromes that differ in oxidation-reduction potential, both because of the nature of the prosthetic group, which creates broad differences, and because of the nature of the peptide surrounding the prosthetic group, which changes both the potential and the specificity toward other reactants.

The general flow of electrons through the cytochromes is believed to be as follows:

$$QH_2 \longrightarrow \text{cytochrome b} \longrightarrow \text{non-heme iron} \xrightarrow{\star} \text{cytochrome } c_1 \longrightarrow$$

$$\text{cytochrome c} \longrightarrow \text{cytochrome a} \longrightarrow \text{cytochrome } a_3 \xrightarrow[\text{site III}]{\star} O_2$$

The electron transfers that are believed to be associated with the generation of ATP are indicated by stars in the above scheme, but this localization is particularly uncertain at site III, because the terminal cytochromes a and a_3 are bound in a complex, often called cytochrome oxidase, that has been particularly difficult to study.

---

*These designations were made in the days when the cytochromes were mainly known as changing absorption bands in the spectrum of light passed through working insect muscles. The unknown compound responsible for the absorption of the longest wavelengths was called cytochrome a, that corresponding to the next longest cytochrome b, and so on. Unfortunately, the order of wavelength does not correspond to the physiological sequence in which they function.

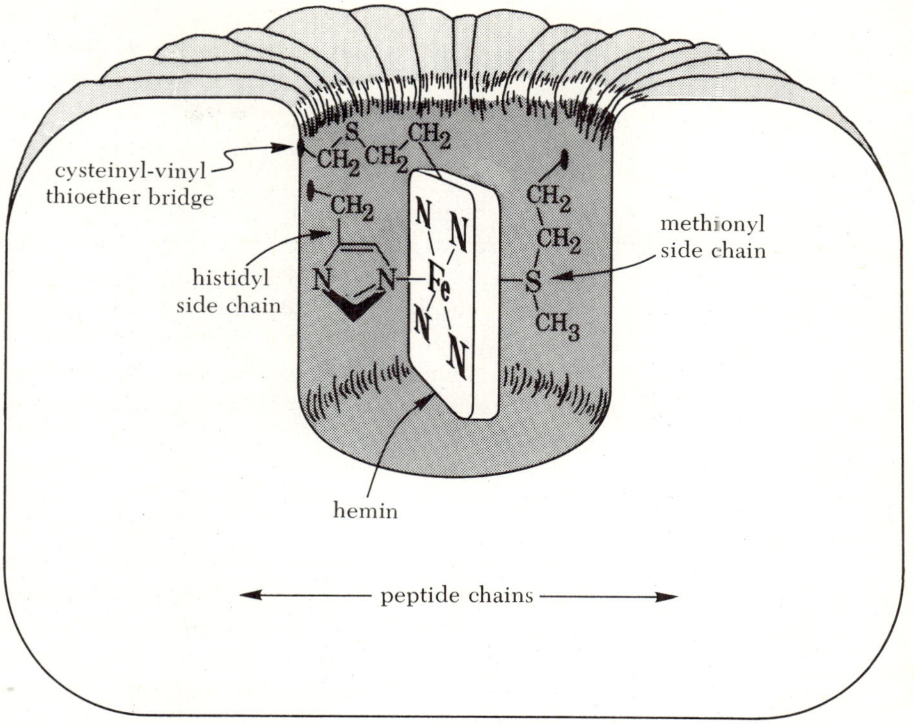

Figure 11-6 Idealized structure of cytochrome c. The peptide chains fold around a hemin molecule, so as to fill the two remaining coordinating positions on the iron of the hemin with the sulfur atom of a methionine residue and a nitrogen atom in a histidyl side chain. The hemin is also covalently bound to the peptides through the formation of a thioether bridge by condensation of cysteinyl sulfhydryl groups with the vinyl side chains of the hemin. Only one of these bridges is shown; the other lies in front of the histidyl side chain.

Actions of Cytochromes. We noted that the cytochromes transfer electrons by the reduction and oxidation of the iron atoms in the associated hemin groups. For example, the initial reaction is something like this:

$$QH_2 + 2\,(Fe^{3+}\text{-porphyrin-protein}_b) \longrightarrow Q + 2\,H^+ + 2\,(Fe^{2+}\text{-porphyrin-protein}_b)$$

in which we are indicating the oxidation of ubiquinol by two hemin groups on cytochrome b, with the resultant reduction of these groups to the heme form in which the associated iron is in the ferrous state.

The next reaction, neglecting the probable participation of non-heme iron, involves the regeneration of the oxidized form of cytochrome b by the transfer of electrons to cytochrome c_1:

$$2\,(Fe^{2+}\text{-porphyrin-protein}_b) + 2\,(Fe^{3+}\text{-porphyrin-protein}_{c_1}) \longrightarrow 2\,(Fe^{3+}\text{-porphyrin-protein}_b) + 2\,(Fe^{2+}\text{-porphyrin-protein}_{c_1})$$

This kind of transfer is repeated on through various cytochromes until the electrons finally reach oxygen.

The Reduction of Oxygen. Each hemin group can only carry one electron at a time, but it requires four electrons to reduce a molecule of oxygen. (Reactions with oxygen are often balanced in a formal way by indicating $\frac{1}{2}\,O_2$, but the element is actually presented as two atoms at a time.) It is still not known how the four electrons are lumped together. The cytochrome oxidase contains one cupric ion for each hemin a, and the copper apparently also participates in the electron transfer by alternating from the cuprous to the cupric state. A complex of cytochromes a and a_3, each with its associated cupric ion, would therefore be able to carry four electrons at one time, but it is not known how they are passed to oxygen. It is unlikely that they are all handled at once, since one molecule of ATP is generated for each pair of electrons transferred and there apparently is only one site at which this is done. We can indicate only the overall reaction from cytochrome c:

$$4\,(Fe^{2+}\text{-porphyrin-protein}_c) + 4\,H^+ + O_2 \longrightarrow 4\,(Fe^{3+}\text{-porphyrin-protein}_c) + 2\,H_2O$$

The requirement of copper for the proper function of the cytochrome oxidase is sufficient in itself to make a supply of the metal absolutely necessary for the survival of most animals and higher plants, and it is also required for the action of other oxidative enzymes. (Copper deficiency can occur in plants growing on deficient soils and in herbivores grazing on these plants, but it is rare in carnivores. An adult human has only two millimoles in his entire body, and it requires no especial precautions to maintain this store in an otherwise approximately normal person.)

The Complete Scheme

The complete pathway for electron transport, according to current information, is laid out in Figure 11–7. As we have seen, the apparent complexity stems only from the necessity of transferring electrons from substrates to oxygen through many steps of smaller chemical potential differences, rather than in one grand burst, so as to conserve the maximum amount of free energy in the form of ATP. Now let us consider how the ATP is created.

THE PHOSPHORYLATIONS

According to the information summarized in Figure 11–7, the generation of ATP from ADP and P_i occurs in association with three electron transfers in the inner membranes of the mitochondria. The passage of a pair of electrons through all three steps causes the generation of three molecules of ATP, and this is the result when electrons from substrates are brought to the inner membrane in the form of NADH. In other words, the P:O ratio is typically 3.0 for mitochondrial oxidations, such as the oxidation of hydroxyl compounds, in which NAD is involved:

$$\text{CH—OH group} + \tfrac{1}{2}\,O_2 + 3\,(ADP^{3-} + P_i^{2-} + H^+) \longrightarrow \text{C=O group} + H_2O + 3\,ATP^{4-}$$

However, the P:O ratio for the mitochondrial oxidation of such things as ethylene groups is only 2.0 because electrons are removed from these groups by ferreflavoprotein dehydrogenases on the inner mitochondrial membrane that transfer the electrons directly to ubiquinone without passage through the first phosphorylation site:

$$CH_2\text{—}CH_2\ \text{group} + \tfrac{1}{2}\,O_2 + 2\,(ATP^{3-} + 2\,P_i^{2-} + H^+) \longrightarrow \text{CH=CH group} + H_2O + 2\,ATP^{4-}$$

In sum, there are three discrete phosphorylation sites on the inner membrane, one of which is involved only in the oxidation of NADH, with the other two involved in the transfer of electrons from all substrates, including NADH.

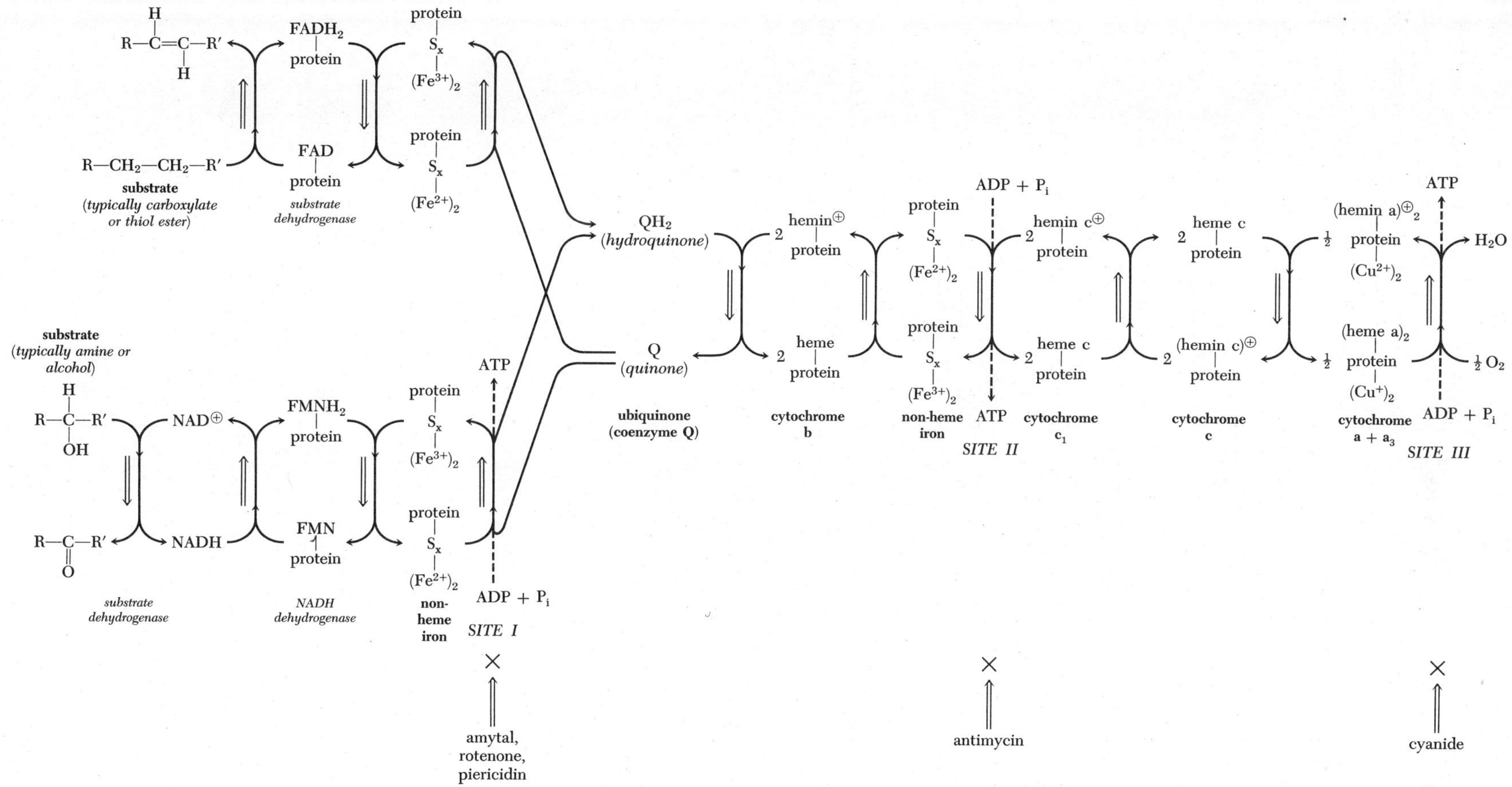

Figure 11-7 The complete electron transport chain. Electrons from substrates of high chemical potential (*bottom left*) pass through one more phosphorylation site on their way to oxygen than do electrons from substrates of lower chemical potential (*top left*). The sites of phosphorylation are those postulated to be most consistent with present experimental data according to the chemical coupling hypothesis.

Mechanism of Phosphorylation

The difficulties of working with the inner membrane are such that we still don't know the mechanism by which the phosphorylations occur, despite hundreds of man-years of work. The chemical potential dissipated by the electron transfers must somehow be "captured" if it is to force the formation of ATP. There is no doubt that the transfers create some sort of high-energy state within the inner membrane. This is so because the electron transfers are known to be capable of driving other energy-requiring events, such as the movement of ions across the inner membrane against a concentration gradient, in place of the formation of ATP. These same events can also be driven experimentally by adding ATP, and in some cases the creation of an ionic concentration gradient has also been shown to result in the formation of ATP. All of this is most readily explained by imagining an undefined high-energy condition within the membrane that is in equilibrium with the oxidized and reduced forms of an electron carrier, with ionic concentration gradients across the membrane, and with ATP and ADP + P_i (Fig. 11–8).

This picture conveys most of the information we shall need to understand metabolism; the electron transfers serve to maintain the adenine nucleotides in the form of ATP, but a part of the resultant free energy may be diverted to maintain concentration gradients and the like. The diversion may occur directly, from the high-energy state without the formation of ATP, or may be at the expense of previously formed ATP. In any event, the bulk of the chemical potential of the reduced electron carriers is utilized for the generation of ATP.

The High-Energy State. Even if we do have most of the information necessary for further reasoning, it is unsatisfactory to have blind faith in a mystical high-energy state. Biochemistry is supposed to be on a sounder basis than parapsychology. There are two main notions on the way this state is created. One is the chemical-coupling hypothesis, the other the chemiosmotic hypothesis.

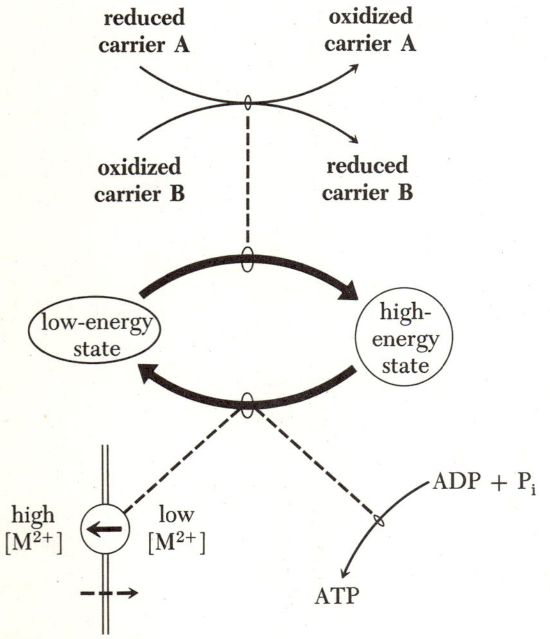

Figure 11–8 The utilization of energy obtained from an oxidation-reduction reaction hinges upon the reaction somehow creating a high-energy state. This state may represent a change in conformation or association of proteins, a change in concentration across membranes, or the formation of new chemical intermediates. Whatever it may be, it is utilized in a variety of ways, and these include driving ion pumps so as to move the ions against concentration gradients, and the phosphorylation of ADP to form ATP.

CHEMICAL COUPLING. According to the chemical-coupling hypothesis, the electron transfers involve the formation of a temporary intermediate with the electron donor:

$$AH_2 + B + I \longrightarrow A\text{—}I + BH_2$$

in which AH_2 is the reduced electron carrier, and B is the oxidized carrier that reacts with it. This intermediate is considered to have a high chemical potential, and to be the precursor of another high-energy intermediate:

$$A\text{—}I + X \longrightarrow A + X\text{—}I$$

This high-energy intermediate is believed to be the form that can drive ion transfers, or support the phosphorylation of ADP:

$$X\text{—}I + P_i \longrightarrow X\text{—}P + I$$
$$X\text{—}P + ADP \longrightarrow ATP + X$$

CHEMIOSMOSIS. According to the chemiosmotic hypothesis, the electron transfers involve the creation of a proton gradient across the inner membrane:

$$A{:} + 2\,H^+(\text{inside}) + B \longrightarrow A + 2\,H^+(\text{outside}) + B{:}$$

The proton gradient represents not only a concentration gradient, but also an electrical potential across the membrane, and according to this hypothesis the sum of these two forces is sufficient to support the formation of high-energy phosphate. The necessary transduction of energy is postulated to involve the use of the high proton concentration to force hypothetical intermediates into their non-ionized, acidic forms, which combine to create the high-energy intermediate:

$$X^- + IO^- + 2\,H^+ \longrightarrow XH + IOH \text{ (on outer surface of membrane)}$$
$$XH + IOH \longrightarrow X\text{—}I + H_2O$$

This removes protons from the region of high concentration, and the X—I then moves to the inner surface of the membrane, where it is utilized to create ATP and at the same time releases protons into the low-concentration region of the matrix:

$$X\text{—}I + P_i + ADP^{3-} \longrightarrow X^- + IO^- + 2\,H^+ + ATP^{4-}$$

According to this scheme, the phosphorylation of ADP therefore relieves the proton gradients created by electron transfers.

Each of these hypotheses has advantages and disadvantages. The chemical-coupling notion with its different sites of phosphorylation is more consistent with our knowledge of the nature of the intermediate carriers of electrons and the order in which they react, and with the known existence of more than one kind of phosphorylating enzyme. The chemiosmotic hypothesis is more consistent with the vectorial nature of the inner membrane, that is, with the fact that the components of the inner membrane, including at least some of the electron carriers and the phosphorylation sites, are unevenly distributed across the membrane. The arguments are not conclusive and we shall have to wait for the true picture.

The Regulation of Oxygen Consumption

Most of the oxygen consumed by organisms is used as the terminal substrate for the processes of oxidative phosphorylation we have been discussing. In other words, oxygen consumption is coupled to phosphorylation. To the extent that this is true, it follows that oxygen cannot be consumed unless there is a supply of ADP and of P_i to be combined into ATP. No phosphorylation, no oxidation in coupled systems.

It further follows that the rate of oxidation of substrates will automatically adjust so as to keep pace with the demand for ATP. When ATP is utilized to drive endergonic processes such as muscular contraction or the synthesis of cellular constituents, it is cleaved with the eventual formation of ADP and P_i. An elevation in the concentration of ADP and P_i causes a more rapid depletion of the high-energy state in the inner membrane, no matter what its nature, so as to create more ATP. The depletion of the high-energy state permits a more rapid transfer of electrons so as to regenerate the high-energy state. The more rapid transfer of electrons results in a more rapid oxidation of fuel metabolites and more rapid oxygen consumption. Therefore, the oxidation of fuels is efficiently matched to the requirements for driving endergonic processes, so long as oxidation is tightly coupled to phosphorylation. The coupling is indeed tight in most aerobic cells under most circumstances, and we might expect this, since a more efficient utilization of fuel ought to convey a great evolutionary advantage. The only exception we might expect is the utilization of oxygen for synthetic reactions, which is usually small.

ATP used outside the mitochondria is also regenerated by oxidative phosphorylation, because the inner mitochondrial membrane has an ADP-ATP translocase that exchanges these nucleotides across the membrane. [The translocase is an example of an antiport (p. 85).] Utilization of ATP outside the mitochondria will cause a fall in its extramitochondrial concentration, and a rise in the concentration of ADP. The result will be an increased rate of movement of ADP into the mitochondria, and ATP out. In other words, utilization of ATP will cause a rise in the concentration of intramitochondrial ADP, regardless of the site of the utilization.

INHIBITORS

Since oxidative phosphorylation is so vital to most aerobic organisms, we might expect that anything interfering with the process will be lethal, and this is so. We die from suffocation because the lack of oxygen prevents the electron transfers necessary for the formation of ATP, and it is the fall in the concentration of ATP that is directly responsible for the failure of cell function. (Organisms that live in the absence of oxygen do so because they have other means of generating ATP.) Any compound affecting any part of the oxidative phosphorylation mechanism has the same metabolic consequences as does suffocation. We would expect such compounds to be dangerously toxic if they can penetrate the mitochondria of living organisms.

Inhibitors of Electron Transfer. The Supreme Court of the United States has recently outlawed one of the practical applications of an inhibitor of mitochondrial electron transfer. The **cyanide** ion coordinates readily with many metallic ions, including the iron atom of heme groups, but it also binds well with copper ions in the cytochrome $a + a_3$ complex, thereby preventing transfer of electrons to oxygen. The small ion diffuses readily and rapidly forms complexes, so a lethal dose acts within a few minutes. This property was formerly used to kill selected felons in some states, and is still used to eliminate rats from ships, moles in lawns, and the like. (The lethal dose of cyanides is of the order of tenths of grams, but the compounds still deserve great respect because of the rapidity of action and the volatility of HCN.)

There are other useful inhibitors of particular electron transfers. For, example, the insecticide **rotenone** and the **barbiturate** sedatives block electron transfer from NADH to ubiquinone.

Many microorganisms, especially fungi, have found it practical to produce antibiotics as protective agents, and in many cases these compounds are lethal to competing organisms because they block some part of the oxidative phosphorylation mechanism. An example is **antimycin A,** which inhibits transfer of electrons from cytochrome b to cytochrome c.

Inhibitors of Phosphorylation. Inhibitors are also known that affect the phosphorylation process. **2,4-Dinitrophenol** can penetrate the hydrophobic regions of the inner membrane in sufficient concentrations to act as a catalyst that causes the spontaneous decomposition of the high-energy intermediate. Since ATP and the electron carriers are both equilibrated with the high-energy intermediate, the destruction of the intermediate by dinitrophenol causes these compounds to react in a direction that forms more intermediate. In other words, ATP will be broken down to ADP and P_i by a reversal of the process by which it is formed, and the electron transfer is accelerated in an attempt to replace the high-energy intermediate. The resultant exorbitant consumption of oxygen is said to result from an **uncoupling** of oxidation and phosphorylation. Some antibiotics act on the phosphorylation mechanism. For example, **oligomycin** inhibits the generation of high-energy phosphate at the expense of the high-energy intermediate.

FURTHER READING

F. M. Harold, Conservation and transformation of energy by bacterial membranes, Bacter. Rev., 36:172 (1972). Despite the title, this well-written review also deals with mitochondria. Much is directed at the professional, but the essential lucidity of this advocate of the chemiosmotic hypothesis shines through in several places.

E. Racker, The two faces of the inner mitochondrial membrane, Essays in Biochemistry, 6:1 (1970). Known for his rabbinical style of writing, this adept in-fighter in biochemical polemics sometimes entraps the unwary with an illusion of even-handed consideration, but it is possible to learn a lot from him.

E. C. Slater, The coupling between energy-yielding and energy-utilizing reactions in mitochondria, Quart. Rev. Biophysics, 4:35 (1971). An intransigent advocate of chemical coupling makes some important points. Slater has the disconcerting habit of being frequently right.

D. E. Green, ed., The mechanism of energy transduction in biological systems, Ann. N.Y. Acad. Sci., vol. 227 (1974). Account of long-overdue discussions of current problems by advocates of various theories. Professional-level articles.

QUESTIONS

1. Mitochondria oxidize compound A to compound B by removing two hydrogen atoms from it. The oxidation is not inhibited by rotenone, but it is inhibited by antimycin A, cyanide, and oligomycin. Without any more information, predict:
   (a) the route by which electrons are transferred from the compound to O_2, and
   (b) the number of molecules of ATP generated per atom of oxygen consumed; explain how you arrived at the conclusions.

2. Explain how the oxygen consumption of a cell may be increased by the formation of either AMP or GDP, either outside or inside the mitochondria.
3. A deficiency of copper in a cell might cause an impairment of oxidative phosphorylation. Why?
4. A deficiency of iron in a cell might cause multiple impairments of oxidative phosphorylation. What sites might be affected?
5. Deficiencies of nicotinamide and riboflavin cause generalized symptoms in animals. However, it is conceivable that a deficiency of riboflavin would impair the oxidation of more substrates in mitochondria than would a deficiency of nicotinamide. Why?
6. Which of the following experimental observations are most consistent with the chemiosmotic hypothesis of oxidative phosphorylation, and which with the chemical coupling hypothesis?
   (a) There is a difference in H^+ concentration between the inside and outside of mitochondria.
   (b) The apparent equilibrium position for the transfer of electrons to cytochrome b shifts drastically when ATP accumulates.
   (c) A coupling of oxidation and phosphorylation has been observed only in particles of the mitochondrial membrane that spontaneously form closed vesicles (small membrane "bubbles").

CHAPTER 12

THE CITRIC ACID CYCLE

THE CONCEPTS

Since most of the ATP is generated by oxidative phosphorylation in aerobic organisms, the processes of fuel combustion must be carried out in such a way that electrons may be fed, one pair at a time, into the membranes carrying out the phosphorylation. This is done by converting nearly all of the fuels to acetyl groups, which are then oxidized to CO_2 and H_2O by a set of reactions known as the citric acid cycle. The citric acid cycle occurs within the mitochondria of eukaryotic cells, and the electrons removed from acetyl groups are directly available for oxidative phosphorylation. Approximately two-thirds of the ATP used by aerobic organisms is generated as a result of the oxidation of acetyl groups in the citric acid cycle.

Coenzyme A and Thiol Esters. **The citric acid cycle involves coenzyme A as a carrier of acyl groups. This coenzyme contains a sulfhydryl group to which acyl groups are attached; thus, it is often abbreviated as CoA-SH. The resultant thiol esters represent high-energy bonds, with free energies of hydrolysis comparable to those of pyrophosphates. The initial metabolism of the various fuels creates acetyl groups in the form of acetyl coenzyme A, which is the initial substrate for the citric acid cycle.**

Reactions of the Citric Acid Cycle. **The formal stoichiometry for the oxidation of acetyl coenzyme A is:**

$$H_3C-\overset{\overset{\displaystyle O}{\|}}{C}-S-CoA + 2\,O_2 \longrightarrow 2\,CO_2 + CoA-SH + H_2O$$

The citric acid cycle is a device for accomplishing the four dehydrogenations by which electrons are removed for transfer to the four oxygen atoms, and the two decarboxylations by which the two molecules of CO_2 are created. The combination of these six events represents the total oxidation of the acetyl group.

Oxaloacetate as a Carrier. **The citric acid cycle hinges on the use of oxaloacetate as a carrier for the acetyl group as it goes through the sequence of reactions. A molecule of oxaloacetate is recovered at the end of the cycle for each molecule that enters, so the citric acid cycle neither consumes or produces oxaloacetate; only acetyl groups and oxygen disappear as a result of its action.**

Types of Reactions. **The citric acid cycle is largely constructed of variants on common types of biochemical reactions, including a main-line sequence and oxidative decarboxylations. The main-line sequence is the oxidation of a saturated carbonyl compound, followed by hydration of the unsaturated product, and further oxidation of the resultant alcohol to a ketone:**

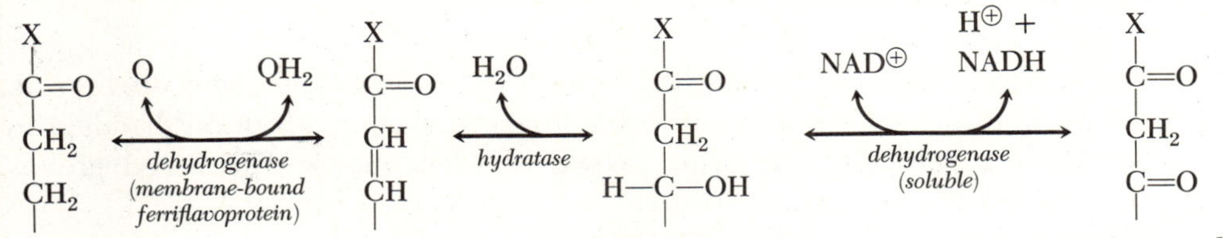

acyl — enoyl — 3-hydroxy acyl — 3-keto acyl

The first oxidation is carried out by a flavoprotein with direct passage of electrons to ubiquinone, and the second oxidation involves an NAD-coupled dehydrogenase.

The oxidative decarboxylations consist of the formation of a transient 3-ketocarboxylic acid, which easily loses CO_2, from the corresponding 3-hydroxy compound:

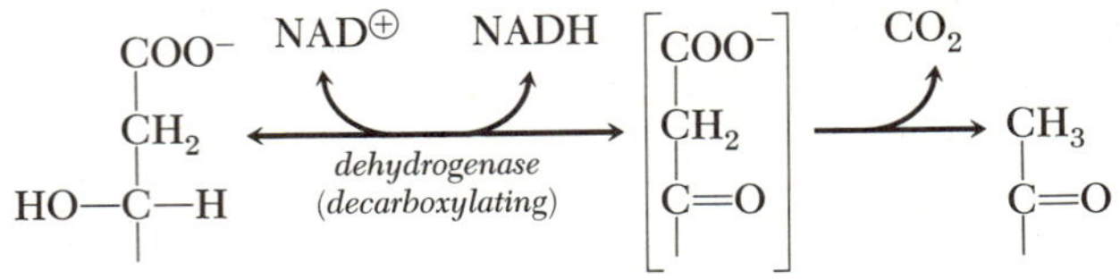

and of the oxidation of a 2-ketocarboxylate by an enzyme complex with the resultant formation of a coenzyme A ester and CO_2.

Arrangement of the Reactions. **The reactions of the cycle are as follows:**

(1) acetyl coenzyme A + oxaloacetate ⟶ citrate + CoA-SH. The loss of the thiol ester bond drives this reaction nearly to completion.
(2) citrate ⟶ isocitrate. A rearrangement to create an oxidizable alcohol group.
(3) isocitrate + NAD ⟶ α-ketoglutarate + CO_2 + NADH. An oxidation accompanied by a decarboxylation of what would be a 3-ketocarboxylic acid.
(4) α-ketoglutarate + NAD + CoA-SH ⟶ succinyl coenzyme A + CO_2 + NADH. Oxidative decarboxylation of a 2-ketocarboxylate is sufficiently exergonic to support formation of a product with a high-energy thiol ester bond.
(5) succinyl coenzyme A + GDP + P_i ⟶ succinate + GTP + CoA-SH. Capture of the energy of the thiol ester bond as a high-energy phosphate bond.
(6) succinate + Q ⟶ fumarate + QH_2. Oxidation of saturated carbon atoms with direct transfer of electrons by a flavoprotein to ubiquinone.
(7) fumarate + H_2O ⟶ L-malate. Hydration of a double bond to create an alcohol.
(8) L-malate + NAD ⟶ oxaloacetate + NADH. Oxidation of an alcohol to a ketone.

Yield of High-Energy Phosphate. **Three of the four pairs of electrons removed during oxidation of an acetyl group are transferred to NAD; oxidation of the resultant 3 NADH by O_2 results in the formation of $3 \times 3 = 9$ ATP. Oxidation of the ubiquinol created by direct transfer of a pair of electrons from succinate results in the formation of an additional 2 ATP. Finally, the molecule of GTP generated by cleavage of succinyl coenzyme A can be used to form an additional molecule of ATP. The total yield of ATP possible from the oxidation of one acetyl group is therefore twelve molecules. With four atoms of oxygen consumed, the P:O ratio for the citric acid cycle is 3.0.**

Regulation of the Cycle. **The principal regulation of the overall rate comes from the necessity of ADP for electron transfers. When ATP is consumed for endergonic processes, ADP is produced, and accelerates the oxidations of reduced coenzymes. The resultant increased supply of NAD and oxidized flavoproteins accelerates dehydrogenations of substrates in the citric acid cycle.**

However, internal regulations of the cycle are also necessary to preserve metabolic balance. Excessive consumption of acetyl coenzyme A to form citrate is prevented by inhibitions of citrate synthase by citrate itself, and by ATP or succinyl coenzyme A. ADP, a signal for increased energy demand, accelerates isocitrate dehydrogenase, but this enzyme is inhibited by NADH, which indicates an overloaded electron transfer system. Succinyl coenzyme A also inhibits α-ketoglutarate dehydrogenase, preventing its own accumulation when there is an inadequate supply of GDP for utilizing the high-energy bond. This inhibition is competitive with free coenzyme A, and therefore is also a safety device for maintaining a supply of the free coenzyme.

GENERAL DESCRIPTION

The combustion of fuels can be sketched very simply if we use only bold strokes (Fig. 12–1). Each kind of major fuel is converted to **acetyl** groups, which are handled by attachment to a particular coenzyme known as **coenzyme A.** The acetyl groups, regardless of source, can then be oxidized to CO_2 and H_2O.

Simple as this sketch is, it describes the major part of metabolic processes in tissues such as muscles and nerves, in which metabolism is mainly geared to the production of ATP for physical movement or for transmission of neural impulses. We shall see

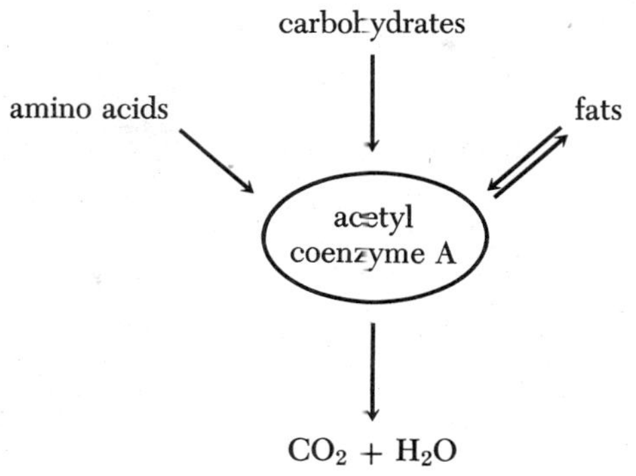

Figure 12–1 Acetyl coenzyme A is formed from carbohydrates, fats, and amino acids. Whatever the source, a large fraction of it is oxidized to CO_2 and H_2O, but any excess may be used to form fats for storage.

later that the oxidation of acetyl groups accounts for roughly two-thirds of the total oxygen consumption and ATP production in most animals.

The sequence of reactions by which acetyl groups are oxidized is known as the citric acid cycle. The reactions function as a unit to remove electrons from acetyl groups within mitochondria and to feed the electrons into the oxidative phosphorylation pathway, with the ultimate transfer to molecular oxygen. The prime purpose of the complete citric acid cycle is the complete oxidation of acetyl groups in a way that will cause the formation of ATP.

The citric acid cycle gets its name because it begins with the formation of **citrate,** the anionic form of citric acid. (The cycle is also known as the Krebs cycle, after Sir Hans A. Krebs, its discoverer, and as the tricarboxylic acid cycle.) Citrate has six carbon atoms, and it is formed by the condensation of the two-carbon acetyl group removed from acetyl coenzyme A with a four-carbon compound, **oxaloacetate** (Fig. 12–2). The sequence proceeds with an oxidation that causes the loss of one carbon atom as CO_2, leaving the five-carbon compound, α-ketoglutarate. A second carbon atom is then lost as CO_2 in another oxidation, and the four-carbon remainder is further oxidized until it is finally transformed into oxaloacetate, which replaces the oxaloacetate originally consumed and completes the cycle.

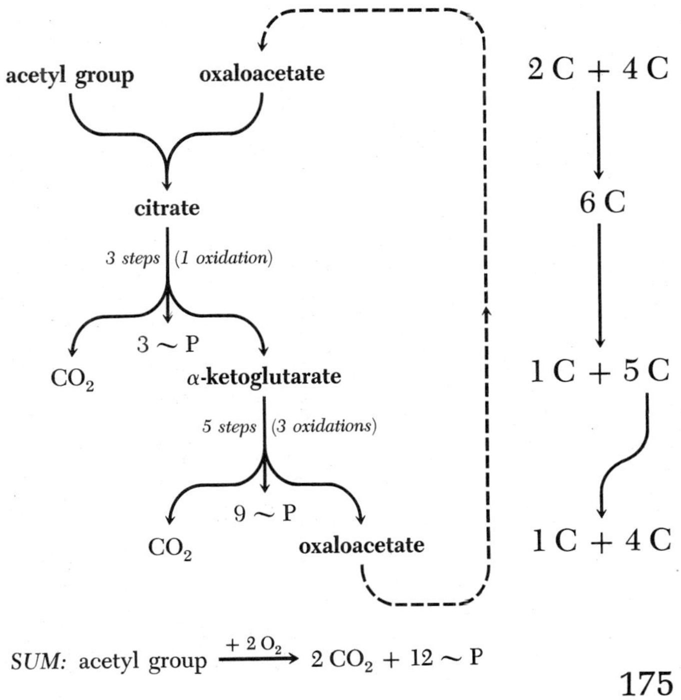

Figure 12–2 Outline of the citric acid cycle. A four-carbon compound, oxaloacetate, acts as a carrier for the two-carbon acetyl group that is oxidized in the cycle. The six-carbon product of their condensation, citrate, undergoes eight consecutive reactions in which two molecules of CO_2 are formed. The cycle ends with the formation of a new molecule of oxaloacetate to replace the original carrier molecule. Two molecules of O_2 disappear along with the acetyl group during the cycle, so the overall result is the same as the direct combustion of the acetyl group, except that the transfers of electrons to O_2 result in the formation of high-energy phosphate.

There are four oxidative steps in the cycle, and the dehydrogenases responsible for these steps catalyze the transfer of hydrogen atoms, including the associated electrons, to NAD or directly to ubiquinone. In either case, the electrons are used for oxidative phosphorylation, so there is a concomitant consumption of oxygen. The overall result of all of this, as we shall see, is the complete combustion of the acetyl group.

The function of the cycle depends upon close association of the enzymes catalyzing its constituent reactions with those catalyzing oxidative phosphorylation. In cells having mitochondria, the enzymes involved in the cycle are also found on the inner membrane or in the matrix. (Some believe that even the enzymes appearing to be in the matrix are really loosely attached to the inner membrane in intact mitochondria.)

COENZYME A

Acyl Thiol Esters. Before taking a closer look at the citric acid cycle, let us consider the nature of coenzyme A. We shall encounter this coenzyme repeatedly, because it is used as a carrier not only for the important acetyl groups, but for acyl groups in general. The way in which coenzyme A serves this purpose is very simple; the coenzyme contains a single sulfhydryl group, which is used to form thiol esters. We can indicate the functional part of the coenzyme by designating it as CoA-SH, so the formula for acetyl coenzyme A is given as:

$$CH_3-\overset{\overset{\displaystyle O}{\|}}{C}-S-COA$$

This handy way of abbreviating the structure properly emphasizes the acyl group being transported and its linkage as a thiol ester, but coenzyme A is actually quite complex, with the functional —SH group occurring at the end of a long chain which presumably permits the group to wave around over an enzyme surface (Fig. 12–3). The other end of the chain is attached to an adenine nucleotide, which provides groups for binding the coenzyme to the appropriate enzymes, including phosphate on both the 3′ and 5′ positions of adenosine.

Pantothenic Acid. The main feature of interest in coenzyme A, beyond the presence of the critical sulfhydryl group, is that it contains the vitamin, D-pantothenic acid. We have already noted that coenzymes frequently contain unusual structures (unusual in the sense that animals have been able to dispense with the ability to synthesize them, and they therefore must be supplied in the diet), but in the case of coenzyme A, the vitamin does not contain the reactive group of the coenzyme. It appears that the unusual branched chain structure of pantothenate acts primarily as a marker for those enzymes making the complete coenzyme from its components. In any event, animals lacking pantothenate die, and it is no consolation to know that some of the enzymes could have functioned with another thiol if it had been at hand. Fortunately, a natural deprivation of pantothenate is very rare because coenzyme A is present in all living cells, and therefore is in the natural food of all animals.

REACTIONS OF THE CITRIC ACID CYCLE

Let us now look at the individual reactions of the citric acid cycle in some detail, not only because of their importance, but also because each and every one is an example

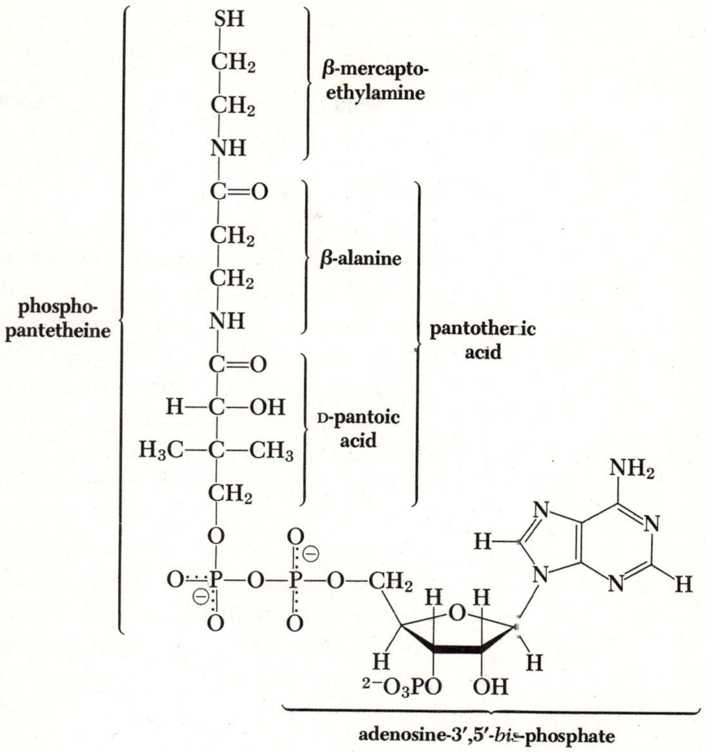

Figure 12-3 The structure of coenzyme A, and the names of some of its constituents.

of an important type of reaction that we shall repeatedly encounter, and gaining a good grasp now will save much later effort.

Formation of Citrate. The cycle begins with the condensation of acetyl coenzyme A and oxaloacetate to form citrate (Fig. 12–4), catalyzed by the enzyme, citrate synthase. As the figure shows, the reaction proceeds in two parts on the enzyme surface; the initial condensation results in the formation of citryl coenzyme A (the coenzyme A thiol ester of citric acid). The citryl coenzyme A is then hydrolyzed to release free citrate and coenzyme A into solution.

The formation of a carbon to carbon bond by the condensation of a carbonyl group with an activated methylene carbon is a common type of reaction in metabolism. These are familiar reactions to the organic chemist, and are variants of the classical **aldol condensation** (Fig. 12–5).

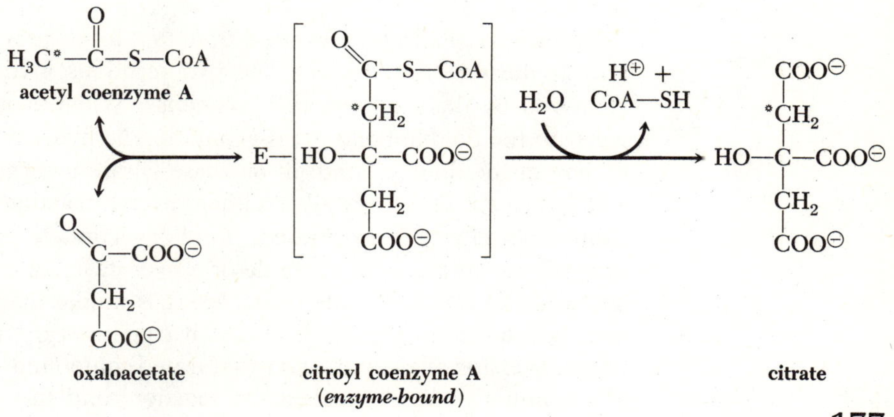

Figure 12-4 The citrate synthase reaction.

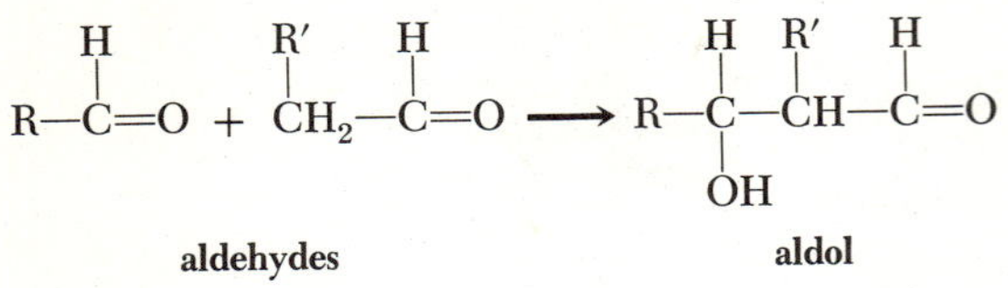

Figure 12-5 The aldol condensation, in which the methylene group of one aldehyde condenses with the carbonyl group of another to form a 3-hydroxy-aldehyde, is a familiar organic reaction. Similar condensations commonly occur in metabolism.

It so happens that free acetate can be made to condense with oxaloacetate, so what is the point of evolving a reaction that utilizes the coenzyme A ester, since it is destroyed before the reaction is over? The answer lies in the position of equilibrium of the reaction. Thiol esters such as acetyl coenzyme A represent "high-energy" compounds, and the hydrolysis of acetyl coenzyme A liberates as much free energy as does the hydrolysis of ATP under the same conditions.

We are therefore dealing here with another example of the coupling of an endergonic and an exergonic process. The condensation of acetate and oxaloacetate by themselves has an equilibrium position such that only relatively high concentrations of the starting materials will result in significant formation of citrate. However, by making acetyl coenzyme A the starting material, we add the highly exergonic hydrolysis of the coenzyme A ester to the reaction, and the sum of these two processes makes the formation of citrate an almost irreversible reaction, so much so that it can readily proceed even when the intramitochondrial concentration of oxaloacetate falls to an estimated 4 micromolar or lower.

Formation of α-Ketoglutarate

Citrate ⟶ Isocitrate. The metabolism of citrate begins by converting it into an alcohol that can be oxidized. The hydroxyl group of citrate is on a tertiary carbon, and could not be attacked without breaking a carbon bond, but rearrangement into the isomer, isocitrate, creates a secondary alcohol group that can be oxidized:

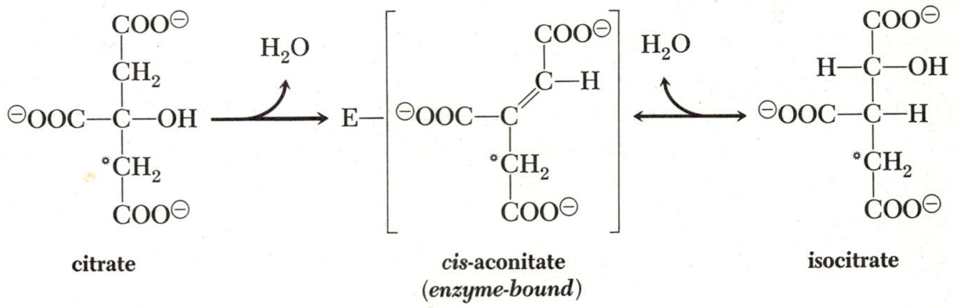

(The formula of citrate is inverted from that in the previous sketch to show the reacting end at the top. So it goes.) The two reactions involved in the rearrangement are catalyzed by the same enzyme, **aconitase.** When aconitase catalyzes the addition of water to the double bond of *cis*-aconitate, the hydroxyl group may be added to either carbon of the double bond: in one case citrate is formed, and in the other, isocitrate. The enzyme will also catalyze either reverse reaction, causing the removal of water from either citrate or isocitrate to form *cis*-aconitate as an intermediate bound on the enzyme. Aconitase is an example of a **hydratase,** an enzyme catalyzing the reversible hydration of double bonds; however, it is unlike many enzymes of this type, which usually require no cofactors, in that it contains Fe^{2+} for binding the substrates. The interconversion of alcohols and unsaturated compounds by addition or removal of water is a common type of biochemical reaction, and the standard free energy change is usually small enough so that the reaction can go in either direction to a biologically significant extent. In this case the equilibrium mixture contains about 91% citrate, 3% *cis*-aconitate, and 6% isocitrate, but the intramitochondrial concentration of citrate is greater than 1 millimolar, so the equilibrium concentration of isocitrate would be of the order of 0.1 mM, which is a reasonable level for metabolic intermediates.

Under ordinary circumstances, the reactions go through the sequence as given: citrate $\longrightarrow$ (aconitate) $\longrightarrow$ isocitrate. There is nothing peculiar about aconitase to cause this; it only catalyzes the attainment of equilibrium. The net flow of metabolites goes in one direction because citrate is constantly being formed by the irreversible citrate synthase reaction, and isocitrate is constantly being removed by the next reaction, in which isocitrate is oxidized.

Oxidative Decarboxylation of Isocitrate. The alcohol group of isocitrate is oxidized by NAD in a reaction catalyzed by an isocitrate dehydrogenase:

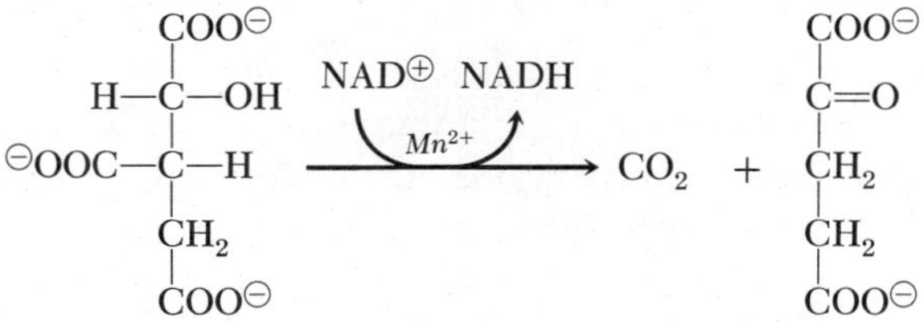

isocitrate **α-ketoglutarate**

This reaction results not only in the conversion of the alcohol to the corresponding ketone, but also in the loss of one of the carboxyl groups as CO_2, so that the remaining carbons are released as α-ketoglutarate. The reaction is therefore an example of an oxidative decarboxylation.

The enzyme we are discussing apparently catalyzes both the oxidation and the decarboxylation in a concerted way, but there are related enzymes that catalyze the two parts separately. When this happens, the initial oxidation of isocitrate by NAD causes the temporary formation of the corresponding ketone known as **oxalosuccinate** on the enzyme:

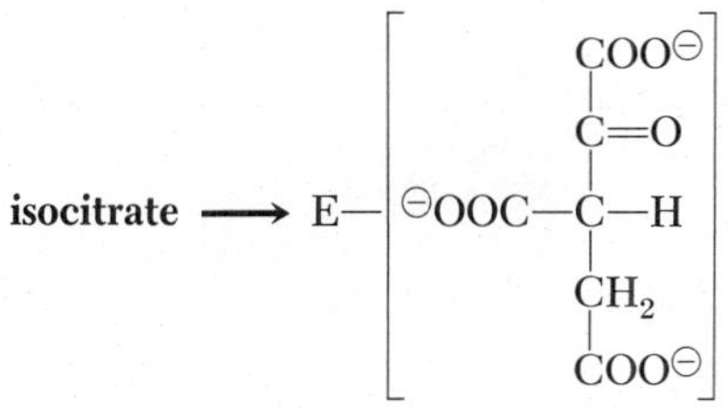

This is a straightforward alcohol dehydrogenase type of reaction, but notice that the carbonyl group of the intermediate oxalosuccinate is in the β-position relative to the middle carboxylate group. (Of course, it is also in the α-position relative to the top carboxylate group, but that is not relevant to our point.) Now, we know from organic chemistry that β-ketoacids are readily decarboxylated:

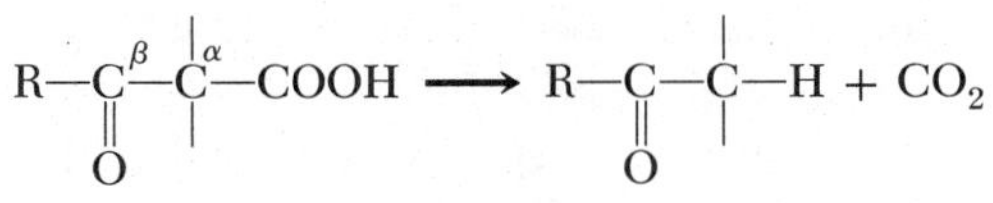

Therefore, we might expect the intermediate oxalosuccinate to readily lose CO_2, and it does. It is quite common, although not obligatory, for the enzymatic oxidation of a hydroxyl group to a carboxylate group to cause the simultaneous loss of CO_2. In the example at hand this not only occurs, but it does so without even a transitory appearance of the intermediate β-keto compound.

ROLE OF Mn^{2+}. Furthermore, the spontaneous decarboxylation of oxalosuccinate in the test tube is accelerated by the presence of metallic ions such as Mn^{2+}, because of the formation of a metal chelate that favors the necessary movement of electrons from the carboxylate group. Isocitrate dehydrogenase requires Mn^{2+} for activity like many enzymes that catalyze β-decarboxylations, and it is believed that the metal performs a similar function in these enzymatic decarboxylations. Enzymes catalyzing simple dehydrogenations without decarboxylation do not require metallic ions for activity.

Oxidative Decarboxylation of α-Ketoglutarate

The next reaction of the citric acid cycle is an oxidation of α-ketoglutarate by NAD in such a way that the first carboxyl group appears as CO_2. The resultant four-carbon succinyl group is transferred onto coenzyme A, thereby capturing part of the energy of the oxidation in the energy-rich thiol ester:

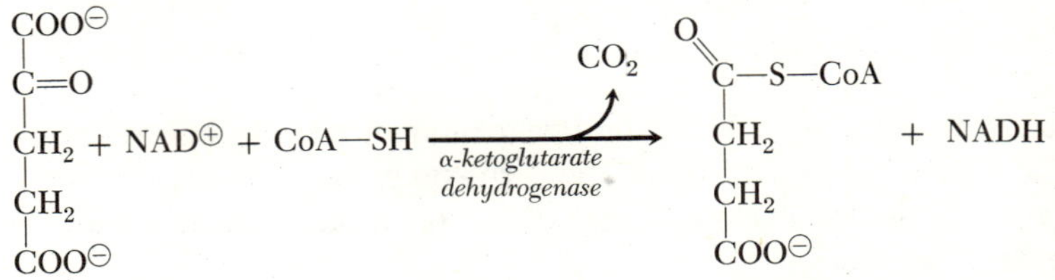

α-ketoglutarate **succinyl coenzyme A**

We see that there are at least three things going on here: decarboxylation, oxidation, and formation of the thiol ester, and all of this is too much to be accomplished by a single enzymatic reaction.

α-Ketoglutarate is an example of a 2-ketocarboxylate, and it is a convenient formalism to regard the oxidation of these compounds as the sum of two organic reactions. One is a simple decarboxylation to produce CO_2 and an aldehyde:

$$\mathrm{R{-}\overset{O}{\overset{\|}{C}}{-}COOH \longrightarrow R{-}\overset{O}{\overset{\|}{C}}{-}H + CO_2}$$

and the other is the oxidation of the aldehyde to form a carboxylate:

$$\mathrm{R{-}\overset{O}{\overset{\|}{C}}{-}H + H_2O + NAD^{\oplus} \longrightarrow R{-}COOH + NADH + H^{\oplus}}$$

These steps could in theory proceed independently, and do so in some microorganisms, but the two steps combined have a standard free negative energy change that is ample for the creation of a high-energy bond, so the reaction is modified to provide for the formation of the coenzyme A ester, rather than the free anion of the carboxylic acid product.

The formation of the high-energy thiol ester bond is quite independent of the concomitant formation of high-energy phosphate by mitochondrial electron transport; it serves to tap the extra free energy available from the oxidative decarboxylation of the 2-ketocarboxylate, which is substantially greater than the free energy released during the oxidation of alcohols. It is even greater than the free energy released during the oxidative decarboxylation of 3-hydroxy compounds such as isocitrate.

α-Ketoglutarate Dehydrogenase Complex. The catalysis of the sequence of reactions involves three separate proteins aggregated into a complex within the mitochondrial matrix (perhaps loosely bound to the inner membrane), and the entire complex constitutes α-ketoglutarate dehydrogenase. Complexes such as this are the next step in organization beyond a single protein. One protein may contain several peptide chains aggregated spontaneously into a stable molecule. Similarly, different proteins can be constructed so that they spontaneously associate in fixed proportions to form complexes. Each of these proteins in α-ketoglutarate dehydrogenase catalyzes a distinct step in the overall reaction, but the association into a single complex makes it possible to lock the three reactions together, because the intermediate forms of the substrate are not released into solution.

THE DECARBOXYLATING DEHYDROGENASE. The first step in the process, the decarboxylation of α-ketoglutarate without the release of the intermediate aldehyde, is accomplished through the use of the coenzyme, **thiamine pyrophosphate,** in the decarboxylating dehydrogenase component of the enzyme complex (Fig. 12–6). Thiamine is another of the compounds of unusual structure whose synthesis has been deleted in the evolution of mammals, and is therefore a vitamin.

The dehydrogenase component of the enzyme complex also catalyzes the transfer

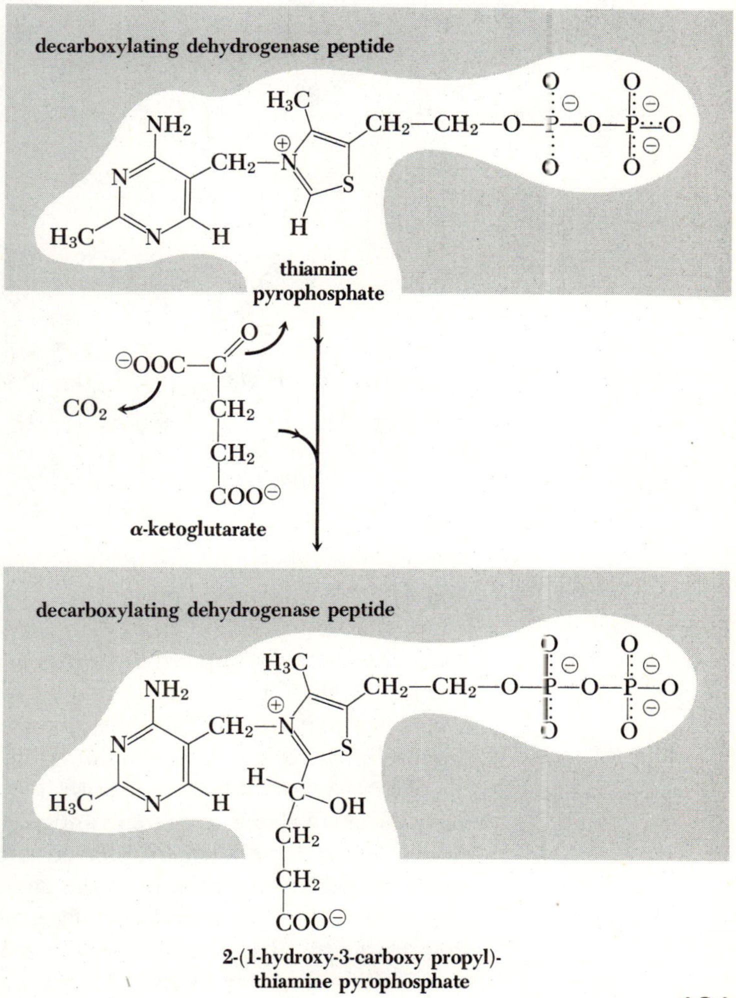

Figure 12–6 The decarboxylation of α-ketoglutarate by reaction with thiamine pyrophosphate that is attached to the dehydrogenase peptide.

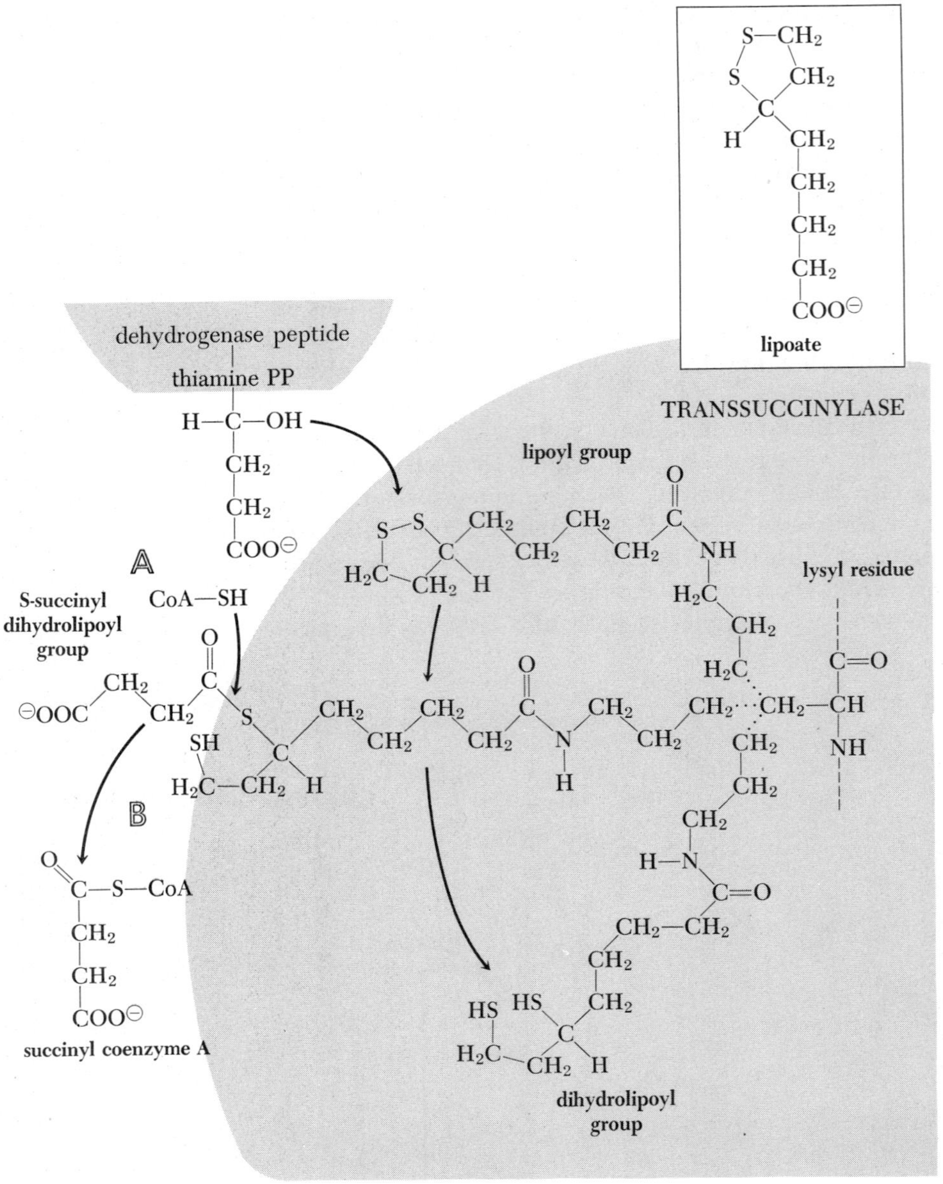

Figure 12–7 *A.* When a succinate semialdehyde group is transferred from thiamine pyrophosphate to a lipoyl group on transsuccinylase, it is oxidized to a succinyl group. The lipoyl group itself is the oxidizing agent. *B.* The succinyl group is then transferred to coenzyme A.

of the succinaldehydate group to the second protein of the complex **transsuccinylase** (Fig. 12–7A). The second protein has a coenzyme **lipoic acid,** which contains a disulfide bond, attached to one of its lysyl groups. The disulfide bond is cleaved to receive the succinaldehydate group, so it itself is acting as an oxidizing agent for the aldehyde. The result therefore is that succinaldehydate becomes succinate, and the lipoyl residue becomes a dihydrolipoyl residue, except the two products are combined as a succinyl dihydrolipoyl residue still remaining on the transsuccinylase peptide.

TRANSFER OF SUCCINYL GROUP TO COENZYME A. At this stage, the substrate has been decarboxylated, oxidized, and converted to a high-energy thiol ester, but the electrons that have been transferred and the thiol ester group are both still present on the dihydrolipoyl residue of the enzyme, rather than in utilizable form. The next step catalyzed by the transsuccinylase component is the transfer of the succinyl group from its dihydrolipoyl residue onto the sulfhydryl group of coenzyme A (Fig. 12–7B).

DIHYDROLIPOATE DEHYDROGENASE. The preceding steps complete the formation of the organic products, and the remaining problem is the disposal of the electrons, which are handled by the third component of the enzyme complex, **dihydrolipoate dehydrogenase.** Dihydrolipoate dehydrogenase is a flavoprotein that catalyzes the oxidation of dihydrolipoyl groups by NAD (Fig. 12–8). The two results are the final restoration of the enzyme to its original form, ready to react with more α-ketoglutarate, and the formation of NADH, which can be reoxidized by the NADH dehydrogenase of the inner mitochondrial membrane. It may seem that electrons are going backwards in being transferred through a flavin to NAD, when they will later be transferred from the resultant NADH to another flavin during oxidative phosphorylation. FAD is probably used because flavins are especially well suited to the single electron mechanisms indicated in Figure 12–8, but the nature of the overall reaction is such that it can support the formation of three more high-energy bonds; hence it is more efficient to transfer the electrons through NAD for disposal by the complete apparatus of oxidative phosphorylation.

The key structural feature making the enzyme complex possible evidently is the long side chain represented by the lipoyllysyl group, which can swing about on the surface of the transuccinylase protein and successively come in contact with the decarboxylase, coenzyme A, and the dihydrolipoate dehydrogenase (Fig. 12–9). The

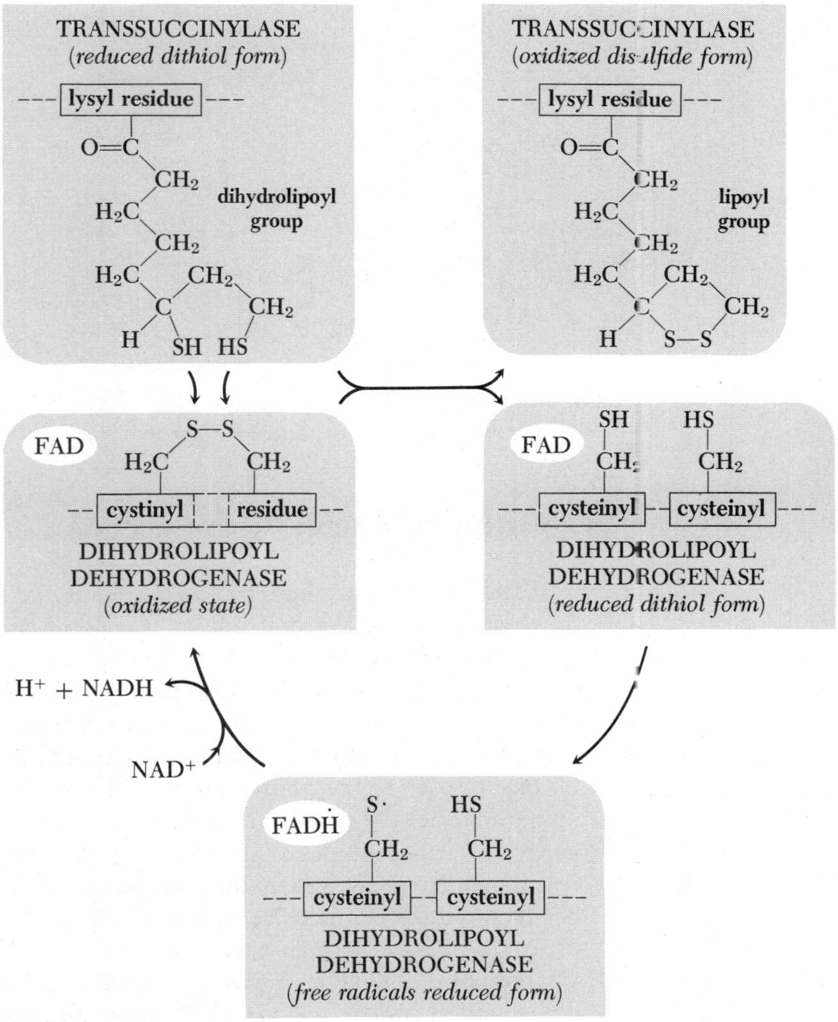

Figure 12–8 The final steps of the α-ketoglutarate dehydrogenase reaction involve the reconversion of the reduced lipoyl group to its oxidized form. The electrons are carried through both an FAD molecule and a disulfide group on the dihydrolipoyl dehydrogenase component of the enzyme complex. The final electron acceptor is NAD.

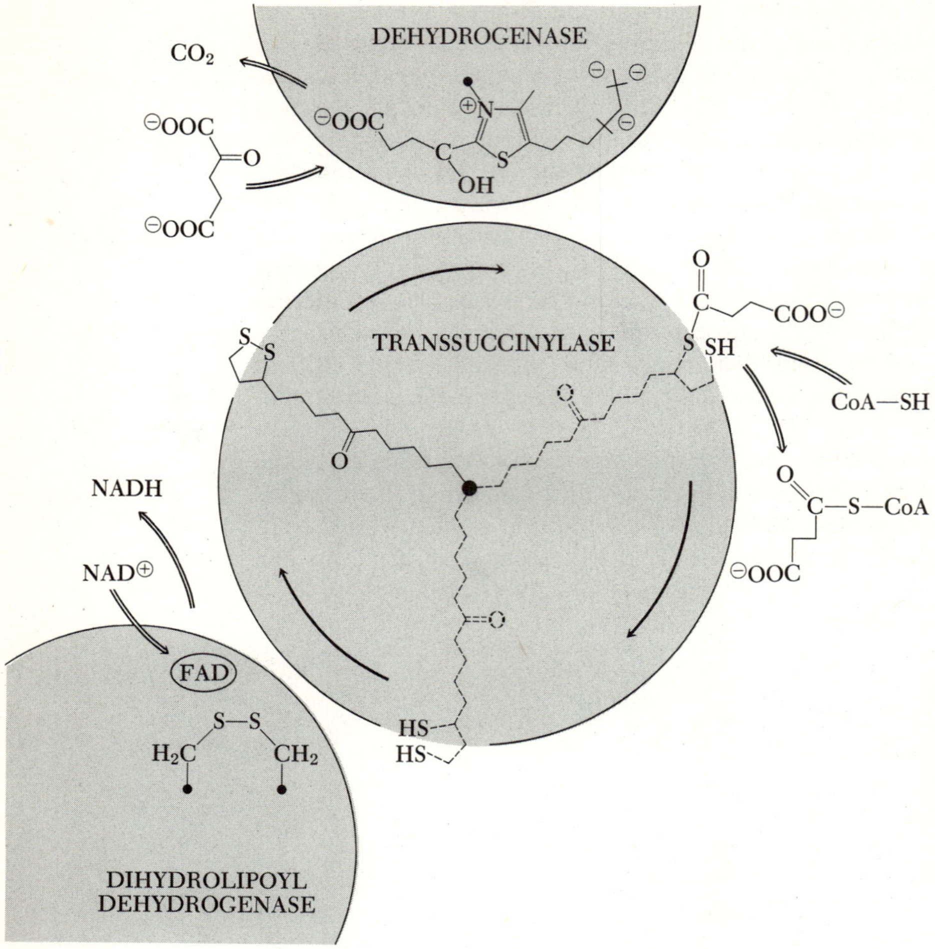

Figure 12-9 The α-ketoglutarate dehydrogenase reaction is believed to depend upon the wide area that can be covered by the long lipoyl-lysyl group (center) on the transsuccinylase peptides.

transuccinylase occupies the core of the complex, and the other components are distributed about it in an organized fashion.

Recovery of Energy from Succinyl Coenzyme A

The next step in the citric acid cycle is the recovery of the potential energy of the thiol ester bond as a high-energy phosphate (Fig. 12–10). Here we have an example of a **substrate-level phosphorylation,** in which a high-energy phosphate is created in a metabolite, rather than being created by electron flow on the mitochondrial membrane. The reaction involves the cleavage of succinyl coenzyme A by P_i on the enzyme surface, perhaps with the formation of an intermediate succinyl phosphate, followed by the transfer of the phosphate onto the imidazole side chain of a histidyl residue on the enzyme. The phosphate is then transferred onto guanosine diphosphate, creating guanosine triphosphate. Why GTP as a product, rather than ATP, which is just as feasible on energetic and mechanistic grounds? We shall see that the answer probably lies in the dual use of GTP as a signal for regulation of metabolism in addition to its use as part of the high-energy phosphate pool. In any event, we already noted in Chapter 10 that GTP and ADP are equilibrated to form GDP and ATP. In addition, mitochondria contain a **GTP:AMP phosphotransferase,** so the high-energy phosphate

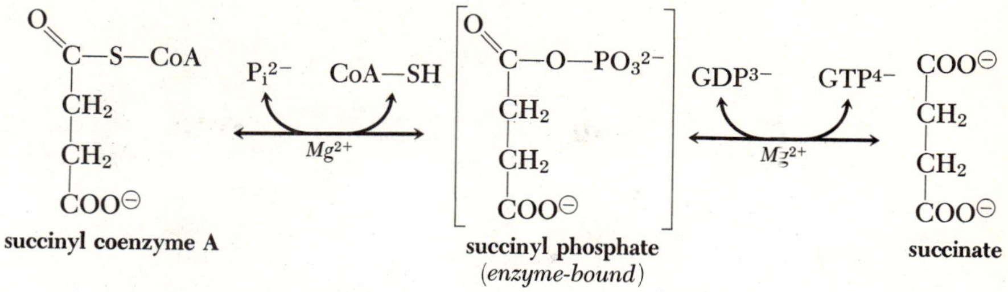

Figure 12-10 The reaction of succinyl CoA synthetase is believed to involve intermediate formation of succinyl phosphate.

created by the cleavage of the succinyl coenzyme A is fully available for all reactions in which ATP is utilized.

Synthetases. The enzyme is named as a synthetase to be consistent with the nomenclature of other enzymes of this type because the reaction is freely reversible, and synthetases are enzymes catalyzing the formation of compounds at the expense of high-energy phosphate. Succinyl coenzyme A synthetase is an example of an enzyme that requires Mg^{2+} for activity. Most enzymes catalyzing the transfer of phosphate groups require this ion, presumably to bind the substrate to the active site of the enzyme.

The Oxidation of Succinate

We have seen that the oxidation of α-ketoglutarate produces the second, and final, molecule of CO_2 released in the citric acid cycle. However, this does not complete the oxidation of the acetyl group, because it is only the second of the necessary four oxidations. In other words, electrons formally derived from the acetyl group are still present. We know this is so, even though two carbon atoms have appeared as CO_2, because succinate is more reduced than the original oxaloacetate carrier. The remainder of the reactions in the cycle are concerned with the recovery of these electrons for oxidative phosphorylation and a concomitant regeneration of oxaloacetate.

Succinate Dehydrogenase. Succinate is oxidized to **fumarate** by succinate dehydrogenase, which is one of the ferreflavoproteins on the inner mitochondrial membrane that transfer electrons directly to ubiquinone, bypassing the first phosphorylation site (Fig. 12–11).

It follows that the overall transfer of electrons from succinate to oxygen will result in the generation of only two high-energy phosphates, as opposed to the three that are generated as a consequence of the oxidations of isocitrate and α-ketoglutarate, in which NADH is formed.

Regeneration of Oxaloacetate. Fumarate is hydrated to form the hydroxycarboxylate, **L-malate,** which then undergoes the final oxidation of the cycle to become

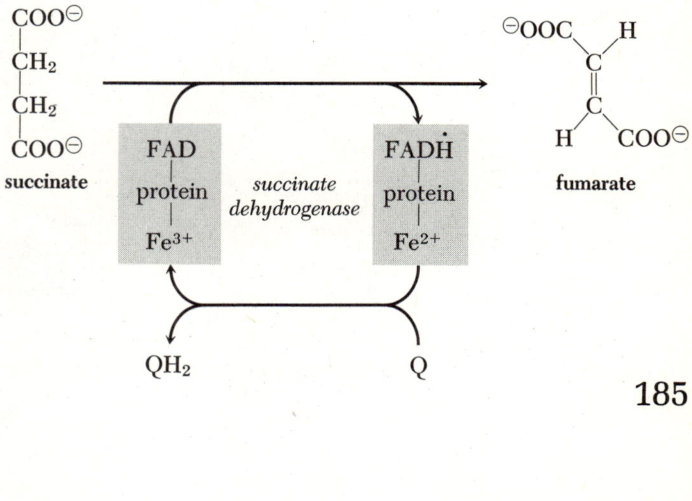

Figure 12–11 Succinate dehydrogenase is a flavoprotein that catalyzes the transfer of electrons from succinate to ubiquinone.

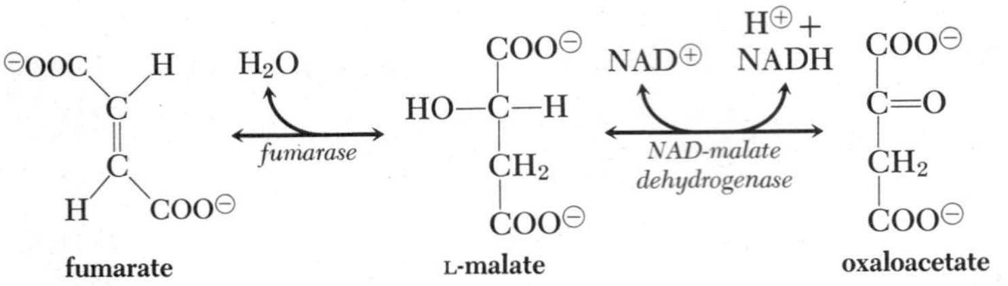

Figure 12-12 Fumarate is equilibrated with oxaloacetate by a hydration followed by an oxidation.

oxaloacetate (Fig. 12–12). We have here typical hydratase and alcohol dehydrogenase reactions. The NADH produced is available for oxidative phosphorylation, and the oxaloacetate replaces the molecule originally used to create citrate.

THE COMPLETE CYCLE

Total Stoichiometry

Now that we have gone over the individual steps, let us survey the complete cycle as it is portrayed in Figure 12–13. If the cycle is really oxidizing the acetyl group of

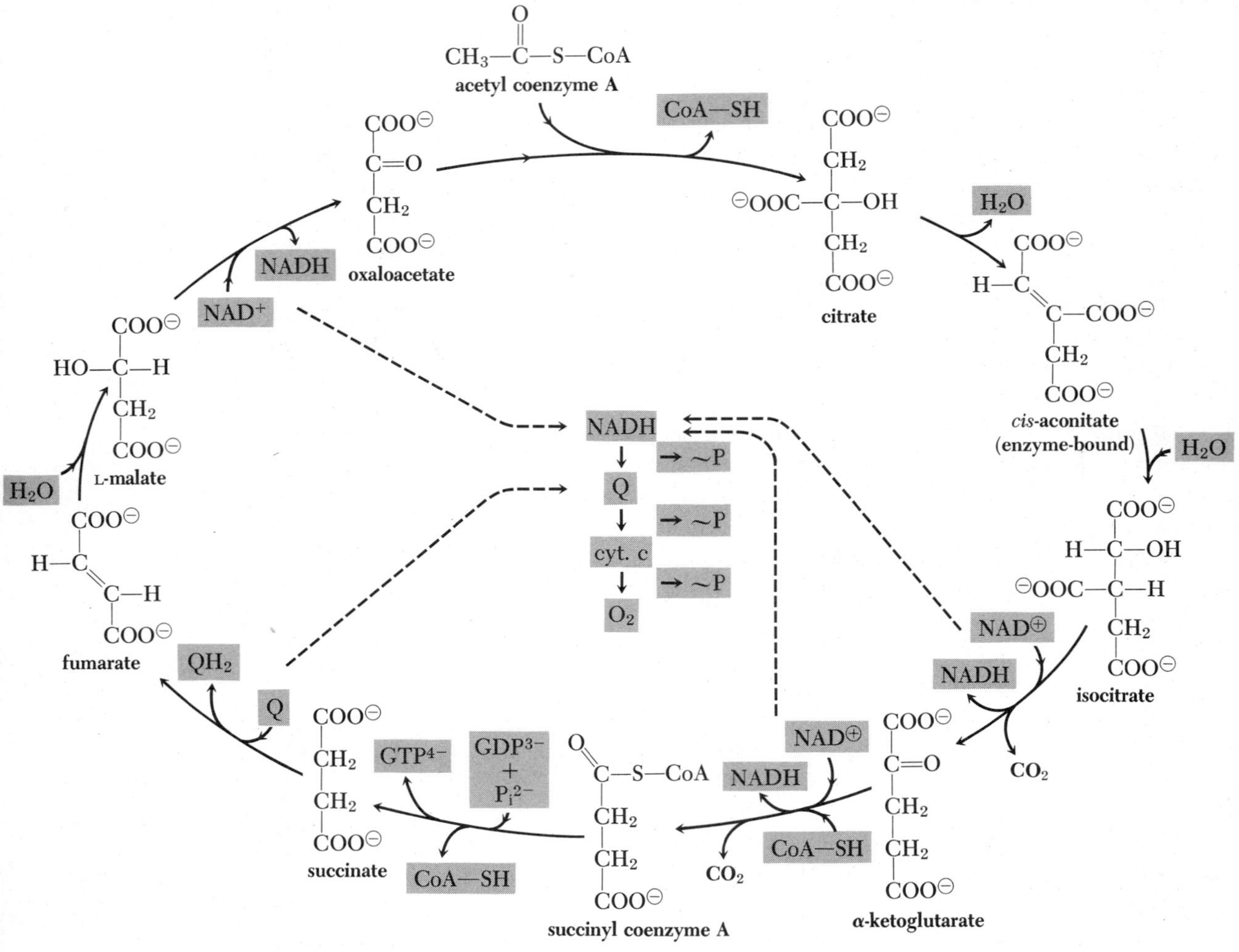

Figure 12-13 The citric acid cycle. Citrate is oriented so as to correspond atom-for-atom with *cis*-aconitate and isocitrate; when pictured this way, the atoms in citrate derived from acetyl coenzyme A are at the bottom of the formula.

acetyl coenzyme A to CO_2 and H_2O, the sum of all the equations for the individual reactions must add up to the formal stoichiometry:

$$H_3C{-}\overset{\overset{\displaystyle O}{\|}}{C}{-}S{-}CoA + 2\,O_2 \longrightarrow 2\,CO_2 + CoA{-}SH + H_2O$$

after any high-energy phosphate that is produced has been utilized and converted back to the starting materials. In this case, if we add all of the reactions in the cycle, we arrive at the sum:

$$H_3C{-}\overset{\overset{\displaystyle O}{\|}}{C}{-}S{-}CoA + 3\,NAD^{\oplus} + Q + GDP^{3-} + P_i^{2-} + 2\,H_2O \longrightarrow$$
$$2\,CO_2 + CoA{-}SH + 3\,NADH + QH_2 + 2\,H^{\oplus} + GTP^{4-}$$

We see here the production of two molecules of CO_2 and the four transfers of pairs of electrons necessary for the oxidation. Neglecting ATP production, electrons will be transferred eventually to oxygen according to the equation:

$$3\,NADH + 3\,H^{\oplus} + QH_2 + 2\,O_2 \longrightarrow 3\,NAD^{\oplus} + Q + 4\,H_2O$$

When GTP is utilized in other reactions, the effect will be:

$$GTP^{4-} + H_2O \longrightarrow GDP^{3-} + P_i^{2-} + H^{\oplus}$$

If we add these two equations to the sum for the cycle we indeed have the formal stoichiometry for the oxidation of acetyl groups.

In addition to showing the oxidation of the acetyl group, there is another important lesson in the stoichiometry. **The citric acid cycle does not involve the net production or consumption of oxaloacetate or of any other constituent of the cycle itself.** The reactions of the citric acid cycle do not provide a route for making oxaloacetate from acetyl groups. Failure to appreciate this point has led intelligent men into serious error in the past, and it must be kept firmly in mind to avoid making the same mistakes in the future.

High-Energy Phosphate Yield. The maximum yield of high-energy phosphate—the amount obtained with perfect coupling between oxidation and phosphorylation—can be easily estimated. The complete oxidation of an acetyl group in the citric acid cycle involves the formation of three molecules of NADH. The oxidation of each of these by O_2 results in the formation of three molecules of ATP from ADP and P_i, for a total of nine molecules of ATP. In addition, one molecule of ubiquinol is directly formed and the oxidation of this by O_2 results in the formation of two more molecules of ATP. Finally, the molecule of GTP formed in the succinyl CoA synthetase reaction is equivalent to an additional molecule of ATP:

$$GTP + ADP \longrightarrow GDP + ATP,$$

so there is a grand total of twelve molecules of ATP that can be formed during complete oxidation of the acetyl group.

Since 2 O_2 are consumed in the citric acid cycle, the P:O ratio, the ratio of high-energy phosphates produced to atoms of oxygen consumed, is 12:4, or 3.00. We shall later have occasion to use this number in assessing the relative energy production obtained from various fuels.

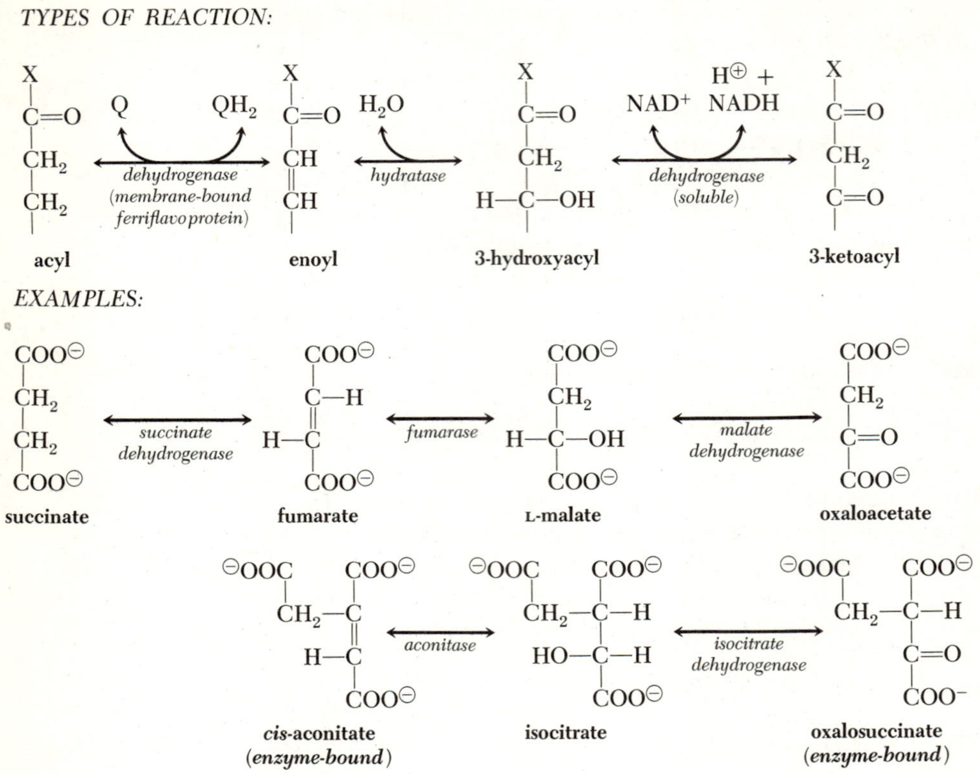

Figure 12-14 The mainline sequence of reactions. This sequence, in which a compound is successively converted to an unsaturated compound, an alcohol, and a carbonyl compound, is common in metabolism. The citric acid cycle is mainly composed of reactions of this sort, as shown in the examples.

Types of Reactions

The Main-Line Sequence. Much of the citric acid cycle is made from a sequence of reactions that occurs again and again in biochemistry, sometimes complete and sometimes as fragments. This sequence begins with the anion or ester of a saturated carboxylic acid, which is successively modified by oxidation to the unsaturated compound, followed by hydration of the double bond to form an alcohol group, and subsequent oxidation of this group to form a keto compound (Fig. 12–14). The figure shows how this sequence occurs in the citric acid cycle, with the formulas of the compounds arranged to match the general scheme.

We have here a good demonstration of the way in which metabolism has evolved so as to accomplish seemingly complex results with only a relatively small number of general types of reactions. However, there are sometimes variations on the general theme. We previously noted that oxidation of 3-hydroxyl carboxylates may cause a simultaneous loss of the carboxyl group as CO_2, as is illustrated by the oxidation of isocitrate to α-ketoglutarate. L-Malate is also a 3-hydroxy carboxylate, but its oxidation in the citric acid cycle by malate:NAD dehydrogenase does not involve a simultaneous decarboxylation. Although the CO_2 could be lost, it is not in this case. Otherwise, there couldn't be any citric acid cycle, because the cycle depends upon the regeneration of the intact oxaloacetate molecule to be used again as a carrier for acetyl groups.

Regulation of the Citric Acid Cycle

Since the citric acid cycle is the major route of oxidative metabolism in many cells, there must be some control of the rate at which it proceeds. It wouldn't do to have the oxidative machinery going full tilt like a runaway boiler at times of rest, nor would it do to have it only sluggishly responsive when there is an immediate demand for ATP.

Stoichiometric Regulation by ADP. Since a major part of the action of the citric acid cycle is the conversion of ADP and P_i to ATP through the mechanism of oxidative phosphorylation, it follows that the cycle won't function unless there is a supply of ADP and P_i. It is the concentration of ADP that is usually limiting in animal tissues. Electrons can't be transferred to O_2 unless the cells are doing something that requires ATP and therefore causes the production of ADP, such as moving, synthesizing proteins, transporting ions, and the like. Oxygen consumption diminishes in resting cells, and the electron carriers accumulate in their reduced form. To be specific, a lack of ADP prevents NADH from being re-oxidized back to NAD. The resultant lack of NAD will slow the oxidations of isocitrate, α-ketoglutarate, and L-malate. Ubiquinol will also accumulate because it cannot be re-oxidized to ubiquinone. The lack of ubiquinone will not only slow the oxidation of NADH, but it will also slow the oxidation of succinate.

We are dealing here with a kind of stoichiometric regulation in which the rate of metabolism is controlled by the availability of the substrate. The oxidized electron carriers are substrates for the dehydrogenases of the citric acid cycle, and the cycle can't proceed without them, but the oxidized carriers can't become available until the reduced forms are re-oxidized through the transfer of electrons to molecular oxygen. This transfer requires ADP as a substrate, and unless it is available, no transfer of electrons, no dehydrogenase reactions, and no citric acid cycle can occur. Automatic adjustment of the rate of the cycle in this way, so as to supply electrons for oxidative phosphorylation only as they are consumed, probably constitutes the major control in consumer cells, such as muscle fibers or neurons.

Regulation by Effectors. There are additional adjustments, involving modifications of enzyme activity through competitive inhibition and allosteric effects, that are used to keep the reactions of the citric acid cycle under control. The most important of these involve the regulation of citrate synthase, isocitrate dehydrogenase, and α-ketoglutarate dehydrogenase, which catalyze essentially irreversible reactions in mitochondria (Fig. 12–15). There is always the danger that an unregulated irreversible reaction will continue until it has used up all available sources of the substrate for the formation of a surfeit of products.

REGULATION OF CITRATE SYNTHASE. The position of equilibrium of the citrate synthase reaction is so far toward the formation of citrate that all available acetyl coenzyme A or oxaloacetate could be converted to citrate, even when the remainder of the citric acid cycle is ticking along at the resting rate. We shall see that there are better uses for superfluous acetyl coenzyme A and oxaloacetate than mere accumulation as citrate—they are stored as fat or carbohydrate for later use. In order to prevent wasteful expenditure of these compounds, citrate synthase is inhibited by citrate, and by succinyl coenzyme A. Let us analyze why this single enzyme is subjected to two different controls.

Inhibition by Citrate. Citrate is an inhibitor that competes with oxaloacetate on citrate synthase. In other words, the rate of the reaction depends on the relative concentrations of the substrate oxaloacetate and the end-product citrate. Less citrate will be formed if the remainder of the citric acid cycle is not operating at an equivalent rate to remove the citrate through isocitrate, and to regenerate oxaloacetate.

Inhibition by Succinyl Coenzyme A. Citrate synthase is inhibited by succinyl coenzyme A, which competes with acetyl coenzyme A, and this appears to be the most important control. The disposal of succinyl coenzyme A depends upon the availability

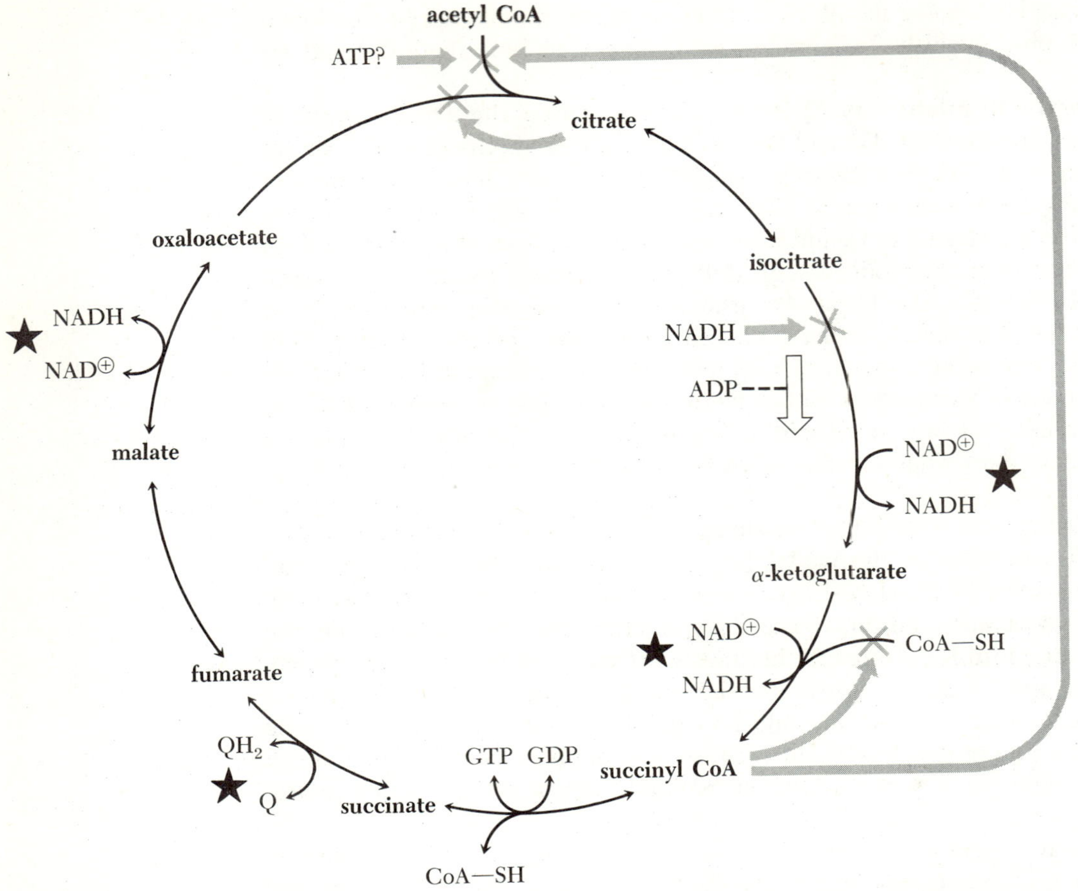

Figure 12-15 Regulation of the citric acid cycle. The starred reactions require oxidized coenzymes; the ratio of oxidized to reduced coenzymes is governed by the availability of ADP and P_i for oxidative phosphorylation, thereby regulating the cycle to demand. However, the nearly irreversible isocitrate and α-ketoglutarate dehydrogenase reactions can still proceed at low NAD levels. They are controlled through inhibition by NADH and succinyl coenzyme A, respectively. Also, isocitrate dehydrogenase is activated by ADP. Finally, when the high-energy phosphate supply is high and GTP accumulates, the accumulating succinyl coenzyme A inhibits the initial citrate synthase reaction in competition with oxaloacetate. This effect also tends to balance the initial part of the cycle that consumes oxaloacetate against the final part that produces oxaloacetate.

of GDP. Since GDP is mainly formed by the transfer of phosphate from GTP to ADP, its concentration probably changes along with the concentration of ADP. Some suspect that the guanosine nucleotides are compartmented in mitochondria in some way so as to give a clearer signal of changes in the energy state. In any event, a decline in the rate of utilization of high-energy phosphate will cause less ADP to be available, and this results in the accumulation of succinyl coenzyme A. The rising concentration of succinyl coenzyme A in turn inhibits the citrate synthase reaction at the beginning of the citric acid cycle.

Why would succinyl coenzyme A be evolved as the inhibitor, rather than succinate or malate? The reason is that it is the product of two essentially irreversible reactions in sequence that are in themselves less sensitive to changes in ADP concentration through its effect on electron transport. Isocitrate and α-ketoglutarate could still be oxidized at a slow rate when the electron carriers are too reduced for continuation of later reactions in the cycle.

There is a further danger in the accumulation of succinyl coenzyme A; as much as 70% of the total coenzyme A in some tissues can be tied up as succinyl coenzyme A. Additional accumulation would leave little of the coenzyme available for the many other reactions in which it is required. As a still further safeguard against this possibility, α-ketoglutarate dehydrogenase is inhibited by succinyl coenzyme A, which is a competitive inhibitor for the free coenzyme A required by this enzyme. The reaction slows as the ratio of [succinyl CoA]/[CoA] rises.

REGULATION OF ISOCITRATE DEHYDROGENASE. Finally, major controls are imposed on the isocitrate dehydrogenase, such as a specific and important activation by ADP, which lowers the K_M for isocitrate. The tendency of this effect is to spur the cycle into faster operation whenever there is more rapid utilization of high-energy phosphate. Here we have a provision in the first irreversible reaction of the cycle—the first committed reaction—for an accelerated injection of metabolites whenever the amount of ADP rises. We have already seen that ADP accelerates electron transport because it is a substrate for oxidative phosphorylation; here we see that it acts as an allosteric modifier to accelerate the provision of sources of these electrons.

Isocitrate dehydrogenase is also inhibited by NADH through binding at allosteric sites. Accumulation of NADH therefore causes the reaction to slow in two ways. One is the allosteric inhibition and the other is a resultant lack of NAD as a substrate. If there is ample supply of ATP, electron transfer is impaired, NADH accumulates, and the isocitrate dehydrogenase slows. This would cause an accumulation of isocitrate, and therefore citrate. We have already seen that the accumulating citrate shuts off the citrate synthase reaction. The regulation of the isocitrate dehydrogenase plugs an additional hole; the substrates can't be drained by an accumulation of α-ketoglutarate.

FURTHER READING

Lowenstein, J. M., The tricarboxylic acid cycle, in D. E. Greenberg, ed., Metabolic pathways, 3rd ed., 1:147 (1967). A detailed discussion by one of the more lucid writers.

The following papers are mainly aimed at the professional:

P. A. Srere, The citrate enzymes: Their structure, mechanisms and biological functions, Curr. Topics Cell Regul., 5:229 (1972). Includes a section on citrate synthase.

———, Is there an organization of Krebs cycle enzymes in the mitochondrial matrix, in M. A. Mehlman and R. W. Hanson, eds., Energy metabolism and the regulation of metabolic processes in mitochondria, p. 79, Academic Press (1972). Other articles in this volume will be of interest to advanced students after further background is obtained.

R. A. Harvey, J. I. Heron, and G. W. E. Plaut, Regulation of diphosphopyridine nucleotide-linked isocitrate dehydrogenase from bovine heart, J. Biol. Chem., 247:1801 (1972). Diphosphopyridine nucleotide (DPN) is an old name for NAD, now becoming camp, but the information in this article is currently valid, even so.

L. J. Reed and D. J. Cox, Multienzyme complexes, in P. D. Boyer, ed., The enzymes, 3rd ed., 1:213, Academic Press (1970). Pages 214–225 consider the 2-ketocarboxylate dehydrogenases.

J. S. Nishimura and F. Grinnell, Mechanism of action and other properties of succinyl coenzyme A synthetase, Advances Enzymol., 36:183 (1972).

T. P. Singer, E. B. Kearney, and W. C. Kenney, Succinate dehydrogenase, Advances Enzymol., 37:189 (1973).

K. F. Lanoue, J. Bryla, and J. R. Williamson, Feedback interactions in the control of citric acid cycle activity in rat heart mitochondria, J. Biol. Chem., 247:667 (1972).

QUESTIONS

1. What reactions in the citric acid cycle fit the main-line sequence of saturated compound $\longrightarrow$ unsaturated compound $\longrightarrow$ alcohol $\longrightarrow$ ketone? Use structural formulas.
2. Which of the reactions in Question 1 requires a flavoprotein as an enzyme? Why?
3. What is the yield of high-energy phosphate expected as the result of the occurrence of each of the above reactions in mitochondria? Explain.
4. Do the individual steps between citrate and α-ketoglutarate sometimes partially fit the main-line sequence? Explain. Do the individual steps between α-ketoglutarate and succinate sometimes fit?
5. Explain why the oxidative decarboxylation of α-ketoglutarate results in the formation of a coenzyme A ester, but the oxidative decarboxylation of isocitrate does not. (It is usually wise to assume that evolution has proceeded so as to gain greatest efficiency.)
6. Prove that oxaloacetate cannot be made from acetyl coenzyme A by the reactions of the citric acid cycle, no matter how much of the latter is available.
7. Show how a fall in the concentration of ADP will in two different ways cause the citrate synthase reaction to slow.
8. We shall later see that two molecules of acetyl coenzyme A are created from one molecule of glucose by both plants and animals. How many molecules of ATP are created by the action of the citric acid cycle during the complete combustion of one molecule of glucose? How many molecules of O_2 are consumed by the action of the citric acid cycle during the complete combustion of one molecule of glucose?

CHAPTER 13

FATS AS FUELS

THE CONCEPTS

Simple straight-chain alkyl carboxylic acids are known as fatty acids because they occur as esters of glycerol in the fats. The fats are triglycerides composed of three molecules of fatty acids esterified to one glycerol molecule, with the fatty acid residues comprising most of the mass. The fatty acids are important fuels for the muscles of most animals, including man, with those containing 16 and 18 carbon atoms in straight chains being most abundant. Some of the fatty acid residues in fats have completely saturated hydrocarbon chains, whereas others contain one or more double bonds in the *cis* configuration spaced at three-carbon intervals. Palmitic acid is the most abundant saturated fatty acid, and is indicated as 16:0, meaning that it has a 16-carbon chain with 0 double bonds. Oleic acid, the most abundant unsaturated fatty acid, has 18 carbons atoms and one double bond (18:1).

The combustion of fatty acids requires their conversion to coenzyme A esters, which is usually driven by a simultaneous cleavage of ATP to AMP and PP_i. The subsequent hydrolysis of PP_i pulls the reaction to completion, so it is effectively driven by the cleavage of two high-energy phosphate bonds. The oxidation of the acyl coenzyme A esters proceeds by the main-line sequence, with dehydrogenation to an unsaturated compound, hydration to form a 3-hydroxy compound, and oxidation of the hydroxyl group to form a ketone.

The 3-ketoacyl coenzyme A compound is then cleaved between C-2 and C-3 by another molecule of coenzyme A, with the first two carbons split off as acetyl coenzyme A, ready to be oxidized in the citric acid cycle. The remaining carbons now have the new molecule of coenzyme A attached to the carbonyl group, and are therefore again in the form of the coenzyme A ester of a fatty acid, except that the carbon chain is two atoms shorter.

The shortened acyl coenzyme A molecule undergoes the same main-line sequence of reactions, followed by splitting still another molecule of acetyl coenzyme A from the resultant 3-ketoacyl coenzyme A compound to produce another coenzyme A ester of a fatty acid, now four carbon atoms shorter than the original molecule.

This repetition of oxidation and cleavage continues until the entire chain has been converted to acetyl coenzyme A. (If the original fatty acid had an odd number of carbon atoms, the final remnant would be propionyl coenzyme A with three carbon atoms, but such fatty acids are not nearly as abundant as those with an even number of atoms.)

The unsaturated fatty acids are handled in much the same way, except that two additional enzymes are necessary to cope with the stereochemical problems introduced by the *cis* double bonds. One is an isomerase that interconverts 3-*cis* and 2-*trans* isomers of enoyl coenzyme A, and the other is a racemase that interconverts D- and L-3-hydroxyacyl coenzyme A isomers. These enzymes come into play when the existing double bonds are approached by the coenzyme A ester group as the chain shortens.

Since the oxidation of fatty acids occurs within mitochondria, it provides electrons for oxidative phosphorylation in addition to those provided by the subsequent oxidation of acetyl coenzyme A in the citric cycle. However, the acyl coenzyme A dehydrogenases are flavoproteins that transfer electrons to ubiquinone, with only two high-energy phosphate bonds generated per pair of electrons, so the overall P:O ratio is near 2.8 for complete combustion of most fatty acids.

Fats are major fuels for animals. Their principal components, the fatty acids, are oxidized in the mitochondria to form acetyl coenzyme A. These oxidations provide electrons for oxidative phosphorylation themselves, and the acetyl coenzyme A that results can feed the citric acid cycle for the production of even greater quantities of high-energy phosphate.

The importance of the oxidation of fatty acids is not limited to the obese or to devotees of greasy foods; it is a critical part of the metabolic economy in the lean as well as the lardy. This is so because fatty acids are stored, and these stores may be created from any ingested fuels, in addition to fats. The fatty acids are then later released to meet the demands for fuel by the tissues, especially the muscles. (The transport of fatty acids will be discussed more fully in Chapter 22, where their storage as fat is considered.)

SATURATED FATTY ACIDS

Nature of Fatty Acids. Fatty acids are simple aliphatic monocarboxylic acids, R—COOH, existing in solution at physiological pH as the ionized alkyl carboxylates, $R—COO^-$. The natural fatty acids vary in size, but the common ones contain an even number (from 14 to 24) of carbon atoms in a straight chain. The hydrocarbon chain may be completely saturated, or it may contain one or more double bonds. We shall first discuss the metabolism of the saturated compounds.

Many of the naturally occurring saturated fatty acids have trivial names in common use; here are some of the examples for the anionic forms:

Formula	Trivial Name	Systematic Name	Type Designation
$CH_3(CH_2)_{12}—COO^-$	myristate	tetradecanoate	14:0
$CH_3(CH_2)_{14}—COO^-$	palmitate	hexadecanoate	16:0
$CH_3(CH_2)_{16}—COO^-$	stearate	octadecanoate	18:0
$CH_3(CH_2)_{18}—COO^-$	arachidate	eicosanoate	20:0

The type designations shown are abbreviations for the number of carbon atoms and double bonds. The most abundant saturated fatty acid in humans, palmitic acid, has sixteen carbon atoms with no double bonds, and is 16:0.

As in the case with nucleic acids, it is common to speak of fatty acids, even though the corresponding anion is the predominant form in aqueous solutions at physiological pH values. We shall sometimes follow custom and at other times refer to the carboxylate form, particularly in dealing with balanced equations.

Fats are Triglycerides. As the name implies, fatty acids are derived from fats, which are esters of glycerol with three molecules, usually different, of fatty acids. These are named from top to bottom when the formula is drawn so as to have a conventional L-configuration. Thus, myristoyl palmitoyl stearoyl glycerol is:

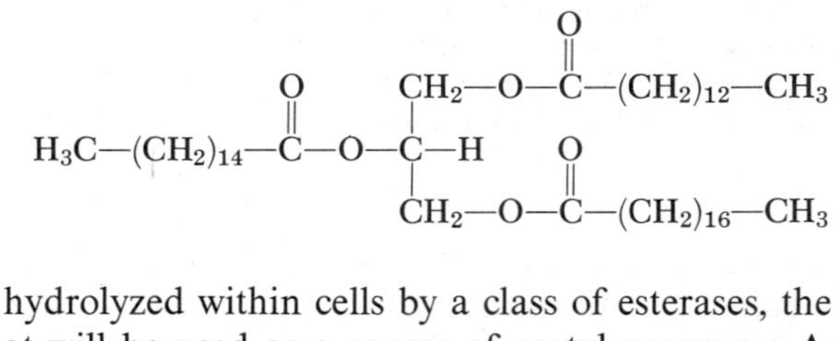

Triglycerides are hydrolyzed within cells by a class of esterases, the lipases, to release the fatty acids that will be used as a source of acetyl coenzyme A:

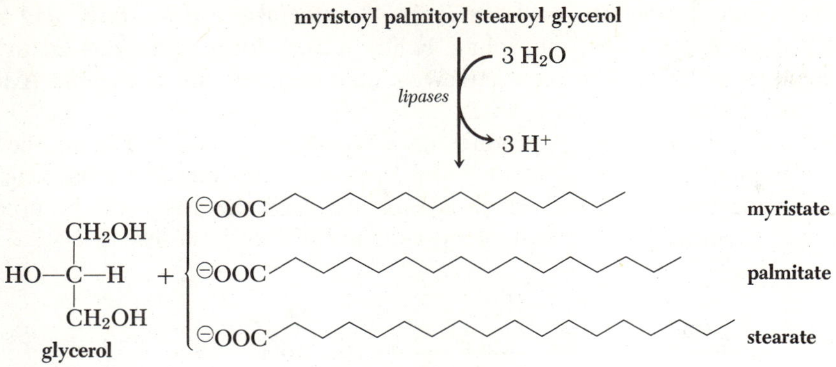

It takes only a glance at this equation to see that the fatty acids constitute by far the major part of the mass of the products; the metabolism of fats is mainly the metabolism of fatty acids in a quantitative sense.

We shall first consider the metabolism of the saturated fatty acids, and then go on to consider the unsaturated compounds.

Oxidation of Saturated Fatty Acids

The fatty acids are oxidized in a straightforward way by the main-line sequence of reaction types we discussed in the previous chapter, but all of this is done with the fatty acids in the form of their coenzyme A esters.

Formation of Acyl Coenzyme A. The acyl coenzyme A compounds with which we are now concerned are identical to acetyl coenzyme A in structure, except that they usually are made from fatty acids with 14 to 20 carbon atoms instead of the two-carbon acetic acid. They are like acetyl coenzyme A in being high-energy thiol esters, with a standard free energy of hydrolysis comparable to that of ATP, and they are made from the free fatty acids at the expense of high-energy phosphate.

FORMATION ON THE ENDOPLASMIC RETICULUM. Fatty acids come into the cell either as the free fatty acids or as triglycerides that are hydrolyzed outside the mitochondria to release the fatty acids. It is desirable to convert the free fatty acids nearly quantitatively to the coenzyme A thiol esters, not only for efficient utilization of the available fuel, but also because their anions are soaps, and detergent action is deleterious to the preservation of membrane structures within the cell. Free fatty acids are known to uncouple oxidation and phosphorylation in mitochondria because of this effect.

The conversion of a fatty acid to its coenzyme A derivative is effectively made irreversible by expending two high-energy phosphate bonds to drive the reaction. The way in which this is done is an example of a general type of reaction for making

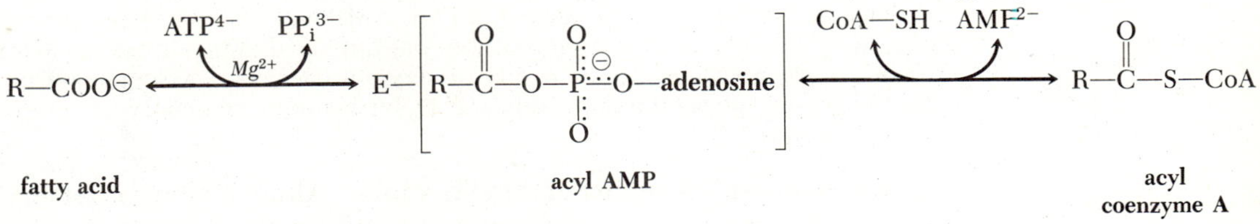

Figure 13-1 The acyl CoA synthetase reaction.

coenzyme A thiol esters. The **acyl coenzyme A synthetase** causes a fatty acid to react with ATP at the internal pyrophosphate bond, initially forming an acyl adenylate on the enzyme (Fig. 13–1). The intermediate is then cleaved with coenzyme A to form the thiol ester, with a release of AMP.

Since this acyl coenzyme A product has a high-energy thiol ester bond, the formation by cleaving one pyrophosphate bond is easily reversible. However, one of the products of the reaction is PP_i, which is hydrolyzed by the action of the ubiquitous inorganic pyrophosphatase so as to keep its concentration at a low level:

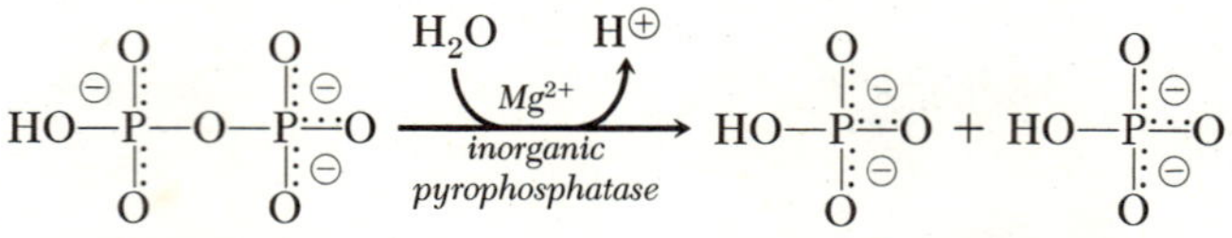

pyrophosphate (PP_i) **2 phosphate (P_i)**

The hydrolysis of PP_i effectively adds the irreversible destruction of an additional high-energy phosphate bond to the overall reaction, making the sum also irreversible:

$$\text{fatty acid}^- + \text{CoA-SH} + \text{ATP}^{4-} \longleftrightarrow \text{acyl coenzyme A} + \text{AMP}^{2-} + \text{PP}_i^{\,3-}$$
$$\text{PP}_i^{\,3-} + \text{H}_2\text{O} \longrightarrow 2\ \text{P}_i^{\,2-} + \text{H}^+$$
$$\text{SUM: fatty acid}^- + \text{CoA-SH} + \text{ATP}^{4-} + \text{H}_2\text{O} \longrightarrow \text{acyl coenzyme A} + \text{AMP}^{2-} + 2\ \text{P}_i^{\,2-} + \text{H}^+$$

The AMP formed in this way is phosphorylated by the action of AMP kinase:

$$\text{AMP}^{2-} + \text{ATP}^{4-} \longleftrightarrow 2\ \text{ADP}^{3-}$$

and we can see that it will require two phosphorylations to convert the resultant two molecules of ADP back to ATP, establishing in a different way that the formation of the acyl coenzyme A was accomplished at the expense of two high-energy phosphate bonds.

FORMATION WITHIN MITOCHONDRIA. Fatty acids can also be converted to acyl coenzyme A compounds within mitochondria. Although the physiological purpose is not clear, the processes are intriguing because the syntheses are carried out at the expense of GTP. One of the acyl coenzyme A synthetases utilizes GTP directly in a reversible reaction:

$$\text{fatty acid}^- + \text{CoA-SH} + \text{GTP}^{4-} \longleftrightarrow \text{acyl coenzyme A} + \text{GDP}^{3-} + \text{P}_i^{\,2-} + \text{H}^+$$

The other utilizes ATP and forms AMP in the same way as does the enzyme on the endoplasmic reticulum. However, AMP in the mitochondrial matrix is converted back to ADP by the action of a GTP:AMP phosphotransferase:

$$\text{GTP}^{4-} + \text{AMP}^{2-} \longleftrightarrow \text{GDP}^{3-} + \text{ADP}^{3-}$$

so one of the high-energy phosphates expended is also derived from GTP by this route.

Sinçe neither the guanine nucleotides nor AMP will cross the inner mitochondrial membrane, the effect is to isolate intramitochondrial fatty acid uptake from the extramitochondrial process. As we noted in the discussion of succinyl coenzyme A synthetase in the citric acid cycle, the guanine nucleotides probably are involved in some regulatory process that we presently do not understand.

Intracellular Transport of Acyl Groups. Although the conversion of fatty acids to the acyl coenzyme A esters occurs mainly on the endoplasmic reticulum, their combustion occurs in the matrix side of the inner membrane of mitochondria. Acyl

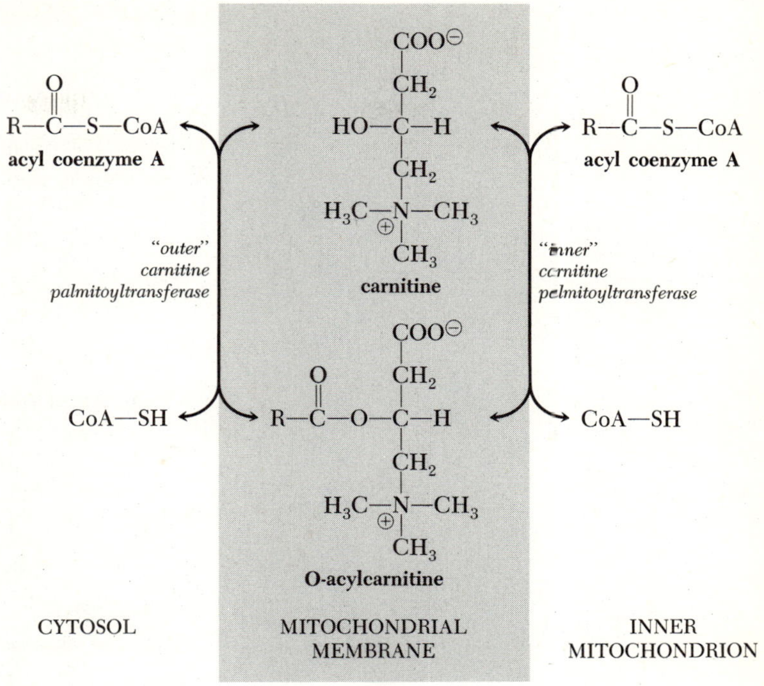

Figure 13–2 Acyl groups are transported through the inner mitochondrial membrane as carnitine derivatives.

groups are moved across the inner membrane of the mitochondria by transferring them from coenzyme A to another compound, **carnitine,** at the outer surface of the membrane. An acyl carnitine can penetrate the inner mitochondrial membrane, so simple equilibration of acyl carnitine and acyl coenzyme A on either side of the membrane will make acyl groups on the outer side of the membrane available to the enzymes of fatty acid oxidation on the inner side (Fig. 13–2).

The Oxidative Reactions. Acyl coenzyme A compounds are oxidized in a straightforward way by animal tissue to provide electrons for oxidative phosphorylation; for example, the initial sequence with palmitoyl coenzyme A is shown at the top of the following page.

All of these reactions are of familiar type, resembling the sequence beginning with succinate in the citric acid cycle. The methylene carbons are oxidized to an unsaturated *trans* configuration, then hydrated to form an L-hydroxycarbonyl compound, followed by oxidation of the alcohol to a ketone.

Of course, the reactions of the acyl coenzyme A compounds are catalyzed by specific enzymes, not by enzymes of the citric acid cycle, but the principles are the same, and the enzymes are also located in the inner compartment of the mitochondria. Let us look at them in more detail.

ACYL COENZYME A DEHYDROGENASES. An acyl coenzyme A is oxidized by a flavoprotein because this reaction, like the oxidation of succinate, will not support the generation of 3 ATP, and it is necessary to bypass the first phosphorylation site by transferring electrons directly from the substrate to ubiquinone. Several of these flavoproteins with varying specificity occur in a mitochondrion, and the number differs from one tissue to another. Some react more rapidly with the longer chain derivatives, even larger than palmitoyl coenzyme A. Some react better with intermediate compounds, and others with short-chain derivatives such as hexanoyl coenzyme A. (Caproyl coenzyme A is the trivial name for this six-carbon acyl ester.)

ELECTRON TRANSFER FLAVOPROTEIN. The acyl coenzyme A dehydrogenases differ from succinate dehydrogenase in that they contain no iron, and transfer electrons within

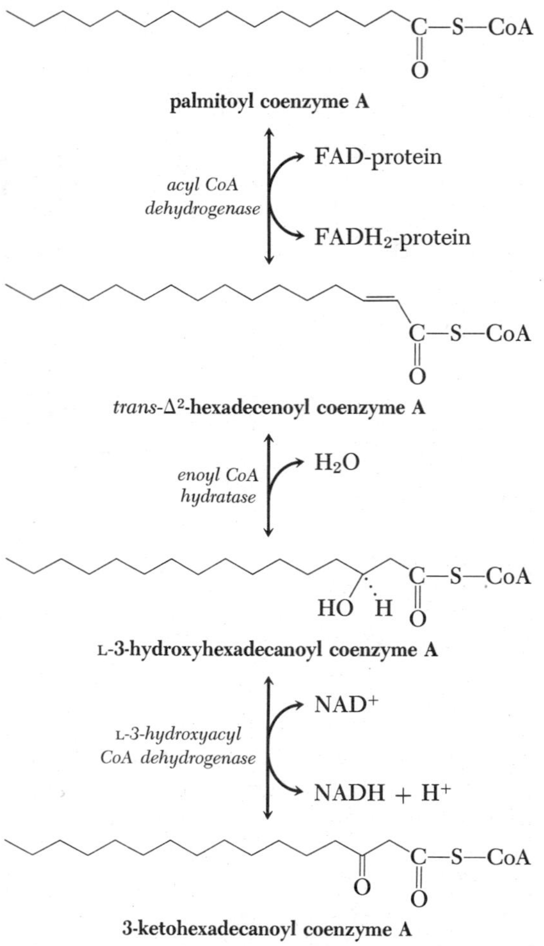

mitochondria to still another flavoprotein, the electron-transfer flavoprotein (ETF), from which the electrons then travel to ubiquinone:

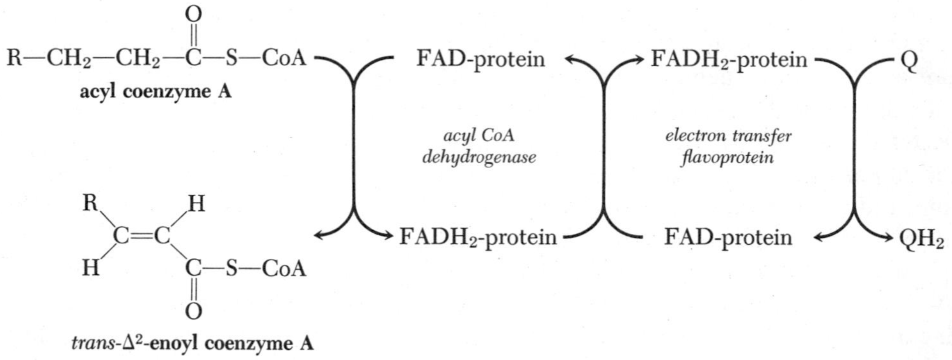

Why this extra flavoprotein is utilized for fatty acid oxidation is not clear, since the end result is similar to that of succinate oxidation: Electrons are introduced into the mitochondrial electron transport chain at the level of ubiquinone with two moles of high-energy phosphate generated per mole of acyl coenzyme A oxidized. The distinctive pathway may enable fatty acids to be oxidized in preference to other fuels at some times, but no direct experimental test of this speculation has been devised.

HYDRATION AND DEHYDROGENATION. The hydration of unsaturated acyl coenzyme A compounds to form the corresponding L-3-hydroxyacyl derivatives is straightforward, quite similar to the hydration of fumarate in the citric acid cycle, but catalyzed by another enzyme.

The oxidation of the alcohol group by NAD also has no unusual features. There is no possibility of an accompanying decarboxylation such as we saw in the oxidation of isocitrate, because there is no free carboxylate group—it is fixed as a coenzyme A ester.

Cleavage by Coenzyme A. The 3-ketoacyl coenzyme A compounds that result from the main-line sequence are split to form acetyl coenzyme A. Esters of 3-keto acids are subject to C—C scission through attack by a nucleophilic reagent, both in the test tube and in biological systems. (The familiar synthesis of ethyl acetoacetate by a Claisen condensation is the reverse of such a reaction.) The biological nucleophilic reagent frequently is coenzyme A, and the cleavage therefore is a thiolysis—a splitting by a thiol. For example, the 3-ketohexadecanoyl coenzyme A formed by the oxidation of palmitoyl coenzyme A is split in this manner:

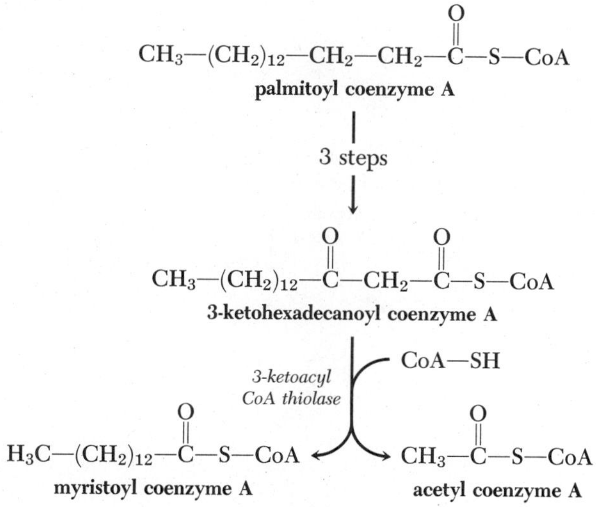

What does this achieve? A molecule of acetyl coenzyme A is formed from the original palmitate molecule in a reaction that is nearly irreversible at intracellular concentrations, and the remaining carbons are now in the form of the coenzyme A ester of myristic acid. Myristoyl coenzyme A is also a substrate for an acyl coenzyme A dehydrogenase, and undergoes the same sequence of reactions as that shown for palmitoyl coenzyme A. It is oxidized, hydrated, oxidized again, and then it, too, is cleaved by coenzyme A, releasing still another molecule of acetyl coenzyme A with the remaining 12 carbon atoms as dodecanoyl coenzyme A.

The Complete Sequence. In short, oxidation of the coenzyme A esters of fatty acids followed by thiolysis removes two carbons as acetyl coenzyme A, but the remaining carbons are still present as coenzyme A esters of fatty acids, which will go through the whole process again. The sequence will be repeated until the final four-carbon chain **(butyryl coenzyme A)** has been oxidized and cleaved, at which point all of the carbons in the original palmitate will have been converted to acetyl coenzyme A (Fig. 13-3).

What an elegant economy of mechanism! Mitochondria use the same sequence of reactions, and chop a random mixture of fatty acids chain into units of acetyl coenzyme A, which is the standard fuel for the citric acid cycle.

ODD-CHAIN FATTY ACIDS. What happens if a fatty acid with an odd number of carbon atoms is introduced into mitochondria? There are such fatty acids in nature,

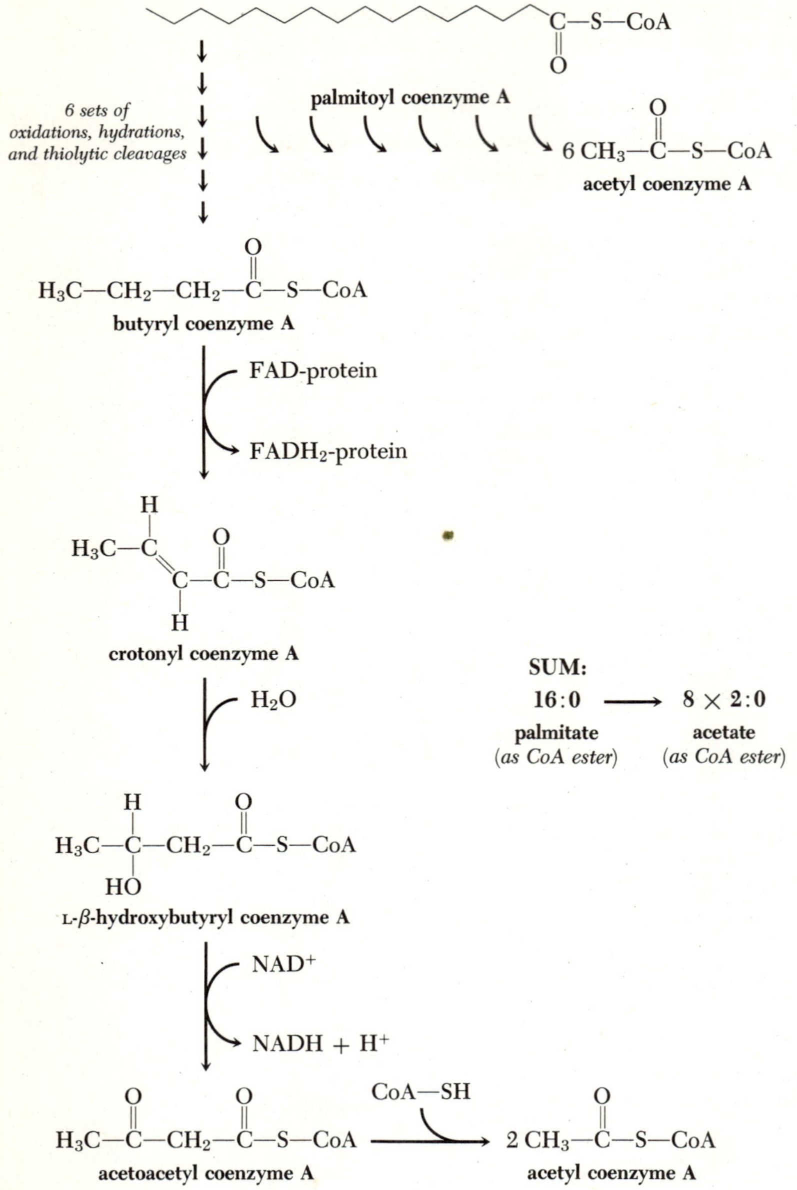

Figure 13-3 Total cleavage of palmitoyl coenzyme A to acetyl coenzyme A.

although they are much less common than those with an even number of carbon atoms. The sequence of reactions proceeds just as before. (We expect this, because it is asking too much to expect an enzyme to be specific for substrates with chains of, say, 14, 16, or 18 carbon atoms without the enzyme also binding those of 15 or 17 carbon atoms.) Acetyl coenzyme A units are successively cleaved from these odd-numbered chains until the very end of the sequence, when the three-carbon remainder is in the form of **propionyl coenzyme A:**

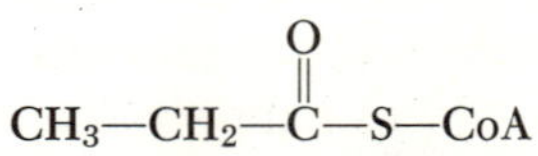

propionyl coenzyme A

This compound is not a substrate for citrate synthase, and therefore does not enter the citric acid cycle. It undergoes a completely different metabolism, which is important in the breakdown of amino acids and will be considered in connection with them (p. 373). The odd-chain fatty acids are only a small fraction of the total, and only the terminal three carbons appear as propionyl coenzyme A. The metabolism of propionyl coenzyme A is therefore not of great quantitative significance in fatty acid oxidation.

OXIDATION OF UNSATURATED FATTY ACIDS

Natural Unsaturated Fatty Acids

More than half of the total acyl residues in the tissues of a typical mammal and even more in plant tissues contain one or more double bonds. Oleic acid is the most abundant of the unsaturated fatty acids. It has a single double bond in the middle of an 18-carbon chain with a *cis* configuration, and is therefore systematically named *cis*-Δ^9-octadecenoate:

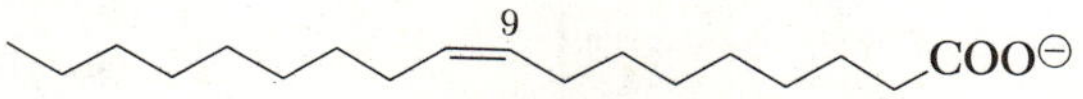

oleate
(18:1)

Most of the natural unsaturated fatty acids have all of the double bonds in *cis* configuration; some of the more common in addition to oleic acid are:

16:1

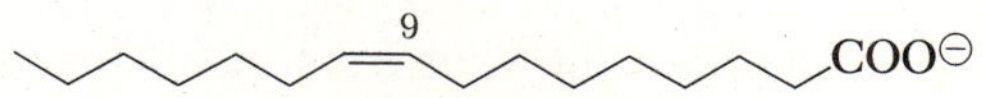

palmitoleate
(*cis*-Δ^9-**hexadecenoate**)

18:2

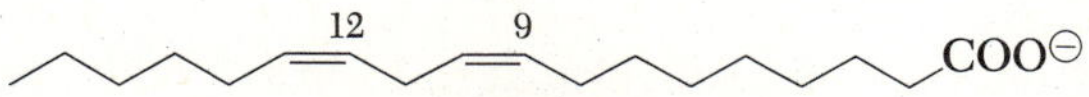

linoleate
(*cis,cis*-$\Delta^{9,12}$-**octadecadienoate**)

18:3

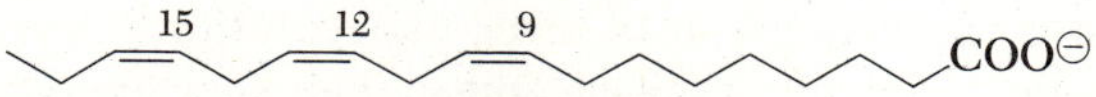

linolenate
(*all cis*-$\Delta^{9,12,15}$-**octadecatrienoate**)

20:4

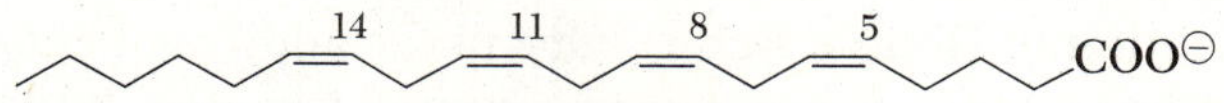

arachidonate
(*all cis*-$\Delta^{5,8,11,14}$-**eicosatetraenoate**)

There are dozens of known examples beyond those shown, but most share the same peculiarity—the double bonds are spaced at three-carbon intervals. The function served by this spacing is not known; it may be structural, since the greatest variety of polyunsaturated residues is found in membrane phospholipids.

Higher animals can make oleoyl residues from stearoyl residues, as we shall discuss in connection with fatty acid synthesis (Chapter 20), but they have lost the necessary enzymes for introduction of double bonds beyond the ninth carbon atom in the chain. Polyunsaturated acids such as linoleic or linolenic acids are essential fatty acids for the survival of animals, and must be supplied in their diets.

Mechanism of Oxidation

Since over half of the fatty acid residues in body lipids are unsaturated, a large part of the high-energy phosphate generated in many tissues must come from the oxidation of this type of compound. The general route includes all of the reactions involved in the oxidation of saturated fatty acids, with the addition of a few more reactions that convert the unsaturated structures into intermediates of the regular pathway.

As an example, let us consider the metabolism of linolenate—*all cis*-$\Delta^{9,12,15}$-octadecatrienoate. The double bonds are well removed from the carboxylate end, so it will begin to be metabolized as if it were an ordinary saturated fatty acid:

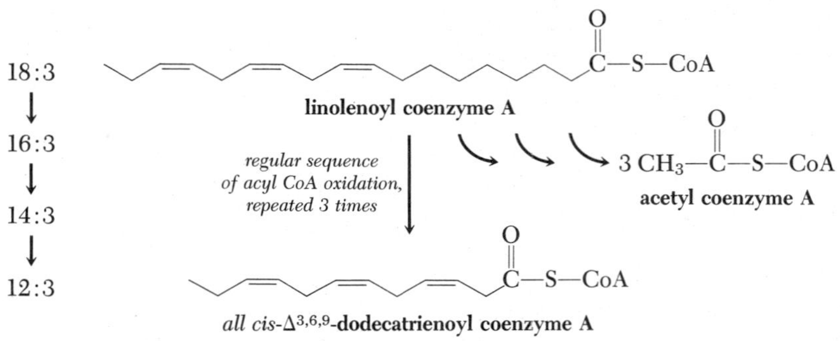

1. Acyl thiokinase catalyzes the formation of linolenoyl coenzyme A.
2. Linolenoyl coenzyme A is oxidized by an acyl coenzyme A dehydrogenase, forming the corresponding trans-Δ^2-enoyl coenzyme A, which, of course, will also have the original three double bonds at carbons 9, 12, and 15, in addition to the newly created one at carbon 2.
3. The new double bond is hydrated to form L-3-hydroxylinolenoyl coenzyme A, which is then oxidized by NAD to form 3-ketolinolenoyl coenzyme A.
4. 3-Ketolinolenoyl coenzyme A is cleaved with coenzyme A, liberating acetyl coenzyme A, and the whole process is repeated.

The sequence can proceed until three molecules of acetyl coenzyme A have been cleaved, but no farther, because the chain is then shortened so that the double bond that was originally on the ninth carbon of linolenate is now on the third carbon of the remaining chain, thereby preventing oxidation by the flavoprotein of acyl coenzyme A dehydrogenase, which attacks carbons 2 and 3.

Isomerization of Double Bond. One of the additional enzymes now comes into play by catalyzing a migration of the double bond from the third to the second carbon atom, and at the same time changing the configuration from *cis* to *trans* (top p. 203). Equilibrium for this reaction is reached with about $^7/_8$ in the *trans* form, so no energy donors or receptors are involved. After migration, the double bond is in the same position and has the same configuration as the regular intermediates of fatty acid oxidation, so the compound will once more enter the general pathway, beginning with a hydration.

Hydration of *cis*-Enoyl CoA. Two more molecules of acetyl coenzyme A can be cleaved from the chain before the carbonyl end becomes only two carbons distant from the second of the original double bonds in linolenate, still in its *cis* configuration. The double bond is then at the same position at which a double bond is created during the regular sequence of oxidation of a saturated chain, with the important qualification that the regular sequence forms the *trans* isomer. However, the enoyl hydratase that catalyzes the addition of water during the regular sequence is not specific for con-

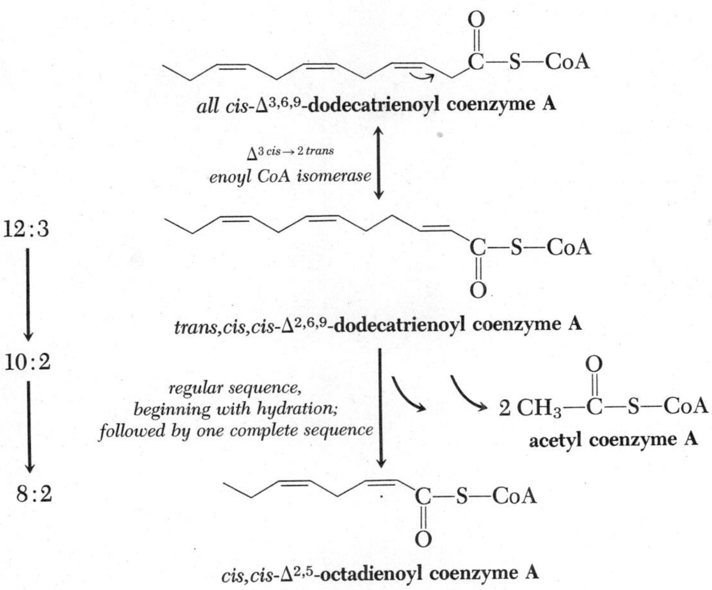

figuration, and it will also cause the addition to the *cis* form.

The rub is that hydration of a *cis*-Δ^2-enoyl coenzyme A by this enzyme results in the formation of a D-3-hydroxyacyl CoA, rather than the L-isomer formed in the regular sequence, and D-3-hydroxyacyl coenzyme A derivatives are not substrates for the L-3-hydroxyacyl CoA dehydrogenases used in the regular route. An additional enzyme, a racemase, exists to catalyze the interconversion of the D- and L-isomers. The L-isomer is constantly removed by the action of the hydroxyacyl CoA dehydrogenase, and the racemase will continue to act to convert more of the D-isomer to the L, so the effect is to divert all of the D-compound into the regular pathway of fatty acid oxidation (Fig. 13–4).

Here is another example of the beautiful economy of organization of metabolism. The introduction of two additional types of enzymes, an enoyl coenzyme A isomerase and a 3-hydroxyacyl coenzyme A racemase, makes it possible to handle any combination of double bonds found in an unsaturated chain through the same route used for saturated fatty acids. (It is an interesting exercise in mental gymnastics to test this on a random assortment of double bonds in a long chain, except that the structure, —C=C=C—, is forbidden. Allenes are rare among natural compounds, being known only as products of the metabolism of a few kinds of microorganisms.)

Mechanism of Hydration. Why do the *cis* and *trans* isomers yield different stereoisomers upon hydration? Hydratases are like other enzymes in that they are constructed to bind substrates in a particular way. If the addition of the elements of water to a *trans* bond create an L-isomer of the resultant hydroxy compound, then

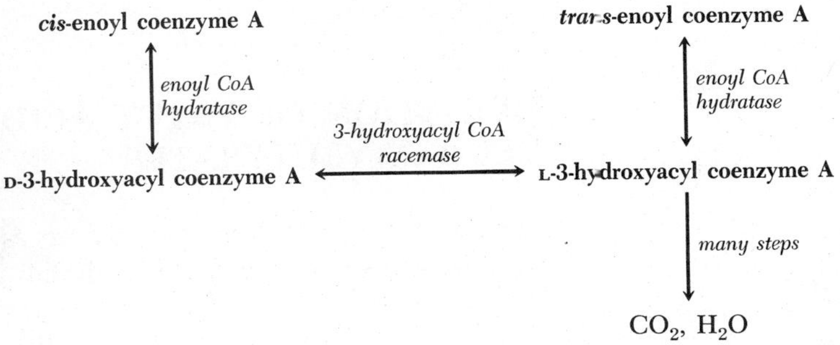

Figure 13–4 Both the *cis*- and *trans*-isomers of 2-enoyl coenzyme A compounds are oxidized to CO_2 and H_2O *via* the intermediate L-3-hydroxyacyl compounds, but metabolism of the *cis*-isomer requires a racemase to equilibrate the D-3-hydroxyacyl derivative resulting from its hydration with the L-isomer.

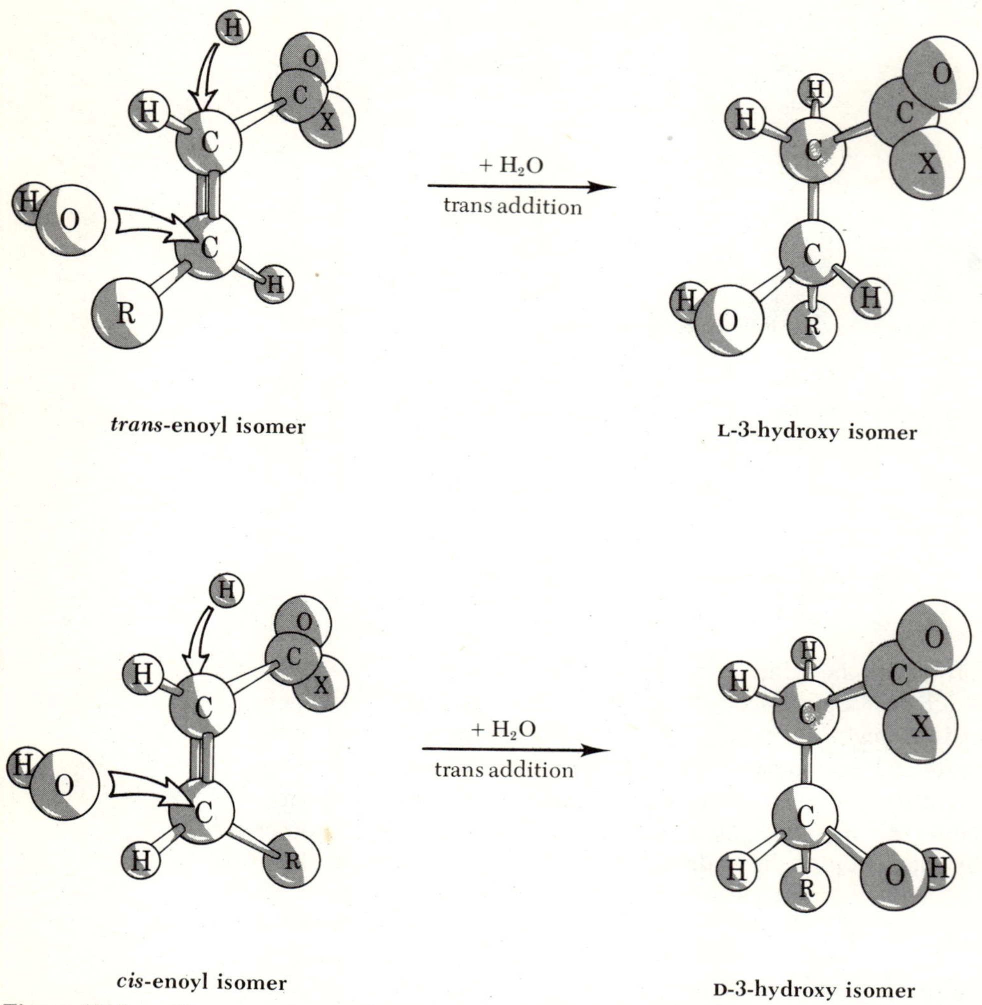

Figure 13-5 If an enzyme catalyzes *trans* addition of the elements of water to a double bond, that is, addition of the H and OH to opposite sides of the bond, so as to convert a *trans*-unsaturated compound to an L-hydroxy compound, the enzyme must catalyze the conversion of the *cis*-unsaturated isomer to a D-hydroxy compound. (Assuming specificity permits reaction with both isomers.)

addition of water in a similar way to a *cis* bond must create a D-isomer. Why this is so is shown in Figure 13-5.

We noted in the previous chapter that hydration of *cis*-aconitate produces D-isocitrate, and hydration of fumarate, which is a *trans* isomer, produces L-malate. The hydration of *cis* to form D and of *trans* to form L is a handy mnemonic in these cases, but it is more of an accident than a general mechanism, and we shall see an important exception to this "rule."

OXIDATION OF FATTY ACIDS VIA 3-OXYBUTYRATES

The major route for utilizing fatty acids as fuels is as outlined in the preceding sections, with the fatty acids being oxidized and cleaved to acetyl coenzyme A, which is then oxidized through the citric acid cycle in the same cell. This route is especially important in animal muscles.

However, there is still another way in which higher animals can oxidize fatty acids to CO_2 and H_2O. This route involves the oxidation of the fatty acids and the cleavage to acetyl coenzyme A in the liver or kidneys by the same reactions we have outlined, but with the conversion of the resultant acetyl groups to acetoacetate (3-oxobutyrate in systematic nomenclature) and 3-hydroxybutyrate, which diffuse into the blood for transport to the peripheral tissues. These 3-oxybutyrates are converted back to acetyl coenzyme A in the peripheral tissues for oxidation in the citric acid cycle:

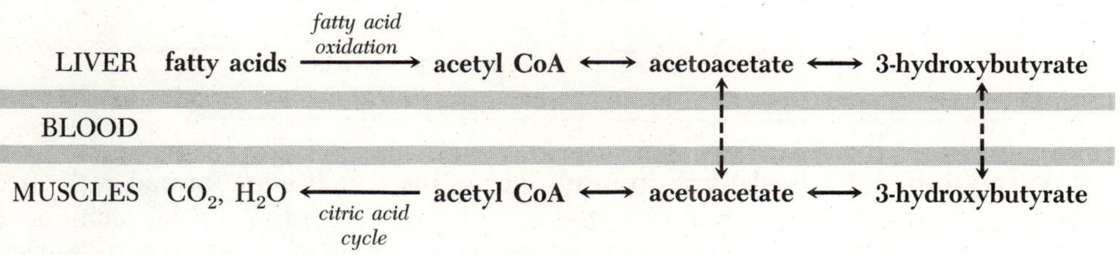

Offhand, it might appear that this circuitous route offers no advantages to the organism over the direct oxidation of the fatty acids in the receptor tissues. The important difference is that the 3-oxybutyrates, unlike the fatty acids, readily enter neurons, and can be utilized as a fuel by nervous tissue in place of the glucose that ordinarily is the major fuel for this tissue. Conditions in which the supply of glucose is impaired, such as starvation, cause an increased production of acetoacetate and D-3-hydroxybutyrate.

Ketone Bodies. Acetoacetate spontaneously decarboxylates to form acetone. This is a slow reaction at physiological pH values, and the amount of acetone formed is a small fraction of the total acetoacetate produced. However, the accumulation of acetoacetate is sometimes great enough, especially in diabetics, to make the odor of acetone detectable in the breath. This is part of the reason that acetoacetate, 3-hydroxybutyrate, and acetone were collectively called the "ketone bodies" by early investigators. The term is still in use. However, acetone is a minor product in quantitative terms, and we shall mainly be concerned with the 3-oxybutyrates.

Formation of Acetoacetate. Acetoacetate is produced in the liver and kidneys by a simple two-step process (Fig. 13-6) in which acetyl coenzyme A and acetoacetyl coenzyme A first condense to form **3-hydroxy-3-methylglutaryl coenzyme A** with the loss of one molecule of coenzyme A, which is then cleaved at a different point to yield free acetoacetate and acetyl coenzyme A in an irreversible reaction. If we think of

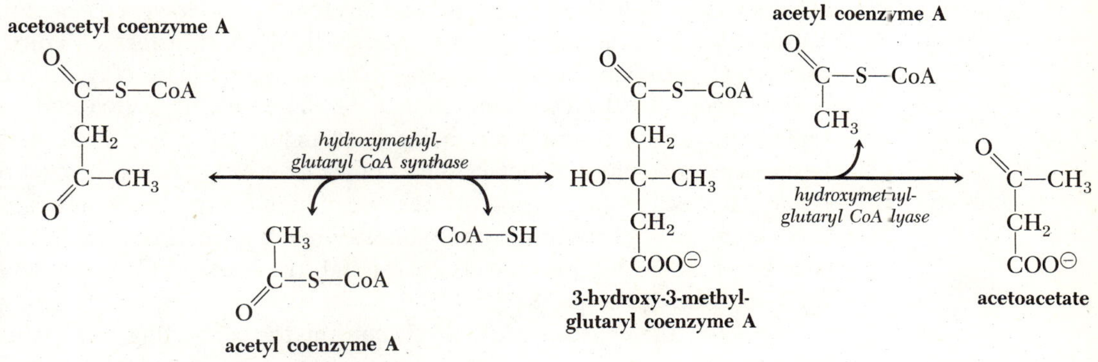

Figure 13-6 The formation of acetoacetate.

acetoacetyl coenzyme A as being analogous to oxaloacetate, we see that the condensation reaction is exactly analogous to the formation of citrate in the first step of the citric acid cycle (p. 177). (However, it is catalyzed by a quite different enzyme, 3-hydroxy-3-methylglutaryl CoA synthase.)

What is the effective result? Since acetyl coenzyme A and acetoacetyl coenzyme A are in equilibrium because of the reaction catalyzed by acetoacetyl coenzyme A thiolase (p. 200), all of the carbons of 3-hydroxy-3-methylglutaryl coenzyme A can be formed from acetyl coenzyme A:

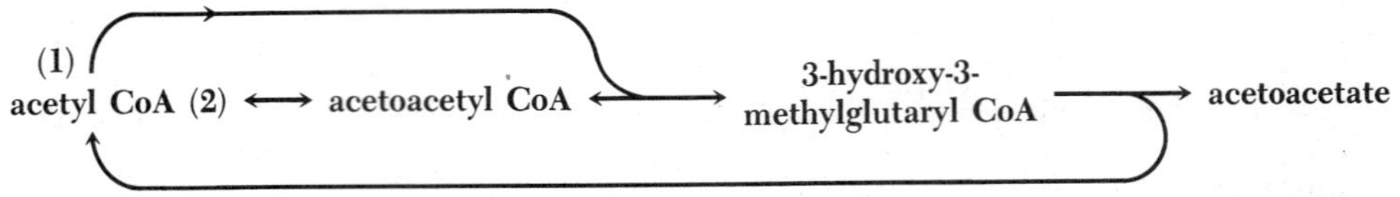

Formation of D-3-Hydroxybutyrate. Part of the acetoacetate formed in the liver is converted to D-3-hydroxybutyrate, because the mitochondrial cristae contain an NAD-coupled D-3-hydroxybutyrate dehydrogenase, which is a typical alcohol dehydrogenase catalyzing the reversible reaction:

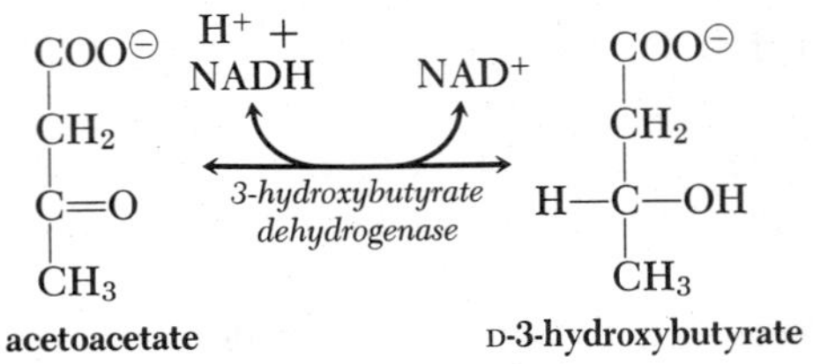

(Why does the dehydrogenase form the D-isomer? Because it is built that way. Why is it built that way? Presumably so as to differentiate the 3-oxybutyrate route from the usual route of fatty acid oxidation, which involves the L-3-hydroxy derivatives.) The amount of conversion of acetoacetate to D-3-hydroxybutyrate is determined by the ratio of NADH to NAD in the mitochondria. Indeed, the relative amounts of the two oxybutyrates produced by the liver is used as an index of the state of reduction of NAD in mitochondria. The formation of hydroxybutyrate is, in effect, withdrawing electrons from the mitochondria to make a more reduced substrate, and later oxidation of the compound in peripheral tissue can produce more high-energy phosphate than does the oxidation of acetoacetate.

Utilization of 3-Oxybutyrates. The 3-oxybutyrates appearing in the blood diffuse into the muscles and the neurons. The mitochondria of these tissues also interconvert D-3-hydroxybutyrate and acetoacetate. However, the mitochondria of muscle also have another enzyme, 3-ketoacid CoA transferase, which catalyzes the transfer of coenzyme A from succinyl CoA to acetoacetate (Fig. 13–7). The reaction is reversible, but the constant removal of the resultant acetoacetyl coenzyme A to replace the acetyl coenzyme A being used in the citric acid cycle makes it proceed in one direction physiologically. The uptake of acetoacetate catalyzed by the transfer occurs, in effect, at the expense of one mole of high-energy phosphate. This is so because it involves the conversion of succinyl coenzyme A to succinate, and GTP would otherwise be obtained by this conversion through the succinyl CoA synthetase reaction in the citric acid cycle (p. 184).

In sum, the muscles have a mechanism for converting D-3-hydroxybutyrate to acetoacetate, and the carbons of acetoacetate obtained in this way and by direct diffusion from the blood are injected into the citric acid cycle in the form of acetyl

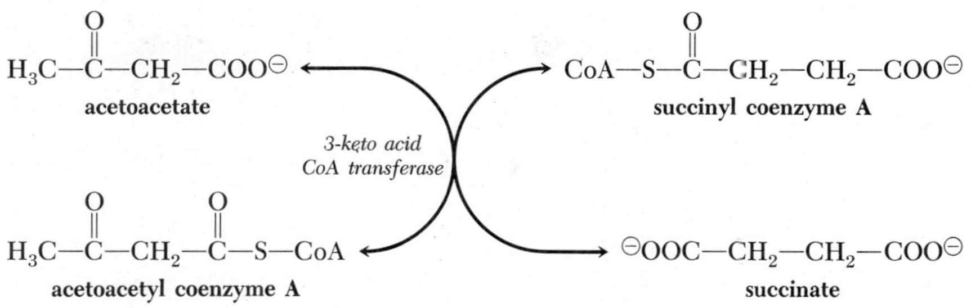

Figure 13–7 Muscles and brain convert acetoacetate to acetoacetyl coenzyme A for use as a fuel by transferring coenzyme A from succinyl coenzyme A.

coenzyme A. Two moles of acetyl coenzyme A are obtained from one mole of acetoacetate (Fig. 13–8).

YIELD OF HIGH-ENERGY PHOSPHATE FROM FATTY ACID OXIDATION

Yield from Direct Combustion. As we saw, each cleavage of acetyl coenzyme A from a saturated acyl chain is preceded by a pair of oxidations, one catalyzed by a flavoprotein and the other by an NAD-coupled alcohol dehydrogenase. Electrons from the flavoprotein are inserted into the mitochondrial electron transport system at the ubiquinone level, and therefore yield two high-energy phosphate bonds per molecule of substrate oxidized. Electrons from NADH go through the complete electron transport mechanism and yield three high-energy phosphate bonds per molecule of substrate oxidized. The sum of the two reactions is therefore five high-energy phosphate bonds generated per acetyl coenzyme A unit cleaved. How many such cleavages occur with a given fatty acid? There is one less than the number of pairs of carbon atoms in the chain, because the cleavage of two carbons from the final four carbon unit in the chain also leaves the terminal two carbons in the form of acetyl coenzyme A. (It only takes $n - 1$ cuts to divide a string into n pieces.)

We must take into account the two high-energy phosphate bonds expended in forming the original coenzyme A ester and the 12 high-energy phosphate bonds formed as a result of the oxidation of each molecule of acetyl coenzyme A in the citric acid cycle. We also must allow for the fact that each double bond already present in the original molecule eliminates one of the acyl coenzyme A dehydrogenase reactions necessary for the oxidation of a saturated compound, and therefore diminishes the high-energy phosphate yield by two.

If we go through the necessary arithmetic, we arrive at equations such as these for the complete oxidation of palmitate, which is the most abundant saturated fatty

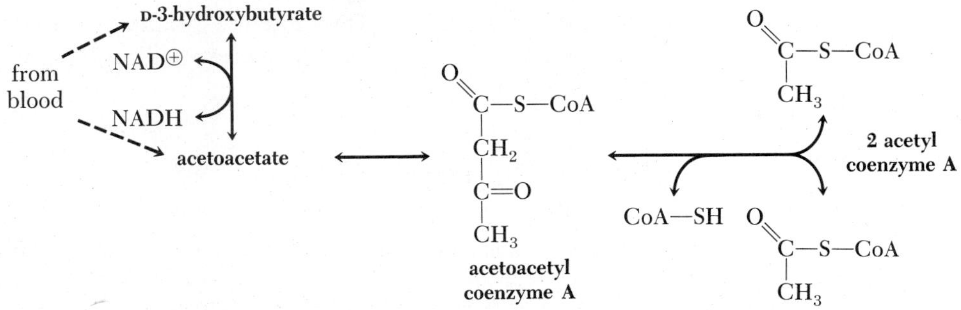

Figure 13–8 Muscles and brain also can equilibrate D-3-hydroxybutyrate with acetoacetate by an NAD-coupled dehydrogenase, and can therefore utilize both acetoacetate and D-3-hydroxybutyrate obtained from the blood.

acid in many plant and animal tissues, and for the complete oxidation of oleate, which is the most abundant of all fatty acid residues in the higher animals:

Palmitate:

$$C_{16}H_{31}O_2^- + 23\ O_2 + 129\ (ADP^{3-} + P_i^{2-}) + 130\ H^+ \longrightarrow 16\ CO_2 + 145\ H_2O + 129\ ATP^{4-}$$

Oleate:

$$C_{18}H_{33}O_2^- + 25\tfrac{1}{2}\ O_2 + 144\ (ADP^{3-} + P_i^{2-}) + 145\ H^+ \longrightarrow 18\ CO_2 + 161\ H_2O + 144\ ATP^{4-}$$

We see that the P:O ratios are 129/46 and 144/51, or 2.80 and 2.82, respectively.

Yield from Combustion *via* 3-Oxybutyrates. The equations just given are those that apply to the complete oxidation of a fatty acid within the mitochondria of one cell. How is the picture changed if the fatty acids are oxidized to acetoacetate or to D-3-hydroxybutyrate in the liver, and these compounds are transported to the peripheral tissues for oxidation? The total balance is changed very little, but the oxidations, and therefore the production of high-energy phosphate, are distributed between the liver and the peripheral tissues. When one mole of palmitate is oxidized *via* acetoacetate, 0.30 of the required total oxygen consumption and 0.26 of the total ATP production occur in the liver; when it is oxidized *via* 3-hydroxybutyrate, 0.22 of the oxygen consumption and 0.17 of the ATP production occur in the liver. In either case, the P:O ratio for oxidation of the oxybutyrate in the peripheral tissues is 2.89, so the peripheral tissues have higher yield of ATP per molecule of O_2 consumed in oxidizing the 3-oxybutyrates than they do when they completely oxidize palmitate. This may be another reason why the brain is adapted to use 3-oxybutyrates, but not fatty acids, thereby conserving its oxygen supply.

REGULATION OF FATTY ACID OXIDATION

The rate of oxidation of the fatty acids to acetyl coenzyme A, like the subsequent oxidation of acetyl coenzyme A *via* the citric acid cycle, hinges on the availability of ADP for coupled oxidative phosphorylation. If there is no demand for high-energy phosphate, then there is no production of ADP, no electron transport, and no fatty acid oxidation. Very simple.

However, given a demand for high-energy phosphate, the primary regulation in animals appears to hinge on the amount of substrates available. The 3-oxybutyrates are preferentially used by peripheral tissues when they are available, and high concentrations of the free fatty acids promote the formation of the 3-oxybutyrates in the liver. We shall have more to say about the relative utilization of fatty acids after we examine the other kinds of fuels available.

FURTHER READING

S. J. Wakil, ed., Lipid metabolism, Academic Press (1970). Detailed summaries of several aspects.

J. T. Brosnan, B. Kopec, and I. B. Fritz, The localization of carnitine palmitoyltransferase on the inner membrane of bovine liver mitochondria, J. Biol. Chem., 248:4075 (1973).

P. B. Garland et al., Interactions between fatty acid oxidation and the TCA cycle, in J. M. Lowenstein, ed., Citric acid cycle, Academic Press (1969).

QUESTIONS

1. What similarities exist in the action of aminoacyl tRNA synthetases and acyl coenzyme A synthetases?
2. What would be the yield of high-energy phosphate from the total combustion of linoleic acid (18:2) after introduction into the cytosol of a cell? What is the P:O ratio?
3. If one micromole of stearate (18:0) is completely converted to acetoacetate in the liver, what will be the yield of high-energy phosphate in the brain from complete oxidation of the resultant acetoacetate?
4. What reactions in the citric acid cycle are mechanistically similar to the initial reactions of fatty acid oxidation? (Use structural formulas to illustrate the point.)
5. Is the yield of high-energy phosphate greater from the oxidation of an unsaturated or a saturated fatty acid? Why?
6. Does the P:O ratio increase, decrease, or remain the same for complete combustion of fatty acids with increasing chain length? Explain.
7. The initial reaction involved in the utilization of acetoacetate as a fuel by skeletal muscles would in itself tend to cause an acceleration of the citric acid cycle beyond any effect of increased availability of acetyl coenzyme A. Why?
8. Show why the complete combustion of oleic acid (Δ^9-18:1) and of vaccenic acid (Δ^{11}-18:1) can be accomplished with the same complement of enzymes. Is the P:O ratio the same or different in the two cases?

CHAPTER 14

THE OXIDATION OF GLUCOSE

THE CONCEPTS

A sugar is a polyhydroxy aldehyde or ketone. The most important sugar, glucose, is an aldohexose, that is, a six-carbon aldehyde sugar. It is completely oxidized by both plants and animals for the generation of ATP by first forming pyruvate in the cytosol of cells; the pyruvate is then oxidized in mitochondria to acetyl coenzyme A as a fuel for the citric acid cycle.

Glucose Uptake. Glucose enters cells by active transport or by facilitated diffusion, and is trapped inside the cell in either case through its irreversible phosphorylation by ATP. The reaction is catalyzed by a hexokinase, and the resultant glucose 6-phosphate does not cross the plasma membrane. Its principal uses include direct consumption as a fuel and conversion to glycogen or starch for storage.

Commitment to Embden-Meyerhof Pathway. The use of glucose 6-phosphate for energy production begins in the soluble cytoplasm with the reactions of the Embden-Meyerhof pathway. The pathway begins with commitment of glucose 6-phosphate by another irreversible phosphorylation. The compound is first changed by the action of an isomerase to the corresponding ketose (ketone sugar), fructose 6-phosphate, in which an alcohol group appears on C-1. This group is then phosphorylated by the action of phosphofructokinase to make fructose 1,6-diphosphate.

Cleavage to Triose Phosphates. Fructose 1,6-diphosphate is reversibly cleaved into three-carbon sugar phosphates: dihydroxyacetone phosphate is a ketotriose phosphate, and glyceraldehyde 3-phosphate is an aldotriose phosphate. Although equal amounts must be formed by the cleavage of fructose 1,6-diphosphate, the two compounds are interconverted by an aldose-ketose isomerase. Therefore, the removal of only the glyceraldehyde 3-phosphate by later reactions will effectively drain all of the carbons of the original hexoses.

Creation of High-Energy Phosphate by Oxidation of Glyceraldehyde 3-Phosphate. A dehydrogenase in the cytosol catalyzes the oxidation of the aldehyde group by NAD. The energy of oxidation is trapped by forming an anhydride with phosphate so that the product is 1,3-diphosphoglycerate rather than 3-phosphoglycerate. The high-energy phosphate on C-1 is made available for general use by transfer to ADP, releasing 3-phosphoglycerate and forming ATP.

Creation of High-Energy Phosphate by Rearrangement of Substituents. The phosphate remaining on 3-phosphoglycerate is converted to a high-energy phosphate by first transferring it to C-2 and then removing the elements of water to form an unsaturated 2-phosphate ester. The phosphate can then be transferred to ADP almost irreversibly because the product becomes the unsaturated alcohol, or enol, form of pyruvate. The keto-enol equilibrium is such that almost all of the enol form spontaneously changes to the keto form, thereby pulling the entire reaction forward.

Oxidation of NADH in the Cytosol. The Embden-Meyerhof pathway utilizes NAD as an oxidizing agent, producing NADH. In order to re-oxidize NADH in the cytosol, it is used to reduce ketones to alcohols, which sometimes pass into mitochondria for further transfer of the electrons. An example is the reduction of dihydroxyacetone phosphate to glycerol 3-phosphate. This converts NADH back to NAD for further use in the Embden-Meyerhof pathway. Glycerol 3-phosphate diffuses into mitochondria, where there is another dehydrogenase transferring electrons directly to ubiquinone. Oxidation is favored by the use of this stronger oxidizing agent, and the resultant dihydroxyacetone phosphate generated in the mitochondria diffuses back into the cytosol. The overall result is the use of dihydroxyacetone phosphate as a carrier for electrons from NADH in the cytosol to ubiquinone in mitochondria, whence they will be transported to O_2 with the generation of 2 ATP. The dihydroxyacetone phosphate used in this way is not consumed.

Oxidation of Pyruvate. Pyruvate readily crosses mitochondrial membranes, and the pyruvate generated in the cytosol by the Embden-Meyerhof pathway therefore is readily accessible to a pyruvate dehydrogenase complex in mitochondria. This complex oxidizes pyruvate to acetyl coenzyme A much in the same way that α-ketoglutarate is oxidized to succinyl coenzyme A. There is the same sort of decarboxylation utilizing thiamine pyrophosphate as a coenzyme, followed by oxidation with a lipoate residue, and transfer of the resultant acetyl group to coenzyme A. There is the same regeneration of an oxidized lipoate group by transfer of electrons through FAD to NAD.

The acetyl coenzyme A produced from pyruvate, like that from fatty acids, is a fuel for the citric acid cycle, and its combustion completes the combustion of glucose.

Thiamine Deficiency and Heavy Metal Poisoning. Pyruvate dehydrogenase is the site most susceptible to damage by low intakes of thiamine in animals, and pyruvate accumulation is a sign of thiamine deficiency. It is also a sign of poisoning by ions like arsenite or mercuric ions that have a high affinity for pairs of thiol groups such as those present in dihydrolipoate residues during the action of the dehydrogenase.

Overall Reaction. The complete equation for the combustion of glucose is

$$\text{glucose} + 6\,O_2 + 36\,(ADP^{3-} + P_i^{2-} + H^+) \longrightarrow 6\,CO_2 + 36\,H_2O + 36\,ATP^{4-}$$

Since the P:O ratio is 3.0, compared to the 2.8 obtained with typical fatty acids, less oxygen must be consumed to generate a given amount of ATP when glucose is the fuel.

Regulation. The rate of triose phosphate utilization is primarily affected by the concentration of ADP in animals (P_i in some protists and plants). The concentration of ADP changes sharply enough in skeletal muscles upon going from rest to maximum O_2 uptake to cause a 200-fold difference in the rate of glucose oxidation.

Corresponding adjustments of triose phosphate production are obtained by regulation of phosphofructokinase. ATP inhibits the enzyme, but AMP relieves the inhibition, and the concentration of AMP is a sensitive indicator of the rate of discharge of high-energy phosphate.

Glucose uptake is partially regulated through the use of isoenzymes, or isozymes of hexokinase, in different tissues, which catalyze the same reaction but differ in molecular composition, and therefore in kinetic properties. One isozyme is associated with insulin sensitivity. The hexokinases are also regulated through inhibition by glucose 6-phosphate, preventing phosphorylation of glucose beyond the capacity of the tissue to utilize it. The liver has still another enzyme, glucokinase, that will phosphorylate glucose only when the concentration is high, as in the portal blood coming from the intestines after a meal.

Pyruvate dehydrogenase is regulated through phosphorylation of the pyruvate decarboxylase peptide in the complex. This covalent modification represents the creation of an isozyme with very little enzymatic activity. The modification is itself the result of the action of a protein kinase in the complex. Since only one molecule of this kinase is required per 10 molecules of the decarboxylase component on which it acts, changes in its activity cause amplified changes in the activity of pyruvate dehydrogenase.

Glucose is a fuel of central importance for nearly every organism. The ultimate supply is from photosynthesis by green plants and some microorganisms; animals obtain their glucose either by eating plants or by producing it from related compounds, such as the amino acids, that also have their ultimate origin in photosynthetic glucose. Whatever its source, both plants and animals completely burn glucose to CO_2 and H_2O in order to generate energy. This combustion is accomplished by first oxidizing glucose to acetyl groups in the form of acetyl coenzyme A, which are then oxidized by the reactions of the citric acid cycle in the same way as are acetyl groups derived from the fatty acids.

THE NATURE OF GLUCOSE

We know from organic chemistry that glucose is a sugar—a compound containing a carbonyl group and several hydroxyl groups. More specifically, it is an **aldohexose,** a sugar with six carbon atoms in which the carbonyl function is present as an aldehyde group. The chemistry of glucose and other carbohydrates is reviewed in more detail in the Appendix (p. 492), but an aspect of immediate significance to us is that glucose spontaneously reacts within itself to form a six-membered ring, or **pyranose** structure

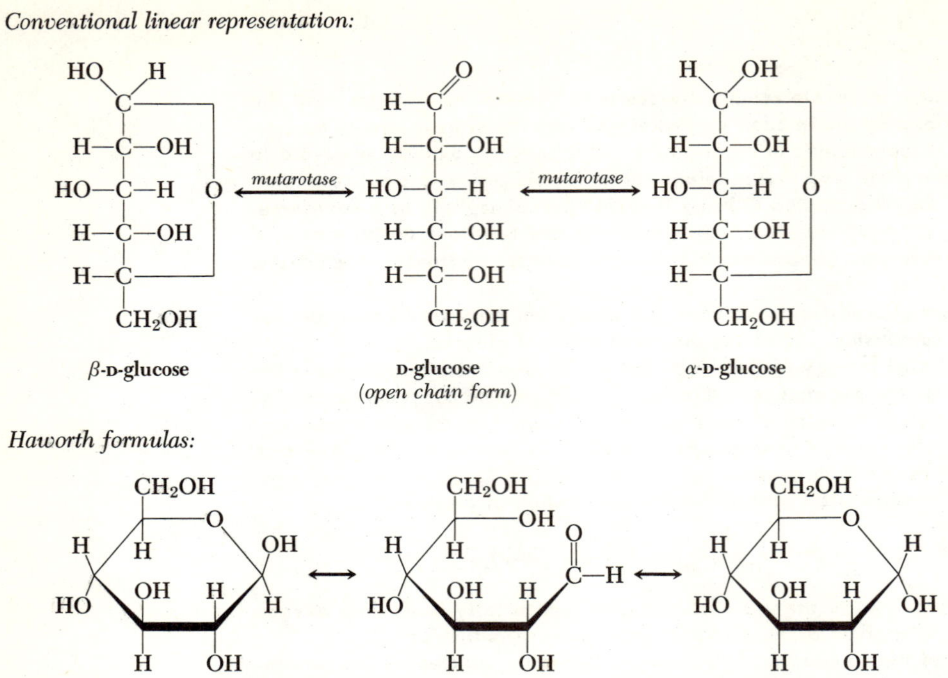

Figure 14-1 The mutarotation of glucose, shown in both conventional linear formulas and the cyclical Haworth formulas. The central aldehyde form may condense with its own C-5 hydroxyl group to create 6-membered pyranose rings. Condensation may occur so that the C-1 oxygen is below or above the plane of the resultant ring, yielding α or β glucopyranose, respectively. Such hemiacetal isomers of sugars are called anomers. Their interconversion occurs spontaneously, but is also catalyzed by mutarotase; mutarotation describes the change in rotation of polarized light that accompanies equilibration of the anomeric forms.

(Fig. 14–1), so that only a small amount of the free aldehyde remains. When the ring closes, the new hydroxyl group may appear on either side. In other words, ring closure gives two isomers that differ only in the configuration of the new hydroxyl groups. Such isomers are said to be **anomers,** designated as α-D-glucose and β-D-glucose. When we talk about a solution of D-glucose, we are really talking about a solution of three distinct compounds—the two anomers, which have differing chemical properties, and the free aldehyde form. However, the anomers spontaneously equilibrate with the aldehyde, and tissues also contain an enzyme to accelerate the interconversion, so in practical terms any reaction of one of the three forms will continue until all of the glucose is eventually equilibrated with the products.

GENERAL PATHWAY OF GLUCOSE OXIDATION

The oxidation of glucose is handled in stages (Fig. 14–2). (1) Metabolism begins with the transport of glucose into cells, where it is captured by converting it to **glucose 6-phosphate.** This is true whether the glucose is to be stored, to be burned, or to be converted to other cellular components. (2) When the glucose unit is to be used as a fuel, glucose 6-phosphate is rearranged and phosphorylated so that it can be split in the middle, making two molecules of **triose phosphate** (trioses are three-carbon sugars). (3) The generation of high-energy phosphate begins by oxidizing and rearranging the triose phosphates to form **pyruvate,** which is a 2-ketocarboxylate. (4) Pyruvate is then oxidized to acetyl coenzyme A, which is further oxidized to CO_2 and H_2O in the citric acid cycle.

The conversion of glucose to pyruvate occurs in the soluble cytoplasm of eukaryotic cells, and this part of the sequence is frequently called the **Embden-Meyerhof pathway,** after its discoverers. The oxidation of pyruvate to acetyl coenzyme A occurs in the mitochondria, so not only are the acetyl groups directly available for oxidation in the

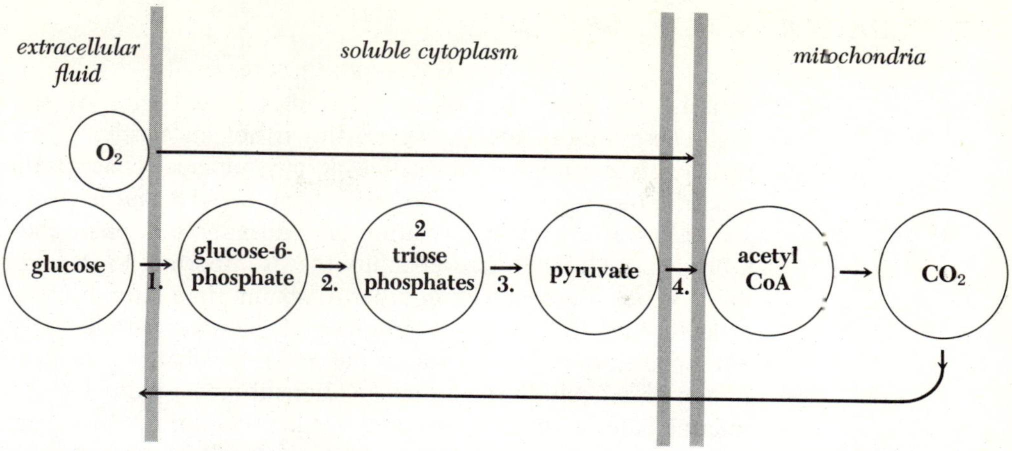

Figure 14-2 General outline of the oxidation of glucose. The numbered segments of the scheme are discussed in the text.

citric acid cycle, but the electrons from the oxidation of pyruvate are also available for generation of ATP by oxidative phosphorylation.

Let us now look at the stages of glucose metabolism in more detail, and then consider the complete pathway.

CELLULAR UPTAKE OF GLUCOSE

Transport

We noted in Chapter 6 that glucose may enter cells either through facilitated diffusion, in which the energy of transport is derived from a concentration gradient between the outside and inside of the cell, or by active transport, in which the movement of glucose is coupled to some other energy-yielding process so that the concentration inside the cell may be made greater than the concentration outside. Cells obtaining glucose from the environment generally capture it by active transport so that they can feed on low external concentrations of the fuel. On the other hand, most cells of the higher plants and animals obtain their glucose from an internal circulation by facilitated diffusion because the circulation has a relatively high concentration of glucose created by other cells in the organism. Thus, we saw that the intestines of animals absorb glucose against a concentration gradient by using a symport mechanism driven by a gradient of Na^+. The resultant high concentration of circulating glucose (4 to 5 mM in humans, for example) permits it to move into cells of other tissues by facilitated diffusion.

However, even movement by facilitated diffusion can continue if, and only if, glucose is being consumed within the cell so as to maintain a lower concentration. It is this consumption of glucose that we now begin to describe.

Phosphorylation of Glucose

The metabolism of glucose begins by transferring a phosphate group to it from ATP:

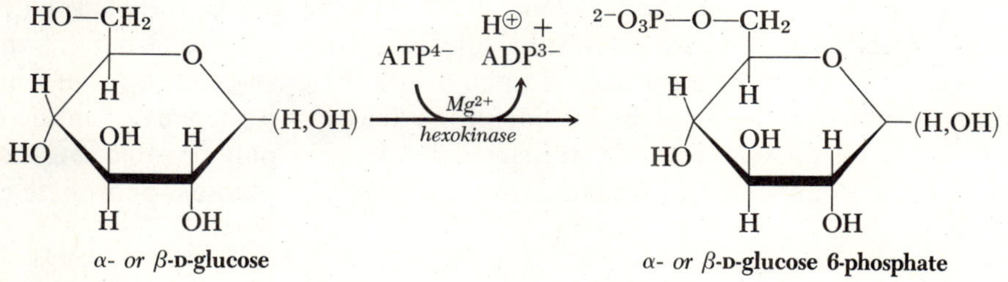

A route for generating high-energy phosphate begins by spending a molecule of high-energy phosphate! However, this is not an accidental quirk of evolution. The reaction is essentially irreversible at physiological concentrations of reactants and products because the pyrophosphate bond of ATP that is cleaved has a much higher standard free energy of formation than does the phosphate ester bond in the glucose 6-phosphate. It is this irreversibility that is important to the organism and justifies an initial expenditure of ATP in order to obtain more later, because glucose 6-phosphate leaks through the plasma membrane only slowly, if at all, and it therefore represents a trapped form of glucose within the cell. (Phosphate esters and anhydrides in general do not pass freely through biological membranes; the phosphorylated derivatives are intermediates of metabolism, and are kept within internal compartments for further reaction.)

The result is that the trapping of glucose in this way is never limited by an approach to equilibrium, and the phosphorylation catalyzed by **hexokinase** maintains a favorable concentration gradient for facilitated diffusion of glucose. There is another important advantage in never having the initial reaction of glucose metabolism approach equilibrium. The enzyme can then always be turned on or off in a decisive way by regulatory effects, as we shall discuss later in the chapter.

THE FORMATION OF TRIOSE PHOSPHATES

The conversion of glucose 6-phosphate into two molecules of pyruvate by the Embden-Meyerhof pathway begins in earnest with the conversion of glucose 6-phosphate into two molecules of triose phosphate (Fig. 14–3). This conversion involves examples of general classes of reactions that occur repeatedly in metabolism, and it is worth looking at these in some detail.

Glucose 6-Phosphate ⟷ Fructose 6-Phosphate. The initial step involves shifting the potential carbonyl group of the glucose residue from C-1 to C-2; there is an isomerization of an aldehyde sugar, an aldohexose, into a ketone sugar, or ketohexose, in the form of the phosphate ester. This freely reversible interconversion of glucose 6-phosphate and fructose 6-phosphate is catalyzed by **glucosephosphate isomerase** through the intermediate formation of an enediol:

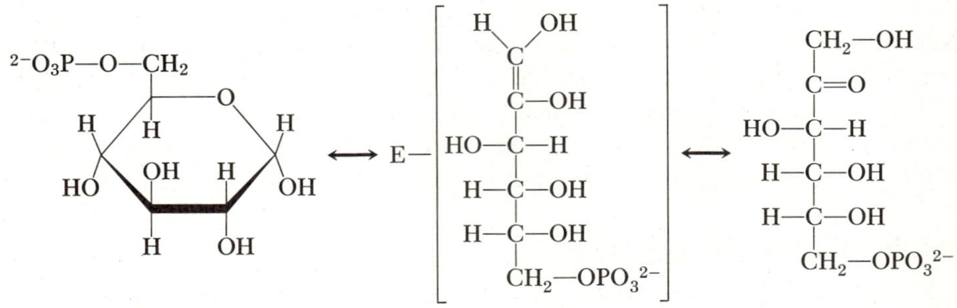

α-D-glucose 6-phosphate | enediol (enzyme-bound) | D-fructose 6-phosphate

We shall later see similar interconversions of other aldose and ketose phosphates by isomerases specific to them. An interesting sidelight of the enzyme at hand is that it interconverts the α-form of glucose 6-phosphate with the open-chain form of fructose 6-phosphate. It is true that a larger fraction of the ketose phosphate exists in the open chain form than is the case with the free sugars because the only possible ring closure is a less-favored five-membered **furanose** ring, but even so, fructose 6-phosphate exists mainly in the ring form at equilibrium.

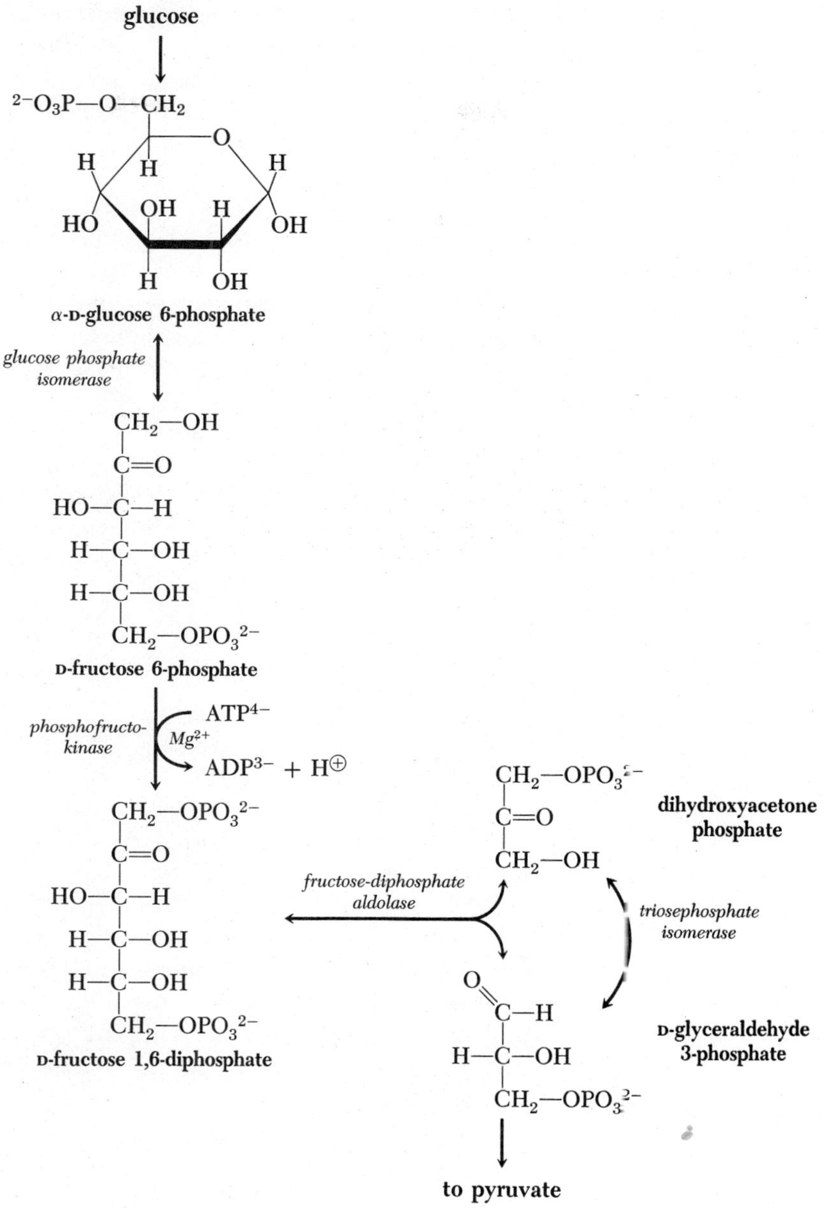

Figure 14-3 Glucose 6-phosphate is converted to two triose phosphates, which are equilibrated by isomerase.

Fructose 6-Phosphate ⟶ Fructose 1,6-Diphosphate. When fructose 6-phosphate is formed, a new primary alcohol group appears on C-1, and the next step in the Embden-Meyerhof pathway is the phosphorylation of this group by transfer from ATP:

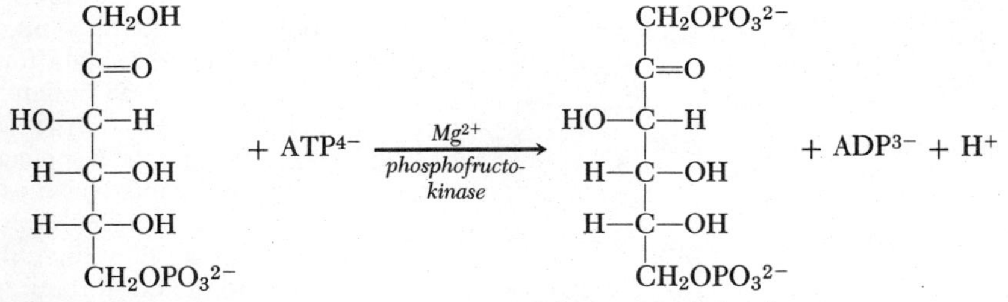

D-fructose-6-phosphate D-fructose-1,6-diphosphate

This reaction, catalyzed by **phosphofructokinase,** is like the phosphorylation of glucose catalyzed by hexokinase in being essentially irreversible under physiological conditions. The action of hexokinase commits the cell to taking up glucose. The action of phosphofructokinase commits it to metabolizing the glucose rather than storing it or converting it to some other hexose, and we shall see that this enzyme is also a key site of regulation.

Fructose 1,6-Diphosphate ⟷ Triose Phosphates. Since fructose diphosphate is a molecule with phosphate groups on both ends, it can be split in the middle to form the two isomeric triose phosphates—the aldose, D-glyceraldehyde 3-phosphate, and the ketose, dihydroxyacetone phosphate. We discussed this freely reversible reaction and the mechanism of the fructosediphosphate aldolase that catalyzed it in Chapter 8 (p. 101) as the most prominent example of several aldol condensations and cleavages occurring in metabolism.

Glyceraldehyde 3-Phosphate ⟷ Dihydroxyacetone Phosphate. The triosephosphates formed by the aldolase reaction in equal amounts are aldose-ketose isomers, and they are interconverted by a **triose phosphate isomerase** in the same way that glucose and fructose phosphates are interconverted by the glucose phosphate isomerase:

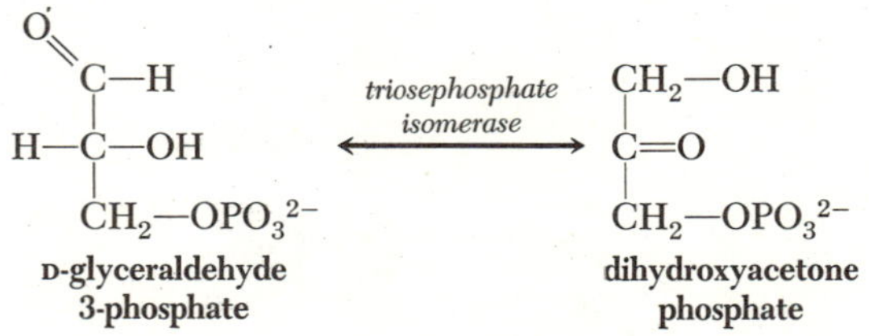

The existence of triose phosphate isomerase makes it possible to divert all of the carbons of glucose into any pathway utilizing one of the triose phosphates. We shall see in the next section that glyceraldehyde 3-phosphate is converted to pyruvate; however, all of the carbons of glucose can be converted to pyruvate owing to the presence of triose phosphate isomerase, and this is true even though the concentration of dihydroxyacetone phosphate is much greater than the concentration of glyceraldehyde phosphate at equilibrium. This is a point that bothers many people, so let us spend a few moments on it. Figure 14–4 represents the pools of compounds in a tissue as tanks, connected by reactions in the form of pipes. Fructose diphosphate and the triose phosphates are equilibrated freely. We can see from the diagram that conver-

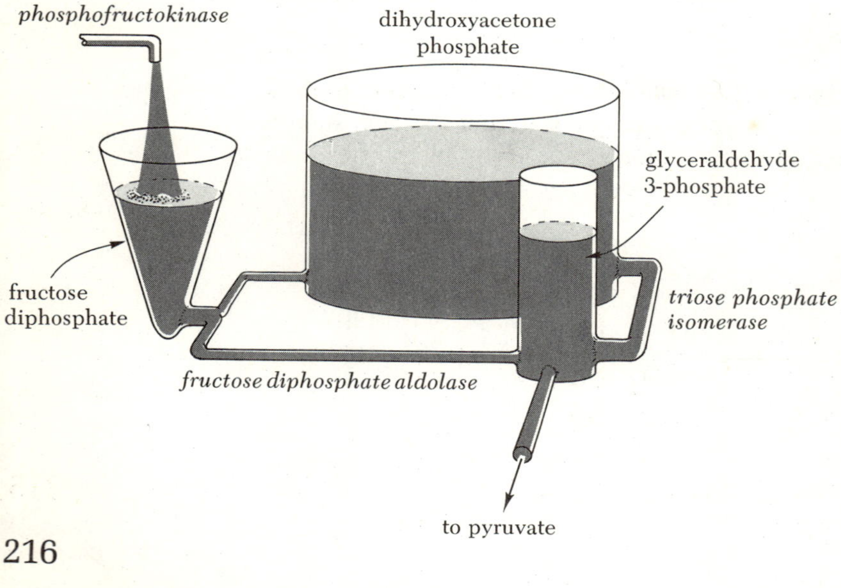

Figure 14–4 Fructose diphosphate and the triose phosphates are maintained near equilibrium concentrations, with dihydroxyacetone phosphate present in the highest concentration. (The proportion of fructose diphosphate increases as the total concentration rises, since it is one molecule in equilibrium with two.) The pool of these three compounds is fed by the irreversible formation of fructose diphosphate. Even though glyceraldehyde 3-phosphate is the direct precursor of pyruvate, its removal causes part of it to be replaced from dihydroxyacetone phosphate in order to maintain equilibrium. The result is that all of the hexose carbons flow toward pyruvate.

sion to pyruvate has the immediate effect of lowering the concentration of glyceraldehyde 3-phosphate, but this will cause replacement of glyceraldehyde 3-phosphate from the dihydroxyacetone phosphate equilibrated with it, which is therefore also being consumed. Both triose phosphates are converted to pyruvate in equal amounts.

THE FORMATION OF PYRUVATE FROM TRIOSE PHOSPHATES

The conversion of the triose phosphates to pyruvate in the soluble cytoplasm of cells initiates the actual recovery of energy from the metabolism of glucose. Since both triose phosphates are involved, two molecules of pyruvate are formed from each molecule of glucose 6-phosphate consumed. Essentially, the sequence involves an oxidation of glyceraldehyde 3-phosphate with capture of the energy as high-energy phosphate, followed by rearrangements that result in the formation of still further high-energy phosphate (Fig. 14–5). The high-energy phosphate is used to form ATP from ADP.

Glyceraldehyde 3-Phosphate ⟷ 3-Phosphoglycerate. The aldehyde group on glyceraldehyde 3-phosphate is oxidized by NAD. Oxidation of an aldehyde normally forms a carboxylic acid, 3-phosphoglyceric acid in this case. However, when we discussed the oxidation of α-ketoglutarate to succinyl coenzyme A in the citric acid cycle (p. 180), we noted that such oxidations have a standard free energy change sufficiently negative to support the formation of a high-energy bond at physiological concentrations. In the example at hand, the energy of oxidation of glyceraldehyde 3-phosphate is captured by causing the simultaneous formation of an anhydride bond between the carboxyl group and phosphate. The products of the reaction catalyzed by **glyceraldehyde 3-phosphate dehydrogenase** are NADH and **1,3-diphosphoglycerate,** and the 1-phosphate anhydride is a high-energy bond. Another enzyme, a **3-phosphoglycerate kinase,** is present to catalyze the reversible transfer of the high-energy phosphate to ADP, forming ATP and releasing the carbon atoms originally obtained from glucose in the form of 3-phosphoglycerate.

Glyceraldehyde-3-phosphate dehydrogenase is like α-ketoglutarate dehydrogenase in creating a thiol ester as the initial high-energy bond, but the participating sulfhydryl group is provided by a residue of cysteine in the enzyme peptide rather than by coenzyme A or dihydrolipoate (Fig. 14–6). The aldehyde group of the substrate reversibly combines with the cysteinyl residue as a thiohemiacetal, which is converted to a high-energy thiol ester upon oxidation with NAD. Phosphorolysis of the ester creates the high-energy phosphate bond and liberates the original sulfhydryl group on the enzyme.

We see that the cysteinyl group doesn't participate in electron transfers in the way that a lipoyl group does during the oxidation of the aldehyde moiety of α-keto acids. However, glyceraldehyde-3-phosphate dehydrogenase is susceptible to inhibition by reagents reacting with thiols. This provided a powerful tool for early investigations in carbohydrate metabolism because treatment of an intact tissue with iodoacetate:

$$\underset{\boxed{\text{peptide}}}{\overset{\text{SH}}{|}} + \text{I—CH}_2\text{—COO}^{\ominus} \longrightarrow \underset{\boxed{\text{peptide}}}{\overset{\text{S—CH}_2\text{—COO}^{\ominus}}{|}} + \text{H}^+ + \text{I}^-$$

stopped metabolism of the triose phosphates at this point. The resultant failure of ATP regeneration made it possible to show that high-energy phosphate is depleted during muscular work.

3-Phosphoglycerate ⟶ Pyruvate. The remaining reactions in the formation of pyruvate rearrange the three-carbon compounds in such a way as to capture the free energy difference between 3-phosphoglycerate and pyruvate in the form of ATP.

MUTASES. The phosphate group is reversibly transferred from C-3 to C-2 of

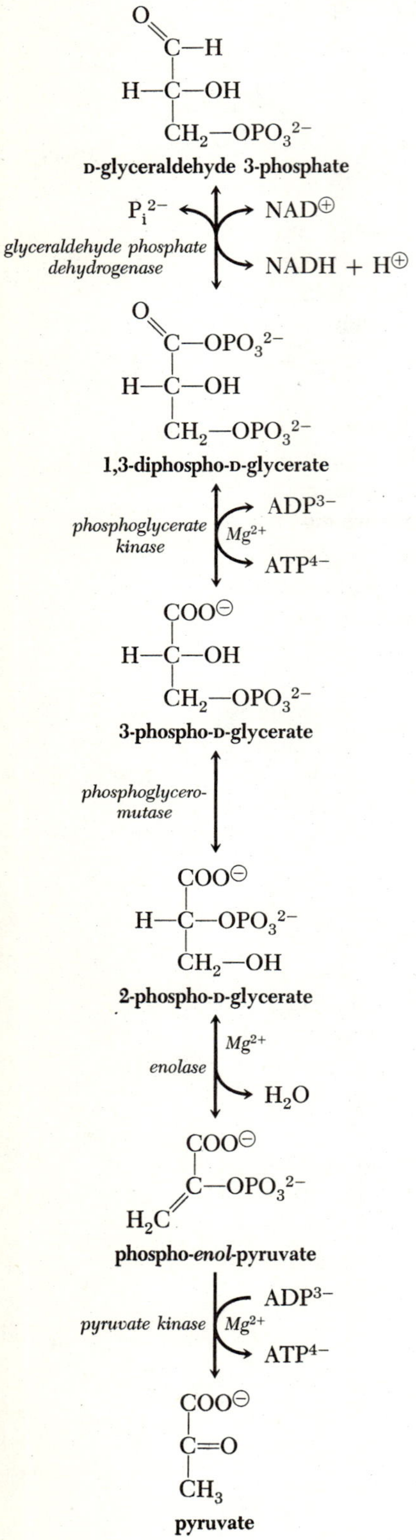

Figure 14-5 The conversion of glyceraldehyde 3-phosphate to pyruvate. For each molecule of pyruvate produced, two molecules of ATP are formed. One molecule of high-energy phosphate is generated by the oxidation of D-glyceraldehyde 3-phosphate, and the other by rearrangement of 3-phosphoglycerate.

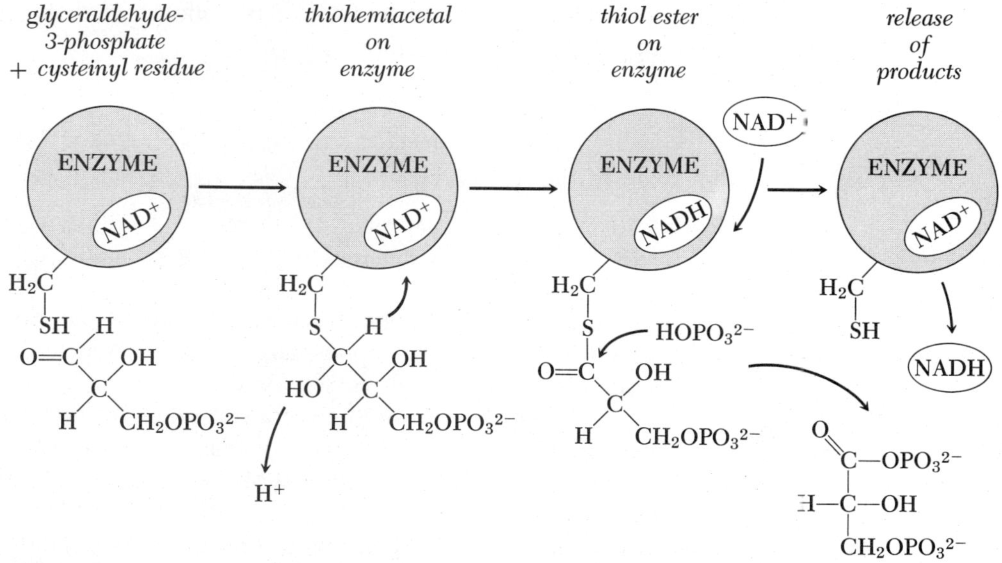

Figure 14-6 The oxidation of glyceraldehyde-3-phosphate involves its combination with a sulfhydryl group on the dehydrogenase peptide, forming a thiohemiacetal. This structure is oxidized by NAD, also on the enzyme, to form a thiol ester, which is cleaved by inorganic phosphate to produce 1,3-diphosphoglycerate. The NADH produced on the enzyme is less tightly bound, and is displaced by a molecule of NAD from the solution.

glycerate. Enzymes catalyzing these intramolecular transfers of phosphate are called mutases, and usually proceed by the kind of mechanism shown in Figure 14–7 for the **phosphoglyceromutase** involved here. The active enzyme contains a phosphorylated seryl residue, and the phosphate is first transferred to either 3- or 2-phosphoglycerate. This forms the transient intermediate, 2,3-diphosphoglycerate, on the enzyme surface, which in turn reacts to transfer one of its phosphate groups back onto the seryl residue. However, either of the phosphate groups may be transferred, and the remaining phosphate on the glycerate may be on either C-2 or C-3, so the effect of a continuation of the process is to bring **2-phosphoglycerate** and 3-phosphoglycerate to equilibrium.

The small concentrations of the intermediate 2,3-diphosphoglycerate necessary in the solution to prime the reaction are made by a diphosphoglycerate mutase in the

Figure 14–7 Mutases, which catalyze intramolecular transfer of phosphate, frequently have mechanisms involving phosphorylation of a seryl group on the enzyme peptide by a double phosphorylated form of the substrate. As is shown in the center, either of the phosphate groups of 2,3-diphosphoglycerate may be transferred to a seryl group. Therefore, either 3-phosphoglycerate or 2-phosphoglycerate may be formed. Since the reactions are reversible, the enzyme will catalyze the interconversion of the phosphoglycerates. A small amount of 2,3-diphosphoglycerate is required initially to prime the enzyme with phosphate groups.

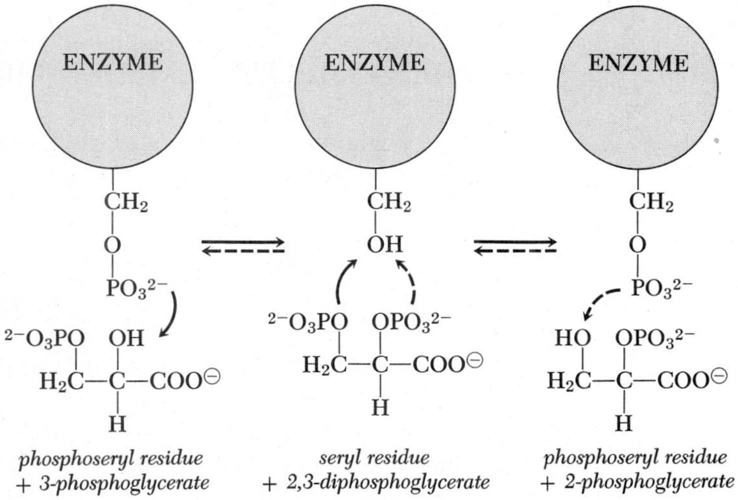

cytoplasm, which catalyzes a transfer of the phosphate from the first to the second carbon of 1,3-diphosphoglycerate:

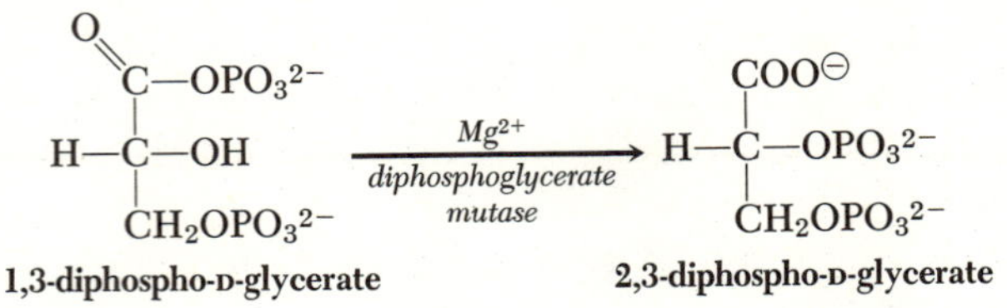

This priming reaction ought not to be confused with the major pathway we are discussing, in which most of the 1,2-diphosphoglycerate is used to form ATP by the phosphoglycerate kinase reaction discussed above.

ENOLASE. The 2-phospho D-glycerate created by the mutase reaction is next dehydrated by the action of an enzyme, enolase, to form **phospho-*enol*-pyruvate.** This appears to be a straightforward removal of the elements of water from an alcohol to form an unsaturated compound, except that the product has a phosphate ester group on one of the unsaturated carbons. Now, unsaturated secondary alcohols are the enol forms of ketones, and the product here is a phosphate ester of the enol form of the keto acid, pyruvate, in its anion form.

Phospho-*enol*-pyruvate contains a high-energy phosphate. The reason is that release of the enol by cleavage of the phosphate allows it to revert spontaneously to the keto form:

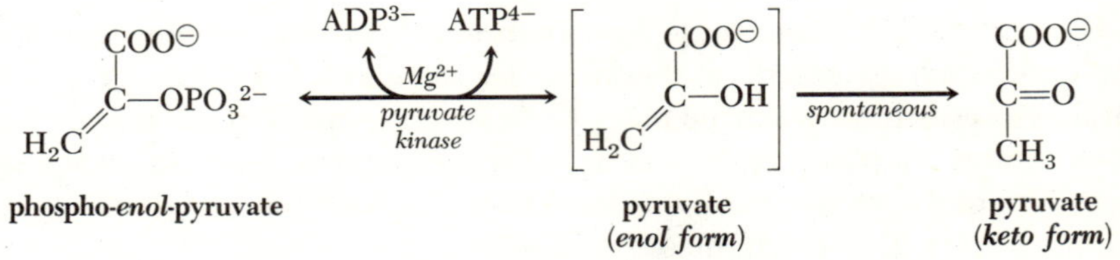

The position of equilibrium is far in the direction of the ketone form of pyruvate, and the large amount of free energy released by this equilibration is added to the free energy of phosphate ester hydrolysis.

PYRUVATE KINASE. The final reaction of the Embden-Meyerhof pathway to pyruvate is the transfer of the high energy phosphate from phospho-*enol*-pyruvate to ADP, thereby forming ATP.

THE COMPLETE EMBDEN-MEYERHOF PATHWAY

If we begin with a molecule of glucose and add all of the reactions involved in its conversion to two molecules of pyruvate according to the Embden-Meyerhof scheme, the result is:

$$\text{glucose} + 2\,\text{NAD}^+ + 2\,(\text{ADP}^{3-} + \text{P}_i^{2-}) \longrightarrow 2\,\text{pyruvate}^- + 2\,\text{NADH} + 2\,\text{ATP}^{4-} + 2\,\text{H}^+ + 2\,\text{H}_2\text{O}$$

(You ought to convince yourself that this is so.) Three things happen simultaneously: glucose is oxidized to pyruvate, NAD is reduced to NADH, and ADP is phosphorylated to form ATP. There can be no Embden-Meyerhof pathway without all three events, which means that ADP, P_i, and NAD, as well as glucose, must be present.

It follows that the rate of the Embden-Meyerhof pathway, like the rate of oxidative phosphorylation (p. 170), is controlled in part by the rate of utilization of ATP. Conversion of one molecule of glucose to two molecules of pyruvate causes a net production of two molecules of ATP from ADP and P_i, and the process will stop when all of the ADP or P_i in the cytosol is exhausted. When the rate of expenditure of ATP increases, the resultant rise in the concentration of ADP and P_i will accelerate the formation of pyruvate and the regeneration of ATP until the rates of utilization and production just balance. (ADP concentration is usually controlling in animal cells, while the concentration of P_i is controlling in at least some protist and higher plant cells.)

Oxidation of Cytoplasmic NADH. Since the Embden-Meyerhof pathway also consumes NAD and produces NADH, it cannot proceed without some means of regenerating the oxidized nucleotide. The NADH of eukaryotic cells cannot enter mitochondria to be oxidized by molecular oxygen through the apparatus of oxidative phosphorylation, and it therefore must be handled in the cytosol. The only significant means of doing this is through displacement of the equilibrium of alcohol dehydrogenases by the increasing concentration of NADH; this isn't difficult because most of the alcohol dehydrogenases have equilibria favoring formation of the alcohol:

$$\mathrm{H{-}\overset{|}{\underset{|}{C}}{-}OH} + \mathrm{NAD}^{\oplus} \rightleftharpoons \mathrm{\overset{|}{\underset{|}{C}}{=}O} + \mathrm{NADH} + \mathrm{H}^{\oplus}$$

But what to do with the accumulating alcohols? They could be excreted as end products in metabolism, and we shall discuss the way some cells use this method of handling the problem in the next two chapters; but many cells, particularly those of the skeletal muscles and nervous tissue, remove one or more of the resulting alcohols by transporting it into mitochondria where it can be oxidized by molecular oxygen. The result is the effective transport of electrons from NADH of the cytosol to oxygen in mitochondria. Let us look at a specific example.

The Glycerol Phosphate Shuttle. The cytosol contains a dehydrogenase that equilibrates glycerol 3-phosphate and dihydroxyacetone phosphate with NAD and NADH (Fig. 14-8). This is a straightforward equilibration of secondary alcohol and the corresponding ketone. (We saw that dihydroxyacetone phosphate is an intermediate in the conversion of glucose to pyruvate, but we are here talking about an entirely different function of the compound.) When the concentration of NADH tends to rise owing to the action of the Embden-Meyerhof pathway, there will be a shift from dihydroxyacetone phosphate to glycerol 3-phosphate that utilizes part of the increased NADH.

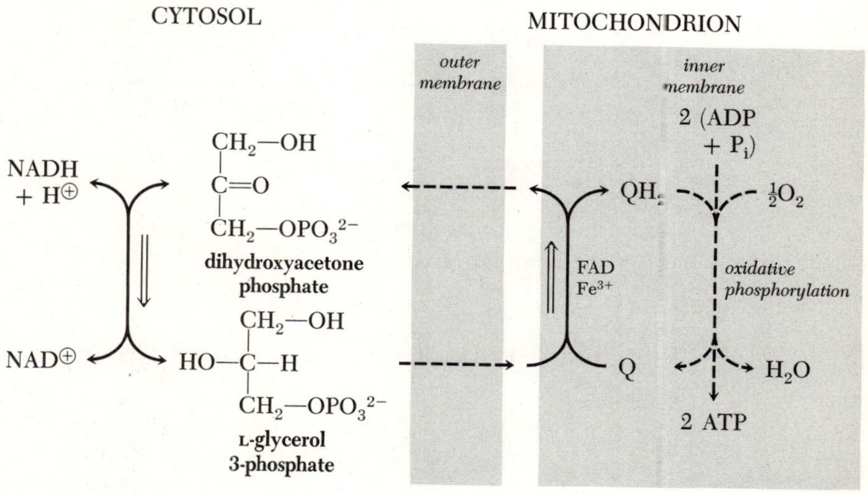

Figure 14-8 The glycerol phosphate shuttle of electrons. NADH and dihydroxyacetone phosphate are equilibrated with NAD and glycerol 3-phosphate in the cytosol. Glycerol 3-phosphate can cross the outer mitochondrial membrane and be irreversibly oxidized back to dihydroxyacetone phosphate by a dehydrogenase in the inner membrane, with transfer of the electrons to ubiquinone. The result is the creation of concentration gradients causing a flow of glycerol phosphate into mitochondria, and of dihydroxyacetone phosphate out. The overall effect is the oxidation of NADH in the cytosol by O_2 in the mitochondria, but only two molecules of ATP are produced, since electrons are transferred to ubiquinone in the mitochondria.

Now, glycerol 3-phosphate can cross the outer mitochondrial membranes and become exposed to the action of a dehydrogenase present on the outer surface of the inner membrane. This dehydrogenase also catalyzes the interconversion of glycerol 3-phosphate and dihydroxyacetone phosphate; however, it is an iron-containing flavoprotein, similar to succinate dehydrogenase, and the use of this stronger oxidizing agent makes the equilibrium strongly favor the formation of the ketone. In addition, the electrons removed are directly transferred to ubiquinone, and the re-oxidation of reduced ubiquinone by O_2 results in the generation of two high-energy phosphate bonds per glycerol 3-phosphate oxidized.

Here we have it. Dihydroxyacetone phosphate acts as a catalytic carrier for electrons in the glycerol phosphate shuttle, much in the way that oxaloacetate acts as a catalytic carrier for acetyl groups in the citric acid cycle. The shuttle occurs because the appearance of NADH tends to raise the ratio [glycerol 3-P]/[dihydroxyacetone P] in the cytosol and the mitochondrial oxidation lowers the same ratio in the mitochondria. Therefore, there is a concentration gradient for glycerol 3-phosphate into mitochondria, and for dihydroxyacetone phosphate out of mitochondria.

Since there is no net consumption or production of dihydroxyacetone phosphate in the shuttle, this function does not detract from utilization of the triose phosphate in the Embden-Meyerhof pathway. The glycerol phosphate shuttle is especially important in white muscle fibers of the higher animals and the flight muscles of insects.

The overall reaction of the glycerol phosphate shuttle is nothing more than:

$$\text{NADH(cytosol)} + \tfrac{1}{2}\,O_2 + 2\,(\text{ADP}^{3-} + \text{P}_i^{2-}) + 3\,\text{H}^+ \longrightarrow \text{NAD}^+ + 2\,\text{ATP}^{4-} + 3\,H_2O$$

When the two molecules of NADH produced in the Embden-Meyerhof pathway are oxidized by the shuttle, the effective result is the oxidation of glucose to pyruvate by O_2.

$$\text{glucose} + O_2 + 6\,(\text{ADP}^{3-} + \text{P}_i^{2-}) + 4\,\text{H}^+ \longrightarrow 2\,\text{pyruvate}^- + 6\,\text{ATP}^{4-} + 8\,H_2O$$

THE OXIDATION OF PYRUVATE

The final steps in the total combustion of glucose by plants and animals involve the diffusion of pyruvate from the cytosol into the mitochondria, where it is oxidized to acetyl coenzyme A, and then to CO_2 and H_2O by the citric acid cycle:

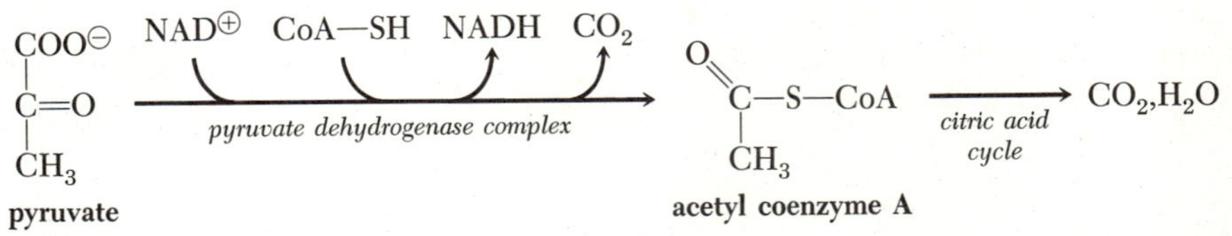

These mitochondrial oxidations account for over 80% of the total ATP obtained from the complete oxidation of glucose.

The Pyruvate Dehydrogenase Complex

Pyruvate is an α-ketocarboxylate, which is oxidized by the same sort of mechanism as is α-ketoglutarate (p. 181). A decarboxylase peptide in the pyruvate dehydrogenase complex catalyzes the removal of CO_2; the remaining two carbons combine with an attached molecule of **thiamine pyrophosphate** as a **hydroxyethyl group** (Fig. 14–9). A

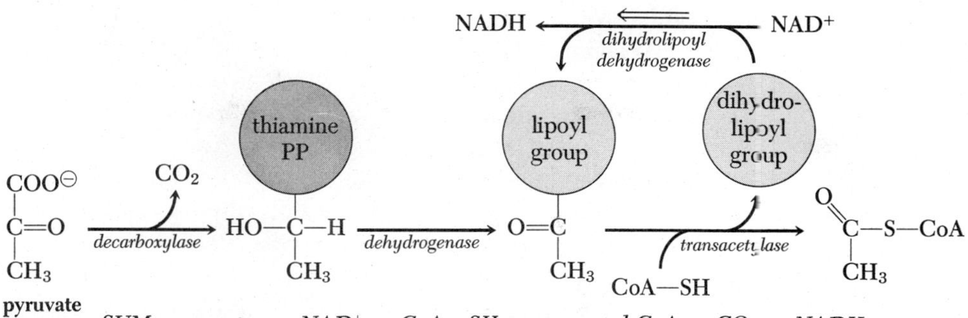

SUM: pyruvate⁻ + NAD⁺ + CoA—SH ⟶ acetyl CoA + CO_2 + NADH

Figure 14-9 The oxidative decarboxylation of pyruvate uses the same kind of mechanism seen with α-ketoglutarate dehydrogenase, except that the enzyme has separate decarboxylase and dehydrogenase peptides. The hydroxyethyl group created by the initial decarboxylation is attached to thiamine pyrophosphate on the decarboxylase peptide, and the dehydrogenase peptide catalyzes its transfer to a lipoyl group on a transacetylase peptide. The resultant acetyl group is then transferred to coenzyme A, and the now-reduced dihydrolipoyl group is re-oxidized by NAD through catalysis by dihydrolipoyl dehydrogenase peptide, a flavoprotein.

dehydrogenase peptide then catalyzes the transfer of the hydroxyethyl group, which is equivalent to acetaldehyde in oxidation state, to a **lipoyllysyl** side chain on still another peptide. The transferred group is thereby oxidized to an **acetyl** group, combined with what is now a dihydrolipoyllysyl side chain. Finally, the acetyl group is tranferred to coenzyme A, and the remaining dihydrolipoyllysyl group is re-oxidized to its disulfide form by transferring electrons through **FAD** to NAD.

The pyruvate dehydrogenase of animal tissues apparently differs from α-ketoglutarate dehydrogenase and the pyruvate dehydrogenase of some bacteria in having the decarboxylase and dehydrogenase activities on separable peptide chains.

Effect of Thiamine Deficiency. Thiamine pyrophosphate is required for the oxidation of pyruvate and for the oxidation of α-ketoglutarate, as well as for other reactions we shall encounter. Animals have lost the ability to make thiamine and depend upon a dietary supply from which to make the necessary enzymes. One or more enzymes will eventually be present in less than adequate amounts for normal metabolism in an animal eating progressively less thiamine.

Evidently, pyruvate dehydrogenase loses thiamine pyrophosphate more readily than does α-ketoglutarate dehydrogenase, which is also necessary for the metabolism of fatty acids and amino acids, because thiamine deficiency appears to affect carbohydrate metabolism preferentially, especially in the brain. The thiamine requirement of a human is dependent upon carbohydrate intake, being about 1.5 micrograms per gram of carbohydrate eaten in the typical mixed diets of this country. Furthermore, thiamine-deficient humans show much greater accumulation of pyruvate than of α-ketoglutarate after they are fed glucose.

When humans remove the hard outer layer and the embryo from seeds before using the soft, starchy interior as food, either directly or as flour, they are also removing the cells containing most of the thiamine pyrophosphate. People heavily dependent upon refined seeds for food, especially in the rice-consuming areas of the Orient, may therefore have a partial deprivation of thiamine that slowly results in an illness called **beri-beri** (failure of the heart, paralysis, abnormal sensations in the limbs).

Humans may also become deficient in thiamine through excessive use of alcohol as a depressant for diminution of unpleasant stimulations. A drunk may live only with his bottle, and eat so little food that an acute deficiency of thiamine develops rapidly. (The resultant **Wernicke's encephalopathy** with severe mental disturbances and loss of motor control was also common in Japanese prisoner-of-war camps during the

Second World War.)

Arsenite and Mercury Poisoning. During the action of pyruvate dehydrogenase, dihydrolipoyl groups are formed which have a closely spaced pair of sulfhydryl groups. Metallic ions with a high affinity for sulfhydryl groups, such as mercuric or arsenite ions, are bound much more tightly to a pair on one molecule than they are to two sulfhydryl groups on separate molecules. For example, trivalent arsenic was formerly in common use by murderers and suicides, essentially because the formation of a dihydrolipoyl–arsenite chelate prevents the re-oxidation of the dihydrolipoyl group necessary for continued activity of the α-keto acid dehydrogenase complexes. Indeed, arsenite poisoning mimics some effects of thiamine deficiency on the nervous system, and causes an accumulation of pyruvate in the blood. An American ambassadress to Rome had her pyruvate dehydrogenase inhibited in this way by her bedroom wallpaper, which had a patrician design partially created with the mellow green of cupric arsenite.

The high affinity of arsenite for compounds containing neighboring thiol groups means that it accumulates in the protein keratin. This constituent of hair, skin, horns, and the like, contains a high concentration of disulfide bonds. Some of the parent sulfhydryl groups tightly bind arsenite during maturation of the protein. Enough of the hair and fingernails survived dissolution in the otherwise well-aged corpse of Charles Francis Hall, an explorer who died in Northern Greenland in 1871 after a two-week illness, to enable proof in 1968 that he had been murdered by his associates, because the hair and nails grown during his last days of life contained high levels of arsenic and older portions did not.

THE COMPLETE PROCESS

We have now seen all of the reactions necessary for the total oxidation of glucose: the oxidation of glucose to pyruvate in the cytosol, the transfer of the resultant electrons from the cytosol to mitochondria, the oxidation of the pyruvate to acetyl coenzyme A in mitochondria, and finally the total oxidation of acetyl coenzyme A by the citric acid cycle in mitochondria. What is the result?

If we add the individual equations, we arrive at an overall stoichiometry:

$$\text{glucose} + 6\ O_2 + 36\ (ADP^{3-} + P_i^{2-} + H^+) \longrightarrow 6\ CO_2 + 36\ ATP^{4-} + 42\ H_2O$$

Thirty-six molecules of high-energy phosphate are generated per molecule of glucose burned, and the P:O ratio is 3.0. Slightly less oxygen is consumed to generate a given quantity of ATP when glucose is burned than is consumed when fatty acids are the fuel (P:O ratio $\sim$ 2.8).

Stoichiometry of High-Energy Phosphate

Let us examine exactly how the figure of 36 high-energy phosphates produced per glucose consumed was obtained. It is important to remember that two moles of triose phosphates are produced from each mole of glucose, so that the stoichiometry for all of the reactions beginning with the oxidation of glyceraldehyde 3-phosphate must be multiplied by two.

1. One high-energy phosphate is consumed to phosphorylate glucose: −1
2. One high-energy phosphate is consumed to phosphorylate fructose 6-phosphate: −1
3. Two high-energy phosphates are produced by oxidative phosphorylation in

mitochondria for each of the two pairs of electrons transported from glyceraldehyde 3-phosphate via NADH and the glycerol phosphate shuttle: +4

4. One high-energy phosphate is gained by transfer to ADP from each of two molecules of 1,3-diphosphoglycerate: +2
5. One high-energy phosphate is gained by transfer to ADP from each of two molecules of phospho-*enol*-pyruvate: +2
6. Three high-energy phosphates are produced by oxidative phosphorylation in mitochondria from reoxidation of each of the two molecules of NADH formed by oxidation of pyruvate: +6
7. Twelve high-energy phosphates are produced by the complete oxidation of each of the two molecules of acetyl coenzyme A in the citric acid cycle: +24

TOTAL +36

Regulation of Glucose Oxidation

The regulation of glucose oxidation consists of two parts. One is the automatic regulation of the rate of ATP generation to the rate of ATP utilization that occurs as a result of the accompanying changes in ADP or P_i concentration. The other is regulation of the uptake and commitment of glucose to the oxidative pathways so as to provide sufficient fuel for the reactions generating ATP. These effects are best illustrated in mammalian skeletal muscle, to which the following discussion applies.

Regulation by Changes in ADP Concentration. To recapitulate what we have noted in this and the preceding chapter (Fig. 14–10), ADP is required for two reactions during the conversion of triose phosphates to pyruvate. It is also required for the maintenance of oxidized coenzymes in mitochondria through the transfer of electrons to oxygen by the processes of oxidative phosphorylation. These oxidized coenzymes are in turn necessary for the oxidation of pyruvate to acetyl coenzyme A, and for the further oxidation of acetyl coenzyme A in the citric acid cycle, as well as for the oxidation of glycerol phosphate used to transfer electrons from the cytosol. In sum, ADP causes an acceleration of the formation of pyruvate in the cytosol, and its total oxidation in the mitochondria.

Although the absolute magnitudes of changes in ADP concentration are kept low in muscles by the presence of phosphocreatine (p. 149), the relative changes are very large as work begins (Fig. 14–11). The ADP concentration will continue to rise, causing greater and greater acceleration of glucose metabolism until the increased rate of ATP production matches the rate of ATP utilization, at which point the concentration of ADP will stop rising. The effects of ADP concentration are huge. The oxygen consumption of human thigh muscles increases some 200-fold upon going from rest to maximum effort, and this is mainly a result of increased concentrations of ADP.

Regulation of Phosphofructokinase. Acceleration of the utilization of triose phosphates by ADP will do no good unless there is a corresponding increase in the rate of their formation, and this is obtained by controlling the rate of the phosphofruc-

Figure 14–10 ADP is required for the conversion of triose phosphates to pyruvate by the Embden-Meyerhof pathway in the cytosol, and for the oxidation of reduced coenzymes in the mitochondria. The formation of pyruvate and its oxidation is therefore automatically adjusted, in part, to the utilization of high-energy phosphate, which produces ADP.

CYTOSOL (glucose $\longrightarrow$ pyruvate):

1,3-diphosphoglycerate + ADP $\longleftrightarrow$ ATP + 3-phosphoglycerate

phospho-*enol*-pyruvate + ADP $\longrightarrow$ ATP + pyruvate

MITOCHONDRION (pyruvate $\longrightarrow$ CO_2, H_2O):

$NADH + Q + ADP \longleftrightarrow ATP + QH_2 + NAD^{\oplus}$

$QH_2 + 2(\text{cyt. c}) + ADP \longrightarrow ATP + 2(\text{reduced cyt. c}) + Q$

$2(\text{reduced cyt. c}) + \frac{1}{2}O_2 + ADP \longrightarrow ATP + H_2O + 2(\text{cyt. c})$

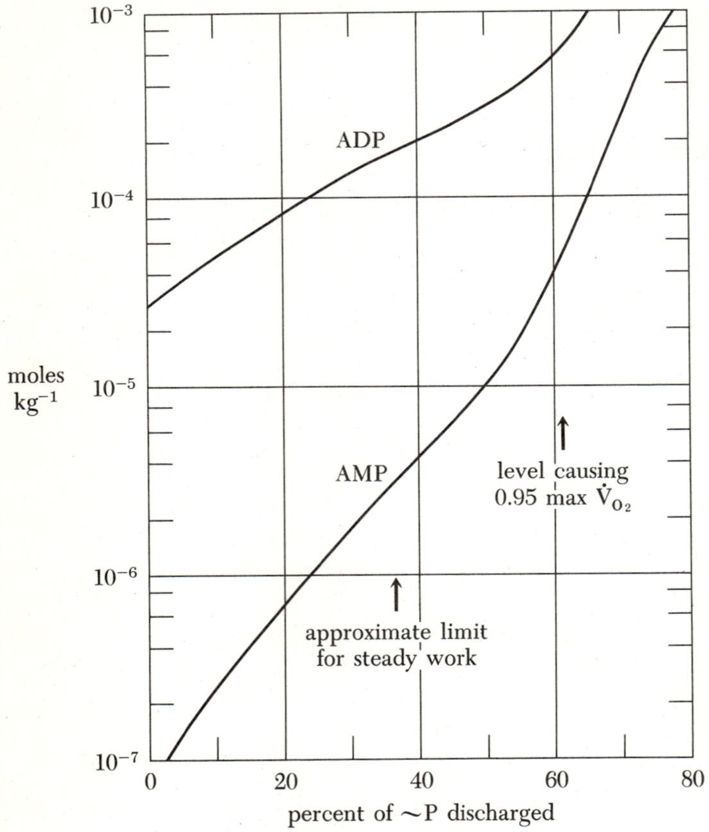

Figure 14-11 The changes in concentrations of ADP and AMP in skeletal muscles at increasing work loads cause an increased discharge of total high-energy phosphate stores. Although the absolute concentrations are low with light activity, the relative changes are very sensitive to changes in power output.

tokinase reaction (p. 215). We already noted that this phosphorylation of fructose 6-phosphate to form fructose 1,6-diphosphate is an irreversible reaction, a step that commits the glucose residue to metabolism. It is obvious that tissues have sufficient enzyme to supply fuel for the most rapid energy production they can achieve—otherwise it wouldn't happen. However, it would not do to have an irreversible reaction going full speed at rest; the whole body would be converted to fructose diphosphate! Hence, phosphofructokinase is tightly regulated through allosteric effects so that it is almost completely inhibited in resting muscles. This is accomplished by blocking the action of phosphofructokinase with physiological concentrations of ATP, which binds to both substrate and regulatory sites on the enzyme. The inhibition is relieved by AMP, but not by the low concentration present in resting muscle. However, the concentration of AMP changes even more rapidly than does the concentration of ADP with increasing rates of work. Any depletion of high-energy phosphate, such as that caused by muscular contraction, results in a prompt elevation of the AMP concentration and activation of phosphofructokinase.

Phosphofructokinase is also inhibited in the test tube by a variety of anions, including citrate and phosphoglycerate. Since an accumulation of citrate would signal a surfeit of substrates for the citric acid cycle, and an accumulation of phosphoglycerate would occur with a similar clogging of the Embden-Meyerhof pathway, it may be that these compounds are also effective in this way in the living muscles.

Regulation Through Isozymes—Glucose Uptake. Since the phosphorylation of glucose is irreversible, hexokinase is another example of an enzyme that must be controlled, in this case to prevent the cell from being swamped with glucose 6-phosphate at times of glucose surfeit. This problem is met simply by making the hexokinases so that they are inhibited by glucose 6-phosphate, their own product. If glucose 6-phosphate is not removed for storage or for use as a fuel, the resultant accumulation will prevent further uptake of glucose.

However, there is an additional problem in the higher animals. Different tissues have different requirements for glucose. For example, it is desirable to have the brain capable of drawing on the glucose supply as long as some is available, while the liver acts mainly as a temporary storehouse for glucose and therefore ought not take up the compound unless there is a plentiful supply. Therefore, these organs are built with different enzymes catalyzing the same phosphorylation of glucose by ATP, which are said to be **isoenzymes,** or **isozymes.** The purpose of the existence of isoenzymes in general is to permit different responses of enzymatic activity to environmental circumstances.

Most tissues contain different isozymes of hexokinase that are characterized by relatively low K_M values for glucose, and are also able to catalyze the phosphorylation of other sugars, such as fructose or mannose. They vary somewhat in their affinity for glucose and for ATP, and are believed to provide fine tuning for regulation of glucose uptake in the tissues. In addition, regulation of glucose transport by insulin is also associated with the presence of one of the hexokinase isozymes.

The liver, on the other hand, contains a glucokinase that is relatively specific for glucose with a much higher K_M for the sugar:

	K_M (ATP)	K_M (glucose)
brain hexokinase	4×10^{-4} M	5×10^{-5} M
liver glucokinase	1×10^{-4} M	2×10^{-2} M

The concentration of ATP in these tissues is held near 0.001 M or greater, which is substantially greater than K_M for either enzyme, and this substrate is therefore not limiting in either case. The brain receives arterial blood in which the concentration of glucose is normally around 5 millimolar, 100 times the K_M of its hexokinase for glucose.

The K_M for glucose of the glucokinase in liver is four times the normal arterial concentration. However, the liver receives blood from the intestine through the portal circulation, and the portal blood has much higher concentrations of glucose during absorption of a meal containing carbohydrate. Therefore, the liver is built with an enzymatic constitution that permits it to store excess glucose when it is available without later competing with the brain and other tissues.

Regulation by Phosphorylation of an Enzyme—Pyruvate Decarboxylase. The activity of the pyruvate dehydrogenase complex determines how much acetyl coenzyme A will be formed from glucose. The pyruvate decarboxylase peptide of the complex catalyzes the initial and rate-determining step, and it is the activity of this peptide that is regulated (Fig. 14–12). (The necessity for regulation may explain why the decarboxylase is present on a separate peptide in the mammalian complexes.) There is regulation by negative feedback—acetyl coenzyme A and NADH inhibit the enzyme and therefore slow the utilization of glucose when the citric acid cycle or oxidative phosphorylation already have a surfeit of substrates.

However, there is an additional kind of regulation involving covalent modification of the enzyme through phosphorylation. We shall see other examples of this general kind of regulation. In effect, the phosphorylation converts the enzyme to an isozyme with a different activity under the same circumstances. In this case, the phosphorylation of the pyruvate decarboxylase peptide makes it inactive. The phosphorylation is catalyzed by still another enzyme, a protein kinase, present in the pyruvate dehydrogenase complex. There is approximately one molecule of this **pyruvate decarboxylase**

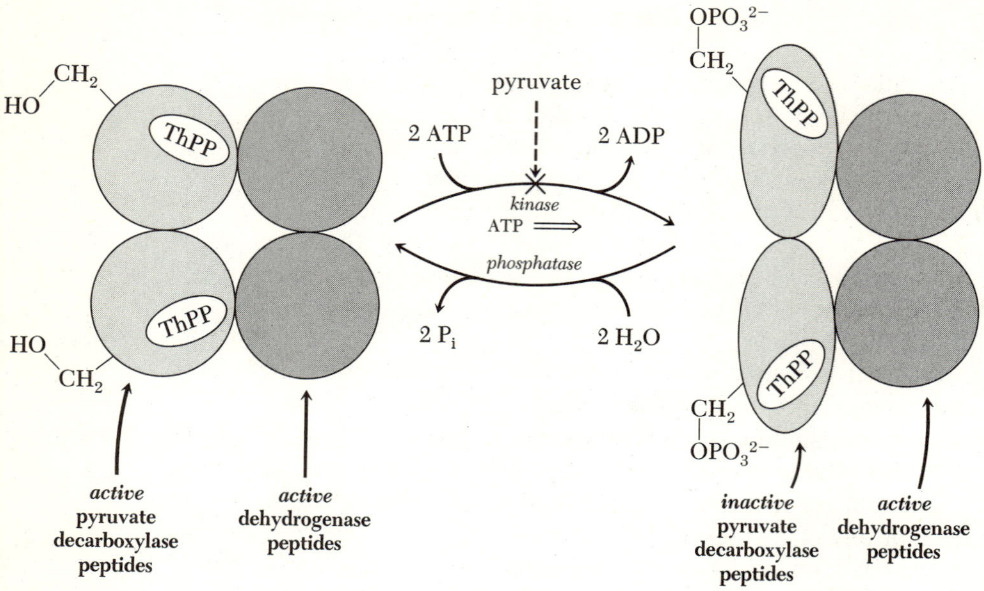

Figure 14–12 The pyruvate dehydrogenase complex contains a regulatory kinase that catalyzes the phosphorylation of a seryl group in the decarboxylase peptide. This causes the decarboxylase peptide to assume an inactive conformation. Since decarboxylation is the first reaction in the series catalyzed by the complex, control of the decarboxylase regulates the entire series, even though the other peptides in the complex remain active. A phosphatase is also present to remove the inactivating phosphate group. The only known effectors controlling the activity of these regulating enzymes are ATP, which activates the kinase, and pyruvate, which inhibits it.

kinase for each 10 decarboxylase peptides. There is also a **phosphatase** present in the complex to catalyze the hydrolysis of the phosphate groups, thereby restoring the activity of pyruvate decarboxylase. The regulation of phosphorylation and dephosphorylation, which in turn control the activity of the pyruvate decarboxylase, is still not clear. It is known that the kinase is allosterically activated by ATP, and the reasoning goes as follows: excess ATP activates pyruvate decarboxylase kinase, which then catalyzes faster phosphorylation of pyruvate decarboxylase, making it less active. Less active pyruvate decarboxylase means a decreased rate of oxidation of pyruvate to acetyl coenzyme A, diminishing further use of glucose when more ATP is not needed.

FURTHER READING

F. Dickens, P. J. Randle, and W. J. Whelan, Carbohydrate metabolism and its disorders, Chaps. 1, 2, 3 in v. 1, Academic Press (1968). Contains detailed discussions of processes in animal tissues.

W. Pigman and D. Horton, eds., The carbohydrates, Academic Press (1972). A yet incomplete multi-volume reference work. Valuable for details of chemistry of carbohydrates.

T. E. Mansour, Phosphofructokinase, Curr. Topics Cell Regul., 5:1 (1972). Detailed discussion of regulation.

L. J. Reed et al., Pyruvate dehydrogenase complex: Structure, function and regulation, p. 253 in M. A. Mehlman and R. W. Hanson, eds., Energy metabolism and the regulation of metabolic processes in mitochondria, Academic Press (1972).

R. W. McGilvery, Use of fuels for muscular exercise, in H. Howald and J. Poortmans, eds., Metabolic adaptation to prolonged physical exercise, Birkhäuser Verlag Basel (1974). A review of regulation by ADP and AMP.

F. K. Paddock, C. C. Loomis, and A. K. Perkons, An inquest on the death of Charles Francis Hall, New Eng. J. Med., 282:784 (1970).

QUESTIONS

1. Are there anomeric forms of D-glucose 6-phosphate? Of D-fructose 6-phosphate?
2. Reasoning by analogy, would the reaction of an enzyme catalyzing the phosphorylation of free glycerol by ATP to form glycerol 3-phosphate be readily reversible under physiological conditions? Why? Would the reaction of an enzyme catalyzing the phosphorylation of free glycerate by ATP to form 1-phosphoglycerate be readily reversible under these conditions? Why?
3. The two phosphate groups on fructose 1,6-diphosphate are separately derived from ATP. In what reactions does the transfer occur? Both of these groups are eventually returned by transfer to ADP. In what reaction is each of the groups returned?
4. At what steps, if any, are coenzymes derived in animals from the following vitamins required for the complete combustion of glucose? (a) Nicotinamide; (b) riboflavin; (c) thiamine; (d) biotin; (e) pyridoxine.
5. What, if any, are the similarities between the oxidation of pyruvate and the oxidation of α-ketoglutarate in mitochondria? Are there any resemblances to the oxidation of glyceraldehyde 3-phosphate?
6. Predict the action of a tetrose 4-phosphate isomerase, or a pentose kinase.
7. Calculate the relative value of glucose and of fatty acids as fuels by estimating the yield of ATP from 50 g of glucose (MW = 180) and 50 g of palmitic acid (MW = 256). How do these relative values compare to estimates based on the heats of combustion of 16 kJ per g of glucose and 40 kJ per g of fat?
8. Explain why it is that pairs of thiol groups on one molecule will form a tighter complex with mercuric ions than will two thiol groups provided by separate molecules? Hint: What are the relative positions of equilibrium of $A + B \longrightarrow AB$ and $A + 2C \longrightarrow AC_2$ at low concentrations of reactants, given equal standard free energies?
9. Name all of the reactions in the complete oxidation of glucose that are directly accelerated by an increased concentration of ADP. Name those that are directly accelerated by an increased concentration of AMP. Which ratio changes most when muscles begin working at a steady pace, [ADP]/[ATP] or [AMP]/[ATP]?
10. Why do tissues such as the brain phosphorylate glucose mostly by the action of hexokinases, when the liver uses a glucokinase for the same purpose?
11. Why doesn't the use of dihydroxyacetone phosphate for transport of electrons from cytosol to mitochondria diminish the amount of pyruvate formed from an increased uptake of glucose?
12. Isozymes of phosphofructokinase have been discovered in different tissues. The action of which regulatory effector is likely to be different in these tissues as a result?
13. How is it that the labeled carbon will appear in pyruvate when glucose labeled with ^{14}C in either C-1 or C-6 is fed to an animal? Trace the path of the isotope through the various intermediates between glucose and pyruvate.

CHAPTER 15

GLYCOLYSIS, GLUCONEOGENESIS, AND GLYOXYLATE

THE CONCEPTS

Glycolysis is a process, complete in itself, for generating ATP by cleaving glucose into two molecules of lactic acid. It occurs by a continuation of the Embden-Meyerhof pathway; pyruvate and NADH react to form lactate while regenerating NAD through the action of lactate dehydrogenase. The necessary glucosyl units for rapid glycolysis are obtained from stored glycogen, and three molecules of ATP are produced at the time that a glucosyl unit is converted to a pair of lactate molecules. This can occur because the initial expenditure of one ATP to take up glucose was made at the time of storage.

The relative amounts of glycolysis and complete combustion of glucosyl units used for the generation of ATP depend upon the relative capacities of the Embden-Meyerhof pathway in the cytosol and the oxidative pathways in mitochondria. For example, white muscle fibers have a potentially rapid Embden-Meyerhof pathway and relatively few mitochondria compared to red fibers. The rapid and strong contractions of which these fibers are capable soon raise the ADP concentration to a point at which it stimulates the production of pyruvate and NADH beyond the capacity of mitochondria to handle them. A further rise in ADP concentration then causes a sharp rise in lactate formation. This capacity for rapid glycolysis enables humans to work two to three times faster than they can by oxidative phosphorylation alone, but only for 30 seconds or so before the resultant acidification of the muscle stops contraction.

Red muscle fibers have more mitochondria and less capacity for the Embden-Meyerhof pathway. Stimulation of these processes by a rising concentration of ADP therefore results in most of the high-energy phosphate being generated by oxidative phosphorylation, with little formation of lactate. Indeed, red muscle fibers are like heart and brain cells in oxidizing lactate to pyruvate and then on to CO_2 and H_2O as a fuel. The higher oxidative capacity of these cells makes the lactate dehydrogenase reaction proceed toward pyruvate. Furthermore, the dehydrogenase of these cells is an isozyme that is inhibited by pyruvate, so the formation of lactate from pyruvate is impeded even when a high pyruvate concentration creates a favorable equilibrium.

Although glycolysis does not require oxygen, it is frequently associated with workloads that also cause a high oxygen consumption. Exceptions occur in diving animals, in which the muscular blood supply is diminished to conserve oxygen, and movement is made possible mainly by glycolysis. On the other hand, insect flight muscles lack lactate dehydrogenase, and they are completely dependent on oxidative metabolism.

White muscles must have the ability to change the rate of formation of triose phosphates from near zero to a very high value. This is accomplished by the creation of a futile cycle in which the fructose diphosphate created by phosphofructokinase in resting muscle is destroyed through hydrolysis by a phosphatase. The phosphatase is inhibited by AMP; since the kinase is activated by AMP, this creates a hair-trigger in which there is no net formation of fructose diphosphate (and therefore triose phosphates) at the AMP concentration found in resting muscle, but with the concentration such that any further increase in AMP results in a massive activation of the kinase and a formation of triose phosphate.

Gluconeogenesis from lactate, in which it is converted to glucose residues, is a major route for its disposal. Gluconeogenesis involves modification of the Embden-Meyerhof pathway so as to introduce additional high-energy phosphate, thereby changing the position of equilibrium

to favor glucose formation from lactate. These modifications include the carboxylation of pyruvate to oxaloacetate, driven by ATP, followed by a decarboxylating phosphorylation to form phospho-*enol*-pyruvate at the expense of GTP. They also include the substitution of irreversible hydrolyses of fructose diphosphate and of glucose 6-phosphate in place of the irreversible formation of these compounds by the respective kinases in the Embden-Meyerhof pathway. The route permits the formation of glucose from lactate, pyruvate, oxaloacetate, phospho-*enol*-pyruvate, or any compound that can be converted to one of these precursors, and is the major means by which glucose is made from amino acids.

The glyoxylate cycle is a device for gluconeogenesis from fatty acids in some plant seeds and microorganisms. Animals cannot convert acetyl coenzyme A to pyruvate or oxaloacetate, and therefore cannot convert fats to glucose. Some other organisms can do this because they possess an isocitrate lyase that cleaves isocitrate into glyoxylate and succinate, and a malate synthase that condenses glyoxylate with acetyl coenzyme A to form malate. The combination of these reactions with those of the citric acid cycle has the effect of causing the formation of succinate from two acetyl groups. Since succinate can be converted to oxaloacetate, which is a precursor of glucose *via* phospho-*enol*-pyruvate, gluconeogenesis from acetyl groups, and therefore from fatty acids, occurs.

GLYCOLYSIS

We saw in the preceding chapter how ATP may be generated through the complete oxidation of glucose; ATP may also be generated by less complete metabolism of glucose, such as occurs in a process known as glycolysis. Glycolysis literally means the splitting of glucose, and the name is apt. Glucose is cleaved to form two molecules of lactic acid according to the formal stoichiometry:

$$\underset{\text{D-glucose}}{C_6H_{12}O_6} \longrightarrow 2\ \underset{\text{L-lactate}}{HO\text{—}\overset{\displaystyle COO^{\ominus}}{\underset{\displaystyle CH_3}{C}}\text{—}H} + 2\,H^{\oplus}$$

The important features of glycolysis are that it produces ATP without consuming O_2 and that it produces H^+.

The Reactions of Glycolysis. Glycolysis is nothing more than the formation of pyruvate by the Embden-Meyerhof pathway, with a further reduction of pyruvate to lactate providing the means for disposal of NADH without the utilization of O_2. We noted that the enzymes of the Embden-Meyerhof pathway, which are especially abundant in the soluble cytoplasm of skeletal muscles, catalyze the conversion of glucose and NAD to pyruvate and NADH, with a concomitant generation of ATP:

$$\text{(1) glucose} + 2\,NAD^+ + 2\,(ADP^{3-} + P_i^{2-}) \longrightarrow$$
$$2\ \text{pyruvate}^- + 2\,NADH + 2\,ATP^{4-} + 2\,H^+ + 2\,H_2O$$

We earlier emphasized the further oxidation of the pyruvate in mitochondria and the removal of electrons from NADH by the glycerol phosphate shuttle. However, the cytosol of mammalian skeletal muscles is rich in a lactate dehydrogenase catalyzing the equilibrium:

$$\underset{\text{pyruvate}}{\overset{\displaystyle COO^{\ominus}}{\underset{\displaystyle CH_3}{C}}\text{=O}} + NADH + H^{\oplus} \xrightleftharpoons[]{\text{lactate dehydrogenase}} \underset{\text{L-lactate}}{HO\text{—}\overset{\displaystyle COO^{\ominus}}{\underset{\displaystyle CH_3}{C}}\text{—}H} + NAD^{\oplus}$$

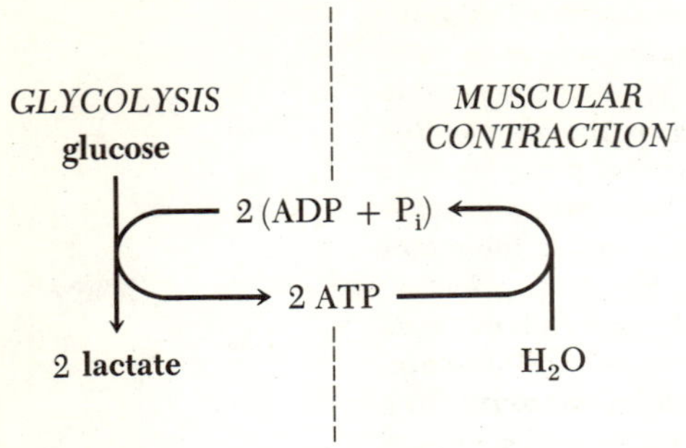

Figure 15-1 The ATP consumed for muscular contraction is partially regenerated by glycolysis, so the major changes in concentration are equivalent to a simple cleavage of glucose into two molecules of lactate, with the formation of two H^+ (not shown).

Now, this reaction is a secondary alcohol-ketone interconversion in which both pyruvate and electrons from NADH are being removed. The reaction is a dead-end; nothing else happens to lactate in most cells, so it is a product of glucose metabolism in the cell in which it is produced, and its formation also regenerates NAD^+ for further attack on glucose:

$$\text{(2)}\ \ 2\ \text{pyruvate}^- + 2\,(\text{NADH} + \text{H}^+) \longrightarrow 2\ \text{lactate}^- + 2\ \text{NAD}^+$$

Adding equations (1) and (2), we now have an overall reaction of:

$$\text{(3)}\ \ \text{glucose} + 2\,(\text{ADP}^{3-} + 2\ \text{P}_i^{\,2-}) \longrightarrow 2\ \text{lactate}^- + 2\ \text{ATP}^{4-} + 2\ \text{H}_2\text{O}$$

Lactate can diffuse out of cells such as the muscles, so this reaction represents a process for the generation of ATP that is complete in itself without the consumption of oxygen.

We have already seen that the Embden-Meyerhof pathway won't proceed unless ATP is being consumed elsewhere, so let us add to the total a twitch of the muscles that will consume ATP (Fig. 15-1):

$$\text{(4)}\ \ 2\ \text{ATP}^{4-} + 2\ \text{H}_2\text{O} \longrightarrow 2\,(\text{ADP}^{3-} + \text{P}_i^{\,2-}) + 2\ \text{H}^+$$

Upon doing this, we are left with the formal stoichiometry of glycolysis:

$$\text{(3)} + \text{(4)}:\ \ \text{glucose} \longrightarrow 2\ \text{lactate}^- + 2\ \text{H}^+$$

Viewing a working muscle over a period of time, we see glucose being consumed and lactate being one of the products that appear, with the muscle acidified as a result.

ROLE OF GLYCOGEN. We have been discussing the metabolism of free glucose, but in fact muscles store glucose as glycogen, and mobilize this stored form as glucose 6-phosphate for use during contractions. The mechanisms of storage and utilization are discussed in Chapters 18 and 19. Suffice it for now to note that a glucose unit in glycogen is converted to glucose 6-phosphate by a simple uptake of inorganic phosphate:

$$\text{glycogen unit} + \text{P}_i \longrightarrow \text{glucose 6-phosphate}$$

The importance of this is that the conversion of glucose 6-phosphate to pyruvate (or lactate) results in the direct formation of 3 ATP per hexose consumed:

$$\textbf{glucose 6-P} \xrightarrow{-\text{ATP}} \textbf{fructose 1,6-diP} \longleftrightarrow \textbf{2 triose P} \xrightarrow{+4\ \text{ATP}} \textbf{2 lactate}$$

$$\textit{NET: } +3\ \text{ATP}$$

(We shall see that additional high-energy phosphates are expended when glycogen is stored, but this enables a higher yield later at the time of contraction.) Therefore, the yield of high-energy phosphate available for work in muscles is 3 ATP per glucosyl unit consumed, or 1.5 ATP per lactate produced. (This does not include the earlier cost of storing glycogen, which would have been covered by increased metabolism at that time.)

Comparison of Glycolysis with the Glycerol Phosphate Shuttle. Glycolysis and the glycerol phosphate shuttle (p. 221) involve similar reactions for disposal of NADH in the cytosol. Both include increased reduction of a ketone group to a secondary alcohol by NADH formed in the Embden-Meyerhof pathway. There the similarity ends. Glycerol phosphate cannot leave the cell across the plasma membrane, except for some small leakage, and there is a second dehydrogenase in mitochondria to re-oxidize the compound. Lactate, on the other hand, freely traverses the plasma membrane and there is no additional lactate dehydrogenase in mitochondria to remove it. There is no net conversion of glucose to glycerol 3-phosphate as a result of the electron shuttle, but there is a net conversion to lactate as a result of glycolysis.

Glycolysis or Complete Combustion?

We see that the metabolism of glucose by the Embden-Meyerhof pathway in mammalian skeletal muscles can lead to two different results, total combustion or glycolysis, depending upon the route of disposal of NADH (Fig. 15–2). If NADH in the cytosol is used to reduce pyruvate to lactate, neither pyruvate nor glycerol phosphate will be available as a source of electrons for oxidative phosphorylation in the mitochondria, and only the relatively small amount of ATP generated in the cytosol per mole of lactate formed will be available to support muscular contraction. What factors determine the extent to which this occurs? First, we ought to examine the nature of skeletal muscle more closely.

Types of Skeletal Muscle. Different skeletal muscles are built to perform different functions, not only from one animal to another, but also within an animal. Muscle fibers vary between two extremes that differ in the molecular structure of their myosin and in their metabolic capacity. Some fibers are built to contract repeatedly for extended periods of time; in order to do this they are constructed for the generation of ATP by oxidative phosphorylation, and the fibers contain many mitochondria and a large concentration of myoglobin to transport oxygen to the mitochondria. These fibers have a deep red color because of the high concentrations of heme proteins.

Other fibers are built for short bursts of very heavy activity, so intense that ATP is used at a much faster rate than could be sustained by mitochondrial oxidations. These fibers have high concentrations of the enzymes of the Embden-Meyerhof pathway in their cytosol; they have mitochondria, but a larger fraction of the oxidative capacity of the mitochondria is taken up with the ubiquinone-coupled glycerol phosphate dehydrogenase that is necessary for the glycerol phosphate shuttle. Since they also contain lower concentrations of myoglobin, as well as of the mitochondrial heme proteins, they appear relatively white. The significance of these structural differences in relation to function is dramatized by a recent finding that the more slowly contracting myosin ordinarily found in red muscle fibers begins to appear in white muscle that is subjected to repeated stimulation.

Many muscles contain both red and white fibers, but others predominantly have one or the other. Extreme examples of these differing types are evident on every platter of cooked chicken. Chickens constantly use their legs to run around in search of food,

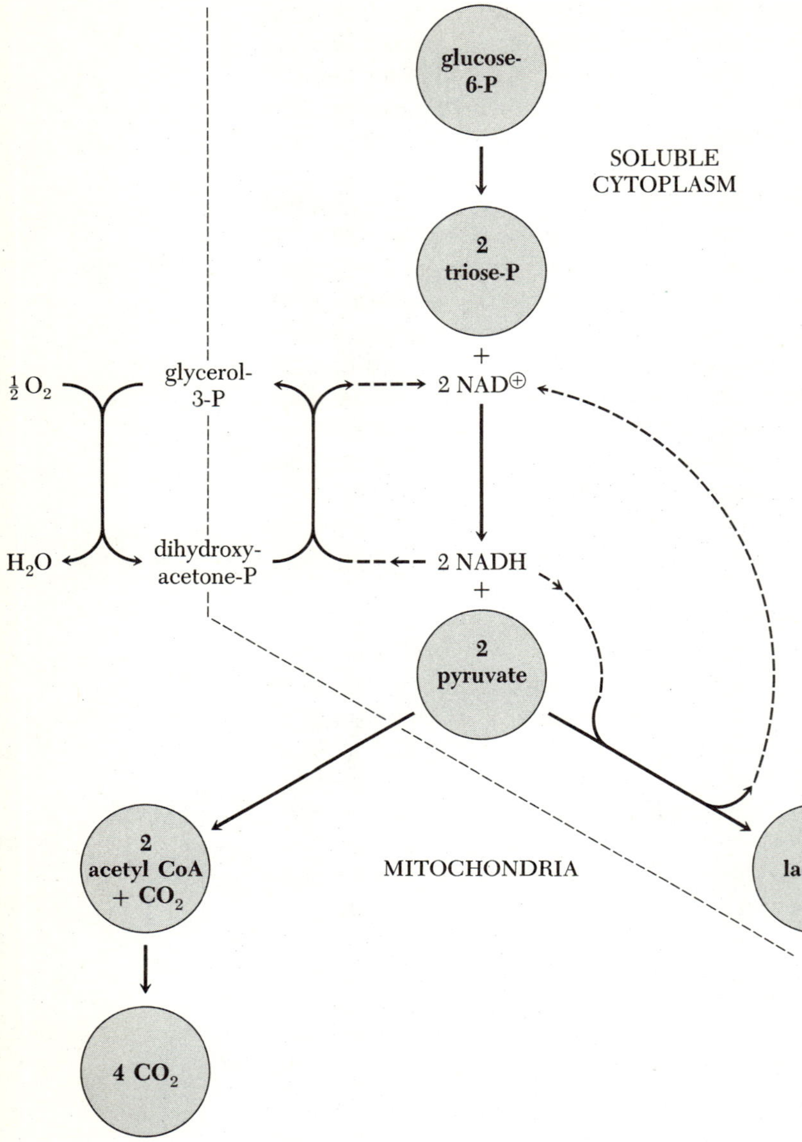

Figure 15–2 The distribution of pyruvate between total oxidation and formation of lactate in working muscles is determined by the ability of the mitochondria to oxidize NADH by the glycerol phosphate shuttle (and by another route to be discussed later (p. 372)) and to oxidize pyruvate to acetyl coenzyme A. When a muscle can produce these compounds in the cytosol faster than the mitochondria can remove them, lactate will be produced. The disparity can result from the inherent enzymatic constitution of the tissue, but it also can be caused by a deprivation of the oxygen supply.

but they only rarely fly, and when they do take to the air, the muscles moving the wing contract rapidly and powerfully to get the heavy carcass off the ground. Therefore, the leg muscles are dark meat with a capacity for sustained oxidative metabolism, whereas the wing muscles are white meat, with a high capacity for rapidly generating ATP by the Embden-Meyerhof pathway, but unable to work for long periods.

Comparative Generation of High-Energy Phosphate. No matter what the type of muscle, the production of ADP due to contraction will increase the rate of all of the reactions in the cytosol that are dependent upon ADP concentration. These include the reactions forming ATP by transfer from phosphocreatine and by transfer from 1,3-diphosphoglycerate and phospho-*enol*-pyruvate in the Embden-Meyerhof pathway, along with the exchange of ADP in the cytosol for ATP in the mitochondria by an antiport mechanism (Fig. 15–3), which in turn accelerates oxidative phosphorylation in the mitochondria.

Which of these processes will be accelerated most? The answer depends upon these factors: the relative sensitivity of the different processes to a given change in ADP, the magnitude of the change in ADP concentration as determined by the rate of work (power output), the concentrations of the enzymes catalyzing the various processes in different muscles, and the availability of substrates.

Mobilization of Phosphagen. It turns out that high-energy phosphate can be transferred from phosphocreatine much more rapidly than it can be generated from the other reactions. Therefore, quick, strong contractions depend upon this transfer, and humans can generate from 6 to 12 times as much power by using phosphocreatine as they can by oxidative phosphorylation. However, such expenditures are one-shot efforts that may continue for only a few seconds at most, with the muscles becoming exhausted before full production of ATP by glucose metabolism has even begun. (Sprinters adapt to training by developing increased stores of phosphocreatine, but no marked change occurs in those trained by longer periods of exercise.)

Use of Glycolysis. When muscles work at something less than a do-or-die pace, the resultant rise in ADP concentration occurs slowly enough to bring the Embden-Meyerhof pathway and oxidative phosphorylation into play. When the power output is low, the ADP concentration need not rise far before the resultant acceleration of the Embden-Meyerhof pathway and oxidative phosphorylation generate ATP as fast as it consumed, thereby preventing a further rise in ADP concentration. The result is

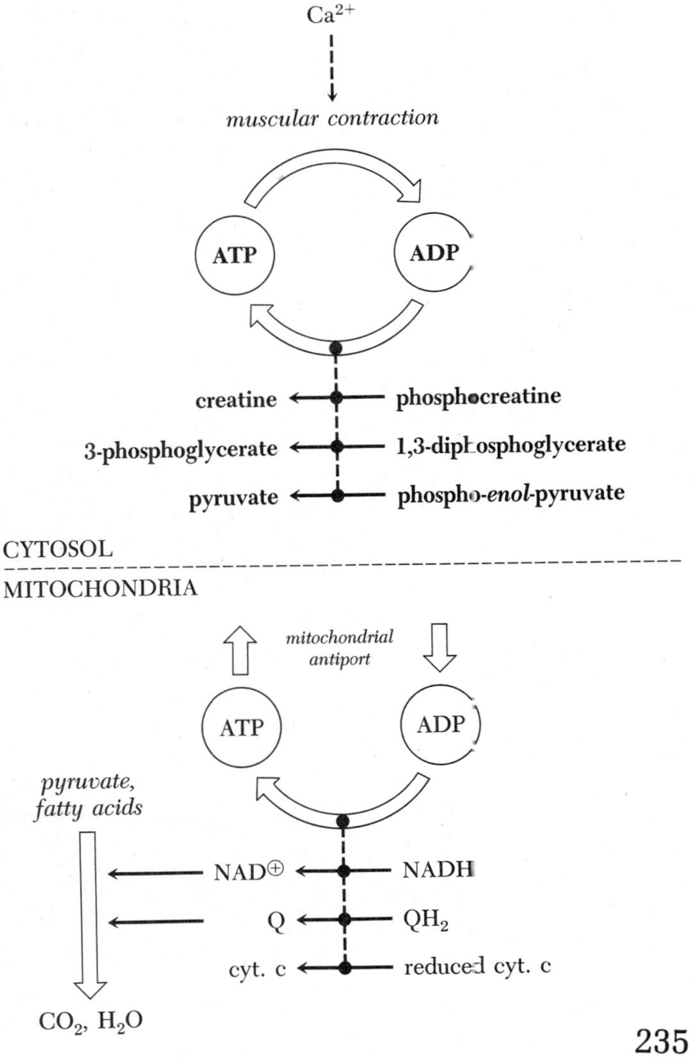

Figure 15-3 The increased concentration of ADP caused by muscular contraction results in an increased depletion of phosphocreatine and an acceleration of the conversion of triose phosphates to pyruvate in the cytosol. It also causes an increased rate of oxidative phosphorylation in the mitochondria, therefore accelerating the oxidation of pyruvate or fatty acids.

an increased total combustion of glucose owing to the work load. However, the ADP concentration will reach a point with larger loads at which it causes the Embden-Meyerhof pathway to go faster than oxidative phosphorylation, owing to its greater capacity in white fibers. The concentrations of pyruvate and NADH begin to rise, and lactate formation increases along with a further increase in the combustion of glucose. Still greater work loads will then cause large increases in lactate output, with oxygen consumption reaching the maximum possible rate (Fig. 15–4).

Even though the yield of ATP from glycolysis is relatively low, typical muscles in humans are constructed to form pyruvate some 25-fold faster than it can be oxidized, and the maximum power output from glycolysis alone is 2- to 3-fold that from oxidative phosphorylation. Glycolysis can also be brought to a maximum rate faster upon stimulation of the muscle. However, this maximum rate can be continued only some 30 seconds before the resultant acidification of the muscle prevents further function. In short, glycolysis, like the use of phosphocreatine, is a device for high-power, but short-term, work in many animals.

RED FIBERS. The red fibers, characteristic of muscles built for long-term continual work, have a capacity for oxidative phosphorylation more nearly matching their capacity for forming pyruvate. They ordinarily produce little lactate, and oxidize both glucose and fatty acids to CO_2 and H_2O.

RUNNERS. Essentially, we are here discussing a mechanism for the commonly known fact that the length of time one can work decreases with increasing rates of work, and an excellent example is provided by foot races of varying length. The sprints are run at a much faster pace than is the marathon. If we plot the world records for various races as the rate of running against the duration of the run (Fig. 15–5), we

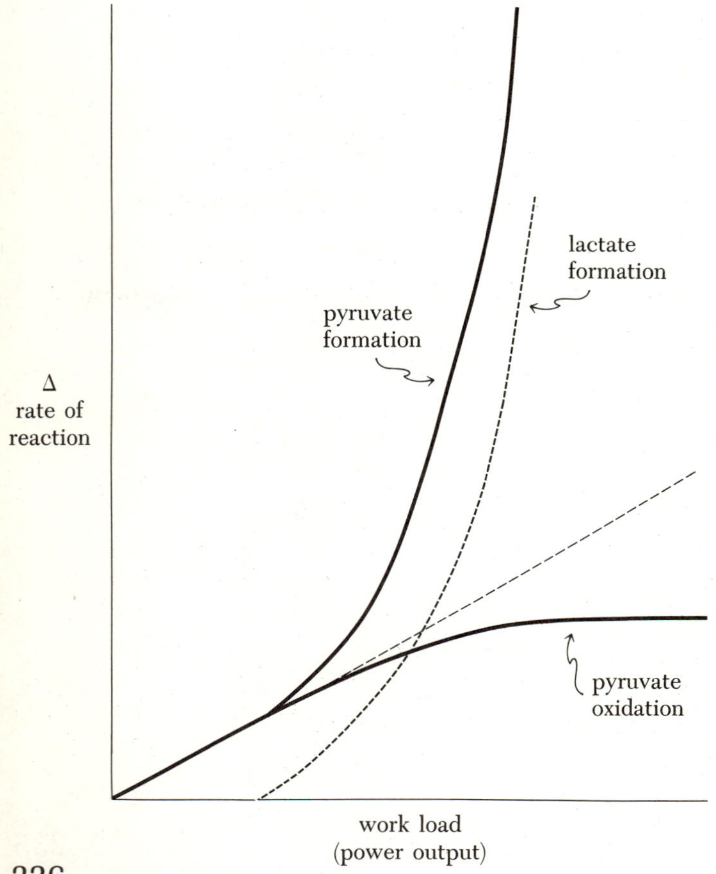

Figure 15–4 As the power output of muscles increases, the consumption of pyruvate at first increases at a steady pace with little change in lactate output, because the acceleration of oxidation of pyruvate by ADP is keeping pace with the acceleration of its production. Working still harder will cause the ADP and AMP concentrations to reach levels at which they accelerate the formation of pyruvate and NADH beyond the capacity of mitochondria to handle them. Since glycolysis produces less high-energy phosphate per pyruvate handled than does oxidation, much larger increases in the flux of pyruvate are required to balance the higher utilization of high-energy phosphate, and large amounts of lactate are formed. The dashed line indicates the rate of pyruvate formation that would occur if oxidative phosphorylation could cope with the total energy demand.

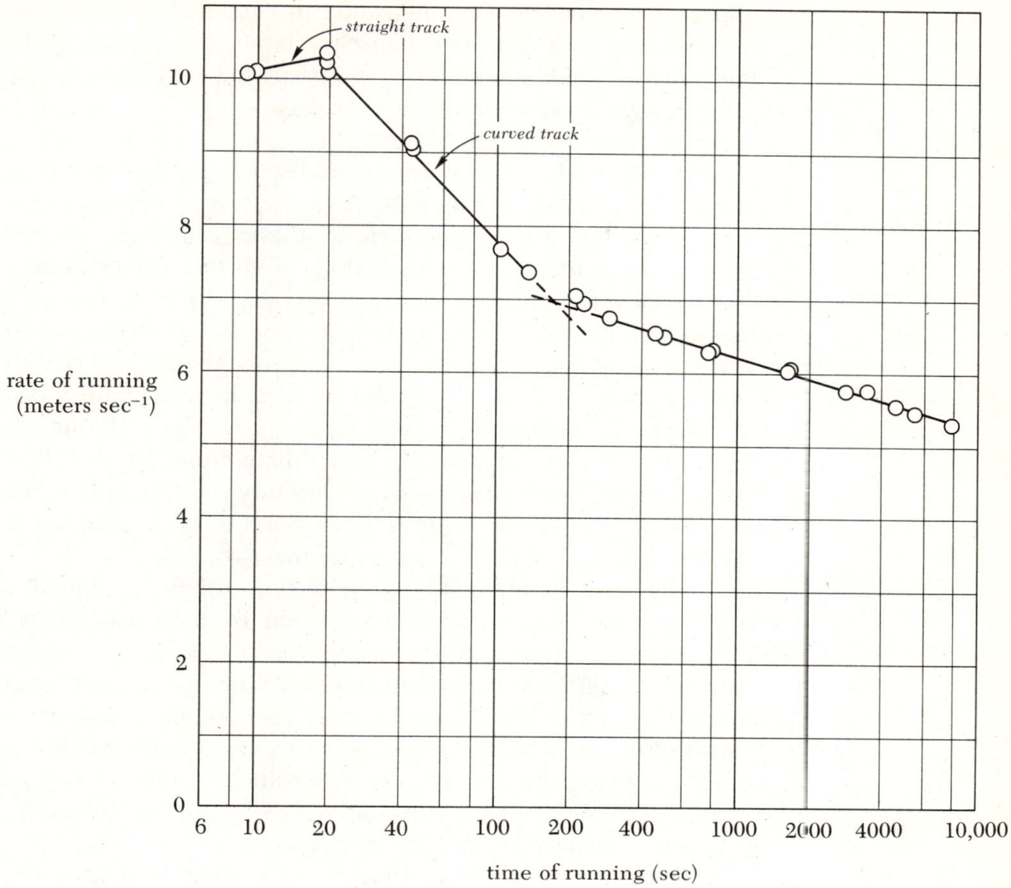

Figure 15-5 World record track performances, plotted to show the intensity of work as a function of the time for which it can be sustained. The data suggest that humans running at their maximum rate exhaust some source of energy in 20 seconds, and that there is some additional source that can be mobilized for only 180 seconds.

see an interesting confirmation of the picture we have developed. The data fall near three intersecting straight lines. The sprinters get along mainly on their high-energy phosphate stores with some contribution from glycolysis, and some of the speedy hold their breath while racing. However, this rapid pace depletes the high-energy phosphate so quickly that there is too little for further effort after 20 seconds or so. If one is to run for a longer period of time, and therefore run farther, he must start at a slower pace so that glycolysis, supplemented by oxidative phosphorylation, can contribute a larger fraction of the total ATP required by the greater total work to be done, and thereby maintain a useable concentration of ATP for a longer time. Glycolysis also has its limits, and if the greater energy obtainable by total oxidation of glucose is to be utilized with little lactate formation, the rate of running must be slowed down further. A run of three minutes or longer can be accomplished only if it is begun at a slow enough rate so that the oxidative metabolism generates nearly all of the high-energy phosphate being expended.

Glycolysis In Other Animals

As we have seen, man and his fellow vertebrates of terrestrial habitat ordinarily increase their production of lactate and their consumption of oxygen together. The appearance of lactate is an indication that the rate of utilization of ATP is exceeding the rate at which oxidative phosphorylation can replace it, and the cause of this imbalance in the land animals is ordinarily the enzymatic constitution of the muscles, rather than a gross deprivation of oxygen.*

However, not all air breathing animals live on the land; some make their way by searching under water for food, and some also dive to escape predators. A diving animal of this kind, lacking gills, closes its own access to oxygen, and the small store it can carry with it is not adequate to sustain its activity for more than a few mintues in most cases; the diver does not differ from the surface-dweller in this respect.

Given muscles with a declining oxygen supply, it is a foregone conclusion that they will produce lactate from glycogen upon excitation because oxidative phosphorylation will be even less adequate for disposal of pyruvate and NADH, and this is precisely what happens. The diving reptiles produce large quantities of lactate and are built to tolerate the associated massive acidosis; the blood H^+ may rise to 200 nanomolar from its normal 40 nanomolar (pH falling from 7.4 to 6.7) as a result of lactate accumulation. The ATP generated in this way is sufficient to permit a fresh-water turtle to survive as long as 12 hours at 22° without oxygen. Even the lizards and snakes can survive as much as 45 minutes under these conditions.

Whether it be mammal, reptile or bird, the diving animal has a brain that is as dependent upon oxidative phosphorylation for survival as is ours, and it can stay below only as long as there is oxygen in the blood circulating through its brain. The animals are able to achieve long dives because they conserve a small amount of oxygen carried within them for use by the vital tissues. This is done by a reflex response to immersion which results in closing the circulation to the skeletal muscles, and a drastic slowing of the frequency of the heart beat. Adaptation of this sort also occurs to a lesser extent in trained human divers; a similar reflex is seen in fetuses during delivery, which frequently involves deprivation of oxygen.

Glycerol Phosphate in Insects. The flight muscles of insects lack lactate dehydrogenase, and therefore do not carry out glycolysis. However, incubation of the muscles in the absence of oxygen causes an accumulation of glycerol 3-phosphate and pyruvate (Fig. 15–6), and it is sometimes said that these are normal end-products of glucose metabolism in insects. However, this is wrong. The flight muscles have a very active oxidative metabolism, including an efficient glycerol phosphate shuttle. Insects couldn't afford to lift the large quantities of fuel that would be required to sustain a long flight by glycolysis, and therefore dropped lactate dehydrogenase. The appearance of glycerol 3-phosphate and pyruvate is an experimental artifact caused by the lack of oxygen. (The same compounds would appear in mammalian muscles in the absence of oxygen if the muscles lacked lactate dehydrogenase; they don't appear because the equilibria are such as to favor the formation of lactate from glycerol 3-phosphate and pyruvate.)

Regulation of Glycolysis by a Futile Cycle

Muscles, such as the white fibers of higher animals, that depend upon glycolysis to supply the energy for rapid and strong contractions must be capable of massive

*Isometric contractions do shut off the blood supply, and therefore can be sustained only by glycolysis.

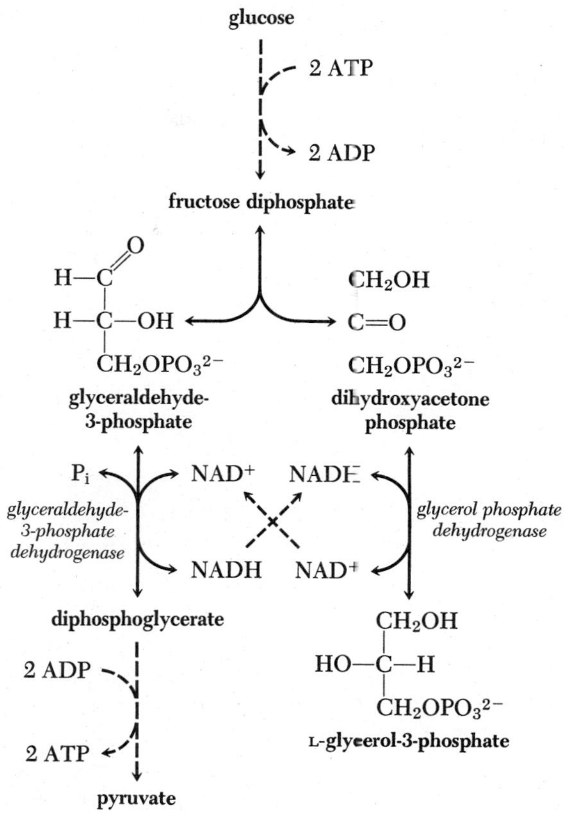

Figure 15-6 The dismutation of glucose to pyruvate and glycerol 3-phosphate. The NADH formed during the production of pyruvate is used to reduce dihydroxyacetone phosphate to glycerol 3-phosphate. There is no net gain of high-energy phosphate; insect muscles are built to avoid significant occurrence of the process through mitochondrial re-oxidation of glycerol 3-phosphate, and mammalian muscles avoid it through the more highly exergonic production of lactate.

acceleration of the Embden-Meyerhof pathway. The flight muscles of insects, although carrying out complete combustion, also have a similar acceleration. Unusual measures are necessary to make the acceleration of triose phosphate formation match the acceleration by ADP of triose phosphate utilization.

The problem is that a simple modulation of phosphofructokinase by AMP or similar effectors such as we discussed in the preceding chapter does not cause a prompt response to early changes in effector concentration (Fig. 15–7). The problem is solved by constructing muscles with a high capability for triose phosphate metabolism to

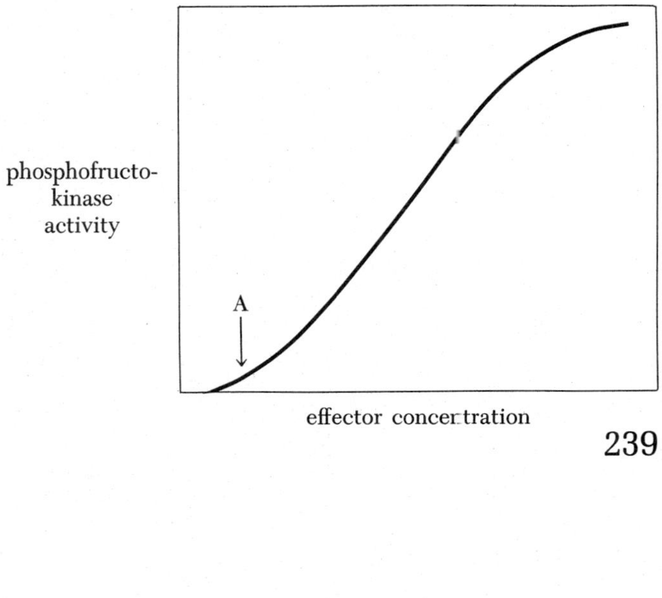

Figure 15-7 An enzyme with a sigmoidal response to effector concentration cannot have a significant increase from zero activity in response to a small change in effector concentration, as indicated at A.

contain **fructose diphosphatase,** an enzyme that catalyzes the hydrolysis of the phosphate on C-1:

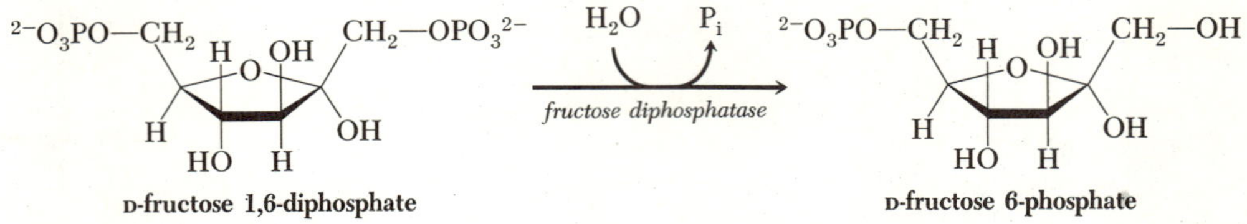

At first glance, this reaction appears to defeat the purpose of the tissue, since the actions of fructose diphosphatase and phosphofructokinase taken together represent a futile cycle in which the substrate is continually phosphorylated and dephosphorylated, so that the net result is nothing but the hydrolysis of ATP.

However, it now appears that the futile cycle is a device for insuring a prompt production of fructose 1,6-diphosphate, and therefore triose phosphates, in response to a demand for more fuel. The fructose diphosphatase of muscles is inhibited by low concentrations of AMP compared to the concentrations necessary for full activation of phosphofructokinase (Fig. 15–8). In addition, the total activity of phosphofructokinase is many-fold (15 to 40 times) greater than the activity of fructose 1,6-diphosphatase, so the concentration of AMP required to make the kinase form fructose 1,6-diphosphate as rapidly as the phosphatase hydrolyzes it is not very high, although it is above the resting level.

The result is that there is no net formation of fructose diphosphate from fructose 6-phosphate in resting muscle, and there will be little change when a muscle begins working until the AMP concentration rises to the point at which the phosphofructokinase activity will exceed the fructose diphosphatase activity. A still further rise in AMP concentration will then cause a very steep acceleration of fructose diphosphate formation. Why? Because there is a high concentration of potential phosphofructokinase activity in these muscles, and the AMP concentration has now risen to a point on the sigmoidal response curve at which the activity of phosphofructokinase is very sensitive to changes in AMP concentration. Furthermore, phosphofructokinase is activated by

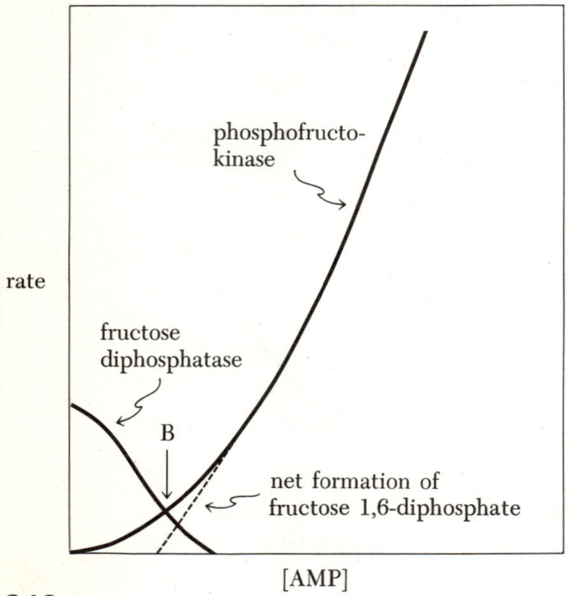

Figure 15–8 The presence of fructose diphosphatase in white muscles enables the maintenance of significant concentration of effector without net production of fructose 1,6-diphosphate, according to the Newsholme hypothesis, because the small increase in the activity of phosphofructokinase is counterbalanced by the remaining activity of fructose diphosphatase. A further increase in AMP concentration beyond point B causes rapid increases in phosphofructokinase activity along the steep portion of the sigmoidal curve, and the sigmoidal character of the response assures that it will be effective over a considerable range of AMP concentrations.

its own product, fructose diphosphate, and the rise in its concentration further accelerates its own production.

Here we have it; the futile cycle is a device permitting phosphofructokinase to be sensitive to changes in AMP concentration at levels not far above the resting level without having fructose diphosphate piling up in the cell. The futile cycle wastes ATP, but the amount involved is small potatoes compared to the expenditure in a fully working muscle. Red muscles contain little fructose diphosphatase because they do not have the extreme changes in rate of glucose metabolism from rest to activity, and ordinary allosteric controls are sufficient.

THE UTILIZATION OF LACTATE: OXIDATION OR GLUCONEOGENESIS

The lactate and lesser amounts of pyruvate diffusing into blood from rapidly contracting muscles represent incompletely oxidized glucose residues, and are potential fuels in themselves. Animals therefore utilize the compounds in other tissues, rather than excreting them.

Combustion of Lactate

One way of disposing of lactate is to oxidize it to pyruvate, and this occurs in red muscle fibers, the heart, and the brain. We have been emphasizing the formation of lactate from pyruvate by the lactate dehydrogenase in rapidly contracting muscles, but the actual direction of the pyruvate-lactate interconversion depends upon the concentrations of the compounds involved. Tissues with a high oxidative capacity, such as the red muscle fibers, heart, and brain, frequently have ratios of [lactate]/[pyruvate] and [NAD]/[NADH] that favor the oxidation of lactate to pyruvate, which is then further oxidized in mitochondria in the usual way.

Lactate Dehydrogenase Isozymes. Muscles with high oxidative capacity also utilize lactate more readily than they form it because they contain a different isozyme of lactate dehydrogenase than do white muscles. Lactate dehydrogenase contains four interchangeable subunits that occur in two principal forms, designated H for heart, and M for muscle. (There is a third kind in spermatazoa, but this is of minor importance in the total fuel economy, whatever its other consequences might be.) The major types of lactate dehydrogenase are H_4, which is predominant in the tissues of high oxidative capacity, and M_4, which is predominant in white muscle fibers and the liver. The three hybrid possibilities, HM_3, H_2M_2 and H_3M, also occur, but in lesser amounts. The H subunit conveys the property of being inhibited by high concentrations of pyruvate. Therefore, the lactate dehydrogenase of the oxidative tissues has most activity when the pyruvate concentration is low.

Conversion of Lactate to Glucose

The other principal route for the disposition of lactate in animals is its conversion back to glucose. Such a formation of glucose from a non-carbohydrate precursor is known as **gluconeogenesis,** and it occurs mainly in the liver and kidneys.

Glycolysis, in which glucose is converted to lactate as outlined earlier, is an irreversible process; otherwise it wouldn't have much value as a means of generating ATP. Something different must be done to convert lactate to glucose, and this something

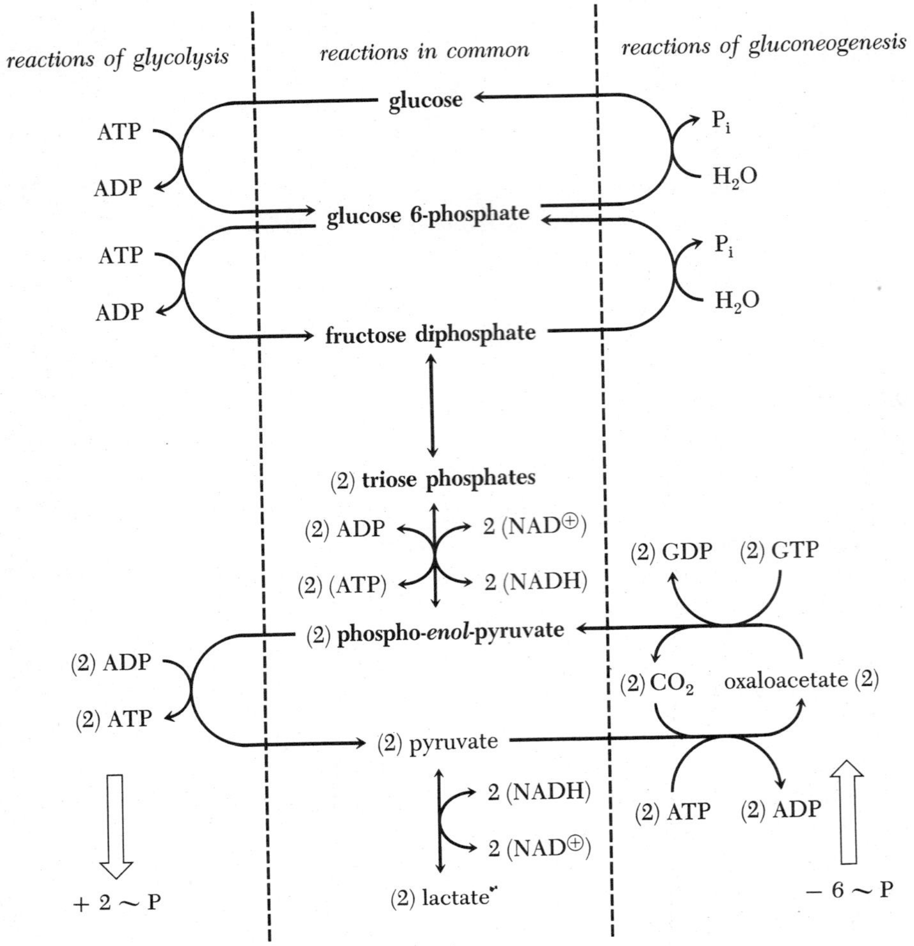

Figure 15–9 The conversion of glucose to lactate by glycolysis is not reversible, and the formation of glucose from lactate requires the presence of different reactions to make the process exergonic.

different must include new reactions creating equilibria favoring gluconeogenesis rather than glycolysis. The general differences between gluconeogenesis and glycolysis are shown in Figure 15–9, and these involve two sets of reactions:

A. The hexokinase and phosphofructokinase used in glycolysis to push glucose toward the triose phosphates are replaced in gluconeogenesis by a pair of phosphatases that catalyze the irreversible removal of the phosphates, pushing the conversion of triose phosphates to glucose.

B. Gluconeogenesis also involves two new reactions inserted between phospho-*enol*-pyruvate and pyruvate. These reactions cause the transient formation of oxaloacetate with the expenditure of an additional molecule of high-energy phosphate per phospho-*enol*-pyruvate formed. The pyruvate kinase reaction of the Embden-Meyerhof pathway, in which phosphate is transferred from phospho-*enol*-pyruvate to ADP, has an equilibrium favoring the formation of pyruvate, but the change in chemical potential is not great enough to support the formation of any more ATP. When the reaction is changed so as to include an additional transfer of high-energy phosphate, the position of equilibrium is changed to favor the reverse reaction in which pyruvate is converted to phospho-*enol*-pyruvate, and gluconeogenesis occurs.

The entire process, in which glucose is converted to lactate in skeletal muscles by glycolysis and the lactate is converted back to glucose in the liver and kidneys by gluconeogenesis, is known as the **Cori cycle,** after Carl F. Cori (Nobel laureate), who first described it clearly.

Let us now look at the distinctive reactions of gluconeogenesis more closely. We shall later see that most of them are also involved in other biological processes.

Mechanism of Gluconeogenesis

Pyruvate ⟶ Oxaloacetate. The formation of phospho-*enol*-pyruvate begins with carboxylation of pyruvate at the expense of ATP to form oxaloacetate:

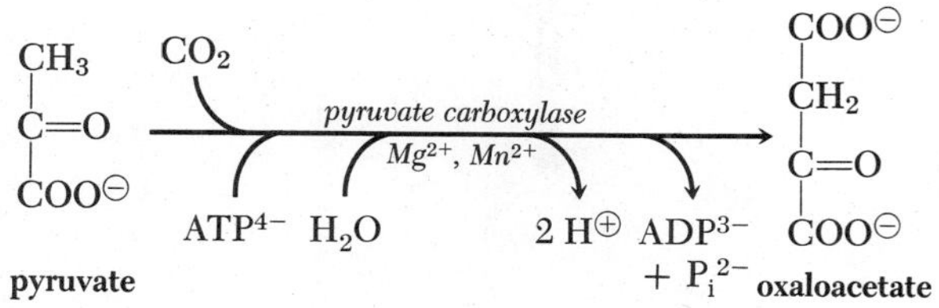

Dissolved CO_2 is in equilibrium with carbonic acid and the bicarbonate ion; the bicarbonate ion is the form actually utilized by this enzyme. We earlier discussed this reaction as an example of the participation of **biotin** as a coenzyme (p. 106).

Pyruvate carboxylase has an absolute requirement for **acetyl coenzyme A** as an activator. This compound is not directly involved in the reaction, but the rate of conversion of pyruvate to oxaloacetate is governed by the extent to which acetyl coenzyme A has accumulated. We can at this point visualize two possible circumstances causing an accumulation (Fig. 15–10). There might be a shortage of oxaloacetate to combine with the acetyl coenzyme A and form citrate. The resultant accumulation of acetyl coenzyme A would tend to provoke increased activity of the pyruvate carboxylase, thereby causing the formation of more oxaloacetate to prime the citric acid cycle.

It is also possible that acetyl coenzyme A accumulates because enough is being formed from fatty acids to supply the energy requirements of the cell. Increasing the conversion of pyruvate to oxaloacetate would then divert the carbons of pyruvate to the formation of glucose, thereby diminishing its oxidation to increase the already abundant concentration of acetyl coenzyme A.

Oxaloacetate ⟶ Phospho-*enol*-pyruvate. Oxaloacetate is converted to phospho-*enol*-pyruvate by phosphorylation with GTP, accompanied by a simultaneous decarboxylation:

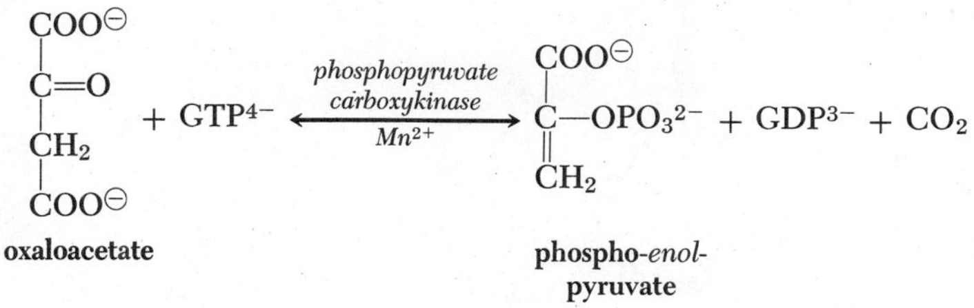

The preceding carboxylation of pyruvate is in effect an increase in the chemical potential of the compound at the expense of ATP. The chemical potential is then discharged by decarboxylation in order to drive the formation of phospho-*enol*-pyruvate.

The **phosphopyruvate carboxykinase** catalyzing this reaction differs from pyruvate carboxylase in mechanism. The reaction does not involve biotin, and CO_2 is not "activated." GTP evidently acts to cleave oxaloacetate with the liberation of CO_2 and the formation of some nucleotide-pyruvate intermediate on the enzyme surface.

Phosphorylation of Pyruvate in Other Species. The two-step process we have just discussed is essentially a device in higher animals for utilizing two molecules of high-energy phosphate in the conversion of pyruvate to phospho-*enol*-pyruvate, but it includes an additional benefit in that it provides a route for making oxaloacetate for other purposes when required, and also for disposing of excess oxaloacetate gen-

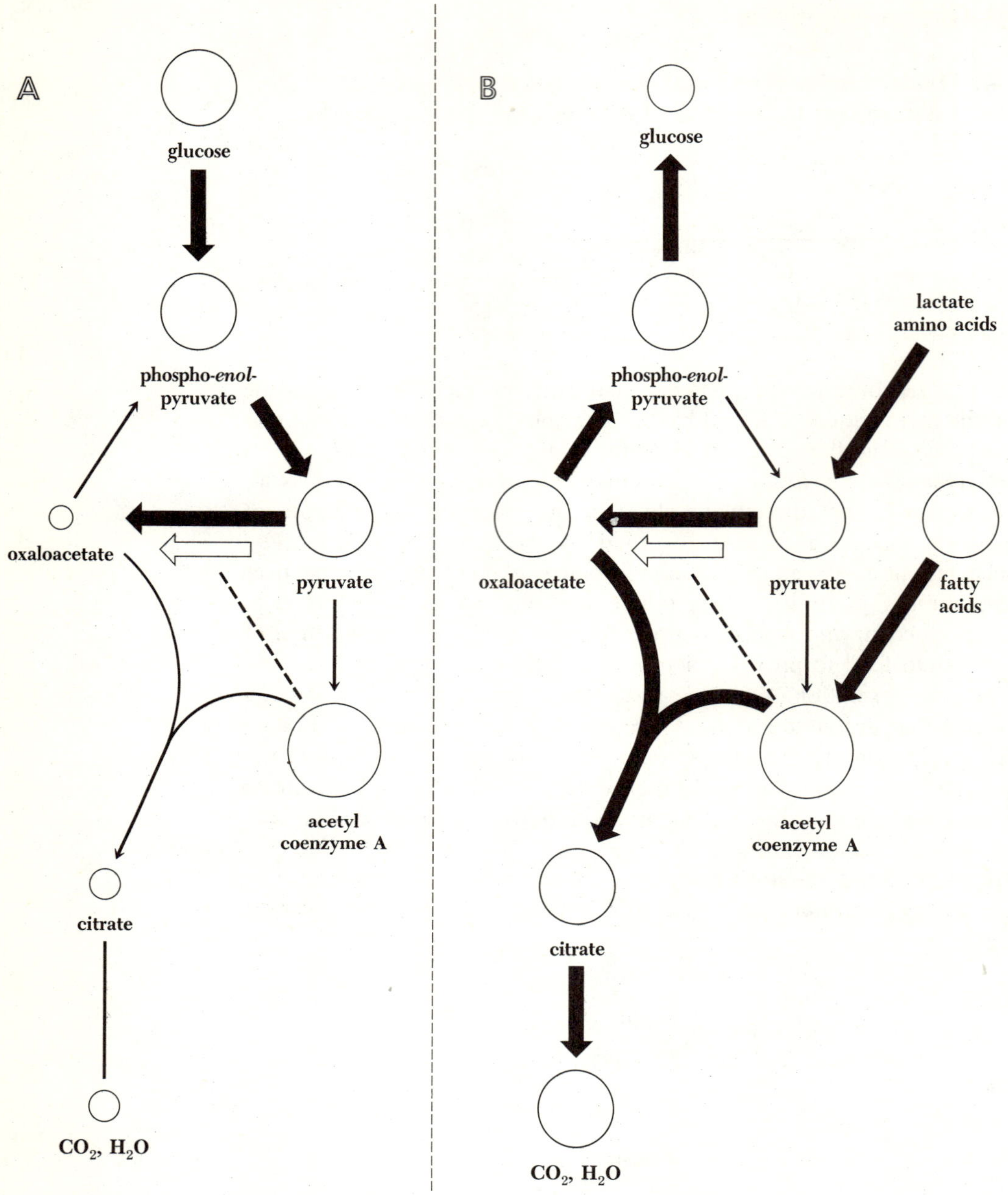

Figure 15-10 Two of the circumstances that might cause an accumulation of acetyl coenzyme A, with a resultant activation of pyruvate carboxylase to accelerate oxaloacetate formation, are (*A*) a deficit of oxaloacetate necessary to remove acetyl coenzyme A as citrate for total combustion, and (*B*) an accumulation of acetyl coenzyme A from high concentrations of fatty acids, so that pyruvate derived from lactate and amino acids is not being oxidized, and is available for gluconeogenesis.

erated by other mechanisms. These additional functions are not so important to organisms such as some protozoa and certain tropical grasses, which include important food plants such as corn and sugar cane. These organisms therefore have evolved a process in which a single enzyme catalyzes the necessary expenditure of two molecules of high-energy phosphate in order to convert pyruvate directly to phospho-*enol*-pyruvate, without the intermediate formation of oxaloacetate:

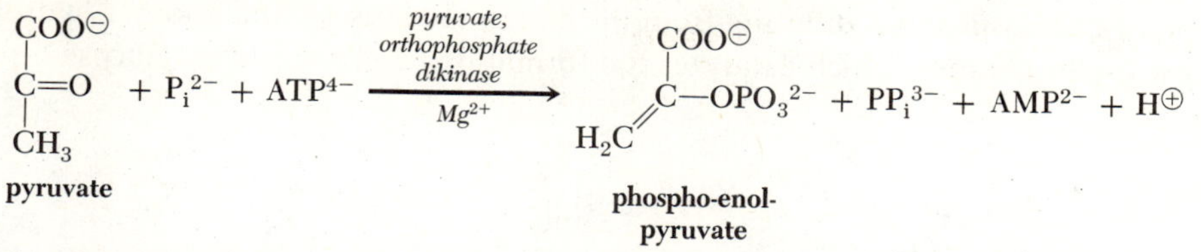

In this unusual reaction, one of the high-energy phosphate groups of ATP is used to phosphorylate inorganic phosphate, forming pyrophosphate, while the second high-energy group is used to phosphorylate pyruvate. The overall reaction is reversible in the test tube, but the constant removal of the resultant inorganic pyrophosphate by the ubiquitous inorganic pyrophosphatase also present in these organisms makes it an effective route for the continual synthesis of phospho-*enol*-pyruvate.

The Phospho-*enol*-pyruvate Futile Cycle. Skeletal muscles lack pyruvate carboxylase and are therefore not able to convert pyruvate or lactate to phospho-*enol*-pyruvate; their metabolism hinges on the opposing pyruvate kinase reaction for the generation of ATP, and the only known control over this reaction in muscles is the availability of ADP to be phosphorylated.

However, the liver and other gluconeogenic organs contain pyruvate kinase for use when the glucose supply is high, in addition to the pyruvate carboxylase and phospho-*enol*-pyruvate carboxykinase necessary for making glucose when the supply is low (Fig. 15-11). The liver therefore has the enzymes present for another futile cycle in which high-energy phosphate is hydrolyzed by turning over phospho-*enol*-pyruvate. The cycle may serve a regulatory function in a way similar to the fructose diphosphate futile cycle of muscles, but such a function has not been analyzed. The cycle is capable of being controlled because the gluconeogenic organs contain a different isozyme of pyruvate kinase, which is completely inhibited by physiological concentrations of ATP, with the inhibition relieved by fructose 1,6-diphosphate. The apparent effect is to accelerate pyruvate kinase as the final reaction of the Embden-Meyerhof pathway when there is abundant glucose available, but complete understanding is yet to be obtained.

Formation of Glucose from Fructose Diphosphate. The conversion of fructose diphosphate to glucose in the liver and other gluconeogenic organs involves an isozyme

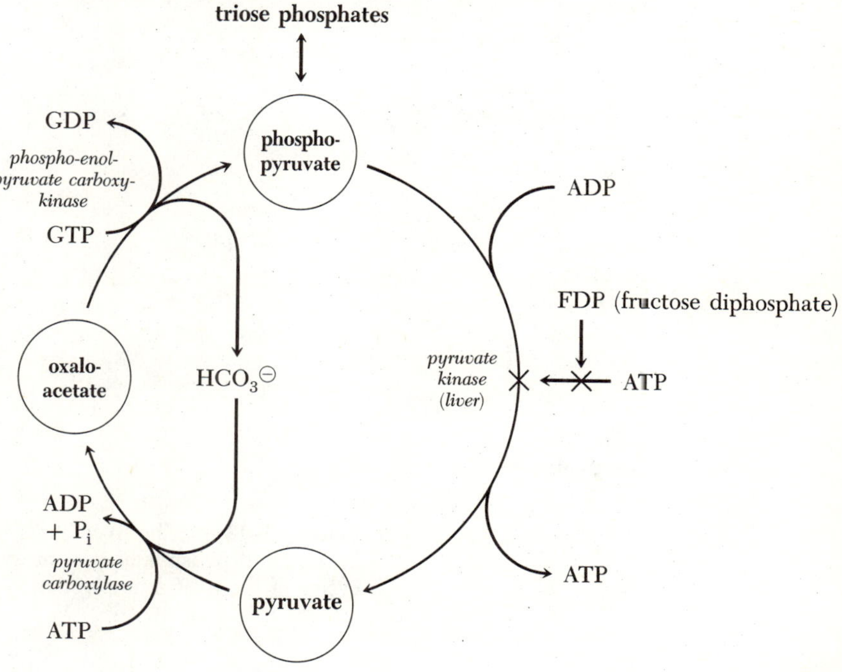

Figure 15-11 Tissues such as the liver that contain both pyruvate carboxylase and pyruvate kinase have the capacity for a futile cycle, with the net effect being the hydrolysis of GTP. The cycle is partially controlled through the presence of a pyruvate kinase that is inhibited by physiological concentrations of ATP, with the inhibition relieved by fructose diphosphate.

of **fructose diphosphatase,** differing from the one in the muscle, and another hydrolase, **glucose-6-phosphatase,** which catalyzes the formation of glucose from glucose 6-phosphate:

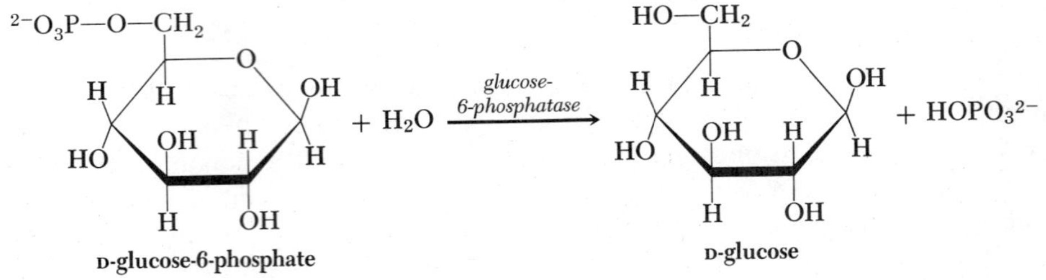

Glucose-6-phosphatase occurs in the endoplasmic reticulum; it is often used as an identifying marker for this organelle. It is missing in all vertebrate muscles, as is pyruvate carboxylase, and this absence of the initial and terminal enzymes necessary for gluconeogenesis from pyruvate explains why the participation of the liver and similar organs is necessary for the completion of the Cori cycle. (Some invertebrate muscles have complete complements of enzymes and may be able to re-utilize their own lactate.)

The liver also contains phosphofructokinase, hexokinase, and glucokinase, and

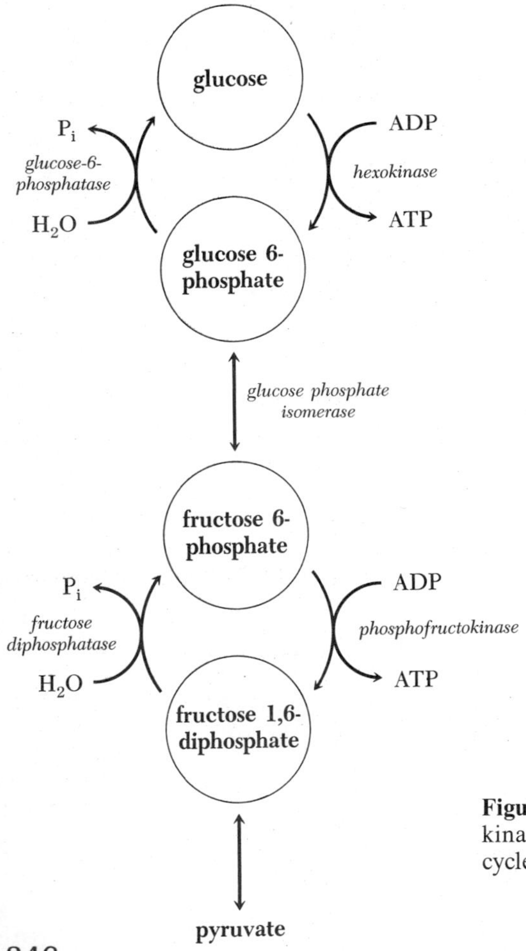

Figure 15–12 The liver has a potential for futile cycles involving the kinases and phosphatases of hexose metabolism. The regulation of these cycles in the liver is not understood.

therefore has two more potential futile cycles not found in red muscle (Fig. 15–12). The regulation of these cycles is still an enigma.

THE GLYOXYLATE CYCLE–GLUCOSE FROM FATS

The higher animals are not able to convert fatty acids to glucose, and therefore require glucose for metabolism. It may be obtained in the diet, or may be made by gluconeogenesis from anything that can be converted to pyruvate, oxaloacetate, or phospho-*enol*-pyruvate. (We shall later see that amino acids are good sources of these compounds.) However, animals cannot make any of these precursors from acetyl coenzyme A; the conversion of pyruvate to acetyl coenzyme A is an irreversible process in the higher animals. This is not so in many microorganisms, in plant seeds, and perhaps in some invertebrate animals, which can utilize fatty acids not only as fuels, but also as sources of glucose and of other compounds synthesized from oxaloacetate because they have two enzymes that are not present in the higher animals.

Isocitrate Lyase. One of the plant enzymes catalyzes a cleavage of isocitrate to form **glyoxylate** and **succinate:**

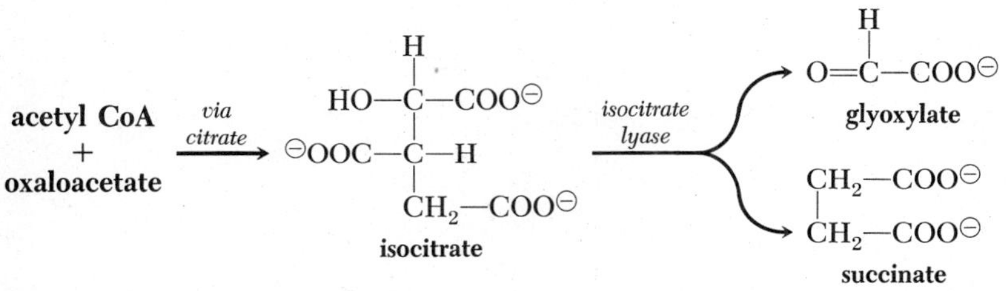

We can see that this reaction resembles the familiar citrate synthase reaction, except that there is no high-energy coenzyme A ester bond to be cleaved. The isocitrate lyase reaction is therefore readily reversible in the test tube, but physiological concentrations are such as to favor the formation of glyoxylate and succinate.

Malate Synthase. The second additional enzyme necessary for the formation of glucose from fats catalyzes the condensation of glyoxylate and acetyl coenzyme A to form malate:

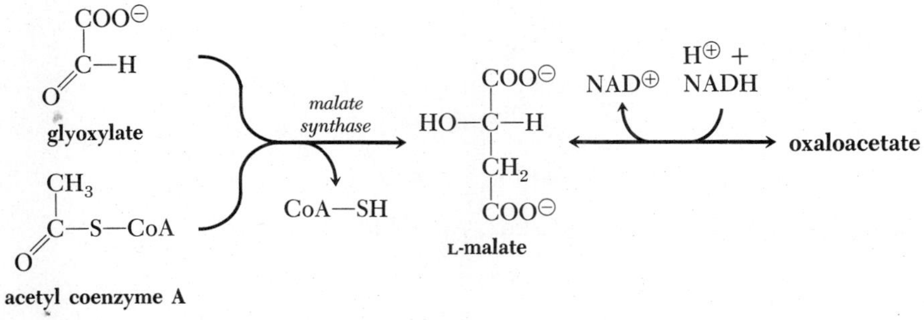

This enzyme has an even closer resemblance to citrate synthase. The reaction is exactly comparable except for the utilization of glyoxylate as the 2-ketocarboxylate substrate in place of oxaloacetate.

The Glyoxylate Cycle. The reactions catalyzed by isocitrate lyase and malate synthase, along with those of malate dehydrogenase, citrate synthase, and aconitase, complete a cycle in which glyoxylate acts as a carrier, much in the way that oxaloacetate acts as a carrier in the citric acid cycle. There is an important distinction; two acetyl

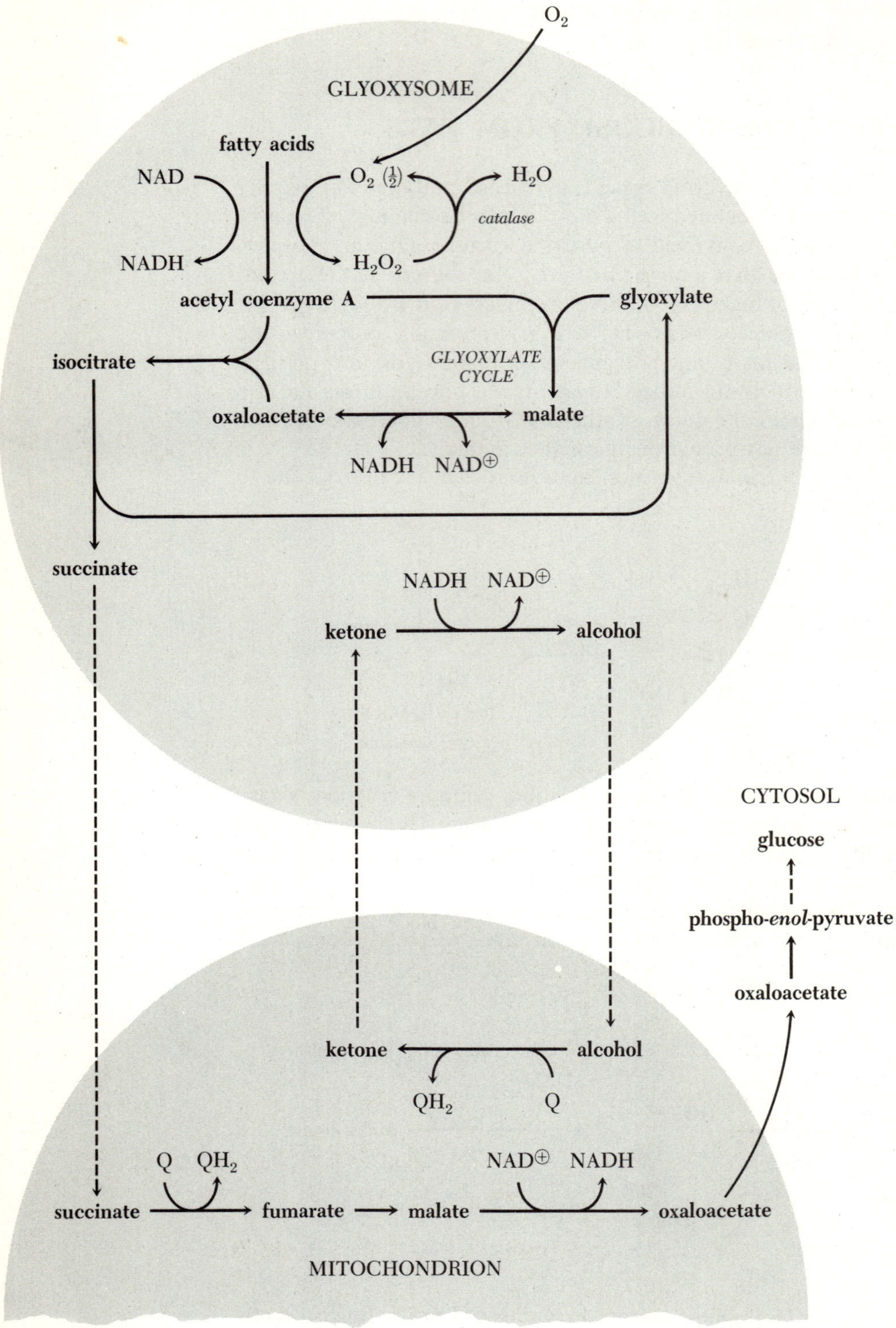

Figure 15-13 Fatty acids are converted to succinate by the glyoxysomes of plant embryonic cells. The process involves a glyoxylate cycle in which glyoxylate acts as a carrier for 2-carbon units, appearing first as malate, and later as citrate and isocitrate. The succinate is oxidized further in the mitochondrion, and the resultant oxaloacetate moiety is transferred to the cytosol as aspartate (not shown) for gluconeogenesis. The NADH in the glyoxysomes may transfer electrons to the cytosol by a shuttle similar to the glycerol phosphate shuttle, but the mechanism has not been established.

groups are successively added, and the resultant four carbons appear as succinate. There is no loss of carbon as CO_2. Succinate can then be converted to oxaloacetate by the same enzymes ordinarily used for the citric acid cycle, and we have already seen how oxaloacetate can be converted to glucosyl residues. Cycles mainly used for synthetic purposes are sometimes called **anaplerotic,** or replenishment cycles.

GLYOXYSOMES. The enzymes necessary for the glyoxylate cycle occur within special organelles, known as glyoxysomes, found in plant seeds that depend upon stored fat for the nutrition of the embryo. The glyoxysomes also carry out most of the familiar reactions of **fatty acid oxidation,** but have none of the apparatus for oxidative phosphorylation. The acyl coenzyme A dehydrogenases of these organelles are flavoproteins, but they resemble flavoproteins used mainly for synthetic purposes or for the disposal of minor waste products, in that they transfer electrons directly from the substrate to molecular oxygen with the formation of hydrogen peroxide. Glyoxysomes contain catalase to catalyze the rapid destruction of H_2O_2 (Fig. 15–13).

Electrons from the NADH formed by the 3-hydroxyacyl coenzyme A dehydrogenases are utilized by the mitochondria, probably by some shuttle mechanism similar to those employed in animal cells for transfer of electrons.

The result of all of this, as shown in the figure, is that glyoxysomes consume fatty acids, O_2 and NAD, and produce succinate, H_2O and NADH as the only products. The succinate is then converted to oxaloacetate by the mitochondria, followed by conversion of the oxaloacetate to phospho-*enol*-pyruvate and then to glucose 6-phosphate in the cytosol.

FURTHER READING

R. Margaria, The sources of muscular energy, Scientific Amer., 227:84 (1972). Readable account by a pioneering authority, although energy yield of glycolysis is misstated.

R. W. McGilvery, Use of fuel for muscular exercise, in H. Howald and J. Poortmans, eds., Metabolic adaptation to prolonged physical exercise. Birkhäuser Verlag Basel (1974). An extension and amplification of the treatment in this author's 1970 textbook.

J. Keul, E. Doll, and D. Keppler, Energy metabolism of human muscle (vol. 7 of Medicine and sport, E. Jokl, ed.), University Park Press (1972). Contains good and quite readable reviews.

H. C. Dessauer, Blood chemistry of reptiles. Physiological and evolutionary aspects, in C. Gans and T. S. Parsons, eds., Biology of the reptiles, Academic Press (1970). Use of glycolysis for diving is covered.

H. T. Andersen, Physiological adaptations in diving vertebrates, Physiol. Rev., 46:212 (1966). Also covers mammals.

E. A. Newsholme, The regulation of phosphofructokinase in muscle, Cardiology, 56:22 (1971). Original re-evaluation of the futile cycle by one of the more creative thinkers.

N. E. Tolbert, Microbodies—peroxisomes and glyoxysomes, Ann. Rev. Plant Physiol., 22:45 (1971). Contains a summary of metabolic routes, as well as references to experimental literature.

QUESTIONS

1. Show why only 1 mole of ATP is formed per mole of lactate made from glucose, when 1.5 moles of ATP are formed per mole of lactate made from one glucosyl unit in glycogen.
2. Show how one mole of glucose 6-phosphate can be converted to one mole each of glycerol 3-phosphate and pyruvate without the net utilization of any other electron donor or acceptor. What is the net yield of ATP from this overall conversion? How far off the ground would a bee get if this conversion were the only source of energy for its flight muscles?

3. Consider the life styles of wild ducks and jackrabbits, and postulate the comparative contents of the following in the duck wing muscles and the jackrabbit leg muscles: (a) myoglobin; (b) phosphocreatine; (c) cytochrome a_3; (d) phosphofructokinase; (e) pyruvate dehydrogenase; (f) enolase; (g) fructose 1,6-diphosphatase.
4. How much ATP could a heart generate per molecule of lactate that it oxidizes to CO_2 and H_2O? (Remember that the conversion of lactate to pyruvate occurs in the cytosol.)
5. Why does gluconeogenesis of glucose from lactate require different enzymes than those required for the Embden-Meyerhof pathway, since all of the intermediates in the Embden-Meyerhof pathway are also intermediates in gluconeogenesis?
6. Gluconeogenesis from lactate requires the reduction of 1,3-diphosphoglycerate to glyceraldehyde 3-phosphate by NADH, forming NAD. Study the route of gluconeogenesis and explain where the NADH comes from in this case.
7. Why doesn't the Cori cycle occur in mammalian muscles alone—why is the liver also necessary?
8. What do plants have that animals don't that enable them to convert palmitate to glucose? Explain how it is that plants are using enzymes of the citric acid cycle to do this when we have repeatedly emphasized that the citric acid cycle will not produce oxaloacetate.

CHAPTER 16

THE FERMENTATIONS

THE CONCEPTS

Fermentations are processes in which microorganisms obtain energy by rearranging organic compounds without consuming oxygen. They are akin to glycolysis in muscles, and some organisms convert glucose to lactate in exactly the same way as do muscles, except that the fermenting organisms survive in the continued absence of oxygen. (These homolactate fermentations also may result in the formation of either D- or L-lactate, or both.) Some bacteria are strict anaerobes and are poisoned in the presence of oxygen, owing to a lack of superoxide dismutase. Other organisms are facultative anaerobes that will burn fuels when oxygen is present or will shift to a fermentation in its absence.

Simple fermentations include, in addition to the homolactate fermentation, an ethanol fermentation in which the Embden-Meyerhof pathway is also used to convert glucose to two pyruvate molecules with the generation of 2 ATP. The organisms do not have lactate dehydrogenase, and pyruvate is decarboxylated to acetaldehyde before reduction by NADH, so the product is ethanol rather than lactate.

The heterolactate fermentation is an example of a more complex process producing both lactate and ethanol. It involves the pentose phosphate pathway, which is also an important route in animal and plant metabolism. The pathway begins by the oxidation of C-1 on glucose 6-phosphate to form 6-phosphogluconolactone, an inner ester. Hydrolysis of the ester bond releases 6-phosphogluconate, which now has a 1-carboxyl group. 6-Phosphogluconate is oxidatively decarboxylated by attack on C-3, converting the remaining five carbons to D-ribulose 5-phosphate, the keto analogue of D-ribose 5-phosphate. The successive oxidations of glucose 6-phosphate in this way remove electrons from glucose for reducing other compounds and also serve as a source of ribose for creating nucleotides, as we shall later see. In the heterolactate fermentation, ribulose 5-phosphate is consumed by converting it to an isomer, D-xylulose 5-phosphate, in which adjacent hydroxyl groups have a *trans* configuration. The important thing about the configuration is that it, like a similar configuration in fructose diphosphate, facilitates a cleavage, which here is a phosphorolytic cleavage. The products from xylulose 5-phosphate are glyceraldehyde 3-phosphate and acetyl phosphate. Glyceraldehyde 3-phosphate is converted to lactate in the same way that it is in mammalian muscle. The acetyl phosphate, which is a high-energy anhydride of the carboxyl group of acetic acid with phosphoric acid, exchanges with coenzyme A to form acetyl coenzyme A, which is then reversibly reduced, first to acetaldehyde, and then to ethanol. The electrons used for these reductions are those gained from the pentose phosphate pathway. The heterolactate fermentation is important to the production of authentic dill pickles and sauerkraut.

The solvent fermentations of clostridia illustrate still more complex processes. The clostridia are strict anaerobes, and the fermentations they carry out illustrate the use of ferredoxin, an iron-sulfide protein of a type widely used by plants and microorganisms for transporting electrons. Ferredoxins are powerful reducing agents. In the case at hand, clostridia produce pyruvate by the regular Embden-Meyerhof pathway, generating ATP and NADH, but pyruvate is oxidized to acetyl coenzyme A by passing the electrons to ferredoxin. Many clostridia pass electrons from reduced ferredoxin to protons in solution, creating hydrogen gas, which is released as one of the products of the fermentation. The two molecules of acetyl coenzyme A formed per molecule of original glucose can then condense to form acetoacetyl coenzyme A by the same kind of reaction used in animals for fatty acid metabolism. Various clostridia differ in the route used for disposal of the acetoacetyl group and of the two NADH molecules still remaining from the original generation of pyruvate. Simple reduction of acetoacetyl coenzyme A to 3-hydroxybutyryl coenzyme A and then to butyryl coenzyme A can dispose of the products, forming butyrate as a product of the fermentation after conversion of the high-energy thiol ester to a phosphate for capture as ATP.

More complex processes frequently occur. One strain discovered by Chaim Weizmann decarboxylates half of the acetoacetyl groups to acetone (after capture of high-energy phosphate) and uses the resultant excess NADH to further reduce the butyryl groups formed from the other half, forming butanol. The British need for solvents during the First World War led to negotiations that established a basis for the later origin of the State of Israel.

The conversion of glucose to lactate in the muscles is essentially a transient process for the generation of ATP; animals mainly depend upon complete combustion to extract the maximum possible amount of utilizable energy out of a given mass of fuel, which they must find and frequently tote around. The oxygen they consume has an even greater mass than the combustible fuel, but it is extracted from the atmosphere with relatively small expenditure of energy for its transport.

Anaerobes and Aerobes—Strict and Facultative. However, some microorganisms make a way of life out of chemical processes, such as glycolysis, that demand no oxygen. If an ecological niche contains compounds that can be rearranged or that react together so as to sustain the generation of ATP, some microorganism will usually occupy the niche. Many microorganisms are like the higher forms in that they are built to take advantage of the greater ATP yield from combustion of fuels by molecular oxygen, if oxygen is available. Some of these have evolved so as to be totally dependent on oxidative phosphorylation, and, like us, are **strict aerobes** that cannot survive in the absence of oxygen.

Other kinds of microorganisms will utilize oxidative phosphorylation when possible, but are capable of surviving in the absence of oxygen. These are **facultative anaerobes.** Still other microorganisms—the **strict anaerobes**—cannot survive in the presence of oxygen; they thrive in airless domains that cannot be invaded by the more efficient aerobes.

Some of the anaerobic bacteria make do by utilizing oxidizing agents other than oxygen; these organisms can use many of the same metabolic processes occurring in strict aerobes, except that electrons removed from substrates are ultimately transferred to compounds like nitrate or sulfate ions so as to produce nitrogen gas or sulfide ions in place of the water formed by aerobes.

However, many of the anaerobic organisms, both facultative and strict, survive in the absence of oxygen by rearranging organic compounds so as to form products of substantially lower chemical potential with a concomitant phosphorylation of ADP, much in the way that animal cells rearrange glucose to lactate. These anaerobic rearrangements are known as **fermentations,** a name that comes from the early days when the known examples were those that created gases among products, with their bubbling evolution creating a ferment in the medium. The name is now used to cover all anaerobic rearrangements of organic compounds by microorganisms, although the best known examples are those in which glucose, or a closely related compound, is the principal starting material.

The Toxicity of Oxygen to Anaerobes. Before going further, let us examine why it is that strict anaerobes won't survive exposure to oxygen. The reason apparently is that they have lost superoxide dismutase. We saw earlier (p. 116) that this enzyme catalyzes the dismutation of superoxide anions:

$$O_2^- + O_2^- + 2\,H^+ \longrightarrow O_2 + H_2O_2$$

which are formed as a byproduct of the action of many metalloflavoprotein oxidases, but may also be generated when other non-heme iron proteins are exposed to oxygen. When an organism is completely committed to life in anaerobic environments, it suffers no harm from loss of the superoxide dismutase genome, and may even gain a small advantage by discontinuing the synthesis of the now superfluous enzyme. However, once the loss occurs, return to aerobic life becomes impossible.

SIMPLE FERMENTATIONS

Since fermentations are rearrangements of organic compounds that can occur without involving oxygen or other inorganic electron acceptors, it follows that all oxidations of intermediates must be accompanied by reductions of other intermediates. The total result must be a balanced chemical equation, and lack of balance is an indication of incomplete information.

Within this constraint, there are many possible ways in which even a single compound, such as glucose, may be rearranged so as to support the generation of ATP, and microbial evolution appears to have thought of them all. Let us look at a few examples.

Homolactate Fermentation

Some microorganisms gain most of their ATP by converting glucose to lactate by exactly the same glycolytic pathway found in muscles:

$$\text{glucose} \xrightarrow{2\,(\text{ADP} + \text{P}_i) \;\rightarrow\; 2\,\text{ATP}} 2\ \text{lactate}^{\ominus}$$

(The charges shown on the phosphate compounds are less than those we use in discussing mammalian metabolism, because most of the lactate fermentations proceed best in more acidic solutions.) Fermentations proceeding in this way are known as **homolactate fermentations,** meaning that lactate is the only important product formed from glucose. We shall shortly talk about **heterolactate** fermentations, in which other products are also formed.

We discussed the important features of this process in the preceding chapter, noting that NADH formed during the conversion of glucose residues to pyruvate is removed by converting pyruvate to lactate. The major difference between glycolysis in muscle

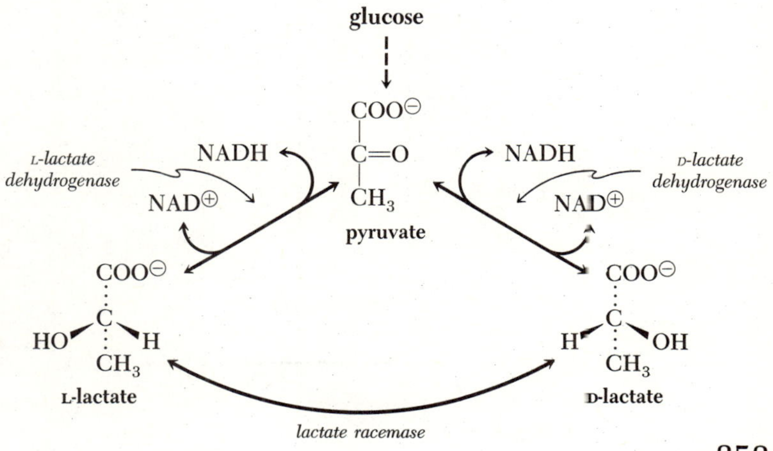

Figure 16-1 Some bacteria produce one isomer of lactate or the other, and some produce both, as a result of the fermentation of glucose by the Embden-Meyerhof pathway, depending upon their enzymatic constitution.

and homolactate fermentation is that the product is the L-isomer of lactate in muscle, whereas it is the D-isomer or a mixture of the D- and L-isomers in many microorganisms. This comes about because there are lactate dehydrogenases of differing specificity, some equilibrating the L-isomer with pyruvate, and others equilibrating the D-isomer. An organism may contain either kind of enzyme, or both. To complicate the story, still other microorganisms produce only one isomer, but contain an additional enzyme, a lactate racemase, to catalyze the interconversion of the two isomers (Fig. 16–1). The effective result is the same in any case—ATP is generated as a result of lactate formation, and it is not known why one isomer or the other is produced by particular species, although the formation of the DL-mixture would make it possible to have a higher concentration of total lactate at equilibrium, since each isomer would be separately equilibrated with pyruvate.

Ethanol Fermentation

The best known of all fermentations is the conversion of glucose to ethanol, especially by yeasts. The consequences of the action of ethanol as a drug have been so appealing to humans over the millenia since they were discovered that its consumption has long been an important part of many social cultures, and its production has been a correspondingly important part of the economy of these cultures.

All of this hinges on a particular method used by some yeasts for disposing of the electrons transferred from glyceraldehyde 3-phosphate to NAD. These yeasts make pyruvate from glucose by the usual Embden-Meyerhof pathway, but instead of reducing the pyruvate directly to lactate, as in homolactate fermentation or glycolysis, they first decarboxylate the pyruvate to form **acetaldehyde.** The electrons of NADH are then transferred to the acetaldehyde, forming **ethanol** and completing the fermentation, as is shown in Figure 16–2.

The **pyruvate decarboxylase** of yeast is very similar in its action to the pyruvate decarboxylase peptide of the pyruvate dehydrogenase complex (p. 222), with **thiamine pyrophosphate** as a coenzyme. The **ethanol dehydrogenase,** commonly called alcohol

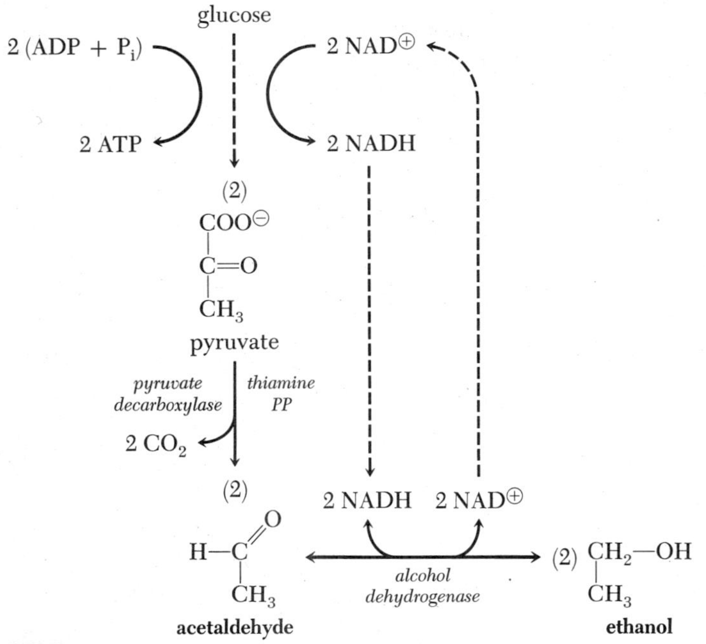

Figure 16–2 The ethanol fermentation of yeasts involves a decarboxylation of pyruvate through the use of thiamine pyrophosphate, and the acetaldehyde formed is reduced to ethanol.

dehydrogenase, is also similar to enzymes catalyzing the same reaction in many species. Indeed, the major route by which a drinking man disposes of his ethanol so as to once more face unadorned reality begins by using alcohol dehydrogenase to oxidize the compound to acetaldehyde in the liver. (The reaction will go in the direction of oxidation for the same reason that the lactate dehydrogenase reaction goes in that direction in liver; the NAD/NADH concentration ratio is relatively high, and the concentration of acetaldehyde is kept low by its further oxidation.)

Balancing Fermentation Equations. Since the same Embden-Meyerhof pathway is used in both homolactate fermentation (glycolysis) and in ethanol fermentation, there is the same net formation of two molecules of ATP per molecule of glucose consumed in both processes. Considering only the fate of the carbons, the alcoholic fermentation can be summarized as:

$$\underset{\textbf{glucose}}{C_6H_{12}O_6} \longrightarrow 2\ \underset{\textbf{ethanol}}{C_2H_6O} + 2\ CO_2$$

The equation balances as it stands; we have already seen that the electrons abstracted from the triose phosphates during pyruvate formation are put back on acetaldehyde to make ethanol, so there is no net oxidation or reduction. However, the stoichiometry does differ from that of the homolactate fermentation in that there are two products. Let us therefore consider in this simple case a more formal approach that is sometimes helpful in rationalizing complex fermentations in which the route of metabolism is not always clear.

In considering oxidation-reduction reactions, we noted that the removal of two hydrogen atoms is electronically equivalent to adding one oxygen atom. Let us now look at the ethanol fermentation in those terms. The starting glucose has two hydrogen atoms and one oxygen atom for each carbon atom; in other words, it is formally $6 \times CH_2O$. However, the ethanol product is formally $2 \times CH_3O_{0.5}$. Ethanol has one more hydrogen atom and one-half less oxygen atom per carbon, or the equivalent of two more hydrogen atoms per carbon than are found in the starting glucose. Right away, we see that ethanol is more reduced than glucose, and we know, without further information, that there must be some other product that is more oxidized than glucose if there is to be a true fermentation in which oxidations balance reductions. Of course, that other product is CO_2, which has two less H and one more O per carbon atom, and is therefore four hydrogen equivalents more oxidized than the carbon in glucose.

We could use that kind of arithmetic to predict the proportion of the products:

> Each carbon atom in ethanol is two hydrogen equivalents more reduced than a carbon atom in glucose.
>
> Each carbon atom in CO_2 is four hydrogen equivalents more oxidized than a carbon atom in glucose.
>
> To balance the oxidations and reductions, two carbon atoms from glucose must appear in ethanol for each carbon atom that appears as CO_2 (2×2 hydrogen equivalents reduced $= 1 \times 4$ hydrogen equivalents oxidized).

HETEROLACTATE FERMENTATION AND THE PENTOSE PHOSPHATE PATHWAY

In the homolactate and ethanol fermentations we have examined, NADH is formed in one reaction, and consumed in one other reaction. Most fermentations are not so straightforward; NADH may be produced or consumed in several reactions, and the fermentations result in a mixture of products.

Let us consider an example of this kind of fermentation, a heterolactate fermentation that results in the production of equal quantities of **lactate, ethanol** and **CO_2.** Admirers of sauerkraut and of dill pickles are indebted to organisms that gain their energy in this way. Cabbages and cucumbers are infested with such organisms along with other less desirable varieties, and it was found long ago that steeping the vegetables with salt promoted the growth of the lactate-forming organisms. (The formation of sauerkraut is especially complex, with heterolactate fermenters growing most rapidly at first, creating a brew bubbling with the evolved CO_2 in which small amounts of flavor-producing esters are also created, followed by ascendancy of homolactate fermenting organisms as the solution grows more acid, and finally succeeded by highly acid-tolerant heterofermenting organisms that finish off the remaining supply of glucose derived from the plant. Our ancestors knew none of this, but they had discovered how to make chopped cabbage behave this way most of the time. Modern processors use their more sophisticated knowledge to gain a higher batting average.)

General Description. Our interest at the moment in the heterolactate fermentation comes from its illustration of metabolic pathways that are important for many purposes. The equimolar mixture of lactate, ethanol and CO_2 is not created by a combination of the enzymes used by other organisms for their separate production, but by the use of a different route known as the **pentose phosphate pathway,** which results in a controlled mixture of products (Fig. 16–3). This pathway involves successive direct oxida-

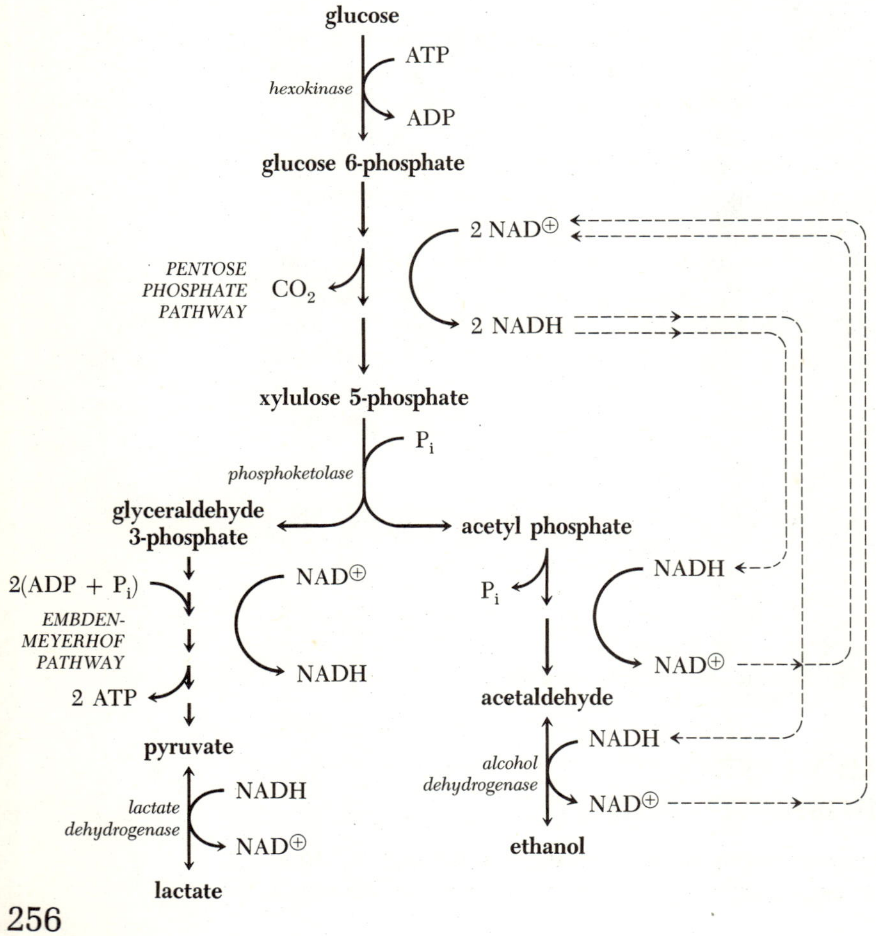

Figure 16–3 Outline of the heterolactate fermentation. Glucose 6-phosphate is oxidatively decarboxylated to xylulose 5-phosphate by a series of reactions of general importance to many organisms that is called the pentose phosphate pathway. The xylulose 5-phosphate is cleaved to glyceraldehyde 3-phosphate, which is converted to lactate by the usual reactions of glycolysis, and to acetyl phosphate. Acetyl phosphate is reduced in 2 steps to ethanol, thereby disposing of the excess NADH created by the earlier pentose phosphate pathway. The result is the conversion of glucose to an equimolar mixture of lactate, ethanol, and CO_2.

tions of glucose 6-phosphate by NAD that cause the loss of one carbon as CO_2, with five carbons remaining as a ketopentose phosphate, **D-xylulose 5-phosphate.** This compound is then split into two pieces: the familiar three-carbon **D-glyceraldehyde 3-phosphate,** and a two-carbon compound, **acetyl phosphate,** which is the anhydride of acetic acid and phosphoric acid.

The molecule of triose phosphate is handled by the conventional Embden-Meyerhof pathway, just as it is in homolactate fermentation or in muscle glycolysis, and is therefore converted to one molecule of **lactate** with the generation of two molecules of ATP. This portion of the fermentation involves the formation of NADH, but it is consumed by the later reduction of pyruvate to lactate in the same process, and therefore does not affect the balance of other reactions. However, the acetyl phosphate is handled in a way that is new in our discussion, in which the two final steps involve successive reductions by NADH, first to **acetaldehyde** and then to **ethanol.** These two steps therefore balance the initial oxidations of glucose 6-phosphate, in which two molecules of NADH are formed.

The overall result now is a true fermentation, with no external oxidizing or reducing agent, but it forms only one molecule of ATP per molecule of glucose consumed:

$$\underset{\textbf{glucose}}{C_6H_{12}O_6} + (ADP^{2-} + P_i^{-}) \longrightarrow \underset{\textbf{lactate}}{C_3H_5O_3} + \underset{\textbf{ethanol}}{C_2H_6O} + CO_2 + ATP^{4-} + H_2O$$

After the organism uses ATP for its various energy requirements, the result is the simple fermentation as it is usually written:

$$\text{glucose} \longrightarrow \text{lactate}^- + \text{ethanol} + CO_2 + H^+$$

Let us now look a little more closely at the routes involved in this fermentation that are new to us.

The Pentose Phosphate Pathway

The oxidative decarboxylation of glucose 6-phosphate by the pentose phosphate pathway is, as we shall see, an important part of the mechanism for fat synthesis in animals, as well as being involved in metabolic pathways in microorganisms other than the one we are considering. The route is also known as the hexosemonophosphate pathway, the pentose shunt, and other permutations of these words.

The Dehydrogenations. The initial steps are straightforward variants of many similar reactions (Fig. 16–4), and the hydroxyl group on C-1 of the pyranose form of glucose 6-phosphate is oxidized by a dehydrogenase utilizing NAD. The result is the formation of a carbonyl group connected to the ring oxygen, in other words, an inner ester or lactone. The parent acid is gluconic acid, so this is the lactone of the 6-phosphate of gluconic acid: **6-phospho-D-gluconolactone.**

The lactone is then hydrolyzed to form the open-chain **6-phospho-D-gluconate,** which is the substrate for a second dehydrogenase. This enzyme utilizes NAD to attack the hydroxyl group on the third carbon atom, forming a carbonyl group. Now, we have emphasized before that 3-ketocarboxylic acids readily lose CO_2 and that oxidations forming such compounds may result in the simultaneous loss of the CO_2. We saw an example in the citric acid cycle; isocitrate is oxidized and decarboxylated by the same enzyme. Here we have another such example: **6-phosphogluconate dehydrogenase** converts C-3 of the substrate to a carbonyl group and thereby causes the loss of the C-1 carboxyl group as CO_2. The carbonyl group now becomes C-2 of the five-carbon

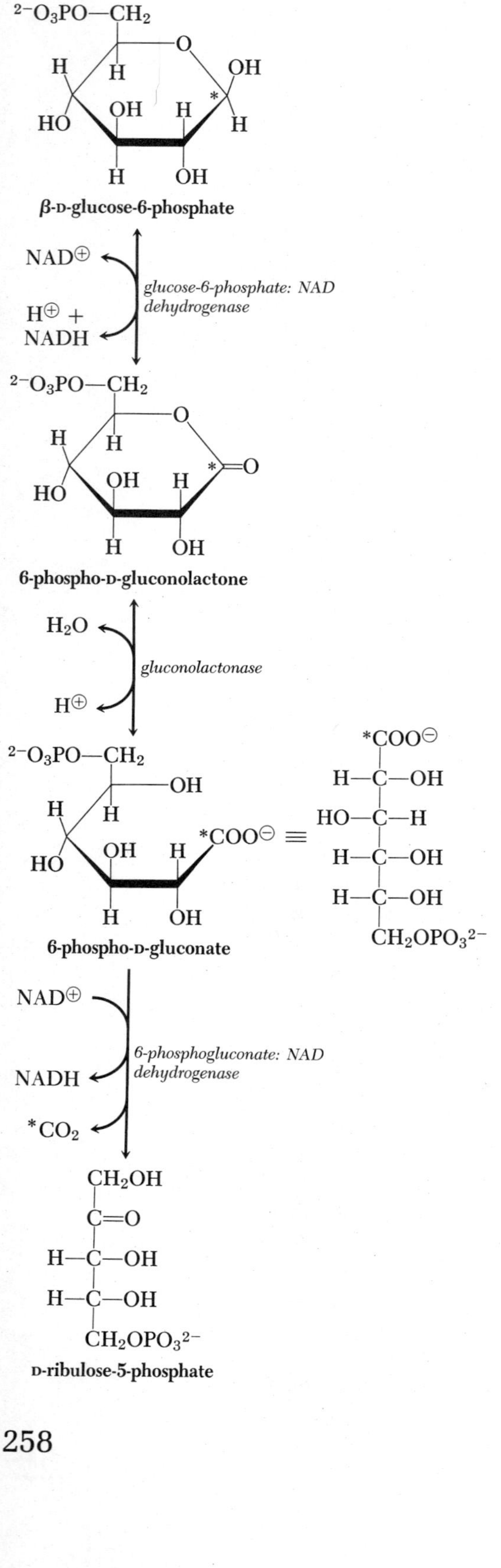

Figure 16-4 The pentose phosphate pathway begins in heterolactate-fermenting bacteria with a pair of NAD-coupled oxidations of glucose 6-phosphate. The first produces a lactone that is hydrolyzed to 6-phosphogluconate, which is the acid corresponding to glucose 6-phosphate, and the second causes an oxidative decarboxylation that forms ribulose 5-phosphate.

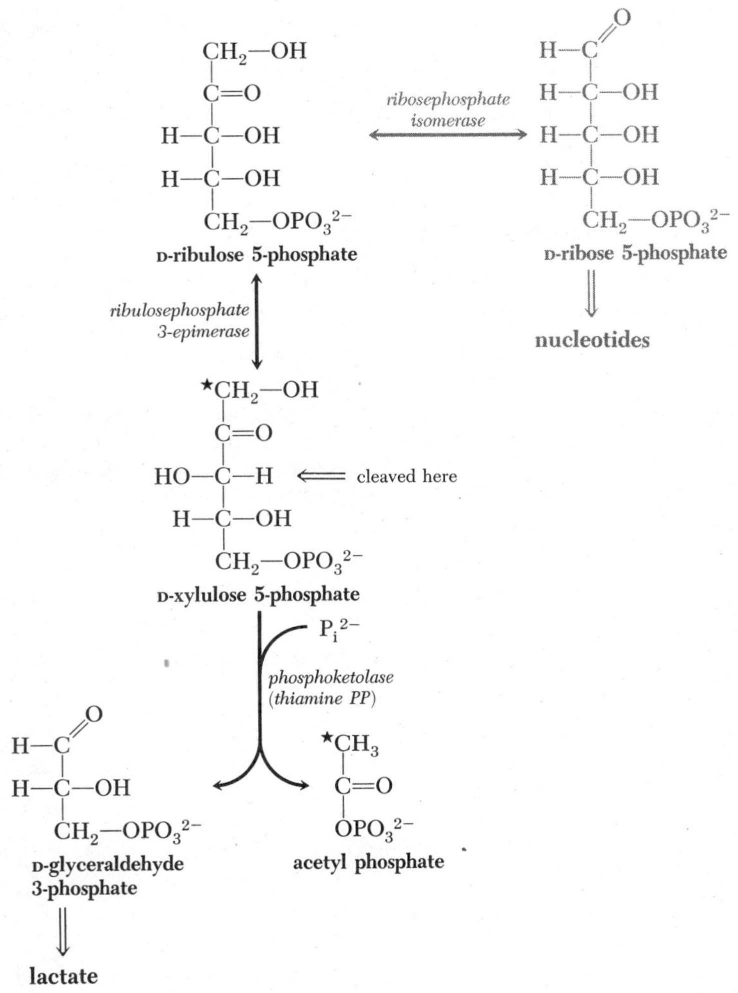

Figure 16–5 The ribulose 5-phosphate formed by the pentose phosphate pathway may be isomerized to form ribose 5-phosphate for incorporation into nucleotides, but the heterolactate fermentation involves epimerization at C-3 to form xylulose 5-phosphate, which is cleaved by phosphorolysis to form glyceraldehyde 3-phosphate and acetyl phosphate.

product, which therefore is the phosphorylated derivative of a ketose, **D-ribulose 5-phosphate.**

Disposition of Ribulose Phosphate. The name ribulose phosphate implies that it is the ketose analogue of ribose phosphate. (If this kind of nomenclature had been started earlier, fructose would be called gluculose; perhaps one could get used to it.) Indeed, there is an isomerase that catalyzes the interconversion of the ribulose and ribose phosphates (Fig. 16–5), and we shall later see that ribulose phosphate can provide a supply of pentose for the formation of nucleotides, including the nucleic acids, by this reaction. Right now, we are concerned with a different route that involves an epimerization, which is a reversal of the order of substitution of the various groups on C-3 of ribulose 5-phosphate to form a different ketopentose phosphate, **D-xylulose 5-phosphate.**

Notice that C-3 of xylulose 5-phosphate has the L-configuration, whereas C-4 has the D-configuration. Nearly all enzymes catalyzing the cleavage of sugar chains require this kind of *trans* arrangement of hydroxyl groups for activity. We have already seen an example; fructose diphosphate, which is cleaved by an aldolase into two triose phosphates (p. 102), has this kind of configuration next to the carbonyl group. In the case at hand, the enzyme **phosphoketolase** cleaves xylulose 5-phosphate next to the carbonyl group, as indicated by the arrow in the figure. The enzyme contains **thiamine pyrophosphate** as a coenzyme, so the cleavage is really related to the pyruvate decar-

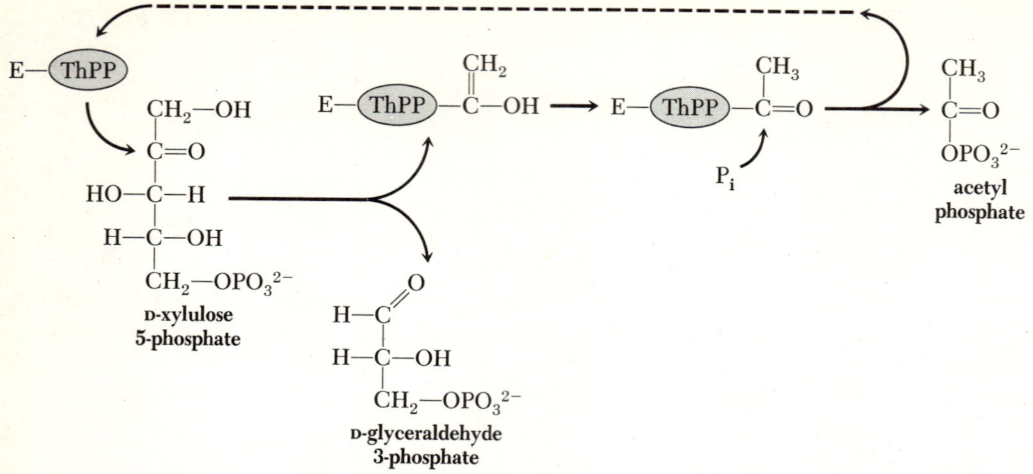

Figure 16-6 The phosphoketolase catalyzing the phosphorolysis of xylulose 5-phosphate contains thiamine pyrophosphate, and the mechanism involves the transfer of a 2-carbon unit from the substrate to the coenzyme, with rearrangement to create an acetyl thiamine intermediate. The intermediate is cleaved with P_i to release acetyl phosphate.

boxylase reaction (p. 223), with an intermediate transfer of the two-carbon group that is to become an acetyl group onto the coenzyme (Fig. 16-6). In terms of oxidation state, a 2-hydroxy aldehyde is equivalent to a carboxylic acid:

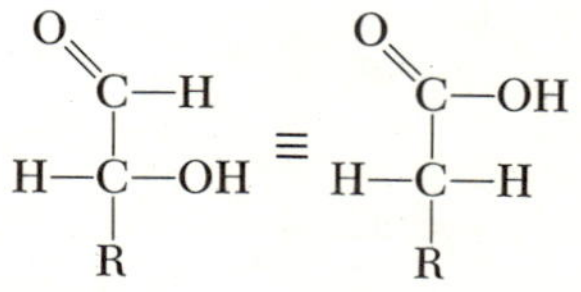

and the rearrangement occurs upon release of the two-carbon group by reaction with inorganic phosphate, forming **acetyl phosphate.**

Fate of Acetyl Phosphate. The final steps of the heterolactate fermentation involve the reduction of acetyl phosphate to form ethanol. Acetyl phosphate is an important intermediate in many microbial processes. It is a high-energy phosphate, and the cells in which it occurs have an enzyme catalyzing the exchange of the phos-

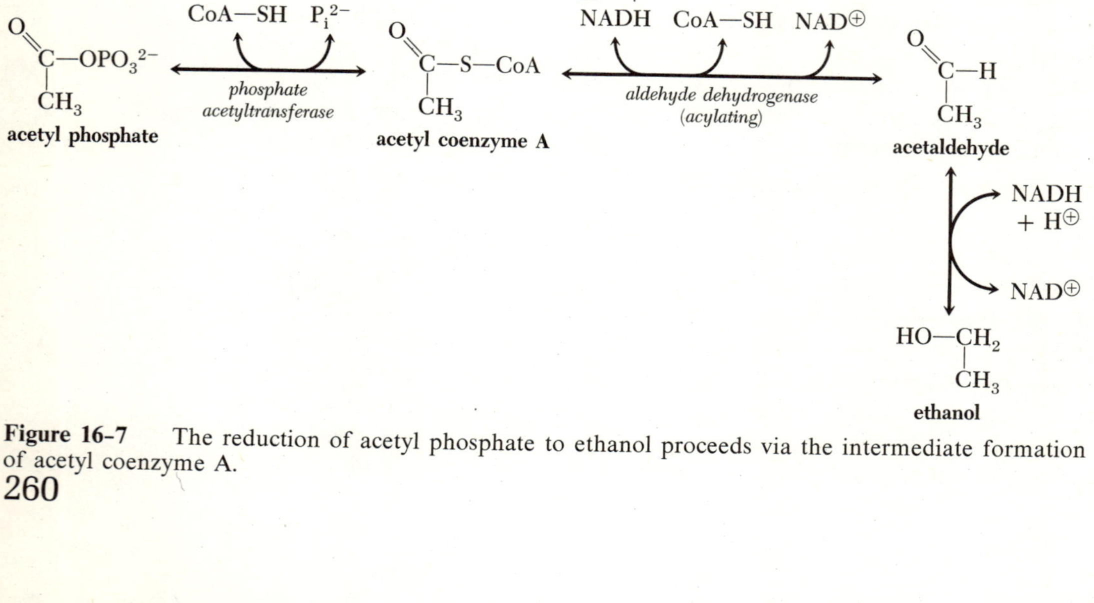

Figure 16-7 The reduction of acetyl phosphate to ethanol proceeds via the intermediate formation of acetyl coenzyme A.

phate for coenzyme A (Fig. 16–7).

A second enzyme catalyzes the NAD-coupled interconversion of **acetyl coenzyme A** and **acetaldehyde.** We have already noted that the oxidation of aldehydes to carboxylic acids is by itself a highly exergonic process, and the reaction is frequently modified so as to create high-energy bonds (the oxidation of glyceraldehyde 3-phosphate to form diphosphoglycerate in the Embden-Meyerhof pathway, p. 217; the oxidative decarboxylation of α-ketoglutarate, with the formation of succinyl coenzyme A, p. 180). The formation of a high-energy bond diminishes the release of free energy, so such oxidations of aldehydes in which no decarboxylation is also involved are freely reversible, and the heterolactate fermenters use the reverse reaction to reduce acetic acid, as the coenzyme A ester, to acetaldehyde. The acetaldehyde is then reduced to ethanol by the familiar alcohol dehydrogenase, and the equilibrium of this reaction is so far toward ethanol that it continually keeps the preceding easily reversible reactions displaced toward ethanol production and NADH removal.

BUTYRATE FERMENTATIONS AND FERREDOXIN

Finally, let us consider some fermentations carried out by organisms from the genus *Clostridium,* in which there is an intermediate formation of **butyrate** from glucose, accompanied by the discharge of $\mathbf{CO_2}$ and $\mathbf{H_2}$ as gases. The clostridia are strict anaerobes and include some formidable adversaries of man; among them are the species causing tetanus, botulinus poisoning, and gas gangrene. They are widely distributed, but their requirement for strictly anaerobic conditions only occasionally permits them to cause trouble.

There are more beneficent clostridia that have been encouraged to pursue their fermentations for the industrial production of solvents, especially acetone and butanol. Indeed, the state of Israel owes its existence to some extent to the behavior of *Clostridium acetobutylicum.* Great Britain desperately needed acetone as a solvent for making nitrocellulose explosives during the First World War. An ardent Zionist, Chaim Weizmann, had isolated a particular strain of this species of *Clostridium* that utilized starch as a source of glucose to produce a mixture of acetone and butanol. This information came to the attention of Winston Churchill, then First Lord of the Admiralty. The result was that the British got their acetone, and Weizmann got a change in the attitude toward Palestine that later made Israel possible, with Weizmann as its president. It could be that Palestinian guerrillas would even now include *Clostridium acetobutylicum* Weizmann among the disease-producing organisms, although the organism has been of declining importance in the economy because the production of acetone, and then of butanol (used in automobile lacquer), became cheaper by nonbiological synthesis. However, we may call again on this or related organisms as our supply of petroleum dwindles.

Glucose ⟶ Acetoacetyl Coenzyme A

The clostridia in question convert glucose to pyruvate by the regular Embden-Meyerhof pathway. Various species form solvents such as **acetone, isopropanol, butyrate,** or **butanol** from **acetoacetyl coenzyme A,** the same compound we encountered as an intermediate in fatty acid oxidation (p. 200). We are primarily interested in the steps by which pyruvate is converted to acetoacetyl coenzyme A, because they illustrate the use of **ferredoxin,** an oxidizing agent we have not discussed previously.

The pyruvate dehydrogenase of clostridia, like the eukaryotic complex we already

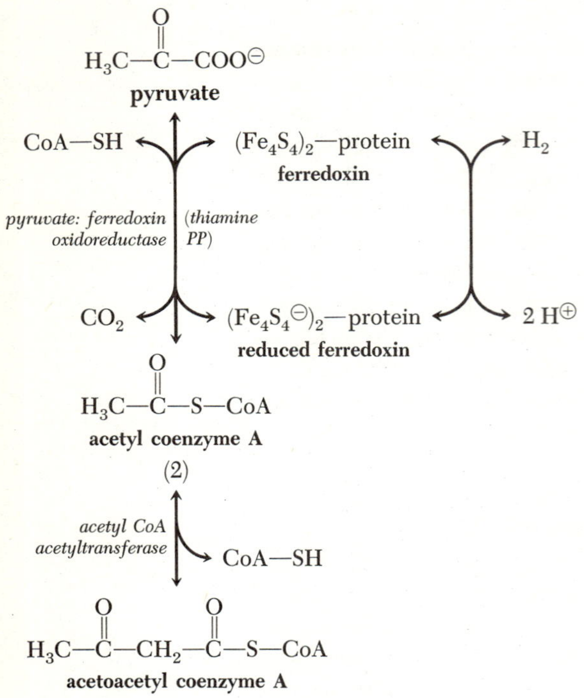

Figure 16-8 The conversion of pyruvate to acetyl coenzyme A and H_2 by clostridia. Acetyl coenzyme A is also in equilibrium with acetoacetyl coenzyme A in these organisms.

considered (p. 222), begins its reaction by transferring the acetaldehyde moiety of pyruvate to **thiamine pyrophosphate** as a hydroxyethyl group, with the release of CO_2. The hydroxyethyl group is then oxidized to an acetyl group that appears as acetyl coenzyme A, but the electrons are transferred to ferredoxin, which is a non-heme iron protein. Finally, two molecules of acetyl coenzyme A are equilibrated with acetoacetyl coenzyme A by the same thiolase reaction used in fatty acid oxidation. The novelty in all of this is the ferredoxin reaction, and let us consider this further.

Ferredoxin. We shall encounter ferredoxins, or similar compounds, that are also involved in photosynthesis, in nitrogen fixation, and even in the formation of mammalian adrenal hormones. They are small proteins containing **iron** and **inorganic sulfide.** For example, the clostridial ferredoxin has eight iron atoms, presumable in ferric state, and eight sulfide atoms, which are arranged in two groups of four, with Fe-S bonds also being formed to **cysteinyl residues** in the apoprotein. (This arrangement was discussed on p. 117 (Fig. 8–15).) The entire complex has a molecular weight of approximately 6000. Each of the two iron-sulfur cages can carry one electron; there is no interaction between the cages, so the second cage takes up an electron as easily as does the first.

The important functional characteristic of the ferredoxin cages is that they retain electrons much less readily than most of the non-heme iron proteins. Why this is so has not been rationalized completely, but in any event, the ferredoxins are among the most powerful reducing agents of all of the known electron carriers; they are so powerful that reduced and oxidized ferredoxins will equilibrate with protons and hydrogen gas under the influence of an enzyme, **hydrogenase** (Fig. 16–8), and this is the source of the hydrogen emitted during clostridial and other microbial fermentations.

Now, the reduction of ferredoxin and the resultant reduction of protons to hydrogen are endergonic processes compared to the reduction of NAD. The mammalian pyruvate dehydrogenase complex can oxidize and decarboxylate pyruvate while reducing NAD to NADH and creating the high-energy acetyl coenzyme A bond. The clostridial pyruvate dehydrogenase likewise oxidizes and decarboxylates pyruvate while creating acetyl coenzyme A, but it also accomplishes the much more endergonic reduction of ferredoxin. This extra endergonic component makes the clostridial reaction reversible, unlike the irreversible mammalian reaction we considered earlier.

The Fate of Acetoacetyl Coenzyme A

The conversion of one molecule of glucose to one molecule of acetoacetyl CoA as we have outlined it involves the formation of two molecules each of NADH, H_2 and CO_2. There must be further reactions to dispose of the NADH, and the simplest route is to reduce acetoacetyl CoA to **butyryl CoA** (Fig. 16-9). This is the reverse of the fatty acid sequence, with the important distinction that NADH is used for both reductions, whereas in fatty acid oxidation, a flavoprotein is used for oxidizing saturated acyl coenzyme A compounds to unsaturated enoyl coenzyme A. The reason is that the reverse reaction is favored by a more powerful reducing agent.

We can see from Figure 16-9 that the conversion of glucose to butyryl coenzyme A constitutes a complete fermentation, except for the formation of the coenzyme A ester. The final necessary step is the release of free butyrate, and this is accomplished by transferring the coenzyme A to acetate. The energy of the thiol ester is then captured,

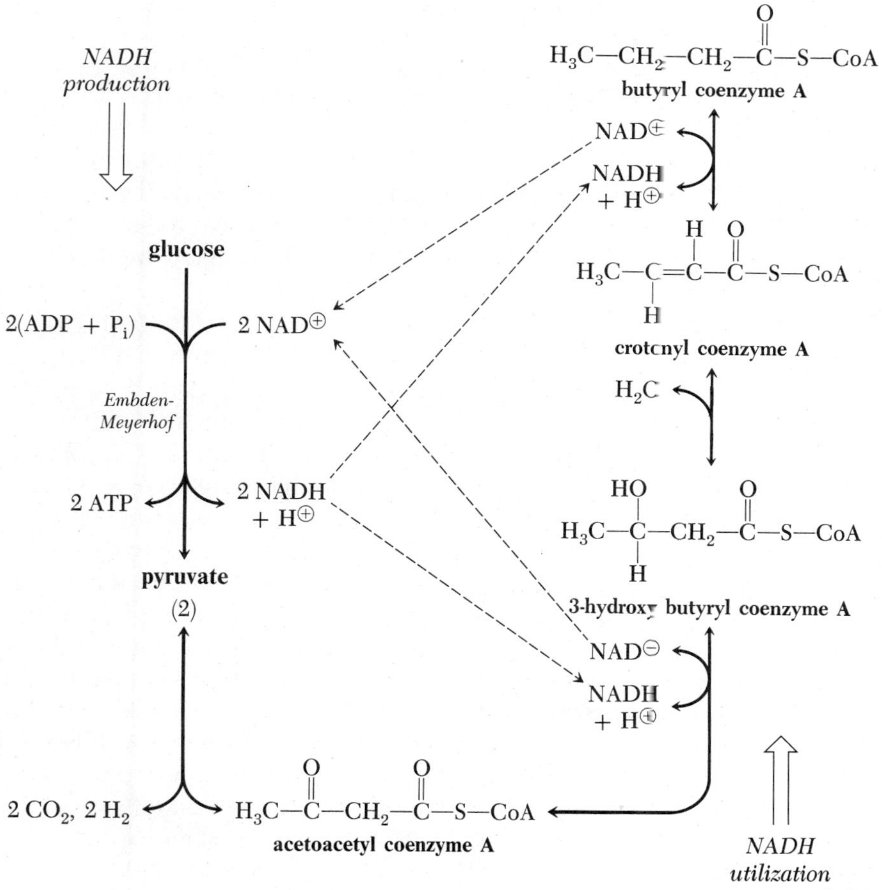

Figure 16-9 The NADH produced by the conversion of glucose to pyruvate in the Embden-Meyerhof pathway of some clostridia is consumed by reducing acetoacetyl coenzyme A to butyryl coenzyme A.

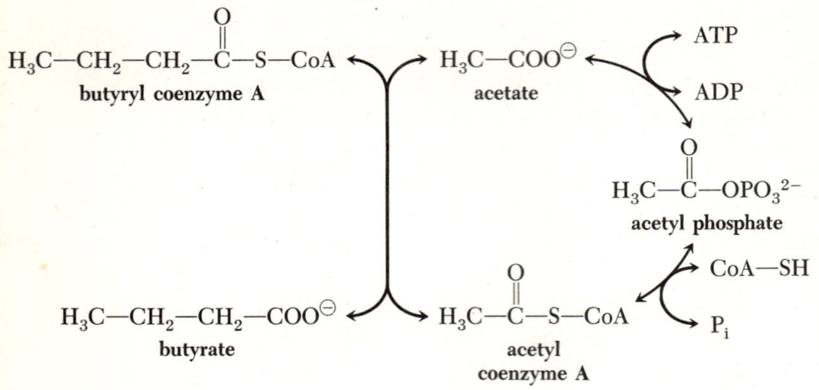

Figure 16-10 Clostridia have a mechanism for capturing the energy of some thiol esters, such as butyryl coenzyme A, by transferring the coenzyme A group to acetate. Cleavage of the resultant acetyl coenzyme A with P_i forms a high-energy phosphate that can be used to phosphorylate ADP to ATP. Butyrate then appears as an end-product of metabolism.

first by forming acetyl phosphate, and then by transferring the phosphate to ADP (Fig. 16-10). The overall result of the fermentation then becomes:

$$\underset{\textbf{glucose}}{C_6H_{12}O_6} + (ADP^{3-} + P_i^{2-} + H^+) \longrightarrow$$

$$\underset{\textbf{butyrate}}{C_4H_7O_2^-} + H^+ + 2\,CO_2 + 2\,H_2 + 3\,(ATP^{4-} + H_2O)$$

(The clostridial fermentations occur at a more neutral pH than the other fermentations we have discussed; hence the designation of the fully ionized forms of the phosphate compounds.)

The Solvent Fermentations

What we have outlined is considerably more complex than unadorned glycolysis, but still logically simple. Unfortunately, the clostridial solvent fermentations are more complex, and frequently form many products. Let us satisfy ourselves that, given time, we could rationalize the most complex events, by advancing one more state in complexity.

The clostridia may release butyrate from butyryl CoA as we outlined above, but there is another alternative. The butyryl CoA may be reduced to **butyraldehyde** much as acetyl CoA may be reduced to acetaldehyde by the heterolactate fermenters we saw earlier in the chapter. The butyraldehyde may then be reduced to **butanol.** We have thus accounted for one of the products of the Weizmann fermentation, but these two reductions required two additional molecules of NADH. Where are they to come from?

In our outline of the butyrate fermentation (Fig. 16-9) we noted that the NADH produced in forming acetoacetyl CoA is consumed in converting acetoacetyl CoA to butyryl CoA. If half of the acetoacetyl CoA is not reduced, NADH will be accumulating and can be used to convert the remainder of the acetoacetyl CoA all the way to butanol. Here, then, is the secret of the acetone-butanol fermentation. Glucose is converted to acetoacetyl CoA with the concomitant formation of 2 NADH per molecule of glucose consumed. Half of the acetoacetyl CoA is converted to acetoacetate, which is then decarboxylated by a specific **acetoacetate decarboxylase** to release **acetone** (Fig. 16-11). The other half of the acetoacetyl CoA is converted to butyryl CoA.

The half of the glucose that is used for acetone production causes excess formation of NADH. The half of the glucose that is used for butyryl CoA formation causes neither consumption nor production of NADH. Therefore, the excess NADH from acetone

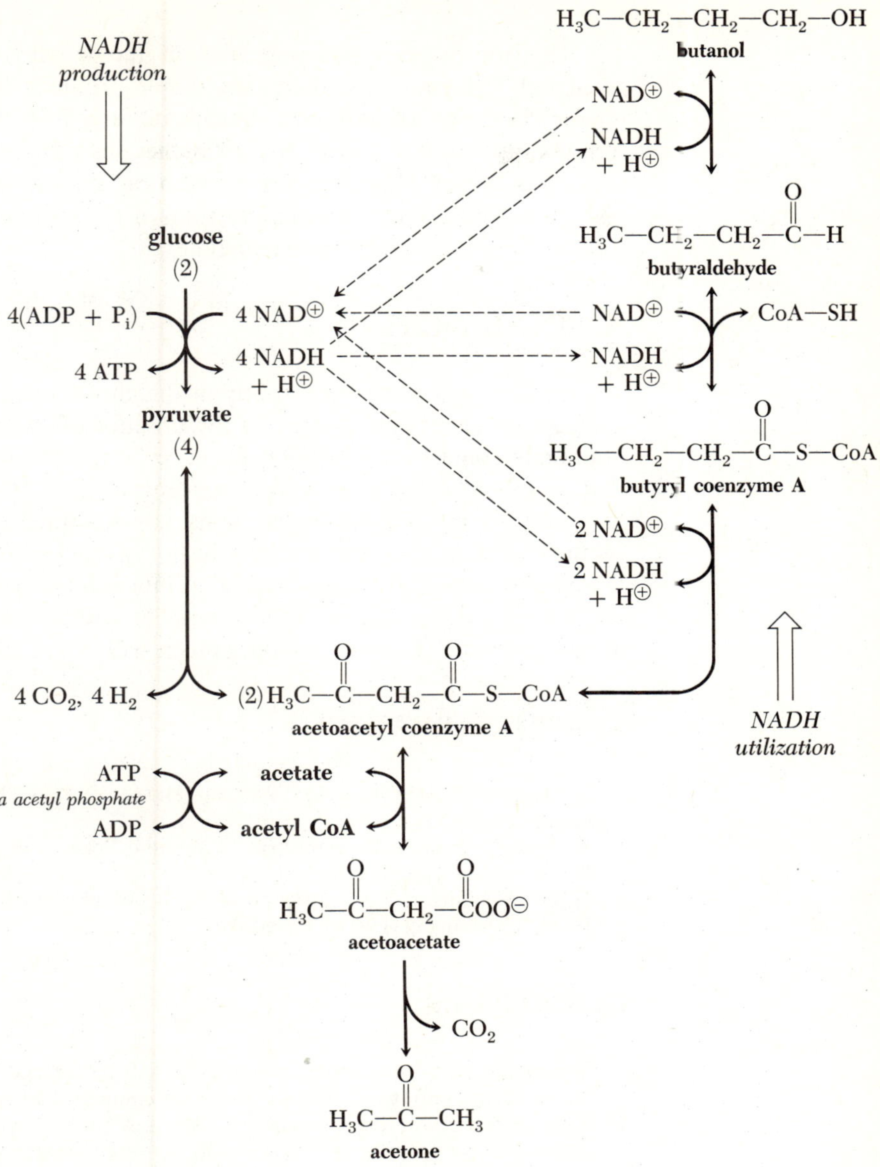

Figure 16–11 Some clostridia utilize the NADH gained from two molecules of glucose in the Embden-Meyerhof pathway to reduce one molecule of acetoacetyl coenzyme A all the way to butanol. (The individual steps between acetoacetyl coenzyme A and butyryl coenzyme A are given in Figure 16–9.) The remaining molecule of acetoacetyl coenzyme A is decarboxylated to acetone after recovery of the energy from the thiol ester bond as acetyl coenzyme A. These organisms produce both butanol and acetone as end-products.

formation can be used to further reduce the butyryl CoA to butanol. The balance is shown on the figure and can also be summarized like this, neglecting ATP turnover:

(1) $2\ C_6H_{12}O_6 + 2\ \text{CoA-SH} + 4\ NAD^+ \longrightarrow$ (**glucose**)

$2\ C_4H_5O_2\text{-(S-CoA)} + 4\ (NADH + H^+) + 4\ CO_2 + 4\ H_2$ (**acetoacetyl CoA**)

(2) $C_4H_5O_2\text{-(S-CoA)} + H_2O \longrightarrow C_3H_6O + CO_2 + \text{CoA-SH}$ (**acetoacetyl CoA** → **acetone**)

(3) $C_4H_5O_2\text{-(S-CoA)} + 2\ (NAD + H^+) \longrightarrow C_4H_7O\text{-(S-CoA)} + 2\ NAD^+ + H_2O$ (**acetoacetyl CoA** → **butyryl CoA**)

(4) $C_4H_7O\text{-(S-CoA)} + 2\ (NADH + H^+) \longrightarrow C_4H_{10}O + 2\ NAD^+ + \text{CoA-SH}$ (**butyryl CoA** → **butanol**)

SUM: $2\ C_6H_{12}O_6 \longrightarrow C_4H_{10}O + C_3H_6O + 5\ CO_2 + 4\ H_2$ (**2 glucose** → **butanol**, **acetone**)

The sum involves two molecules of glucose per complete fermentation sequence. In actual fermentations, there are minor products beyond those shown, including ethanol, isopropanol, and some short-chain fatty acids. In addition, some of the reduced ferredoxin is used to create NADH rather than H_2, so the equations do not balance exactly as shown. However, anyone who can handle the logic of the balance we have just made would find the rationalization of the more complicated fermentations to be well within reach, given sufficient time.

A FINAL NOTE

We see that organisms vary widely in the choice of products to form from glucose as a means of generating energy in the absence of oxygen. Part of the differences undoubtedly come from evolution for survival in the face of competition. An organism that adapts to survival at a high concentration of H^+ can kill off many competitors by producing H^+. Similar explanations may account for the diversity of solvents created by the clostridia. Our account here has only touched the surface of a complex subject. Given any persistent, nearly neutral, dilute aqueous solution of an organic compound containing reduced carbon atoms, with or without the presence of oxygen, it seems almost certain that some microorganism will adapt to utilize the compound.

FURTHER READING

B. D. Davis et al., Microbiology, 2nd ed., Harper & Row (1973). See Chapter 3 of this monumental textbook.

H. W. Doelle, Bacterial metabolism, Academic Press (1969). Contains some out of date biochemistry, but valuable factual reference.

W. H. Orme-Johnson, Iron-sulfur proteins. Structure and function, Ann. Rev. Biochem., 42:159 (1973). Contains review of ferredoxins.

QUESTIONS

1. How many additional molecules of ATP will be formed per molecule of glucose in homolactate fermentations producing D-lactate compared to those producing L-lactate?
2. What enzyme would you expect to be present in oxygen-tolerant anaerobes—those not utilizing oxygen but able to survive its presence—but not in strict anaerobes?
3. Is the following conversion a balanced fermentation?

$$\text{glucose} \longrightarrow \text{lactate}^- + H^+ + \text{acetaldehyde} + CO_2 + H_2$$

4. The presence of what compound among the reaction products of a fermentation makes it almost certain that the responsible organism is utilizing ferredoxin?
5. What reaction in the Embden-Meyerhof pathway is most nearly analogous to the acetaldehyde dehydrogenase (CoA acylating) reaction that equilibrates acetaldehyde and acetyl coenzyme A in the presence of NAD and NADH?
6. What is the two-carbon unit carried by thiamine pyrophosphate in each of the following reactions or processes, and what is the final product made from the two-carbon unit in each case? (a) The oxidation of pyruvate by NAD in a strict aerobe; (b) the conversion of glucose to ethanol by a yeast; (c) the phosphoketolase reaction of a heterolactate-fermenting lactobacillus; (d) the oxidation of pyruvate by ferredoxin in a clostridium.
7. The recovery of energy from acetyl coenzyme A involves the formation of acetyl phosphate, followed by transfer of the phosphate to ADP. Could ATP also be generated by a similar transfer of phosphate from D-xylulose 5-phosphate? Explain.
8. Bonus question: Construct a metabolic pathway, using known bacterial reactions, that would require a fermentation to proceed precisely according to this equation:

$$2\ \text{glucose} \longrightarrow 2\ \text{lactate}^- + 2\ H^+ + \text{butanol} + 2\ CO_2 + H_2O$$

CHAPTER 17

PHOTOSYNTHESIS

THE CONCEPTS

Photosynthesis includes all processes by which the energy of absorbed light is used to drive biological syntheses, but it usually means the light-driven reduction of CO_2 to glucose by green plants, in which water is oxidized to release O_2. This process occurs in chloroplasts, which contain the light-absorbing pigments and the necessary enzymes. Chloroplasts are like mitochondria in having stacked layers of inner membranes in which electron transfers are associated with phosphorylations, and they also have their own DNA and apparatus for protein synthesis. Chloroplasts make glucose residues and store them as starch during daylight hours; mitochondria oxidize pyruvate from glucose residues, especially during the night, to provide energy for the plant.

Reaction Centers. Chloroplasts contain compounds with highly resonant structures, carotenes and chlorophylls, to absorb much of the sunlight. The energy of excitation is passed from one pigment to another until it arrives at a reaction center, where chlorophyll a complexes occur in association with other proteins necessary for utilization of the energy. Chlorophyll a in the reaction center loses excitation energy and becomes oxidized by transferring electrons to an acceptor.

Cyclic Photophosphorylation. Plants contain type I reaction centers in which electrons displaced by photo-excitation are transferred from their receptors back to oxidized chlorophyll. The transfer occurs through several intermediate carriers so that it can be used to generate high-energy phosphate. In this mechanism, electrons displaced by absorbed light are continually coming back to the parent chlorophyll, but the recombination occurs through the apparatus of oxidative phosphorylation.

Formation of O_2. The electrons necessary to restore oxidized chlorophyll of photosystem I to its initial state may also be supplied by water. In order to do this, light is absorbed by another type of reaction center, type II, in which the oxidized chlorophyll left after removal of an electron will react with hydroxide ions of water and release O_2. Electrons are also transferred from photosystem II to photosystem I through part of the apparatus of oxidative phosphorylation so that at least one high-energy phosphate is generated per pair of electrons transferred.

Reduction of Ferredoxin. The use of water as an electron donor permits electrons to be removed from the system for other purposes, leaving O_2 behind. The immediate acceptor of electrons from photosystem I is a ferredoxin-reducing substance, and the reduced ferredoxin generated by it is primarily used in green plants to reduce NADP to NADPH.

Reduction of CO_2. Glucose is made from CO_2 by utilizing the NADPH and ATP generated by the photochemical processes. CO_2 is fixed by combining it with ribulose 1,5-diphosphate and cleaving to form two molecules of 3-phosphoglycerate, followed by reduction to triose phosphate with NADPH. The pentose carrier for CO_2 is regenerated by rearrangement of part of the triose phosphates formed, with the remainder forming glucose 6-phosphate for use as a fuel. The entire sequence constitutes the Calvin cycle, in which ATP is used to drive the formation of ribulose diphosphate and to form 1,3-diphosphoglycerate for reduction to triose phosphate.

The operation of the Calvin cycle hinges on the isomerization and epimerization of pentose phosphates, along with a transketolase reaction in which two carbon units are transferred *via* thiamine pyrophosphate from a donor ketose to an acceptor aldose.

Hatch-Slack Pathway. Chloroplasts are constructed so that the rate of the Calvin cycle changes with atmospheric CO_2 concentration. A plant that diminishes water loss to circulating air by closing leaf stomata also curtails its supply of CO_2, but some plants evolved to survive hot, dry conditions by utilizing ATP to concentrate CO_2. The resultant Hatch-Slack pathway involves carboxylation of pyruvate to oxaloacetate at the expense of ATP in an external ring

of mesophyll cells, followed by reduction by NADPH to malate. Malate diffuses into an inner ring of bundle sheath cells, where it is oxidatively decarboxylated by NADP to form pyruvate and a high concentration of CO_2 for use in the Calvin cycle.

Changing Atmosphere. **Photosynthesis is responsible for the oxidation-reduction represented by the accumulation of reduced carbon compounds in sediments at the expense of carbonates and the accumulation of oxygen in the atmosphere at the expense of water. Alterations in the balance of CO_2 and O_2 are today somewhat self-compensating, and the system is so massive that catastrophic changes owing to interference by man are not likely from simple perturbations of the stoichiometry of the system.**

GENERAL DESCRIPTION

We come now to the present-day major source of chemical potential for living organisms, the processes lumped together as photosynthesis. Photosynthesis includes the photochemical reactions and associated processes that occur in green plants, algae, and some bacteria following the absorption of light quanta. Most people know that plants in the sunlight can use carbon dioxide and water to form carbohydrate and oxygen; some can even specify the carbohydrate as glucose, or as its stored polymer, starch:

$$6\,CO_2 + 6\,H_2O \xrightarrow{\text{sunlight}} C_6H_{12}O_6 + 6\,O_2$$

Although this simple equation is an accurate appraisal of the end-result of photosynthetic processes in plants, it summarizes many complicated events. Even so, photosynthesis of all kinds, bacterial or plant, is not difficult to understand if it is appreciated that it consists of two mechanistically separated sequences of reactions, of which only one involves the absorption of light.

The Light Reactions

Electron Transfers. The light quanta absorbed by the photosynthetic apparatus are used to drive an oxidation-reduction reaction in a direction away from its normal equilibrium position:

$$2\,NADP^+ + 2\,H_2O \xrightarrow{h\nu} 2(NADPH + H^+) + O_2$$

Here we have the creation of both molecular oxygen and a strong reducing agent (NADPH). Except for the use of NADP instead of NAD (the two nucleotides have nearly identical chemical potentials for electron transfers), this is a reversal of the reaction used in mitochondria for the generation of ATP:

$$2\,NADH + 2\,H^+ + O_2 \longrightarrow 2\,NAD^+ + 2\,H_2O + 6\,{\sim}P$$

In other words, the absorption of light during photosynthesis is equivalent, per molecule of O_2 released, to an injection of energy greater than the energy released by hydrolyzing six high-energy phosphate bonds. This injection of energy is used to transfer electrons from water to NADP, forming NADPH and releasing O_2. (Some protists remove electrons from donors other than water to form oxidized products other than O_2, but the principle is the same—absorbed photons drive the reaction in the reverse of its spontaneous direction.)

The Dark Side of Photosynthesis

There are several ways in which the energy captured by photochemical electron transfers can be utilized for other purposes (Fig. 17–1). These energy-utilizing processes can occur in the absence of light, given a supply of reduced coenzymes, and are therefore sometimes referred to as dark reactions. However, it is wrong to think that they occur in plants in the middle of the night, because their continuation depends upon further formation of reduced coenzymes by the photochemical processes.

Photophosphorylation. The photochemical reactions involve the formation of strong reducing and oxidizing agents. Much of our discussion of metabolism to this point has centered on the generation of energy in mitochondria by transferring electrons from strong reducing agents to strong oxidizing agents. Photosynthesis involves this same process of oxidative phosphorylation, which appears to proceed in exactly the same way as it does in mitochondria, with the same uncertainties and arguments over mechanism. We shall see that some high-energy phosphate is formed during the electron shifts that generate NADPH and O_2 in green plants and algae. Photosynthetic organisms in general also often carry out a cyclic photophosphorylation, in which electrons travel directly back from the photochemically-formed reducing agent for the purposes of oxidative phosphorylation only. The photochemical system is then constantly turning over without the generation of another oxidized or reduced product, such as NADPH or O_2.

Gluconeogenesis by Reduction of CO_2. The major use of photochemical energy is the conversion of CO_2 to glucose. The process by which this occurs is often called CO_2 fixation, or carbon fixation, but we shall see that it is akin to other mechanisms

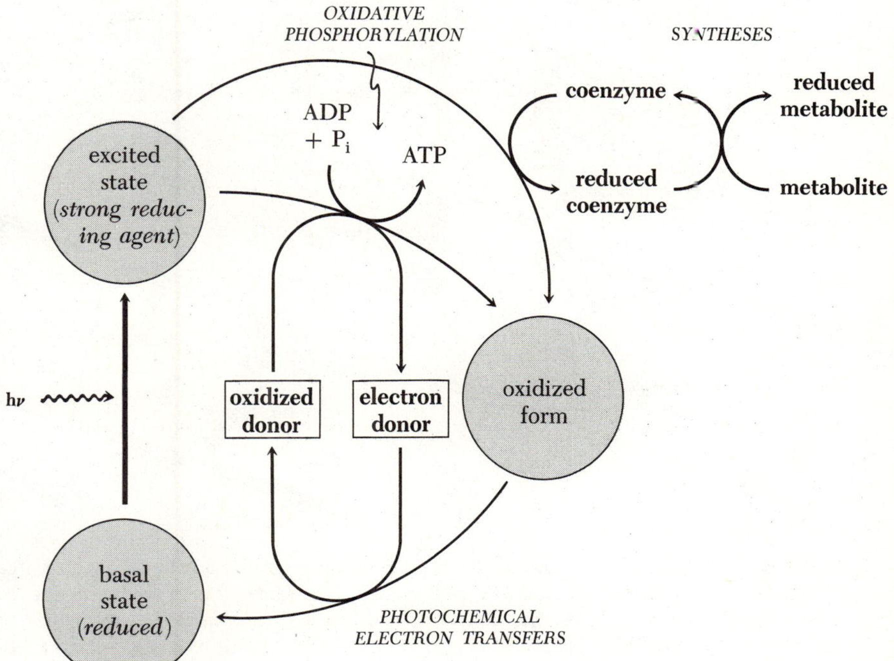

Figure 17–1 The absorption of photons converts the chlorophyll of reaction centers into a powerful reducing agent. The electrons may be transferred through carriers to coenzymes such as NADP, with the resultant NADPH used to create reduced metabolites. They may also be used to create an electron donor that will convert the oxidized chlorophyll back to its original state, and this cyclical flow of electrons can be used to generate ATP.

of gluconeogenesis. It requires both NADPH and ATP formed as a result of the photochemical electron transfers.

PLANT ANATOMY

Chloroplasts. Before going on, we ought to note the anatomical structures that are involved in photosynthesis. The green plants and many algae have chloroplasts, which are discrete organelles that contain the complete apparatus of photosynthesis. The components of this apparatus include the necessary pigments and enzymes for the photochemical electron transfers and subsequent oxidative phosphorylation, along with the enzymes necessary for gluconeogenesis. (The few bacteria that are photosynthetic contain the photochemical apparatus in vesicles associated with the plasma membrane.) In other words, higher plants have chloroplasts for photosynthesis and the photochemically driven oxidative phosphorylation; they have mitochondria for substrate oxidation and the associated oxidative phosphorylation.

The chloroplast has many features in common with a mitochondrion, including its own DNA and associated mechanism for protein synthesis. It contains **thylakoids,** which are stacks of flattened membrane sacs known as **grana.** Thylakoids resemble miniature stacks of coins, except that the stacks are interconnected with membrane tubules (Fig. 17–2). The thylakoid membranes contain the pigments necessary for light absorption. In addition, they are studded on one side with small granules that appear

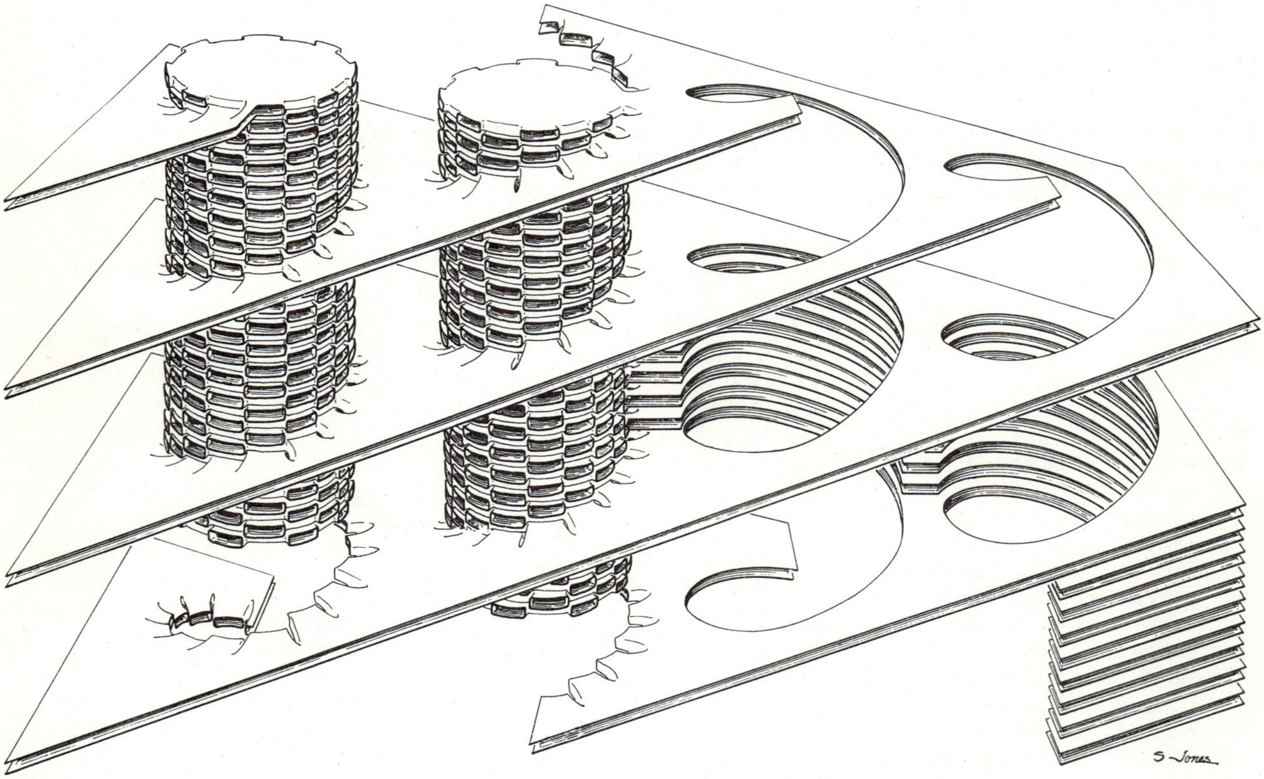

Figure 17–2 The inner membrane of chloroplasts is organized into a complex structure that appears to be totally interconnected. Sac-like grana are stacked into thylakoids, around which sheet-like lamella (only two shown) are connected in helical positions, according to an interpretation by D. A. Paolillo, Jr. (From J. Cell Science, 6:246 (1970) by permission of the Company of Biologists, Ltd., publishers, and the author.)

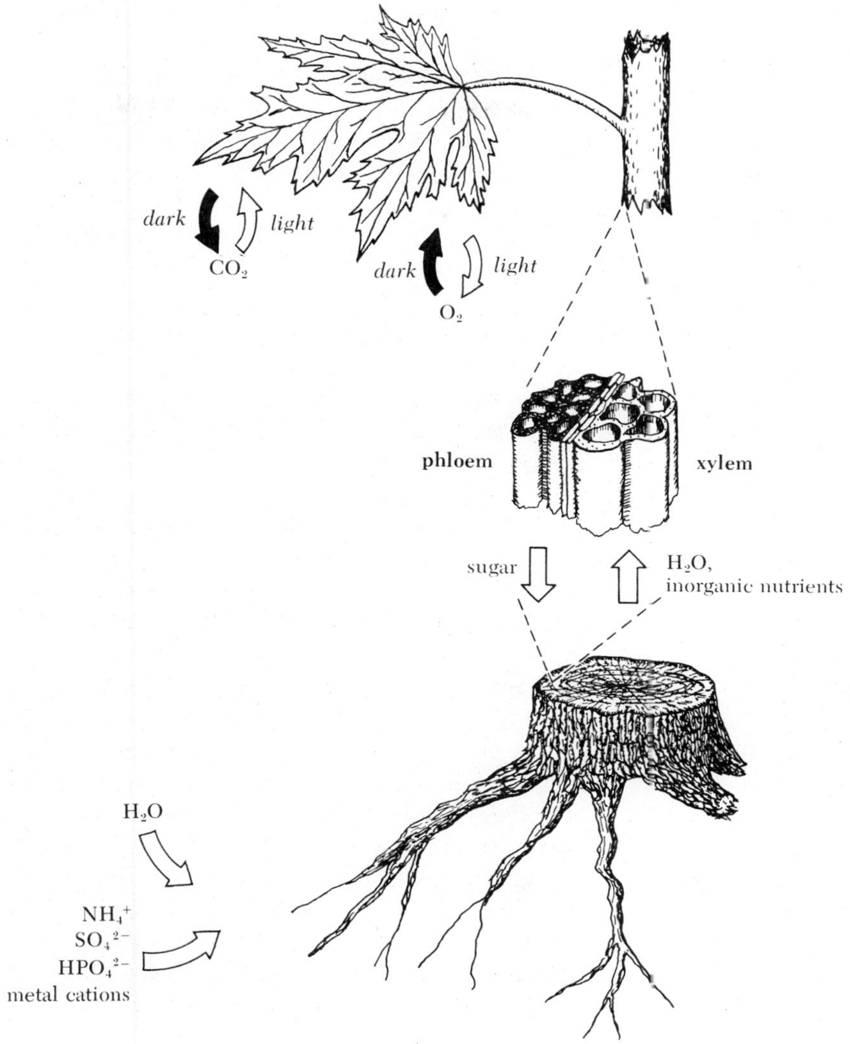

Figure 17-3 Plant nutrients are transported from the roots through the xylem tubules to the leaves. The leaves take up CO_2 and discharge O_2 during the light as a result of photosynthesis. During the dark, they take up O_2 for combustion of fuels and discharge CO_2 in the same way as do other aerobic organisms. The carbohydrate formed in the leaves by photosynthesis is transported for use as a fuel to other tissues through the phloem.

to contain the proteins necessary for oxidative phosphorylation, and are therefore much like the granules found in mitochondrial cristae in both structure and function.

Nutrient Circulation. Land plants depend upon a root system for the absorption of water and of inorganic salts containing all of the elements used in forming plant tissue except carbon and oxygen. Nitrogen is absorbed as ammonium or nitrate ions, sulfur as sulfate, phosphorus as phosphate, and so on (Fig. 17-3). Carbon dixoide and oxygen exchange with the atmosphere through the leaves. When the leaves are illuminated, carbon dioxide is absorbed and oxygen is discharged owing to photosynthesis in the chloroplasts. Oxygen is absorbed and carbon dioxide is discharged in the dark, owing to the oxidative metabolism of the mitochondria.

The transport of absorbed nutrients from the roots to the leaves through the **xylem** and the reverse transport through the **phloem** of fuels created by photosynthesis in the leaves, especially sucrose, hinge upon movement of relatively large volumes of water. Most of the flow occurs from the roots owing to evaporation of water from the leaves. There is no pulsatile tissue like the animal heart, and the driving force for the circulation is developed solely by intermolecular forces in the solvent and between the solvent and the tubules in which it moves.

THE PHOTOCHEMICAL REACTIONS

Light Frequency and Quantum Energy. Photochemical reactions are caused by the absorption of quanta of light—photons—with sufficient energy to excite bonding electrons to a higher quantum level. Physics tells us that the energy of a quantum of light increases directly with its frequency:

$$E = h\nu$$

where h is Planck's constant and ν is the frequency. Ultraviolet light has much greater energy per photon than does infrared light, which has a lower frequency and longer wavelength.

In order for a photon to be absorbed through excitation of electrons, its energy must match the increment in energy necessary to change the bonding electrons from one quantum state to another—intermediate levels aren't permitted. The energy levels available for the *sp* electrons in ordinary single bonds are so widely spaced that only quanta of high energy corresponding to the far ultraviolet are absorbed. The presence of a double bond, with its π electrons, creates more closely spaced energy states and shifts the region of light absorption to somewhat longer ultraviolet wavelengths (lower frequency). There are even more available states if double bonds are conjugated so that resonance can occur; a large number of conjugated bonds will make the difference in energy between quantum states small enough so that photons in the visible region, even up into the near infrared, will have sufficient energy to shift orbital electrons.

If plants are to use sunlight efficiently, they must contain molecules capable of absorbing even the near infrared, since the long wavelength light will penetrate a murky atmosphere and therefore be available more often. But in order to do this, the absorbing molecules in the plant must be excited by relatively low-energy quanta, so they must be highly conjugated molecules with many closely spaced energy levels. It also means that they are colored, since they absorb visible light.

Reaction Centers and Chlorophyll. The compounds that actually undergo photochemical reaction are chlorophyll-protein complexes. There is more than one kind, but we are especially interested in the chlorophyll a (Fig. 17–4) that occurs in the reaction centers of green plants—the protein complexes where excited chlorophyll causes a photochemical oxidation-reduction reaction. We see that the molecule has a **phytyl** group, which is a long branched hydrocarbon tail that gives it stronger affinity for the lipid-filled thykaloid membrane. (We shall find the phytyl group attached to other structures for similar reasons.) The working part of the molecule is the porphyrin ring, present as a magnesium chelate, and it is this highly conjugated ring that provides the closely spaced quantum levels necessary for the absorption of red light. The exact wavelengths absorbed will be determined also by the character of the protein to which chlorophyll is attached, much in the same way that the reactivity of heme groups in the cytochromes, hemoglobin, and other pigments is determined by the associated protein.

Accessory Pigment. Reaction centers alone would absorb only a small fraction of the incoming light, because the photosynthetic apparatus requires the presence of many proteins, which are transparent to visible light and therefore dilute the light-absorbing chlorophyll. Additional pigments are present in the thykaloids to make the process more efficient, especially in dim light. For example, additional chlorophyll occurs outside the reaction center, but even this is not enough for efficient light utilization, because chlorophyll does not absorb the most abundant photons in the sunlight, which have frequencies in the middle of the visible region. Since chlorophyll is green, it obviously is not absorbing green light.

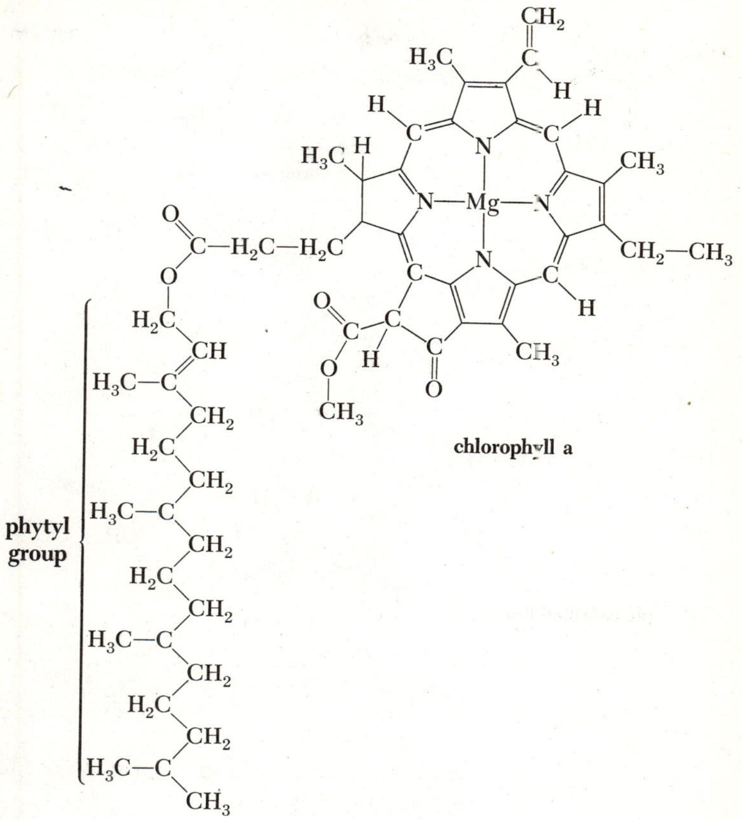

Figure 17-4 Chlorophyll a is a magnesium porphyrin with a long phytyl tail.

The higher plants and photosynthetic bacteria contain another class of compounds, the **carotenes** (Fig. 17–5), which do absorb light in the middle frequencies of the visible spectrum. Since those photons have greater energy than photons of red light, it follows that carotene gains more energy upon excitation than does chlorophyll excited by red light. The carotene molecules therefore have enough energy to excite nearby chlorophyll molecules, and energy can be transferred among the chlorophyll molecules until it reaches a reaction center (Fig. 17–6). (This kind of intermolecular transfer functions efficiently only at relatively high concentrations of pigments, but the total pigment concentration in the thykaloid membranes is of the order of 0.1 M, which is very high indeed for these large molecules.)

For those with a more thorough grounding in orbital theory, we may note that the absorbed quanta promote electrons to an excited singlet stage, which rapidly decays through small steps to a relatively long-lived triplet stage in which paired electrons are rotating in the same direction. The triplet-triplet transitions have a lower energy differential, so there is more overlap in states available to the carotenes and chlorophylls; the greater the overlap, the more efficient the energy transfer.

Figure 17–5 also gives the structure of a **phycobilin,** a different kind of pigment found in some algae that accomplishes the same purpose as do the carotenes. This compound represents a porphyrin ring that has been broken open at one point. We shall later see quite similar structures for porphyrin degradation products that are excreted by animals in the bile, which gives rise to the "bilin" part of the name.

The Primary Photochemical Reaction. An electron is tranferred from excited chlorophyll to an acceptor molecule in the primary event. The acceptor has not been fully characterized in any photosynthetic system; however, we need not know its

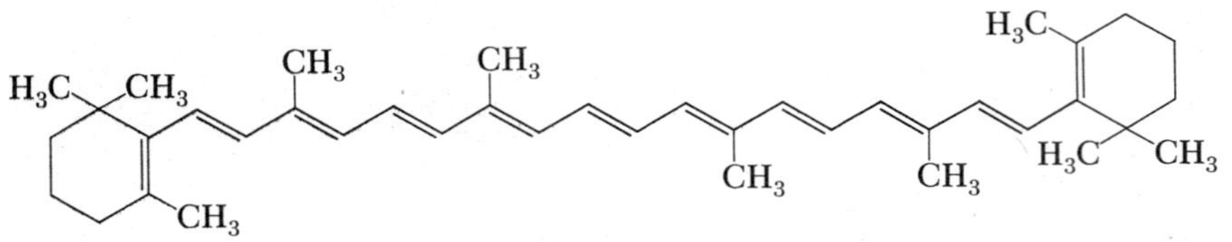

β-carotene

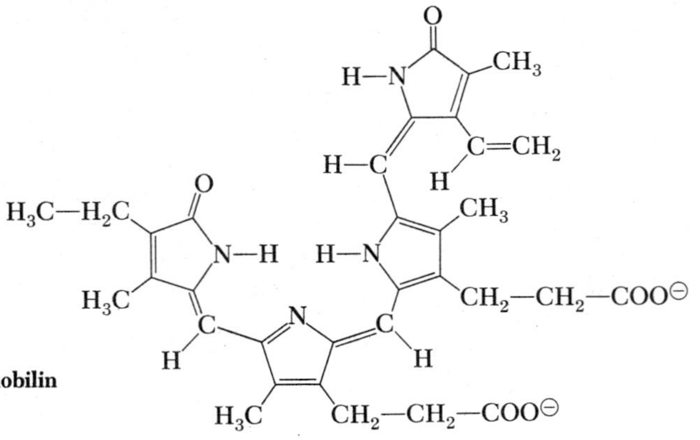

phycocyanobilin

Figure 17-5 Accessory pigments for increased absorption of light include carotenes and cyanobilins, as well as chlorophylls outside of the reaction centers.

structure to understand what it does. One of the important acceptors is a ferredoxin-reducing substance:

Chl a_1* (P-700) +	FRS^+	⟶	Chl a_1^+ +	FRS
excited chlorophyll a_1	**ferredoxin-reducing substance** (oxidized)		**oxidized chlorophyll a_1**	**ferredoxin-reducing substance** (reduced)

This is the photochemical reaction occurring at the first reaction center in the chloroplasts. P-700 is another designation for the particular chlorophyll pigment that is also designated a_1 in that center. (Excitation causes changes in the spectrum of the molecule at 700 nm.) Since the product of the transfer is, as the name implies, capable of reducing

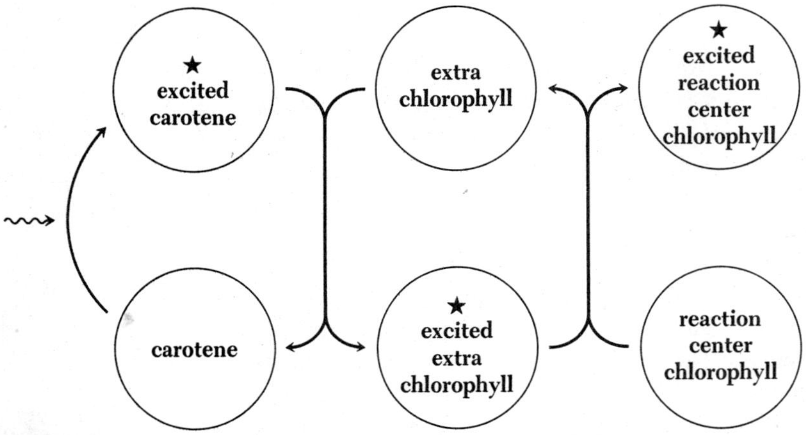

Figure 17-6 The excited carotene created by absorption of a photon has sufficient energy to excite free chlorophyll, which in turn can excite the chlorophyll of the reaction center.

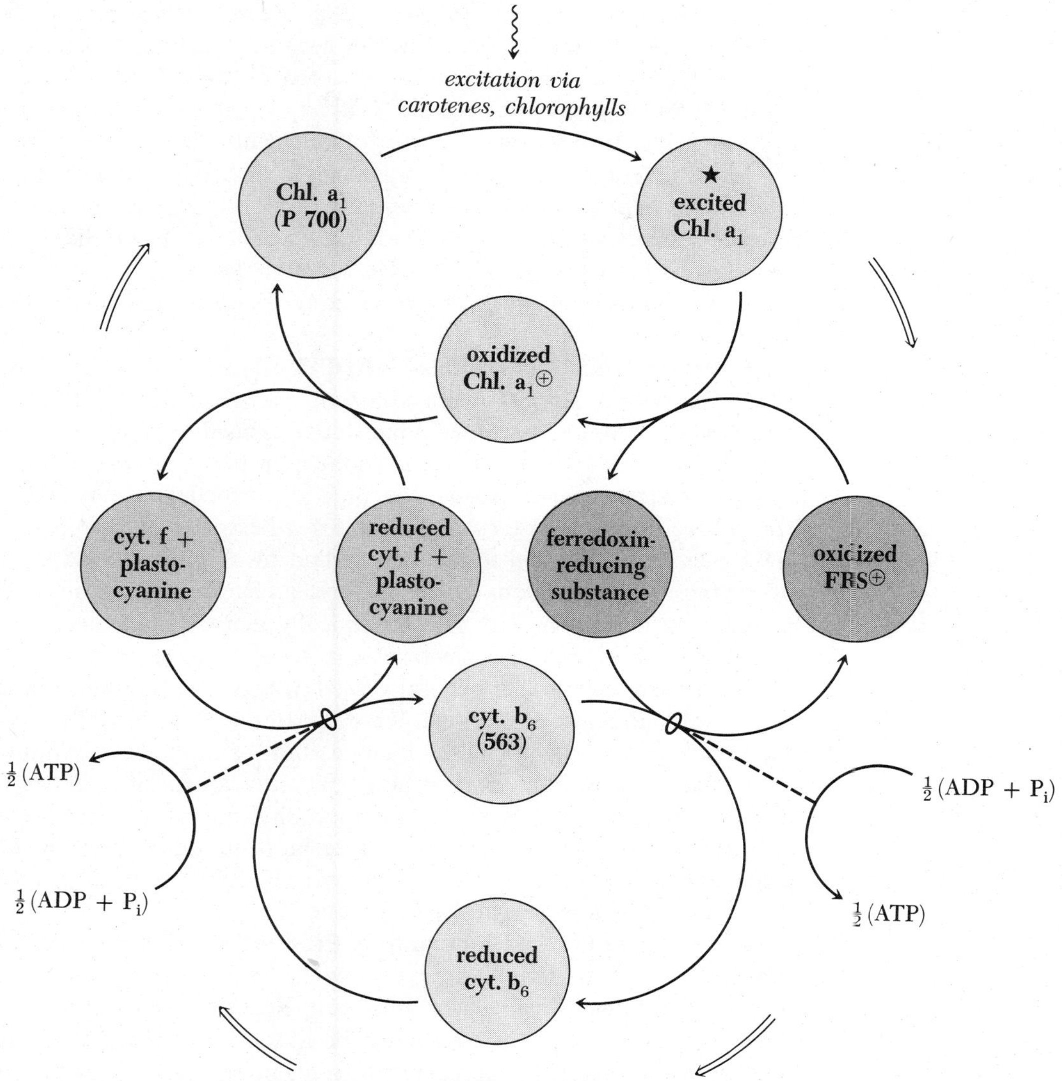

Figure 17–7 Cyclic photophosphorylation. Electrons are transferred from excited chlorophyll a_1 through a succession of carriers before returning to the chlorophyll. The transfers result in the formation of ATP. Transfers through similar carriers in mitochondria generate one ATP per electron, as shown, but some believe the photosynthetic transfers create only one ATP per pair of electrons.

ferredoxin, and we saw in the preceding chapter that reduced ferredoxin is capable of generating H_2 from protons, it is evident that this reaction has used the energy of excitation of chlorophyll a_1 to create a very powerful reducing substance, indeed.

Cyclic Photophosphorylation. The reoxidation of a reducing agent as powerful as ferredoxin-reducing substance ought to be capable of liberating large amounts of free energy, even more than the corresponding reactions of NADH that we saw in connection with oxidative phosphorylation. Many photosynthetic organisms use the ferredoxin-reducing substance for just this purpose, and cause the electrons to be transferred from it back to oxidized chlorophyll a in small steps, with a concomitant generation of high-energy phosphate (Fig. 17–7). At least two cytochromes are involved, a chloroplast variant of **cytochrome b,** and **cytochrome f,** which has an oxidation-reduction potential similar to that of cytochrome c. Cytochrome f is associated with

plastocyanin, a protein containing Cu^{2+} that is also involved in electron transfer. Figure 17–7 indicates the generation of two molecules of ATP per pair of electrons passing through the cycle; this number is accepted by people who believe that oxidative phosphorylation occurs by chemical coupling (p. 169). Those who believe in chemiosmotic coupling usually assign lower fractional numbers to the ATP yield.

In any event, photosynthetic organisms of all kinds are capable of using the energy of absorbed light solely for the generation of high-energy phosphate through the cyclic transfer of electrons that we have outlined. Essentially, the mechanism uses light energy for displacing an oxidation-reduction reaction far from equilibrium, with the later reaction of the components back toward equilibrium being used to generate high-energy phosphate.

Photosynthetic Reductions—NADPH. The name of ferredoxin-reducing substance implies its second major function, the reduction of ferredoxins to provide electrons for synthetic purposes. Plant ferredoxins differ from the clostridial molecule in having only one pair of ferric and sulfide ions per molecule, so that they can transfer only one electron per molecule, but they also function as powerful reducing agents. The reduced ferredoxin created by photosynthesis can be employed in two ways. We saw reactions in bacterial fermentations that result in the formation of reduced ferredoxin; these same reactions can be made to go backwards in photosynthetic organisms by reducing ferredoxin with photochemically derived electrons.

More importantly, the electrons can be transferred from reduced ferredoxin to NADP, a coenzyme that is generally used in reductive syntheses in all kinds of organisms—animal, plant, and protist. We shall later see how NADPH is used as the source of electrons for reducing CO_2 to glucose, and for other photosynthetic reductions. In the meantime, it is important to note that the transfer of electrons from ferredoxin-reducing substance to NADP leaves chlorophyll in the oxidized state. The formation of NADPH therefore requires that there be some other electron donor available to return the chlorophyll to its normal reduced form in order for photosynthesis to continue. Let us now see how this is done.

The Second Photosystem and O_2 Production. The ultimate source of electrons within chloroplasts is the OH^- ion of water, and oxygen gas is released when these electrons are removed. However, removing electrons from water is in itself an endergonic process, and light quanta must be absorbed to provide the necessary energy. Another photosystem in the chloroplast, commonly known as photosystem II, is involved. Electrons from water first pass through photosystem II and then through photosystem I on their way to ferredoxin and NADP.

The active pigment in photosystem II also contains chlorophyll a as the prosthetic group, but it is evidently attached to a different protein, because it has a slightly different spectrum, and more importantly, it becomes a very strong oxidizing agent when an electron is removed, strong enough to remove electrons from water. It is designated as chlorophyll a_2 or P-689, to distinguish it from the a_1 (or P-700) pigment in photosystem I. The sequence of events in the photochemical reaction is much like the one we saw in photosystem I (Fig. 17–8). Upon activation by absorbed photons, the chlorophyll pigment loses an electron to an acceptor, which is an uncharacterized compound known as the **quenching substance,** or **Q** (not to be confused with Q for ubiquinone).

The loss of an electron from chlorophyll a_2 converts it to a powerful oxidizing agent that will remove an electron from still another uncharacterized intermediate, designated as **X** in Figure 17–8. This intermediate is associated in some way with manganese ions, which are obligatory for the transfer, but the function of these ions is also uncharacterized. It is embarrassing to be so ignorant, but the important thing is that X must also be a powerful oxidizing agent when it loses an electron, because it reacts with hydroxide ion to form oxygen. Now, four electrons must be transferred to create one molecule of O_2, and chlorophyll a_2 only moves one electron at a time.

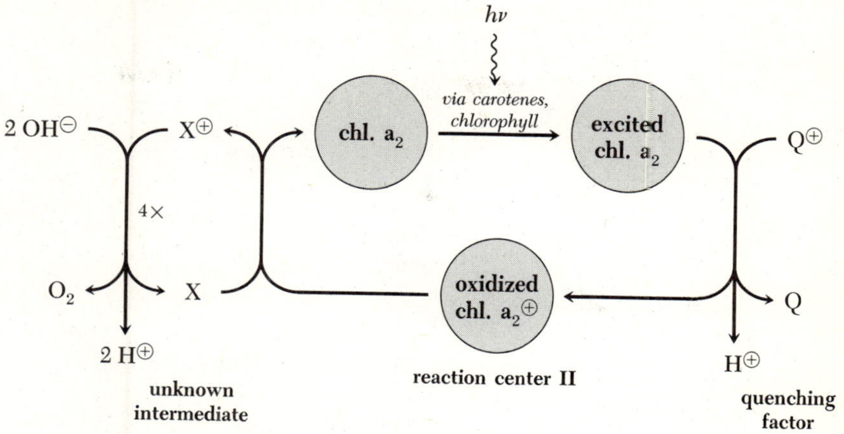

Figure 17-8 Reaction center II uses the energy of excitation to pump electrons from water to reaction center I. Excited chlorophyll a_2 transfers an electron to a quenching substance. The resultant oxidized form of chlorophyll a_2 can abstract electrons from hydroxyl ions and create molecular oxygen.

It is believed that molecules of X and the chlorophyll are associated in tandem, so that pairs of electrons are moved in adjacent channels; in any event, it is believed that the reduction of oxygen goes in steps, and the system returns to its original condition only when four electrons have been transferred.

Transfer of Electrons from Photosystem II to Photosystem I. We have just seen how electrons are moved by photosystem II from water to form a reduced quenching factor. We earlier saw how photosystem I moves electrons to ferredoxin-reducing substance, leaving oxidized chlorophyll a_1. The remaining steps involve the coupling of these two systems by moving the electrons from reduced quenching factor to oxidized chlorophyll a_1. The successive transfers between photosystems II and I go through increasingly stronger oxidizing agents (Fig. 17–9), concluding with the same cytochrome f-plastocyanin couple used in cyclic photophosphorylation. The steps are much like the transfers in mitochondrial electron transport, and there is also at least one associated phosphorylation per pair of electrons. (Some claim two phosphorylations, but this seems unlikely on energetic grounds. One advocate of chemiosmotic mechanism has tried to fit observations with a scheme that postulates movement of 2 H^+ across the membrane per electron transferred and generation of one high-energy phosphate for 3 H^+ moved. This would give an overall yield of $1\frac{1}{3}$ ATP per NADPH ultimately produced.)

The Overall Photochemical Process. Figure 17–10 summarizes the sequence of events in the two photosystems of chloroplasts. The overall reactions are something like this:

$$\text{photochemical reactions: } 2\,\text{NADP}^+ + 2\,H_2O + 8\,h\nu \longrightarrow 2\,\text{NADPH} + O_2 + 2\,H^+$$

$$\text{phosphorylation(s): } 2\text{-}4\,(\text{ADP}^{3-} + P_i^{2-} + H^+) \longrightarrow 2\text{-}4\,\text{ATP}^{4-} + 2\text{-}4\,H_2O$$

Another common way of indicating the flow of electrons in the process is to diagram the successive carriers on a scale of standard reduction potential or free energy changes (Fig. 17–11).

Having now seen how NADPH and ATP are generated in the photochemical reactions, let us now see how they are used by the chloroplasts for synthetic purposes.

GLUCONEOGENESIS IN THE CHLOROPLAST

The most common pathway by which NADPH and ATP are used as sources of the necessary electrons and chemical potential for converting CO_2 to glucosyl residues is usually called the Calvin cycle, after Melvin Calvin, the Nobel laureate. Other contributors to the development of the cycle are also sometimes honored by talking about

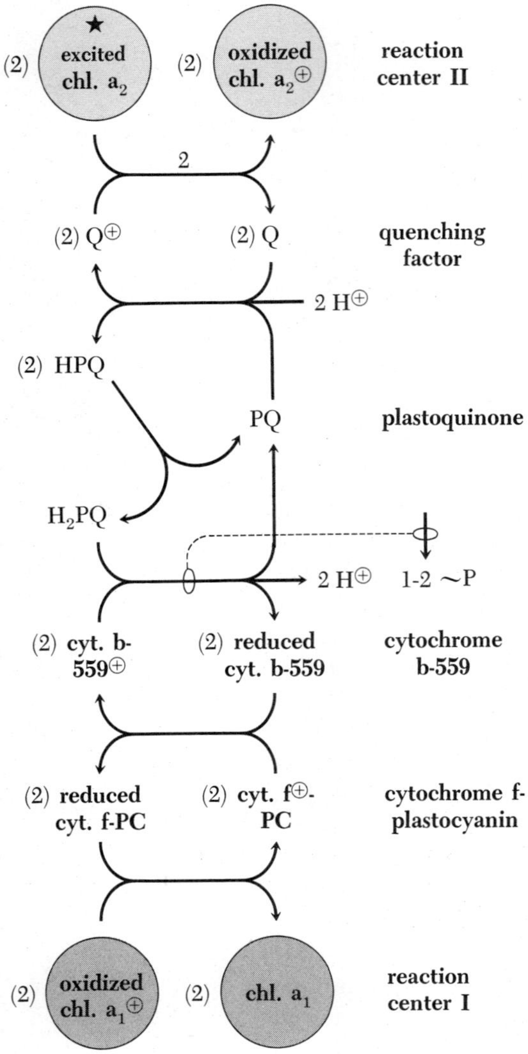

Figure 17–9 The reduced quenching factor created by transfer of electrons from excited chlorophyll a_2 in reaction center II is used to reduce oxidized chlorophyll a_1 created in reaction center I. The transfers are made through several intermediate carriers with the generation of ATP. By analogy with comparable mitochondrial carriers, one ATP ought to be formed per pair of electrons, but some believe two are formed. The intermediate plastoquinone, which is similar to ubiquinone, may carry one electron at a time through the formation of an intermediate free radical.

the Benson-Calvin or Calvin-Bassham cycle. The Calvin pathway occurs in most green plants and in some bacteria.

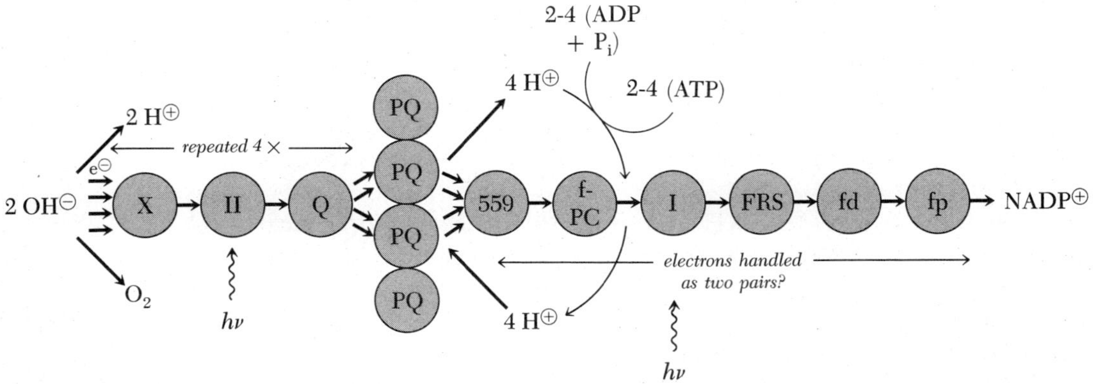

Figure 17–10 The overall view of photosynthetic electron transfers. Two quanta are absorbed at the reaction centers II and I for each electron transferred from water to NADP. According to the chemiosmotic view, ATP is generated by the discharge of a proton concentration gradient that the electron transfers create across the membrane.

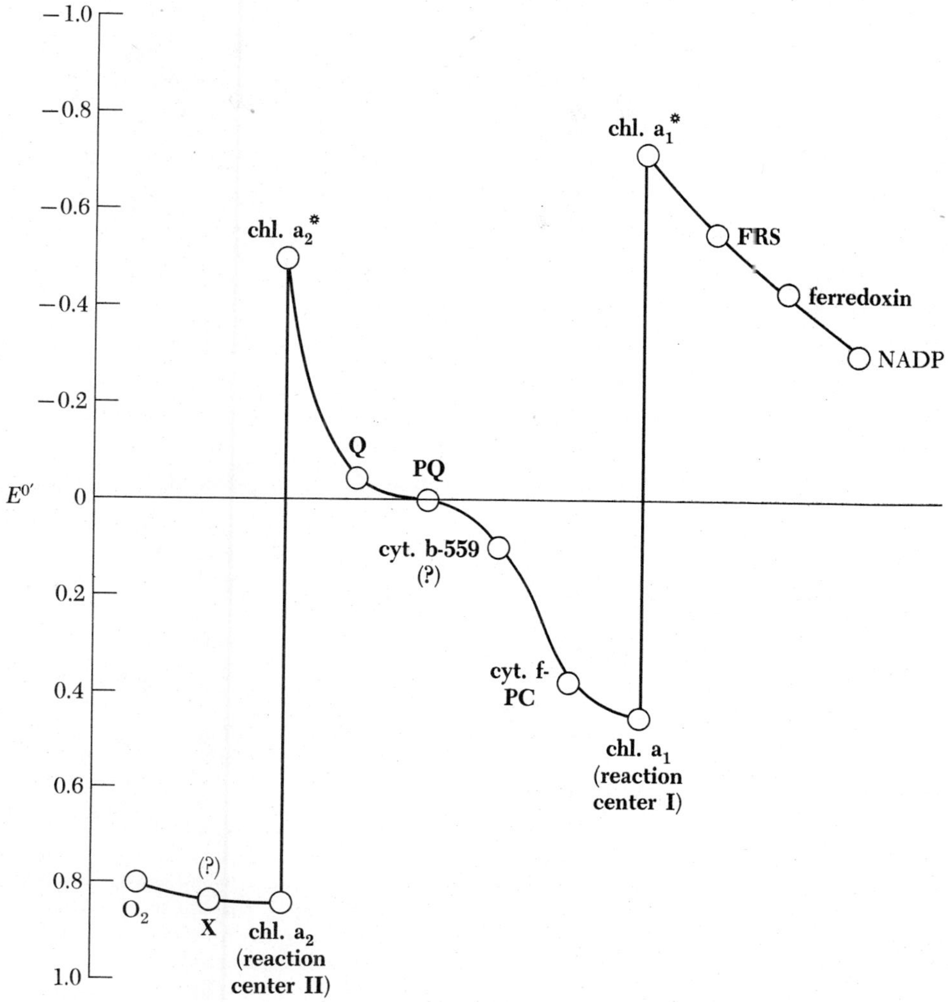

Figure 17-11 A plot of successive electron carriers in photosynthesis according to their standard oxidation-reduction potentials, which are measures of the standard free energy change for transfer of electrons from the reduced form. Two quanta are necessary to energize the reduction of NADP by water, but there is sufficient additional energy to sustain the generation of ~P upon electron transfer between reaction centers.

The Reductive Step

The conversion of CO_2 to glucose requires two molecules of NADPH per carbon atom converted:

$$6\ CO_2 + 12\ (NADPH + H^+) \longrightarrow C_6H_{12}O_6 + 6\ H_2O$$

This is the formal stoichiometry, neglecting associated phosphate transfers. The sole means of introducing electrons from NADPH to accomplish the stoichiometry in the Calvin cycle is a reversal of the glyceraldehyde phosphate dehydrogenase reaction. We have seen this reaction in the forward direction as an important part of glycolysis (p. 218), and in the reverse direction as a part of gluconeogenesis (p. 242). Now we see it playing a key role in photosynthesis.

The glyceraldehyde 3-phosphate dehydrogenase from chloroplasts differs in an important respect from the corresponding enzyme found in the cytosol of plant and animal tissues (Fig. 17-12). The enzyme is specific for NADP and NADPH, when the NADPH concentration is relatively high! When the sun rises, and NADPH is created by photochemical reactions in the leaves, glyceraldehyde 3-phosphate dehydrogenase becomes specific for this nucleotide. Since photosynthesis creates a high

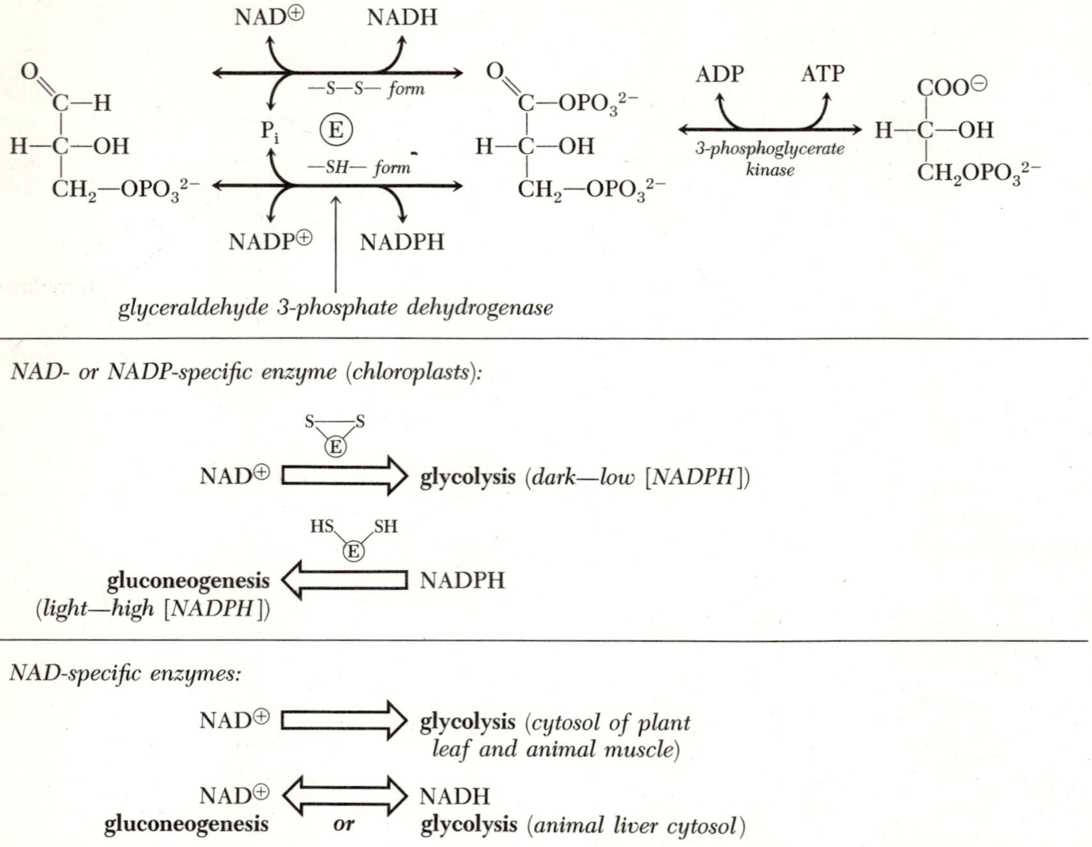

Figure 17-12 The glyceraldehyde 3-phosphate dehydrogenase of chloroplasts exists in a disulfide form that is specific for NAD and a sulfhydryl form that is specific for NADP. The sulfhydryl form is created when the leaves are illuminated, and promotes the formation of glyceraldehyde 3-phosphate at the expense of NADPH, which is created by photosynthesis. In contrast, the enzymes of the cytosol in plants and animals are specific for NAD. The reversible use of the enzyme in animal livers depends upon the relative concentrations of the reactants rather than a change in specificity.

[NADPH]/[NADP] ratio, the change in specificity, along with the higher concentration of ATP generated by photophosphorylation, shifts the position of equilibrium and pushes 3-phosphoglycerate back to the triose phosphate stage.

Control of Specificity. The specificity of glyceraldehyde 3-phosphate dehydrogenase is evidently changed through the action of a light-activated **disulfide reductase,** which uses NADPH to reduce some intermediate disulfide with the eventual formation of new sulfhydyl groups on the enzyme (Fig. 17–13). When the light is off and NADPH is no longer created, the enzyme reverts to a specificity of NAD and NADH. This

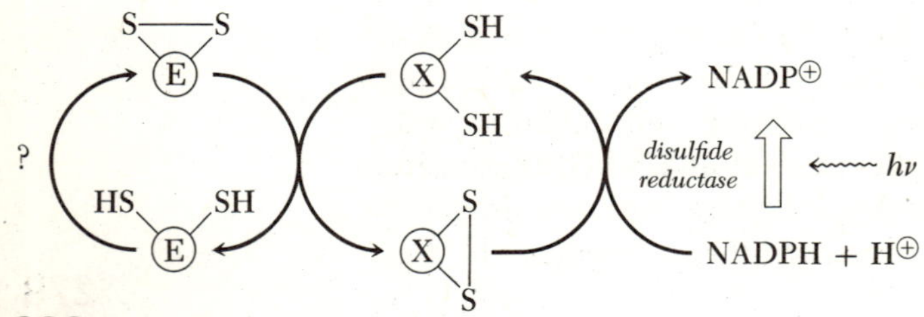

Figure 17-13 The mechanism of shifting glyceraldehyde 3-phosphate dehydrogenase from the disulfide to the sulfhydryl form involves the light-activated reduction of an intermediate protein by NADPH.

more oxidized couple, along with a declining supply of ATP, favors reaction in the direction of glycolysis, so as to maintain the supply of ATP in the dark.

Here we see an illustration of the reason for the presence of two kinds of nicotinamide nucleotides. In both plants and animals, the NADPH/NADP pair is kept in a highly reduced state for use in syntheses, whereas the NADH/NAD pair is kept more oxidized for use in substrate oxidations. This is accomplished by having different sets of enzymes that are specific for the respective nucleotides. (For example, there is no ferredoxin:NAD reductace in chloroplasts.)

CO_2 Fixation

The changing specificity of the glyceraldehyde phosphate dehydrogenase accounts for the use of NADPH as a reducing agent, but it does not explain how this reaction results in the reduction of CO_2 to glucose residues. The way in which this is done is to combine a pentose diphosphate with CO_2; a transient six-carbon intermediate is formed, which is cleaved into two molecules of 3-phosphoglycerate, each of which may then be phosphorylated by ATP and reduced by NADPH to glyceraldehyde 3-phosphate. This is it. The resultant two molecules of triose phosphate can be converted *via* fructose 1,6-diphosphate and fructose 6-phosphate to glucose 6-phosphate in the same way that this conversion is accomplished during gluconeogenesis in other organisms (Fig. 17–14).

The details of this important reaction sequence are shown in Figure 17–15. We see that the sequence begins with ribulose 5-phosphate, which we encountered in heterolactate fermentations (p. 258), and shall encounter again in other connections. The reaction sequence is driven by expenditure of a molecule of ATP to form **ribulose 1,5-diphosphate,** which makes it possible to form a carboxylated compound that can be cleaved into two molecules of phosphoglycerate. The enzyme responsible for the addition of CO_2 is a **ribulose diphosphate carboxylase;** its reaction is the sole mechanism for introducing the CO_2 from which glucose is made into the Calvin cycle. The carboxylation does not involve biotin or any other cofactor, but the enzyme molecule contains one atom of Cu^{2+} of unknown function.

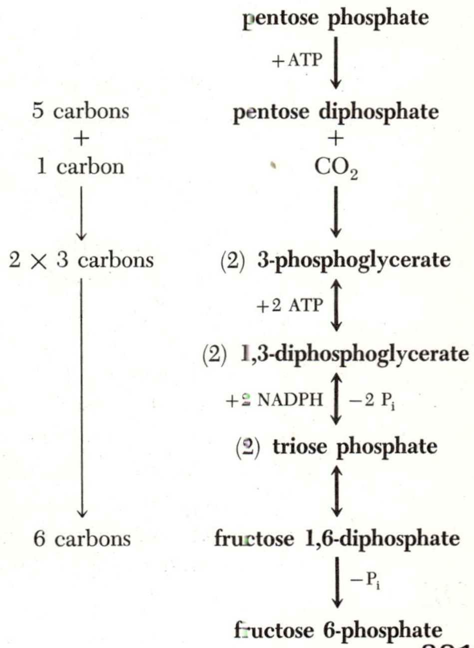

Figure 17–14 The conversion of CO_2 to glucose residues involves its addition to a pentose diphosphate, with cleavage to form two molecules of 3-phosphoglycerate. ATP is expended to convert these to 1,3-diphosphoglycerate, which is then reduced by NADPH to glyceraldehyde 3-phosphate. The necessary pentose diphosphate is created by phosphorylation of a pentose phosphate. The reactions summarized here include all in which electrons and ATP are used to drive the formation of carbohydrate from CO_2.

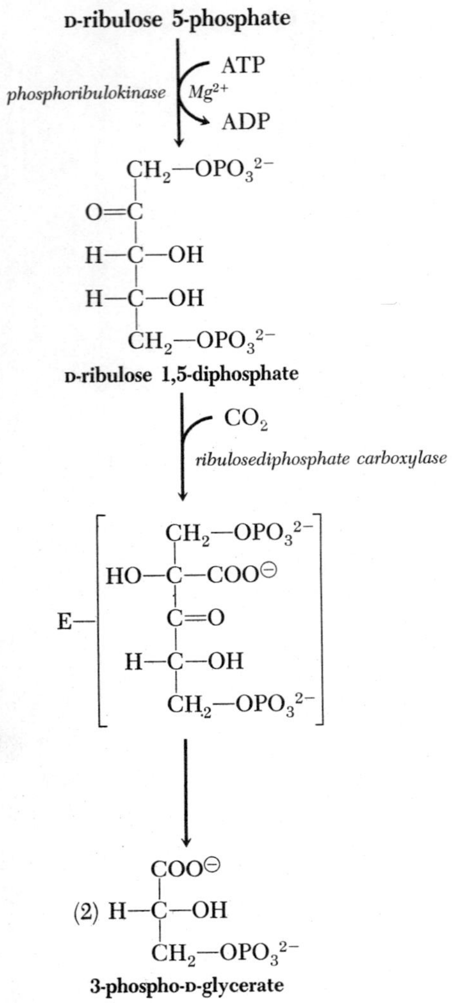

Figure 17-15 The fixation of CO_2 in photosynthesis.

Generation of Ribulose Phosphate

So far we have covered the creation of glucose 6-phosphate from a pentose phosphate and CO_2. In order to make a complete molecule of glucose, six molecules of CO_2 must be supplied, and the pentose phosphate must be replaced.

The way in which all of this is accomplished by the remainder of the Calvin cycle appears to many people to be a trick, but it really isn't. The chloroplasts have enzymes that will convert triose phosphates to pentose phosphates. Once we prove this, everything is plain.

According to the reactions we have reviewed, a pentose phosphate and CO_2 are consumed to form two molecules of triose phosphate. Doing this six times makes a total of 12 molecules of triose phosphate from six molecules each of CO_2 and pentose phosphate. Ten of these molecules of triose phosphate ($10 \times 3 = 30$ carbon atoms) are then used to replace the six molecules of pentose phosphate ($6 \times 5 = 30$ carbon atoms). The two remaining molecules of triose phosphate then can be converted to fructose diphosphate and on to glucose 6-phosphate (Fig. 17–16). Since the pentose phosphate molecules have been replaced, the only carbon compounds disappearing are the six CO_2 molecules, and the only organic product formed is the glucose phosphate. Q.E.D. The glucose residue is completely made from CO_2.

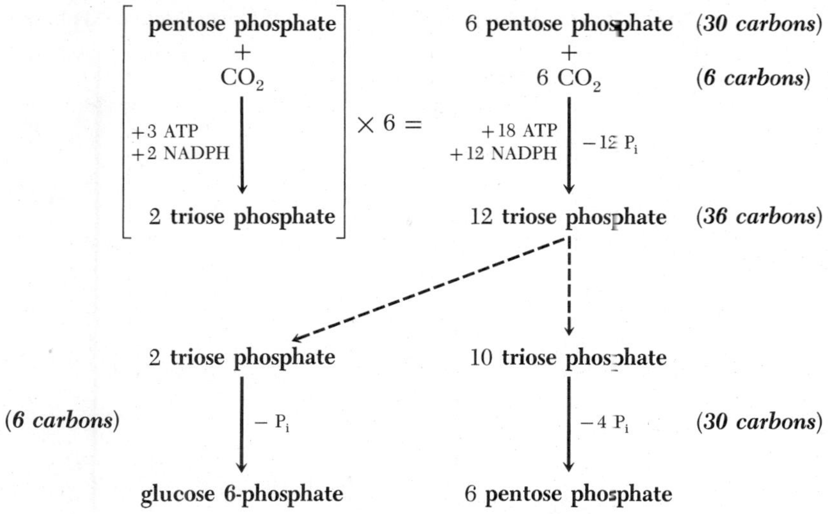

SUM: $6\ CO_2 + 12\ NADPH + 18\ ATP^{4-} + 11\ H_2O \longrightarrow$
$\text{glucose 6-P}^{2-} + 12\ NADP^{\oplus} + 18\ ADP^{3-} + 17\ P_i^{2-} + 6\ H^{\oplus}$

Figure 17-16 The conversion of six CO_2 to one glucose residue involves the consumption of six pentose phosphate. These are regenerated from 10 of the 12 triose phosphates that are formed, leaving two triose phosphates from which to gain net formation of glucose phosphate.

Use of Transketolase. The mechanism of conversion of triose phosphate to pentose phosphate actually hinges upon the action of a transketolase, which reversibly transfers a two-carbon unit from ketose phosphates to aldose phosphates (Fig. 17-17).

6 + 3 = 4 + 5. To begin, we have shown that chloroplasts make fructose 6-phosphate from two molecules of triose phosphate. Now, transketolase can transfer two carbons from the fructose 6-phosphate onto another molecule of glyceraldehyde 3-phosphate (Fig. 17-18). The gain of two carbons by the triose phosphate converts it into the pentose, D-xylulose 5-phosphate, which is equilibrated with D-ribulose 5-phosphate in the same epimerase reaction involved in bacterial metabolism of pentose phosphates (p. 259).

4 + 3 = 7. The four carbons of fructose 6-phosphate remaining after transfer are present as **D-erythrose 4-phosphate,** which is utilized by condensing it with still another molecule of triose phosphate (Fig. 17-19), first forming **sedoheptulose 1,7-diphosphate,**

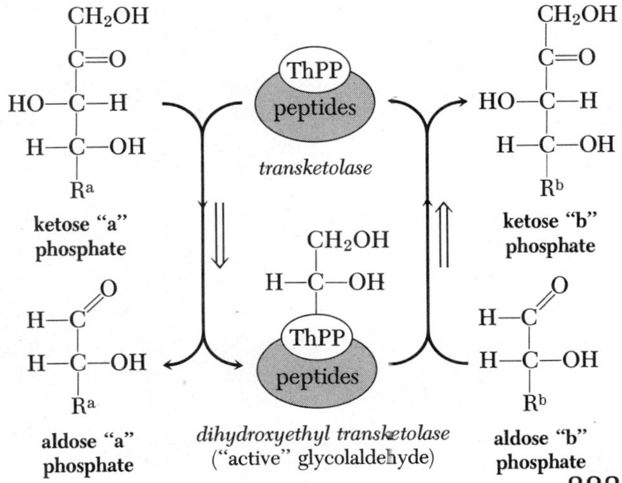

Figure 17-17 The recovery of pentose phosphates in photogluconeogenesis (the Calvin cycle) involves the action of transketolase, which transfers 2-carbon units from a ketose to an aldose, with intermediate formation of a dihydroxyethyl group on thiamine pyrophosphate.

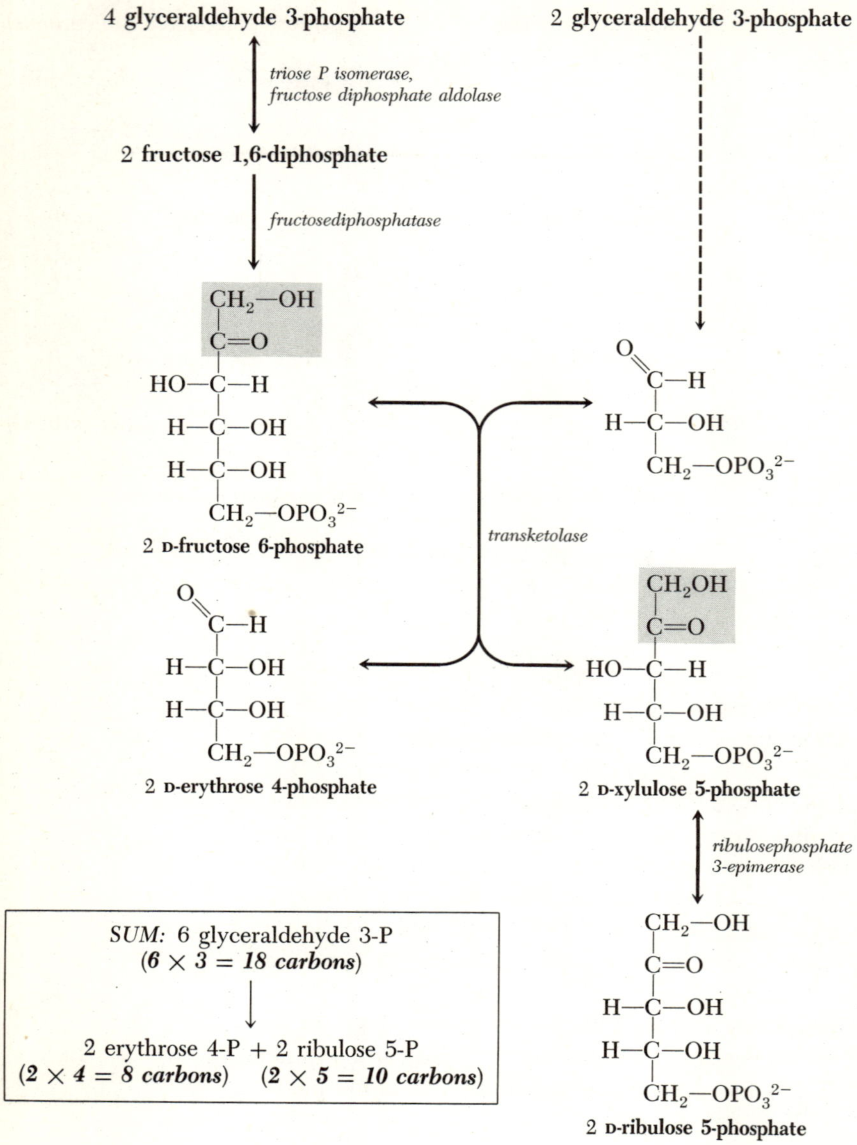

Figure 17–18 Two molecules of ribulose 5-phosphate can be created from six molecules of glyceraldehyde 3-phosphate via the intermediate formation of fructose 6-phosphate and the action of transketolase. The fate of the remaining eight carbons, present as erythrose 4-phosphate, is shown in the next figure.

and then sedoheptulose 7-phosphate. These reactions are handled by the same aldolase and fructose diphosphatase that catalyze the ordinary sequence:

$$\text{2 triose phosphates} \longleftrightarrow \text{fructose 1,6-diphosphate} \longrightarrow \text{fructose 6-phosphate}$$

7 + 3 = 5 + 5. Two carbons of the sedoheptulose 7-phosphate are then transferred to a final molecule of glyceraldehyde 3-phosphate by the action of transketolase, leaving ribose 5-phosphate, and forming xylulose 5-phosphate. Both of these pentose phosphates are equilibrated with ribulose 5-phosphate through the respective actions of ribose 5-phosphate isomerase and ribulose 5-phosphate 3-epimerase.

Sum. If we multiply each of these sequences by two, we have from Figure 17–18:

$$\text{6 (glyceraldehyde 3-phosphate)} \longleftrightarrow \text{2 (erythrose 4-phosphate)} + \text{2 (ribulose 5-phosphate)};$$

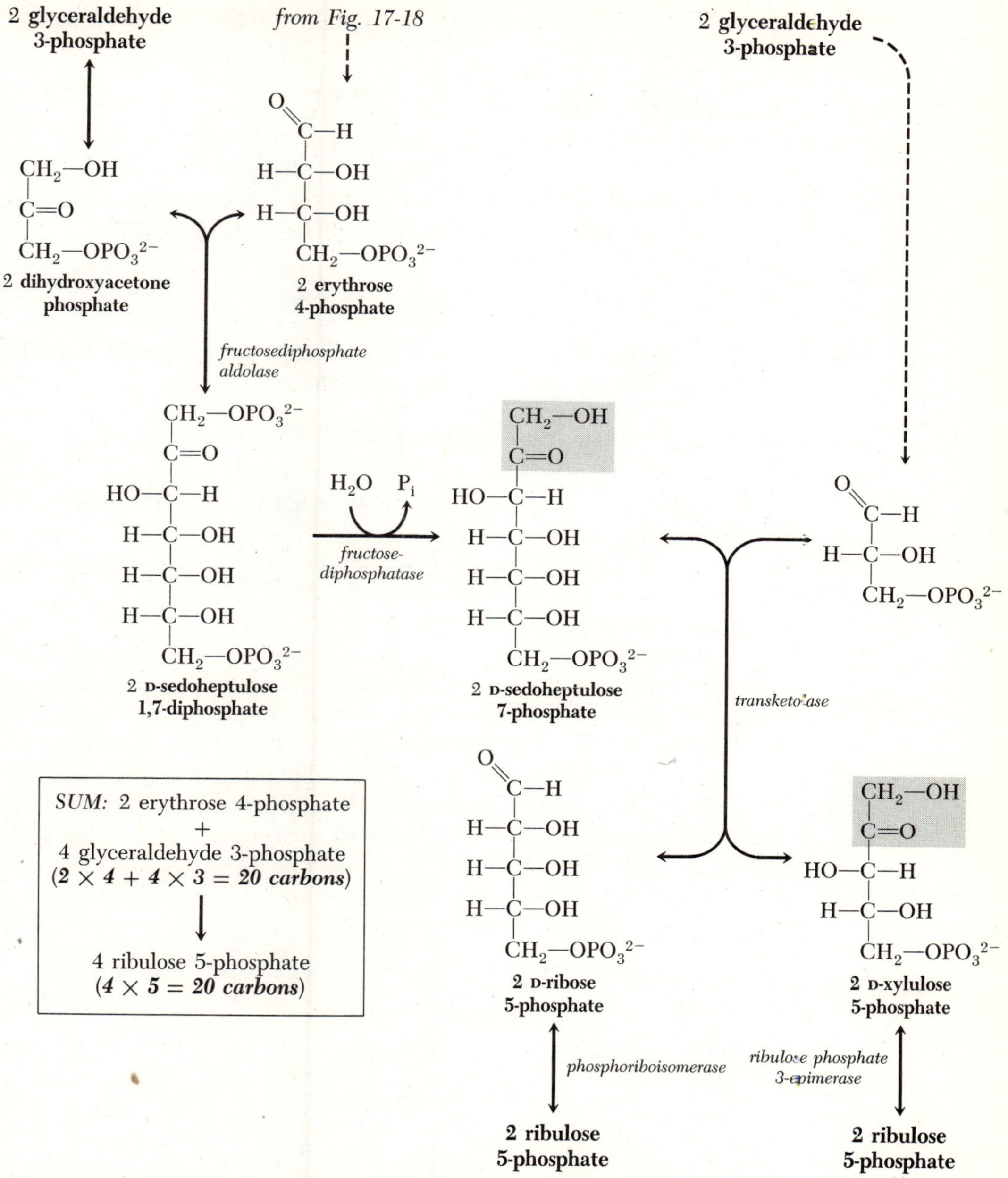

Figure 17-19 Two molecules of erythrose 4-phosphate and four more molecules of glyceraldehyde 3-phosphate are converted to four molecules of ribulose 5-phosphate by a combination of an ordinary aldolase condensation and the action of transketolase, along with isomerization of pentoses. This completes the generation of six molecules of ribulose 5-phosphate from 10 molecules of triose phosphate.

from Figure 17-19:

4 (glyceraldehyde 3-phosphate) + 2 (erythrose 4-phosphate) $\longleftrightarrow$ 4 (ribulose 5-phosphate);

SUM: 10 (glyceraldehyde 3-phosphate) $\longleftrightarrow$ 6 (ribulose 5-phosphate)

and we have completed the regeneration of the pentose phosphates necessary for fixing CO_2.

The Total Calvin Cycle. The grand total for the gluconeogenic reactions of the chloroplast is:

$$6\ CO_2 + 12\ NADPH + 18\ ATP^{4-} + 11\ H_2O \longrightarrow (\text{glucose 6-phosphate}^{2-}) + 12\ NADP^+ + 18\ ADP^{3-} + 17\ P_i^{2-} + 6\ H^+$$

If we take a liberal view of ATP yield per photon of light absorbed, the necessary photochemical generation of the NADPH results in (p. 277):

$$12\ NADP^+ + 12\ (ADP^{3-} + P_i^{2-}) + 48\ h\nu \longrightarrow 6\ O_2 + 12\ NADH + 12\ ATP^{4-}$$

which supplies the electrons, but not enough ATP. The additional high-energy phosphate can be supplied by cyclic photophosphorylation:

$$6\ (ADP^{3-} + P_i^{2-} + H^+) + 6\ h\nu \longrightarrow 6\ ATP^{4-} + 6\ H_2O$$

Our grand total of the minimum cost of the Calvin cycle then is:

$$6\ CO_2 + P_i^{2-} + 5\ H_2O + 54\ h\nu \longrightarrow \text{glucose 6-phosphate}^{2-} + 6\ O_2$$

or nine quanta per carbon atom fixed.

Regulation. The Calvin cycle is like other metabolic routes in containing irreversible reactions that require regulation. One means of regulation is by use of the light-activated disulfide reductase that makes glyceraldehyde 3-phosphate dehydrogenase specific for NADP rather than NAD. The same enzyme apparently also activates ribulose phosphate kinase and ribulose diphosphate carboxylase (Fig. 17–20).

There is a further internal regulation that probably serves to balance the rates of various parts of the Calvin cycle to each other and to other metabolic processes.

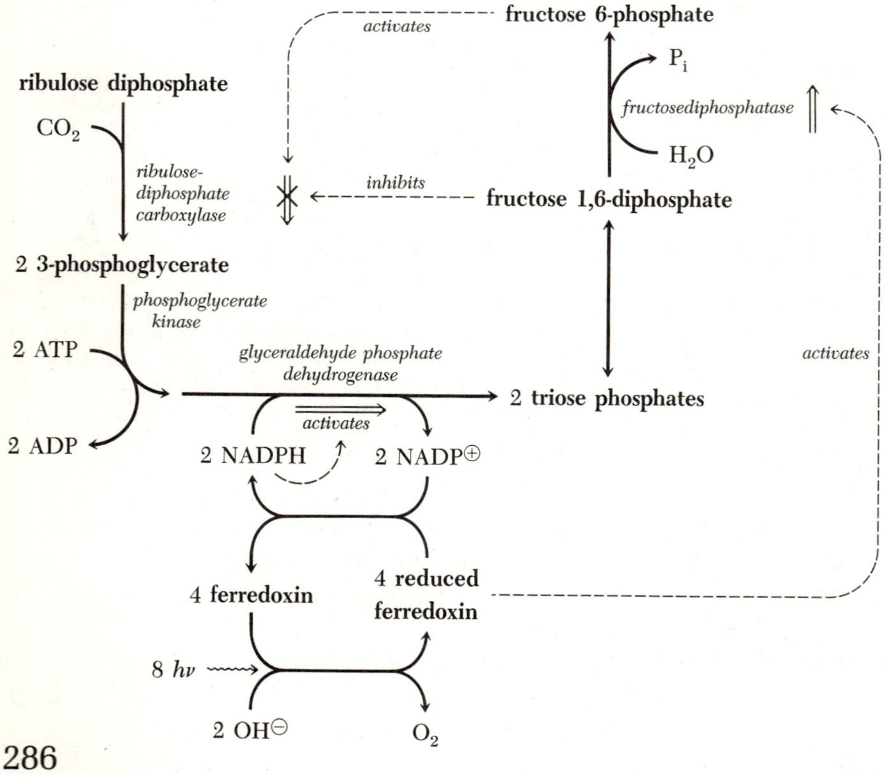

Figure 17–20 The photosynthetic process and its regulation.

The fructose diphosphatase of plant chloroplasts is activated by reduced ferredoxin, which in turn is created by the photochemical reactions. This tends to balance the commitment of triose phosphates to glucose synthesis with the availability of electrons for forming triose phosphates from CO_2. In addition, the fructose 6-phosphate produced by the phosphatase increases the affinity of ribulose 5-phosphate carboxylase for CO_2, which, as we shall see in the next section, is frequently the limiting factor in photosynthesis.

CARBON DIOXIDE CONCENTRATION

The rate of photosynthesis is dependent upon the concentration of available carbon dioxide. In most plants, cells conducting photosynthesis simultaneously respire, so that they have a competing production of CO_2 and consumption of O_2. (We do not have a satisfactory rationalization of this photo-respiration, but that does not prevent it from occurring.) The break-even point at which the consumption of CO_2 by photosynthesis has been slowed to match the rate at which it is produced by respiration usually occurs near 50 ppm (parts per million) of CO_2 in the atmosphere surrounding the cells. As the concentration is raised above this level toward the normal value of 320 ppm in free-moving air near the earth's surface, the rate of photosynthesis increasingly exceeds the rate of respiration. However, the carboxylase system is not completely saturated with CO_2 even at this level, so most plants have a rate of photosynthesis that responds under natural conditions to changes in the CO_2 content of the atmosphere.

However, some plants have evolved to live in arid tropical climates (dry, hot, and bright), and a critical part of the necessary adaptations is a diminution of water loss through the leaves. This in turn necessitates a restriction of the free circulation of the atmosphere to the photosynthetic cells—the same movement of air that brings CO_2 will remove H_2O. Restriction of free circulation means that the concentration of CO_2 will fall from the atmospheric value. The plants that grow under these unfavorable conditions do so because they have developed means of using CO_2 at lower concentrations. These include nearly complete elimination of photo-respiration, thereby diminishing the loss of laboriously fixed carbon, and the utilization of different reactions in which there is additional discharge of free energy to increase the temporary fixation of CO_2.

The Hatch-Slack Pathway. Some plants capture CO_2 at low concentrations by a carboxylation of pyruvate to oxaloacetate, followed by interconversions with malate that result in the delivery of both CO_2 and electrons to cells carrying out the Calvin cycle. Such plants include the tropical grasses, and before anyone starts complaining about relevance, let him consider that the tropical grasses include corn, sugar cane, and other food crops. The route is variously known as the Hatch-Slack pathway, the C-4 pathway, or the dicarboxylic acid pathway. (M. D. Hatch and C. R. Slack are Australians who were hired by a refinery to study sugar cane; they served both us and the refinery well.)

Plants with the Hatch-Slack pathway have a different anatomy; the leaves are made from concentric cylinders of cells, with an innermost bundle of phloem tubules to carry away newly synthesized fuel. The fuel is made by a surrounding cylinder of **sheath** cells, which carry out the Calvin cycle and store starch. Finally, there is an outermost layer of **mesophyll** cells that can trap atmospheric CO_2 at lower concentrations for transport to the sheath cells, where it is released to create a higher concentration (Fig. 17–21). The trapping of CO_2 in the mesophyll cells requires expenditure of high-energy phosphate to convert pyruvate to phospho-*enol*-pyruvate, which then reacts with CO_2 to form oxaloacetate (Fig. 17–22). The phosphorylation occurs by the pyruvate-phosphate dikinase reaction (p. 244), which has the effect of expending both high-energy

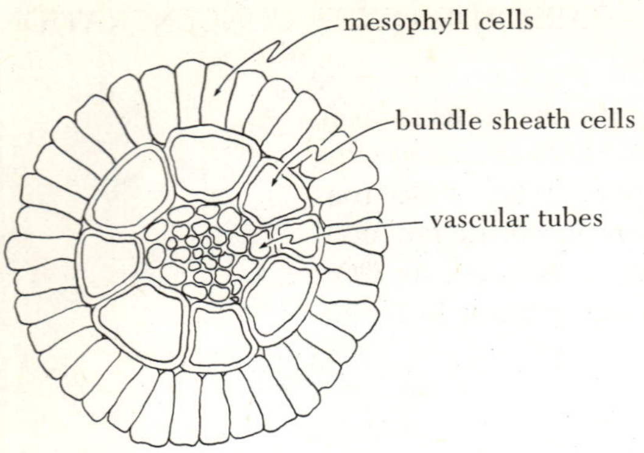

Figure 17-21 Some plants living in sporadically arid tropical regions have the cells carrying out photosynthesis arranged in bundles around the vascular tubes through which circulation occurs. The outer mesophyll cells utilize ATP to trap CO_2 and transport it to the inner bundle sheath cells for use in the Calvin cycle. Both types of cells have chloroplasts to generate NADPH and ATP by photosynthesis.

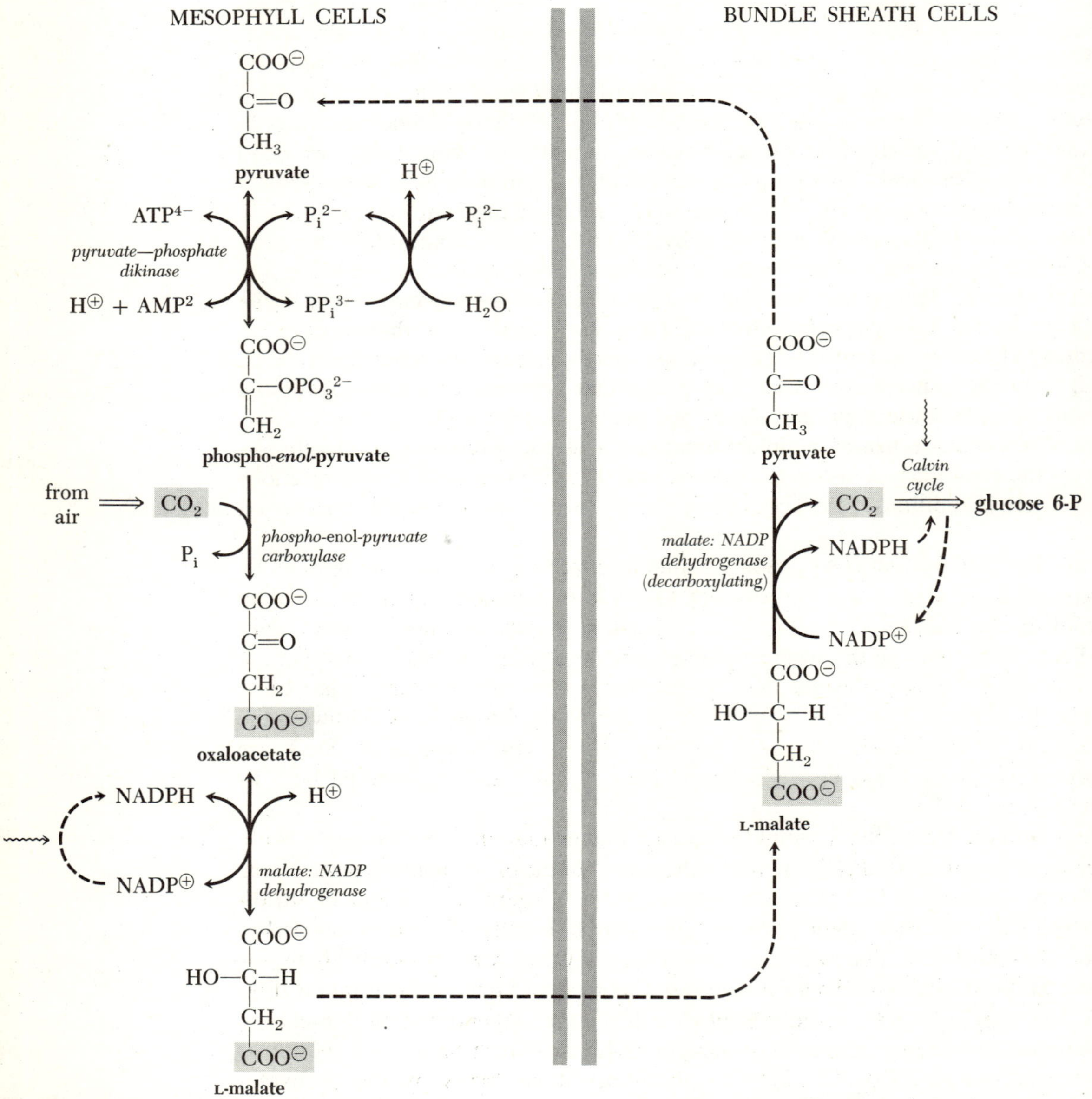

Figure 17-22 The Hatch-Slack pathway involves the use of malate to transport electrons and CO_2 from mesophyll cells to bundle sheath cells.

bonds in ATP to form the single high-energy bond of phospho-*enol*-pyruvate. This high-energy phosphate is also discharged upon formation of oxaloacetate, so the uptake of CO_2 in mesophyll cells is directly driven by two cleavages of high-energy phosphate bonds that do not occur in cells depending upon diffusion from the atmosphere. (Of course, this means that the Hatch-Slack pathway is less efficient in terms of yield of glucose per quantum of light absorbed, since it requires additional cyclic photophosphorylation, but it enables greater efficiency in terms of yield attainable at given CO_2 concentrations.)

The mesophyll chloroplasts have a malate dehydrogenase that interconverts malate and oxaloacetate; however, it is specific for NADP, and can therefore utilize the high NADPH/NADP ratio created in mesophyll chloroplasts to convert oxaloacetate to malate. Malate can cross the cell membranes where oxaloacetate cannot, and therefore diffuses from the mesophyll cells into the bundle sheath cells. The malate is in effect carrying both CO_2 and photo-electrons from the mesophyll cells.

The chloroplasts of the sheath cells have another NADP-specific malate dehydrogenase. However, this enzyme catalyzes a simultaneous decarboxylation of the intermediate oxaloacetate, so the products are pyruvate and CO_2. The position of equilibrium of this reaction favors the oxidation of malate owing to the additional loss of chemical potential caused by the decarboxylation. Therefore, the reaction can be used to raise the concentration of CO_2 within the bundle sheath cells. At the same time, it is supplying one of the two NADPH molecules required per CO_2 to form glucose. The pyruvate that remains diffuses back into the mesophyll cells for further use as a carrier.

Other Mechanisms. Still other plants, such as the sedums and other members of the family Crassulaceae, utilize the phospho-*enol*-pyruvate carboxylation mechanism in a different way. During the dark hours when photosynthesis cannot occur, they continue to take up CO_2 by using part of the previously stored starch to generate pyruvate, which is then converted to malate in the same way that it is in the Hatch-Slack pathway. Malate, along with lesser amounts of other citric acid cycle intermediates, accumulates in the leaves. The plant is in this way storing CO_2 during the dark for use in the daylight when the malate is broken down to pyruvate and CO_2. The pyruvate can be converted directly to glucose residues, and the CO_2 is used in photosynthesis to generate more of these residues.

PHOTOSYNTHESIS AND THE ENVIRONMENT

The discussion of photosynthesis completes our survey of energy generation, and before we go on it is fitting that we take note of the role of photosynthesis in the maintenance of our atmosphere, and the present concern about the degree to which man is disturbing that role. Major aspects of our culture are being questioned, involving difficult decisions that it would be impertinent to raise here. However, there are some fundamental principles within our scope that are imperative for rational judgment. To appreciate these principles, it may be helpful to review the present understanding of the history of the carbon cycle (Fig. 17–23).

History of Carbon Cycle

The primitive earth is believed to have had an atmosphere rich in CO_2 but lacking O_2, so that the sea could contain dissolved ferrous salts. There was little absorption of ultraviolet light in the atmosphere, and high-energy quanta arrived at the surface of the sea, causing photochemical reactions. These reactions induced an organic evolu-

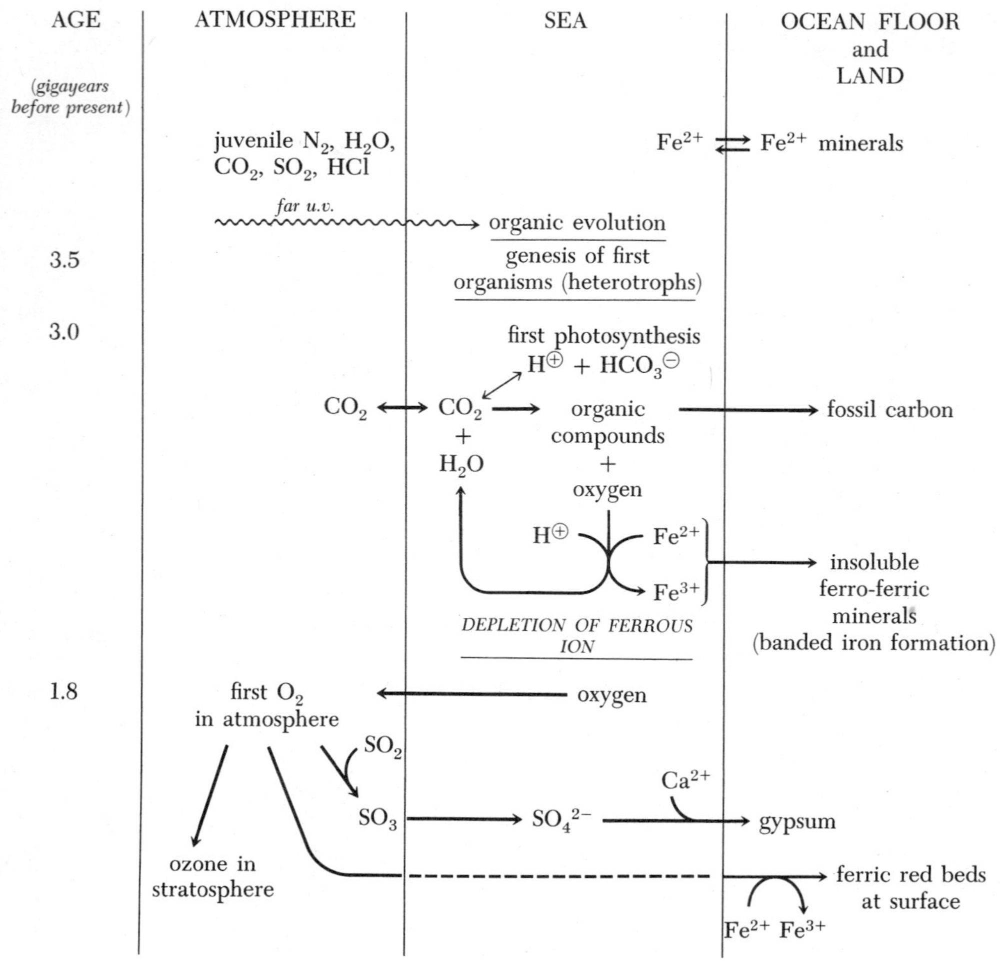

Figure 17–23 Important events in the evolution of the earth's surface. When photosynthesis began and fossil carbon was deposited, the net loss of electrons was made good by oxidizing ferrous iron. As the ferrous iron was depleted, the electrons were supplied by a net oxidation of water to oxygen. Oxygen will accumulate from photosynthesis only when there is also a net accumulation of organic compounds. Adapted from P. E. Cloud, Jr.

tion—a creation of new mixtures of compounds—from which the first organisms formed to begin biological evolution. These organisms were almost certainly heterotrophs, gaining their energy supply by utilizing the pre-formed organic compounds, but at some time around 3000 million years ago, the first photosynthetic organisms appeared.

The beginning of photosynthesis meant the beginning of the production of oxygen; this event is marked in the fossil record by the appearance of both fossil carbon and ferro-ferric minerals in the deposited rocks. The formation of oxygen is indicated by the sudden appearance of the insoluble ferric compounds, and the origin of the oxygen from photosynthetic processes is indicated by the simultaneous deposition of carbon. Here we have an important point. Carbon more reduced than CO_2 can accumulate from photosynthesis only if there is a simultaneous production of oxygen; the electrons necessary for reduction are, as we have seen, abstracted from water. The corollary is true: There can be a net production of oxygen from the photosynthetic process only if the carbon products also accumulate. Therefore, the most likely explanation for this part of the geological record is that photosynthesis had begun, with production of reduced carbon compounds and oxygen, but the oxygen was being consumed by the oxidation of ferrous salts so the carbon compounds accumulated.

When the supply of ferrous iron ran out, liberated oxygen gas started to appear in the atmosphere to match the accumulation of reduced carbon in new sediments. Some of it would be used to oxidize sulfur compounds to sulfate, and it wasn't long after this time that deposits of calcium sulfate began to appear in the strata. The atmospheric oxygen also completed the oxidation of iron salts in uplifted strata, thereby creating the one-time bonanza of iron ores that we now mine.

With the appearance of oxygen in the atmosphere, the protective layer of ozone that absorbs high-energy ultraviolet quanta began to be formed, and this permitted evolution of organisms living at the surface of the sea, and eventually on land. (Of course, the appearance of oxygen also demanded the synthesis of superoxide dismutase and catalase for protection against autoxidation of cellular components [p. 252].)

A major point in all of this for our purposes is that photosynthesis can create oxygen in the atmosphere only to the extent that there is a simultaneous deposition of reduced carbon (or some equivalent reduced compound). This is not the fate of most of the carbon formed by photosynthesis today. We have a balance between photosynthesis and respiration (Fig. 17–24) in which the carbon atoms constantly recirculate.

Since photosynthesis is frequently limited by the CO_2 concentration in the atmosphere, but respiration is rarely limited by the O_2 concentration, there is some automatic regulation of the cycle in addition to the buffering power of the large deposits of carbonates that we noted in our preliminary outline of the carbon cycle (p. 134). Suppose we could stop the combustion of compounds by man and other animals. The result would be a rising concentration of O_2 and a declining concentration of CO_2 in the atmosphere, but the declining CO_2 would slow photosynthesis and slow O_2 production, so that the result would be a new steady state in which there was somewhat *less* living tissue present. Most of the combustion is ordinarily carried out by soil organisms, anyway, and we can't avoid the conclusion that whatever may be the other deleterious effects of burning current plant products, such as paper, they do not include any dangerous alteration of the O_2 and CO_2 balance.

However, another major point in our discussion is that most of the accumulation of fossil carbon was counterbalanced by the oxidation of ferrous salts and sulfur compounds; much less was associated with the accumulation of atmospheric oxygen. It follows that the quantity of fossil carbon greatly exceeds the quantity of atmospheric oxygen, mole for mole. It is therefore formally possible that all of our oxygen could be used to burn coal and oil. Is it likely? We can dismiss this, because all of the minable

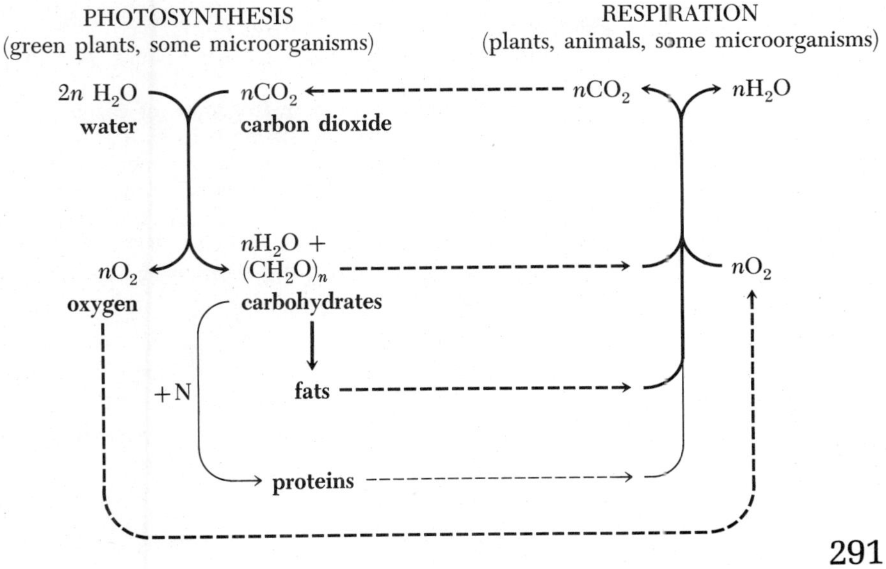

Figure 17–24 The carbon cycle appears to be substantially balanced today, with the oxygen and organic compounds formed by photosynthesis almost completely used in respiration.

coal and oil would require less than 2% of the atmospheric oxygen for combustion; most of the fossil carbon is so thinly disseminated in the ancient formations that the energy required to mine it exceeds the energy available from its combustion.

In short, we can, through the application of simple logic, dismiss from our mind the possibility that we shall cause major alterations in the total supply of oxygen in the atmosphere by our present activities, and concentrate on our real problems.

FURTHER READING

O. Björkman and J. Berry, High-efficiency photosynthesis, Scientific Amer., 229:80 (1973). Despite the misleading title, this is an informative survey of the Hatch-Slack pathway and the rationale for its evolution.

H. T. Witt, Functional membrane of photosynthesis, Quart. Rev. Biophys., 4:365 (1971). Exposition of concepts of multiple paths of electron flow.

A. Trebst, Energy conservation in photosynthetic electron transport of chloroplasts, Ann. Rev. Plant Physiol., 25:423 (1974). Summary of current views.

B. B. Buchanan and D. I. Arnon, Ferredoxins, Adv. Enzymol., 33:119 (1970). Includes lucid discussion of role in photosynthesis.

M. Zucker, Light and enzymes, Ann. Rev. Plant Physiol., 23:133 (1972). Review of regulatory responses to illumination.

J. A. Basham, The control of photosynthetic carbon metabolism, Science, 172:526 (1971). Review.

P. E. Cloud, Jr., Atmospheric and hydrospheric evolution on the primitive earth, Science, 160:729 (1968).

QUESTIONS

1. When the absorption of quanta of light is used to drive cyclic photophosphorylation, why is no oxygen evolved? Why is no NADPH produced?
2. Why does a transfer of electrons from photosystem II to photosystem I diminish cyclic photophosphorylation?
3. Why is it reasonable to expect less high-energy phosphate produced per pair of electrons transferred from photosystem II to photosystem I than is produced per pair of electrons transferred during cyclic photophosphorylation?
4. What are the similarities and what are the differences between the conversion of ribulose 5-phosphate to two molecules of triose phosphate during the Calvin cycle and the conversion of fructose 6-phosphate to two molecules of triose phosphate by the Embden-Meyerhof pathway?
5. Would you expect plant cells to have the Embden-Meyerhof pathway? Explain.
6. What things start happening in a chloroplast during the dawn's early light to promote a faster rate of conversion of CO_2 to glucose?
7. Explain why the Hatch-Slack pathway is not used by all plants. What are its advantages and disadvantages?
8. Does the malate:NADP dehydrogenase of the mesophyll cells or the malate:NADP dehydrogenase of the bundle sheath cells most closely resemble in action the malate:NAD dehydrogenase of mammalian muscle mitochondria? Which most closely resembles in action the 6-phosphogluconate dehydrogenase of the pentose phosphate pathway?
9. Explain how it is that the author of this book can assert that it will make little difference to the long-term balance of O_2 and CO_2 in the atmosphere if the trees of the Amazon basin are chopped down, and can still claim to be a long-standing advocate of strict conservation.

PART 4

STORAGE OF FUELS

CHAPTER 18

STORAGE OF GLUCOSE AS GLYCOGEN AND STARCH

THE CONCEPTS

Glycogen in animals and starch in plants are polymers of glucose serving as storage reservoirs of the fuel. The principal structural unit is the amylose chain in which successive glucosyl groups are linked by ether bonds from C-1 to C-4 on the next group. Pure amylose chains, which are part of starch particles, form a helix that can be detected because it gives a blue complex with I_2. In glycogen and in the amylopectin portion of starch particles, the 1,4-α-chains are modified by creating branches through attachment of glucosyl units on C-6 of every fourth residue, from which new 1,4-chains grow outwards and are in turn branched. The result is a globular molecule with a high affinity for water, which only gives a red-violet color with I_2.

The principal stores of glycogen in vertebrates occur in the liver and skeletal muscles. Humans have approximately 40 g (dry weight) per kg of liver and 14 g per kg of muscle, for a total store of approximately 3 moles of glucose residues.

Glycogen is built by the addition of one residue of glucose at a time; each glucosyl group is obtained by transfer from uridine diphosphate glucose (UDP-glucose) to the ends of existing amylose chains until an average of about 20,000 residues per glycogen molecule is attained. The UDP-glucose is formed from glucose 6-phosphate, first by the phosphoglucomutase reaction in which the phosphate is shifted to C-1, and then by reaction of the resultant glucose 1-phosphate with UTP.

Branches in the chains are made by transferring a piece of amylose chain, seven residues in length, onto a C-6 hydroxyl group in a neighboring segment. The shortened chain from which the piece was removed can then be rebuilt by transfer from UDP-glucose, and the new branch that is created can be lengthened in the same way. (A pure amylose chain has only one site at which it can grow, but glycogen can grow at the tip of each branch.) When the new branches grow too long, they also will be pruned to provide still more branches.

Glycogen is utilized through a phosphorolytic cleavage of 1,4-α-bonds, catalyzed by glycogen phosphorylase. Since the glucose 1-phosphate produced in this way is interconverted

with glucose 6-phosphate, the 1,4-α- groups of glycogen become directly available as a fuel within the cell. Special means are used to remove the 1,6-linked groups at the branches. The action of glycogen phosphorylase stops short of the branches, and a debranching complex does two things; it transfers the remaining 1,4-stub from the 1,6-linked residue, thereby exposing it, and it hydrolyzes the residue to free glucose. Only about 1 in 14 residues of glycogen is released in this way as glucose.

Leaf chloroplasts create and mobilize starch in much the same way, except that they use adenosine diphosphate glucose (ADP-glucose) rather than UDP-glucose as the glucosyl donor for this purpose. However, they do mobilize glucosyl residues for use elsewhere by also making UDP-glucose and reacting it with fructose 6-phosphate to form sucrose 6-phosphate. The phosphate group is removed by hydrolysis. Sucrose, which has no free potential carbonyl group, is transported through the phloem to non-photosynthetic cells in the plant. These cells maintain concentrations of UDP, P_i and PP_i such that sucrose is converted *via* UDP-glucose to starch by a simple reversal of reactions ordinarily proceeding in the opposite direction in other cells.

Insects utilize trehalose as a storage and transport sugar. Trehalose contains two glucosyl groups with ether linkage from C-1 to C-1, and therefore resembles sucrose in having no potential carbonyl group. The disaccharide is made by transfer of a glucosyl group from UDP-glucose to glucose 6-phosphate, followed by hydrolysis of the 6-phosphate. Insects store high concentrations in the blood, and later obtain the glucose residues for use as fuel by simple hydrolysis.

Organisms are frequently unable to acquire fuels at the moment they are needed. The sun doesn't always shine, the grass isn't always long, and the prey doesn't always fall to the sting. Plants, animals, and many protists have therefore devised means of storing fuels at times of plenty for later use. We have emphasized the metabolism of glucose, and the reservoirs of glucose stored in the form of glycogen or starch constitute the most readily available fuel to most plant and animal cells. Glycogen is the simpler molecule, so let us consider it first.

THE NATURE OF GLYCOGEN

In a formal sense, glycogen contains glucose residues joined by ether linkages. The linkages always occur between the α-configuration of a hemiacetal hydroxyl on C-1 of one glucose residue and another hydroxyl group on a second glucose residue. Most of the bonds in glycogen are formed to C-4 on the second residue (Fig. 18–1A). A polymer of glucose containing nothing but α-1,4 linkages is known as **amylose;** a glycogen molecule is therefore partially constructed from segments of amylose chains. (More systematically, amylose is a **1,4-α-glucan.**) Portions of starch particles are made of nearly pure amylose chains, which form a bright blue complex with iodine.

However, glycogen gives a less intense red-violet color with iodine because it is made up of segments of amylose chains interspersed with many branches. These branches are formed by additional glucosidic bonds with the hydroxyl group on C-6 (Fig. 18–1B) so that the interior of the molecule has 1,6-bonds at an average spacing of four 1,4-linked residues. The resultant arrangement is sketched in cross-section in Figure 18–1C.

Occurrence. Glycogen appears as discrete particles in cells (Fig. 18–2), evidently composed of aggregates of molecules with molecular weights ranging around 10^7, of which at least two-thirds is water (the many hydroxyl groups make the molecule quite polar). The particles also contain the enzymes concerned with the formation and the breakdown of glycogen.

Concentration. The amount of glycogen varies widely among different tissues in animals. Liver and muscles contain the largest stores, but the amount depends upon the nature of the diet and the activity of the animal. We shall mainly be concerned

A. Glycogen contains linear amylose chains made by linking carbons 1 and 4 of glucose through oxygen.

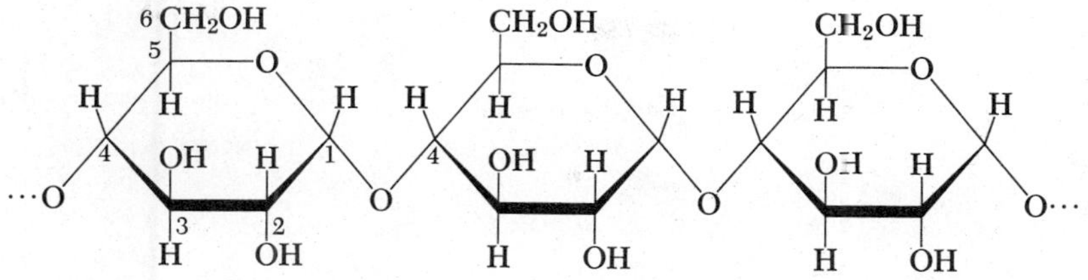

B. Branches occur in the amylose chains where carbon 6 of a residue is also linked through oxygen to the C-1 terminal of another chain segment.

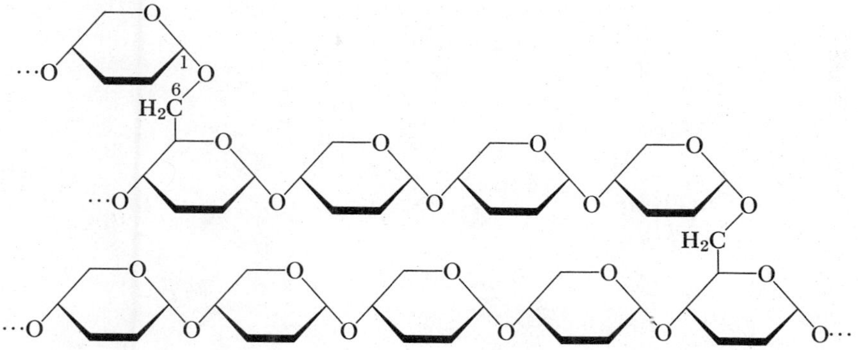

C. A cross section through glycogen showing the tree-like structure created by branched amylose chains. The short inner segments are actually part of branches extending above and below the cross-section. The circles represent glucosyl residues; only one residue (arrow) doesn't have C-1 attached to an ether linkage so that it may assume an open-chain form and mutarotate.

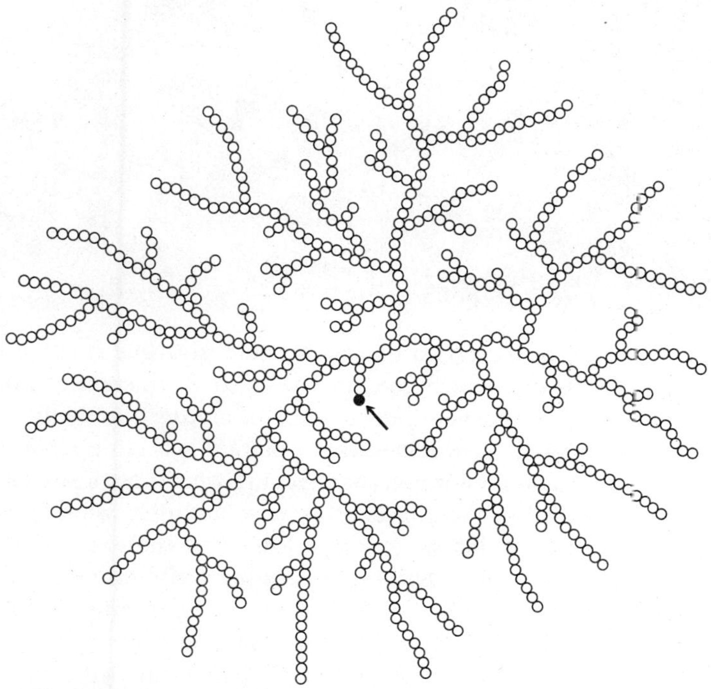

Figure 18-1 The structure of glycogen.

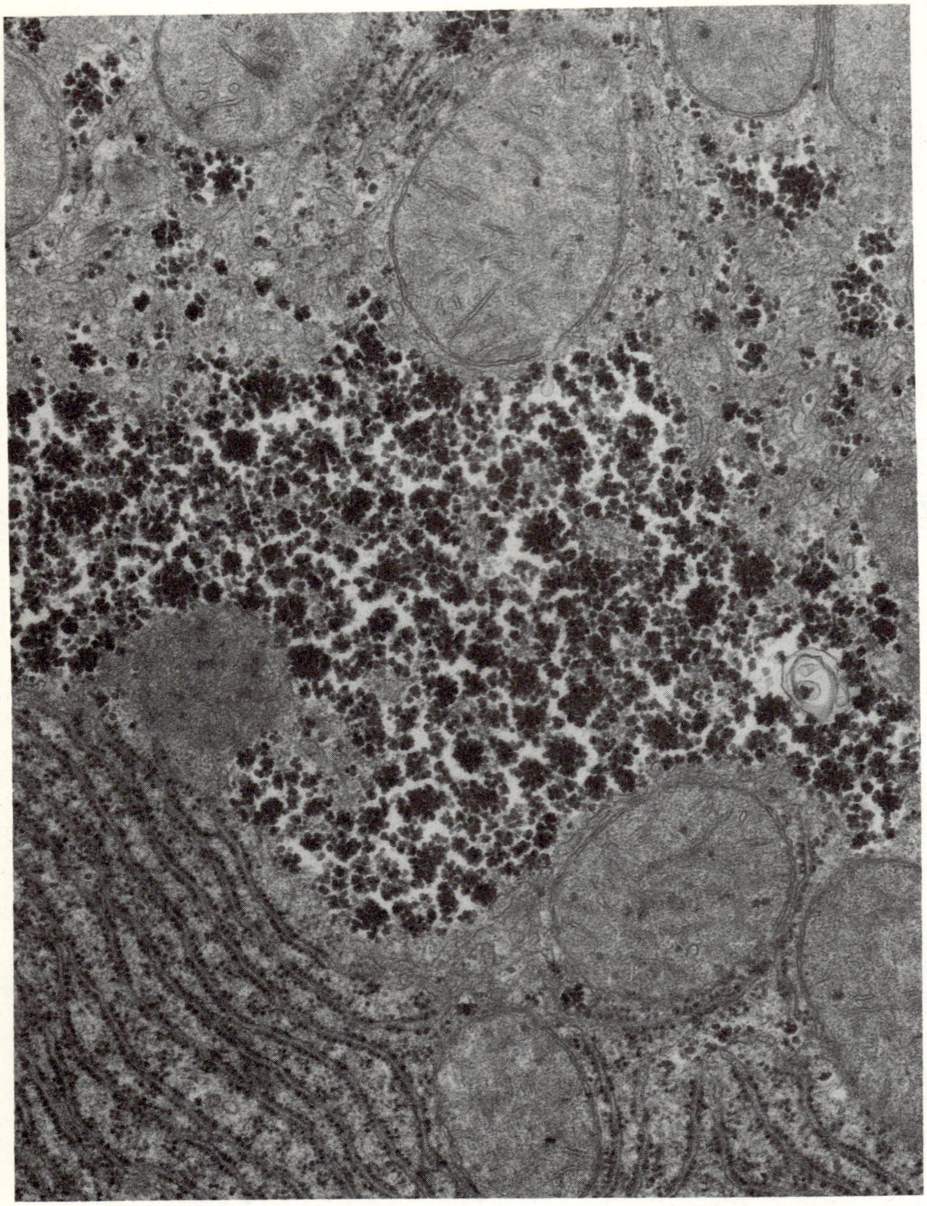

Figure 18–2 Dense clumps of glycogen fill the center of this view of the liver of a rat fed a high-carbohydrate diet. The large organelles are mitochondria. Rough endoplasmic reticulum and associated ribosomes are at the lower left; smooth endoplasmic reticulum is at the upper right. Magnification 31,000 X. (Courtesy of Dr. Robert R. Cardell, Jr.)

with these two tissues, because glycogen is usually at a lower concentration in other tissues, which contain only a small fraction of the total in the body.

In general, the content of glycogen in the liver will vary promptly with diet, while that in the muscles will be more slowly affected. We have data from studies with humans made in more recent years in Sweden. Stoical students donated small pieces of muscle to show the effects of exercise and diet, while liver samples were taken from patients undergoing surgery for ulcers. The content in muscles varied from 10 to 20 grams per kilogram of tissue from resting well-fed individuals, depending upon the proportion of white fibers in the tissue. Trained athletes on a high carbohydrate diet had the highest levels. Exercising a muscle depleted its glycogen to unmeasurable levels.

The content in human liver varied from 10.6 g per kg of tissue after 24 hours of starvation to 73.3 grams per kg of tissue in well-fed individuals also receiving an intravenous infusion of 100 g of glucose.

We can estimate from these data median values for well-fed humans:

Liver glycogen: 40 g (dry weight/kg wet tissue)
Muscle glycogen: 14 g (" " " " ")

However, a young man weighing 70 kilograms will have about 30 kilograms of muscle, but only 1.6 kilograms of liver. Therefore, approximately 420 grams of his glycogen store, dry weight, will be in his muscles, but only 64 grams in his liver. A glucose residue in glycogen, $C_6H_{10}O_5$, has a formula weight of 162, so the total store in both tissues is on the order of 3.0 moles of glucose equivalents.

MECHANISM OF GLYCOGEN STORAGE

Glycogen is made by adding one glucosyl residue at a time, creating amylose chains that are then rearranged to make branches. This is mostly done by enlarging already existing molecules. However, it isn't necessary to pass precursor molecules of glycogen from parent to daughter cells; new molecules can slowly arise through the action of the same enzymes we are about to describe, but simple chance favors extension of existing chains when they are abundant.

The glycosyl residues that are transferred come from a nucleotide, **uridine diphosphate glucose (UDP-glucose),** which in turn is derived from glucose 6-phosphate. The overall process is conveniently thought of in three stages: (1) the conversion of glucose 6-phosphate to UDP-glucose; (2) the transfer of glucosyl units from UDP-glucose onto terminal glycogen chains, so as to make a growing amylose chain composed of 1,4-linkages; and (3) the creation of branches by shifting a portion of the chain onto the C-6 hydroxyl group of an adjacent chain.

The Formation of UDP-Glucose. Since it is the C-1 of glucose that will later be attached to glycogen, the sequence begins by transferring the phosphate group of glucose 6-phosphate to form glucose 1-phosphate (Fig. 18–3). This freely reversible reaction is catalyzed by **phosphoglucomutase,** which utilizes the corresponding diphosphate compound in small concentrations as an intermediate (compare phosphoglycerate mutase, p. 219).

Glucose 1-phosphate then reacts with UTP to form UDP-glucose and inorganic pyrophosphate. As is the case with other reversible reactions involving pyrophosphate, its constant removal through hydrolysis by inorganic pyrophosphatase pulls the reaction in the direction of UDP-glucose formation. The UTP utilized in this reaction is generated by a **nucleoside diphosphokinase** reaction:

$$ATP^{4-} + UDP^{3-} \longleftrightarrow ADP^{3-} + UTP^{4-}$$

so that the ultimate source of the high-energy phosphate is ATP.

Formation of Amylose Chains. UDP-glucose acts as a donor of glucose residues used for extending the terminal branches of glycogen in a reaction catalyzed by glycogen synthase. The reaction is specific for the hydroxyl group on C-4 of the glycogen residues, so the new glucosyl residue simply extends the 1,4-chain (Fig. 18–4). Since the nature of the chain is not changed by extension, the **glycogen synthase** reaction can be repeated indefinitely. A molecule of UDP is released for each glucosyl residue added.

Formation of Branches. If nothing else happened, the result of the glycogen synthase reaction would be long amylose chains composed only of 1,4-bonds. However, cells storing glycogen also have a branching enzyme, a **glycosyl 4:6-transferase,** that

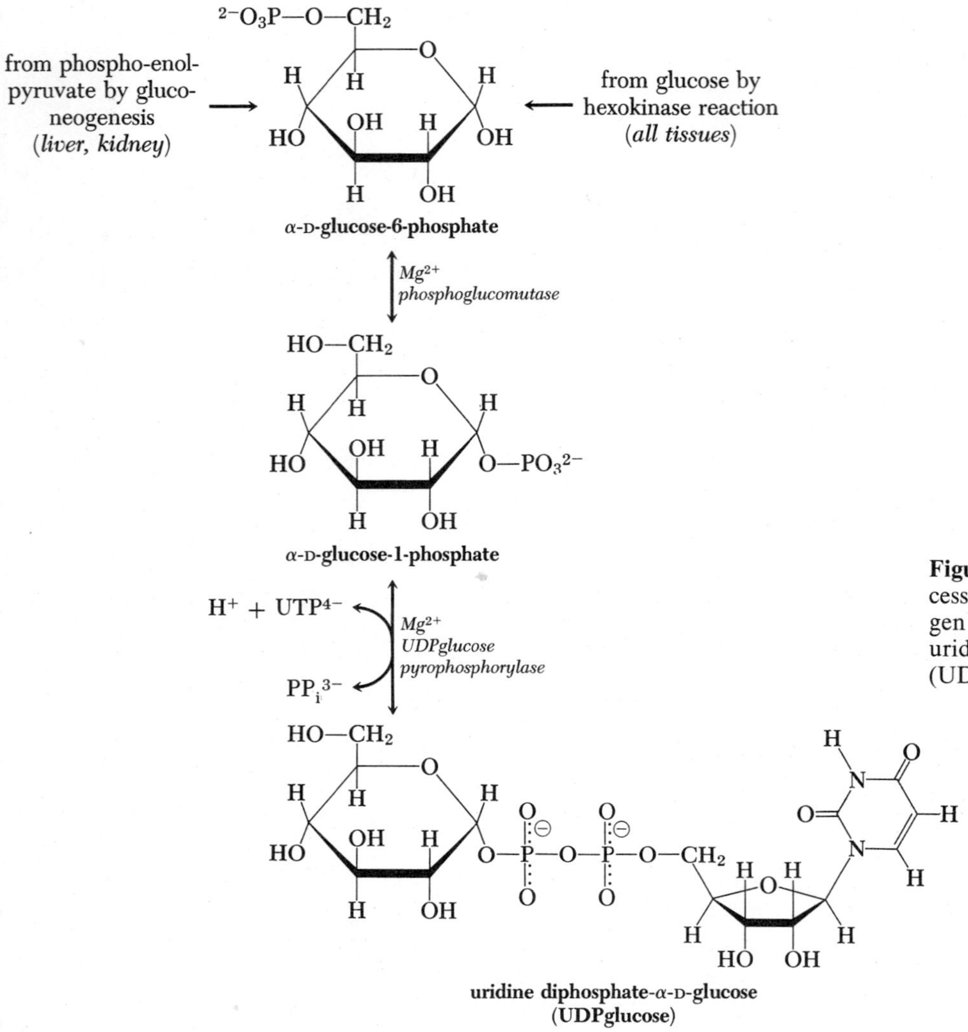

Figure 18-3 Storage of excess glucose residues as glycogen involves the formation of uridine diphosphate glucose (UDP-glucose).

catalyzes the transfer of a segment of amylose chain onto the C-6 hydroxyl of a neighboring chain (Fig. 18-5). This enzyme moves a block of seven 1,4-residues from a chain at least 11 residues in length, and transfers it onto another segment of amylose chain at a point four residues removed from the nearest branch. (Transfer of seven residues is favored, but specificity is not absolute.) The new branch is therefore seven residues in length, and the remaining stub from which it was removed is at least four residues in length, but more commonly six to nine residues long. 1,6-Glucosides have about 4800 joules per mole less standard free energy content than do 1,4-glucosides, so the equilibrium of reaction favors branching.

Further Growth. The new branch and the remaining stub from which it was obtained can grow in length by addition of more 1,4-glycosyl residues from UDP-glucose through the action of glycogen synthase. When enough have been added to extend them to at least 11 residues beyond the branch, a further transfer by the branching enzyme may create still another branch, which can grow in length. What limits the size of the molecule is not known. There is little information to justify speculation, although large glycogen particles appear to be made of subunits of approximately the theoretical limit for tightly packed spheres. What is certain is that

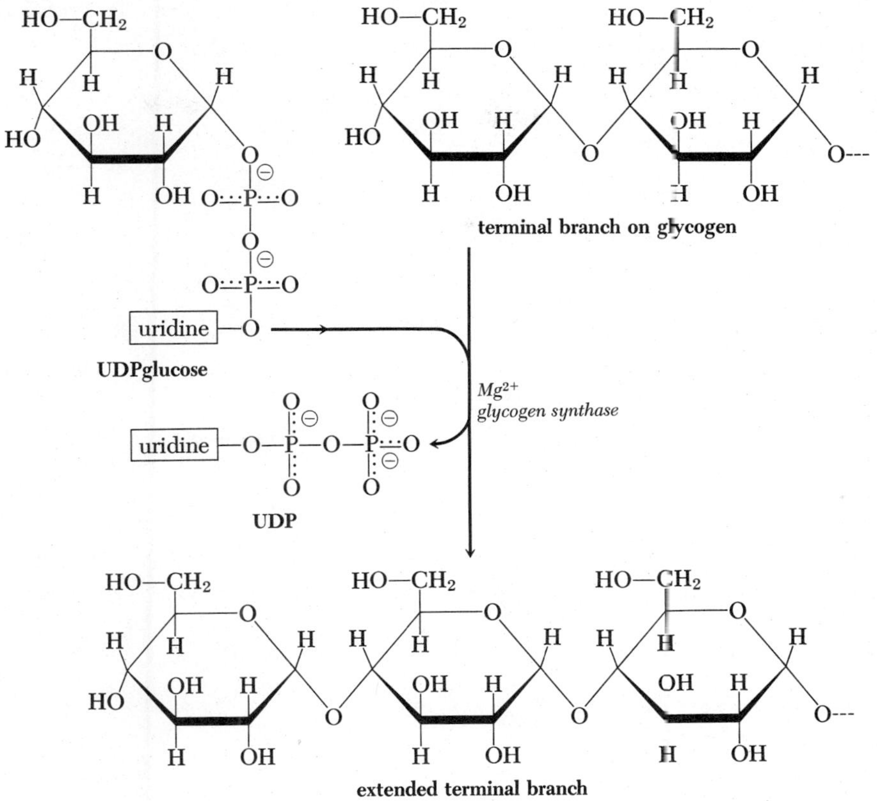

Figure 18–4 Terminal amylose chains on glycogen are extended by transfer of glucosyl residues from UPD-glucose to the C-4 hydroxyl groups of the chains. The extended branches can react repeatedly in this way with additional molecules of UDP-glucose, successively adding more glucosyl residues.

skeletal muscle does not accumulate glycogen indefinitely, even with a high concentration of blood glucose. The content of glycogen in the liver can rise markedly under heavy dietary loading, but even in this tissue glucose is absorbed slowly enough with more usual conditions so that an increased fraction of the excess supply is used for making fat (Chapter 20) after the glycogen content rises above 50 to 60 grams per kilogram of tissue. The mashed livers of force-fed Strasbourg geese, from which the pâté de foie gras favored by epicures is made, owe their special properties to high contents of both glycogen and fat.

UTILIZATION OF GLYCOGEN

Phosphorolytic Cleavage. Glycogen is mainly degraded by a simple phosphorolysis of the 1,4-glucosidic bonds to form glucose-1-phosphate, accompanied by reactions to remove the 1,6-branches. The primary reaction, catalyzed by **glycogen phosphorylase,** cleaves the terminal 1,4-glucosidic bonds with inorganic phosphate so as to shorten the chain by one residue (Fig. 18–6). The reaction is freely reversible, with the equilibrium ratio of P_i to glucose-1-phosphate concentrations near 3.5. However, the concentration of P_i in the liver is some 30-fold greater than the concentration of glucose-1-phosphate, so the reaction always proceeds in the direction of formation of glucose-1-phosphate.

When a glucose residue is removed by phosphorolysis, the shortened 1,4-branch on the glycogen molecule can be attacked again to remove another residue, followed by further attack on the remainder. However, phosphorylase by itself will not catalyze the removal of all of the terminal residues. In anthropomorphic terms, it won't go near

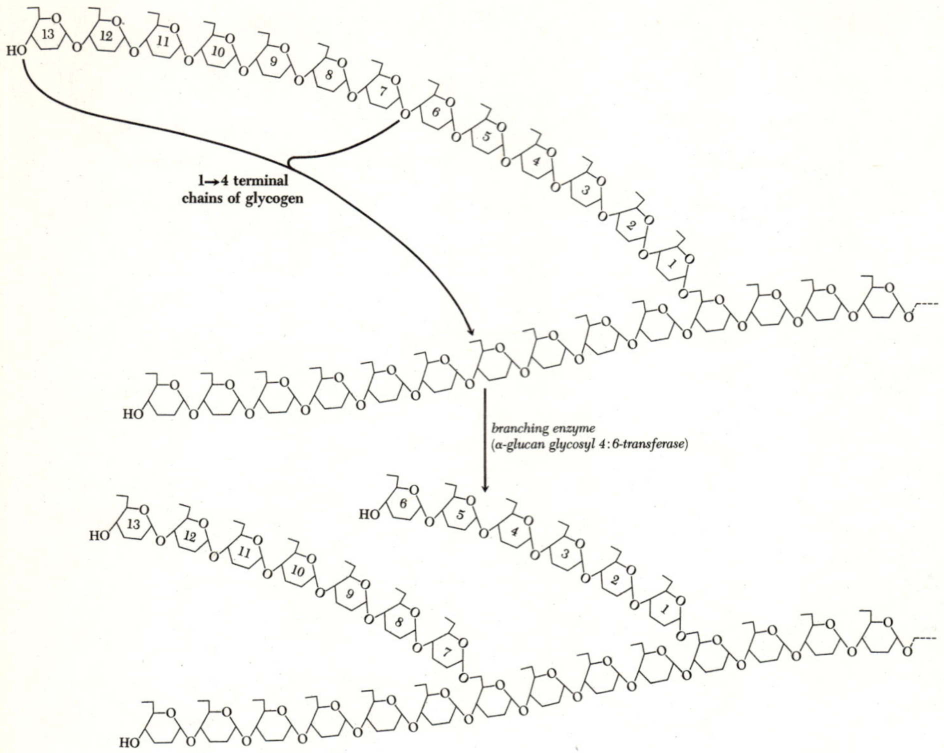

Figure 18-5 Branches are created in glycogen by transferring seven-residue segments of amylose terminal chains to hydroxyl groups on carbon 6 of a glucosyl residue that is four residues removed from an existing branch. A terminal branch must be at least 11 residues long before a segment is transferred from it.

the branches. Expressed more mechanistically, the specificity of the enzyme is such that the 1,4-bond attacked must be at least four residues removed from a 1,6-branch. Therefore, phosphorylase alone will not make the outer branches any shorter than four glycosyl residues. The function of this specificity is not clear. Glycogen completely sheared by phosphorylase to the four-residue stubs is called the phosphorylase limit

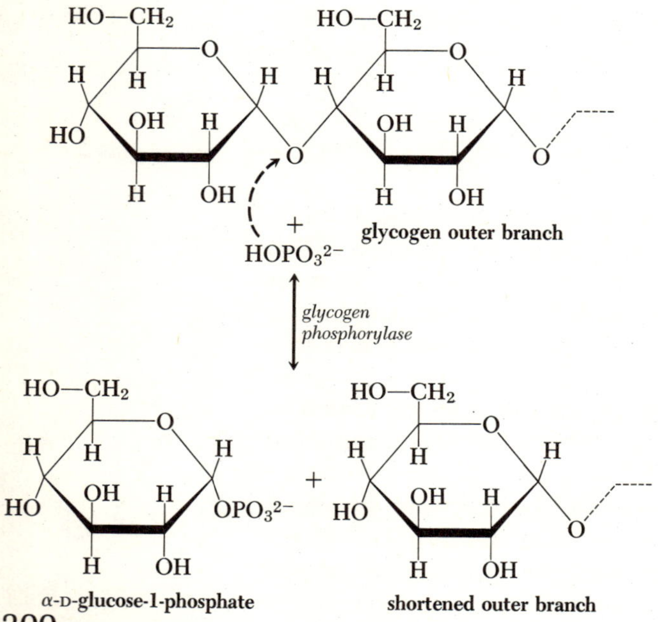

Figure 18-6 The recovery of the glucosyl residues stored as glycogen begins with phosphorolysis of terminal glucosidic bonds to form glucose 1-phosphate. Glucose 1-phosphate is in equilibrium with glucose 6-phosphate (not shown) and can supply the Embden-Meyerhof pathway in all cells or be used to replenish the blood glucose from the liver.

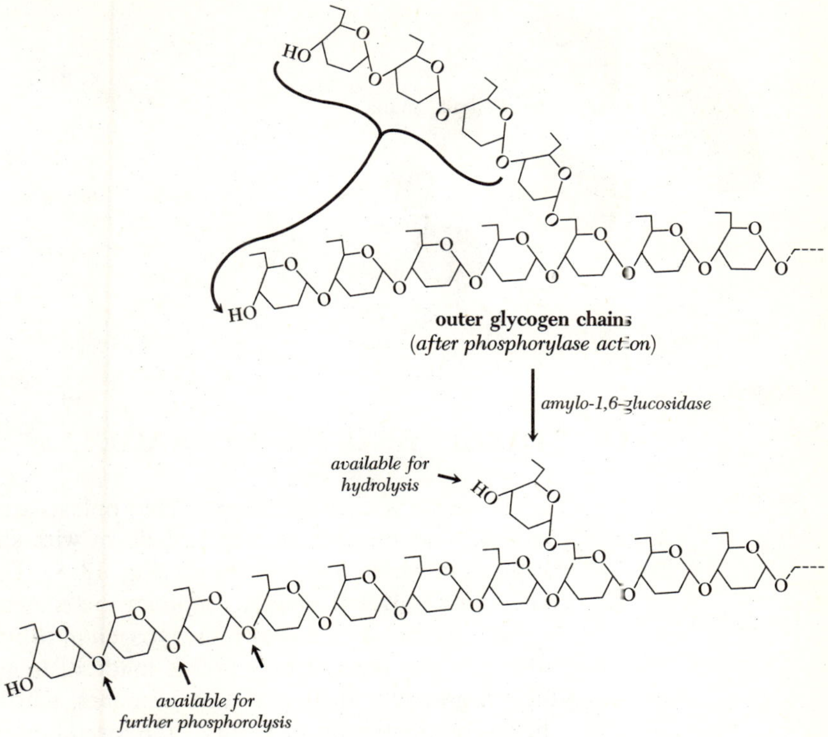

Figure 18-7 Phosphorylase removes glucosyl residues no closer than four residues from a branch point in glycogen. Another enzyme, amylo-1,6-glucosidase, catalyzes the transfer of three residues from the stubs of branches to the C-4 hydroxyl group of amylose stubs. The same enzyme then catalyzes the hydrolysis of the exposed 1,6-linked residue. Further attack by phosphorylase on the extended 1,4-amylose chain then removes the three added glucosyl residues.

dextrin, or Φ-dextrin. (Dextrin is a term borrowed from starch chemistry, describing partially hydrolyzed glucose homopolymers, and it is widely used for describing intermediates obtained during chemical investigation of structure, but this does not imply the occurrence of these discrete types of molecules in cells.)

Removal of Branches. Further degradation of glycogen requires a second enzyme, **amylo-1,6-glucosidase.** This enzyme catalyzes two successive reactions. In the first reaction, it acts as a **glucosyl transferase** akin to the branching enzyme functioning during glycogen synthesis, but differing in that it transfers three glucosyl residues from a branch onto a chain terminus so as to lengthen it (Fig. 18–7). Suppose that phosphorylase has adjacent chains shortened as much as possible at a branch. Each will be four glucosyl residues in length. The glucosyl 4:4-transferase activity catalyzes the removal of three of the residues of the stub of the branch, leaving a single residue attached to C-6, and transfers the three-residue package to the end of the other stub, which now has seven residues in 1,4-linkage and can therefore be attacked again by phosphorylase.

The amylo-1,6-glucosidase then catalyzes hydrolysis of the single residue remaining on C-6 at the branch to yield free glucose. The hydrolytic activity is absolutely specific for a 1,6-linkage to a single residue, thereby protecting longer branches on glycogen from internally disruptive attack by this enzyme.

Removal of the single branched residue exposes a straight chain of 1,4-linked residues down to the next branch, so phosphorylase can catalyze the removal of more residues as glucose 1-phosphate before reaching its limit of four residues next to a branch. What is the result? The whole sequence causes a continual stripping of glucosyl residues as glucose 1-phosphate, except for the single residues at branches that are removed as free glucose. The degree of branching is such that 11 to 14 molecules of glucose 1-phosphate are formed for each molecule of free glucose released.

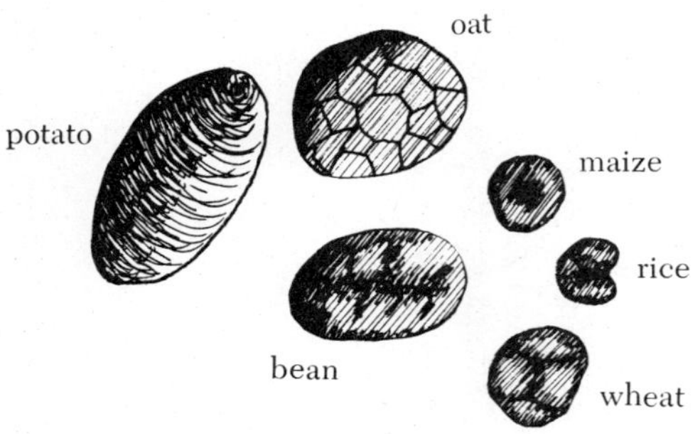

Figure 18-8 Starch granules from various sources have characteristic appearances.

STARCH AND ITS STORAGE

The starch particles found in plant chloroplasts are more complex than animal glycogen particles. They are larger, and laid down with shapes and striations characteristic of the plant in which they are found (Fig. 18–8). The starch particles, like glycogen, are coated with a protein sheath including the enzymes necessary for their formation and degradation, but they differ from glycogen in containing two kinds of glucose polymers. From 10 to 30 percent of starch is made of long amylose chains of several hundred glucosyl groups with few, if any, branches, which curl into a helix (Fig. 18–9). (It is a helical configuration that causes the formation of a bright blue complex when starch is treated with iodine.)

The other glucose polymer is a highly branched configuration, called **amylopectin,** which resembles glycogen, but which has terminal branches about 20 residues long.

The Formation of Starch

Starch is made in the chloroplasts of many plants by a mechanism similar to the one we outlined for glycogen synthesis. The principal difference is that the glucosyl groups are transferred from ADP-glucose, rather than UDP-glucose:

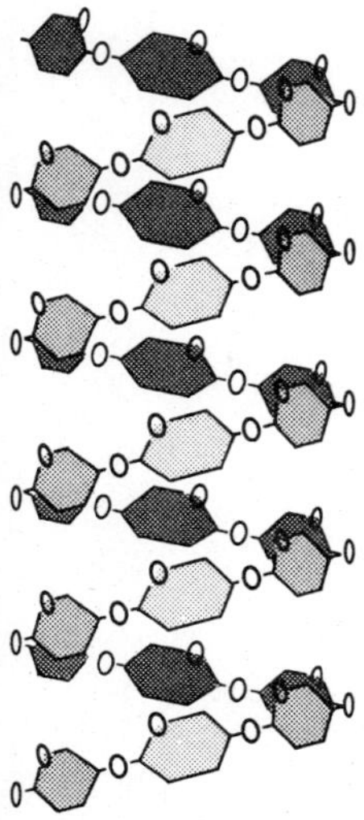

Figure 18-9 The long amylose chains in starch form a helix.

$$\text{Calvin cycle} \longrightarrow \text{glucose 6-phosphate} \longleftrightarrow \text{glucose 1-phosphate}$$

$$\text{glucose 1-phosphate} + \text{ATP}^{4-} + \text{H}^+ \xleftrightarrow{\textit{ADP-glucose pyrophosphorylase}} \text{ADP-glucose}^{2-} + \text{PP}_i^{3-}$$

$$\text{ADP-glucose}^{2-} + \text{amylose chain} \xrightarrow{\textit{starch synthase}} \text{extended amylose chain} + \text{ADP}^{3-} + \text{H}^+$$

$$\text{extended amylose chain} \xrightarrow{\textit{“branching enzyme”}} \text{branched chain in amylopectin}$$

However, starch is also laid down in plant cells that do not carry out photosynthesis. This secondary storage of starch apparently occurs by a reversal of the phosphorylase reaction:

$$\text{glucose 1-phosphate} + \text{amylose chain} \xleftrightarrow{\textit{starch phosphorylase}} \text{extended amylose chain} + \text{P}_i^{2-}$$

How is it that an enzyme ordinarily used for degradation of starch can now be used for synthesis? There must be some alteration in reactant concentrations in the cells where that occurs, and such is the case. It turns out that most plants transport sugar in the form of sucrose, and the cells using sugar and cells making sugar have different patterns of metabolite concentrations.

Formation of Sucrose for Transport. The role of sucrose is presently being vigorously investigated, but we can examine a likely interpretation of its function. The chloroplasts of some cells convert glucose 1-phosphate to ADP-glucose, and then store the glucose residues as starch by the route we noted. Whether this happens or not, nearly all chloroplasts of the higher plants also have the ability to convert glucose 1-phosphate to UDP-glucose and to use it with fructose 6-phosphate to form the disaccharide sucrose (Fig. 18–10). The initial formation of sucrose phosphate occurs by a reversible reaction in these cells, but the reaction is driven to completion by the essentially irreversible hydrolysis of the phosphate group, leaving free sucrose. Sucrose

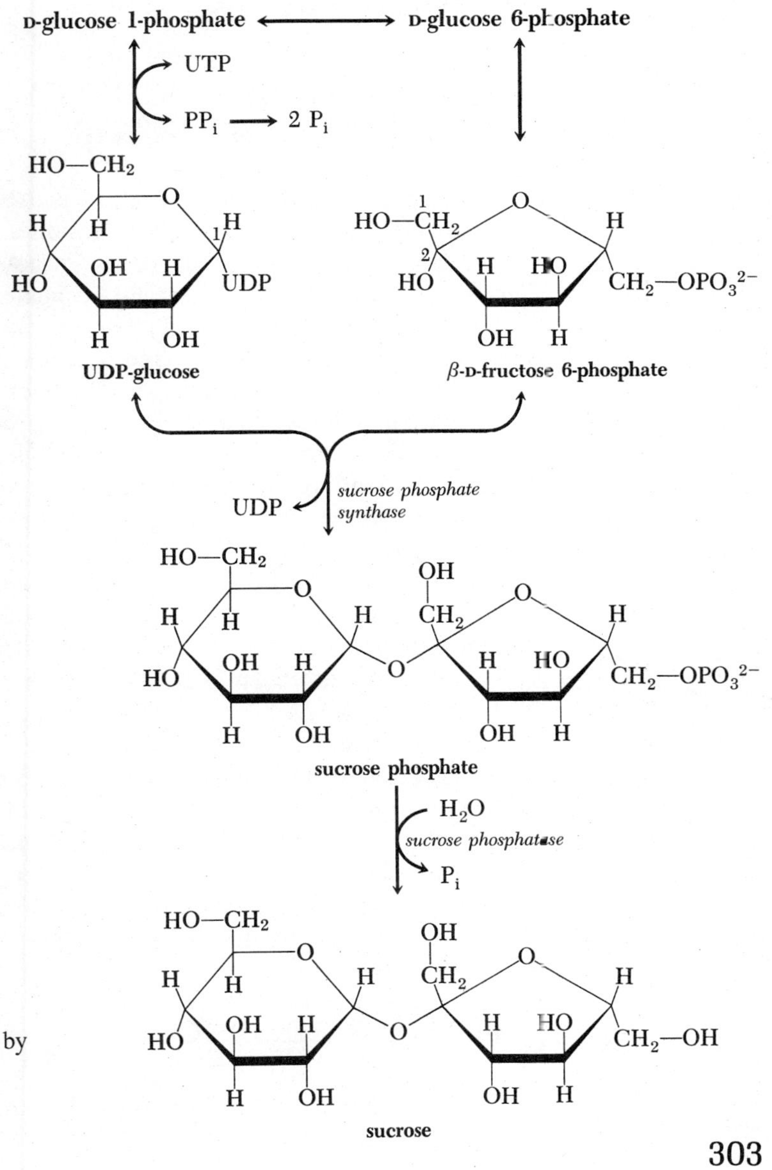

Figure 18–10 The formation of sucrose by chloroplasts.

is somewhat of an oddity, in that both of the potential carbonyl groups are linked together, but the important functional point is that sucrose is discharged into the phloem as a means of moving glucose residues from the cells in which they are synthesized to other cells of the plant for use as a fuel and as a raw material for constructing cellular components.

Utilization of Transported Sucrose. The cells that receive sucrose have a high concentration of an enzyme that cleaves the free disaccharide with UDP to form UDP-glucose. The other product in this case is free fructose. Now, this is also a reversible reaction requiring inorganic pyrophosphate. How can it occur, since we have been emphasizing the maintenance of a low PP_i concentration by the action of pyrophosphatase? It so happens that the cells being fed from the phloem in this way appear to have relatively little inorganic pyrophosphatase, so they can maintain the concentration of PP_i at a relatively high level, while the concentration of P_i is relatively low. The successive reversible reactions of UDP-glucose pyrophosphorylase and starch phosphorylase therefore proceed in the direction of formation of starch, which is contrary to the "normal" direction of these reactions in plant cells, and comparable reactions in animal cells.

TREHALOSE AS A STORAGE AND TRANSPORT SUGAR

Still another disaccharide, trehalose, is used in some animals and protists as a means of storing and transporting glucose residues. The formation of this compound resembles the formation of sucrose in plants, except that a glucosyl group is transferred from UDP-glucose to C-1 of glucose 6-phosphate. The result is trehalose 6-phosphate, which is then hydrolyzed by a specific phosphatase to form free trehalose, a disaccharide that is like sucrose in having no free potential carbonyl group.

The function of trehalose has been especially well described in insects. The concentration in insect hemolymph ranges from 15 to 150 millimolar, or the equivalent of 30 to 300 milimolar stored residues of glucose. (Compare this to the 3 to 5 millimolar glucose found in the blood of most vertebrates.) This substantial store is readily available to the flight muscles, which contain an active trehalase for hydrolyzing the compound to glucose.

Why do the insects make trehalose rather than simply raising the glucose concentration in the body fluids? A likely explanation is that a high glucose concentration would impede the absorption of glucose from ingested foods.

In any event, there is some evidence obtained in recent years that trehalose may have a more general function. Trehalase, the enzyme hydrolyzing the disaccharide, has been demonstrated in mammalian intestinal mucosa and kidney tubules. These are the tissues that transport glucose against a concentration gradient. One might surmise that the intestinal enzyme is present to hydrolyze trehalose in the food; after all, some insects are delicacies to many people. Caution is indicated, because the kidney cells are also able to synthesize trehalose. There is a remote possibility that the formation of this sugar may turn out to be a part of the mechanism for active transport of glucose across some membranes, but don't hold your breath.

FURTHER READING

C. T. Greenwood, Starch and glycogen, 2B:471 in W. Pigman and D. Horton, The carbohydrates, Academic Press (1970). Authoritative discussion of the chemistry.

R. Piras and H. G. Pontis, eds., Biochemistry of the glycosidic linkage, Academic Press (1972). The section on disaccharides (pp. 239–314) includes material difficult to find elsewhere. Other papers are also valuable.

F. Dickens, P. J. Randle, and W. J. Whelan, Carbohydrate metabolism and its disorders, Academic Press (1968). See chapter 4 in vol. 1.

B. E. Ryman and W. J. Whelan, New aspects of glycogen metabolism, Adv. Enzymol., 34:283 (1971). Updates preceding reference. Both are more readable than most, but still technical.

J. E. Frederick, ed., Storage polyglucosides, Ann. N. Y. Acad. Sci., vol. 210 (1973). Several papers on structure and metabolism. Includes scanning electron micrographs of starch particles.

QUESTIONS

1. Add all of the reactions necessary for the conversion of glucose to glycogen in a liver cell. Include the nucleoside diphosphokinase reaction for replacement of expended UTP with ATP. What is the cost in high-energy phosphate bonds destroyed per glucosyl unit stored?
2. Why can't animal cells make glycogen by direct transfer of glucosyl units from glucose 1-phosphate when some plant cells make starch by this route?
3. Similarly, how can animal cells make UDP-glucose from glucose 1-phosphate when some plant cells carry out the reverse of the identical reaction?
4. How many moles of ATP could be generated by the complete combustion of all of the glycogen stored in a typical well-fed and resting human?
5. How many moles of ATP could be generated by converting that same quantity of glycogen to lactate?
6. What enzymes would not be required for the formation of pure amylose that are required for the formation and degradation of glycogen? Suggest one or more advantages that the organism gains from making glycogen that justify the presence of additional enzymes.
7. Compare trehalose and sucrose in chemical composition and in the routes of synthesis and utilization.
8. Why are segments of amylose chain transferred during both the synthesis and the degradation of glycogen?

CHAPTER 19

REGULATION OF GLYCOGEN STORAGE

THE CONCEPTS

The activities of glycogen synthase and glycogen phosphorylase are closely regulated to avoid a rapid futile cycle and to permit the presence of enough enzyme for rapid metabolism when the need occurs without unnecessary reaction at other times. The existence of these enzymes in active or inactive conformation is determined by a combination of allosteric binding of metabolites along with phosphorylations of the enzyme proteins that fix them in one conformation or the other.

Glycogen phosphorylase is stimulated to break down glycogen faster by combination with AMP, which signals an existing deficiency of high-energy phosphate. It is also stimulated by other signals that cause phosphorylation of the enzyme by ATP, catalyzed by a glycogen phosphorylase kinase. For example, this kinase is stimulated by Ca^{2+}. Therefore, the release of these ions to cause muscular contraction also causes an increased phosphorylation of glycogen phosphorylase, which in turn mobilizes the fuel that will be required by the working muscle.

Glycogen phosphorylase kinase in turn is affected by additional signals because it itself can be phosphorylated to a more active form by a protein kinase. This kinase consists of a catalytic C-peptide and an inhibitory regulator (R-) peptide. The inhibitory peptide binds cyclic adenosine monophosphate (cyclic AMP) more tightly than it does the catalytic peptide, so the presence of cyclic AMP causes the release of free catalytic peptide of the protein kinase, ready to phosphorylate glycogen phosphorylase kinase, which in turn phosphorylates glycogen phosphorylase and promotes the breakdown of glycogen.

Cyclic AMP contains ester bonds between a single phosphate group and the 3′ and 5′ hydroxyl groups of a single adenosine residue. It is formed from ATP in a reaction catalyzed by adenyl cyclase that is regulated in this way: The adenyl cyclase of each cell produces cyclic AMP that eventually results in the destruction of glycogen, but the cyclase is located in the plasma membranes of cells. The membranes of cells are built so that the cyclase is active only when other effectors, such as hormones brought through the blood stream, are also attached to specific sites on the membrane. Different kinds of cells differ in the kinds of receptors in their membranes, and they therefore differ in the chemical signals to which they will respond by activating adenyl cyclase. Cyclic AMP may be regarded as a "second messenger" within the cell for these external signals.

The adenyl cyclase of skeletal muscles is built to respond to low concentrations of the hormone adrenaline, which is released by the adrenal medulla at times of excitement. Adrenaline signals an emergency, and it causes the release of cyclic AMP and the consequent mobilization of glucosyl groups from glycogen in preparation for action.

The adenyl cyclase of the liver is built, on the other hand, to respond to low concentrations of a peptide hormone, glucagon, which is released by cells in the pancreas in response to a fall in blood glucose concentration. The adenyl cyclase of muscles does not respond to glucagon, so the physiological effect of the hormone is to cause a breakdown of glycogen in the liver to stem the fall in blood glucose concentration without affecting the glycogen in muscles. Glycogen synthase is regulated by similar signals. It is phosphorylated to an inactive form by the same protein kinase that activates glycogen phosphorylase kinase. Therefore, the increased concentration of cyclic AMP caused by adrenaline in the muscles or by glucagon in the liver will result in decreased activity of glycogen synthase.

Insulin in some way causes an increase in the activity of glycogen synthase in the liver and muscles. Therefore, when the pancreas secretes more insulin in response to a rise in blood

glucose concentration, the storage of the increased amount of glucose as glycogen will be promoted.

The activities of the phosphatases and kinases responsible for changes in glycogen metabolism are also controlled through allosteric effects. For example, glucose forms a complex with the liver isozyme of glycogen phosphorylase-P (the phosphorylated form) that is inactive, but this is not true of the muscle enzyme. The effect is to prevent the breakdown of glycogen to more glucose in the liver when the blood glucose concentration is high, but not to prevent full mobilization of fuel in the muscles. Similarly, glycogen forms an inhibitory complex with glycogen synthase phosphatase, and therefore causes glycogen synthase to be held in the inactive phosphorylated form.

Regulation of the synthesis of starch involves an activation of ADP-glucose pyrophosphorylase by 3-phosphoglycerate, thereby preventing storage of fuel unless the demands of the Embden-Meyerhof pathway and other routes of utilization are being met. The enzyme is also inhibited by P_i, presumably as an indicator of a deficit of high-energy phosphate.

We outlined in the preceding chapter the steps by which glycogen is formed and those by which it is degraded for utilization as a fuel. Since any normal cell in which glycogen is stored contains the enzymes necessary to catalyze both its formation and its degradation, it has the potential for a major futile cycle in which glucose residues are rapidly being added to and stripped from glycogen. The ultimate result of such a cycle is nothing more than the hydrolysis of ATP (Fig. 19–1), and the possibility of this major wastage of chemical potential may have been sufficient in itself to have required the evolution of regulatory mechanisms preventing simultaneous full-velocity synthesis and degradation.

Beyond all of this, the different functions of various organs in the higher animals demand different controls over the deposition and mobilization of their respective glycogen stores. For example, most of the blood circulating through the small bowel passes into the liver by way of the **portal veins** (Fig. 19–2), and only then is it returned

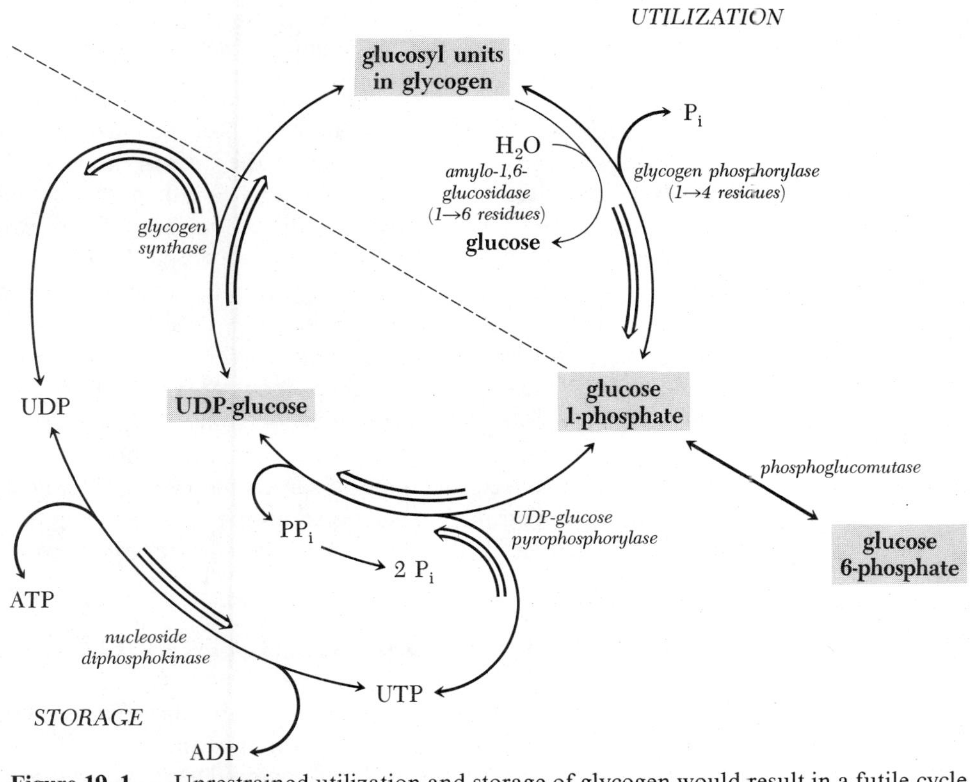

Figure 19–1 Unrestrained utilization and storage of glycogen would result in a futile cycle causing the net hydrolysis of ATP.

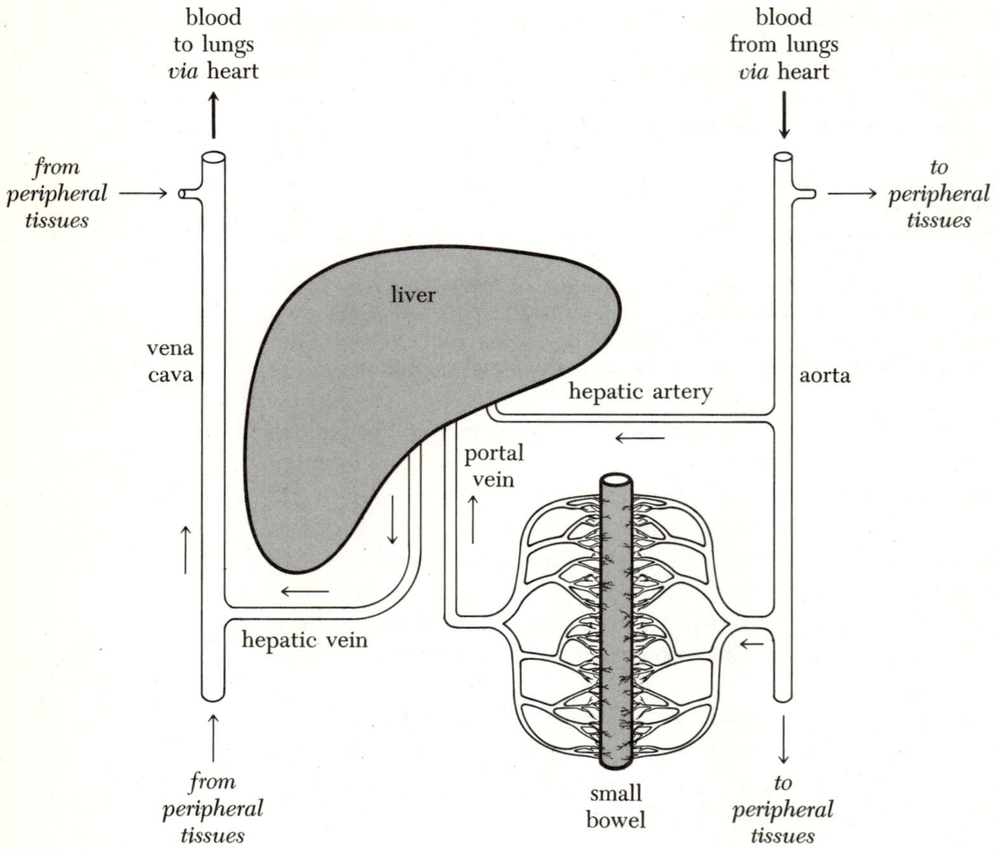

Figure 19-2 The liver receives some blood directly from the heart through the hepatic artery, but much of its supply first passes through the small bowel into the portal vein.

to the heart and lungs for general circulation. The glucose absorbed from a meal in the small bowel therefore first traverses the liver, where some of it is taken up and stored as glycogen. The balance leaves the liver in the venous return to the heart, and is then distributed to the peripheral tissues either for immediate use as a fuel, as in the brain, or for further storage as glycogen, as in the skeletal muscles. We see that under these conditions of plentiful glucose supply both the liver and muscles must be storing glycogen; something must occur in both tissues to promote the action of UDP-glucose pyrophosphorylase and glycogen synthase while slowing the reactions catalyzed by glycogen phosphorylase and amylo-1,6-glucosidase.

Between meals, the situation is changed. Liver glycogen is mobilized to maintain the concentration of glucose in the blood going to the peripheral tissues, so the enzymes degrading glycogen in the liver must be activated while the enzymes catalyzing synthesis are inhibited. Muscles may at the same time be responding differently. When circumstances call for strong contractions, glycogen is degraded to provide fuel, especially in the white fibers, with the glycogen rebuilt during times of rest.

CONTROL BY PHOSPHORYLATION OF ENZYMES

The primary control over glycogen metabolism involves regulation of synthesis by changes in the activity of glycogen synthase, and regulation of degradation by changes in the activity of glycogen phosphorylase. These changes result from the existence of the respective enzymes in active and inactive conformations. The conformations may be made to change by direct interaction of the enzymes with some metabolites, but the principal cause of a shift in conformation is a phosphorylation of peptides in the respective enzymes, much in the way that the decarboxylase peptide of pyruvate dehydrogenase is phosphorylated to regulate enzymatic activity (p. 227). The phosphate groups are added by transfer from ATP in reactions catalyzed by kinases, and they are removed by hydrolysis in reactions catalyzed by phosphatases (Fig. 19–3).

Phosphorylation May Inhibit or Activate. Now comes the important point. Efficient metabolism seems to require that synthesis of glycogen diminishes when degradation accelerates, and vice versa. If glycogen phosphorylase becomes more active, then the glycogen synthase in the same cell ought to become less active. The activities of glycogen synthase and glycogen phosphorylase must therefore change in opposite directions in response to the same environmental stimulus. Translating this into molecular terms, if control is exerted because some stimulus causes phosphorylation of these enzymes, the phosphorylation must make one enzyme more active and the other enzyme less active than the corresponding nonphosphorylated forms, and this is exactly how it happens.

Let us designate the forms of these enzymes with free seryl side chains as glycogen synthase (free) and glycogen phosphorylase (free), and designate the corresponding phosphate ester forms as glycogen synthase-P and glycogen phosphorylase-P, analogous to the nomenclature of other ester phosphates. (Some name the latter forms as phosphosynthase, or phosphophosphorylase, to be consistent with the general designation of phosphoprotein.)

Under most conditions:

Glycogen synthase (free) is more active than glycogen synthase-P.
Glycogen phosphorylase (free) is less active than glycogen phosphorylase-P.

Glycogen metabolism is regulated by controlling the addition or removal of phosphate groups to these two enzymes. Addition promotes degradation of glycogen; removal promotes synthesis of glycogen.

The mechanism for regulating these interconversions of active and inactive conformations of enzymes involved in glycogen metabolism are considerably more complex than anything we have encountered before. They differ somewhat from one tissue to another, so to get a coherent picture, let us first dissect the circumstances in mammalian skeletal muscles.

REGULATION OF GLYCOGEN PHOSPHORYLASE

Effects of Metabolites

The proportion of active and inactive conformations of glycogen phosphorylase may be changed by three fundamentally different mechanisms (Fig. 19–4). Some

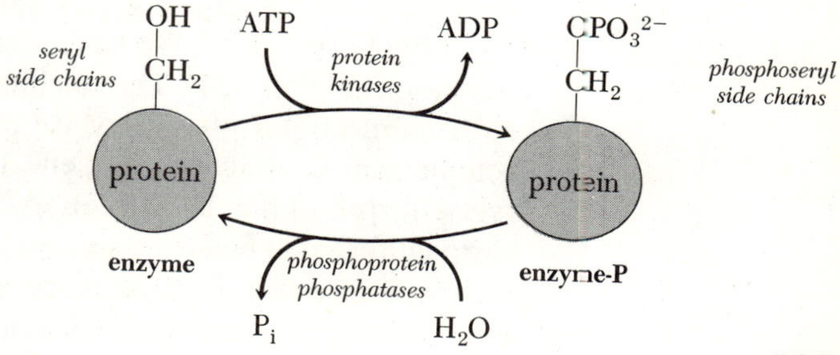

Figure 19–3 Some enzymes are regulated by changing their conformation through a phosphorylation and dephosphorylation of seryl residues.

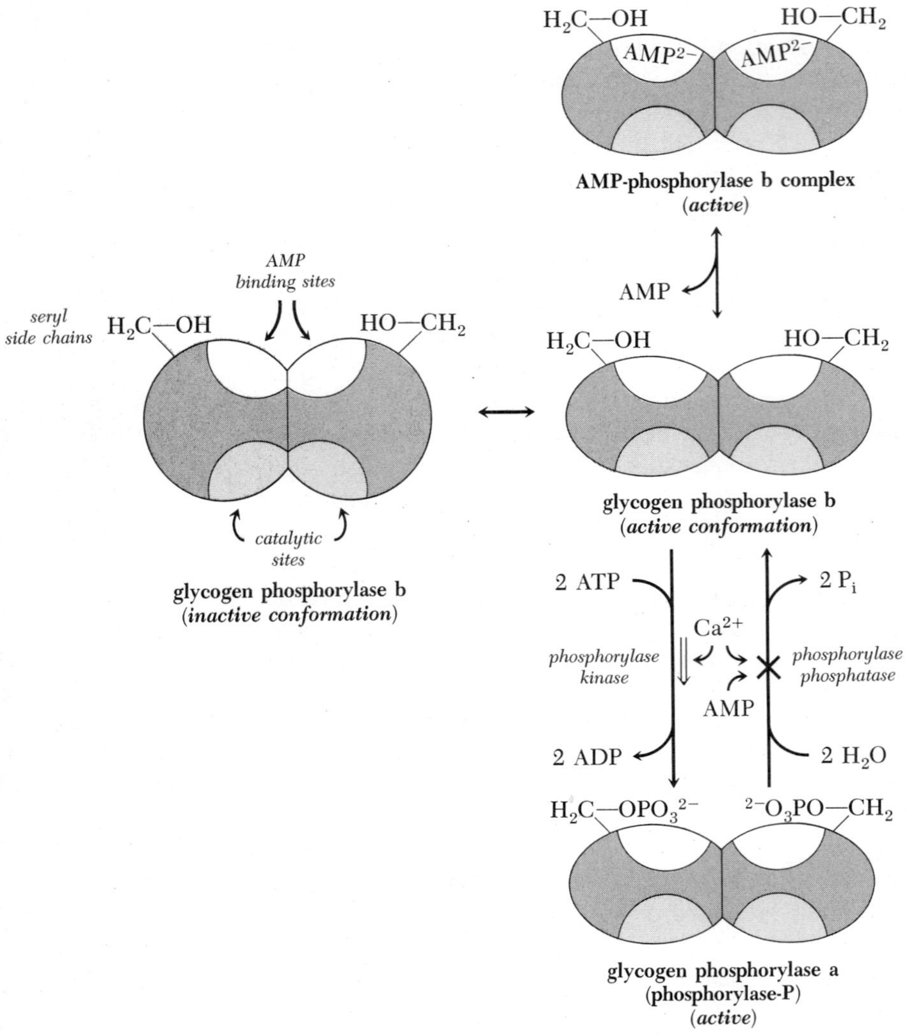

Figure 19-4 The glycogen phosphorylase b of skeletal muscles is a dimer existing in an inactive conformation. The active conformation may be stabilized by combination with AMP (*top right*), or through phosphorylation of a seryl group on each monomeric unit to form phosphorylase a (*bottom right*). The kinase catalyzing the phosphorylation is activated by Ca^{2+}, and the phosphatase catalyzing the dephosphorylation is inhibited by Ca^{2+} and AMP. Both of these agents therefore promote the breakdown of glycogen.

intracellular metabolite may bind so as to favor one conformation. The activity of the kinase that catalyzes the conversion of phosphorylase (free) to phosphorylase-P may be altered. Finally, the activity of the phosphatase that catalyzes the hydrolysis of the phosphate groups from phosphorylase-P may be altered. All of these effects occur.

Direct Binding with AMP. The active conformation of glycogen phosphorylase binds AMP without loss of activity. The inactive conformation has a lower affinity for AMP, and an increase in the AMP concentration will therefore increase the activity of glycogen phosphorylase. Since a rising AMP concentration is a sensitive indicator of a fall in high-energy phosphate content (p. 226), its effect on glycogen phosphorylase may well be a major means of adjusting the mobilization of glycogen as a fuel to fit the demand for high-energy phosphate.

Effects of Ca^{2+}. We have seen that muscular contraction is precipitated by the release of Ca^{2+} (p. 154). The calcium ions that are released also activate phosphorylase kinase and inhibit phosphorylase phosphatase, thereby causing a metabolic event to complement contraction. The effect of these changes is to cause the ratio [phosphorylase-P]/[phosphorylase (free)] to rise until the rates of phosphorylation and dephosphorylation again balance a new steady state condition. In short, the activity of glycogen phosphorylase rises because more of it is fixed in its active form by phosphorylation. The apparent physiological function of this effect is to cause the mobilization of glycogen upon receipt of the signal that causes contraction of the muscle without waiting for the resultant fall in high-energy phosphate concentration. This would be especially important for white fibers.

Indirect Effect of AMP. The binding of AMP has no effect on enzymatic activity of the already-active glycogen phosphorylase-P. However, it does make the phosphoprotein a poor substrate for the phosphorylase phosphatase. AMP not only makes glycogen phosphorylase (free) active, but it also stabilizes the active phosphorylated form against loss of its phosphate by hydrolysis.

Adrenaline and Cyclic AMP

Efficient use of glycogen as a fuel involves a coordination of events in different tissues, especially the liver and skeletal muscles. The coordination is obtained by the use of hormones as signals to the different tissues, and part of the regulation of glycogen metabolism consists of responses to the appearance of particular hormones in the circulation. Adrenaline is such a hormone, and one of its important effects is to increase the formation of glycogen phosphorylase-P.

When an animal is confronted with an emergency that may demand prompt and strenuous physical activity—flee or fight—it is advantageous for it to mobilize glucose 1-phosphate rapidly from glycogen in its skeletal muscles so as to have the fuel available even before the signal for contraction is given. The advantage is achieved because emergencies of this sort are recognized in the central nervous system, with a resultant stimulation of the adrenal medulla (the tissue in the core of the adrenal glands) to release adrenaline and the related noradrenaline into the blood stream:

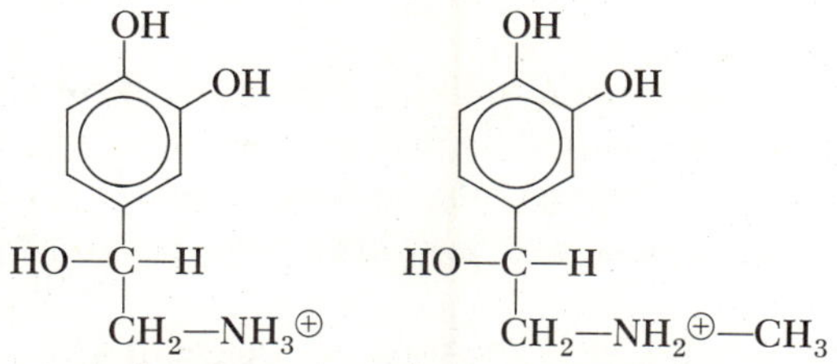

noradrenaline **adrenaline**

(Adrenaline is called epinephrine in some American medical circles because the former term used to be a trade name. Adrenaline is the name used in Chemical Abstracts, and is more widely understood, so let us use it. There is no point in being deliberately mysterious.)

Human adrenal medullas release more adrenaline than noradrenaline, but the reverse is true in some mammals. Both compounds have similar effects on metabolism in many, but not all cells, and they are frequently lumped together for pharmacological discussion as catecholamines.

Adenyl Cyclase and Cyclic AMP. Many of the metabolic effects of adrenaline occur because it combines with receptors on the plasma membrane of target cells so as to activate an enzyme, adenyl cyclase. Adenyl cyclase catalyzes an intramolecular condensation of ATP to produce **adenosine 3′,5′-monophosphate,** more familiarly known as cyclic AMP (Fig. 19–5). (The compound is sometimes designated as **3′,5′-AMP,** and sometimes as **cAMP.**) Cyclic AMP acts as a "second messenger," conveying the signal received in the form of adrenaline on the plasma membrane to the responsive enzymes within the cell. It does so by activating a relatively non-specific protein kinase in muscle

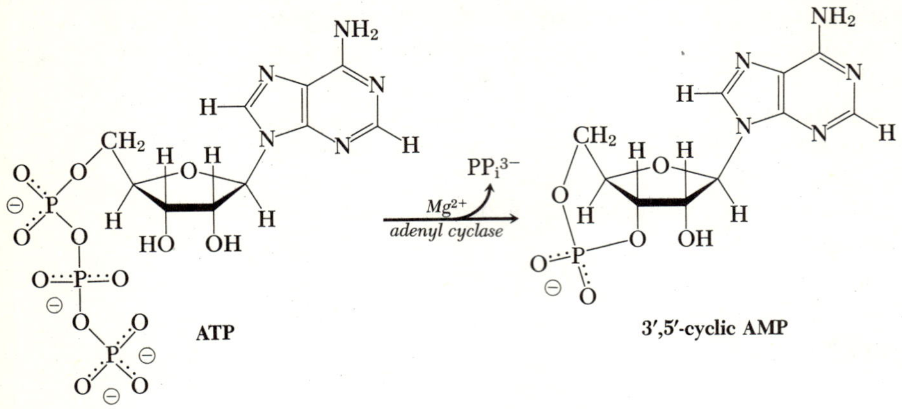

Figure 19-5 The formation of cyclic AMP from ATP.

fibers, and this is perhaps its most important effect in all cells in which it serves as a mediator of endocrine responses.

Activation of Protein Kinase. The important changes in the activity of the cyclic AMP sensitive protein kinase occur because it contains two peptides, one of which has catalytic activity **(C-peptide),** and the other of which serves as a regulator **(R-peptide).** The combination of the two peptides has no enzymatic activity, so the regulatory peptide is an inhibitor. However, the regulatory peptide will also bind cyclic AMP at a site that prevents binding with the catalytic peptide. In other words, cyclic AMP and the catalytic peptide compete for binding with the regulator peptide (Fig. 19–6). When cyclic AMP concentration rises, it forms more of the complex with regulator peptide, thereby leaving more active catalytic peptide free in the solution. When the cyclic AMP concentration falls, more regulator peptide will be available to inhibit the catalytic peptide by combining with it.

Effect of Protein Kinase on Glycogen Phosphorylase Kinase. The protein kinase acts on many different enzymes, but we are now concerned with its direct effects on glycogen metabolism. It so happens that glycogen phosphorylase kinase also exists in free and phosphorylated forms, and the phosphorylated form is activated by lower concentrations of Ca^{2+}.

What we are dealing with here is a cascade sequence in which an enzyme activated by cyclic AMP acts on an enzyme that acts on an enzyme, and the cyclic AMP is the product of still another enzyme activated by adrenaline. Let us summarize the activating events here and in Figure 19–6:

1. A small amount of adrenaline stimulates adenyl cyclase to produce larger amounts of cyclic AMP.
2. The cyclic AMP removes an inhibiting peptide from a protein kinase. The protein kinase converts glycogen phosphorylase kinase to its phosphorylated form, which is more active than the free enzyme.
3. The newly activated glycogen phosphorylase kinase causes the phosphorylation of glycogen phosphorylase (free), which is active only in the presence of AMP, to glycogen phosphorylase-P, which has even greater activity, even in the absence of AMP.
4. The more active glycogen phosphorylase catalyzes the formation of orders of magnitude more glucose 1-phosphate from glycogen.

Since there is a magnification by successive enzyme action, a minute amount of adrenaline has a very large effect, so large that 500 μg is a potent dose for humans. The normal blood concentration of adrenaline is in the nanomolar range. It has been estimated that a rise in the concentration of cyclic AMP to 1 micromole per kg of muscle causes the formation of 25,000 times as much glucose 1-phosphate per minute.

Reversal of Adrenaline Action. When the stimulus disappears and adenyl cyclase

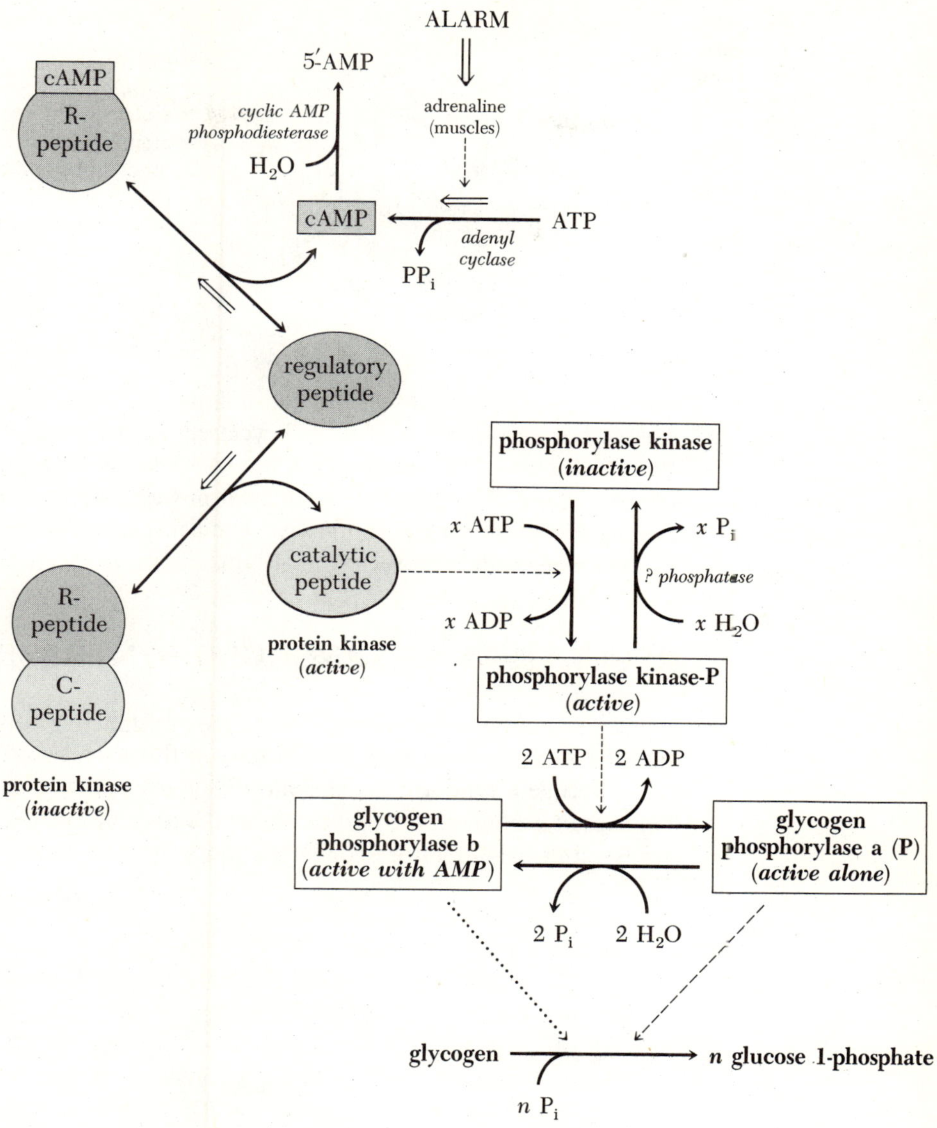

Figure 19-6 The adenyl cyclase of skeletal muscles is activated by adrenaline (*top center*) to form cyclic AMP, which reacts with an inhibiting regulatory peptide and prevents it from combining tightly with the catalytic peptide of protein kinase (*left*). The free and active protein kinase then catalyzes the phosphorylation of phosphorylase kinase, making it active (*left center*), and the active phosphorylase kinase catalyzes the conversion of glycogen phosphorylase to its active phosphorylated form. The active phosphorylase then catalyzes the breakdown of glycogen to glucose 1-phosphate. Each of these steps is reversed through the action of a specific hydrolase that removes the phosphate groups from the peptides or hydrolyzes cyclic AMP to 5′-AMP.

is no longer activated, the effects disappear as a result of the action of phosphatases, also shown in Figure 19-6. A **cyclic phosphodiesterase** catalyzes the hydrolysis of cyclic AMP to ordinary 5′-AMP. (This enzyme is inhibited by **caffeine** and related stimulatory purines, resulting in an increased concentration of cyclic AMP. Coffee appeals to us for this reason.)

Removal of cyclic AMP releases the regulatory peptide for inhibition of protein kinase. The phosphorylated forms of glycogen phosphorylase and glycogen phosphorylase kinase are then formed at a slower rate than they are attacked by phosphatases, and they are converted to their free forms.

Specificity of Adrenaline Action. It is important to realize that the formation of cyclic AMP is not a specific indication of the presence of adrenaline. A cell may have receptors for other hormones that activate adenyl cyclase, and the effects of a change in cyclic AMP concentration will be the same, regardless of the hormone that caused the change.

The specificity of the effect of a hormone acting through cyclic AMP arises from the specificity of the receptor sites in the target cells. In the case at hand, striated muscle

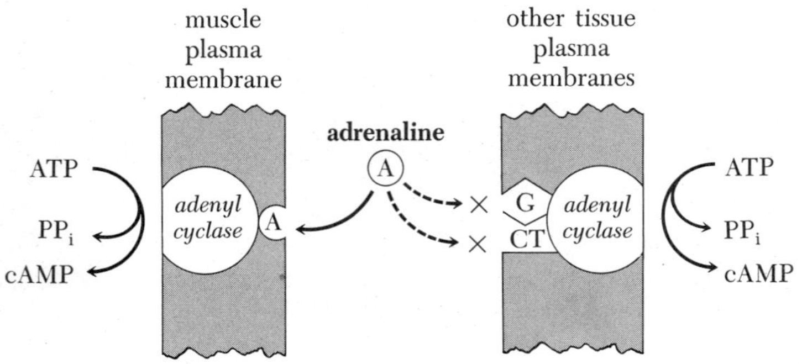

Figure 19–7 The plasma membrane of muscles has a site that specifically binds adrenaline to activate adenyl cyclase. The plasma membranes of other tissues have sites that fit other hormones, such as glucagon or corticotropin, and some have no sites that fit adrenaline. Adrenaline therefore does not activate the adenyl cyclase of those tissues.

fibers have receptor sites with a high affinity for catecholamines, and binding at these sites causes an activation of adenyl cyclase with the production of an increased concentration of cyclic AMP within the fibers. Adrenaline therefore acts as a hormone stimulating cyclic AMP formation in skeletal muscles, while it will not do so in other cells lacking receptors for the compound, even though such cells may have adenyl cyclase in their plasma membranes (Fig. 19–7).

REGULATION OF GLYCOGEN SYNTHASE

Glycogen synthase also exists with active and inactive conformations in muscles, and it is the inactive form that is stabilized in this case by phosphorylation.

Glycogen synthase is phosphorylated by the action of the same cyclic AMP-dependent protein kinase that catalyzes the phorphorylation of glycogen phosphorylase kinase, and it is therefore converted to its inactive form by the action of adrenaline.

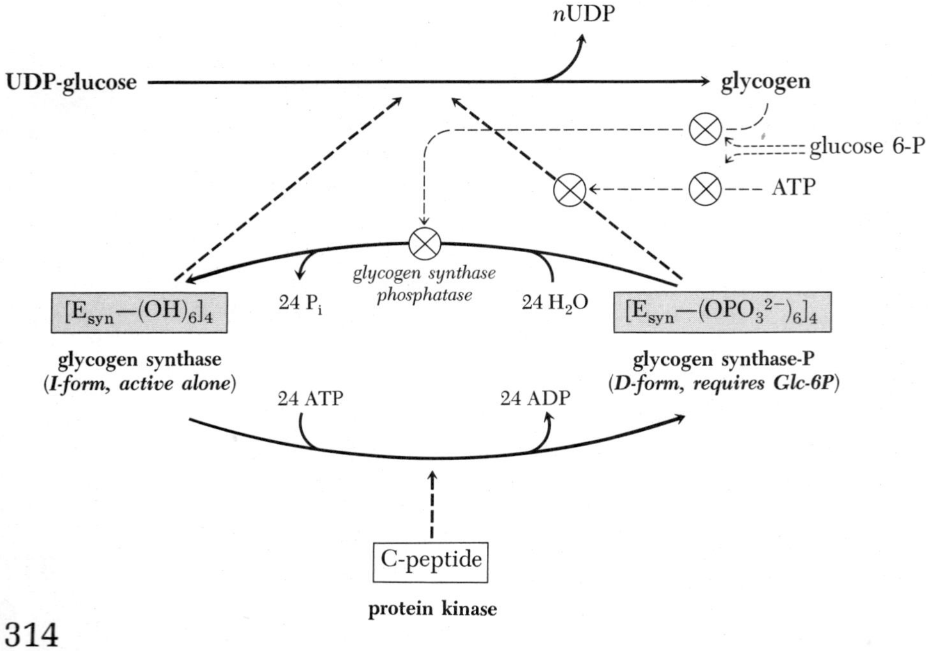

Figure 19–8 Glycogen synthase in the dephosphorylated form is active. The phosphorylated form is inhibited by physiological concentrations of ATP, but this inhibition can be relieved by glucose 6-phosphate. The phosphorylation is catalyzed by the same cAMP-activated protein kinase that acts on glycogen phosphorylase kinase. The phosphate groups are removed by a phosphatase that is inhibited by glycogen, but this inhibition is also prevented by glucose 6-phosphate. The effect of these regulatory devices is to promote the synthesis of glycogen when there is a surfeit of glucose 6-phosphate and a peaceful environment, but to prevent its synthesis when there is excess glycogen or when glycogen is being mobilized by active phosphorylase.

This makes sense; adrenaline promotes the breakdown of glycogen and blocks its synthesis in skeletal muscles.

Regulation by Glucose 6-Phosphate. Glycogen synthase-P is sensitive to inhibition by normal physiological concentrations of ATP, but glucose 6-phosphate competes for the binding site and prevents the inhibition (Fig. 19–8). Glycogen synthase (free) is active without the presence of glucose 6-phosphate, and is therefore said to be the independent (I) form, whereas glycogen synthase-P is active only in the presence of glucose 6-phosphate, and is therefore said to be the dependent (D) form. It seems likely that this effect would be useful for gathering up glucose 6-phosphate and storing the glucosyl group as glycogen at any time an accumulation of the compound isn't being utilized for energy production. This interpretation is disputed by many for mammalian muscle, but it so happens that frogs have a glycogen synthase with an absolute requirement for glucose 6-phosphate for activity, even in the free form, and it is therefore difficult to doubt the physiological relevance of the effect to the croakers.

Regulation by Glycogen Concentration. Glycogen inhibits the glycogen synthase phosphatase. As glycogen accumulates in the muscle, it therefore shuts off its own production by increasing the conversion of glycogen synthase to its less active phosphorylated form. This effect is the most likely explanation of why animals on high carbohydrate diets don't store massive quantities of glycogen in their muscles.

TROPONIN

Phosphorylation and dephosphorylation may also be used to control the activity of the contractile apparatus itself in skeletal muscles. Phosphorylase kinase also causes a phosphorylation of the inhibitory component of troponin (p. 154). Since the kinase is activated by Ca^{2+} directly and by adrenaline indirectly, its action may be a physiological device for promoting increased contraction of the actomyosin complex upon stimulation. It has also been shown that the phosphate groups are removed from troponin-P by phosphorylase phosphatase, which further supports the notion of a physiological role for the phosphorylation-dephosphorylation sequence.

GLYCOGEN METABOLISM IN THE LIVER

The turnover of glycogen in the liver is regulated through the same kind of mechanism seen in striated muscles. A protein kinase is activated by cyclic AMP, and it in turn phosphorylates glycogen synthase and a glycogen phosphorylase kinase; glycogen phosphorylase kinase then phosphorylates glycogen phosphorylase. However, the enzymes involved are different isozymes than those seen in the muscle, and are regulated by metabolites in different ways. In addition, the activating receptors for adenyl cyclase on the hepatic cell plasma membrane respond to different hormones. Let us first consider the endocrine effects.

Glucagon and Insulin

Secretion by Pancreas. The pancreas of higher animals is both a digestive organ that elaborates enzymes to digest food, and an endocrine organ that secretes hormones into the blood. The pancreas contains nests of cells known as the **islets of Langerhans,** which play a major role in regulating metabolism by secreting two hormones, insulin and glucagon. We have already encountered insulin, which consists of two peptide chains linked by disulfide bonds, as an example of modification of a peptide after its synthesis (p. 49); the cells forming insulin are known as beta cells. Glucagon is also

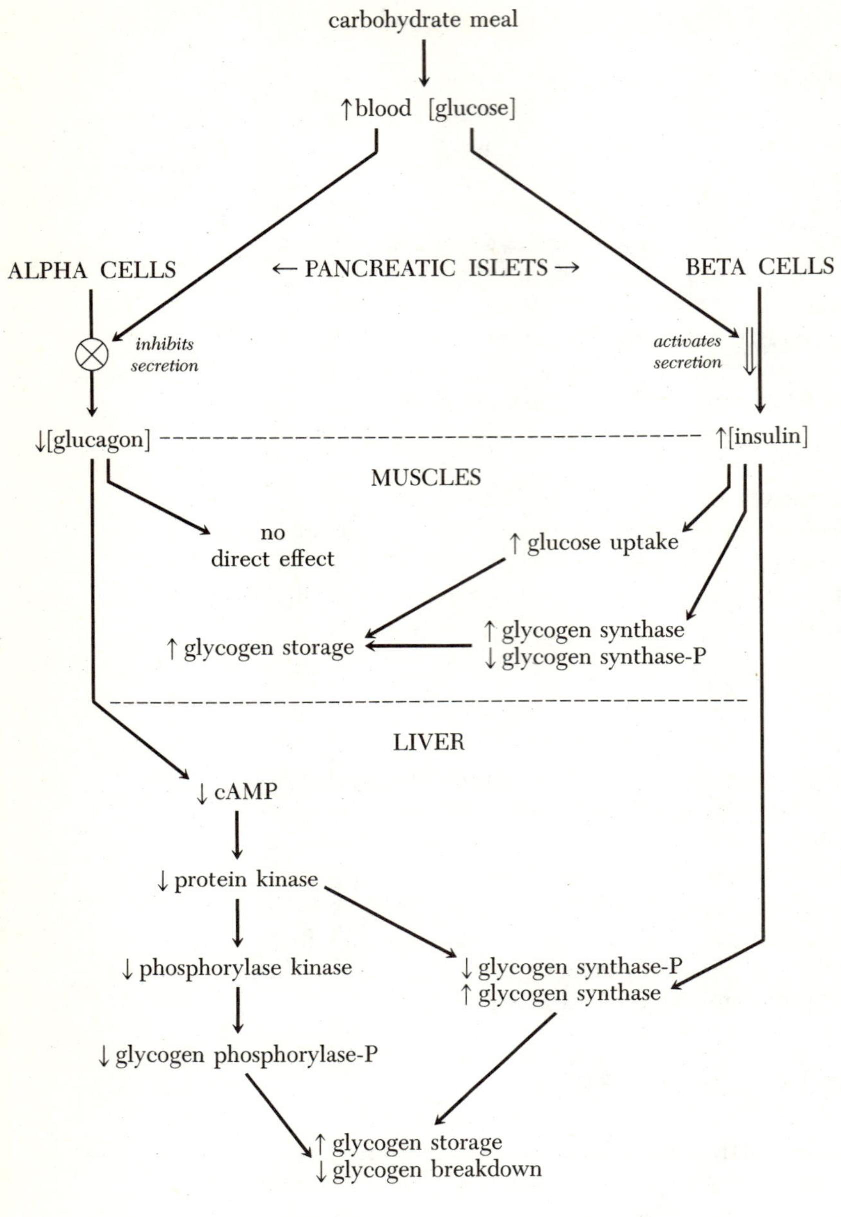

Figure 19-9 The regulation of glucose metabolism by secretion of glucagon or insulin. An increased supply of glucose causes decreased secretion of glucagon and increased secretion of insulin. The increased supply of insulin promotes uptake of glucose and storage of glycogen in the liver and muscles. The decreased supply of glucagon results in less active adenyl cyclase in the liver, with declining activities of the regulated protein kinase and phosphorylase kinase, so as to inhibit mobilization of liver glycogen. When the glucose supply is low, the reverse occurs, and the high glucagon activates adenyl cyclase in the liver, and promotes the breakdown of glycogen to replenish the blood glucose supply.

a peptide, but with only some 29 residues in the known examples, and it is secreted by different cells in the islets, the alpha cells.

These hormones have opposing effects on glucose metabolism. The alpha cells are stimulated to release glucagon when the blood glucose concentration falls, and glucagon activates the adenyl cyclase in liver to cause an increased rate of degradation of glycogen. The glucose 6-phosphate thus produced from liver glycogen is hydrolyzed by glucose 6-phosphatase to release free glucose for transport to the peripheral tissues. Glucagon has no effect on the adenyl cyclase of muscles; it does not control the utilization of glucose, but rather its production by the liver.

Insulin, on the other hand, promotes the storage of glucose in both liver and the skeletal muscles. It does so in the muscles by permitting more rapid transport of glucose, but it also augments the maintenance of glycogen synthase in its active free form in both the muscles and the liver. The mechanism of these effects is unknown. Some think it does so by activating the phosphodiesterase that attacks cyclic AMP. Others invoke some unknown "second messenger," comparable to cyclic AMP, that in some way makes the protein kinase less active. The 50th anniversary of the announcement of the discovery of insulin has now passed, and we still don't know how the hormone works. However, we can say positively that insulin promotes the storage of glycogen in both the muscles and the liver. The beta cells are stimulated to secrete insulin when the blood glucose concentration rises, and the insulin causes the excess glucose to be laid down as glycogen. In general, insulin secretion rises when the secretion of glucagon falls and vice versa (Fig. 19–9).

Metabolite Regulation

Perhaps the most important modulation of enzyme activity in the liver is due to a combination of glycogen phosphorylase-P with glucose (Fig. 19–10). The combination is enzymatically inactive, which means that elevated glucose concentration will prevent the breakdown of liver glycogen to form more glucose. In addition, the glucose–phosphorylase-P complex is a better substrate for glycogen phosphorylase phosphatase than is phosphorylase-P alone, so the presence of glucose accelerates the conversion of glycogen phosphorylase to its less active free form.

The resultant loss of glycogen phosphorylase-P not only slows down the degradation of glycogen, but it also accelerates synthesis in the liver, because glycogen phosphorylase-P is an inhibitor of glycogen synthase-P phosphatase!

Isn't this getting to be a bag of worms! The active form of glycogen phosphorylase, the P-form, inhibits the conversion of the inactive form of glycogen synthase, which is also the P-form, to its active free state. Glucose enables the formation of the active free state of glycogen synthase by accelerating the removal of the active P-form of glycogen phosphorylase.

SUMMARY OF GLUCOSE HOMEOSTASIS

Let us pull all of this together by recapitulating the events that occur when the blood glucose concentration rises and falls.

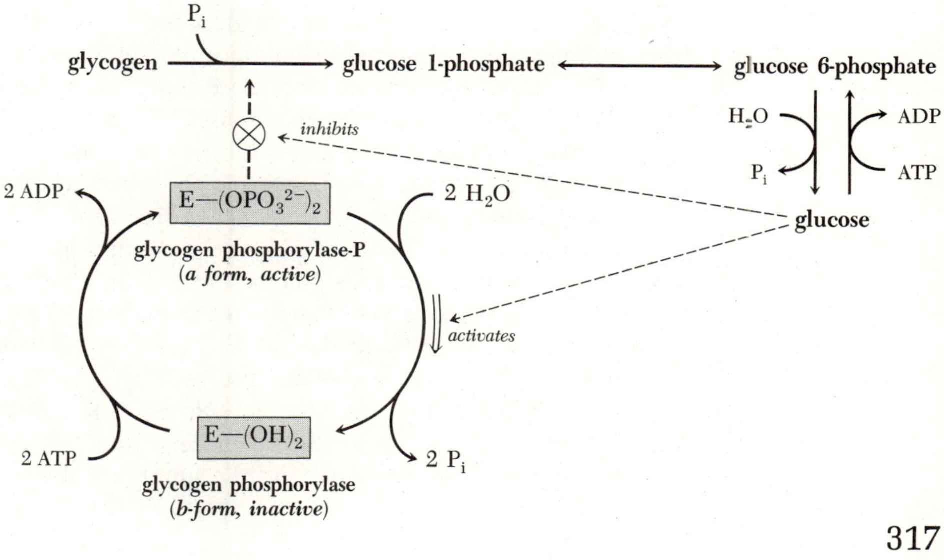

Figure 19–10 The glucose concentration has a direct effect on the mobilization of liver glycogen. High concentrations inhibit glycogen phosphorylase and activate the dephosphorylation of the enzyme to its inactive form.

Excess Glucose

We eat and the blood glucose concentration rises. There are three important direct results:

1. The pancreatic islets put out less glucagon and more insulin. Less glucagon means less cyclic AMP formed in the liver, and less active protein kinase. With less active protein kinase, there is less formation of active glycogen phosphorylase, and of inactive glycogen synthase. More insulin also results in more active glycogen synthase in both the liver and the muscles and more rapid transport of glucose into the muscles.

2. Glucose combines with glycogen phosphorylase in the liver. This causes increased loss of active glycogen phosphorylase, and also promotes the formation of active glycogen synthase.

3. Increased blood glucose concentration results in the net formation of glucose 6-phosphate in the liver, since the liver glucokinase is not saturated with substrate, and therefore can respond to changes in blood glucose concentration.

All of these things taken together mean an elevation in blood glucose concentration is itself a sufficient signal to cause further storage of glucose as glycogen in both the liver and the muscles. We mentioned only the increased glycogen synthase activity in the muscles, but don't forget that this will cause increased removal of glucose 6-phosphate: glucose 6-P $\longleftrightarrow$ glucose 1-P $\longrightarrow$ UDP-glucose $\longrightarrow$ glycogen. Since glucose 6-phosphate is an inhibitor of its own formation by the hexokinase reaction (p. 226), its increased removal to form glycogen will also tend to promote increased uptake of glucose in the muscle.

The deposition of glycogen in the muscles will proceed only until a characteristic level is reached even if elevated concentrations of glucose persist. However, the liver will continue to store more glycogen, although at an increasingly slower rate. We shall see in the following chapters that more and more glucose is converted to fat for storage as the glycogen reserves begin to be filled.

Deprivation of Glucose

The blood concentration falls as more time elapses from the preceding meal. Here we have the opposite effects:

1. The pancreatic islets put out more glucagon and less insulin. More glucagon means more cyclic AMP formed in the liver, and a more active protein kinase. The protein kinase causes the conversion of glycogen synthase to its inactive phosphorylated form, and the conversion of glycogen phosphorylase to its active phosphorylated form.

2. The fall in the amount of glucose slows the hydrolysis of glycogen phosphorylase-P in the liver because phosphorylase-P without glucose is a poorer substrate for phosphorylase-P phosphatase than is the glucose complex of the phosphoprotein. The resultant higher concentration of glycogen phosphorylase-P also inhibits the conversion of inactive glycogen synthase-P to its active free form.

3. The low concentration of glucose results in a low rate of the liver glucokinase reaction, so that the liver adds glucose to the blood, rather than removing it.

What are the results? The changes in enzyme activity in the liver stop the formation of glycogen and accelerate its degradation. The resultant rise in the concentration of glucose 6-phosphate will accelerate the hydrolysis of this compound to form free glucose, which will diffuse into the blood to prevent a further drop in concentration. The maintenance of the blood glucose concentration will enable the brain to continue using this fuel at its normal rate, and the supply for this purpose is conserved by the simultaneous slowing of glucose uptake and of glycogen formation in the muscles, owing to the declining insulin levels.

CONTROL OF STARCH SYNTHESIS IN PLANTS

Much less is known about the mechanisms of regulation of starch turnover in plants than is known about glycogen metabolism in animals. It may be that there is less to be known—plants appear to get through their days in a much less frantic fashion, and they may not have intricate mechanisms for controlling the rate of storage and recall of glucosyl residues. We ought not count on this, however, and it may well be that we know less because plant metabolism has been subjected to less intensive investigation, and also because the relative slowness of plant metabolism and circulation makes it more difficult to study the mechanisms of regulation.

One thing does seem clear—the major site of regulation of starch synthesis in chloroplasts appears to be ADP-glucose pyrophosphorylase, the enzyme forming ADP-glucose. This means that plants, unlike animals, regulate the formation of the donor of glucosyl residues for extending the amylose chains, rather than the transfer itself of glucosyl residues. (Animals may control the later step because UDP-glucose, their glucosyl donor, is used as a source of other kinds of polysaccharides and sugar derivatives, as well as glycogen; regulating UDP-glucose formation would regulate the formation of all of these, rather than specifically controlling glycogen formation.)

The mode of this regulation is simple. The first major product of CO_2 fixation, 3-phosphoglycerate, is used to activate the ADP-glucose pyrophosphorylase, thereby promoting the formation of starch (Fig. 19–11). If 3-phosphoglycerate is being drained off elsewhere as fast as it is formed from CO_2, to supply the Embden-Meyerhof pathway for example, no starch will be stored to compete with these other demands. As the compound accumulates, its rising concentration accelerates its own ultimate storage as starch. Beyond all this, the fructose phosphates appear to serve as weaker, secondary

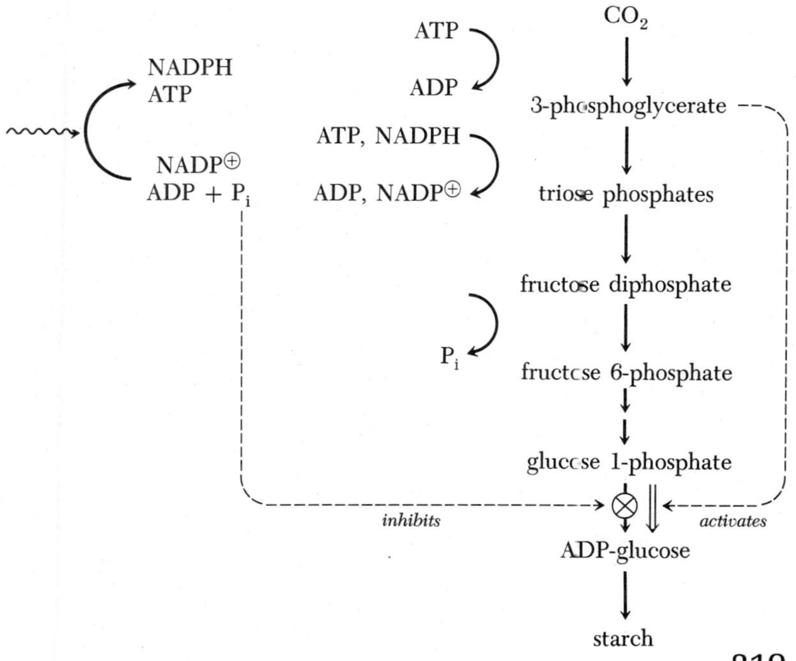

Figure 19–11 The synthesis of starch in plants is apparently regulated through metabolite inhibition and activation of the formation of ADP-glucose.

activators, so any accumulation of the hexose phosphates will also tend to accelerate starch storage.

The ADP-glucose pyrophosphorylase is also inhibited by P_i, and this presumably serves as an additional means of shutting off fuel storage when there is an inadequate supply of ATP; the less the amount of phosphorylation of adenine nucleotides, the greater the amount of inorganic phosphate.

FURTHER READING

See the general references at the end of Chapter 18, in addition to the following:

E. H. Fischer, L. M. G. Heilmeyer, Jr., and R. H. Haschke, Phosphorylase and the control of glycogen degradation, Curr. Topics Cell Regul., 4:211 (1971).

C. Villar-Palasi, J. Larner, and L. C. Shen, Glycogen metabolism and the mechanism of action of cyclic AMP, Ann. N.Y. Acad. Sci., 185:74 (1971).

J. P. Jost and H. V. Rickenberg, Cyclic AMP, Ann. Rev. Biochem., 40:741 (1971). 1971 was a vintage year for reviews on regulation of glycogen metabolism, but even these occasionally assume prior knowledge.

QUESTIONS

1. If a child is born with a lack of protein kinase in its liver, would you expect it to show unusual changes in the amount of glycogen in its liver? Explain.
2. How does a change in glucose concentration affect the activity of enzymes in glycogen metabolism through direct effects on the target cell and through indirect effects resulting from changes in hormone secretion?
3. How is glycogen metabolism matched to muscular activity? Consider advance mobilization, activation of contraction, and adjustment to the demand for high-energy phosphate.
4. Explain how less than 1 milligram of adrenaline can cause massive changes in glycogen metabolism in a human weighing 70 kilograms.

CHAPTER 20

STORAGE OF FATTY ACIDS: FORMATION OF THE CARBON CHAIN

THE CONCEPTS

The combination of fatty acid residues with glycerol to form triglycerides is the major means of storing fuel in many animals. The triglycerides are deposited as fat droplets, mainly in muscle and liver cells in lower vertebrates, but in a specialized adipose tissue in the higher animals. The fatty acids may be derived from dietary fats or they may be made from excess glucose.

The formation of fatty acids involves the condensation of eight acetyl groups and reductions by NADPH to create a molecule of palmitate (16:0). Other fatty acids are created from palmitate by addition of more acetyl groups and by creation of double bonds in the chain.

Fatty acids are synthesized in the form of acyl groups attached to an acyl carrier peptide, which is a separate protein in many protists, but is a part of a fatty acid synthase complex in animals. The acyl groups are bound to sulfhydryl groups contained in phosphopantetheine residues.

In order to create a favorable equilibrium for condensation, acetyl groups are first carboxylated to form malonyl coenzyme A at the expense of ATP. A head-to-tail condensation of acetyl groups then occurs by displacing the newly attached CO_2 from the malonyl group by the methyl carbon of another acetyl group. The energy of loss of the carboxyl group is thus driving the condensation, which forms an acetoacetyl group.

The acetoacetyl group is reduced to a butyryl group on the enzyme by two reactions with NADPH in which the equilibrium permits formation of the saturated carbon chain.

The butyryl group is then used to displace CO_2 from another molecule of malonyl coenzyme A, forming a six-carbon chain, which is reduced to the six-carbon fatty acid residue. The process of addition of two carbon units by decarboxylation of malonyl coenzyme A, followed by reduction to a saturated chain, continues until the 16-carbon palmitoyl group has been constructed. Free palmitate is released as the product. Completed fatty acid chains may be further lengthened by use of malonyl coenzyme A in the endoplasmic reticulum and by use of acetyl coenzyme A in mitochondria.

Fatty acids may also be modified by oxidation to form double bonds. The desaturases are examples of mixed function oxidases; they use NADH to half-reduce O_2, activating it so that it will attack an acyl coenzyme A and form a double bond. (Mixed function oxidases are not used to generate ATP.) Plants create double bonds at three-carbon intervals throughout the length of the chain, but animals can add double bonds only at three-carbon intervals beginning at C-9 and proceeding toward C-1. Animals therefore can synthesize residues of oleic acid (18:1) by chain lengthening (16:0 $\longrightarrow$ 18:0) followed by oxidation, but they cannot synthesize residues of linoleic acid (18:2), which has a double bond at C-12 in addition to one at C-9.

A method of nomenclature for fatty acids has been invented to clarify the existence of families of fatty acids with related origins. The number of carbon atoms in the tail of a fatty acid after the last double bond is designated by a numeral following an ω. Thus, oleic acid is $18{:}1\omega9$ and linoleic acid is $18{:}2\omega6$. The advantage is that the ω number stays the same as the chain is lengthened, because lengthening occurs at the carboxyl end.

Fatty acid synthesis is regulated by controlling the carboxylation of acetyl coenzyme A. The carboxylase is activated by an accumulation of citrate, which is an indicator of a surfeit of fuel. The carboxylase is inhibited by an accumulation of its end-product, malonyl coenzyme

A. Desaturation of fatty acids is regulated in some unknown fashion to adjust the melting points of triglycerides so as to be somewhat below the environmental temperatures, thereby keeping the intracellular globules in a mobile state.

NATURE AND DISTRIBUTION OF FAT STORES

Fat is a fuel that is laid down for long-term storage in organisms with an ample supply of oxygen; glycogen and starch are fuels for short-term use, or for the maintenance of organisms in the presence of limited amounts of oxygen. The human epitomizes this dual usage; the ordinary adult has only enough glycogen to maintain activity for one day or less, but he can live from his fat for nearly a month. He is built for a daily routine in which he oxidizes glucose residues for energy immediately after meals, while maintaining his glycogen reserves and converting any excess glucose to fatty acids. As the time of the last meal recedes, more and more of his energy is obtained by oxidizing previously stored fatty acids. Even the overnight fast is sufficient to result in twice the amount of oxygen being used for the oxidation of fatty acids from fats as is used for the oxidation of glucose from glycogen.

The great advantage of fat as a stored fuel, which we shall discuss more fully in Chapter 22, is that it is light in weight, and the appearance of organisms with large stores evidently coincided with the development of ability to move over relatively long distances without an intake of food. Salmon and ducks are alike in building up large stores of fat before they begin their long migrations, but vertebrates of more fixed domicile, along with many insects, also can store fat for less dramatic exertion.

Location of Fat. Most people have a vague idea of the character of animal fat and give it an equally diffuse anatomical role. Let us take a moment to discuss the sites of deposition so that we can more fully appreciate the biochemistry of these tissues. Fat deposition began to be important with the evolution of vertebrates, and the liver was the initial site of deposition. Modern sharks frequently have massive livers containing cells loaded with triglycerides. With the appearance of bony fish, fat began to be deposited to a greater extent in and around the muscle fibers, creating the oily flesh we see in salmon and sardines. Insects went on another pathway, and created a multi-purpose organ with many of the functions of the vertebrate liver, but which contains so much fat that it is known as the **fat body.** The advanced vertebrates, beginning with some fish, developed a discrete **adipose tissue** by modifying the same kind of cells from which the blood cells are derived. These **adipocytes** contain globules of triglyceride that may constitute 90 per cent or more of the mass of the cell.

Adipose tissue appears relatively formless and is difficult to handle experimentally because of its high content of fat, but it is a well-organized tissue with a rich blood supply, nerve endings for stimulation, and an active metabolism appropriate for its important function as an internal larder. Adipose tissue can become the largest in the body, comprising half or more of the total mass of some individuals. Humans can become tubs of lard. Such people are objects of humor, disdain, or concern in our society, but in societies subject to famine they may be happily living on their own fat while burying the last of their formerly trim companions.

The distribution of adipose tissue differs from species to species; it is frequently especially prevalent under the skin, around deep blood vessels, and in the abdominal cavity.

Plants also store fat, especially in the tissues surrounding the embryos in seeds. The light weight of this kind of a fuel no doubt aids in the dispersal of many kinds of seeds, but fat is also the predominant stored fuel in large seeds, where its hydrophobic character may be of primary importance in protecting the embryo until time for development. In any event, we have seen that plant embryos have an advantage over animals—they can convert stored fatty acids to carbohydrate via the glyoxylate pathway.

THE ORIGIN OF FATTY ACIDS

Some of the fatty acids that are laid down in fat stores are obtained directly from the diet; this is becoming increasingly true of modern Americans, for whom the fats in the diet now represent the largest source of chemical potential. However, most animals other than carnivores still ingest far more carbohydrate than fat, and animals in general synthesize fatty acids from glucose for long-term storage. The synthesis of fatty acids will occupy our attention in this and the following chapter. Synthesis occurs in both the liver and the adipose tissue of the common experimental animals, but we do most of our conversion of glucose to fatty acids in the liver, although the products are stored in our adipose tissue.

The Overall Mechanism. The fatty acid chain is constructed by condensing acetyl groups obtained by transfer from acetyl coenzyme A. The conversion of acetyl groups to fatty acids is in a sense the reversal of the processes of oxidation of the fatty acids, in which electrons are removed for oxidative phosphorylation. Therefore, electrons must be added back in order to form the alkyl chains. Although the routes of oxidation and synthesis have some similarities, the processes are quite separate, both in mechanism and in physical location. We saw that the oxidation of fatty acids to acetyl groups for use as a fuel occurs in mitochondrial inner membranes; however, the synthesis of fatty acids from acetyl groups occurs in the cytosol. Now, the source of these acetyl groups is pyruvate derived from glucose by the Embden-Meyerhof pathway, which also occurs in the soluble cytoplasm, but the formation of the acetyl groups from pyruvate occurs in the mitochondria. Therefore, synthesis of fatty acids also involves the transport of acetyl groups from the mitochondria to the cytosol (Fig. 20–1). Finally, as the figure shows, electrons must be supplied in the form of NADPH in the cytosol for the reduction of acetyl groups to the fatty acid chain. The next chapter will be concerned with the supply of the necessary NADPH, and we shall see that the transport of the acetyl groups from the mitochondria to the cytosol is also tied in with this supply. For now, let us concentrate on the mechanism by which the chain is assembled.

Assembly of the Carbon Chain

Activation of Acetyl Groups by Carboxylation. The fatty acid chains are assembled by transfer of one acetyl group at a time from coenzyme A. The synthesis is driven by a carboxylation of acetyl coenzyme A at the expense of ATP, followed

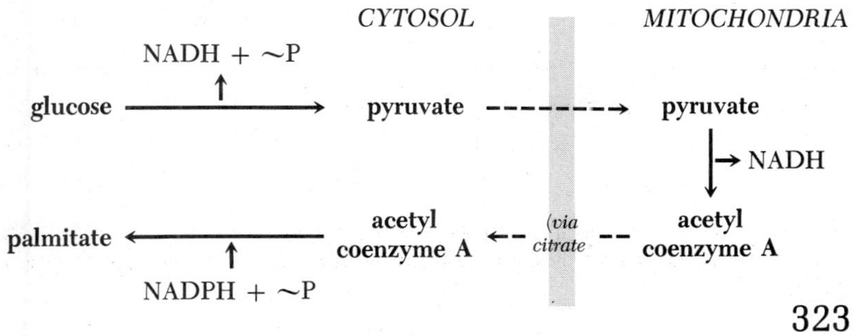

Figure 20–1 The conversion of glucose to fatty acids involves the formation of acetyl groups in mitochondria and their transport to the cytosol as citrate.

by a decarboxylation that drives what would otherwise be an unfavorable condensation reaction. We already saw in our discussion of fatty acid oxidation that the equilibrium for a simple cleavage of 3-ketoacyl compounds by coenzyme A favors the cleavage of the compounds, rather than their formation.

The initial carbons of what is to be a fatty acid are provided by the acetyl group of acetyl coenzyme A or the butyryl group of butyryl coenzyme A. The remainder of the carbons are supplied in the form of malonyl coenzyme A, which is made by carboxylation of acetyl coenzyme A in the cytosol:

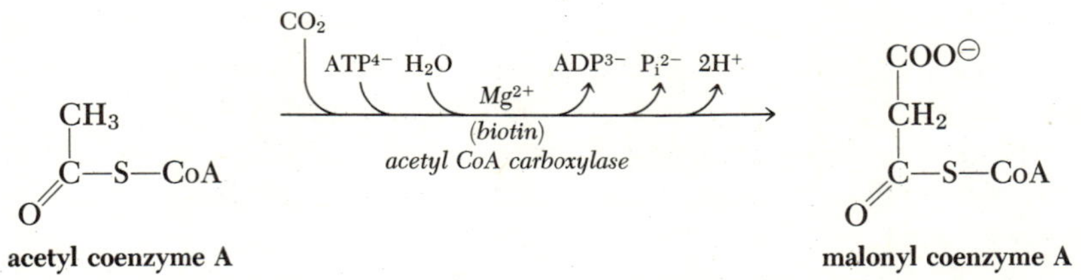

This is straightforward, with CO_2 activated by attachment to a **biotin** residue on the **acetyl CoA carboxylase,** using energy supplied by the hydrolysis of ATP. (Some bacteria have a small peptide that carries biotin for use in several carboxylation reactions, but biotin is bound directly to the specific peptide catalyzing carboxyl transfer in animals.)

Phosphopantetheinyl Groups as Acyl Carriers. During the construction of a new fatty acid chain, the growing acyl residues are attached to a peptide chain as thiol esters. The necessary sulfhydryl group is provided by a residue of phosphopantetheine, the same structure found in coenzyme A, but attached in this case to a seryl residue of the peptide (Fig. 20–2). This peptide is a separate small protein, the **acyl carrier protein,** in bacteria, but it is a part of a large enzyme complex, the **fatty acid synthase,** in eukaryotes. The phosphopantetheine residue serves the same acyl-carrying function in all of these organisms that coenzyme A does during fatty acid oxidation. The reactive part of the molecule is the same in either case, except that coenzyme A has phospho-

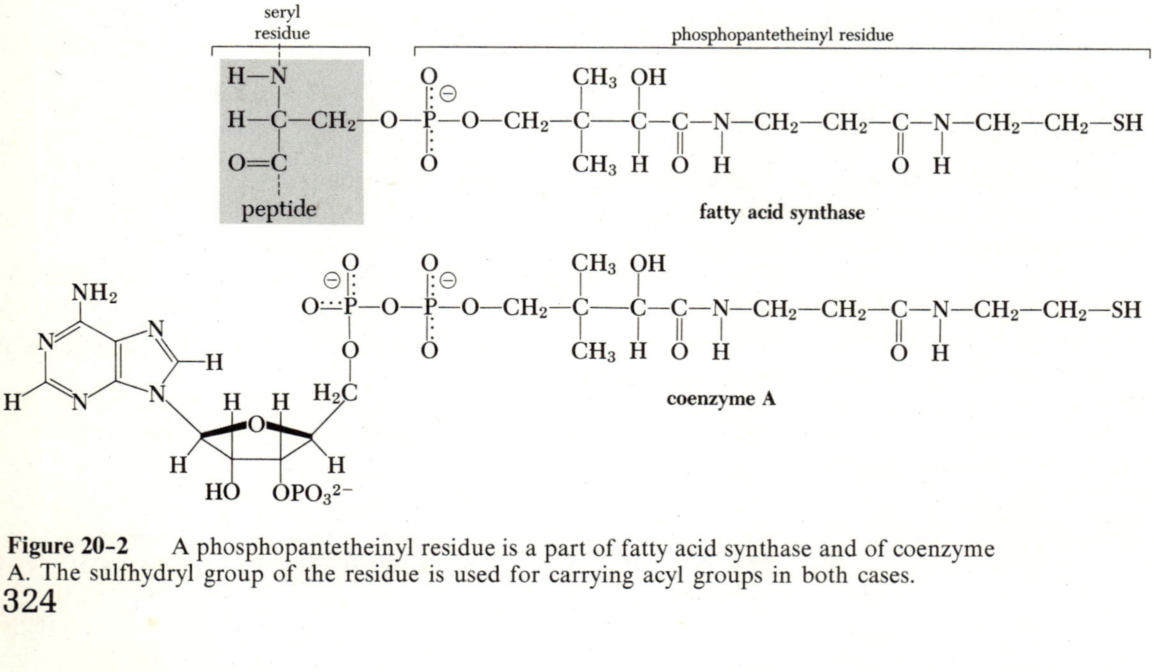

Figure 20–2 A phosphopantetheinyl residue is a part of fatty acid synthase and of coenzyme A. The sulfhydryl group of the residue is used for carrying acyl groups in both cases.

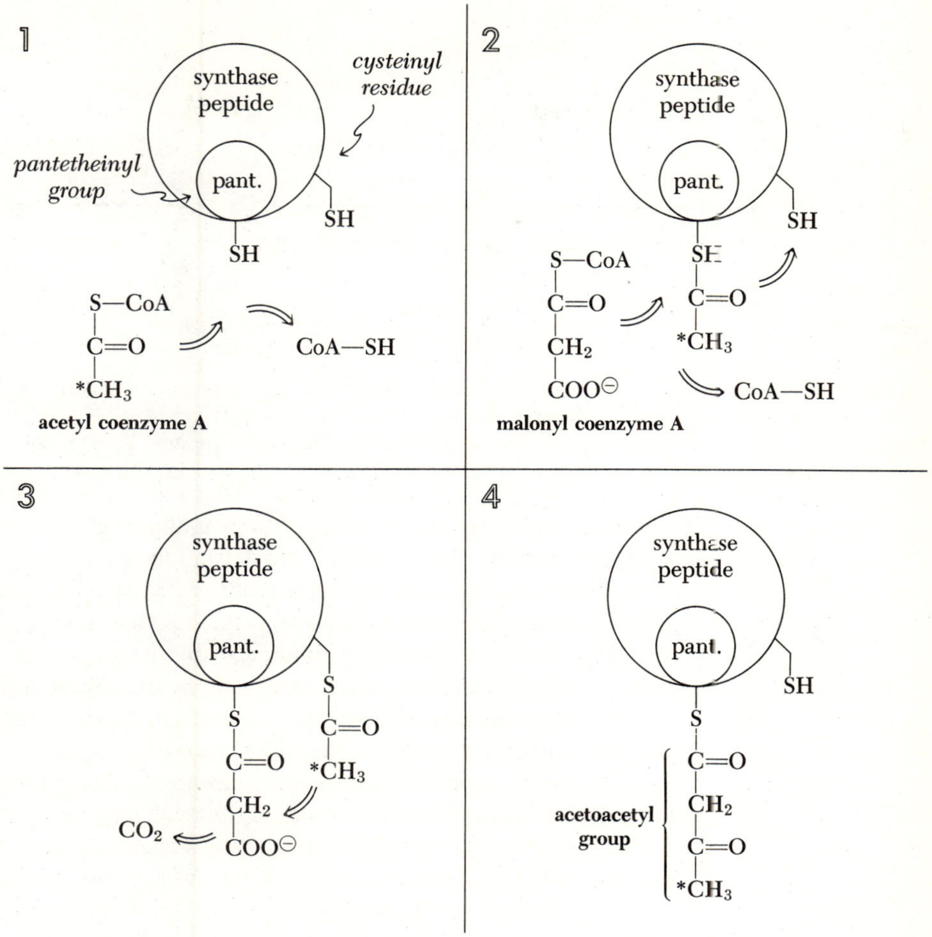

Figure 20-3 The chain-lengthening process in fatty acid synthesis. The figure shows the initial addition of 2-carbon units, but the same mechanism is involved for later additions.

1. A priming acetyl group is attached to the pantetheinyl group with release of coenzyme A.

2. The acetyl group moves to a cysteinyl residue, and its place is taken by a malonyl group.

3. The acetyl group condenses with the methylene carbon of the malonyl group. CO_2 is liberated.

4. The result is an acetoacetyl group attached to the pantetheinyl group on the enzyme.

pantetheine attached to a relatively small 3′,5′-*bis*phosphoadenosyl group and is therefore free to migrate from one enzyme to another.

The many individual steps in fatty acid synthesis, which we shall shortly examine, are catalyzed by separate proteins in at least some bacteria, but a large fatty acid synthase is responsible for all of them in eukaryotes, and it has not yet been possible to dissect the synthase complex into individual active peptides. We shall treat it as a unit, but it appears to consist of a large doughnut-shaped association in which the long phosphopantetheine chains sweep around the center to bring attached acyl groups into successive contact with the necessary catalytic sites.

The Condensations. Synthesis begins with either acetyl coenzyme A (bacteria, yeast, mammalian adipose tissue) or butyryl coenzyme A (mammalian liver, mammary glands). The end result is the same with either primer, so let us describe events beginning with acetyl coenzyme A. The first step is the transfer of an acetyl group from coenzyme A onto the phosphopantetheine residue attached to fatty acid synthase (Fig. 20-3). (This and the following transfers probably involve the intermediate formation of esters of a seryl group at the transferase active site.) The fatty acid synthase then makes use of another sulfhydryl group provided by a cysteine residue in its peptides. This group is used as a storage site at a fixed location for acetyl groups, contrasting with the mobile site on the phosphopantetheine residue. When the acetyl group is then moved onto the cysteinyl residue, a malonyl group is transferred onto the newly liberated phos-

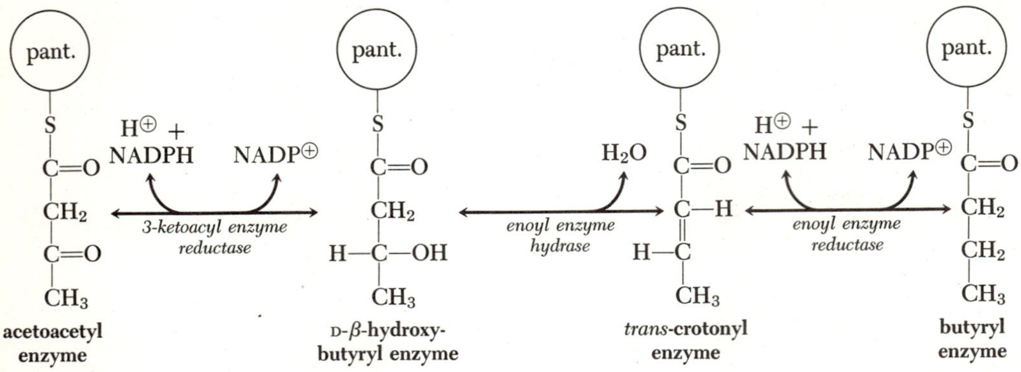

Figure 20–4 The reduction of 3-ketoacyl groups, in this case an acetoacetyl group, to saturated acyl groups during fatty acid synthesis resembles the reversal of fatty acid oxidation, except that NADPH is used as a donor of electrons for both reductions, and the acyl groups are attached to a phosphopantetheinyl group on a carrier peptide in the fatty acid synthase complex.

phopantetheinyl group. The acetyl and malonyl groups are now both attached to the synthase, and the stage is set for condensation. In effect, the acetyl group is transferred to displace CO_2 from the malonyl group, forming a carbon-to-carbon bond. The result is a four-carbon acetoacetyl group attached to phosphopantetheine on the enzyme.

The Reductions. The remainder of the transformation involves the reduction of the 3-keto compound to the saturated hydrocarbon chain in the reverse of the sort of route seen in fatty acid oxidation. The same principles that apply to reductions of acetoacetyl coenzyme A by clostridia also apply here.

Where the oxidative mechanism employs a flavoprotein for oxidation of the alkyl chain because the thermodynamics of the reaction requires this stronger oxidizing agent (p. 114), the reverse reaction requires a strong reducing agent, and a reduced nicotinamide nucleotide is used as the electron donor for both reductive steps (Fig. 20–4). The actual sequence of changes by which the acetoacetyl group is reduced is quite similar to a reversal of the steps in oxidation of fatty acids, except that the group remains attached to the phosphopantetheinyl residue on the fatty acid synthase. NADPH is used for both reductions in most organisms, in accord with the general principle that NADPH is maintained in a highly reduced form, and is used for syntheses.

The figure shows another distinctive feature of fatty acid synthesis. Synthesis involves the D-3-hydroxyacyl compound, which is dehydrated to the *trans*-enoyl derivative. The reaction is an exception to the usual interconversion of L and *trans* isomers.

Chain Growth. The product of the initial set of reductions is a butyryl phosphopantetheinyl group on the enzyme. Now, the butyryl group can be moved onto the storage cysteinyl group and replaced by an incoming malonyl group in the same way that an acetyl group was replaced in the initial steps of synthesis (Fig. 20–3). The butyryl group will then be transferred onto the methylene carbon of the malonyl group, displacing CO_2 and forming a carbon-to-carbon bond. The resultant 3-ketohexanoyl group will go through the same cycle of reductions by NADPH to form the saturated six-carbon hexanoyl group. This in turn can be displaced by a new malonyl group, and so on, making a growing fatty acid chain in which all but the terminal pair of carbons have passed through malonyl coenzyme A.

Chain Termination. The chain grows on the fatty acid synthase until seven pairs of carbon atoms have been added from malonyl coenzyme A onto the original pair from acetyl coenzyme A, thereby producing a 16-carbon palmitoyl residue. The final step is the release of the chain as free palmitate. It is not known how chain lengthening is limited to the 16-carbon saturated fatty acid, or how the residue is released from the protein.

In any event, the stoichiometry for the formation of palmitate from acetyl coenzyme A, allowing for the intermediate formation of seven moles of malonyl coenzyme A, becomes:

(1) 7 (acetyl-S-CoA) + 7 CO_2 + 7 ATP^{4-} + 7 H_2O ⟶
7 (malonyl-S-CoA)$^-$ + 7 ADP^{3-} + 7 P_i^{2-} + 14 H^+

(2) (acetyl-S-CoA) + 7 (malonyl-S-CoA)$^-$ + 14 NADPH + 20 H^+ ⟶
(palmitate)$^-$ + 7 CO_2 + 14 $NADP^+$ + 8 CoA-SH + 6 H_2O

SUM: (3) 8 (acetyl-S-CoA) + 7 ATP^{4-} + 14 NADPH + 6 H^+ + H_2O ⟶
(palmitate)$^-$ + 7 ADP^{3-} + 7 P_i^{2-} + CoA-SH + 14 $NADP^+$

MODIFICATION OF THE FATTY ACID CHAIN

Both the triglycerides and the membrane lipids of cells contain residues of a variety of fatty acids. These residues are created for the most part by elongating the palmitoyl carbon chain, and by introducing double bonds. The **oleoyl** group is the most abundant fatty acid residue in mammalian fat, and it is formed from palmitate by the addition of two carbons and the creation of one double bond. Animals have a much smaller proportion of polyunsaturated fatty acids obtained from the diet, or of modifications of these acids that they cannot make. Let us see how changes, both of newly synthesized palmitate and of dietary fatty acids, are made.

Chain Elongation

Elongation on Endoplasmic Reticulum. Palmitate is converted to palmitoyl coenzyme A, and the chain is then elongated by the addition of one or more acetyl groups from malonyl coenzyme A. The sequence of reaction is exactly the same as we outlined for the action of fatty acid synthase (Fig. 20–5), except that the elongation enzymes are located on the endoplasmic reticulum. Two carbon units can be added to various saturated or unsaturated fatty acids by this system until the total length of the chain reaches 24 carbon atoms. However, the specificity is such that saturated chains are most easily elongated if they contain 16, or fewer, carbon atoms, so the principal saturated product is stearoyl coenzyme A (18:0). Increasing the number of double bonds makes it easier to lengthen the chain, so the residues with 24 carbon atoms are mainly polyunsaturated.

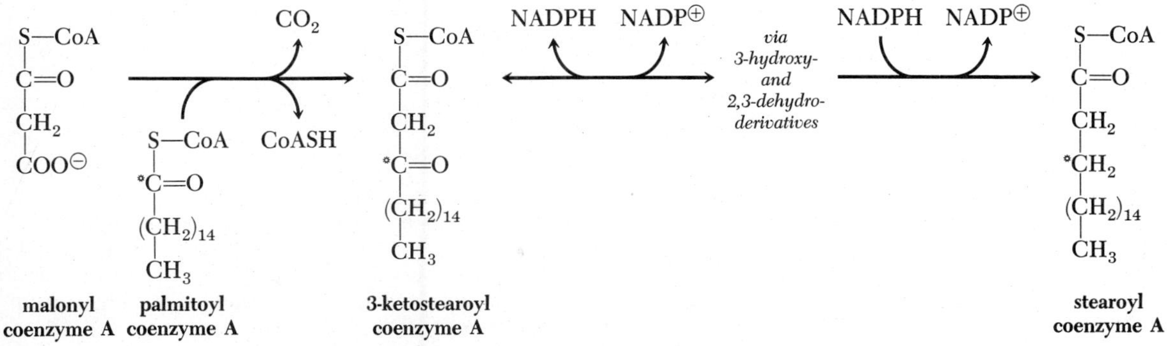

Figure 20–5 The elongation of fatty acids, such as the conversion of palmitoyl groups to stearoyl groups, proceeds by steps similar to those occurring during fatty acid synthesis, except that different enzymes are involved, which use the coenzyme A derivatives as substrates.

Elongation in Mitochondria. There is also a chain elongation system in mitochondria, which presumably produces the fatty acid residues necessary for the formation of structural lipids in that organelle. The lower $[NAD^+]/[NADH]$ ratio in the mitochondria makes it possible to use some of the enzymes of fatty acid oxidation for chain elongation. That is, enough 3-hydroxyacyl coenzyme A remains at equilibrium with 3-ketoacyl coenzyme A to provide significant concentrations of enoyl CoA, which is the substrate for the one additional enzyme that is required, an NADH-coupled enoyl coenzyme A reductase. This sequence is sufficient to provide the relatively small amounts of acyl residues required for making structural lipids.

Chain Desaturation

Plants can introduce double bonds at any three-carbon interval throughout the length of a fatty acid residue. Animals have taken advantage of this almost unfailing supply by dropping their ability to introduce double bonds beyond the C-10 position. Animals therefore have no problem in making oleoyl coenzyme A from stearoyl coenzyme A (Fig. 20–6), or in putting an additional double bond toward the carbonyl group to make $\Delta^{6,9}$-octadecadienoyl coenzyme A, but they cannot make linoleoyl coenzyme A ($\Delta^{9,12}$-octadecadienoyl coenzyme A).

Mixed-Function Oxidases. Both plants and animals introduce double bonds through the action of enzymes belonging to the class of mixed-function oxidases. These are enzymes that simultaneously oxidize two substrates, one of which is usually a

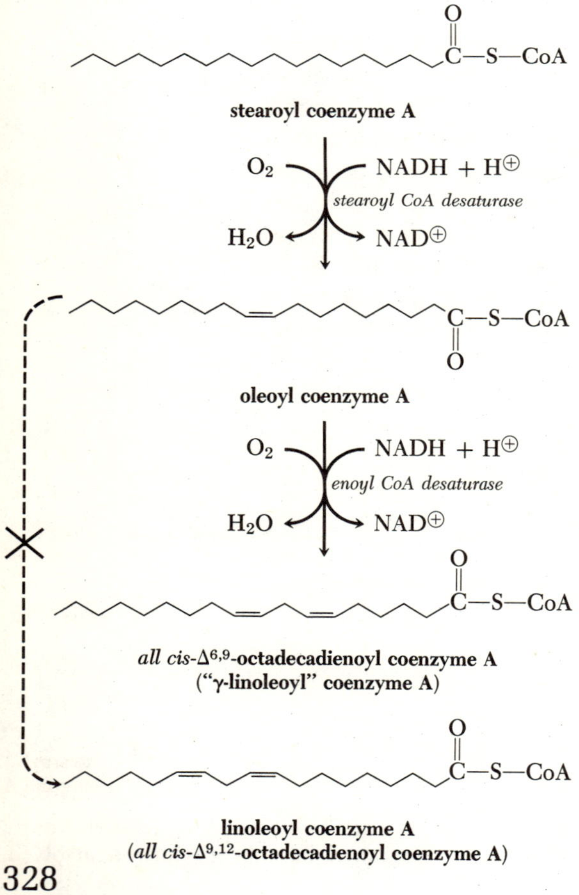

Figure 20–6 Double bonds can be introduced into coenzyme A esters of fatty acids by oxidation at C-9 and at successive 3-carbon intervals toward the carboxyl end. The mammalian enzyme cannot introduce double bonds beyond C-9, and therefore cannot form linoleate.

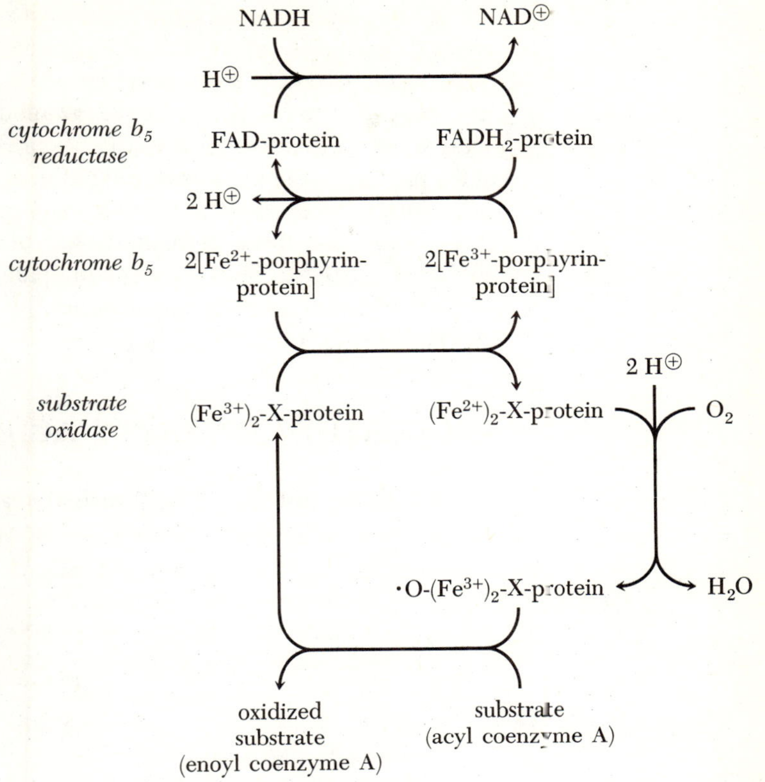

Figure 20–7 The desaturation of acyl coenzyme A derivatives involves an electron transport system in the endoplasmic reticulum, which utilizes electrons from NADH to activate O_2 by partial reduction for attack on the substrate. Enzymes that use a reduced substrate or coenzyme to activate oxygen so that it will oxidize a second substrate are said to be mixed function oxidases. This particular oxidase system utilizes an uncharacterized electron carrier designated X.

reduced coenzyme that serves to "activate" molecular oxygen for attack on the second substrate. We shall see many examples in our later discussions, because the mixed-function oxidases are frequently employed to modify structural components, hormones, and other compounds involved in the function of the cell, but which are outside of the mainstream of fuel metabolism.

Electron Flow. The exact route of electron flow is not known for either the plant or the animal **acyl CoA desaturase.** The best known plant system requires NADPH, ferredoxin, and molecular oxygen to convert stearoyl acyl carrier protein to oleoyl acyl carrier protein; the NADPH is simultaneously oxidized to NADP and the oxygen is reduced to water. In other words, acyl groups are both formed and modified while attached to the separate acyl carrier protein in these organisms.

The acyl CoA desaturases of animal tissues are found in the endoplasmic reticulum. Electron transfer in the endoplasmic reticulum is used only for modification of substrates; there is no associated phosphorylation or other means of capturing the released energy. In general, electrons are transferred from NADH or NADPH to a special cytochrome, either cytochrome b_5 or cytochrome P-450, and the reduced cytochrome in some way contributes electrons for activation of molecular oxygen. The acyl coenzyme A desaturases employ NADH and cytochrome b_5 (Fig. 20–7). As the figure shows, some uncharacterized intermediate is also involved in these transfers.

Families of Fatty Acids. Since animals introduce double bonds into fatty acids at regular three-carbon intervals, proceeding toward the carbonyl end, lipid chemists have found it convenient to invent a new way of designating unsaturated fatty acids in which the number of carbons and the number of double bonds are stated in the usual way (18:1 for oleic acid, for example) followed by the Greek letter ω and the number of carbon atoms in the hydrocarbon tail beyond the last double bond. Thus, oleic acid is 18:1ω9, linoleic acid is 18:2ω6, and linolenic acid is 18:3ω3.

The value of this system is seen when tracing the origin of longer chain polyunsaturated acids. Since animals cannot introduce double bonds beyond the 9-10 position of palmitoyl CoA, forming 16:1ω7, any fatty acid with a terminal number less than ω7 must have originated by modifying a dietary fatty acid of plant origin. Thus, dietary linoleate (18:2ω6) can be converted to **arachidonate,** 20:4ω6, the precursor of the prostaglandin hormones, but palmitate cannot (Fig. 20–8). The closest the animals can come is to begin with palmitoleoyl coenzyme A (16:1ω7) and successively add carbons and desaturate to create 20:4ω7, or to begin with oleoyl coenzyme A and create 20:4ω9 (Fig. 20–9). (The pathway from palmitoyl CoA creates residues of **vaccenic acid,** 18:1ω7, which is a common constituent of animal fats, although not as abundant as oleoyl residues, 18:1ω9.)

REGULATION OF FATTY ACID SYNTHESIS

Chain Synthesis. The principal regulation over fatty acid synthesis involves acetyl CoA carboxylase, because the conversion of acetyl coenzyme A to malonyl

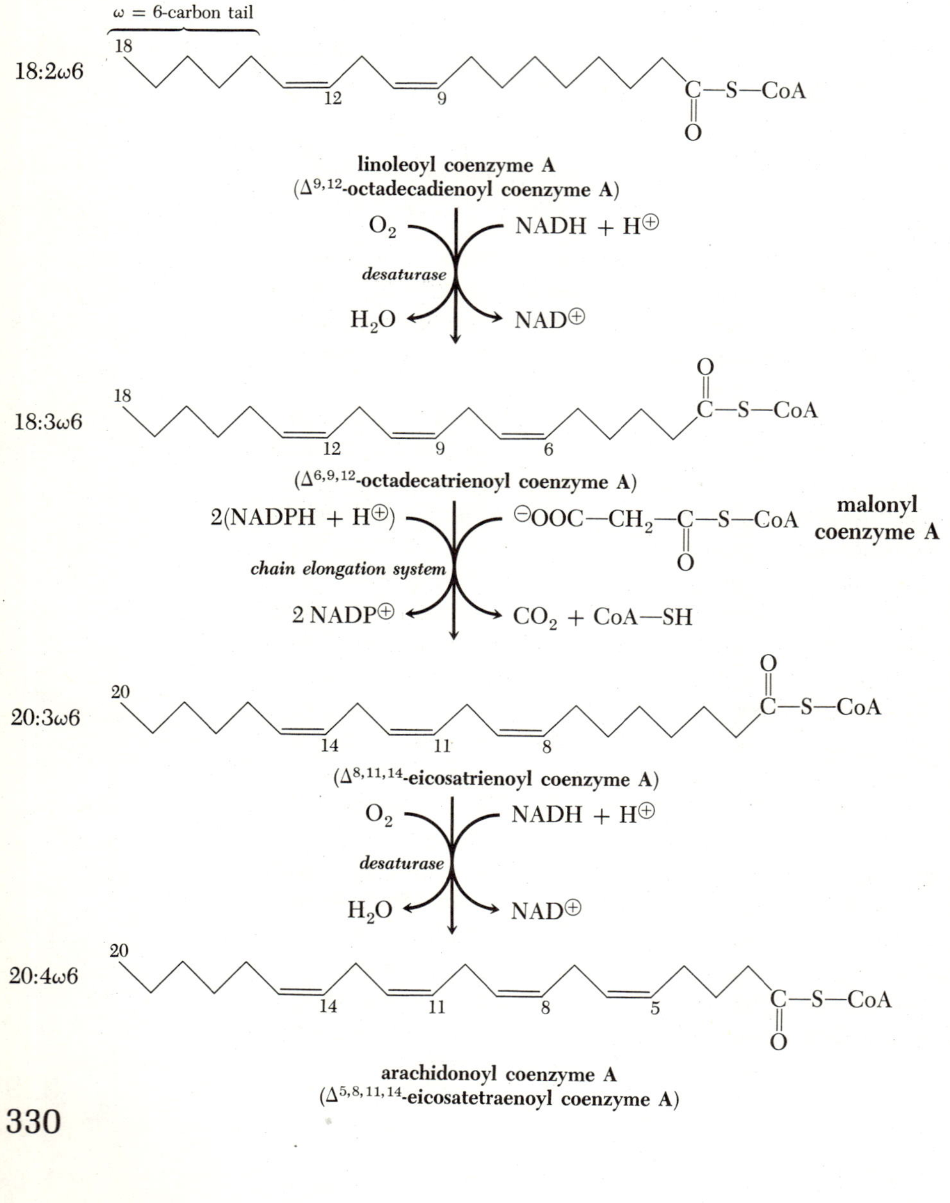

Figure 20–8 The synthesis of arachidonyl coenzyme A from linoleoyl coenzyme A involves a combination of chain lengthening and further desaturation toward C-1. The ω-nomenclature designates the number of carbons from the methyl tail to the nearest double bond; it is valuable because the ω-number does not change when unsaturated fatty acids are modified by the mechanisms shown here.

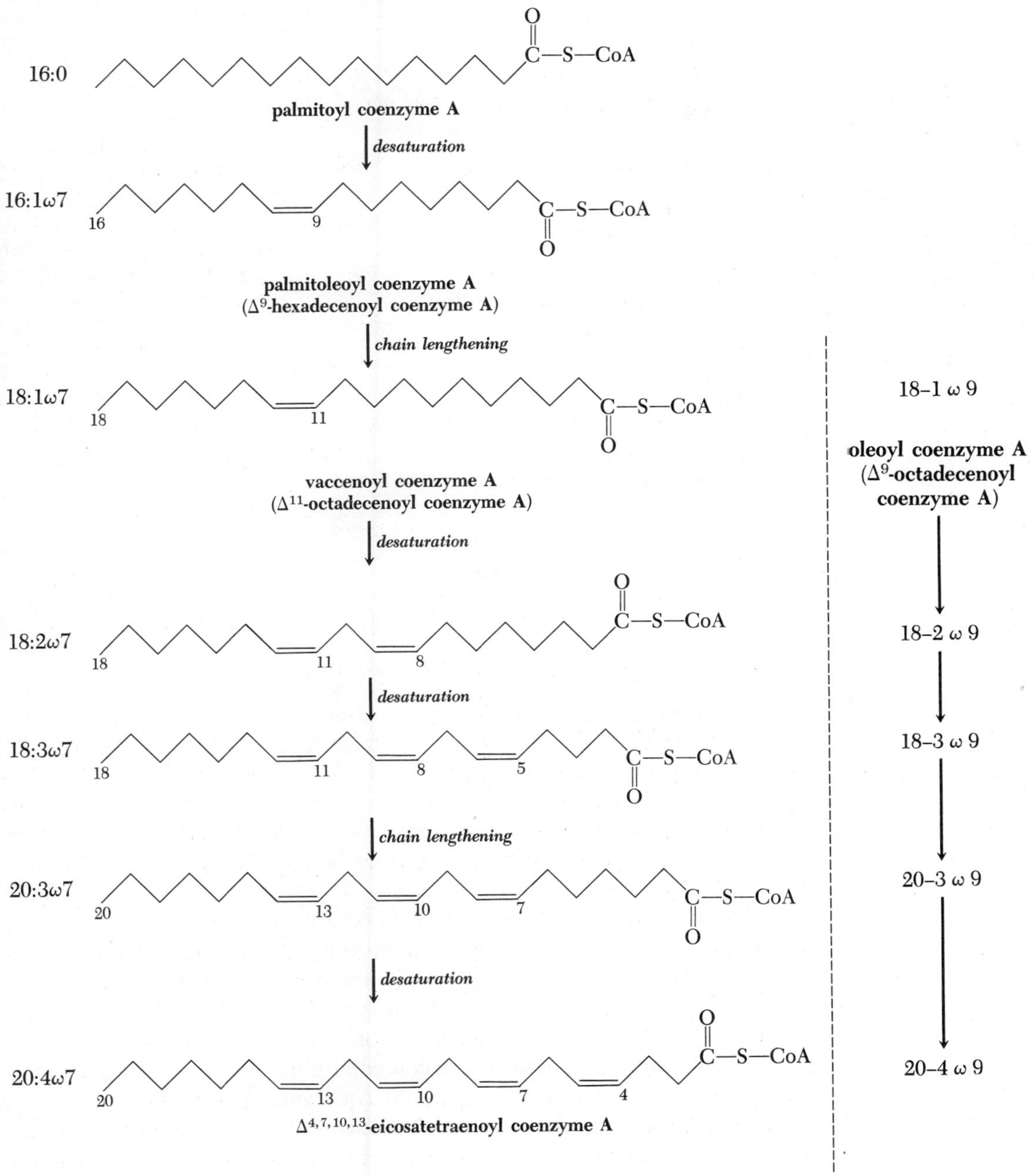

Figure 20-9 When the diet lacks ω-6 fatty acids, ω-7 substitutes will be synthesized in increased amounts for incorporation into membrane lipids.

coenzyme A commits the carbon atoms to the formation of fatty acids or related compounds. This enzyme has a nearly absolute requirement for citrate (or isocitrate) as an activator. The binding of citrate appears to change the conformation so as to bring the biotinyl prosthetic group into effective proximity to the substrate. (The conformational change also results in a striking association of enzyme molecules into long threads, but the fundamental significance, if any, of this association is obscure.)

The point is that there must be a sufficient supply of both acetyl coenzyme A and of oxaloacetate to raise the citrate level, if fatty acid synthesis is to proceed. An active

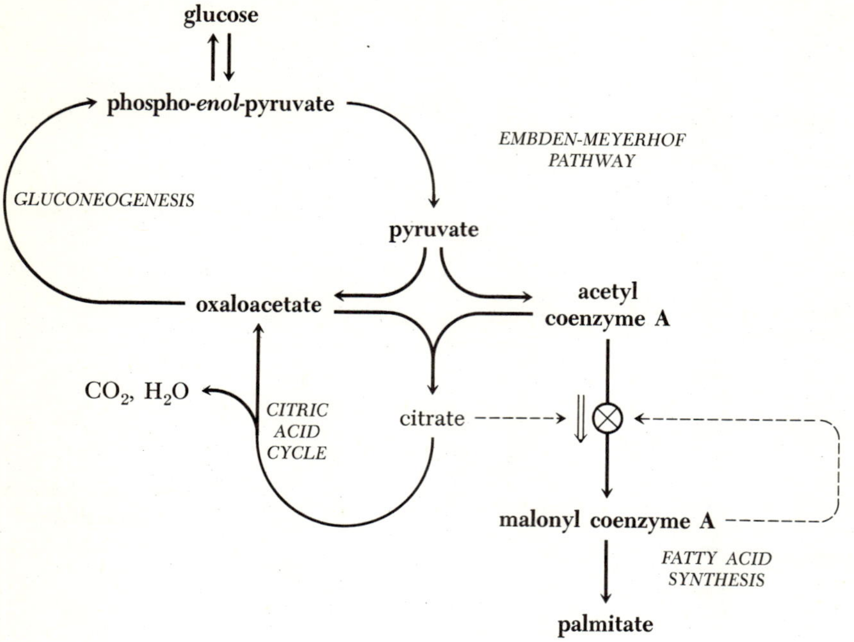

Figure 20-10 Acetyl groups are removed for fatty acid synthesis only when there is an accumulation of citrate to activate acetyl CoA carboxylase. Fatty acids are not synthesized when oxaloacetate is being drained for gluconeogenesis, or acetyl groups are being oxidized to CO_2 and H_2O at a rapid rate by the citric acid cycle. Fat synthesis is therefore truly a device for storing excess fuel. Also, wasteful accumulation of malonyl coenzyme A is prevented by its inhibition of its own formation.

citric acid cycle, a lack of ample supply of pyruvate as a precursor of acetyl coenzyme A, or a depletion of oxaloacetate for gluconeogenesis would stop the carboxylation of acetyl coenzyme A, and therefore stop fatty acid synthesis (Fig. 20–10).

The acetyl coenzyme A carboxylase is also inhibited by an accumulation of malonyl coenzyme A, the end-product of its reaction, and it is reasonable to expect some means of preventing malonyl coenzyme A from being formed at a rate faster than it can be handled by the fatty acid synthase.

Desaturation. The mechanism of control of the rate of introduction of double bonds into the fatty acid chains is unknown, but the effects are clear. More double bonds appear in the stored triglycerides and in the structural lipids when the environmental temperature falls. Since double bonds lower the melting point, this provides a mechanism to prevent crystallization of the lipids in the tissue.

Furthermore, polyunsaturated compounds of the ω7 and ω9 series—those that can be completely synthesized from acetyl coenzyme A—are not formed if there is an adequate dietary supply of linoleate and linolenate, or some other ω6 and ω3 precursors. These essential fatty acids will be preferentially used for the construction of structural lipids when they are available; when they are not, more of the ersatz synthetic substitutes will be formed.

FURTHER READING

J. J. Volpe and P. R. Vagelos, Saturated fatty acid biosynthesis and its regulation, Ann. Rev. Biochem., 42:21 (1973). Review by experts on bacterial enzymes.

F. Lynen, The role of biotin-dependent carboxylations in biosynthetic reactions, Biochem. J., 102:381 (1967). A lucid exposition by an expert on eukaryotic synthesis.

S. L. Wakil and E. M. Barnes, Jr., Fatty acid metabolism, 185:57 in M. Florkin and E. H. Stotz, eds., Comprehensive biochemistry (Elsevier, 1971).

QUESTIONS

1. The physical location of fat stores is in itself an indication that they are geared for use in slower, steady work rather than in rapid bursts of maximum effort. Why?
2. What are the differences between the routes by which a molecule of acetoacetyl coenzyme A is converted to two acetyl coenzyme A molecules during fatty acid oxidation and by which two acetyl coenzyme A molecules are converted to an acetoacetyl group during fatty acid synthesis?
3. If the acyl carrier during fatty acid synthesis is described as a phosphopantetheinyl peptide, what is the corresponding description of the acyl carrier used during fatty acid oxidation? The formation of both by animals depends upon the presence of what vitamin?
4. What resemblance is there between the routes for converting pyruvate to phospho-*enol*-pyruvate during gluconeogenesis and for converting two acetyl groups to an acetoacetyl group during fatty acid synthesis?
5. Suggest a reason why it would not be advantageous to an organism to carry out gluconeogenesis and fatty acid synthesis simultaneously, and explain why regulation of fatty acid synthesis by citrate concentration may aid in preventing this from happening.
6. Explain the purpose of a mixed-function oxidase, since it consumes oxygen and NADH (or NADPH) without generating high-energy phosphate.
7. Draw structural formulas for a 20:4ω6 fatty acid and explain why it probably can be made by animals from dietary fats containing linoleate, but not by synthesis from glucose.
8. Animals can synthesize ω7 fatty acids. How? (Hint: The same desaturase that attacks stearoyl coenzyme A will also attack palmitoyl coenzyme A.)

CHAPTER 21

THE SUPPLY OF ELECTRONS FOR FATTY ACID SYNTHESIS

THE CONCEPTS

The NADPH necessary for reducing acetyl groups to fatty acids is obtained from two principal sources; one is the concerted action of a pair of malate dehydrogenases that effect a transfer of electrons from NADH to NADP, and the other is the pentose phosphate pathway.

The cytosol of cells synthesizing fatty acids contains an NADP-coupled malate dehydrogenase that causes an oxidative decarboxylation of malate to pyruvate. The cytosol also contains the familiar NAD-coupled malate dehydrogenase that catalyzes the equilibration of malate and oxaloacetate, in which the formation of malate and NAD from oxaloacetate and NADH is favored. The combined reactions of the two enzymes cause the conversion of oxaloacetate to pyruvate and CO_2, with the energy of decarboxylation driving a transfer of electrons from NADH to NADP, creating NADPH.

Since glucose is metabolized by the Embden-Meyerhof pathway for fatty acid synthesis, pyruvate and NADH are both produced in the cytosol. The NADH is used to form NADPH by the malate dehydrogenase route, and pyruvate is oxidized to acetyl coenzyme A in mitochondria. The transfer of the resultant acetyl groups to the cytosol for use in fatty acid synthesis is accomplished by a citrate–pyruvate cycle that both moves acetyl groups and provides the oxaloacetate necessary for electron transfers *via* malate. The cycle is designed so that cleavage of two ATP molecules drives the transfer of both acetyl groups and electrons.

The combination of the Embden-Meyerhof pathway and the citrate–pyruvate cycle forms one NADPH per acetyl coenzyme A utilized. However, 14 NADPH are required to convert eight acetyl groups to palmitate; the remaining 6 NADPH are provided by the pentose phosphate pathway. This pathway has the same oxidation of glucose 6-phosphate and oxidative decarboxylation of 6-phosphogluconate to ribulose phosphate occurring in heterolactate fermentation, except that animals employ the pathway as a source of electrons for syntheses, and therefore utilize NADP as the oxidizing agent with the dehydrogenases. Two NADPH molecules are produced for each CO_2 formed. The ribulose 5-phosphate formed in the pathway is rearranged to hexose and triose phosphates by a series of reactions so that the net result is an appearance of three CO_2, six NADPH, and one triose phosphate for each glucose 6-phosphate consumed. The necessary rearrangements involve two-carbon transfers by transketolase, and a three-carbon transfer by a transaldolase.

The utilization of one molecule of glucose 6-phosphate by the pentose phosphate pathway and $3\frac{1}{2}$ molecules by the Embden-Meyerhof pathway will provide the requisite eight molecules of pyruvate and 14 molecules of NADPH for synthesis of a molecule of palmitate.

We saw in the previous chapter that the reduction of acetyl coenzyme A to fatty acids is accomplished by oxidizing NADPH to NADP. How is NADP then reduced back to NADPH? That is the question at hand.

We know that NADP is structurally and mechanistically very similar to NAD; therefore, we might predict the actual circumstance. NADP is converted to NADPH by being used in specific dehydrogenase reactions that oxidize hydroxyl groups. These dehydrogenases provide electrons for reductive syntheses, and are therefore functionally distinct from the NAD-specific dehydrogenases that provide electrons for oxidative phosphorylation.

MALATE DEHYDROGENASES AND ACETYL TRANSFER

Generation of NADPH. We have already noted (p. 287) that plants utilizing the Hatch-Slack pathway of CO_2 fixation take advantage of an NADP-specific malate dehydrogenase that catalyzes the oxidation of L-malate with a simultaneous decarboxylation to pyruvate so that the intermediate oxaloacetate does not appear. The cytosol of animal cells also contains an enzyme catalyzing the same reaction:

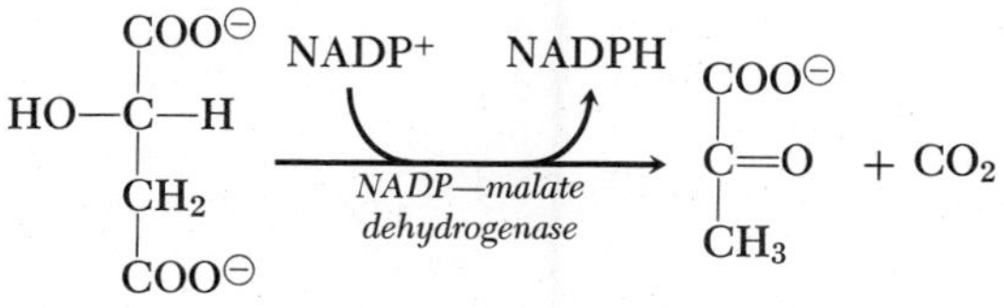

L-malate **pyruvate**

We pointed out that 3-ketocarboxylates are easily decarboxylated, and that reactions producing them may, or may not, involve the simultaneous loss of CO_2. The NAD-coupled malate dehydrogenase of mitochondria produces oxaloacetate without decarboxylation, but the NADP-coupled enzyme of the cytosol causes the simultaneous decarboxylation to pyruvate.

This reaction is an important source of NADPH in adipose tissue when fatty acids are being synthesized from glucose, and it presumably is of equal value in the human liver. Its importance comes from the fact that the cytosol also contains the usual malate:NAD dehydrogenase that equilibrates malate and oxaloacetate. The two reactions in combination provide a means for transferring electrons from NADH to NADP in the cytosol, with the transfer driven by the simultaneous decarboxylation of oxaloacetate to pyruvate and CO_2:

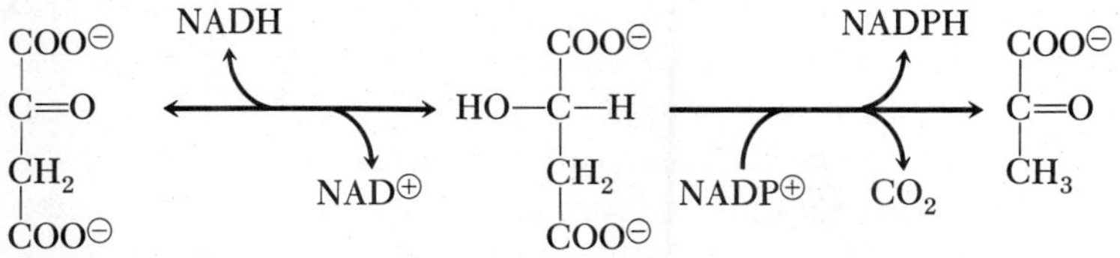

oxaloacetate **L-malate** **pyruvate**

SUM: NADH + NADP$^{\oplus}$ + oxaloacetate $\longrightarrow$ NAD$^{\oplus}$ + NADPH + pyruvate + CO_2

Malate acts only as a transient intermediate in this process. (By the way, this is a third route for the disposal of NADH created in the cytosol of animal tissues by the Embden-Meyerhof pathway. We have seen that muscles may use NADH to reduce pyruvate to lactate or to reduce dihydroxyacetone phosphate to glycerol 3-phosphate. Now we see that the liver and adipose tissue can remove NADH from the cytosol by reducing oxaloacetate to malate.)

The transfer of electrons just described fits very smoothly into the overall mecha-

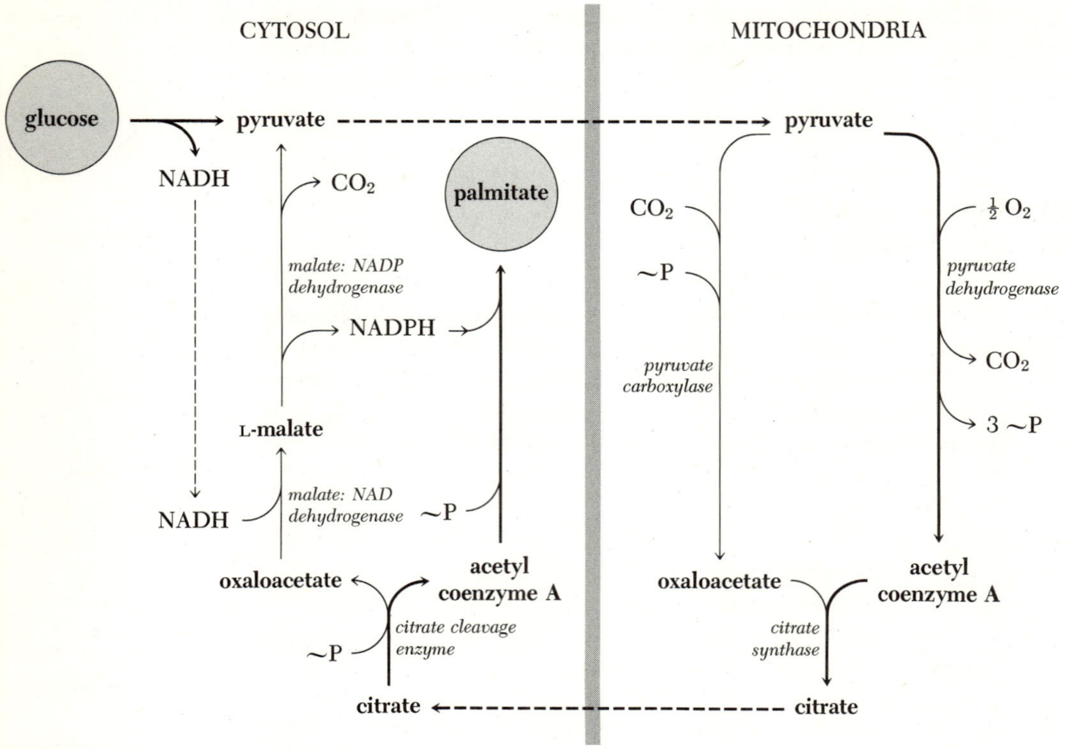

Figure 21–1 The citrate-pyruvate cycle involves the addition of acetyl groups to oxaloacetate for transport out of mitochondria and the addition of hydride ions from NADH to oxaloacetate for transfer to NADP in the cytosol.

nism of fatty acid synthesis. The conversion of glucose to fatty acids begins with the formation of pyruvate and NADH by the Embden-Meyerhof pathway in the cytosol. Pyruvate is oxidized to acetyl coenzyme A as the source of carbons for the fatty acid chain. Since the malate dehydrogenases provide a means of utilizing NADH in the cytosol to form NADPH, glucose therefore is supplying both carbon atoms in the form of acetyl groups and some of the electrons in the form of NADPH for fatty acid synthesis.

Transfer of Acetyl Groups. The malate dehydrogenases fit into the synthetic scheme in still another way. We must keep an eye on the requirement for NADPH, but synthesis also requires a transfer of acetyl groups from the mitochondria, where they are formed by the oxidation of pyruvate, to the cytosol. This is done by an ingenious scheme in which citrate is formed in the mitochondria and transported to the cytosol, where its cleavage not only supplies acetyl groups for the fatty acid chain, but also provides the oxaloacetate for driving electron transfer via malate (Fig. 21–1). In this scheme, citrate is formed from oxaloacetate and acetyl coenzyme A by the familiar citrate synthase reaction of the citric acid cycle in mitochondria. Instead of being oxidized, it is transported to the cytosol by exchange for P_i or other anions. It is cleaved to form acetyl coenzyme A and oxaloacetate in the cytosol by a separate enzyme, and the cleavage occurs at the expense of ATP.

The Citrate–Pyruvate Cycle. Now comes the clever part of the mechanism. The acetyl coenzyme A released in the cytosol from the cleavage of citrate is used to create fatty acid chains. The oxaloacetate that is also released is used by the malate dehydrogenase route for transfer of electrons from NADH to NADP, and it is converted to pyruvate and CO_2 as a result. The original source of the oxaloacetate was in the mitochondria, where it was used to make citrate. We have seen before that oxaloacetate is made in the mitochondria by carboxylation of pyruvate:

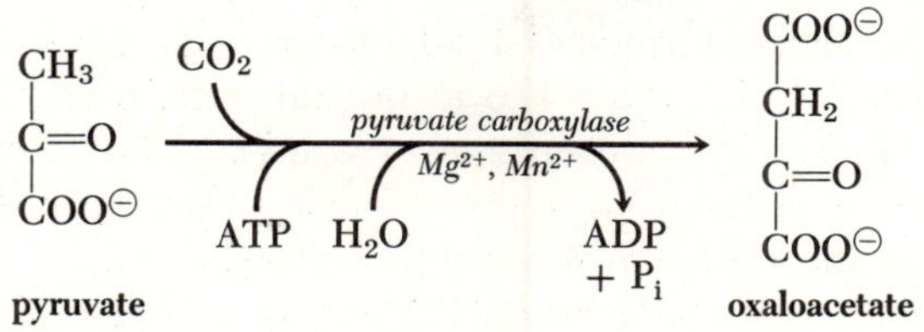

Therefore, the pyruvate formed in the cytosol by the sequence citrate ⟶ oxaloacetate ⟶ pyruvate can diffuse into mitochondria to replace the pyruvate used in the sequence pyruvate ⟶ oxaloacetate ⟶ citrate!

The citrate–pyruvate cycle simultaneously moves an acetyl group from mitochondria to the cytosol and shifts a pair of electrons from NADH to NADP. Two molecules of ATP are expended per turn of the cycle, one in carboxylating pyruvate and the other in cleaving citrate.

Integration of Citrate–Pyruvate Cycle and Fatty Acid Synthesis. This is a fascinatingly interwoven set of reactions; let us go through it again, this time in a step-by-step analysis (the corresponding reactions are listed in Fig. 21–2):

1. An excess supply of glucose to the liver or adipose tissue causes an accelerated formation of pyruvate and NADH in the cytosol by the Embden-Meyerhof pathway.
2. Pyruvate diffuses into mitochondria. Part is oxidized to acetyl coenzyme A, and

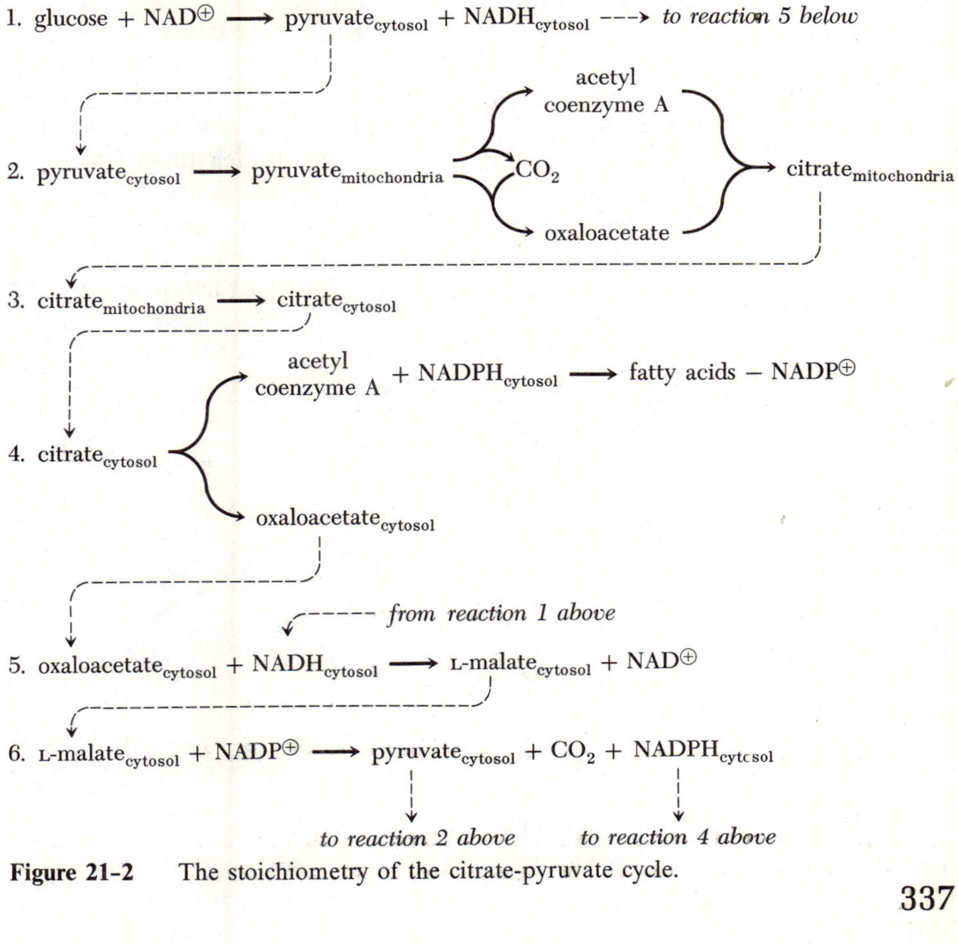

Figure 21–2 The stoichiometry of the citrate-pyruvate cycle.

part is carboxylated to form oxaloacetate. Acetyl coenzyme A and oxaloacetate condense to form citrate.

3. Tissues synthesizing fatty acids from glucose have a relatively slow citric acid cycle, and most of the citrate formed is available for exchange into the cytosol.

4. Citrate is cleaved in the cytosol to form oxaloacetate and acetyl coenzyme A at the expense of ATP. The acetyl coenzyme A is utilized for fatty acid synthesis.

5. The oxaloacetate released from citrate in the cytosol is reduced to malate by the NADH formed in the Embden-Meyerhof pathway.

6. The malate is oxidatively decarboxylated to form NADPH, pyruvate and CO_2. The NADPH is utilized in forming fatty acids.

7. The pyruvate produced from malate mixes with the pyruvate directly formed by the Embden-Meyerhof pathway. When it moves into mitochondria, it is effectively replacing the pyruvate formerly utilized to make oxaloacetate, so the only pyruvate now missing is that which was oxidized to form acetyl coenzyme A.

The sum of all of the reactions involved shows that the conversion of eight molecules of triose phosphate to palmitate *via* eight molecules of acetyl coenzyme A will also form all but six of the 14 molecules of NADPH required. Let us now consider how these additional six molecules of NADPH are obtained.

THE PENTOSE PHOSPHATE PATHWAY

We examined the pentose phosphate pathway earlier in connection with heterolactate fermentation (p. 256). To recapitulate, the pathway involves an oxidation of glucose 6-phosphate, hydrolysis of 6-phosphogluconolactone, and an oxidative decarboxylation of the resultant 6-phosphogluconate, which forms ribulose 5-phosphate. This is the same route used in animal tissue, and by many other organisms, for the generation of NADPH (Fig. 21-3). The important distinction is that the glucose 6-phosphate dehydrogenase and 6-phosphogluconate dehydrogenase of these cells are built to use NADP, rather than NAD, as oxidizing agents.

The result of the pentose phosphate pathway in animals therefore is an oxidation of glucose to provide electrons for the reduction of other compounds. The sequence generates two molecules of NADPH for each molecule of CO_2 produced from glucose

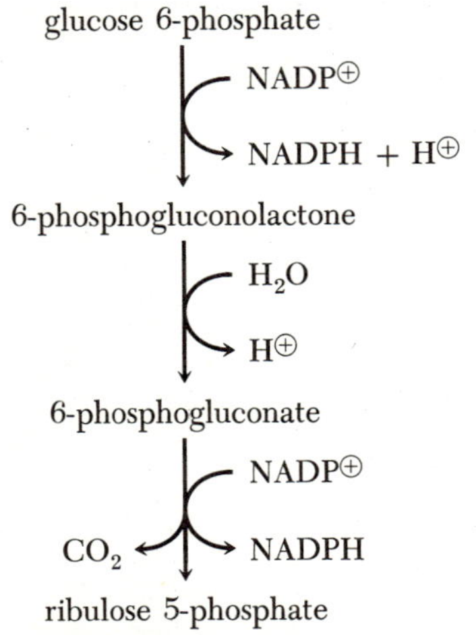

SUM: glucose 6-phosphate + 2 NADP$^{\oplus}$ + H_2O $\longrightarrow$
ribulose 5-phosphate + CO_2 + 2 NADPH + 2 H$^{\oplus}$

Figure 21-3 The pentose phosphate pathway is used in many cells, including those synthesizing fatty acids, as a means of generating NADPH through the oxidation of glucose 6-phosphate to ribulose 5-phosphate.

6-phosphate. The remainder of the pathway involves the rearrangement of ribulose 5-phosphate, which contains five out of the six carbons originally present in glucose 6-phosphate.

Disposition of the Pentose Phosphates

In handling the pentose phosphates, the problem solved by evolution is essentially one of reshuffling the carbons so as to wind up with hexose and triose phosphates. The redistribution is accomplished mainly through the action of transketolase, which catalyzes the transfer of two-carbon units from one sugar to another (p. 283), and a transaldolase, which catalyzes the transfer of three-carbon units.

5 + 5 = 3 + 7. The early reactions are much like those we discussed in connection with heterolactate fermentation and photosynthesis (pp. 259 and 282). Transketolase requires an aldose phosphate and a ketose phosphate with *trans*-hydroxyl groups as substrates. Ribulose 5-phosphate is converted to ribose 5-phosphate (the aldose phosphate) and to xylulose 5-phosphate (the ketose phosphate), thereby providing both substrates (Fig. 21–4). Transketolase can then transfer a two-carbon unit from the ketose to the aldose phosphate, forming the seven-carbon sedoheptulose 7-phosphate and leaving behind glyceraldehyde 3-phosphate.

3 + 7 = 6 + 4. Sedoheptulose 7-phosphate and glyceraldehyde 3-phosphate are in turn substrates for transaldolase, which is an enzyme that catalyzes the transfer of a three-carbon unit from the ketose phosphate. The products are fructose 6-phosphate and erythrose 4-phosphate.

What do we have now? Two molecules of the original ribulose 5-phosphate have been consumed, and their 10 carbon atoms have been converted to a molecule each of fructose 6-phosphate and erythrose 4-phosphate. The fructose phosphate is in equilibrium with glucose 6-phosphate, and therefore represents full rehabilitation, as it were, of six carbons derived from pentose phosphates. However, four carbons still remain in the form of erythrose 4-phosphate. What to do with these?

5 + 4 = 3 + 6. Erythrose 4-phosphate is an aldose phosphate, and therefore is also an acceptor substrate for transketolase, becoming fructose 6-phosphate after the transfer of a two-carbon unit and, again, fructose 6-phosphate is interconverted with glucose 6-phosphate. The donor of the two carbons once more is xylulose 5-phosphate, derived from ribulose 5-phosphate, and a molecule of glyceraldehyde 3-phosphate remains after the transfer. This represents the consumption of a third molecule of ribulose 5-phosphate.

Now what do we have? Beginning with three molecules of ribulose 5-phosphate, two molecules of glucose 6-phosphate and one molecule of glyceraldehyde 3-phosphate have been formed by the following transformations:

$$
\begin{array}{lrcl}
 & 5C + 5C & \longrightarrow & 3C + 7C \text{ (transketolase)} \\
 & 3C + 7C & \longrightarrow & 6C + 4C \text{ (transaldolase)} \\
 & 5C + 4C & \longrightarrow & 3C + 6C \text{ (transketolase)} \\
\text{SUM:} & 5C + 5C + 5C & \longrightarrow & 6C + 6C + 3C
\end{array}
$$

Total Stoichiometry of the Pentose Phosphate Pathway. Each of the ribulose 5-phosphate molecules that we have disposed of so neatly was derived from a molecule of glucose 6-phosphate, with a concomitant generation of CO_2 and two molecules of NADPH. The original problem was to generate six molecules of NADPH so as to

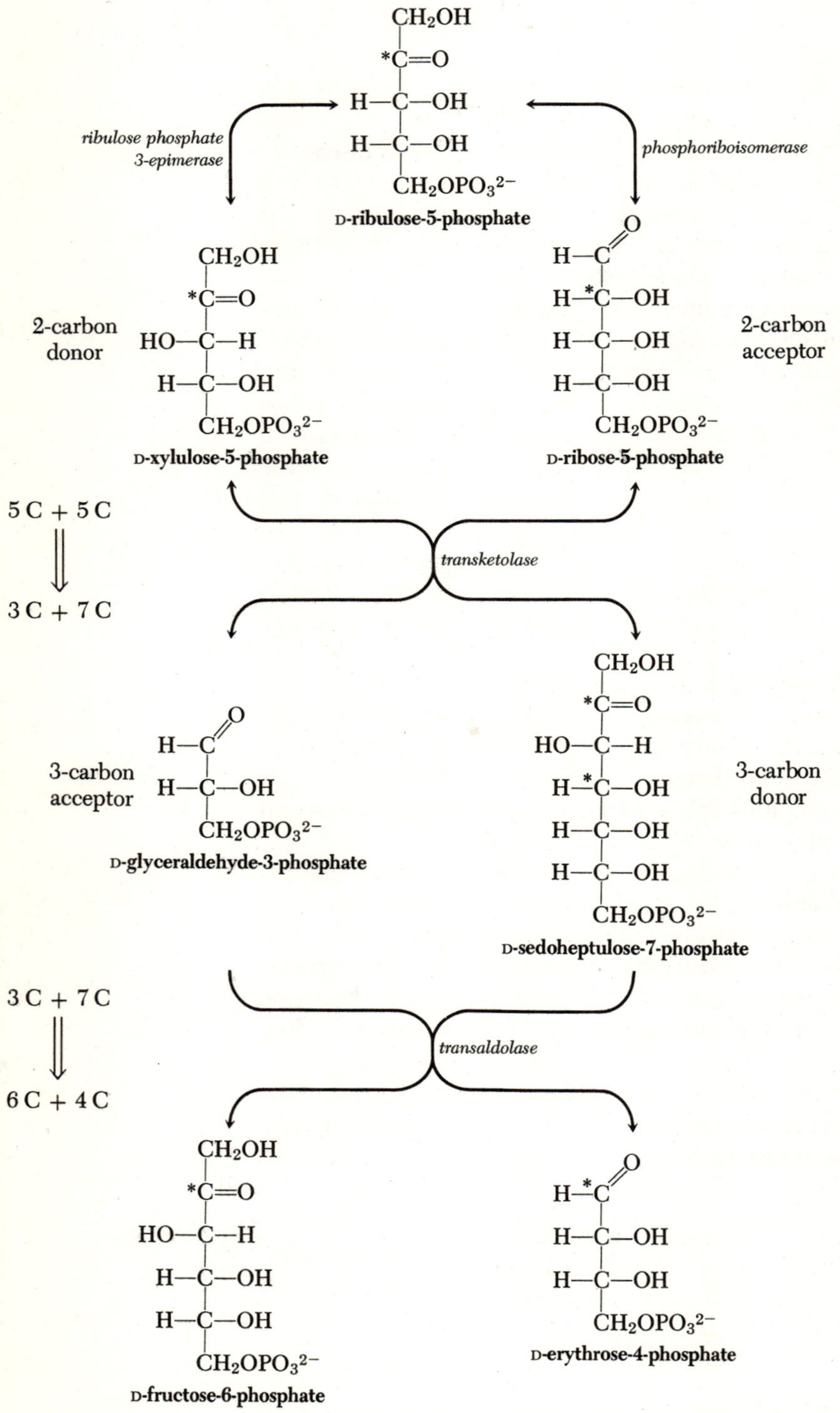

Figure 21-4 Two molecules of ribulose 5-phosphate formed in the pentose phosphate pathway are converted to fructose 6-phosphate and erythrose 4-phosphate. (*Continued on next page.*)

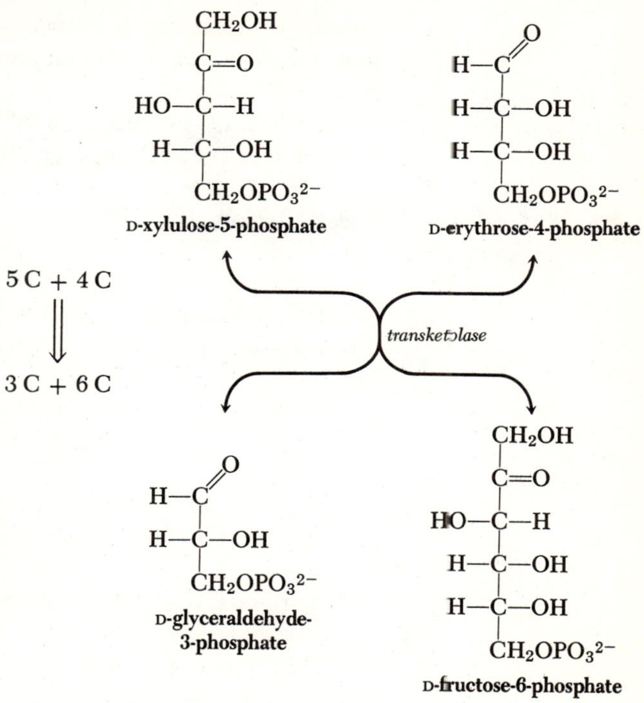

Figure 21-4, continued A third molecule of pentose 5-phosphate reacts with erythrose 4-phosphate to form glyceraldehyde 3-phosphate and fructose 6-phosphate. This completes the conversion of three molecules of pentose phosphate to two molecules of hexose phosphate and one molecule of triose phosphate.

complete the formation of palmitate from glucose (p. 338). In order to do this, three molecules of glucose 6-phosphate must be oxidized by the pentose phosphate pathway:

$$3\ (\text{glucose 6-phosphate})^{2-} + 6\ \text{NADP}^+ + 3\ H_2O \longrightarrow 3\ (\text{ribulose 5-phosphate})^{2-} + 3\ CO_2 + 6\ \text{NADPH} + 6\ H^+$$

We have just seen that three molecules of ribulose 5-phosphate are converted to one molecule of glyceraldehyde 3-phosphate and two molecules of glucose 6-phosphate:

$$3\ (\text{ribulose 5-phosphate})^{2-} \longrightarrow 2\ (\text{glucose 6-phosphate})^{2-} + (\text{glyceraldehyde 3-phosphate})^{2-}$$

This equation tells us that the three ribulose phosphate molecules are used to replace two of the original glucose 6-phosphate molecules, with the remaining carbons appearing as triose phosphate. When we add the two equations for the overall process, the result therefore is:

$$(\text{glucose 6-phosphate})^{2-} + 6\ \text{NADP}^+ + 3\ H_2O \longrightarrow (\text{glyceraldehyde 3-phosphate})^{2-} + 3\ CO_2 + 6\ \text{NADPH} + 6\ H^+$$

This is the final stoichiometry for the complete pentose phosphate pathway. The effect is the oxidation by NADP of half of a glucose residue to CO_2 and H_2O. The remaining carbons that appear as glyceraldehyde 3-phosphate can be used in the ordinary Embden-Meyerhof pathway.

THE TOTAL STOICHIOMETRY OF FATTY ACID SYNTHESIS

Having examined routes for supplying the necessary NADPH, we are now in a position to cast the complete balance for the conversion of glucose to fatty acids. Let us go through this one step at a time, not because the process is something to be memorized in detail, but rather so we can see that it is indeed possible to reason about complicated pathways.

To begin, one molecule of palmitate is made from eight molecules of acetyl coenzyme A (neglecting ionic charges, water, and H^+ for the moment) (p. 327):

$$\text{8 acetyl-S-CoA} + \text{7 ATP} + \text{14 NADPH} \longrightarrow \text{palmitate} + 7\,(\text{ADP} + \text{P}_i) + 14\,\text{NADP}^{\oplus}$$

The eight molecules of acetyl coenzyme A are provided in the cytosol along with a transfer of hydrogen from NADH to NADP by the pyruvate–citrate cycle (p. 336):

$$\text{8 acetyl-S-CoA}_{(\text{mitoch.})} + \text{8 NADH} + 8\,\text{NADP}^+ + \text{16 ATP} \longrightarrow \text{8 acetyl-S-CoA}_{(\text{cytosol})} + 8\,\text{NAD}^+ + \text{8 NADPH} + 16\,(\text{ADP} + \text{P}_i)$$

These acetyl coenzyme A molecules in the mitochondria are formed by oxidizing pyruvate with a concomitant oxidative phosphorylation:

$$\text{8 pyruvate} + 4\,\text{O}_2 + 24\,(\text{ADP} + \text{P}_i) \longrightarrow \text{8 acetyl-S-CoA} + 8\,\text{CO}_2 + \text{24 ATP}$$

The pyruvate in turn arises from glyceraldehyde 3-phosphate by the Embden-Meyerhof pathway (p. 218):

$$\text{8 glyceraldehyde 3-phosphate} + 8\,\text{NAD}^+ + 16\,(\text{ADP} + \text{P}_i) \longrightarrow \text{8 pyruvate} + \text{8 NADH} + \text{16 ATP}$$

One molecule of glyceraldehyde phosphate, along with the remaining six molecules of NADPH that are required, are formed by the pentose phosphate pathway:

$$\text{glucose 6-phosphate} + 6\,\text{NADP}^+ \longrightarrow \text{glyceraldehyde 3-phosphate} + 3\,\text{CO}_2 + \text{6 NADPH}$$

The other seven molecules of glyceraldehyde phosphate are formed by the usual initial steps of the Embden Meyerhof pathway:

$$3\tfrac{1}{2}\,\text{glucose 6-phosphate} + 3\tfrac{1}{2}\,\text{ATP} \longrightarrow \text{7 glyceraldehyde 3-phosphate} + 3\tfrac{1}{2}\,\text{ADP}$$

Finally, a total of $4\frac{1}{2}$ molecules of glucose 6-phosphate are made from glucose:

$$4\tfrac{1}{2}\,\text{glucose} + 4\tfrac{1}{2}\,\text{ATP} \longrightarrow 4\tfrac{1}{2}\,\text{glucose 6-phosphate} + 4\tfrac{1}{2}\,\text{ADP}$$

Adding all of these steps together, we get a grand total (with the ionic forms now inserted):

$$4\tfrac{1}{2}\,\text{glucose} + 4\,\text{O}_2 + 9\,(\text{ADP}^{3-} + \text{P}_i^{2-}) + 8\,\text{H}^+ \longrightarrow (\text{palmitate})^- + 11\,\text{CO}_2 + 9\,\text{ATP}^{4-} + 20\,\text{H}_2\text{O}$$

How about that! Everything works out, and there is even a small production of ATP to sustain the later conversion of fatty acids to triglycerides. Twenty-seven carbons in the form of glucose are consumed to create 16 carbons in the form of palmitate. The flow of carbons and electrons is recapitulated in Figure 21–5.

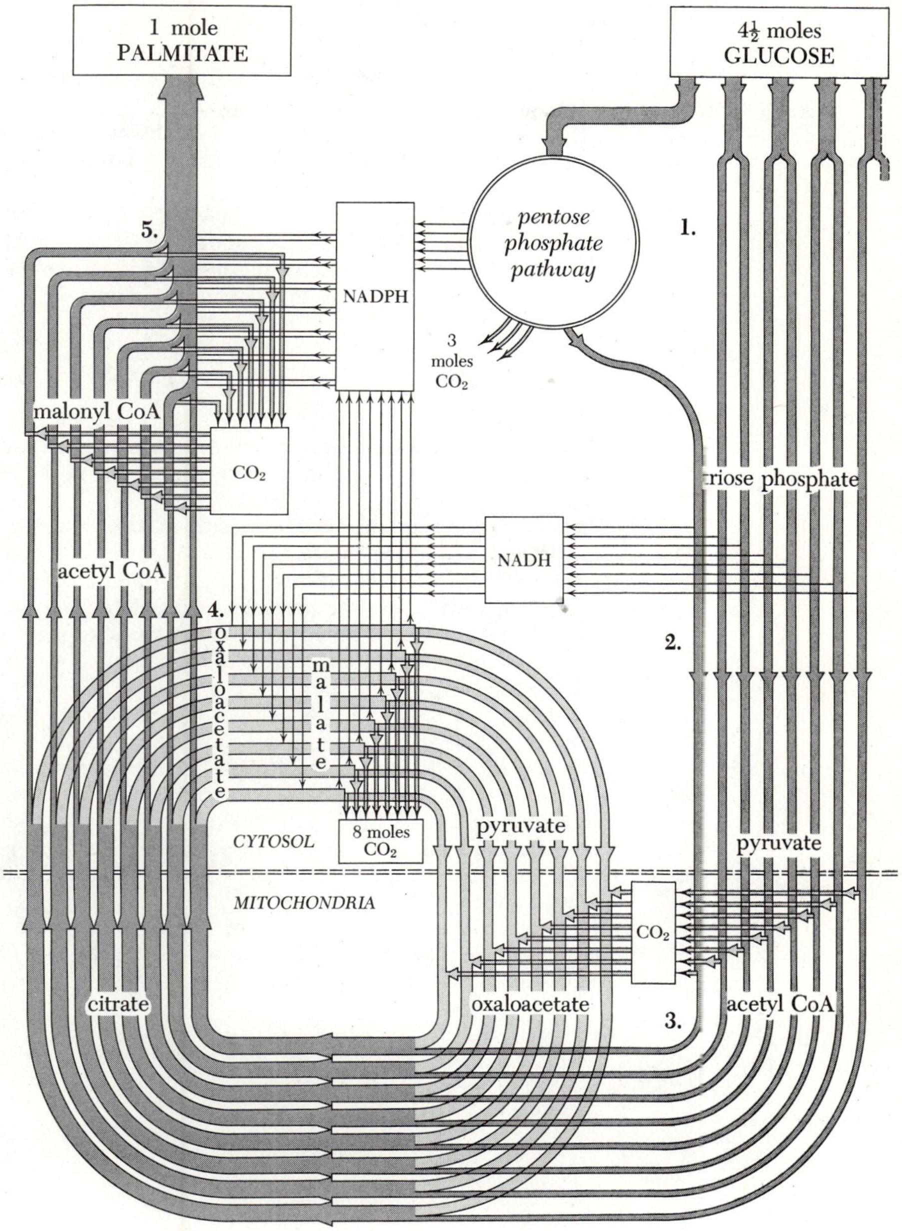

Figure 21-5 Flow sheet for the synthesis of palmitate from glucose. The flow of carbons appearing in palmitate is shown by heavy shading. Lighter shading indicates the recycling of oxaloacetate via pyruvate from the cytosol to the mitochondria. Transfers of electrons are indicated by narrow arrows.

1. Four and a half moles of glucose are required to make one mole of palmitate; one of these passes through the pentose phosphate pathway to generate six moles of NADPH. The remainder are converted directly to triose phosphates by the Embden-Meyerhof pathway.

2. The eight moles of triose phosphates created in step 1 are converted to pyruvate by the Embden-Meyerhof pathway, with the formation of eight moles of NADH.

3. Eight moles of pyruvate are oxidized to acetyl coenzyme A in the mitochondria, and the acetyl coenzyme A combines with oxaloacetate to form citrate (8 moles).

4. The citrate passes from the mitochondria into the cytosol, where it is cleaved to acetyl coenzyme A and oxaloacetate. The oxaloacetate is reduced to malate, using the eight moles of NADH formed in step 2. The malate is then oxidized to pyruvate by the NADP-coupled dehydrogenase, to form an additional eight moles of NADPH. The pyruvate diffuses back into the mitochondria, where it is carboxylated to regenerate oxaloacetate consumed in step 3.

5. The eight moles of acetyl coenzyme A transported into the cytosol as citrate are carboxylated (7 moles) and condensed to form palmitate. The necessary reductions consume the NADPH generated in steps 1 and 4.

FURTHER READING

S. Rous, The origin of hydrogen in fatty acid synthesis, Adv. Lipid. Res., 9:73 (1971). Discussion from experimental point of view.

B. L. Horecker, Pentose phosphate pathway, 1:139 in F. Dickens, P. J. Randle, and W. J. Whelan, Carbohydrate metabolism and its disorders, Academic Press (1968). Description by a pioneer in the field.

J. M. Lowenstein, Effect of (−)-hydroxycitrate of fatty acid synthesis by rat liver in vivo, J. Biol. Chem., 246:629 (1971). Description of evidence for the role of citrate cleavage enzyme in fatty acid synthesis by one of the more lucid writers in biochemistry.

Also see the general references at the end of Chapter 20.

QUESTIONS

1. What are the resemblances and differences, if any, in the use of both NAD and NADP-specific malate dehydrogenases in fatty acid synthesis and in the Hatch-Slack pathway of photosynthesis?
2. What is there about the NADP-specific malate dehydrogenase (decarboxylating) and the dehydrogenases of the pentose phosphate pathway that makes it possible to create a relatively high [NADPH]/[NADP] ratio compared to the ratio of [NADH]/[NAD] that can be maintained in the cytosol in the presence of lactate dehydrogenase?
3. Show how electrons removed from glucose 6-phosphate can appear in oleic acid residues by two routes, one of which involves formation of glyceraldehyde 3-phosphate before the electrons are transferred, and one after.
4. A deficiency of thiamine may cause a loss of activity of two enzymes directly required for synthesis of fatty acids from glucose. What are they?
5. Compare the actions of transketolase and transaldolase with that of fructose diphosphate aldolase (p. 102). Which of these enzymes would you expect to have a mechanism involving the formation of a Schiff's base between a lysyl group and a dihydroxyacetone residue?
6. Compare the route of forming hexose phosphates from pentose phosphates in the pentose phosphate pathway with the route of forming pentose phosphates from hexose phosphates in the Calvin cycle.
7. Glucose containing 27 carbon atoms must be consumed to create palmitate containing 16 carbon atoms. The other 11 carbon atoms appear as CO_2. Why is this? Why can't all of the carbon atoms of glucose appear as palmitate?

CHAPTER 22

DEPOSITION AND DEGRADATION OF FATS IN VERTEBRATES

THE CONCEPTS

Fatty acids are converted to triglycerides both for transport and for storage. The triglycerides are built by successive transfers of acyl groups from coenzyme A to a glyceryl backbone, which is provided as dihydroxyacetone phosphate and may be reduced to glycerol 3-phosphate either before or after the first acylation. Transfer of a saturated fatty acid residue onto C-1 and of an unsaturated residue onto C-2 creates a phosphatidate, or phosphate ester of a diglyceride. The third acylation follows removal of the phosphate group by hydrolysis.

The triglycerides are transported through the blood as micelles stabilized by external layers of protein and phospholipid, such as the relatively large chylomicrons passed from the intestine through the lymph into the blood and smaller, very-low-density lipoproteins used to transport triglycerides from the liver. Other tissues, including muscle and adipose tissue, hydrolyze the triglyceride in the micelles through the action of a lipoprotein lipase. The absorbed fatty acids are then rebuilt into triglycerides by the recipient cells.

The stored fatty acids are mobilized for use as fuels through hydrolysis by lipases. The rate-determining step is the initial removal of an acyl group because the resultant diglyceride is attacked more rapidly, and this initial step is catalyzed by a lipase controlled through phosphorylation and dephosphorylation. The lipase is activated by phosphorylation catalyzed by the cyclic AMP-sensitive protein kinase of adipose tissue. The formation of cyclic AMP is accelerated in adipose tissue by the presence of catecholamines, glucagon, and peptide hormones, including corticotropin (ACTH). Fatty acids are therefore mobilized from the stored triglycerides at the same time that glycogen is mobilized in the muscles or liver, and are also mobilized in response to other stresses. The free fatty acids liberated from adipose tissue by the lipases are transported to the muscles as complexes with serum albumin. Insulin, on the other hand, inhibits the hydrolysis of triglycerides in some way, and also accelerates the synthesis of fatty acids from glucose so as to take advantage of the high blood glucose concentration that causes insulin to be secreted.

Young mammals are likely to contain a specialized brown adipose tissue that is rich in mitochondria, in which stored fatty acids are mobilized and oxidized to generate heat without an accompanying phosphorylation. The mechanism by which oxidation and phosphorylation are uncoupled is not known.

FORMATION OF TRIGLYCERIDES

We outlined in the preceding chapters how fatty acids are synthesized from glucose in the liver or adipose tissue; they are also formed by hydrolysis of dietary fat in the intestinal lumen and absorbed by the intestinal mucosa. In all of these cases, the free fatty acids are converted to triglycerides by the same mechanisms for transport to, or deposition in, the adipose tissue. This is done by making the coenzyme A thioesters of the fatty acids, and then transferring the acyl groups to the hydroxyl groups of glycerol. The glycerol is initially provided in the form of dihydroxyacetone phosphate, which can be reduced to glycerol 3-phosphate before or after the addition of the first acyl group. The phosphate group is removed to permit attachment of the third and final acyl group (Fig. 22–1). Let us look at these processes in more detail.

The Initial Acylation. Figure 22–2 illustrates the two routes for placing an initial acyl group on what will be the glyceryl backbone of a triglyceride. The ultimate source of the glycerol residue is glucose in either case, but the enzymes and coenzyme used for reducing the dihydroxyacetone are different in the two cases. The product is trivially named as a **lysophosphatidate.** (The lyso- prefix is given by analogy with lysolecithin, a monoacyl glyceryl phosphate ester of choline that has the property of causing lysis of cells by its detergent action. Phosphatidic acids are diacyl glycerol esters of phosphoric acid.)

It might as well be admitted at once that there is much to be learned about triglyceride synthesis in various tissues and organisms. We do know that the initial acylation preferentially involves a saturated fatty acid. This is true when dihydroxyacetone phosphate or glycerol 3-phosphate is the acceptor for the acyl group, and Figure 22–2 shows a palmitoyl group, the most common residue on position 1, being transferred.

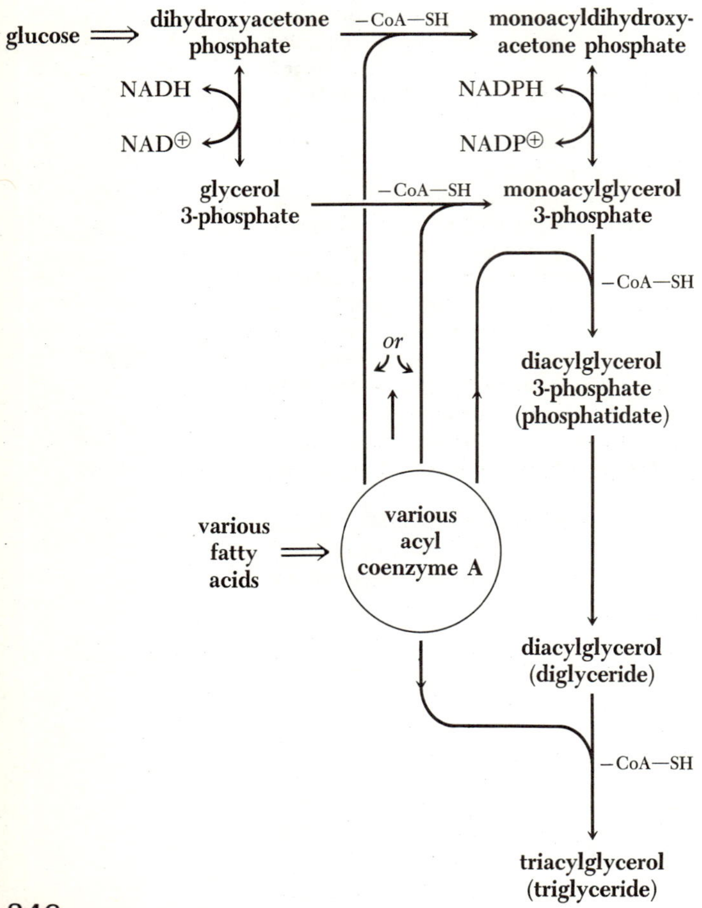

Figure 22–1 Triglycerides are built by successive transfers of acyl groups from their coenzyme A derivatives. The first transfer may occur to glycerol 3-phosphate created by the reduction of dihydroxyacetone phosphate, or to dihydroxyacetone phosphate followed by reduction of the monoacyl compound.

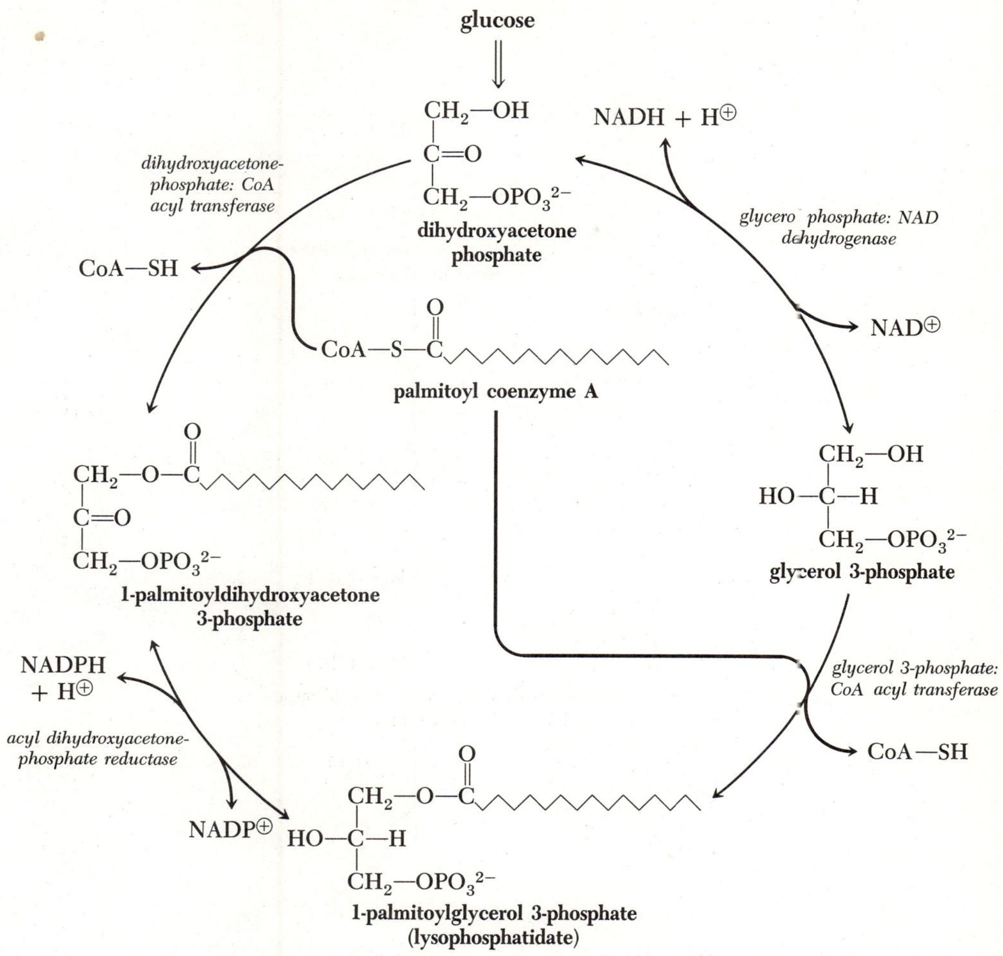

Figure 22-2 The initial acylation in fat synthesis usually involves a saturated acyl group, such as the palmitoyl group. The product is sometimes named as a lysophosphatidate because analogous phosphocholine derivatives (lysolecithins) are powerful detergents that lyse (break open) red blood cells.

Since the ultimate precursors and products appear to be the same in the two routes, except for the electron carriers, it is not clear why both exist. The route using dihydroxyacetone phosphate has been known only in recent years, and the exact proportion of triglycerides and other lipids made in this way is not known, although it appears to be more than trivial.

The Second and Third Acylations. Unsaturated fatty acid residues are transferred from their coenzyme A derivatives to the remaining free hydroxyl group at position 2 of a lysophosphatidate (Fig. 22-3). The resultant phosphatidate is then attacked by a specific phosphatase to expose the final hydroxyl group of the glyceryl backbone. Still another acyl transferase, this one specific for the free diglyceride acceptor, can then add the final fatty acid residue, which may be either saturated or unsaturated.

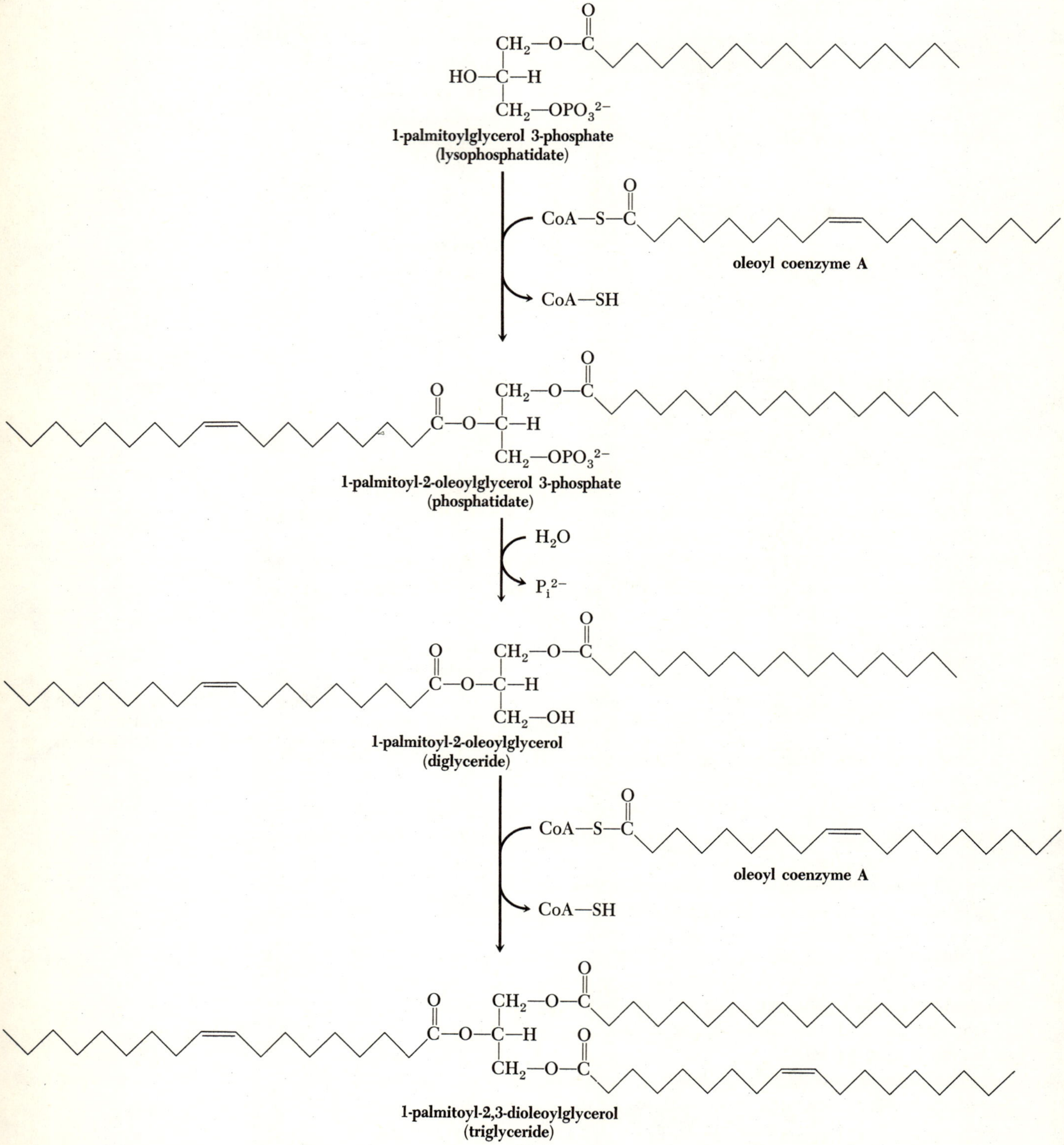

Figure 22-3 The second and third acylations during triglyceride synthesis frequently involve the transfer of unsaturated acyl groups, such as the oleoyl group.

Why are the phosphorylated compounds used during the initial acylations in place of free glycerol and monoglycerides? One possibility is that the low molecular weight materials might escape from the cell without the phosphate group. Another is economy of mechanism, because phosphatidates are also precursors for separate classes of structural lipids, in addition to being intermediates in triglyceride synthesis.

Whatever the explanation, triglycerides are made by the route outlined, and the result in a typical human will be a mixture of compounds with the following acyl groups comprising the bulk of the total:

20%	16:0	(palmitoyl)
7%	16:1	(palmitoleoyl)
50%	18:1	(oleoyl and vaccenyl)
10%	18:2	(linoleoyl)

TRANSPORT OF FATS

Triglycerides are moved from the small intestine and the liver to adipose tissue and the muscle for storage or utilization. However, triglycerides have a low solubility in water. In order to transport them from one tissue to another, they must be combined with other compounds carrying a sufficient number of polar groups to interact with neighboring water molecules. These polar groups are supplied in some instances by association with specific proteins and phospholipids, and in other cases by compounds with a detergent action, which combine in a non-specific way with the fats to form micelles, in which a central hydrophobic region is surrounded by a film of polar groups to create a stable complex.

Intestinal Absorption

Dispersion and Hydrolysis of Typical Fats. Ingested fats are partially hydrolyzed for absorption by a lipase secreted from the pancreas. Before this can occur, the fat must be converted to a micelle. The dispersion of the fats begins with the action of **bile salts** (p. 451), which are detergents secreted from the liver into the upper small intestine. The presence of the bile salts aids in breaking up the fat into small enough droplets—an emulsion—so that the **pancreatic lipase** can begin to function. The action is not simply one of making a large surface for the enzyme to attack, although this helps. The lipase is like most enzymes in that it has no particular affinity for hydrophobic compounds, and is actually damaged by contact with pure fats. The bile salts form a charged surface on the fat droplets, thereby enabling the lipase to come into contact with them without disruption of its active conformation.

Once hydrolysis begins, the presence of free fatty acid anions (soaps) and monoglycerides, which have detergent action themselves, facilitates the formation of true micelles from the much larger emulsified droplets. Hydrolysis proceeds rapidly in the micelles (Fig. 22–4). The pancreatic lipase can catalyze the hydrolysis of all of the acyl residues from a triglyceride, but it is much more active toward the outer, or primary ester, groups. The result is that the major products of digestion of a triglyceride are two fatty acid anions and a 2-monoglyceride, and these can be absorbed by the intestinal mucosa from the micelles. Once safely inside the cell, the fatty acids are converted to the coenzyme A esters and reattached to 2-monoglycerides, making a new assortment

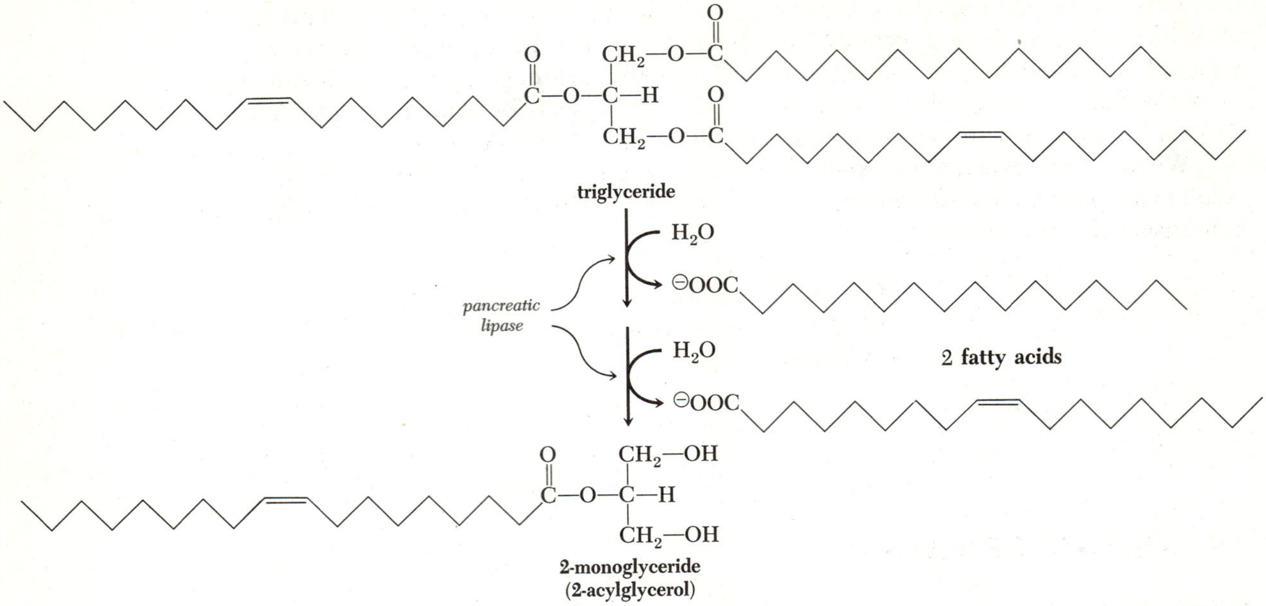

Figure 22–4 Pancreatic lipase catalyzes the hydrolysis of the terminal acyl groups from dietary fats, liberating free fatty acid anions (soaps) and 2-monoglycerides.

of triglycerides. (The chance of an acyl group being put back on the same glyceryl backbone from which it was removed during digestion is negligible.)

Digestion of Medium-Chain Fats. Triglycerides containing fatty acids with 10 or fewer carbon atoms can be hydrolyzed in the absence of bile salts because of their higher solubility and greater ease of emulsification, and the resultant fatty acid anions are absorbed rapidly. Even the triglycerides can be absorbed, and then be hydrolyzed within the mucosa cells. In either case, the resultant fatty acid anions are transported as such in the portal blood draining the intestines. Artificial mixtures of "medium-chain triglycerides" are therefore used to feed humans with defects in bile formation or intestinal function that impair the absorption of the longer-chain triglycerides that constitute the fat of most natural foods.

Transport in Blood

Chylomicrons. The triglycerides formed in the intestinal mucosa from the absorbed fatty acids and monoglycerides are extruded in the form of droplets, typically 1.5 to 4 micrometers in diameter, that are stabilized by the presence of small amounts of protein, phospholipids, and cholesterol (p. 82). These droplets, known as chylomicrons, are elaborated into the lymphatic drainage of the gut, and the lymph travels through the thoracic duct into the venous circulation. The separated plasma from a sample of blood taken after a fat-rich meal appears milky because of its high chylomicron content.

Plasma Lipoproteins. The liver produces three types of lipoproteins found in blood plasma. They are frequently designated according to electrophoretic mobility, with the α-lipoprotein moving faster, a pre-β lipoprotein next most rapidly, and a β-lipoprotein least rapidly (chylomicrons do not migrate). These proteins are also commonly classified by density. The pre-β lipoprotein has the most lipid, and is therefore also known as a **very-low-density lipoprotein.** This is the protein of greatest interest to us now, because it contains some 50 to 80% triglyceride, and is the form in which triglycerides synthesized in the liver are transported to other tissues. The protein is also stabilized by the presence of phospholipids and cholesterol, but it is of molecular dimensions and is freely soluble in the blood plasma.

Uptake of Triglycerides by Tissues. Chylomicrons are removed from the blood by many tissues, including the liver, muscles, and adipose tissue. Very-low-density lipoproteins are also removed by the muscles and adipose tissue. Uptake of either the chylomicrons or the very-low-density lipoproteins involves the action of a **lipoprotein lipase,** which hydrolyzes the triglycerides bound in these complexes, forming free fatty acid anions for transport into the acceptor cells. The lipase is specific for lipoprotein-triglyceride complexes at the cell surface and therefore doesn't attack already stored triglycerides within the cells. Once the fatty acids have crossed the cell membrane, they are again converted to triglycerides, which become part of the internal fat globules.

MOBILIZATION OF FATTY ACIDS

The fatty acids stored as triglycerides in adipose tissue are made available for use as a fuel by hydrolysis. The hydrolysis is catalyzed by a battery of lipases, the first one of which acts on triglycerides, and perhaps also on diglycerides, but not on monoglycerides. There also appears to be a specific diglyceride hydrolase, and there certainly is an enzyme hydrolyzing monoglycerides (Fig. 22–5).

Fatty Acid–Albumin Complexes. The fatty acid anions that are released by the hydrolases cross the plasma membrane into the blood, where they are transported mainly in combination with **serum albumin,** the most abundant protein in the blood. Even though approximately 40 grams of albumin are in each liter of blood, the amount of free fatty acid transported at one time is not great, ranging around 2 milligrams of fatty acid per gram of albumin, or substantially less than 1 millimole per liter of blood. However, the turnover is so rapid that some 25 grams, or 0.1 mole, of free fatty acids are easily shuttled through the blood from the adipose tissue each hour.

Fate of Glycerol. The adipose tissue cannot re-utilize free glycerol released from triglycerides; it utilizes dihydroxyacetone phosphate as a source of the glyceryl residue. Hence, glycerol passes into the blood along with fatty acids and it is converted to glycerol 3-phosphate by the action of a **glycerol kinase** in the liver. The liver can utilize it to

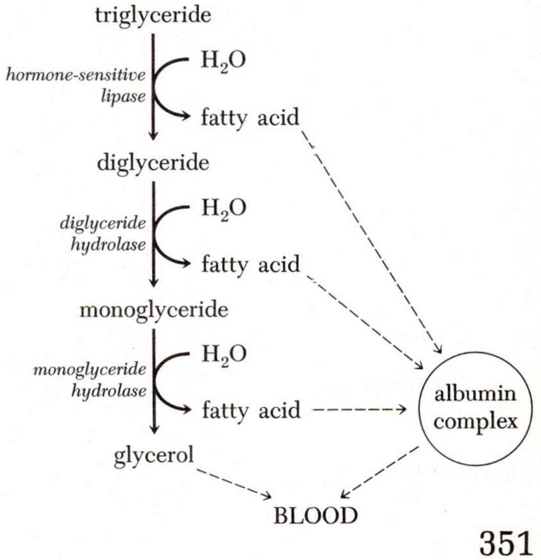

Figure 22-5 The mobilization of fatty acids from the triglycerides in adipose tissue is triggered by a hormone-sensitive lipase. Once the first acyl group is removed, the other enzymes catalyze the rapid hydrolysis of the remaining acyl groups. The fatty acids are transported in the blood as albumin complexes and the liberated glycerol is transported in solution.

make triglycerides. However, circumstances causing mobilization of fat also frequently cause increased gluconeogenesis, and glycerol 3-phosphate can also act as a precursor of glucose *via* dihydroxyacetone phosphate.

Regulation of Fat Mobilization

The mobilization of fat involves the same kind of regulation encountered in glycogen metabolism. It would not do to have the stored triglycerides constantly broken down in the absence of any need for more fuel. Consequently, the adipose tissue lipase that acts on triglycerides is constructed to be activated through the action of a cyclic AMP-sensitive protein kinase. Fatty acid residues are mobilized from adipose tissue triglycerides in somewhat the same way that glucose residues are mobilized from liver or muscle glycogen.

The plasma membrane of adipocytes has receptors for various hormones that cause an activation of adenyl cyclase (Fig. 22–6). The resultant increase in concentration of cyclic AMP displaces the catalytic peptide of protein kinase from its inhibiting regulator peptide. The free kinase then catalyzes the phosphorylation of adipose tissue lipase, converting it to an active form that hydrolyzes an acyl group from a triglyceride molecule. The initial hydrolysis of triglycerides is the rate-determining step in their utilization because one acyl group must be removed before other glyceride hydrolases will act to strip off the remaining two groups. The mobilization of fat is like the mobilization of glycogen in that activation of adenyl cyclase initiates a sequence of events that make the fuel totally available.

Activators of Adipose Tissue Adenyl Cyclase. Adenyl cyclase in adipose tissue is activated by catecholamines, either the hormone **adrenaline** arriving from the blood stream, or **noradrenaline** released by the sympathetic nervous system within the tissue. It is activated by **glucagon.** Taken together, these effects will result in a mobilization of fatty acids from adipose tissue at times that glycogen is being mobilized in the liver and skeletal muscles as a result of hormonal action.

The adipose tissue adenyl cyclase also responds to other signals, including a variety of peptide hormones secreted by the pituitary gland. The most important of these is **corticotropin** (adrenocorticotrophic hormone, ACTH), which is elaborated under conditions of stress with the principal function of causing the adrenal glands to secrete cortisol, which we will discuss in a later chapter. The corticotropin serves also to counteract stress by mobilizing more fuel from the adipose tissue.

Insulin and Adipose Tissue. Insulin is necessary for the uptake of glucose by adipose tissue, thereby directly promoting the formation of triglycerides, since glucose is a precursor of the dihydroxyacetone phosphate used to make the glyceryl group to which fatty acyl residues are attached. Insulin also counteracts in some way the promotion of lipolysis (fat degradation) caused by hormones that stimulate adenyl cyclase.

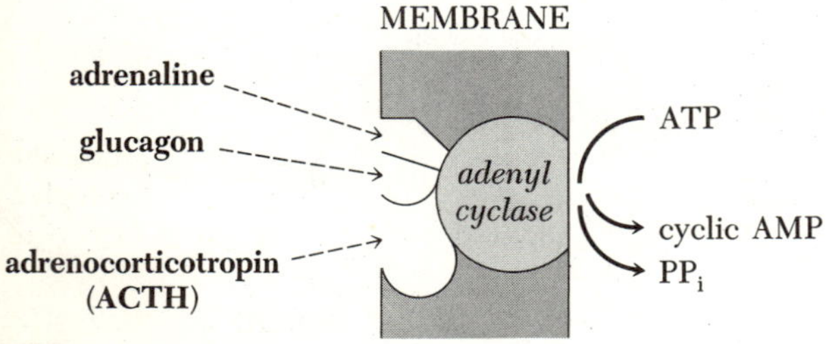

Figure 22-6 The plasma membranes of cells in adipose tissue (adipocytes) have receptor sites for several hormones that stimulate adenyl cyclase to form cAMP for activation of the sensitive lipase.

We shall have to wait for more data on mechanisms, but this ought not obscure the ultimate action of insulin on adipose tissue, which is to promote fat storage and inhibit fat mobilization.

These effects of insulin make physiological sense. It is elaborated when glucose is plentiful, and if there is an ample supply of glucose with its storage as glycogen being promoted, there is no reason for mobilizing fatty acids. Quite the contrary, if the glycogen reserves are becoming saturated, the increasing concentration of glucose in the presence of high insulin levels will promote both the conversion of glucose to fatty acids in either the liver or the adipose tissue, and the storage of these fatty acids as triglycerides in the adipose tissue.

Other Effects of Cyclic AMP in Adipose Tissue. According to reports from one laboratory, acetyl CoA carboxylase is also phosphorylated and dephosphorylated, at least in rat adipose tissue, apparently in response to activation of protein kinase by cyclic AMP. It seems reasonable for the same signal that causes a mobilization of fatty acids and of glucose for use as fuels to suppress the synthesis of fatty acids from glucose, and other laboratories will undoubtedly test this hypothesis shortly.

THE ECONOMY OF FAT STORAGE

Expense of Making Triglycerides. When fatty acids are obtained from the diet, the cost of storing them as triglycerides is relatively low; two ~P must be used for each passage across a cell membrane in order to convert the fatty acid to the coenzyme A ester. Since there may be only two such passages, one in the intestinal mucosa and another in adipose tissue, the total cost of storage may be as little as 3 per cent ($^4/_{129}$) of the potential yield of ~P, which is a low price for the advantages obtained.

Expense of Storing Glucose as Fat

A typical triglyceride, 1-palmitoyl-2,3-dioleoyl glycerol, can be formed from glucose according to the equation:

$$15.42 \text{ glucose} + 15\ O_2 + 27.5\ (ADP + P_i) \longrightarrow \text{1-palmitoyl-2,3-dioleoyl glycerol} + 37.5\ CO_2 + 27.5\ ATP$$

(This represents the sum of the equations for converting glucose to the individual fatty acids as the coenzyme A esters, for transferring them to the glyceryl backbone, and for creating the glyceryl group from glucose.)

High-Energy Phosphate Yield. When this triglyceride is later mobilized and oxidized to CO_2 and H_2O, 437 molecules of ~P will be generated per molecule of triglyceride—129 from palmitate, 144 each from oleate, and 20 from glycerol. How does this compare with direct utilization of the 15.42 moles of glucose required to form one triglyceride molecule?

High-energy phosphate yield by various routes of utilization of 15.42 moles of glucose:

a. Direct oxidation to CO_2 and H_2O (15.42 × 36)	555 ~P
b. Storage as glycogen before oxidation to CO_2 and H_2O (15.42 × (−2 + 37))	540 ~P
c. Storage as triglyceride before oxidation to CO_2 and H_2O (calculated above)	437 ~P

We see that storage as fat causes a loss of 21% of the possible energy yield from ingested glucose, whereas storage as glycogen costs only 3%. (It costs two high-energy phosphates, one as ATP and one as UTP, to store a glucosyl unit in glycogen, but 37 are regained when that glucosyl unit is later burned.)

Oxygen Consumption. We have noted before that the P:O ratio is lower for the oxidation of fatty acids than it is for the oxidation of glucose; 3.08 molecules of ~P are formed for each atom of oxygen consumed in the combustion of a glucosyl residue from glycogen, while only 2.81 molecules are formed for each atom of oxygen consumed in the combustion of our typical triglyceride. The result is that an individual burning fats must consume more oxygen to do the same amount of work, and this theoretical calculation reflects the actual circumstances observed in working humans.

The Advantage of Fat Storage. Considering the lower efficiency of fat storage in terms of energy yield from either the food or the oxygen consumed, along with the less rapid mobilization of fat, why is excess carbohydrate ever stored as fat? The answer is that the many hydroxyl groups protruding on glycogen molecules cause an obligatory association with water, so that the combined mass of glycogen and its bound water per mole of potential ~P is approximately 13 grams. A typical triglyceride is hydrophobic, and little extra mass is required when it is stored, other than the small amount represented by the active substance of the adipocytes. Therefore, no more than 2.4 grams of mass are added per mole of potential ~P in this form.

Put another way, our typical 25-year old American male with his 7.7 kilograms of triglyceride would be walking around with an additional 34 kilograms or more of body mass if his fat store was replaced by glycogen with equal potential yield of ~P.

Fat and Desert Animals. More water is obtained by combustion of fat than is obtained by the combustion of an equal mass of carbohydrate. This is often advanced as an explanation of the use of fat stores by desert animals. However, it turns out that the combustion of fat produces less water per molecule of O_2 consumed or of ATP generated. The apparent advantage of fat as a source of water could only be gained by uncoupling oxidation and phosphorylation, thereby adding even more heat to be eliminated by the animal.

BROWN ADIPOSE TISSUE

Animals have another type of adipose tissue that has a high content of mitochondria, giving it a distinctly brown hue. Adult humans have little of this tissue, but it is prominent in the newborn, who have it in the upper torso and neck. It is also common in adults of animals that hibernate. The tissue acts as a means of producing heat, which is quite different from the function of ordinary adipose tissue as a reservoir of potential energy.

Larger animals appear to be limited in the rate of metabolism by the difficulty in disposing of heat. George Gamow has estimated that an elephant would be literally red-hot if its metabolic rate equalled that of a mouse. The point here is that the limitations on the elephant's metabolism come not from some inherent theoretical limit of the metabolic scheme, but from a built-in regulation adjusting its energy metabolism to its capacity for heat disposal. However, infants of a given species, including humans, have a high ratio of surface area to tissue mass as compared to adults, and are more vulnerable to cold. They are equipped with brown adipose tissue in which metabolism is deliberately inefficient, so that the rate of oxidation, and therefore the rate of heat production, is not geared to the utilization of high-energy phosphate by other metabolic processes. The mitochondria of brown adipose tissue apparently have a nearly total lack of coupling between oxidation and phosphorylation in the electron transport chain when the tissue is stimulated to maximum heat production. How this happens is not known. Small amounts of high-energy phosphate are produced by substrate level phosphorylations, such as the single mole created from each mole of succinyl CoA in the citric acid cycle, and this is apparently sufficient to maintain cell function.

The result is that the rate of oxidation is no longer influenced by the concentration of ATP and ADP in mitochondria. The regulating factor is unknown, but it may be the availability of fatty acids determined by the rate of breakdown of triglycerides, which in turn is regulated by neural or endocrine stimulation much as in ordinary white adipose tissue.

This tissue then is an example of a lipid store used for maintenance of body temperature when the ordinary metabolic processes together with increased metabolism caused by shivering are inadequate. The fact that it exists makes belief in the efficiency of the metabolism of other tissues much stronger. If they were inefficient, their metabolism could also be used for heat production, and there would be no need for a specialized brown adipose tissue.

FURTHER READING

R. M. S. Smellie, ed., Plasma lipoproteins, Biochem. Soc. Sympos. No. 32, Academic Press (1972).

P. Desnuelle, The lipases, 7:575 in P. D. Boyer, ed., The enzymes, 3rd ed. Academic Press (1972). Technical account.

J. C. Khoo, D. Steinberg, B. Thompson, and S. E. Mayer, Hormonal regulation of adipocyte enzymes. J. Biol. Chem., 248:3823 (1973). Effects of adrenaline and insulin on cyclic AMP.

Also see general references in Chapter 20.

QUESTIONS

1. What is different about the intermediates in the complete hydrolysis of a triglyceride and the intermediates in the formation of a triglyceride? Would these differences aid in the prevention of a futile cycle involving diglycerides and triglycerides?
2. Fatty acids may occur in the blood as a complex with albumin or in the form of triglycerides. What is the difference in the physical state and in the physiological role of the two forms?
3. Why must adipose tissue have either glucose or some precursor of glucose in order to store triglycerides brought to it through the blood?
4. The ingestion of medium-chain triglycerides causes a higher blood concentration of acetoacetate than does the ingestion of an equal weight of long-chain triglycerides. Why? (Hint: Medium-chain triglycerides are not stored in human adipose tissue.)
5. Explain what advantages storage of fat may have to an animal living in a hot desert over storage of carbohydrate.
6. All animals lose more water than they take in. (Why?) Would the action of brown adipose tissue exaggerate or diminish this effect? Why?

THE NITROGEN CYCLE

PART 5

AMINO ACIDS AS FUELS

CHAPTER 23

AMINO ACIDS: REMOVAL AND DISPOSAL OF NITROGEN

THE CONCEPTS

Amino acids are constantly being destroyed by animals. There is a basal excretion of nitrogen that requires an equal consumption by adults to maintain nitrogen equilibrium. An additional intake is necessary to lay down more tissue in the young or convalescent who are in positive nitrogen balance. The sick and injured are in negative nitrogen balance because they are metabolizing proteins from their own tissues in addition to those from the diet. After the needs for maintenance and growth of tissue are met, normal animals respond to increased intake of nitrogen by an increased excretion so as to maintain nitrogen balance. The excess carbon skeletons are used as fuel.

Direct deamination (removal of the amino group) of a saturated alkylamino acid to form a double bond is not a thermodynamically feasible reaction. However, it becomes feasible when C-3 has additional substituents causing further loss of free energy during the reaction. Serine and threonine can lose NH_4^+ directly because there is a concomitant dehydration of their 3-hydroxyl groups and a rearrangement to form 2-ketoacids. Histidine, phenylalanine, tyrosine, and aspartate can lose NH_4^+ directly because the resultant double bond is conjugated with resonant substituents in the C-3 substituent as well as with the C-1 carboxylate group.

The nitrogen of the amide groups of glutamine and asparagine is released as NH_4^+ by simple hydrolysis. However, the most common routes for removal of nitrogen from amino acids involve transaminations with α-ketoglutarate to form glutamate. The nitrogen is then removed by glutamate dehydrogenase, which uses NAD to form α-ketoglutarate and NH_4^+. The combined action of the aminotransferases and glutamate dehydrogenase makes it possible to have nitrogen from one amino acid appear as another or as NH_4^+. Since the reactions are reversible, it is also possible to synthesize some amino acids from NH_4^+ and the common 2-keto acid intermediates of metabolism.

The flexible interconversions of amino acids such as glutamate, aspartate, and alanine

simplify the development of effective means of nitrogen excretion. Organisms have evolved accelerated rates of formation of otherwise minor metabolic products as a means of creating products for excretion. For example, organisms make purines for incorporation into nucleotides by utilizing the nitrogen of amino acids, but the arthropods, birds, and reptiles divert nearly all of their excess amino acid nitrogen into the formation of purines, and then excrete insoluble purine derivatives. This permits disposal of the excess without great loss of water. The mammals, on the other hand, divert their excess amino acid nitrogen into the formation of arginine beyond the amount required for incorporation of the amino acid into tissue proteins, and hydrolyze the excess arginine to form urea, which is excreted in the urine. Ornithine is the other product of urea formation, and arginine is re-made from it by adding back one carbon and two nitrogen atoms. The carbon and one nitrogen are contributed by CO_2 and NH_4^+ in the form of carbamyl phosphate. The other nitrogen is obtained from aspartate, releasing its carbon skeleton as fumarate.

Ornithine therefore acts as a carrier for the carbon and nitrogen atoms from which urea is made, much in the way that oxaloacetate acts as a carrier for the carbons of acetyl groups. Aspartate, CO_2, NH_4^+ and four high-energy phosphate bonds are consumed to form urea and fumarate. The excretion of nitrogen as purines also consumes aspartate, CO_2 and NH_4^+, along with glycine, so all animals convert much of their amino acid nitrogen to aspartate and NH_4^+ for disposal. This is easy to do through the action of specific aminotransferases, including a powerful aspartate aminotransferase, and glutamate dehydrogenase.

Animals have a constant stream of organically-bound nitrogen passing through them. They ingest the 20 common amino acids in various proportions, depending upon the nature of the proteins in their customary foods, and use these nitrogen-containing substances as the precursors with which to build their own proteins. The amino acids are also the raw materials for the formation of other nitrogenous constituents, which include the purines and pyrimidines of nucleic acids, the porphyrins, and many less-abundant compounds that are still important to the function of the organism.

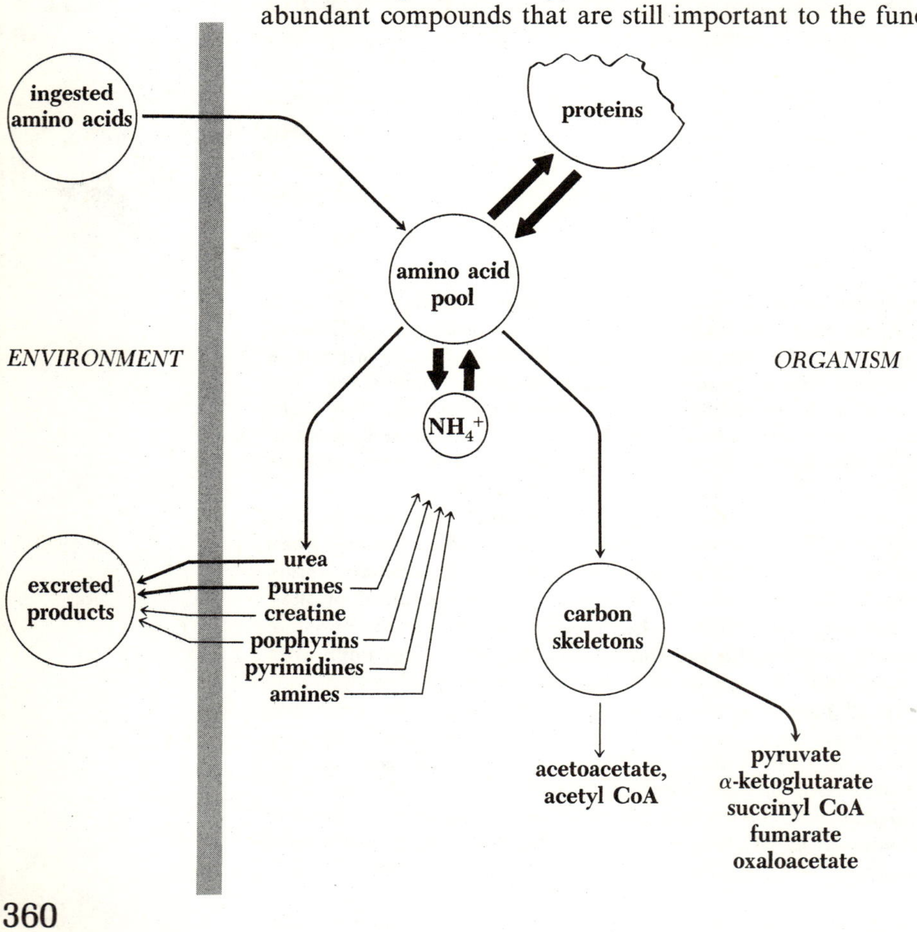

Figure 23-1 Animals absorb amino acids obtained from proteins in their food, and incorporate them into a free amino acid pool. Proteins are constantly synthesized from the pool and degraded to add to it. The pool is also used to form other nitrogenous compounds (*lower left*), some of which are degraded to form excreted products, and others to form NH_4^+. Some amino acids can be reformed from NH_4^+ and carbon skeletons, but there is a constant loss from the pool, with the carbon skeletons being converted to familiar intermediates in the oxidative metabolism of fats and carbohydrates.

The flow of nitrogen is outlined in Figure 23–1, which indicates that the first task of an organism is to rearrange its supply of amino acids so as to meet its own internal needs. An organism requires enough fuel to meet its daily energy demands, but it also needs sufficient amino acids with which to make new proteins and other nitrogenous components. The amino acid composition of the food does not always coincide with the optimum proportions for internal utilization by the tissues; hence, the organisms have a capacity for utilizing part of the ingested organic nitrogen to make new amino acids, thereby creating "pools" of free amino acids within the organism of proper composition for maintaining normal nitrogen metabolism.

Nitrogen Balance. Adult animals characteristically maintain nearly constant body composition over extended periods of time; they are said to be in **nitrogen equilibrium,** although they always show some variation in nitrogen content from one time to another.

A growing baby constantly accumulates more protein, nucleic acids, and so on, and therefore has a **positive nitrogen balance** in which the intake exceeds the losses. An injured or infected adult, on the other hand, has an increased rate of destruction of tissues; he therefore loses more nitrogen than he ingests, and is in **negative nitrogen balance.**

MAINTENANCE OF NITROGEN EQUILIBRIUM. Even without the formation of additional tissue, a dietary supply of nitrogen is necessary to maintain nitrogen equilibrium. This is so because the proteins and other compounds are constantly being broken down and remade. Some of the products of metabolism are not re-utilized and are excreted, for example in the urine of higher animals. Such inevitable losses of nitrogen must be replaced in the diet.

Animals are also prepared to cope with intakes of nitrogenous compounds that far exceed their minimal, or even optimal, needs. Where protists and plants can selectively absorb what they need from dissolved external mixtures of compounds, animals ingest single mouthfuls of tissues that contain their fuel supply and their nitrogen supply. It would be wasteful for any of these materials to pass into the feces unabsorbed. Hence, animals are built to utilize the carbon skeletons of amino acids as fuels while maintaining nitrogen equilibrium by excreting excess nitrogen. It is this removal and disposal of nitrogen that we shall now consider. The use of the carbon skeletons is taken up in the next chapter.

DEAMINATION OF AMINO ACIDS

Direct Deamination

Compounds containing amino groups could in theory lose ammonia by a direct deamination analogous to the dehydration of an alcohol:

$$\underset{\oplus NH_3}{\underset{|}{R{-}CH}}{-}CH_2{-}R' \xrightarrow{?} NH_4^{\oplus} + R{-}CH{=}CH{-}R'$$

(Note that the product is given as NH_4^+, rather than NH_3. There is 100 times as much ammonium ion as free ammonia at pH 7.4.) The position of equilibrium for such direct deaminations of simple amines is unfavorable, and removal in this way of the 2-amino group from amino acids is possible only when the amino acids contain other structures causing an additional loss of chemical potential during the reaction. Structures facilitating direct loss of ammonium ion include hydroxyl groups and resonant substituents on C-3 of the amino acid.

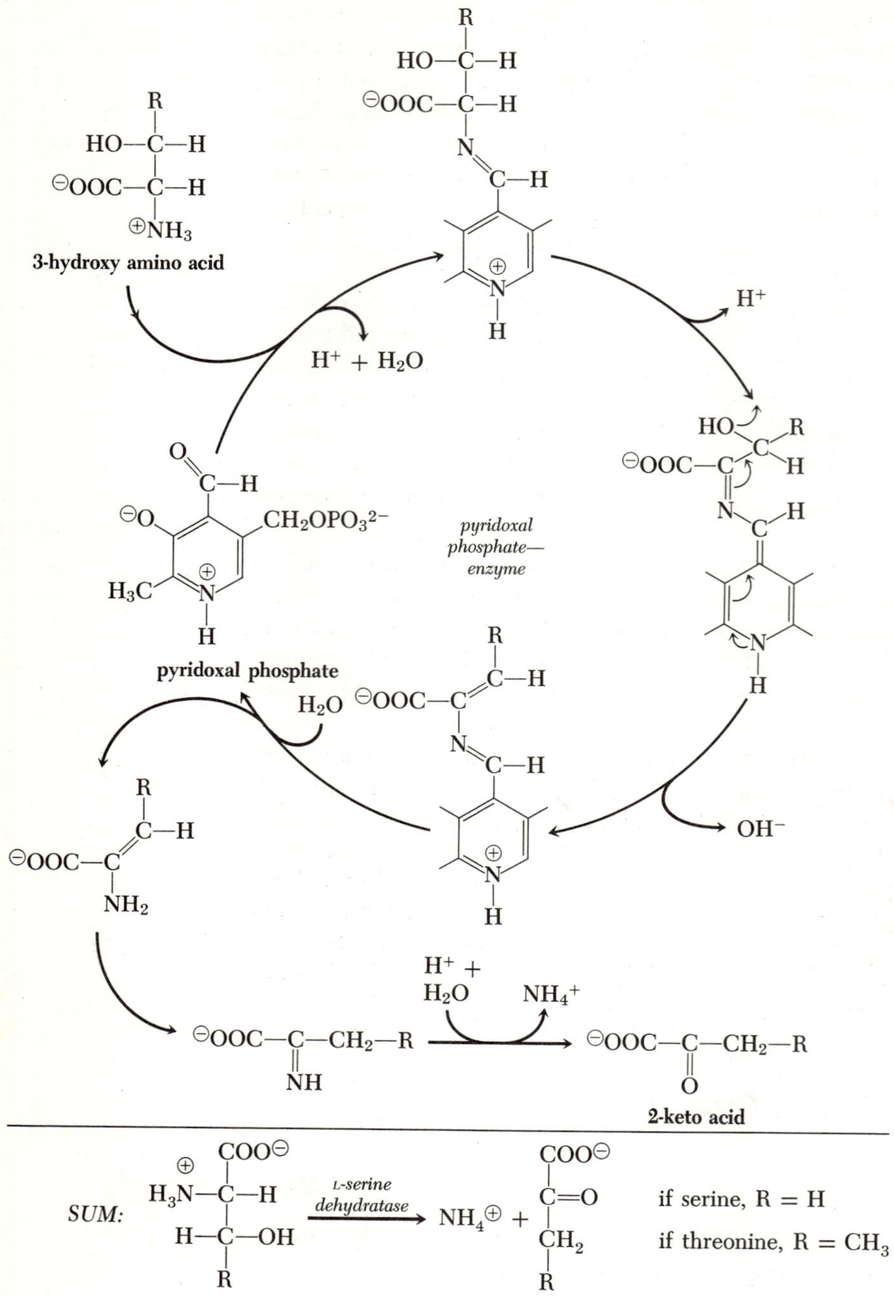

Figure 23-2 The deamination of hydroxy amino acids by dehydratases involves a combination of the amino group with the aldehyde group of pyridoxal phosphate on the enzyme to form an imine, or Schiff's base (*top center*). A series of electron shifts results in the elimination of the water, leaving an unsaturated imine (*bottom center*). Hydrolysis of the imine bond regenerates the aldehyde group of the coenzyme and liberates an unstable unsaturated amine, which spontaneously rearranges and hydrolyzes to yield NH_4^+ and the 2-keto analogue of the original amino acid.

Deamination of Serine and Threonine. Ammonium ions can be removed directly from serine and threonine, because these amino acids contain hydroxyl groups that participate in the reaction so that the ultimate products, in addition to NH_4^+, are pyruvate from serine and 2-ketobutyrate from threonine (Fig. 23-2). The presence of the hydroxyl group permits the formation of an intermediate unsaturated amine that rearranges to drive the reaction.

Use of Pyridoxal Phosphate. Serine dehydratase is one of several enzymes that make use of pyridoxal phosphate as a coenzyme for catalysis of amino acids. The reaction in each case involves the formation of a Schiff's base (aldimine) in which the double bond is conjugated with the pyridine ring of the coenzyme, and it is possible

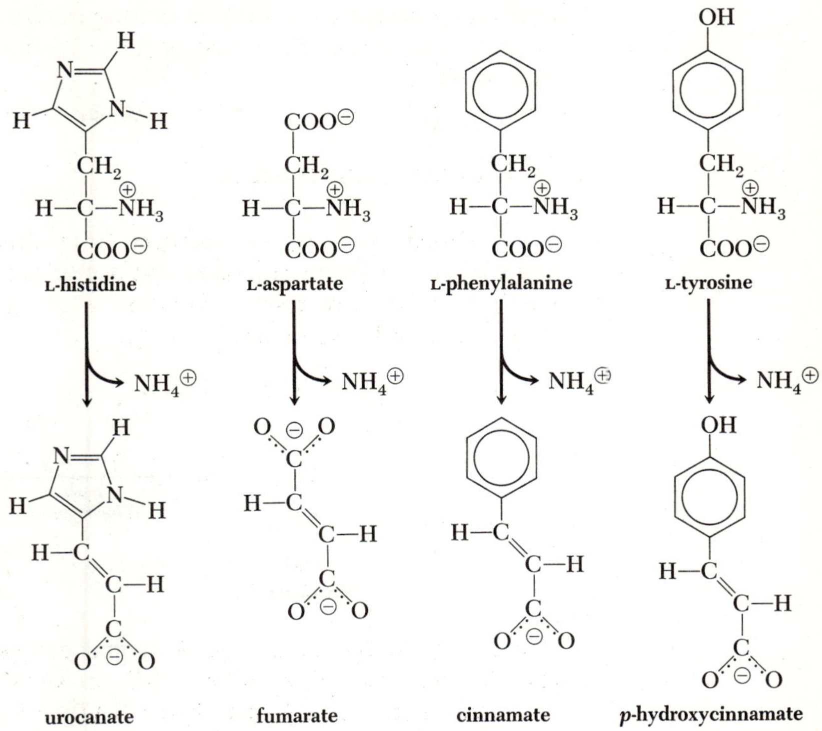

Figure 23-3 Simple deamination of histidine, aspartate, phenylalanine, and tyrosine is feasible because of the increased energy release caused by resonance of the products, but not all are handled this way in particular organisms.

to rearrange the conjugate in a variety of ways. (We shall encounter other examples.) The enzyme at hand is correctly named as a **dehydratase,** since its action involves the removal of the elements of water from the coenzyme-substrate complex.

Deamination of Histidine, Aspartate, Phenylalanine and Tyrosine. Direct deamination of amino acids containing resonant substituents on C-3, such as carboxylate groups or aromatic rings, is possible because the resultant double bond is conjugated with the C-1 carboxylate group as well as with the C-3 substituent (Fig. 23-3). The additional loss of free energy owing to resonance stabilization of the product makes the reaction feasible. However, animals degrade only histidine by this route. Some protists will use histidine or aspartate as fuels in this way. Direct deamination of phenylalanine and tryosine mainly occurs in plants to provide structural precursors (p. 461).

Hydrolysis of Amide Groups

Nitrogen atoms occur as amide groups in glutamine and asparagine, and these groups are directly hydrolyzed to NH_4^+ and glutamate or aspartate (Fig. 23-4). In

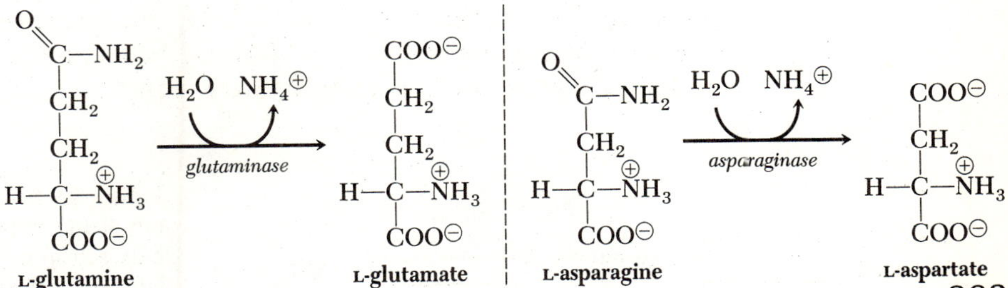

Figure 23-4 The amide nitrogen of glutamine and asparagine is released by simple hydrolysis.

addition, some nitrogen atoms occurring in tryptophan and histidine are converted to amide groups during the course of metabolism of the amino acids, and also removed by hydrolysis.

Oxidative Deamination

It is possible to remove nitrogen from almost any amino acid by an oxidation. There are many lesser examples, but one of the most important reactions in nitrogen metabolism is the reversible oxidation of glutamate by a nicotinamide nucleotide to form NH_4^+ and α-ketoglutarate:

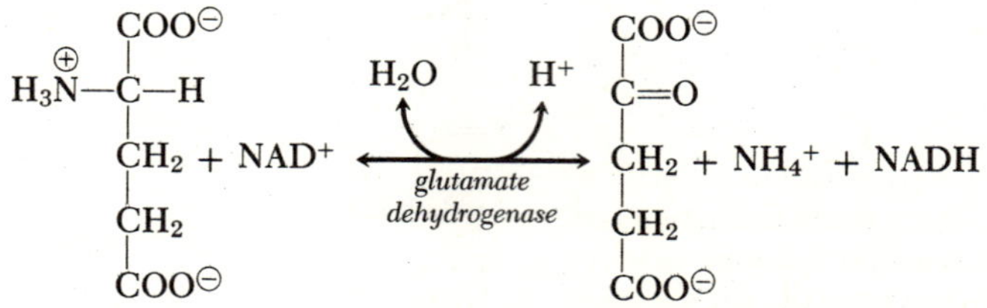

L-glutamate **α-ketoglutarate**

The glutamate dehydrogenase of animal tissues occurs in the inner matrix of mitochondria and will utilize either NAD or NADP. Since the NAD of mitochondria is somewhat more oxidized than is the NADP, it may be that the use of one nucleotide or the other permits glutamate dehydrogenase to be used for both degradation and synthesis of glutamate. Plants and protists frequently contain isozymes specific for either NAD or NADP that presumably function for one purpose or the other, but not both.

Transamination

Nitrogen is most commonly removed from amino acids by transferring the amino group to α-ketoglutarate. What was an amino acid is now a 2-keto acid, and α-ketoglutarate becomes glutamate. The overall strategy for this major process is shown in Figure 23–5. Transamination permits the exchange of nitrogen between many members of the amino acid pool and glutamate, and glutamate nitrogen is reversibly exchanged with ammonium ion by glutamate dehydrogenase, as we saw in the preceding section. The combined actions of the transaminases and glutamate dehydrogenase are therefore responsible for much of the flexibility of composition of the amino acid pool, and provide a common route for removing or introducing nitrogen.

Aspartate Aminotransferase. We discussed the mechanism of this enzyme in Chapter 8 to illustrate the use of pyridoxal phosphate. It equilibrates aspartate and α-ketoglutarate with oxaloacetate and glutamate (Fig. 23–6). The action of this enzyme is of central importance in nitrogen metabolism. Applying the general strategy, we see that the combined action of the aminotransferase and glutamate dehydrogenase makes it possible for aspartate N to appear as NH_4^+, or for aspartate to be formed from NH_4^+ and oxaloacetate. (NADPH or NADH will be an additional product.) Aspartate may be formed or removed, as circumstances require.

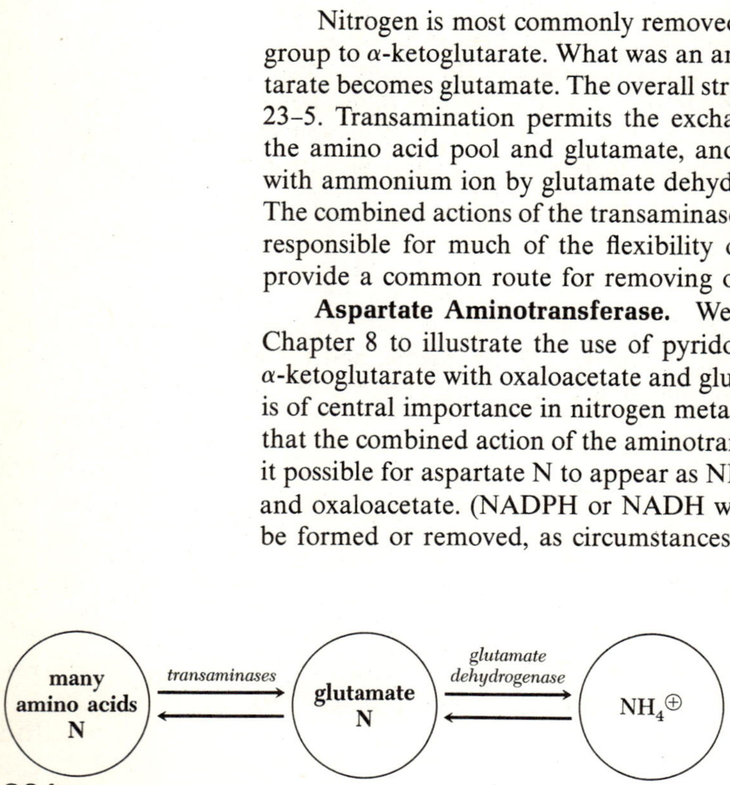

Figure 23–5 The strategy of nitrogen metabolism involves the exchange of nitrogen between many amino acids and glutamate by aminotransferases (transaminases), and the equilibration of that nitrogen with NH_4^+ by glutamate dehydrogenase.

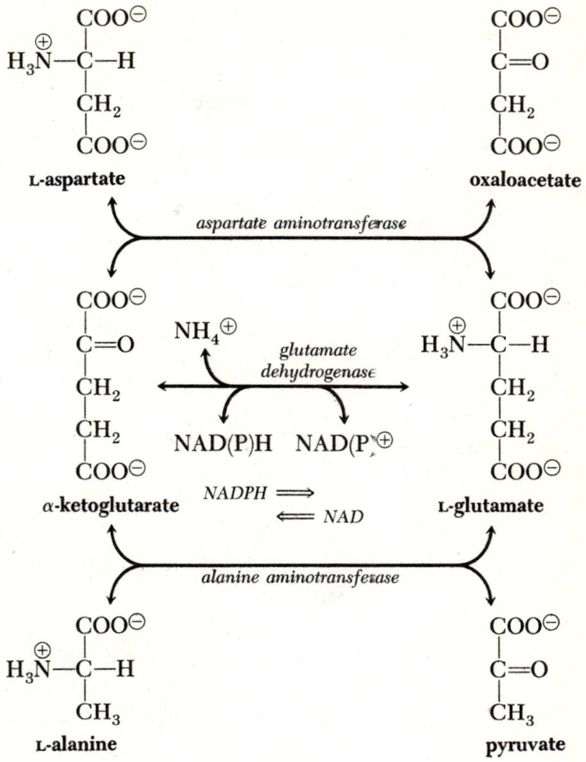

Figure 23-6 The metabolism of aspartate and alanine is of general importance. The amino acids and their keto analogues, oxaloacetate and pyruvate, are equilibrated by specific aminotransferases with glutamate and α-ketoglutarate. Glutamate dehydrogenase utilizes either NAD for removing NH_4^+ from glutamate, or NADPH for synthesizing glutamate from NH_4^+ and α-ketoglutarate. These routes make it possible to degrade or to synthesize aspartate and alanine.

Alanine Aminotransferase. Alanine is also of central importance in amino acid metabolism, and it is equilibrated with its corresponding 2-keto acid, pyruvate, through transamination with α-ketoglutarate. Studying Figure 23–6 more closely, we see that it is not only possible to interconvert the nitrogen of alanine with that of NH_4^+ through the combined action of the aminotransferase and glutamate dehydrogenase, but it is also possible to move nitrogen between aspartate and alanine without going through NH_4^+!

Other Aminotransferases. Aminotransferases specific for a variety of other compounds also occur. The transfers sometimes form alanine, rather than glutamate, as the second product, but the general principle is the same: the nitrogen can eventually appear as glutamate, and then as either aspartate or NH_4^+.

EXCRETION OF NITROGEN

Evolution of Routes

Simple marine animals have no problem in disposing of excess nitrogen; they produce $\mathbf{NH_4^+}$, which diffuses (as NH_3) into the surrounding sea and becomes rapidly diluted. It may well be that the primitive ancestors of these animals evolved so that not only their nitrogen economy, but their sensitivity to ions hinged on the presence of low concentrations ($<100\ \mu M$) of NH_4^+. In any event, modern animals will not tolerate high concentrations, and an important consequence was that species capable of surviving outside of the sea appeared only after mechanisms evolved for converting ammonia to less dangerous compounds that can be excreted in batches.

Uricotelism and Ureotelism. Nitrogen excretion was achieved in land animals by the modification of already existing metabolic reactions, frequently of minor quan-

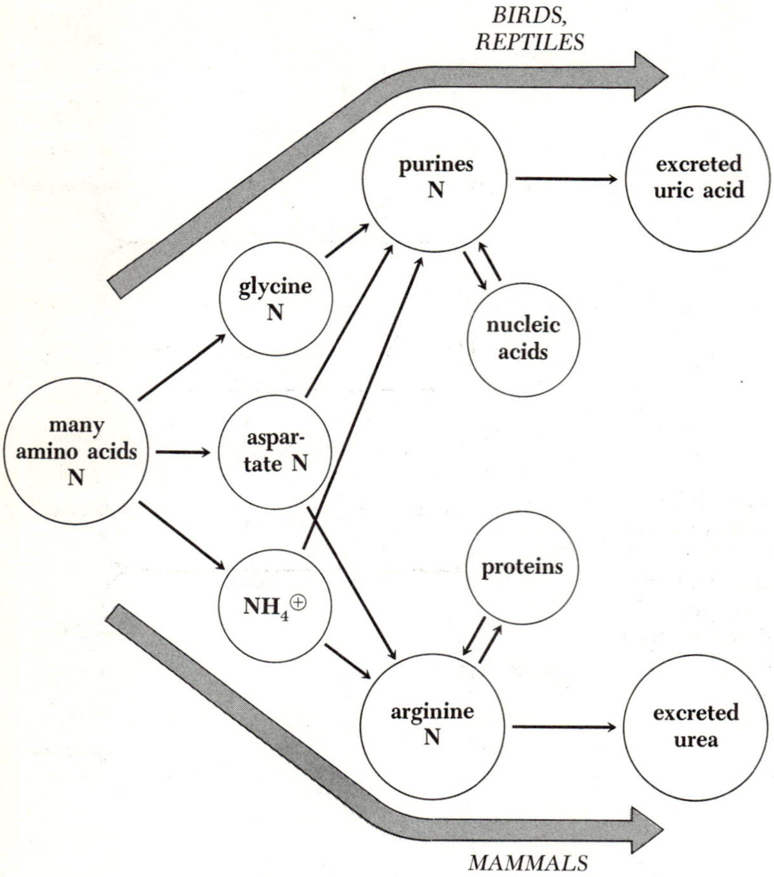

Figure 23-7 Animals such as birds and reptiles eliminate excess nitrogen by converting it to glycine, aspartate and NH_4^+, from which purines are formed in amounts exceeding the requirements for maintaining nucleic acids and other nucleotides. The excess is converted to uric acid for excretion. Mammals utilize aspartate and NH_4^+ to synthesize arginine in excess of the amounts required for maintaining proteins, and this excess is hydrolyzed to form urea for excretion.

titative significance, in marine animals. (Of course, their kidneys also evolved to handle the compounds.) For example, the two most widely used routes for elimination of nitrogen by present animals involve the formation of excess purines or excess arginine (Fig. 23-7). Birds, reptiles, and terrestrial arthropods utilize excess nitrogen to form **purines** in quantities far beyond the amount necessary to maintain the stores of ATP, GTP, nucleic acids, and the like. The excess is converted to some insoluble product such as **guanine** or **uric acid,** and excreted with little loss of water. (The animal is said to be uricotelic if uric acid is the product.) Other animals also make excreted derivatives of purines, but only in the small quantities representing normal wear and tear of the nucleotide stores. The purine excretors have magnified this customary route to handle nearly all of their nitrogen flux.

On the other hand, mammals have evolved to magnify the synthesis of **arginine,** an amino acid, as a means of eliminating nitrogen. The excess nitrogen is hydrolyzed in a way that will form **urea,** and this highly soluble compound with a low toxicity is stored in solution for excretion. Mammals are therefore ureotelic. Birds and reptiles also make arginine, but only in the quantity required to maintain their tissue proteins, and they have lost the ability to degrade arginine to urea.

Sources of Excreted Nitrogen

The formation of uric acid requires nitrogen from glycine, aspartate, and NH_4^+; the formation of arginine also requires nitrogen from aspartate and NH_4^+. Excess nitrogen must therefore be diverted into these compounds from the general amino acid pool for excretion. We shall consider the formation of the purines in Chapter 26, and consider only the disposal of nitrogen as urea *via* arginine now.

Formation of Aspartate and NH_4^+. We have already seen the basis for converting excess nitrogen to aspartate and NH_4^+. Some amino acids yield at least one molecule of NH_4^+ directly, and these include serine, threonine, asparagine, glutamine, and histidine. Other amino acids do so indirectly, through the combined action of aminotransferases and glutamate dehydrogenase. These routes for producing NH_4^+ are indicated to the left in Figure 23–8. However, the intermediate glutamate also is equilibrated with aspartate by its aminotransferase, as is shown to the right in Figure 23–8. It is therefore possible to have the nitrogen from all amino acids converted to both NH_4^+ and aspartate in any proportions.

Formation of Urea

Urea is actually formed by cleaving the amidinio group from the side-chain of arginine (Fig. 23–9). The synthesis of urea therefore requires replacement of the amidinio group of arginine, with its one carbon and two nitrogen atoms. The remainder of the arginine molecule, which appears as ornithine when urea is formed, acts only as a carrier for this process, much in the way that oxaloacetate acts as a carrier for acetyl groups in the citric acid cycle. (Ornithine is an amino acid, but there are no codons specifying it; hence it is not incorporated into proteins. This is also true of the other intermediate amino acids in urea synthesis, except for arginine itself.)

Synthesis of Carbamyl Phosphate. The first step in the rebuilding of arginine from ornithine involves the combination of NH_4^+ and CO_2 as carbamyl phosphate, which contains a high-energy phosphate bond. Many organisms that do not excrete nitrogen as urea make carbamyl phosphate for other purposes by a reversible cleavage of one molecule of ATP. The animals we are considering, which do excrete urea, couple the synthesis of carbamyl phosphate to the cleavage of two molecules of ATP in order to make the reaction effectively irreversible. It is this irreversibility that enables the concentration of NH_4^+ to be kept at low levels.

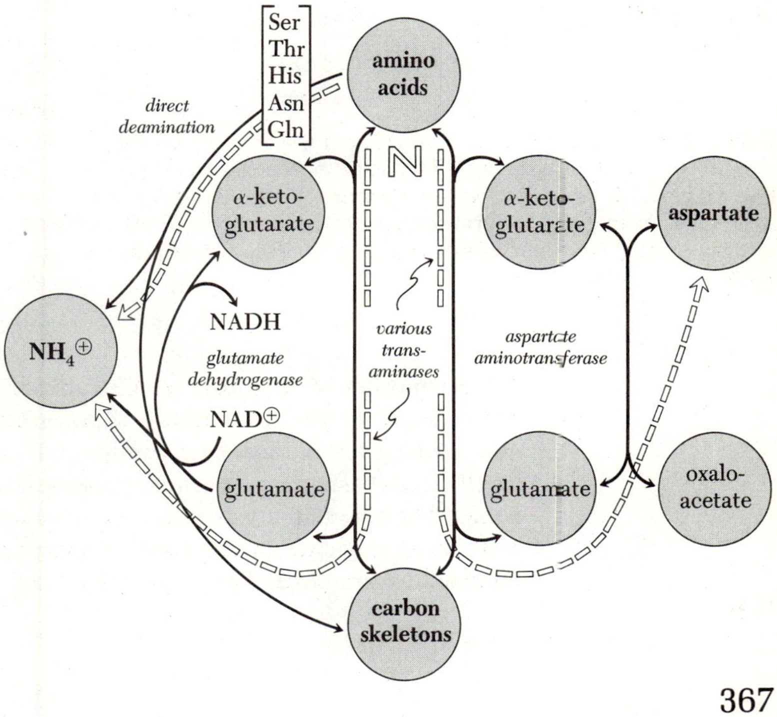

Figure 23-8 The conversion of amino acid nitrogen to aspartate and NH_4^+ for disposal as urea. Some NH_4^+ is formed by direct deamination of amino acids (*upper left*); the balance is made by transamination to form glutamate, which is oxidatively deaminated by glutamate dehydrogenase. Aspartate is formed by transamination to form glutamate, followed by another transamination that yields aspartate (*right*).

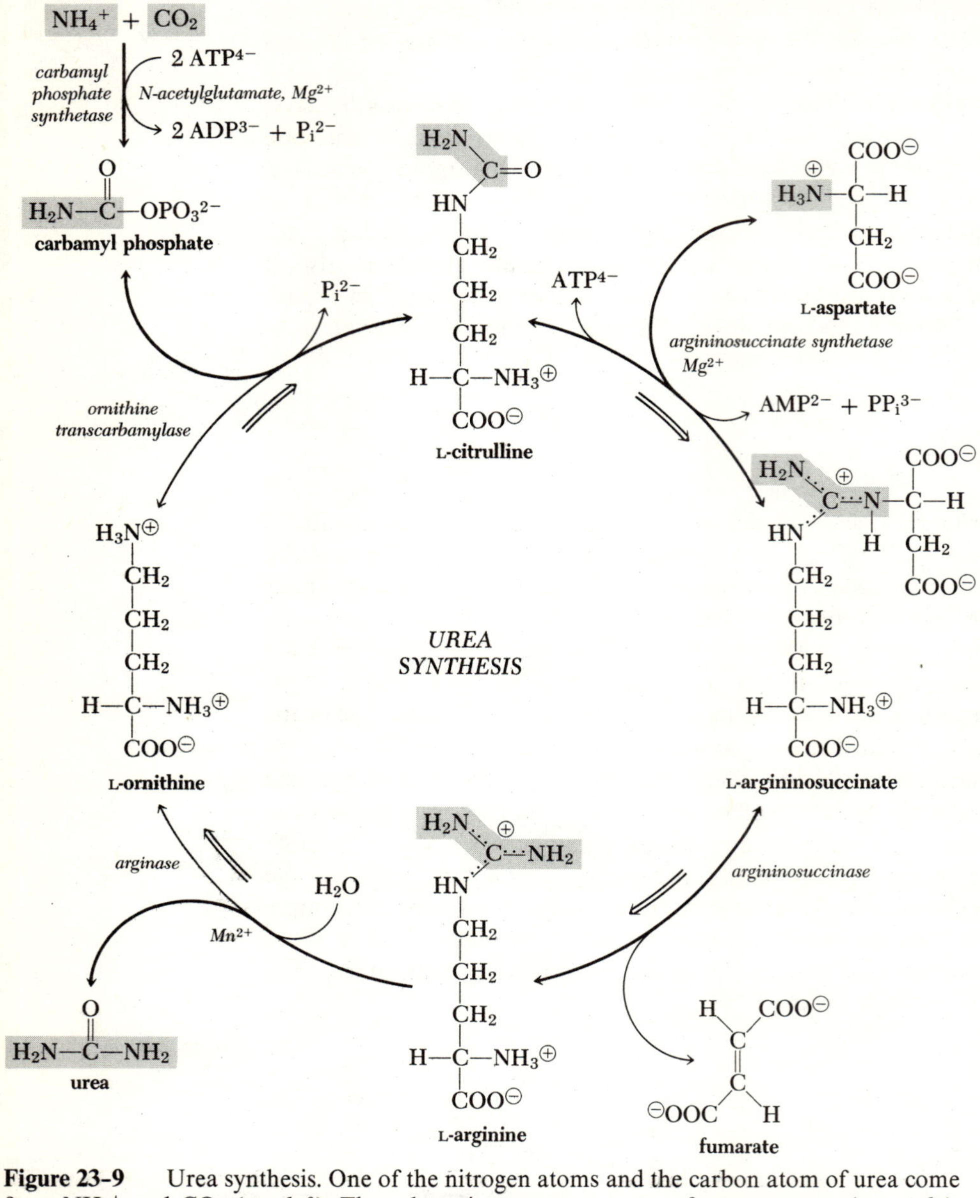

Figure 23-9 Urea synthesis. One of the nitrogen atoms and the carbon atom of urea come from NH_4^+ and CO_2 (*top left*). The other nitrogen atom comes from aspartate (*top right*). The amino acid, ornithine, acts as a carrier for the groups, and it is converted to arginine. Arginine is hydrolyzed to form urea, with the liberation of the ornithine carrier. The entire process is driven by the ultimate cleavage of four high-energy phosphate bonds, including the hydrolysis of PP_i.

Formation of Arginine *via* Citrulline. The carbamyl group of carbamyl phosphate is transferred to ornithine to form citrulline. Citrulline then gains a nitrogen atom from aspartate to form arginine. This is accomplished by a condensation of citrulline and aspartate driven by the expenditure of two more high-energy phosphate bonds. The resultant argininosuccinate is cleaved so as to leave the nitrogen atom that came from aspartate in the form of arginine. The remaining atoms of aspartate are liberated as fumarate. The effect of this sequence is to form a —C=N—C— bridge on one side of the central nitrogen atom, and cleave it on the other; the condensation and cleavage effectively transfer the nitrogen from aspartate to citrulline.

Complete Cycle. In sum, the formation of one molecule of urea requires the consumption of one molecule each of NH_4^+, aspartate, and CO_2, with a cleavage of four high-energy phosphate bonds. A molecule of fumarate is produced in addition to a molecule of urea, and we shall see in the next chapter how this and other carbon skeletons are metabolized.

Urea synthesis was the first biochemical cycle to be discovered. The route was worked out by Hans A. Krebs, a physician with good biochemical training. He later elucidated the citric acid cycle as the second major example of a cyclical process. A Nobel prize and subsequent English knighthood were something of an anticlimax after all of this. Formally retired, he is still in the first rank of biochemists solving problems of metabolic control.

FURTHER READING

R. W. McGilvery, Biochemistry, W. B. Saunders (1970). More detailed discussions of the metabolic routes are in Chapter 17; the nitrogen economy is discussed in Chapters 22 and 27.

A. Meister, Biochemistry of the amino acids, 2nd ed., Academic Press (1965). Authoritative two-volume source for details on reactions.

J. W. Campbell, ed., Comparative biochemistry of nitrogen metabolism, Academic Press (1970). Detailed technical accounts.

J. W. Campbell and L. Goldstein, eds., Nitrogen metabolism and the environment, Academic Press (1972). Somewhat more up-to-date and more lucid than preceding reference.

QUESTIONS

1. Why is the direct deamination of some naturally occurring amino acids feasible?
2. Predict whether these reactions are possible:

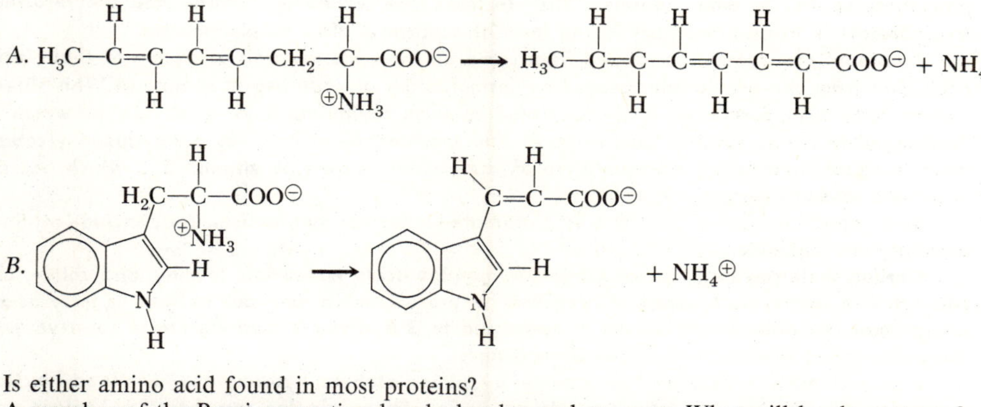

Is either amino acid found in most proteins?

3. A member of the Pepsi generation breaks her leg and recovers. What will be the status of her nitrogen balance during this time? Explain.
4. Show how the nitrogen of tyrosine may appear as NH_4^+ by the combined action of tyrosine aminotransferase and glutamate dehydrogenase.
5. Show how the nitrogen of excess tyrosine can be equally partitioned between aspartate and NH_4^+.
6. How many high-energy phosphate bonds must be cleaved to excrete one atom of nitrogen as urea?
7. Why is the formation of urea accompanied by the formation of fumarate?
8. Explain why the toxicity of ammonia may necessitate the expenditure of two high-energy phosphate bonds during the formation of carbamyl phosphate.

CHAPTER 24

AMINO ACIDS: DISPOSAL OF THE CARBON SKELETONS

THE CONCEPTS

The carbon skeletons of most amino acids are converted to pyruvate or intermediates of the citric acid cycle, such as α-ketoglutarate, succinyl coenzyme A, fumarate, and oxaloacetate. The amino acid skeletons therefore contribute to any process utilizing malate and oxaloacetate as intermediates, including gluconeogenesis and fatty acid synthesis. Gluconeogenesis is of special importance because amino acids sometimes are the only available precursors of glucose, whereas fatty acid synthesis proceeds only when there is already an excess of fuel in the form of glucose.

The components of the citric acid cycle are mostly produced from the amino acids in mitochondria, and transferred to the cytosol in the form of malate or aspartate for further metabolism. Malate is a good precursor of glucose through the route malate ⟶ oxaloacetate ⟶ phospho-*enol*-pyruvate ⟶ triose phosphate. The carbon skeleton of aspartate is converted to malate when its nitrogen is removed for urea synthesis (aspartate ⟶ fumarate ⟶ malate). The transport of aspartate across the mitochondrial membranes is also involved in an electron shuttle that serves the same function in red muscles that is played by the glycerol phosphate shuttle in white muscles. The electrons are carried as malate, and the resultant oxaloacetate is transported back in the form of aspartate, after transamination.

Propionyl coenzyme A is formed from some amino acids, as well as from odd-chain fatty acids and from the propionate created by fermentation of cellulose in ruminants. This three-carbon fatty acid derivative is carboxylated to form methylmalonyl coenzyme A, which is rearranged to create succinyl coenzyme A. The rearrangement involves deoxyadenosylcobalamin, a cobalt-containing representative of compounds known as vitamin B_{12}, which has an otherwise unusual carbon-cobalt bond.

Some amino acids are converted to glutamate for further metabolism. They include proline, arginine, and histidine.

Carbon skeletons from the branched chain amino acids, isoleucine, leucine, and valine, are converted to coenzyme A esters of branched fatty acids, which are metabolized as fatty acids, except that the skeleton of leucine is converted to 3-hydroxy-3-methylglutaryl coenzyme A, the precursor of acetoacetate, at an early stage.

Phenylalanine is oxidized to tyrosine by phenylalanine hydroxylase, a mixed-function oxidase that activates O_2 with tetrahydrobiopterin. (Phenylalanine can therefore replace any tyrosine requirement in the diet.) Tetrahydrobiopterin is a coenzyme related to folate (next chapter) and to pterin pigments found in insect wings.

Tyrosine is degraded by an oxygenase that adds O_2 across a double bond; there is a simultaneous decarboxylation and shift of the side chain. The product, known as homogentisate, is attacked by another oxygenase that opens the aromatic ring with O_2, forming new carbonyl groups in a straight-chain compound that is cleaved to fumarate and acetoacetate.

Representative fates of the carbon skeletons of amino acids are:

pyruvate from: alanine, cysteine, glycine, serine, tryptophan;

α-ketoglutarate from: arginine, glutamate, histidine, proline;

succinyl coenzyme A from (*via* methylmalonyl coenzyme A): isoleucine, methionine, threonine, valine:

fumarate from: aspartate, phenylalanine, tyrosine;

acetoacetate from: leucine, phenylalanine, tyrosine;
acetyl coenzyme A from: isoleucine, lysine.

When proteins are used as fuel, the yield of high-energy phosphate per unit mass is about that from carbohydrates, but more oxygen must be consumed. Although tissue proteins may be consumed as fuels when the supply of fat is depleted, the loss of function can be serious in a short time because the yield of high-energy phosphate per unit mass is only about 0.1 as much.

The destruction of amino acids also includes disposition of the carbon atoms. The organism uses these carbon skeletons as fuel in the same way that it uses fats or carbohydrates. The fraction of the fuel economy represented by amino acids varies between species and from day to day. For example, amino acids may easily represent as much as one-half of the potential energy in the diet of carnivores, while a starving animal is forced to destroy only a small amount of amino acids in order to keep its cellular constituents in repair. (However, it is of some importance to the starving animal to recover whatever energy it can from this small amount.)

GENERAL ROUTES

Metabolism as Citric Acid Cycle Components

Most carbon atoms of most amino acids appear as pyruvate and as constituents of the citric acid cycle after removal of the nitrogen atoms. We have already seen the formation of **α-ketoglutarate** from glutamate, **oxaloacetate** or **fumarate** from aspartate, and pyruvate from alanine or serine. Other amino acids are precursors of the same compounds, or are converted to the same amino acids for disposal. Still other amino acids are precursors of **succinyl coenzyme A.**

Most of the degradation of amino acids occurs in the liver of mammals. The intermediates of the citric acid cycle formed from amino acids are subject to the same reactions seen with the same compounds derived from other sources. α-Ketoglutarate and succinyl coenzyme A formed from amino acids are also oxidized to malate and oxaloacetate. We have already seen that malate and oxaloacetate are involved in somewhat intricate ways with the synthesis of glucose and fatty acids in liver.

Here then is the general strategy for the disposal of most amino acid skeletons (Fig. 24–1). They are converted in the liver to pyruvate, malate, and oxaloacetate, which are used as precursors of phospho-*enol*-pyruvate when the liver is carrying out gluconeogenesis, and as precursors of acetyl groups, with a coincident formation of NADPH, when the liver is synthesizing fatty acids.

Seen in these terms, a grand logic in chemical evolution begins to take shape. The particular amino acids that are used to make a bewildering variety of proteins have structures that also facilitate their metabolism through the same routes used for general fuel metabolism. Which was the determining factor—the character of the amino acids necessary to create particular proteins, or the structures that could be handled by general routes of metabolism? We don't know, but whatever might have been the primitive condition, the two characteristics now complement each other.

Use in Gluconeogenesis. More attention is given to the use of amino acids as a source of glucose, because it provides the only supply to a starving animal. It becomes significant even during the overnight fast, and it is also important to carnivores and others eating a diet with little carbohydrate. (Glucose is used as a precursor of many cellular constituents, in addition to its function as fuel.)

Gluconeogenesis from amino acids hinges on transport of citric acid cycle interme-

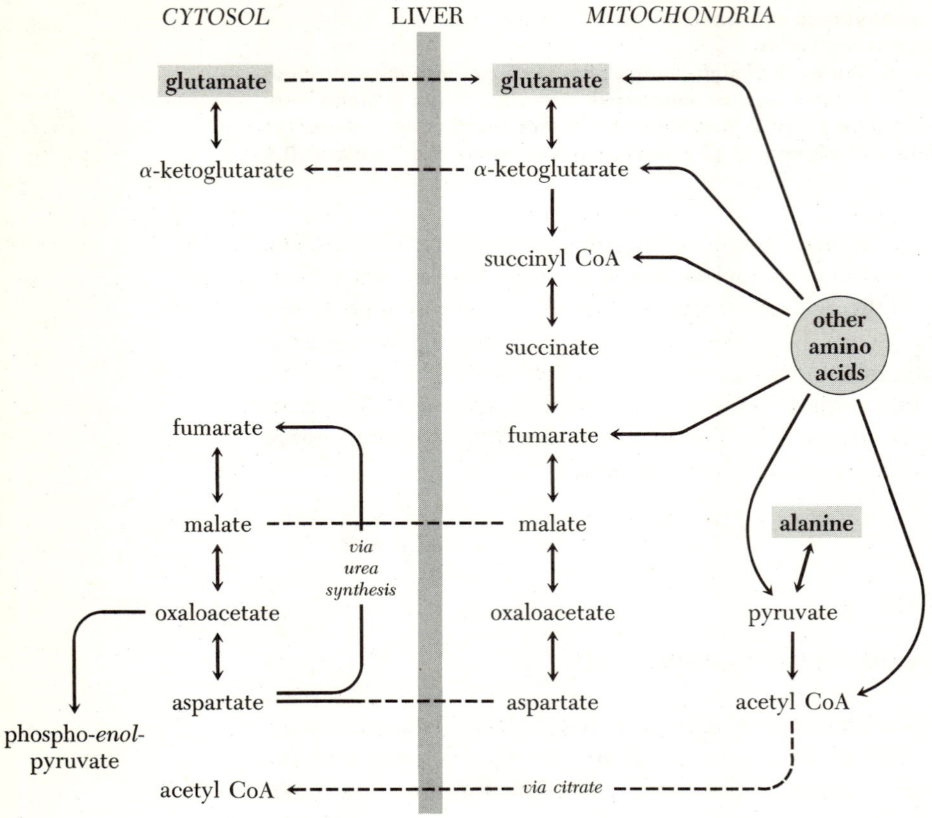

Figure 24–1 The carbon skeletons of amino acids are converted to intermediates of the citric acid cycle, pyruvate or acetyl coenzyme A. They may be moved from the cytosol as malate or aspartate. Aspartate is converted to fumarate in the cytosol by its participation in urea synthesis. Malate and fumarate are converted to phospho-*enol*-pyruvate *via* oxaloacetate.

diates from the mitochondria into the cytosol, and their conversion to phospho-*enol*-pyruvate via oxaloacetate (Fig. 24–2). Glucose 6-phosphate is then made in the usual way (Chap. 15). Several of the constituent compounds in the citric acid cycle can be transported into the cytosol, but the greatest flux of carbons for gluconeogenesis is believed to occur in the form of **malate** and **aspartate.** Malate is the paradigm precursor of glucose. It is converted to oxaloacetate by an oxidation that generates NADH. NADH is then available for the required reversal of the Embden-Meyerhof pathway to form triose phosphates, and malate therefore can be converted to a triose phosphate and CO_2 without any other oxidation or reduction.

Similarly, when aspartate is transported into the cytosol to be used in urea synthesis, the carbons appear as fumarate, which is equilibrated in the cytosol with malate, and can therefore be used directly as a precursor for three carbons in glucose.

Use in Fatty Acid Synthesis. The carbons from amino acids appearing as malate, oxaloacetate, and pyruvate may also be used to form fatty acids when the liver has an excess supply of glucose. The likely route here involves the use of the NADP-coupled malate dehydrogenase to generate pyruvate (Fig. 24–3). It has not been intensively studied because the conditions under which it will occur also make the amino acids of minor importance as a fuel.

Aspartate-Malate Shuttle in Electron Transport. Amino acids are also involved in transport of electrons from the cytosol to the mitochondria in fibers of red muscles and the heart. We have already discussed transport by the glycerol phosphate shuttle in white muscles. The other muscles get electrons into mitochondria by reducing oxaloacetate to malate in the cytosol, transporting the malate into mitochondria, and re-oxidizing it within the mitochondria. Oxaloacetate won't cross the membranes, and it is returned to the cytosol in the form of aspartate (Fig. 24–4). The nitrogen is added

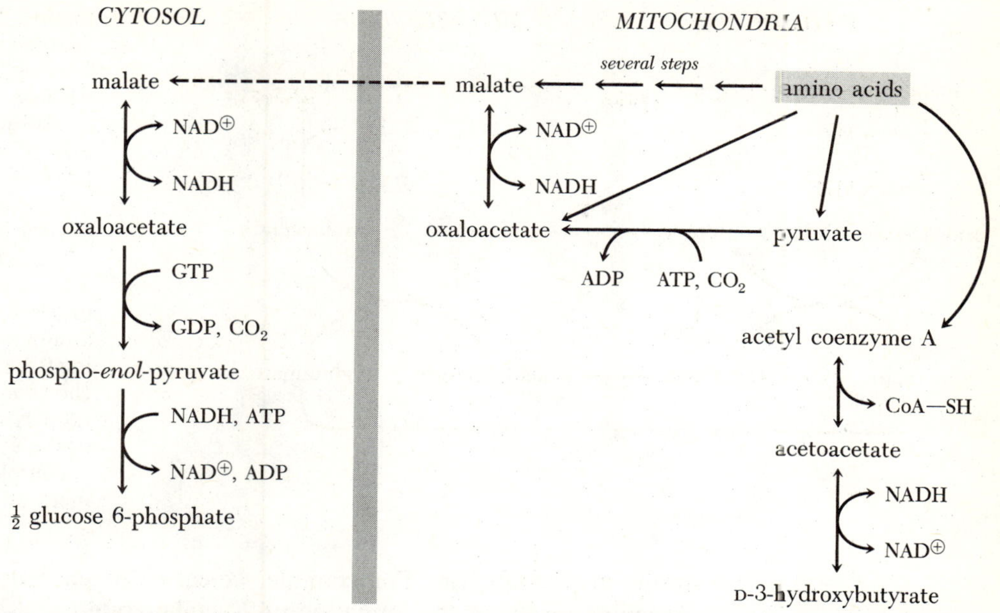

Figure 24-2 Gluconeogenesis from the carbon skeletons of amino acids *via* malate is usually accompanied by ketogenesis from the acetyl groups also produced.

and removed by a concomitant transamination with α-ketoglutarate and glutamate. Energy is somehow pumped into this system when glutamate is exchanged for aspartate, so it is probable that one high-energy phosphate is expended for the three later obtained by oxidation of NADH, with the same net yield of two ATP molecules per pair of electrons transferred that is obtained by the glycerol phosphate shuttle.

Propionyl Coenzyme A and Cobalamins

Propionyl Coenzyme A from Amino Acids. Carbon atoms from some amino acids, including threonine, isoleucine, and methionine, appear as propionyl coenzyme

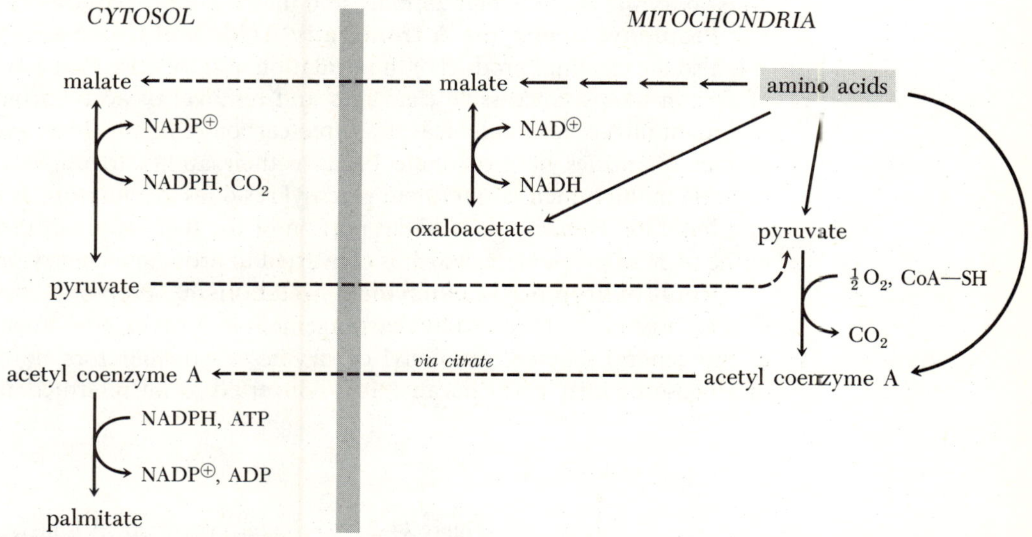

Figure 24-3 The carbon skeletons of amino acids can also be used to synthesize fatty acids at times when glucose is plentiful.

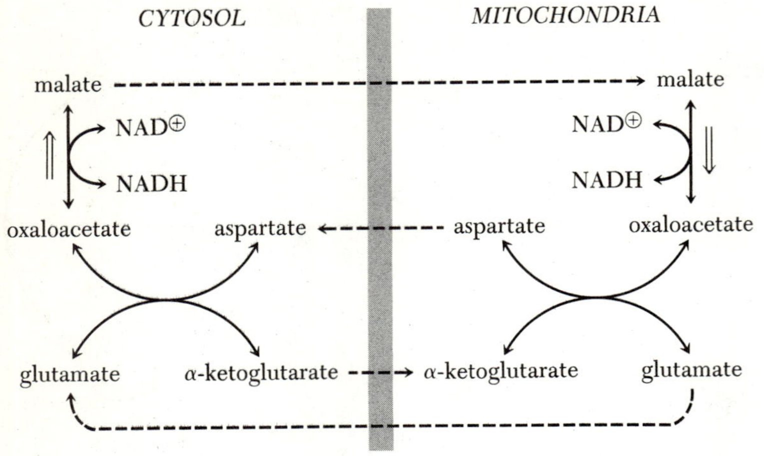

Figure 24-4 The aspartate-malate electron shuttle. Malate is used as a means of transporting electrons from NADH in the cytosol to NAD in the mitochondria of cardiac muscle and the red fibers of skeletal muscles. Oxaloacetate is transported back to the cytosol in the form of aspartate, which is exchanged for glutamate. This exchange appears to be driven by high-energy phosphate, and provides the energy for creating more NADH in the mitochondria, where the NADH/NAD ratio is already higher than it is in the cytosol. The entire process is completed by a reverse movement of α-ketoglutarate.

A during their catabolism. For example, we earlier noted that the direct deamination of threonine results in the formation of **2-ketobutyrate** (p. 362). This compound is a typical 2-ketocarboxylate, the next higher homologue of pyruvate, and it is attacked by pyruvate dehydrogenase in an exactly analogous way, complete with decarboxylation, oxidation by a lipoyl group, and transfer of the resultant acyl group to coenzyme A. The only difference is that the product has one more carbon atom; it is propionyl coenzyme A:

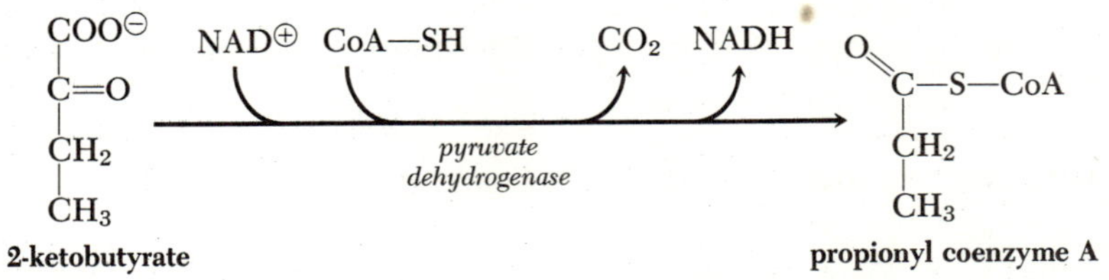

(This oxidative decarboxylation is an irreversible reaction; there is no route for forming 2-ketobutyrate in the higher animals, and they therefore require threonine in their diet.)

Propionyl Coenzyme A from Fatty Acids and Glucose. Propionyl coenzyme A is also the terminal product of the oxidation of fatty acids that contain an odd number of carbon atoms. Successive cleavages and removal of acetyl groups from these less-abundant fatty acids finally leaves a three-carbon remnant. The ruminants handle even greater quantities of propionate because their ability to utilize cellulose hinges on bacteria in the rumen that ferment glucosyl residues to a mixture of acetate, propionate, and butyrate. Hence, a substantial portion of the fuel supply of these animals appears in the form of propionate, which is converted to propionyl coenzyme A for metabolism.

Route of Propionyl Coenzyme A Metabolism. Propionyl coenzyme A is handled by a carboxylation followed by rearrangement to form succinyl coenzyme A. According to the general scheme, propionyl coenzyme A can therefore be used as a precursor of glucose or fatty acids because it is converted to an intermediate in the citric acid

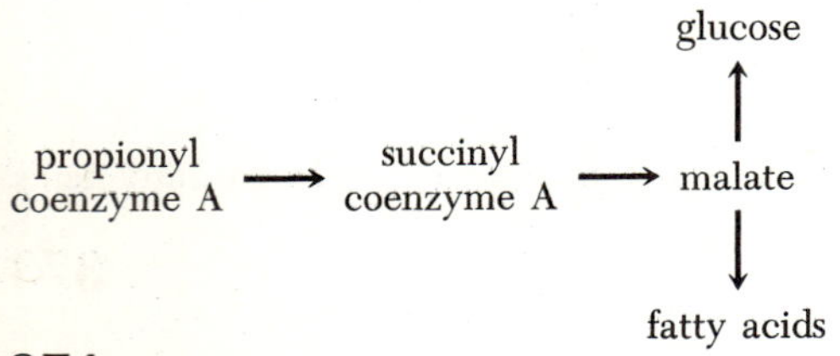

Figure 24-5 Propionyl coenzyme A is metabolized by converting it to succinyl coenzyme A, which may be converted to glucose or to fatty acids.

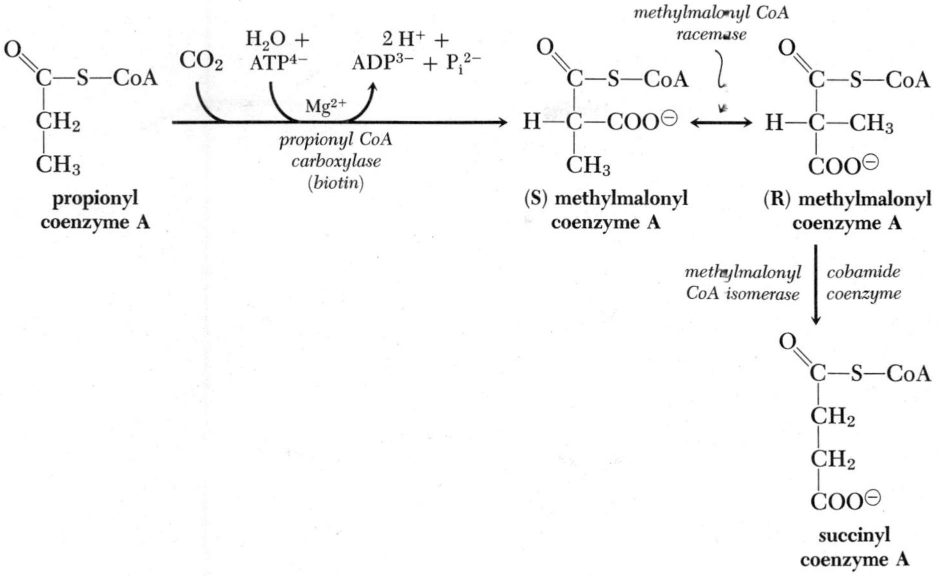

Figure 24-6 The conversion of propionyl coenzyme A to succinyl coenzyme A involves a carboxylation driven by ATP, and a rearrangement that requires the presence of deoxyadenosylcobalamin.

cycle (Fig. 24-5). (It follows that odd-chain fatty acids are an exception to our general dictum that glucose can not be made from fatty acids by the higher animals; however, only three carbons of each molecule can be used to make glucose. Given the low occurrence of odd-chain fatty acids, the exception becomes trivial in terms of the total metabolic economy.)

Some of the details of propionyl group metabolism are too important to be neglected. The initial carboxylation by a biotin-containing enzyme at the expense of ATP is straightforward. The methylmalonyl coenzyme A formed is asymmetric, and a racemase is present to interconvert the stereoisomers (Fig. 24-6). (It is not clear why enzymes have not evolved so as to use only one of the isomers.) Methylmalonyl coenzyme A is also formed by metabolism of the amino acid valine without intermediate formation of propionyl coenzyme A.

It is the final step shown in Figure 24-6 that is unusual. Methymalonyl coenzyme A is rearranged to form succinyl coenzyme A. The necessary scission of C—C bonds requires the presence of **deoxyadenosylcobalamin,** a coenzyme we have not discussed earlier.

Cobalamins. The cobalamins, otherwise known as vitamin B_{12}, are large compounds containing **cobalt** in a **corrin** ring (Fig. 24-7). (The corrin ring resembles the porphyrin ring in many ways, and is formed from similar precursors.) The cobalamins are peculiar to animals and some bacteria, and they account for the cobalt requirement of these organisms. Plants and most bacteria get along nicely without cobalt because they do not use cobalamins as coenzymes. Even the animals require only minute amounts, something like 4 nanomoles per day being an adequate supply for human adults. (The large cobalamin molecule requires the presence of a glycoprotein secreted by the stomach for absorption, and a different protein is present in the blood to transport it to the tissues.)

The particular cobalamin derivative that is involved in the methylmalonyl CoA mutase reaction has a molecule of adenosine bound directly to the cobalt atom by its 5′ carbon. It is this unusual cobalt-carbon bond that is broken and reformed during the rearrangement of the substrates. (The mechanism of the reaction is not known; most proposals involve a transfer of hydrogen from methylamalonyl coenzyme A to the deoxyadenosyl group of the coenzyme, followed by the formation of a cobalt-carbon bond between the substrate and coenzyme.)

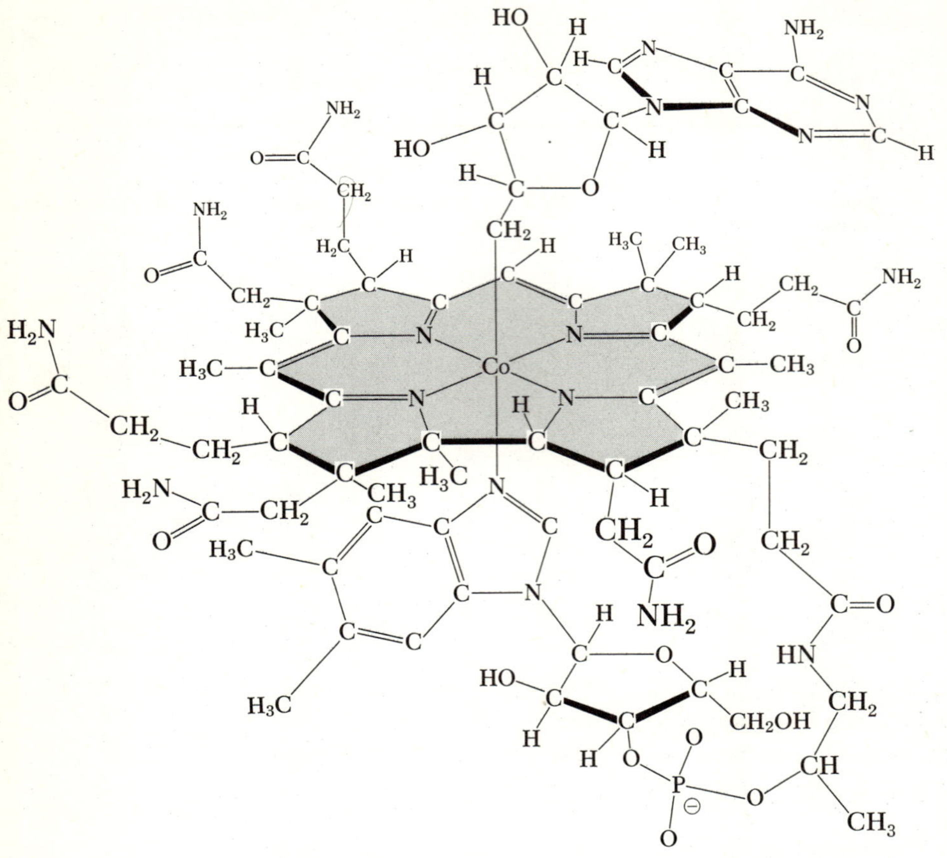

Figure 24-7 The structure of cobamide coenzyme. The large ring seen on edge around the central cobalt atom, resembling a porphyrin ring with one methylene group missing, is the corrin ring. The corrin-cobalt complex complete with the various side chains on the ring and including the ribosyl group attached through a 3′-phosphate diester bond (*bottom right*) is cobamide. The further combination with a dimethylbenzimidazole ring, viewed face-on below the corrin ring and with three of its substituent hydrogen atoms removed for clarity, constitutes a cobalamin. The final coordination position of cobalt is usually occupied by another group, in this case 5′-deoxyadenosine combined through a carbon atom; cobamide coenzyme is 5′-deoxyadenosylcobalamin. Commercially available vitamin B_{12} has a cyanide group attached and is cyanocobalamin. The figure is an idealization of a true projection of the spatial position of the atoms.

DEGRADATION OF INDIVIDUAL AMINO ACIDS

It is possible to get some understanding of the routes of metabolism of many of the amino acids without a detailed treatment of each. We have already covered the metabolism of **alanine, serine, threonine, aspartate, glutamate, asparagine,** and **glutamine** (Fig. 24-8), which give rise to intermediates in the citric acid cycle, or to pyruvate, which can be converted to glucose. These amino acids are therefore said to be **glucogenic**—they will cause increased formation of glucose in an animal lacking carbohydrate.

Amino Acids Giving Rise to Glutamate. Several amino acids are metabolized by being converted to glutamate. These include **arginine** (the ornithine portion of the molecule), **proline,** and **histidine.** Here again is a collection of amino acids that convey diverse properties to proteins in which they are incorporated, but which are built to be metabolized by a common route (Fig. 24-9).

Branched-Chain Amino Acids

Isoleucine, leucine, and **valine** have branched hydrocarbon side chains and are noteworthy in that they are mainly metabolized by the muscles of higher animals. The reason for this is not apparent. The metabolism of all three begins with a transamina-

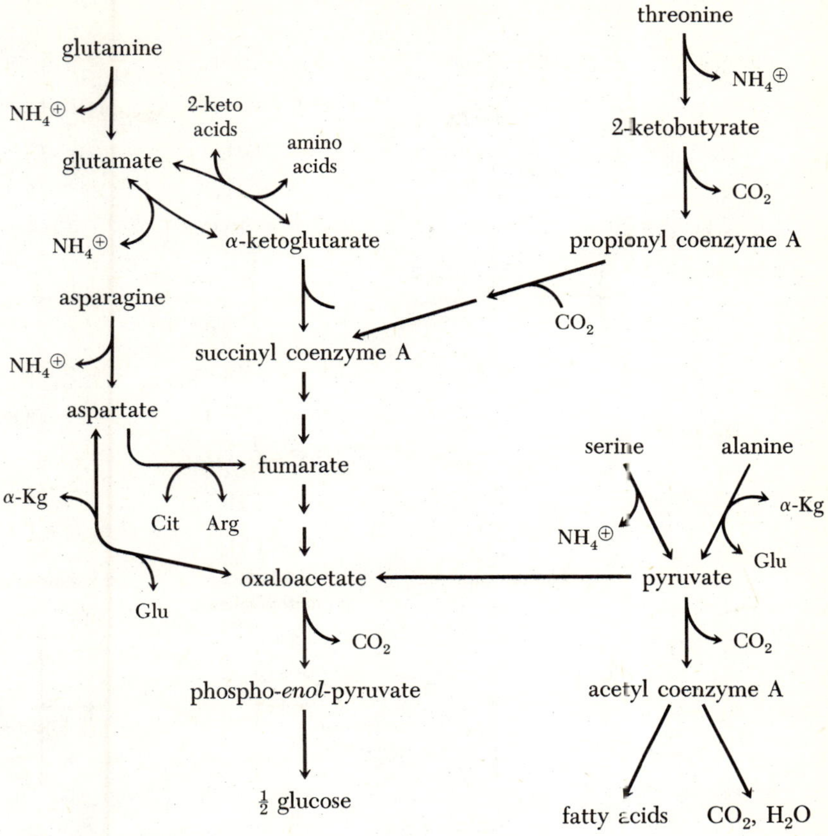

Figure 24-8 The metabolism of some glucogenic amino acids.

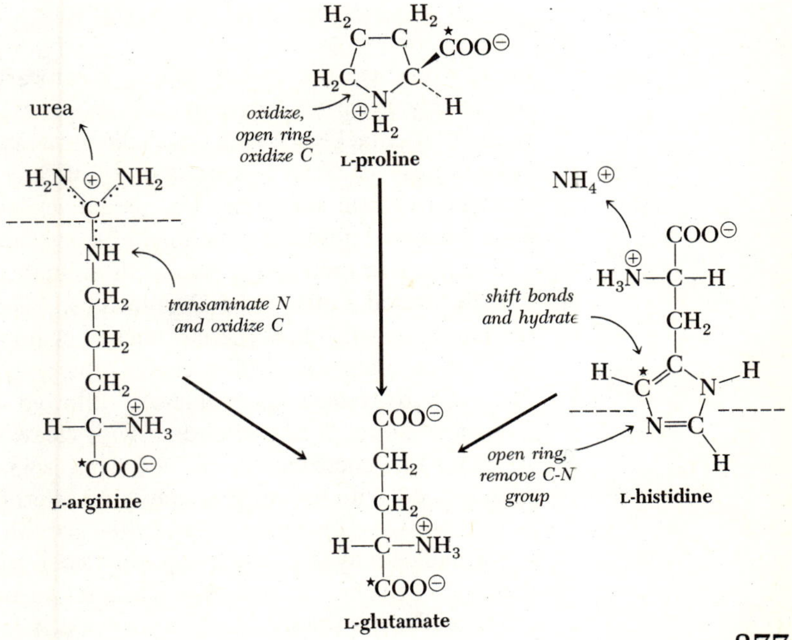

Figure 24-9 Glutamate is formed from five carbon atoms and one nitrogen atom of arginine, proline, or histidine.

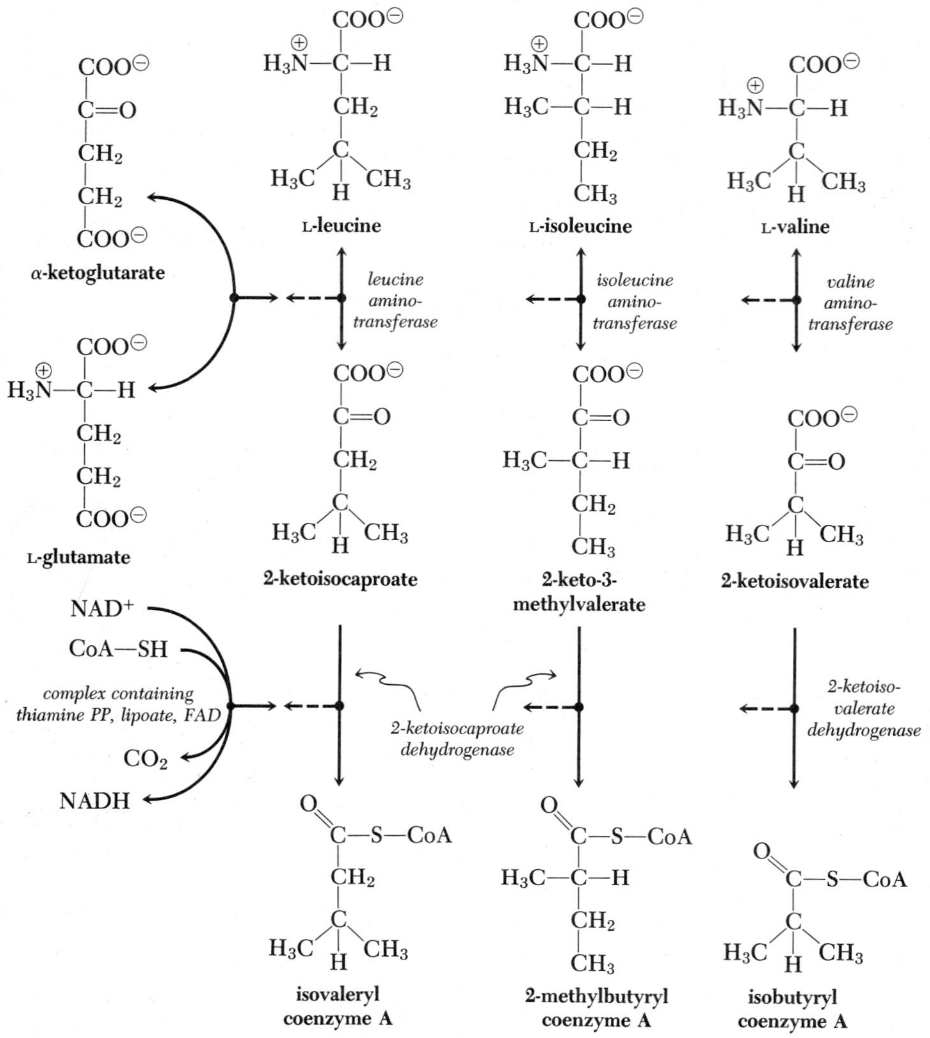

Figure 24–10 The catabolism of the branched chain amino acids begins with a transamination, followed by oxidative decarboxylation of the resultant 2-keto carboxylate. The oxidative decarboxylation proceeds by the same mechanism as do similar reactions with pyruvate and α-ketoglutarate, catalyzed by a multi-peptide complex containing thiamine pyrophosphate, lipoate, and FAD.

tion to produce the corresponding 2-ketocarboxylates (Fig. 24–10), which are then oxidatively decarboxylated by dehydrogenase complexes in mitochondria much like those that attack pyruvate or α-ketoglutarate. The products are acyl coenzyme A compounds—coenzyme A derivatives of fatty acids, except that the fatty acids have branched carbon skeletons. The oxidative decarboxylations are irreversible, and the 2-ketocarboxylates cannot be made by any other route in animals. Isoleucine, leucine, and valine are therefore essential in animal diets.

Branched Fatty Acid Derivatives. The enzymes of fatty acid metabolism in the mitochondria attack these branched chain acyl compounds as far as they can. That is, a flavoprotein will oxidize each to the enoyl compound, which is hydrated to form the L-3-hydroxyacyl coenzyme A, followed by oxidation with NAD to form the 3-oxoacyl compound, and ending with cleavage by coenzyme A.

The acyl coenzyme A derived from isoleucine undergoes the complete sequence as described, with the carbons emerging as propionyl coenzyme A and acetyl coenzyme A (Fig. 24–11). The derivative of valine goes along as far as the 3-oxo compound, which is the half-aldehyde of methylmalonyl coenzyme A, and is then converted to methylmalonyl coenzyme A and on to succinyl coenzyme A.

Finally, the branched acyl coenzyme A formed from leucine cannot undergo the

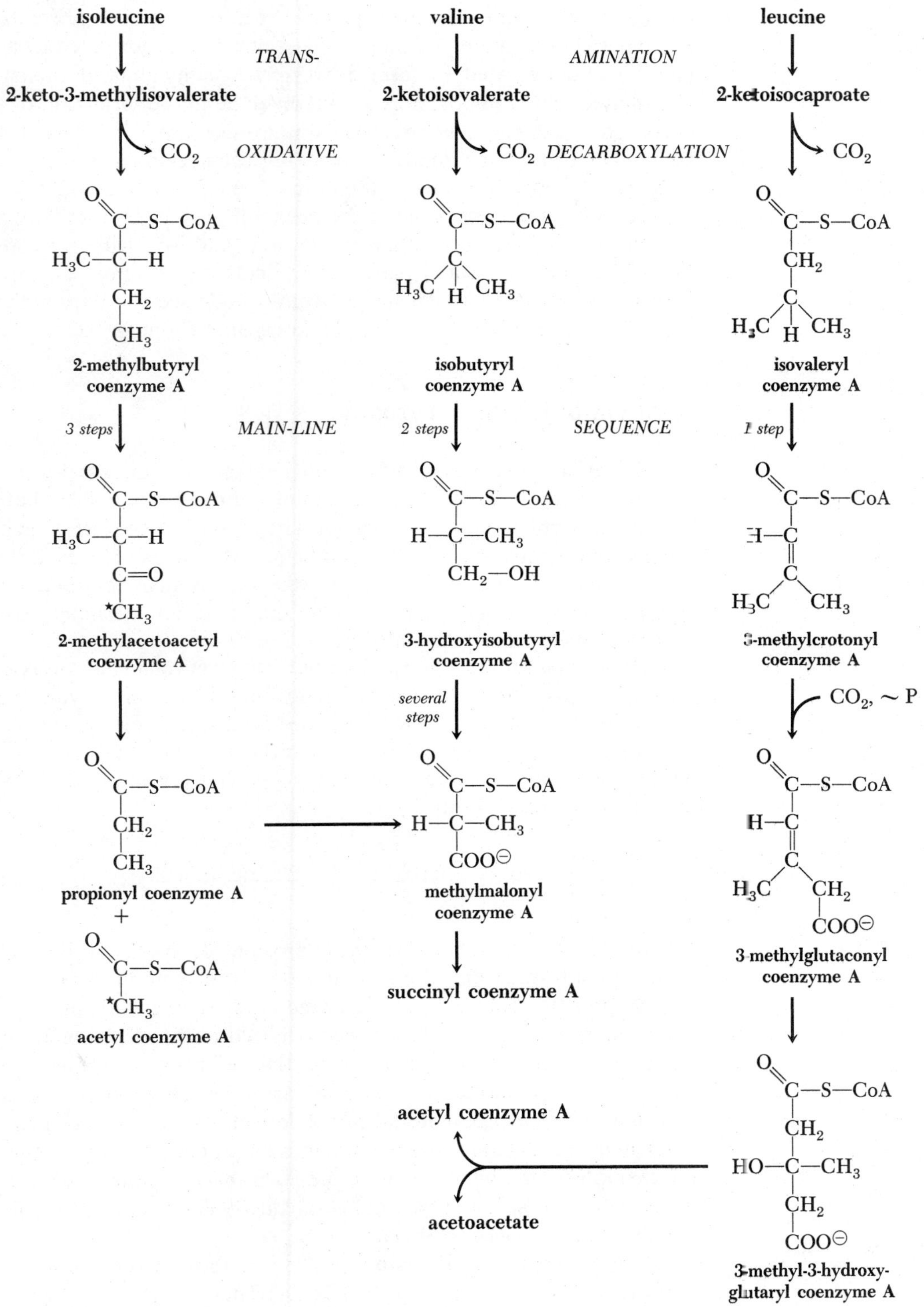

Figure 24-11 The branched chain acyl coenzyme A derivatives initially undergo the same reactions as do the straight chain fatty acid derivatives. The derivative of valine requires an additional oxidation to form methylmalonyl coenzyme A, and the derivative of leucine is carboxylated before hydration to form 3-hydroxy-3-methylglutaryl coenzyme A, the precursor of acetoacetate.

complete fatty acid oxidation sequence because the branch prevents formation of the 3-oxo derivative. Therefore, the carbon skeleton is carboxylated by a biotin-containing enzyme and hydrated to form 3-hydroxy-3-methylglutaryl coenzyme A. We have already seen this compound as an intermediate in the formation of acetoacetate from acetyl groups in the liver (p. 205). Now we encounter it in the skeletal muscles and heart, where it is apparently cleaved to acetoacetate and acetyl coenzyme A at a sufficient rate to permit the metabolism of leucine. (The amounts of leucine involved are relatively small compared to the metabolism of glucose or fatty acids by muscles.)

In sum, some carbon atoms from valine and isoleucine are converted to methylmalonyl coenzyme A, and these amino acids are therefore glucogenic. Atoms from leucine, and also from isoleucine, are converted to acetyl groups or directly to acetoacetate, and can therefore be said to be **ketogenic** (forming "ketone bodies").

Phenylalanine and Tyrosine

Phenylalanine is Essential. Phenylalanine is converted to tyrosine by an irreversible oxidation. There are other minor routes of metabolism, but they also include irreversible steps, so phenylalanine must be supplied in the diet of higher animals. There are also irreversible steps in the metabolism of tyrosine; however, if there is an excess of phenylalanine in the diet beyond the requirement for maintenance of nitrogen balance, the need for tyrosine is diminished and may disappear completely, because it can be made from phenylalanine.

Hydroxylation of Phenylalanine. The **phenylalanine hydroxylase** that produces tyrosine is an example of a mixed-function oxidase, an enzyme that uses a reduced coenzyme to activate O_2 for attack on a substrate. We previously encountered an example of this class of enzymes in the acyl coenzyme A desaturases. The hydroxylases are another type that cause an atom of activated oxygen to combine with the substrate, creating a hydroxyl group:

$$R{-}H + O_2 + X{-}H_2 \xrightarrow{\textit{hydroxylase}} R{-}OH + X + H_2O$$

in which R—H is the substrate being hydroxylated, and $X{-}H_2$ is the reduced coenzyme, or second substrate, that donates electrons for activation of O_2.

Biopterin. The reduced coenzyme used by phenylalanine hydroxylase is tetrahydrobiopterin (Fig. 24–12), which is oxidized to dihydrobiopterin while reducing O_2 and is regenerated by a second enzyme that utilizes NADPH as a reducing agent. We would give the molecule short shrift in our survey, except that we shall encounter other pteridine coenzymes that are folic acid derivatives, and discuss their reactions in some detail in the next chapter. The compounds have been known for some time as pigments, for example in the wings of butterflies. The basis for their chemistry was laid down in the late 1800's, but it was not until the 1930's that evidence for more profound metabolic roles began to appear.

Degradation of Tyrosine. The catabolism of tyrosine begins with a straightforward transamination (Fig. 24–13). The corresponding 2-ketocarboxylate is then attacked by a remarkable oxygenase, which simultaneously catalyzes (a) the oxidative decarboxylation of the pyruvate side chain in the 2-keto compound, (b) migration of the resultant acetyl group on the aromatic ring, and (c) hydroxylation of the ring. This complex reaction sets the stage for the action of a second oxygenase, which cleaves the aromatic ring to form two carbonyl groups. The second enzyme is a more typical oxygenase, which is an enzyme that adds both atoms of O_2 to compounds with double

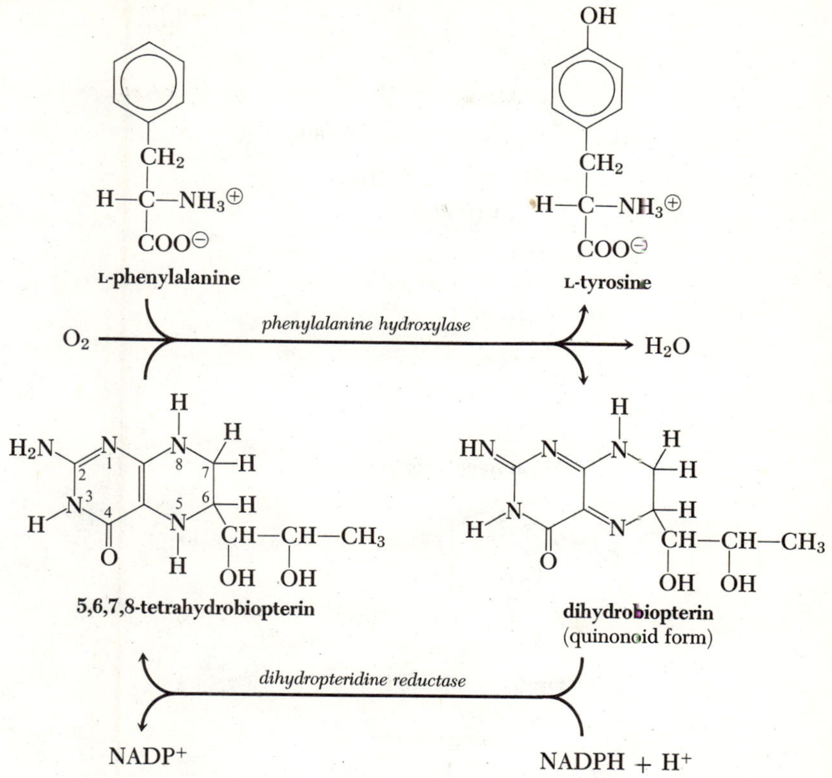

Figure 24-12 Phenylalanine is converted to tyrosine by a mixed function oxidase that uses tetrahydrobiopterin as an electron donor to activate molecular oxygen. The tetrahydrobiopterin is regenerated by electrons from NADPH.

bonds or aromatic rings. The effect commonly is to cleave the bond or ring and form a pair of carbonyl groups:

$$\text{R—CH=CH—R}' + O_2 \xrightarrow{\textit{oxygenase}} \text{R—CH=O} + \text{O=CH—R}'$$

(Oxygenases often require Fe^{2+} or heme for activity.)

The result of opening the ring in this case is to create an eight-carbon straight-chain compound that is easily cleaved to yield fumarate and acetoacetate! (I have looked at this I don't know how many times, and still get great satisfaction from seeing the familiar ingredients of the citric acid cycle and fatty acid metabolism appear when the aromatic ring is broken. Does the fact that it takes place this way explain why proteins contain phenylalanine rather than phenylglycine or phenylaminobutyrate as their amino acids? Who knows?)

The result is that tyrosine, and also phenylalanine through its conversion to tyrosine, is both a glucogenic and a ketogenic amino acid.

TOTAL CATABOLISM OF PROTEIN

Approximately three out of every ten young adult males in the United States consume amino acids containing 1.4 or more moles of nitrogen each day. If the amino acid mixture has a composition approximating that of meat proteins, it represents at least 1 mole of amino acids. What is the quantitative result? We have seen that it is not possible to predict the exact route of metabolism of the amino acids. Some carbon skeletons will be used to form glucose for storage, some will be used to form fatty acids, and others will be oxidized, depending upon the nutritional state of the individual and his

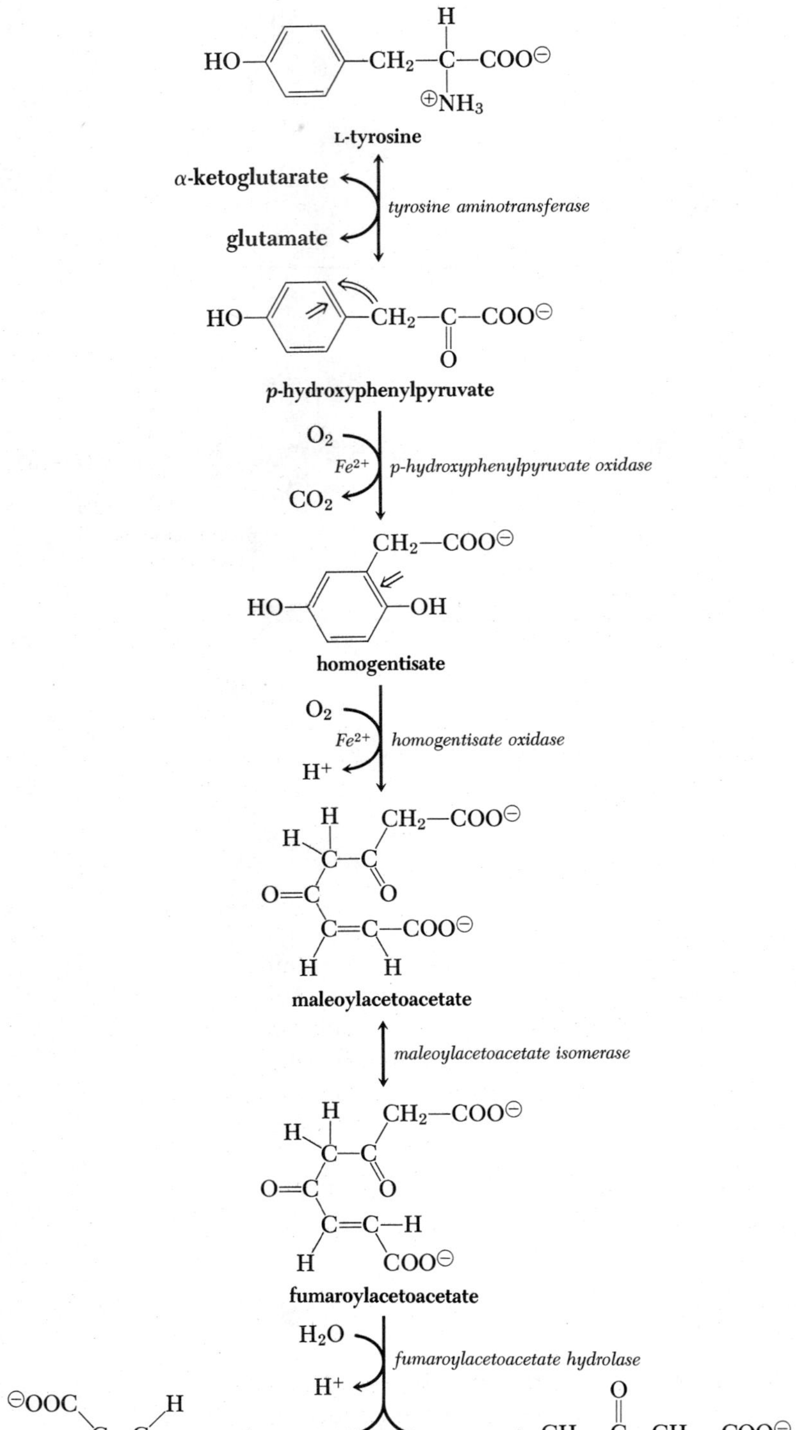

Figure 24-13 The major route of tyrosine metabolism utilizes oxygenases to oxidize the side chain and open the ring.

activity. We can, however, make a fairly good approximation of the extent to which protein can alleviate the effects of fasting in a normal individual. Under such circumstances, as many carbon atoms as possible will be diverted to the production of glucose, like this:

$$1000\,(\text{amino acids}) + 1500\ O_2 \longrightarrow$$
$$700\,(\text{urea}) + 400\,(\text{glucose}) + 600\,(\text{acetyl groups}) + 35\ SO_4^{2-} + 600\ CO_2 + ca.\,2200 \sim P$$

The equation is given in millimoles of compound per day. Acetoacetate and acetyl coenzyme A have been lumped together in the formulation. The sulfate comes from the metabolism of cysteine and methionine, which is treated in the next chapter.

Two important points emerge. About 0.4 mole equivalent of glucose can be formed from mixed amino acids, or 72 grams from the 110 grams of protein consumed by our well-fed young adults. Secondly, later combustion of the glucose and the acetyl groups, along with the high-energy phosphate already generated, results in about the same total production of high-energy phosphate from complete catabolism of amino acids as is obtained from the combustion of an equal weight of glucose. However, the P:O ratio is only 2.4, compared to 2.8 for fats and 3.1 for glycogen, so amino acids are not a good fuel for maximum power production. Their best use is as a transient source of relatively small quantities of glucose to tide the brain over periods between meals, and also to supply glucose as a precursor for synthesis of cellular constituents in other cells. Gluconeogenesis from amino acids is a normal supplement in this way to the mobilization of fats for fuels. Body proteins are consumed at an increasing rate as a principal source of fuel when the fat stores begin to be depleted by longer periods of starvation. A deficit of fuel intake that causes a 5 kg loss of fat would require the loss of roughly 50 kg of tissue, mostly skeletal muscle, when protein becomes the principal fuel.

FURTHER READING

B. Safer, C. M. Smith, and J. R. Williamson, Control of the transport of reducing equivalents across the mitochondrial membrane in perfused rat heart, J. Mol. Cardiology, 2:11 (1971). Discussion of the malate–aspartate shuttle.

H. A. Barker, Corrinoid-dependent enzymatic reactions. Ann. Rev. Biochem., 41:55 (1972). Discussion of reactions of cobalamins.

S. Kaufman, The phenylalanine-hydroxylating system from mammalian liver, Adv. Enzymol., 35:245 (1971). Technical review.

B. Lindblad, G. Lindstedt, and S. Lindstedt, The mechanism of enzymatic formation of homogentisate from *p*-hydroxphenylpyruvate, J. Amer. Chem. Soc., 92:7446 (1970). A postulated mechanism for this complicated reaction, and a discussion of related reactions.

C. R. Scriver and L. E. Rosenberg, Amino acid metabolism and its disorders, Saunders (1973). General discussion as well as information in abnormalities.

Also see references at end of Chapter 23.

QUESTIONS

1. Show how carbons from glutamate can be used to form glucose and to form palmitate.
2. If circumstances in a liver are such that pyruvate is mainly being converted to glucose and acetyl groups are mainly appearing as acetoacetate or 3-hydroxybutyrate, how many molecules of glucose and of the 3-oxybutyrates will be formed by the catabolism of 100 molecules of valine? of isoleucine? of leucine? of phenylalanine?

3. It could be that an increased consumption of phenylalanine will cause an increased rate of the pentose phosphate pathway. Why?
4. A dietary deficiency of a certain vitamin will cause an excretion of methylmalonic acid in the urine. Predict the vitamin.
5. The transfer of electrons from the cytosol to the mitochondria by the malate–aspartate shuttle causes the formation of NADH within the mitochondria. Why is it believed that the shuttle results in the formation of two ATP molecules per pair of electrons rather than the three that usually result from the oxidation of NADH?
6. The ATP yield from the combustion of fat is approximately 2.3 times that from the combustion of an equal mass of protein. Why then would a starving man brought to the point where he consumes his own proteins lose mass at a rate 10 times greater than one burning stored fat?

CHAPTER 25

THE ONE-CARBON POOL

THE CONCEPTS

Single-carbon groups that are more reduced than carboxylate groups are transferred for such diverse purposes as the formation of purine rings and the methylation of amines and alcohols. Methyl groups ($—CH_3$) are equivalent in oxidation state to methanol, methylene groups ($—CH_2—$) and hydroxymethyl groups ($—CH_2OH$) are equivalent to formaldehyde, and methylidyne groups ($—CH=$) or formyl groups ($—CH=O$) are equivalent to formate.

All of these groups are carried by attachment to nitrogen atoms in tetrahydrofolate (H_4folate), a coenzyme containing a reduced pteridine ring. 5,10-Methylene-H_4folate is formed by transfer of the hydroxymethyl group from serine, leaving glycine, but the same compound is also formed by oxidation of glycine itself, and by combination of H_4folate with formaldehyde, which is obtained during the oxidative catabolism of N-methyl compounds. The formyl- and methylidyne-H_4folate used for purine synthesis can be obtained by oxidation of methylene-H_4folate, by catabolism of histidine, and by direct combination with formate.

Methionine is the principal donor of methyl groups for synthesis of cellular constituents; it is first converted to S-adenosylmethionine by transfer of the adenosyl group from ATP. S-Adenosylmethionine has a positively charged sulfonium group in which three carbon atoms are attached to the sulfur. It therefore represents a high-energy compound for cleavage of a C—S bond, and transfer of the methyl group to leave S-adenosylhomocysteine is an irreversible reaction.

The greatest uses of methyl groups in most animals are the formations of creatine and of choline. Creatine is made by transferring the amidinio group of arginine to glycine, and then methylating the resultant guanidinioacetate. Choline is made as phosphatidylcholine by methylating phosphatidylethanolamine three times. There is a constant turnover of choline and ethanolamine, with the phosphatidyl compounds hydrolyzed to form free bases, and the free bases converted to CDP-derivatives for re-incorporation into phospholipids. (The ethanolamine moiety is created from serine through reactions involving lipid derivatives.) Methyl groups are lost by excretion of creatinine and other methylamines or methoxy compounds, and by oxidation to formaldehyde. These losses must be made good by dietary supplies of methyl compounds or by synthesis of transferrable methyl groups.

Both methionine and choline are ingested in the diet. The methyl group of excess methionine can be utilized to synthesize other compounds, but the supply is usually limited, and the methyl group must be replaced on homocysteine from other sources, with the homocysteine residue acting as a cyclical carrier of methyl groups. After choline is oxidized to a carboxylic acid, transfer of one of its three methyl groups causes sufficient loss of free energy to permit transfer to homocysteine, regenerating methionine. The other two methyl groups are oxidized to formaldehyde.

If the dietary supplies of both methionine and choline are inadequate, methyl groups are made by reducing methylene-H_4folate to 5-methyl-H_4folate. The methyl group is then transferred to homocysteine in a reaction involving aquocobalamin as a coenzyme; it is the failure of this reaction in vitamin B_{12} deficiency that causes most of the symptoms.

The sulfur atom from excess homocysteine is used to make cysteine, which is degraded to pyruvate and sulfate; the carbon skeleton of homocysteine appears as 2-ketobutyrate, which is converted to propionyl coenzyme A. Dietary methionine therefore acts as a source of methionine for incorporation into proteins, as a source of sulfur for making cysteine and other sulfur-containing compounds, and as a source of methyl groups for making phosphatidyl choline, which is necessary for construction of membranes and for transport of lipids.

Groups containing single carbon atoms are transferred for many different purposes, including the introduction of carbon atoms into purine rings and the formation of methyl groups on compounds such as choline, creatine, and the bases of nucleic acids. Of course, we have already seen many examples of the utilization or formation of CO_2 through carboxylations and decarboxylations, but we are now concerned with the transfer of carbon atoms in a less fully oxidized state. It is convenient to lump together the sources of these more reduced carbon groups as the one-carbon pool, since they are somewhat interconvertible, but it will become apparent as the story unfolds that the pool is more like a series of interconnected basins, and the different kinds of one-carbon groups are not fully exchangeable.

NATURE OF ONE-CARBON GROUPS

What precisely are we talking about? Single carbon atoms can exist in various oxidation states, which are represented by the series of simplest organic compounds: methane, methanol, formaldehyde, formate, and carbon dioxide. It is possible to incorporate carbon units at each of these oxidation states, except that of methane, into other compounds by the formal elimination of water. The results are given in Figure 25-1. All of the possible structures of one-carbon groups shown in the figure are found in biological compounds. The figure uses the general R- designation for substituents on the one-carbon units, but the actual nature of the groups that can undergo such interchanges is limited by their chemical potential in most cases to those containing N, O, or S atoms. Furthermore, the figure includes carbonic acid, the hydrated form of CO_2, for completeness even though compounds at this oxidation state are handled by carboxylation and decarboxylation, not by the reactions of the one-carbon pool.

Figure 25-1 is organized so that each row differs from its neighbors by the equivalent of two electrons; it follows that the rows are interconvertible only by oxidations or reductions. Those groups on the same row are of equivalent oxidation-reduction state, and are interconvertible by removal or addition of the elements of water.

The division of the one-carbon groups according to oxidation state also divides them according to their typical types of reactions. For example, we have already seen

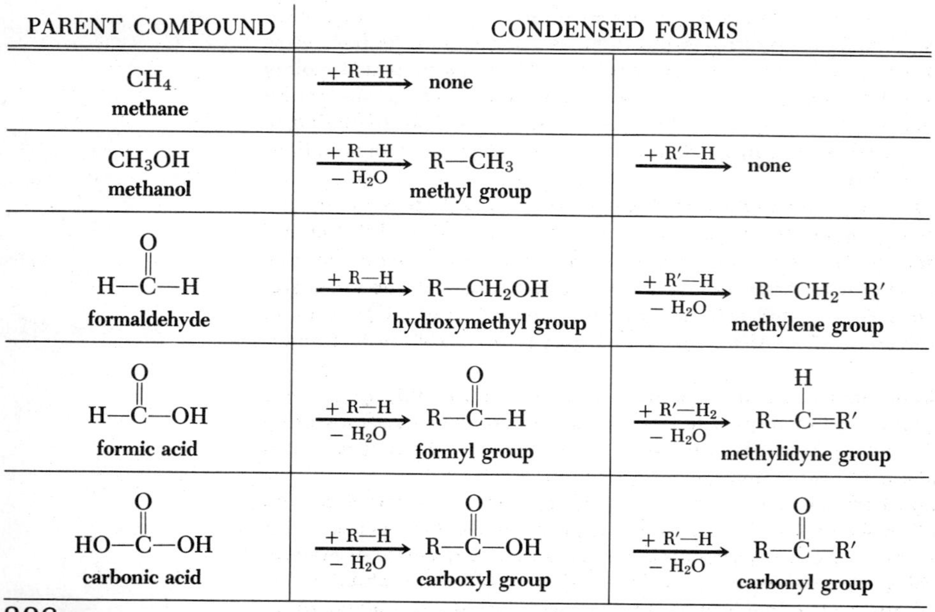

Figure 25-1 One-carbon compounds of various oxidation states and their formal relationship to one-carbon groups of the same oxidation states.

that CO_2 is carried by biotin for the formation of carboxylate groups. Now we shall see a pteridine compound, tetrahydrofolate, used for the transfer of single carbon groups equivalent in oxidation state to formate, formaldehyde, and sometimes methanol. That is, tetrahydrofolate carries methylidyne groups, methylene groups, and sometimes methyl groups.

Finally, we shall see how methyl groups, the most reduced of the transferrable single-carbon groups, are usually derived from an activated form of the amino acid methionine.

TETRAHYDROFOLATE

Tetrahydrofolate is a reduced pteridine like tetrahydrobiopterin (p. 381), but it has the specific function of carrying one-carbon units, and does not participate in mixed-function oxidase reactions. Plants and many protists can synthesize the pteridine ring from simple precursors and combine it with *p*-aminobenzoic acid to form **pteroic acid** (Fig. 25–2), followed by conjugation of the tetrahydro derivative with a molecule of glutamate to make **tetrahydropteroylglutamate,** which is a more systematic name for tetrahydrofolate. Still more molecules of glutamate may be attached through the 5-carboxyl group to make tetrahydropteroyl polyglutamates. Animals, including us, usually depend upon plants for the principal supply, although the protists are sometimes of importance. (Rats, for example, disgust us by eating their own feces, but this enables them to use the folate and other vitamins synthesized by their intestinal bacteria. We

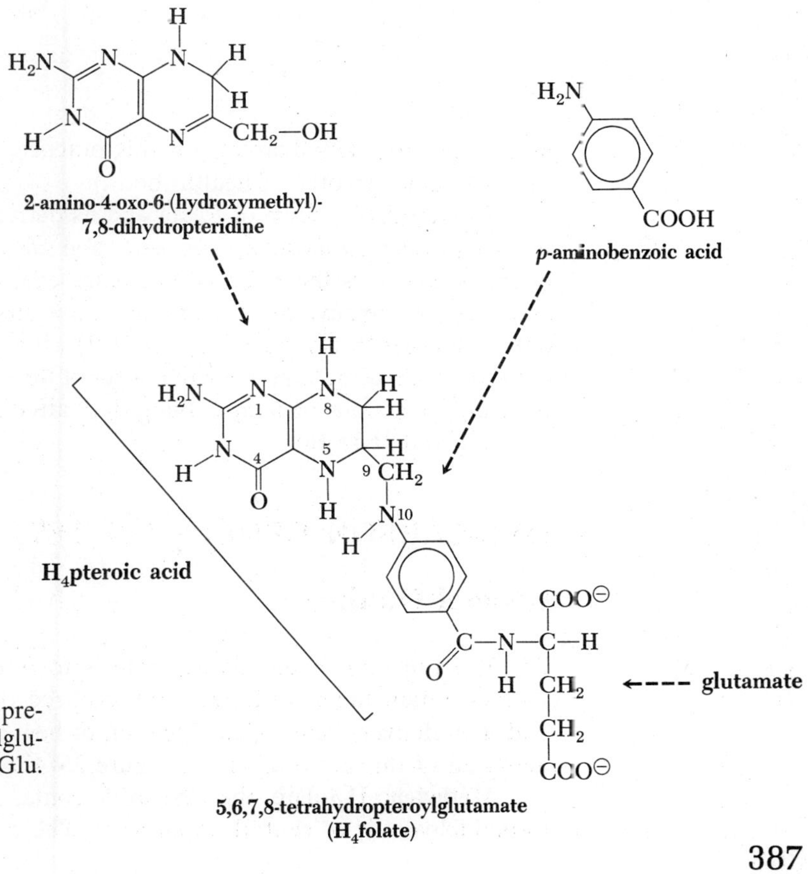

Figure 25–2 Tetrahydrofolate and its precursors. It is also named tetrahydropteroylglutamate, sometimes abbreviated as H_4PteGlu.

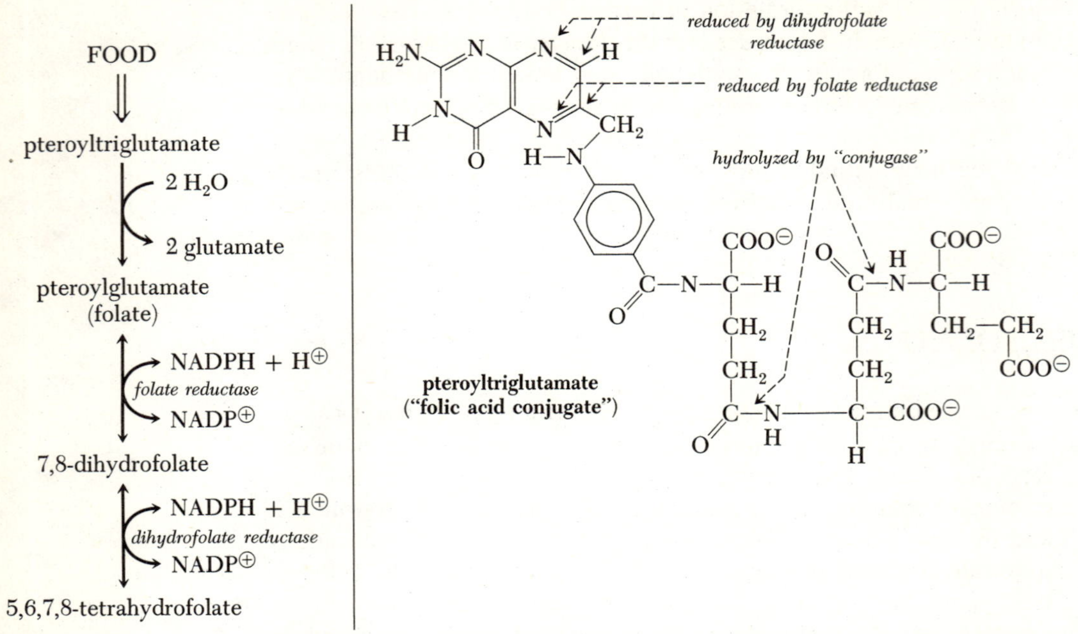

Figure 25-3 The tetrahydropteroylglutamates of foodstuffs usually become oxidized before absorption. The intestinal mucosa removes all but one glutamyl residue from pteroylpolyglutamates, and reduces the resultant folate to its tetrahydro form in two steps.

aren't built to take advantage of this practice, and it is not recommended, even for the most avid devotee of health foods.)

The tetrahydro form of folate and its derivatives is readily oxidized to folate and its derivatives by atmospheric oxygen upon release from intact cells during preparation of foods, and it is these forms that reach the intestinal mucosa. The intestines have enzymes that remove all but one glutamyl group from polyglutamyl forms, leaving only folate which is reduced by NADPH after absorption, first to dihydrofolate, and then to tetrahydrofolate, the active form of the coenzyme (Fig. 25-3). For convenience in writing reactions or in specifying derivatives, the reduced forms are designated as H_2folate and H_4folate.

ONE-CARBON GROUPS ON TETRAHYDROFOLATE

General Outline

The function of tetrahydrofolate is to receive one-carbon groups from various sources, retain them while they are oxidized or reduced from one form to another, and then deliver them for the creation of new compounds. The general pathways for doing all of this are outlined in Figure 25-4.

Methylene-H_4folate, the derivative containing a group at the oxidation level of formaldehyde, is of central importance. The methylene group may be derived from formaldehyde itself, but the major sources are the amino acids serine and glycine. Serine donates a methylene group, thereby becoming glycine, and glycine is a source of an additional methylene group.

The methylene groups are used to form the side chains of thymine incorporated into DNA (next chapter), and are sources of methyl groups (by reduction) and methylidyne groups (by oxidation).

Methylidyne-H_4folate and the equivalent formyl-H_4folate are made by oxidation of methylene-H_4folate and by combination of H_4folate with formate. Formate is not only ingested by ant-fanciers, but it also is a normal intermediate of metabolism. Histidine, too, is a source of a methylidyne group.

Methylidyne and formyl H_4folate are obligatory precursors of the purines.

Methyl-H_4folate is made by reduction of methylene-H_4folate and is used to regenerate methyl groups on methionine, which is the precursor of most methylated metabolites of the sort we shall consider later in this chapter. The degradation of such compounds results in the oxidation of the methyl groups to formaldehyde, which is recovered by combination with H_4folate.

Let us now look at some of the details of transfer of one-carbon units *via* H_4folate.

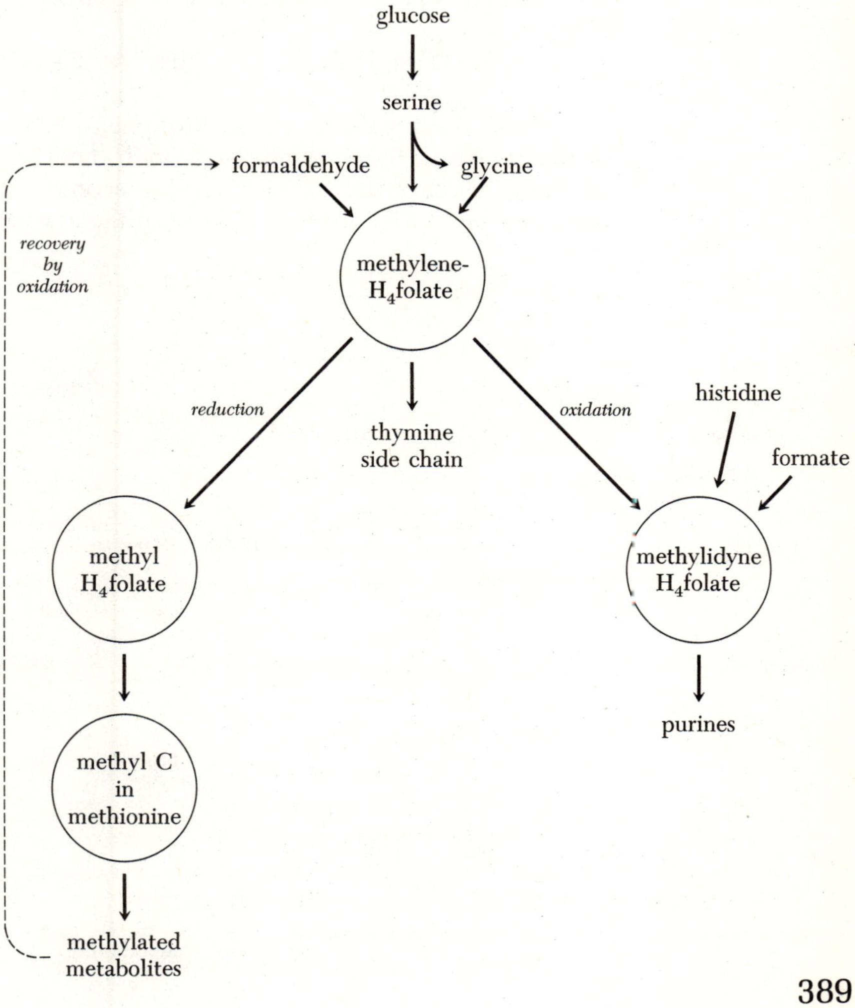

Figure 25–4 Glucose is the ultimate source of one-carbon groups, which are formed *via* serine and glycine. The principal uses of the groups are to form methylated compounds, the side chain of thymine, and carbons in the purine ring. One-carbon groups can be recovered by oxidation to formaldehyde or formate, or by direct transfer from histidine.

Methylene Groups

Role of Serine. Serine is a metabolically active amino acid that is the precursor of several cellular constituents in addition to being a major component of proteins. Animals have therefore preserved the ability to synthesize the amino acid from glucose, using routes that perforce differ from the irreversible deamination used in catabolism (Fig. 25–5). For example, serine can be made from 3-phosphoglycerate by simple oxidation at C-2 and transamination, followed by hydrolysis of the phosphate group. The use of serine as a source of methylene groups therefore provides a means of making them from glucose or other precursors of 3-phosphoglycerate.

Methylene Groups from Serine and Glycine. Serine combines with **pyridoxal phosphate** on a **hydroxymethyl transferase,** which transfers the group to nitrogen atoms at positions 5 and 10 of H_4folate (Fig. 25–6). The other product is glycine, and the equilibration of serine and glycine in this way is one of the most important reactions in nitrogen metabolism:

$$\text{serine} + H_4\text{folate} \longleftrightarrow \text{glycine} + 5,10\text{-methylene-}H_4\text{folate}$$

This reaction is rapid enough in most animals to provide their needs for glycine, which is therefore not an essential amino acid for them.

Glycine is degraded by a reaction sequence that is equivalent to an oxidative deamination with an associated decarboxylation:

$$\text{glycine} + NAD^+ + H_4\text{folate} \longrightarrow NH_4^+ + CO_2 + 5,10\text{-methylene-}H_4\text{folate} + NADH$$

When there is a high demand for one-carbon units, it may be met by converting serine to glycine, by oxidizing glycine, or by both processes. (The reactions also provide a means of converting excess glycine to serine in the absence of a demand for one-carbon groups. The resultant serine can then be catabolized *via* pyruvate.)

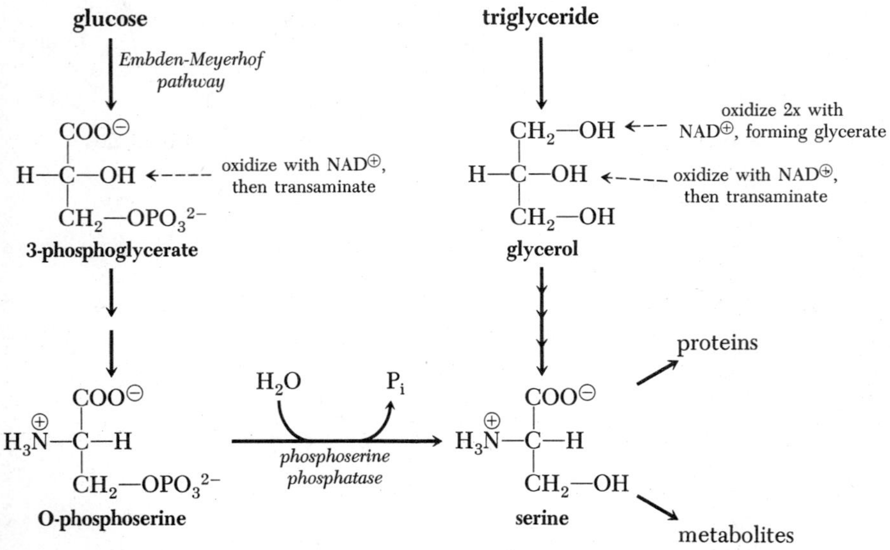

Figure 25–5 Two of the routes for synthesizing serine from glucose. One is an oxidation and transamination of phosphoglycerate; the other involves three oxidations of the glycerol unit of triglycerides, followed by transamination.

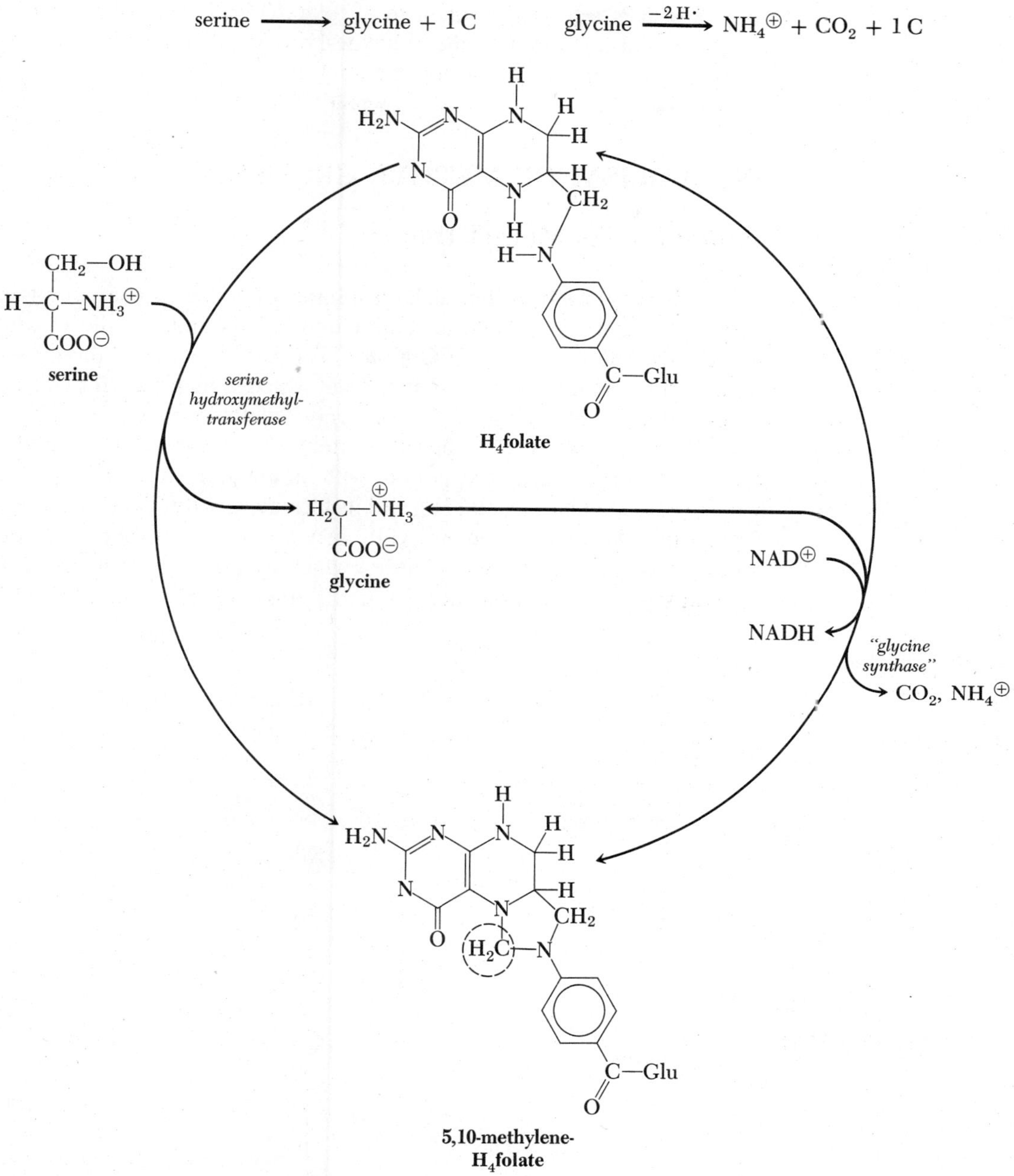

Figure 25–6 A methylene group can be transferred reversibly from serine to H_4folate, forming glycine. Glycine can be oxidized to form another methylene group, along with CO_2 and NH_4^+.

Methylidyne Groups

5,10-Methylidyne-H_4folate is equilibrated with 5,10-methylene-H_4folate by a dehydrogenase that uses NADP as a coenzyme (Fig. 25–7). Carbon atoms from serine, glycine, or formaldehyde can be made available by this route for use in the construction of purine nucleotides. The figure also shows how free formate is utilized.

Formation from Histidine. We noted in Chapter 24 that the catabolism of histidine begins with a deamination and ends with the formation of glutamate. Intermediate reactions involve opening the imidazole ring, and doing this creates **N-formiminoglutamate.** The formimino group is the nitrogen analogue of a formyl group, and it is transferred intact to H_4folate (Fig. 25–8), followed by loss of NH_4^+ and cyclization to form 5,10-methylidyne-H_4folate. The reaction is interesting, but it is not a major part of one-carbon metabolism.

METABOLISM OF METHYL GROUPS

Methionine As Methyl Donor

S-Adenosylmethionine. A large number of biological compounds contain methyl groups that have been added to some parent compound, usually by attachment to O or N atoms, but sometimes to C atoms. The usual source of these methyl groups is the methyl thioether group of methionine, which is activated for transfer by forming S-adenosylmethionine (Fig. 25–9). S-Adenosylmethionine is formed by transfer of the adenosyl group from ATP to the sulfur atom of methionine, which makes a **sulfonium** group. It is a high-energy compound, with an apparent K'_{eq} of 2×10^4 for hydrolysis to adenosine, methionine, and H^+, and its formation is driven in effect by the hydrolysis of all of the phosphate bonds in ATP, since the initial transfer of the adenosyl group liberates inorganic triphosphate (PPP_i) which is rapidly hydrolyzed to PP_i and P_i.

Transfer of Methyl Groups. When methyl groups are transferred from S-adeno-

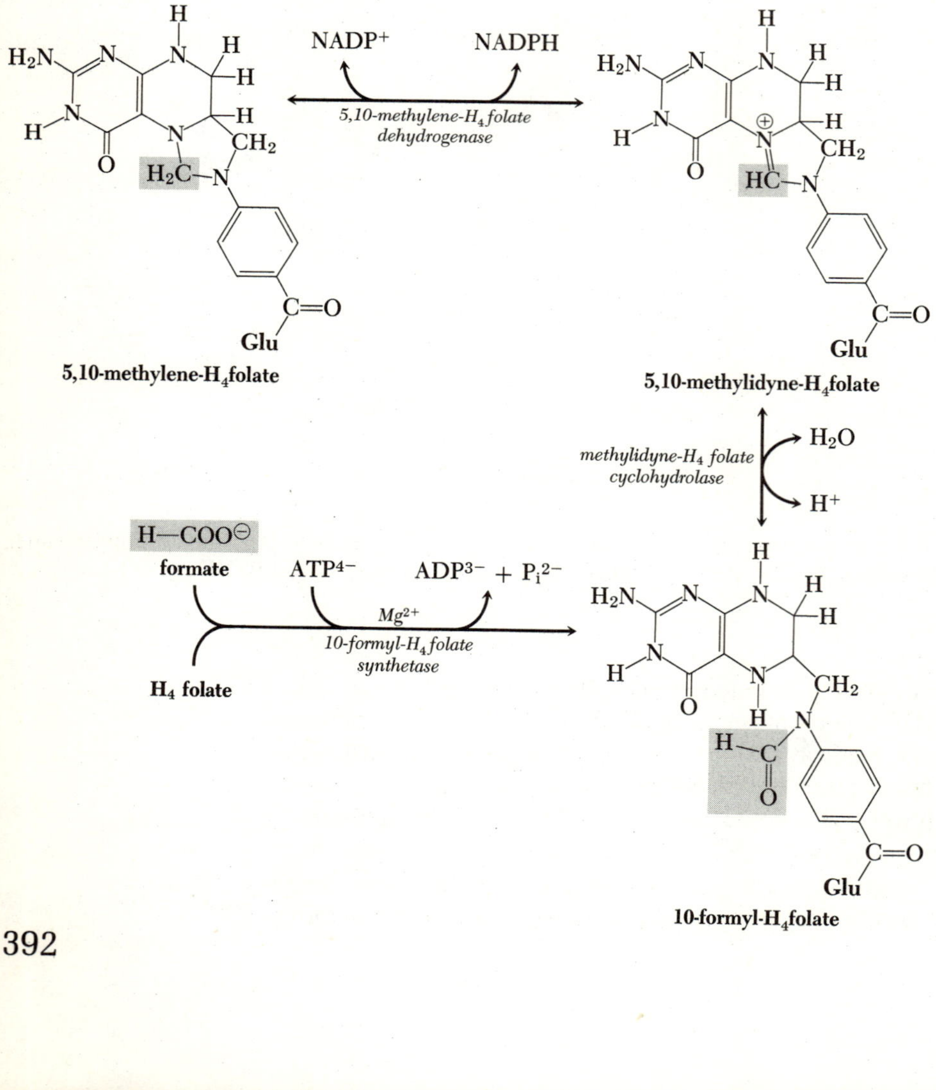

Figure 25–7 5,10-Methylene-H_4folate can be oxidized by NADP to form 5,10-methylidyne-H_4folate in a reversible reaction. The methylidyne compound and 10-formyl-H_4folate are interconvertible by the action of a second enzyme, catalyzing a simple hydrolysis. 10-Formyl-H_4folate can also be formed by the combination of formate with H_4folate at the expense of high-energy phosphate.

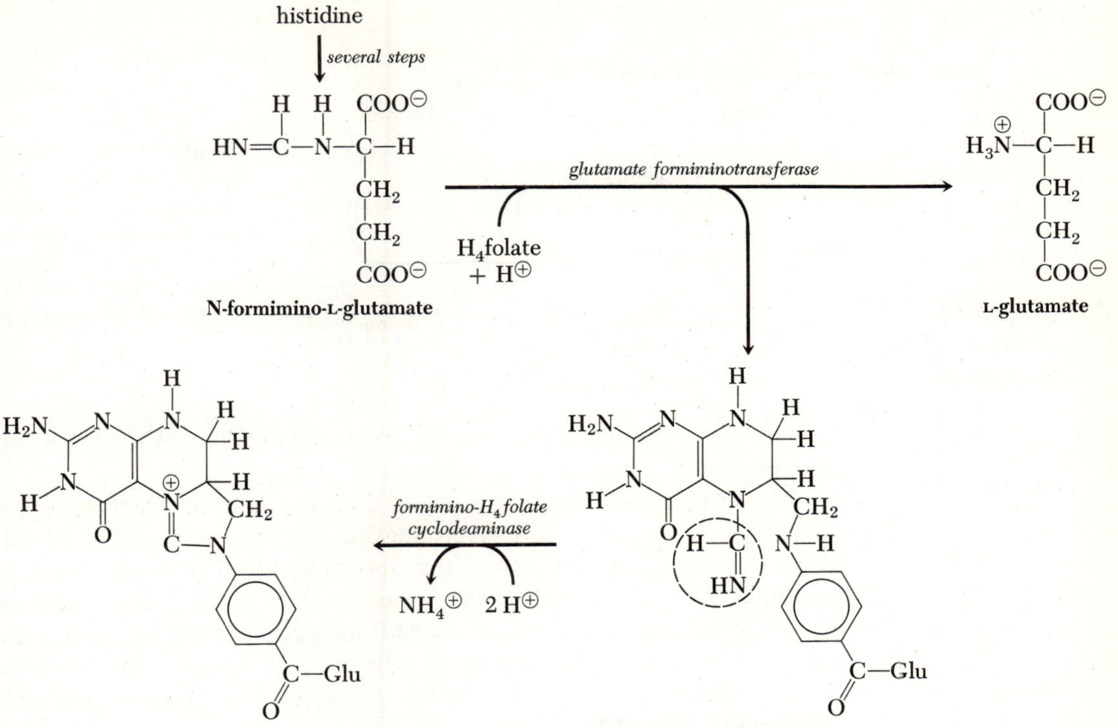

Figure 25-8 One carbon from the imidazole ring of histidine is transferred to H_4folate as a formimino group. Cyclization with the loss of NH_4^+ creates 5,10-methylidyne-H_4folate.

sylmethionine to an acceptor, such as an amine or alcohol (Fig. 25-10), the remaining **S-adenosylhomocysteine** no longer has a charged sulfonium group. It is a simple thioether, analogous to methionine, and the resultant loss of free energy makes the methyl transfers essentially irreversible. Let us now consider important examples of these transfers.

Formation of Creatine

Creatine is made by transfer of a methyl group from S-adenosylmethionine to **guanidinioacetate** (Fig. 25-11). The guanidinioacetate is formed by transfer of an

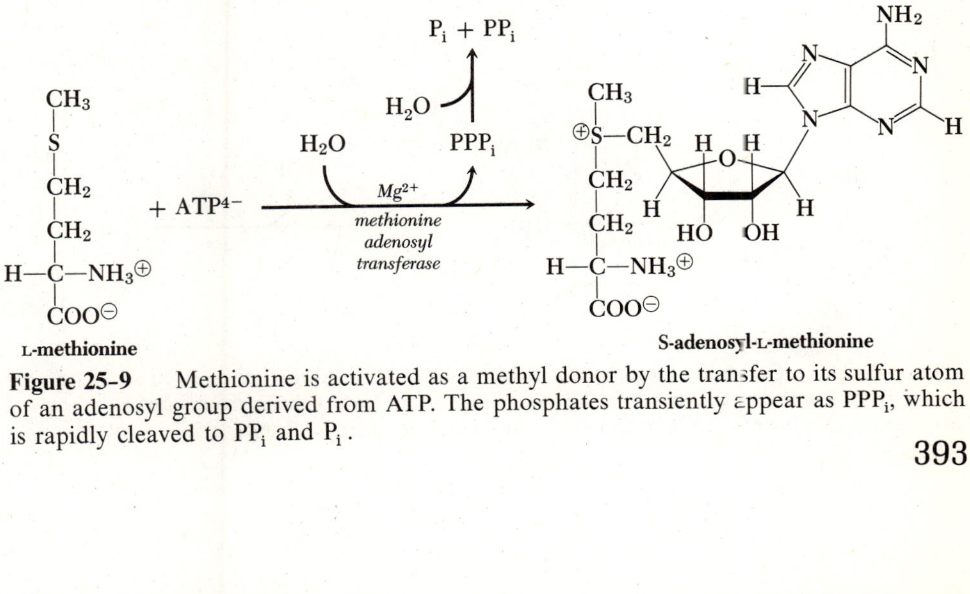

Figure 25-9 Methionine is activated as a methyl donor by the transfer to its sulfur atom of an adenosyl group derived from ATP. The phosphates transiently appear as PPP_i, which is rapidly cleaved to PP_i and P_i.

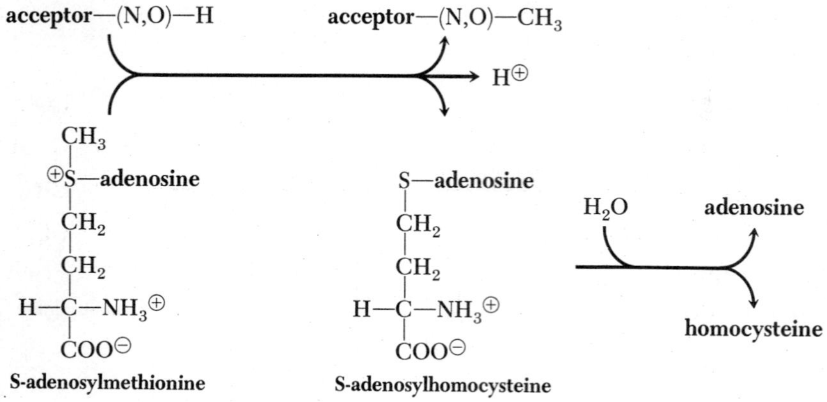

Figure 25-10 Methyl groups are transferred from S-adenosylmethionine to various acceptors, usually groups containing N or O atoms. The S-adenosylhomocysteine that remains is hydrolyzed to release adenosine and homocysteine.

amidinio group from arginine to glycine, leaving ornithine. Creatine is therefore made from fragments of three amino acids.

The formation of creatine provides a means of storing high-energy phosphate in muscles, but it also represents a constant drain on the organism's supply of methionine. This is true because phosphocreatine spontaneously cyclizes at a slow rate to form **creatinine,** which is excreted in the urine. The rate of loss is dependent only upon the total phosphocreatine content at constant temperature and pH, and is therefore quite constant from day to day in a given individual. A typical adult male excretes about 15 millimoles per day. It is the methyl group, not the glycine or the amidinio group, that is most difficult to replace.

Choline and Phospholipids

Choline is the most abundant N-methyl compound in most organisms, where it mainly occurs as an ester of phosphatidates (Fig. 25-12). It is also qualitatively important as the precursor of **acetylcholine,** which is a transmitter in some nerves, but only

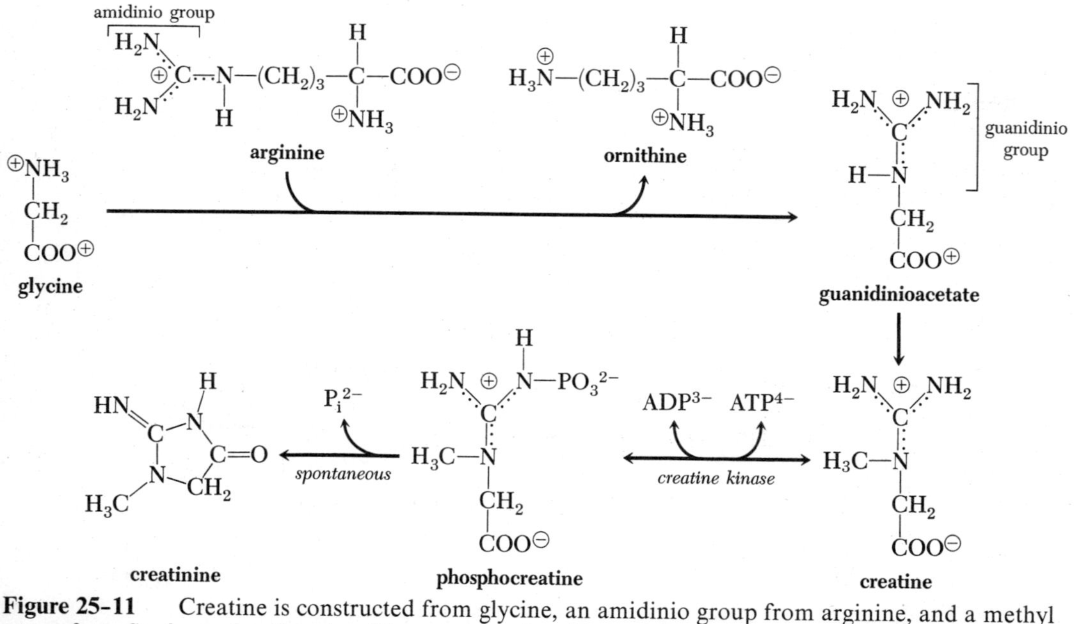

Figure 25-11 Creatine is constructed from glycine, an amidinio group from arginine, and a methyl group from S-adenosylmethionine. There is a continual loss of these groups owing to the spontaneous cyclization of phosphocreatine to creatinine, which is excreted in the urine.

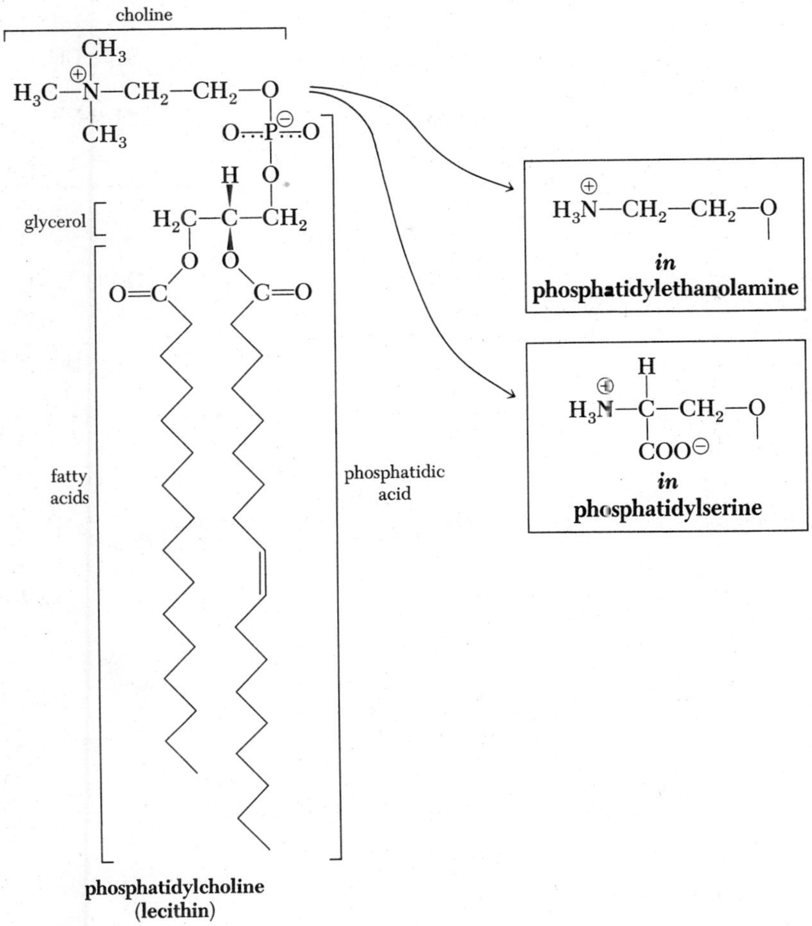

Figure 25-12 The principal phospholipids are derivatives of diacylglycerol phosphate (phosphatidate) in which the phosphate is further esterified with the hydroxyl group of choline, ethanolamine, or serine.

a small amount is required for this purpose. **Phosphatidylcholines** and the related **phosphatidylethanolamines** and **phosphatidylserines** are major components of the lipid fraction of membranes and of transport lipoproteins. (There are many different kinds, depending upon the particular fatty acid residues present.)

Use of Free Bases. Because of the wide occurrence of the phospholipids, choline and ethanolamine can be obtained from most foods. They are also released during the internal turnover of phospholipids within an organism. The free compounds are incorporated intact into phospholipids by reactions involving the formation of esters with **cytidine diphosphate** (Fig. 25-13).

Synthesis of Choline. The diet does not always contain sufficient choline and ethanolamine to sustain the normal turnover of phospholipids, and animals have retained the ability to synthesize the phosphatidyl derivatives from amino acids. Phosphatidylethanolamine is methylated three times to form phosphatidylcholine (Fig. 25-14). (Ethanolamine is obtained from serine by reactions involving the formation of phosphatidyl serine or the combination of serine with palmital. The end result is a decarboxylation of serine in either case, and the details need not concern us here.)

Sources of Methyl Groups

Synthesis from Methylene-H$_4$folate. An animal obtains methyl groups in the form of methionine and choline in the diet, but it usually also requires the formation

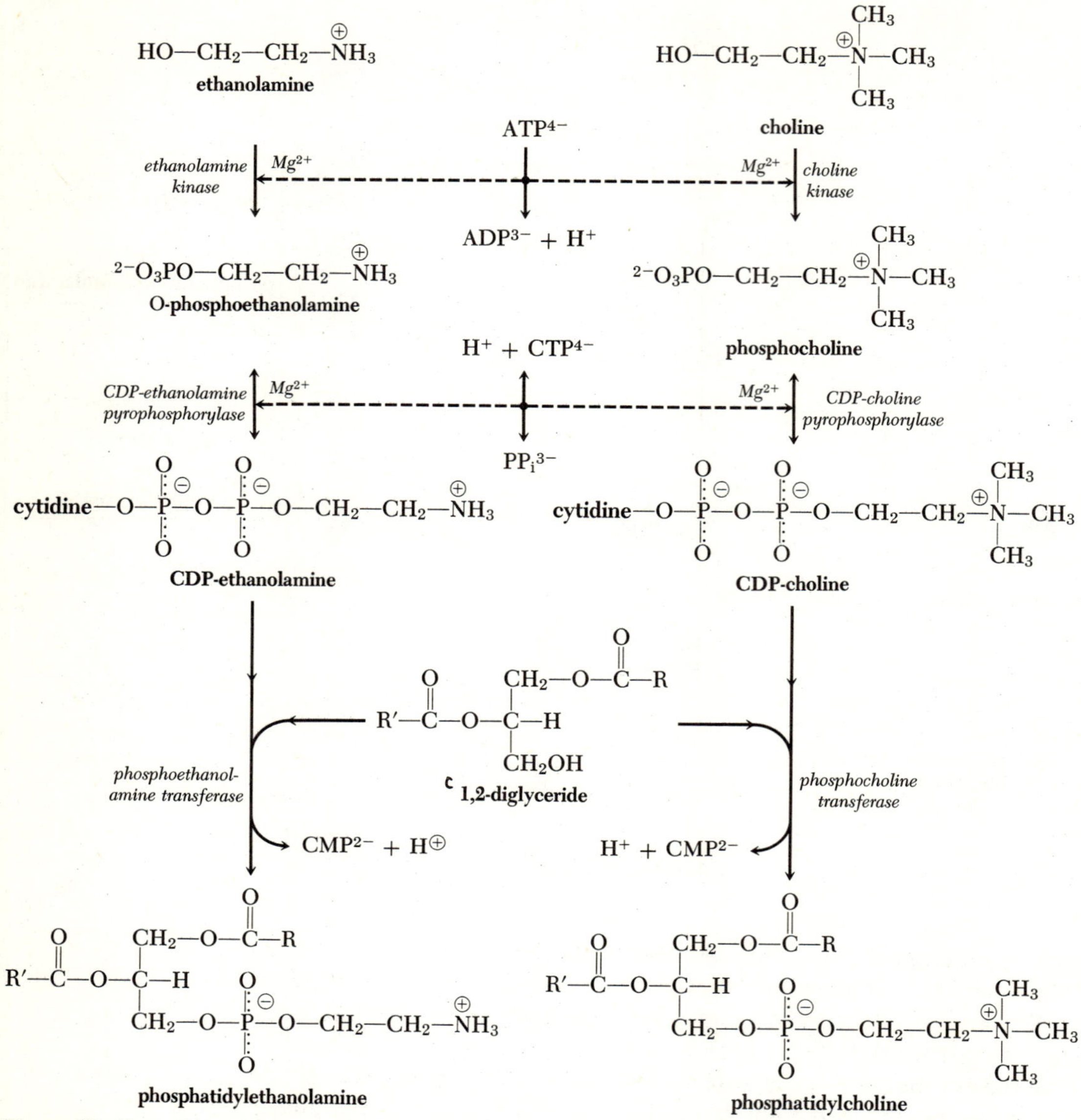

Figure 25-13 Phosphatidylcholine and phosphatidylethanolamine can be made from the free bases by converting them to the CDP-derivatives, from which phospho-base moieties are transferred to 1,2-diglycerides.

of methyl groups from the one-carbon pool. This is accomplished by an irreversible reduction of 5,10-methylene-H_4folate to 5-methyl-H_4folate (Fig. 25-15). The methyl group is then transferred to homocysteine, regenerating methionine.

The enzyme responsible for transferring the methyl group to homocysteine requires **aquocobalamin** as a coenzyme, rather than the deoxyadenoxylcobalamin necessary for methylmalonyl CoA mutase (p. 375). Many of the deleterious effects of a deficiency of vitamin B_{12} are believed to result from a failure of this critical transfer of methyl groups.

Recovery of Methyl Groups from Choline. It is possible to salvage one of the methyl groups from an excessive supply of choline for use elsewhere. This is done by raising the chemical potential of choline through an oxidation of its alcohol group to a carboxylate group (Fig. 25-16). This creates a **betaine** ("bay-tah-een"), an N,N,N-trimethylamino acid. The loss of free energy upon removing one methyl group from the quaternary nitrogen is sufficient to support a transfer of the group to homocysteine.

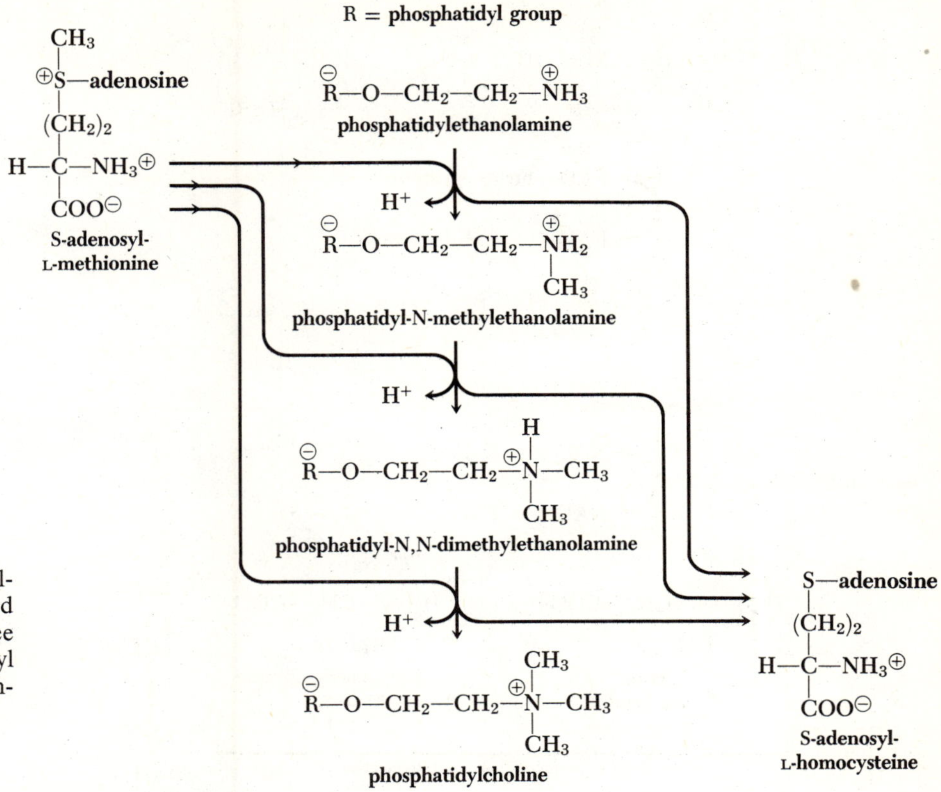

Figure 25-14 Phosphatidylethanolamine can be converted to phosphatidylcholine by three successive transfers of methyl groups from S-adenosylmethionine.

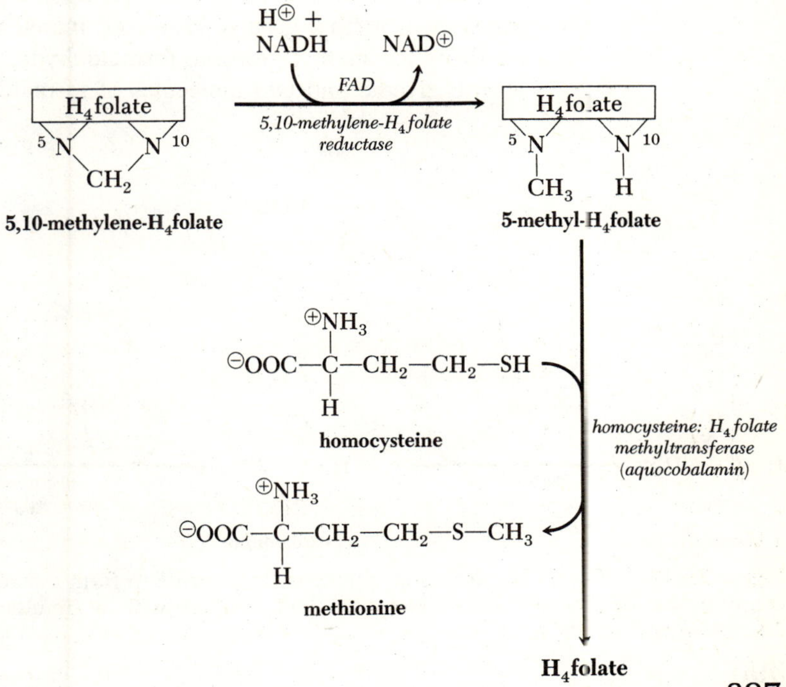

Figure 25-15 The methyl group of methionine may be synthesized by transfer from 5-methyl-H_4folate to homocysteine. This diminishes the demand for methionine in the diet of animals, which cannot synthesize the homocysteine chain. The transfer of the methyl group requires cobalamin.

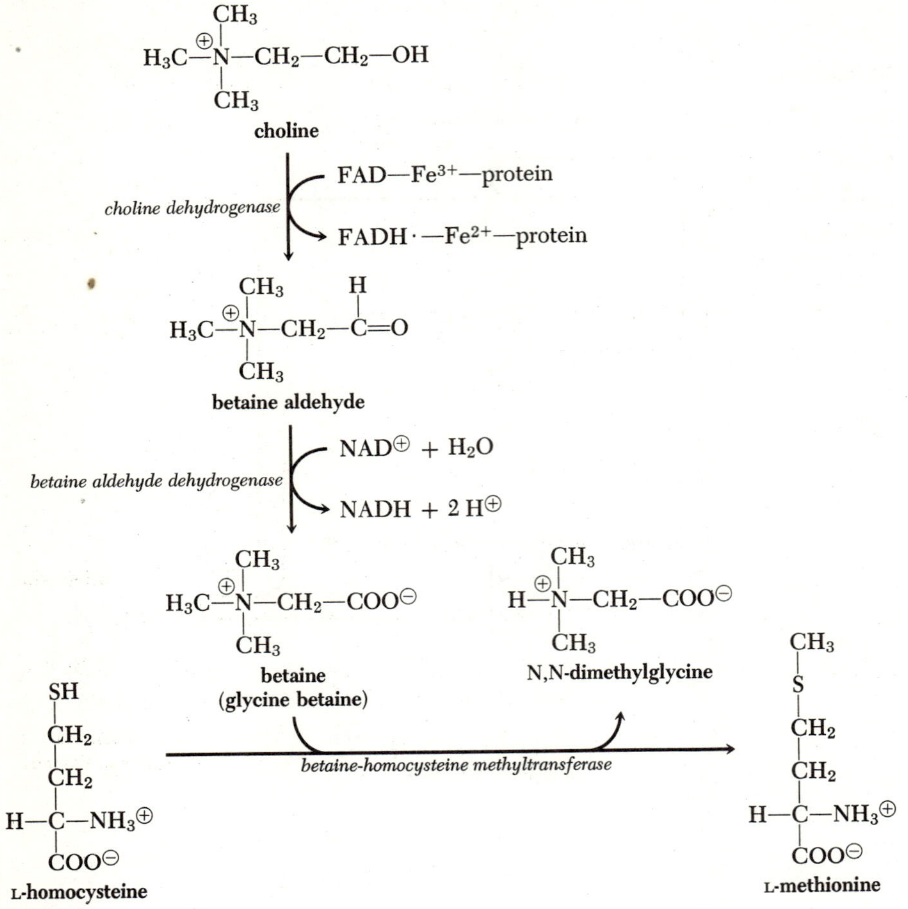

Figure 25-16 Excess choline is metabolized by oxidation to a betaine, which has a high enough chemical potential to make the transfer of a methyl group to homocysteine possible.

The remaining tertiary amino group has too little free energy to support additional transfers of methyl groups. However, many N-methyl compounds are catabolized by oxidizing the methyl group to formaldehyde, and **dimethyl glycine** is converted in this way to glycine and two molecules of formaldehyde.

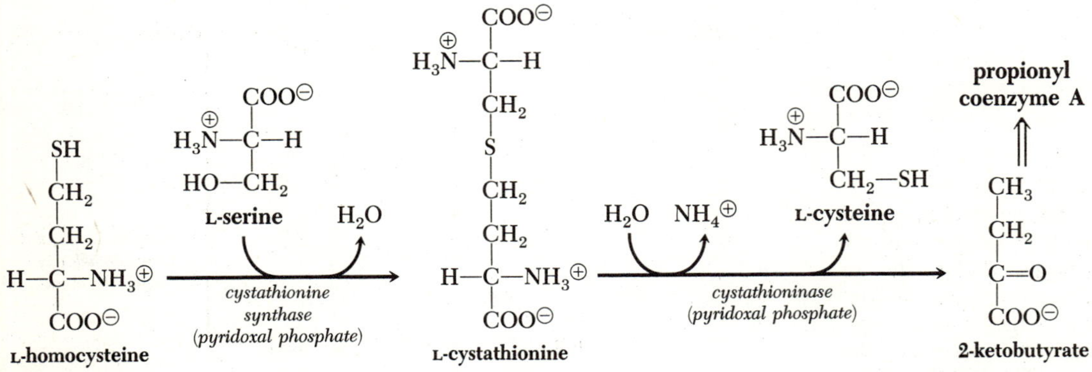

Figure 25-17 Excess homocysteine combines with serine to form cystathionine, which is cleaved on the opposite side of the sulfur atom to yield cysteine with a simultaneous deamination to form 2-ketobutyrate and NH_4^+.

Degradation of Homocysteine

Only part of the homocysteine released by methylations is converted back to methionine; the balance is degraded. The route involves a condensation of the sulfhydryl group with serine to form an intermediate thioether, **cystathionine,** which is then cleaved on the opposite side of the sulfur atom to form cysteine and 2-ketobutyrate (Fig. 25–17). Cysteine therefore is not an essential amino acid if there is sufficient methionine in the diet. 2-Ketobutyrate is degraded *via* propionyl coenzyme A (p. 374), and cysteine is metabolized by routes that involve the oxidation of the sulfur atom to sulfate, and the release of the carbon skeleton as pyruvate.

The important point in all of this is that methionine has at least a triple function from what we have seen so far. It is required for the synthesis of proteins, in which it plays an important structural role; it is required for the transfer of methyl groups; and finally, it is a donor of a sulfur atom for the synthesis of cysteine.

FURTHER READING

R. W. McGilvery, Biochemistry, Saunders (1970). Chap. 18 has a more extensive discussion than given here, and Chap. 19 illustrates methylation of biologically active amines.

G. M. Brown, The biosynthesis of pteridines, Adv. Enzymol., 35:35 (1971). *Also* Biogenesis and metabolism of folic acid, 4:383, in D. M. Greenberg, ed., Metabolic pathways, Academic Press (1970).

Nutrition Society Symposium, Evolution of present concepts concerning the action of lipotropic agents, Federation Proc., 30:130 (1971). Discussion of formation and utilization of methyl groups, and relation to fat transport.

QUESTIONS

1. What are the similarities and the differences in the use of UDP-glucose in the formation of glycogen, and of CDP-choline in the formation of phosphatidylcholine?
2. What structural features necessary for function as a one-carbon carrier are lacking in the coenzyme of phenylalanine hydroxylase?
3. A large fraction of the total folate in a human is present as 5-methyl-H_4folate in the extracellular fluids. Suggest a reason why a deficiency of cobalamin may also cause the effects of a deficiency of folate.
4. Because phospholipids are necessary for the transport of triglycerides from the liver (in what form?), any disturbance of phospholipid formation may cause a fatty liver. Without making a search of the literature, suggest how the appearance of a fatty liver might be influenced by the dietary content of each of the following: methionine, cysteine, choline, folate, cobalamin, creatine. (Deficiencies may cause other disturbances, so one cannot say with absolute assurance that a fatty liver will or will not appear without experimental confirmation.)
5. Show how the methyl group in creatine can be obtained from glucose.
6. Show how the nitrogen atoms in creatine can be obtained from NH_4^+.

PART 6

SYNTHESIS OF NITROGENOUS COMPOUNDS

CHAPTER 26

THE TURNOVER OF NUCLEOTIDES

THE CONCEPTS

The nucleotides, including the nucleic acids, are constantly turning over so that their concentrations may be adjusted by regulation of the rate of synthesis or degradation. Synthesis is no problem, for both the purine and the pyridimidine nucleotides are made from common cellular constituents. The purine ring is assembled on a ribose phosphate unit by use of a molecule of glycine, along with nitrogen atoms from glutamine and aspartate, and carbon atoms from CO_2 and the one-carbon pool. The result is inosine 5′-phosphate, a nucleotide that may be converted to either AMP or GMP by further use of nitrogen atoms from aspartate and glutamine, and an oxidation in the case of GMP.

The enzyme catalyzing the initial step in purine synthesis is inhibited by both adenine and guanine nucleotides, thereby regulating the total concentration of purine nucleotides formed. The relative amounts of the two nucleotides are then controlled by modulating the enzymes catalyzing their formation from inosine 5′-phosphate, with each kind of purine tending to suppress its own formation and stimulate the formation of the other.

The pyrimidine ring is assembled by a condensation of carbamyl phosphate and aspartate, followed by an oxidation to form a carboxylate-substituted pyrimidine, orotate. Orotidine 5′-phosphate is formed by combination with phosphoribosyl pyrophosphate, and UMP is made from it by decarboxylation. The cytidine nucleotides are made, usually as CTP, by transfer of a nitrogen from glutamine to the uracil residue.

The carbamyl phosphate used for pyrimidine synthesis by eukaryotes is generated in the cytosol by an enzyme that transfers nitrogen from glutamine, which is therefore distinct from

the mitochondrial enzyme used for arginine synthesis. This permits the formation of carbamyl phosphate to be inhibited in the cytosol by UTP without disturbing the mitochondrial reaction, which is necessary for the synthesis of urea.

The nature of the regulation of RNA formation is not clear. DNA molecules to be used as templates for RNA must also provide some identification of the type of RNA to be formed, perhaps through sites for binding specific regulatory proteins. RNA is synthesized as primitive molecules containing extra sequences of nucleotides on the ends beyond the functional segments. The transformation of primitive ribosomal RNA into finished molecules by selective hydrolysis was discussed in Chapter 3. Messenger RNA and transfer RNA molecules also are the products of partial hydrolysis of precursors. In addition, mRNA contains as many as 170 consecutive AMP residues that are later added for recognition purposes.

Turnover of DNA is limited to repair processes during the life of a cell. The deoxyribonucleotide triphosphates necessary for DNA synthesis during cell division, and in a limited way for repair during resting phases of the cell cycle, are made as the diphosphates by reducing the corresponding ribonucleotide diphosphates, except that dUDP is produced instead of the needed deoxythymidine phosphate. The thymine nucleotide is made as the monophosphate by transfer of a methylene group from H_4folate. There is a simultaneous reduction of the transferred group to a methyl group, forming dTMP. The corresponding oxidized product is H_2folate, so dividing cells must reduce H_2folate to H_4folate at a faster rate than do resting cells in order to maintain the supply of functional coenzyme.

Ribonucleic acids are hydrolyzed to their constituent nucleoside 5′-phosphates through the action of a group of enzymes that are not fully characterized. Some are cyclizing enzymes that hydrolyze 5′-phosphate bonds to form cyclic 2′,3′-esters. These ribonucleases will not attack DNA, which lacks the 2′-hydroxyl position. Other enzymes are 3′-phosphodiesterases that form 5′-nucleotides.

Degradation of the nucleotides includes the hydrolytic deamination of cytidine, adenosine, and guanosine compounds, which may occur in different species with the nucleotide, the nucleoside or the free base. The pyrimidine ring is further degraded through reduction and successive hydrolyses to return the nitrogen and carbon atoms to the general metabolic pool, but it is the fate of the purine ring that is of the most interest. Although primitive organisms completely degrade the purines to gain reutilizable products, the gain is small, and many organisms have evolved so as to dispense with some of the reactions necessary for total degradation of purines. We have already noted how the formation of insoluble uric acid is of value to some organisms for conservation of water, and some birds, reptiles, and arthropods divert their major nitrogen flow into purine synthesis for disposal in this way. Those organisms that form more soluble nitrogenous waste products from the amino acids also usually degrade the purines sufficiently to form soluble products. This avoids the tendency to deposit crystals of urate in the joints, causing the inflammatory condition known as gout. The primates, however, have reverted to excretion of excess purines as urate, even though they form soluble urea as the major end-product of other nitrogenous compounds. The reason is unknown, but it may be related to an apparent correlation between high concentrations of urate in the blood and an aggressive, driving personality.

The nucleotides of a cell are constantly being broken down and remade. We have seen how they serve as reactants in general metabolic reactions and as precursors of the nucleic acids, and now let us consider how they are made. The synthesis of purine nucleotides first forms **inosine 5′-phosphate,** from which both AMP and GMP are made (Fig. 26–1). The synthesis of pyrimidine nucleotides first forms UMP, a portion of which is then converted to CTP. The 2′-deoxyribonucleotides required for DNA formation are made by reduction of both the purine and the pyrimidine ribonucleotides. The dUMP included among the products is then modified to form dTMP.

All of the precursors of nucleic acids are built from common metabolites that we have already considered. For example, the **purines** are built with atoms derived from **glycine, aspartate, glutamine, CO_2,** and **one-carbon units** attached to tetrahydrofolate. The **pyrimidines** are made from **aspartate, glutamine, CO_2,** and **one-carbon units.** The source of the **pentose** moiety is **ribose 5-phosphate,** which is obtained from glucose by the pentose phosphate pathway.

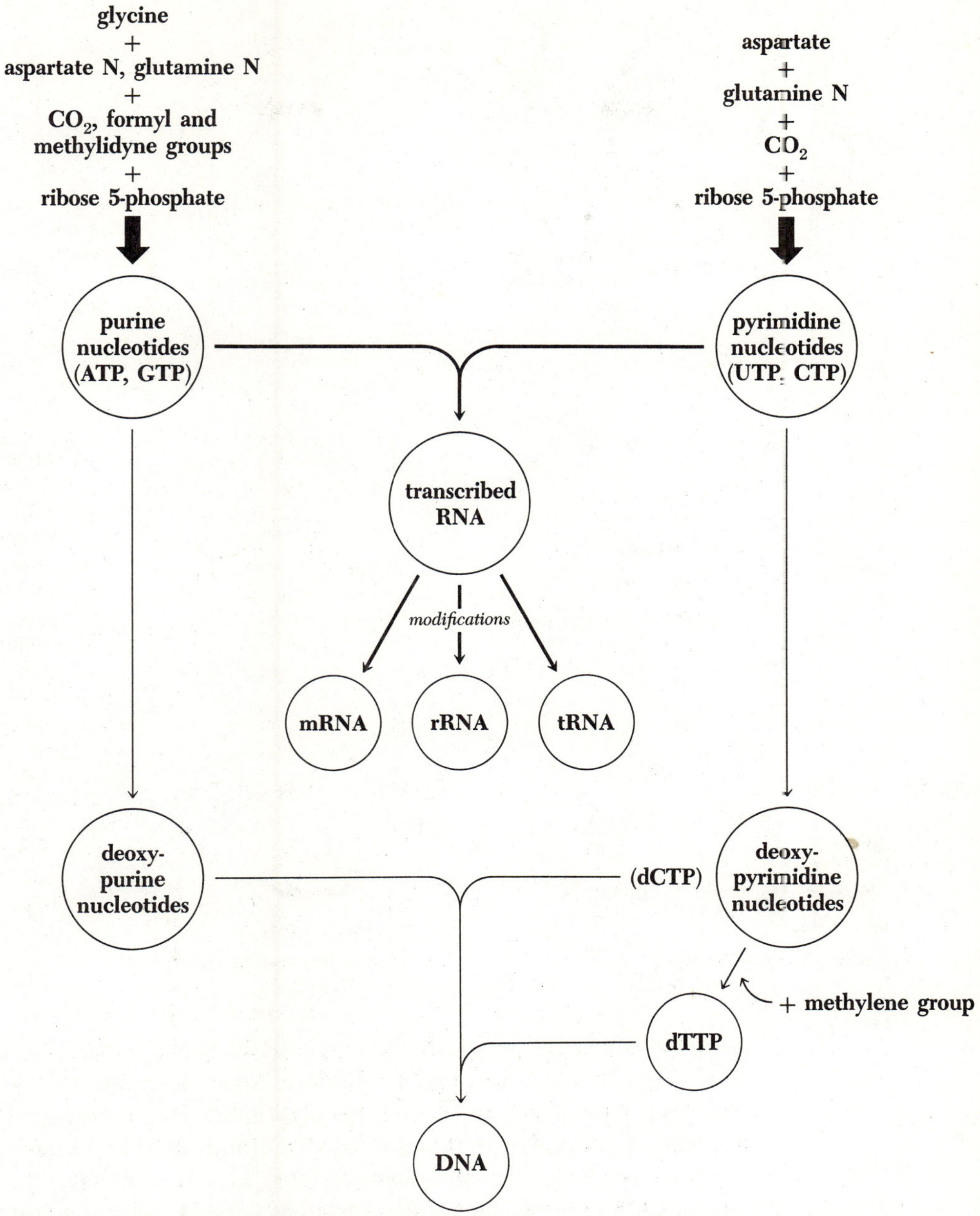

Figure 26-1 The purine and pyrimidine nucleotides that are used as metabolic intermediates and as precursors of RNA are formed from readily available metabolites. The deoxyribonucleotide precursors of DNA are formed by reduction of the ribonucleotides, except that a methylene group is transferred from H_4folate to create the methyl group of thymine residues.

SYNTHESIS OF PURINE NUCLEOTIDES

The general scheme for the synthesis of the purine nucleotides is shown in Figure 26–2. Let us first look at the formation of inosine 5′-phosphate, and then examine how it is converted to AMP or GMP.

The Initial Committed Step. The parent compound for the pentose residue in all ribonucleotides is **5-phospho-α-D-ribosyl pyrophosphate,** which is made from ribose 5-phosphate by a transfer of pyrophosphate from ATP. The first distinctive step in the

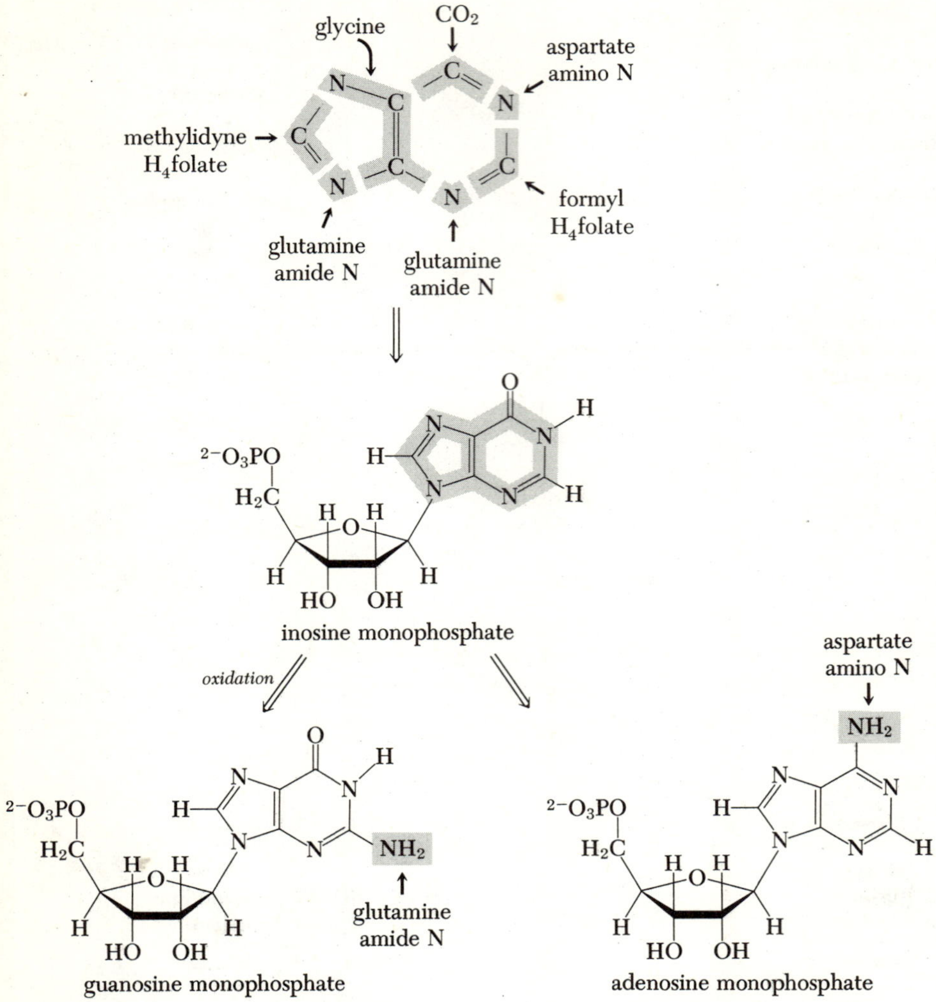

Figure 26–2 Sources of the atoms of purines. The ring is assembled on a ribose-5-phosphate residue obtained from 5-phosphoribosylpyrophosphate (not shown), forming inosine monophosphate as a common precursor of both GMP and AMP. The formation of GMP involves an oxidation and the transfer of the substituent amino group from glutamine. AMP is formed by transfer of the substituent amino group from aspartate.

synthesis of purine nucleotides, as opposed to the formation of other kinds of nucleotides, begins with a transfer of nitrogen from glutamine to C-1 of 5-phosphoribosyl pyrophosphate, and the loss of the pyrophosphate makes the reaction effectively irreversible (Fig. 26–3). Animals use this route only for the formation of the purine compounds; since the intermediates that are formed have no other function, it is advantageous for all subsequent reactions to be capable of going faster than the initial reaction. This permits the regulation of the entire sequence of reactions by controlling the rate of the first reaction in the sequence, and this is accomplished through an inhibition by one or more guanine or adenine nucleotides. In other words, an increased concentration of purine nucleotides shuts off their own synthesis. (The nucleotides giving most effective inhibition differ from one species to another.)

We shall see that glutamine is used as a donor of nitrogen atoms for many purposes in addition to purine synthesis. The amino group is frequently transferred to carbonyl or aromatic carbon atoms, and often with a concomitant discharge of high-energy phosphate.

Building the Imidazole Ring. A purine contains fused 5- and 6-membered rings. After the first nitrogen atom of the purine-to-be is in place, the components of the 5-membered ring are assembled around it, along with an additional nitrogen atom that provides a position for later assembly of the 6-membered ring. The 5-membered ring

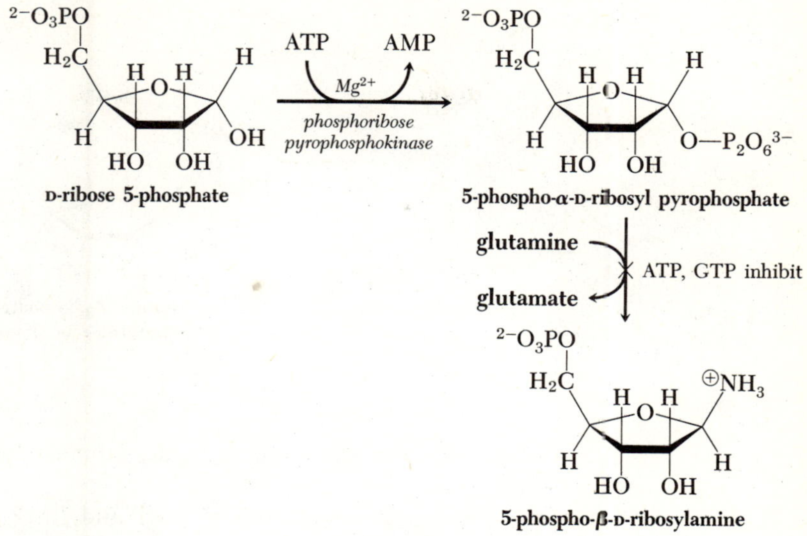

Figure 26-3 The ribose phosphate moiety of all nucleotides is formed from 5-phosphoribosyl pyrophosphate, which is made from ribose 5-phosphate. The first committed step in purine synthesis is the transfer of the amide nitrogen from glutamine to form 5-phosphoribosylamine. Purine synthesis is controlled through an inhibition of this reaction by ATP and GTP.

is then closed (Fig. 26–4). Three of the steps are driven by a concomitant hydrolysis of ATP, and the resultant irreversibility of the reactions, together with the relatively high activity of the responsible enzymes, prevents accumulation of intermediates.

Completing the Purine Ring. An additional molecule of ATP is expended to drive the assembly of the remaining portion of the purine ring (Fig. 26–5). A transfer of a nitrogen atom from aspartate is of special interest because it is accomplished by a mechanism similar to the one we saw in the conversion of citrulline to arginine (p. 368). A carbon atom in the nucleotide condenses with the nitrogen of aspartate to form a —C—N—C— bridge. The bridge is then cleaved on the opposite side of the nitrogen atom to release fumarate (Fig. 26–6).

Differentiating the Purines. The final steps of purine nucleotide synthesis convert inosine 5′-phosphate to either guanosine 5′-phosphate or adenosine 5′-phosphate (Fig. 26–7). AMP is formed by another transfer of nitrogen from aspartate, involving the intermediate formation of adenylosuccinate and the subsequent release of fumarate. The condensation is driven in this case by hydrolysis of GTP to GDP and P_i.

The formation of GMP from IMP requires an initial oxidation of the **hypoxanthine** ring to a **xanthine** ring, followed by an ATP-driven transfer of nitrogen. The nitrogen

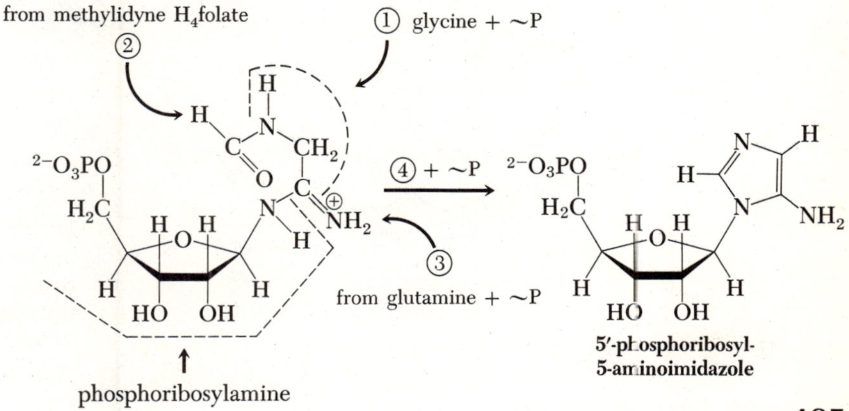

Figure 26–4 The formation of the imidazole ring of purine nucleotides.

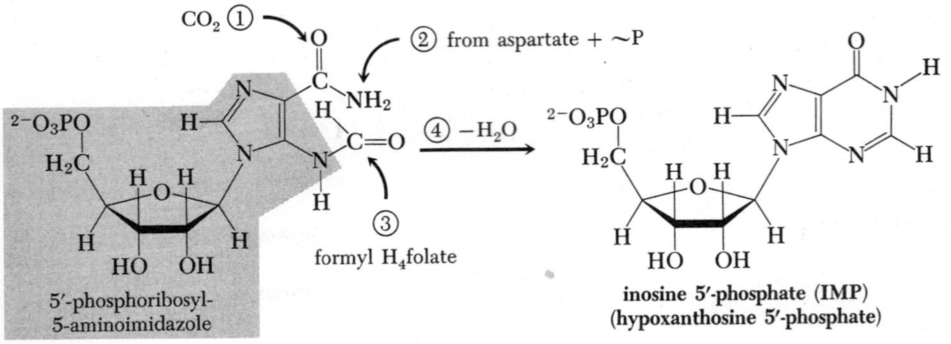

Figure 26-5 The completion of the purine ring forms inosine 5′-phosphate.

is derived from glutamine in higher animals, but at least some protists directly utilize NH^{4+}.

The relative proportion of AMP and GMP produced is closely regulated, although the mechanism of regulation differs somewhat from one kind of organism to another. In general, the first step in the synthesis of AMP from IMP is inhibited by AMP and stimulated by GTP (Fig. 26–7), whereas the first step in GMP synthesis is inhibited by GMP and stimulated by ATP.

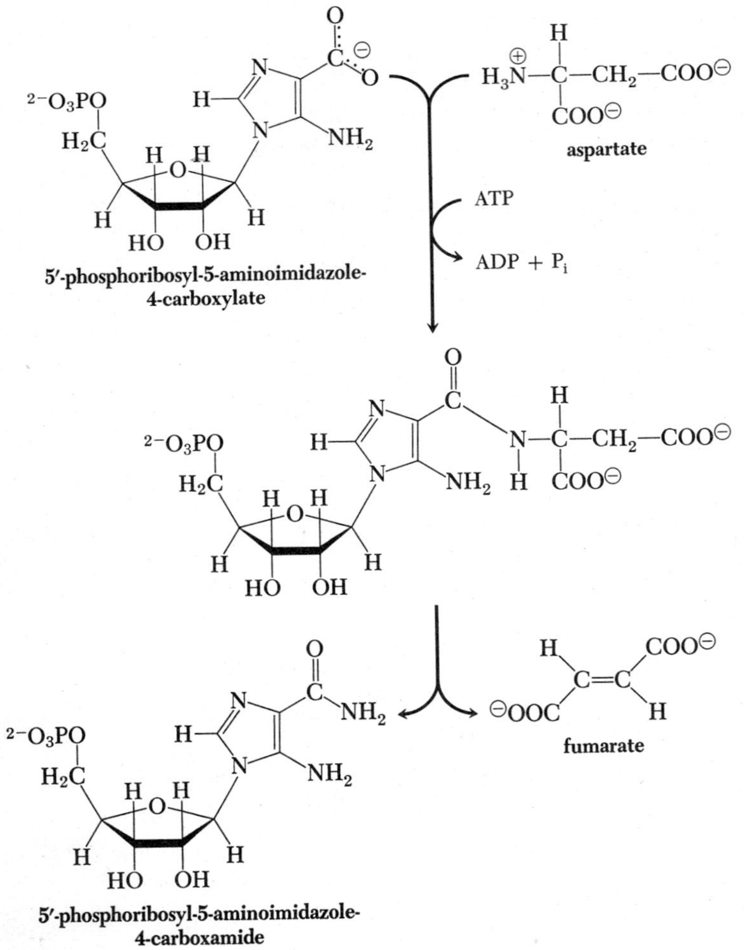

Figure 26-6 The nitrogen of aspartate is transferred for the formation of the purine ring in the same way that it is transferred for the formation of arginine—through a condensation, followed by cleavage on the opposite side of the nitrogen atom to release fumarate.

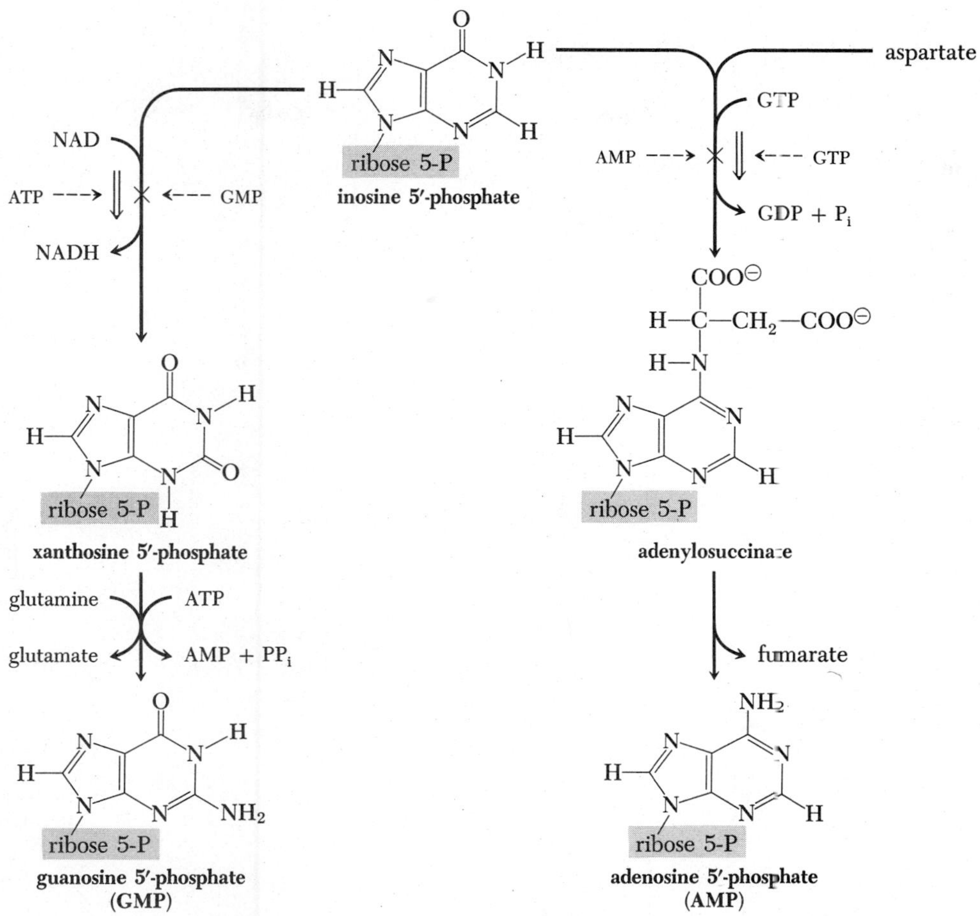

Figure 26–7 The nitrogen of aspartate is also transferred to inosine 5′-phosphate to form adenosine 5′-phosphate. Guanosine 5′-phosphate is formed by an oxidation, followed by a transfer of the amide nitrogen of glutamine. The initial step in each case is inhibited by the end product of the sequence (GMP or AMP), and the inhibition is relieved by the other purine nucleoside triphosphate.

SYNTHESIS OF PYRIMIDINE NUCLEOTIDES

The synthesis of the pyrimidine ring is a relatively simple operation, involving nothing more than a combination of aspartate and carbamyl phosphate to create a dihydropyrimidine, followed by an oxidation to remove the extra hydrogen atoms. The resultant pyrimidine is **orotate,** the salt of **orotic acid** (Fig. 26–8).

There is a catch. Carbamyl phosphate is also required for the formation of arginine, and therefore of urea, in the higher animals. In order to prevent a competition for this compound between pyrimidine synthesis and urea synthesis, the carbamyl phosphate used to make pyrimidine nucleotides is generated in the cytosol of animal tissues by a different enzyme which uses glutamine as the source of the nitrogen of the carbamyl group. This enzyme, unlike the mitochondrial enzyme used for urea synthesis, is inhibited by uridine triphosphate. Here is another example of regulation of the initial committed step in a synthetic sequence through feedback inhibition by an ultimate product of the sequence.

Protists don't make large quantities of urea but they sometimes use carbamyl phosphate in other ways, involving the recovery of its high-energy phosphate. As a result, the first committed step in pyrimidine synthesis in these organisms is the later

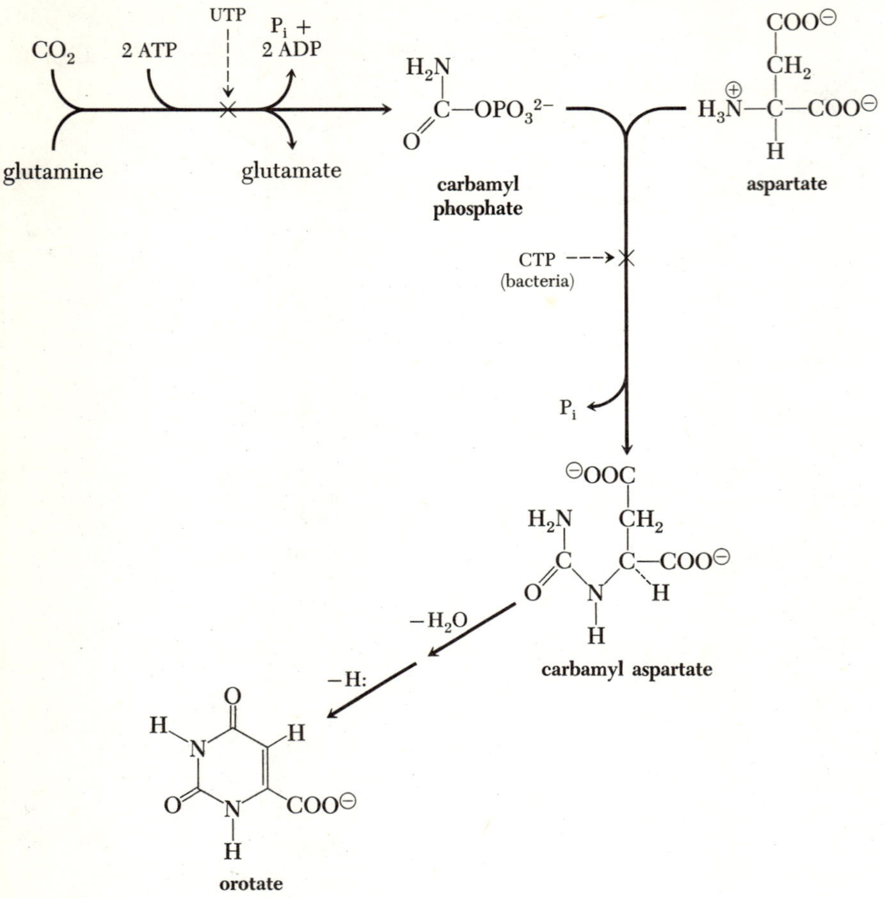

Figure 26-8 The formation of the pyrimidine ring by condensation of aspartate and carbamyl phosphate. Carbamyl phosphate is formed for this purpose by utilizing the amide nitrogen of glutamine in the cytosol. The closure of the ring first forms dihydroorotate, which is oxidized to orotate, the carboxylated analogue of uracil.

aspartate transcarbamylase reaction, which they control through inhibition by CTP.

Formation of Pyrimidine Nucleotides. Orotate combines with 5-phosphoribosyl pyrophosphate to form a nucleotide, **orotidine 5′-phosphate.** Simple decarboxylation produces uridine 5′-phosphate, which is partially converted to cytidine nucleotides by an ATP-driven transfer of nitrogen from glutamine (Fig. 26-9). (UMP is converted to UTP for this transfer in most organisms.) The transfer is regulated by a complex interplay of activations and inhibitions designed to maintain a balanced supply of all of the ribonucleotides.

SYNTHESIS OF RIBONUCLEIC ACIDS

We discussed the transcription of genetic information into the form of RNA in Chapter 3. The overall process is clear; nucleoside triphosphates are polymerized as complements of the deoxyribonucleotide sequence in DNA. However, at least three distinct classes of RNA are formed: messenger RNA, ribosomal RNA, and transfer RNA. There must be some signals in DNA that are included in RNA to prevent confusion of function. For example, the primordial ribosomal RNA is not taken as instruction for the synthesis of a polypeptide chain even though it has the same linear polynucleotide structure as does the primordial mRNA.

Nature of the Signals for RNA Function. Much of a DNA molecule consists of spacer segments, whose complements do not appear in the finished RNA molecules.

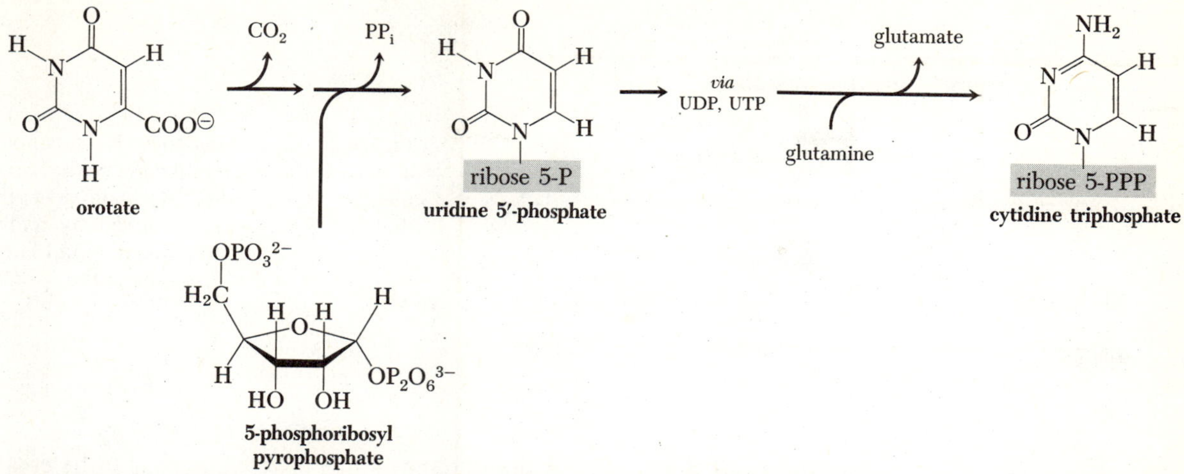

Figure 26-9 Orotate is converted to uridine 5′-phosphate by condensation with phosphoribosylpyrophosphate and decarboxylation. Cytidine is formed as the triphosphate by transfer of the amide nitrogen of glutamine to UTP.

Part of the "extra" sequence is transcribed into segments of RNA that are removed by hydrolysis before functional RNA appears. Other parts of the spacer segments may not even be replicated. For example, some of the DNA is reiterative, that is, the same polynucleotide sequence appears in more than one spacer segment.

These spacer segments are believed to be the sites that convey recognition of the types of RNA to be formed, and at which the initiation of formation of different RNA molecules is regulated. One important implication is that some amino acid sequences may never appear in proteins. If certain sequences of nucleotides convey recognition of RNA types, it may be that the sequences are never used to code for the sequence of amino acids that is also represented. However, the problem may be avoided by having recognition occur on a segment of untwisted double helix in the DNA adjacent to the single chain being transcribed. It is conceivable that a protein required for recognition would fit the exposed surfaces of particular bases on two strands of the double helix. This "signal" would therefore be composed of two linear fragments of DNA chain in a fixed three-dimensional conformation, so that the occurrence of the same nucleotide sequence elsewhere in the chain to designate amino acid sequence would not be confused with the signal for RNA initiation.

Discrimination by RNA Polymerases. Whatever the nature of the signal for specific transcription may be, its interpretation may depend to some extent upon the specificity of the RNA polymerases. The mammalian cell contains at least two different enzymes, one located in the nucleolus for the synthesis of ribosomal RNA, and the other located in the nucleoplasm for the synthesis of messenger RNA. Presumably, the segments of DNA bearing instructions for formation of ribosomal RNA have distinctive adjacent spacer segments that aid their movement, by unknown means, into the nucleolus for transcription.

Since the prokaryotes lack a nucleus and nucleolus for compartmentation of rRNA formation, they evidently resort to changes in the specificity of RNA polymerase itself as a means of identifying the RNA to be formed. The RNA polymerase of at least some prokaryotes contains three different peptides necessary for catalytic activity, and the chain composition is expressed as $\alpha_2\beta\beta'$. However, these peptides constitute only the catalytic core of the enzyme, and the utilization of this catalytic capability hinges upon the attachment of regulatory peptides. The best-known of these, the σ-peptide, leads to the formation of mRNA. There is evidence for a ψ-peptide that creates RNA polymerase activity for synthesis of rRNA.

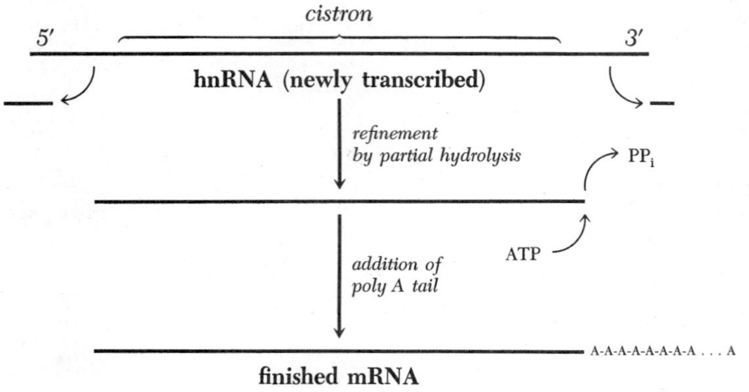

Figure 26–10 Messenger RNA is first made as an overly-large molecule in heterogenous nuclear RNA (hnRNA). Some of the redundant groups are removed by hydrolysis, but a polyadenosine phosphate tail is created by transfer of AMP groups to the 3′-end from ATP.

Perfection of RNA. All of the different kinds of RNA appear to be created as raw molecules containing extra nucleotide sequences on both ends. We have already discussed the refinement of ribosomal RNA by removal of spacers and end pieces (Chapter 3).

Messenger RNA first appears in the nucleus as heavier molecules designated **hnRNA** for **heterogeneous nuclear RNA,** which contain as many as 200 extra nucleotides on their 5′-ends, and a somewhat smaller number on the 3′-ends, with the cistron specifying amino acid sequence between. These extra nucleotides are partially removed by hydrolysis, but at some point a structure appears that is recognized by another enzyme, which catalyzes the successive addition of as many as 170 adenosine phosphate groups to the 3′-end (Fig. 26–10). This poly-A sequence only appears in messenger RNA. It may be involved, along with the extra terminal nucleotide sequences, in recognition for ribosomal attachment, but it also may be used as a site for attachment of proteins involved in the translation process.

Similarly, the various transfer RNA molecules are also made with extra sequences of nucleotides on both ends, which are removed before the molecules become functionally active.

Modification of the Bases. The ribosomal and transfer RNAs are further modified through chemical alterations of some of the constituent nucleosides. Methyl groups are added to a variety of positions in both the ribose and the base moieties, using S-adenosylmethionine as a methyl donor. Sulfur atoms are transferred from cysteine to create thiol-substituted bases. The purpose of these, and several other alterations, may be to facilitate recognition of sites on the nucleic acids by particular proteins. The alterations are made by enzymes of varying specificity, peculiar to the organism in which they occur, so the modifications are also different in different organisms.

SYNTHESIS OF DEOXYRIBONUCLEIC ACIDS

We know that DNA is synthesized by polymerizing deoxynucleotide triphosphates, specifically dATP, dGTP, dCTP, and dTTP, but where do these nucleotides come from? The first three are created by reducing the 2′-position of the corresponding ribonucleotides. This reduction is a prerequisite for cell division to occur. The mechanism of reduction and the particular form of the nucleotide that is reduced vary from one organism to another.

The electrons required for reduction are derived from NADPH by transfer to a small disulfide-containing protein, **thioredoxin.** The disulfide group is thereby converted to two sulfhydryl groups (Fig. 26–11), which are then used to reduce the ribonucleotides

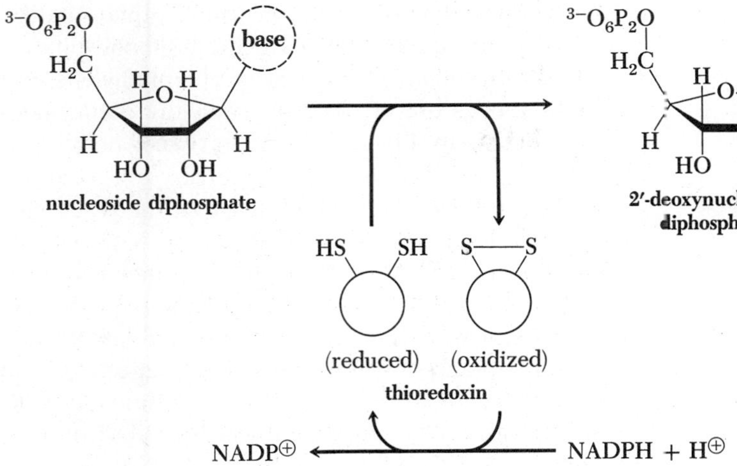

Figure 26-11 The reduction of nucleoside diphosphates to 2′-deoxynucleoside diphosphates.

to deoxyribonucleotides. A few microorganisms, for reasons that are not clear, require deoxyadenosylcobalamin as a coenzyme in the reduction, but this is not true in most organisms. The active substrates are usually the nucleoside diphosphates, although some of the cobalamin-requiring organisms utilize the triphosphates.

Formation of Deoxythymidine Phosphates. We have already noted that RNA contains uracil nucleotides, whereas DNA contains thymine nucleotides. The ribo-

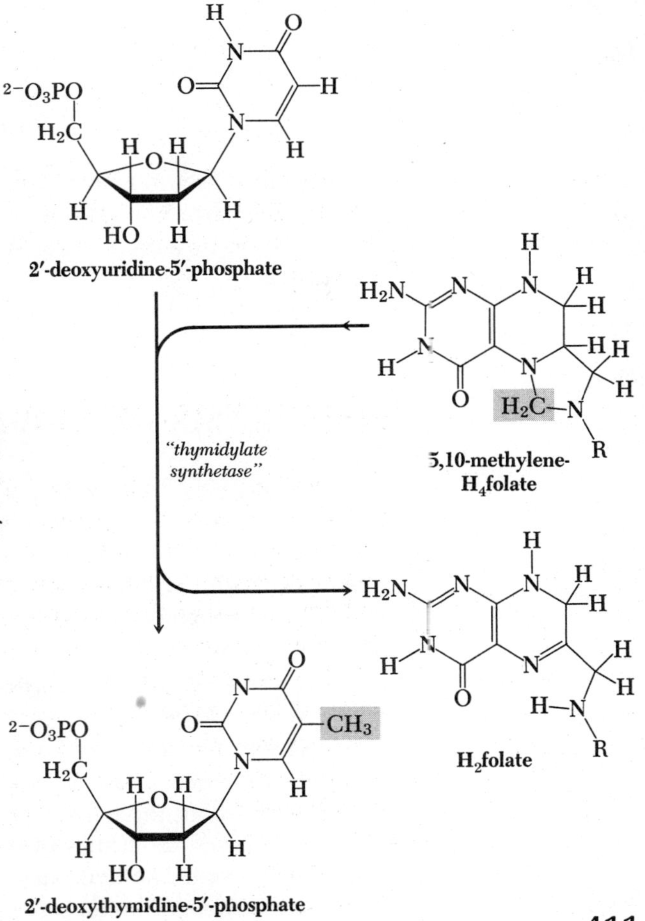

Figure 26-12 The deoxythymidine phosphate found in DNA is created by transfer of methylene groups from H_4folate to 2′-deoxyuridine 5′-phosphate. The H_4folate moiety also acts as a reducing agent to convert the methylene group to a methyl group, resulting in the release of H_2folate as a product.

nucleotide reductases do act on uridine diphosphate, forming deoxyuridine diphosphate, which is in equilibrium with the monophosphate. However, dUMP is converted to dTMP; this involves the transfer of a methylene group from tetrahydrofolate, with the simultaneous use of electrons from the coenzyme to reduce the methylene group to a methyl group (Fig. 26–12). We have seen nothing like this before. The tetrahydrofolate is being used both as a group carrier and as an electron carrier, and it is converted to dihydrofolate as a consequence of the reaction.

It follows that the use of methylene tetrahydrofolate in making the thymine groups required for DNA synthesis, unlike other uses of the one-carbon pool, is associated with an obligatory requirement for the reduction of dihydrofolate to tetrahydrofolate. (Otherwise, all of the limited supply of folate would shortly be in the partially reduced form.) A practical consequence is that effective deficiencies of tetrahydrofolate can be created in actively dividing cells by administration of inhibitors of the reductase enzyme in concentrations that have much less effect on resting cells. Compounds of this sort, such as methotrexate:

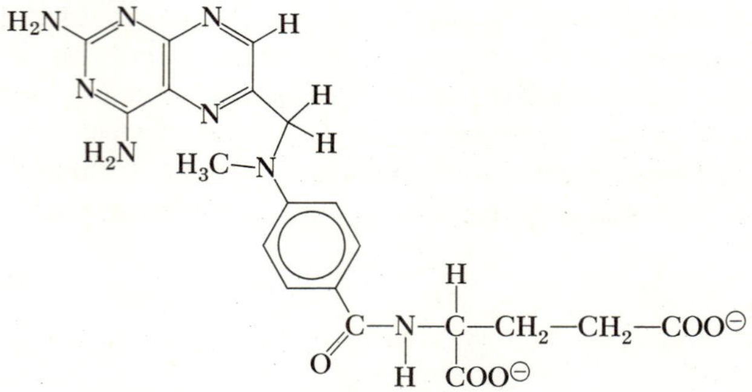

methotrexate
(4-deoxy-4-amino-10-methylfolate)

are for this reason sometimes of value in treating certain kinds of malignancies. (Such agents also harm normal cells that divide rapidly, like those in the intestinal mucosa and in blood-forming tissues, and the resultant side-effects limit the dosage that can be used.)

HYDROLYSIS OF NUCLEIC ACIDS

The destruction of ribonucleic acids by hydrolysis is a necessary part of the constant turnover required for maintenance and regulation of cellular function. On the other hand, complete destruction of the genetic instructions represented by DNA is not consistent with the maintenance of normal function, and it does not occur until the cell dies, although there is occasional removal and replacement of damaged portions. Our major concern therefore is with the metabolism of the ribonucleotides.

We know the general reactions of the hydrolases attacking RNA, but we still lack detailed knowledge of the sequence of events. There appear to be several different ribonucleases within a cell. Some enzymes must be specific for the removal of inactive terminal sequences present on all newly synthesized RNA, but there is little specific information about these hydrolases, or about those responsible for controlled turnover of the functional molecules of mRNA, tRNA, and rRNA.

In any event, the hydrolases attacking interior bonds in RNA are of two classes. Some are cyclizing ribonucleases that always form a 3′-nucleotide as a product. These

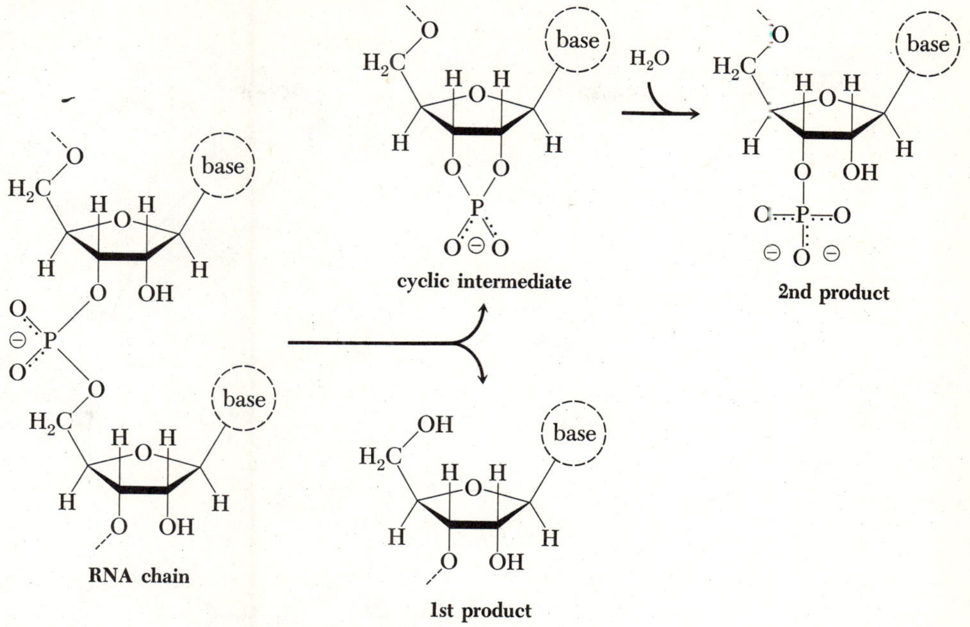

Figure 26-13 The mechanism of cyclizing ribonucleases involves the formation of an intermediate with a 2′,3′-phosphodiester group.

enzymes do not require a metal ion, and form 2′,3′-cyclic phosphate esters as intermediates in the hydrolysis (Fig. 26-13). They therefore cannot attack DNA, which lacks 2′-hydroxyl groups for participation in the cyclization mechanism, and this inherent defense against destruction may be one of the reasons for the creation of DNA as the relatively permanent store of genetic information.

The second group of RNA hydrolases, the phosphodiesterases, always require an activating cation, usually Mg^{2+}, and catalyze the direct hydrolysis of a phosphate ester bond, often the 3′-bond, so that one product is a 5′-nucleotide. Some phosphodiesterases attack interior bonds, while others hydrolyze only the terminal nucleotides in a polymer.

The concerted effect of the action of the various hydrolases is believed to result mainly in the formation of the nucleoside 5′-phosphates AMP, GMP, UMP, and CMP, and the products of RNA degradation therefore become part of the nucleotide pools involved in ordinary metabolic reactions.

DEGRADATION OF NUCLEOTIDES

The general pathway for the metabolism of the nucleoside 5′-phosphates involves the removal of the 5′-phosphate by hydrolysis, followed by the liberation of free purines or pyrimidines, which may then be further metabolized. In this scheme, the substituent amino groups of adenine, guanine, and cytosine residues are removed by simple hydrolysis at different points, depending upon the compound involved. For example, the amino group of adenine is removed while it is still combined in the form of AMP.

The hydrolysis of adenosine 5′-phosphate, catalyzed by **AMP deaminase,** creates inosine 5′-phosphate. The reaction is unquestionably a part of the route for disposal of excess adenine nucleotides, but the enzyme is too active for this to be its only function, especially in skeletal muscles. It is believed to participate in a cycle involving the regeneration of AMP from IMP at the expense of aspartate (Fig. 26-14), so that the end result is the conversion of aspartate to NH_4^+ and fumarate.

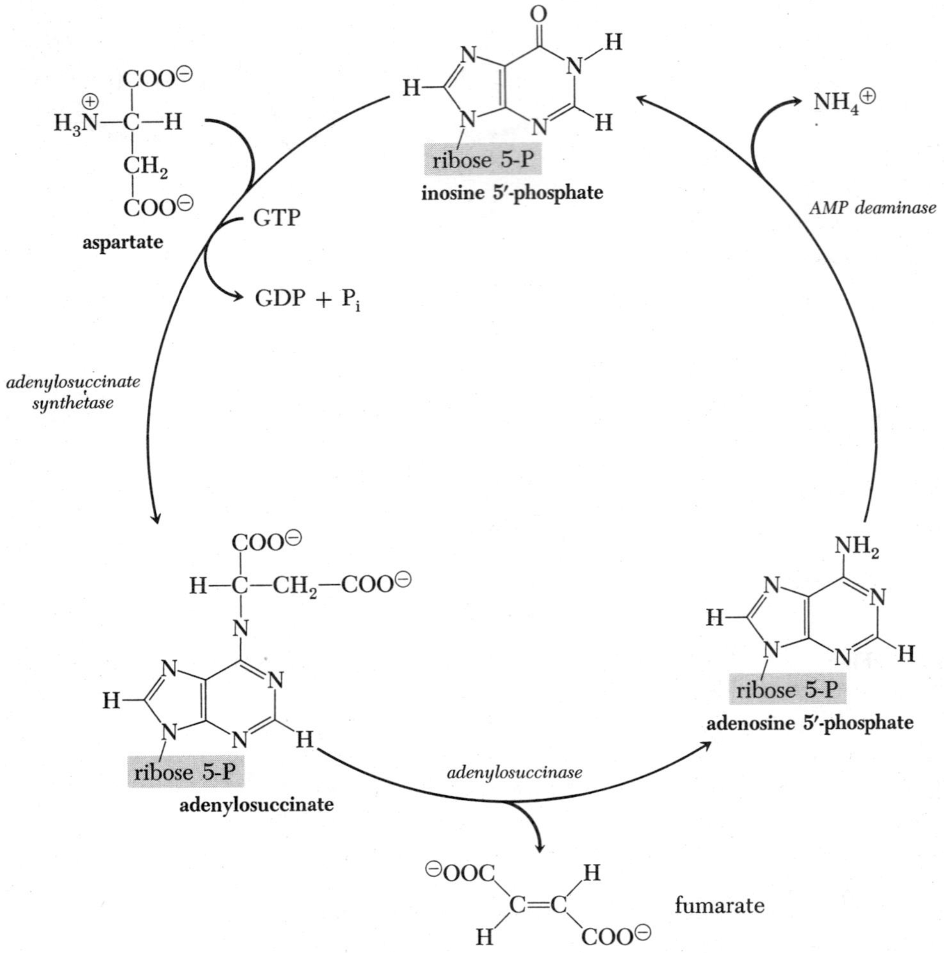

Figure 26–14 The purine nucleotide cycle of J. L. Lowenstein. The deamination of AMP to IMP, together with the resynthesis of AMP by use of aspartate nitrogen, may be a device for deaminating aspartate to fumarate and NH_4^+ in skeletal muscles.

Disposal of the Purine Nucleotides. The phosphate groups are removed from inosine 5′-phosphate and guanosine 5′-phosphate by the action of a **5′-nucleotidase.** Inosine and guanosine are substrates for **phosphorylases** that cleave the base-sugar bond with inorganic phosphate so as to form **ribose 1-phosphate** and liberate free hypoxanthine or guanine. (The ribose 1-phosphate is recovered by the action of a mutase that interconverts it with ribose 5-phosphate.)

The relationship between these degradative reactions and the synthetic reactions considered earlier is summarized in Figure 26–15, which also depicts the subsequent degradation of the free purines. It is especially important to recognize that the turnover of the purine nucleotides represents a continual flow of nitrogen atoms from the precursor amino acids to the excreted products of purine degradation. This flow is only a small, although indispensable, part of the total nitrogen economy in animals that excrete waste nitrogen as ammonium ion or urea. However, those animals that utilize purine degradation as the major route for excreting nitrogen synthesize and degrade purines at a rate much greater than is required for simple maintenance of the metabolic pool of nucleotides.

Catabolism of the Purines. The free bases released from nucleosides are in part recovered, as discussed later, and are in part metabolized to excreted products. The most primitive organisms have the most extensive degradation, involving in some cases the release of the nitrogen atoms of the purine ring as NH_4^+. Subsequent evolution

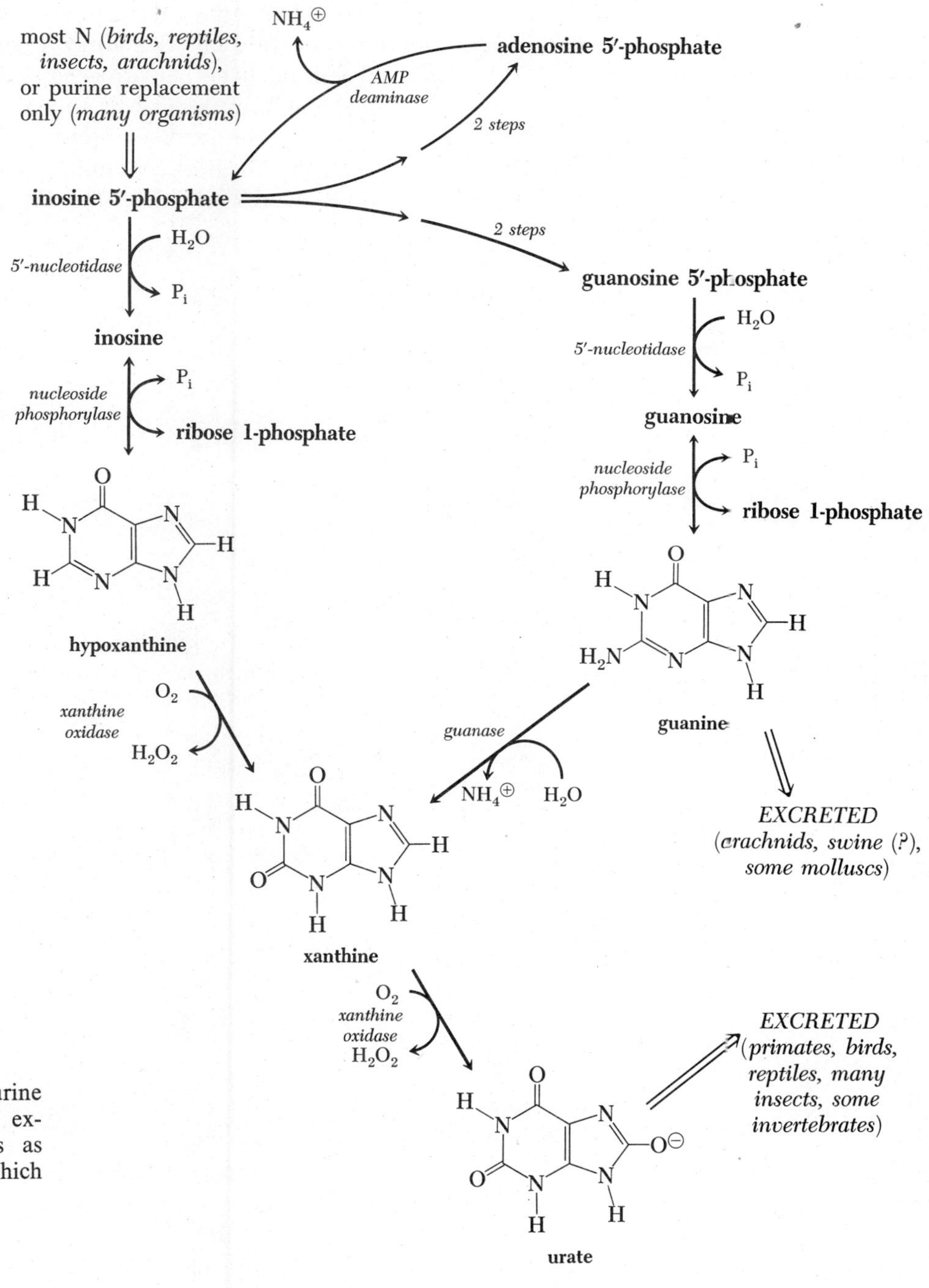

Figure 26-15 The purine moiety of nucleotides is excreted by some animals as guanine or uric acid, which have a low solubility.

caused the loss of enzymes catalyzing the final reactions of the sequence, so that higher animals excrete various partially degraded derivatives of the original purines.

Indeed, some organisms, especially the spiders, excrete guanine as the major end-product of purine metabolism. However, most animals convert both hypoxanthine and guanine to xanthine (Fig. 26–15); this can be done by a simple deamination of guanine. Hypoxanthine is oxidized to xanthine through the action of **xanthine oxidase,** which contains both ferric and molybdate ions, in addition to sulfide and flavin adenine dinucleotide. (This, and a related aldehyde dehydrogenase, account for a small, but definite, requirement for molybdenum in the diet of animals.)

The same oxidase also catalyzes the further oxidation of xanthine to uric acid, which is present as urate ion at physiological concentrations of H^+. Uric acid is the excreted end product of purine metabolism in several classes of invertebrates and vertebrates, including the primates.

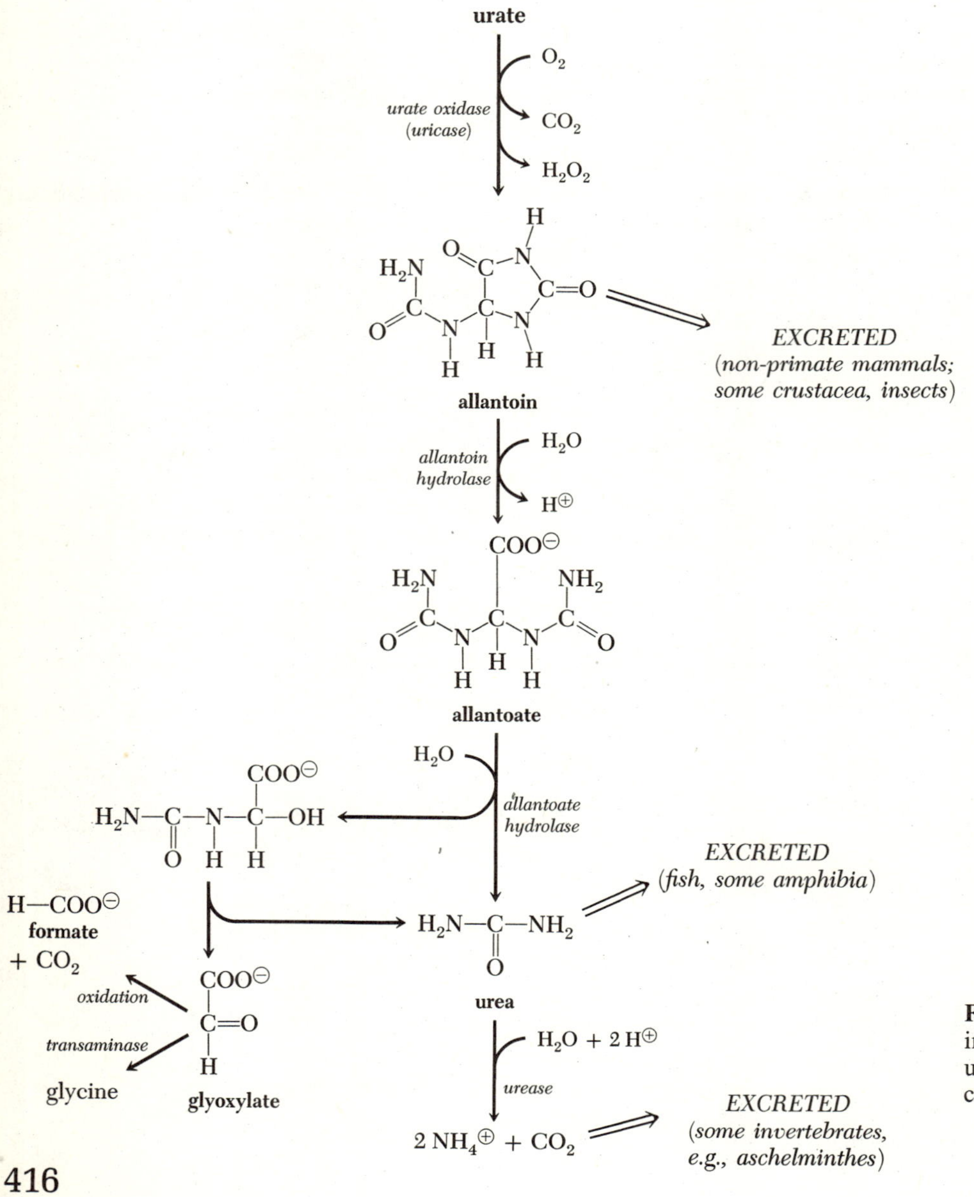

Figure 26-16 Many animals further degrade urate to more soluble compounds for excretion.

Degradation of Urate. Urate is degraded further by many animals, beginning with an oxidation that involves opening one ring and losing CO_2 to form **allantoin.** This reaction, catalyzed by **urate oxidase** (known as **uricase** in the older literature), occurs in all of the mammals except the primates. The mammals lack enzymes to attack allantoin, which they excrete as the end-product of their purine metabolism.

Many invertebrates degrade allantoin further through a series of hydrolyses outlined in Figure 26–16. The initial products are molecules of urea, which some animals excrete as such; but primitive forms have a urease catalyzing hydrolysis to NH_4^+ and bicarbonate. The other two carbons of allantoin appear as glyoxylate, the carbonyl analogue of glycine, which may be further oxidized to formate, or transaminated to glycine.

RATIONALE OF PURINE DEGRADATION

Relation to Environment. We ought to ask why it is that there are such great differences among animals in the nature of the excreted products of purine degradation. Part of the answer lies in the changing environment during evolution, as we discussed in Chapter 23. The sea is still used today by many aquatic organisms as a cesspool for the ammonia derived from purines and pyrimidines, as well as ammonia from amino acids. Simple organisms form urea from both arginine and the purines, but the urea is hydrolyzed to NH_4^+ and CO_2 through the action of urease, a hydrolase.

Those animals that diminished the requirement for water by synthesizing purines as the major end-products of nitrogen metabolism obviously handle the purines derived from nucleotide turnover in the same way. All of the birds, and the land dwellers among the reptiles and the arthropods (spiders and insects), discarded the enzymes involved in the disruption of the purine ring, beginning with urate oxidase, so that urate became the end product of purine metabolism. The spiders went a step further in eliminating the enzymes of purine metabolism. Somehow, they avoid oxidizing xanthine to uric acid, and excrete their excess nitrogen as guanine, which is even less soluble than uric acid (39 mg of guanine per liter of saturated solution at 40°, compared to 65 mg of uric acid).

PURINES AND PERSONALITY. Even those land animals that maintained urea synthesis as a major route for nitrogen excretion were also free to discard the enzymes of purine degradation. That is, the use of arginine turnover for handling most excess nitrogen in no way necessitated the conversion of the relatively small excess of purines to urea. In fact, many of the enzymes were discarded even before the development of urea synthesis (Table 26–1), and we find some invertebrates that excrete both uric acid and NH_4^+. However, the vertebrates that excrete either ammonia or urea as major end-products frequently maintain some of the enzymes of purine degradation so that the purine end-product is also a soluble compound, such as allantoin or urea, rather than uric acid or guanine. Why is this so?

Gout. The excretion of uric acid or guanine has the advantage of minimizing water loss, but the low solubility from which this advantage stems also creates problems of its own. Unless the internal concentration of these compounds is maintained below the saturation level, crystals will tend to form in the organs, especially in the joints, and the result is a painful and life-shortening condition known as gout. The great toe is frequently affected. (The crystals are monosodium urate in the uric acid excretors. It has a solubility of only 70 mg per liter of human blood serum, owing to the high Na^+ concentration in the blood.)

TABLE 26-1

	Typical Products Excreted From Metabolism of:	
	Amino Acids	Purines
Protozoa	NH_4^+	hypoxanthine
Platyhelminthes (flatworms)	NH_4^+ or urea	uric acid
Aschelminthes (nematodes)	NH_4^+ or urea	NH_4^+
Molluscs	NH_4^+	hypoxanthine, guanine, or uric acid
Annelids	NH_4^+ or urea	uric acid
Arthropods:		
Crustacea	NH_4^+	NH_4^+, allantoate, allantoin, or uric acid
Arachnids	guanine	guanine
Insects	uric acid	uric acid
Pisces (fish)	NH_4^+ or urea	urea
Amphibia	NH_4^+ (aquatic) or urea (terrestrial)	urea
Reptilia	uric acid (terrestrial)	uric acid
Aves (birds)	uric acid	uric acid
Mammalia	urea	allantoin (except uric acid in primates)

Note: Only a few species have been studied in some invertebrate phyla.

Gout occurs in alligators and in birds. It also occurs in humans even though they only excrete excess purine nitrogen as uric acid. Nearly all of the mammals oxidize urate to the more soluble allantoin, but the primates do not; they have discarded urate oxidase during their evolution. (The Dalmatian dog is often cited as another exception; however, it has urate oxidase. Something has happened to its liver that affects the ability of the kidneys to eliminate uric acid. Mongrel livers transplanted to Dalmatians make them uric acid excretors, whereas the Dalmatian liver prevents excretion in a mongrel.)

Why have primates discarded the enzyme that prevents dangerous accumulation of urate? There is a long standing notion that people with gout are likely to be superior folk. There has been little basis for this other than the propensity to take special note when the mighty are felled by sore toes. The idea is also repellent to some because high blood urate concentrations and gout are primarily afflictions of the male and of post-menopausal women.

However, we now have a study of male high school students that appears to support the old notion. The general conclusion is not that high levels of urate are associated with greater intellectual ability, but that they are associated with more drive and ambition; people with high urate levels are over-achievers compared to the bulk of their fellows, more likely to utilize their abilities to the utmost. If this is so, we have at least the possibility that part of the seeming superiority of primates is really the result of a constant provocation to activity caused by their purine metabolism, even though it is difficult to visualize how urate affects mental behavior. It is at least possible that the dangers and inconvenience of gout are compensated by a more general benefit.

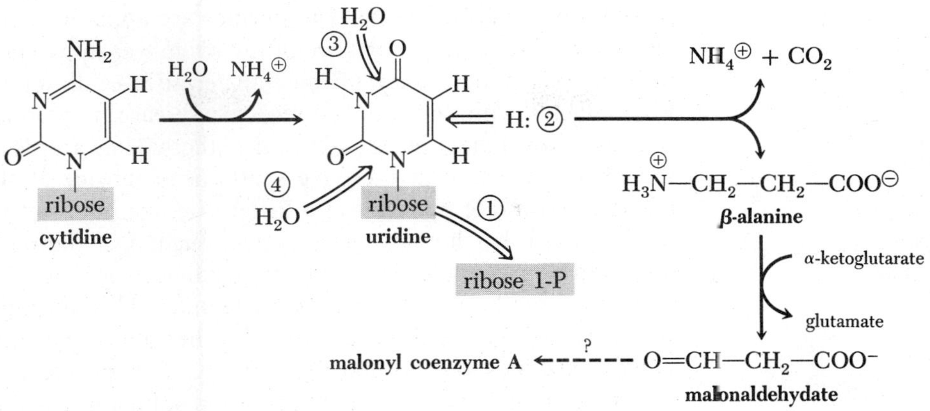

Figure 26-17 The nitrogen of pyrimidines is recovered for further use, and the carbon skeleton may appear in part as malonyl coenzyme A, or be decarboxylated to acetyl coenzyme A (not shown).

PYRIMIDINE DEGRADATION

The pyrimidine nucleotides, like the purine compounds, are converted to nucleosides, and then undergo phosphorolysis to release free pyrimidines (Fig. 26-17). In most organisms, cytidine is deaminated to form uridine before phosphorolysis, so uracil is the major free pyrimidine formed. Uracil is then reduced, followed by a hydrolytic cleavage of the ring. The route of degradation is a reversal of the route of synthesis, except that synthesis involves the carboxylate analogues, dihydroorotate and orotate. The nitrogen of pyrimidines is eventually recovered in the form of NH_4^+ and glutamate, and the carbons may be converted to malonyl coenzyme A. In any event, the turnover of pyrimidines is, like the turnover of the purines in ureotelic animals, a small part of the total nitrogen economy, although the nitrogen of pyrimidines is recovered rather than being excreted, and there are no insoluble end-products to cause trouble.

SALVAGE OF FREE BASES

Not all of the purines and pyrimidines released by phosphorolysis of nucleosides are degraded. Enzymes are present for recovering the bases, along with those absorbed from the diet, by attaching 5-phosphoribosyl units derived from 5-phosphoribosyl

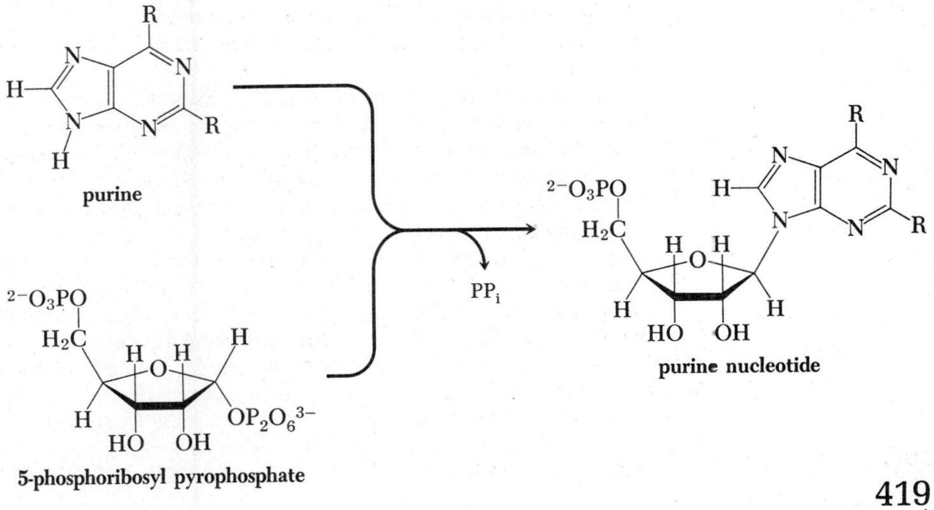

Figure 26-18 A sizeable fraction of the purines liberated by degradation of nucleotides is salvaged by condensation with phosphoribosyl pyrophosphate to regenerate the nucleotides in other cells.

pyrophosphate (Fig. 26–18). The purines are apparently recovered more readily than the pyrimidines; the importance of the route was appreciated only after the discovery of a hereditary deficiency of the transferase specific for hypoxanthine and guanine. Boys afflicted with this X-linked recessive disease frequently have uncontrolled aggressiveness toward themselves and toward others. They are also afflicted with gout, because the condition results in excessive synthesis of inosine 5′-phosphate, and the resultant formation of urate proceeds at a faster rate, considering the body size, than has been seen in any other humans. The overproduction of purines is believed to be due to a diversion of 5-phosphoribosyl pyrophosphate from the salvage route to the first step of de novo synthesis of the purine nucleotides. This interpretation of the origin of gout is augmented by the discovery of still other gouty patients who have normal purine salvage enzymes and normal regulation of the specific steps of purine synthesis, but who apparently have a failure of regulation of the rate of phosphoribosyl pyrophosphate synthesis, thereby causing the unusually high intracellular concentrations of the compound.

FURTHER READING

J. F. Henderson and A. R. P. Paterson, Nucleotide metabolism, Academic Press (1973). Logical, somewhat detailed summary.

J. N. Davidson, The biochemistry of the nucleic acids, 7th ed., Academic Press (1972). Includes chapter on the hydrolytic enzymes.

M. J. Chamberlin, The selectivity of transcription, Ann. Rev. Biochem., 43:721 (1974). Specifically discusses the problems of initiation of RNA formation.

J. B. Stanbury, J. B. Wyngaarden, and D. S. Frederickson, The metabolic basis of inherited disease, 3rd ed., McGraw-Hill (1972). See Part VI for a discussion of disorders of purine and pyrimidine metabolism, including gout and Lesch-Nyhan disease.

QUESTIONS

1. The amino groups substituted on the rings of cytosine and guanosine phosphates are derived from ammonia, but they are irreversibly released as ammonia when the nucleotides are degraded. How is the unfavorable equilibrium overcome to create the amino groups from ammonia?
2. Why is the transfer of nitrogen from glutamine to phosphoryibosyl pyrophosphate the rate-controlling step in purine nucleotide synthesis, rather than the formation of phosphoribosyl pyrophosphate from ribose 5-phosphate?
3. What are the similarities and differences, if any, in the formation of adenylosuccinate and argininosuccinate?
4. The use of urate as a means of excreting amino acid nitrogen by birds hinges upon the ability to derive the nitrogen atoms in the purine from amino acids. For example, show how it might be theoretically possible for the nitrogen in an excessive supply of serine to be used as a precursor for all of the nitrogen atoms in urate.
5. Since the formation of uridine phosphates and arginine both require carbamyl phosphate, why don't their concentrations rise and fall together?
6. Why do urea excretion and allantoin excretion frequently appear together? What advantage is gained by not degrading allantoin further so that its nitrogen is also excreted as urea?
7. Why might the development of cyclizing ribonuclease make the protection of genetic information in the form of 2′-deoxyribonucleic acids feasible?
8. Gouty people are frequently treated with an inhibitor of xanthine oxidase so as to prevent accumulation of high concentrations of urate. However, some untreated people who have high urate concentrations do not develop gout. Suggest an ethical study that might aid in detecting any direct effect of urate concentration on personality.
9. What purine will accumulate if xanthine oxidase is inhibited?

CHAPTER 27

THE TOTAL SYNTHESIS OF AMINO ACIDS

THE CONCEPTS

The ultimate precursors of amino acids are nitrogen and carbon dioxide from the air, and water. Plants are able to make all of the amino acids; they derive the carbon skeletons by reductions of CO_2 that are driven by photosynthesis, and they derive the amino groups from ammonium ions. The ammonium ions are made, directly or indirectly, by reductions of atmospheric N_2 carried out by microorganisms, or by reduction of nitrate ions, derived from atmospheric oxidations.

Many microorganisms can fix nitrogen from the air by a direct reduction to ammonium ions. They include free-living species and symbiotic species that live in specialized nodules on the roots of legumes and other plants. The nitrogenase catalyzing this reaction contains non-heme iron and molybdate; the electrons are obtained from reduced ferredoxin, and the transfer to N_2 is driven by expenditure of ATP, somewhat like a reversal of oxidative phosphorylation. The mechanism of nitrogenase appears to be similar in all species, but the electrons supplied as reduced ferredoxin may be derived from anaerobic metabolism of pyruvate, from oxidative electron transfers, or from photosynthetic reductions, depending upon the organism involved.

The soil contains nitrifying bacteria, which do not fix nitrogen themselves, but utilize the NH_4^+ as a fuel to be oxidized for generation of high-energy phosphate. Some oxidize ammonium ions to nitrite ions, while others oxidize nitrite ions to nitrate ions. Many higher plants benefit from the process, because they absorb nitrate ions faster than they do ammonium ions. The plants then reduce the absorbed nitrate back to ammonium ions for incorporation into amino acids.

Oxides of nitrogen are also created by direct fixation of N_2 when air is heated to high temperatures for brief periods, as in lightning flashes and in gasoline engines. However, most of the non-biological fixation of nitrogen occurs during industrial production of ammonia, much of which is returned to the soil in fertilizers. Before the industrial age, the amount of fixed nitrogen was kept in balance by denitrifying bacteria in the soil, which use nitrite and nitrate ions as final electron acceptors in place of oxygen during oxidative phosphorylation. The ions are reduced to N_2 as a result, which returns to the atmosphere. This grand nitrogen cycle is apparently unbalanced by industrial fixation, and there has been a worrisome increase in nitrate levels in ground water as a result.

The ammonium ion made available to plants as a result of nitrogen fixation may be incorporated into glutamate by a simple reversal of the glutamate dehydrogenase reaction, but plants also carry out a more effective ATP-driven reductive transfer of the amide nitrogen of glutamine to α-ketoglutarate. Ammonium ion can then be added to the resultant glutamate to form glutamine. Transaminations permit the utilization of glutamate or glutamine nitrogen with carbon skeletons obtained from glucose to form many amino acids—alanine, aspartate, asparagine, proline, arginine, serine, and glycine. Animals depend upon plants to make many of the remaining amino acids. For example, plants can modify and reduce the terminal carbon of aspartate to form threonine and methionine. The aromatic acids are made by making a 6-membered ring from phospho-*enol*-pyruvate and erythrose 4-phosphate, followed by further additions of familiar metabolites to create the remainder of the molecules. Histidine is made in a seemingly odd way, with one nitrogen and one carbon derived from an adenine ring, another nitrogen from glutamine, and five carbons from ribose.

Cysteine is made from sulfide ions and serine; the sulfide is obtained by reducing sulfate in the form of 3′-phosphoadenosine 5′-phosphosulfate, which is a high-energy mixed anhydride

of sulfate with AMP. (An additional 3′-phosphate group is added during synthesis to drive the reaction toward completion.)

Other nitrogenous compounds in living organisms are made from the amino acids. For example, a number of amines are formed by decarboxylating amino acids. Porphyrins are made by condensing succinyl coenzyme A with glycine to form porphobilinogen, a monopyrrole. The condensation of four molecules of porphobilinogen and subsequent oxidations create the porphyrins.

NITROGEN FIXATION

All of the reactions of nitrogen-containing compounds that we have considered in the preceding chapters involve nitrogen that is equivalent in oxidation state to ammonia. Yet, the great reserve of nitrogen at the surface of the earth is the molecular nitrogen present in the atmosphere. The existence of all organisms hinges on the conversion of nitrogen gas to ammonium ion, which can be used to construct amino acids. The conversion is an example of nitrogen fixation, a term describing any conversion of N_2 to more reactive forms.

General Processes of Nitrogen Fixation. Some protists can reduce nitrogen directly to ammonia:

$$N_2 + 6H^{\oplus} + 6e^{\ominus} \longrightarrow 2NH_3$$

These include free-living organisms, and other bacteria that must live in plant tissues. The latter symbiotic bacteria are of special importance in legumes (alfalfa, peas, soybeans, locust, and the like), where they dwell in nodules formed in the roots. The conversion of N_2 to ammonia by organisms probably accounts for half of the total rate of nitrogen fixation on the earth's surface.

Atmospheric nitrogen is also fixed through industrial reactions, mostly by reduction to ammonia with hydrogen gas derived from natural gas. A substantial amount of this nitrogen is delivered to the soil as fertilizer, mostly as ammonia, ammonium salts, urea, or ammonium nitrate. (The nitrate ion is created by oxidizing part of the ammonia.) Industrial processes now represent perhaps a third of the total nitrogen fixation.

Finally, something less than one-tenth of nitrogen fixation results from the combination of nitrogen and oxygen in the atmosphere in response to high temperatures. The necessary conditions are commonly created by lightning flashes in the open atmosphere, and in more recent years by the explosion of gasoline in internal combustion engines. The resultant mixture of nitrogen oxides dissolves in water to form nitrate and nitrite ions.

Utilization of Fixed Nitrogen for Energy. While some microorganisms fix nitrogen, still other microorganisms in the soil profit from their labor by using the fixed nitrogen in their major fuel economy. The advantage gained is the generation of ATP. The fixed nitrogen is a substrate for oxidative phosphorylation in the same way that fatty acids are substrates for oxidative phosphorylation in mammalian muscle. For example, the oxidation of ammonia by molecular oxygen is an exergonic process, and some Nitrosomonas use this reaction as a source of electrons for oxidative phosphorylation:

$$NH_3 + \frac{3}{2}O_2 \longrightarrow NO_2^{\ominus} + H_2O + H^{\oplus}$$

Still other microorganisms, the Nitrobacter, use the nitrite generated in this way as a fuel by oxidizing it further to nitrate:

$$NO_2^{\ominus} + \frac{1}{2}O_2 \longrightarrow NO_3^{\ominus}$$

Use of Nitrate by Plants. Many higher plants have evolved so as to take advantage of the microbial reactions in the soil by preferentially absorbing nitrate ions. Ammonium ions complex fairly tightly with soil minerals, so that the concentration of the free ions in the soil water is very low. On the other hand, nitrate ions complex poorly and are easily leached out of the soil. The plant that rapidly absorbs nitrate therefore will not lose as much of its nitrogen supply into the ground water. In addition, the steady oxidation of ammonium ion released from the soil complexes will provide a steadier and longer-term supply of nitrogen in the form of nitrate.

The nitrogen assimilated as nitrate must be reduced within the plant to ammonia before it can be used in the synthesis of amino acids and other nitrogenous constituents. The reduction is done in steps, first to nitrite, and then to ammonia. **Nitrate reductase** contains molybdate and non-heme iron to transfer electrons from NADPH:

$$NO_3^{\ominus} + NADPH + H^{\oplus} \xrightarrow[\text{nitrate reductase}]{Mo^{+6},\ Fe\text{—}S} NO_2^{\ominus} + NADP^{\oplus}$$

In the following steps, nitrite is reduced, first to hydroxylamine, and then to ammonia:

$$NO_2^{\ominus} \xrightarrow[5H^{\oplus}]{4e^{-} \qquad H_2O} [NH_2OH] \xrightarrow[3H^{\oplus}]{2e^{-} \qquad H_2O} NH_4^{\oplus}$$

Finally, the ammonia is used for the synthesis of amino acids by routes we shall examine shortly.

Use of Nitrate by Microorganisms. Some soil microorganisms, the **denitrifying organisms,** compete with the plants for nitrate and nitrite by using the ions as oxidizing agents in place of oxygen. These organisms have the same sort of fuel metabolism seen in most organisms and use an electron transport scheme for the generation of ATP, but they differ from the aerobic organisms in that the electrons are ultimately transferred to either nitrite or nitrate, which is commonly reduced to nitrogen gas. Whereas the Nitrosomonas and Nitrobacter merely convert one form of fixed nitrogen to another, without causing its loss from the soil, the denitrifying organisms cause the return of nitrogen to the atmosphere.

THE NITROGEN CYCLE

The interconversions of atmospheric nitrogen, ammonium ions, and nitrate ions are summarized in Figure 27–1. We see that they do represent a grand cycle. It seems likely that this cycle was balanced at the start of the industrial age, with the denitrifying bacteria of the soil returning nitrogen to the atmosphere at about the same rate it was removed by fixation. With the development of industrial nitrogen fixation, the addition of fertilizer nitrogen to the soil began to rival biological fixation in magnitude, and the total amount of fixed nitrogen on the earth appears to be steadily rising.

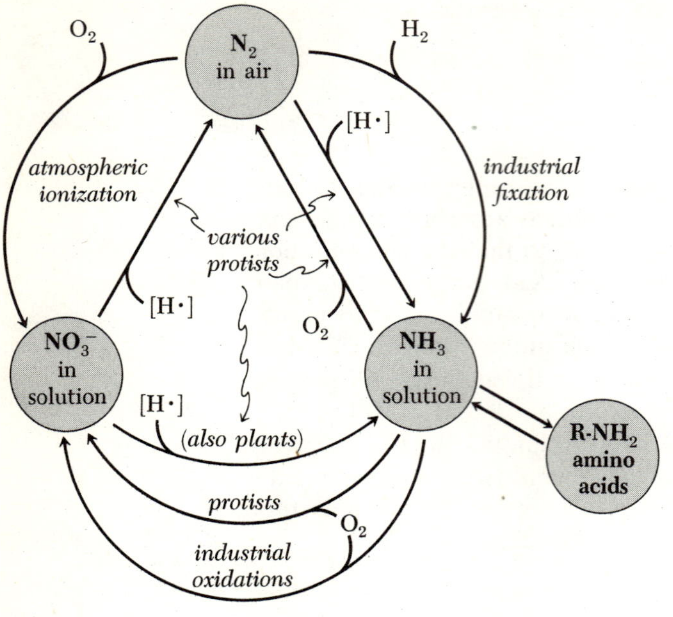

Figure 27-1 The nitrogen cycle. Nitrogen in the atmosphere may be oxidized to nitrate in heated or ionized air, or it may be reduced to NH_4^+ by biological nitrogen fixation or industrial processes. Plants also make NH_4^+ by reduction of absorbed nitrates. Some protists use NH_4^+ as a fuel, and oxidize it to nitrogen or its oxides. Other protists use nitrate and nitrite as substitutes for oxygen in oxidative phosphorylation, creating nitrogen or NH_4^+.

Toxicity of Nitrate. Increased nitrogen in the soil may cause serious problems in some localities because of the toxicity of nitrate. For example, the water in the Sangamon River, which drains the rich cornfields of central Illinois and is used as the source of water for Decatur, already contains over 0.7 of the maximum permissible level of nitrate according to the standards of the Public Health Service for drinking water.

The necessity for clear vision in approaching this problem is emphasized by the recent misfortune of an infant who was fed 500 ml of carrot juice and had over half of its hemoglobin oxidized to methemoglobin (the ferric-porphyrin form) because of the nitrite in the carrot juice. Stored plants that contain nitrate sometimes reduce part of it to nitrite, and this proved to be the case in the example at hand. The local supermarket had obtained carrots from California, where they were grown by heavy feedings of nitrogen-containing fertilizers, and from Florida, where they were grown on Everglades muck without the addition of nitrogen-containing fertilizer. Let all devotees of organic gardening take heed: the carrots with high levels of nitrate and nitrite were those grown on native Everglades muck. The chemically-fed California specimens had negligible quantities. Here is another example of the fallibility of gut reactions in developing serviceable solutions to real environmental problems.

General Role of Nitrogen Fixation. From the standpoint of general biochemistry, the important function of nitrogen fixation is in supplying a source of ammonia for the synthesis of the amino acids, which in turn are used as precursors for the nucleic acids and most other compounds containing nitrogen in living tissues.

We see that most of the nitrogen is primarily fixed by microorganisms as ammonia. When this occurs in the root nodules of legumes, the nitrogen can be used more or less directly by the host plant. When it is fixed in the soil, the nitrogen frequently is first used as an energy supply through oxidation to nitrate, and the plants then remove nitrate and reduce it to ammonia.

Animals obtain their nitrogen originally from the plants, followed perhaps by passage through several species before reaching the ultimate predator. In the end, both the plants and animals die, and their tissues reach the soil to replenish its supply of ammonium ion.

Since the soil nitrogen is constantly being depleted by the denitrifying organisms, the entire population of living organisms ultimately depended on the ability of some microorganisms to convert nitrogen to ammonia before the advent of industrial nitrogen fixation. Let us see how this is done.

Mechanism of Nitrogen Fixation

The reduction of nitrogen to ammonia is catalyzed by an enzyme complex known as nitrogenase. This complex consists of two kinds of electron-transferring proteins. One of these contains only non-heme iron, that is, iron atoms and associated sulfide ions. The other contains molybdate ions along with non-heme iron.

The exact mechanism of action of nitrogenase is not known. The electron donor is reduced ferredoxin in all cases, and the nitrogen-fixing organisms differ mainly in the means used to reduce ferredoxin. That is, they differ in the original electron donor whose oxidation is coupled to the reduction of nitrogen (Fig. 27–2). For example, some clostridia use the reduced ferredoxin generated by the phosphoroclastic reaction of pyruvate—the conversion of pyruvate to acetyl phosphate (p. 262)—to reduce nitrogen rather than using it to produce H_2 as we discussed earlier. Still other microorganisms have a photosynthetic apparatus resembling the photosystem I of plants, and use light quanta to provide energy for the production of reduced ferredoxin, with the electrons being removed from fuel metabolites. Finally, the most important of the nitrogen-fixing bacteria use electrons derived from the oxidation of fuels, that is, electrons from the ordinary electron transport chain, to reduce ferredoxin. These include the free-living Azotobacter, which are the major sources of fixed nitrogen for many plants, and the Rhizobia, which are the symbionts found in the root nodules of legumes.

The reduction of nitrogen by ferredoxin is driven by ATP. This reductive dephosphorylation is somewhat akin to the reversal of oxidative phosphorylation, and there is a similar uncertainty over the mechanism and the number of high-energy phosphates required per pair of electrons transferred, with estimates ranging from two to four. The overall balance for nitrogen fixation therefore becomes:

$$N_2 + 6(\text{reduced ferredoxin}) + 6\text{-}12\ \text{ATP} \longrightarrow 2\ NH_4^{\oplus} + 6(\text{ferredoxin}) + 6\text{-}12\ (\text{ADP} + P_i)$$

SYNTHESIS OF AMINO ACIDS

The amino acids are like other components of living organisms in that the original materials are inorganic compounds that are used by plants or protists to construct

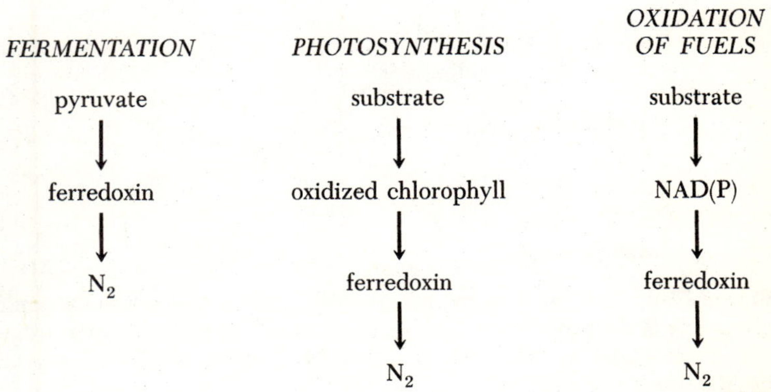

Figure 27-2 The reduced ferredoxin necessary for biological nitrogen fixation may be obtained directly from substrates, as in clostridia, by photosynthetic transfer of electrons from some substrate donor, as in photosynthetic bacteria, or by transfer of electrons from substrates through nicotinamine nucleotides, especially NADP.

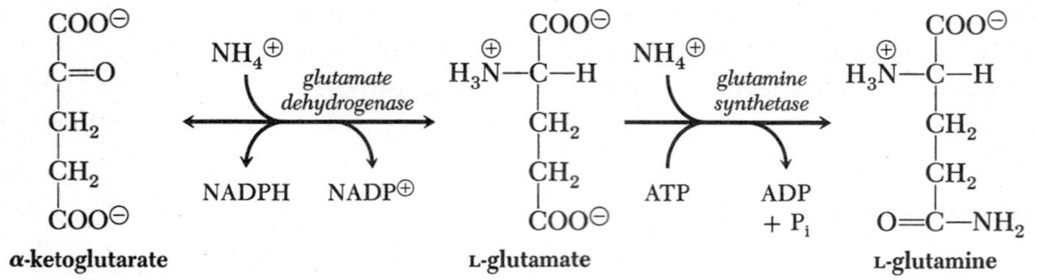

Figure 27-3 Ammonium ions are taken up for the synthesis of amino acids in many organisms by a reversal of the glutamate dehydrogenase reaction, using NADPH as the reducing agent, and by the conversion of glutamate to glutamine. Either glutamate or glutamine serves as a nitrogen donor for the synthesis of other amino acids.

organic compounds upon which animals depend. We shall see that the pathway of synthesis for amino acids begins with carbon skeletons derived from glucose. The conversion of CO_2 to glucose by photosynthesis and the formation of NH_4^+ by nitrogen fixation therefore enable the production of amino acids from inorganic precursors.

Universally Synthesized Amino Acids

Animals and many protists have lost the ability to make some of the amino acids because they depend upon plant tissues as a source of food, and the plants can make all of the amino acids. There was no evolutionary pressure for the maintenance of the necessary synthetic enzymes in the case of those amino acids required mainly for the synthesis of proteins.

However, all organisms have retained the ability to make the amino acids that have important metabolic roles in addition to their function as precursors of proteins. We have already seen how amino acids such as glutamate, aspartate, and alanine act as carriers of amino groups for transfer from one carbon skeleton to another; the routes of transfer often include within themselves the means of creating the amino acids from ammonia, glucose and water as the original sources of the constituent atoms. Let us summarize and extend these routes.

Glutamate and Glutamine. All of the nitrogen used in the synthesis of amino acids is derived from either glutamate or glutamine, with the sole exception of the single nitrogen atom in arginine that is obtained from carbamyl phosphate. This means

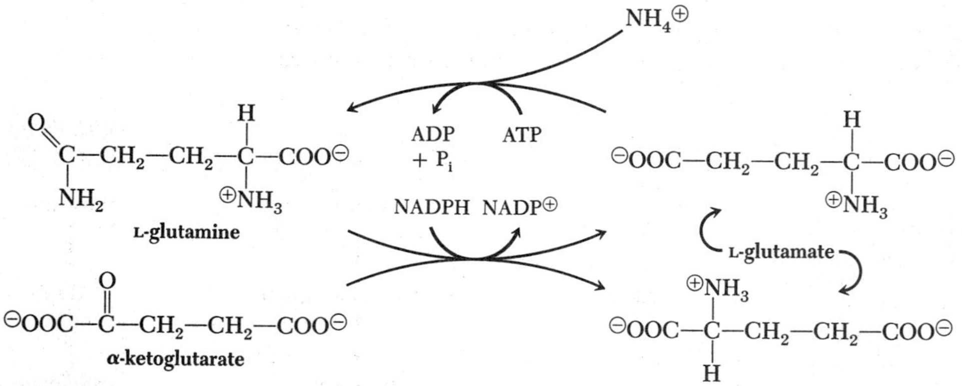

Figure 27-4 Some bacteria take up NH_4^+ for the synthesis of amino acids by forming glutamine at the expense of ATP, and then transferring the amide nitrogen to α-ketoglutarate, with a simultaneous reduction to glutamate. The net result is a reductive amination driven by high-energy phosphate.

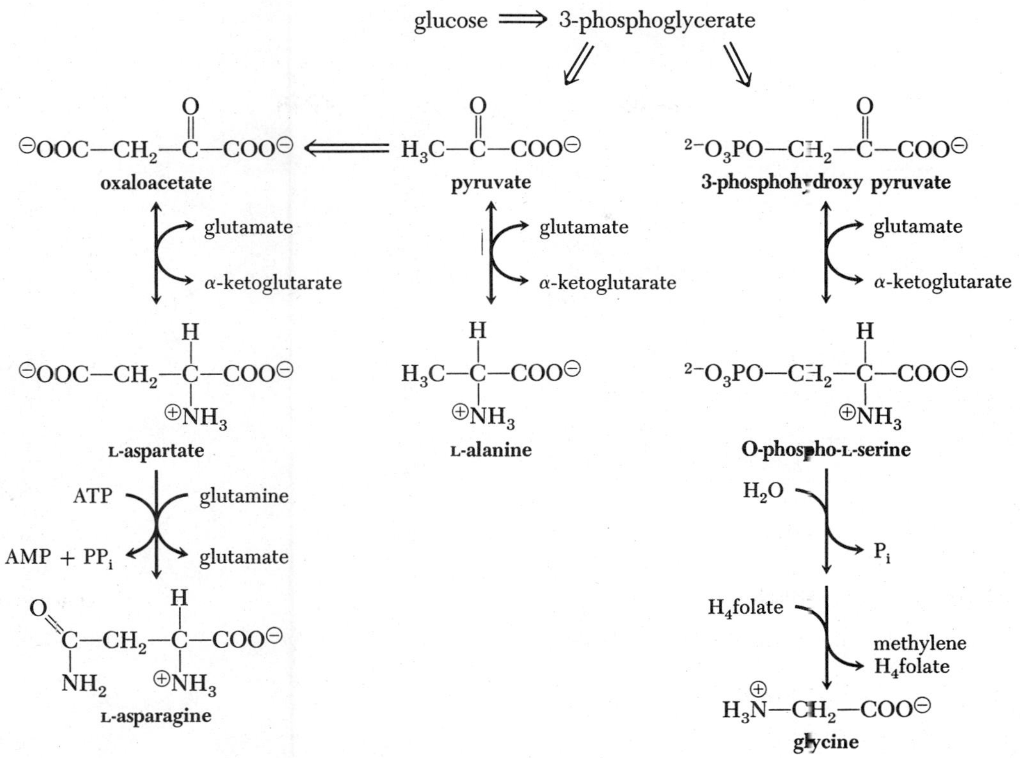

Figure 27-5 Aspartate, asparagine, alanine, serine, and glycine are readily made from intermediates of the Embden-Meyerhof pathway.

that the NH_4^+ made by nitrogen fixation is first incorporated into glutamate and glutamine before it is used to form other amino acids. We already know one way in which this is done. Glutamate dehydrogenase can catalyze the reductive amination of α-ketoglutarate by NADPH to form glutamate, and ammonia is added to glutamate to form glutamine at the expense of ATP (Fig. 27-3). The necessary α-ketoglutarate can be formed by the condensation of oxaloacetate and acetyl coenzyme A, both of which can be made from pyruvate.

Some microorganisms, including many that fix nitrogen, form glutamate by a transfer of the amide nitrogen from glutamine to α-ketoglutarate, with a simultaneous reduction by NADPH (Fig. 27-4). The glutamine is then regenerated by the glutamine synthetase reaction, so the overall process becomes an ATP-driven reductive amination of α-ketoglutarate, capable of forming glutamate at low concentrations of ammonium ion.

Other Metabolically Active Amino Acids (Fig. 27-5). We know that **alanine** and **aspartate** are readily made from pyruvate and oxaloacetate by transamination with glutamate; **asparagine** is made from aspartate. Similarly, **serine** is made from hydroxypyruvate, either free or phosphorylated, by transamination; the hydroxypyruvate is derived from glucose via 3-phosphoglycerate. **Glycine** can be formed from serine.

Proline and Arginine. Glutamate is a precursor of ornithine and proline, evidently through the intermediate formation of glutamic semialdehyde (Fig. 27-6). Direct reduction of the carboxylate to an aldehyde is not feasible, but the nature of the intermediate step is not known in many organisms. It may involve the formation of some high-energy intermediate, perhaps an anhydride phosphate, which will be cleaved

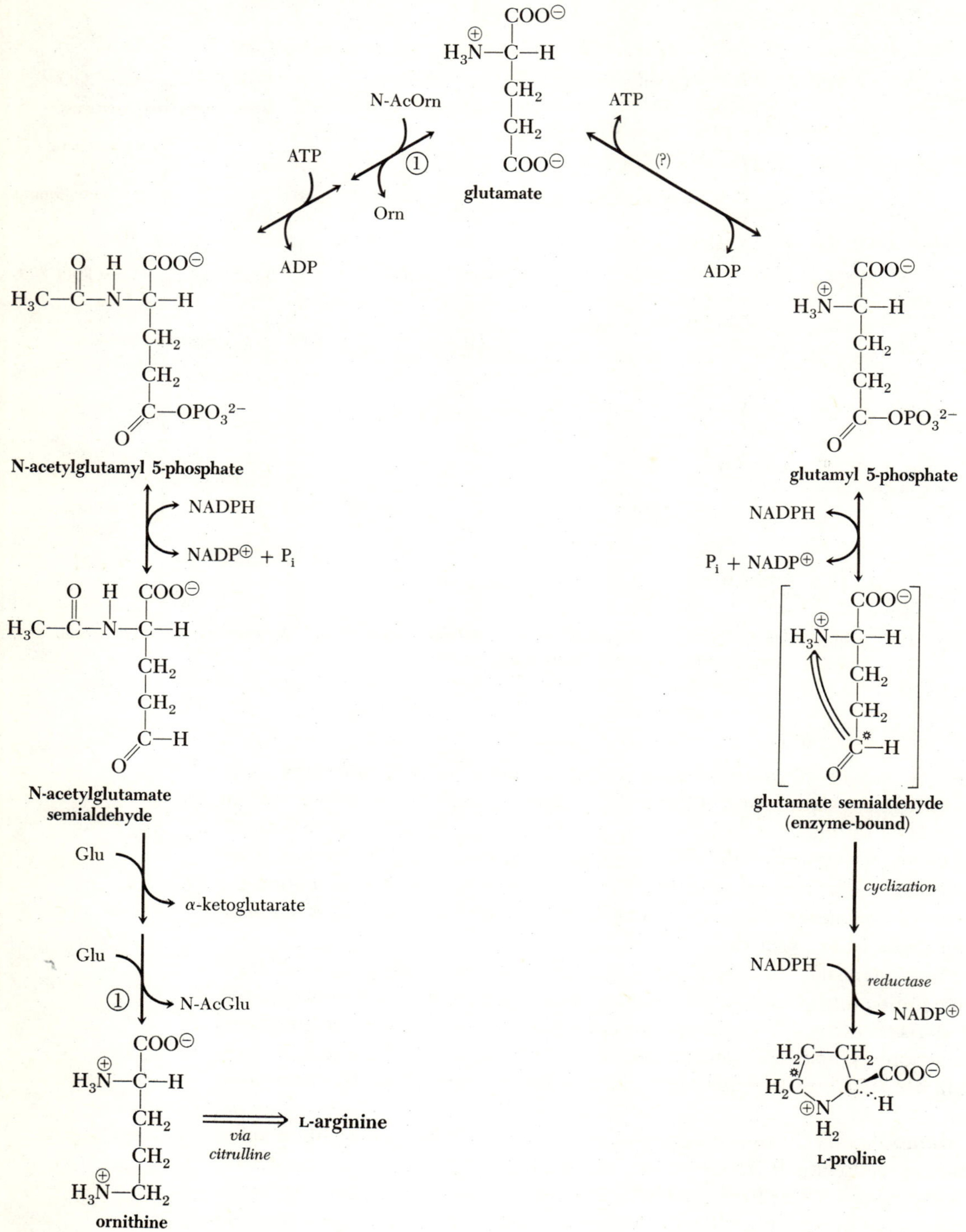

Figure 27-6 Glutamate is converted to proline in plants by reducing the side-chain carboxylate group to an aldehyde, followed by cyclization and reduction. The formation of the aldehyde is driven by cleavage of a high-energy phosphate. The formation of ornithine also involves reduction to an aldehyde, but with the 2-amino group blocked by an acetyl group to prevent cyclization. The aldehyde is then converted to an amine by transamination.

so as to drive the reduction, in the same way that 1,3-diphosphoglycerate is reduced during gluconeogenesis (p. 280), or acetyl coenzyme A is reduced during some fermentations (p. 260).

In any event, cyclization of the aldehyde and further reduction creates proline. Alternatively, transamination of the aldehyde forms ornithine, which can be converted to arginine by the same reactions used in urea synthesis. (The only difference is that protists and plants use glutamine, rather than NH_4^+, as the source of carbamyl phosphate for both arginine and pyrimidine synthesis.)

The Aspartate Family

Now let us turn to a consideration of the amino acids that cannot be synthesized by most animals. Obviously, the plants have enzymes catalyzing reactions that are not found in animals and that we have not previously discussed. These include a sequence

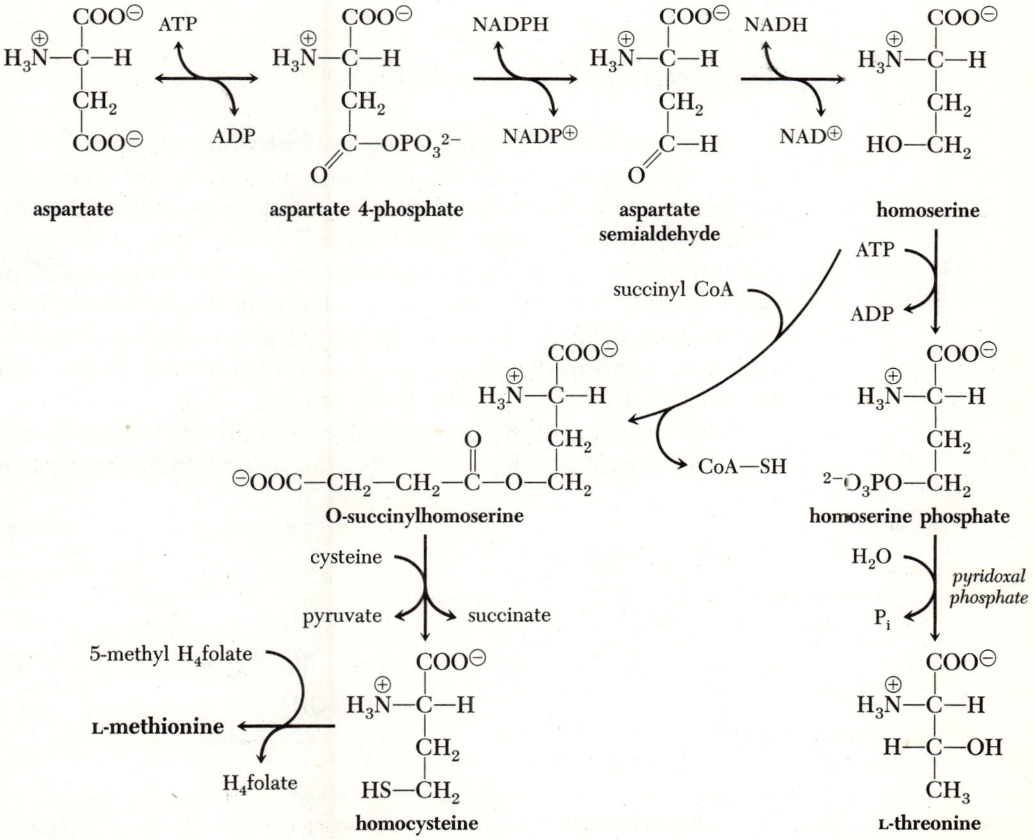

Figure 27-7 The side chain carboxylate group of aspartate is reduced to an aldehyde in a reaction driven by cleavage of high-energy phosphate, and the aldehyde is the precursor of the homocysteine portion of methionine and of threonine. The sulfur atom of homocysteine is obtained by transfer from cysteine, driven by cleavage of a succinyl ester bond.

that begins with aspartate, and results in the formation of **threonine, methionine,** and **lysine.** (There is an alternate route for the synthesis of lysine in certain protists that we shall also consider.)

Threonine. The conversion of aspartate to threonine begins with a reduction of the 4-carboxylate group to an aldehyde, with the intermediate formation of a phosphate anhydride to drive the reaction (Fig. 27–7). The resultant aldehyde is equilibrated with the corresponding alcohol, which is **homoserine.** Homoserine is then rearranged to threonine by the intermediate formation of a phosphate ester. (The rearrangement involves removal of the phosphate from homoserine phosphate to form a double bond, followed by the addition of the elements of water in such a way as to put the hydroxyl group on C-3. All of this takes place while the amino acid is attached to pyridoxal phosphate, which is a coenzyme for the reaction.)

Methionine. Homoserine is also an intermediate in the formation of methionine (Fig. 27–7). Succinyl coenzyme A is used to make an ester group, which is cleaved by a transfer of sulfur from cysteine so as to form homocysteine. We already know that homocysteine can be converted to methionine by transfer of a methyl group from methyl tetrahydrofolate. We shall discuss the origin of the cysteine later in the chapter.

Lysine. Finally, aspartate semialdehyde is the source of four of the carbons and one of the nitrogens in lysine synthesized by green plants and many protists (Fig. 27–8). The route involves a condensation of aspartate semialdehyde with pyruvate to form a ring which is then opened to create the keto-analogue of 2,6-diaminopimelate. This 7-carbon, diamino-dicarboxylic acid is decarboxylated to give lysine.

The Branched Amino Acids

The carbon skeletons for **valine** and **isoleucine** are created by enzymes containing thiamine pyrophosphate, which react with pyruvate to form the hydroxyethyl derivative of the coenzyme ("active acetaldehyde") in the same way as does pyruvate dehydrogenase or pyruvate decarboxylase (pages 222 and 254). One of the enzymes catalyzes the transfer of the acetaldehyde group to another molecule of pyruvate; the other enzyme catalyzes the transfer to a molecule of 2-ketobutyrate, which is obtained by direct deamination of threonine. Each of these transfers involves an aldol condensation to form a 2-hydroxyketone, which is then reduced in a novel reaction that constitutes the "trick" of branched chain synthesis (Fig. 27–9).

The reduction of the hydroxyketones to dihydroxy compounds is accompanied by a shift of a carbon side chain. This kind of **acyloin rearrangement** wasn't known in

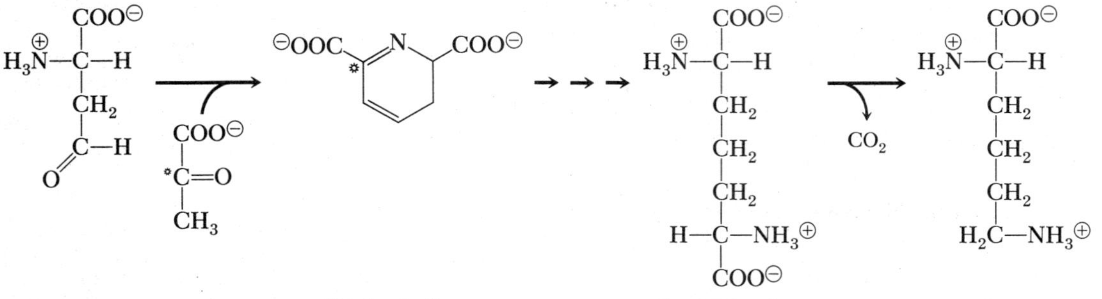

aspartate semialdehyde | pyruvate | dihydropicolinate | diaminopimelate | L-lysine

Figure 27–8 Aspartate semialdehyde is also the precursor of lysine in green plants and many prokaryotes.

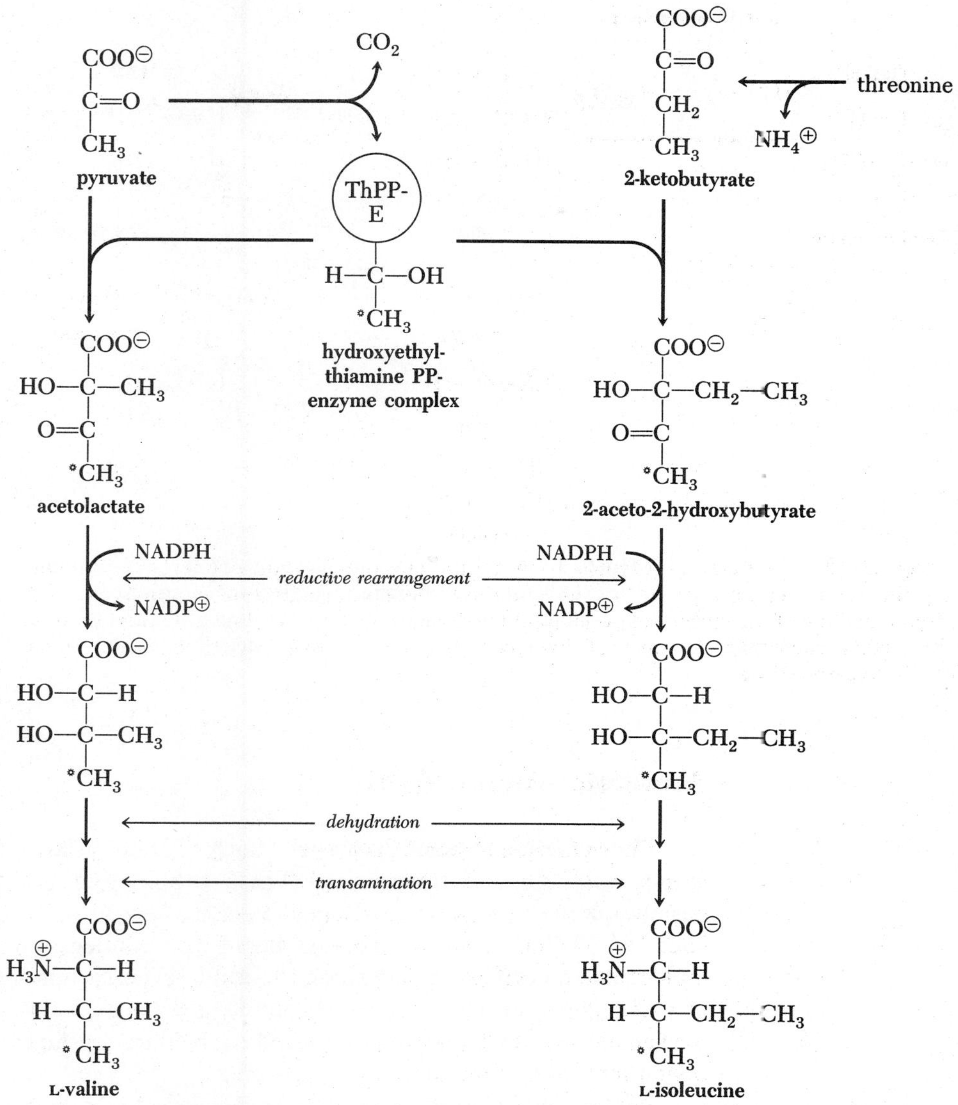

Figure 27-9 The formation of the branched chain amino acids involves a condensation of an "active acetaldehyde" group carried on thiamine pyrophosphate with pyruvate or 2-ketobutyrate. The side chain of each product is shifted with a simultaneous reduction of the carbonyl group to create a dihydroxy compound, which is dehydrated to the keto analogue of the final amino acid.

organic chemistry until relatively recently. Actually, it is another example of the sort of intramolecular oxidation and reduction, accompanied by side chain migration, seen in the well-known pinacol and benzilic acid rearrangements. In the enzymatic reaction, the rearrangement presumably is immediately followed on the enzyme surface by reduction of the carbonyl group to form the dihydroxy product.

Simple dehydration of the dihydroxy compound yields the 2-keto analogues of valine and isoleucine, which are converted to the amino acids by transamination. The dehydration is analogous to the conversion of 3-phosphoglycerate to pyruvate, except that no phosphate group is involved.

Leucine Formation. Leucine is also formed from 2-ketoisovalerate. The additional carbon is furnished by a condensation with acetyl coenzyme A (Fig. 27–10), which is another example of the kind of mechanism used to form citrate from oxaloacetate and acetyl coenzyme A. A shift of the hydroxyl group and an oxidative decarboxylation form the 2-keto analogue from which leucine is made by transamination.

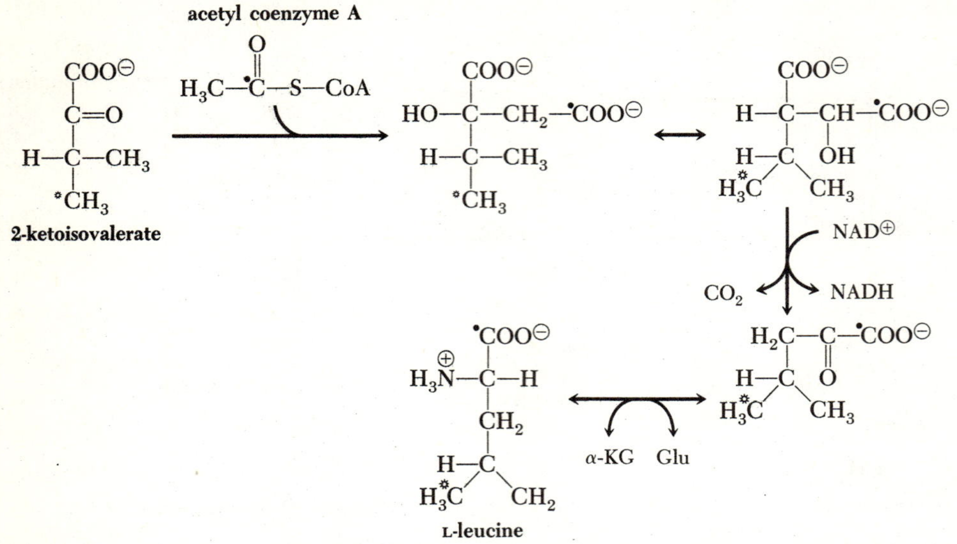

Figure 27-10 Leucine is formed by an additional condensation of the keto analogue of valine with acetyl coenzyme A. This and the following reactions are reminiscent of the initial reactions of the citric acid cycle up to the formation of α-ketoglutarate (condensation with acetyl coenzyme A, shift of hydroxyl group, oxidative decarboxylation of the 3-hydroxycarboxylate).

Aromatic Amino Acids

Phenylalanine and Tyrosine. Each of these amino acids contains nine carbon atoms, including an aromatic ring. These carbon atoms are supplied by two molecules of phospho-*enol*-pyruvate and one molecule of erythrose 4-phosphate, with one carbon later lost as CO_2. The proceedings begin with condensation of one phosphopyruvate molecule and erythrose phosphate to form a seven-carbon intermediate, which cyclizes to make the forerunner of the aromatic ring (Fig. 27-11). The ring is studded with oxygen atoms, which are later removed by dehydrations to create the conjugated double bonds formally comprising a phenyl ring.

Before the aromatic character is developed, condensation occurs with a second molecule of phosphopyruvate to create **chorismate.** (The name chorismic acid was modified from a Greek word meaning separation, because the routes for formation of phenylalanine and tyrosine separate from the route for the formation of tryptophan after this compound.) Chorismate rearranges to bring the additional three carbons into position to form the aliphatic chain of phenylalanine. This is followed by a final dehydration to form the aromatic ring, with or without an additional oxidation to introduce a hydroxyl group, producing the 2-keto analogues of phenylalanine and tyrosine.

Tryptophan. Chorismate can be rearranged in another way, not fully understood, involving the transfer of the amide nitrogen from glutamine and the loss of the pyruvate moiety just added (Fig. 27-12). Perhaps the purpose of this seemingly circuitous route will someday be more obvious.

In any event, the resultant **anthranilate** reacts with 5-phosphoribosyl pyrophosphate to form a nucleotide. The nucleotide has only a transient existence, for an enzyme catalyzes the opening of the ribose ring with the formation of a double bond. A new ring closure involving the existing phenyl ring and the double bond occurs, and the

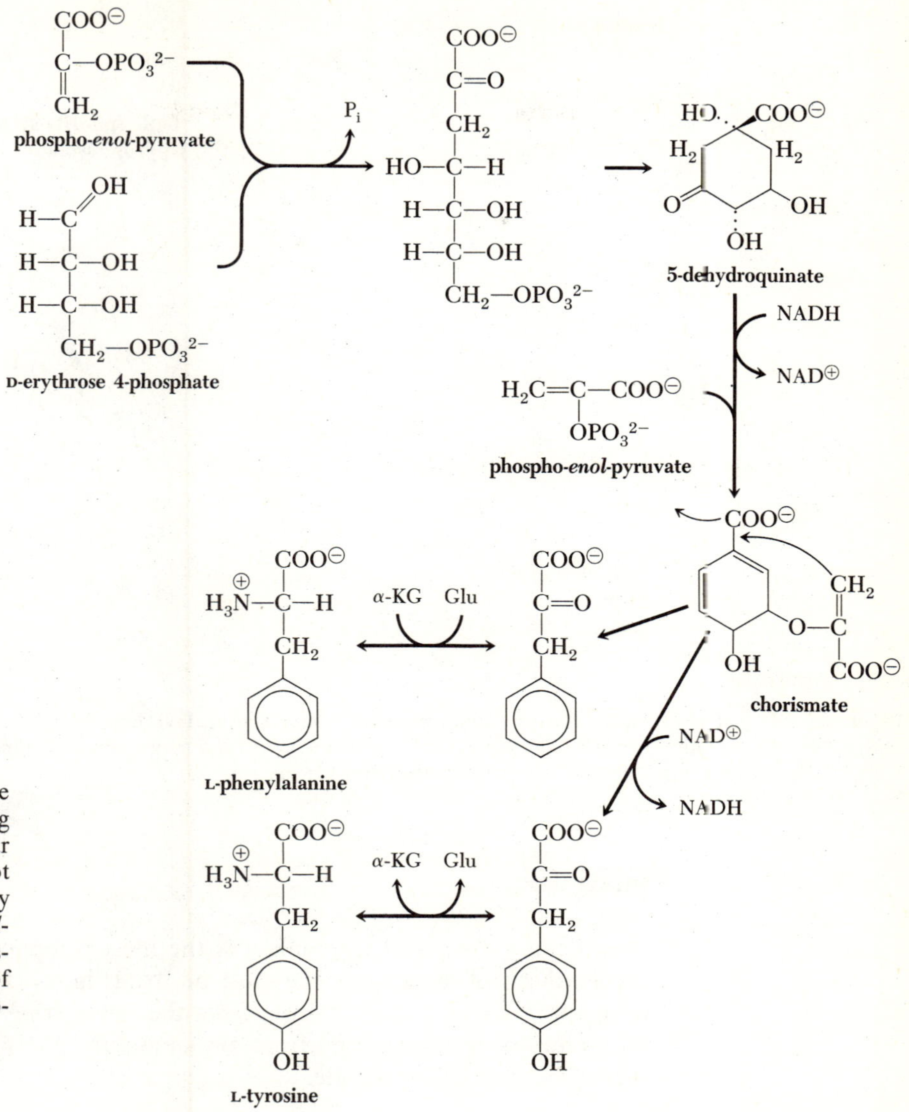

Figure 27-11 Phenylalanine and tyrosine are created by ring closure of a seven-carbon sugar derivative (several steps are not shown), which is made by condensation of phospho-*enol*-pyruvate and erythrose 4-phosphate. An additional molecule of phospho-*enol*-pyruvate contributes the side chain on the ring.

result is the formation of the indole ring of tryptophan attached to a three-carbon glycerol-phosphate moiety. Finally, the indole ring is transferred from this three-carbon chain to a molecule of serine to form tryptophan without further ado.

This is perhaps the most complicated of all of the amino acid syntheses. The formation of tryptophan involves the consumption of serine, ribose phosphate, glutamine, erythrose phosphate, and two molecules of phospho-*enol*-pyruvate. The final product contains all of the N and C atoms of serine and all four carbons of the erythrose phosphate, along with the glutamine N, but it contains only two carbons from one molecule of phosphopyruvate, and none from the other molecule, and only two carbons from ribose phosphate. However, nothing is really wasted, because only one carbon appears as CO_2. The other six appear as pyruvate and glyceraldehyde 3-phosphate, ready for re-use.

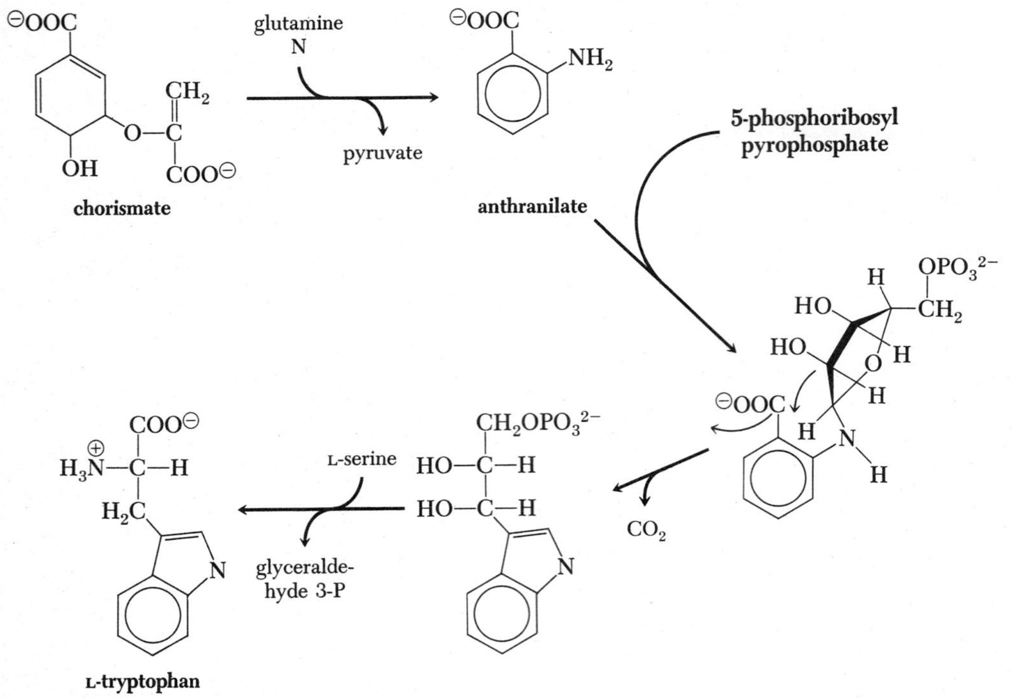

Figure 27–12 The synthesis of tryptophan involves a spectacular deviation from the route of synthesis of the other aromatic amino acids, in which some of the ring atoms are supplied by a ribose moiety, and the side chain is made from serine.

Histidine

If the synthesis of tryptophan is the most complicated among the amino acids, the synthesis of histidine is the most bizarre (Fig. 27–13). It involves the abstraction of a nitrogen and a carbon atom from the purine ring of ATP, which are used with an additional nitrogen atom from glutamine and the five carbon atoms of ribose to create the histidine molecule.

Cysteine

Plants make cysteine from serine, using sulfur originally obtained from inorganic sulfate. The initial problem is one of reducing sulfate to sulfide, which is the oxidation state of sulfur in cysteine. The substrate for the first critical reduction is a high-energy sulfate anhydride, **3′-phosphoadenosine 5′-phosphosulfate** (Fig. 27–14), which we shall later see is also used as a source of sulfate groups for incorporation into various compounds.

The formation of the anhydride bond involves a reaction of ATP with inorganic sulfate to liberate PP_i and to form adenosine 5′-phosphosulfate. The equilibrium is unfavorable, although the maintenance of a low concentration of PP_i makes the reaction feasible in most cells. In order to drive the reaction further, another molecule of ATP is used to phosphorylate the 3′-carbon of the ribose moiety, making the formation of 3′-phosphoadenosine 5′-phosphosulfate irreversible. This compound, often abbreviated as **PAPS,** is reduced by NADPH in plants to release **sulfite.** (The adenosine 3′,5′-*bis*phosphate also formed is hydrolyzed to recover 5′-AMP and P_i.)

Plants reduce sulfite to **sulfide,** presumably in three steps, and the incorporation

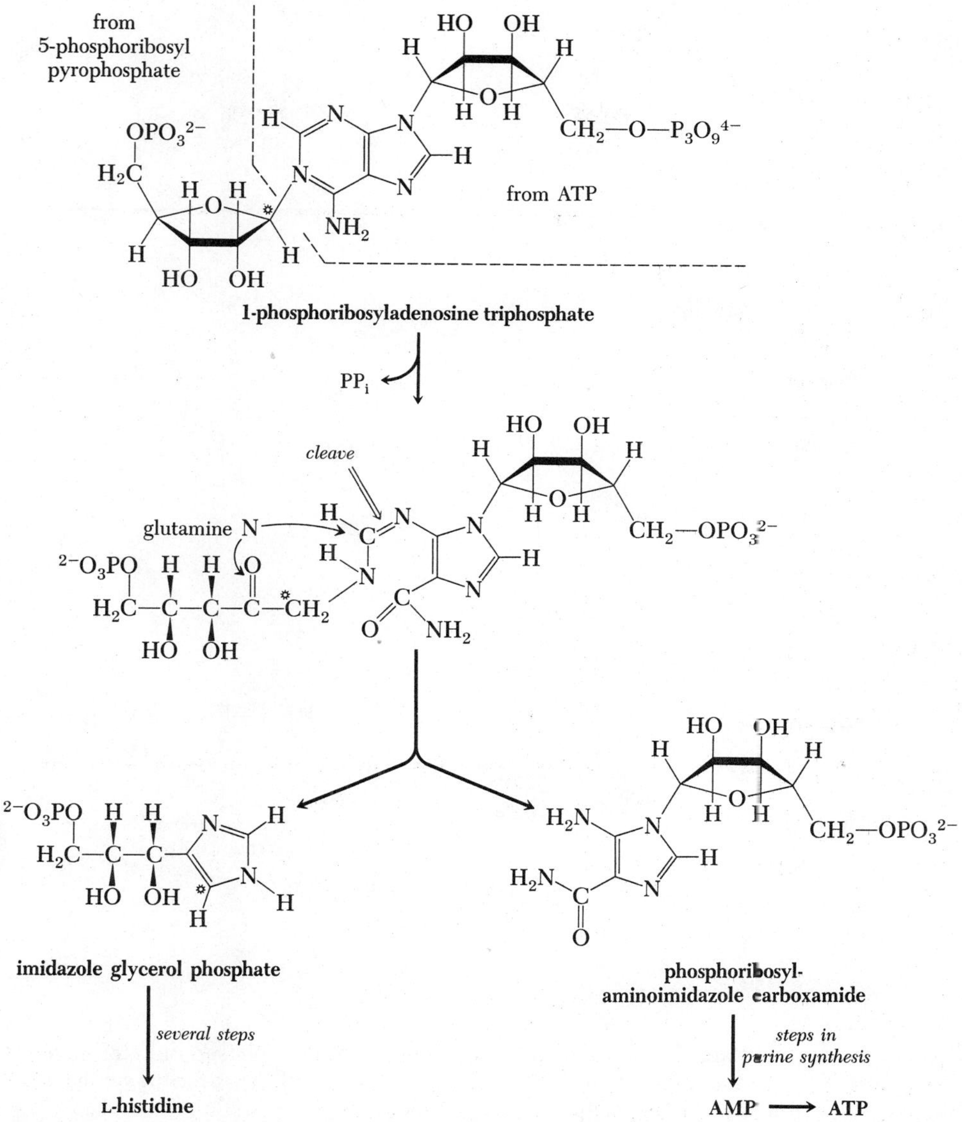

Figure 27-13 The formation of histidine involves the attachment of an additional phosphoribose group to a ring nitrogen in ATP. The ring is cleaved in such a way that one each of its carbon and nitrogen atoms, together with an amide nitrogen from glutamine, cyclize on the ribose skeleton to make an imidazole ring. The side chain is then converted to the histidine structure. The remaining piece of the adenine ring is an intermediate in purine synthesis, and is converted back to ATP.

of the sulfide into cysteine involves a simple exchange for an acetyl group on O-acetyl serine, which is made by reaction of acetyl coenzyme A with serine.

SYNTHESIS OF OTHER NITROGENOUS CONSTITUENTS

The amino acids act as precursors of a variety of nitrogen-containing compounds that we do not have time to examine in detail. We can only sketch some of the more important routes.

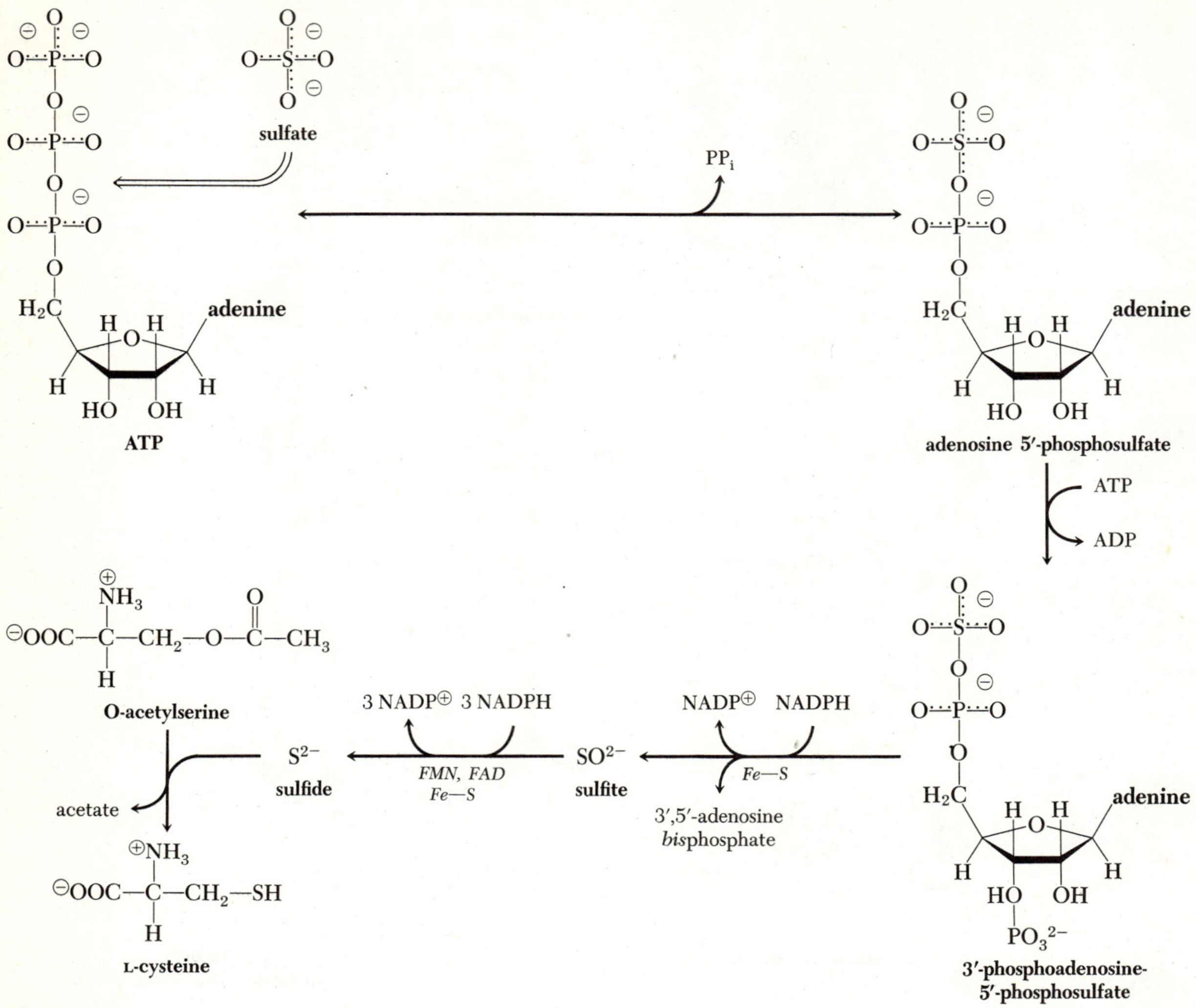

Figure 27-14 Sulfate is converted to 3′-phosphoadenosine-5′-phosphosulfate as the primary donor of sulfate groups for forming other compounds. It is also used as a source of sulfur for the synthesis of cysteine, which requires four reductions of the sulfate group to create sulfide ions. The sulfide is exchanged for an acetyl group on the carbon skeleton of serine.

Amines

A variety of physiologically important amines are generated by removal of the carboxylate group from amino acids (Fig. 27-15). The amino acid decarboxylases catalyzing these reactions contain pyridoxal phosphate as a coenzyme.

Porphyrins

Each substituted pyrrole and connecting methylene bridge in a porphyrin is derived from one molecule each of succinyl coenzyme A and glycine (Fig. 27-16). Four of the porphobilinogen molecules are united to make the skeleton, and subsequent oxidations and decarboxylations create a finished porphyrin. The porphyrins in animals are degraded by opening the ring to form tetrapyrrole pigments known as the bile pigments. (They are the principal sources of the color in bile, and also in the feces and urine.)

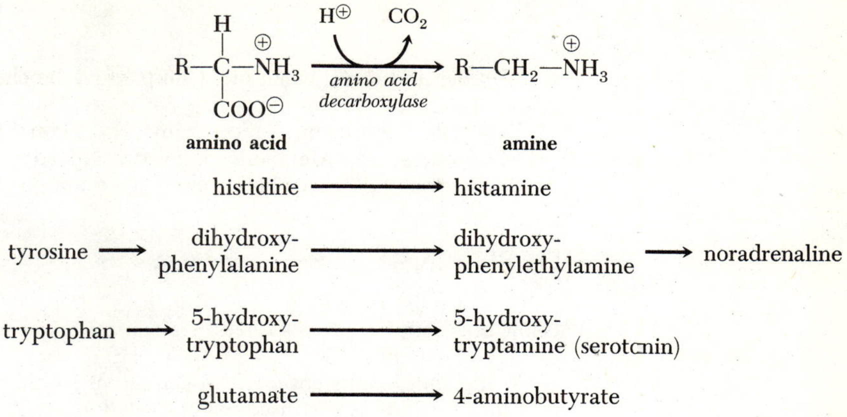

Figure 27-15 Many physiologically active amines are synthesized by decarboxylating amino acids. All of these decarboxylases contain pyridoxal phosphate as a coenzyme.

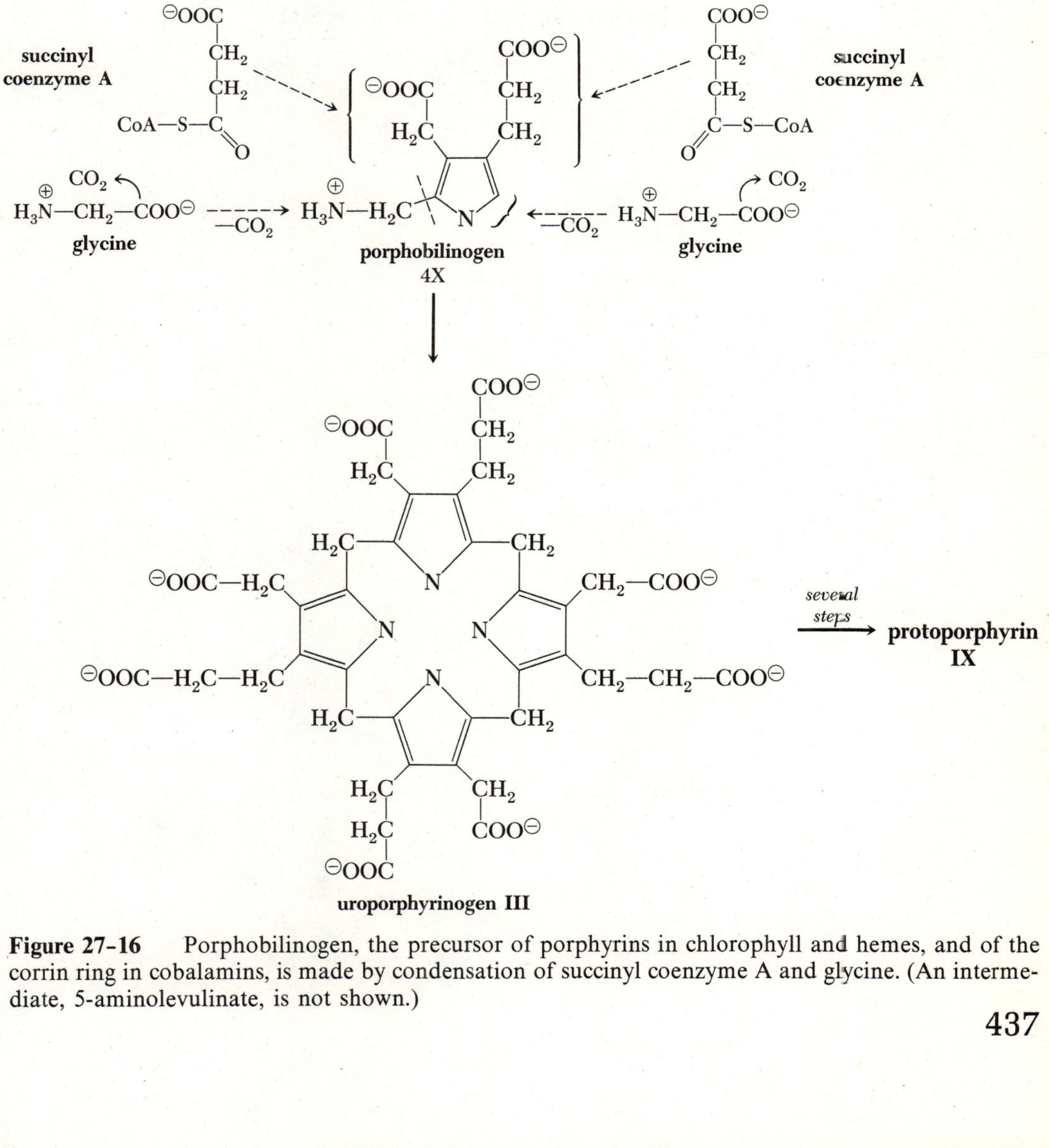

uroporphyrinogen III

Figure 27-16 Porphobilinogen, the precursor of porphyrins in chlorophyll and hemes, and of the corrin ring in cobalamins, is made by condensation of succinyl coenzyme A and glycine. (An intermediate, 5-aminolevulinate, is not shown.)

FURTHER READING

S. L. Streicher and R. C. Valentine, Comparative biochemistry of nitrogen fixation, Ann. Rev. Biochem., 42:279 (1973).
M. J. Dilworth, Dinitrogen fixation, Ann. Rev. Plant Physiol., 25:81 (1974).
D. M. Greenberg, ed., Metabolic pathways, 3rd ed., vol. 3, Amino acids and tetrapyrroles, Academic Press (1969). Contains chapter on amino acid synthesis.

QUESTIONS

1. Show how nitrate ions absorbed by a spinach plant may be used to create the amino group on C-2 of arginine.
2. Show the additional steps the nitrogen atoms would have to undergo to appear in the same location if nitrate is first used as an oxidizing agent by denitrifying bacteria.
3. Why must aspartate by phosphorylated in order to permit reduction of the 4-carboxylate group to an aldehyde group?
4. Show how all of the carbons of methionine can be obtained from glucose.
5. What steps in the formation of leucine and of lysine are reminiscent of the steps in the citric acid cycle?
6. Show how the carbon skeleton of one of the branched-chain amino acids is made from glucose.
7. Show how stored fatty acids can be used by a plant embryo to form an aromatic amino acid. (Hint: Don't forget the glyoxylate cycle.)

SPECIALIZED METABOLISM

PART 7

CHAPTER 28

POLYPRENYL COMPOUNDS

THE CONCEPTS

Many natural compounds are made by condensing five-carbon isoprene units, or prenyl groups. The resultant polyprenyl compound may remain as a linear hydrocarbon chain, with branched methyl groups on every fourth carbon atom, or it may cyclize to varying extents. That is, successive addition of prenyl groups will create derivatives of geraniol (10 carbons), farnesol (15 carbons), and geranylgeraniol (20 carbons), but these may cyclize respectively to form the cyclic terpenes, sesquiterpenes, and diterpenes that occur in plants.

Other compounds may be made by tail-to-tail condensation of two polyprenyl compounds. Two 20-carbon units condense to a precursor of the carotenes in this way. The carotenes are used by animals as a precursor of the light-sensitive pigments in the eye, which contain 11-*cis*-retinal, the aldehyde form of half of a carotene. Animals store the alcohol form, retinol, which is also known as vitamin A, as fatty acid esters.

Tail-to-tail condensation of 15-carbon units creates squalene, the precursor of steroids, which contain four fused rings. Two reactions are required for the cyclization of squalene, creating lanosterol in animals, and cycloartenol in plants, as precursors of the other steroids. Lanosterol is modified to form cholesterol, which is a prominent constituent of the lipid phase of membranes and of some lipoproteins.

Cholesterol is the precursor of various steroid hormones. The formation of the hormones involves removal of part, or all, of the cholesterol side chain, and oxidations to create hydroxyl or carbonyl groups at various locations on the steroid rings. Pregnenolone is an intermediate precursor of all of the steroid hormones, and a particular endocrine gland may form several hormones from it. For example, the adrenal glands, the ovaries, and the testes can form progesterone, a steroid that promotes development of the uterus during the reproductive cycle, but the adrenal glands remove the progesterone to form cortisol, and the testes remove it to form testosterone. The effect of each gland therefore depends upon the relative amounts of the various steroids that it secretes.

The major fraction of the cholesterol is excreted as such or in the form of bile salts, which contain oxidized derivatives of cholesterol with strong detergent properties, and which are necessary for normal digestion and absorption of fats.

Every organism contains compounds made by condensing prenyl groups, otherwise known as isoprene groups:

$$-CH_2-\overset{\overset{\displaystyle CH_3}{|}}{C}=CH-CH_2-$$

For example, two prenyl groups combine to make a terpene (10 carbon atoms), such as geraniol:

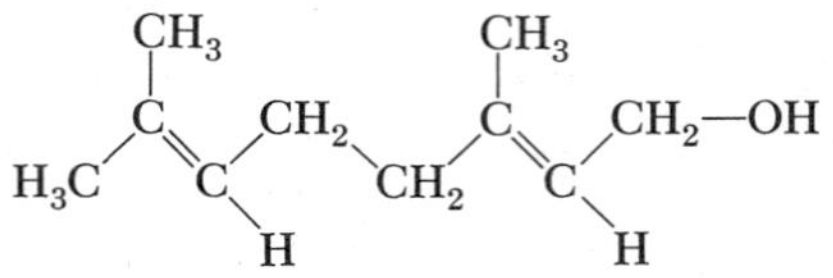

or the terpene may be closed into a ring, such as is seen in limonene, or pinene:

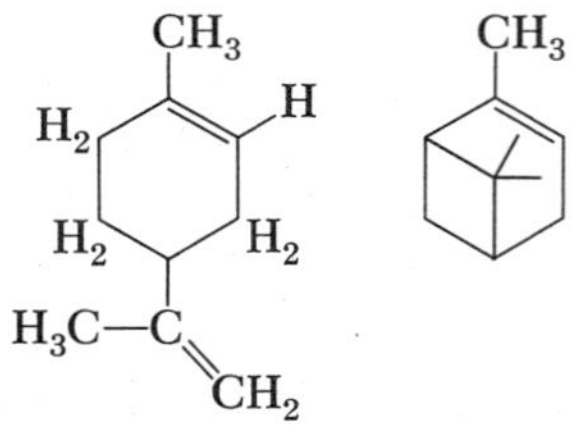

limonene **α-pinene**

Three prenyl groups make a sesquiterpene (15 carbon atoms) and four make a diterpene (20 carbon atoms), and so on. Examples of these various terpenes abound in plants, but the polyprenyl compounds best known to mammalian biochemists are the steroids, of which we shall have a great deal to say. Other important polyprenyl compounds include (a) precursors of the side chains of ubiquinone and chlorophyll, (b) carotenes and their derivatives, such as vitamin A, (c) rubber, and (d) various plant and insect hormones. In sum, the simple five-carbon branched chain of a prenyl group serves as a precursor for a large variety of complex compounds.

THE ORIGIN OF PRENYL GROUPS

Prenyl groups are created from **3-hydroxy-3-methylglutaryl coenzyme A,** the same compound that acts as a precursor of acetoacetate (p. 205). The initial reaction, which has no other function than to initiate the formation of polyprenyl compounds, is a reduction of the thiol ester group to the corresponding alcohol with the consumption of two molecules of NADPH (Fig. 28–1).

The product of the reduction, **mevalonate,** is converted to the pyrophosphate ester by two successive additions of a phosphate group from ATP (Fig. 28–2). Creating the pyrophosphate in this way, rather than by a single addition of a pyrophosphate group, drives the reaction farther forward, since two phosphate anhydride bonds are being cleaved by the transfers. Still another phosphate is transferred from ATP to mevalonate pyrophosphate, this time to the 3-hydroxyl group, and this transfer causes a concerted

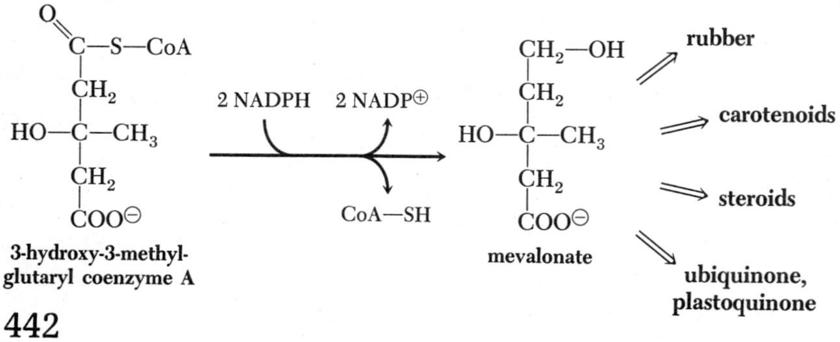

Figure 28–1 Mevalonate is made from 3-hydroxy-3-methylglutaryl coenzyme A as the precursor of polyprenyl compounds.

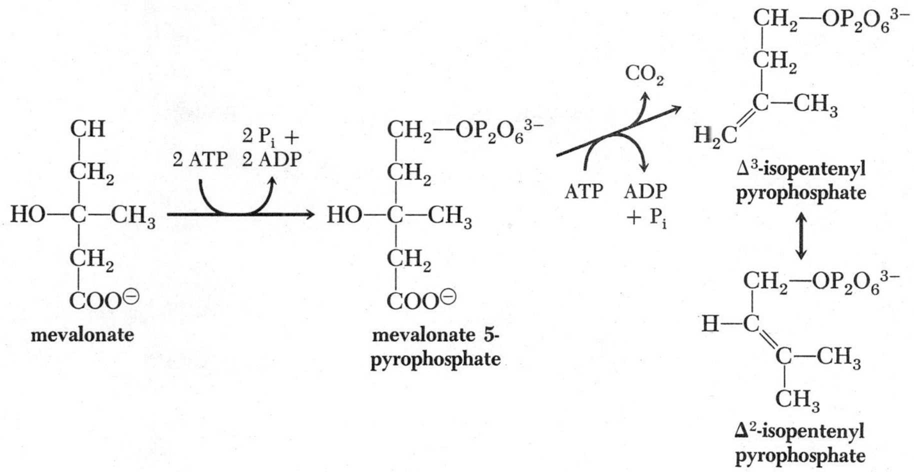

Figure 28-2 Mevalonate is converted to the pyrophosphate ester, which is then decarboxylated and dehydrated to form prenyl groups.

loss of CO_2 with elimination of the phosphate group, as shown in the figure. The result is the formation of **Δ³-isopentenyl pyrophosphate,** which is equilibrated with **Δ²-isopentenyl pyrophosphate,** also known as **dimethylallyl pyrophosphate.** Here we have authentic prenyl groups. Now let us see how they are used.

FORMATION OF POLYPRENYL CHAINS

The polyprenyl compounds are built by the sequential addition of isopentenyl groups obtained from Δ³-isopentenyl pyrophosphate (Fig. 28–3). For example, the transfer of a single group to Δ²-isopentenyl pyrophosphate forms the pyrophosphate ester of **geraniol,** which is the precursor of terpenes; the transfer of an additional group to geranyl pyrophosphate forms **farnesyl pyrophosphate,** the precursor of sesquiterpenes, and transfer of still another group forms **geranylgeranyl pyrophosphate,** the precursor of diterpenes.

Carotenes. Polyprenyl compounds may themselves combine. For example, the tail-to-tail combination of two molecules of geranylgeranyl pyrophosphate forms the precursor of the carotenes (Fig. 28–4). There are some 400 known carotenes that occur

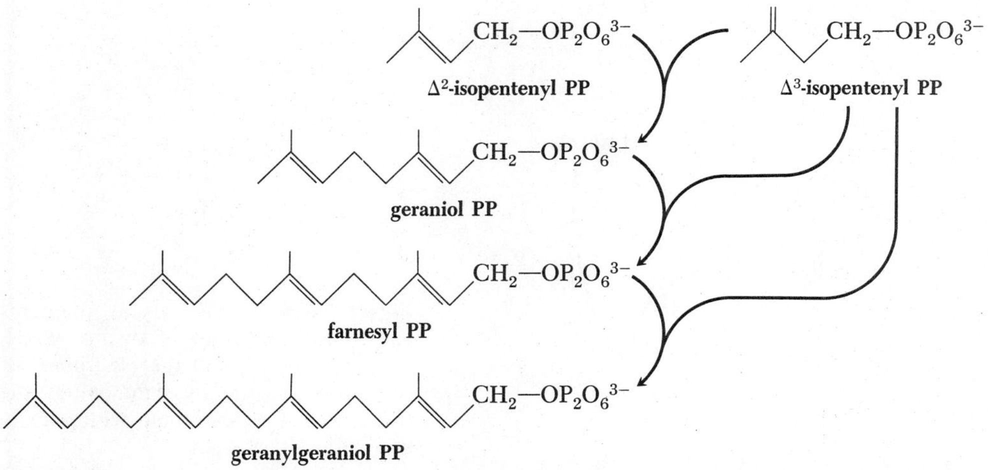

Figure 28-3 Successive additions of prenyl groups form the di-, tri-, and tetraprenyl pyrophosphates in plants.

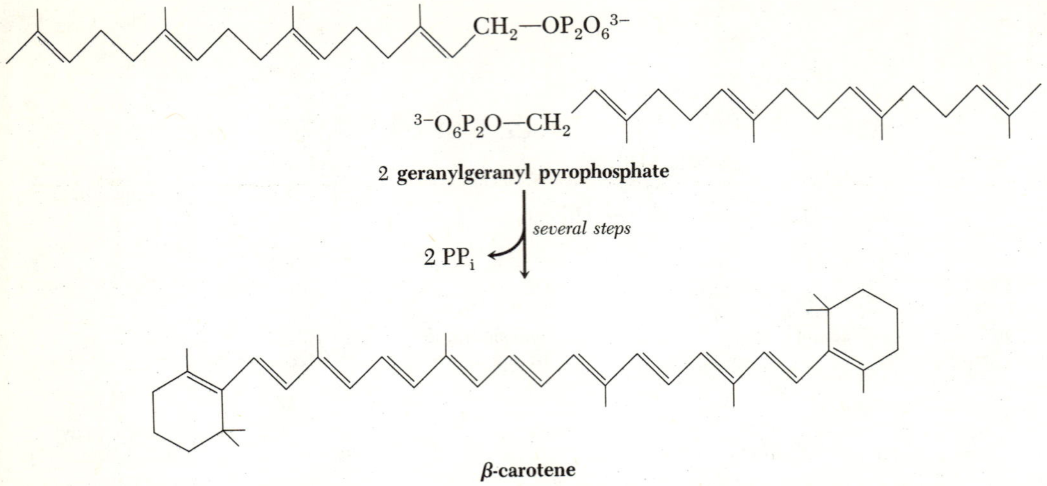

Figure 28-4 Tail-to-tail condensation of two tetraprenyl pyrophosphates results in the formation of carotenes, such as β-carotene, in plants.

in plants. One of the more common is the **β-carotene** shown in the figure; it is easy to visualize the oxidations and ring closure necessary to form this compound from the parent 40-carbon polyprenyl chain.

VISUAL PIGMENT AND VITAMIN A. The principal function of the carotenes is to act as auxiliary pigments for capture of photons during photosynthesis, but some carotenes also have the important function of acting as precursors of the visual pigments in animals. These pigments in the retina of the eye consist of an isomer of a polyprenyl aldehyde known as **retinal** (Fig. 28-5) combined with an **opsin,** which is a lipid-associated protein that binds retinal so as to modify its light absorption spectrum. The color-blind, but dim-light-sensitive rods of the retina are receptors with one kind of opsin, and therefore one visual pigment, known variously as **visual purple** and **rhodopsin.** The color-sensitive cones are receptors that appear to have at least three opsins so as to create three different visual pigments for color differentiation.

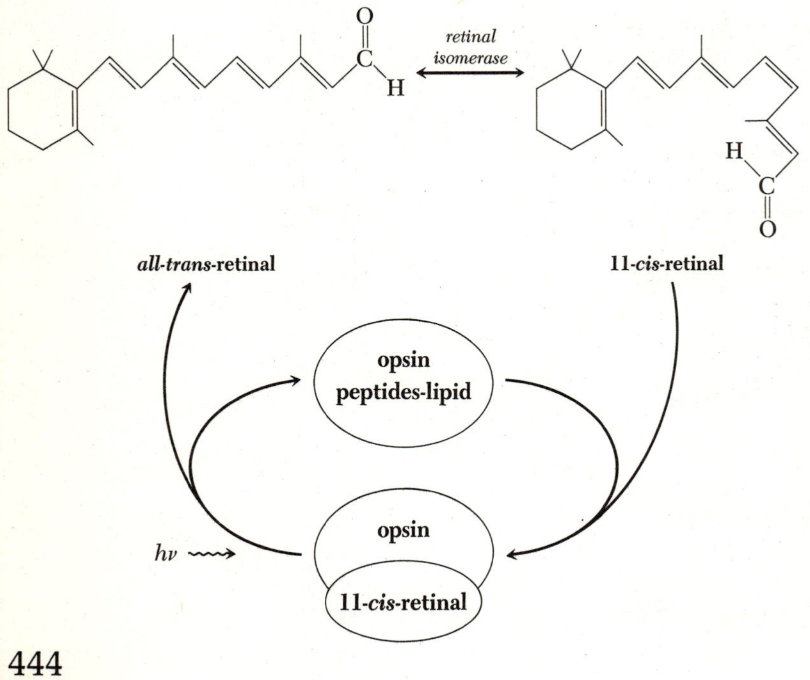

Figure 28-5 The visual pigments consist of complexes of opsins, which are lipoproteins, and the *cis* isomer of retinal. Excitation by light causes the formation of *trans*-retinal, which has a low affinity for opsin.

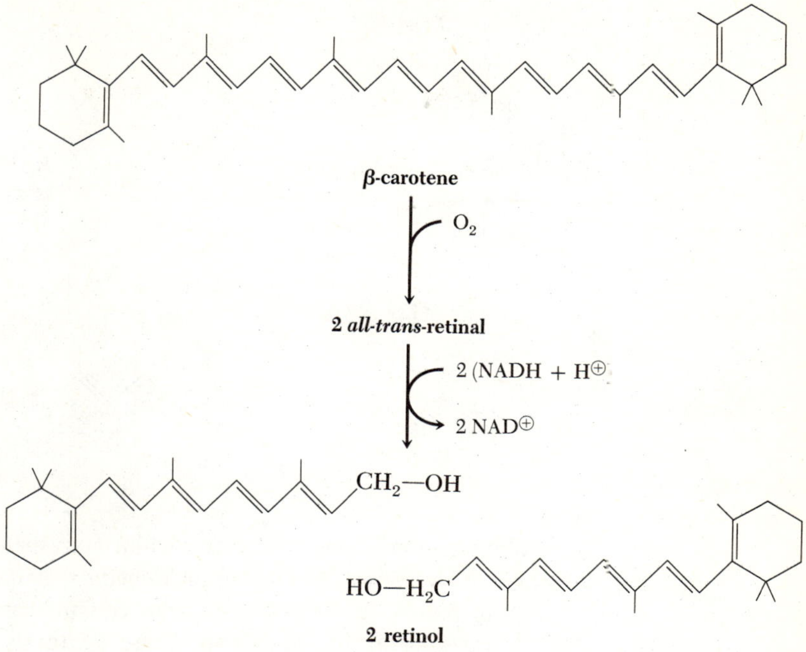

Figure 28-6 Carotenes in the diet are cleaved by an oxygenase in the intestinal mucosa to form two aldehydes. The symmetrical β-carotene yields two molecules of *trans*-retinal, which are reduced by an alcohol dehydrogenase to retinol, and transported as a palmitoyl ester (not shown). Equilibration of the alcohol with the aldehyde form in the retina enables formation of the visual pigment.

As Figure 28–5 shows, the absorption of light causes the 11-*cis* isomer of retinal to dissociate and become the more stable *all-trans* isomer. However, the affinity of opsin for the 11-*cis* isomer is so great in the absence of light that the visual pigment re-forms, even though the concentration of that isomer is very low.

The retinal of the eye is formed by oxidation of **retinol,** the corresponding alcohol, which is otherwise known as vitamin A. Animals obtain retinol by eating other animals, or by cleaving particular carotenes by oxidation (Fig. 28–6). The carotenes of appropriate structure are common in leafy vegetables, and both the carotenes and retinol (as fatty acid esters) can accumulate in tissues, so deficiencies of vitamin A are not common in people with an otherwise adequate diet. Indeed, grossly excessive intakes of retinol are toxic, causing mental disturbances sometimes diagnosed as schizophrenia, and even death.

FORMATION OF STEROIDS

The fundamental steroid skeleton contains 30 carbon atoms, representing the condensation of six prenyl groups:

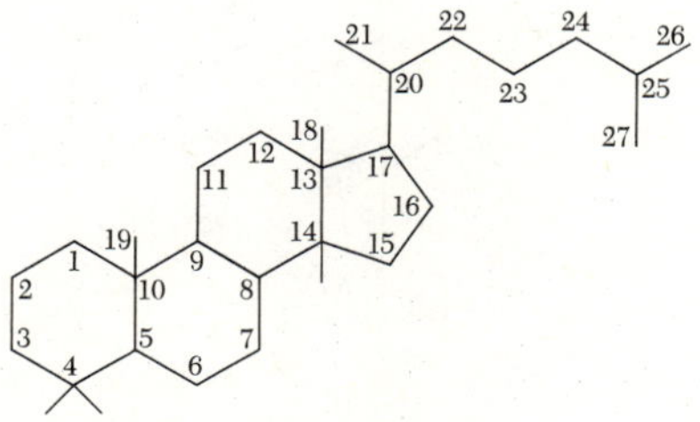

This skeleton constitutes a relatively rigid platform often used by organisms for the development of rather specific biological activities. That is, it provides a means of spacing hydroxyl groups, carbonyl groups, altered side chains, and so on in ways that

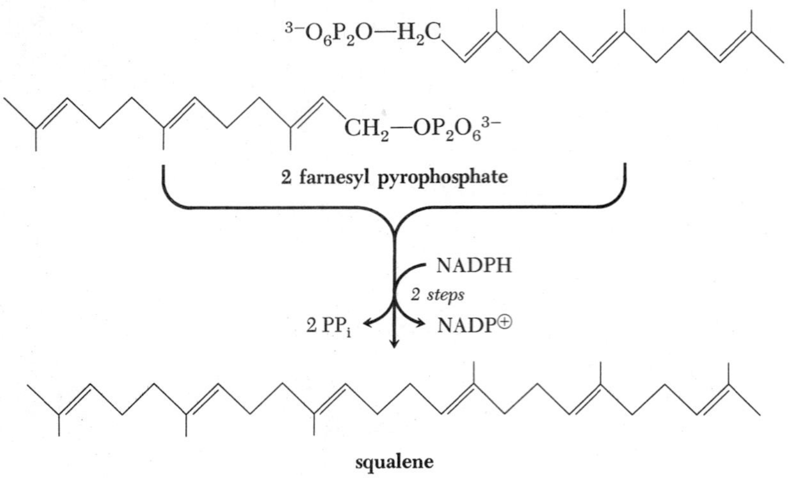

Figure 28-7 Animals and plants create squalene, the precursor of steroids, by tail-to-tail condensation of two triprenyl pyrophosphate molecules.

will cause combination with particular active sites. Hence, we shall see that the steroids include a variety of hormones produced to regulate metabolic processes, both in animals and in plants, as well as important constituents of cell lipids.

Formation of Squalene. The synthesis of steroids begins with a tail-to-tail combination of two molecules of farnesyl pyrophosphate with a simultaneous reduction to form the 30-carbon hydrocarbon, squalene (Fig. 28-7). (Squalene got its name from its occurrence in the liver of sharks of the genus *Squalus*.)

Formation of Lanosterol. Squalene is oxidized by a mixed function oxidase to

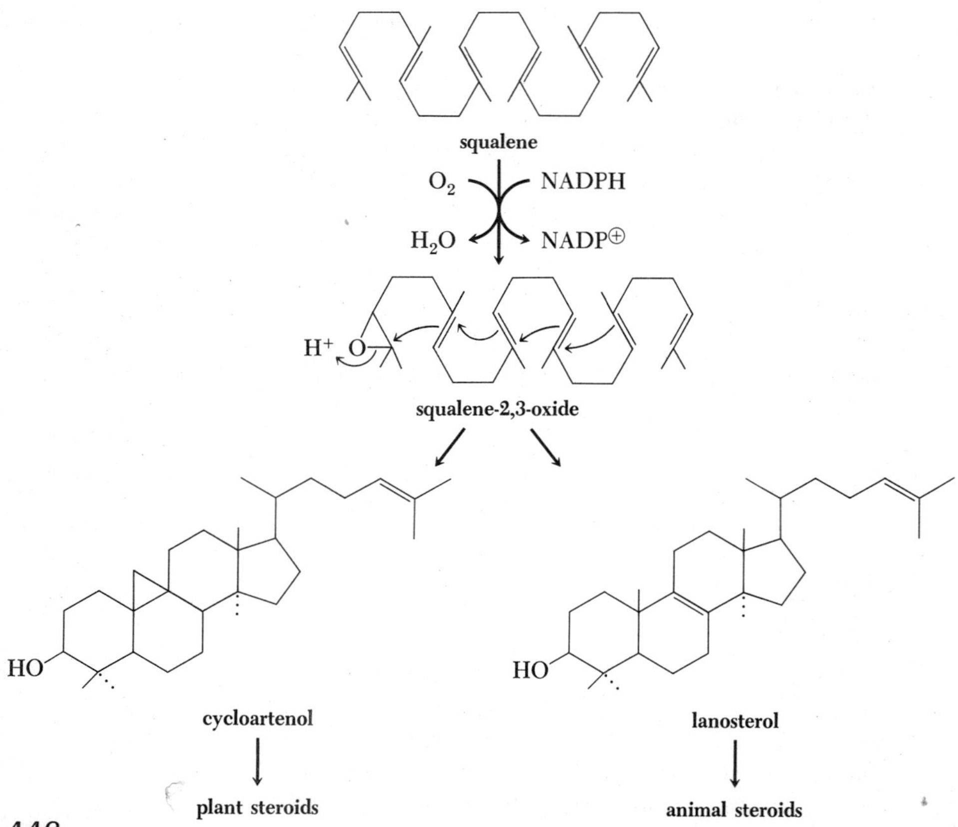

Figure 28-8 Squalene is converted to an oxide by a mixed-function oxidase. The oxide cyclizes to form steroid rings, which differ in plants and animals.

create a cyclic oxide, which is then cyclized to form either lanosterol or **cycloartenol** (Fig. 28–8). Lanosterol (named for its occurrence in wool fat; lana = wool; lanosterol = wool-steroid-alcohol) is the precursor from which the other steroids are made in animals and some protists. Cycloartenol is the precursor of plant steroids. Cyclization involves a migration of methyl groups, but the products still have 30 carbon atoms.

Conversion of Lanosterol to Cholesterol. Lanosterol differs from cholesterol in having three more methyl groups, and a double bond in the side chain. The methyl groups are removed by the action of mixed function oxidases, perhaps a single enzyme, that successively perform the three oxidations necessary to produce a transient carboxyl group, which is removed as CO_2 (Fig. 28–9). The side-chain double bond of lanosterol is removed by a simple reduction with NADPH. The transformation to cholesterol also involves the elimination of the double bond at C-8, and the creation of a new double bond at C-5. As the figure shows, this involves the transient formation of **$\Delta^{5,7}$-cholestadienol,** which has additional importance because it is the natural precursor of vitamin D, as we shall see in the next chapter. However, most of the cholestadienol is transformed into cholesterol, which is the precursor of all other steroids in animals, in addition to being an important constituent of structural lipids in its own right.

Structural Role of Cholesterol. The bulk of the cholesterol in animals, and of related steroids in plants, is found in the lipid mixtures of membrane cores and in circulating lipoproteins. There is no question that inclusion of varying amounts of cholesterol in artificial lipid membranes causes pronounced changes in their properties, but the precise role being played by the steroid in natural membranes is still debated.

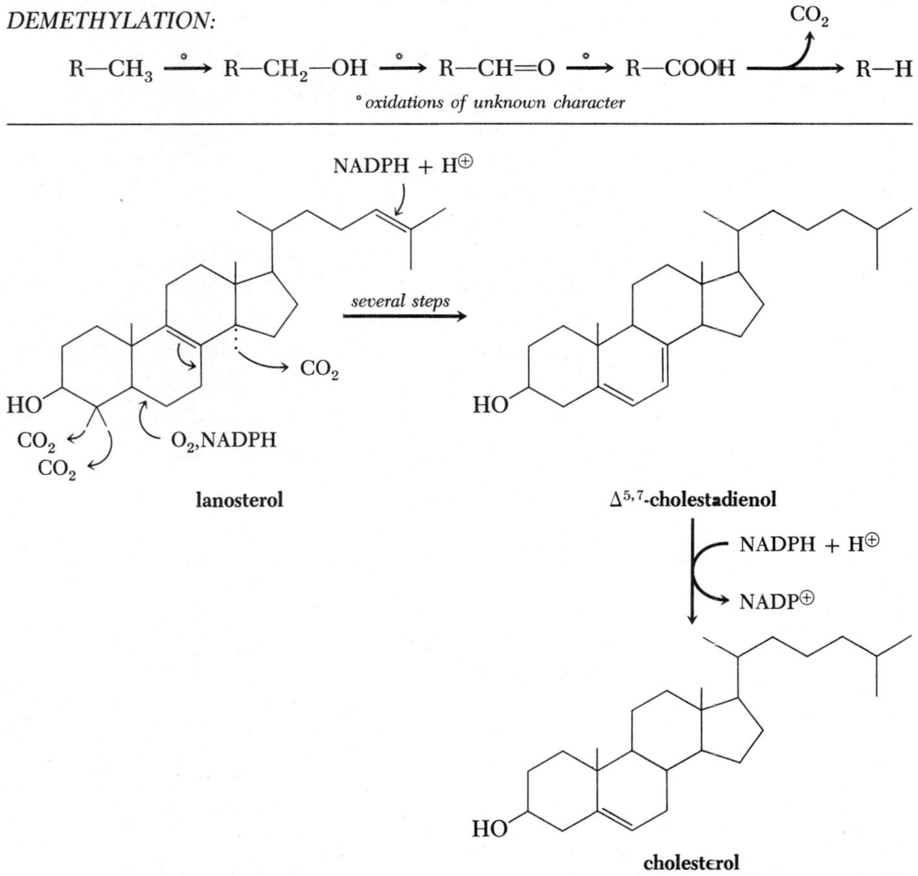

Figure 28–9 The formation of cholesterol from lanosterol involves three oxidative demethylations of unknown mechanism, and a shift of the ring double bond through formation of an intermediate cholestadienol, as well as reduction of the double bond in the side chain.

Presumably, the nearly planar steroid tends to slide on edge among the columns of fatty acid side chains extending into a membrane from the phospholipids. Interpretations of the purpose range from a more precise structural role, such as stabilizing a particular radius of curvature for the membrane, to a more general modification of physical properties, such as preventing the viscosity of the lipid phase from becoming exceptionally high or low. (The importance of "filler" molecules in establishing radius of curvature can be seen by drawing phospholipid tails around a curve. If the tails are in close contact on the inside, they are far apart in the center.)

FORMATION OF STEROID HORMONES

There are many natural steroids with complex metabolic interrelationships, but only a few kinds of reactions account for nearly all of their transformations. We can remove much of the mystery and apprehension (hopefully without losing reasonable awe) by examining in detail the formation of only a few examples.

Formation of Pregnenolone. The synthesis of all mammalian steroid hormones involves the removal of part of the side-chain of cholesterol to form **pregnenolone** (Fig. 28-10). This is accomplished by three successive oxidations catalyzed by mitochondrial hydroxylase systems, which probably occur in the outer membranes. These hydroxylases use NADPH as the second electron donor to activate oxygen, but the electrons are transferred by a flavoprotein through a particular cytochrome (P-450) and a small iron-sulfide protein known as adrenodoxin.

The final oxidation in the series results in the cleavage of a carbon-carbon bond, which liberates six carbons as a branched-chain aldehyde. (The aldehyde is handled by oxidation to form isocaproyl coenzyme A, followed by metabolism as a fatty acid. It is a trivial contribution to fuel metabolism.)

Formation of Progesterone. Pregnenolone can be converted to a hormone by oxidizing the alcohol group to a carbonyl group, and shifting the double bond to C-4 (Fig. 28-11). Here are two more important kinds of reactions in steroid chemistry: the simple equilibration of alcohols and ketones by sterol dehydrogenases, and the shifting of double bonds by isomerases.

The progesterone formed by these reactions has the property of promoting maturation of the uterus to receive a fertilized ovum, and its continued development to nurture the embryo after implantation. It also supresses further ovulation. Now, progesterone is formed by the adrenal cortex, by the testis in males, and by the corpus luteum in females. (The corpus luteum is the tissue developing in an ovarian follicle after it has ruptured to release an ovum.) Yet, only the corpus luteum causes the characteristic responses to progesterone in normal individuals. Why is this so?

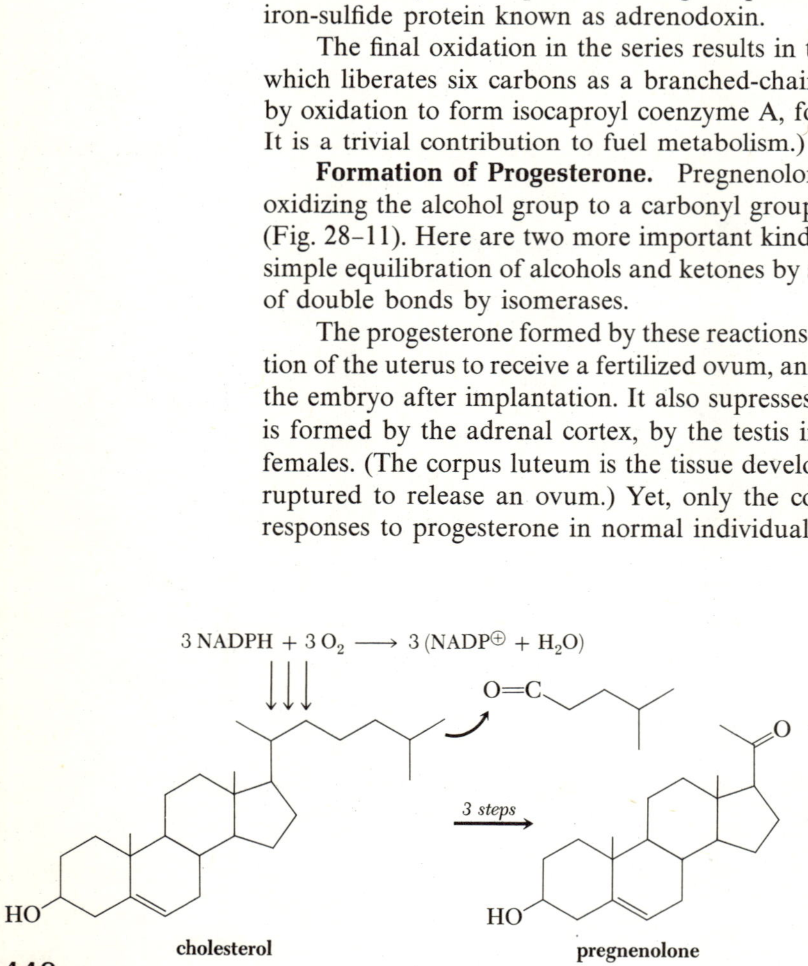

Figure 28-10 Part of the side chain of cholesterol is removed to form pregnenolone, the precursor of steroid hormones.

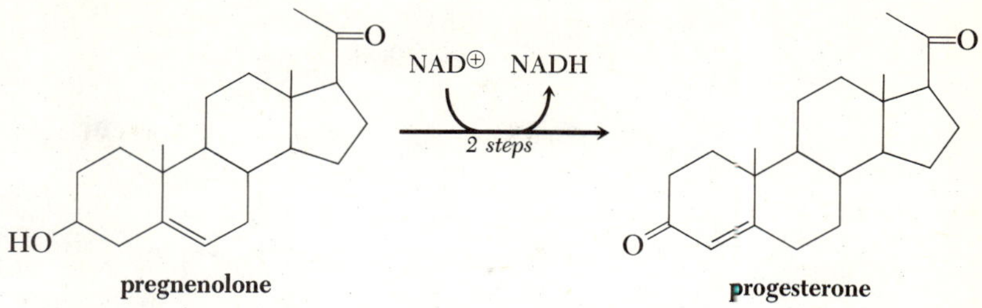

Figure 28-11 Progesterone is formed by an oxidation of the ring hydroxyl group and a shift of the double bond in pregnenolone.

Progesterone is an intermediate in the formation of other steroid hormones in the adrenal cortex and the testis, so these tissues remove it at a rate sufficient to keep its concentration low, whereas it is a terminal product of steroid metabolism in the corpus luteum, which releases it into the blood stream in physiologically effective quantities.

Here we have an illustration of an important principle in considering endocrinology. The endocrine glands are frequently not absolutely specific in the kinds of steroids they form, and the specificity of functions comes only from the production of much larger quantities of some steroids than of others.

Formation of Cortisol. The progesterone produced in the adrenal cortex is converted to cortisol by three successive hydroxylations (Fig. 28-12). (The formation of progesterone and the first hydroxylation occur in the endoplasmic reticulum. The final two hydroxylations occur in the mitochondria.)

These hydroxylations also illustrate another variable by which different functions can be created. The hydroxyl group on C-11 of cortisol has a β-configuration, meaning that it is above the plane of the paper as drawn, whereas the hydroxyl group on C-17 has an α-configuration, meaning that it lies behind the plane of the paper.

The physiological effects of cortisol, also known as hydrocortisone, will be discussed in Chapter 30.

Formation of Testosterone. The testes contain cells that form progesterone from cholesterol via pregnenolone, and then hydroxylate the progesterone in the same way we have described for the adrenal cortex. However, the 17-hydroxyprogesterone is attacked in the testis by another mixed function oxidase, which removes the side chain, leaving a carbonyl oxygen (Fig. 28-13). This ketone is then reduced to the corresponding alcohol, which is testosterone. Testosterone is an end-product of the testes and is elaborated in the male to promote the development of secondary sexual characteristics. The effects are most prominent at puberty, but testosterone must also be present during early development for adequate adult expression of machismo. Testosterone is also produced in maturing ovarian follicles, but these tissues use it as a precursor for forming estradiol, a steroid hormone producing typical female secondary characteristics and promoting the normal sexual cycle (Fig. 28-14).

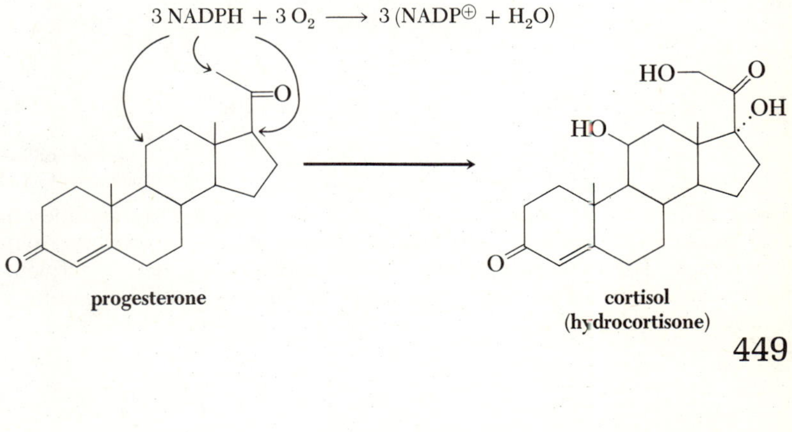

Figure 28-12 The action of three mixed-function oxidases in the adrenal cortex converts progesterone to cortisol.

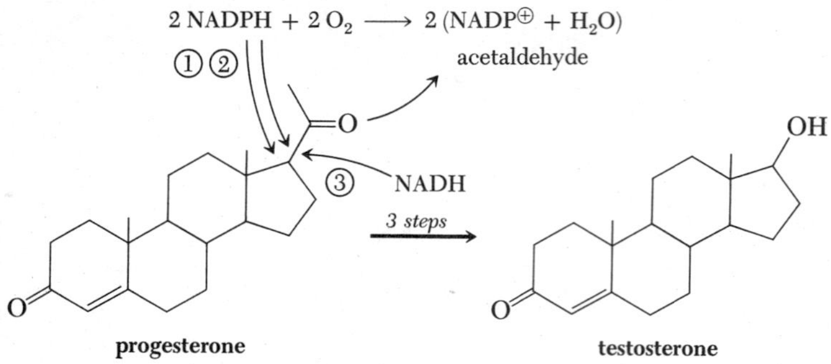

Figure 28-13 Testosterone is formed in the Leydig cells of the testes by oxidative scission of the side chain, followed by reduction of the resultant carbonyl group to an alcohol.

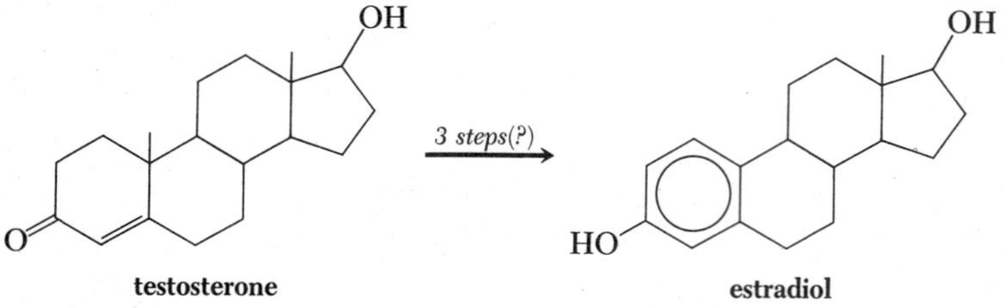

Figure 28-14 Ovarian follicles create an aromatic ring in testosterone to form estradiol.

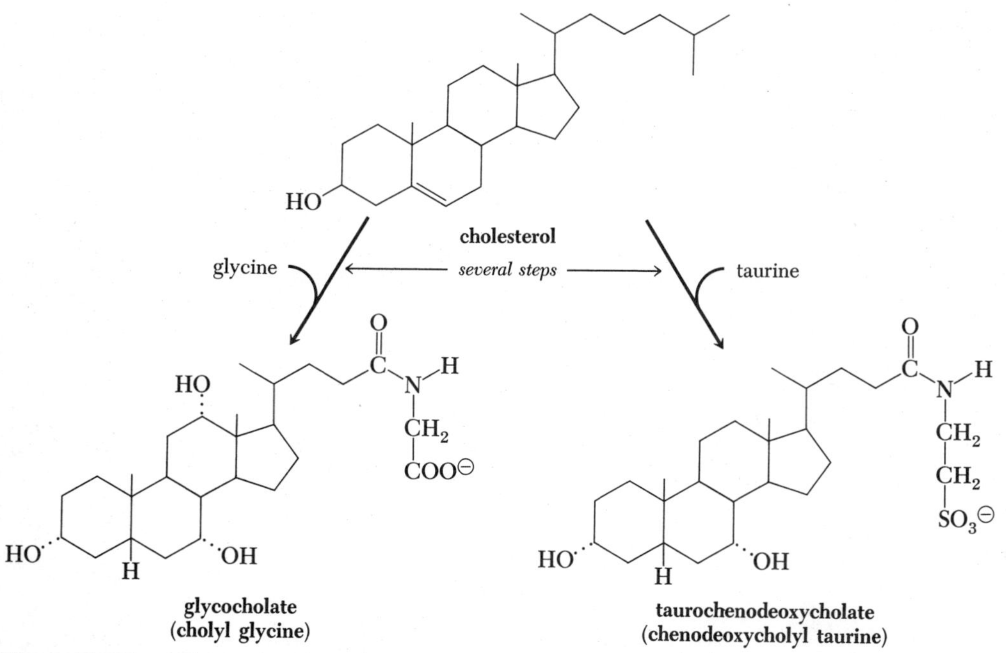

Figure 28-15 The major products of cholesterol metabolism are bile acids produced in the liver by oxidative scission of part of the side chain to form a carboxylate group and hydroxylation of the rings. The coenzyme A esters of the resultant bile acids react with glycine or taurine to form bile salts. These conjugates are powerful detergents that are necessary for digestion of fats.

BILE SALTS

The steroid hormones are of major importance in qualitative terms, but are minor products of cholesterol metabolism in terms of quantity. The major metabolic products of cholesterol in vertebrates are compounds known as the **bile acids,** which are produced in the liver by partial cleavage of the side chain and by α-hydroxylations (Fig. 28–15). These bile acids are converted to the coenzyme A esters, and react with either glycine or taurine to form bile salts, which are secreted into the small intestine from the liver. (**Taurine** is produced from cysteine by oxidation of the sulfur and decarboxylation.)

We have already mentioned the bile salts in connection with fat absorption. They have a detergent action that promotes the formation of micelles from dietary fat.

The bile also contains free cholesterol, and this, along with the bile salts, is the principle route by which cholesterol leaves the body. Most of the cholesterol and the bile salts are reabsorbed, but a portion, including excess dietary cholesterol, is not, and is excreted in the feces.

FURTHER READING

T. W. Goodwin, ed., Aspects of terpenoid chemistry and biochemistry, Academic Press (1971).

W. H. Sebrell, Jr., and R. S. Harris, The vitamins, 2nd ed., Academic Press (1971). See Chap. 1 in vol. 1 for a discussion of vitamin A and the carotenes.

S. J. Wakil, ed., Lipid metabolism, Academic Press (1970). Includes chapters on steroid and isoprenoid metabolism.

F. J. Barnes, A. A. Qureshi, E. J. Semmler, and J. W. Porter, Prelycopersene pyrophosphate and lycopersene, J. Biol. Chem., 248:2768 (1973). This and the preceding paper discuss key steps in carotenoid and steroid biosynthesis.

A. White, P. Handler, and E. L. Smith, Principles of biochemistry, 5th ed., McGraw-Hill (1973). This compendium includes chapters on steroid hormones.

QUESTIONS

1. The wavelength of excitation usually increases as the number of conjugated double bonds in a molecule increases. Suggest a reason for the use of carotenes rather than oxidized derivatives of squalene in photosynthetic plants. Why must retinal combine with a protein to form an effective visual pigment? (Hint: Vitamin A has a light yellow color.)
2. Why would a failure in cholesterol synthesis affect the ability to absorb fatty acids from the intestine?
3. What are the essential differences in structure between the bile acids and the steroid hormones?
4. Explain how it might be that some tumors of the adrenal gland cause men to develop feminine characteristics, and other tumors cause women to develop masculine characteristics.
5. Investigators have been trying to develop a connection between high levels of fat and high levels of cholesterol in the blood. What reason might there be to suspect a correlation between synthesis of fats (or failure to oxidize them), and synthesis of cholesterol?

CHAPTER 29

FIBERS AND MATRIX

THE CONCEPTS

Many organisms create structural components from fibers surrounded by a matrix of different material, which may distribute stresses or otherwise improve the mechanical characteristics of the fibers. The connective tissue of animals, for example, frequently contains fibers of collagen in a matrix of chondroitin sulfate. The chondroitin sulfates are proteoglycans, or protein-polysaccharides, in which linear polysaccharides are attached to a peptide core, like bristles on a brush.

Chondroitin is an example of a heteropolysaccharide constructed from alternating sequences of an N-acetylhexosamine and a hexuronate. The osamines are hexoses in which the C-2 hydroxyl group has been replaced by an amino group; chondroitin contains N-acetylgalactosamine residues transferred from UDP-N-acetylgalactosamine, created by epimerization of UDP-N-acetylglucosamine. The osamines originate as glucosamine 6-phosphate, which is made from fructose 6-phosphate by a transfer of the amide nitrogen of glutamine.

The hexuronates are hexoses in which C-6 has been oxidized to a carboxylate group, and chondroitin contains glucuronate residues derived from UDP-glucuronate. A protein polysaccharide in skin, dermatan sulfate, contains residues of L-iduronate derived from UDP-iduronate, which is made by epimerization of UDP-glucuronate at C-5.

As the chondroitin chain is built, sulfate residues are attached in ester linkage to C-4 or C-6 of the N-acetylgalactosamine residues. The sulfate is obtained by transfer from 3′-phospho-adenosine-5′phosphosulfate. The sulfate residues and the carboxylate groups of the glucuronate residues represent a massive negative charge that keeps the polysaccharide chains separated and heavily hydrated, and these conditions are believed to contribute to the resilience of tissues like cartilage.

Bone is a tissue like cartilage in which much of the protein-polysaccharide is replaced by deposits of hydroxyapatite, $Ca_5OH(PO_4)_3$, to give it hardness and rigidity. Deposition depends upon the development of local concentrations of the constituent ions that exceed the solubility product for the mineral. The transport of calcium requires the presence of 1,25-dihydroxychole-calciferol, or related compounds. Cholecalciferol is formed in the skin by the action of ultraviolet light on cholestadienol, an intermediate in cholesterol synthesis, and it is further hydroxylated by enzymes in the liver and kidneys. It, or similar compounds with vitamin D activity, must be supplied in the diet of children who are not exposed to sunlight. The concentration of transported calcium is controlled by the opposing actions of two peptide hormones; parathyroid hormone promotes mobilization of bone to raise the concentration of circulating calcium, and calcitonin promotes deposition of calcium to lower its concentration.

Another fiber and matrix combination is seen in the cuticles of invertebrates, where fibers are formed by polymerizing N-acetylglucosamine residues to make chitin, and are buried in a tanned protein known as sclerotin. Tanning consists of forming covalent linkages between peptide chains through the use of polyphenols. The dimensions and composition of the cuticle can be varied to give different mechanical properties, and extra hardness is obtained by depositing calcium minerals in an interior layer, as in crab shells.

The wood of plants is made from still another fiber and matrix. The fibers are cellulose, composed of glucose residues linked in β-1,4 configuration to form side-by-side, but anti-parallel, chains. The matrix is lignin, in which an important component is a polymer of polyphenols derived from phenylalanine or tyrosine. The complex structure of lignin has not been fully elucidated.

The structural components of organisms include many examples of combinations of fibers embedded in, or surrounded by, an amorphous matrix. These combinations have mechanical properties not found in either the fibers or the matrix alone. The Mosaic chronicles cite the difficulties of making bricks without straw, but biochemical evolution uncovered the advantages of that sort of combination long before.

COLLAGEN AND CHONDROITIN SULFATE

The connective tissues of the vertebrates are mainly built from fibers of a protein, collagen, embedded in a matrix of polysaccharide sulfate. These components are synthesized by fibroblasts, or other related cells built to form particular connective tissues. We discussed collagen in Chapter 4 as a typical example of a fibrous protein, noting that it is made from triple helices cross-linked by covalent bonds. The resultant stiff rods are used to give rigidity to a variety of tissues, but collagen is accompanied by varying quantities of polysaccharides, which usually contain esterified sulfate groups.

The polysaccharides of vertebrate connective tissue are **heteropolysaccharides,** meaning that they are composed of more than one kind of sugar. Furthermore, they are **proteinpolysaccharides,** or **proteoglycans,** meaning that the polysaccharide constituents are covalently linked to peptide chains. The polysaccharide is the major constituent of the proteinpolysaccharides, whereas the peptide chains comprise the bulk of the molecule in **glycoproteins.**

Osamines and Uronates

In order to understand the nature of the proteinpolysaccharides and glycoproteins, we must first understand the nature of the constituent groups from which they are constructed. Sugars are modified in several ways to produce the constituents of heteropolysaccharides, and we shall consider three processes of major importance: Osamines are formed by the replacement of a hydroxyl group of a sugar with an amino group. Uronic acids, present as uronate anions, are formed by the oxidation of the terminal carbon, C-6, of a hexose to a carboxyl group. Finally, epimers are formed at one or more carbon atoms.

Epimers. Epimers are stereoisomers in which the mirror image is formed on only one asymmetric atom; the effect is as if the H— and HO— are interchanged on one atom, and we have already noted the epimerization of D-ribulose 5-phosphate to form xylulose 5-phosphate (p. 259). Let us consider another simple example more pertinent to the heteropolysaccharides. Some proteins contain attached residues of glucose, obtained by transfers from UDP-glucose as a donor in the same way that they are obtained for the construction of glycogen (p. 298). However, proteins often contain residues of D-galactose, which differs from glucose only in the configuration at C-4. Galactose is therefore an epimer of glucose, and galactosyl residues are obtained for transfer in the form of UDP-galactose by a simple epimerization of UDP-glucose (Fig.

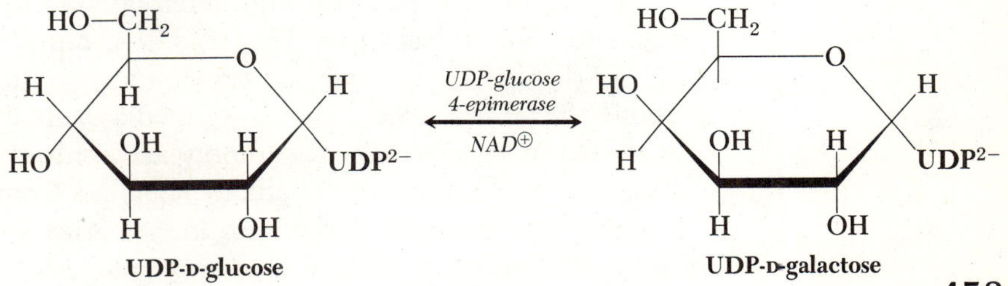

Figure 29-1 UDP-galactose is formed from UDP-glucose by changing the configuration on C-4.

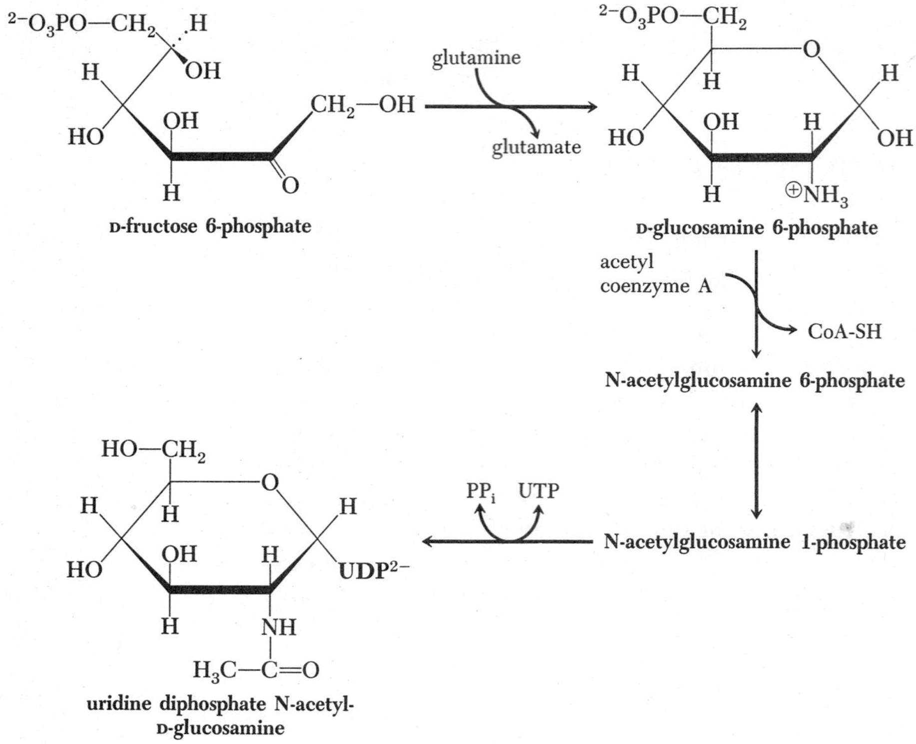

Figure 29-2 Glucosamine 6-phosphate is formed from fructose 6-phosphate by transfer of the amide nitrogen from glutamine. An intermediate acetylation converts it to the N-acetyl derivative. Otherwise, the conversion of glucosamine 6-phosphate to UDP-N-acetylglucosamine involves the same steps seen in the conversion of glucose 6-phosphate to UDP-glucose.

29–1). (This epimerase requires catalytic amounts of NAD, and its mechanism is believed to involve oxidation of the affected alcohol group to a ketone, followed by reduction to the epimer of the alcohol.)

Formation of Osamines. **D-Glucosamine** is often found in heteropolysaccharides in the form of its N-acetyl derivative. It is made by a transfer of nitrogen from glutamine to fructose 6-phosphate (Fig. 29–2). After acetylation of the amino group with acetyl coenzyme A, the N-acetylglucosamine 6-phosphate is converted successively to the 1-phosphate and then to the UDP derivative, much in the way that glucose 6-phosphate is converted to UDP-glucose.

UDP-N-acetylglucosamine is the donor of N-acetylglucosamine residues for incorporation into heteropolysaccharides. In addition, it is a substrate for an epimerase that acts on C-4 to form **UDP-N-acetylgalactosamine** in many connective tissue cells. The epimerization is closely analogous to the interconversion of UDP-glucose and UDP-galactose.

Formation of Uronates. The uronates, with their charged carboxylate group, are created for incorporation into heteropolysaccharides by initially oxidizing UDP-glucose to UDP-glucuronate. This oxidation requires the reduction of two molecules of NAD (Fig. 29–3), and yet the reaction appears to be catalyzed by a single enzyme without the appearance of the intermediate aldehyde. The glucuronate residue is transferred by specific enzymes to polysaccharide chains; it still contains the potential aldehyde group of the original glucose, and can form the same sort of glycosidic bond.

UDP-glucuronate is also subject to epimerization at C-5 to form another precursor of polysaccharides, as is also shown in Figure 29–3. Mechanistically, this is not much

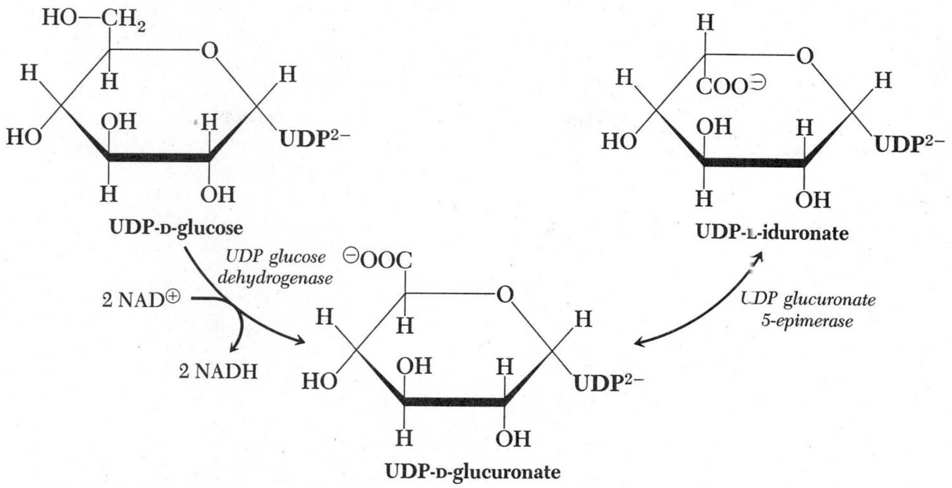

Figure 29-3 C-6 of UDP-glucose is oxidized to form UDP-glucuronate. Inversion of the configuration on C-5 creates UDP-L-iduronate.

different from the other epimerizations, but it causes a convulsion in the nomenclature. We assign hexoses to the D- or L- family depending upon the configuration at C-5, which is the final asymmetric carbon atom in the chain. Therefore, an epimerization at C-5 changes the nomenclature from D- to L-. It so happens that the resultant uronic acid has a configuration corresponding to the aldohexose, L-idose, so the product of the epimerization is named L-iduronate (the anion of L-iduronic acid).

Xylose Residues. One other reaction of UDP-glucuronate is of interest. The carboxyl group can be removed through the action of a decarboxylase (Fig. 29–4). The remaining five carbons represent a residue of an aldopentose, D-xylose, in the form of UDP-xylose. This residue is frequently transferred to peptide chains as a "starter" for the growth of polysaccharides on the peptide.

Formation of Chrondroitin-Protein Chains

The initial step in the construction of the protein-polysaccharide matrix by fibroblasts is the formation of peptide chains, some 300 nm long, by the apparatus of protein synthesis. These chains act as the core on which polysaccharides are to be constructed, and they contain 60 to 65 seryl groups that act as sites for this purpose. The construction begins through recognition of these sites by a peptide:UDP xylosyl transferase, which attaches xylosyl groups to the seryl residues in the peptide.

The xylosyl-peptide groups act in turn as substrates for another transferase, which causes the attachment of a galactosyl group obtained from UDP-galactose. The successive attachment of sugar residues, each creating a specific substrate for the attachment

Figure 29–4 UDP-xylose is formed by decarboxylation of UDP-glucuronate.

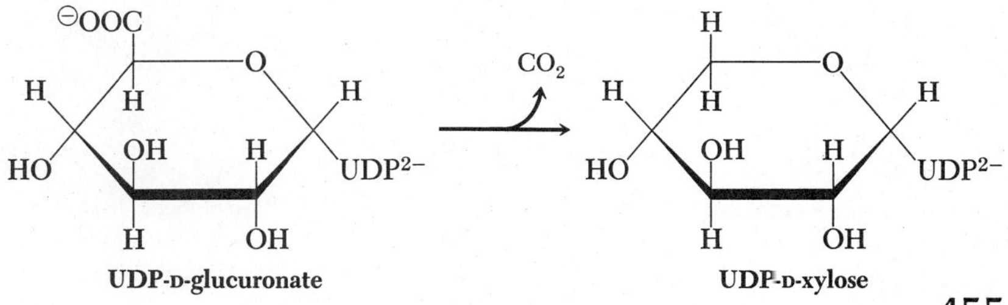

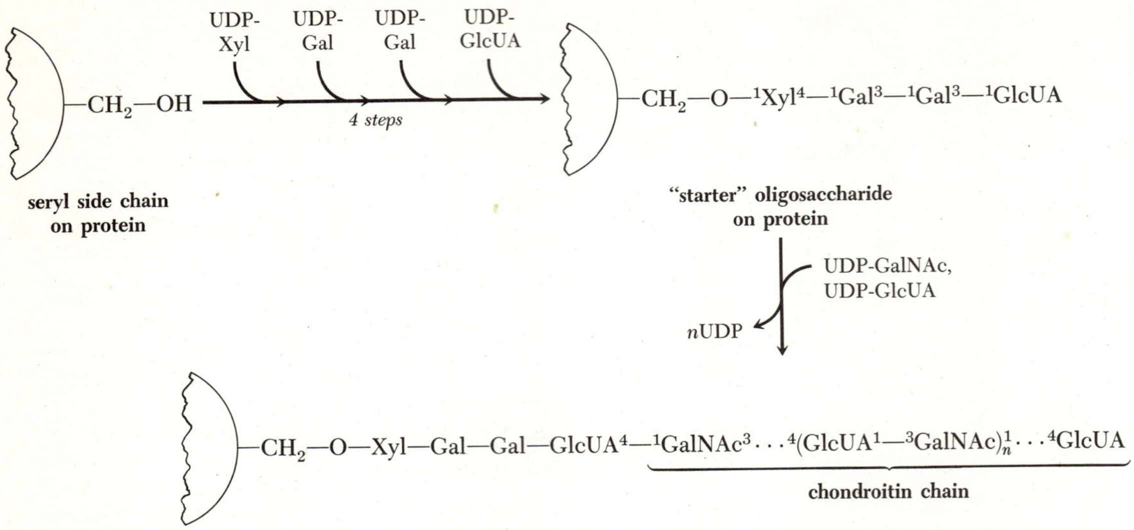

Figure 29–5 The formation of many glycoproteins begins with the transfer of a xylose residue to a seryl side chain on the protein. The protein polysaccharide, chondroitin sulfate, is made by the further addition of two residues of galactose and one of glucuronate, followed by alternate addition of N-acetylgalactosamine and glucuronate residues. The UDP-derivatives are the donors of all of these residues.

of the next residue, continues until the sequence is glucuronate-galactose-galactose-xylose-serine (Fig. 29–5). This sequence acts as a foundation upon which the main part of the heteropolysaccharide is built. The main chain consists of alternating sequences of glucuronate and N-acetylgalactosamine residues, added by the alternate action of two transferases using the corresponding UDP derivatives as substrates until over a hundred pairs of residues are added.

Addition of Sulfate. As the chondroitin chain grows, sulfate groups are added. The source of the sulfate groups is 3′-phosphoadenosine-5′-phosphosulfate (PAPS), which is the source of sulfide for making cysteine in plants (p. 434), but which acts primarily as a sulfate donor in animals, much in the way that ATP acts as a phosphate donor for kinase reactions. Connective tissue cells contain two kinds of transferases reacting with chondroitin. One adds sulfate groups to C-6, and the other to C-4, of growing chondroitin chains (Fig. 29–6), so that some kinds of cells make chondroitin 4-sulfate, and others chondroitin 6-sulfate. (The other product in either case is adenosine-3′,5′-*bis*-phosphate, which is hydrolyzed to form AMP.)

Dermatan Sulfate. This major protein polysaccharide sulfate of the skin, where it is found in the basal layers, is like chondroitin sulfate except that it contains residues

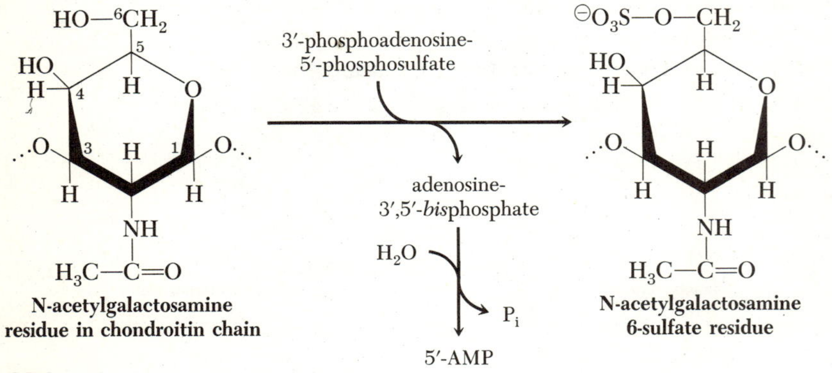

Figure 29–6 Chondroitin sulfate is made by the transfer of sulfate groups to the growing polysaccharide chain from 3′-phosphoadenosine-5′-phosphosulfate. The sulfate groups are placed on C-6 of N-acetylgalactosamine residues in some cells, and on C-4 in others.

of L-iduronate rather than of D-glucuronate, alternating with N-acetylgalactosamine residues. It is also found in lesser quantities in other tissues.

Function of the Proteinpolysaccharide Sulfates

The contribution of the protein polysaccharides to the function of connective tissue is not completely clear, but we can get some notion from the characteristics of cartilage, which is mainly composed of collagen and chondroitin sulfate. The chondroitin sulfate molecules resemble bottle brushes, with a central peptide core to which bristles of heteropolysaccharide are attached. The bristles are prevented from close association because they bear an abundance of negative charges. Nearly every constituent residue is either a uronate residue with its charged carboxylate group, or an N-acetylglucosamine residue with an attached charged sulfate group.

Furthermore, these charged groups and the other polar groups in the sugar derivatives can bond water molecules. The combination of open structure due to charge repulsion and strongly hydrophilic character results in a molecule with a large domain; that is, it occupies a relatively large volume of solution compared to a molecule of equal mass with a compact structure.

It is believed that the collagen fibers—rigid and strong—form a lattice that traps the bulky chondroitin sulfate molecules, and the presence of these molecules gives the lattice resilience. The resilience is believed to result from the loss of some of the water in the domain of chondroitin sulfate molecules when they are subjected to compression. An outside force squeezes the polysaccharide chains together, expelling water, until the repulsive forces of the charged chains balance the outside force. When the outside force is removed, water moves in again to separate the like charges and to diminish the internal repulsive forces.

BONE

Cartilage has collagen for strength and rigidity, and chondroitin sulfate for resilience. If much of the chondroitin sulfate is replaced by crystals of a calcium hydroxyphosphate, hydroxyapatite ($Ca_5OH(PO_4)_3$), the result is bone. The resilience of cartilage is replaced by the hardness of bone. Bone formation can to some extent be regarded as a mineralization of a loose cartilage, with the mineral derived from calcium and phosphate ions in the body fluids. Bone mineral can't be laid down unless the concentrations of these ions, and hydroxide ion, exceed the solubility product for calcium hydroxyphosphate at the site of bone formation. That is, $[Ca^{2+}]^5 \times [PO_4^{3-}]^3 \times [OH^-]$ must be greater than the value obtained in a saturated solution if the mineral phase is to grow. The cells responsible for bone growth and dissolution probably determine the actual concentrations at the mineral interface, but bone growth is determined to some extent by the concentrations of these ions in the general body fluids. For example, a drop in $[OH^-]$ usually results in solution of bone mineral, with a resultant rise in $[Ca^{2+}]$ in the blood. A retention of inorganic phosphate, which is normally secreted by the kidney, tends to cause a deposition of mineral and a fall in blood $[Ca^{2+}]$. The metabolism of bone is therefore inextricably mixed with the general metabolism of calcium and phosphate ions. Even adult bones are constantly being destroyed by osteoclasts, which burrow small tunnels through the bone by dissolving mineral and degrading collagen, and are constantly being rebuilt by osteoblasts, which form new collagen networks and lay down new deposits of calcium hydroxyphosphate within them.

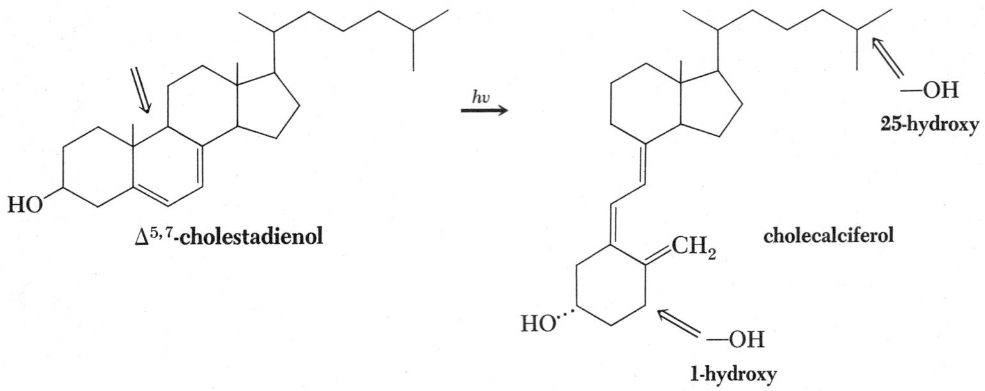

Figure 29–7 Cholecalciferol is formed by the photochemical scission of $\Delta^{5,7}$-cholestadienol, which is also an intermediate in cholesterol synthesis. Hydroxylation to create 25-hydroxycholecalciferol, and further hydroxylation to create 1,25-dihydroxycholecalciferol, form the biologically active compounds with vitamin D activity.

Cholecalciferol and Calcium Transport. The transport of calcium from the intestines and at the sites of calcium exchange in the bones requires the presence of hydroxylated metabolites of a steroid derivative known as cholecalciferol. This, and compounds with similar activities, are known as **vitamin D.**

Cholecalciferol is formed from $\Delta^{5,7}$-cholestadienol by the action of ultraviolet light in the skin. (We previously encountered cholestadienol as an intermediate in the formation of cholesterol (p. 447).) Cholecalciferol is hydroxylated, first at the 25-position by an enzyme in the liver, and then by an enzyme in the kidney (Fig. 29–7). The **1,25-dihydroxycholecalciferol** is absolutely required for the absorption of calcium ions by the intestinal mucosa, and also for calcium transport at the bones. The mechanism of its action is not clear.

Formation of these cholecalciferol derivatives from cholestadienol requires exposure to sunlight, and normal function of the skin, the liver, and the kidneys. If formation of adequate quantities fails at any stage, deficiency of calcium will result. The results are usually more obvious in the very young, who have not developed large mineral deposits, and are rapidly developing bones; the loss of normal bone formation leads to a condition known as rickets.

Rickets can be prevented even without adequate exposure to sunlight, if the diet contains cholecalciferol or some related compound from which it can be made. However, compounds with vitamin D activity are toxic in excess, so uncontrolled dietary supplementation may be risky.

Endocrine Regulation of Calcium Metabolism. The concentration of calcium ions in the blood is closely regulated, usually within $\pm 10\%$. The tight control results from the opposing action of two hormones, both of which are small peptides. The **parathyroid glands** (the name implies their location near the thyroid gland in the neck) respond to a decline in the free Ca^{2+} concentration in the blood by elaborating a peptide that combines with receptors in the plasma membrane of particular target cells and causes an activation of adenyl cyclase, much in the same way that adrenaline or glucagon activate adenyl cyclase in their respective target cells. The cells affected by parathyroid hormone are those responsible for the reabsorption of phosphate ions from the filtrate in the kidney and those responsible for the mobilization of mineral in the bones. The effects of the increased 3′,5′-AMP concentrations in these cells are to increase the loss of phosphate in the urine, and to increase the solution of bone mineral, a process that is also aided by the declining blood phosphate concentrations. These effects taken together make more calcium ions available to eliminate the deficit that first caused the parathyroid glands to secrete hormone.

Other kinds of cells in both the parathyroid and thyroid glands secrete another type of peptide, **calcitonin,** in response to elevated calcium ion concentrations. Calcitonin, also known as thyrocalcitonin, increases the deposition of bone mineral, thereby decreasing the blood calcium concentration, although the mechanism by which it does this is not known. In any event, the parathyroid hormone and calcitonin, with their opposing effects, prevent large fluctuations in the calcium ion concentration.

CHITIN AND SCLEROTIN

We have so far been dealing with internal connective tissue in the vertebrates; now let us turn to another arrangement of fibers and matrix used to create entirely different properties in the integument of invertebrates, especially the arthropods. The cuticle of crustaceans, insects, spiders, and the like, is a complex tissue composed of several layers. The strength of the tissue comes from fibers, but the fibers are composed in this case of chitin, a homopolysaccharide, which consists of chains of N-acetylglucosamine joined by $\beta(1\rightarrow4)$ linkages (Fig. 29–8).

Sclerotin. The toughness and water impermeability of the arthropod cuticle come from the matrix in which the chitin fibers are embedded in the outer layers of the cuticle. This matrix is a tanned protein complex, sclerotin. The process of tanning, which we usually think of as something humans do to skins flayed from other animals, involves the generation of cross-links between proteins. Tanned skins are stronger because it takes much more force to break the additional covalent bonds. The cross-links are established by multiple bonding with polyphenols, and these polyphenolic compounds are created from tyrosine (Fig. 29–9). They act as fasteners that link several peptide chains in a 3-dimensional lattice.

Variations in Cuticle Composition. The arthropods vary the nature of their cuticle by varying both the proportion of chitin and proteins, and the degree of tanning. Very hard cuticles, such as those in beetles, are heavily tanned in thick layers, whereas soft-skinned insects may have relatively little tanning. Furthermore, the crustaceans frequently develop shells in which an outermost layer is heavily tanned, and an inner layer represents a modified form with deposits of calcium carbonate among the chitin fibers, much in the way that bone represents a modified cartilage in vertebrates.

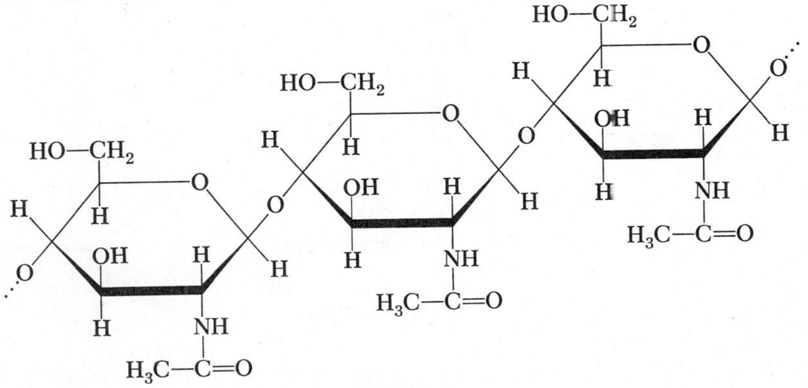

Figure 29–8 The exoskeleton of arthropods gains its strength from fibers of chitin, a homopolymer of N-acetylglucosamine.

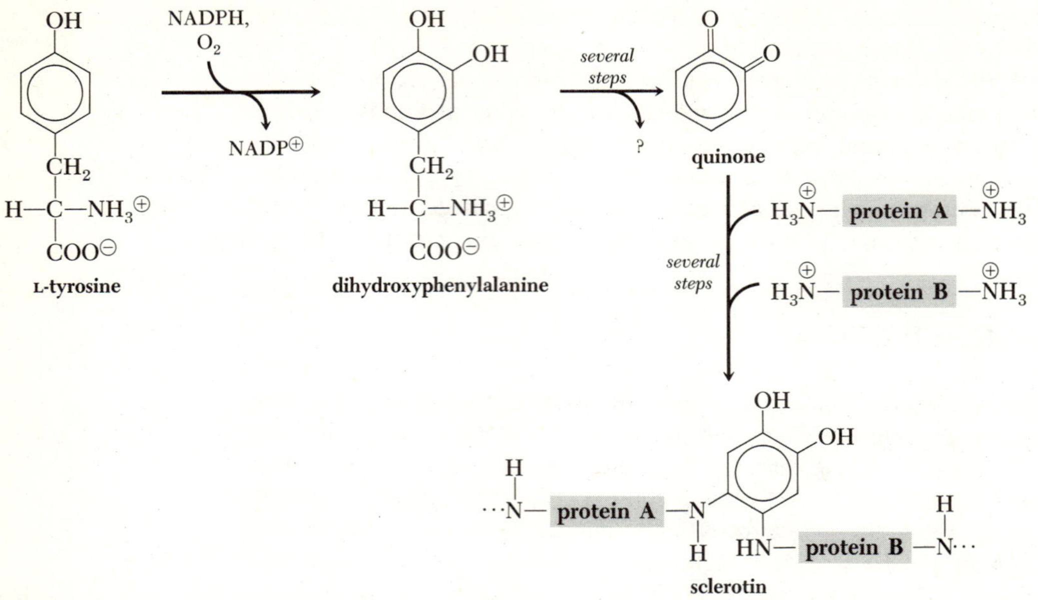

Figure 29-9 The chitin fibers of arthropod cuticles are buried in a matrix of sclerotin, a tanned protein. The tanning agents are quinones obtained by the oxidation of tyrosine. Tanning involves condensation of the quinones with amino groups on the proteins to create a lattice structure.

CELLULOSE AND LIGNIN

The higher plants, like vertebrate animals, have a connective tissue made from fibers of homopolysaccharide and surrounding matrix. However, the polysaccharide is cellulose, and the matrix is lignin, and the result is wood. (Wood, like all of the other connective tissues we are considering, contains many minor components, but its physical properties to a large extent stem from its cellulose and lignin components.)

Cellulose is made from chains of glucosyl residues in $\beta(1\rightarrow4)$ linkages (Fig. 29-10), which lie side by side in anti-parallel orientation to form fibers. The glucosyl residues are apparently added from **GDP-glucose,** rather than the UDP-glucose used for most purposes, although there is some dispute on this point. The GDP-glucose is presumably made from a reaction of GTP with glucose 1-phosphate in the same way that UTP is used to form UDP-glucose.

The **xylem** is the channeled woody core of plants; as its maturation proceeds, lignin begins to be formed around the cellulose fibers. Lignin is a polymer of phenolic derivatives made from phenylalanine and tyrosine. Unlike the sclerotin made to harden

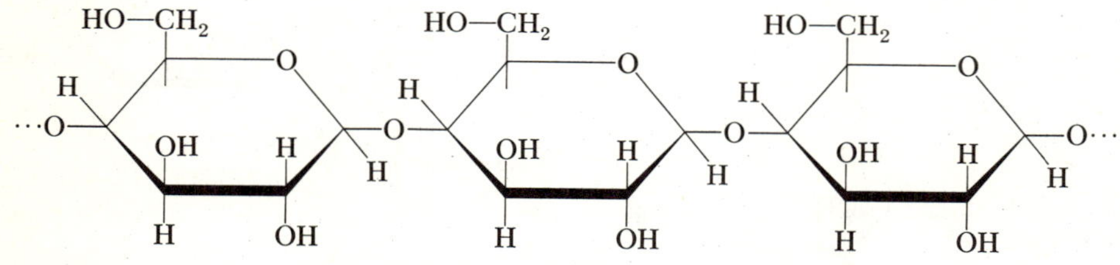

Figure 29-10 Cellulose is made of chains of glucose residues linked by β-1,4 bonds. (The linkage is shown here in a closer approximation of the actual conformation than is apparent in the usual Haworth formulations.)

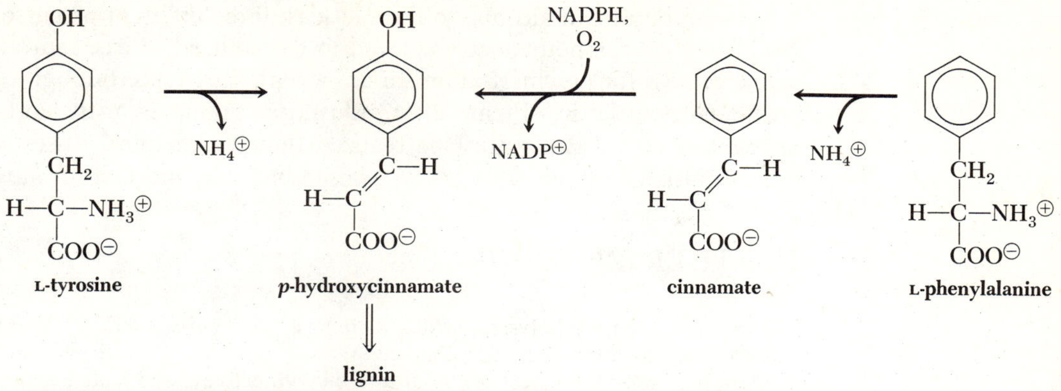

Figure 29-11 The *p*-hydroxycinnamate that is a precursor of lignin may be formed from tyrosine or from phenylalanine.

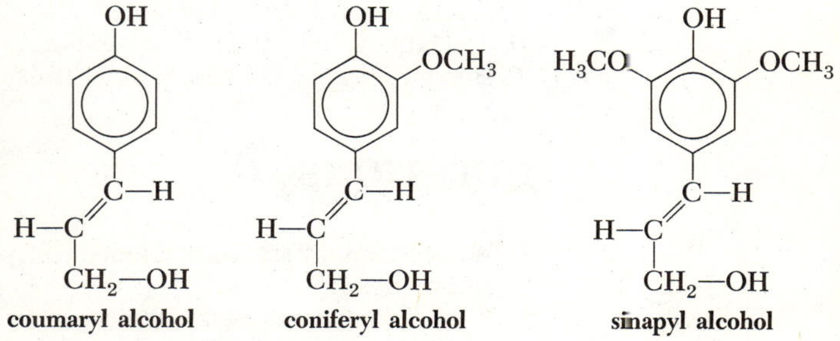

Figure 29-12 The components of lignin are formed from *p*-hydroxycinnamate by reduction of the carboxylate group to an alcohol, by further hydroxylation of the ring, and by methylation of some of the hydroxyl groups.

invertebrate cuticle, lignin contains little protein; its three-dimensional lattice is formed completely from the phenols.

Precursors of Lignin. The formation of lignin begins with a direct deamination of phenylalanine or tyrosine (Fig. 29-11). In the end, it makes little difference which is used, for cells deaminating phenylalanine also contain a cinnamate 4-hydroxylase that creates the same **4-hydroxycinnamate** resulting from the deamination of tyrosine. 4-Hydroxycinnamate is modified by a succession of reactions, including further hydroxylation, the conversion of hydroxyl groups to methoxyl groups (—OCH_3) by transfer of methyl groups from S-adenosylmethionine, and the reduction of the car-

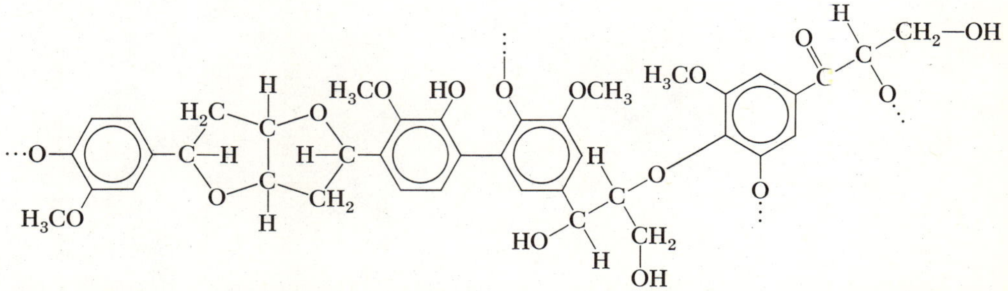

Figure 29-13 An illustration of some of the types of condensation by which lignin is formed. The particular example is a spruce lignin made from coniferyl alcohol.

boxylate group to an alcohol, to form at least three different precursors of lignin (Fig. 29–12). These compounds are believed to be oxidized to free radicals so as to create active centers for polymerization. In any event, they unite through covalent bonds to create a strong lattice. Figure 29–13 illustrates examples of the sort of bonding that appears to occur, but it must be realized that the chemical dissection of lignin is a difficult task, one might almost say a miserable task, and there is much to be learned.

FURTHER READING

S. Kirkwood, Unusual polysaccharides, Ann. Rev. Biochem., 43:401 (1974). This contains a clear discussion of the fiber-matrix concept.

M. Schubert and D. Hamerman, A primer on connective tissue biochemistry, Lea and Febiger (1968). A lucid introduction, but not simple-minded.

M. Florkin and E. Stotz, eds., Comprehensive biochemistry, vols. 26A-C, Extracellular and supporting structures, Elsevier (1968–1971).

W. Pigman and D. Horton, eds., The carbohydrates, 2nd ed., Academic Press (1970). Includes chapters on cellulose and on heteropolysaccharides (mucopolysaccharides).

R. H. Wasserman and R. A. Corradino, Vitamin D, calcium, and protein synthesis, Vitamins and Hormones, 31:43 (1973).

H. F. DeLuca, Vitamin D: the vitamin and the hormone, Feder. Proc., 33:2211 (1974).

T. Higuchi, Formation and biological degradation of lignins, Adv. Enzymol., 34:207 (1971).

QUESTIONS

1. What is the difference in function of polyphenol compounds in the formation of sclerotin and of lignin?
2. What is the important difference between the polysaccharide chains forming a matrix, as in chondroitin sulfate, and those forming fibers, as in cellulose or chitin?
3. Extending the principles seen in this chapter, what would be the product of epimerization at C-4 of UDP-glucuronate? What would be the product of epimerization at C-4 of UDP-N-acetylgalactosamine? What would be the product of decarboxylation of UDP-L-iduronate?
4. What is the important difference in structure between cellulose and amylose?
5. Would a failure to excrete excess phosphate ions tend to increase or decrease the concentration of blood calcium ions, assuming no concomitant change in the concentration of H^+? Why?
6. It has been suggested that cholecalciferol and its hydroxylated derivatives are more properly designated as hormones rather than vitamins. What justification is there for this view?
7. It has been suggested that the darker pigmentation of people indigenous to the lower latitudes is a necessary device for protection against vitamin D poisoning. Explain.

CHAPTER 30

METABOLIC REGULATION

THE CONCEPTS

The many enzymatic reactions comprising metabolism are kept in balance by adjusting the catalytic activity of individual enzyme molecules, or by changing the number of enzyme molecules. The signal causing these responses may be an alteration in metabolite concentration within a cell, or in multicellular organisms it may be a change in the concentration of a hormone sent from some other tissue.

The most common regulation is the alteration in enzymatic activity by changing substrate concentrations, such as the changes in the rate of fuel metabolism caused by changes in ADP concentration. Other examples include the balancing of the rate of the pentose phosphate pathway against the rate of synthesis of fatty acid chains; the two processes are coupled through the formation and utilization of NADPH. Also, the rate of carbamyl phosphate formation, and therefore of urea synthesis, automatically adjusts to the rate of NH_4^+ production through acceleration by any rise in NH_4^+ concentration.

Enzymatic activity is also altered through the binding of effectors; these are usually metabolites, but may also be peptides having various effects. The regulating protein kinase is inhibited by a peptide that also binds cAMP. The tryptophan synthase of *E. coli* is composed of two peptides that catalyze individual steps in the synthesis, but that have more activity when they associate. The lactose synthase of mammary gland contains a modifying protein that changes the specificity of the enzyme so that it synthesizes lactose, the carbohydrate of milk, rather than the carbohydrate moiety of a glycoprotein made by the enzyme when it occurs alone.

The activity of enzymes may also be changed by covalent modifications, as in the phosphorylation of the enzymes of glycogen metabolism. Some enzymes are modified by the formation of a seryl ester with an AMP group, rather than P_i, but the principle is the same. Covalent alteration by hydrolysis is common for activation of extracellular enzymes, but the intracellular significance as a regulatory mechanism is less clear.

Changes in the number of molecules of an enzyme in a cell usually occur in prokaryotes by induction or repression of the synthesis of the enzyme, and the affected step is often the transcription of mRNA. For example, the metabolism of less common sugars by *E. coli* requires certain enzymes. The transcription of mRNA coding for these enzymes is often prevented by the presence of repressor proteins bound to a double stranded regulatory segment of DNA, or operator region, near the affected cistrons. However, the repressor proteins are built to lose their affinity for the operators when they combine with the special sugars. The result is that the presence of the sugars permits the formation of enzymes necessary for their metabolism.

The mechanism for changing enzyme concentrations in eukaryotes is less well understood, although the effects are clear. The enzymatic pattern in tissues of omnivorous mammals undergoes massive changes, especially in the liver, as the animals shift from one kind of diet to another. Those enzymes peculiar to the conversion of glucose to fatty acids increase when the diet is rich in carbohydrate, while those peculiar to gluconeogenesis decline. (Enzymes used in both circumstances do not change to a large extent.) The opposite changes occur when the animal eats a diet rich in fats and low in carbohydrates. Diets rich in protein cause an increase in the enzymes necessary for removing and transferring nitrogen, along with the enzymes of urea synthesis. Adaptations of enzyme content also occur in response to changes in the intake of minor components of the diet; the enzymes of cholesterol synthesis decline when the diet contains adequate supplies of cholesterol.

The hormones secreted by one tissue may affect the enzymatic activity in other tissues by acting as a modulating metabolite or by modifying the rate of synthesis or destruction of specific enzymes. Several hormones act as activators or inhibitors of adenyl cyclase in the plasma membrane of receptor cells. These include not only adrenaline, glucagon, and perhaps insulin,

but also prostaglandins, which are recently discovered derivatives of polyunsaturated fatty acids with widespread functions. The hormones that modify the rate of protein synthesis include several of the steroid hormones, such as the androgens, estrogens, and cortisol.

Blood draining from the hypothalamus in the base of the brain passes to the anterior pituitary gland. The hypothalamus secretes several small peptides acting as specific releasing factors or inhibitory factors to control the release of peptide hormones from the anterior pituitary gland. For example, neural signals to the hypothalamus of emotional or physical stress cause the appearance of a corticotropin releasing factor, which in turn provokes the release of corticotropin from the anterior pituitary gland. Corticotropin travels through the general circulation to the adrenal glands, where it causes an accelerated formation of cortisol from pregnenolone. Finally, cortisol acts on many tissues, especially the muscles and viscera, to mobilize protein for use as a fuel and to suppress the utilization of glucose. It also diminishes inflammation. The concentration of cortisol is controlled through negative feedback, presumably by inhibition of the appearance of corticotropin releasing factor from the hypothalamus.

Other peptide hormones secreted by the anterior pituitary include somatotropin, which indirectly affects carcass growth, and thyrotropin, which stimulates the release of thyroxine from the thyroid gland. Thyroxine is formed by iodination of residues of tyrosine in a particular protein, thyroglobulin. It is necessary for normal development, and increases the metabolic rate in some unknown way.

We shall summarize in this chapter the processes by which metabolism is controlled. Control involves changes in the rates of enzymatic reactions, which may be made in two general ways. The rate of catalysis by existing molecules of enzymes may be altered, or the number of molecules of enzyme may be altered.

Control mechanisms may also be subdivided according to the signal causing a response. Some controls hinge upon changes in metabolite concentrations within the cell being regulated. Multicellular organism have another dimension of control through the action of hormones that are secreted by one tissue as a means of altering the metabolic activities of other tissues.

Either kind of signal may be used with either mechanism. That is, changes in internal metabolite concentration or changes in the level of circulating hormones may alter the effectiveness of given molecules of enzyme or may cause the enzyme to be synthesized or destroyed faster.

CHANGES IN SUBSTRATE CONCENTRATION

The simplest way to alter the rate of any enzyme is to change the concentration of one of its substrates. We have discussed the principle and cited examples, but experience shows that simple principles are sometimes forgotten in the excitement of tackling new problems, and this is especially true in the field of metabolic regulation. Let us consider a few examples to reinforce the principle.

Utilization of Fuels. Let us first emphasize again that the primary regulation of the rate of utilization of the major fuels comes from the effects of changes in ADP concentration on the rates of reactions utilizing ADP as a substrate. This is true of both aerobic and anaerobic processes. When more high-energy phosphate is used, more ADP is produced, and a higher ADP concentration accelerates the reactions that utilize ADP and produce ATP. All other regulatory mechanisms in fuel metabolism appear to be secondary adjustments superimposed on this primary regulation.

Pentose Phosphate Pathway. The rate of the pentose phosphate pathway in animals and in many protists is probably controlled by the availability of NADP. The rate-limiting step in the pathway is the initial glucose 6-phosphate dehydrogenase reaction, and measurements indicate that the concentration of NADP limits the rate of the dehydrogenase. Now, the pentose phosphate pathway converts NADP to

NADPH, and NADPH is used for various synthetic reactions, in which it is converted back to NADP. The result is that the rate of the pentose phosphate pathway is automatically adjusted so as to replace the NADPH being consumed. When the pathway has created a high NADPH/NADP ratio, it slows down and will remain slow until some synthetic process lowers the ratio by consuming NADPH and creating a higher concentration of NADP.

For example, a major process utilizing NADPH in animals is the synthesis of fatty acids from acetyl coenzyme A. An animal actively synthesizing fatty acids ought to have a higher concentration of NADP (and lower NADPH) than an animal that is supplied pre-formed fat. Experiments show that the NADP content in the livers of rats fed a high-glucose diet is indeed some seven times greater than the NADP content of the livers of rats fed a high-fat diet, or starved. The highest concentrations are still below the K_M value of glucose 6-phosphate dehydrogenase, meaning that the rate of the dehydrogenase is influenced by the concentration of NADP over the entire range.

Urea Synthesis. The rate-limiting step in the formation of urea is the synthesis of carbamyl phosphate. Is this step controlled by the concentration of NH_4^+? We have evidence suggesting that it is. Some children are born with genetic defects in the formation of carbamyl phosphate synthetase, causing the content of the enzyme to be low. (Total loss would be lethal.) These children have a dangerous hyperammonemia, that is, a high concentration of NH_4^+ in their blood, but they still excrete most of their excess nitrogen as urea. This is what would be expected if the NH_4^+ concentration controls the rate of urea synthesis, and let us analyze why.

Normal individuals have the capability of removing ammonium ion much faster than it is produced; that is, they contain sufficient carbamyl phosphate synthetase so that its V_{max} is much greater than the rate of NH_4^+ production. Only a small fraction of that V_{max} is necessary for removal of NH_4^+ to equal its formation. Therefore, NH_4^+ will be depleted to form urea until its concentration has dropped to a low concentration, well below the K_M for the synthetase, before the rate of urea formation is slowed enough to balance the rate of NH_4^+ production.

The children who lack the ability to make normal amounts of carbamyl phosphate synthetase have a substantially lower V_{max} for the enzyme. The enzyme must be operating at a much greater than normal fraction of V_{max} in order to make the removal of ammonium ion balance its production, which means that the NH_4^+ concentration cannot fall as far as it does in normal individuals. Q.E.D. The rate of urea formation is normal because the NH_4^+ concentration will rise until the rate of its removal by the smaller amount of enzyme equals the rate of its production.

MODULATION OF ENZYME ACTIVITY

Regulation of the synthesis of body constituents and secondary adjustments in fuel metabolism are principally made by altering the activity of enzymes, through changes in either the nature or the quantity of the enzyme molecules. The nature of an enzyme—its ability to bind substrates and catalyze reactions—can be changed in several ways.

Modulation by Effectors

We have seen many examples of regulation of an enzyme through binding of a metabolite at a regulatory site. The result may be a competitive inhibition of a simple enzyme, or a more complex allosteric activation or inhibition of an enzyme with multiple catalytic sites. These modulations serve to adjust the rate of syntheses to the need for the product, or to mobilize stored materials when the time for their utilization has arrived.

Peptides as Effectors. Alterations in enzyme activity can also be caused by combination with other proteins. For example, we saw that a cyclic AMP-binding peptide will associate with a protein kinase when cyclic AMP is absent, and inhibit the kinase (p. 312). One enzyme may affect another; glycogen phosphorylase a combines with glycogen synthase phosphatase and inhibits it (p. 317).

TRYPTOPHAN SYNTHASE. An even better example of protein interaction is seen with the tryptophan synthase of *E. coli,* which is composed of two peptides. One forms indole:

$$\text{indoleglycerol 3-phosphate} \longrightarrow \text{indole} + \text{glyceraldehyde 3-phosphate.}$$

The other utilizes indole:

$$\text{indole} + \text{serine} \longrightarrow \text{tryptophan.}$$

When they combine, the reaction becomes the sum of the two separate reactions:

$$\text{indoleglycerol 3-phosphate} + \text{serine} \longrightarrow \text{tryptophan} + \text{glyceraldehyde 3-phosphate,}$$

but the important point is that the combined reaction goes at a much faster rate than does either of the individual reactions when catalyzed by the separated peptides. (Some organisms improve on the arrangement by synthesizing a single long peptide that contains both enzymatic activities in different domains.)

LACTOSE SYNTHESIS. The lactose synthase in the mammary gland is an example of an enzyme that catalyzes different reactions in the presence and absence of a modulating protein. The enzyme catalyzes the transfer of galactosyl groups from

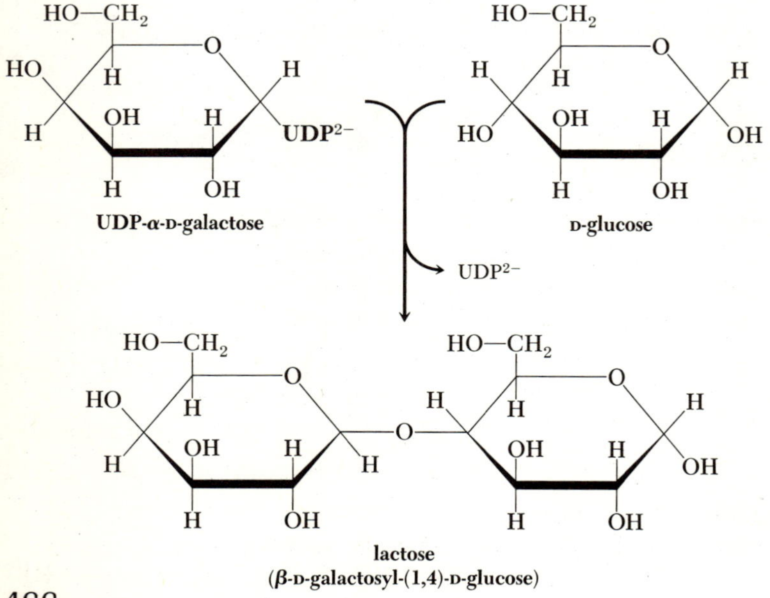

Figure 30-1 The synthesis of lactose.

Figure 30–2 Residues of L-fucose (6-deoxy-L-galactose) commonly occur on the end of carbohydrate chains in glycoproteins, but they also occur as part of the milk sugar in monotremes.

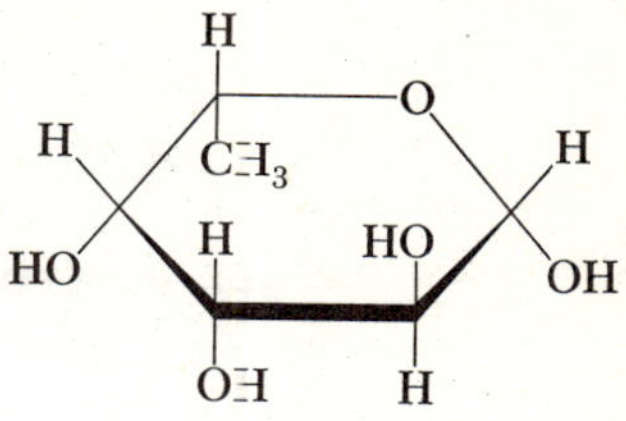

UDP-galactose to N-acetylglucosamine, and it is related to the enzymes that construct the relatively short polysaccharide chains on glycoproteins. However, the enzyme combines with α-lactalbumin, another protein synthesized by the mammary gland when milk production begins, and the combination changes the specificity of the enzyme so that it transfers galactosyl groups to glucose to form lactose (Fig. 30–1), which is the principal carbohydrate in milk.

It appears reasonable to conclude that the evolution of the mammary gland involved a modification of an already existing enzyme used in constructing glycoproteins so that it would produce an unusual disaccharide as a major fuel for the suckling infant. (The advantage of the unusual sugar is that its formation can be regulated independently of the maternal glucose metabolism.) This view is strongly reinforced by recent examination of the milk of the echidna and the platypus. These Antipodean monotremes are near the bottom of the mammalian evolutionary ladder, and the carbohydrates in their milk are a fucosylgalactosylglucose (fucosyllactose), and a fucosylfucosylgalactosylglucose (difucosyllactose), respectively. The L-fucose residue (Fig. 30–2) is formed by all kinds of animals, but it was formerly known only as a terminal residue on the carbohydrate chains of some glycoproteins. Its occurrence in milk sugars buttresses the idea that they were created by a modification of an enzyme used for making glycoproteins.

Modulation by Covalent Alteration

Phosphorylation. The activity of an enzyme molecule may be altered in a definitive way by some covalent reaction. We have seen several examples in which seryl residues are phosphorylated to change the activity of particular enzymes: Phosphorylation activates glycogen phosphorylase, glycogen phosphorylase kinase, and perhaps adipose tissue lipase. It inhibits glycogen synthase, pyruvate dehydrogenase, and acetyl CoA carboxylase, and counteracts the effect of the inhibitory component of troponin.

Adenylylation. The glutamine synthetase of *E. coli* is regulated by a variant of the phosphorylation mechanism in which an AMP residue, rather than a phosphate

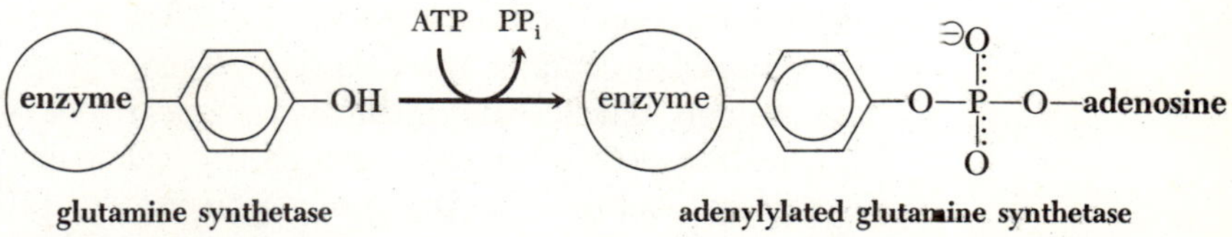

Figure 30–3 The glutamine synthetase of *E. coli* is regulated by attachment of an AMP group, rather than a phosphate group, and attachment is made to the phenolic hydroxyl group of a tyrosine residue.

group, is attached to the enzyme protein by transfer from ATP. The attachment is made to a tyrosyl side chain (Fig. 30–3), and has been termed adenylylation by derivation from adenylic acid, the old term for AMP. The transferase catalyzing the attachment is subject to an extraordinary number of complex controls that is beyond the scope of our discussion, all apparently designed to insure a balanced production of glutamate and glutamine in the cell.

Hydrolysis of Peptides. We have already shown how many hydrolytic enzymes are formed through hydrolysis of proenzymes. This is a clear example of modulation of enzyme activity; its importance as a means of adjusting intracellular metabolism has not been demonstrated.

CHANGES IN ENZYME CONCENTRATION

Enzymes, like other cellular constituents, are constantly being made and destroyed. The amount of an enzyme may therefore be changed by altering the rate of synthesis or the rate of destruction. The half-life of an enzyme is minutes in some cases and days in others, and comparable times will be required for substantial changes in its concentration. Enzymes most susceptible to control in this way are likely to have the shortest half-lives.

Changes in the rate of synthesis of an enzyme appear to be more common than changes in the rate of destruction. We know more of the mechanism by which this is done in some prokaryotic cells, but have a better picture of the general metabolic patterns in the eukaryotic mammals. Much less is known about the regulation of enzyme content in the higher plants, except that there is now evidence for the kinds of controls seen in prokaryotes.

Induction and Repression in Prokaryotes

The DNA of prokaryotes frequently is arranged so that the transcription of mRNA for several related enzymes is regulated as a single unit, or **operon.** That is, the cistrons for different enzymes involved in the same process sometimes follow one another on DNA, and the entire group is headed by an additional sequence of nucleotides that includes a controlling site. This controlling site has a region of DNA (the **operator**) that specifically binds a protein acting as a signal. Some of the protein-operator combinations cause an initiation of mRNA formation that will not occur in the absence of the protein. In such cases the protein is said to be an **activator** of the operon, which is under positive control. Other operators combine with a protein to prevent mRNA formation. In such cases the protein is an inhibitor, or **repressor,** of the operon, which is under negative control. Let us look at some actual examples to see how these systems work.

The *lac* Operon. One of the most thoroughly studied operons in *E. coli* controls the synthesis of enzymes responsible for metabolizing lactose. This operon contains the information for transcription of mRNA coding for three different proteins; that is, the operon contains three structural genes (Fig. 30–4). The relationship of one of the proteins to lactose metabolism is not clear. The others are a protein that participates in the transport of lactose through the cell membrane, and a β-galactosidase that hydrolyzes lactose to its constituent glucose and galactose. In other words, the operon codes for the proteins responsible for bringing external lactose into the cell and for beginning its metabolism.

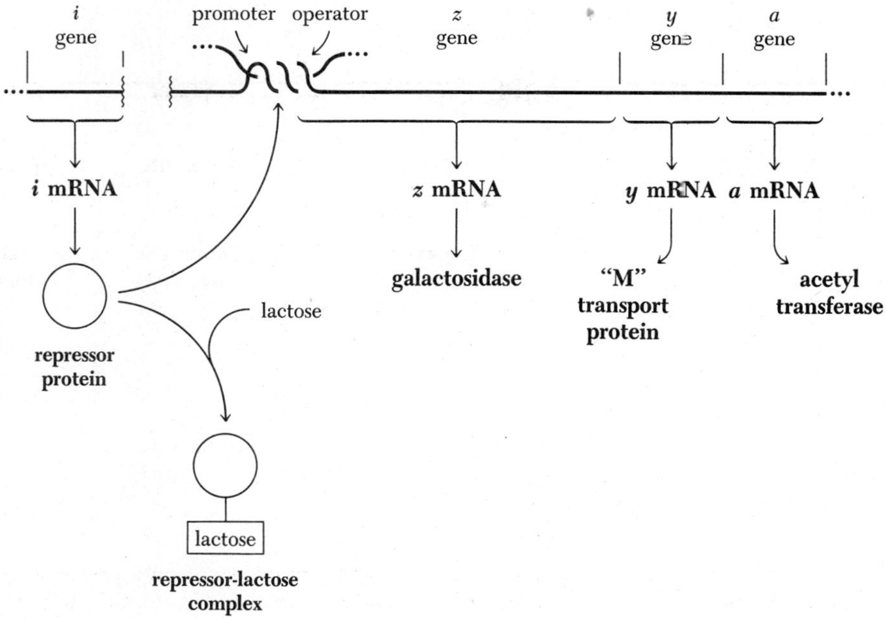

Figure 30–4 The *lac* operon of *E. coli* contains three structural genes that code for mRNA formation, and an operator and promoter region. A separately located gene codes for an mRNA from which an inhibitory protein is synthesized. This repressor protein will bind with the operator region of the *lac* operon and prevent transcription unless lactose is present. The lactose-repressor complex is not inhibitory.

The *lac* operon is regulated by the presence or absence of a repressor protein, which is synthesized in response to mRNA transcribed from another part of the *E. coli* DNA. This repressor, which is a protein of approximately 160,000 M.W., apparently has a protrusion of some 50 amino acid residues that specifically bind to the operator region of the *lac* operon, and prevent mRNA initiation. The binding is very tight; the dissociation constant for the repressor-DNA complex is approximately 10^{-13} M. However, the repressor protein has a second binding site with an affinity for β-galactosides, such as lactose. The combination of lactose with the protein alters its conformation so that it no longer effectively combines with the *lac* operon. Lactose is therefore an inducer of the formation of the three structural proteins coded by the operon, because it prevents attachment of the repressor protein.

The Arabinose Operon. Now let us consider an example of both negative and positive control. *E. coli* is capable of metabolizing a variety of odd sugars; one of these is L-arabinose. The three enzymes utilized for this purpose have no other function, and it is therefore economical to make them only when L-arabinose is available.

The arabinose operon is also regulated through the binding of a protein that is made in response to information from another regulatory gene (Fig. 30–5), and the protein switches between two conformations, depending upon the presence or absence of L-arabinose. However, in this case both conformations of the regulatory protein are active regulators. The conformation existing in the absence of arabinose combines with the operator as an inhibitor. The conformation created by combination with arabinose will not bind effectively with the operator, but it does bind with the initiator region, and this binding is required for initiation of mRNA transcription.

Cyclic AMP and Transcription. The regulation of gene transcription in prokaryotes also involves the action of adenyl cyclase. Initiation of mRNA formation in the *lac* or arabinose operons, and in operons necessary for handling other unusual fuels, requires the presence of a "catabolite-activator-protein" that contains bound cyclic AMP. Unless the adenyl cyclase of these organisms is functioning, they cannot make the enzymes necessary for handling many fuels. Now, their adenyl cyclase is inhibited by metabolites of carbohydrate metabolism. The result is that organisms in a medium

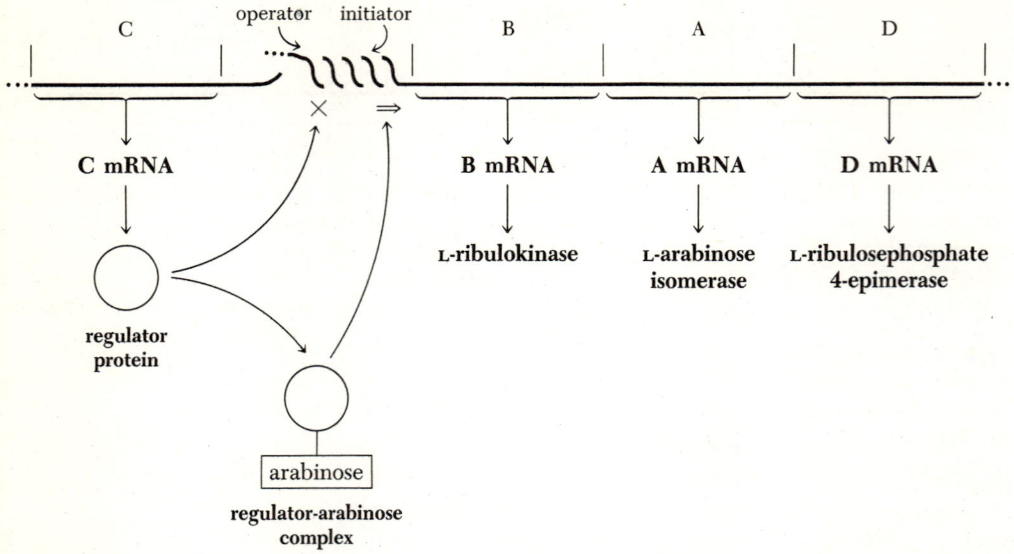

Figure 30-5 Binding of L-arabinose to a regulator protein not only prevents the inhibition of the arabinose operon ordinarily seen in the absence of L-arabinose, but the complex is also required for initiation of transcription of the three structural genes.

containing ample glucose will not make cyclic AMP, and therefore cannot induce the formation of enzymes for the metabolism of lactose and the like, even if these fuels are also present. The organism has no need for expending energy to develop the capability of handling other fuels when it has ample glucose. It has only so much room for enzymes, and gluttony in a rich environment might be lethal.

Enzymatic Adaptations in Mammals

Animals also respond to altered biochemical environments by changes in enzyme content. This is especially true of omnivorous mammals, such as rats and men, that are built to live on widely different diets. In the absence of detailed information on the mechanism by which these changes occur, it is safer to use adaptation, a noncommittal term, to describe them.

Adaptations to Dietary Fuels. The changes in enzyme content occurring in response to alterations in the intake of fuels are like most enzymatic adaptations in that they appear to be secondary adjustments to changing circumstances, rather than primary regulating events. Most changes are what one would predict are necessary for efficient utilization of the fuels. The concentrations of enzymes are increased as necessary to handle increased intakes of a fuel, and excessive amounts of other enzymes that are not being used to capacity are discarded. The changes are most prominent in the visceral tissues.

Although the fuel content of an animal's diet may be described by the individual amounts of fat, carbohydrate, and protein, it is more common to describe the fuel consumption in terms of potential energy production, such as kilojoules per day, and then specify the fraction of that potential represented by the individual types of fuel (only two must be specified to define the third, if the total is known. A diet cannot be simultaneously high in carbohydrate, fat, and protein.)

The Effects of Carbohydrate *vs.* Fat Diets. When the diet of an omnivore changes so that fat replaces carbohydrate as the major fuel, or *vice versa,* many-fold changes occur in the content of enzymes involved in synthesizing fat from carbohydrate and in synthesizing glucose from amino acids. For example, the changes occurring in the liver of rats upon shifting from a low-carbohydrate diet to one in which glucose is the major fuel are as follows (Fig. 30–6):

The content of **glucokinase** increases, as is necessary to cope with the higher concentrations of glucose in the portal blood following a high-carbohydrate meal. However, the content of the **hexokinases** does not change significantly; these enzymes are believed to be responsible for taking up glucose for maintenance purposes, such as the formation of osamines, uronates, pentoses, and so on.

Since most of the other enzymes in the Embden-Meyerhof pathway are involved in the formation of glucose by gluconeogenesis as well as in its conversion to pyruvate for fatty acid synthesis when it is plentiful, their contents also do not change strikingly upon shifting fuels, except for the content of **pyruvate kinase,** which is used in the formation of pyruvate, but not in gluconeogenesis. The content of pyruvate kinase increases to aid in the conversion of phospho-*enol*-pyruvate to pyruvate, and thence to acetyl coenzyme A. On the other hand, the content of **phospho-*enol*-pyruvate carboxykinase,** which forms phospho-*enol*-pyruvate from oxaloacetate during gluconeogenesis, declines.

The amounts of all of the enzymes peculiar to fatty acid synthesis increase in a rat eating ample supplies of a high-glucose diet. These include **acetyl CoA carboxylase, fatty acid synthase,** the **citrate cleavage enzyme,** and the **NADP-specific malate dehydrogenase** of the cytosol. (The NAD-specific enzyme does not change; it is also necessary for amino acid metabolism, and for gluconeogenesis.) The contents of the

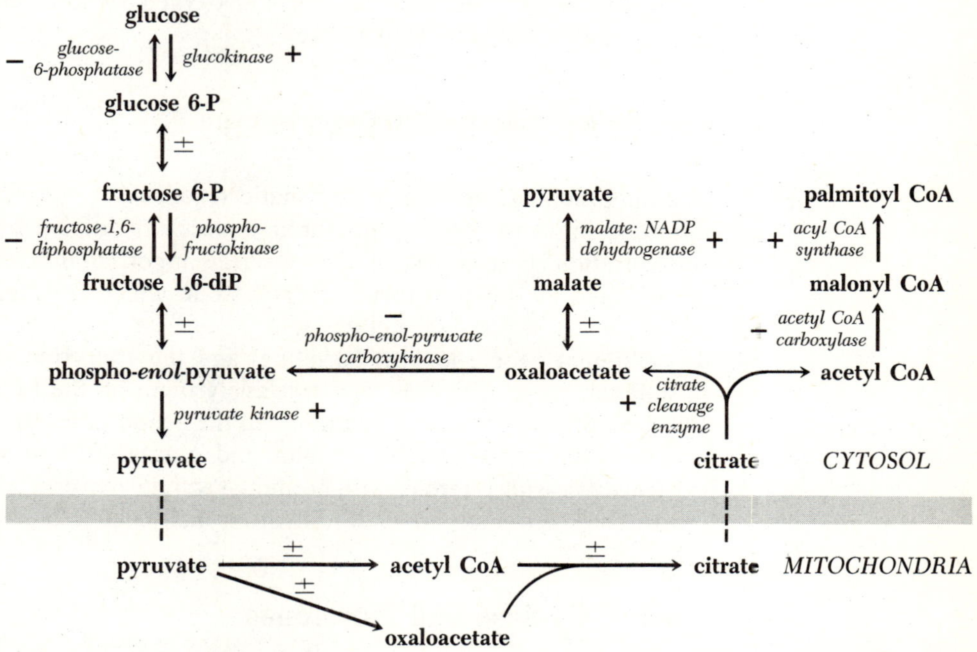

Figure 30–6 Metabolic adaptations to a diet rich in glucose or starch include an increased synthesis of enzymes necessary for the synthesis of fatty acids from glucose, shown by bold plus signs, a decreased synthesis of enzymes necessary for gluconeogenesis, shown by bold minus signs. Those enzymes necessary both for fatty acid synthesis and for gluconeogenesis do not change, and are shown by ± symbols.

NADP-specific **glucose 6-phosphate** and **6-phosphogluconate dehydrogenases** also increase on a high-glucose diet to insure ability to meet the increased demand for NADPH created by more rapid fatty acid synthesis.

Finally, the key enzymes of gluconeogenesis decline in activity. There is no point in maintaining a high capacity to synthesize glucose in an animal eating large quantities in its diet, and the amounts of **glucose 6-phosphatase** and of **fructose 1,6-diphosphatase,** as well as of phospho-*enol*-pyruvate carboxykinase, fall.

Adaptations to Altered Protein Intake. Variations in the consumption of protein cause corresponding variations in the content of many enzymes involved in nitrogen metabolism. For example, the contents of enzymes required for **urea synthesis** rise or fall as the dietary protein intake rises or falls. Enzymes involved with the metabolism of individual amino acids also may change with dietary intake. The **aminotransferases** in the liver cytosol adapt, but those in the mitochondria do not, because they are also involved in more general metabolic transformations.

Other Dietary Adaptations. Some cellular components occur in the food, but they may be synthesized when the dietary supply is inadequate. In such cases, the enzymes are made by the cells only when supplementation of the dietary supply is necessary. For example, **cholesterol** may be absorbed from the food, or synthesized from acetyl coenzyme A. The first step peculiar to cholesterol synthesis, and the rate-limiting step, is the reduction of 3-hydroxy-3-methylglutaryl coenzyme A to mevalonate. The amount of the reductase synthesized in the liver is controlled by the cholesterol concentration. More cholesterol, less reductase. Therefore, an adequate dietary supply will diminish internal synthesis.

Similarly, the first reaction in **heme** synthesis is the condensation of succinyl coenzyme A and glycine catalyzed by 5-aminolevulinate synthase. The content of this enzyme appears to adapt to the amount of uncombined end-product present. If there is insufficient apoprotein present to combine with heme, then heme will accumulate and be converted to hemin by reaction with oxygen. Hemin then represses the formation of more 5-aminolevulinate synthase.

REGULATION BY HORMONES

The alteration of the rate of enzymatic reactions by hormones is accomplished by the same kinds of mechanisms through which regulation by changes in metabolite concentration is accomplished. However, the important difference is that the hormones are secreted by different tissues than those in which the regulation occurs, and they act as signals in place of metabolites.

Different people look at hormones and the endocrine glands that secrete them in different ways. Chemists tend to classify them on the basis of chemical structure. For example, we have already examined the action of certain **amines** (adrenaline and noradrenaline) and **peptides** (insulin and glucagon), and we have mentioned the existence of various **steroids** with hormonal activity (cortisol, aldosterone, progesterone, testosterone, estradiol, and 1,25-dihydroxycholecalciferol).

Adenyl Cyclase and Hormones

Cell physiologists tend to look at hormones in terms of the mechanism of their action. The mechanisms fall in two classes. Some peptides and amines combine with specific receptor sites in the plasma membranes of target cells, so as to modify the activity of adenyl cyclase. We have noted several examples of hormone action depending upon a stimulation of adenyl cyclase. Changes caused by hormones of this sort will also occur after any other stimulus of adenyl cyclase activity in the target cell, with a resultant change in the concentration of 3′,5′-AMP.

We have noted that the specificity of such hormones in affecting some cells and not others results solely from differences in the plasma membranes of the various kinds of cells. The membranes are built to bind particular hormones and not others, and the specificity of the hormone action comes from specific recognition by the target cells.

Protein Synthesis and Hormones

The second mechanism of hormone action is a combination of hormone, usually a steroid, with specific receptor proteins inside the cell, so as to cause in some way a change in the rate of synthesis of particular proteins. Changes in protein synthesis may be due to a specific interaction with some chromosomal component, thereby altering the rate of synthesis of mRNA by transcription of DNA, or it may be due to an extra-nuclear interaction that changes the effectiveness of mRNA as a messenger, causing more or less peptide to be translated per unit time from a given mRNA molecule.

The steroids that affect specific tissue development, such as **testosterone, progesterone,** and **estradiol,** appear to act through mechanisms of this sort. Target cells, such as those in the genitalia or those responsible for development of secondary sexual characteristics, are stimulated to grow by the appropriate gonadal hormone through alterations in the rate of protein synthesis, primarily by accelerating the rate of formation of mRNA. The stimulation involves the combination of the steroid hormone, or some modified form like **dihydrotestosterone,** with a receptor protein built specifically to interact with the particular hormone.

Adrenal Cortex and Pituitary Function

Some hormones act primarily on other endocrine glands, providing another dimension of control. We can appreciate this best by tracing the sequence of events involved in causing the adrenal cortex to secrete cortisol (Fig. 30–7).

Hypothalamus. The chain of stimulation for the adrenal cortex begins in the hypothalamus, a part of the base of the brain near the pituitary gland. Some of the cells of the hypothalamus receive impulses signalling stress, such as anxiety, injury, or pain, and translate them into chemical terms by releasing a small peptide known as **corticotropin releasing factor** into blood vessels that go from the hypothalamus to part of the pituitary gland. (These blood vessels constitute a portal circulation, analogous to the portal circulation leading from the intestines to the liver.)

Anterior Pituitary Gland. The pituitary gland, or hypophysis, is like the adrenal gland in being two distinct tissues. The anterior pituitary gland (adenohypophysis) contains some cells with specific receptor sites for the corticotropin releasing factor arriving from the hypothalamus, and combination of the releasing factor with those sites activates adenyl cyclase. The resultant increase in the concentration of 3′,5′-AMP causes the release of a peptide hormone, **corticotropin.** In other words, the signal for the ultimate secretion of cortisol appears as corticotropin releasing factor, then as 3′,5′-AMP, and finally as corticotropin within specific cells of the anterior pituitary gland.

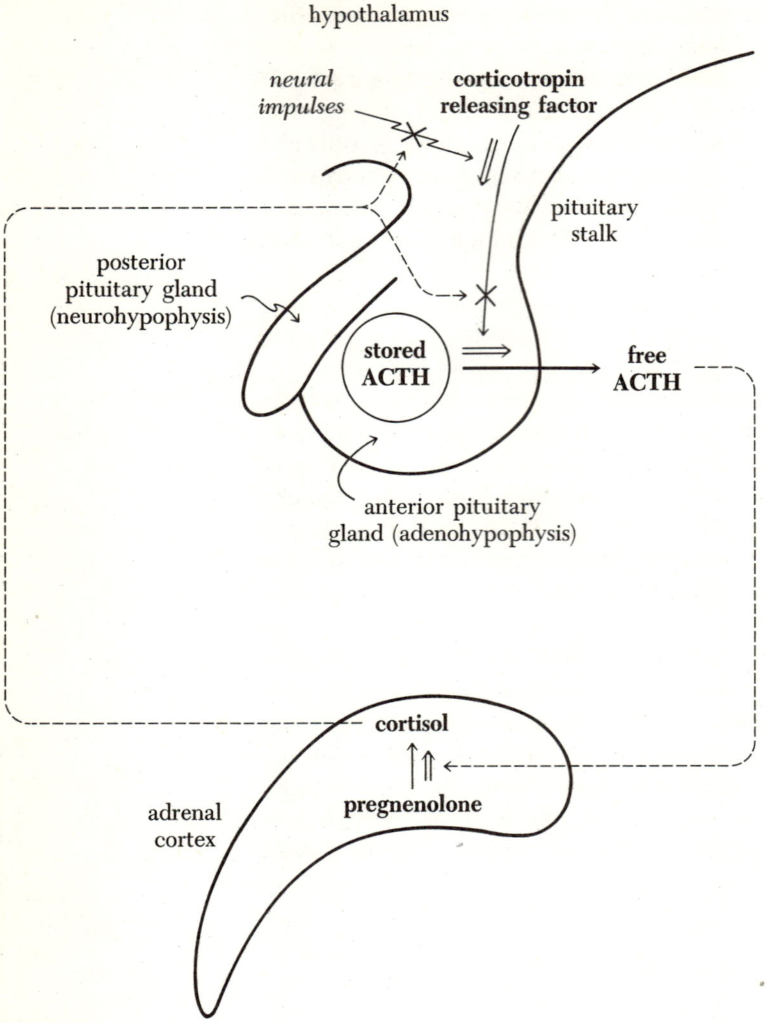

Figure 30–7 The pituitary-adrenal axis. Neural impulses cause the release of corticotropin-releasing factor from the pituitary stalk and its transport to the anterior pituitary gland through a portal circulation, unless inhibited by already high concentrations of cortisol. The releasing factor stimulates the release of corticotropin (ACTH), which travels through the circulation and stimulates the cortex of the adrenal gland to convert pregnenolone to cortisol. As the cortisol level rises, it progressively inhibits the steps necessary for its own formation, through its action in the pituitary stalk.

Action of Corticotropin. Corticotropin contains only 39 amino acid residues, but it has two distinct properties. It forms tight complexes with specific binding sites on target cells, and it activates adenyl cyclase in those cells. Among these target cells are the **adipocytes** of adipose tissue, and we have already noted that corticotropin, like glucagon or adrenaline, causes a release of fatty acids because it activates adenyl cyclase in adipose tissue. The mobilization of fat for use as a fuel is therefore one of the responses to the original neural signal of stress to the hypothalamus.

However, the most important sites of action of corticotropin are in the **adrenal cortex.** It gets its name, a shortened version of adrenocorticotropin (ACTH), because it stimulates the formation of **cortisol** from pregnenolone. Most of the responses to the original signal in the central nervous system therefore are the effects of cortisol on its target tissues.

Action of Cortisol. Cortisol acts to alter the rate of synthesis of particular proteins in its target tissues. The details of the mechanism are not known, except that it involves combination with a specific receptor protein within the target cell.

The important targets for cortisol include the muscles and the viscera, in which it causes an increase in the activity of enzymes responsible for the degradation of proteins, and it suppresses the utilization of glucose. The result is an increase in the glycogen stores of the body, both because of increased formation from the amino acids of the body's own stores, and because of its decreased utilization. Steroids with these effects are known as **glucocorticoids.**

Cortisol also dimishes inflammation from various causes, and this is the reason for most of its therapeutic uses. Treatment with it is not undertaken lightly, in part because of a rebound phenomenon that disturbs the endocrine balance in a potentially dangerous way. This is due to a control by cortisol of its own production through negative feedback to the hypothalamus, suppressing the transfer of corticotropin releasing factor to the anterior pituitary gland. When cortisol is administered, it therefore slows down its own formation, owing to diminished levels of corticotropin (ACTH). If the cortisol administration is suddenly stopped, the resultant precipitous drop in its concentration causes a sharp stimulation of corticotropin formation, affecting not only the adrenal cortex, but also other tissues.

Other Functions of the Anterior Pituitary. There are many specialized cells in the anterior pituitary, each secreting a peptide hormone in response to specific signals from the hypothalamus in the form of small peptides. (These peptides act as releasing factors in most cases, but the formation of **prolactin,** which stimulates the secretion of milk by the mammary gland, is inhibited by its controlling hypothalamic peptide; the hypothalamus signals "Don't secrete" to the prolactin-forming cells instead of the usual positive signal.) Let us summarize the function of some of these hormones.

SOMATOTROPIN. Somatotropin, or growth hormone, contains 190 amino acid residues in the human. The hormone is specifically bound to the liver, the kidney, and the zona glomerulosa of the adrenal cortex, but the major action of interest is the stimulation of the formation of still another peptide, **somatomedin** (molecular weight approximately 2000), by the liver. This appears to be the ultimate active factor, with the property of promoting division and growth of cells involved in formation of the skeleton and its attached muscles. Somatotropin also causes the mobilization of fat from adipose tissue. People who lack the capacity to make the hormone tend to be short and fat.

THYROTROPIN. Thyrotropin is also released from specific cells in the pituitary in response to a hypothalamic factor, which is a modified tripeptide: pyroglutamylhistidylprolineamide (Fig. 30–8). The molecule is surprisingly small for such a specific function, but the terminal pyroglutamyl and amide groups presumably are distinctive enough for good recognition by the pituitary cell receptors. Thyrotropin binds to the plasma membrane of cells in the thyroid gland, activating adenyl cyclase. The resultant increased concentration of 3′,5′-AMP causes a release of thyroxine.

Thyroxine is an iodinated derivative of tyrosine (Fig. 30–9), formed in a particular protein, **thyroglobulin,** by the thyroid gland. This protein has a conformation such that particular tyrosyl groups are in positions facilitating iodination and subsequent coupling

Figure 30–8 The structure of thyrotropin releasing factor.

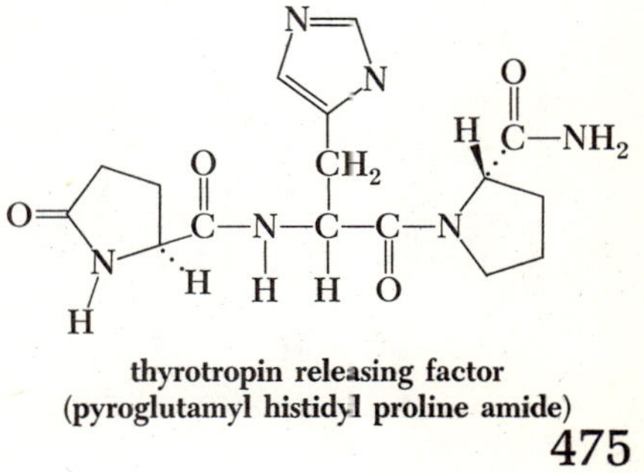

thyrotropin releasing factor
(pyroglutamyl histidyl proline amide)

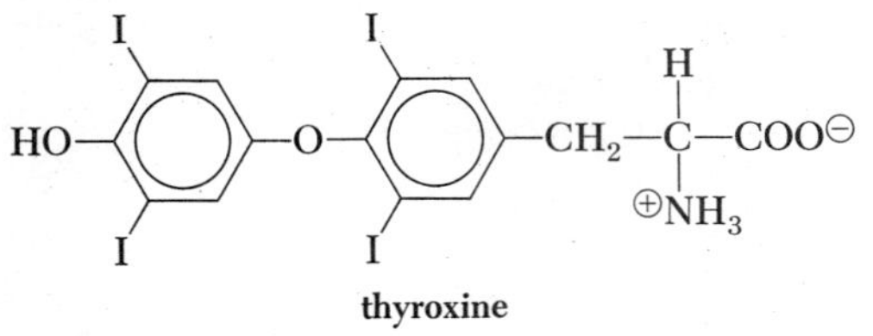

Figure 30-9 Thyroxine is also named as 3,5,3′,5′-tetraiodothyronine.

of two of the residues to make a thyroxine residue in the protein. (Some thyroxine can be formed by iodination of non-specific proteins. The yield is small because of the unfavorable spacing of the tyrosyl residues in most proteins.)

The mode of action of thyroxine is still unknown. It is required for the normal development of young animals. Tadpoles won't change into frogs, and human embryos won't grow into normal children unless some thyroxine is present. In adults, thyroxine causes an increased metabolic rate, that is, it results in a more rapid oxygen consumption. We think of hyperthyroid people as thin and overactive, whereas people lacking thyroid function are lethargic, but the mechanism of these effects is not clear.

PROSTAGLANDINS

Many animal tissues have the capacity to convert 20-carbon polyunsaturated fatty acids into related cyclic and hydroxylated derivatives known as prostaglandins (Fig. 30–10). The parent fatty acids can be made only from polyunsaturated fatty acids in the diet, which may be the major reason why polyunsaturated fatty acids are essential in the diet.

Some six major kinds of prostaglandin are known. The compounds were originally discovered in seminal fluid (hence the name), but their functions are now known to be important for nearly all, if not all, mammalian cells. Most of the actions appear to involve bindings of the hormones to membranes. For example, they block the activation of adenyl cyclase in adipose tissue by other hormones, thereby diminishing release of fatty acids, but they activate adenyl cyclase in many other tissues, including the thyroid and anterior pituitary glands.

One effect of prostaglandins is to promote inflammation. Aspirin inhibits the formation of prostaglandins, and therefore has an anti-inflammatory effect.

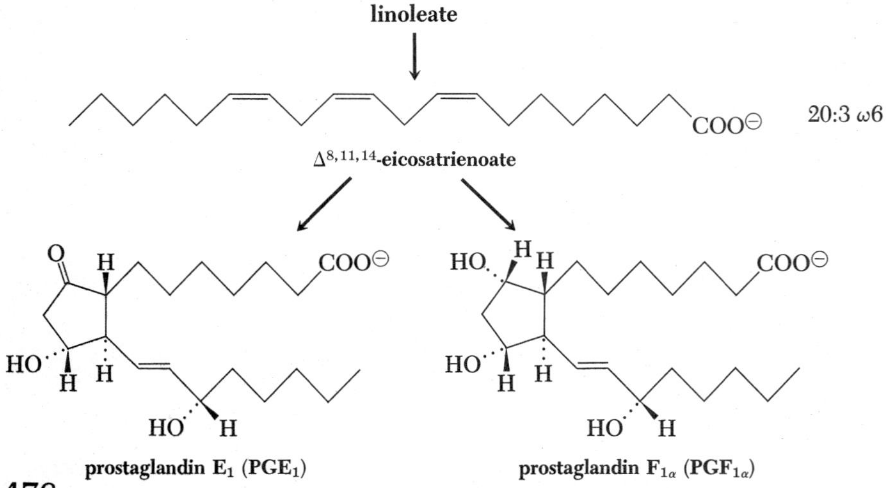

Figure 30–10 The 20-carbon precursors of prostaglandins are synthesized from dietary linoleate. Arachidonate (20:4ω6) is a precursor of additional prostaglandins (not shown).

FURTHER READING

H. J. Vogel, ed., Metabolic Pathways, vol. 5, Metabolic regulation, Academic Press (1971). Detailed accounts of some aspects of modulation by effectors, and induction or repression of mRNA formation.
McGilvery, R. W., Biochemistry, Chap. 23, W. B. Saunders Company (1970). Expanded discussion of some aspects of regulation in mammals.
Guillemen, R., Hypothalamic releasing factors, Ann. Rev. Physiol., 35:357 (1973).
H. V. Rickenberg, ed., Biochemistry of hormones, University Park Press (1974).

QUESTIONS

1. Is the end result of the action of a repressor or activator protein on an operator in *E. coli* a modification of enzymes with respect to their K_M, their V_{max}, both, or neither? Explain.
2. A certain commune subsists mainly on seed vegetables and lean chicken, but one of its members occasionally backslides into an orgy of marbled steak and a continental cuisine that leans heavily on butter and cream as ingredients. Explain why it is reasonable to assume that the amounts of some enzymes in his liver will be higher, some lower, and some about the same when he returns compared to what they were when he left.
3. Why is the occurrence of fucosyl residues in the sugar of monotreme milk of more general significance?
4. Explain why the action of adenyl cyclase in prokaryotes causes changes in the quantity of enzymes present rather than the activity of a given quantity, whereas the reverse is often true in eukaryotic tissues.
5. At what stages between the generation of a neural signal and the changes in glucose utilization is cyclic AMP involved in the production of glucocorticoid action?
6. Why can't prostaglandins be made by total synthesis from acetyl coenzyme A in mammals?

APPENDIX

CHAPTER 31

ANALYSIS AND CHEMICAL PROPERTIES OF BIOLOGICAL COMPOUNDS

The purpose of this appendix is to give additional information on some chemical properties of amino acids, sugars, and fatty acids, and some of the techniques presently being used for their study in the laboratory. It does not give a comprehensive review of the structure and chemical reactions of all natural compounds. The references at the end give more complete accounts of both the organic and analytical chemistries of natural compounds. Modern textbooks of organic chemistry also treat some natural products.

AMINO ACIDS AND PEPTIDES

Structural Formulas (See p. 480)

Acid-Base Behavior

Consider the simplest amino acid, glycine. It can equilibrate with H^+ in two ways:

$$^{\oplus}H_3N{-}CH_2{-}COOH \underset{K_1 = 10^{-2.35}}{\overset{H^{\oplus}}{\rightleftarrows}} {}^{\oplus}H_3N{-}CH_2{-}COO^{\ominus} \underset{K_2 = 10^{-9.78}}{\overset{H^{\oplus}}{\rightleftarrows}} H_2N{-}CH_2{-}COO^{\ominus}$$

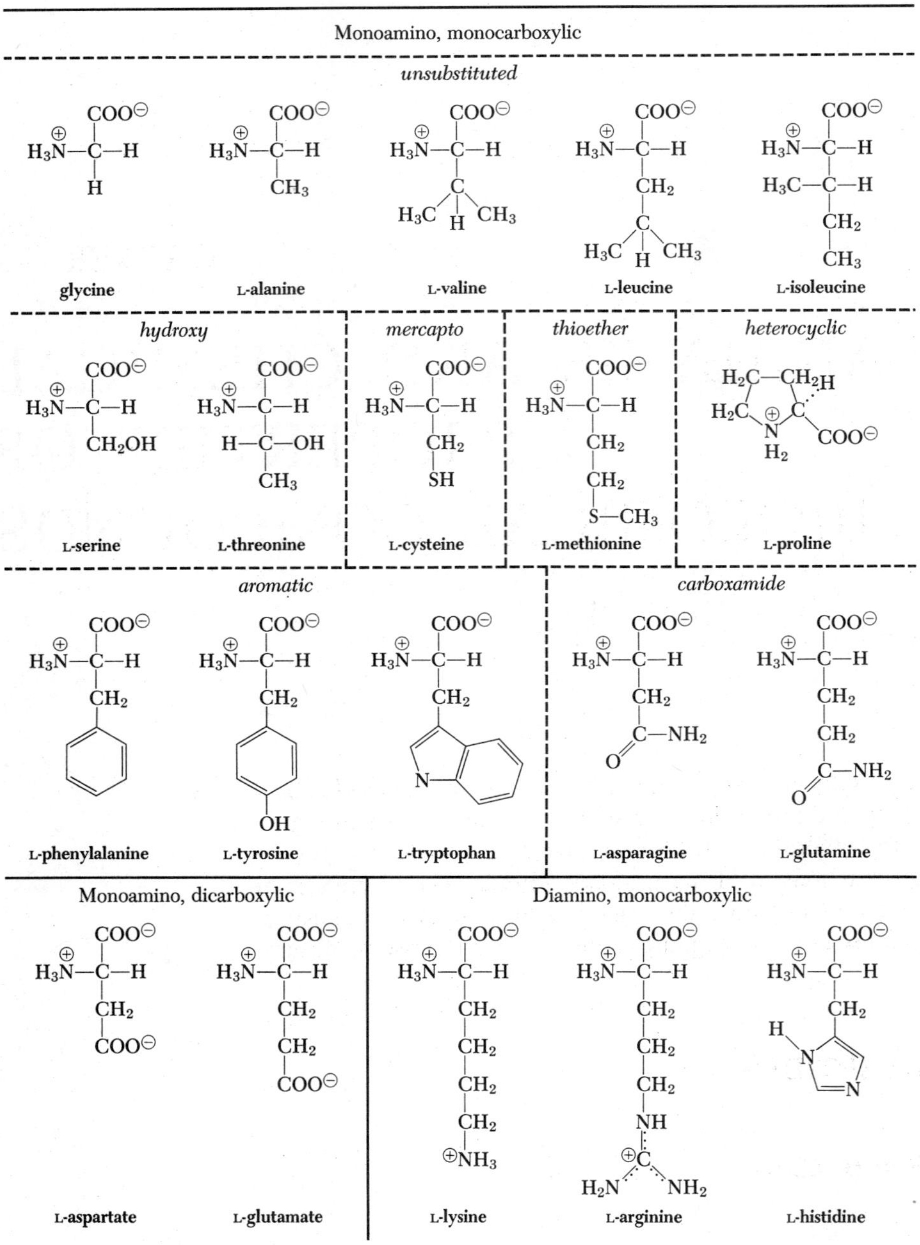
Monoamino, monocarboxylic
unsubstituted
glycine
L-alanine
L-valine
L-leucine
L-isoleucine
hydroxy
L-serine
L-threonine
mercapto
L-cysteine
thioether
L-methionine
heterocyclic
L-proline
aromatic
L-phenylalanine
L-tyrosine
L-tryptophan
carboxamide
L-asparagine
L-glutamine
Monoamino, dicarboxylic
L-aspartate
L-glutamate
Diamino, monocarboxylic
L-lysine
L-arginine
L-histidine

The form shown in the middle is a zwitterion, meaning hermaphrodite ion, that has no net charge because it has equal numbers of positive ammonium groups and negative carboxylate groups. This form can be crystallized as such and is what one has in a bottle of glycine. Suppose one adds HCl to a solution of the zwitterion form. Nothing will happen to the ammonium group; it already has H^+ affixed to the nitrogen. However, the increasing concentration of H^+ will cause the carboxylate group to pick up H^+ to form the undissociated carboxylic group to an extent that is defined by the dissociation constant:

$$\frac{[\text{R—COO}^-][\text{H}^+]}{[\text{R—COOH}]} = K_1 = 10^{-2.35}$$

When $[H^+]$ equals K_1, half the glycine will be in the zwitterion form (designated Z in the figure below), and half will be in the acidic form (designated *A*). Since the acidic form has a net positive charge, it cannot be isolated as such, but must be associated with some anion; in our example, it could be precipitated as glycine hydrochloride if the H^+ concentration is high enough to convert most of the amino acid to that form.

If H^+ is removed from a solution of the zwitterion, for example, by adding NaOH, H^+ will dissociate from the ammonium group to an extent defined by a second dissociation constant:

$$\frac{[\text{R—NH}_2][\text{H}^+]}{[\text{R—NH}_3^+]} = K_2 = 10^{-9.78}$$

As in the first dissociation, the concentration of the basic form (designated *B* in the figure below) will equal the concentration of the zwitterion when $[H^+]$ equals K_2. The basic form still has the negative charge of the carboxylate group, and therefore can be isolated only as the salt of a cation, in this case as sodium glycinate.

The fraction of the zwitterion present at a given H^+ concentration is shown in this graph:

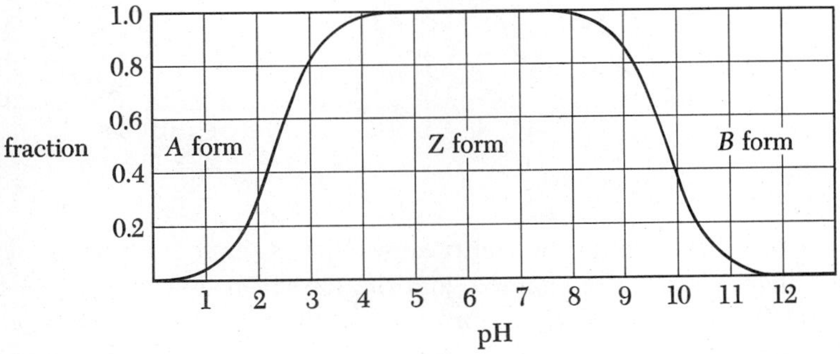

We see that glycine exists mostly as a zwitterion over a broad range centered near 10^{-6} M H^+. The curves at the end are almost the shape of titration curves showing the change in $[H^+]$ of a solution of glycine as one adds successive increments of a strong acid or strong base (reading from the top down); the titration curve isn't quite the same because it takes a little extra reagent to titrate water to the extreme pH values at which glycine is present mostly in the acidic or basic forms.

According to the equations given above for the two dissociations, there must be at least a small loss of H^+ from the ammonium group and a small uptake of H^+ by the carboxylate group at any concentration of H^+, leaving some molecules with net negative and positive charges, respectively. We see from the graph that there must be some [H^+] at which these changes are just balanced so that most of the molecules are zwitterions with no net charge and the very small balance is evenly divided between molecules with net negative and positive charges. This [H^+] is the isoelectric point of glycine, commonly expressed as a pH, at which there will be no net movement of the molecules through an electric field, and it is equal to $\sqrt{K_1K_2}$. pI = ½($pK_1 + pK_2$). This can be shown by setting [R—NH_2] equal to [R—COOH] in the two equations, and solving for [H^+].

The description we have given of the ionization of glycine applies to all of the monoamino, monocarboxylic acids, and most of them have ionization constants close to those of glycine. Now let us consider the amino acids that have additional ionizable groups on their side chains, such as aspartate:

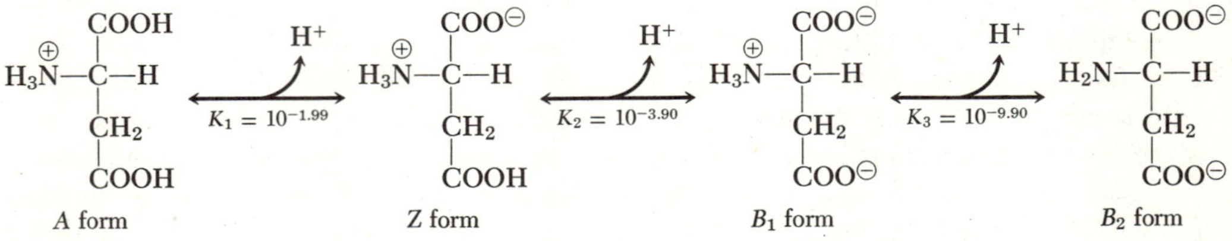

Here we have three distinct equilibria. The ammonium group doesn't behave much differently than the ammonium group of glycine, but the side-chain carboxylic group is a weaker acid and the 1-carboxylic group is a stronger acid than the group on glycine. The way in which the proportion of these forms shifts with [H^+] is shown on the following graph:

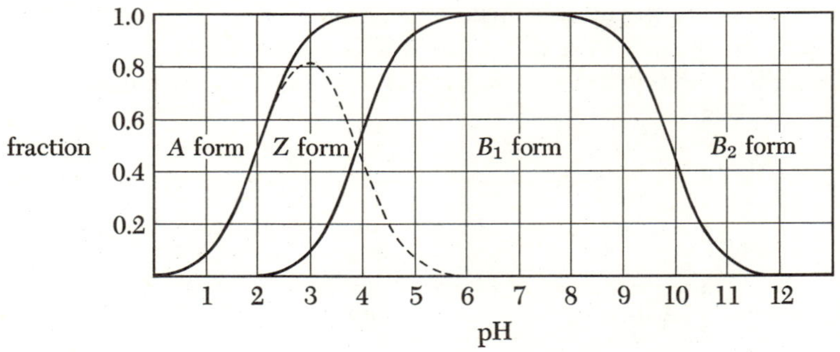

The bell-shaped solid curve in the center shows the fraction existing as the B_1 form, in which all of the groups are charged, and the dashed bell-shaped curve to the left shows the fraction existing as the Z form, in which one of the carboxylic groups is not ionized and the remaining negative charge of the other carboxylate group neutralizes the positive charge of the ammonium group. The other solid curve to the left shows the fraction of the total that is not in the A form (that is, it shows the sum of the Z and B_1 forms). Here we see that aspartate carries one negative charge over a broad range near the physiological pH values.

What is the isoelectric point of aspartic acid? It will be the [H^+] at which there is an average of one negative charge to balance the positively charged ammonium group. This balance will occur when the number of molecules with no negative charges (form A) equals the number with two negative charges (form B_1). When we solve the equilibrium equations for this condition, we find again that the isoelectric [H^+] = $\sqrt{K_1K_2}$, which is $10^{-2.94}$ M in this case. If we want to crystallize aspartic acid, we ought to bring the solution to pH 2.94 so that there will be no charges to attract other ions. If we add one mole of NaOH to a solution of aspartic acid, the [H^+] will fall to $10^{-6.90}$, and if we now precipitate the compound, we will isolate monosodium aspartate. (The $[H^+]$ of a solution of the monosodium salt is equal to $\sqrt{K_2K_3}$ for all practical purposes. The first dissociation constant can be neglected because it is 100-fold greater than the second, which means that near neutral pH the amount of compound with no undissociated carboxylic groups will be only 0.01 that of the amount with one undissociated carboxylic group. This approximation can't be made for multibasic acids in which the dissociation constants are more nearly equal.)

The same kind of reasoning we have applied here can also be used in treating the diamino, monocarboxylic acids such as lysine and arginine. The zwitterion of these compounds will exist at low concentrations of H^+ because there are two acidic forms and only one basic form. (The K' values for lysine are $10^{-2.16}$, $10^{-9.18}$, and $10^{-10.79}$.) The isoelectric point of these compounds is $\sqrt{K_2K_3}$.

Stereoisomers

Let us briefly review what organic chemistry tells us about stereoisomers as it applies to the amino acids. All of the amino acids that are introduced into peptide chains by protein synthesis have one carbon (C-2) that is bonded to four different groups, except glycine, which has two H atoms. There are two possible arrangements of groups around such an asymmetric center:

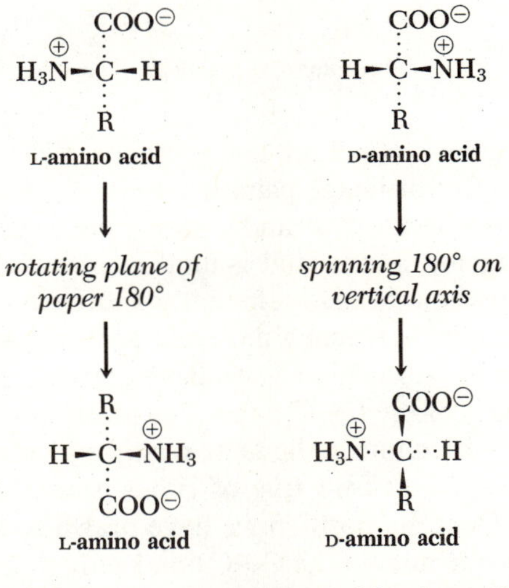

Amino acids having one of the arrangements are said to have the L-configuration; those with the other have the D-configuration. The two configurations are mirror images of each other, and like all mirror images of asymmetric objects cannot be superimposed no matter how they are turned. We have noted that the natural amino acids used for protein synthesis have the L-configuration.

D and L isomers have the same chemical and physical properties in many cases. Many chemical reactions involve reagents with symmetrical molecules that can approach a molecule of either the D or the L isomer at an orientation that will make contact with the same reacting groups. However, this is not true of an asymmetrical reacting compound. It is not possible to set down models of D and L isomers on a sheet of paper so that the contacts are identical, and this is the reason many enzymes catalyze the reaction of only one stereoisomer.

D and L isomers also differ in their effect on polarized light passing through the compound. Each isomer has a spatial sense analogous to the sense of a screw; a right-hand screw is still a right-hand screw if one views it from the opposite end. The spatial sense represents a different order of arrangement of electron fields in the compounds, and the result is that a D-isomer oscillates to shift the electric vector of the light quantum in one direction and the L-isomer causes it to shift an equal amount in the opposite direction. We see the result as a change in the plane of polarization of linearly polarized light, and the measurement of this ***optical activity*** can be used to measure the relative amounts of D and L isomers in a solution. (A helix also has a spatial sense and causes changes in the optical activity of a peptide compared to that of a random arrangement of the same primary structure.)

It is common to designate a stereoisomer in structural formulas by a convention in which all vertical bonds are directed behind the plane of the paper and all horizontal bonds are directed in front of the plane of the paper. Some of the ways in which L-alanine can be written according to this convention were illustrated on p. 6. A useful rule of thumb is that interchanging any two substituents on each asymmetric carbon in a conventional structural formula gives a representation of the other stereoisomer; making any two such interchanges gives another representation of the same stereoisomer.

Diastereoisomers. Some amino acids have more than one asymmetric carbon atom. Consider L-threonine, which has four possible stereoisomers:

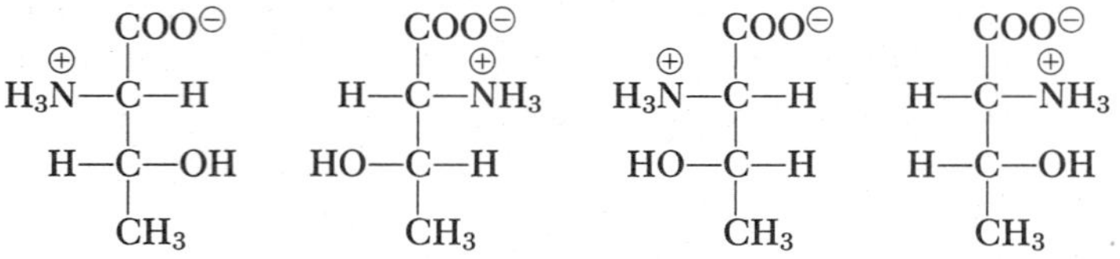

L-threonine D-threonine L-allothreonine D-allothreonine

Each of the four is a different compound, and only one, L-threonine, occurs naturally in proteins. There are two mirror-image pairs represented, and the two pairs are given different names. This is so because D- and L-threonine have similar behavior with symmetrical chemical reagents, and D- and L-allothreonine have similar behavior, but L-threonine and L-allothreonine behave differently and have different melting points, solubilities, and so on. Imagine a reacting molecule approaching the region of the two asymmetric carbon atoms in L-threonine as we have drawn it. The —NH_3^+ and —OH groups are on opposite sides of the C—C bond. The same reagent, if it is symmetrical, can rotate and approach D-threonine in the same region and encounter the same groups at exactly the same spacing. This isn't true of either isomer of allothreonine. If one of the carbons is rotated from the position we have drawn so as to place the —NH_3^+ and —OH groups on opposite sides of the C—C bond, either the —COO^- or the —CH_3 group will also be rotated into the position formerly occupied by —H, and this will change the reactivity toward a reagent. Since most organic chemists deal with symmetrical reagents, they note this different reactivity of the two pairs of the four different compounds and give one pair one name and the other pair another name. The names also point up the difference in optical activity, because it is only the mirror images that cause equal and opposite rotation of plane polarized light. L-Threonine and L-allothreonine cause different amounts of rotation.

DESIGNATING ROTATION. We designate all of the amino acids having the same arrangement of groups around C-2 found in L-alanine as L-amino acids regardless of the arrangement about other asymmetric centers. Some L-amino acids cause a rotation of a plane polarized light to the left, others to the right. The direction of rotation is shown when desired by lower case italic letters (*d*) or (*l*) in parentheses to designate dextro- or levorotatory, respectively. (It can also be shown by (+) for dextro- and (−) for levo-.) The older literature is confusing in this respect because there was a time of transition when the lower case letters were used for configurational family as well as for actual rotation.

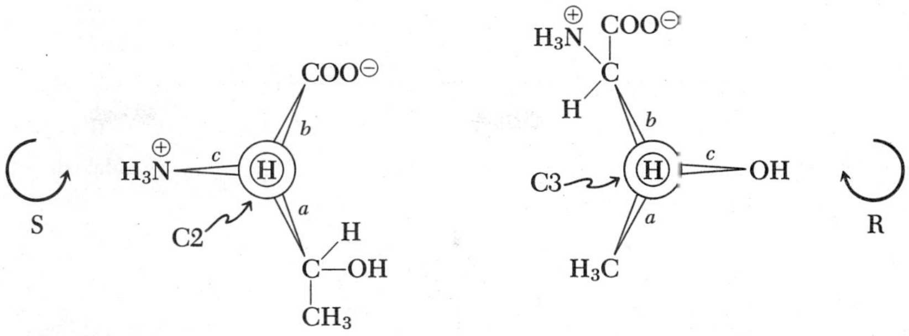

Figure 31-1 Configuration in the (R) and (S) system can be determined by looking down on an asymmetric atom arranged so that the substituent of lowest atomic number is facing the viewer. In the example on the left, one is looking past the substituent H atom at C-2 of L-threonine. In order to go from the lowest to the highest substituent among the remaining three, one must go in a left-hand circle (COO outranks CH-OH(CH_3) because it has two O atoms attached to the carbon, and these higher atomic number atoms outrank the single O and C in the other group; the directly attached N of the amino group has a higher atomic number than C and therefore outranks both of the other groups). The left-hand circle is designated as (S) configuration.

The example on the right shows the configuration about C-3 of L-threonine. One is again looking down on H as the substituent of lowest rank order in terms of atomic number. In this case, the methyl group is the lowest ranking of the remaining three substituents, and the hydroxyl group is the highest. Traveling in a right-hand circle carries one from lowest to highest ranking substituent, so this carbon has an (R) configuration.

R and S Nomenclature. Because of the difficulty sometimes created in designating configurational family with many types of compounds, a new nomenclature has been invented. Briefly, each of the four constituent groups about an asymmetric carbon is arranged in order of increasing atomic number of the nearest constituent atom or in order of increasing valence electron density. (N ranks higher than C, and O higher than N; ethylene carbons rank higher than saturated carbons, a —CH_2—COO^- group ranks higher than a —CH_2—CH_3 group, and so on.) One looks at the asymmetric center in such a way as to peer directly down on the substituent of lowest rank order, which is frequently —H with the amino acids. When this is done, the remaining three substituents will be arranged as spokes on a wheel, and one goes around the wheel from the lowest rank order to the highest. If this is a clockwise direction, the configuration is **rectus** or **(R):** if it is counterclockwise, the configuration is **sinistrus** or **(S).** The process is repeated for each asymmetric center. Designating the isomers does take some practice in visualization of the structures, but the nomenclature has the advantage of creating an unambiguous designation of the absolute configuration, no matter how many asymmetric centers there are. Under this system, L-threonine is (2S:3R)-threonine, or more systematically, (2S:3R)-2-amino-3-hydroxybutyrate (Fig. 31-1).

Qualitative Detection of Amino Acids

A widely used reaction for detecting the presence of amino acids in general involves heating with **ninhydrin (triketohydrindene hydrate).** This causes an oxidative decarboxylation and deamination; the liberated ammonia then condenses with hydrindantin, which is the reduced form of ninhydrin created in the initial reaction, and with a second molecule of ninhydrin (Fig. 31-2). The condensation product has a bright blue color

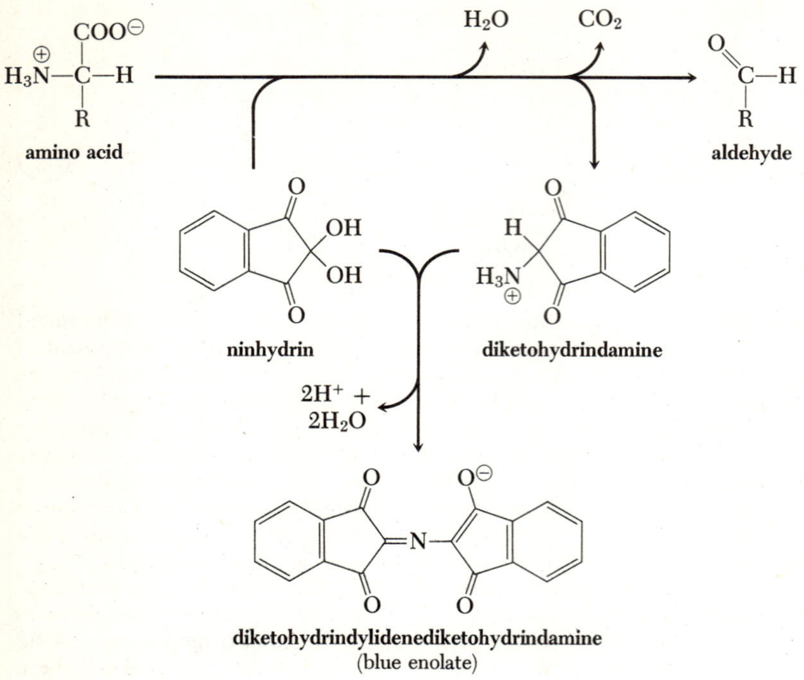

Figure 31-2 The ninhydrin reaction involves an oxidative decarboxylation of an amino acid, and a condensation of a second molecule of ninhydrin with the reduced product formed in the first step and NH_4^+.

that can be detected when nanomolar quantities of amino acids on a solid support are sprayed with ninhydrin and heated in an oven. This technique is sometimes used by police for developing fingerprints on porous materials, but it is more commonly used in the laboratory for the detection of amino acids that have been separated by **paper chromatography** or similar methods. In these methods, a small sample is spotted on the corner of a sheet of filter paper or on a plate coated with a thin layer of cellulose, silica gel, or other adsorbent. An edge of the sheet or plate near the spot is then dipped in a solvent, typically an acidic organic solvent-water mixture. As the solvent rises across the sample spot because of capillary action, it dissolves different amounts of the various amino acids in the sample. Those that go readily into the solvent will be carried farther as the solvent moves across fresh adsorbent before they are adsorbed. There is a continuous succession of solution of the compound by fresh solvent arising from below and removal from solution by fresh adsorbent. The result is a series of spots of amino acids spaced up the sheet in the direction of the solvent front (Fig. 31-3). Each amino acid will move a specific fraction, designated as R_F, of the total distance traversed by the solvent front. Not all of the amino acids are separated in one dimension, and more complete separation can be achieved by drying the sheet and then turning it 90° so that the band of spots is down. It is then dipped into a different solvent system, such as NH_3-water-organic solvent, that will separate those amino acids moving together in the first system. The second solvent carries the amino acids at right angles to their original direction of motion so that the final result is a sheet with a roughly diagonal scatter of spots. After drying, spraying with a ninhydrin solution, and heating, the presence of particular amino acids in the original sample becomes known through the appearance of blue spots. (The color varies somewhat, and proline gives a yellow spot.)

Quantitative Analysis

Ion-Exchange Chromatography. Quantitative analysis of the amino acid composition of a sample is usually done by separating the amino acids through ion-exchange

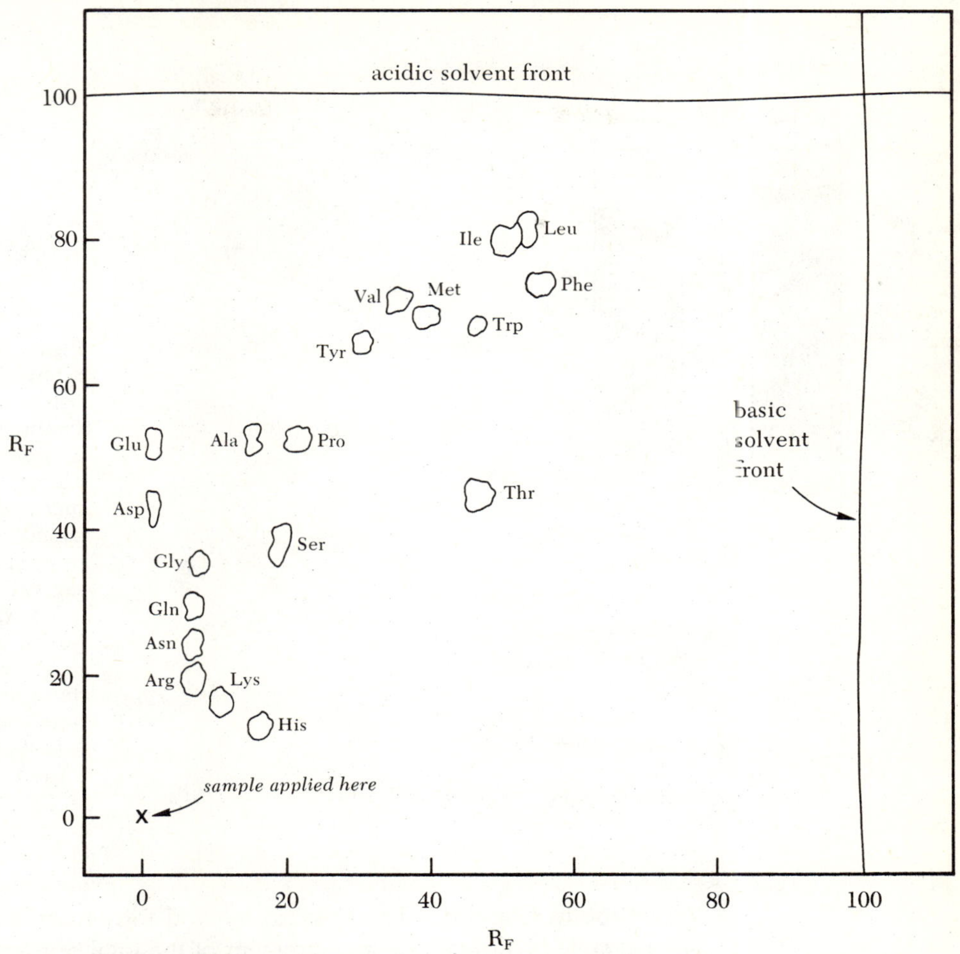

Figure 31-3 A separation of a mixture of amino acids by thin-layer chromatography. The sample was applied at the bottom left and dipped in an acidic solvent mixture until the solvent had risen nearly to the top of the plate. The plate was dried, turned 90°, and dipped in a basic solvent. After development in this solvent, the plate was dried and sprayed with a ninhydrin reagent. The R_F value is the fraction of the distance from the point of sample application to the solvent front traversed by a particular amino acid.

chromatography and measuring the amount of color each develops upon treatment with ninhydrin. The separation involves the use of insoluble resins substituted with ionized groups that will attract ions of opposite charges from solution. The resins are typically polymers of styrene with variable amounts of cross-links between the linear polystyrene chains. The charged groups incorporated into the resin include substituted ammonium groups for binding anions (negative ions) and carboxylate or sulfonate groups for binding cations (positive ions). The sulfonic cation exchange resins are most widely used for chromatography of amino acids.

The separation of compounds on ion-exchange resins hinges upon their selective displacement by other ions. For example, consider a cation exchange resin placed in a cylindrical column and loaded with a mixed sample of cations, such as an acidic solution of amino acids. If the column is washed with a solution containing another cation, the weakly-bound cations will move down the column and appear most rapidly in the effluent from the column (Fig. 31-4). By manipulation of the composition of the eluting solution and the temperature, and the use of different columns, it is possible to separate all of the amino acids. **Amino acid analyzers** for performing the separation and carrying out a quantitative ninhydrin reaction are commercially available.

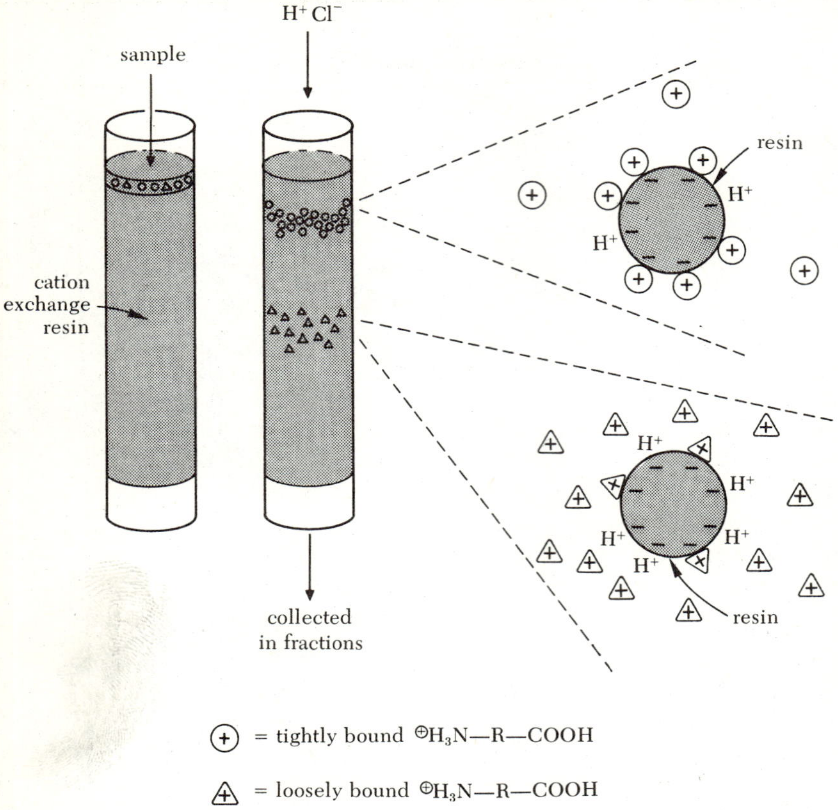

Figure 31-4 Column chromatography on ion exchange resins involves the application of the acidic sample to a cation exchange resin in a column. (The fittings and plumbing are not shown.) The resin is a polymer containing anionic groups, such as sulfonate groups, that bind cations to its surface. As a solution containing cations, such as HCl, is passed across the sample, the more tightly bound amino acids will resist displacement from resin particles by H^+, and remain near the top of the column. More weakly cationic amino acids will be readily displaced and be moved in solution toward the bottom of the column.

Protein Content. The classical method for determining the amount of protein in a sample is through the measurement of the total nitrogen by the **Kjeldahl method.** This involves digesting the sample in boiling sulfuric acid, which converts most of the nitrogen to ammonium ion. The amount of ammonium ion is then determined by colorimetric analysis, or by titration following distillation. The Kjeldahl method has the advantage of being applicable to insoluble materials such as most foodstuffs, and the disadvantage of not distinguishing proteins from other sources of nitrogen such as nucleic acids, urea, and the like.

A quick estimate of both the protein and the nucleic acid content of soluble samples can be made by measuring the **light absorption** at **260** and **280 nanometers.** The nucleosides have maximum absorption near 260 nanometers, and tyrosyl and tryptophanyl residues of the proteins have a maximum absorption near 280 nanometers. By solving the simultaneous equations for the relative absorption of each compound at the two wavelengths, factors can be obtained for determining the amount of each. This method is good only as a relative guide to the content of protein in mixed samples because it depends upon the amino acid composition of the protein.

The most widely used procedure for estimating protein content is the **Lowry method,** in which the sample is treated with an alkaline reagent containing cupric, phosphotungstate, and phosphomolybdate ions. The presence of peptide chains causes color to develop in two ways. Polypeptides react with alkaline Cu^{2+} to form a violet color (the **biuret** reaction), and the complex phosphotungstate and phosphomolybdate ions are reduced to blue compounds by tyrosyl and tryptophanyl groups in the peptide. The resultant light absorption is approximately proportional to the content of peptides in the sample.

Determination of the Primary Structure of Proteins

The Ideal. If a protein forms exactly defined chelates with a heavy metal, and if these chelates can be made to grow into large, stable, and nearly perfect crystals, it may be possible to shine an X-ray beam through the crystals onto a photographic plate in such a way as to create diffracted spots at regular positions from which the location and nature of all atoms in the entire skeleton of the peptide can be calculated. However, the dreams of X-ray crystallographers are rarely realized in so easy a fashion, and the primary structure of most proteins has been determined in more tedious and prosaic ways, with X-ray diffraction providing the final tool for specifying the three-dimensional geometry after determination of the primary peptide structure. Let us now examine the stages by which the primary structure is ordinarily determined.

Chain Composition. A protein molecule may contain one or several kinds of peptide chains. Some clue as to the number can often be obtained by end-group analysis, in which a protein is treated with a reagent that will react with the terminal amino acid groups, such as the free amino group at the N-terminus of the peptide. **Dansyl chloride** (1-dimethylaminonaphthalene-5-sulfonyl chloride) is such a reagent (Fig. 31–5). When a protein that has been treated with dansyl chloride is hydrolyzed to its constituent amino acids, those originally present at the N-terminus of chains will have dansyl-substituted α-amino groups, and they can be identified by comparing their behavior upon chromatography with known dansylated amino acids. (Dansyl groups also remain on the side chain amino group of lysine and on the phenolic group of tyrosine during the procedure, but these derivatives are also identifiable.) The strong fluorescence of the dansyl group makes it possible to detect as little as 100 picomoles of compound in a spot on a chromatogram, and if more than one α-dansylamino acid is found, there must be more than one kind of peptide chain in the sample.

SDS-POLYACRYLAMIDE GEL ELECTROPHORESIS. Different peptide chains can often be detected by first dissociating the chains in a protein molecule, and then separating them by electrophoresis. Dissociation is accomplished by treating the sample with mercaptoethanol to reduce disulfide bonds to the sulfhydryl form, followed by addition of **sodium dodecyl sulfate** (SDS), a powerful detergent. The solution of separated peptide chains in SDS is then subjected to electrophoresis in a gel made by polymerizing acrylamide under controlled conditions, so that proteins can migrate through it, but not too easily. The distance traveled by peptides in the gel depends mainly upon their molecular weights, so peptides of different size in a protein sample will appear as separate bands in the gel after electrophoresis and staining with a dye. The gel can also be calibrated with known proteins so that the molecular weight of the peptide chains can be estimated with fair precision.

Separation of Peptide Chains. Further analysis of a protein depends upon preparation of samples of the individual peptide chains. This is often accomplished by dissociating the protein with **guanidine** or **urea** in high concentrations, which prevent normal development of interchain forces, and then separating the chains by ion-exchange chromatography or by molecular sieving.

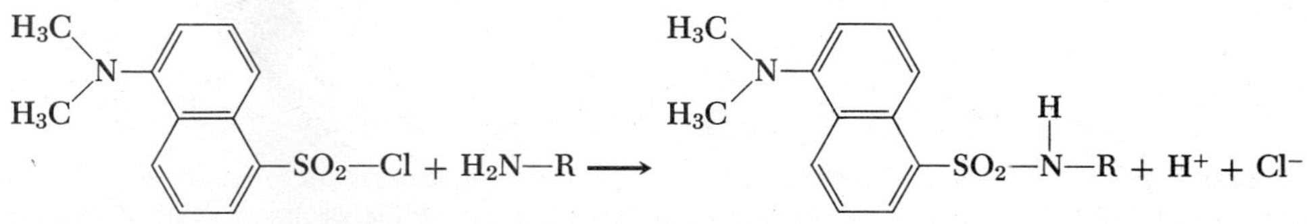

Figure 31–5 The use of dimethylaminonaphthalene-5-sulfonyl chloride (dansyl chloride) for labeling amino terminal residues.

Molecular sieving frequently uses **dextrans,** which are 1,6 polymers of glucose with frequent branching, and which are made by microorganisms. Dextrans hydrate to form a gel-like structure with domains that are resistant to penetration by large molecules. Dextrans are commercially available under the trade name Sephadex with various sizes of lattice structure, so that one grade excludes molecules of rather small size, and another excludes only very large molecules, with other grades in between. A column packed with beads of one of these dextrans separates molecules according to their ability to penetrate the beads. This means that a given grade of dextran is effective for separating molecules of a particular range of molecular weights. Molecules too large to enter will be washed through early, and those much smaller than the lattice openings will not appear in the effluent until they have equilibrated with the water within the beads. Those of intermediate size are the ones that will appear at varying positions, depending upon the amount of water in the beads that is available to them.

Determination of Amino Acid Composition. Having isolated an individual peptide, the next step is to determine the relative amount of each amino acid that it contains. This is done by hydrolyzing the peptide, usually by heating in dilute acid, and determining the composition of the hydrolyzate with an amino acid analyzer. (Some amino acids, such as tryptophan, serine, and threonine, are at least partially destroyed by acid hydrolysis, and special measures are necessary for their determination.) End-group analysis of the individual peptides is also valuable information.

Fragmentation of the Peptides. Given a purified peptide of approximately known amino acid composition, determination of the primary structure can begin in earnest. Since peptides may easily have 100 to 200 residues, or even more, it is usually necessary to break them into identifiable pieces in a reproducible fashion. If the peptide chain contains several lysyl and arginyl residues, hydrolysis by **trypsin** may be valuable. Since the enzyme catalyzes only the hydrolysis of **lysyl** and **arginyl bonds,** it will form a reproducible mixture of products, each of which terminates in a lysyl or arginyl residue except the original C-terminal residue (Fig. 31-6).

A peptide chain may also be reproducibly cleaved by treating it with **cyanogen bromide** (Fig. 31-7), which causes the rupture of **methionyl peptides.**

Peptide Map. When the original peptide is cleaved into smaller pieces, the number of fragments is determined by a procedure known as **fingerprinting.** The sample is spotted on one corner of a sheet of filter paper and a one-dimensional chromatogram

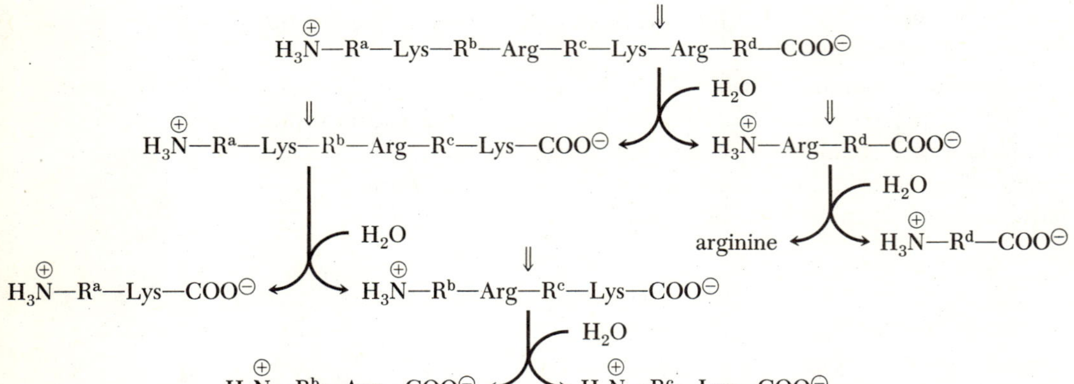

Figure 31-6 Trypsin is a valuable tool in the determination of the primary structure of proteins because it specifically hydrolyzes lysyl and arginyl peptide bonds, creating smaller fragments of the chains in a reproducible fashion. In the example given, the chain is cleaved into five fragments, one of which is a free molecule of arginine.

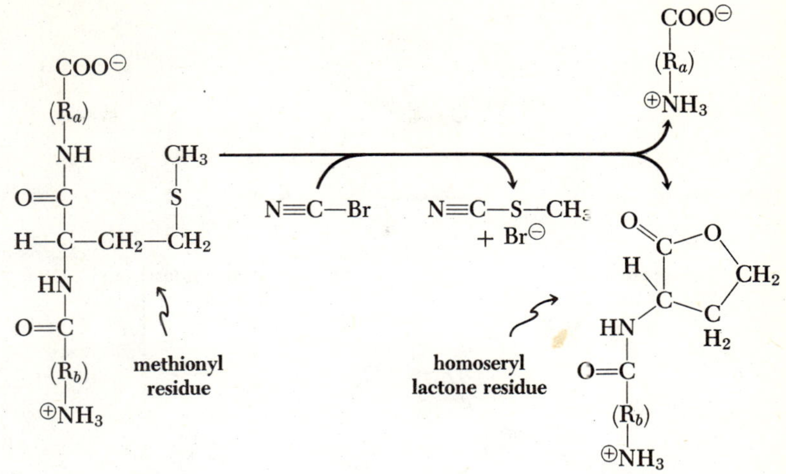

Figure 31-7 Cyanogen bromide cleaves peptides of methionine.

is developed by flowing solvent over it. The paper is then subjected to electrophoresis in the second dimension, which gives greater resolution with most mixtures of peptides than can be obtained by further chromatography. Not only does the number of spots fix the minimum number of peptide fragments, but their shape and position (the "fingerprint" is characteristic of the particular peptide in the original sample. (Mutations of a known protein can often be identified by a change in position of one spot in its fingerprint.)

With the peptide map as a guide, the mixture of smaller peptides is again separated by ion-exchange chromatography or molecular sieving until each fragment has been obtained in pure form. Each is also analyzed for end-groups and for amino acid composition. Some may be small enough to proceed directly with sequence determination. Others may be too large, and require further cleavage by a different procedure, such as the use of a different proteolytic enzyme, to produce sufficiently small pieces for further work.

Sequence Determination. The most powerful tool for sequence determination is the **Edman degradation** using **phenyl isothiocyanate,** which combines with amino groups in alkaline solution to form thiocarbamyl derivatives (Fig. 31-8). When these derivatives are treated with anhydrous acid (heptafluorobutyric acid), the terminal amino acid derivative is cleaved from the remaining peptide by a cyclization that forms an anilinothiazolinone compound. This heterocyclic derivative can be extracted with an organic solvent without removing the remaining peptide, which now has the next amino acid exposed in a terminal position. The shortened peptide can then be treated with fresh phenyl isothiocyanate and be carried through the entire procedure to release the second amino acid of the original peptide as its anilinothiazolinone derivative. Commercial instruments (sequenators) are now available for carrying out the procedure through as many as 40 repetitions, delivering solutions of the derivatives of each successive amino acid residue. The derivatives are treated with aqueous acid to convert them to stable **phenylthiohydantoins** that can be identified by chromatographic methods.

The Edman degradation has enormously simplified the problem of determination of primary structure, and has greatly improved its practical accuracy, since it is now easy for the careful investigator to determine sequence after cleaving his original peptides in more than one way, so that the fragments created by one method overlap the points of cleavage in the other method, thereby providing a check on the sequence.

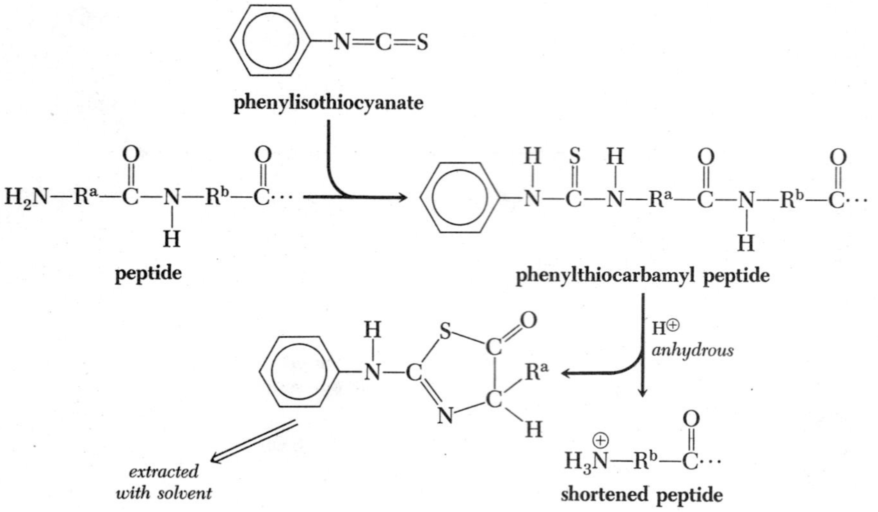

Figure 31-8 The Edman degradation involves the reaction of a peptide with phenyl isothiocyanate to form the phenylthiocarbamyl derivative of the N-terminal amino acid residue. Treatment with anhydrous acid causes this residue to be cleaved as an anilinothiazolinone derivative, which can be extracted by an organic solvent. The shortened peptide can be carried through the procedure again to isolate the derivative of the next amino acid residue, and so on.

SUGARS

The sugars by definition are polyhydroxy aldehydes or ketones. The simplest aldose and ketose are glyceraldehyde and dihydroxyacetone. In a formal sense, all of the other sugars are considered to be derivatives of either D- or L-glyceraldehyde, made by adding the elements of formaldehyde to the aldehyde carbon. For example, adding one formaldehyde unit would create the tetroses:

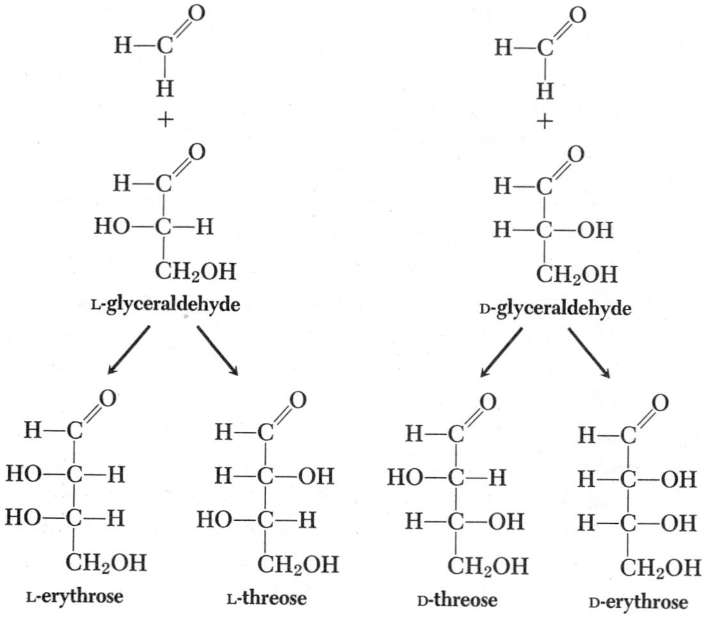

Looked at in this way, the configurational family (D- or L-) is determined by the configuration of the asymmetric center most distant from the aldehyde group. We also see that the addition of the equivalent of a formaldehyde unit to the structure creates two new mirror-image pairs, each given a different name. Thus, there is only one pair of aldotrioses, two of aldotetroses, four of aldopentoses, and eight of aldohexoses.

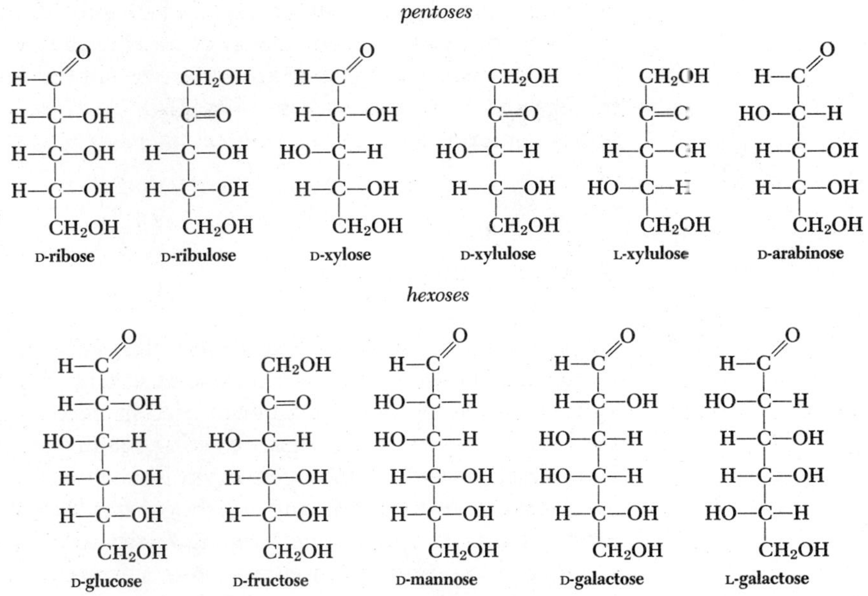

Figure 31-9 Common pentoses and hexoses.

The ketoses could have the carbonyl group on any of the central carbon atoms, but most of the natural ketoses have it on C-2. Some of the ketoses, such as fructose, have trivial names of their own, but many are named by combining the prefix of the name of the corresponding aldose with the suffix -ulose. Some of the common aldoses and ketoses are illustrated in the Figure 31–9.

We have already seen that sugars tend to form internal hemiacetals, creating the **furanose** or **pyranose** forms. This cyclization creates another asymmetric center, and the isomers formed in this way are known as the **α** or **β anomers** of the sugar. Which name applies depends upon the configurational family. If the configuration of the anomeric carbon is the same as that of the final asymmetric center (the center that determines D- or L- designation) it is the α-anomer; if not, it is the β-anomer. In other words, mirror images will have the same anomeric designation. The anomers are really different compounds in the same way that glucose and galactose are different compounds, and the only reason they aren't given different trivial names is because they are so freely interconvertible in solution.

The furanose and pyranose forms of the sugars are usually depicted as pentagons or hexagons lying on edge, as is done in this book. These Haworth formulations are not very accurate representations of the true configuration of the molecule because

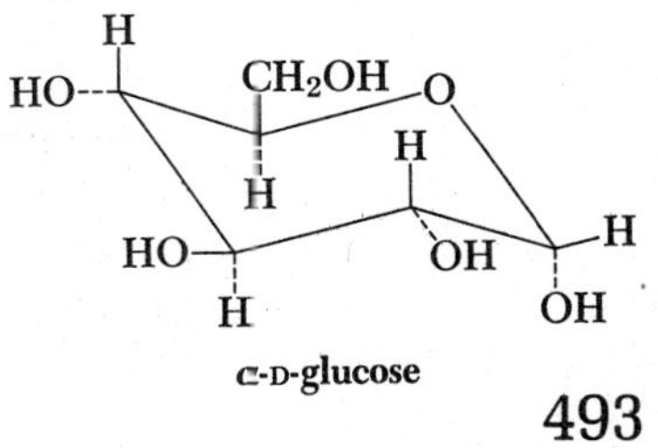

Figure 31-10 Glucose exists in a puckered conformation that is more accurately represented by the type of formula shown here.

the ring atoms do not lie in a plane, and the substituent hydroxyl groups are not above or below the plane, but equatorial or axial to the center of the molecule. The conformation in which the hydroxyl groups are equatorial is usually favored. The use of these conformational representations (Fig. 31–10) will undoubtedly become common as the actual conformations of the residues in natural compounds become more generally known.

Reducing Sugars

α-Hydroxy aldehydes and ketones are more easily oxidized than ordinary aldehydes and ketones, which is the same as saying that they are more powerful reducing agents. This property has long been used in making both qualitative and quantitative analyses of sugars. Even sugars existing mainly in furanose or pyranose forms have a sufficient amount of the open-chain isomer present to have the property. Reagents for determination of reducing sugars contain **cupric ion** associated with a chelating agent, usually tartrate, or they contain **ferricyanide** as the oxidizing agent. The amount of the reduced agent, either cuprous ion or ferrocyanide ion, formed upon heating with the sample is usually determined by colorimetric analysis using phosphomolybdate or phosphotungstate.

The determination of reducing sugar was formerly widely employed for the estimation of glucose in the blood and urine. However, the method does not distinguish between the various reducing sugars or between sugars and other compounds that will reduce cupric ions or ferricyanide, and it has been largely replaced by more convenient methods utilizing a glucose oxidase from microorganisms that catalyzes the specific oxidation of glucose to gluconate with the production of hydrogen peroxide. The peroxide is then determined by the action of a peroxidase on an organic amine to produce a colored compound.

Determination of reducing sugar is still of value in structural analysis of oligo- and polysaccharides. Compounds in which another group is attached to the anomeric hydroxyl group of a sugar residue cannot form an open-chain isomer, and therefore are not susceptible to oxidation. Glycogen, for example, has very little reducing power because there is only one unbound anomeric carbon in the entire molecule. All of the other glucosyl residues are linked through C-1. Lactose, on the other hand, has roughly half as much reducing power per glycosyl residue as does free glucose or galactose, because its glucose residue can form the open chain (Fig. 31–11).

This kind of information on an unknown oligosaccharide can give important clues to structure. The fact that sucrose is not a reducing sugar was an important clue for deducing that its unusual structure involves an anomeric carbon to anomeric carbon bond.

Analysis of Total Polysaccharide

There are no good methods for analyzing the total content of carbohydrate polymers in a biological sample. Heating a soluble sample in a strongly acidic solution of **anthrone** or **phenol** produces a color with many glycosyl compounds, as well as the free sugars; even the pentosyl residue of nucleoside derivatives will react, but quantitative application requires some knowledge of the kind of carbohydrate involved. Glycogen and starch are relatively stable in strong alkali, and digestion of tissues under these drastic conditions was formerly employed as a preliminary to their determination.

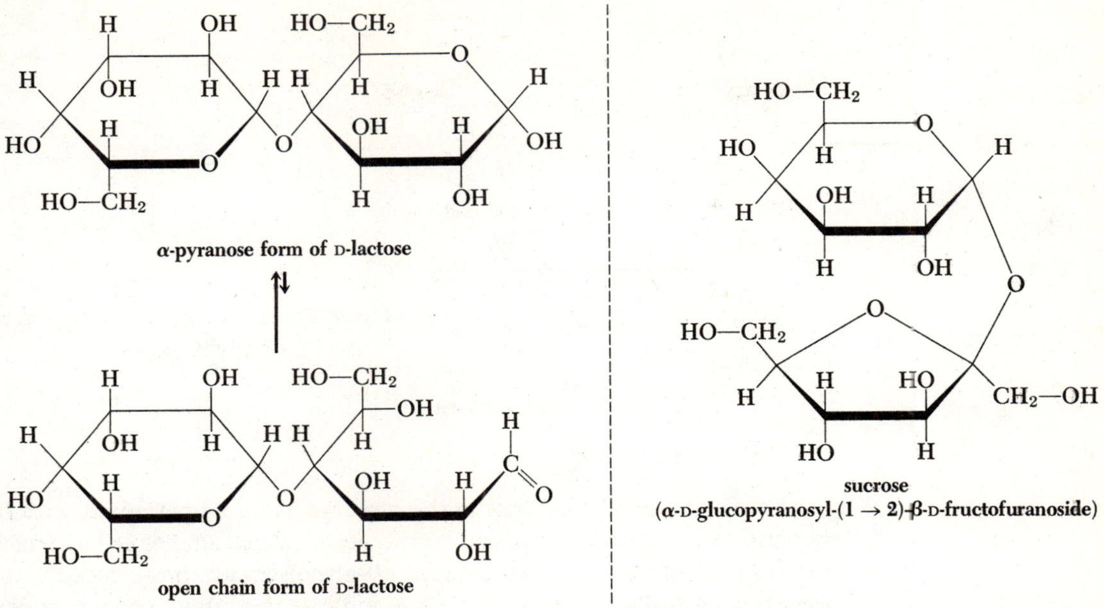

Figure 31-11 D-Lactose is a disaccharide in which the hexose residues are linked by a 1,4 bond, leaving C-1 free on one residue to form the open-chain form. Lactose is a reducing sugar and shows mutarotation. Sucrose, however, is linked between C-1 of glucose and C-2 of fructose, so neither residue is free to assume the open-chain form. Sucrose therefore is not a reducing sugar and does not undergo mutarotation.

Estimation of the heteropolysaccharides usually hinges upon colorimeteric determination of the uronate or osamine content.

The structural analysis of heteropolysaccharides is a complicated business—beyond the scope of our discussion. Among the techniques that may be used are partial acid hydrolysis with attempted identification of the various fragments that are produced, attack by a variety of hydrolytic enzymes that will remove specific groups, specific tests for particular sugars, and a number of organic reactions that will degrade the sugars so as to enable identification of the linkages between the residues, such as the periodate oxidation.

Periodate Oxidation

Periodic acid oxidizes compounds that have one oxygen atom on each of adjacent carbon atoms to cause a C—C cleavage. For example, periodic acid causes two successive cleavages of glycerol (Fig. 31-12). Reactions of this kind are valuable in determining the structure of carbohydrates. (Periodic acid will also attack compounds in which one or both of the requisite oxygen atoms is replaced by an amino group, as in the osamines, but not if the amino group is combined in amide linkage, as in the N-acetylosamines.)

Here are two examples of the kind of information that can be obtained:

1. Furanosides and pyranosides can be distinguished by the number of moles of periodate consumed in their oxidation (Fig. 31-13).

2. The number of end-groups in some homopolysaccharides can be determined by noting the number of moles of formic acid produced. Consider the oxidation of one terminal chain in glycogen (Fig. 31-14). Formic acid is released only from the terminal residue because the presence of bonds on the 1 and 4 carbons of the internal residue prevents further oxidation to release formic acid.

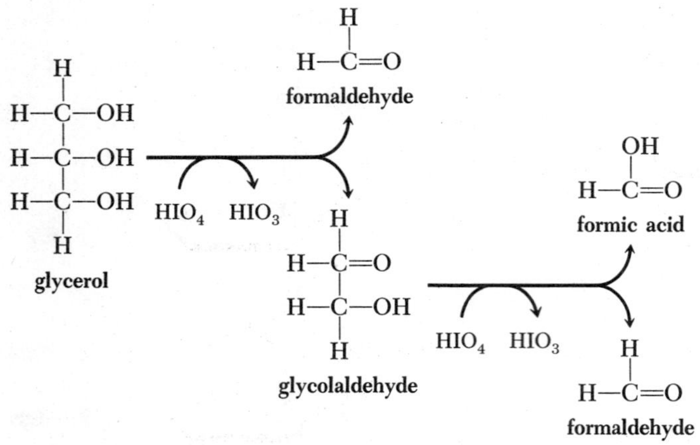

Figure 31-12 Glycerol is cleaved into three fragments by periodate.

Lead tetraacetate also acts in the same way as does periodate, with the additional property of being soluble in organic solvents, which makes it more useful for some preparative purposes. It also attacks *cis*-glycols much more rapidly than the *trans* isomers, so it can sometimes be used to indicate the relative configuration of adjacent hydroxyl groups in sugars having a ring structure. However, lead tetraacetate is less useful than periodate in applications requiring quantitative analysis.

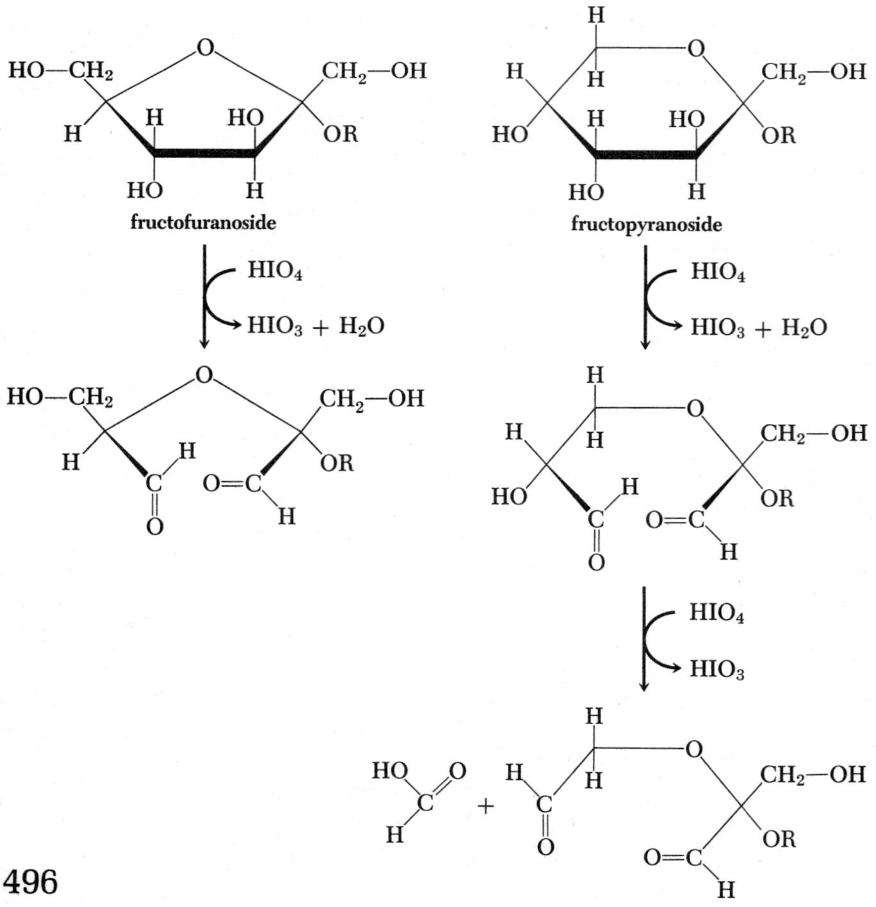

Figure 31-13 Periodate cleavage enables discrimination of fructofuranosides from fructopyranosides, and it is used to make similar distinctions with other sugar residues.

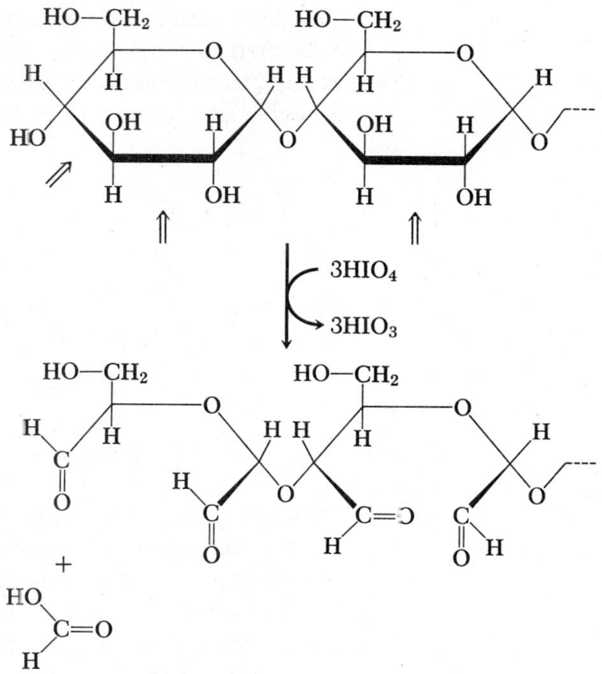

Figure 31-14 Only terminal residues of a glucose polymer yield formic acid upon periodate cleavage.

Oxidized and Reduced Derivatives of Sugars

The **oxidation** of C-1 of an aldose forms an aldonic acid; this is readily accomplished by the action of bromine in acid solution. Oxidation at C-6 forms an alduronic acid; although this can be done chemically in one step, the yields are very small, and other routes are employed for realistic synthesis. The aldonic and alduronic acids are named after the parent aldose:

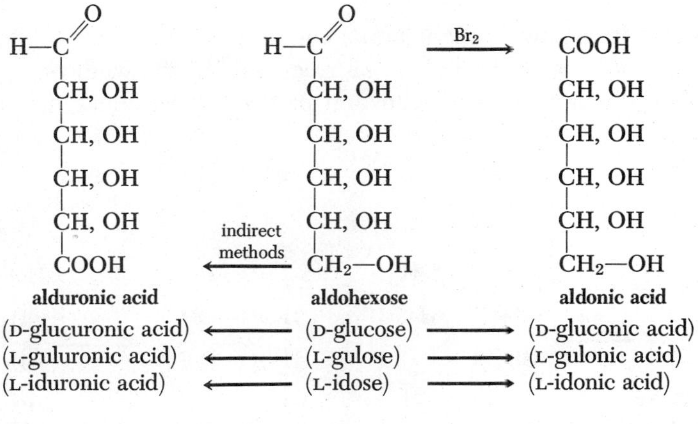

The reduction of the carbonyl group of sugars by agents such as sodium borohydride forms an alcohol group:

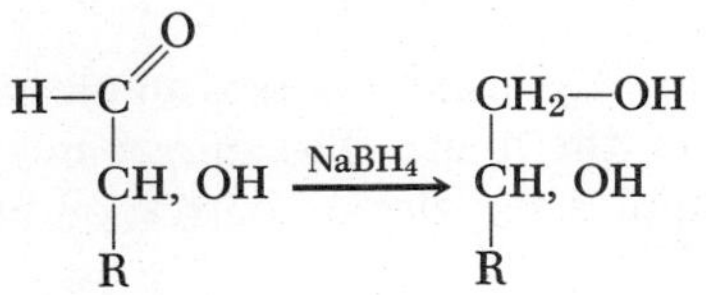

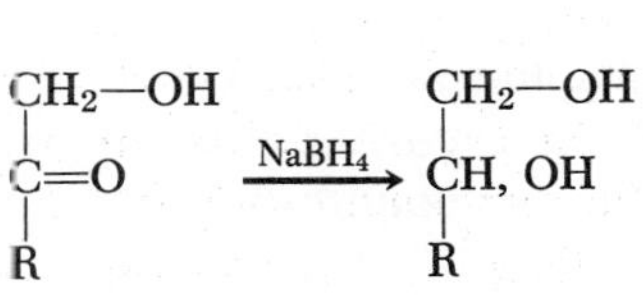

This leads into a sticky problem of nomenclature. Since the product of monosaccharide reduction is a polyhydric alcohol without distinguishing groups at either end, there is no inherent reason for looking at it from a particular end, and D- and L- nomenclature becomes ambiguous. Consider the alcohol formed by reducing glucose:

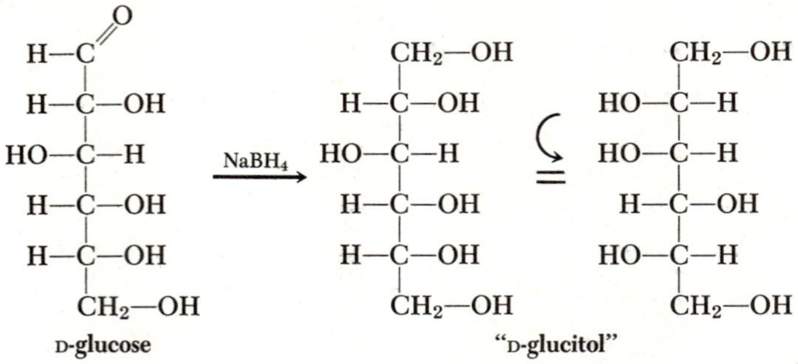

We see that merely turning the molecule end-for-end changes it in a conventional sense from a derivative of D-glucose to a derivative of the sugar, L-gulose. Indeed, the reduction of either of these aldoses forms the same compound. What shall we call the hexitol? D-Glucitol or L-gulitol? It is sometimes called D-glucitol, but it was originally named **sorbitol** because of its occurrence in the mountain ash, *Sorbus aucuparia,* along with a corresponding ketose, L-sorbose:

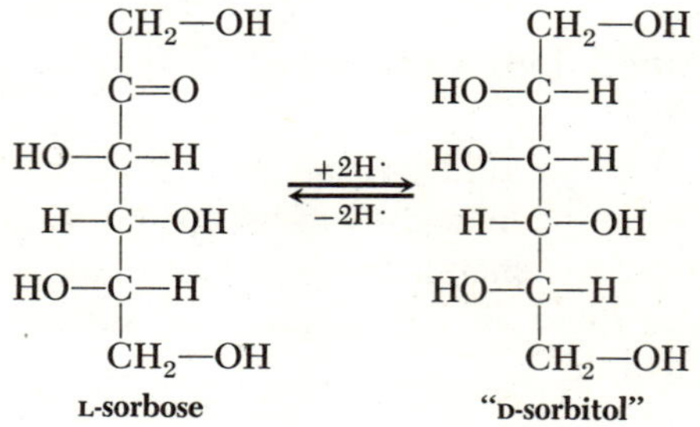

You would think from this it might be known as L-sorbitol, but no, it is frequently designated even today as D-sorbitol, so all rules are out the window.

The alcohol obtained by the reduction of D-galactose illustrates an interesting point:

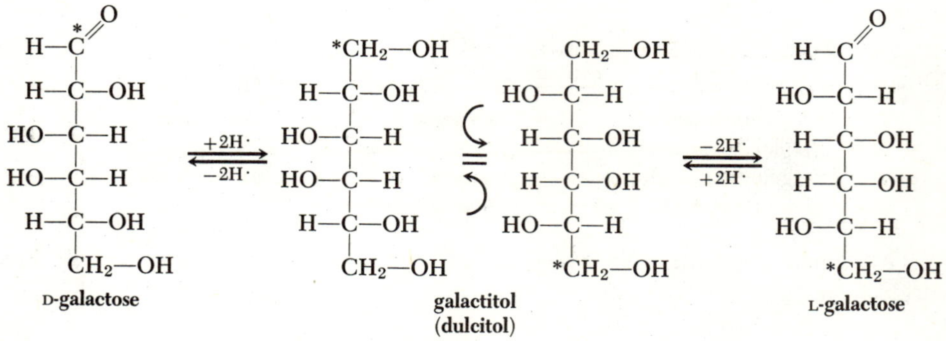

This galactitol, also known as dulcitol, has no optical activity because it is symmetrical. We can see this by turning it end-for-end, as is done in the figure. The mirror image is the compound itself. It follows from this that galactitol is the alcohol corresponding to both D- and L-galactose.

The reduction of the aldehyde group of an alduronic acid also causes difficulties in nomenclature. The rules for naming these compounds require one to view the aldehyde carbon of the alduronic acids as C-1 and the carboxylic carbon of the aldonic acids as C-1. Therefore, when one reduces an alduronic acid to an aldonic acid, what was C-1 becomes C-6, and vice versa. This makes the simple reaction appear more formidable than it actually is because it usually necessitates a change in the type name and sometimes in configurational designation from reactant to product. For example, D-glucuronate is reduced to L-gulonate, a shift of names that confuses the fact that the actual configuration has not been changed on a single asymmetric carbon atom:

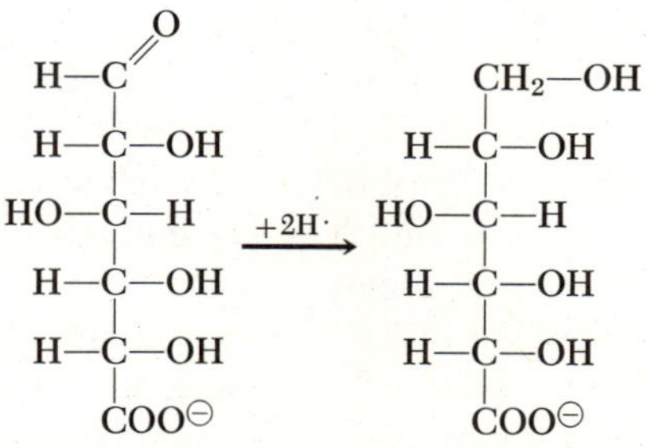

D-glucuronate L-gulonate

LIPIDS

The salient property of the lipids that is exploited for their isolation and determination is their greater solubility in non-polar solvents. Hydrocarbon solvents such as *n*-hexane extract triglycerides from aqueous suspensions and also extract free fatty acids if the pH is low enough to suppress their ionization. Simple titration of extracted fatty acids will give an estimate of their concentration, and can also be used to determine the fatty acids liberated from triglycerides by hydrolysis.

The phospholipids require more polar solvents such as a chloroform-methanol mixture, but even these leave the carbohydrates and proteins behind. The initial step in the determination of the distribution of lipids in a tissue therefore is an extraction with this sort of solvent, usually with great care to exclude oxygen so as to avoid destruction of the unsaturated compounds. Various techniques are available for further fractionation, and ion exchange chromatography is a useful first step for separating triglycerides and other relatively uncharged lipids from the phospholipids. This procedure employs a derivative of cellulose: **diethylaminoethylcellulose (DEAE-cellulose)** as an anion exchanger because it can be used with non-polar solvents that attack the polystyrene in the more common types of resin ion exchange materials. (DEAE-cellulose is also a very useful material for fractionating proteins in aqueous solution.) The various groups of lipids separated by ion-exchange chromatography can then be further fractionated on silicic acid columns. For example, the neutral fraction can be divided into triglycerides, sterols, and sterol esters in this way.

Gas-Liquid Chromatography (GLC)

The fatty acid constituents of the various types of lipids can be liberated by hydrolysis and the nature of the fatty acids determined by a method that has revolutionized lipid chemistry: gas-liquid chromatography. This is a method that hinges upon the conversion of the components of a sample to a gas, and it can be applied to any compound that can be converted to stable volatile derivatives. There are even methods for converting amino acids and sugars to volatile derivatives, but gas-liquid chromatography is especially applicable to the fatty acids because of their inherent low reactivity and the ease with which they are converted to volatile derivatives. The mixture to be analyzed is converted to the methyl esters by reaction with diazomethane and is then introduced into a heated column that contains a layer of some non-volatile solvent such as various silicones, hydrocarbon greases, or organic polymers.

The principle is to hold the non-volatile solvent in position, and pass a current of inert gas, such as helium, over it to sweep along the gaseous sample. Those compounds in the sample having the lowest vapor pressure at the operating temperature and the greatest solubility in the stationary solvent will tend to remain behind.

The stationary phase is created in the column by suspending the non-volatile solvent on materials like crushed fire-brick or diatomaceous earth, or by coating the walls of a long piece of capillary tubing. The gas emerging from the column is passed through an ionization detector that creates a signal when ionizable molecules appear in the gas stream. The application of gas chromatography has made available for the first time routine and reliable assays of the amounts of the individual fatty acids in natural lipids, and it is this technique that has made it possible to follow changes in the composition of human adipose tissue by analysis of the small samples obtained by plunging a needle through the skin of very much alive subjects.

FURTHER READING

S. Colowick and N. O. Kaplan, eds., Methods in enzymology, Academic Press. The many volumes of this work, of which the first appeared in 1955 and the last is yet to come, contain excellent discussion of the applications as well as procedural details on ion exchange chromatography, paper chromatography, thin-layer chromatography, gas-liquid chromatography, general and specific analyses, and the procedures used in determining structure of proteins and complex polysaccharides.

W. W. Pigman and D. Horton, The carbohydrates, 2nd ed., Academic Press (1970). General treatise with several volumes slowly appearing.

G. Rouser et al., Lipid composition of beef brain, beef liver, and the sea anemone: two approaches to quantitative fractionation of complex lipid mixtures, J. Am. Oil Chem. Soc., 40:425 (1963).

R. S. Cahn, C. K. Ingold, and V. Prelog, The specification of asymmetric configuration in organic chemistry, Experientia, 12:81 (1956). The definition of (R) and (S) nomenclature.

CHAPTER 32

THE NOMENCLATURE OF ENZYMES

Until this decade, the creation of names for enzymes was mainly the responsibility of the discoverer, subject to modification by later investigators and to the taste of the various editors of the scientific journals. Decision between alternative names was a matter for the marketplace; those that weren't used disappeared. The only agreement was that all enzyme names ought to have the suffix *-ase,* but this might be preceded by the name of a substrate, the name of a product, or the type of reaction catalyzed.

After 1956, an effort was made by a commission of the International Union of Biochemistry to create a more systematic nomenclature. The proposals, like the systematic nomenclature for organic compounds, had a mixed reception in terms of actual usage, even after revision in 1964. A new revision was made in 1972 that faced reality by making the common trivial names the recommended names, wherever possible, but grouped within a systematic framework for classifying enzymes. Readers of this book ought to be familiar with some of the principles of the systematic classification, if for no other reason that the intelligent exercise of their power to decide the accepted nomenclature through usage. Perhaps the Commissions, like the rest of us, tend to oscillate too wildly between strict and dictatorial regimentation and unrestrained chaos.

General Classes

The IUB nomenclature uses six type designations as the final part of an enzyme name:

1. Oxidoreductases. These are enzymes catalyzing all of the reactions in which one compound is oxidized and another compound is reduced:

dehydrogenases
reductases
oxidases
peroxidases
hydroxylases
oxygenases

2. Transferases. These are enzymes catalyzing reactions not involving oxidation and reduction in which a group containing C, N, P, or S is transferred from one substrate to another:

transferases
trans—ases (such as transaminase, transketolase, transaldolase, transmethylase)

3. Hydrolases. These are enzymes catalyzing hydrolytic cleavages or their reversal. (They do not include enzymes catalyzing the addition or removal of water from one compound, such as fumarase or enolase.) This includes all of the enzymes named as:

esterases
amidases
peptidases
phosphatases
glycosidases

4. Lyases. These are enzymes catalyzing the cleavage of C—C, C—O, C—N bonds, etc., without a hydrolysis or oxidation-reduction:

decarboxylases
aldolases
synthases (but not properly named synthetases)
cleavage enzymes (such as citrate or 3-hydroxy-3-methylglutaryl CoA cleavage enzymes)
hydrases or **hydratases** or **dehydratases**
deaminases
nucleotide cyclases

5. Isomerases. These are enzymes catalyzing intramolecular rearrangements not involving a net change in the concentration of compounds other than the substrate:

isomerases
racemases
epimerases
mutases

6. Ligases. These are enzymes catalyzing all of the reactions involving the formation of bonds between two substrate molecules that are coupled to the cleavage of a pyrophosphate bond in ATP or another energy donor. They include all of the enzymes now named as synthetases, except in cases where this name has been misapplied. The name synthetase was originally defined to include those enzymes now being defined as ligases, but it was later applied to enzymes catalyzing the formation of compounds by other mechanisms. Thus, one sometimes sees glycogen synthetase or δ-aminolevulinate synthetase even though the reactions catalyzed by these enzymes do not involve the cleavage of a high-energy phosphate bond. The term synthase was later coined to cover these enzymes, which are lyases in the IUB nomenclature.

Individual Enzymes

Within each type of enzyme, further subdivisions are made and given group numbers. The groups are divided into numbered sub-groups, and the individual enzymes within a sub-group are given another number. Thus, each enzyme is designated by four numbers. Some examples will make it clear, and also show advantages and disadvantages of the systematic nomenclature. The recommended trivial name is shown in italics.

1. Oxidoreductases
  1. Acting on the CH—OH group of donors
    1. With NAD or NADP as acceptor
      27. L-lactate:NAD oxidoreductase
          EC 1.1.1.27 (*lactate dehydrogenase*)

2. Transferases
   4. Glycosyltransferases
      1. Hexosyltransferases
         18. α-1,4-Glucan:α-1,4-glucan 6-glycosyltransferase
             EC 2.4.1.18 (*1,4-α-glucan branching enzyme*)

   7. Transferring phosphorus-containing groups
      1. Phosphotransferases with an alcohol group as acceptor
         2. ATP:D-glucose 6-phosphotransferase
            EC 2.7.1.2. (*glucokinase*)

3. Hydrolases
   4. Acting on peptide bonds
      21. Serine proteases
         4. no systematic name given
            EC 3.4.21.4 (*trypsin*)

4. Lyases
   2. Carbon-oxygen lyases
      1. Hydro-lyases
         13. L-Serine hydro-lyase (deaminating)
             EC 4.2.1.13 (*serine dehydratase*)

5. Isomerases
   1. Racemases and epimerases
      3. Acting on carbohydrates and derivatives
         1. D-Ribulose-5-phosphate 3-epimerase
            EC 5.1.3.1 (*ribulosephosphate 3-epimerase*)

6. Ligases
   2. Forming C—S bonds
      1. Acid-thiol ligases
         3. Acid:CoA ligase (AMP-forming)
            EC 6.2.1.3 (*acyl CoA synthetase*)

FURTHER READING

Enzyme Nomenclature, Elsevier (1973). This report of the 1972 recommendations of the IUB is a valuable, even though Anglicized, reference work for more general purposes than nomenclature.

INDEX

Page numbers in boldface indicate that the item is illustrated, or referred to, in a figure on that page. As is common in the biochemical literature, names are indexed letter-by-letter; that is, Acetylamino, Acetylcholine, Acetyl CoA, and Acetyl coenzyme A appear in that order. Isomeric designations are neglected in the primary alphabetization. Thus, *cis*-Aconitate, S-adenosyl-L-methionine, L-Alanine, and *p*-Aminobenzoate are listed as beginning with A.

ABBREVIATIONS

A adenosine
ACTH adrenocorticotropic hormone (corticotropin)
ADP adenosine diphosphate
Ala alanyl
AMP adenosine monophosphate
Arg arginyl
Asn asparaginyl
Asp aspartyl
ATP adenosine triphosphate
ATPase adenosine triphosphatase

C cytidine
cAMP 3′,5′-cyclic AMP
CDP cytidine diphosphate
CMP cytidine monophosphate
CoA coenzyme A (in names of compounds)
CoA-SH coenzyme A (in reactions)
CTP cytidine triphosphate
Cys cysteinyl
cyt cytochrome

dAMP 2′-deoxyadenosine monophosphate
dATP 2′-deoxyadenosine triphosphate
dCMP 2′-deoxycytidine monophosphate
dCTP 2′-deoxycytidine triphosphate
dGMP 2′-deoxyguanosine monophosphate
dGTP 2′-deoxyguanosine triphosphate
DNA deoxyribonucleic acid(s)
DOPA dihydroxyphenylalanine
dTMP 2′-deoxythymidine monophosphate
dTTP 2′-deoxythymidine triphosphate
dUMP 2′-deoxyuridine monophosphate

E enzyme
EDTA ethylenedinitrilotetraacetate

FAD(H_2) flavin adenine dinucleotide (reduced)
FDP fructose 1,6-diphosphate
Fru fructosyl
FMN(H_2) riboflavin 5′-phosphate (reduced)

G guanosine
Gal galactosyl
GalNAc N-acetylgalactosamine
GDP guanosine diphosphate
Glc glucosyl
Glc 6-P glucose 6-phosphate
GlcNAc N-acetylglucosamine
GlcUA glucuronate
Gln glutaminyl
Gly glycyl
GMP guanosine monophosphate
GSH, GSSG glutathione (reduced and oxidized)
GTP guanosine triphosphate

Hb hemoglobin
HbO_2 oxyhemoglobin
HDL high-density lipoprotein
His histidyl
hnRNA heterogenous nuclear RNA

I inosine
Ig immunoglobulin
Ile isoleucyl
IMP inosine monophosphate

K_M Michaelis constant

LDL low-density lipoprotein
Leu leucyl
Lys lysyl

Met methionyl
MgATP magnesium ATP
mRNA messenger RNA
M.W. molecular weight

NAD (NADH) nicotinamide adenine dinucleotide (reduced)
NADP (NADPH) nicotinamide adenine dinucleotide phosphate (reduced)

~P high-energy phosphate
P_i inorganic phosphate
PAPS phosphoadenosine phosphosulfate
PCr phosphocreatine
pI isoelectric pH

Phe phenylalanyl
P : O high-energy phosphate/atom of oxygen consumed
PP_i inorganic pyrophosphate
$PP\cdots P_i$ inorganic polyphosphates

RNA ribonucleic acids
R.Q. respiratory quotient
rRNA ribosomal RNA

S Svedberg unit
S substrate
SDS sodium dodecyl sulfate
Ser seryl

T thymidine (ribosylthymine)
ThPP thiamine pyrophosphate

tRNA transfer RNA
Trp tryptophanyl
Tyr tyrosyl

U uridine
UDP uridine diphosphate
UMP uridine monophosphate
UTP uridine triphosphate

V_{max} maximum velocity
VAL valyl
VLDL very-low-density lipoprotein

XMP xanthosine monophosphate
Ψ pseudouridine